D1230997

THE ENGLISH AND SCOTTISH
POPULAR BALLADS

THE

ENGLISH AND SCOTTISH

POPULAR BALLADS

EDITED BY

FRANCIS JAMES CHILD

IN FIVE VOLUMES

VOLUME V

NEW YORK
DOVER PUBLICATIONS, INC.

This Dover edition, first published in 1965, is an unabridged and unaltered republication of the work originally published by Houghton, Mifflin and Company, as follows:

Vol. I—Part I, 1882; Part II, 1884
Vol. II—Part III, 1885; Part IV, 1886
Vol. III—Part V, 1888; Part VI, 1889
Vol. IV—Part VII, 1890; Part VIII, 1892
Vol. V—Part IX, 1894; Part X, 1898.

This edition also contains as an appendix to Part X an essay by Walter Morris Hart entitled "Professor Child and the Ballad," reprinted *in toto* from Vol. XXI, No. 4, 1906 [New Series Vol. XIV, No. 4] of the *Publications of the Modern Language Association of America.*

Library of Congress Catalog Card Number: 65-24347

Manufactured in the United States of America

Dover Publications, Inc.
180 Varick Street
New York, N.Y. 10014

ADVERTISEMENT TO PART IX

NUMBERS 266–305

THE delay of the publication of this Ninth Part of the English and Scottish Ballads has been occasioned partly by disturbances of health, but principally by the necessity of waiting for texts. It was notorious that there was a considerable number of ballads among the papers of Charles Kirkpatrick Sharpe, and it was an important object to get possession of these, the only one of the older collections (with a slight exception) which I had not had in my hands. An unexpected opportunity occurred upon the sale of Sharpe's manuscripts last year. All the ballads, including, besides loose sheets, several sets of pieces, were secured by Mr Macmath, and turned over to me (mostly in transcripts made by his own hand) with that entire devotion to the interests of this undertaking which I have had so frequent occasion to signalize. A particularly valuable acquisition was the "old lady's complete set of ballads," mentioned by Scott in his correspondence with Sharpe, which was the original of most of the pieces in the Skene MS.

This Ninth Part completes the collection of English and Scottish ballads to the extent of my knowledge of sources, saving that William Tytler's Brown-MS. has not been recovered. Copies, from Mrs Brown's recitation, of all the pieces in this MS. are, however, elsewhere to be found, excepting in a single instance, and that of a ballad which is probably a variety of one or another here given in several forms (No 99 or No 158).

I have to thank Mr MACMATH once more for his energetic and untiring co-operation; the Rev. WILLIAM FINDLAY, of Sabine, for permission to make use of his ballad-gatherings; the Rev. S. BARING-GOULD, Mr P. Z. ROUND, Mr WILLIAM WALKER, and Mr R. BRINLEY JOHNSON, for texts; Professor WOLLNER, of Leipzig, for the most liberal assistance in Slavic matters; Mr KAARLE KROHN, of the University of Helsingfors, for a minute and comprehensive study of the Esthonian and Finnish forms of No 95; Dr AXEL OLRIK for Scandinavian texts and information relating thereto; Professor KITTREDGE for notes; and Mr R. B. ARMSTRONG, of Edinburgh, Dr ÅKE W:SON MUNTHE, of Upsala, Miss M. H. MASON, of London, Mr ALFRED ROGERS, of the Library of the University of Cambridge, Mr H. L. KOOPMAN, late of Harvard College, and Mrs MARIA ELLERY MACKAYE, for kind help of various descriptions.

It is intended that Part X (completing the work) shall contain a list of sources, a full and careful glossary, an index of titles and matters and other indexes, and a general preface.

F. J. C.

APRIL, 1894.

ADVERTISEMENT TO PART X

FOR texts, information, or correction of errors, I have the pleasure of expressing my indebtedness to the following gentlemen in Europe: Mr ANDREW LANG; Mr J. K. HUDSON of Manchester; Professsor J. ESTLIN CARPENTER of Oxford; Messrs W. MACMATH and DAVID MACRITCHIE of Edinburgh; Mr W. WALKER of Aberdeen; Dr AXEL OLRIK of Copenhagen; and in America to the following ladies and gentlemen: Miss MARY C. BURLEIGH of Massachusetts; Miss LOUISE PORTER HASKELL of South Carolina; Professor KITTREDGE, Dr W. H. SCHOFIELD, Dr W. P. FEW and Mr E. E. GRIFFITH of Harvard College; Professor W. U. RICHARDSON of the Harvard Medical School; Dr F. A. MORRISON of Indiana, and Mr W. W. NEWELL, editor of the Journal of American Folk-Lore. The services of Mr LEO WIENER of Harvard College have been at my full command in Slavic matters, and had time been at my disposal would have been employed for a much wider examination of the very numerous collections of Slavic popular songs. Mr G. F. ARNOLD, late of Harvard College Library, obligingly undertook the general bibliographical index at the end of this volume; but the labor proving too great for his delicate health, this index was completed by my friend Miss CATHARINE INNES IRELAND, who besides has generously devoted a great deal of time to the compilation or correction of all the other indexes and the preparation of them for the press. Still further favors are acknowledged elsewhere. In conclusion I would recognize with thanks and admiration the patience, liberality and consideration shown me by my publishers from beginning to end.

F. J. C.

[The manuscript of this Tenth and final Part of the English and Scottish Ballads (including the Advertisement), was left by Professor Child substantially complete, with the exception of the Bibliography, and nearly ready for the press. The Bibliography, which Miss Ireland had in hand at the time of Professor Child's death, has been completed by her, with some assistance. In accordance with Professor Child's desire, and at the request of his family, I have seen the present Part through the press. My own notes, except in the Indexes and Bibliography, are enclosed within brackets, and have been confined, in the main, to entries in the Additions and Corrections. Acknowledgments are due to Mr MACMATH, Professor LANMAN, and Dr F. N. ROBINSON for various contributions, and to Mr W. R. SPALDING for reading the proof-sheets of the music. Mr LEO WIENER, Instructor in Slavic Languages in Harvard University, has had the great kindness to revise the Slavic titles in the List of Ballads, the List of Collections of Ballads, and the Bibliography. To Miss IRELAND I am especially indebted for material assistance of various kinds, especially in the proof-reading.

G. L. K.]

JANUARY, 1898.

CONTENTS OF VOLUME V

———•———

JOHN THOMSON AND THE TURK

A. 'John Thomson and the Turk,' Buchan's Ballads of the North of Scotland, II, 159 ; Motherwell's Minstrelsy, Appendix, p. ix. 'John Tamson,' Motherwell's MS., p. 615.

B. Leyden's Glossary to The Complaynt of Scotland, p. 371, four stanzas.

LEYDEN (1801) says that he had "heard the whole song when very young." * Motherwell's copy was probably given him by Buchan.

John Thomson has been fighting against the Turks for more than three years, when he is surprised by receiving a visit from his wife, who walks up to him in a rich dress, as if Scotland were just round the corner. The lady stays several days, and then gives her husband to understand that she is going home. He recommends her to take a road across the lea, for by doing this she will escape wild Hind Soldan and base Violentrie. It is not so much an object with the lady to avoid these Turks as John Thomson supposes. The Soldan, it turns out, has been slain ; but she goes straight to Violentrie. After a twelvemonth John Thomson sends a letter to Scotland, "to see about his gay lady." An answer is returned that her friends have not laid eyes on her in all that time. John Thomson disguises himself as a palmer and hies to Violentrie's castle, where he finds his lady established. Learning that the palmer has come from the Scots' army in Greece, she asks whether one of the chieftains has seen his wife lately, and is told that it is long since the knight in question parted with his wife, and that he has some

fear lest the lady should have been captured by his foes. The lady declares that she is where she is by her own will, and means to stay. The palmer throws off his disguise, begs to be hidden from Violentrie, and is put down in a dark cellar. Violentrie soon arrives and calls for his dinner, casually remarking that he would give ten thousand sequins for a sight of the Scot who has so often put him to flight. The lady takes him at his word, and calls up John Thomson. The Turk demands what he would do if their positions were exchanged. "Hang you up," the Scot replies, with spirit, "and make you wale your tree." Violentrie takes his captive to the wood. John Thomson climbs tree after tree, ties a ribbon to every branch, and puts up a flag as a sign to his men : all which the Turk thinks no harm. Then John Thomson blows his horn. Three thousand men come tripping over the hill and demand their chief. The Turk begs for mercy, and gets such as he would have given : they burn him in his castle, and hang the lady.

This ridiculous ballad is a seedling from an ancient and very notable story, which has an extensive literature, and has of late been subjected to learned and acute investigation.† It may be assumed with confidence that the

---

* He has introduced the main points of the story (in fact **B** 2, 3) into his ballad of 'Lord Soulis,' Scott's Minstrelsy, 1833, IV, 244.

† Especially by A. Vesselofsky, Slavic Tales concerning Solomon and Kitovras, etc., St Petersburg, 1872 (in Russian) ; Neue Beiträge zur Geschichte der Salomonssage,

Archiv für Slavische Philologie, VI, 393 ff., 548 ff., 1882 ; V. Jagić, Archiv, etc., I, 103 ff., 1876 ; F. Vogt, Salman und Morolf, 1880, Zur Salman-Morolfsage, Paul und Braune's Beiträge, VIII, 313 ff., 1882. See these for tales containing portions of the same matter in various combinations, and for a discussion of an Oriental derivation.

story was originally one of King Solomon and his queen, of whom it is related in Russian, Servian, and German. In the course of transmission, as ever has been the wont, names were changed, and also some subordinate circumstances; in Portuguese, Solomon is replaced by Ramiro II, king of Leon; in a French romance by the Bastard of Bouillon. It is, however, certain that the Solomon story was well known to the French, and as early as the twelfth century.* Something of the same story, again, is found in König Rother and in the Cligès of Crestien de Troies, both works of the twelfth century, and in various other poems and tales.

The tale of the rape of Solomon's wife and of the revenge taken by Solomon is extant in Russian in three *byliny* (or, we may say, ballads), taken down from recitation in this century, and in three prose versions preserved in MSS of the sixteenth, seventeenth, and eighteenth centuries. The *byliny* † relate that Tsar Vasily of Constantinople (or Novgorod), while feasting with his nobles, demands of them to find him a wife who shall be his fair match in stature, beauty, wit, and birth. One of the company undertakes to get for his master Salamanija (Salomonida), the beautiful wife of Salomon, Tsar of Jerusalem (or of Constantinople), and effects the business by enticing her on board of a ship to see fine things, an artifice of frequent occurrence in ballads. Salomon sets out to retrieve his wife, attended by a large army (which he conceals in a grove), presents himself at Vasily's palace as a pilgrim (or other humble personage), is recognized by his wife, and shut up in a box. When Vasily comes back from hunting, Salamanija tells him what has chanced, and advises the instant execution of Salomon, which is resolved on. Salomon is to be beheaded, but he begs that he may be hanged, and that three nooses, of rope, bast, and silk, may be provided. Under the gallows Salomon asks to be allowed to sound his horn. Salamanija objects, but is overruled. He blows thrice;

his army comes at the third sounding. Vasily is hanged in the silken noose, Salamanija in the rope, and the man that carried her off in the bast.

One of the prose tales narrates these transactions as follows. The wife of Solomon, king of Jerusalem, is stolen from him by his brother Kitovras, through the agency of a magician, who, in the character of a merchant, excites Solomon's admiration for a magnificent purple robe. Solomon buys the robe, and invites the seeming merchant to his table. During the repast the magician envelops the king and his people in darkness, brings a heavy slumber upon the queen and her people, and carries her off in his arms to his ship. Solomon, learning that his wife is in the possession of Kitovras, proceeds against him with an army, which he orders to come to his help when they shall hear his horn sound the third time. Clad as an old pilgrim or beggar, he enters Kitovras's garden, where he comes upon a girl with a gold cup, who is about to draw water. He asks to drink from the king's cup. The girl objects, for, if reported to the king, such a thing would be the death of both of them; but the gift of a gold ring induces her to consent. The queen sees the ring on the girl's hand, and asks who gave it to her. An old pilgrim, she replies. No pilgrim, says the queen, but my husband, Solomon. Solomon is brought before the queen, and asked what he has come for. To take off your head, he answers. To your own death, rejoins the queen; you shall be hanged. Kitovras is sent for, and pronounces this doom. Solomon reminds Kitovras that they are brothers, and asks that he may die in regal style; that Kitovras and the queen shall attend the execution, with all the people of the city; and that there shall be ample provision of food and drink: all which is granted. At the gallows he finds a noose of bast; he begs that two other nooses may be provided, one of red silk, one of yellow, so that he may have a choice, and this whim is complied with. Al-

* G. Paris, in Romania, VII, 462, IX, 436; Cligès, ed. Foerster, p. xix.

† Rybnikof, II, Nos 52, 53, III, No 56. See Jagić, as

above, pp. 103–6; Miss I. F. Hapgood, Epic Songs of Russia, p. 282, who combines the three texts.

ways urging their brotherhood, Solomon, at three successive stages, asks the privilege of blowing his horn. The army is at hand upon the third blast, and is ordered to kill everybody. Kitovras and the queen are hanged in the silken nooses, the magician in the bast.*

The variations of the other versions are mostly not material to our purpose. In one, King Por takes the place of Kitovras; in the third, the king of Cyprus. In the latter, Solomon asks to be hanged upon a tree, a great oak. The king of Cyprus begs for a gentle death, and his veins are opened. The queen is dismembered by horses.

A Servian popular tale runs thus. Solomon's wife fell in love with another king, and not being able to escape to him on account of the strict watch which was kept over her, made an arrangement with him that he should send her a drink which should make her seem to be dead. Solomon, to test the reality of her death, cut off her little finger, and seeing no sign of feeling, had her buried. The other king sent his people to dig her up, restored animation, and took her to wife. When Solomon found out what had been done, he set out for the king's palace with a body of armed men, whom he left in a wood, under orders to hasten to his relief when they heard the blast of a trumpet, each man with a green bough in his hand. The king was out a-hunting, the queen at home. She wiled Solomon into a chamber and locked him up, and when the king came back from the chase told him to go into the room and cut Solomon down, but to enter into no talk, since in that case he would certainly be outwitted. Solomon laughed at the king and his sword: that was not the way for a king to dispose of a king. He should take him to a field outside the city, and let a trumpet sound thrice, so that everybody that wished might witness the spectacle; then he would find that the very greenwood would come to see one king put another to death. The king was curious to know whether the wood would come, and adopted Solomon's suggestion. At the first sound of the trum-

pet, Solomon's men set forward; at the second they were near at hand, but could not be distinguished because of the green boughs which they bore.† The king, convinced that the wood was coming, ordered a third blast. Solomon was rescued; the king and his court were put to the sword.‡

A Little Russian story of Solomon and his wife is given by Dragomanof, Popular Traditions and Tales, 1876, p. 103, translated in Revue des Traditions Populaires, II, 518, by E. Hins. Solomon takes a wife from the family of a heathen tsar. She hates him, and concerts an elopement with a heathen tsarevitch. She pretends to be dead. Solomon burns her hands through and through with a red-hot iron. She utters no sound, is buried in the evening, and immediately disinterred and carried off by her paramour. Solomon goes to the tsarevitch's house, attended by three armies, a black, a white, and a red (which are, of course, kept out of sight), and furnished with three pipes. The tsarevitch has a gallows set up, and Solomon is taken out to be hanged. He obtains liberty first to play on his pipes. The sound of the first brings the white army, that of the second the red, that of the third the black. The tsarevitch is hanged, the tsaritsa dragged at a horse's tail.

A like story is narrated in German in a passage of about two hundred and fifty verses, which is appended to the Wit-Combat, or Dialogue, of Solomon and Morolf; and again, with much interpolation and repetition, in a later strophic poem of more than four thousand lines. Both pieces are extant in manuscripts and print of the fifteenth century, but their original is considerably earlier.

In the briefer and earlier of the two German versions, Solomon's wife has bestowed her love on a nameless heathen king, and wishes to escape to him, but cannot bring this about. She feigns to be sick, and the heathen (with whom she has been in correspondence) sends two minstrels to her, who pretend to be able to cure sick folk with their music. They obtain admission to the queen,

---

* Jagić, Archiv, I, 107 f.; Vesselofsky, the same, VI, 406.
† Cf. **B** 3⁴. Methinks I see a coming tree.

‡ Karadschitsch, Volksmärchen der Serben, 1854, No 42, p. 233.

give her an herb which throws her into a death-like sleep, and carry her off to their master. Morolf, at King Solomon's entreaty, sets forth to find the queen, and, after traversing many strange lands, succeeds. Solomon, under his guidance and advice, and properly supported by an armed force, goes to the castle where the queen is living; leaves his men in an adjoining wood, under command to come to him when they hear his horn blow; and, disguised as a pilgrim, begs food at the castle. His wife knows him the moment she lays eyes on him, and tells the heathen that it is Solomon. The heathen, overjoyed, says to Solomon, If I were in your hands, what should be my death? Would God it were so! answers the king. I would take you to the biggest wood, let you choose your tree, and hang you. So shall it be, says the heathen, calls his people, takes Solomon to the wood, and bids him choose his tree. I shall not be long about that, says Solomon; but, seeing that I am of kingly strain, grant me, as a boon, to blow my horn three times. The queen objects; the heathen says, Blow away. At the third blast Morolf arrives with Solomon's men. The heathen and all his people are slain; the queen is taken back to Jewry, and put to death by opening her veins in a bath.*

The longer poem has several additional incidents which recur in our ballad, and others which link it with other forms of the story. Salme, Solomon's wife, is daughter of an Indian king (Cyprian, cf. the third Russian prose tale), and has been stolen from her father by Solomon. Fore, a heathen king, in turn steals Salme from the king of Jerusalem. Morolf is not the sharp-witted boor of the other piece, but Solomon's brother. When Solomon goes to Fore's castle, he is kindly received by that king's sister, and she remains his fast friend throughout. He tells her that

he is a sinful man, upon whom has been imposed a penance of perpetual pilgrimage. Brought before the queen, Solomon tries to make Salme come back to him. She lets him know that she loves Fore three times as well as him, and to Fore will she stick. Solomon is put into some side room. Fore comes home and sits down to table with Salme, and she informs him that Solomon is in his power. The army consists of three divisions, a black, a white, and a wan (bleich), nearly as in the Little Russian tale. The reason which Solomon alleges for wishing to blow his horn is to give notice to St Michael and the angels to come and take his soul in charge. Fore is hanged. Salme is disposed of as before, but not until after she has eloped with another king. Solomon marries Fore's sister after Salme's death.†

The adventure of Solomon will be recognized in what is recounted in Portuguese genealogies of the fourteenth century concerning King Ramiro Second of Leon († 950).‡ King Ramiro, smitten with passion for a beautiful Moorish lady, got himself invited to the castle of her brother Alboazar, at Gaya, and plumply asked for her. He would make her a Christian and marry her. Alboazar replied that Ramiro had a wife and children already. Ramiro could not deny this, but his queen was, it seems, conveniently near of kin to him, and Holy Church would allow a separation. The Moor swore that he never would give his sister to Ramiro. Ramiro, under cover of a darkness produced by an astrologer in his service, carried her off to Leon and had her baptized with the name Artiga. Alboazar, in revenge, availed himself of a favorable opportunity to lay hands on Aldora, Ramiro's queen, and took her to his castle of Gaya. Ramiro, with five galleys crowded with his vassals, ran in at San João de Foz, near Gaya. He had taken the precaution to cover his gal-

---

* Von der Hagen u. Büsching, Deutsche Gedichte des Mittelalters, 1808, I, 62, vv. 1605–1848.

† Vogt, Salman und Marolf.

‡ Os livros de Linhagens, in Portugaliæ Monumenta Historica, Scriptores, 1856, I, 180 f., 274–7. The latter account was printed by Southey in the preface to his ballad 'King

Ramiro' (1802), Poetical Works, 1853, VI, 122, and a passage from the other.

Kemble, Salomon & Saturnus, p. 19, 1848, remarks on the resemblance of the story of Ramiro to that of Solomon. For historical names and facts in the Portuguese sage, see Baist in Zs. f. romanische Philologie, V, 173

leys with green cloth, and he laid them under the boughs of trees with which the place was covered, so that they were not to be seen. Having landed his men, he left them under the command of his son, D. Ordonho, with directions that they should keep well hidden and not stir from the spot till they should hear his horn, but then come with all speed, and himself putting on mean clothes (panos de tacanho, de veleto) over sword, mail, and horn, went and lay down at a spring near the castle. One of the queen's women came out to fetch water for her mistress. Ramiro, feigning to be unable to rise, asked her for a drink, which she offered him. He put into his mouth the half of a ring which he had divided with his queen, and dropped it into the vessel. The queen saw the half-ring and knew it, and elicited from her maid that she had met a sick beggar, who had asked for a drink. The man was sent for. 'What brings you here, King Ramiro?' demanded the queen. 'Love for you,' said he. 'No love for me; you care more for Artiga,' she retorted. Ramiro was put into a back room, and the door was locked. Presently Alboazar came into the queen's chamber. The queen said to him, What would you do to Ramiro if you had him here? Put him to death cruelly (What he would do to me, kill him), responded the Moor. He is locked up in that room, said the queen, and you can proceed at your will.

Ramiro heard all this, and saw that he had never had more need to use his wits. He called in a loud voice to Alboazar: I wronged you by carrying off your sister. I confessed my sin to my priest, and he required of me as penance to go to you in this vile garb, and put myself in your power; and if you wished to take my life, I was to submit to death in a shameful place, and the fact and cause of my death were to be proclaimed by a

horn to all your people. Now I have to ask that you would collect your sons, your daughters, your kinsfolk, and the people of this town, in a cattle-yard (curral), put me up high, and let me blow this horn that I wear, until breath and life fail. So you will have your revenge, and I shall save my soul. Alboazar began to feel compassion for Ramiro. Aldora exclaimed at his weakness and folly. Ramiro, she said, was revengeful and cunning, and sparing him was rushing into destruction; whereby the Moor was brought to say, You know that if you had me in your hands, I should not escape. I will do what you ask, for the salvation of your soul. So Alboazar took Ramiro to the yard, which had high walls and but one gate, and the queen, her dames and damsels, the Moor's sons and kinsfolk, and the town's people, were there. Ramiro was put on a pillar, and told to blow till life left his body; and he blew with all his might. D. Ordonho came with the king's vassals and beset the gate. Ramiro drew his sword and split Alboazar's head. The queen and her ladies were spared, but every other creature in the yard was slain, including four sons and three daughters of Alboazar, and no stone was left standing in Gaya. Ramiro put the queen and her women aboard the galleys. Aldora was found weeping. Ramiro asked the cause. Because you have killed the Moor, a better man than yourself, was her answer. This was thought too much to be borne. The queen was tied to a millstone and thrown into the sea. Ramiro married Artiga.*

There is a poem on this theme by João Vaz (Lisbon, 1630, reprinted by Braga, 1868), which points to a different source than the genealogies. Ramiro takes the sister of King Almanzor captive in war, and becomes enamored of her, in consequence of which Gaya, Ramiro's wife, elopes with Almanzor. Gaya receives Ramiro with feigned kindness when

---

* There is nothing about the fair Moor in the first and briefer account, or of the penance given Ramiro. Ortiga is there the name of the servant who comes to fetch water. Ramiro is brought before the Moor and told that he is to die. But I should like to ask you, says the Moor, what manner of death mine should be if you had me in your hands. The

king was very hungry, and he answered, I would give you a stewed capon and a loaf, and make you eat them, and then wine and make you drink, and then open the gates of my cattle-yard and have all my people called to see you die, and make you mount on a pillar and blow your horn till your breath was gone.

he comes to the castle, then betrays him (as in the French romance).*

Almeida-Garrett composed a little romance out of the story as here given, with the name Zahara for Alboazar's sister, and Gaia for Ramiro's wife, and making Ramiro cut off Gaia's head before he throws her into the water: 'Miragaia,' Romanceiro, I, 181, ed. 1863. He informs us that he has interwoven in his poem some verses from popular tradition. A ballad of Ramiro, or at least some remnant of one, appears still to be in existence. Madame de Vasconcellos (1880) had heard two lines of it.

Li Bastars de Buillon, a romance of the fourteenth century, repeats the chief incidents of the foregoing accounts, agreeing in details sometimes with one, sometimes with another.† Ludie, daughter of the emir of Orbrie, is to marry Corsabrin, king of Mont Oscur. The Bastard of Bouillon, who has heard of the beauty of the Saracen princess, conceives a sudden fancy for her. He besieges and takes the city of Orbrie, kills the emir, and compels Ludie to submit to baptism and to marriage with himself. She takes advantage of an absence of the Bastard to escape to Corsabrin, who makes her his queen. The Bastard, bent on vengeance, sails to Mont Oscur, and in the adjacent woods lights on a charcoal-man who is going to the castle in the way of his business. He kills the charcoal-man and puts on his clothes, and in this habit, with a well-blackened face, has no difficulty in obtaining entrance to the residence of Corsabrin. His men he has left in the wood under command of his counsellor and lieutenant, Hugh. Corsabrin is hawking, but the Bastard falls in with Ludie, who affects to be glad of his coming, and offers to go off with him if he will forgive her and do her no harm. A bath would seem to be in order. Ludie has one prepared for the Bastard, and while he is engaged in taking it, sends for Corsabrin, who comes in upon the young Frank with sixty men. Ludie enjoins her rightful husband to show no mercy. The Saracen will not do so

infamous a thing as to put his enemy to death in a bath, but assures his wife that the Bastard shall die à guise de martir. A rich dress is furnished the Bastard, and Corsabrin then says, On your oath, now, what death should I die, were I in your power? Sire, says the Bastard, why should I dissemble? I promise you, I would take you to a wood, and I would hang you to the highest tree I could find. By Mahound! says the king, so will I do with you. The Bastard is taken to a wood, with a rope round his neck. Corsabrin's people look out the highest tree. The Bastard is made to go up, higher and higher, the hangman drawing the rope all too tight the while, till the king says, Now. At the last moment the Bastard calls out to Corsabrin that he is a knight of high birth, and ought not to die like a rogue, but as a man of mark dies among the Franks. And how is that? asks the Saracen. They give him a horn, and he blows four or five times to summon the angels to come for his soul. Then he says a prayer. Then they strangle him or behead him. A horn is sent up to the Bastard, and he blows lustily. Hugh hears, and rides in hot haste to the call. The Bastard makes the most of his grace; his prayer is very long. He sees that a fight is going on below, and knocks the hangman dead from the tree with his fist, then comes down from the tree and joins in the fray. Hugh runs Corsabrin through with a lance, Ludie is taken captive, and every other living being in the castle is slain. Hugh begs as a reward for his services that he may have the disposal of Ludie. The Bastard accords the boon, with a recommendation to mercy: 'arse fu li royne c'on appella Ludie.'

The escaping to a lover by taking a drug which causes apparent death, and the test of molten lead or gold, in the German poems, and in Cligès, 6000 ff., are found in 'The Gay Goshawk,' No 96, II, 355 ff. The test is also employed in one form of the Russian prose narratives: Vesselofsky, in the Slavic Archiv, VI, 409.

---

* Madame Michaëlis de Vasconcellos, in Paul u. Braune's Beiträge, VIII, 315 f.

† Ed. Scheler, Bruxelles, 1877; vv. 4503-6253.

A portion of the story is preserved in Scandinavian ballads, with very distinct marks of Russian origin.

Swedish. 'Jungfru Solfager,' Arwidsson, I, 177, No 25 : A from a MS. of the sixteenth century, B from recitation.

A. Solfager is a handsome woman, so handsome as to endanger her husband Sir David's life. Fearing that she may be carried off, David in some way marks or stamps her hand with a gold cross, that she may be known thereby. As Solfager is standing at the castle gate, Novgorod's (Nougård's) king comes riding up. He asks if her husband is at home; Sir David went away the day before, and will not come back for a year. The king tells her that if she will plight herself to him she shall always wear gold shoes; Solfager answers that she loves David dearly. The king gives her a drink, two drinks; she swoons, and falls to the ground; she is laid on a bier, taken to the kirk-yard, and buried. The king (David in the text, absurdly) has kept his eye on their doings; he digs her up, and carries her out of the land. David, disguised as a pilgrim, goes to the king of Novgorod's palace, and asks to be housed as a poor pilgrim. The king invites him in. David takes his place with other pilgrims; Solfager breaks bread for them. [Her hand is gloved.] David asks why she does not break bread with a bare hand; she calls him an old fool, and bids him eat or go. The king, from his bed, inquires what the pilgrim is saying. 'Lie down, my lord,' answers Solfager; 'what a fool says is no matter.' They all fall asleep in their places; Solfager follows Sir David home.

B. Solfot looks at her face in the water. 'God help me for my beauty!' she exclaims, 'surely I shall come to a strange land.' Her husband, the Danish king, tells her that he shall write a cross in her right hand, by which he shall find her again. While Solfot is combing her hair out of doors, the Ormeking asks her if she has a golden crown to put on it; she has four and five, all the gift of the king of the Danes. Ormeking gives her a drink which turns her black and blue; Solfot is laid in the ground; Ormeking knows well where,

takes her up, carries her off to his own place, and gives her seven drinks; she stands up as good as ever. Daneking dons pilgrim's clothes and goes to Ormeking's. Solfot, as northern ladies wont, is combing her hair out of doors. Daneking asks for a pilgrim's house; there is one on the premises, where poor pilgrims use (like King Claudius) to take their rouse. The pilgrims stand in a ring; Solfot is to dispense mead to them in turn. Daneking dashes his gloves on the board : 'Is it not the way here that ladies deal mead with bare hands?' Ormeking dashes his gloves on the board: 'That was a bold word for a pilgrim!' 'If that was a bold word for a pilgrim,' says Daneking, 'it was bolder yet to dig Solfot out of the ground.' Then he puts Solfot on his horse and rides away.

There are also two unprinted nineteenth-century copies in Professor G. Stephens's collection.

Norwegian. 'Sólfager og Ormekongin,' Landstad, p. 503, No 56, from a woman's singing. They stamp a gold cross on (or into? the process is not clear) Sólfager's hand, that she may be recognized in a strange country. The Ormeking (or King Orm) comes riding while Sólfager is sunning her hair. 'Trick King David,' he says, 'and bind yourself to me.' 'Never shall it be,' she replies, 'that I give myself to two brothers.' He administers to her three potions, she swoons; word comes to King David that she is dead; they bury her. Ormeking does not fail to carry off the body. King David goes to Ormeking's land in pilgrim's garb, with pilgrim's staff; as he enters the court Sólfager is undoing her hair. [Then there is a gap, which may be easily filled up from the Swedish story.] 'Is it the custom here to cut bread with gloved hand?' She takes off his pilgrim's hat, and takes his yellow locks in her hand. 'When you say you are a pilgrim, you must be lying to me.' 'Even so,' he answers, 'but I am your dear husband, as you easily may see. Will you go home with me?' 'Gladly,' she says, 'but I am afraid of Ormeking.' King David takes Ormeking's horse and rides home with his wife. When Ormeking comes back, Sólfager is away. (A final stanza does not belong to the story.)

There are other unprinted copies which will appear in a contemplated edition of Norwegian ballads by Sophus Bugge and Moltke Moe.

Danish. Eight unprinted MS. copies of the seventeenth century and a flying sheet of the date 1719. The ballad will be No 472 of Danmarks gamle Folkeviser.* A fragment of five stanzas (of dialogue relative to the gloved hand) is given by Kristensen, Jyske Folkeminder, X, 331, No 82.

It will be observed that the ravisher is king of Novgorod in Swedish A, as in one of the Russian epics, and that he is the brother of King David in the Norwegian ballad as he is of King Solomon in the Russian prose tale. The sleeping-draught, burial, and digging up are in the Servian tale, and something of them in the Little Russian tale, as also in the earlier German poem.

For the boon of blowing the horn see No 123, 'Robin Hood and the Curtal Friar,' and No 140, 'Robin Hood rescuing Three Squires,' III, 122, 177, ff.; also Heiðreks Saga, Rafn, Fornaldar Sögur, I, 458–61 (14), 529 f. (9); Vesselofsky, in the Slavic Archiv, VI, 404 f.; and Wollner's note, Abschiedblasen, Brugman's Litauische Märchen, p. 552.

August 1, 1586, there was allowed to Yarrat James as one of six ballads 'A merrie jest of John Tomson and Jakaman his wife,' Arber, Stationers' Registers, II, 450. This ballad is preserved in the Roxburghe collection, I, 254, 255, Ballad Society's edition, II, 136, and, so far as I have observed, there only. It is subscribed M. L., initials which Mr Chappell was unable to identify, and it

was imprinted at London for Edward Wright. The Roxburghe copy was reprinted by R. H. Evans, Old Ballads, 1810, I, 187. The title is

'A merry Iest of Iohn Tomson and Jakaman his wife,
Whose jealousie was justly the cause of all their strife.'

It is dated in the Museum catalogue 1635?. This is an extremely vapid piece, and has no manner of connection with 'John Thomson and the Turk.' In Halliwell's Notices of Popular English Histories, p. 91, Percy Society, vol. xxiii, there is one, No 108, of 'John Thompson's Man, or a short survey of the difficulties and disturbances that may attend a married life,' etc., 24 pp., 12°. There is a copy in the Abbotsford Library.

'To be John Thomson's man' † is a Scottish proverb signifying to be submissive to a wife, or, more generally, to be complaisant. "John Thomson's men" are "still ruled by their wives:" Colville's Whig's Supplication, or, The Scotch Hudibras, cited by Motherwell. "Samson was the greatest fool that ever was born, for he revealed his secrets to a daft hussie. Samson, you may well call him Fool Thompson, for of all the John Thomson's men that ever was he was the foolest:" The Scotch Presbyterian Eloquence, etc., London, 1692 (cited by Motherwell, from the edition of 1768, in a MS. note, Appendix, p. x, in a copy of the Minstrelsy which belonged to Mr R. A. Ramsay.) Some begging verses of Dunbar to the King have the refrain, 'God gif ye war Johne Thomsoneis man.' (Other quotations in Leyden, p. 370, Motherwell, Appendix, p. ix.) ‡

---

* I am indebted to Dr Axel Olrik for information concerning the Solfager ballads, and for transcripts of Danish and Swedish versions not received in time for notice here. See p. 280.

† Originally, no doubt, as Motherwell suggests, Joan Thomson's man, or husband.

‡ "One John Thomson is mentioned as an officer in the army of Edward Bruce in Ireland. After Bruce's death, he led back to Scotland the remnant of his army. In 1333, he held for David Bruce the castle of Lochdoun in Carrick. Sir W. Scott thus characterizes him: 'John Thomson, a man of obscure birth and dauntless valor, the same apparently who led back from Ireland the shattered remainder of Edward Bruce's army, held out for his rightful sovereign.' History of Scotland, I, 181." Note by Motherwell in Mr Ramsay's copy of the Minstrelsy, Appendix, p. ix.

A

Buchan's Ballads of the North of Scotland, II, 159;
Motherwell's MS., p. 615; Motherwell's Minstrelsy, Appendix, p. ix.

1 JOHN THOMSON fought against the Turks
    Three years into a far country,
And all that time, and something more,
    Was absent from his gay lady.

2 But it fell ance upon a time,
    As this young chieftain sat alane,
He spied his lady in rich array,
    As she walkd oer a rural plain.

3 'What brought you here, my lady gay,
    So far awa from your own country?
I 've thought lang, and very lang,
    And all for your fair face to see.'

4 For some days she did with him stay,
    Till it fell ance upon a day,
' Farewell for a time,' she said,
    ' For now I must bound home away.'

5 He 's gien to her a jewel fine,
    Was set with pearl and precious stone;
Says, My love, beware of these savages bold,
    That 's on your way as ye go home.

6 Ye 'll take the road, my lady fair,
    That leads you fair across the lee;
That keeps you from wild Hind Soldan,
    And likewise from base Violentrie.

7 With heavy heart these two did part,
    And minted as she would go home;
Hind Soldan by the Greeks was slain,
    But to base Violentrie she 's gone.

8 When a twelvemonth had expired,
    John Thomson he thought wondrous lang,
And he has written a broad letter,
    And seald it well with his own hand.

9 He sent it along with a small vessel
    That there was quickly going to sea,
And sent it on to fair Scotland,
    To see about his gay ladie.

10 But the answer he received again,
    The lines did grieve his heart right sair;

None of her friends there had her seen
    For a twelvemonth and something mair.

11 Then he put on a palmer's weed,
    And took a pikestaff in his hand;
To Violentrie's castle he hied,
    But slowly, slowly he did gang.

12 When within the hall he came,
    He joukd and couchd out-oer his tree:
' If ye be lady of this hall,
    Some of your good bountieth give me.'

13 ' What news, what news, palmer?' she said,
    ' And from what countrie came ye?'
' I 'm lately come from Grecian plains,
    Where lys some of the Scots army.'

14 ' If ye be come from Grecian plains,
    Some more news I will ask of thee;
Of one of the chieftains that lies there,
    If he have lately seen his gay ladie.'

15 ' It is twelve months and something more
    Since we did part in yonder plain;
And now this knight has begun to fear
    One of his foes he has her taen.'

16 ' He has not taen me by force nor might,
    It was all by my own free will;
He may tarry in the fight,
    For here I mean to tarry still.

17 ' And if John Thomson ye do see,
    Tell him I wish him silent sleep;
His head was not so cozelie
    Nor yet so well as lies at my feet.'

18 With that he threw [aff] his strange disguise,
    Laid by the mask that he had on;
Said, Hide me now, my ladie fair,
    For Violentrie will soon be home.

19 ' For the love I bare thee once,
    I 'll strive to hide you if I can;'
Then put him down to a dark cellar,
    Where there lay mony a new slain man.

20 But he hadna in the cellar been
    Not an hour but barely three,
Till hideous was the sound he heard;
    Then in at the gates came Violentrie.

21 Says, I wish yon well, my lady fair,
　　It's time for us to sit and dine;
　Come, serve me with the good white bread,
　　And likewise with the claret wine.

22 'That Scots chieftain, our mortal foe,
　　So oft from field has made us flee,
　Ten thousand sequins this day I'd give
　　That I his face could only see.'

23 'Of that same gift would ye give me,
　　If I could bring him unto thee?
　I fairly hold you at your word;
　　Come ben, John Thomson, to my lord.'

24 Then from the vault John Thomson came,
　　Wringing his hands most piteouslie;
　'What would ye do,' the Turk he cried,
　　'If ye had me, as I have thee?'

25 'If I had you, as ye have me,
　　I'll tell you what I'd do to thee;
　I'd hang you up in good greenwood,
　　And cause your own hand wile the tree.

26 'I meant to stick you with my knife,
　　For kissing my beloved wife;'
　'But that same weed ye've shaped for me,
　　It quickly shall be sewed for thee.'

27 Then to the wood they both are gone,
　　John Thomson clamb from tree to tree;
　And aye he sighd, and said, Ohon!
　　Here comes the day that I must die!

28 He tied a ribbon on every branch,
　　Put up a flag his men might see;
　But little did his false foe ken
　　He meant them any injurie.

29 He set his horn to his mouth,
　　And he has blawn baith loud and shrill;
　And then three thousand armed men
　　Came tripping all out-oer the hill.

30 'Deliver us our chief!' they all did cry,
　　'It's by our hand that ye must die!'
　'Here is your chief,' the Turk replied,
　　With that fell on his bended knee.

31 'O mercy, mercy, good fellows all,
　　Mercy I pray you'll grant to me!'
　'Such mercy as ye meant to give,
　　Such mercy we shall give to thee.'

32 This Turk they in his castle burnt,
　　That stood upon yon hill so hie;
　John Thomson's gay lady they took,
　　And hangd her on yon greenwood tree.

———◆———

B

Leyden's Glossary to The Complaynt of Scotland, p. 371.

1 O cam ye in by the House o Rodes,
　　Or cam ye there away?
　Or have [ye] seen Johne Tamson?
　　They say his wife has run away.
　　*　　*　　*　　*　　*　　*

2 'O what wad ye do, Johne Tamson,
　　Gin ye had me as I hae thee?'

'I wad tak ye to the gude green-wood,
　　And gar your ain hand weil the tree.'
　*　　*　　*　　*　　*　　*　　*

3 Johne Tamson peeped and poorly spake
　　Untill he did his ain men see;
　'O by my sooth,' quo Johne Tamson,
　　'Methinks I see a coming tree.'
　*　　*　　*　　*　　*　　*　　*

4 And they hae hanged that grim Soudan,
　　For a' his mirth and meikle pride,
　And sae hae they that ill woman,
　　Upon a scrogg-bush him beside.

———◆———

15¹. two months *in all the copies; cf.* 8¹.
19⁴. lye.
*Motherwell's MS. has a few variations, but these
　may be attributed to Motherwell. All except-
　ing one, which is an error of the pen, appear
　in the Minstrelsy.*

5⁴. in your.　14⁴. has.　15². part on.
16³. into the.　19⁴. lay.　20³. Then.
(20⁴. *Minstrelsy,* When.)　20⁴. gate.
21². sit to.　22³. I'll.
25¹. have, *error of the pen.*　25⁴. wale.
26². ladie *for* wife, *to avoid couplets.*　28³. foes.

267

THE HEIR OF LINNE

A. 'The Heir of Lin,' Percy MS., p. 71; Hales and Furnivall, I, 174.

B. a. 'The Heir of Linne,' Buchan's MSS, I, 40; Motherwell's MS., p. 630; Dixon, Scottish Traditional Versions of Ancient Ballads, p. 30, Percy Society, vol. xvii. **b.** 'The Weary Heir of Linne,' Buchan's MSS, II, 114. **c.** 'The Laird o Linne,' Christie's Traditional Ballad Airs, I, 112.

THE three stanzas cited by Motherwell, Minstrelsy, Introduction, p. lxviii, note 15 (wrongly as to 2⁴), and repeated from Motherwell by Chambers, p. 310, Whitelaw, p. 81, Aytoun, II, 342, are from **B a.**

A. The heir of Linne, a Scots lord, took to cards, dice, and wine, sold his lands to John o the Scales, and went on in dissolute ways for three fourths of a year longer; then he was forced to go to Edinburgh and beg his bread. Some gave him, some refused him, some bade him go to the devil. Brooding over his destitution, he remembered that his father had left him a paper which he was not to look into till he should be in extreme need. This paper told him of a castle wall in which stood three chests of money. Filling three bags with gold, he went to John o Scales's house. John's wife wished herself a curse if she trusted him a penny. One good fellow in the company offered to lend him forty pence, and forty more, if wanted. John o Scales tendered him his lands back for twenty pounds less than they had been sold for. The heir of Linne called the lords present to witness, threw John a penny to bind the bargain, and counted out the money from his bags. Then he gave the good fellow forty pounds, and made him keeper of his forest, and beshrewed himself if ever he put his lands in jeopardy again.

B. The heir of Linne stands at his father's gates, and nobody asks him in. He is hungry, wet, and cold. As he goes down the town, gentlemen are drinking. Some say, Give him a glass; some say, Give him none. As he goes up the town, fishermen are sitting. Some say, Give him a fish; some say, Give him a fin. He takes the road to Linne,* and on the way begs of his nurse a slice of bread and a bottle of wine, promising to pay them back when he is laird of Linne; which he will never be, she says. A score of nobles are dining at Linne. Some say, Give him beef, some say, Give him the bone; some say, Give him nothing at all. The new laird will let him have a sip, and then he may go his gate. At his wits' end, he now recalls a little key given him by his mother before she died, which he was to keep till he was in his greatest need. This key fits a little door somewhere in the castle. He gets gold enough to free his lands. He returns to the company of nobles. The new laird offers him Linne back for a third of what had been paid for it. He takes the guests to witness, and tells the money down on a table. He pays the nurse for her bread and wine. His hose had been down at his ankles; now he has fifteen lords to escort him. †

Percy, Reliques, 1765, II, 309, 1794, II, 128 (with some readings of his manuscript

---

* Cane in hand, 10³, 22³. This is bad enough, but not quite so bad as the woman with cane in hand, 'Tam Lin,' III, 505, **O** 16², and 'The Kitchie-Boy,' No 252, **E** 6². The mantle and cane are a commonplace. See also **E** 14 of No 252, No 76, **G** 3, and No 97, **B** 20².

† The Gallowgate port of **B a** 35 belongs to Aberdeen.

restored in the later edition), as he puts it, revised and completed A by " the insertion of supplemental stanzas," " suggested by a modern ballad on a similar subject." In fact, Percy made a new ballad,* and a very good one, which, since his day, has passed for ' The Heir of Linne.' (Herd, 1769, p. 227, but afterwards dropped; Ritson, Scotish Songs, II, 129; Ritson, Ancient Songs and Ballads, 1829, II, 81, with a protest; even Chambers, p. 310, Aytoun, II, 342; for the Scottish version had not been printed when these collections appeared.)

The modern ballad on a similar subject used by Percy was ' The Drunkard's Legacy,' † an inexpressibly pitiable ditty, from which Percy did not and could not take a line, but only, as he says, a suggestion for the improvement of the story. In this, a gentleman has a thriftless son given over to gaming and drunkenness. The father, foreseeing his ruin, builds a cottage on a waste plat of land, with one door, fastened by a spring-lock. On his death-bed he sends for his son, tells him of the cottage, and directs him, after he has lost all his friends and pawned his lands, to break open the door, for he shall find something within to end his troubles. After the father's death the son spent all his ready money, and then pawned his lands to the keeper of a tavern which he had frequented, who, in the end, kicked him out of doors. Recalling now his father's injunction, the son broke open the cottage, hoping to find money. He saw only ' a gibbet and a rope,' and a stool under the rope. He mounted the stool, put the rope round his neck, and jumped off. The ' gibbet ' broke, and a thousand pound in gold came tumbling about his ears. The young man, with a blessing on his father, vowed to give up drinking. He went to the vintner's, and getting a rough reception, complained of his so treating a man who had pawned to him for three hundred pounds lands bringing in eight score pounds' rent, and besides had spent the money in that shop. The vintner told him to bring a hundred pounds the next

day and take the lands back. The young man asked a note to this effect, which was unsuspectingly given. He then went and fetched the money, bringing with him a comrade, ' who had made him drink when moneyless.' The vintner declared that he had spoken in jest, but ' this young man's friend ' urged that the written agreement would ' cast ' him in law; so the vintner had to take the hundred pounds and give up the deeds, and he cut his throat for mortification. From that time the prodigal lived a sober, charitable life.

Percy's introduction of the lonesome lodge, the hanging, the bursting ceiling, and the father's double admonition, is an improvement too striking to require or bear much comment. It is very far from certain that a young reprobate, who has spent everything in riotous living, will be turned into better courses by simply coming upon more money, as in the traditional ballad; whereas there is a very fair chance that the moral shock received in the other might be efficacious.

There are several Oriental stories which closely resemble that of ' The Drunkard's Legacy,' or of Percy's ' Heir of Linne.'

(1.) Sinadab was left by his father's will free to dispose of a large property, with the exception of a diminutive garden, at the end of which was a small house. This he was on no account to part with. He indulged in reckless profusion, and in about two years everything was spent. The friends of his affluent days abandoned him, — all but one, who gave him ten sequins. With only this in hand he set out on a voyage which led to adventures which may be passed over. They ended in his coming again to extreme poverty. He then remembered the little garden which he had been forbidden to sell. He found a small box in the house, and eagerly broke it open. There was nothing in it but a rope, with a writing in his father's hand, rebuking him for his dissipation, and suggesting that, if he had sufficient resolution, he might put an end to his troubles by use of the rope.

---

* Of the 212 lines of Percy's ballad, some 80, or the substance of them, occur in the MS. copy, and half a dozen more of the 216 lines of the 4th edition.

† Reprinted by Dixon, Ancient Poems, Ballads, etc., p. 151, Percy Society, vol. xvii, from a chap-book.

Sinadab accordingly got up on a stool, fastened the rope to the ceiling, adjusted a noose about his neck, and pushed back the stool. The ceiling gave way, and he was covered with a shower of gold pieces, which proved to be only a trifling part of riches concealed above. His career after this was serious and prudent. Gueulette, ' Les mille et un quart d'heure,' Contes Tartares, Cabinet des Fées, XXI, 66–70, 89–93.

(2.) **Turkish.** A merchant took his son to a certain house, and said, If you waste the wealth I leave, do not beg, but get a rope and hang yourself from this ring. The son squandered his inheritance with sycophants, who reviled him after he was stripped. He got a rope, went to the house, mounted a stool, fastened one end of the rope to the ring, the other about his neck, and threw himself from the stool. A board in which the ring was fastened gave way, the young man fell to the ground, and gold and jewels came pouring upon him. He repented of his profligacy, and reformed his ways. ' The Forty Vezirs,' Gibb, p. 244; Behrnauer, p. 253.

(3.) **Arabic.** A man charged his son not to beg if he should come to want, for he had hidden a treasure in his house, which, however, he was not to resort to until compelled by dire necessity. After his father's death, the son, without delay, broke into the place where the treasure had been said to be concealed, but found only an empty room, with a rope hanging from the ceiling. Under the rope was a pile of bricks, and a paper recommending him to get up on the bricks and hang himself. The young man went off, and with the assistance of parasites, was soon rid of all his wealth. After a taste of the sharpness of poverty and of the baseness of summer friends, he went to the room where he had expected to find the treasure, stepped on the pile of bricks, tied the rope round his neck, and kicked away the bricks. The rope parted, and a quantity of precious things tumbled from overhead. His false friends promptly returned with prosperity, but were put to shame. Tausend und eine Nacht, Deutsch von Habicht, v. d. Hagen u. Schall, 1840, XIV, 65–68.

(4.) The same story, with some of the details of both 2 and 3, in Pauli's Schimpf und Ernst, Oesterley, p. 400, from the edition of 1533. In Pauli's tale, the young man, after a year of exemplary life in the world, gives all his goods to the poor and turns hermit.

(5.) **Persian.** Atalmulc's extravagances cause his father great anxiety. The father, when near his end, charges his son, if he should be so unhappy as to dissipate the fortune he will receive, to hang himself to a branch of a tree in the middle of the garden. The bough breaks, and the trunk is found to be full of precious stones. Petis de la Croix, Les Mille et un Jour, Cabinet des Fées, XIV, 457.

There is another and seemingly an independent story, summarized in two distichs in the Greek Anthology (IX, 44, 45, translated by Ausonius, Epigrammata, 22, 23), how a man, who was about to hang himself, found some money, and left his rope behind, and how the owner of the money, coming for it and not finding it, hanged himself with the rope.* La Fontaine's fable, ' Le Trésor et les deux Hommes,' IX, 16, is this story, with a wall falling, not by precontrivance, but from its ruinous condition.

The eighth tale in the ninth decade of Giraldi Cinthio's Hecatommithi, 1565, II, 563, is a modification of what may be called the Greek story. " Chera hid a treasure. Elisa, going about to hang herself, and tying the halter about a beam, found that treasure, and in place thereof left the halter. Philene, the daughter of Chera, going for that treasure, and busily searching for the same, found the halter, wherewithal, in despair, she would have hanged herself, but," etc. (Painter's argument to his translation of Cinthio's tale in the Palace of Pleasure, 2d Tome (1567), 11th novel, ed. Jacobs, II, 264.)

The Greek Syntipas has another variety. A man, reduced to want, takes a sword and goes to a lonely place to end his misery. He finds in a deep hole or fosse a quantity of gold which has been hidden there by a cy-

---

* 44. Χρυσὸν ἀνὴρ εὑρὼν ἔλιπε βρόχον· αὐτὰρ ὁ χρυσὸν ὃν λίπεν οὐχ εὑρὼν ἧψεν ὃν εὗρε βρόχον.

clops, takes it, and goes back to his house very happy. The cyclops, coming to the spot and not finding his gold, but seeing the sword lying about, slays himself. Matthæi, Syntipæ Fabulæ, 1781, p. 38, μη; Coray, Æsop, p. 246, No 384.*

A tale in Anvár-i Suhailí has been cited in connection with the foregoing, which has only a general and remote resemblance to 'The Heir of Linne.' A wise king, perceiving that his two unpromising sons would misuse his treasures, buries them in a hermitage. After his death, his sons quarrel about the succession. The younger is worsted, and brought so low that he abandons the world, and selects this hermitage for his retirement. Here he learns wisdom that is better than riches, and also discovers the buried treasure. Both the elder brother and a king with whom he is at variance are killed in a fight, and the younger is offered a double kingdom. (Chapter I, story II, Eastwick, p. 74; also, Contes et Fables Indiennes de Bidpaï et de Lokman (Galland), Cabinet des Fées, XVII, 122; The Fables of Pilpay, London, 1818, p. 51.)

Percy's ballad is translated by Bodmer, II, 117, and by Knortz, Lieder und Romanzen Alt-Englands, p. 78.

A

Percy MS., p. 71; Hales and Furnivall, I, 174.

1 OFF all the lords in faire Scotland
    A song I will begin;
    Amongst them all there dweld a lord
    Which was the vnthrifty lord of Linne.

2 His father and mother were dead him froe,
    And soe was the head of all his kinne;
    To the cards and dice that he did run
    He did neither cease nor bl[i]nne.

3 To drinke the wine that was soe cleere,
    With euery man he wold make merry;
    And then bespake him Iohn of the Scales,
    Vnto the heire of Linne sayd hee.

4 Sayes, How dost thou, Lord of Linne?
    Doest either want gold or fee?
    Wilt thou not sell thy lands soe brode
    To such a good fellow as me?

5 'Ffor . . I . . ' he said,
    'My land, take it vnto thee;'
    'I draw you to record, my lord[ë]s all;'
    With that he cast him a god's peny.

6 He told him the gold vpon the bord,
    It wanted neuer a bare penny:
    'That gold is thine, the land is mine,
    The heire of Linne I wilbee.'

7 'Heere's gold inoughe,' saithe the heire of
        Linne,
    'Both for me and my company:'
    He drunke the wine that was soe cleere,
    And with euery man he made merry.

8 With-in three quarters of a yeere
    His gold and fee it waxed thinne,
    His merry men were from him gone,
    And left him himselfe all alone.

9 He had neuer a penny left in his pursse,
    Neuer a penny [left] but three,
    And one was brasse, and another was lead,
    And another was white mony.

10 'Now well-aday!' said the heire of Linne,
    'Now welladay, and woe is mee!
    For when I was the lord of Linne,
    I neither wanted gold nor fee.

11 'For I haue sold my lands soe broad,
    And haue not left me one penny;

---

* All the above tales, except Pauli's, have been cited, in one connection or another, by Dunlop, History of Fiction, (II, 201, of Wilson's late edition); by Benfey, Pantschatantra, I, 97 f.; or by Liebrecht, Göttingische Gelehrte Anzeigen, 1868, p. 1891. Oesterley, in his note to Pauli, 16, p. 552 f., refers to three sixteenth-century story-books which I have not seen. Robert, Fables Inédites, etc., II, 232, in his note to La Fontaine, IX, 16, refers to other fabulists. Clouston, Popular Tales and Fictions, II, 55, gives from some old magazine a story after the pattern of the Greek distich.

I must goe now and take some read
 Vnto Edenborrow, and begg my bread.'

12 He had not beene in Edenborrow
 Not three qwarters of a yeere,
But some did giue him, and some said nay,
 And some bid 'to the deele gang yee!

13 'For if we shold hang any landles feer,
 The first we wold begin with thee.'
'Now welladay!' said the heire of Linne,
 'No[w] welladay, and woe is mee!

14 'For now I have sold my lands soe broad,
 That mery man is irke with mee;
But when *that* I was the lord of Linne,
 Then on my land I liued merrily.

15 'And now I have sold my land soe broade
 That I haue not left me one pennye!
God be with my father!' he said,
 'On his land he liued merrily.'

16 Still in a study there as he stood,
 He vnbethought him of [a] bill;
He vnbethought him of [a] bill
 Which his father had left with him.

17 Bade him he shold neuer on it looke
 Till he was in extreame neede,
'And by my faith,' said the heire of Linne,
 'Then now I had neuer more neede.'

18 He tooke the bill, and looked it on,
 Good comfort *that* he found there;
Itt told him of a castle wall
 Where there stood three chests in feare.

19 Two were full of the beaten gold,
 The third was full of white mony;
He turned then downe his baggs of bread,
 And filled them full of gold soe red.

20 Then he did neuer cease nor blinne
 Till Iohn of the Scales house he did winne.
When *that* he came to Iohn of the Scales,
 Vpp at the speere he looked then.

21 There sate three lords vpon a rowe,
 And Iohn o the Scales sate at the bord's
  head,
And Iohn o the Scales sate at the bord's head,
 Because he was the lord of Linne.

22 And then bespake the heire of Linne,
 To Iohn o the Scales' wiffe thus sayd hee:
Sayd, Dame, wilt thou not trust me one shott
 That I may sitt downe in this company?

23 'Now, Christ's curse on my head,' shee said,
 'If I doe trust thee one pennye;'
Then be-spake a good fellowe,
 Which sate by Iohn o the Scales his knee.

24 Said, Haue thou here, thou heire of Linne,
 Forty pence I will lend thee;
Some time a good fellow thou hast beene;
 And other forty if neede bee.

25 Thé dru[n]ken wine *that* was soe cleere,
 And euery man thé made merry;
And then bespake him Iohn o the Scales,
 Vnto the lord of Linne said hee.

26 Said, How doest thou, heire of Linne,
 Since I did buy thy lands of thee?
I will sell it to thee twenty pound better cheepe
 Nor euer I did buy it of thee.

27 'I draw you to recorde, lord[ë]s all,'
 With that he cast him [a] god's penny;
Then he tooke to his baggs of bread,
 And they were full of the gold soe redd.

28 He told him the gold then over the borde,
 It wanted neuer a broad pennye:
'*That* gold is thine, the land is mine,
 And the heire of Linne againe I wilbee.'

29 'Now welladay!' said Iohn o the Scales' wife,
 'Welladay, and woe is me!
Yesterday I was the lady of Linne,
 And now I am but Iohn o the Scales' wiffe!'

30 Saies, Haue thou heere, thou good fellow,
 Forty pence thou did lend me,
Forty pence thou did lend me,
 And forty pound I will giue thee.

31 'Ile make thee keeper of my forrest
 Both of the wild deere and the tame,'
 · · · · · · ·
 · · · · · · ·

32 But then bespake the heire of Linne,
 These were the words, and thus said hee,
Christs curse light vpon my crowne
 If ere my land stand in any ieopardye!

B

a. Buchan's MSS, I, 40. b. Buchan's MSS, II,
114. c. Christie's Traditional Ballad Airs, I, 112.

1 ‘THE bonny heir, and the well-faird heir,
    And the weary heir o Linne,
  Yonder he stands at his father's yetts,
    And naebody bids him come in.

2 ‘ O see for he gangs, an see for he stands,
    The weary heir o Linne !
  O see for he stands on the cauld casey,
    And nae an bids him come in !

3 ‘But if he had been his father's heir,
    Or yet the heir o Linne,
  He wadna stand on the cauld casey,
    Some an woud taen him in.’

4 ‘Sing ower again that sang, nourice,
    The sang ye sung just now ; ’
  ‘I never sung a sang in my life
    But I woud sing ower to you.

5 ‘O see for he gangs, an see for he stands,
    The weary heir o Linne !
  O see for he stands on the cauld casey,
    An nae an bids him come in !

6 ‘But if he had been his father's heir,
    Or yet the heir o Linne,
  He woudna stand on the cauld casye,
    Some an woud taen him in.

7 ‘When his father's lands a selling were,
    His claise lay well in fauld,
  But now he wanders on the shore,
    Baith hungry, weet, and cauld.’

8 As Willie he gaed down the town,
    The gentlemen were drinking ;
  Some bade gie Willie a glass, a glass,
    And some bade him gie nane,
  Some bade gie Willie a glass, a glass,
    The weary heir o Linne.

9 As Willie he came up the town,
    The fishers were a’ sitting ;
  Some bade gie Willie a fish, a fish,
    Some bade gie him a fin,
  Some bade gie him a fish, a fish,
    And lat the palmer gang.

10 He turned him right and round about,
    As will as a woman's son,
  And taen his cane into his hand,
    And on his way to Linne.

11 His nourice at her window lookd,
    Beholding dale and down,
  And she beheld this distressd young man
    Come walking to the town.

12 ‘Come here, come here, Willie,’ she said,
    ‘ And rest yoursel wi me ;
  I hae seen you in better days,
    And in jovial companie.’

13 ‘Gie me a sheave o your bread, nourice,
    And a bottle o your wine,
  And I ’ll pay you it a’ ower again,
    When I ’m the laird o Linne.’

14 ‘Ye ’se get a sheave o my bread, Willie,
    And a bottle o my wine,
  But ye ’ll pay me when the seas gang dry,
    For ye ’ll neer be heir o Linne.’

15 Then he turnd him right and round about,
    As will as woman's son,
  And aff he set, and bent his way,
    And straightway came to Linne.

16 But when he came to that castle,
    They were set down to dine ;
  A score o nobles there he saw,
    Sat drinking at the wine.

17 Then some bade gie him beef, the beef,
    And some bade gie him the bane ;
  And some bade gie him naething at a’,
    But lat the palmer gang.

18 Then out it speaks the new-come laird,
    A saucy word spake hee ;
  ‘Put round the cup, gie my rival a sup,
    Let him fare on his way.’

19 Then out it speaks Sir Ned Magnew,
    Ane o young Willie's kin ;
  ‘This youth was ance a sprightly boy
    As ever lived in Linne.’

20 He turned him right and round about,
    As will as woman's son,
  Then minded him on a little wee key,
    That his mother left to him.

21 His mother left [him] this little wee key
    A little before she died ;
And bade him keep this little wee key
    Till he was in maist need.

22 Then forth he went, these nobles left,
    All drinkin' in the room,
Wi walking rod intill his hand,
    He walked the castle roun.

23 There he found out a little door,
    For there the key slipped in,
And there [he] got as muckle red gowd
    As freed the lands o Linne.

24 Back through the nobles then he went,
    A saucy man was then :
' I 'll take the cup frae this new-come laird,
    For he neer bade me sit down.'

25 Then out it speaks the new-come laird,
    He spake wi mock an jeer ;
' I 'd gie a seat to the laird o Linne,
    Sae be that he were here.

26 ' When the lands o Linne a selling were,
    A' men said they were free ;
This lad shall hae them frae me this day,
    If he 'll gie the third pennie.'

27 ' I take ye witness, nobles a',
    Guide witnesses ye 'll be ;
I 'm promisd the lands o Linne this day,
    If I gie the third pennie.'

28 ' Ye 've taen us witness, Willie,' they said,
    ' Guide witnesses we 'll be ; '

' Buy the lands o Linne who likes,
    They 'll neer be bought by thee.'

29 He 's done him to a gaming-table,
    For it stood fair and clean ;
There he tauld down as much rich gowd
    As freed the lands o Linne.

30 Thus having done, he turnd about,
    A saucy man was he ;
' Take up your monie, my lad,' he says,
    ' Take up your third pennie.

31 ' Aft hae I gane wi barefeet cauld,
    Likewise wi legs full bare,
An mony days walkd at these yetts
    Wi muckle dool and care.

32 ' But now my sorrow 's past and gane,
    And joy 's returned to me,
And here I 've gowd enough forbye,
    Ahin this third pennie.'

33 As Willie he gaed down the town,
    There he crawd wonderous crouse ;
He calld the may afore them a',
    The nourice o the house,

34 ' Come here, come here, my nurse,' he says,
    ' I 'll pay your bread and wine ;
Seas ebb and flow [as] they wont to do,
    Yet I 'm the laird o Linne.'

35 As he gaed up the Gallowgate port,
    His hose abeen his sheen ;
But lang ere he came down again
    Was convoyed by lords fifeteen.

———◆———

A. 2. *The third and fourth lines are fourth and third.*
  3. *There is probably a gap after the second line.*
  5¹. Ffor *wanting : supplied from the bottom of the preceding page.*
  5⁴. a good-se. 7¹. Lime.
  8¹, 9², 12², 18⁴, 19², 21¹. 3. 13¹. Land selfeer.
  16² *has* bis *prefixed to it.* 19¹. 2. 20¹. blime.
  20³. Scalels : *misprint ?* 21² *has* bis *prefixed.*
  20, 21, *are written together.*

24²·⁴, 30²·³. 40. 26³. 20!:. 28⁴, 32¹. Lime.
30² *marked* bis. 30⁴. 40!.
B. a. 9². a; b, all. 14². o your.
  14⁴. But ye 'll : *cf.* b.
  23². For there ; *perhaps simply* For (= Where).
  b. 1 *wanting.* 2³. on that. 2³, 3³, 5³, 6³, causey.
  4¹. that sang again.
  6¹. if ye, *wrongly.* 13, 14 *follow* 6.
  7 *wanting.* 9². were all.
  9⁵. And some : gie 'm. 10–12 *wanting.*

13¹. twa sheaves.   13². And ae glass.

13³. And I will pay you them back again.

13⁴. The day I'm heir of.   14¹. get three sheaves.

14². And twa glass.

14³. But I'll be paid : sea gangs. 14⁴. For ye'll.

15–19 *wanting.*

20¹, ². As Willie was sitting one day alane,
     And nae body him wi.

20³. He minded on.

20⁴. That's mither to him did gie.

20⁵, ⁶. Bade him never open a lock wi it
     Ere the greatest strait he could see.

21, 22 *wanting.*

23. Then he did spy a little wee lock,
     And the key gied linking in,
   And he got goud and money therein
     To pay the lands o Linne.

24–32 *wanting.*

35, 33, 34, *for* 33–35.

33¹, ². When Willie he came to the ha,
     There he cried out wonderous crouse.

34¹. Come down, come down, nourice, he said.

34². Ere I pay you your.

34³. For ye will be paid ere the seas gang dry.

34⁴. For this day I'm heir.

35¹. As Willie he gied down the town.

35³. But when that he came up again.

*Both Motherwell in copying the ballad (which
he in all likelihood received from Buchan),
and Dixon in printing it, made a few changes :
as (Motherwell) the northern for in 2¹, ³, to
whare, but not in 29², where for also=where.*

C. "The editor can trace the air and ballad here
given as far back as 1775, through an aged relative who died in 1842 in her eightieth year,
and who had it from her mother." *Christie
neither professed nor practised a rigid fidelity to texts, and this copy, at best not a valuable one, is given for the little it may be
worth.*

1 O yonder he stands, and there he gangs,
    The weary heir o Linne,
 Yonder he stands on the cauld causey,
    And nane bids him come in.

2 But it fell ance upon a day
    The sheets were laid in fauld,
 And poor Willie found he had nae friends,
    And it was wondrous cauld.

3 'Oh, one sheave o your bread, nourice,
    And one glass o your wine,

And I will pay you oer again
    When I am laird o Linne.'

4 'Oh, one sheave o my bread, Willie,
    And one glass o my wine,
 But the seas will be dry ere ye pay me again,
    For ye'll never be laird o Linne.'

5 But he mind't him up, and he mind't him down,
    And he mind't him oer again,
 And he mind't him on a little wee key
    That his mother gae to him.

6 He did him to the house o Linne,
    He sought it up and down,
 And there he found a little wee door,
    And the key gaed slippin in.

7 And he got gowd, and he got gear,
    He got gowd stord within,
 And he got gowd, and he got gear,
    Thrice worth the lands o Linne.

8 He did him to the tavern straight,
    Where nobles were drinking therein ;
 The greatest noble among them a'
    Was near to Willie o kin.

9 And some of them bade him fish to eat,
    And some of them bade him a fin,
 And some of them bade him nothing at a',
    For he'd never be father's son.

10 But out it spake an aged knicht,
    And vow but he spake slie !
 'I'll sell you your father's land back again
    All for the third pennie.'

11 'I take witness upon you here,' he says,
    'I take witness upon thee,
 That you will sell me my father's land again
    All for the third pennie.'

12 Then he took out a little wee coffer,
    And he set it on his knee,
 And he told the goud down on the table roun,
    Says, Tak up your third pennie.

13 'Come ben, come ben, my good nourice,
    I'll pay you when you come ben ;
 For the seas are not dry, and I'll pay you back
    again,
    For I'm again the laird o Linne.'

14 Poor Willie that night at eight o'clock
    Had his stockings abeen his sheen,
 But ere the morrow at twelve o'clock
    He was convoyd by lords sixteen.

APPENDIX

—◆—

(From a Broadside among Percy's Papers.)

THE DRUNKARD'S LEGACY

IN THREE PARTS

PART I

1 YOUNG people all I pray draw near,
And listen to my ditty here,
Which subject shews that drunkenness
Brings many mortals to distress.

2 As for example now I can
Tell you of one, a gentleman,
Who had a very good estate ;
His earthly travels they were great.

3 We understand he had a son
Who a lewd wicked race did run ;
He daily spent his father's store,
When moneyless he came for more.

4 The father oftentimes with tears
Would sound this alarm in his ears :
' Son, thou dost all thy comforts blast,
And thou wilt come to want at last.'

5 The son these words did little mind ;
To cards and dice he was inclind,
Feeding his drunken appetite
In taverns, which was his delight

6 The father, ere it was too late,
He had a project in his pate,
Before his aged days were gone
To make provision for his son.

7 Near to his house, we understand,
He had a waste plat of land,
Which did but little profit yield,
On which he had a cottage built.

8 ' The Wise-Man's Project ' was its name ;
There was few windows in the same ;
Only one door, substanti[a]l thing,
Shut by a lock went by a spring.

9 Soon after he had playd this trick,
It was his lot for to fall sick ;
As on his bed he did lament,
Then for his drunken son he sent.

10 Who, sent for, came to his bed-side ;
Seeing his son, he then reply'd,
' I sent for you to make my will,
Which do you faithfully fulfil.

11 ' To such one cottage is one door ;
Neer open it, do thou be sure,
Until thou art so poor that all
Do then despise you, great and small.

12 ' For to my grief I do perceive
When I am dead this life you live
Will soon melt all thou hast away :
Do not forget these words, I pray.

13 ' When thou hast made thy friends thy foes,
Pawnd all thy lands, and sold thy cloaths,
Break ope the door, and there depend
To find something thy grief to end.'

14 Thus being spoke, the son did say,
Your dying words I will obey ;
Soon after this his father dear
Did die and buried was, we hear.

PART II

15 Now pray observe the second part,
And you shall hear his sottish heart :
He did in taverns so frequent
Till he three hundred pounds had spent.

16 This being done, we understand
He pawnd the deeds of all his land
Unto a tavern-keeper, who
When poor did him no favour shew.

17 For to fulfil his father's will
He did command this cottage still ;
At length great sorrow was his share,
Quite moneyless, with garments bare.

18 Being not able for to work,
He in the tavern there did lurk,
From box to box, among rich men,
Who often times revil'd him then.

19 To see him sneak so up and down,
The vintner on him he did frown,
And one night kickd him out of door,
Charging him to come there no more.

20 He in a stall did lie all night,
In this most sad and w[r]etched plight ;
Then thought it was high time for he
His father's legacy to see.

21 Next morning, then, opprest with woe,
This young man got an iron crow,
And, as in tears he did lament,
Unto this little cottage went.

22 When he this door had open got,
This poor distressëd drunken sot,
Who did for store of money hope,
He saw a gibbet and a rope.

23 Under this rope was plac'd a stool,
    Which made him look much like a fool,
    Crying, Alas, what shall I do !
    Destruction now appears in view.

24 ' As my father foresaw this thing,
    What sottishness to me would bring,
    As moneyless and free of grace,
    This legacy I will embrace.'

25 So then, opprest with discontent,
    Upon the stool he sighing went,
    And then, his precious life to check,
    Did place this rope about his neck.

26 Crying, Thou God, who sittst on high,
    Who on my sorrows hast an eye,
    But thou knowst I have not done well,
    Preserve my precious soul from hell.

27 ' 'T is true the slighting of thy grace
    Brought me to this most wretched case,
    And as thro folly I 'm undone,
    I 'll now eclipse my morning sun.'

28 When he with sigh had these words spoke,
    Jumpt off, and down the gibbet broke ;
    In falling, as it plain appears,
    Droppd down about this young man's ears,

29 In shining gold, a thousand pound,
    Which made the blood his ears surround :
    Tho in amaze, he cry'd, I 'm sure
    This golden salve will heal the sore.

30 ' Blest be my father,' then he cry'd,
    ' Who did this portion for me hide,
    And while I do alive remain
    I never will be drunk again.'

Part III

31 Now by [the] third part you will hear
    This young man, as it does appear,
    With care he then secur'd his chink,
    And to this vintner went to drink.

32 When the proud vintner did him see,
    He frownd on him immediately,
    And said, Begone, or else with speed
    I 'll kick thee out of doors indeed.

33 With smiles the young man he did say,
    Thou cruel knave, tell me, I pray,
    As I have here consum'd my store,
    What makes thee kick me out of door ?

34 To me thou hast been too severe ;
    The deeds of eight-score pounds a year
    I pawnd them for three hundred pound ;
    Which I spent here ; what makes thee frown ?

35 The vintner said unto him, Sirrah,
    Bring me one hundred pounds tomorrow
    By nine o'clock, take them again :
    So get you out of doors till then.

36 He answerd, If this chink I bring,
    I fear thou wilt do no such thing ;
    He said, I 'll give under mine hand
    A note that I to this will stand.

37 Having the note, away he goes,
    And straightway went to one of those
    Who made him drink when moneyless,
    And did the truth to him confess.

38 They both went to this heap of gold,
    Wherre in a bag he fairly told
    A thousand pounds in yellow boys,
    And to this tavern went their ways.

39 This bag they on the table set,
    Which made the vintner for to fret,
    And said, Young man, this will not do,
    For I was but in jest with you.

40 So then bespoke this young man's friend,
    And [said], Vintner, thou mayst depend
    In law this note it will you cast,
    And he must have his land at last.

41 This made the vintner to comply,
    Who fetchd the deeds immediately ;
    He had one hundred pounds, and then
    The young man got his deeds again.

42 At length, the vintner, for to think
    How he was foold out of his chink,
    Said, When 't is found how I came off
    My neighbours will me game and scoff.

43 So, to prevent their game and laughter,
    The vintner, in a few days after,
    Being void of grace, as will appear,
    He cut his throat from ear to ear.

44 Thus he untimely left the world,
    Who to this young man prov'd a churl ;
    Now he who followd drunkenness
    Lives sober and [does] his lands possess.

45 Instead of wasting all his store,
    As formerly, resolves no more
    To act the same, but does inde[e]d
    Poor fatherless and mother- feed.

46 ' And let all young men, for my sake,
    Take care how you such havock make,
    For drunkenness, you plain may see,
    Was near my ruin for to be.'

Printed and sold in Bow-Church-Yard, London.

268

THE TWA KNIGHTS

Buchan's Ballads of the North of Scotland, II, 271.

A KNIGHT and a squire, sworn brothers, have a talk about fair women. 'There's nae gude women but nine,' says the squire. 'My luck is the better,' replies the knight, 'that one of them is mine.' The squire undertakes to win the knight's wife within six months, if the husband will go over seas for that time; the knight is willing to give him nine months. The knight's lands are wagered (21) against the squire's life (23). As soon as the knight is at sea, the squire comes to the lady with an offer of money. If you were not my lord's brother, says the lady, I would hang you on a pin before my door. The squire betakes himself to his foster-mother, sets forth his case, and offers her a heavy bribe for her aid. The false carline goes to the lady and opens her business; the lady will never wrong her lord. The carline (who is the wife's foster-mother as well) now pretends concern about the lady's health, which is in danger for want of sleep. She turns all the people out of the castle, lulls the dame to sleep, and introduces the squire. He wakes the lady, and tells her that she is in his power. The lady has presence of mind; it would, she says, be a sin to defile her husband's bed, but she will come to the squire's bed at night. She then offers her niece five hundred pounds to go to the squire in her place. The young woman was never so much disposed to say nay, but goes, notwithstanding. When the squire has had his will, he cuts off 'her ring but and her ring-finger.' The maids come from the hay, the young men from the corn, and the lady tells them all that has passed. She will tie her finger in the dark, and hopes to loose it in the light. The knight returns, and is greeted

by the squire as a landless lord. The ring and ring-finger are exhibited in proof. Thereupon the knight gives a dinner, to which he asks the squire and his wife's parents. He throws his charters across the table and bids his wife farewell forever. It is now time for the lady to loose in the light the finger which she had tied in the dark. Come here, my lord, she says. No smith can join a finger. My niece 'beguiled the squire for me.' They lay before the niece a sword and a ring, and she is to have her choice, to stick the squire with the sword, or to wed him with the ring. Thrice she puts out her hand as if to take the sword, but she ends with taking up the ring.

This ballad can have had no currency in Scotland, and perhaps was known only through print. A similar one is strictly traditional in Greece, and widely dispersed, both on the mainland and among the islands.

Romaic. **A.** Νεοελληνικὰ' Ἀνάλεκτα, I, 80, No 16, 75 vv., Melos. **B.** 'Τὸ στοίχημα τοῦ βασιλιᾶ καὶ τοῦ Μαυριανοῦ,' Jeannaraki, p. 231, No 294, 76 vv., Crete. **C.** 'Ὁ Μαυριανὸς καὶ ὁ βασιλεύς,' Zampelios, p. 719, No 6, 61 vv., Corcyra (?); repeated in Passow, p. 355, No 474, Kind's Anthologie, p. 56. **D.** 'Τοῦ Μαυριανο-πούλου,' Manousos, II, 56, 51 vv., Corcyra (?). **E.** 'Ὁ Μαυριανὸς κ' ὁ βασιλεᾶς,' Pappadopoulos in Πανδώρα, XV, 417, 23 vv., Cargese, Corsica; repeated in Legrand, p. 302, No 136. **F.** Δελτίον τῆς ἱστορικῆς καὶ ἐθνολογικῆς ἑταιρίας τῆς Ἑλλάδος, I, 551, No 5, 35 vv., Peloponnesus. **G.** 'Ὁ Σταυριανὸς καὶ ὁ βασιλιᾶς,' Melandrakes, in the same, III, 345, 54 vv., Patmos. **H.** 'Τὸ Στοίχημα,' Kanellakes, Χιακὰ ἀνάλεκτα, p. 8, No 5, 50 vv., Chios. **I** a. Bartholdy, Bruch-stücke zur nähern Kenntniss des heutigen

Griechenlands, 1805, p. 434, 78 vv., translation without text. b. 'Maurogène,' Lemercier, I, 167, translation without text, neighborhood of Arta. J. 'Στοίχημα Διονῦ καὶ Χαντσαρλῆ,' Chasiotes, p. 142, No 14, 26 vv., Epirus.

The personages are Μαυριανός, B-E, Μαυγιανός, A, Mavrogeni, I, Σταυριανός, G, Γιάννος, F, Κωσταντῆς, H; his sister, A-I, 'Αρετή, D, Μάρω, F, Λιερή, G, and in I b (unless the name is supplied by the editor), Cymodore; a king, anonymous except in J, Διονύς, in which also the other two parties are husband (ὁ χαντσιαρλῆς, the chancellor) and wife.

At the king's table there is talk of women fair or foul. Maurianos extols his sister (the chancellor his wife, I), whom gifts cannot seduce. What shall be your forfeit, asks the king, if I seduce her? Maurianos stakes his head, A-I, and the girl is to be the king's slave, H; the king, his kingdom and crown, A, B, his property, C, F. There is a mutual wager of nine towers of silver, J. The young man is to be a prisoner till the morning, I. The king begins, in A, B, by engaging the services of witches eighteen, witches fifteen, or bawds eighteen, witches fifteen. They ply their magic early and late: forty days to get up her stair, other four-and-forty to get sight of the girl, A. They address her with flatteries, but are rebuffed, A, B. The king sends rich presents, A, C-I; beasts laden with silver and money, nine, twelve, twenty and again ten. The girl receives them with professions of pleasure; her brother will return the compliment to the giver. It is explained that no return is looked for; the presents are from the king, who desires to pass the night with her. (In J the king goes straight to the wife, and says that he has her husband's permission.) The lady affects to put herself at the king's disposition. She appeals to her maid-servants, A, B; first her "nurses," then her maids, C; one servant, and then another, H. Which of them will enable her to keep her word, change clothes with her, and pass the night with the king? Only Maria, the youngest of all (of forty, B), is willing to stead her mistress in this strait, A-C. In D-G, I, J, there is but one nurse or servant, and she as-

sents, or follows her mistress's directions as a matter of course. The servant is to have the king's present in D. The substitute is elaborately combed and dressed, with a gold band round her hair, and a beautiful ring on her finger. At midnight, or before dawn, the king cuts off the finger that has the ring, A, I, her finger, B, F, G, H (fingers, B, v. 43), little finger, D, E; takes the ring from her finger, C, all the rings from her fingers, J. He also cuts off her hair (braid), with its golden band, B (braids, v. 43), C, I, her hair (braid), with the golden flowers, A, with the pearl, H, right braid, D, braid, F, G, I, extremity of her braid, E. These are to serve as tokens; he puts them in his handkerchief, A, D. He takes his trophies to the assembly. Maurianos has lost his wager, and is to be hanged. Where is Maurianos, the braggart, and where his precious sister, whom no gifts could seduce? Word comes to the sister. She dresses herself beautifully, and makes her way into the assembly; she would fain know why they are to hang Maurianos. 'I have seduced his sister,' says the king, 'and I will hang Maurianos.' The girl demands tokens. 'I cut off her finger, with the golden sapphire; I cut off her hair, with the golden flowers (band).' She extends her hand; the earth is filled with sapphires. 'See, lords! are fingers of mine wanting?' She flings out her hair; the earth is filled with flowers. 'See, lords! is a braid of mine wanting?' (A, B, and the rest to the same effect.) Then she turns to the king. 'It fits you no more to play the king,' A, B. 'You have slept with my slave, and my slave you shall be,' C-I. 'Take my mule and go fetch wood.' In A, B, the king has to marry Maria. In F, John becomes king (as a consequence of winning the wager). In I, the people depose the king and make Maurianos's sister queen.

There are numerous tales in which a man wagers heavily upon a woman's (generally his wife's) constancy, and, upon plausible evidence, which in the end proves to be nugatory, is adjudged to have lost.* We are con-

---

* The cutting off the hair from a woman substituted occurs in the fabliau 'Des Tresces,' Barbazan et Méon, IV, 393,

cerned only with a small section of these stories, characterized by the circumstances that the woman whose virtue is questioned puts another woman in her place in the encounter with the assailant, and that the proofs of success offered are a finger, finger-ring, and head, or braid, of hair * (one of these, or more).

A rhymed tale of the thirteenth century, ' Von zwein Kaufmannen,' by Ruprecht von Würzburg,† has the following story, evidently French by origin. Bertram, a merchant of Verdun, who has been happily married for ten years, is required in the course of business to go to a fair at Provins. While he is sitting at table in an inn with other merchants, Hogier, the host, sets his guests to talking of their wives, and three of them give a very bad account of their domestic experiences. Bertram, when urged to take his turn, professes himself the most fortunate of men, for his wife (Irmengard) is, for beauty, sense, modesty, manners, the flower of womankind. The host declares that the man is mad, and offers to stake all his goods against Bertram's that he will seduce this peerless wife within six months. The wager is accepted, and Bertram, to afford an opportunity, sends his wife word that he shall be gone from home longer than he had intended. Hogier goes to Verdun and takes a lodging opposite to Bertram's house. He begins with presents and messages to Irmengard; she treats these with con-

tempt, and threatens to make a complaint to her friends. He gives bounties to the servants, who sing his praises to their mistress till they are told that they will be thrashed if they continue. He then gives a pound to Irmengard's favorite maid, Amelin, and commissions her to offer a hundred mark if he may have his will ; and the wife proving to be both firm and indignant, he raises his offer to two hundred mark, and finally to a thousand for one night. Not only the maid, but Irmengard's own father and her husband's father, to whom she successively appeals, urge her to take this large sum, and assure her that she will incur her husband's resentment if she does not. A way out of her difficulties now occurs to her (which the author of the poem represents as an express suggestion from God). She asks the maid if she will give Hogier a night for the consideration of a hundred mark ; Amelin is ready so to do for half the money. Hogier is told to pay in his thousand, and an appointment is made. Irmengard receives him in Amelin's garb, and Amelin in Irmengard's. In the morning Hogier asks for some jewel as a keepsake, and the maid having nothing to give him, he cuts off one of her fingers. He now calls upon Bertram to pay his forfeit. Bertram has some doubt whether he has not been tricked. It is mutually agreed that the matter shall be settled at a banquet which Bertram is to give at Verdun. Ber-

---

Montaiglon et Raynaud, IV, 67, and Méon, Nouveau Recueil, I, 343, Montaiglon et Raynaud, V, 132 (a different version) ; Boccaccio, Decameron, VII, 8 ; ' Der verkêrte Wirt,' von der Hagen's Gesammtabenteuer, II, 337, No 43 : all varieties of one story. See also ' Der Reiger,' p. 157 of the same volume of von der Hagen, No 31, and the literary history of No 43, at p. XLII. — Bédier, Les Fabliaux, p. 149 ff., refers to several other examples.

* The more important of the stories which lack the distinctive traits of the Scottish and Romaic ballads are : Roman de la Violette, thirteenth century (ed. Michel, 1834) ; Roman du Comte de Poitiers, thirteenth century (ed. Michel, 1831) ; Li Contes du Roi Flore et de la bielle Jehane, thirteenth century, Moland et d'Héricault, 1856, p. 85, and Monmerqué et Michel, Théâtre Français au Moyen Age, 1842, p. 417 ; Miracle de Nostre Dame, Conment Ostes, roy d'Espaingne, perdi sa terre par gagier contre Berengier, etc., Monmerqué et Michel, as before, p. 431, and Miracles de Nostre Dame, G. Paris et U. Robert, IV, 319 ; an episode in Perceforest, vol. iv, cc. 16, 17, retold by Bandello, Part I, Nov. 21 (R. Köhler, in Jahrbuch für Rom. u. Eng. Lit., VIII, 51 ff.) ;

the story of Bernabò da Genova da Ambruogiuolo ingannato, Boccaccio, Decameron, II, 9, repeated in Shakspere's Cymbeline and many other pieces. Popular tales with the wager are : Campbell, West Highlands, II, 1, No 18 ; J. W. Wolf's Deutsche Hausmärchen, p. 355 ; Simrock, Deutsche Märchen, p. 235 (ed. 1864), No 51 ; Pröhle, Kinder- und Volksmärchen, No 61, p. 179 (see also p. XLII) ; Das Ausland, 1856, p. 1053, Roumanian ; Miklosich, Märchen u. Lieder der Zigeuner der Bukowina, p. 49, No 14 ; Bernoni, Fiabe veneziane, p. 1, No 1 ; Gonzenbach, I, 38, No 7 ; Pitrè, Fiabe, Novelle e Racconti siciliani, II, 142, 165, Nos 73, 75 ; Imbriani, Novellaja fiorentina, p. 483. (Some of these have been cited by Köhler, some by Landau.) See, in general, the Grimms, Altdeutsche Wälder, I, 35 ff., II, 181 f. ; von der Hagen's Gesammtabenteuer, introduction to No LXVIII, especially III, XCI–CIX ; R. Köhler, as above, and in Orient u. Occident, II, 315 ; Landau, Quellen des Dekameron, 1884, p. 135 ff. ; R. Ohle, Shakespeares Cymbeline und seine romanischen Vorläufer, Berlin, 1890.

† Altdeutsche Wälder, I, 35 ; von der Hagen, Gesammtabenteuer, III, 357.

tram, upon his return home, cannot conceal a deep depression. His wife asks him the cause, and he opens his mind to her; she bids him be of good cheer, for all Hogier's goods are theirs. At the banquet Hogier states his case, and produces the finger in confirmation of his claim. Irmengard, asked what answer she has to make, humorously replies that she is sorry for her misbehavior, but all her friends, there present, had advised her to commit it. She then shows her hands, both unmarred. Amelin comes in and complains of the treatment she has received. Hogier owns that he has lost, and desires to become Bertram's 'poor man.' Amelin is given him as wife, with her hundred mark for a dowry. Here we have wager, substitution, finger cut off, as in the Scottish ballad and most of the Romaic versions, and the loser marries the maid, as in the Scottish ballad and Romaic A, B.

The Mabinogi of Taliesin, "in its present form not older than the thirteenth century," has the incidents of the substitution of the maid-servant, the finger and finger-ring, with the modification that the wife's general high character, and not simply her continence, is impugned and vindicated.

At a Christmas feast in the palace of King Maelgwn, the company were discoursing of the unequalled felicity of the king, upon whom heaven had bestowed, with every other good gift, a queen whose virtues exceeded those of all the noble ladies in the kingdom. Elphin, Maelgwn's nephew, said, None but a king may vie with a king; otherwise he would say that his own wife was as virtuous as any lady in the kingdom. Maelgwn was not there to hear this boast, but it was duly reported to him, and he ordered Elphin to be thrown into prison, pending a test of Elphin's wife which he deputed his graceless son, Rhun, to make. Taliesin, Elphin's bard, warned the lady that Rhun would try to put some disgrace upon her, and advised that one of the servants should personate her mistress when Rhun came to the house. Accordingly, a kitchen-maid was dressed up in her mistress's clothes, and was seated at the supper-table, her hands loaded with rings. Rhun made his appear-

ance and was welcomed by the disguised menial. He fell to jesting with her, put a powder into her drink, which cast her into a sound sleep, and cut off her little finger, on which was Elphin's signet-ring. The king assembled his councillors, had Elphin brought in from prison, and showed him the finger, which (so Rhun had averred) had been cut from his wife's hand the preceding night, while she was sunk in a drunken sleep. Elphin could not deny that the ring was his, but he gave three incontrovertible reasons why the finger could not be his wife's, one of these being that the ring was too large to stay on his wife's thumb, yet too small to go over the joint of the little finger of the hand from which it had been cut; and the fact was put beyond question by Taliesin's afterwards bringing in Elphin's wife at a state-dinner, and displaying her unmutilated hand.[*]

A lively play of Jakob Ayrer's (about 1600) has the wager, the substitution, the ring offered in evidence (as in Romaic C, G), the marriage with the maid.

Claudius, master of the hunt to the Prince of Calabria, on the eve of his departure on a voyage, is heard by two courtiers, Leipolt and Seübolt, soliloquizing on the excellences of his wife, Frigia, her housekeeping, virtue, and love for him. They wager all their goods against his that they will bring the woman to do their will. One undertakes to present her wedding-ring, the other her necklace, in proof of the achievement. Leipolt and Seübolt, always acting severally, attempt to buy the services of Jahn Türck, a quick-witted and loyal servant of Claudius. He tells everything to his mistress, and by his advice she dresses two of her maids in her clothes and lets them meet the men, warning them to keep within bounds. Leipolt and Seübolt, each finding the supposed lady coy, are content to secure the means of winning their wager, and, by Frigia's connivance (who, it seems, had come to knowledge of the wager through Jahn), one of them receives her ring,

* Lady Charlotte Guest's Mabinogion, Part VII, pp. 364–83, or p. 477 ff. of the edition of 1877 ; an abstract in E. Jones's Bardic Museum, p. 19.

the other her necklace, as pretended love-tokens. Claudius comes home. Leipolt informs the prince of the wager, and asks Claudius whether he knows the ring and will pay; Seübolt brings out the necklace. Claudius gives all for lost. The prince sends for Frigia. She challenges the courtiers to say that she has misbehaved with them. They own that they have never laid eyes on her, but they recognize the maids when they are brought in, still in their mistress's clothes. Frigia explains in detail. The prince addresses his councillors (for such they are) in terms of exemplary severity, and adjudges them to marry the maids, making over one third of their property to these and another to Claudius, or to lose their heads. (Compare the Scottish ballad at the end.) They prefer to keep their heads.*

A Danish ballad, very popular in the sixteenth and seventeenth centuries, has the wager (only on the part of the assailant), but the story takes a different turn from the foregoing, for the irresistible knight has simply a conversation with the lady, in which he meets with a definitive repulse.

'Væddemaalet,' 'Herr Lave og Herr Iver Blaa,' Grundtvig, IV, 302, No 224, A-L, Kristensen, I, 319, No 118, X, 137, No 36;

Prior, III, 28, No 104. Lange (Lave) and Peder (Iver) sit at the board talking of wives and fair maids. Peder asserts that the maid lives not in the world whom he cannot cajole with a word. Lange knows the maid so virtuous that neither words nor gold can beguile. Peder wagers life (gold, goods, house, land) and neck (halsbane) that she shall be his by the morrow. He rides straightway to Ingelil, Thorlof's daughter, and makes love to her in honorable phrase. Ingelil reminds him of two ladies who have received the same professions from him and been betrayed. If she will be his dear, every finger shall wear the red gold: her father has nine gold rings, and would give them all to her if she wished. If she will be his, she shall have a train of servants, out and in: she is not halt or blind, and can go out and in by herself. If he cannot have his will with her, it will cost him his white halsbane: much better so than that he should cheat her, or any honorable maid. Peder rides away sorrowful, for lost is gold and his white halsbane besides.† We have already had the Scottish counterpart of this ballad, with variations for better or worse, in 'Redesdale and Wise William,' IV, 383, No 246, A-C.

---

1 THERE were twa knights in fair Scotland,
   And they were brothers sworn;
   They made a vow to be as true
   As if they'd been brothers born.

2 The one he was a wealthy knight,
   Had lands and buildings free;
   The other was a young hynde squire,
   In rank of lower degree.

3 But it fell ance upon a day
   These squires they walkd alone,

And to each other they did talk
About the fair women.

4 'O wed a may,' the knight did say,
   'For your credit and fame;
   Lay never your love on lemanry,
   Bring nae gude woman to shame.'

5 'There's nae gude women,' the squire did say,
   'Into this place but nine;'
   'O well falls me,' the knight replied,
   'For ane o them is mine.'

---

* Ayrers Dramen, herausgegeben von A. von Keller, IV, 2279, No 30; Comedia von zweyen fürstlichen räthen die alle beede umb eines gewetts willen umb ein weib bulten, u. s. w.

† There is another Danish ballad in which two knights

wager on a maid's fidelity, but it is of entirely different tenor, the maid being lured by a magical horn: 'Ridderens Runeslag,' Grundtvig, II, 285, No 73, A-B, 'Ridder Oles Lud,' Kristensen, II, 108, 353, No 34, A-C; Prior, III, 34, No 105.

6 'Ye say your lady 's a gude woman,
  But I say she is nane ;
I think that I could gain her love
  Ere six months they are gane.

7 'If ye will gang six months away,
  And sail upon the faem,
Then I will gain your lady's love
  Before that ye come hame.'

8 'O I 'll gang till a far countrie,
  And far beyond the faem,
And ye winna gain my lady's love
  Whan nine lang months are gane.'

9 When the evening sun did set,
  And day came to an end,
In then came the lady's gude lord,
  Just in at yon town's end.

10 'O comely are ye, my lady gay,
   Sae fair and rare to see ;
I wish whan I am gane away
   Ye keep your mind to me.'

11 She gae 'm a bason to wash in,
   It shin'd thro a' the ha ;
But aye as she gaed but and ben
   She loot the saut tears fa.

12 'I wonder what ails my gude lord
   He has sic jealousie ;
Never when we parted before,
   He spak sic words to me.'

13 When cocks did craw, and day did daw,
   This knight was fair at sea ;
Then in it came the young hynde squire,
   To work him villanie.

14 'I hae a coffer o gude red gowd,
   Another o white monie ;
I woud gie you 't a', my gay lady,
   To lye this night wi me.'

15 'If ye warna my lord's brother,
   And him sae far frae hame,
Even before my ain bower-door
   I 'd gar hang you on a pin.'

16 He 's gane frae the lady's bower,
   Wi the saut tear in his ee,

And he is to his foster-mother
  As fast as gang coud he.

17 'There is a fancy in my head
   That I 'll reveal to thee,
And your assistance I will crave
   If ye will grant it me.

18 'I 've fifty guineas in my pocket,
   I 've fifty o them and three,
And if ye 'll grant what I request
   Ye 'se hae them for your fee.'

19 'Speak on, speak on, ye gude hynde squire,
   What may your asking be ?
I kenna wha woud be sae base
   As nae serve for sic a fee.'

20 'O I hae wagerd wi my brother,
   When he went to the faem,
That I woud gain his lady's love
   Ere six months they were gane.

21 'To me he laid his lands at stake
   Tho he were on the faem,
I wudna gain his lady's love
   Whan nine lang months were gane.

22 'Now I hae tried to gain her love,
   But finds it winna do ;
And here I 'm come, as ye her know,
   To seek some help frae you.

23 'For I did lay my life at stake,
   Whan my brother went frae hame,
That I woud gain his lady's love
   Whan he was on the faem.'

24 But when the evening sun was set,
   And day came to an end,
In it came that fause carline,
   Just in at yon town's end.

25 'O comely are ye, my gay lady,
   Your lord is on the faem ;
Yon unco squire will gain your love,
   Before that he come hame.'

26 'Forbid it,' said the lady fair,
   'That eer the like shoud be,
That I woud wrang my ain gude lord,
   And him sae far at sea.'

27 'O comely are ye, my gay lady,
  Stately is your fair bodie;
Your lovely visage is far chang'd,
  That is best known to me.

28 'You 're sair dune out for want o sleep
  Sin your lord went to sea;
Unless that ye do cease your grief,
  It will your ruin be.

29 'You 'll send your maids unto the hay,
  Your young men unto the corn;
I 'll gar ye sleep as soun a sleep
  As the night that ye were born.'

30 She sent her maids to ted the hay,
  Her men to shear the corn,
And she gard her sleep as soun a sleep
  As the night that she was born.

31 She rowd that lady in the silk,
  Laid her on holland sheets;
Wi fine enchanting melodie,
  She lulld her fast asleep.

32 She lockd the yetts o that castle
  Wi thirty locks and three,
Then went to meet the young hynde squire
  To him the keys gae she.

33 He 's opend the locks o that castle,
  Were thirty and were three,
And he 's gane where that lady lay,
  And thus to her said he.

34 'O wake, O wake, ye gay lady,
  O wake and speak to me;
I hae it fully in my power
  To come to bed to thee.'

35 'For to defile my husband's bed,
  I woud think that a sin;
As soon as this lang day is gane,
  Then I shall come to thine.'

36 Then she has calld her niece Maisry,
  Says, An asking ye 'll grant me,
For to gang to yon unco squire
  And sleep this night for me.

37 'The gude red gowd shall be your hire,
  And siller 's be your fee;

Five hundred pounds o pennies round,
  Your tocher it shall be.'

38 She turnd her right and round about,
  And thus to her did say;
O there was never a time on earth
  So fain 's I woud say nay.

39 But when the evening sun was set,
  And day drawn to an end,
Then Lady Maisry she is gane,
  Fair out at yon town-end.

40 Then she is to yon hynde squire's yates,
  And tirled at the pin;
Wha was sae busy as the hynde squire
  To lat that lady in!

41 He 's taen her in his arms twa,
  He was a joyfu man;
He neither bade her meat nor drink,
  But to the bed he ran.

42 When he had got his will o her,
  His will as he lang sought,
Her ring but and her ring-finger
  Away frae her he brought.

43 With discontent straight home she went,
  And thus lamented she;
Says, Wae be to yon young hynde squire!
  Sae ill as he 's used me.

44 When the maids came frae the hay,
  The young men frae the corn,
Ben it came that lady gay,
  Who thought lang for their return.

45 'Where hae ye been, my maidens a',
  Sae far awa frae me?
My foster-mother and lord's brother
  Thought to hae beguiled me.

46 'Had not she been my foster-mother,
  I suckd at her breast-bane,
Even before my ain bower-door,
  She in a gleed shoud burn.

47 'The squire he thought to gain my love,
  He 's got but Lady Maisry;
He 's cutted her ring and her ring-finger,
  A love-token for to be.

48 'I 'll tie my finger in the dark,
     Where nae ane shall me see;
I hope to loose it in the light,
     Amang gude companie.'

49 When night was gane, and birds did sing,
     And day began to peep,
The hynde squire walkd alang the shore,
     His brother for to meet.

50 'Ye are welcome, welcome, landless lord,
     To my ha's and my bowers;
Ye are welcome hame, ye landless lord,
     To my lady white like flowers.'

51 'Ye say I am a landless lord,
     But I think I am nane,
Without ye show some love-token
     Awa frae her ye 've tane.'

52 He drew the strings then o his purse,
     And they were a' bludie;
The ring but and the ring-finger
     Sae soon as he lat him see.

53 'O wae be to you, fause hynde squire,
     Ane ill death mat ye dee!
It was too sair a love-token
     To take frae my ladie.

54 'But ae asking of you, hynde squire,
     In your won bowers to dine;'
'With a' my heart, my brother dear,
     Tho ye had asked nine.'

55 Then he is to his lady's father,
     And a sorrow man was he:
'O judge, O judge, my father dear,
     This judgment pass for me.

56 'What is the thing that shoud be done
     Unto that gay lady
Who woud gar her lord gae landless,
     And children bastards to be?'

57 'She shoud be brunt upon a hill,
     Or hangd upon a tree,
That woud gar her lord gang landless,
     And children bastards be.'

58 'Your judgment is too rash, father;
     Your ain daughter is she
That this day has made me landless;
     Your squire gaind it frae me.

59 'Yet nevertheless, my parents dear,
     Ae favour ye 'll grant me,
And gang alang to my lost ha's,
     And take your dine wi me.'

60 He threw the charters ower the table,
     And kissd the yates o tree;
Says, Fare ye well, my lady gay,
     Your face I 'll never see.

61 Then his lady calld out to him,
     Come here, my lord, and dine;
There 's nae a smith in a' the land
     That can ae finger join.

62 'I tied my finger in the dark,
     Whan nae ane did me see;
But now I 'll loose it in the light,
     Amang gude companie.

63 'Even my niece, Lady Maisry,
     The same woman was she;
The gude red gowd shall be her hire,
     And likeways white monie.

64 'Five hundred pounds o pennies round
     Her tocher then shall be,
Because she did my wills obey,
     Beguild the squire for me.'

65 Then they did call this young hynde squire
     To come right speedilie,
Likeways they calld young Lady Maisry.
     To pay her down her fee.

66 Then they laid down to Lady Maisry
     The brand but and the ring;
It was to stick him wi the brand,
     Or wed him wi the ring.

67 Thrice she minted to the brand,
     But she took up the ring;
And a' the ladies who heard o it
     Said she was a wise woman.

269

LADY DIAMOND

A. 'Lady Daisy,' Aytoun's Ballads of Scotland, II, 173, 1859.

B. 'Lady Dayisie,' from an old lady's collection formerly in possession of Sir Walter Scott,* now belonging to Mr Macmath, Edinburgh.

C. Sharpe's Ballad Book, p. 12, 1823.

D. 'Lady Diamond,' Buchan's MSS, II, 164; 'Lady Diamond, the King's Daughter,' Buchan's Ballads of the North of Scotland, II, 206; 'Ladye Diamond,' Dixon, Scottish Traditional Versions of Ancient Ballads, p. 71, Percy Society, vol. xvii.

E. 'Robin, the Kitchie-Boy,' Joseph Robertson, "Adversaria," p. 66.

DIAMOND (Daisy, Dysmal, Dysie), only daughter of a great king, is with child by a very bonny kitchen-boy. The base-born paramour is put to death, and, by the king's order, his heart is taken to the princess in a cup of gold. She washes it with the tears which run into the cup, A, B, C, and dies of her grief. Her father has a sharp remorse, A, C; his daughter's shame looks pardonable, when he considers the beauty of the man he has slain, A.

B is blended with 'Willie o Winsbury,' No 100; cf. B 4–9, and No 100, A 2–7, B 1–5, etc. In 'Willie o Winsbury', B, the princess's name is Dysmill. A 12, B 11 of 'Lady Diamond' also recall 'Willie o Winsbury.'

In C, D, the kitchen-boy is smothered between two feather-beds.

Isbel was the princess's name in a copy obtained by Motherwell, but not preserved. Motherwell's Note-Book, p. 7; C. K. Sharpe's Correspondence, II, 328.

The ballad is one of a large number of repetitions of Boccaccio's tale of Guiscardo and Ghismonda, Decamerone, IV, 1. This tale was translated in Painter's Palace of Pleasure, 1566 (ed. Jacobs, I, 180), and became the foundation of various English poems and plays.† Very probably it was circulated in a

chap-book edition in Great Britain, as it was in Germany (Simrock, Volksbücher, VI, 153).

Prince Tancredi has an only daughter (cf. A, B, C, 1), whose name is Ghismonda (Diamond, C, Dysmal, B, Dysie, D, Daisy, A). She has a secret amour with a young man of inferior condition (valetto, di nazione assai umile; giovane di vilissima condizione, says Tancredi), sunk in the ballad to the rank of kitchen-boy. This young man, Guiscardo, is, however, distinguished for manners and fine qualities; indeed, superior in these to all the nobles of the court. In the ballad he is a very bonny boy (preferred to dukes and earls, B, C). Guiscardo is strangled (or suffocated); the bonny boy is smothered between two feather-beds in B 8, C 7. The bonny boy's heart is cut out and sent to the king's daughter in a cup of gold, in the ballad; she washes it with the tears that run from her eyes into the cup. Ghismonda, receiving Guiscardo's heart in a gold cup, sheds a torrent of tears over it, pours a decoction of poisonous herbs into the cup (ove il cuore era da molte delle sue lagrime lavato), and drinks all off, then lies down on her bed and awaits her death. Tancredi, repenting too late of his cruelty, has the pair buried with honors in one tomb.‡

Italian. A. 'Il padre crudele,' Widter und

---

* See a letter from Scott to C. K. Sharpe, in Mr Allardyce's edition of Sharpe's letters, II, 264.

† See Dunlop's History of Fiction, ed. Wilson, II, 91; von der Hagen's Gesammtabenteuer, I, cxxii f.; Clarence Sher-

wood, Die neu-englischen Bearbeitungen der Erzählung Boccaccios von Ghismonda und Guiscardo, Berlin, 1892; Varnhagen in Literaturblatt, December, 1892, p. 412 ff.

‡ The too late repentance and the burial of the two lovers

Wolf, Volkslieder aus Venetien, p. 72, No 93. A king has an only daughter, Germonia. She has twelve servants to wait upon her, and other twelve to take her to school, and she falls in love with the handsomest, Rizzardo. They talk together, and this is reported to the king by Rizzardo's fellow-servants. The king shuts Rizzardo up in a room, bandages his eyes, cuts his heart out, puts it in a gold basin, and carries it to his daughter. 'Take this basin,' he says; 'take this fine mess, Rizzardo's heart is in it.' Germonia reproaches him for his cruelty; he tells her, if he has done her an offence, to take a knife and do him another. She does not care to do this; however, if he were abed, she would. In a variant, she goes out to a meadow, and 'poisons herself with her own hands.'

B. 'Flavia,' Sabatini, Saggio di Canti popolari romani, in Rivista di Letteratura popolare, Rome, 1877, p. 17 f., and separately, 1878, p. 8 f. Flavia has thirteen servants, and becomes enamored of one of these, Ggismónno. His fellows find out that the pair have been communing, and inform the king. 'Ságra coróna' orders them to take Ggismónno to prison, and put him to death. They seat him in a chair of gold, and dig out his heart, lay the heart in a basin of gold, and carry it to Flavia, sitting at table, saying, Here is a mess for you. She retires to her chamber, lies down on her bed, and drinks a cup of poison.

C. 'Risguardo belo e Rismonda bela,' Bernoni, Tradizioni pop. veneziane, p. 39. A count has an only daughter, Rismonda. She has twelve servants, and falls in love with the handsomest, who waits at table, — the handsome Risguardo. She asks him to be her lover; he cannot, for if her father should come to know of such a thing he would put him to death in prison. The knowledge comes to the father, and Risguardo is put into prison. One of his fellows looks him up after a fortnight, and after a month cuts out his heart, and takes it to Rismonda; 'here is a fine dish, the heart of Risguardo.' Rismonda, who is

in one grave occur, also, in Decameron, IV, 9, presently to be spoken of.

sitting at table, goes to her chamber; her father comes to console her; she bids him leave her. If I have done you wrong, he says, take this sword and run it through me. She is not disposed to do this; she will write three letters and die.

All these come from the Decameron, IV, 1. The lover is sunk to a serving-man, as in the Scottish ballad. The names are fairly well preserved in A, C; in B the lover gets his name from the princess, and she is provided with one from the general stock.

Swedish. 'Hertig Fröjdenborg och Fröken Adelin,' broadside, 48 stanzas, Stockholm, 1757; Afzelius, I, 95, No 19, ed. Bergström och Höijer, I, 81, No 18, 47 sts; Lagus, Nyländska Folkvisor, I, 30, No 8 a, 47 sts; Djurklou, Ur Nerikes Folkspråk, p. 96, 22 sts; Dybeck, Runa, 1869, p. 34, 37 sts, of which only 8 are given; Lagus, as above, b, 2 sts, c, 1 st.; Aminson, Bidrag, I, 1st heft, p. 31, No 6, 2d heft, p. 16, 1 st. each; unprinted fragments, noted by Olrik, Danmarks gamle Folkeviser, V, II, 216 f. The broadside is certainly the source or basis of all the printed copies, and probably of an unpublished fragment of twenty-eight stanzas obtained by Eva Wigström in 1882 (Olrik); some trifling variations are attributable to editing or to tradition.

Adelin is in the garden, making a rose chaplet for Fröjdenborg, who, seeing her from his window, goes to her and expresses the wish that she were his love. Adelin begs him not to talk so; she fears that her father may overhear. False maid-servants tell the king that Fröjdenborg is decoying his daughter; the king orders him to be put in chains and shut up in the dark tower. There he stays fifteen years. Adelin goes to the garden to make Fröjdenborg a garland again. The king sees from his window what she is about, orders her into his presence (he has not cared to see her for fifteen years), and angrily demands what she has been doing in the garden. She says that she has been making a rose garland for Fröjdenborg. 'Not forgotten him yet?' 'No; nor should I, if I lived a hundred years.' 'Then I will put a stop to this love.'

Fröjdenborg is taken out of the tower; his hair and beard are gray, but he declares that the fifteen years have seemed to him only a few days. They bind Fröjdenborg to a tree, and kill him as boors slaughter cattle. They lay him on a board, and gut (slit) him as boors gut (slit) a fish. The false maids take his heart and dress the lady a dainty dish. She has a misgiving, and asks what she has eaten. They tell her it is her lover's heart; then, she says, it shall be my last meal. She asks for drink: she will drink to Fröjdenborg, she will drink herself dead. Her heart breaks; word is carried to her father; God a mercy! he cries, I have betrayed my only child. The two are buried in one grave, from which springs a linden; the linden grows over the church ridge; one leaf enfolds the other.

Danish. 'Hertug Frydenborg,' in about forty copies from recent tradition and a broadside of the eighteenth century, but not found in old manuscripts: Olrik, Danmarks gamle Folkeviser, V, II, 216, No 305, **H-A**, and Kristensen, XI, 117, No 46. Of these, **E i**, obtained in 1809, had been printed by Nyerup og Rasmussen, Udvalg af danske Viser, II, 238, No 71. Others are in Kristensen's Skattegraveren, I, 33, No 113, III, 148, Nos 835–38, and in Kristensen's Jyske Folkeminder, II, 207, No 61 **A-D** ('Ridderens Hjærte'), and X, 213, 385, 360, No 52 **A-E**, No 94 **B**.

One half of these texts, as Olrik remarks, are of Swedish origin, and even derived from the Swedish broadside; others have marks of their own, and one in particular, which indicates the ultimate source of the story in both the Swedish and the Danish ballad. This source appears to be the Decameron, IV, 1, as in the Scottish and Italian ballads. The points of resemblance are: A princess, an only daughter, has a lover; her father disapproves, and throws the lover into prison (where he remains fifteen years in the ballad, only a day or two in the tale). The lover is taken from

prison and put to death, and his heart is cut out. (The heart is not sent to the princess in a golden vessel, as in the Decameron, IV, 1, and the Scottish and Italian ballads, but is cooked, and given her to eat, and is eaten; and she says, when informed that she has eaten her lover's heart, that it shall be her last food.) In most of the Scandinavian ballads the princess calls for wine (mead), and 'drinks herself to death.' But in **C** it is expressly said that she drinks poisoned wine, in **E a, c, k**, poisonous wine, in **D** that she puts a grain of poison in the cruse. (In **E l** they mix the lover's blood in wine; she takes two draughts, and her heart bursts.)

A husband giving his wife her lover's heart to eat is a feature in an extensive series of poems and tales, sufficiently represented for present purposes by the ninth tale in the fourth day of the Decameron, and no further explanation is required of the admixture in the Scandinavian ballad.*

In Danish **A a, b, h, o, B b**, two lilies spring from the common grave of the lovers, and embrace or grow together. In **E k, l, F b, e, f**, and Kristensen, XI, No 46, the lovers are buried apart (she south, he north, of kirk, etc.), a lily springs from each, and the two grow together.

Low and High German, Dutch. **A.** 'Brennenberg,' 12 stanzas, Uhland, I, 158, No 75 A, Niederdeutsches Liederbuch, No 44, conjectured to be of the beginning of the seventeenth century. 'Der Bremberger,' Böhme, p. 87, No 23 B (omitting sts 3, 4); Simrock, Die deutschen Volkslieder, p. 14, No 5, Die geschichtlichen deutschen Sagen, p. 325, No 105 (omitting sts 1–4, and turned into High German). **B.** 'Ein schöner Bremberger,' 8 stanzas, flying-sheet, 8°, Nürnberg, Valentin Newber, about 1550–70, Böhme, No 23 A; Wunderhorn, ed. Erk, 1857, IV, 41, modernized. **C.** 'Van Brandenborch,' 6 stanzas, Antwerpener Liederbuch, 1544, ed.

---

* There is a mixture of Decameron, IV, 1 and 9 (with arbitrary variations), in Palmerin of England (ch. 87, II, 328, of Southey's edition of the English translation). Artibel visited the Princess Brandisia in a tower, ascending by a rope. One night he was taken. He was shut up till the princess was delivered of a child (cf. the Scottish ballad). Then the father took Artibel's heart and sent it to Brandisia in a cup. She filled the cup with her tears, and sent the cup of tears to her father, reserving the heart, dressed herself in her bravest apparel, and cast herself headlong from the tower.

Hoffmann, p. 120, No 81 ; Hoffmann's Niederländische Volkslieder, 1856, p. 34, No 7
(omitting st. 6) ; Uhland, No 75 B.   D a.
Grasliedlin, 1535, one st., Bohme, No 23 a ;
Uhland, No 75 C.   b. The same, heard on
the Lower Rhine, 1850, Bohme, No 23 b.

'Brunenborch,' Willems, No 53, p. 135,
21 stanzas, purports to be a critical text, con-
structed partly from copies communicated to
the editor (" for the piece is to this day sung
in Flanders "), and partly from C, A, D a,
and Hoffmann, No 6.* It is not entitled to
confidence.

All the versions are meagre, and A seems to
be corrupted and defective at the beginning.†

A youth, B 2, has watched a winter-long
night, brought thereto by a fair maid, A 1, 3,
B 1, to whom he has devoted his heart and
thoughts, and with whom he wishes to make
off, A, B. Ill news comes to the maid, B 2,
that her lover is a prisoner, and has been
thrown into a tower. There Brennenberg
(A, der Bremberger, B, Brandenborch, C, der
Brandenburger, D a) lay seven years or more,
till his head was white and his beard was gray.
They laid him on a table and slit him like a
fish,‡ cut out his heart, dressed it with pepper, and gave it to the fairest, A, the dame, B,
the dearest, C, to eat. 'What have I eaten
that tasted so good ?' 'Brennenberg's heart,'
A. 'If it is his heart, pour wine for me, and
give me to drink.' She set the beaker to her
mouth, and drank it to the bottom, B. The
first drop she drank, her heart broke into a
dozen bits, A, C. (Their love was pure, such
as no one could forbid, A 11 ; the same implied in A 12, C 5.)

The German-Dutch ballad, though printed
two hundred years before any known copy
of the Swedish-Danish, is much less explicit.
The lady is certainly a maid in B, and she is
a maid in A if the first stanza is accepted
as belonging to the ballad. Then it should
be her father who proceeds so cruelly against
her. The wine-drinking, followed by speedy
death, may come, as it almost certainly does
in some of the Scandinavian ballads, from
the story of Ghismonda ; and therefore the
German-Dutch ballads, as they stand, may
perhaps be treated as a blending of the first
and the ninth tale of Boccaccio's fourth day.
But there is a German meisterlied, printed,
like B, C, D a, in the sixteenth century, which
has close relation with these ballads, and
much more of Boccaccio's ninth tale in it :
'Von dem Brembergers end und tod,' von der
Hagen's Minnesinger, IV, 281, Wunderhorn,
1808, II, 229, epitomized in the Grimms'
Deutsche Sagen, II, 211, No 500. The knight
Bremberger has loved another man's wife.
The husband cuts off his head, and gives his
heart to the lady to eat. He asks her if she
can tell what she has eaten. She would be
glad to know, it tasted so good. She is told
that it is Bremberger's heart. She says she
will take a drink upon it, and never eat or
drink more. The lady hastens from table to
her chamber, grieves over Bremberger's fate,
protesting that they had never been too intimate, starves herself, and dies the eleventh
day. The husband suffers great pangs for
having 'betrayed'§ her and her deserving
servant, and sticks a knife into his heart.‖
The incident of a husband giving his wife

---

* This is a Dutch ballad of Brennenberg without the ex-
traction of the heart, MS. of the end of the fifteenth century.
(Sts 1, 2 resemble, A 3, 4.) A fair lady offers Brunenburch
a rose garland ; a knight observes this, goes to his master,
and tells him, Brunenburch has been sleeping with your wife.
Brunenburch is imprisoned in a tower, and after a time sent
to the gallows. The lady rides to the gallows. She has
seven bold brothers, who will avenge his death. Brunenburch affirms and reaffirms his innocence. The lady vows
never to braid her hair, etc. (Cf. II, 156 f.) Frydenborg is
hanged in Danish **A d, n, E b**, and his heart then taken
out.

† In **A** 3, 4, which (as also **A** 1 and **B** 1) are in the first
person, a fair maid offers the singer a rose garland. This

warrants no inference of community with the Scandinavian
ballad. The passage probably does not belong in the ballad.
Compare the beginning of Hoffmann, No 6, and a song of
John I of Brabant, Willems, p. 13, No 5.

'Recht so einem wildenschwin,' **A** 8, brings to mind
'quel cuor di cinghiare,' in Decameron, IV, 9, but, considering the 'recht wo einen visch' of **A** 7, may be judged an
accidental correspondence.

§ It is to be noted that the father reproaches himself for
'betraying' his only child in the Swedish ballad, and in
Danish **A 1, F a, c, d.**

‖ A meisterlied, of about 1500 (Böhme), noted by Goedeke, Grundriss, § 139, No 7 c, has not been reprinted.

her lover's heart to eat occurs in a considerable number of tales and poems in literature, and in all is obviously of the same source.

Ysolt, in the romance of Tristan, twelfth century, sings a lai how Guirun was slain for love of a lady, and his heart given by the count to his wife to eat. (Michel, III, 39, vv. 781–90.)

Ramon de Castel Rossillon (Raimons de Rosillon) cut off the head of Guillems de Cabestaing, lover of his wife, Seremonda (Margarita), took the heart from the body, 'fetz lo raustir e far pebrada,' and gave it to his wife to eat. He then told her what she had been eating (showing her Cabestaing's head), and asked her if it was good. So good, she said, that she would never eat or drink more; hearing which, her husband rushed at her with his sword, and she fled to a balcony, let herself fall (threw herself from a window), and was killed. (Chabaneau, Les Biographies des Troubadours en langue provençale, pp. 99–103, MSS of the thirteenth and the fourteenth century.) Nearly the same story, 'secondo che raccontano i provenzali,' in the Decameron, IV, 9, of Messer Guiglielmo Rossiglione and Messer Guiglielmo Guardastagno. The lady says that she liked very much the dish which she had eaten, and the husband, No wonder that you should like when it was dead the thing which you liked best of all when it was living: what you have eaten was Guardastagno's heart. God forbid, replies the lady, that I should swallow anything else after so noble a repast; then lets herself drop from a high window.

In Konrad von Würzburg, 'Das Herz,' 'Das Herzmäre,' 1260–70, five or six hundred verses, a knight and a lady are inflamed with a mutual passion (tugendhafter mann, reines weib). The lady's husband conceives that he may break this up by taking her to the Holy Land. In that case, the knight proposes to follow; but the lady prevails upon him to go before her husband shall take this step, with the object of lulling his jealousy and stopping the world's talk. The knight goes, and dies of the separation. As his end was approaching, he had ordered his attendant

to take out his heart, embalm it, enclose it in a gold box, and carry it to the lady. The husband lights upon the emissary, takes away the box, directs his cook to make a choice dish of the heart, and has this set before his wife for her exclusive enjoyment. He asks her how she finds it, and she declares that she has never eaten anything so delicious. She is then told that she has eaten the knight's heart, sent her by him as a token. God defend, she exclaims, that any ordinary food should pass my mouth after so precious victual, and thereupon dies (von der Hagen's Gesammtabenteuer, I, 225). The same story is introduced as an "example" in a sermon-book: 'Quidam miles tutpiter adamavit uxorem alterius militis.' * The lady kills herself.

Again, in a romance of eight thousand verses, of the Châtelain de Couci and la Dame de Faiel (of the end of the thirteenth or the beginning of the fourteenth century), with the difference that the châtelain takes the cross, is wounded with a poisoned arrow, and dies on his way to France. (Jakemon Sakesep, Roman du Châtelain de Couci, etc., ed. Crapelet, 1829.) From this romance was derived The Knight of Curtesy and the Fair Lady of Faguell (in which the lady is chaste to her lord as is the turtle upon the tree), five hundred verses, Ritson's Metrical Romanceës, III, 193, from an edition by William Copland, "before 1568;" also a chap-book, curiously adapted to its time, 'The Constant but Unhappy Lovers,' London, 1707 (cited by Clouston, Popular Tales and Fictions, II, 191).

Descending to tradition of the present time, we find in the adventures of Rájá Rasálu, as told in verse and prose in the north of India, surprising agreements with Boccaccio's tale: a. Temple's Legends of the Panjâb, I, 64 f., 1883. b. The same, III, 240 f., 1886. c. Swynnerton in the Folk-Lore Journal, I, 143 ff., 1883, and in The Adventures of Rájá Rasálu, 1884, pp. 130–35. d. Clouston, Popular Tales and Fictions, II, 192, from a book

* Sermones Parati, No 124, ninth Sunday after Trinity: cited by M. Gaston Paris, Histoire Littéraire de la France, XXVIII, 382 f.

privately printed, 1851. Rájá Rasálu kills
his wife's lover, tears out his heart, a, heart
and liver, d, takes of his flesh, b, c, roasts and
gives to his wife to eat. She finds the meat
is very good, a, no venison was ever so dainty,
c. The king retorts, You enjoyed him when
he was living; why should you not relish his
flesh now that he is dead? and shows her the
body of his rival. She leaps from the palace
wall and is killed (c only). (Rájá Rasálu is
assigned to our second century.)

A Danish ballad in Syv's collection, 1695,
has one half of the story. A king has a man
for whom his wife has a fancy chopped up
and cooked and served to the queen. She
does not eat. ('Livsvandet,' Grundtvig, II,
504, No 94 A, Prior, I, 391.)

Very like the Indian and the Provençal
sage, but with change of the parts of husband
and wife, is what Mme d'Aulnoy relates as
having been enacted in the Astorga family,
in Spain, in the seventeenth century. The
Marchioness of Astorga kills a beautiful girl
of whom her husband is enamored, tears out
her heart, and gives it to her husband in a
stew. She asks him if the dish was to his
taste, and he says, Yes. No wonder, says the
wife, for it was the heart of the mistress whom
you loved so much; and then produces the
gory head. (Mémoires de la Cour d'Espagne,
La Haye, 1691, I, 108.)

Going back to the twelfth century, we come,
even at that early date, upon one of those extravagances, not to say travesties, which are
apt to follow successful strokes of invention.
Ignaure loves and is loved by twelve dames.
The husbands serve his heart to their twelve
wives, who, when they are apprised of what
has passed, duly vow that they will never eat
again after the precious mess which they
have enjoyed. (Lai d'Ignaurès, ed. Monmerqué et Michel.) There are relics of a
similar story in Provençal and in German,
and a burlesque tale to the same effect was
popular in Italy: Le Cento Novelle Antiche,
of about 1300, Biagi, Le Novelle Antiche,
1880, p. 38, No 29.*

A kitchen-boy plays a part of some consequence in several other ballads. A kitchen-
boy is the hero of No 252, IV, 400, a very
poor ballad, to be sure. There is a bad tell-
tale of a kitchen-boy in 'Lady Maisry,' A,
No 65, II, 114, and there is a high-minded
kitchen-boy in 'The Lady Isabella's Tragedy.'† 'A ballett, The Kitchen-boyes
Songe' (whatever this may be), is entered
as licensed to John Alde in the Stationers'
Registers, 1570–71, Arber, I, 438. In about
half of the versions of 'Der grausame Bru-
der' (see II, 101 f.), the king of England presents himself as a küchenjung to the brother
of a lady whom he asks in marriage after a
clandestine intimacy.

A is translated by Knortz, Schottische Balladen, p. 22, No 9.

---

* The older literature is noted, with his usual fulness, by
von der Hagen, Gesammtabenteuer, I, cxvi–xxi. See, also,
Dunlop's History of Fiction, ed. Wilson, II, 95 f. M. Gaston Paris has critically reviewed the whole matter, with
an account of modern French imitations of the romance of
the Châtelain de Couci, in Histoire Littéraire de la France,
XXVIII, 352–90. See, also, his article in Romania, XII,
359 ff.

† See Percy's Reliques, 1765, III, 154, and Ebsworth,
Roxburghe Ballads, VI, 650. It is in many of the collections of black-letter broadsides besides the Roxburghe, as
Pepys, Wood, Crawford, etc. Though perhaps absolutely
the silliest ballad that ever was made, and very far from

silly sooth, the broadside was traditionally propagated in
Scotland without so much change as is usual in such cases:
'There livd a knight in Jesuitmont.' Scotch Ballads, Materials for Border Minstrelsy, No 22 e, Abbotsford, in the
handwriting of William Laidlaw, derived from Jean Scott;
'The Knight in Jesuite,' Campbell MSS, II, 63; 'There was
a knight in Jessamay,' Motherwell's MS., p. 399, from Agnes
Laird, of Kilbarchan. Percy's ballad is translated by
Bodmer, I, 167, and by Döring, p. 91. The tragedy is said
to be localized at Radcliffe, Lancashire: Harland, Ballads
and Songs of Lancashire, ed. 1879, p. 46, Roby's Traditions of Lancashire, 1879, I, 107, both citing Dr Whitaker's
History of Whalley.

A

Aytoun's Ballads of Scotland, II, 173, 1859, from the recollection of a lady residing at Kirkaldy.

1 THERE was a king, and a very great king,
   And a king of meikle fame ;
   He had not a child in the world but ane,
   Lady Daisy was her name.

2 He had a very bonnie kitchen-boy,
   And William was his name ;
   He never lay out o Lady Daisy's bower,
   Till he brought her body to shame.

3 When een-birds sung, and een-bells rung,
   And a' men were boune to rest,
   The king went on to Lady Daisy's bower,
   Just like a wandering ghaist.

4 He has drawn the curtains round and round,
   And there he has sat him down ;
   'To whom is this, Lady Daisy,' he says,
   'That now you gae so round ?

5 'Is it to a laird ? or is it to a lord ?
   Or a baron of high degree ?
   Or is it William, my bonnie kitchen-boy ?
   Tell now the truth to me.'

6 'It 's no to a laird, and it 's no to a lord,
   Nor a baron of high degree ;
   But it 's to William, your bonnie kitchen-boy :
   What cause hae I to lee ? '

7 'O where is all my merry, merry men,
   That I pay meat and fee,
   That they will not take out this kitchen-boy,
   And kill him presentlie ? '

8 They hae taen out this bonnie kitchen-boy,
   And killd him on the plain ;
   His hair was like the threads o gold,
   His een like crystal stane ;
   His hair was like the threads o gold,
   His teeth like ivory bane.

9 They hae taen out this bonnie boy's heart,
   Put it in a cup o gold ;
   'Take that to Lady Daisy,' he said,
   'For she 's impudent and bold ; '
   And she washd it with the tears that ran from
      her eye
   Into the cup of gold.

10 'Now fare ye weel, my father the king !
   You hae taen my earthly joy ;
   Since he 's died for me, I 'll die for him,
   My bonnie kitchen-boy.'

11 'O where is all my merry, merry men,
   That I pay meat and wage,
   That they could not withold my cruel hand,
   When I was mad with rage ?

12 'I think nae wonder, Lady Daisy,' he said,
   'That he brought your body to shame ;
   For there never was man of woman born
   Sae fair as him that is slain.'

B

From "The Old Lady's Collection," formerly in the possession of Sir Walter Scott, No 41.

1 THER was a king, an a worthy king,
   [An a king] of birth an fame ;
   He had an only dear daughter,
   An Dayesie was her name.

2 Ther was a boy about the house,
   Bold Roben was his name ;
   He would not stay out of Dayese's bour,
   Till he brought her body [to] shame.

3 When bells was rung, ...
   An a' man bon to rest,

The king went up to Lady Dayese's bour,
   He was an unwelcom gast.

4 'O Lady Dayesë, dear, d[ea]r Dayisie,
   What gars ye gae sae round ?
   We yer tua sides high an yer bellie bige,
   Fra yer face the couller is gane.'

5 'O have ye loved ? or have ye lang-sought ?
   Or die ye goo we barn ? '
   'It 's all for you, fair father,
   That ye stayed so long in Spain.'

6 'It 's aff ye take yer berry-broun goon,
   An ye lay it on a ston,

An I will tell you in a very short time
  If ye loued any man or no[n].'

7 It 's aff she has tane her berry-broun goon,
  An laid it on a ston;
We her tua sides high, her belley turned bigg,
  Fra her face the couller was gane.

8 'O is it to lord? or is to lard?
  Or till a man of mean?
Or is it to Bold Roben, the kittchen-boy?
  Nou, Dayisie, dinne lea[n].'

9 'It 's no to leard, nor [to] lord,
  Nor to a man of mean,
But it 's to Bold Robien, our kittchen-boy;
  Fatt neads me for to lea[n]?'

10 . . . . . .

  It 's the morn befor I eat or drink
  His heart-blude I sall see.'

11 He 's tean Bold Robien by the **hand**
  Lead him across the green;

His hear was leak the very threeds of goud,
  His face shone leak the moon.

12 He 's tane out this bonny boy's hear[t]
  Into a cupe of gold,
Had it to Lady Dayese's bour,
  Says, No[u], Dayesë, behold!

13 'O welcom to me my heart's delight!
  Nou welcom to me my joy!
Ye have dayed for me, an I 'll day for ye,
  Tho ye be but the kittchen-boy.'

14 She has taen out the coup of gold,
  Lead it belou her head,
An she wish it we the tears ran doun fra her
    eays,
  An or midnight she was dead.

15 She has tean out the coup of gold,
  Laid it belou her hear,
An she wish it we the tears ran don fra her
    eays,
  An alass! spak never mare.

C

Sharpe's Ballad Book, No 4, p. 12, as sung by Mary
Johnston, dairy maid at Hoddam Castle.

1 THERE was a king, and a glorious king,
  And a king of mickle fame,
And he had daughters only one,
  Lady Dysmal was her name.

2 He had a boy, and a kitchen-boy,
  A boy of mickle scorn,
And she lovd him lang, and she loved him aye,
  Till the grass oergrew the corn.

3 When twenty weeks were gone and past,
  O she began to greet!
Her petticoat grew short before,
  And her stays they wadna meet.

4 It fell upon a winter's night
  The king could get nae rest;
He cam unto his daughter dear,
  Just like a wandring ghaist.

5 He cam into her bed-chalmer,
  And drew the curtains round:
'What aileth thee, my daughter dear?
  I fear you 've gotten wrong.'

6 'O if I have, despise me not,
  For he is all my joy;
I will forsake baith dukes and earls,
  And marry your kitchen-boy.'

7 'Go call to me my merry men all,
  By thirty and by three;
Go call to me my kitchen-boy,
  We 'll murder him secretlie.'

8 There was nae din that could be heard,
  And neer a word was said,
Till they got him baith fast and sure
  Between twa feather-beds.

9 'Go cut the heart out of his breast,
  And put it in a cup of gold,
And present it to his Dysmal dear,
  For she is baith stout and bold.'

10 They 've cut the heart out of his breast,
    And put it in a cup of gold,
And presented it to his Dysmal dear,
    Who was baith stout and bold.

11 'O come to me, my hinney, my heart,
    O come to me, my joy!
O come to me, my hinney, my heart
    My father's kitchen-boy!'

12 She 's taen the cup out of their hands,
    And set it at her bed-head;

She washd it wi the tears that fell from her
    eyes,
    And next morning she was dead.

13 'O where were ye, my merry men all,
    Whom I paid meat and wage,
Ye didna hold my cruel hand
    When I was in my rage?

14 'For gone is a' my heart's delight,
    And gone is a' my joy;
For my dear Dysmal she is dead,
    And so is my kitchen-boy.'

D

Buchan's MSS, II, 164.

1 THERE was a king, and a curious king,
    And a king of royal fame,
He had ae daughter, he had never mair,
    Lady Diamond was her name.

2 She 's fa'en into shame, and lost her good name,
    And wrought her parents 'noy;
And a' for her layen her love so low,
    On her father's kitchen-boy.

3 One night as she lay on her bed,
    Just thinking to get rest,
Up it came her old father,
    Just like a wandering ghaist.

4 'Rise up, rise up, Lady Diamond,' he says,
    'Rise up, put on your gown;
Rise up, rise up, Lady Diamond,' he says,
    'For I fear ye go too roun.'

5 'Too roun I go, ye blame me no,
    Ye cause me not to shame;
For better love I that bonny boy
    Than all your well-bred men.'

6 The king 's calld up his wall-wight men,
    That he paid meat and fee:
'Bring here to me that bonny boy,
    And we 'll smore him right quietlie.'

7 Up hae they taken that bonny boy,
    Put him between twa feather-beds;
Naething was dane, naething was said,
    Till that bonny boy was dead.

8 The king 's taen out a broad, broad sword,
    And streakd it on a strow,
And thro and thro that bonny boy's heart
    He 's gart cauld iron go.

9 Out he has taen his poor bloody heart,
    Set it on a tasse of gold,
And set it before Lady Diamond's face,
    Said, Fair lady, behold!

10 Up she has taen this poor bloody heart,
    And holden it in her hand:
'Better loved I that bonny, bonny boy
    Than all my father's land.'

11 Up she has taen his poor bloody heart
    And laid it at her head;
The tears away frae her eyes did fly,
    And ere midnight she was dead.

E

Joseph Robertson, "Adversaria," p. 66; noted down from
a female servant, July 15, 1829.

1 IT was a king, and a verra greit king,
    An a king o muckle fame,

An he had a luvelie dauchter fair,
    An Dysie was her name.

2 She fell in love wi the kitchie-boy,
    An a verra bonnie boy was he,

An word has gane till her father dear,
   An an angry man was he.

3 'Is it the laird? or is it the lord?
   Or a man o high degree?
 Or is it to Robin, the kitchie-boy?
   O Dysie mak nae lee.'

4 'It's nae the laird, nor is it the lord,
   Nor a man o high degree,
 But it's to Robin, the kitchie-boy;
   What occasion hae I to lee?'

5 'If it be to Robin, the kitchie-boy,
   As I trust weel it be,
 The morn, afore ye eat meal or drink,
   Ye'll see him hanged hie.'

6 They have taen Robin out,
   His hair was like threads o gold;
 That verra day afore it was night,
   Death made young Dysie cold.

B. *Written without division into stanzas or verses.*
  3². to bed.
  8⁴. didde lea.
C. "Mary Johnston, our dairymaid at Hoddam
  Castle, used to sing this. It had a very
  pretty air, and some more verses which I

have now forgot." Sharpe's Ballad-Book,
  1880, p. 128.
D. *A little scotticized by Buchan in printing, and
  still more by Dixon.*
  9². tasse *is* tarse *in my transcript; probably
  miscopied.*

270

THE EARL OF MAR'S DAUGHTER

'The Earl of Mar's Daughter,' Buchan's Ballads of the North of Scotland, I, 49; Motherwell's MS. p. 565.

THE Earl of Mar's daughter spies a dove on a tower, and promises him a golden cage if he will come to her. The dove lights on her head, and she takes him into her bower. When night comes, she sees a youth standing by her side. The youth explains that his mother, a queen versed in magic, had transformed him into a dove that he might charm maids. He is a dove by day, a man at night, and will live and die with her. In the course of seven years seven sons are born, all of whom are successively committed to the care of the queen their grandmother. After the twenty-third year a lord comes to court the lady. She refuses him: she will live alone with her bird. Her father swears that he will kill this bird, and Cow-me-doo prudently takes refuge with his mother, who welcomes home her 'young son Florentine,' and calls for dancers and minstrels. Cow-me-doo Florentine will have none of that; the situation is too serious. The morrow the mother of his seven sons is to be wedded; instead of merry-making, he desires to have twenty stout men turned into storks, his seven sons into swans, and himself into a goshawk. This feat is beyond his mother's (quite limited) magic, but it is done by an old woman who has more skill. The birds fly to Earl Mar's castle, where the wedding is going on. The storks seize some of the noble guests, the swans bind the bride's best man to a tree, and in a twinkling the bride and her maidens are carried off by the birds. The Earl of Mar reconciles himself with his daughter.

There is a Scandinavian ballad which

Grundtvig has treated as identical with this, but the two have little in common beyond the assumption of the bird-shape by the lover. They are, perhaps, on a par for barrenness and folly, but the former may claim some age and vogue, the Scottish ballad neither.

Danish. ' Ridderen i Fugleham,' Grundtvig, II, 226, No 68, A-C (C is translated by Prior, III, 206) ; 'Herr Jon som Fugl,' Kristensen, I, 161, No 59, X, 23, No 11, A, B. In Grundtvig's A (MS. of the sixteenth century), the son of the king of England wooes a maid, sending her rich presents. Her mother says he shall never have her daughter, and this message his envoys take back to him. He is angry, and has a bird's coat forged for him out of nine gold rings (but his behavior thereafter is altogether birdlike). He sits on the ridgepole of the maid's bower and sings. The maid exclaims, Christ grant thou wert mine ! thou shouldst drink naught but wine, and sleep in my arms. I would send thee to England, as a gift to my love. She sits down on the ground; the bird flies into her bosom. She takes the bird into her bower ; he throws off his bird-coat, and is recognized. The maid begs him to do her no shame. ' Not if you will go to England with me,' he answers, takes her up, and wings his way thither. There he marries her, and gives her a crown and a queen's name.

In Grundtvig B, the bird is a falcon. The maid will have no man that cannot fly. Master Hillebrand, son of the king of England, learns this fact, and has a bird's coat made for him, enters the room where man had never been before, sleeps under white linen, and in the morning is a knight so braw. (Here the story ends.)

In C, the maid will have no man that cannot fly, and Master Hillebrand orders a bird's coat to be made for him (what could be more mechanical!), flies into the maid's bower, and passes the night on the pole on which she hangs her clothes. In the morning he begins to sing, flies to the bed, and plays with the maid's hair. If you could shed your feathers, says the maid, I would have no other man. Keep your word, says the bird ; give me your

hand, and take my claw. She passes her word ; he throws off his feathers, and stands before her a handsome man. By day, says the maid, he is to fly with the birds, by night to sleep in her bed. He perches so long on the clothes-pole that Ingerlille has a girl and a boy. When her father asks who is their father, she tells him the positive truth; she found them in a wood. When the bird comes back at night, she says that he must speak to her father ; further concealment is impossible. Master Hillebrand asks the father to give him his daughter. The father is surprised that he should want a maid that has been beguiled; but if he will marry her she shall have a large dowry. The knight wants nothing but her.

Kristensen's copies do not differ materially. 11 A in his tenth volume (a very brief ballad) drops or lacks the manufacture of the bird-coat. Grundtvig's D-G drop the bird quite.

The ballad occurs in Swedish, but in the form of a mere abstract; in Arwidsson, II, 188, No 112, MS. of the sixteenth century. A maid will have no man but one that can fly. A swain has wings made from five gold rings; he flies over the rose-wood, over the sea, sits on a lily-spray and sings, flies till he sleeps in the maid's bosom.

A Färöe copy is noted by Grundtvig as in the possession of Hammershaimb, resembling his B, but about twice as long.

The lover in bird-shape is a very familiar trait in fiction, particularly in popular tales.

In Marie de France's Lai d'Yonec, a lover comes in at his mistress's window in the form of a hawk; in ' Der Jungherr und der treue Heinrich,' von der Hagen, Gesammtabenteuer, No 64, III, 197, MS. of 1444, as a bird (by virtue of a stone of which he has possessed himself).* In Hahn, No 102, II, 130 (Albanian), a dove flies in at a princess's window, and is changed to man's shape by dipping in a dish of milk; Hahn, No 7, I, 97 = Pio, No 5, dove (through a hole in the ceiling, dips in a basin of water); Δελτίον τῆς ἱστορικῆς καὶ ἐθνολογικῆς ἑταιρίας τῆς Ἑλλάδος, I, 337, golden eagle

---

* The ' Vogelritter ' mentioned by Prior, III, 207, is this same story. See Mone, Uebersicht der niederländischen Volksliteratur, p. 90, No 59.

(through a window, in rose water); Schneller, No 21, p. 49, dove (dips in a basin of water); Coelho, Contos pop. portuguezes, No 27, p. 65, bird (dips in a basin of water); Braga, Contos tradicionães, No 31, I, 68, bird (dips in a basin of water); Pitrè, Fiabe, etc., No 18, I, 163, green bird (pan of milk, then pan of water); Bernoni, Fiabe, No 17, p. 87 (milk and water, milk, rose-water); Visentini, No 17, p. 95, dove; Gonzenbach, No 27, I, 167, green bird (through a hole in the wall); Nicolovius, p. 34, Asbjørnsen, Norske Folke-

eventyr, Ny Samling, 1871, No 10, p. 35 = Juletræet, 1851, p. 52, falcon; Grundtvig, Danske Folkeæventyr, No 14, p. 167, Madsen, Folkeminder, p. 19 ('The Green Knight'), bird; Berntsen, Folke-Æventyr, No 13, II, 86, bird; Comtesse d'Aulnoy, L'Oiseau bleu,' Cabinet des Fées, II, 67, king turned into bird for seven years.[*]

Translated by Gerhard, p. 44; Knortz, Lieder u. Romanzen Alt-Englands, p. 207, No 62.

---

1   It was intill a pleasant time,
        Upon a simmer's day,
    The noble Earl of Mar's daughter
        Went forth to sport and play.

2   As thus she did amuse hersell,
        Below a green aik tree,
    There she saw a sprightly doo
        Set on a tower sae hie.

3   'O Cow-me-doo, my love sae true,
        If ye 'll come down to me,
    Ye 'se hae a cage o guid red gowd
        Instead o simple tree:

4   'I 'll put gowd hingers roun your cage,
        And siller roun your wa;
    I 'll gar ye shine as fair a bird
        As ony o them a'.'

5   But she hadnae these words well spoke,
        Nor yet these words well said,
    Till Cow-me-doo flew frae the tower
        And lighted on her head.

6   Then she has brought this pretty bird
        Hame to her bowers and ha,
    And made him shine as fair a bird
        As ony o them a'.

7   When day was gane, and night was come,
        About the evening tide,
    This lady spied a sprightly youth
        Stand straight up by her side.

8   'From whence came ye, young man?' she
            said;
    'That does surprise me sair;

My door was bolted right secure,
        What way hae ye come here?'

9   'O had your tongue, ye lady fair,
        Lat a' your folly be;
    Mind ye not on your turtle-doo
        Last day ye brought wi thee?'

10 'O tell me mair, young man,' she said,
        'This does surprise me now;
    What country hae ye come frae?
        What pedigree are you?'

11 'My mither lives on foreign isles,
        She has nae mair but me;
    She is a queen o wealth and state,
        And birth and high degree.

12 'Likewise well skilld in magic spells,
        As ye may plainly see,
    And she transformd me to yon shape,
        To charm such maids as thee.

13 'I am a doo the live-lang day,
        A sprightly youth at night;
    This aye gars me appear mair fair
        In a fair maiden's sight.

14 'And it was but this verra day
        That I came ower the sea;
    Your lovely face did me enchant;
        I 'll live and dee wi thee.'

15 'O Cow-me-doo, my luve sae true,
        Nae mair frae me ye 'se gae;'

[*] Most of the above are cited by R. Köhler, notes in Warnke's ed. of Marie's Lais, p. LXXXVIII f. For the dipping in water, etc., see Tam Lin, I, 338.

'That's never my intent, my luve,
  As ye said, it shall be sae.'

16 'O Cow-me-doo, my luve sae true,
    It's time to gae to bed;'
  'Wi a' my heart, my dear marrow,
    It's be as ye hae said.'

17 Then he has staid in bower wi her
    For sax lang years and ane,
  Till sax young sons to him she bare,
    And the seventh she's brought hame.

18 But aye as ever a child was born
    He carried them away,
  And brought them to his mither's care,
    As fast as he coud fly.

19 Thus he has staid in bower wi her
    For twenty years and three;
  There came a lord o high renown
    To court this fair ladie.

20 But still his proffer she refused,
    And a' his presents too;
  Says, I'm content to live alane
    Wi my bird, Cow-me-doo.

21 Her father sware a solemn oath
    Amang the nobles all,
  'The morn, or ere I eat or drink,
    This bird I will gar kill.'

22 The bird was sitting in his cage,
    And heard what they did say;
  And when he found they were dismist,
    Says, Wae's me for this day!

23 'Before that I do langer stay,
    And thus to be forlorn,
  I'll gang unto my mither's bower,
    Where I was bred and born.'

24 Then Cow-me-doo took flight and flew
    Beyond the raging sea,
  And lighted near his mither's castle,
    On a tower o gowd sae hie.

25 As his mither was wauking out,
    To see what she coud see,
  And there she saw her little son,
    Set on the tower sae hie.

26 'Get dancers here to dance,' she said,
    'And minstrells for to play;
  For here's my young son, Florentine,
    Come here wi me to stay.'

27 'Get nae dancers to dance, mither,
    Nor minstrells for to play,
  For the mither o my seven sons,
    The morn's her wedding-day.'

28 'O tell me, tell me, Florentine,
    Tell me, and tell me true,
  Tell me this day without a flaw,
    What I will do for you.'

29 'Instead of dancers to dance, mither,
    Or minstrells for to play,
  Turn four-and-twenty wall-wight men
    Like storks in feathers gray;

30 'My seven sons in seven swans,
    Aboon their heads to flee;
  And I mysell a gay gos-hawk,
    A bird o high degree.'

31 Then sichin said the queen hersell,
    'That thing's too high for me;'
  But she applied to an auld woman,
    Who had mair skill than she.

32 Instead o dancers to dance a dance,
    Or minstrells for to play,
  Four-and-twenty wall-wight men
    Turnd birds o feathers gray;

33 Her seven sons in seven swans,
    Aboon their heads to flee;
  And he himsell a gay gos-hawk,
    A bird o high degree.

34 This flock o birds took flight and flew
    Beyond the raging sea,
  And landed near the Earl Mar's castle,
    Took shelter in every tree.

35 They were a flock o pretty birds,
    Right comely to be seen;
  The people viewd them wi surprise,
    As they dancd on the green.

36 These birds ascended frae the tree
    And lighted on the ha,

And at the last wi force did flee
  Amang the nobles a'.

37 The storks there seized some o the men,
  They coud neither fight nor flee ;
  The swans they bound the bride's best man
  Below a green aik tree.

38 They lighted next on maidens fair,
  Then on the bride's own head,
  And wi the twinkling o an ee
  The bride and them were fled.

39 There's ancient men at weddings been
  For sixty years or more,

But sic a curious wedding-day
  They never saw before.

40 For naething coud the companie do,
  Nor naething coud they say
  But they saw a flock o pretty birds
  That took their bride away.

41 When that Earl Mar he came to know
  Where his dochter did stay,
  He signd a bond o unity,
  And visits now they pay.

271

THE LORD OF LORN AND THE FALSE STEWARD

A. 'Lord of Learne,' Percy MS., p. 73; Hales and Furnivall, I, 180.

B. 'A pretty ballad of the Lord of Lorn and the Fals Steward.' a. Wood, 401, fol. 95 b.   b. Roxburghe, I, 222; Roxburghe Ballads, ed. Chappell, II, 55.   c. Pepys, I, 494, No 254.

———◆———

ALSO in the Roxburghe collection, III, 534, without printer's name; Ewing, Nos 264, 265; Crawford, No 716. All the broadsides are of the second half of the seventeenth century.

'The Lord of Lorne and the false Steward' was entered, with two other ballads, to Master Walley, 6 October, 1580 ; 'Lord of Lorne' to Master Pavier and others (among 128 pieces), 14 December, 1624. Arber, II, 379 ; IV, 131.*

A. The young Lord of Lorn, when put to school, learns more in one day than his mates learn in three. He returns home earlier than was expected, and delights his father with the information that he can read any book in Scotland. His father says he must now go to France to learn the tongues. His mother is anxious that he should have a proper guardian if he goes, and the 'child' proposes the steward, who has impressed him as a man of fidelity. The Lady of Lorn makes the steward a handsome present, and conjures him to be true to her son. If I am not, he answers, may Christ not be true to me. The young lord sails for France, very richly appointed. Once beyond the water, the steward will give the child neither penny to spend nor meat and drink. The child is forced to lie down at some piece of water to quench his thirst ; the

* Edward Guilpin, in his Skialethia, or A Shadow of Truth, 1598, has this couplet :

  Yet like th' olde ballad of the Lord of Lorne,
  Whose last line in King Harrie's days was borne.
           Chappell, Popular Music, p. 228.

It is possible that Guilpin meant that the last line (stanza ?)

showed the ballad to be of Henry VIII's time ; but he may have meant exactly what he says, that the last line was of Henry VIII's time. We do not know what the last line of the copy intended by Guilpin was, and all we learn from the couplet is that 'The Lord of Lorn' was called an old ballad before the end of the sixteenth century.

steward pushes him in, meaning to drown him. The child offers everything for his life; the steward pulls him out, makes him put off all his fine clothes and don a suit of leather, and sends him to shift for himself, under the name of Poor Disaware. A shepherd takes him in, and he tends sheep on a lonely lea.

The steward sells the child's clothes, buys himself a suit fit for a lord, and goes a-wooing to the Duke of France's daughter, calling himself the Lord of Lorn; the duke favors the suit, and the lady is content. The day after their betrothal, the lady, while riding out, sees the child tending his sheep, and hears him mourning. She sends a maid to bring him to her, and asks him questions, which he answers, not without tears. He was born in Scotland, his name is Poor Disaware; he knows the Lord of Lorn, a worthy lord in his own country. The lady invites him to leave his sheep, and take service with her as chamberlain; the child is willing, but her father objects that the lord who has come a-wooing may not like that arrangement. The steward comes upon the scene, and is angry to find the child in such company. When the child gives his name as Poor Disaware, the steward denounces him as a thief who had robbed his own father; but the duke speaks kindly to the boy, and makes him his stablegroom. One day, when he is watering a gelding, the horse flings up his head and hits the child above the eye. The child breaks out, Woe worth thee, gelding! thou hast stricken the Lord of Lorn. I was born a lord and shall be an earl; my father sent me over the sea, and the false steward has beguiled me. The lady happens to be walking in her garden, and hears something of this; she bids the child go on with his song; this he may not do, for he has been sworn to silence. Then sing to thy gelding, and not to me, she says. The child repeats his story, and adds that the steward has been deceiving both her and him for a twelvemonth. The lady declares that she will marry no man but him

that stands before her, sends in haste to her father to have her wedding put off, and writes an account of the steward's treachery to the old lord in Scotland. The old lord collects five hundred friends of high degree, and goes over to France in search of his son. They find him acting as porter at the duke's palace. The men of worship bow, the serving-men kneel, the old lord lights from his horse and kisses his son. The steward is just then in a castle-top with the duke, and sees what is going on below. Why are those fools showing such courtesy to the porter? The duke fears that this means death for one of them. The castle is beset; the steward is captured, is tried by a quest of lords and brought in guilty, is hanged, quartered, boiled, and burned. The young Lord of Lorne is married to the duke's daughter.

B. B is an abridgment of an older copy. The story is the same as in A in all material particulars. The admiration of the schoolmaster and the self-complacency of his pupil in A 2, 3, B 3, are better justified in B by a stanza which has perhaps dropped out of A:

> There 's nere a doctor in all this realm,
>   For all he goes in rich array,
> [But] I can write him a lesson soon
>   To learn in seven years day.

The last six stanzas are not represented in A, and the last two are glaringly modern; but there is a foundation for 62–64 in a romance from which the story is partly taken, the History of Roswall and Lillian.*

'Roswall and Lillian.' Roswall was son to the king of Naples. Happening one day to be near a prison, he heard three lords, who had been in durance many years for treason, putting up their prayers for deliverance. He was greatly moved, and resolved to help them out. The prison-keys were always hidden for the night under the king's pillow. Roswall possessed himself of them while his father was sleeping, set the lords free, and replaced the keys. The escape of the prisoners was

---

* 'A Pleasant History of Roswall and Lillian,' etc., Edinburgh, 1663, reprint by David Laing, Edinburgh, 1822. Edited, with collation of the later texts and valuable con-

tributions to the traditional history of the tale, by O. Lengert, Englische Studien, XVI, 321 ff., XVII, 341 ff.

reported the next morning, and the king made a vow that whoever had been instrumental to it should be hanged ; if he came within the king's sight, the king would even slay him with his own hands. It soon came to light that the guilty party was none other than the prince. The queen interceded for her son, but the king could not altogether disregard his vow : the prince must be kept out of his sight, and the king promptly decided that Roswall should be sent to reside with the king of Bealm, under charge of the steward, a stalwart knight, to whom the queen promised everything for good service. As the pair rode on their way, they came to a river. The prince was sore athirst, and dismounted to take a drink. The steward seized him by the feet as he bent over the water, and vowed to throw him in unless he would swear an oath to surrender his money and credentials, and become servant where he had been master. To these hard terms Roswall was forced to consign. When they were near the king of Bealm's palace, the steward dropped Roswall's company, leaving him without a penny to buy his dinner; then rode to the king, presented letters, and was well received. Roswall went to a little house hard by, and begged for harbor and victuals for a day. The mistress made him welcome. She saw he was from a far country, and asked his name. Dissawar was his name; a poor name, said the old wife, but Dissawar you shall not be, for I will help you. The next day Roswall was sent to school with the dame's son. He gave his name as Dissawar again to the master ; the master said he should want neither meat nor teaching. Roswall had been a remarkable scholar at home. Without doubt he astonished the master, but this is not said, for the story has been abridged here and elsewhere. In about a month, the steward of the king of Bealm, who had observed his beauty, courtesy, and good parts, carried him to the court of Bealm, where Roswall made himself a general favorite. The princess Lillian, only child of the king of Bealm, chose him to be her chamberlain, fell in love with him, and frankly offered him her heart, an offer which

Roswall, professing always to be of low degree, gratefully accepted.

At this juncture the king of Bealm sent messengers to Naples proposing marriage between his daughter Lillian and the young prince who had been commended to him. The king of Naples assented to the alliance, and deputed lords and knights to represent him at the solemnity. The king of Bealm proclaimed a joust for the three days immediately preceding the wedding. Lillian's heart was cold, for she loved none but Dissawar. She told Dissawar that he must joust for his lady; but he said that he had not been bred to such things, and would rather go a-hunting. A-hunting he went, but before he got to work there came a knight in white weed on a white steed, who enjoined him to take horse and armor and go to the jousting, promising that he should find plenty of venison when he came back. Roswall toomed many a saddle, turned the steward's heels upward, made his way back to the wood, in spite of the king's order that he should be stopped, resumed his hunting-gear, took the venison, which, according to promise, was waiting for him, and presented himself and it to his lady. The order is much the same on the two succeeding days. A red knight equips Roswall for the joust on the second day, a knight in gold on the third. The steward is, on each occasion, put to shame, and in the last encounter two of his ribs are broken.

When Roswall came back to the wood after the third jousting, the three knights appeared together and informed him that they were the men whom he had delivered from prison, and who had promised to help him if help he ever needed. They bade him have no fear of the steward. Lillian had suspected from the second day that the victor was Roswall, and when he returned to her from his third triumph she intimated that if he would but tell the whole truth to her father their mutual wish would be accomplished. But Roswall kept his counsel — very whimsically, unless it was out of respect to his oath — and Lillian was constrained to speak for herself, for the marriage was to be celebrated on the fourth day. She asked her father in plain terms to give her Dissawar for her husband. The king replied, not unkindly, that she could not marry below her rank, and therefore must take the prince who had been selected for her; and to the steward she was married, however sorely against her will. In the course of the wedding-dinner, the three Neapolitan lords entered the hall, and saluted the king, the queen, and Lillian, but not the bridegroom. The king asked why they did no homage to their prince; they replied that they did not see their prince, went in search of Roswall, and brought him in. The force of the oath, or the consciousness of an obligation, must have been by this time quite extinct, for Roswall divulged the steward's treacherous behavior, and announced himself as the victor at the jousts. The steward was hanged that same day; then they passed to the kirk and married Roswall and Lillian. There was dancing till supper and after supper, the minstrels played with good will, and the bridal was kept up for twenty days.

Roswall and Lillian belongs with a group of popular tales of which the original seems to have been characterized by all or many of the following marks: (1) the son of a king liberates a man whom his father has imprisoned; (2) the penalty for so doing is death, and to save his life the prince is sent out of the country, attended by a servant; (3) the servant forces the prince to change places and clothes with him; (4) presents himself at a king's court as prince, and in his assumed quality is in a fair way to secure the hand of the king's daughter; (5) the true prince, figuring the while as a menial (stable-groom, scullion, gardener's lad), is successful, by the help of the man whom he has liberated, in a thrice-repeated contention (battle, tourney, race), or task, after which he is in a position to make known his rank and history; (6) the impostor is put to death, and the prince (who has, perhaps, in his humbler capacity,

already attracted her notice and regard) marries the princess.[*]

Two Slavic tales, a Bosnian and a Russian, come as near as any to the story of our romance.

A king who has caught a wild man shuts him up, and denounces death to any one that shall let him out. The king's son's bedroom is just over the place in which the wild man is confined. The prince cannot bear to hear the continual wailings which come up, and he sets the prisoner free. The prince confesses what he has done; the king is persuaded by his advisers to banish his son rather than to enforce the penalty which he had decreed; the prince is sent off to a distant kingdom, attended by a servant. One day the prince was seized with thirst while travelling, and wished to get a drink from a well; but there was nothing to draw water with, and he ordered his servant to let him down to the surface of the water, holding him the while by the legs. This was done; but when the prince had drunk to his satisfaction, the servant refused to draw him up until he had consented to change places and clothes, and had sworn besides to keep the matter secret. When they arrived at the court of the king designated by the father, the sham prince was received with royal honors, and the true prince had to consort with servants. . . . After a time, the king, wishing to marry off his daughter, proclaimed a three days' race, open to all comers, the prize to be a golden apple, and any competitor who should win the apple each of the three days to have the princess. Our prince had fallen in love with the young lady, and was most desirous to contend. The wild man had already helped him in emergencies here passed over, and did not fail him now. He provided his deliverer with fine clothes and a fine horse. The prince carried off the apple at each of the races, but disappeared as soon as he had the prize in hand. All the efforts of the king to find out the victor were

---

[*] The Grimms have indicated some of the tales belonging to this group, in their notes to No 136 and No 89. Others have been added by Lengert in Englische Studien. A second group, which has several of the marks of the first, is treated by Köhler, with his usual amplitude, in Archiv für Litteraturgeschichte, XII, 142–44. Abstracts of many tales of both groups, including all that I have cited, are given by Lengert. — See further in Additions, p. 280 f.

to no purpose, but one day the princess met the prince in his serving-man's dress, and saw the apples shining from his breast. She told her father. The prince did not feel himself bound to further secrecy ; he told everything ; the king gave him the princess, and the servant was properly disposed of.*

Ivan, the tsar's son, releases from confinement Bulat, a robber, whom the tsar has kept in prison three and thirty years. Bulat tells Ivan to call him by name in case of future need, and he will not fail to appear. Ivan travels in foreign countries with his servant, and feeling thirsty of a warm day tells his servant to get him water from a deep well to which they have come ; Ivan will hold him by a rope tied firmly about him, so that he can go down into the well without danger. The servant represents that he is the heavier of the two, too heavy for his master to hold, and that for this reason it would be better for Ivan himself to go for the water. Ivan is let down into the well, and having drunk his fill calls to his servant to draw him up. The servant refuses to draw him up unless Ivan will swear to give him a certificate in writing that he is master, and Ivan servant. The paper is given ; they change clothes, and proceed on their journey, and come to Tsar Pantui's kingdom. Here the servant is received as a tsar's son, and when he tells Tsar Pantui that the object of his coming is to woo his daughter, the tsar complies with much pleasure. Ivan, at the servant's suggestion, is put to low work in the kitchen. Before long the kingdom is invaded, and the tsar calls upon his prospective son-in-law to drive off the enemy, for which service he shall receive the princess, but without it, not. The false Ivan begs the true Ivan to take the invaders in hand, and he assents without a word. Ivan calls for Bulat : one attacks the hostile army on the right, the other on the left, and in an hour they lay a

hundred thousand low. Ivan returns to his kitchen. A second invasion, and a third, on a larger and larger scale, ensue, and Ivan and Bulat repulse the enemy with greater and greater loss. Ivan each time goes back to his kitchen ; his servant has all the glory, and after the third and decisive victory marries the princess. Ivan gets permission from the cook to be a spectator at the wedding-banquet. The tsar's daughter, it must now be observed, had overheard the conference between the pseudo-prince and Ivan, and even that between Ivan and Bulat, and had hitherto, for inscrutable reasons, let things take their course. But when she saw Ivan looking at the feast from behind other people, she knew him at once, sprang from the table, brought him forward, and said, This is my real bridegroom and the savior of the kingdom ; after which she entered into a full explanation, with the result that the servant was shot, and Ivan married to the tsar's daughter.†

Other tales of the same derivation, but deficient in some points, are : (A.) Radloff, Proben der Volkslitteratur der türkischen Stämme Süd-Sibiriens, IV, 385, ' Der Peri.' (B.) Straparola, Piacevoli Notti, v, 1 (' Guerrino, son of the king of Sicily '). (C.) Grimms, K.- und Hausmärchen, No 136, II, 242, ed. 1857, ' Der Eisenhans.' (D.) Sommer, Sagen, Märchen und Gebräuche aus Sachsen und Thüringen, p. 86, No 2, ' Der eiserne Mann.' (E.) Milenowsky, Volksmärchen aus Böhmen, p. 147, ' Vom wilden Manne.' ‡

(1) The son of a king liberates a prisoner (peri, wild or iron man), A-E. (The keys are under his mother's pillow, B, C.) (2) The prince goes to another kingdom, A-D with attendance, E without. (3) His attendant forces the prince to change places and clothes, only A. (Advantage is taken of the helplessness of the hero when let down into the well to force exchange of parts, in the Servian

---

* ' Kraljev sin,' ' The King's Son,' Bosanske narodne pripovjedke, 1870, No 4, p. 11, Serbian Folk-Lore, Madam Csedomille Mijatovies, ' One good turn deserves another,' p. 189.

† Dietrich, Russische Volksmärchen, No 10, p. 131 ; Vogl, Die ältesten Volksmärchen der Russen, p. 55. ' Słogobyl,' Gliński, Bajarz polski, I, 166, ed. 1862, Chodzko, Contes

des paysans et des patres slaves, p. 193, is an abridged form of the same story, with a traditional variation at the beginning, and in the conclusion a quite too ingenious turn as to the certificate.

‡ Also, Waldau, Böhmisches Märchenbuch, p. 50, after Franz Rubeš.

Tales of Dj. K. Stefanović, 1871, p. 39, No 7, Jagić, Archiv, I, 271 ; Meyer, Albanian Tales, No 13, in Archiv für Litteraturgeschichte, XII, 137 ; Franzisci, Cultur-Studien in Kärnten, p. 99, and, nearly the same, Dozon, Contes Albanais, No 12, p. 83.) (5) The hero, serving as kitchen-boy or gardener's lad, C, D, E, defeats an invading army, C, D, E, wins a prize three successive days, C, E, is successful in three tasks, A, B ; and all these feats are performed by the help of the prisoner whom he set free. The variation of the color of armor and horses occurs in C, E, an extremely frequent trait in tales and romances ; see Ward, Catalogue of Romances, etc., 734 f., Lengert, XVII, 361. (Very striking in the matter of the tournaments is the resemblance of the romance of Ipomedon to Roswall and Lillian. Ipomedon, like Roswall, professes not to have been accustomed to such things, and pretends to go a-hunting, is victorious three successive days in a white, red, black suit, on a white, bay, black steed, vanishes after the contest, and presently reappears as huntsman, with venison which a friend had been engaged in securing for him.) (6) The treacherous attendant is put to death, A. The hero of course marries the princess in all the tales.

The points in the romance which are repeated in the ballad are principally these: The young hero is sent into a foreign country under the care of his father's steward. The steward, by threatening to drown him while he is drinking at a water-side, forces him to consent to an exchange of positions, and strips him of his money ; then passes himself off as his master's son with a noble personage, who eventually fixes upon the impostor as a match for his only daughter. The young lord, henceforth known as Dissawar,* is in his extremity kindly received into an humble house, from which he soon passes into the service of the lady whose hand the steward aspires to gain.

The lady bestows her love upon Dissawar, and he returns her attachment. In the upshot they marry, the false steward having been unmasked and put to death.

What is supplied in the ballad to make up for such passages in the romance as are omitted is, however, no less strictly traditional than that which is retained. Indeed, were it not for the name Dissawar, the romance might have been plausibly treated, not as the source of the ballad, but simply as a kindred story ; for the exquisite tale of 'The Goose Girl' presents every important feature of 'The Lord of Lorn,' the only notable difference being that the young lord in the ballad exchanges parts with the princess in the tale, an occurrence of which instances have been, from time to time, already indicated.

In 'Die Gänsemagd,' Grimms, No 89, II, 13, ed. 1857, a princess is sent by her mother to be wedded to a bridegroom in a distant kingdom, with no escort but a maid. Distressed with thirst, the princess orders her maid to get down from her horse and fetch her a cup of water from a stream which they are passing. The maid refuses; she will no longer be servant, and the princess has to lie down and drink from the stream. So a second and a third time: and then the servant forces her mistress, under threat of death, to change horses and clothes, and to swear to keep the matter secret at the court to which they are bound. There the maid is received as princess, while the princess is put to tending geese with a boy. The counterfeit princess, fearing that her mistress's horse, Falada, may tell what he has observed, induces the young prince to cut off Falada's head. The princess has the head nailed up on a gate through which she passes when she takes out the geese, and every morning she addresses Falada with a sad greeting, and receives a sad return. The goose-boy tells the old king of this, and the next day the king hides behind the gate and hears what

---

* I can make no guess that I am willing to mention as to the derivation and meaning of Dissawar. The old woman in the romance, v. 249 ff., says, 'Dissawar is a poor name, yet Dissawar you shall not be, for good help you shall have ; ' and the schoolmaster, v. 283 ff., says, 'Dissawar, thou shalt want neither meat nor laire.' It would seem that they understood the word to mean, "in want." Some predecessor of the romance may by and by be recovered which shall put the meaning beyond doubt.

passes between the goose-girl and Falada.
The king asks an explanation of the goose-
girl when she comes back in the evening, but
the only answer he elicits is that she has taken
an oath to say nothing. Then the king says,
If you will not tell me your troubles, tell
them to the stove; and the princess creeps
into the oven and pours out all her grief:
how she, a king's daughter, has been made
to change places with her servant, and the
servant is to marry the bridegroom, and she
reduced to tend geese. All this the king
hears from outside of the room through the
stovepipe, and he loses no time in repeating
it to his son. The false maid is dragged
through the streets in a barrel stuck full with
nails, and the princess married to the prince
to whom she had been contracted.

The passage in the ballad in which the
Lord of Lorn relates to the gelding, within

hearing of the duke's daughter, the injuries
which he had sworn to conceal has, perhaps,
suffered some corruption, though quibbling
as to oaths is not unknown in ballads. The
lady should be believed to be out of earshot,
as the king is thought to be by the goose-girl.
Unbosoming one's self to an oven or stove
is a decidedly popular trait; "the unhappy
and the persecuted betake themselves to the
stove, and to it bewail their sufferings, or con-
fide a secret which they may not disclose to
the world."* An entirely similar passage (but
without an oath to secrecy) occurs in Basile's
Pentamerone, II, 8, where a girl who has been
shamefully maltreated by her uncle's wife tells
her very miserable story to a doll, and is accidentally overheard by the uncle. The conclusion of the tale is quite analogous to that
of the goose-girl.

A

Percy MS., p. 73, Hales and Furnivall, I, 180.

1 IT was the worthy Lord of Learen,
   He was a lord of a hie degree;
  He had noe more children but one sonne,
   He sett him to schoole to learne curtesie.

2 Lear[n]ing did soe *proceed* w*i*th that child,
   I tell you all in veretie,
  He learned more vpon one day
   Then other children did on three,

3 And then bespake the schoole-m*a*ster,
   Vnto the Lo*r*d of Learne said hee,
  I thinke thou be some stranger borne,
   For the holy gost remaines w*i*th thee.

4 He said, I am noe stranger borne,
   Forsooth, m*a*ster, I tell it to thee;
  It is a gift of Almighty God
   W*hi*ch he hath giuen vnto mee.

5 The schoole-m*a*ster turnd him round about,
   His angry mind he thought to asswage,

For the child cold answer him soe quicklie,
   And was of soe tender yeere of age.

6 The child he caused a steed to be brought,
   A golden bridle done him vpon;
  He tooke his leaue of his schoolfellows,
   And home the child that he is gone.

7 And when he came before his father,
   He ffell low downe vpon his knee:
  'My blessing, father, I wold aske,
   If Christ wold grant you wold gine it me.'

8 'Now God thee blesse, my sonne and my heire,
   His servant in heauen *tha*t thou may bee!
  What tydings hast thou brought me, child,
   Thou art comen home so soone to mee?'

9 'Good tydings, father, I haue you brought,
   Goo[d tydings] I hope it is to thee;
  The booke is not in all S[c]ottlande
   But I can read it before your eye.'

10 A ioyed man his father was,
   Euen the worthy Lord of Learne:

---

* Grimm, Deutsche Mythologie, 1875, I, 523 and note.
"In 1585, a man that had been robbed, and had sworn silence,
told his story to a stove in a tavern." A boy who has come

to knowledge of a plot, and has been sworn to secrecy on
pain of death, unburdens his mind to a stove. Grimm,
Deutsche Sagen, No 513, II, 231.

'Thou shalt goe into Ffrance, my child,
The speeches of all strange lands to learne.'

11 But then bespake the child his mother,
The Lady of Learne and then was shee;
Saies, Who must be his well good guide,
When he goes into that strange country?

12 And then bespake that bonnie child,
Vntill his father tenderlie;
Saies, Father, I 'le haue the hend steward,
For he hath beene true to you and mee.

13 The lady to concell the steward did take,
And counted downe a hundred pound there;
Saies, Steward, be true to my sonne and my
heire,
And I will giue thee mickle mere.

14 'If I be not true to my master,' he said,
'Christ himselfe be not trew to mee!
If I be not true to my lord and master,
An ill death that I may die!'

15 The Lord of Learne did apparell his child
With bruche, and ringe, and many a thinge;
The apparrell he had his body vppon,
Thé say was worth a squier's liuinge.

16 The parting of the younge Lord of Learne
With his ffather, his mother, his ffellows
deere,
Wold haue made a manis hart for to change,
If a Iew borne that he were.

17 The wind did serue, and thé did sayle
Over the sea into Ffrance land;
He vsed the child soe hardlie,
He wold let him haue neuer a penny to spend.

18 And meate he wold let the child haue none,
Nor mony to buy none, trulie;
The boy was hungry and thirsty both;
Alas! it was the more pitty.

19 He laid him downe to drinke the water
That was soe low beneathe the brime;
He [that] was wont to haue drunke both ale
and wine
Then was faine of the water soe thinne.

20 And as he was drinking of the water
That ran soe low beneath the brime,

Soe ready was the false steward
To drowne the bonny boy therin.

21 'Haue mercy on me, worthy steward!
My life,' he said, 'lend it to mee,
And all that I am heire vpon,'
Saies, 'I will giue vnto thee.'

22 Mercy to him the steward did take,
And pulld the child out of the brime;
Euer alacke, the more pittye!
He tooke his clothes euen from him.

23 Saies, Doe thou me of that veluett gowne,
The crimson hose beneath thy knee,
And doe me of thy cordiuant shoone,
Are buckled with the gold soe free.

24 'Doe thou me off thy sattin doublett,
Thy shirtband wrought with glistering gold,
And doe mee off thy golden chaine,
About thy necke soe many a fold.

25 'Doe thou me off thy veluett hat,
With fether in that is soe ffine;
All vnto thy silken shirt,
That 's wrought with many a golden seam.'

26 The child before him naked stood,
With skin as white as lilly flower;
For [t]his worthy lords bewtie
He might haue beene a ladye's paramoure.

27 He put vpon him a lether cote,
And breeches of the same beneath the knee,
And sent that bony child him froe,
Service for to craue, truly.

28 He pulld then forth a naked sword
That hange full low then by his side;
'Turne thy name, thou villaine,' he said,
'Or else this sword shall be thy guide.'

29 'What must be my name, worthy steward?
I pray thee now tell it me:'
'Thy name shalbe Pore Disaware,
To tend sheepe on a lonelye lee.'

30 The bonny child he went him froe,
And looked to himselfe, truly;
Saw his apparrell soe simple vppon;
O Lord! he weeped tenderlye.

31 Vnto a shepard's house *that* childe did goe,
    And said, S*ir*, God you saue and see!
Doe you not want a servant-boy,
    To tend y*our* sheepe on a lonelie lee?

32 'Where was thou borne?' the shepard said,
    'Where, my boy, or in what country?'
'S*ir*,' he said, 'I was borne in fayre Scottland,
    That is soe farr beyond the sea.'

33 'I haue noe child,' the shepard sayd;
    'My boy, thoust tarry and dwell w*ith* mee;
My liuinge,' he sayd, 'and all my goods,
    I'le make thee heire [of] after mee.'

34 And then bespake the shepard's wife,
    To the L*ord* of Learne thus did she say;
'Goe thy way to our sheepe,' she said,
    'And tend them well both night and day.'

35 It was a sore office, O L*ord*, for him
    That was a lord borne of a great degree!
As he was tending his sheepe alone,
    Neither sport nor play cold hee.

36 Let vs leaue talking of the L*ord* of Learne,
    And let all such talking goe;
Let vs talke more of the false steward,
    That caused the child all this woe.

37 He sold this L*ord* of Learne's his clothes
    For fiue hundred pound to his pay [there],
And bought himselfe a suite of apparrell
    Might well beseeme a lo*rd* to weare.

38 When he *that* gorgeous apparrell bought,
    That did soe finelie his body vppon,
He laughed the bony child to scorne
    That was the bonny L*ord* of Learne.

39 He laughed *that* bonny boy to scorne;
    L*ord*! pitty it was to heare;
I haue herd them say, and soe haue you too,
    That a man may buy gold to deere.

40 When *that* he had all *that* gorgeous apparrell,
    That did soe finelie his body vpon,
He went a woing to the Duke's daughter of
       France,
    And called himselfe the L*ord* of Learne.

41 The Duke of Ffrance heard tell of this,
    To his place *that* worthy lo*rd* was come,
    truly;

He entertaind him w*ith* a quart of red Renish
    wi[ne],
    Saies, L*ord* of Learne, thou art welcome
    to me.

42 Then to supp*er* that they were sett,
    Lords and ladyes in their degree;
The steward was sett next the Duke of France;
    An vnseemlye sight it was to see.

43 Then bespake the Duke of Ffrance,
    Vnto the L*ord* of Leearne said hee there,
Sayes, L*ord* of Learne, if thou'le marry my
    daught[er],
    I'le mend thy liuing fiue hundred pound a
    yeere.

44 Then bespake *that* lady fayre,
    Answered her ffather soe alone,
That shee would be his marryed wiffe
    If he wold make her lady of Learne.

45 Then hand in hand the steward her he tooke,
    And plight *that* lady his troth alone,
That she shold be his marryed wiffe,
    And he wold make her the ladie of Learne.

46 Thus *that* night it was gone,
    The other day was come, truly;
The lady wold see the robucke run,
    Vp hills and dales and forrest free.

47 Then shee was ware of the younge L*ord* of
       Learne
    Tending sheepe vnder a bryar, trulye.

.   .   .   .

.   .   .   .

48 And thus shee called vnto her maids,
    And held her hands vp thus an hie;
Sayes, Feitch me yond shepard's boy,
    I'le know why he doth mourne, trulye.

49 When he came before *that* lady fayer,
    He fell downe vpon his knee;
He had beene so well brought vpp
    He needed not to learne curtesie.

50 'Where wast thou borne, thou bonny boy?
    Where or in what countrye?'
'Madam, I was borne in faire Scottland,
    That is soe farr beyond the sea.'

51 'What is thy name, thou bonny boy?
I pray thee tell it vnto mee;'
'My name,' he sayes, 'is Poore Disaware,
That tends sheepe on a lonely lee.'

52 'One thing thou must tell mee, bonny boy,
Which I must needs aske of thee,
Dost not thou know the young Lord of Learne?
He is comen a woing into France to me.'

53 'Yes, *that* I doe, madam,' he said,
And then he wept most tenderlie;
'The Lord of Learne is a worthy lord,
If he were at home in his oune country.'

54 'What ayles thee to weepe, my bonny boy?
Tell me or ere I part thee froe:'
'Nothing but for a freind, madam,
That's dead from me many a yeere agoe.'

55 A loud laughter the ladie lought,
O Lord! shee smiled wonderous hie:
'I haue dwelled in France since I was borne;
Such a shepard's boy I did neuer see.

56 'Wilt thou not leaue thy sheepe, my child,
And come vnto service vnto mee?
And I will giue thee meate and fee,
And my chamberlaine thou shalt bee.'

57 'Then I will leaue my sheepe, madam,' he sayd,
'And come into service vnto thee,
If you will giue me meate and fee,
Your chamberlaine *that* I may bee.'

58 When the lady came before her father,
Shee fell low downe vpon her knee;
'Grant me, father,' the lady said,
'This boy my chamberlaine to be.'

59 'But O nay, nay,' the duke did say,
'Soe my daughter it may not bee;
The lord *that* is come a woing to you
Will be offended with you and mee.'

60 Then came downe the false steward,
Which called himselfe the Lord of Learne,
trulie;
When he looked that bonny boy vpon,
An angry man i-wis was hee.

61 'Where was thou borne, thou vagabond?
Where?' he sayd, 'and in what country?'
Says, I was borne in fayre Scotland,
That is soe far beyond the sea.

62 'What is thy name, thou vagabond?
Haue done qu[i]cklie, and tell it to me;'
'My name,' he sayes, 'is Poore Disaware,
I tend sheep on the lonelie lee.'

63 'Thou art a theefe,' the steward said,
'And soe in the end I will prooue thee;'
. . . .
. . . .

64 Then be-spake the ladie fayre,
'Peace, Lord of Learne! I doe pray thee;
Ffor if noe loue you show this child,
Noe favor can you haue of mee.'

65 'Will you beleeue me, lady faire,
When the truth I doe tell yee?
Att Aberdonie, beyond the sea,
His father he robbed a hundred three.'

66 But then bespake the Duke of France
Vnto the boy soe tenderlie;
Saies, Boy, if thou loue harsses well,
My stable-groome I will make thee.

67 And thus *that that* did passe vppon
Till the twelve monthes did draw to an ende;
The boy applyed his office soe well
Euery man became his freind.

68 He went forth earlye one morning
To water a gelding at the water soe free;
The gelding vp, and with his head
He hitt the child aboue his eye.

69 'Woe be to thee, thou gelding,' he sayd,
'And to the mare *that* foled thee!
Thou hast striken the Lord of Learne
A litle tinye aboue the eye.

70 'First night after I was borne, a lord I was,
An earle after my father doth die;
My father is the worthy Lord of Learne,
And child he hath noe more but mee;
He sent me over the sea with the false steward,
And thus that he hath beguiled mee.'

71 The lady [wa]s in her garden greene,
    Walking with her mayds, trulye,
  And heard the boy this mourning make,
    And went to weeping, trulie.

72 ' Sing on thy song, thou stable groome,
    I pray thee doe not let for mee,
  And as I am a true ladie
    I wilbe trew vnto thee.'

73 ' But nay, now nay, madam ! ' he sayd,
    ' Soe *that* it may not bee ;
  I am tane sworne vpon a booke,
    And forsworne I will not bee.'

74 ' Sing on thy song to thy gelding,
    And thou doest not sing to mee ;
  And as I am a true ladie
    I will euer be true vnto thee.'

75 He sayd, Woe be to thee, gelding,
    And to the mare *that* foled thee !
  For thou hast strucken the Lord of Learne
    A litle aboue mine eye.

76 First night I was borne, a lord I was,
    An earle after my father doth dye ;
  My father is the good Lord of Learne,
    And child he hath noe other but mee ;
  My father sent me over [the sea] with the
    false steward,
    And thus *that* he hath beguiled mee.

77 ' Woe be to the steward, lady,' he sayd,
    ' Woe be to him verrily !
  He hath beene about this twelve months day
    For to deceiue both thee and mee.

78 ' If you doe not my councell keepe,
    That I haue told you with good intent,
  And if you doe it not well keepe,
    Ffarwell ! my life is at an ende.'

79 ' I wilbe true to thee, Lord of Learne,
    Or else Christ be not soe vnto me ;
  And as I am a trew ladye,
    I 'le neuer marry none but thee.'

80 Shee sent in for her father, the Duke,
    In all the speed *that* ere might bee ;
  ' Put of my wedding, father,' shee said,
    ' For the loue of God, this monthës three.

81 ' Sicke I am,' the ladye said,
    ' O sicke, and verry like to die !
  Put of my wedding, father Duke,
    Ffor the loue of God, this monthës three.'

82 The Duke of France put of this wedding
    Of the steward and the lady monthës three,
  For the ladie sicke shee was,
    Sicke, sicke, and like to die.

83 Shee wrote a letter with her owne hand,
    In all the speede *that* euer might bee ;
  Shee sent [it] over into Scottland,
    That is soe ffarr beyond the sea.

84 When the messenger came beffore the old
    Lord of Learne,
  He kneeled low downe on his knee,
  And he deliuered the letter vnto him,
    In all the speed *that* euer might bee.

85 [The] first looke he looked the letter vpon,
    Lo ! he wept full bitterly ;
  The second looke he looked it vpon,
    Said, False steward, woe be to thee !

86 When the Ladye of Learne these tydings
    heard,
  O Lord ! shee wept soe biterlye :
  ' I told you of this, now good my lord,
    When I sent my child into that wild
    country.'

87 ' Peace, Lady of Learne,' the lord did say,
    ' For Christ his loue I doe pray thee ;
  And as I am a christian man,
    Wroken vpon him *that* I wilbe.'

88 He wrote a letter with his owne hand,
    In all the speede *that* ere might bee ;
  He sent it into the lords in Scottland,
    That were borne of a great degree.

89 He sent for lords, he sent for k*nigh*ts,
    The best that were in the countrye,
  To go with him into the land of France,
    To seeke his sonne in *that* strange country.

90 The wind was good, and they did sayle,
    Fiue hundred men into France land,
  There to seeke *that* bonny boy
    That was the worthy Lord of Learne.

91 They sought the country through and through,
    Soe farr to the Duke's place of Ffrance
      land;
    There they were ware of *that* bonny boy,
    Standing with a porter's staffe in his hand.

92 Then the worshippfull, thé did bowe,
    The serving-men fell on their knee,
    They cast their hatts vp into the ayre
    For ioy *that* boy *that* they had seene.

93 The Lord of Learne then he light downe,
    And kist his child both cheeke and chinne,
    And said, God blesse thee, my sonne and my
      heire!
    The blisse of heauen *that* thou may winne!

94 The false steward and the Duke of France
    Were in a castle-topp, trulie;
    ' What fooles are yond,' says the false steward,
    ' To the porter makes soe lowe curtesie?'

95 Then bespake the Duke of Ffrance,
    Calling my Lord of Learne, trulie;
    He sayd, I doubt the day be come
    That either you or I must die.

96 Thé sett the castle round about,
    A swallow cold not haue flone away;
    And there thé tooke the false steward
    That the Lord of Learne did betray.

97 And when they had taken the false steward,
    He fell lowe downe vpon his knee,
    And craued mercy of the Lord of Learne
    For the villanous dedd he had done, trulye.

98 ' Thou shalt haue mercy,' said the Lord of
      Learne,
    ' Thou vile traitor, I tell to thee,
    As the lawes of the realme they will thee
      beare,
    Wether it bee for thee to liue or dye.'

99 A quest of lords *that* there was chosen,
    To goe vppon his death, trulie;
    There thé iudged the false steward,
    Whether he was guiltie, and for to dye.

100 The forman of the iury he came in,
     He spake his words full lowd and hie;

    Said, Make thee ready, thou false steward,
    For now thy death it drawes full nie.

101 Sayd he, If my death it doth draw nie,
     God forgiue me all I haue done amisse!
     Where is *that* lady I haue loued soe longe?
     Before my death to giue me a kisse.

102 ' Away, thou traitor!' the lady said,
     ' Auoyd out of my company!
     For thy vild treason thou hast wrought,
     Thou had need to cry to God for mercye.'

103 First they tooke him and h[a]ngd him halfe,
     And let him downe before he was dead,
     And quartered him in quarters many,
     And sodde him in a boyling lead.

104 And then they tooke him out againe,
     And cutten all his ioynts in sunder,
     And burnte him eke vpon a hyll;
     I-wis thé did him curstlye cumber.

105 A loud laughter the lady laught,
     O Lord! she smiled merrylie;
     She sayd, I may praise my heauenly king
     That euer I seene this vile traytor die.

106 Then bespake the Duke of France,
     Vnto the right Lord of Learne sayd he
      there;
     Says, Lord of Learne, if thou wilt marry my
      daught[er]
     I 'le mend thy liuing fiue hundred a yeere.

107 But then bespake *that* bonie boy,
     And answered the Duke quicklie,
     I had rather marry your daughter with a ring
      of go[ld]
     Then all the gold *that* ere I blinket on with
      mine eye.

108 But then bespake the old Lord of Learne,
     To the Duke of France thus he did say,
     Seeing our children doe soe well agree,
     They shalbe marryed ere wee goe away.

109 The Lady of Learne shee was sent for
     Throughout Scottland soe speedilie,
     To see these two children sett vpp
     In their seats of gold full royallye.

B

a. Wood, 401, fol. 95 b. b. Roxburghe, I, 222, III, 534 ;
Roxburghe Ballads, ed. Chappell, II, 55. c. Pepys, I, 494,
No 254 (from a transcript in Percy's papers).

1 It was a worthy Lord of Lorn,
　　He was a lord of high degree,
　　He sent [his son] unto the schoole,
　　　To learn some civility.

2 He learned more learning in one day
　　Then other children did in three ;
　　And then bespake the schoolmaster
　　　Unto him tenderly.

3 ' In faith thou art the honestest boy
　　That ere I blinkt on with mine eye ;
　　I hope thou art some easterling born,
　　　The Holy Ghost is with thee.'

4 He said he was no easterling born,
　　The child thus answered courteously ;
　　My father is the Lord of Lorn,
　　　And I his son, perdye.

5 The schoolmaster turned round about,
　　His angry mood he could not swage ;
　　He marvelled the child could speak so wise,
　　　He being of so tender age.

6 He girt the saddle to the steed,
　　The bridle of the best gold shone ;
　　He took his leave of his fellows all,
　　　And quickly he was gone.

7 And when he came to his father dear
　　He kneeled down upon his knee ;
　　' I am come to you, fathe[r],' he said,
　　　' God's blessing give you me.'

8 ' Thou art welcome, son,' he said,
　　' God's blessing I give thee ;
　　What tidings hast thou brought, my son,
　　　Being come so hastily ? '

9 ' I have brought tidings, father,' he said,
　　' And so likëd it may be,
　　There 's never a book in all Scotland
　　　But I can read it, truly.

10 ' There 's nere a doctor in all this realm,
　　For all he goes in rich array,
　　I can write him a lesson soon
　　　To learn in seven years day.'

11 ' That is good tidings,' said the lord,
　　' All in the place where I do stand ;
　　My son, thou shalt into France go,
　　　To learn the speeches of each land.'

12 ' Who shall go with him ? ' said the lady ;
　　' Husband, we have no more but he ; '
　　' Madam,' he saith, ' my head steward,
　　　He hath bin true to me.'

13 She cal'd the steward to an account,
　　A thousand pound she gave him anon ;
　　Sayes, Good Sir Steward, be as good to my
　　　　child,
　　　When he is far from home.

14 ' If I be fals unto my young lord,
　　Then God be [the] like to me indeed ! '
　　And now to France they both are gone,
　　　And God be their good speed.

15 They had not been in France land
　　Not three weeks unto an end,
　　But meat and drink the child got none,
　　　Nor mony in purse to spend.

16 The child ran to the river's side ;
　　He was fain to drink water then ;
　　And after followed the fals steward,
　　　To put the child therein.

17 ' But nay, marry ! ' said the child,
　　He asked mercy pittifully,
　　' Good steward, let me have my life,
　　　What ere betide my body.'

18 ' Now put off thy fair cloathing
　　And give it me anon ;
　　So put thee of thy s'lken shirt,
　　　With many a golden seam.'

19 But when the child was stript naked,
　　His body white as the lilly-flower,
　　He might have bin seen for his body
　　　A prince's paramour.

20 He put him in an old kelter coat
　　And hose of the same above the knee,
　　He bid him go to the shepherd's house,
　　　To keep sheep on a lonely lee.

21 The child did say, What shall be my name ?
　　Good steward, tell to me ;

'Thy name shall be Poor Disawear,
  That thy name shall be.'

22 The child came to the shepheard's house
  And asked mercy pittifully ;
Sayes, Good sir shepheard, take me in,
  To keep sheep on a lonely lee.

23 But when the shepheard saw the child,
  He was so pleasant in his eye,
'I have no child, I 'le make thee my heir,
  Thou shalt have my goods, perdie.'

24 And then bespake the shepheard's wife,
  Unto the child so tenderly ;
'Thou must take the sheep and go to the field,
  And keep them on a lonely lee.'

25 Now let us leave talk of the child,
  That is keeping sheep on a lonely lee,
And we 'l talk more of the fals steward,
  And of his fals treachery.

26 He bought himself three suits of apparrell,
  That any lord might a seem[d] to worn,
He went a wooing to the Duke's daughter,
  And cal'd himself the Lord of Lorn.

27 The duke he welcomed the yong lord
  With three baked stags anon ;
If he had wist him the fals steward,
  To the devill he would have gone.

28 But when they were at supper set,
  With dainty delicates that was there,
The d[uke] said, If thou wilt wed my daughter,
  I 'le give thee a thousand pound a year.

29 The lady would see the red buck run,
  And also for to hunt the doe,
And with a hundred lusty men
  The lady did a hunting go.

30 The lady is a hunting gon,
  Over le and fell that is so high ;
There was she ware of a shepherd's boy,
  With sheep on a lonely lee.

31 And ever he sighed and made moan,
  And cried out pittifully,
'My father is the Lord of Lorn,
  And knows not wha[t] 's become of me.'

32 And then bespake the lady gay,
  And to her maid she spake anon,
'Go fetch me hither the shepherd's boy ;
  Why maketh he all this moan ? '

33 But when he came before the lady

. . . .

  He was not to learn his courtesie :

34 'Where was thou born, thou bonny child ?
  For whose sake makst thou all this mone ? '
'My dearest friend, lady,' he said,
  'Is dead many years agon.'

35 'Tell thou to me, thou bonny child,
  Tell me the truth and do not lye,
Knost thou not the yong lord of Lorn,
  Is come a wooing unto me ? '

36 'Yes, forsooth,' then said the child,
  'I know the lord then, veryly ;
The young lord is a valliant lord
  At home in his own country.'

37 'Wilt leave thy sheep, thou bonny child,
  And come in service unto me ? '
'Yes, forsooth,' then said the child,
  'At your bidding will I be.'

38 When the steward lookt upon the child,
  He bewraild him villainously :
'Where wast thou born, thou vagabone ?
  Or where is thy country ? '

39 'Ha don ! ha don ! ' said the lady gay,
  She cal'd the steward then presently ;
'Without you bear him more good will,
  You get no love of me.'

40 Then bespake the false steward
  Unto the lady hastily :
'At Aberdine, beyond the seas,
  His father robbëd thousands three.'

41 But then bespake the lady gay
  Unto her father courteously,
Saying, I have found a bonny child
  My chamberlain to be.

42 'Not so, not so,' then said the duke,
  'For so it may not be,

For that young L[ord] of Lorn that comes
    a wooing
Will think somthing of thee and me.'

43 When the duke had lookt upon the child,
    He seemd so pleasant to the eye,
'Child, because thou lovst horses well,
    My groom of stables thou shalt be.'

44 The child plied the horses well
    A twelve month to an end;
He was so courteous and so true
    Every man became his fri[e]nd.

45 He led a fair gelding to the water,
    Where he might drink, verily;
The great gelding up with his head
    And hit the child above the eye.

46 'Wo worth thee, horse!' then said the child,
    'That ere mare foalëd thee!
Thou little knowst what thou hast done;
    Thou hast stricken a lord of high degree.'

47 The d[uke's] daughter was in her garden
    green,
She heard the child make great moan;
    She ran to the child all weeping,
And left her maidens all alone.

48 'Sing on thy song, thou bonny child,
    I will release thee of thy pain;'
'I have made an oath, lady,' he said,
    'I dare not tell my tale again.'

49 'Tell the horse thy tale, thou bonny child,
    And so thy oath shall savëd be;'
But when he told the horse his tale
    The lady wept full tenderly.

50 'I 'le do for thee, my bonny child,
    In faith I will do more for thee;
For I will send thy father word,
    And he shall come and speak with me.

51 'I will do more, my bonny child,
    In faith I will do more for thee,
And for thy sake, my bonny child,
    I 'le put my wedding off months three.'

52 The lady she did write a letter,
    Full pittifully with her own hand,

She sent it to the Lord of Lorn
    Whereas he dwelt in fair Scotland.

53 But when the lord had read the letter
    His lady wept most tenderly:
'I knew what would become of my child
    In such a far country.'

54 The old lord cal'd up his merry men,
    And all that he gave cloth and fee,
With seven lords by his side,
    And into France rides he.

55 The wind servd, and they did saile
    So far into France land;
They were ware of the Lord of Lorn,
    With a porter's staff in his hand.

56 The lords they moved hat and hand,
    The servingmen fell on their knee;
'What folks be yonder,' said the steward,
    'That makes the porter courtesie?'

57 'Thou art a false thief,' said the L[ord] of
    Lorn,
'No longer might I bear with thee;
By the law of France thou shalt be ju[d]gd,
    Whether it be to live or die.'

58 A quest of lords there chosen was,
    To bench they came hastily,
But when the quest was ended
    The fals steward must dye.

59 First they did him half hang,
    And then they took him down anon,
And then put him in boyling lead,
    And then was sodden, brest and bone.

60 And then bespake the Lord of Lorn,
    With many other lords mo;
'Sir Duke, if you be as willing as we,
    We 'l have a marriage before we go.'

61 These children both they did rejoyce
    To hear the lord his tale so ended;
They had rather to day then to morrow,
    So he would not be offended.

62 But when the wedding ended was
    There was delicious dainty cheer;
I 'le tell you how long the wedding did last,
    Full three quarters of a year.

63 Such a banquet there was wrought,
   The like was never seen;
The king of France brought with him then
   A hundred tun of good red wine.

64 Five set of musitians were to be seen,
   That never rested night nor day,
Also Italians there did sing,
   Full pleasantly with great joy.

65 Thus have you heard what troubles great
   Unto successive joyes did turn,
And happy news among the rest
   Unto the worthy Lord of Lorn.

66 Let rebels therefore warnëd be
   How mischief once they do pretend;
For God may suffer for a time,
   But will disclose it in the end.

———◆———

A.   2[4]. on 3.   5[4]. agee.   9[2]. to mee.
    10[4]. to learne the speeches of all strange lands.
    13[2]. 100[li]. 16[3]. ? mams *in MS.* Furnivall.
    19[2]. brimn.   19[4]. thime.   22[3]. euen alacke.
    24[3]. *a long* s *in the MS. between* me *and*
    off. F.
    25[2]. thats.   25[4]. golden swaine. **B.** seam.
    35[3]. tenting.   36[3]. falst.
    37[2]. 500[li]: pay [there]. *Cf.* 43[2], 105[2].
    43[4]. 500[l]. 46[3]. rum.
    47[1,2], 48[1,2], *make a stanza in the MS., and*
    52[3,4], 53, *are written together. 47–53 have*
    been arranged upon the supposition that
    two verses (about the boy's mourning) have
    dropped out after 47[1,2].
    48[1,2]. *A tag after* d *in* maids, hands *may not*
    mean s. F.
    53[4]. *One stroke too many for* oune *in MS.* F.
    54[1]. *One stroke too many for* bony, *or too few*
    for bonny, *in the MS.* F.
    60[4]. I-wis.   61[1]. thou was.
    63[1,2], 64, *are written together in the MS.*
    64[1]. he spake.   65[4]. 100: 3.   67[2]. 12.
    69[4]. the knee. *Cf* .68[4], 75[4].
    70[4]. his child. *Cf.* 76[4].
    74[4]. euer. *Either* ieuer *in MS. or the letter*
    before e *crossed out.* F.
    75[1,2] *are written with* 74, 75[3,4] *with* 76[1,2], *in*
    the MS.
    75[1]. to thy. 76[5]. *Cf.* 70[5]. 77[1]. to thee.
    77[3]. beene aboue: 12.
    79[2]. soe *may be* true: *half the line is pared*
    away. F.
    80[4], 81[4], 82[2]. 3. 90[2]. 500. 92[2]. knees.
    92[4]. *Perhaps* did see. 93[3]. chime.
    93[4]. wiine. 95[3]. daubt.
    98[3]. they. *The* y *is in a modern hand.* F.
    100[2]. hiye. 106[4]. 500.
    107[4]. mine. *One stroke too few in the MS.* F.

    109[1]. They: for sent.
    109[3]. 2. And *for* & *always.*
B.   The tune is Green Sleeves.
  a. Printed for F. Coles, T. Vere, and W. Gil-
    bertson.
  b. Printed by and for A. M[ilbourne], and sold
    by the booksellers of London.
  c. Printed for J. Clarke, W. Thackeray, and
    T. Passinger.
  a, b, c. 1[3]. b, c. sent his son.
    2[1]. b, c. learning *wanting.*
    2[3]. b, c. And thus. 2[4]. c. To him.
    3[2]. b, c. with my. 4[3]. a. Lord of Lord.
    5[2]. b. he thought to asswage.
    5[4]. b. so tender of.
    6[2]. a. of his (?) gold. b, c. of the best gold.
    7[2]. c. on his. 7[4]. b. give to.
    8[1]. b, c. my son. 8[2]. c. I the give.
    9[2]. b. if that well liked. 9[3,4]. b, c. *Wanting.*
    10[1]. b, c. all the. 11[3]. b. to France.
    12[2]. b, c. have none. 12[3]. b. said he.
    13[3]. b, c. as *wanting.* 13[4]. b, c. while he.
    14[1]. b. false to.
    14[2]. b. may God justly punish me indeed.
    c. the like.
    15[2]. b, c. to an. 16[1]. b, c. run. b. river.
    16[2]. b. the water. 17[4]. b. eer else.
    19[2]. b, c. as white. 19[4]. b. princess's.
    20[1]. b, c. him on. 20[2]. a. thee.
    20[4]. a. love lodely: b. keep them on a love
    lovely : c. love lovely.
    21[1]. b, c. child said.
    21[3]. a, b, c. poor dost thou wear. A. dis-
    aware.
    22[3]. b, c. sir *wanting.*
    22[4], 24[4], 25[2], 30[4]. a, b, c. love lovely. A.
    lonelye lee. *Perhaps*, lone, lone, lee.
    23[2]. b, c. in the.
    24[1]. a. wise. b, c. bespoke.

24². c. thee sheep. b. to field.
24⁴. a, c. And get. b. keep.
25¹. b, c. talking. 25³. c. we will.
26². b. a lord. b, c. have seemd.
27³. c. himself. 27⁴. b, c. he should.
28². b, c. were. 28³. b. you will.
28⁴. b, c. pounds. 29³. b, c. an.
30². a, c. Feansell. b. feanser.
30³. b, c. aware.
31¹. b. And often: made great moan.
31⁴. c. what is.
32². b, c. unto her maid anon.
33¹,⁴. a, b, c. *Two lines wanting.*
34¹. b. wast born. c. wast thou born.
35¹. b. to *wanting.* 35². c. the *wanting.*
35⁴. b, c. he is.
36¹. a. foorsooth. c. forsooth saith the.
37³. c. the *wanting.*
38². b, c. bewailed. c. villaniously.
38³. b, c. vagabond.
39¹. a, b, c. Ha down. b, c. gay *wanting.*
40¹. a. stewardly. 41¹. c. than.

42³. b. the Lord. c. young D.
42⁴. b, c. think no good. b. of me nor thee.
43¹. b. had *wanting.* 43². b. in the.
43⁴. b, c. stable.
44⁴. a, c. become. b. became.
45². a. may. b, c. might.
45³. b, c. great *wanting.* b. his heel.
46¹. a. thou horse. b. thee. c. the.
46². b, c, ever. 47¹. a, c. D. daughter.
49¹. a. Mell: lonny. 49⁴. b, c. wept most.
50³,⁴, 51¹,². b, c. *Wanting.*
52¹. b, c. she *wanting:* letter then.
52⁴. a. dwells. b, c. dwelt.
54⁴. b. unto.
55³. b. aware. 56⁴. c. maketh.
57¹. b, c. quoth the. 59². b. they *wanting.*
60². a. more. b, c. mo. 61³. b, c. than.
62². b, c. delicate, dilicate.
63. a. *Before* 63: Such a banquet there was
  wrought, the like was seen I say.
64¹. a. fet. b, c. set.
65¹. b, c. how troubles. 65³. b, c. amongst.

272

THE SUFFOLK MIRACLE

'The Suffolk Miracle.' a. Wood, E. 25, fol. 83. b. Roxburghe, II, 240; Moore's Pictorial Book of Ancient
Ballad Poetry, p. 463.

ALSO Pepys, III, 332, No 328; Crawford, No 1363; Old Ballads, 1723, I, 266.

A young man loved a farmer's daughter, and his love was returned. The girl's father sent her to his brother's, forty miles off, to stay till she should change her mind. The man died. A month after, he appeared at the uncle's at midnight, and, as he came on her father's horse and brought with him her mother's travelling gear, he was allowed to take the girl away with him. As they rode, he complained of headache, and the girl bound her handkerchief about his head; he was cold as clay. In two hours they were at her father's door. The man went to put up the horse, as he said, but no more was seen of him. The girl knocked, and her father came down, much astonished to see her, and still more astonished when she asked if her lover, known by the father to be dead, had not been sent to bring her. The father went to the stable, where the girl said the man would be; there was nobody there, but the horse was found to be 'all on a sweat.' After conferences, the grave was opened, and the kerchief was found about the head of the mouldering body. This was told to the girl, and she died shortly after.

This piece could not be admitted here on its own merits. At the first look, it would be classed with the vulgar prodigies printed for hawkers to sell and for Mopsa and Dorcas to buy. It is not even a good specimen of its kind. Ghosts should have a fair reason for walking, and a quite particular reason for riding. In popular fictions, the motive for their leaving the grave is to ask back plighted troth, to be relieved from the inconveniences caused by the excessive grief of the living, to put a stop to the abuse of children by stepmothers, to repair an injustice done in the flesh, to fulfil a promise ; at the least, to announce the visitant's death. One would not be captious with the restlessness of defeated love, but what object is there in this young man's rising from the grave to take his love from her uncle's to her father's house ? And what sense is there in his headache ?

I have printed this ballad because, in a blurred, enfeebled, and disfigured shape, it is the representative in England of one of the most remarkable tales and one of the most impressive and beautiful ballads of the European continent. The relationship is put beyond doubt by the existence of a story in Cornwall which comes much nearer to the Continental tale.*

Long, long ago, Frank, a farmer's son, was in love with Nancy, a very attractive girl, who lived in the condition of a superior servant in his mother's house. Frank's parents opposed their matching, and sent the girl home to her mother ; but the young pair continued to meet, and they bound themselves to each other for life or for death. To part them effectually, Frank was shipped for an India voyage. He could not write, and nothing was heard of him for nearly three years. On All-hallows-Eve Nancy went out with two companions to sow hemp-seed. Nancy began the rite, saying :

> Hemp-seed, I sow thee,
> Hemp-seed, grow thee!
> And he who will my true-love be
> Come after me
> And shaw thee.

This she said three times, and then, looking back over her left shoulder, she saw Frank indeed, but he looked so angry that she shrieked, and so broke the spell. One night in November a ship was wrecked on the coast, and Frank was cast ashore, with just enough life in him to ask that he might be married to Nancy before he died, a wish which was not to be fulfilled. On the night of his funeral, as Nancy was about to lock the house-door, a horseman rode up. His face was deadly pale, but Nancy knew him to be her lover. He told her that he had just arrived home, and had come to fetch her and make her his bride. Nancy was easily induced to spring on the horse behind him. When she clasped Frank's waist, her arm became stiff as ice. The horse went at a furious pace ; the moon came out in full splendor. Nancy saw that the rider was in grave-clothes. She had lost the power of speech, but, passing a blacksmith's shop, where the smith was still at work, she recovered voice and cried, Save me ! with all her might. The smith ran out with a hot iron in his hand, and, as the horse was rushing by, caught the girl's dress and pulled her to the ground. But the rider held on to the gown, and both Nancy and the smith were dragged on till they came near the churchyard. There the horse stopped for a moment, and the smith seized his chance to burn away the gown with his iron and free the girl. The horseman passed over the wall of the churchyard, and vanished at the grave in which the young man had been laid a few hours before. A piece of Nancy's dress was found on the grave. Nancy died before morning. It was said that one or two of the sailors who survived the wreck testified that Frank, on Halloween, was like one mad, and, after great excitement, lay for hours as if dead, and that when he came to himself he declared that if he ever married the woman who had cast the spell, he would make her suffer for drawing his soul out of his body.†

* Mr W. E. A. Axon, in his Lancashire Gleanings, p. 261, speaks of the story of the Spectre Bridegroom as having been current in the neighborhood of Liverpool in the last century, both in an oral and a printed form. But it is plain that what was current, either way, was simply ' The Suffolk Miracle.' Of this I have a copy learned in the north of Ireland in 1850 (and very much changed as to form), in which the scene is laid "between Armagh and County Clare."

† Popular Romances of the West of England, collected and edited by Robert Hunt, First Series, pp. 265–72, dating from about 1830.

A tale of a dead man coming on horseback to his inconsolable love, and carrying her to his grave, is widely spread among the Slavic people (with whom it seems to have originated) and the Austrian Germans, was well known a century ago among the northern Germans, and has lately been recovered in the Netherlands, Denmark, Iceland, and Brittany. Besides the tale in its integrity, certain verses which occur in it, and which are of a kind sure to impress the memory, are very frequent, and these give evidence of a very extensive distribution. The verses are to this effect:

> The moon shines bright in the lift,
> The dead, they ride so swift,
> Love, art thou not afraid?

to which the lovelorn maid answers,

> How fear, when I am with thee? *

There are also ballads with the same story, one in German, several in Slavic, but these have not so original a stamp as the tale, and have perhaps sprung from it.

The following will serve as specimens of the tale in question; many more may certainly be recovered:

Great Russian. 1–5, Sozonovič, Appendix, Nos 1, 2, 7, 8, 9.† **Little Russian.** 6–8, Trudy, II, 411, 413, 414, Nos 119–21; 9, Dragomanof, p. 392; 10–15, Sozonovič, Appendix, Nos 4–6, 10–12; 16, Bugiel, in the Slavic Archiv, XIV, 146. **White Russian.** 17, 18, Sozonovič, Appendix, No 3; Dobrovolskij, Ethnographical Collection from Smolensk, p. 126, No 58. **Servian.** 19, Krauss, in Wisła, IV, 667. **Croat.** 20, 21, Strohal,

pp. 114, 115, Nos 20, 21. **Croat-Slovenian.** 22–24, Valjavec, Narodne Pripovjedke, p. 239; Plohl-Herdvigov, I, 127, 129. **Slovenian.** 25, 26, Krek, in the Slavic Archiv, X, 357, 358. **Polish.** 27, Zamarski, p. 121; 28, Grudziński, p. 15; 29, Lach-Szyrma, Pamiętnik Naukowy, 1819, I, 358; 30, Kolberg, Lud, XIV, 181; 31, Treichel, in Zeitschrift für Volkskunde, II, 144; 32, Chełchowski, II, 40–42, No 59; 33, Siarkowski, in Zbiór wiadomości do antropologii krajowéj, III, III (21). **Bohemian.** 34, Sumlork, I, 608; 35, Erben, Kytice z básní, p. 23 (ballad founded on tale). **Slovak.** 36, Dobšinsky, pp. 23–30 (three versions). **Wendish.** 37, Schulenburg, Wendische Volkssagen, p. 137 (fragment). **Lithuanian.** 38, Leskien u. Brugman, p. 160, No 2, p. 497, No 43. **Magyar.** 39, Pap, Palóc Népköltemények, p. 94, also Arany and Gyulai, I, 207, No 52, and 569, Aigner, in Gegenwart, 1875, No 12. **Gypsy.** 40, Wlisłocki, Volksdichtungen der siebenbürgischen u. südungarischen Zigeuner, p. 283, No 43. **German,** High and Low. 41, Sztodola, in Herrmann, Ethnologische Mittheilungen aus Ungarn. col. 341 f. (Ofen); 42–45, Vernaleken, Mythen u. Bräuche des Volkes in Oesterreich, pp. 76 f., 79 f., Nos 6–9 (Lower Austria); 46–48, A. Baumgarten, Aus der volksmässigen Ueberlieferung der Heimat (Geburt, Heirat, Tod), pp. 135, 136, 136 f. (Upper Austria); 49, Boeckel, in Germania, XXXI, 117 (Baden); 50, 51, Jahn, Volkssagen aus Pommern u. Rügen, pp. 404, 406, No 515, I, II; 52, J. F. Cordes, in The Monthly Magazine, 1799, VIII, 602 f. (Glandorf, Lower Saxony); 53, Müllenhof, Sagen, etc., p. 164, No 224 (Ditmarsch). **Nether-**

---

* A portion (or portions) of a Low German tale of this class, the verses and a little more, was the basis of Bürger's 'Lenore,' composed in 1773. (As to the particulars of the traditional basis, Erich Schmidt seems to me undoubtedly right: Charakteristiken, p. 219 f.) At the end of the last century, when 'Lenore' became well known in England through half a dozen translations, it was maintained that Bürger had taken the idea of his ballad from 'The Suffolk Miracle,' with which he was supposed to have become acquainted through the copy in Old Ballads, 1723. See The Monthly Magazine, 1796, II, 603. But it is nearly certain that Bürger had not seen, and never saw, the "Old Ballads" of 1723. In 1777 Boie made him acquainted with a book of that title, but this was in all probability Evans's first col-

lection, which appeared in that year. See Strodtmann, Briefe von und an G. A. Bürger, II, 85, 87. Bürger knew 'Sweet William's Ghost' from Percy's Reliques, and took a hint or two from that, besides the lover's name.

† I. Sozonovič, Bürger's 'Lenore,' and the related matter in European and Russian popular poetry, Warsaw, 1893 (in Russian). Professor Wollner has furnished me translations of some twenty-five pieces in Sozonovič. See, for German versions of many of the Slavic tales and ballads, Wollner, in Archiv für slavische Philologie, VI, 243–59; Krek, in the same, X, 357–59, and in Magazin für die Litteratur des In- u. Auslandes, 1887, CXII, 629–32, 650–54; Grudziński, Lenore in Polen, 1890, p. 13 ff.; Treichel, in Zeitschrift für Volkskunde, II, 144.

landish. 54–56, Pol de Mont, in Volkskunde, II, 129–31. **Danish.** 57, Grundtvig, Danmarks g. Folkeviser, III, 873. **Icelandic.** 58, Árnason, Íslenzkar þjóðsögur, I, 280 ff.; Maurer, Isländische Volkssagen, p. 73 f.

A lover, who has long been unheard of, but whose death has not been ascertained, roused from his last sleep by the grief of his mistress (which in some cases drives her to seek or accept the aid of a spell), comes to her by night on horseback and induces her to mount behind him. As they ride, he says several times to her, The moon shines bright, the dead ride swift, art not afraid? Believing him to be living, the maid protests that she feels no fear, but at last becomes alarmed. He takes her to his burial-place, and tries to drag her into his grave; she escapes, and takes refuge in a dead-house (or house where a dead man is lying). The lover pursues, and calls upon the dead man within the house to give her up, which in most cases, for fellowship, he prepares to do. At the critical moment a cock crows, and the maid is saved.

Some of the tales are brief and defective, some mixed with foreign matter. The predominant traits, with a few details and variations, may be briefly exhibited by a synoptical analysis.

A pair of lovers are plighted to belong to each other in life and death, 50, 51, 57; whichever dies first is to visit the other, 48; the man, at parting, promises to come back, alive or dead, 25, 26. The man dies in war, 1, 2, 10, 14, 15, 17, 20–22, 25–29, 31, 32, 36, 39, 42, 45–52; the maid, her lover not returning, grieves incessantly, 4, 6–13, 15–18, 28, 29, 32, 49, 53. (The return of the lover is enforced by a spell, recommended or conducted by an old woman, 22, 28, 36, 39, 41, 45, advised by a priest, 20, 21, worked by the maid, 33; a dead man's head, bones, carcass, boiled in a pot, 15–17, 20, 21, 22, 27, 39, a piece of the man's clothing, 28, a cat burned in a red-hot oven, 33.) The man comes on horseback, mostly at night; she mounts with him, 1–5, 8–12, 14–23, 25–32, 36–44, 46, 48–53, 56–58, taking with her a bundle of clothes, smocks, etc., 1, 6, 7, 9, 16,

17, 21, 23, 24, 26, 32, 35, 36, 38. (There are two horses, 45; they go off in coach or wagon, 6, 7, 13, 24, 33; stag for horse, 47; afoot, 35, 54.) As they go, the man says or sings once or more, The moon shines bright, the dead ride fast, art thou afraid? and she answers that with him she has no fear. The verses occur in some form in all copies but 2, 3, 9, 11, 13, 15, 29, 32, 33, 38, 40, 51, and are mostly well preserved. (It is a voice from the churchyard in 38.)

Arrived at a grave in a churchyard, the man bids the maid to go in, 2, 4–6, 8, 10–17, 20, 21, 23, 24, 26, 32, 36, 39; she says, You first, 2, 4–6, 8, 11–17, 23, 24, 32, 36, 39; she will first throw him her things, and then come, 14; she throws in her bundle of things, 1, 5, 23, 24, 26, 32, 36; hands them to him one after another, 6, 7, 16, 17; tells him to take her by the hands, and reaches out to him the sleeves of her gown, 2, 12; gives him the end of a piece of linen or of a ball of thread to pull at, 16, 19; asks him to spread her kerchief in the grave to make the frozen ground softer, 27, all this to gain time. He tears her things in the grave, 9, 13, 24; he seizes her apron, clutches her clothes, to drag her in, 4, 8, 21, 22, 25, 43, 44, 47, 48 (in 4 she cuts the apron in two, in 8 tears her gown off, in 25, 43, 44, 48, her apron parts); she runs off, 1–9, 11, 13–17, 20–27, 29, 30, 35, 36, 38, 39, 41, 45, 46, 48, 50; she throws down articles of dress to delay his pursuit, he tears them, 9, 13, 18, 38.

The maid takes refuge in a dead-house (or house in which there is a dead body, or two, or three), 1–4, 6, 8, 11–15, 17, 18, 20–22, 24–27, 29, 30, 32, 34–36, 38, 39, 41, 45, 46 (malt-kiln, 5, house of vampire, 16). She climbs on to the stove, or hides behind it, 6–8, 11, 13–16, 21, 24, 26, 32, 34, 36, 39, 41. The dead lover calls to the dead in the house to open, hand her out, 4, 6, 8, 11, 17, 20–22, 25, 26, 27, 29, 30, 32, 35, 36, 38, 39, 41, 45, 46, 48, 50, 57 (to seize the girl, 11; to tear her to pieces, 24); the dead man within is disposed to help his comrade, makes an effort so to do, 11, 29, 34, 41, 45, 46; opens the door, 6, 21, 36, 39; is prevented from helping because the maid has laid her cross,

scapular, on his coffin, 4, 17 ; (two dead, because she has laid her rosary on the feet of
one, her prayer-book on the feet of the other,
32 ;) the maid throws at him beads from her
rosary, which check his movements until the
string is exhausted ; the maid puts up three
effectual prayers, 35 ; Ave sounds, 48 ; by
the maid's engaging his attention with a
long tale, 38 ; because his wife or a watcher
knocks him on the head, and orders him to
lie where he is, 20, 30 ; because his wife has
turned him over on his face, 57. In a few
cases the dead man within inclines to protect
the maid, 1, 22, 25 ; the two get into a fight,
1, 13–15, 17, 26, 36 (quarrel, 7). The cock
crows, and the dead fall powerless, return to
their places, turn to pitch, vanish, 1, 2, 3, 5,
8, 10, 11, 13–15, 17, 24, 26, 27, 29, 30, 32,
34–36, 39, 41, 45, 46, and the maid is saved.*

In some of the tales of this section the
maid is not so fortunate : in 6, the two dead
take her by the legs and tear her asunder ;
in 21, the lover tears her, the dead man in
the house having surrendered her. In 39, the
lover, having been let in, says to the other
dead man, Let us tear her to pieces, and is
proceeding to do so, but is stopped by the
cock. She dies of shock, or after a few days,
8, 11, 13, 16, 17, 29, 31, 32, 36.

The maid's escape assured, in one way or another, the man calls to her, Your good luck :
I would have taught you to weep for the dead
(he had been tearing her things in the grave,
and her shift, which she had dropped to delay his pursuit), 9. Your body would have
been rent into as many bits as your smocks
(a bit was found on every grave in the church-
yard), 22, 35. I would have torn you into
a thousand tatters. I was all but saved, and
have had to come so far ! Then he warned
her never again to long for the dead, 42. I
would have taught you to disturb the dead,
41. It was her luck, for she would have been
torn into a thousand bits, like her apron. Let

this be a warning to you, says Our Lady to
the girl, never to mourn so much again for
the dead, for he had a hard journey to make,
43. He tore a portion of her gown into a
thousand pieces, and laid one on every grave,
saying, You were not so much a simpleton
to mourn for me as I was not to tear you to
pieces, 30. There was on every grave a bit
of her gown, from which we may see how it
would have fared with her, 31.

Resentment for the disturbance caused by
the maid's excessive grief is expressed also
in 6, Since you have wept so much for me,
creep into my grave ; in 12, she has troubled
him by her perpetual weeping, he will take
her where he dwells ; in 20, Another time
do not long for my dead body ; in 27, You
have mourned for me, now sleep with me ; in
32, the maid's continual weeping is a burden
to her lover in his grave. In 40, the remon-
strance is affectionate and like (suspiciously
like) that of Helgi and of Sir Aage (II, 235).

In some copies the story closes at the grave,
2, 10, 19, 23, 28, 40, 43, 44, 47, 49, 51, 52,
54, 56, 58 ; many of these, however, are brief
and defective. The man lays himself in the
grave, which closes, she flies, 23 ; he descends
into the grave and tries to draw her in by her
apron, the apron tears, she faints, and is found
lying on the ground the next morning, 43 ;
he descends into the grave and tries to draw
her after him, she resists, the grave closes,
and she remains without, 47 ; he disappears,
she is left alone, 49, 52. She goes into the
grave, remains there, and dies, 10 ; the grave
opens, he pushes or drags her in, 54 ; both
disappear in the grave, 56 ; the horse rushes
three times round in a ring, and they are
nowhere, 53 ; she is killed by the man, her
flesh torn off, and her bones broken, 51.

The maid finds herself in a strange land,
44, 47 ; she is among people of different language, 26, 28, 29, 45 ; nobody knows of the
place which she says she came from, 27 ; she

---

* 30, 31, 32, 50, have curious popular traits. In 30, 32,
the dead man (men) within being unable to render aid, the
lover calls to yarn spun on Thursday (on Thursday after
the evening meal) to open. A watchman tells the yarn to
stay where it was hanged ; the girl cuts the skein in two
with an axe. In 31 there is no corpse in the house ; the

lover calls on a ball of thread and a broom, 'ohne Seele'
(with no centre-piece, no handle) to open. In 50 the dead
man within cannot help the man without because a broom is
standing on its handle ; so the man without calls on a skein
of yarn, a pot-hook, a ball of thread, to open. For various
reasons these appeals prove bootless.

is a long time in getting home, and nobody knows her then, 25; she is years in going home (from two to nine), 20, 22, 28, 46.

The man and woman are a married pair in 2, 3, 23, 44, 45; in 44, the woman has married a second time, contrary to a mutual agreement. 10, 12, 16, 18, 19, have a taint of vampirism, and in 2 a stake is driven through the body of the man after he has returned to his grave, as was done with vampires.

In 31, the maid throws herself from the horse, the man, holding to her gown, tears off a large piece of it, and bits of the gown are found on every grave the next day; so in the Cornish tale, when the maid is pulled from the horse, the man retains a portion of her gown, and a piece is found on his grave. In 27, the maid's kerchief is found in the man's grave, and serves to corroborate her story; so in the Suffolk tale, with the handkerchief which the maid had bound round the man's head. 55, a brief and corrupted copy, compares very well with the Suffolk tale for pointlessness. The man comes on his father's horse, takes the girl on, and rides with her all round the village. Towards morning he brings the maid back to her chamber, and the horse to the stable, and goes where he came from.

Ballads. **Little Russian.** 1, 2, Golovatsky, I, 83, No 40; II, 708, No 12. **Slovenian.** 3, Valjavec, as before, preface, p. IV. **Polish.** 4, Grudziński, p. 25, 'Helene,' Galicia; 5, Max Waldau (G. v. Hauenschild) in Deutsches Museum, 1851, I, 136, No 5, Kreis Ratibor, Oberschlesien; 6, Mickiewicz, 'Ucieczka' (Works, Paris, 1880, I, 74), based on a ballad sung in Polish in Lithuania. **Bohemian, Moravian.** 7, Erben, 1864, p. 471; 8, Bartoš, 1882, p. 150; 9, 10, Sušil, p. 791, p. 111, No 112. **Gypsy.** 11, Wlislocki, as before, p. 104, South Hungary. **German.** 12, Schröer, Ein Ausflug nach Gottschee, Wiener Akademie, Sitzb. d. phil.-hist. Classe, LX, 235.*

As I have already said, the ballads seem less original than the tales; that is, to have been made from tales, as 'The Suffolk Miracle' was. 5, 7, 10, are of the vulgar sort, like the English piece, 7 having perhaps received literary touches. In none of them does the maid fly and the man pursue; the catastrophe is at the grave.

The lovers have sworn mutual faith, 5, 10; the maid wishes that the man may come back, dead or living, 3, 10, 12; even from hell, 6.

The man has fallen in war, 1, 2, 6, 7, 8, 9, 12.

A spell is employed to bring him back, 1, 2, 6, 9.

He comes on a horse, 3, 4, 6–8, 11, 12; in a wagon, 5, 10; on foot, 1, 2, 9.

The verses found in the tales occur in 3 (three times), 4, 5, 6, 12; in 10, a voice from the clouds cries, What hast thou done, to be going off with a dead man?

She is taken to a graveyard. The grave closes over the man, she is left without, 3, 5, 8, 10, 12; both go into the grave, 4, 6, 7, 11.

She breathes out her soul on the grave, 3; she finds herself in the morning in a strange land, of different speech, is seven years in going home, 12.

1, 2, 9, are varieties of one ballad. The man asks the maid to go out with him to the dark wood, 1; to the cherry-tree (trees), 2, 9. After a time, he tells her to go back, he is no longer her lover, but a devil; she turns to dust, 1; the cock crows, he tells her to go home and not look round, to thank God for the cock, because he should have cut off her head, he is no longer her lover but a devil, 2. In 9, the man says his head aches badly, for, after mouldering six years, she had forced him to rise by her spell. The maid tells her mother that her lover is buried under the cherry-trees, mass is said for him; he returns to give thanks for his redemption from hell.†

Reverting now to the English tales, we perceive that the Cornish is a very fairly well-

---

* For German versions of most of the Slavic pieces, Grudziński, as before, p. 27; Wollner, as before, pp. 250, 255 f., 258; Krek, as before, p. 652. 7 also in A. Waldau's Böhmische Granaten, II, 254, No 354.

'Lenore' in Wunderhorn, II, 19, 1808, is to be rejected as spurious, on internal and external evidence. See Pröhle,

G. A. Bürger, Sein Leben und seine Dichtungen, 1856, p. 100 f.

† In 11 we have to do with a married pair, as in several of the tales. In tale 44 the woman has been twice married, and her first husband comes for her.

preserved specimen of the extensive cycle which has been epitomized. Possibly the full moonshine is a relic of the weird verses which occur in so many copies. The hemp-seed rite is clearly a displacement and perversion of the spell resorted to in five Slavic and two German copies to compel the return of the dead man. It has no sense otherwise, for the maid did not need to know who was to be her lover; she was already bound to one for life and death. The ballad was made up from an imperfect and confused tradition. In pointlessness and irrationality it easily finds a parallel in the 55th tale, as already remarked. The hood and safeguard brought by the ghost represent the clothes which the girl takes with her in numerous copies. Remembering the 9th ballad, where the *revenant* complains of a headache, caused by the powerful enchantment which had been brought to bear on him, we may quite reasonably suppose that the headache in ' The Suffolk Miracle,' utterly absurd to all appearance, was in fact occasioned by a spell which has dropped away from the Suffolk story, but is retained in the Cornish.

M. Paul Sébillot has recently (in 1879) taken down, in that part of Brittany where French is exclusively spoken, a tale which is almost a repetition of the English ballad, and which for that reason has been kept by itself, ' Les Deux Fiancés,' Littérature orale de la Haute-Bretagne, p. 197. A young man and a maid have plighted themselves to marry and to be faithful to one another even after death. The young man, who is a sailor, goes on a voyage, and dies without her learning the fact. One night he leaves his tomb, and comes on a white mare, taken from her father's stable, to get the girl, who is living at a farm at some distance from her own home. The girl mounts behind him: as they go he says, The moon is bright, death is riding with you, are you not afraid? and she answers, I am not afraid, since you are with me. He complains of a headache; she ties her handkerchief round his head. They arrive at the girl's home; she gets down and knocks. To an inquiry, Who is there? she replies, Your

daughter, whom you sent for by my husband that is to be. I have come on horseback with him, and lent him my handkerchief on the way, since he had none. He is now in the stable attending to the horse. They go to the stable and find the mare in a sweat, but no man. The girl then understands that her lover is dead, and she dies, too. They open the man's grave to bury the two together, and find the girl's handkerchief on his head. This is the English ballad over again, almost word for word, with the difference that the lover dies at sea, and that the substance of the notable verses is preserved.

In marked and pleasing contrast with most of the versions of the tale with which we have been dealing, in so many copies grotesque and ferocious, with a lover who, from impulses not always clear, from resentment sometimes that his comfort has been disturbed by her unrestrained grief, sometimes that she has been implicated in forcing him by magic to return to the world which he had done with, is bent on tearing his lass to pieces, is a dignified and tender ballad, in which the lovers are replaced by brother and sister. This ballad is found among the Servians, Bulgarians, Greeks, and Albanians, and is very common among the Greeks, both of the mainland and the islands.

Servian. Karadžić, II, 38, No 9, ' Yovan and Yelitza;' Talvj, Volkslieder der Serben, 1853, I, 295; Dozon, Chansons p. bulgares, p. 321; Bowring, Servian Popular Poetry, p. 45. Davidović, pp. 10–14, ' Yovo and Mara,' No 7; Krek, in Magazin f. d. Litt. d. In- u. Auslandes, p. 652, No 8.

Bulgarian. Dozon, Chansons p. bulgares, p. 130, No 7, p. 319. Kačanovskij, p. 120, No 48; Krek as above, p. 653 f., No 10, ' Lazar and Yovana.' Miladinof, 1861, 1891, p. 145, No 100, ' Lazar and Petkana;' Krek, p. 653, No 9. Miladinof, p. 317, No 200, ' Elin Doika;' Rosen, Bulgarische Volksdichtungen, p. 247, No 103. ' Elin Doina,' Popov, in Periodičesko Spisanie, II, 162, lacks the last half; Krek, p. 654, No 11. ' Yana,' Miladinof, p. 339, No 229, Rosen, p. 116, No 32, diverges considerably from the others.

Romaic. Twenty copies, including all previously published, Polites, in Δελτίον τῆς ἱστορ. κ. ἐθνολ. ἑταιρ. τ. Ἑλλάδος, II, 193–261, 552–57, 1885–87. Kanellakes, Χιαχὰ Ἀνάλεκτα, p. 37, No 27, p. 58, No 49, 1890. Ζωγραφεῖος Ἀγών, I, 308, No 30, 397, No 17, 1891. ' Constantine and Arete ' (mostly). C. B. Sheridan, The Songs of Greece, p. 207; C. C. Felton, in English and Scottish Ballads, Boston, 1860, I, 307; Lucy M. J. Garnett, Greek Folk-Songs, etc., 1885, p. 126.

Albanian. (' Garentina,' = Arete.) De Rada, Rapsodie, etc., p. 29 (I, xvii); Dozon, Ch. p. bulgares, p. 327, De Grazia, C. p. albanesi, p. 138. Camarda, Appendice al Saggio, etc., p. 98 (fragment, last half), p. 102. Dora d' Istria, Revue des Deux Mondes, LXIII, 407. La Calabria, II, 55, 1890. — Tale, Metkos, Ἀλβανικὴ Μέλισσα, p. 189, No 12, translated in Dozon, Contes albanais, p. 251.*

A mother has nine sons and an only daughter. The daughter is sought in marriage; the mother and eight of her sons wish to match her in their neighborhood, but the youngest son (whom it will be convenient to call Constantine) has his way, and she is given to a suitor from a distant country (often Babylon). The brothers are to visit their sister often (Slavic); Constantine promises to bring her to his mother should there be special occasion. A fatal year comes, and all the brothers die of the plague (in a few cases they are killed in war). The mother chants laments at the graves of the eight, strews flowers, burns candles, gives alms for their souls; at Constantine's grave she tears her hair. She curses Constantine for the distant marriage, and demands of him her daughter. God takes pity (on mother, sister, or son). The stone over his grave (his coffin, a board for the grave, his shroud, a cloud) is turned into a horse; he goes to his sister and informs her that she is wanted by her mother. The sister will put on gold for joy or black for grief; she is to come as she stands. (He tries to prevent her going, in the Servian copies, where his object is to pay the promised visit.) On the way the sister notes that Constantine is gray with mould, he smells of earth, his skin is black, his eyes are dull, his hair is dusty, his hair or teeth fallen out; why is this? He has been at work in the ground, has been building nine white houses, there has been dust, wind, and rain on the road, he has had long watches, sore sickness. He smells of incense, too; that is because he has been at church lately. Birds call out in human voice as they pass, What wonder is this, the living travelling with the dead! (Thrice in Romaic, 9, 10, and the Albanian tale, twice in Romaic 13.) The sister asks Constantine if he hears what the birds are saying; he hears, they are birds, let them talk. They near their mother's house; a church is hard by. Constantine bids his sister go on; he must say a prayer in the church, or pay a votive candle, find a ring which he lost there, see to his horse; he disappears. The house is locked, the windows shut, there is every sign of desolation and neglect. The daughter knocks; the mother, from within, cries, Avaunt, Death! I have no more children! The daughter cries, It is I.† Who brought you? Constantine. Constantine is dead; (has been dead three days, forty days, five months, twelve years!) The mother opens, they die in a mutual embrace (the mother dies, one dies within, one without).

' Le Frère de Lait,' Villemarqué, Barzaz Breiz, No 22, p. 163, ed. 1867, has no claim to be associated with these ballads, the only feature in which it has similarity not being genuine. Compare ' La Femme aux deux Maris,' Luzel, Gwerziou Breiz-Izel, I, 266–71, two versions, and II, 165–69, two more; and see Luzel, De l'authenticité des chants du Barzas-Breiz, p. 39.

---

* No filiation is implied in the above arrangement of the ballads.

† The mother demands tokens of her identity, Romaic 11, 12 21, 22, Albanian 4, 5. Cf. II, 215.

1 A WONDER stranger ne'r was known
  Then what I now shall treat upon.
  In Suffolk there did lately dwell
  A farmer rich and known full well.

2 He had a daughter fair and bright,
  On whom he plac'd his chief delight;
  Her beauty was beyond compare,
  She was both virtuous and fair.

3 A young man there was living by,
  Who was so charmëd with her eye
  That he could never be at rest,
  He was with love so much possest.

4 He made address to her, and she
  Did grant him love immediately;
  Which when her father came to hear,
  He parted her and her poor dear.

5 Forty miles distant was she sent,
  Unto his brother's, with intent
  That she should there so long remain
  Till she had chang'd her mind again.

6 Hereat this young man sadly grievd,
  But knew not how to be relievd;
  He sighd and sobd continually
  That his true love he could not see.

7 She by no means could to him send
  Who was her heart's espousëd friend;
  He sighd, she grievd, but all in vain,
  For she confin'd must still remain.

8 He mournd so much that doctor's art
  Could give no ease unto his heart;
  Who was so strang[e]ly terrified,
  That in short time for love he dyed.

9 She that from him was sent away
  Knew nothing of his dying-day,
  But constant still she did remain;
  To love the dead was then in vain.

10 After he had in grave been laid
   A month or more, unto this maid
   He comes about middle of the night,
   Who joyd to see her heart's delight.

11 Her father's horse, which well she knew,
   Her mother's hood and safeguard too,
   He brought with him to testifie
   Her parents' order he came by.

12 Which when her unckle understood,
   He hop't it would be for her good,
   And gave consent to her straightway
   That with him she should come away.

13 When she was got her love behind,
   They passd as swift as any wind,
   That in two hours, or little more,
   He brought her to her father's door.

14 But as they did this great haste make,
   He did complain his head did ake;
   Her handkerchief she then took out,
   And tyed the same his head about.

15 And unto him she thus did say:
   'Thou art as cold as any clay;
   When we come home, a fire wee'l have;'
   But little dreamt he went to grave.

16 Soon were they at her father's door,
   And after she ne'r see him more;
   'I'le set the horse up,' then he said,
   And there he left this harmless maid.

17 She knockt, and strait a man he cryed,
   'Who's there?' ''T is I,' she then replyed;
   Who wondred much her voice to hear,
   And was possest with dread and fear.

18 Her father he did tell, and then
   He stared like an affrighted man:
   Down stairs he ran, and when he see her,
   Cry'd out, My child, how cam'st thou here?

19 'Pray, sir, did you not send for me,
   By such a messenger?' said she:
   Which made his hair stare on his head,
   As knowing well that he was dead.

20 'Where is he?' then to her he said;
   'He's in the stable,' quoth the maid.
   'Go in,' said he, 'and go to bed;
   I'le see the horse well littered.'

21 He stared about, and there could hee
   No shape of any mankind see,
   But found his horse all on a sweat;
   Which made him in a deadly fret.

22 His daughter he said nothing to,
   Nor no one else, though well they knew
   That he was dead a month before,
   For fear of grieveing her full sore.

23 Her father to his father went
Who was deceasd, with this intent,
To tell him what his daughter said ;
So both came back unto this maid.

24 They askd her, and she still did say
'T was he that then brought her away ;
Which when they heard they were amaz'd,
And on each other strang[e]ly gaz'd.

25 A handkerchief she said she tyed
About his head, and that they tryed ;
The sexton they did speak unto,
That he the grave would then undo.

26 Affrighted then they did behold
His body turning into mould,
And though he had a month been dead,
This kercheif was about his head.

27 This thing unto her then they told,
And the whole truth they did unfold ;
She was thereat so terrified
And grievd, she quickly after dyed.

28 Part not true love, you rich men, then ;
But, if they be right honest men
Your daughters love, give them their way,
For force oft breeds their lives' decay.

The Suffolk Miracle, or, A relation of a young man who a month after his death appeared to his sweetheart and carryed her behind him fourty miles in two hours time and was never seen after but in the grave.
To the tune of My bleeding heart, etc.
London : Printed for W. Thackery and T. Passenger. [1689. *The date added by Wood.*]
Roxburghe and Crawford : Printed by and for A. M[ilbourne], and sold by the booksellers of Pye-corner and London-bridge.

Pepys : Printed for F. C[oles], T. V[ere], J. W[right], J. C[lark], W. T[hackeray], T. P[assinger].

a. 14³, 25¹. handcherchief.
16⁴. he set (O. B. left).   17². whose.
22¹. too.   24⁴. others.   25⁴. undoe.
b. 3¹. There was a young man.
4¹. addresses.   4³. But when.
16⁴. he set.   19¹. did not you.
19³. hair stand.   27². did *wanting*.

273

KING EDWARD THE FOURTH AND A TANNER OF TAMWORTH

a. Wood, 401, fol. 44, Bodleian Library.

b. Douce, I, 109, Bodleian Library.

c. Roxburghe, I, 176, 177 ; Chappell, Roxburghe Ballads, I, 529.

THE ballad is also in the Pepys collection, II, 129, No 113, and there are two copies in the Euing collection, Nos 273, 274.

The following entries occur in the Stationers' Registers :

1564, September or October, William Greffeth licenced to print a book intituled ' The story of Kynge Henry the IIIJth and the Tanner of Tamowthe.'   Arber, I, 264.

1586, August 1, Edward White, ' A merie

songe of the Kinge and the Tanner.' Arber, II, 451.*

1600, October 6, William White, by the consent of Widow Danter, 'A merye, pleasant and delectable history betwene Kinge Edward the IIIJth and a Tanner of Tamworthe,' and, by like consent of the Widow Danter, "the bal[l]ad of the same matter that was printed by her husband John Danter." Arber, III, 173.

1615, December 9, John Trundle, for a ballad of 'The King and the Tanner.' Arber, III, 579.

1624, December 14, Master Pavier, John Wright, and others, a ballad, 'King and Tanner.' Arber, IV, 131.

The ballad mentioned in the entry under the year 1600 is unquestionably our ballad, or an earlier form of it. No copy from the first half of the seventeenth century is known to be preserved. The "delectable history" entered under the same date is extant in an edition of 1596, printed by John Danter, and in one of 1613, printed by William White.† The ballad, as we have it, was made by abridging the fifty-six stanzas of the history to thirty-nine, with other changes. The history itself has its predecessor, and, as Ritson remarks, its undoubted original, in 'The King and the Barker,' ‡ between which and the history, though the former has come down to us in a sadly mutilated condition, and has been freely treated in the remodelling, there still remain a few verbal correspondences. Several good points are added in the history, and one or two dropped.

'King Edward the Fourth and Tanner of Tamworth,' in Percy's Reliques, 1765, II, 75, was compounded from Danter's history, 1596, and a copy "in one sheet folio, without date, in the Pepys collection." §

King Edward, while out a-hunting, sees a tanner coming along the way, and takes a fancy to accost him. Leaving his lords under a tree, he rides forward and asks the tanner the way to Drayton Basset; the tanner directs him to turn in at the first pair of gallows. The king presses for a civil answer; the tanner bids him be gone; he himself has been riding all day and is fasting. The king promises meat and drink of the best for his company to Drayton Basset; the tanner makes game of the offer, and tries to get away, but in vain. The king now proposes to change his horse for the tanner's mare; the tanner demands a noble to boot, nor shall a cowhide which he is riding on go with the mare. The cowhide thrown on to the king's saddle frightens the horse and the tanner is pitched off; after this he will not keep the horse, but the king in turn exacts a noble to boot. Then the king sounds his horn, and his attendants come riding in; the tanner takes the whole party to be strong thieves, but when he sees the suite fall on their knees he would be glad to be out of the company. 'A collar! a collar!' cries the king (to make the tanner esquire, but this is inadvertently left out in the

---

* 1599, August 28, two plays, being the first and second part of [Thomas Heywood's] 'Edward the IIIJth and the Tanner of Tamworth,' etc. Arber, III, 147.

† See an appendix to this ballad. White's edition has verbal variations from the earlier, and supplies three lines and a half-line which have been cut off in the Bodleian copy of Danter. Heber had a copy of 'King Edward 4th and the Tanner,' printed by Edward Allde (1602–23), whether the "history" or the "ballad" does not appear.

‡ Printed by Ritson, Pieces of Ancient Popular Poetry, 1791, p. 57. Given in an appendix.

§ "Seemingly," says Mr Chappell, "not one bound up with the collection of ballads."

Selden, in the second edition of his Titles of Honor (for so he chooses to spell), 1631, p. 836, remarks: Nor is that old pamphlet of the Tanner of Tamworth and King Edward the Fourth so contemptible but that wee may thence note also an observable passage wherein the use of making

Esquires by giving collars is expressed. He then quotes two stanzas from the history :

'A coller ! a coller !' our king gan cry ;
　Quoth the tanner, It will breed sorrow ;
For after a coller commeth a halter,
　I trow I shall be hangd to morrow.

'Be not afraid, tanner,' said our king;
　'I tell thee, so mought I thee,
Lo, here I make thee the best esquire
　That is in the North Countrie !'

(This passage is not in the first edition, of 1614, as I am informed by Mr Macmath, who has copied it for me.) Percy says that he has "restored" one of his stanzas from the last of these two. The restoration might as well have been made from Danter's history, which he was using. There is a trifling variation from Danter in the fourth verse, as given by Selden and repeated by Percy, which is found in White's edition.

ballad). 'After a collar comes a halter,' exclaims the unhappy tanner. But the king is graciously pleased to pay for the sport which he has had by conferring on the tanner an estate of three hundred pound a year; * in return for which his grateful liegeman engages to give him clouting-leather for his shoon if ever he comes to Tamworth.

Next to adventures of Robin Hood and his men, the most favorite topic in English popular poetry is the chance-encounter of a king, unrecognized as such, with one of his humbler subjects. Even in the Robin Hood cycle we have one of these meetings (in the seventh and eighth fits of the Little Gest), but there the king visits Robin Hood deliberately and in disguise, whereas in the other tales (except the latest) the meeting is accidental.

The most familiar of these tales are ' The King and the Tanner,' and ' The King and the Miller;' the former reaching back beyond the sixteenth century, the latter perhaps not beyond the seventeenth, but modelled upon tales of respectable antiquity, of which there is a specimen from the early years of the thirteenth century.†

In the history or "ballad" of 'The King and the Miller,' or, more specifically, ' King Henry Second and the Miller of Mansfield,' the king, while hunting in Sherwood, loses his nobles and is overtaken by night; he meets a miller, and after some colloquy is granted a lodging; is entertained with bag-puddings and apple-pies, to which is added a course of ' light-foot,' a pasty of the king's deer, two or three of which, the miller tells his guest in confidence, he always keeps in store. The nobles recover

the king at the miller's the next morning; the miller looks to be hanged when he sees them fall on their knees; the king dubs him knight. The king has relished his night with the miller so much that he determines to have more sport out of him, and commands the attendance of the new knight with his lady and his son Dick at court on St. George's day. The three jet down to the king's hall on their mill-horses. In the course of the dinner the king expresses a wish for some of their light-foot; Dick tells him that it is knavery to eat of it and then betray it. Sir John Cockle and Dick dance with the court-ladies, and the buffoonery ends by the king's making the miller overseer of Sherwood, with a stipend of three hundred pound, to which he attaches an injunction to steal no more deer.‡

Of the older poems, 'John the Reeve' (910 vv.) may be noticed first, because it has a nearly complete story, and also resemblance in details with ' The King and the Tanner,' or ' The King and the Miller,' which two others of perhaps earlier date have not. ' John the Reeve' is now extant only in the Percy MS. (p. 357, Hales and Furnivall, II, 550). Since there had been but three kings of the name of Edward (v. 16), it must have been composed, as Mr Hales has remarked, between the death of Edward III and the accession of Edward IV, 1376–1461, and forms of language show that the Percy text must be nearer the end than the beginning of this period.§

Edward Longshanks, while hunting, is separated from all his train but a bishop and an earl. Night comes on, and they know not where they are, and the weather is cold and

---

* ' The King and the Barker' is less extravagant and more rational here; the king simply orders the barker ' a hundred shilling in his purse.' But both the esquiring (knighting) and the estate are found in still older poems which remain to be mentioned.

† A pervasive boorishness, with some coarse pleasantry, distinguishes the seventeenth-century tales disadvantageously from the older ones.

‡ There is an entry of ' Miller and King' (among 128 ballads), December 14, 1624; another entry, June 30, 1625 : Stationers' Registers, Arber, IV, 131, 143. The broadside is in many of the collections : ' A pleasant ballad of King Henry second and the Miller of Mansfield,' Roxburghe, I, 178, 228, III, 853, the first reprinted by Chappell, Rox-

burghe Ballads, I, 537; Pepys, I, 528, No 272; Bagford, II, 25; Wood, 401, fol. 5 b, ' A pleasant new ballad of the Miller of Mansfield in Sherwood and K. Henry the Second,' Wood, 254, iv, ' The pleasant history of the Miller of Mansfield,' etc., dated 1655; Crawford, No 491. Also, ' Kinge and Miller,' Percy MS., p. 235, Hales and Furnivall, II, 147 (see Appendix); Percy's Reliques, 1765, III, 179, the MS. copy " with corrections" from the Pepys. — Not in the ballad-stanza.

§ John the Reeve is mentioned (in conjunction with Rauf Coilyear) by G. Douglas, Palice of Honour, 1501, Small, I, 65, v. 3, and by Dunbar, about 1510, Small, I, 105, v. 33; John the Reeve again by Lindsay, The Complaynt of the Papingo, 1530, Chalmers, I, 318.

rough. As they stand considering which way to turn, a stout carl rides by; they beg him to take them to some harbor. The fellow will at first have nothing to do with them, but finally shows a disposition to be accommodating if they will swear to do him no harm; all that he can promise them, however, is beef and bread, bacon a year old, and sour ale; as for a good fire, which the king would particularly like, they cannot have that, for fuel is dear. They ride on to a town, light at a comely hall, and are taken into a room with a bright fire and candles lighted. The carl, who has already described himself as John the Reeve, husbandman and the king's bondman, inquires of the earl who the long fellow may be, and who the other in the sark: the first, he is told, is Piers, the queen's chief falconer, the other a poor chaplain, and the earl himself a sumpter-man. 'Proud lads, and I trow penniless,' is John's comment; he himself, though not so fine, has a thousand pound and more. They move on to the hall, and are civilly received by the goodwife. John marshals the company, now increased by two daughters of the house, and by Hodge and Hob, two neighbors, setting the three strangers and his wife at the head of the table, his daughters farther down, and taking the end himself with his neighbors. Bean-bread, rusty bacon, lean salt beef a year old, and sour ale are brought in, and every one has a mess. The king murmurs, John says, Thou gettest no other; the king coaxes, John will not give them a morsel unless they swear never to tell of him to Edward. All three pledge their troth, and then come in fine bread, wine red and white, in silver cups, the boar's head, capons, venison, — everything that king could have or crave. After the supper, John, Hob, and Hodge perform a rustic dance; King Edward (who gets his shins kicked) never had so merry a night. In the morning they hear mass and eat a good breakfast, for which they promise warison, and then the king takes leave and rides to Windsor. The lords have a good story to tell the queen; she prays the king to send for the

reve. John is convinced that he has been beguiled by his guests, but arms himself with such as he has, and, after a huge libation with Hodge and Hob, sets forth. The porter at the palace will not let him in; John knocks him over the crown and rides into the hall. Neither before this nor then will he vail hat or hood. [The passage in which the reve discovers that Piers falconer was the king has dropped out.] John bears himself sturdily; the king can punish him, but the king is honorable and will keep his word, and may remember the promised warison. The king gives thanks for the hot capons and good wine, the queen urges that the reve should be promoted. The king, nothing loath, makes John a gentleman, and gives him his manor, a hundred pound and a tun of wine yearly, then takes a collar and creates him knight. John blenches a little at the collar; he has heard that after a collar comes a rope; but he recovers his nerve after supping off a gallon of wine at the table. It is now the bishop's turn to do something; he promises his good offices for John's two sons and two daughters; these, in the end, are well disposed of, and Hodge and Hob are made freemen. John ever after keeps open board for all guests that God sends him.

The tale of Rauf Coilyear,* shortly after 1480, has for its personages Charles the Great and a charcoal-burner. Charles, on his way to Paris from St Thomas, is isolated from his cortége by a fierce storm; night has come on and he is in a strait for shelter. By good luck Rauf makes his appearance, a churl of prodigious inurbanity, but ready to take in any good fellow that is 'will of his way.' Arrived at his house, Rauf calls to his wife to make a fire and kill capons. When supper is dight, the guest is told to give the goodwife his hand and take the head of the table. Charles hangs back; the churl, who has once before criticised his manners, hits him under the ear and sends him sprawling to the floor. There is a plenteous supper, in which venison is not lacking. The carl tells the king that the

---

* Reprinted in Laing's Select Remains of the Ancient Popular Poetry of Scotland, from the edition of St Andrews, 1572; thence in Charlemagne Romances, No 6, ed.

S. J. Herrtage, Early English Text Society, 1882. As to the date, see Max Tonndorf, Rauf Coilyear, Halle a. S. 1893, p. 13 ff.

foresters have threatened to send him to Paris for deer stealing, but he means to have enough for himself and a guest in spite of them. Then after wine they sit by the fire and the collier tells many a tale. Charles is affable; Rauf asks him his name and where he lives; Wymond is his name, and he lives with the queen, in fact, is of her bed-chamber; if Rauf will come to court he shall have the better sale for his fuel. Charles is put to bed in a handsome room, and rises so early that he has to waken his host to take leave. He is urged not to go so soon, but to-morrow is Yule and every officer of the court must be at his post. He wishes to pay the goodwife for her good entertainment; Rauf will not hear of such a thing. Come to court to-morrow, says the king; I want coals myself. Roland and Oliver and a thousand more have been wandering all night in search of their lord, and thank God when they recover him on the road to Paris. Rauf sets out for the court with his coals, according to appointment; the king has him in mind, and sends out Roland to bring in such man as he may meet. Roland finds the collier intractable, and has to return without him. The king is displeased, and Roland is on the point of going again, when he learns from a porter that there is a man with a horse and baskets at the gate who will not be turned away. Rauf is let in; he gives his horse in charge to the porter, and pushes into the hall to find Wymond, and after being shoved about a good deal, gets sight of him, dressed in cloth of gold, and clearly a much greater man than he had called himself; he is daunted by all the splendor; if he could but get away, nothing should bring him to the court again. The king then tells the story of his night at Rauf's, not pretermit-

ting the carl's rough behavior. The lords laugh, the knights are for hanging him; the king thinks he owes better thanks, and dubs Rauf knight, assigns him three hundred a year, and promises him the next fief that falls vacant.*

'King Edward Third and the Shepherd,' MS. of about 1450, Cambridge University Library, Ff. 5. 48 b, 1090 vv.†

The king, while taking his pleasure by a river-side one morning, meets Adam, a shepherd, and engages in talk with him. The shepherd complains of the king's men, who help themselves to his beasts, sheep, hens, and geese, and at best pay with a tally. Edward is concerned for the king's good fame; he is a merchant, but has a son with the queen who can get any boon of her, and the shepherd shall have what is due him. That is four pound two, says Adam, and you shall have seven shillings for your service. It is arranged that the shepherd shall come to court the next day and ask the porter for Joly Robyn. The king is kept a long time by the shepherd's stories, but not too long, for when he is invited to come home and take a bit to eat he accepts with pleasure. They see many a coney, hart, and hind, on their way, and the king tries to put up Adam, who has been bragging of his skill with the sling, to kill a few; but the man, as he says, knows very well the danger of poaching, and never touches anything but wild fowl. Of these they have all sorts at their meal, and two-penny ale. Before they set to drinking, Adam instructs the king in an indispensable form: he that drinks first must call out 'passilodion,' and the respondent 'berafrynd.' Edward praises the dinner, but owns to a hankering for a little game. Can you keep a

---

* So far 767 verses of 975: the rest is not pertinent and is very poor stuff. 'Rauf Coilyear' is a clever piece, but I cannot think with Mr Herrtage that it is "quite original." Its exaggerations suggest a second hand; the author means to pepper higher with his churl's discourtesy than had been done before. The 'marshalling' in 183–86 recalls 'John the Reeve,' 342–50.

† Printed in Hartshorne's Ancient Metrical Tales, p. 35. Professor Kittredge has called my attention to a stanza of Occleve's which shows that the belief that Edward III went

about in disguise among his subjects prevailed not long after the king's death.

> O worthy kyng benigne, Edwarde the laste,
> Thow hadest ofte in thyne hart a drede impressede
> Whiche that thyne humble goste fulle sore agaste,
> And to knowe yf thow cursed were or blessede,
> Amonge the peple ofte hast thow the dressede
> Into the contrey, in symple aray alone,
> To heere what men seide of thy persone.
>
> Occleve, De Regimine Principum,
> ed. Wright (Roxb. Club), p. 92.

secret? asks the shepherd; indeed he can. Upon this assurance, Adam fetches pasties of rabbits and deer; of these he is wont to kill more than he himself needs, and sends presents to gentlemen and yeomen, who in return furnish him with bread, ale, and wine. Wine follows: Edward calls 'passilodion;' Adam is ready with 'berafrynd.' The king now takes leave, but before he goes the shepherd shows him a room underground well stored with venison and wine, and they have one draught more. The next day the shepherd goes to court and asks the porter for Joly Robyn. The king has prepared his lords for the visit, and directed them to call him by that name. Adam is paid his four pound two, and offers Robyn the promised seven shillings for his mediation. Robyn will take nothing; he would do much more than that for love; Adam must dine with him, and is placed at the head of a table. The king sends the prince to Adam for a bout of passilodion; Adam says the merchant has betrayed him, and wishes he were out of the place. A squire is now ordered to tell Adam that Joly Robyn is the king. Adam puts down his hood, which up to this time he would do for nobody,* falls on his knees, and cries mercy. The rest is wanting, but we may be certain that Adam was knighted and presented with an estate.

'King Edward and the Hermit,' MS. Ashmole 6922, of about 1450, a fragment of 522 vv.†

The king, hunting in Sherwood, follows a remarkably large deer till he loses himself. By the favor of St Julian, he discovers a hermitage; he asks quarters for the night; the hermit lives on roots and rinds, and such a lord would starve with him, but he yields to urgency. The guest must take such as he finds, and that is bread and cheese and thin drink. King Edward expresses his surprise that the hermit should not help himself out

with the deer; the hermit is much too loyal for that, and besides, the peril is to be considered. Still the king presses for venison; no man shall know of it; the hermit, convinced that he is safe with his company, brings out venison, salt and fresh, and then a four-gallon pot. The king is taught to drink in good form; when one calls 'fusty bandyas,' the other must come in with 'stryke pantere;' and thus they lead holy life. Such cheer deserves requital; if the hermit will come to court, where his guest is living, he has only to ask for Jack Fletcher, and they two will have the best that is there; the 'frere,' though not eager to close with this proposal, says he will venture a visit. To show Jack more of his privity he takes him into his bedroom and gives him a bow to draw; Jack can barely stir the string; the frere hauls to the head an arrow an ell long. Then, wishing that he had a more perfect reliance on Jack's good faith, the hermit exhibits his stock of venison, after which they go back to their drinking, and keep it up till near day. They part in the morning; the king reminds his host of the promised visit, and rides straight for home. His knights, who have been blowing horns for him all night in the forest, are made happy by hearing his bugle, and return to the town. This is all that is preserved, but again we may be confident that King Edward made the hermit an abbot.

That the hermit had some habilitation for such promotion appears from a story told by Giraldus Cambrensis two hundred years before the apparent date of any of these poems.‡

King Henry Second, separated from his men in hunting, came to a Cistercian house at nightfall and was hospitably received, not as king (for this they knew not), but as a knight of the king's house and retinue. After a handsome supper, the abbot asked his help in some business of the fraternity on which

---

* So John the Reeve; five or six times in each.

† Printed in The British Bibliographer, IV, 81, thence in Hartshorne's Metrical Tales, p. 293, and, with some improvements from the MS., in Hazlitt's Early Popular Poetry, I, 11. 'The King and the Hermit' is told as 'the romans says,' v. 15. It is, as Scott has explained, the source of a

charming chapter (the sixteenth of the first volume) of 'Ivanhoe.' There are many agreements with 'The King and the Shepherd.'

‡ Giraldi Cambrensis Opera, ed. Brewer, Speculum Ecclesiæ, IV, 213–15, about 1216.

he was to visit the king the next day, and this was readily promised. The abbot, to improve his guest's good disposition, had his health drunk in many a cup of choice wine, after the English fashion; but instead of the customary salutation or challenge 'wes heil!' * called 'pril!' The king, who would have answered 'drinc heil!' was at a loss how to respond; he was told that 'wril!' was the word. And so with 'pril' and 'wril' they pursued their compotation, monks, freres, guests, servants, deep into the night. The next morning the king rejoined his party, who had been much alarmed at losing him. Order was given that when the abbot came he should be immediately admitted, and it was not long before he made his appearance, with two of his monks. The king received him graciously, all that he asked was granted; the abbot begged leave to retire, but the king carried him off to luncheon and seated him by his side. After a splendid meal, the king, lifting a big cup of gold, called out, 'Pril, father abbot!' The abbot, staggering with shame and fear, begged his grace and forgiveness. The king swore by God's eyes that as they had eaten and drunk together in good fellowship the night before, so should it be to-day; and it should be 'pril' and 'wril' in his house as it had been at the convent. The abbot could not but obey, and stammered out his 'wril,' and then king and abbot, knights and monks, and, at the king's command, everybody in hall and court, kept up unremittingly a merry and uproarious interchange of 'pril' and 'wril.'

Of all the four old poems we may repeat what Percy has said of 'John the Reeve,' that "for genuine humor, diverting incidents, and faithful pictures of rustic manners, they are infinitely superior to all that have been since written in imitation," meaning by these the broadside ballads or histories.† A brief account of such of these as have not been spoken of (all of very low quality) is the utmost that is called for.

'The Shepherd and the King.'‡ King Alfred, disguised in ragged clothes, meets a shepherd, and all but demands a taste of his scrip and bottle. The shepherd will make him win his dinner, sword and buckler against sheephook. They fight four hours, and the king cries truce; 'there is no sturdier fellow in the land than thou,' says the king; 'nor a lustier roister than thou,' says the shepherd. The shepherd thinks his antagonist at best a ruined prodigal, but offers to take him as his man; Alfred accepts the place, is equipped with sheep-hook, tar-box, and dog, and accompanies his master home. Dame Gillian doubts him to be a cut-throat, and rates him roundly for letting her cake burn as he sits by the fire.§ Early the next morning Alfred blows his horn, to the consternation of Gill and her husband, who are still abed. A hundred men alight at the door; they have long been looking for their lord. The shepherd expects to be hanged; both he and his wife humbly beg pardon. Alfred gives his master a thousand wethers and pasture ground to feed them, and will change the cottage into a stately hall.

'King James and the Tinker.' ‖ King James, while chasing his deer, drops his nobles, and

---

* See Geoffrey of Monmouth, Hist. Reg. Brit., vi, 12, Wace, Roman de Brut, 7111–44, ed. Le Roux de Lincy, I, 329, Layamon's Brut, 14297–332, Madden, II, 174 f.; and for other drinking-calls besides these, Wace, Roman de Rou, Part iii, 7357–60, ed. Andresen, II, 320.

† Preface to 'The King and Miller of Mansfield.'

‡ 1578, September 25, licensed to Ric. Jones, 'A merry Songe of a Kinge and a Shepherd:' Arber, II, 338.

1624, December 14, to Master Pavier and others, among 128 ballads, 'King and Shepperd:' Arber, IV, 131.

Wood, 401, fol. 1 b; Douce, I, fol. 1 b; Euing, Nos 331, 332; Pepys, I, 76, No 36, I, 506, No 260; Crawford, No 648; Roxburghe, I, 504, printed by Chappell, III, 210.

§ This is as old as Asser; Annales, Wise, Oxford, 1722, p. 30.

‖ 'King James and the Tinker,' Douce, III, fol. 126 b, fol. 136 b; no printer, place, or date. 'King James the First and the Tinker,' Garland of Mirth and Delight; no place or date. The same: 'King James and the Tinkler,' Dixon, in Richardson's Borderer's Table-Book, VII, 7, and Ancient Poems, Ballads, and Songs, etc., p. 109, Percy Society, vol. xvii. 'James V. and the Tinker,' A. Small, Interesting Roman Antiquities recently discovered in Fife, p. 283. 'King James the First and the fortunate Tinker,' The King and Tinker's Garland, containing three excellent songs, Sheffield, 1745, Halliwell, Notices of Fugitive Tracts, p. 29, No 36, Percy Society, vol. xxix (not seen). 'The King and the Tinker,' a *rifacimento*, in Maidment's Scotish Ballads and Songs, 1859, p. 92; Kinloch MSS, V, 293.

rides to an ale-house in search of new pleas-
ures, finds a tinker there, and sets to drinking
with him. The tinker has never seen the
king, and wishes he might; James says that
if he will get up behind him he shall see the
king. The tinker fears that he shall not
know the king from his lords; the nobles will
all be bare, the king covered. When they
come to the greenwood the nobles gather about
the king and stand bare; the tinker whispers,
'they are all gallant and gay, which, then, is
the king?' 'It must be you or I,' answers
James, for the rest are all uncovered. The
tinker falls on his knees, beseeching mercy;
the king makes him a knight with five hundred a year. (Compare the story of James
Fifth of Scotland and John Howieson, Scott's
Tales of a Grandfather, ch. 27.)

'The King and the Forester.' * King William the Third, forbidden to hunt by a forester who does not recognize him, tries in vain
to bribe the man, makes himself known, presents the forester with fifty guineas, and ap-
points him ranger.

'The Royal Frolick, or, King William and
his Nobles' Entertainment at the Farmer's
House on his return from the Irish wars.' †
King William, 'returning to London from
Limerick fight,' stops at a farm-house 'for
merriment sake,' and asks country cheer for
himself and his nobles. The farmer and his
wife have gone to the next market-town to
see the king pass, and their daughter alone is
at home. She serves bacon and eggs, all that
she has; the king throws her ten guineas,
and one of his lords adds two for loyal sentiments which the girl had expressed. In a
Second Part the farmer and his wife, when
they return, learn that the king is at their
house, are ordered into his presence, and are

rewarded for the meal which had been furnished.‡

'The King and the Cobbler' (a prose history). § King Henry Eighth, visiting the
watches in the city, makes acquaintance with
a cobbler, and is entertained in the cobbler's
cellar; invites the cobbler to court, directing
him to inquire for Harry Tudor, etc.; settles
upon him land in the Strand worth fifty pound
a year, which land is to be called Cobler's
Acre.

Campbell, West Highland Tales, IV, 142,
says that he has a Gaelic tale like 'The Miller of Mansfield.'

A Belgian story of the Emperor Charles
Fifth and a broom-maker has all the typical
points of the older cycle, and, curiously
enough, Charles Fifth instructs the broom-
maker to bring a load of his ware to the palace to sell, as Charles the Great does in the
case of Rauf Coilyear: Maria von Ploennies, Die Sagen Belgiens, p. 251.

The same collection, p. 246 f., has the story
of the man who wished to see the king (an
anecdote of Charles Fifth and a peasant). This
story turns up again in Thiele's 'Kongen og
Bonden,' Danmarks Folkesager, I, 62 (1843).
Christian the Fourth, after a long walk, takes
a seat in the cart of a countryman who is on
his way to the castle. The countryman wishes
that he might see the king; the king will be
the only man to keep his hat on; the countryman says, It must be you or I.

After the older pattern is this Russian
story, Afanasief, VII, 233, No 32 (given me
by Professor Wollner). A tsar who has lost
himself while hunting passes the night with a
deserter in a robbers-hut in a wood. They
draw lots who shall stand guard, and the lot

* 'The Loyal Forrister, or Royal Pastime,' printed for
C. Bates in Pye-Corner (c. 1696), Euing, No 156. 'King
William and his Forrester,' no imprint, c. 1690–94, Craw-
ford, No 1421. 'The King and the Forrester,' Roxburghe,
III, 790, Ebsworth VII, 763 (Bow Church-Yard ?). 'King
William going a hunting,' Motherwell's MS., p. 101, from
tradition.

† 'The Royal Frolick,' etc., Pepys, II, 313, in Ebsworth's
Roxburghe Ballads, VII, 756.

‡ 'The Royal Recreation, or A Second Part, containing
the passages between the Farmer and his Wife at their re-

turn home, where they found the King with his Noble Retinue.' Pepys, II, 326, Roxburghe, II, 397, Ebsworth, VII,
761.

§ 'The King and the Cobler.' Charles Dennison, at the
sign of the Stationers' Arms within Aldgate (1685–89, Chappell). Wood, 254, xi; Pepys, Penny Merriments, vol. i;
Halliwell, Notices of Popular Histories, p. 48, Percy Society, vol. xxiii, Newcastle, without date; Manchester
Penny Histories (last quarter of the eighteenth century),
Liebrecht, Zur Volkskunde, p. 482, No 6.

falls to the tsar, to whom the soldier gives his side-arms. Notwithstanding many warnings, the tsar dozes on his post, and at last the soldier, first punishing him a little, packs him off to sleep. The robbers come, one by one, and are shot by the soldier. The next day the deserter shows the tsar his road, and afterwards pays the tsar a visit at court, discovers who his comrade was, and is made general.

The Emperor Maximilian Second, while walking in a wood, comes upon a charcoal-burner; they have a talk, and the emperor is invited to share the man's dumplings. Maximilian asks the charcoal-burner to pay him a visit when he comes to the city, lets him see the princes and the empress, and gives him a luncheon. There is no *éclaircissement* at the time. In the end the charcoal-burner

and his family are employed in the imperial garden.*

Robert Dodsley made a very pleasing little sentimental drama out of ' The King and the Miller of Mansfield' (1737), and from this play (perhaps through a translation, 'Le Roi et le Meunier,' made before 1756), Sédaine took the substance of 'Le Roi et le Fermier,' 1762, and Collé the idea of 'La Partie de Chasse de Henri IV, 1774.' Goldoni's musical drama, 'Il re alla caccia' (King Henry IV of England), produced a year after Sédaine's play, seems to have been suggested by it: vol. 37 of the edition of Venice, 1794.

Percy's ballad is translated by Bodmer, I, 172.

---

1 In summer time, when leaves grew green,
  and birds were singing on every tree,
  King Edward would a hunting ride,
  some pastime for to see.

2 Our king he would a hunting ride,
  by eight a clock of the day,
  And well was he ware of a bold tanner,
  came riding on the way.

3 A good russet coat the tanner had on,
  fast buttoned under his chin,
  And under him a good cow-hide,
  and a mare of four shilling.

4 ' Now stand you here, my good lords all,
  under this trusty tree,
  And I will wend to yonder fellow,
  to know from whence came he.

5 ' God speed, God speed,' then said our king;
  ' thou art welcome, good fellow,' quoth he;

'Which is the way to Drayton Basset
  I pray thee shew to me.'

6 ' The ready way to Drayton Basset,
  from this place as thou dost stand,
  The next pair of gallows thou comst to
  thou must turn up [on] thy right hand.'

7 ' That is not the way,' then said our king,
  ' the ready way I pray thee shew me ; '
  'Whether thou be thief or true man,' quoth
  the tanner,
  ' I'm weary of thy company.

8 ' Away, with a vengeance,' quoth the tanner,
  ' I hold thee out of thy wit,
  For all this day have I ridden and gone,
  And I am fasting yet.'

9 ' Go with me to Drayton Basset,' said our
  king,
  ' no daintyes we will lack ;

---

* Kulda, Moravské n. pohádky, etc., 1874, I, 56, No 20, in Wenzig, Westslavischer Märchenschatz, p. 179.

Tonndorf, in the dissertation already cited, remarks with truth that meetings of king and subject (or the like) are quite regularly a sequel or incident of a hunt, and refers to Grimms, Deutsche Sagen, Nos 550, 563, 566 ; Cardonne, Mélanges de Littérature orientale, pp. 68, 87, 110 ; Grässe,

Gesta Romanorum, cap. 56, I, 87, Anhang, No 16, II, 198 ; Othonis Melandri Ioco-Seria, No 338, p. 292, ed. Frankfort, 1617. In four of these cases the noble person loses his way, and has to seek hospitality. In Deutsche Sagen, No 566, we have a charcoal-burner who relieves a prince's hunger and is afterwards entertained at the prince's table.

We 'l have meat and drink of the best,
  And I will pay the shot.'

10 ' Godamercy for nothing,' said the tanner,
  ' thou shalt pay for no dinner of mine ;
I have more groats and nobles in my purse
  then thou hast pence in thine.'

11 ' God save your goods,' then said the king,
  ' and send them well to thee ! '
' Be thou thief or true man,' quoth the tanner,
  ' I am weary of thy company.

12 ' Away, with a vengeance,' quoth the tanner,
  ' of thee I stand in fear ;
The aparrell thou wearst on thy back
  May seem a good lord to wear.'

13 ' I never stole them,' said our king,
  ' I swear to thee by the rood ; '
' Thou art some ruffian of the country,
  thou rid'st in the midst of thy good.'

14 ' What news dost thou hear ? ' then said our
    king,
  ' I pray what news do you hear ? '
' I hear no news,' answered the tanner,
  ' but that cow-hides be dear.'

15 ' Cow-hides ? cow-hides ? ' then said our king,
  ' I marvell what they be ; '
' Why, art thou a fool ? ' quoth the tanner,
  ' look, I have one under me.'

16 ' Yet one thing now I would thee pray,
  so that thou wouldst not be strange ;
If thy mare be better then my steed,
  I pray thee let us change.'

17 ' But if you needs with me will change,
  As change full well may ye,
By the faith of my body,' quoth the tanner,
  ' I look to have boot of thee.'

18 ' What boot wilt thou ask ? ' then said our
    king,
  ' what boot dost thou ask on this ground ? '
' No pence nor half-pence,' said the tanner,
  ' but a noble in gold so round.'

19 ' Here 's twenty good groats,' then said the
    king,
  ' so well paid see you be ; '

' I love thee better then I did before,
  I thought thou hadst nere a peny.

20 ' But if so be we needs must change,
  as change thou must abide,
Though thou hast gotten Brock my mare,
  thou shalt not have my cow-hide.'

21 The tanner took the good cow-hide,
  that of the cow was hilt,
And threw it upon the king's saddle,
  That was so fairly guilt.

22 ' Now help me, help me,' quoth the tanner,
  ' Full quickly that I were gone,
For when I come home to Gillian my wife
  she 'l say I 'm a gentleman.'

23 The king took the tanner by the leg,
  he girded a fart so round ;
' You 'r very homely,' said the king,
  ' were I aware, I 'd laid you o th' ground.'

24 But when the tanner was in the king's saddle
  astonëd then he was ;
He knew not the stirrops that he did wear,
  whether they were gold or brass.

25 But when the steed saw the black cow-tale wag,
  for and the black cow-horn,
The steed began to run away,
  as the divel the tanner had born.

26 Untill he came unto a nook,
  a little beside an ash ;
The steed gave the tanner such a fall
  his neck was almost brast.

27 ' Take thy horse again, with a vengeance,' he
    said,
  ' with me he shall not abide ; '
' It is no marvell,' said the king, and laught,
  ' he knew not your cow-hide.

28 ' But if that we needs now must change,
  as change that well we mought,
I 'le swear to you plain, if you have your mare,
  I look to have some boot.'

29 ' What boot will you ask ? ' quoth the tanner,
  ' What boot will you ask on this ground ? '
' No pence nor half-pence,' said our king,
  ' but a noble in gold so round.'

30 'Here 's twenty [good] groats,' said the tanner,
      'and twenty more I have of thine ;
   I have ten groats more in my purse,
      we 'l drink five of them at the wine.'

31 The king set a bugle-horne to his mouth,
      that blew both loud and shrill,
   And five hundred lords and knights
      came riding over a hill.

32 " Away, with a vengeance,' quoth the tanner,
      ' with thee I 'le no longer abide ;
   Thou art a strong thief, yonder be thy fellows,
      they will steal away my cow-hide.'

33 'No, I protest,' then said our king,
      ' for so it may not be ;
   They be the lords of Drayton Basset,
      come out of the North Country.'

34 But when they came before the king
      full low they fell on their knee ;
   The tanner had rather then a thousand pound
      he had been out of his company.

35 'A coller ! a coller ! ' then said the king,
      'a coller ! ' then did he cry ;
   Then would he have given a thousand pound
      he had not been so nigh.

36 'A coller ? a coller ? ' then quoth the tanner,
      ' it is a thing which will breed sorrow ;
   For after a coller commeth a halter,
      and I shall be hanged tomorrow.'

37 'No, do not fear,' the king did say ;
      ' for pastime thou hast shown me,
   No coller nor halter thou shalt have,
      but I will give thee a fee.

38 'For Plompton Park I will give thee,
      with tenements three beside,
   Which is worth three hundred pound a year,
      to maintain thy good cow-hide.'

39 'Godamercy, Godamercy,' quoth the tanner ;
      ' for this good deed thou hast done,
   If ever thou comest to merry Tamworth,
      thou shalt have clouting-leather for thy
         shone.'

———◆———

a, b. A pleasant new ballad of King Edward the
      Fourth and a Tanner of Tamworth, as he
      rode a hunting with his nobles towards (b,
      to) Drayton Bass[et]. To an excellent new
      tune.
   a. Printed for F. Coles, T. Vere, and W. Gil-
      bertson.
   b. London, printed for F. Coles, T. Vere, and
      J. Wright.
   c. A pleasant new ballad betweene King Edward
      the Fourth and a Tanner of Tamworth, as
      hee rode upon a time with his nobles on
      hunting towards Drayton Basset. . . . Lon-
      don, Printed by A. M. (*probably* Alexander
      Milbourne, 1670–97).
   a. 1[1]. grow. 1[2]. birds sitting. 7[3], 36[1]. qd.
      8[2], 37[4]. the. 13[4]. of the.
      18[8]. no half pence said our king.
      20[4]. shalt noo. 23[2]. guirded. 29[2]. in this.
      29[4]. gould. 30[3]. groat.
      35[1]. A choller, a coller.
      35[2], 36[1,3], 37[3]. choller. 38[2]. besides.
   b. 1[1]. grow. 1[2]. birds were singing.
      2[1]. he *wanting*. 3[2]. to his. 6[4]. up on.

7[3]. be a: or a. 11[1]. said our. 13[4]. the wood.
14[2]. pray thee: dost thou. 16[2]. would.
17[1]. if thou. 17[4]. have some boot.
18[1]. boot will you have.
18[8]. nor half pence said the tanner.
19[1]. said our. 19[2]. see thou. 20[4]. not have.
21[2]. off. 22[1]. Now help me up, quoth.
22[8]. For *wanting*. 23[2]. guirded. 23[4]. I had.
24[1]. But *wanting*. 24[2]. astonished.
25[2]. and before the. 26[1]. into. 26[2]. an oak.
26[4]. almost broke. 28[1]. now *wanting*.
28[2]. change well now we might. 29[2]. on this.
30[1]. twenty good. 30[3]. groats. 34[3]. he gave a.
35[1,2], 36[1,3], 37[3]. collar. 36[1]. then *wanting*.
36[2]. which *wanting*. 38[2]. beside.
39[4]. clout-leather.
   c. 1[1]. grew. 1[2]. birds sitting. 2[4]. come.
      4[1]. good my lords. 5[4]. pray you shew it to.
      6[1]. ready *wanting*. 6[2]. this way.
      6[4]. upon the left. 7[2]. readiest.
      8[8]. all *wanting*. 9[8]. For wee 'l. 9[4]. for the.
      10[1]. quoth the. 11[1]. our king. 11[8]. said the.
      13[2]. to you. 13[4]. of thy. 14[1]. doe you.
      16[1]. thing of thee I. 16[2]. would.

16⁴. pray you.   17¹. thou needs: wilt.
18¹. the king.   18². wilt thou.
18³. nor half pence said the tanner.
19². see that you.   20¹. we must needs.
20². we must.   20⁴. not have.   21¹. he tooke.
22¹. helpe, helpe me up.   23². girded.
23³. then said.   23⁴. I'de a laid.
24². that he.
28¹. wee must needs now change here.
28³. well that we mote.   28⁴. I doe looke.
29¹. wilt thou.   29². wilt thou : on this.
29³. said the.   29⁴. but in gold twenty pound.
30¹. twenty groats.   30². I had.   30³. groats.
31³. Then five.   34³. a hundred.
34⁴. of their.   35¹,², 36¹,³, 37³. coller.
35². that he did cry.   36¹. then *wanting*.
36². that is a thing will.   38¹. will thee give.
38². with the : beside.   38³. five hundred.

The Pepys copy was printed for J. W[right],
J. C[larke], W. T[hackeray], *and* T. P[as-
singer].   *Euing, No* 273, *for* F. Coles, T.
Vere, J. Wright, *and* J. Clarke ; *No* 274,
for F. Coles, T. Vere, *and* W. Gilbertson
(*as* a).   *Heber's copy for* F. Coles (1646–
74).

——◆——

APPENDIX

——◆——

I

THE KING AND THE BARKER

Library of the University of Cambridge, MS. Ee.
iv, 35. 1, fol. 19 b.   Written mostly in couplets of
long lines, sometimes in stanzas of four short lines,
with omissions, transpositions, and other faults.

It will be observed that neither in this tale nor
in the " history " which follows does the tanner become aware that he has been dealing with " our
kyng."   In both he calls the king " good fellow "
to the very last.   What happens at the meeting
with Lord Basset, 30, is not made quite intelligible.
It must be that Lord Basset and his men fall on
their knees, but the conviction that " this " is the
king seems to make no great difference in the tanner's bearing.

1 WELL yow here a god borde
   to make yow all low,

How het ffell apon a tyme,
   or eney man het know ?

2 The kyng rod a hontyng,
   as þat tyme was ;
Ffor to hont a dere
   Y trow hes hope was.

3 As he rode, he houer-
   toke yn the wey
A tannar off Dantre,
   yn a queynte araye.

4 Blake kow-heydes sat he apon,
   the hornys heyng be seyde ;
The kyng low and had god game
   to se the tannar reyde.

5 Howre kyng bad hes men abeyde,
   and he welde sper of hem the wey ;
' Yffe Y may here eney now tythyng,
   Y schall het to yow saye.'

6 Howre kyng prekyd *and* seyde,
   Ser, God the saffe !
The tannar seyde,
   Well mot yow ffare !

7 ' God ffellow,' seyde yowre kyng,
   ' offe on thyng Y þe pray ;
To Drayton Baset well Y reyde,
   wyche ys the wey ? '

8 ' That can Y tell the
   ffro hens þat Y stonde ;
When þow comest to the galow-tre,
   torne vpon þe lyft honde.'

9 ' Gramercy, ffellow,' seyde owre kyng,
   ' withowtyn eney wone,
I schall prey the lord Baset
   thanke the sone.

10 ' God ffellow,' seyde owre kyng,
   ' reyde þow with me
Tell Y com to Drayton Baset,
   Now Y het se.'

11 ' Nay, be mey ffeyt,'
   seyde the barker thoo,
' Thow may sey Y were a ffole,
   and Y dyd so.

12 ' I hast yn mey wey as well
   as þow hast yn theyne ;
Reyde ffforthe *and* seke they wey ;
   þi hors ys better nar meyne.'

13 The tanner seyde,
  What maner man ar ye ?
  ‘ A preker abowt,’ seyd þe kyng,
  ‘ yn maney a contre.’

14 Than spake the tanner,
  ffoll scrodeley ayen ;
  Y had a brother vowsed the same,
  tell he cowde never the[n].

15 Than yowre kyng
  smotley gan smeyle :
  ‘ Y prey the, ffelow,
  reyde wiþ me a meyle.’

16 ‘ What, devell ! ’ quod the tanner,
  ‘ art þou owt off they wet ?
  Y most hom to mey deynere,
  ffor I am ffastyng yet.’

17 ‘ Good ffelow,’ seyde owre kyng,
  ‘ Care þe not ffor no mete ;
  þou schalt haffe mete ynow to neyʒt,
  and yeffe þou welt ette.’

18 The tanner toke gret skorne of hem,
  and sware be Creystys pyne,
  Y trow Y hafe more money yn mey pors
  nar thow hast yn theyne.

19 ‘ Wenest thow Y well be owt on neyʒt ?
  nay, and God beffore ;
  Was Y neuer owt a-neyt
  sen Y was bore.’

20 The tanner lokyd a bake tho ;
  the heydes began to ffall ;
  He was war of the keynges men,
  where they cam reydyng all.

21 Thes ys a theffe, thowt the tanner,
  Y prey to God geffe hem care ;
  He well haffe mey hors, mey heydes,
  and all mey chaffare.

22 ‘ Ffor ffeleyschepe,’ seyde the tannar,
  ‘ y[e]t well Y reyde wiþ the ;
  Y wot, ware Y mete wiþ the affterward,
  thow mast do as meche ffor me.’

23 ‘ God amar[sey],’ seyde owre kyng,
  ‘ wiþowt eney wone,
  Y schall prey þe lord Baset
  to thanke the sone.’

24 Owre kyng seyde, What now tydyng
  herest [þou] as þou [dost] ryd ?
  I wolde ffayne wot,
  ffor þow reydest weyde.

25 ‘ Y know [no] now teytheyng,’ þe tanner seyde,
  herke and þou schalt here ;
  Off al the chaffar that Y know,
  kow-heydys beyt dere.’

26 Owre keyng seyde, On theyng
  on mey loffe Y the prey ;
  What herest sey be the lord Baset
  yn thes contrey ?

27 ‘ I know hém not,’ seyde the tanner,
  ‘ wiþ hem Y hafe lytyll to don ;
  Wolde he neuer bey of me
  clot-lether to clowt wiþ schon.’

28 Howre kyng seyde, Y loffe the well,
  of on thyng I þe praye ;
  Thow hast harde hes servantes speke,
  what wolde þey saye ?

29 ‘ Ye, ffor God,’ seyde the tanner,
  ‘ þat tell Y can ;
  Thay sey thay leke hem well,
  ffor he ys a god man.’

30 Thos they reyd together talkyng,
  for soyt Y yow tell,
  Tell he met þe lord Baset ;
  on kneys downe þey ffell.

31 Alas, the tanner thowt,
  the kyng Y leue thes be ;
  Y schall be honged, well Y wot,
  at men may me se.

32 He had no meynde of his hode nor cape
  nere a dell [more],
  Al ffor drede off hes leyffe
  he wende to haffe lore.

33 The tanner wolde a stole awey,
  whyle he began to speke ;
  Howre kyng had yever an ey on hem,
  that he meyt not skape.

34 ‘ God ffelow’, seyd owre kyng,
  ‘ wiþ me thow most abeyde,
  Ffor þow and Y
  most an hontyng reyde.’

35 Whan they com to Kyng Chas,
  meche game þey saye ;
  Howre kyng seyde, Ffelow, what schall Y do,
  my hors ys so hey ?

36 ‘ God ffelow,’ [seyde owre kyng,]
  lend þow me theyne,
  . . . .
  and hafe here meyne.’

37 Tho the tannar leyt do[w]ne
    and cast a downe hes heydys ;
Howre kyng was yn hes sadell,
    no leyng*ger* he beydes.

38 Alas, *þ*eyn the tanner thowt,
    with mey hors he well reyde awey ;
Y well aft*er*,
    to get hem *and* Y may.

39 He welde not leffe his heydys beheynde
    ffor no theyng . . . ;
He cast them yn the kyng*es* schadyll ;
    *þ*at was a neys seyte.

40 *Þ*o he sat aboffe them,
    as Y [y]ouw saye,
He prekyd ffast aft*er*,
    and ffond *þ*e redey wey.

41 The hors lokyd abowt hem,
    and sey on eu*er*y seyde
.   .   .   .   .
    the kow-hornes blake *and* wheyte.

42 The hors went he had bor*e*
    *þ*e deuell on hes bake ;
The hors prekyd as he was wode,
    het mestoret to spor hem not.

43 The barker cleynt on hem ffast,
    he was sor*e* afferde ffor to ffall ;
.   .   .   .   .   .
  .   .   .   .   .

44 The kyng lowhe [and had gode game,]
    and was glad to ffollow *þ*e chas ;
Lest *þ*e tann*er* wolde ber*e* hem downe
    yette he was agast.

45 The hors sped hem sweythyli,
    he sped hem wonderley ffast ;
Ayen a bow of an oke
    the tann*er*es hed he brast.

46 W*ith* a stombellyng as he rode,
    *þ*e tann*er* downe he cast ;
The kyng lowhe *and* had god game,
    and seyde, Ser, *þ*ou rydyst to ffast.

47 The kyng lowhe and had god game,
    and swar*e* be Sent John,
Seche another horsman
    say Y neuer*e* none.

48 Owr*e* kyng lowhe *and* had god bord,
    and sware be Sent Jame,
Y most nedys lawhe,
    and thow were mey dame.

49 ' Y bescro the same son,'
    seyde the barker tho,
' *þ*at seche a bord welde haffe
    to se hes dame so wo.'

50 When her hontyng was ydo,
    *þ*ey changyd hors agen ;
*þ*o the barker had hes howyn,
    *þ*eyrof he was ffayne.

51 ' God a marsey,' seyd owr*e* kyng,
    ' of *þ*ey ser*u*eyse to daye ;
Yeffe thow hafe awt to do w*ith* me,
    or owt to saye,

52 ' They ffrende schall Y yeffor be,
    Be God [*þ*at] ys bet on ;
.   .   .   .   .   .
  .   .   .   .   .

53 ' God a marsey,' seyde *þ*e barker *þ*o,
    ' thow semyst a ffelow god ;
Yeffe Y met the yn Dantre,
    *þ*ow schalt dreynke, be [*þ*e] rode.'

54 ' Be mey ffeyt,' seyde owr*e* kyng,
    ' or els were Y to blame,
Yeffe Y met the yn Lecheffelde,
    *þ*ow sch*a*lt hafe the same.'

55 *þ*us they rode talkyng togeder
    to Drayton Hall ;
Tho the barker toke hes leffe
    of the lordes all.

56 Owr*e* kyng comand *þ*e barker
    yn that tyde
A c. s*t*. yn hes pors,
    to mend hes kow-heydys.

57 Ther*e* owr*e* kyng and the barker
    partyd ffeyr*e* atwyn ;
God *þ*at set yn heffen so hey
    breyng os owt of sen !

      Explycyt *þ*e Kyng *and* the Barker.

1^2. lawhe all. *For* low, *cf.* 4^3 ; lowhe, 44^1, 46^3,
    47^1, 48^1.
6^4. ffare. *Read, perhaps, with rhyme*, haffe.
7^1, 15^1. yowr*e* = owr*e* : *cf.* yever, yeffor, 33^3, 52^1.
9^2. eney woyt : *see* 23^2. 9^3. they.
11^1. be meyt; *cf.* 54^1. 12^1. I haffe hast ?
14^1, 25^1, 31^1, 33^1, 37^1, 38^1, 46^2. thanner, thannar
    (*the* th *caught from the preceding* the).
14^3. yow (*struck through*) vowsed (*that is*, used).
19^2. be ffore. 22^3. y not : methe.
25^1. no *has been inserted because it occurs in the*

other versions, but now (new), *simply, makes some sense.*

26². as mey. *Perhaps,* as thow me loffe.

27⁴. schoys. 28². of 1.

34¹,². God ffelow *with* me thow most abeyde seyd owre kyng.

38². he well reyde awey *with* mey hors.

39¹. le leffe.

39². *Words seem to have dropped out at the end.*

42. *The rhyme might be restored thus :*

> The hors went the deuell
>   on hes bake he had bore ;
> The hors prekyd as he was wode,
>   het mestoret not hem to spor.

44³,⁴. yeffe he was agast lest þe tann*er* wolde ber*e* hem downe.

45³. a noke. 45⁴. thann*er*es : barst.

48². Jane. 48³. nedyst. 50⁴. of ffayne.

55¹. to gederff.

II

KING EDWARD THE FOURTH AND A TANNER OF TAMWORTH

A merrie, pleasant and delectable Historie, betweene King Edward the Fourth and a Tanner of Tamworth, etc.
a. London, John Danter, 1596, Bodleian Library, 4°, C. 39. Art. Seld. **b.** London, W. White, 1613, Corpus Christi College Library, X. G. 2. 11. 4th tract.

1 IN summer-time, when leaues grou greene,
    and blossoms bud on euery tree,
  King Edward would a hunting ride,
    some pastime for to see.

2 With hawke and hound he made him bound,
    with horne and eke with bow ;
  Toward Drayton Basset he tooke his way,
    whosoeuer doth it know.

3 But as our king on his way rode forth,
    by eight a clocke of the day,
  He was ware of a tanner of mery Tamworth,
    was in a quaint aray.

4 A good russet coat the tanner had on,
    he thought it mickle pride ;
  He rode on a mare cost foure shillings,
    and vnder him a good cow-hide.

5 A paire of rough mittens the tanner did weare,
    his hood was buckled vnder his chin ;
  ' Yonder comes a good fellow,' said our king,
    ' that cares not whether he lose or win.'

6 The tanner came singing on his mare,
    with one so merry a note ;
  He sung out of tune, he was past care,
    he had no neede to grease his throte.

7 ' Stand you here still, my lordes now,
    vnder the greene wood spray,
  And I will ride to yonder fellow,
    to wit what he will say.

8 ' God speede, good fellow,' said our king ;
    ' thou art welcom, sir,' quoth he ;
  ' Which is the way to Drayton Basset,
    I pray thee tell to me.'

9 ' Marry, that I will,' quoth the tanner,
    ' right as here I stand ;
  The next paire of gallows that thou comes to,
    turne in vpon thy right hand.'

10 ' It is an vnready way,' said our king,
    ' I tell you, so mote I thee ;
  I pray you show me the readiest way
    the towne that I may see.'

11 ' Go play the great jauel !' quoth the tanner,
    ' I hold thee out of thy wit ;
  All day haue I ridden on Brocke, my mare,
    and I am fasting yet.'

12 ' Why, we will to the towne,' said our king,
    ' and of dainties [we will none lacke] ;
  We will eate and drinke and fare of the best,
    and I will pay for the shot.'

13 ' God haue mercy for nothing,' quoth the tanner,
    ' thou paiest for none of mine,
  For I haue as many nobles in my purse
    as thou hast pence in thine.'

14 ' God giue you ioy of yours,' said our king,
    ' and send thee well to priefe ; '
  The tanner would faine haue beene away,
    for he wend he had beene a thiefe.

15 ' What art thou, good fellow? ' quoth the tanner,
    ' of thee I am in great feare,
  For the clothes that thou wearest on thy back
    are not for a lord to weare.'

16 ' I neuer stole them,' said our king,
    ' I tell you, sir, by the rood ; '
  ' No, thou plaiest as many an vnthrift doth,
    thou standst in the mids of thy good.'

17 ' What tidings heare you,' said our king,
    ' as you ride farre and neare? '
  ' I heare no tidings,' quoth the tanner,
    ' but that cow-hides are deare.'

18 'Cow-hides? cow-hides?' then said our king,
  'I know not what they be ;'
'Lo, here thou maist see one;' quoth the tanner,
  'here lyeth one vnder me.

19 'Knowst thou not a cow-hide,' quoth the tanner,
  'and hast gone so long to schoole?
If euer thou come to dwell in the country,
  thou wilt be made a foole.'

20 'What craftsman are you?' said our king,
  'I pray you tell me now ;'
'I am a barker,' quoth the tanner,
  ['What craftsman art thou? ']

21 'I am a courtier,' said our king,
  'forth of seruice I am worne ;
Full faine I would be your prentise,' he said,
  'your cunning for to learne.'

22 'Marrie, God forbid,' quoth the tanner,
  'that such a prentise I should haue ;
He wold spend me more than he would get
  by fortie shillings a yere.'

23 'One thing would I wit,' said our king,
  'if you will not seeme strange;
Thou my horse be better than your mare,
  with you faine would I change.'

24 'Nay, there thou liest yet,' quoth the tanner,
  'by Christ, thou shalt abide ;
For, if thou haue Brocke, my mare,
  thou gets not my good cow-hide.'

25 'I will not haue it,' said our king,
  'I tell thee, so mote I thee;
I will not carrie it away
  though you would giue it me.'

26 'Why, then we must change,' quoth the tanner,
  'as needs me thinke thou woot ;
But if you haue Brocke, my mare,
  I will looke to haue some boote.'

27 'That were against reason,' said our king,
  'I tell you, so mote I thee ;
My horse is much better than your mare,
  and that you may well see.'

28 'Avise a vous now,' sayd the tanner,
  'whether thou wilt or no,
For my mare is gentle and will not kicke,
  but softlie she will go.

29 'And thy horse is vnhappie and vnwieldie,
  [and will neuer goe in rest,]
But alwaies skipping here and there,
  and therefore my mare is best.'

30 'What boot will you haue?' then said our king,
  'tell me now in this tide ;'
'Neuer a single pennie,' quoth the tanner,
  'but a noble of gold so red.'

31 'Why, there is your noble,' said our king,
  'well paid looke that you be ;'
'I would haue sworne on a book,' quoth the tanner,
  'thou hadst not one pennie.'

32 Now hath the king the tanner's mare,
  she is nothing faire, fat nor round,
And the tanner hath the king's good steede,
  the saddle is worth fortie pound.

33 The tanner tooke vp the good cowhide,
  off the ground where he stood,
He threw it vpon the king's steede,
  in the saddle that was so good.

34 The steed stared vpon the hornes,
  vnder the greene wood spraie ;
He had weende the diuell of hell had bin come,
  to carrie him thence away.

35 The tanner looked as fast on the stirrops,
  astonied sore he was ;
He meruailed greatly in his minde
  whether they were gold or bras.

36 'Help me [vp], good fellow,' quoth the tanner,
  'lightly that I were gone ;
My wife and my neighbours more and lesse
  will say I am a gentleman.'

37 The king tooke the tanner by the leg,
  and lift him vp a loft ;
The tanner girded out a good round fart,
  his belly it was so soft.

38 'You make great waste,' said our king,
  'your curtesie is but small ;'
Thy horse is so high,' quoth the tanner againe,
  'I feare me of a fall.'

39 But when the tanner was in the saddle
  the steede began to blow and blast,
And against the roote of an old tree
  the tanner downe he cast.

40 'Abide, good fellow,' said our king,
  'ye make ouer great hast ;'
'Thou shalt haue thy horse, with, a vengeance,
  againe,
for my necke is well nigh brast.'

41 'Why then we must change,' said our king,
  'as me thinke needs thou woot ;

But if you haue your mare againe
I will looke to haue some boote.'

42 'What boote wilt thou haue?' quoth the tanner,
'tell me in this stound;
'Neuer a groat nor pennie,' said our king,
'but of thy gold twentie pound.'

43 'Nay, here is thy noble,' quoth the tanner again,
'and Christ's blessing and mine;
'Yea, here is twentie good groats more,
goe drinke them at the wine.'

44 'So mote I thee,' then said our king,
'it shall not slacke my woe;
For when a noble is in small monie
full soone it is agoe.'

45 'Dost thou loue to keepe gold?' quoth the tanner,
the king answered and said, Ye;
'Then I would thou were my neere kinsman,
for I thinke thou wilt thriue and thee.'

46 Now hath the tanner Brocke, his mare,
and vnder him his good cowhide,
Our noble king his horse againe,
which was a well faire steede.

47 'Now farewell, good fellow,' quoth the tanner,
'I will bide no longer with thee;'
'Tarrie yet a little while,' said our king,
'and some pastime we will see.'

48 Our king set a bugle to his mouth,
and blew a blast lowd and small;
Seuen score lords, knights, squires and yeomen
came riding ouer a dale.

49 'Now out alas!' quoth the tanner,
'that euer I saw this tide;
Thou art a strong thiefe, yonder be thy fellowes,
will haue my mare and my cowhide.'

50 'They are no theeues,' then said our king,
'I tell you, so mote I thee;
It is my lord of Drayton Basset
is come a hunting to me.'

51 But when before the king they came,
they fell downe on their knees;
The tanner had leuer than a thousand pound
he had beene from their companies.

52 'A coller! a coller!' our king gan call,
quoth the tanner, It will breede sorrow;
For after a coller commeth a halter,
I trow I shall be hangd tomorrow.

53 'Be not afraid, tanner,' said our king,
'I tell thee, so mote I thee;
Lo, here I make thee the best esquier
in all the North Countrie.

54 'And Plumton Parke I will giue thee,
and Iacie in [t]his tide —
It is worth three hundred pounds by yeare —
to prepare thy good cowhide.'

55 'God a mercie, good fellow,' quoth the tanner,
'for this that thou hast done;
The next time thou comest to Tamworth town,
thou shalt haue clouting-leather for thy shon.'

56 Now God aboue speed well the plough,
and keepe vs from care and woe,
Vntill euerie tanner in [t]his countrie
[doe ride a hunting so.]

A merrie, pleasant and delectable Historie, be-
tvveene King Edvvard the fourth and a Tanner
of Tamworth, as he rode vpon a time with his
nobles a (b, on) hunting toward Drayton Basset:
Verie pleasant and merrie to read.

a. Printed at London by John Danter, 1596. (8
    pages.)

b. At London, printed by W. White, 1613. (8
    pages.)

b *has for a heading* The King and the Tanner.

a. 3^4. quaint of aray. 11^1. play thee.
    12^2. *Defect supplied from* b.
    20^4. *Cut off; supplied from* b.
    26^2. thou wilt.   *Cf.* 41^2.
    29^2, 56^4. *Cut off; supplied from* b. 43^1. quath.
b. 3^1. as the. 3^2. eight of the. 3^4. quaint of ray.
    6^1. tanner he. 7^1. here *wanting*. 8^4. tell it me.
    9^4. vp vpon. 10^2. so might. 11^1. play thee.
    12^2. we will none lacke. 13^1. Godamercy.
    15^2. I stand. 16^4. middes. 18^4. lies.
    19^3. thou happen. 20^4. what craft-man art thou.
    22^3. than I should. 23^1. I wish. 23^2. thou wilt.
    23^3. then thy. 23^4. would I faine.
    25^2, 27^2, 44^1, 50^2. mought. 25^4. thou wouldst.
    26^2. thinkes thou wilt. 26^3. if thou.
    27^3. than thy. 29^2. and will neuer goe in rest.
    31^1. Why heere: said the. 31^3. would asworne.
    33^3. king's faire steed. 35^2. sore that he.
    36^1. me up. 38^3. so hie. 40^4. welnie.
    41^2. mee thinkes: thou wilt. 45^2. yea. 45^3. wert.
    46^2. and *wanting*. 47^2. will no longer abide.
    48^2. and he. 50^1. then *wanting*.
    51^1. when they all before the king came.
    51^3. had rather. 53^2. might. 53^4. that is in the.
    54^2. Jackie in this. 56^3. Till: in this.
    56^4. doe ride a hunting so.

III

KING HENRY II AND THE MILLER OF MANSFIELD

a. 'Kinge and Miller,' Percy MS., p. 235; Hales and Furnivall, II, 147. b. The Pleasant History of the Miller of Mansfield, in Sherwood, and Henry the Second, King of England, etc., Wood, 254, iv. Small octavo of twelve pages. Printed for F. Coles, J. Wright, T. Vere, and William Gilbertson, 1655.

1 HENERY, our royall king, wold goe a huntinge,
  To the greene fforrest soe pleasant and fayre ;
To haue the harts chased, the daintye does tripping,
  To merry Sherwood his nobles repayre ;
Hauke and hound was vnbound, all things prepared
For the same to the game with good regard.

2 All a longe summers day rode the king pleasantlye,
  With all his princes and nobles eche one,
Chasing the hart and hind and the bucke gallantlye,
  Till the darke euening inforced them turne home.
Then at last, ryding fast, he had lost quite
All his lords in the wood in the darke night.

3 Wandering thus wearilye, all alone vp and downe,
  With a rude miller he mett att the last ;
Asking the ready way vnto fayre Nottingham,
  'Sir,' quoth the miller, 'I meane not to iest,
Yett I thinke what I thinke ; truth for to say,
You doe not lightlye goe out of your way.'

4 'Why, what dost thou thinke of me ? ' quoth our
    king merrily,
  'Passing thy iudgment vpon me soe breefe.'
'Good faith,' quoth the miller, 'I meane not to flat-
    ter thee,
  I gesse thee to bee some gentleman-theefe ;
Stand thee backe in the darke ! light not adowne,
Lest I presentlye cracke thy knaues cro[wn]e !'

5 'Thou doest abuse me much,' quoth our king,
    'saying thus ;
  I am a gentleman, and lodging doe lacke.'
'Thou hast not,' quoth the miller, 'a groat in thy
    pursse ;
  All thine inheritance hanges on thy backe.'
'I haue gold to discharge for that I call ;
If itt be forty pence, I will pay all.'

6 'If thou beest a true man,' then said the miller,
  'I sweare by my tole-dish I 'le lodge thee all night.'
'Heere's my hand,' quoth our king, 'that was I
    euer.'
  'Nay, soft,' quoth the miller, 'thou mayst be a
    sprite ;
Better I 'le know thee ere hands I will shake ;
With none but honest men hands will I take.'

7 Thus they went all alonge vnto the millers house,
  Where they were seething of puddings and souce.
The miller first entered in, then after went the king ;
  Neuer came he in soe smoakye a house.
'Now,' quoth hee, 'let me see heere what you are ;'
Quoth our king, Looke you[r] fill, and doe not
    spare.

8 'I like well thy countenance ; thou hast an honest
    fac[e] ;
  With my sonne Richard this night thou shalt lye.'
Quoth his wiffe, By my troth, it is a good hansome
    yout[h] ;
  Yet it is best, husband, to deale warrilye.
Art thou not a runaway ? I pray thee, youth, tell ;
Show vs thy pasport and all shalbe well.

9 Then our king presentlye, making lowe curtesie,
  With his hatt in his hand, this he did say :
I haue noe pasport, nor neuer was seruitor,
  But a poore courtyer, rode out of the way ;
And for your kindnesse now offered to me,
I will requite it in euerye degree.

10 Then to the miller his wiffe whispered secretlye,
   Saing, It seemeth the youth is of good kin,
Both by his apparell and by his manners ;
   To turne him out, certainely it were a great sin.
'Yea,' quoth hee, 'you may see hee hath some
    grace,
When as he speaks to his betters in place.'

11 'Well,' quoth the millers wiffe, 'younge man,
    welcome heer !
   And tho I say 't, well lodged shalt thou be ;
Fresh straw I will lay vpon your bed soe braue,
   Good browne hempen sheetes likwise,' quoth
    shee.
'I,' quoth the goodman, 'and when that is done,
Thou shalt lye [with] noe worse then our owne
    sonne.'

12 'Nay first,' quoth Richard, 'good fellowe, tell me
    true,
   Hast thou noe creepers in thy gay hose ?
Art thou not troubled with the scabbado ?'
   'Pray you,' quoth the king, 'what things are
    those ?'
'Art thou not lowsye nor scabbed ?' quoth hee ;
'If thou beest, surely thou lyest not with me.'

13 This caused our king suddenly to laugh most
    hartilye
   Till the teares trickled downe from his eyes.
Then to there supper were thé sett orderlye,
   To hott bag-puddings and good apple-pyes ;
Nappy ale, good and stale, in a browne bowle,
Which did about the bord merrilye troule.

14 'Heere,' quoth the miller, 'good fellowe, I 'le drinke
    to thee,
    And to all the courtnolls *that* curteous bee.'
'I pledge thee,' quoth our k*in*g, 'and thanke thee
    heartilye
    For my good welcome in eu*er*ye degree;
And heere in like manner I drinke to thy sonne.'
'Doe then,' saies Rich*ar*d, 'and quicke let it come.'

15 'Wiffe,' quoth the miller, 'feitch me forth light-
    foote,
    That wee of his sweetnesse a litle may tast.'
A faire venson pastye shee feiched forth present-
    lye.
    'Eate,' quoth the miller, 'but first, make noe
    wast;
Heer is dainty lightfoote.' 'Infaith,' quoth our
    k*in*g,
'I neu*er* before eate of soe dayntye a thinge.'

16 'Iwis,' said Richard, 'noe dayntye att all it is,
    For wee doe eate of it eu*er*ye day.'
'In what place,' sayd our k*in*g, 'may be bought
    lik to th[is?]'
    'Wee neu*er* pay peennye for it, by my fay;
From merry Sherwood wee feitch it home heere;
Now and then we make bold w*i*th our kings deere.'

17 'Then I thinke,' quoth our k*in*g, '*that* it is venison.'
    'Eche foole,' quoth Richard, 'full well may see
    that;
Neu*er* are we w*i*thout two or three in the rooffe,
    Verry well fleshed and exellent ffatt.
But I pray thee say nothing where-ere thou goe;
We wold not for two pence the k*in*g shold it know.'

18 'Doubt not,' said our k*in*g, 'my promised secresye;
    The k*in*g shall neu*er* know more on 't for mee.'
A cupp of lambes woole they dranke vnto him,
    And to their bedds thé past presentlye.
The nobles next morning went all vp and downe
    For to seeke the k*in*g in eu*er*ye towne.

19 At last, att the millers house soone thé did spye
    him plaine,
    As he was mounting vpon his faire steede;
To whome thé came presentlye, falling downe on
    their knees,
    Which made the millers hart wofullye bleed.
Shaking and quaking before him he stood,
Thinking he shold be hanged by the rood.

20 The k[ing] perceiuing him fearfully tremblinge,
    Drew forth his sword, but nothing he said;
The miller downe did fall crying before them all,
    Doubtinge the k*in*g wold cut of his head.
But he, his kind curtesie for to requite,
Gaue him great liuing, and dubd him a k*nigh*t.

21 When as our noble k*in*g came from Nottingam,
    And w*i*th his nobles in Westminster lay,
Recounting the sports and the pastime thé had tane
    In this late progresse along on the way,
Of them all, great and small, hee did protest
The miller of Mansfeild liked him best.

22 'And now, my lords,' quoth the k*in*g, 'I am deter-
    mined,
    Against St Georges next sumptuous feast,
That this old miller, our youngest confirmed k*nigh*t,
    With his sonne Richard, shalbe both my guest;
For in this merryment it is my desire
To talke w*i*th this iollye k*nigh*t and the younge
    squier.'

23 When as the noble lords saw the k*in*gs merriment,
    Thé were right ioyfull and glad in their harts;
A pursiuant thé sent straight on this busines,
    The w*hi*ch oftentimes vsed those p*ar*ts.
When he came to the place where he did dwell,
His message merrilye then he did tell.

24 'God saue yo*u*r worshippe,' then said the messenger,
    'And grant yo*u*r ladye her owne harts desire;
And to yo*u*r sonne Rich*ar*d good fortune and
    happinesse,
    That sweet younge gentleman and gallant squier!
Our k*in*g greets you well, and thus doth say;
You must come to the court on St Georges day.

25 'Therfore in any case fayle not to be in place.'
    'I-wis,' quoth the miller, 'it is an odd iest!
What shold wee doe there?' he sayd, 'infaith I am
    halfe afraid.'
    'I doubt,' quoth Richard, 'to be hanged att the
    least.'
'Nay,' quoth the messenger, 'you doe mistake;
Our k*in*g prepares a great feast for your sake.'

26 'Then,' said the miller, 'now by my troth, mes-
    senger,
    Thou hast contented my worshipp full well:
Hold! there is three farthings to quite thy great
    gentlenesse
    For these happy tydings w*hi*ch thou dost me tell.
Let me see! hearest thou me? tell to our k*in*g,
Wee 'le wayte on his mastershipp in eu*er*ye thing.'

27 The pursivant smyled at their simplicitye,
    And making many leggs, tooke their reward,
And takeing then his leaue w*i*th great humilitye
    To the k*in*gs court againe hee repayred,
Showing vnto his Grace in eu*er*ye degree
The k*nigh*ts most liberall giffts and great bountye.

28 When hee was gone away, thus can the miller say;
    Heere comes expences and charges indeed!

Now must wee needs be braue, tho wee spend all
    wee haue ;
For of new garments wee haue great need.
Of horsses and serving-men wee must haue store,
With bridles and sadles and twentye things more.

29 'Tushe, Sir Iohn,' quoth his wiffe, ' neither doe
    frett nor frowne,
    You shall bee att noe more charges for mee ;
For I will turne and trim vp my old russett gowne,
    With euerye thing else as fine as may bee ;
And on our mill-horsses full swift wee will ryd,
With pillowes and pannells as wee shall prouyde.'

30 In this most statelye sort thé rod vnto the court,
    Their lusty sonne Richard formost of all,
Who sett vp by good hap a cockes fether in his
    cappe ;
And soe thé ietted downe towards the kings hall,
The merry old miller with his hands on his side,
His wiffe like Maid Marryan did mince at that tyde.

31 The king and his nobles, that hard of their coming,
    Meeting this gallant knight with this braue traine,
' Welcome, Sir Knight,' quoth hee, ' with this your
    gay lady !
Good Sir Iohn Cockle, once welcome againe !
And soe is this squier of courage soe free.'
Quoth Dicke, A botts on you ! doe you know me ?

32 Quoth our king gentlye, How shall I forgett thee ?
    Thou wast my owne bed-fellow; well that I wot.'
' But I doe thinke on a tricke,' — ' Tell me, pray
    thee, Dicke ! '
' How with farting we made the bed hott.'
' Thou horson [un]happy knaue,' the[n] quoth the
    knight,
' Speake cleanly to our [king,] or else goe shite ! '

33 The king and his councellors hartilye laugh at this,
    While the king tooke them by the hand.
With ladyes and their maids, like to the queene of
    spades
The millers wiffe did most orderlye stand,
A milkemaids curtesye at euerye word ;
And downe these folkes were set to the bord.

34 Where the king royally, with princely maiestye,
    Sate at his dinner with ioy and delight ;
When he had eaten well, to jesting then hee fell,
    Taking a bowle of wine, dranke to the knight.
' Heere's to you both ! ' he sayd, ' in ale, wine, and
    beere,
Thanking you hartilye for all my good cheere.'

35 Quoth Sir Iohn Cockle, I 'le pledge you a pottle,
    Were it the best ale in Nottingam-shire.
' But then,' said our king, ' I thinke on a thinge ;
    Some of your lightfoote I wold we had heere.'

' Ho, ho ! ' quoth Richard, ' full well I may say it ;
It 's knauerye to eate it and then to bewray it.'

36 ' What ! art thou angry ? ' quoth our king merrilye,
    ' Infaith I take it verry vnkind ;
I thought thou woldest pledg me in wine or ale
    heartil[y].'
' Yee are like to stay,' quoth Dicke, 'till I haue
    dind.
You feed vs with twatling dishes soe small ;
Zounds ! a blacke pudding is better then all.'

37 ' I, marry,' quoth our king, ' that were a daintye
    thing,
    If wee cold gett one heere for to eate.'
With that, Dicke straight arose, and plucket one
    out of his h[ose,]
Which with heat of his breech began for to
    sweate.
The king made profer to snatch it away ;
' It 's meate for your master, good sir, you shall
    stay ! '

38 Thus with great merriment was the time wholy
    spent,
    And then the ladyes prepared to dance.
Old Sir Iohn Cockle and Richard incontinent
    vnto this practise the king did advance ;
Where with the ladyes such sport thé did make,
The nobles with laughing did make their heads ake.

39 Many thankes for their paines the king did giue
    them then,
    Asking young Richard if he wold be wed :
' Amongst these ladyes faire, tell me which liketh
    thee.'
Quoth hee, Iugg Grumball with the red head,
Shee 's my loue ; shee 's my liffe ; her will I wed ;
Shee hath sworne I shall haue her maidenhead.

40 Then Sir Iohn Cockle the king called vnto him ;
    And of merry Sherwood made him ouerseer,
And gaue him out of hand three hundred pound
    yearlye :
' But now take heede you steale noe more of my
    deere,
And once a quarter let 's heare haue your vew ;
And thus, Sir Iohn Cockle, I bid thee adew ! '

a. 5⁶. 40. 7¹. into. 7². seeding.
   17³. 2 or 3. 17⁶. 2. 18¹. saiy.
   26³. 3. 28⁶. 20ᵗ́ᵉ. 29². charges of.
   31⁶. abotts. 34³. resting. b, jesting.
   36¹. hungry. b, angry. 40³. 300ᶫ́ᶦ.
b. 1¹. would ride. 1³. hart : and dainty. 1⁴. Unto.
   2⁴. him turn. 2⁶. late in dark.
   3⁴. miller, your way you have lost.
   3⁶. not likely. 4¹, 5¹, 13¹. the king.
   4⁴. but some. 4⁵. light thee not down.

4^6. Lest that : knock thy. 5^2. I lack.

5^3. one groat. 5^5. discharge all that. 6^6. I will.

7^1. unto. 7^2. seething.

7^8. after him the. 8^8. good *wanting.*

8^4. for to. 8^5. prethee. 8^6. Shew me.

9^2. thus he. 9^4. of my. 9^5. here offered.

10^2. this youth's. 10^8. and eke by. 10^5. Yes.

10^6. When he doth speak. 11^8. wil have laid on.

11^4. hempten. 11^6. with no. 12^2. within.

12^8. Or art. 12^4. I pray, quoth. 12^5. or.

13^4. With a hot bag-pudding. 14^1. I drink thee.

14^2. courtnols where ever they be.

14^8. Ile pledge you : thank you. 14^4. For your.

14^5. to your. 14^6. Do so, quoth Richard, but.

15^8. pasty then brought she forth. 15^4. but fir.

15^5. then said our. 17^1. said our.

17^2. said Richard. 17^4. wondrous fat.

17^5. But prethee. 18^1. not then said.

18^8. him then. 18^6. seek out. 19^1. they espy'd.

19^6. should have been. 20^1. fearfull and.

20^4. would have cut off.

20^5. But his kind curtesie there to.

20^6. him a living. 21^1. came home.

21^8. and pastime. 21^4. this his progresse along by.

21^5. this he. 21^6. Mansfields sport.

22^8. our last. 22^4. both be my guests.

22^6. with this. 23^1. kings pleasantnesse.

23^8. there was sent : on the.

23^4. Which had many times been in.

23^6. message orderly. 24^2. owne *wanting.*

24^4. gallant young. 24^5. he greets you all.

25^2. this is. 25^8. said, faith. 25^4. to be *wanting.*

26^8. here 's : great *wanting.* 26^5. to your.

27^5. in each. 27^6. gift : great *wanting.*

28^1. When as : thus did.

28^8. we must : though wee sell. 29^2. charges for.

29^4. else *wanting.* 30^1. rode they. 30^5. hand.

31^2. his brave. 32^1. how should. 32^2. mine own.

32^8. doe *wanting :* me that prethee Dick.

32^4. How we : did make. 32^5. happie : then.

32^6. our king. 33^1. laught. 33^2. both by.

33^4. so orderly.

33^6. the folks were sate at the side-board.

34^1. in princely. 34^8. jesting then they.

34^5. wine, ale.

34^6. you all for your country cheere.

35^8. I doe think. 35^6. 'T is.

36^1. Why, art thou angry. 36^8. ale and wine.

36^4. Y' are. 37^2. If a man could get one hot.

37^8. hose. 37^4. for *wanting.* 37^5. made a.

37^6. 'T is : you must. 38^5. Here with.

38^6. their hearts. 39^1. did the king give.

39^8. ladies free. 39^5. she will. 40^6. bid you.

b *is printed with the long lines broken into two.*

274

OUR GOODMAN

A. Herd's MSS, I, 140; Herd's Ancient and Modern Scottish Songs, 1776, II, 172.

B. 'The Merry Cuckold and Kind Wife,' a broadside : Printed and Sold at the Printing-Office in Bow Church-Yard, London.

———◆———

THE copy in Ritson's Scotish Song, I, 231, is from Herd, 1776; that in the Musical Museum, No 454, p. 466, is the same, with change of a few words. In Smith's Scotish Minstrel, IV, 66, the piece is turned into a Jacobite ballad. The goodwife says she is hiding her cousin McIntosh; 'Tories,' says the goodman.

B was reprinted by Dixon in Ancient Poems, Ballads, and Songs of the Peasantry of England, p. 211, Percy Society, vol. xvii, ' Old Wichet and his Wife,' from a copy "obtained in Yorkshire" and " collated" with the Aldermary broadside. The fifth adventure (in the closet) is lacking. Two or three staves, with variations for the better, are given from memory in Notes and Queries, First Series, VI, 118, as communicated by Mr R. C. Warde, of Kidderminster. (See the notes.)

Percy made B over in two shapes, whether for simple amusement or for the projected extension of the Reliques : ' Old Wichet's Discoveries,' 'Old Wichard's Mistakes,' among Percy's papers.

A. Our goodman, coming home, sees successively a saddle-horse, pair of jack-boots, sword, powdered wig, muckle coat, finally a man, where none such should be. He asks the goodwife how this came about without his leave. She responds contemptuously that the things he has supposed himself to see are, respectively, a sow (milch-cow), a pair of water-stoups, a porridge-spurtle, a clocken-hen, a pair of blankets, a milking-maid, which her mother has sent her. Far has he ridden, but a saddle on a sow's (cow's) back, siller

spurs on water-stoups, etc., long-bearded maidens, has he never seen.

B. In B Old Wichet comes upon *three* horses, swords, cloaks, pairs of boots, pairs of breeches, hats, and in the end three men in bed. Blind cuckold, says the wife, they are three milking-cows, roasting-spits, mantuas, pudding-bags, petticoats, skimming-dishes, milking-maids, all presents from her mother. The like was never known, exclaims Old Wichet ; cows with bridles and saddles, roasting-spits with scabbards, etc., milking-maids with beards !

A song founded on this ballad was introduced into the play of " Auld Robin Gray," produced, according to Guest's History of the Stage, at the Haymarket, July 29, 1794. This song is a neat résumé of the ballad, with a satisfactory catastrophe.* See an appendix.

A Gaelic copy, taken down by Rev. Alexander Stewart, of Ballachulish, from the recitation of an old man in his parish whose father had been in the way of singing it sixty years before, is plainly based upon A. The goodman, coming home unexpectedly, finds a boat on the beach, a horse at the door, etc. These and other things are explained by his wife as gifts from her mother. Far has he wandered, but never saw a saddle on a cow, etc. Alexander Stewart, 'Twixt Ben Nevis and Glencoe, 1885, p. 76 ff.

A ballad known and sung throughout Flemish Belgium, ' Mijn man komt thuis,' is formed upon the pattern of A, and must have been

* I am indebted for information concerning this song, and for a copy, to Mr P. Z. Round.

derived from **A**, unless the two have a common source. Two copies are given in Volkskunde (Tijdschrift voor Nederlandsche Folklore), II, 49–58, by the editors, Messrs A. Gittée and Pol de Mont, a third by Pol de Mont, V, 20. A man comes home late, and sees in his bedroom a strange hat, overcoat, and other articles of clothing, and asks whose they are. His wife answers that they are a water-pot, a straw mattress, etc., which her mother has sent her. Travel the world round, he has never seen a water-pot with a band about it, a straw mattress with two sleeves, etc. In the last adventure of the first copy, the husband finds a man in the room, and his wife flatly answers, it is a lover my mother has sent me. The second copy ends a little better, but not well. The man is explained to be a foster-child sent by his wife's mother, and so in the third. The husband has travelled the world round, but a foster-child with whiskers has he never seen. The wife packs out of the house. He has travelled the world round, but a wife like his he wishes never to see again.

Friedrich Wilhelm Meyer, in 1789, turned B into German in very happy style, furnishing a *dénoûment* in which the man gives his wife a beating and explains his cuffs as caresses which her mother has sent her. Meyer's ballad was printed in 1790, in the Göttingen Musenalmanach, p. 61 ff., and the same year in Lieder für fröhliche Gesellschaften, p. 37 (Hamburg). It had great and immediate success, was circulated as a broadside, and was taken up by the people, in whose mouth it underwent the usual treatment of ballads traditionally propagated.* From Germany it spread into Scandinavia and Hungary, and perhaps elsewhere. German varieties are: 'Des Mannes Heimkehr,' Hoffmann u. Richter, p. 225, No 195; 'Wind über Wind,' Simrock, p. 375, No 241; 'Des Ehemannes Heimkehr,' Ditfurth, Fränkische Volkslieder, IIᵣ Theil, p. 61, No 61; Firmenich, Germa-

* Hoffmann von Fallersleben, Unsere Volksthümlichen Lieder, No 478. It begins:

Ich ging in meinen Stall, da sah ich, ei ! ei !
An Krippen standen Pferde, eins, zwei, drei.

niens Völkerstimmen, III, 66; 'Der Bauer u. sein Weib,' Erlach, IV, 90; 'Der betrogene Ehemann,' Pröhle, p. 143; Walter, p. 97; 'O Wind, O Wind, O Wind !' Zurmühlen (Dülkener Fiedler), p. 101. (The last four lack the beating.)

The only Scandinavian copy that I have seen is the Swedish 'Husarerna,' in Bergström och Nordlander, Sagor, Sägner och Visor, 1885, p. 93. For indication of others, Danish, Norwegian, and Swedish (including a broadside as early as 1799), see, particularly, Olrik, Danmarks gamle Folkeviser, V, II, 211 f., and note ***; also, Dybeck's Runa, 1ª Samlingen, 1865, I, 89 (where the beginnings of two stanzas are cited); Afzelius, ed. 1880, II, 285.

Magyar (Szekler), Kríza, Vadrózsák, p. 242, No 483; Aigner, p. 149.

French. A similar ballad is common in France, especially in the south.

Poésies pop. de la France, MSS: II, fol. 54, 'Marion;' III, 60 (printed in Revue des Traditions pop., II, 66), 62, 64, Puy-de-Dôme; 68, Auvergne; 69, 'Zjean et Mariou,' Bourbonnais; 71, Pays de Caux; 72, 'Le jaloux,' environs de Toulouse; 74, Gascogne (Rolland, II, 211); 75, Languedoc; 76, 'Lo surprero,' Limousin (Rolland, II, 212); 78, 'Le mari de Marion,' Normandie; 80, 66, 'Le mari jaloux,' Bouches-du-Rhône; 82, 'Marion,' Provence; 83, Loiret; 84, 'La rusade,' Limousin;' 87, 'Lou jolous' (Rolland, II, 213, Revue des Trad. pop., I, 71), Limoges; VI, 381 vo, 'Jeannetoun' (Rolland, II, 214), Quercy. 'Lou jalous,' Arbaud, Chants pop. de la Provence, II, 152. 'Lou galant,' Atger, Revue des Langues romanes, VI, 261, and Poésies pop. en Langue d'oc, p. 53. 'Las finessos de la Marioun,' Moncaut, Littérature pop. de la Gascogne, p. 316 = Bladé, Poésies pop. de la Gascogne, II, 116 f. Revue des Traditions pop., II, 64, Cévennes. Daudet, Numa Roumestan, ed. 1881, p. 178, Provence = Revue des Tr. pop., II, 65, Ouest de la France. 'Lou Tsalous, Daymard, Bulletin de la Société des Études,' etc., du Lot, IV, 100, 1878, Vieux chants pop. rec. en Quercy, 1889, p. 92. 'Las rebirados de Marioun,' Soleville,

Chants pop. du Bas-Quercy, p. 22 ; partly, in Pouvillon, Nouvelles réalistes, ed. 1878, p. 151. Victor Smith in Romania, IX, 566–68, three copies, Forez, Velay, bas-limousin. 'Le mari soupçonneux,' Tarbé, Romancero de Champagne, II, 98, Ardennes. 'La chanson de la bergère,' Puymaigre, Chants pop. rec. dans le Pays messin, 1865, p. 215, 1881, I, 263. 'Les répliques de Marioun,' Almanach des Traditions pop., 1882, p. 86, in Rolland, II, 208, No 162 a, environs de Lorient. 'Las respounsos de Marioun,' Laroche, Folklore du Lauraguais, p. 211. "Le Chroniqueur du Périgord et du Limousin, Périgueux, 1853, p. 109." "Le Pélerinage de Mireille, p. 173." (The last two I have not seen.)

For the most part, the colloquy runs in this wise : 'Where were you last evening, Marion?' 'In the garden, picking a salad.' 'Who was it you were talking with?' 'A gossip of mine' (camarade, voisine, cousine, sœur, servante, etc.). 'Do women wear a sword?' 'It was no sword, but a distaff.' 'Do women wear breeches?' 'She was kilted up.' 'Have women a moustache?' 'She had been eating mulberries.' 'It is too late for mulberries.' 'They were last year's' (an autumn branch, etc.). 'I will cut off your head.' 'And what will you do with the rest?' 'Throw it out of the window.' 'Les corbeaux (cochons, chiens, chats, mouches, couteliers, capucins, anges, etc.) en feront fête.' In a few instances, to end the more smartly, the husband is made to promise (or the wife to ask) forgiveness for this time, and the wife adds, aside, 'and many more.' 'You will play off no more tricks on me.' 'Forgive this, and I will, a good many.' (Rolland.) 'Pardon this fault; to-morrow I will commit another.' (Victor Smith.) 'Get up: I pardon you.' 'What dolts men are! What can't we make them believe!' (MSS, III, 78.) Etc.

In some half dozen copies, Marion has been at the spring (not in the garden), and has stayed suspiciously long, which she accounts for by her having found the water muddied. After this, and in a few copies which have no garden or spring, the matter is much the same as in the English ballad; there is a sword on the mantel-shelf (a gun on the table), boots (cane) behind the door, a man where nae man should be. Nearest of all to the English is one of Victor Smith's ballads, Romania, IX, 566 : 'Whose horse was that in the stable last night?' 'No horse, but our black cow.' 'A cow with a saddle?' 'No saddle ; it was the shadow of her horns.' 'Whose breeches, boots, sabre, hat?' 'qui était couché à ma place?' The mulberries are nearly a constant feature in the French ballad.

There is an approach to a serious termination in MSS, III, 87 : 'Say your prayers, without so much noise.' 'At least put my bones in the ground.' And in Puymaigre : 'I will take you to Flanders and have you hanged.' 'Leave the gallows for the great robbers of France.' The copies, MSS, III, 62, 71, end, prosaically, 'Jamais je n'ai vu ni fille ni femme qui sent la putain comme toi ; ' 'Femme qui m'a trompé la mort a méritée ! '

The lace-makers of Vorey are wont to recite or sing this ballad winter evenings as a little drama : V. Smith, Romania, IX, 568, note. So the young girls in Lorraine during carnival, Puymaigre, I, 263 ; and the young fellows in Provence, Arbaud, II, 155 f.

Italian. 'Le repliche di Marion,' Nigra, Canti popolari del Piemonte, p. 422, No 85, A, B, C. The Piedmontese copies follow the French closely, beginning with picking salad in the garden, and ending with 'your peace is made,' as in Poésies p. de la France, MSS, III, 64. 'Il marito geloso' (incomplete), Ferraro, Canti p. monferrini, p. 93, No 70. 'La sposa colta in fallo,' Bernoni, Canti p. veneziani, puntata ix, No 8, p. 12. (Mariù goes on her knees and asks pardon, and is told to get up, for pardoned she is.) 'Bombarion,' Ferrari, first in Giornale di Filologia romanza, III, No 7, p. 74, 1880, and then in Archivio per le Tradizioni popolari, Canti p. in San Pietro Capofiume, VII, 398, 1888 (peace is made). All the Italian versions keep near to the French, having nothing original but an unimportant insertion, 'Chi ti farà la minestra?' etc., just before the end.*

* 'O Violina, tu hai le gote rosse,' a very pretty little *contrasto* bundled by Tigri with his *rispetti* (Canti p. toscani,

Catalan. 'La Trapassera,' Briz y Saltó, Cants pop. catalans, II, 69. Father hears daughter talking with lover in the garden; the usual questions and replies; improved, or corrupted, at the end.

For serious ballads, Scandinavian, Spanish, etc., exhibiting similar questions and evasions, see 'Clerk Saunders,' No 69 F, and the remarks at II, 157 f., 512 a, III, 509 a, IV, 468 a. The romance 'De Blanca-Niña' oc-curs in the Cancionero de Romances of 1550. The oldest Scandinavian ballad of the class is one of Syv's, printed in 1695.

Herd, 1776, is translated by Wolff, Halle der Völker, I, 96, Hausschatz, p. 230; by Fiedler, Geschichte der schottischen Lieder-dichtung, I, 32; by Knortz, Schottische Balladen, p. 82.

———◆———

A

Herd's MSS, I, 140.

1 HAME came our goodman,
   And hame came he,
   And then he saw a saddle-horse,
   Where nae horse should be.

2 'What 's this now, goodwife?
   What 's this I see?
   How came this horse here,
   Without the leave o me?'

   Recitative. 'A horse?' quo she.
   'Ay, a horse,' quo he.

3 'Shame fa your cuckold face,
   Ill mat ye see!
   'T is naething but a broad sow,
   My minnie sent to me.'

   'A broad sow?' quo he.
   'Ay, a sow,' quo shee.

4 'Far hae I ridden,
   And farer hae I gane,
   But a sadle on a sow's back
   I never saw nane.'

5 Hame came our goodman,
   And hame came he;
   He spy'd a pair of jack-boots,
   Where nae boots should be.

6 'What 's this now, goodwife?
   What 's this I see?
   How came these boots here,
   Without the leave o me?'

   'Boots?' quo she.
   'Ay, boots,' quo he.

7 'Shame fa your cuckold face,
   And ill mat ye see!
   It 's but a pair of water-stoups,
   My minnie sent to me.'

   'Water-stoups?' quo he.
   'Ay, water-stoups,' quo she.

8 'Far hae I ridden,
   And farer hae I gane,
   But siller spurs on water-stoups
   I saw never nane.'

9 Hame came our goodman,
   And hame came he,
   And he saw a sword,
   Whare a sword should na be.

10 'What 's this now, goodwife?
   What 's this I see?
   How came this sword here,
   Without the leave o me?'

   'A sword?' quo she.
   'Ay, a sword,' quo he.

p. 284, No 1023, ed. 1856), is a skirmish between father and daughter, after the fashion of our ballad. ('My cheeks are stained with mulberries.' 'Show me the mulberries.' 'They are on the hedges.' 'Show me the hedges.' 'The goats have eaten them.' 'Show me the goats,' etc.) Ferrari, in an excellent paper in the journal referred to above, tries to make out some historical relation between the two. He seems to me to take 'La Violina' quite too seriously.

11 'Shame fa your cuckold face,
　　Ill mat ye see !
　It 's but a porridge-spurtle,
　　My minnie sent to me.'

　　'A spurtle ? ' quo he.
　　'Ay, a spurtle,' quo she.

12 'Far hae I ridden,
　　And farer hae I gane,
　But siller-handed spurtles
　　I saw never nane.'

13 Hame came our goodman,
　　And hame came he ;
　There he spy'd a powderd wig,
　　Where nae wig shoud be.

14 'What 's this now, goodwife ?
　　What 's this I see ?
　How came this wig here,
　　Without the leave o me ? '

　　'A wig ? ' quo she.
　　'Ay, a wig,' quo he.

15 'Shame fa your cuckold face,
　　And ill mat you see !
　'T is naething but a clocken-hen,
　　My minnie sent to me.'

　　'Clocken hen ? ' quo he.
　　'Ay, clocken hen,' quo she.

16 'Far hae I ridden,
　　And farer hae I gane,
　But powder on a clocken-hen
　　I saw never nane.'

17 Hame came our goodman,
　　And hame came he,
　And there he saw a muckle coat,
　　Where nae coat shoud be.

18 'What 's this now, goodwife ?
　　What 's this I see ?

How came this coat here,
　　Without the leave o me ? '

　　'A coat ? ' quo she.
　　'Ay, a coat,' quo he.

19 'Shame fa your cuckold face,
　　Ill mat ye see !
　It 's but a pair o blankets,
　　My minnie sent to me.'

　　'Blankets ? ' quo he.
　　'Ay, blankets,' quo she.

20 'Far hae I ridden,
　　And farer hae I gane,
　But buttons upon blankets
　　I saw never nane.'

21 Ben went our goodman,
　　And ben went he,
　And there he spy'd a sturdy man,
　　Where nae man shoud be.

22 'What 's this now, goodwife ?
　　What 's this I see ?
　How came this man here,
　　Without the leave o me ? '

　　'A man ? ' quo she.
　　'Ay, a man,' quo he.

23 'Poor blind body,
　　And blinder mat ye be !
　It 's a new milking-maid,
　　My mither sent to me.'

　　'A maid ? ' quo he.
　　'Ay, a maid,' quo she.

24 'Far hae I ridden,
　　And farer hae I gane,
　But lang-bearded maidens
　　I saw never nane.'

B

A broadside : Printed and Sold at the Printing-Office in
Bow Church-Yard, London.

1 O I went into the stable,
　and there for to see,
And there I saw three horses stand,
　by one, by two, and by three.

2 O I calld to my loving wife,
　and ' Anon, kind sir ! ' quoth she :
' O what do these three horses here,
　without the leave of me ? '

3 ' Why, you old cuckold, blind cuckold,
　can't you very well see ?
These are three milking-cows,
　my mother sent to me.'

4 ' Heyday ! Godzounds ! Milking-cows with
　bridles and saddles on !
the like was never known ! '
Old Wichet a cuckold went out,
　and a cuckold he came home.

5 O I went into the kitchen,
　and there for to see,
And there I saw three swords hang,
　by one, by two, and by three.

6 O I calld to my loving wife,
　and ' Anon, kind sir ! ' quoth she :
' O what do these three swords do here,
　without the leave of me ? '

7 ' Why, you old cuckold, blind cuckold,
　can't you very well see ?
They are three roasting-spits,
　my mother sent to me.'

8 ' Heyday ! Godzounds ! Roasting spits with
　scabbards on !
the like was never known ! '
Old Wichet a cuckold went out,
　and a cuckold he came home.

9 O I went into the parlour,
　and there for to see,
And there I saw three cloaks hang,
　by one, by two, and by three.

10 O I calld to my loving wife,
　and ' Anon, kind sir ! ' quoth she :
' O what do these three cloaks do here,
　without the leave of me ? '

11 ' Why, you old cuckold, blind cuckold,
　can't you very well see ?
These are three mantuas,
　my mother sent to me.'

12 ' Heyday ! Godzounds ! Mantuas with capes
　on !
the like was never known ! '
Old Wichet a cuckold went out,
　and a cuckold he came home.

13 I went into the pantry,
　and there for to see,
And there I saw three pair of boots hang,
　by one, by two, and by three.

14 O I called to my loving wife,
　and ' Anon, kind sir ! ' quoth she
' O what do these three pair of boots do here,
　without the leave of me ? '

15 ' Why, you old cuckold, blind cuckold,
　can't you very well see ?
These are three pudding-bags,
　my mother sent to me.'

16 ' Heyday ! Godzounds ! Pudding-bags with
　spurs on !
the like was never known ! '
Old Wichet a cuckold went out,
　and a cuckold he came home.

17 I went into my closet,
　and there for to see,
And there I saw three pair of breeches lie,
　by one, by two, and by three.

18 O I calld to my loving wife,
　and ' Anon, kind sir ! ' quoth she :
' O what do these three pair of breeches do
　here,
　without the leave of me ? '

19 ' Why, you old cuckold, blind cuckold,
　can't you very well see ?
These are three petticoats,
　my mother sent to me.'

20 'Heyday! Godzounds! Petticoats with waist-
        bands on!
   the like was never known!'
   Old Wichet a cuckold went out,
       and a cuckold he came home.

21 I went into the dairy,
       and there for to see,
   And there I saw three hats hang,
       by one, by two, and by three.

22 I calld to my loving wife,
       and 'Anon, kind sir!' quoth she:
   'Pray what do these three hats do here,
       without the leave of me?'

23 'Why, you old cuckold, blind cuckold,
       can't you very well see?
   They are three skimming-dishes,
       my mother sent to me.'

24 'Heyday! Godzounds! Skimming-dishes with
        hat-bands on!
   the like was never known!'

Old Wichet a cuckold went out,
    and a cuckold he came home.

25 I went into the chamber,
       and there for to see,
   And there I saw three men in bed lie,
       by one, by two, and by three.

26 I called to my loving wife,
       and 'Anon, kind sir!' quoth she:
   'O what do these three men in bed,
       without the leave of me?'

27 'Why, you old cuckold, blind cuckold,
       don't you very well see?
   They are three milking-maids,
       my mother sent to me.'

28 'Heyday! Godzounds! Milking-maids with
        beards on!
   the like was never known!'
   Old Wichet a cuckold went out,
       and a cuckold he came home.

———————

A. 1¹. *Or*, Our goodman came hame at een.
    2¹. *Or*, How came this horse here?
    2². *Or*, How can this be?
    3¹. *Or*, Ye ald blind dottled carl.
    3². *Or*, Blind mat ye be!
    3³. *Or*, a bonny milk-cow.
    3⁴. My minny *is an alternative and necessary
        reading for* The miller.
    4¹. *Or*, travelld.
    4². *Or*, And meikle hae I seen.
    4⁴. [*Or*,] Saw I.
    5¹. *Or*, Our goodman came hame.
    7⁴. The cooper sent.
    9–12. *At the end, with a direction as to
        place: not completely written out.*
    9¹. Hame, etc.
    10³. O how.
    12^{1,2}. Weel far hae I travelled,
            And muckle hae I seen.
    12⁴. Saw I never nane.
    *The regular readings have been inserted or
        substituted. In printing, Herd gave some-
        times the alternative readings, sometimes
        not.*

B. *Printed in seven staves, or stanzas, of eight
        long lines.*
    1¹, 2¹. Oh. 15³, 19³. the three.
    Notes and Queries, First Series, VI, 118
        ("Shropshire Ballad").

I went into the stable,
    To see what I could see;
I saw three gentlemen's horses,
    By one, by two, by three.

I called to my loving wife,
    'Coming, sir!' says she:
'What meaneth these three horses here,
    Without the leave of me?'

'You old fool! you blind fool!
    Can't you, won't you, see?
They are three milking-cows,
    That my mother sent to me.'

'Odds bobs, here's fun! Milking-cows with
        saddles on!
    The likes I never see!

I cannot go a mile from home
But a cuckold I must be.'

I went into the parlour,
To see what I could see ;
I saw there three gentlemen,
By one, by two, by three.

I called to my loving wife,
' Coming, sir ! ' said she :
' What bringeth these three gentlemen here,
Without the leave of me ? '

' You old fool ! you blind fool !
Can't you, won't you, see ?
They are three milking-maids,
That my mother sent to me.'

' Odds bobs, here 's fun !   Milking-maids with
breeches on !
The likes I never see !

I cannot go a mile from home
But a cuckold I must be.'

The unhappy husband next wanders into the
pantry, and discovers ' three pairs of hunting-
boots,' which his spouse declares are

' . . . milking-churns,
Which my mother sent to me.'

' Odds bobs, here 's fun !   Milking-churns with
spurs on !
The likes I never see !
I cannot go a mile from home
But a cuckold I must be.'

The gentleman's coats, discovered in the
kitchen, are next disposed of, but here my
memory fails me.

APPENDIX

—•—

' 'T was on Christmas Day,' found on a slip, " Sold
at No 42 Long Lane," in a volume in the British
Museum, 1876. e (not paged, but at what would be
p. 57), and again in The New Covent Garden Con-
cert, London, Printed and sold by J. Evans, No
41 Long-Lane, West Smithfield, Br. Mus. 1077.
g. 47 (4), dated in the catalogue "1805 ? "

'T was on Christmas Day
Father he did wed ;
Three months after that
My mother was brought to bed.
My father he came home,
His head with liquor stord,
And found in mother's room
A silver-hilted sword.
Fiddle de dum de de, etc.

' How came this sword here ? '
My mother says, says she,

' Lovee, 't is a poker
Antee sent to me.'
Father he stumbld and star'd ;
'T was the first, I ween,
Silver-headed poker
He had ever seen.

Father grumbled on,
But getting into bed
Egad ! as luck fell out,
A man popd up his head ;
' That 's my milk-maid,' says she ;
Says dad, ' I never heard
In all my travels yet
A milk-maid with a beard.'

My father found a whip,
And very glad was he ;
' And how came this whip here,
Without the leave of me ? '
' Oh ! that 's a nice strap-lace
My antee sent to me ; '
Egad ! he lac'd her stays,
And out of doors went she.

275

GET UP AND BAR THE DOOR

A. a. 'Get up and bar the Door,' Herd, The Ancient and Modern Scots Songs, 1769, p. 330; Ancient and Modern Scottish Songs, 1776, II, 159. **b.** [Pinkerton], Select Scotish Ballads, 1783, II, 150.

B. 'John Blunt,' Macmath MS., p. 74.

C. 'Johnie Blunt,' Johnson's Museum, IV, 376, No 365, 1792.

THE copy in Johnson's Museum, volume three, No 300, p. 310, 1790, is **A a** with two slight changes; that in Ritson's Scotish Song, I, 226, 1794, is **A a.** **A b** is substituted for **A a** in the third edition of Herd, 1791, II, 63. Christie, II, 262, who follows **A a**, but with changes, gives as a refrain, " common in the North of Scotland from time immemorial,"

> And the barring o our door,
> Weel, weel, weel !
> And the barring o our door, weel!

A, B. A housewife is boiling puddings anight; a cold wind blows in, and her husband bids her bar the door; she has her hands in her work and will not. They come to an agreement that whoever speaks first shall bar the door. Two belated travellers are guided to the house by the light which streams through an opening. They come in, and, getting no reply to their questions or response to their greetings, fall to eating and drinking what they find; the goodwife thinks much, but says naught. One of the strangers proposes to the other to take off the man's beard, and he himself will kiss the goodwife. Hot water is wanting (for scalding), suggests the second; but the boiling pudding-bree will serve, answers the first. The goodman calls out, Will ye kiss my wife and scald me ? and having spoken the first word has to bar the door.

C. In C man and wife are in bed, and the travellers haul the woman out and lay her on the floor : this makes the husband give tongue.

Stenhouse notes that this ballad furnished Prince Hoare with the principal scene in his musical entertainment of " No Song, no Supper," produced in 1790, and long a favorite on the stage. (Musical Museum, 1853, IV, 292.)

This tale is one of a group which may or may not have had a single archetype. Of the varieties, that which comes nearest is the first story in Straparola's Eighth Day. Husband and wife are sitting near the entrance of their house one night ; the husband says, It is time to go to bed, shut the door ; she says, Shut it yourself. They make a compact that the one who speaks first shall shut the door. The wife, tired of silence and growing sleepy, goes to bed ; the husband stretches himself on a bench. A gentleman's servant, whose lantern has been put out by the wind, seeing the door open, asks for a light. There is no reply. Advancing a little way into the house, he finds the man lying on the bench with his eyes open, but can get no word from him though he shakes him. Looking round, he sees the woman in bed and addresses her, but she is as dumb as her husband ; he gets into the bed. The woman says nothing till the intruder goes away ; then calls out, A pretty man you, to leave the door open all night and let people get into your bed. Fool, he says, now go shut the door. The same, with insignificant divergences, in L'Élite des Contes du Sieur d'Ouville, Rouen, 1699, I, 159.

A wedding-feast over, neither bridegroom nor bride will consent to shut the street-door ;

the lady proposes that the one who speaks first shall do this, to which the bridegroom agrees. They sit looking at each other in silence for two hours. Thieves, seeing the door open, come in, pillage the house, and even strip the young pair of everything valuable that they have on them, but neither says a word. In the morning a patrol of police find the house door open, enter, and make an inspection. The chief demands an explanation of the state of things; neither man nor woman vouchsafes a response, and he orders their heads off. The executioner is beginning with the husband; the wife cries out, Spare him! the husband exclaims, You have lost, go shut the door. (The Arabian tale of Sulayman Bey and the Three Story-Tellers, cited by Clouston, Popular Tales and Fictions, II, 29.)

Hemp-eaters, who have found a sequin and bought a mass of food, quarrel about fastening the gate of a tomb to which they have retired, to gorge unmolested. They come to an agreement that the man who first speaks shall close the gate. They let the victuals stand and sit mute. A troop of dogs rush in and eat all up clean. One of the party had secured some of the provender in advance of the rest, and bits are sticking to his mouth. A dog licks them away, and in so doing bites the lip of the fellow, who, in his pain, raps out a curse on the dog. The rest shout, Get up and shut the gate! (Turkish, Behrnauer, Die vierzig Veziere, p. 175 f.; Gibb, The History of the Forty Vezirs, p. 171 f.)

In the second Pickelheringsspiel, in the first part of Engelische Comedien und Tragedien, 1620, a married pair contend again about the shutting of a door. (R. Köhler; not seen by me.)

In other cases, speaking first entails a penalty different from shutting a door.

A young pair, lying in bed the first night after marriage, engage that whichever of the two gets up first or speaks first shall wash the dishes for a week. The husband, pretending to make his will by the process of expressing by signs his acceptance or rejection of the suggestions of a friend, bequeaths away from his wife a handsome article of

dress belonging to her. The wife utters a protest, and has to wash the dishes. (Novelle di Sercambi, ed. d'Ancona, p. 16, No 3, 'De simplicitate viri et uxoris.')

A man complains of dry bread which his wife has given him for his supper. She tells him to get up and moisten it; he bids her do this, but she refuses. It is finally settled that the one that speaks first shall moisten the bread. A visitor comes in and can make neither of them say a word. He kisses the wife, gives the husband a blow on the cheek; no word from either. He makes complaint to the kází; the husband will say nothing when brought before the kází, and is condemned to be hanged. At the moment of execution the wife ejaculates, Alas, my unfortunate husband! You devil, says he, go home and moisten the bread! (An Arabian story in Beloe's Oriental Apologues, cited by Clouston, II, 21.)

A shoemaker and his wife agree that the one who speaks first shall carry back a frying-pan that they have borrowed. A soldier who requires a girth for his horse asks the shoemaker to cut him one, but gets no answer, though he threatens to take off the man's head. Enraged at last, he seizes the shoemaker by the head to do what he had menaced, when the wife cries out, For mercy's sake, don't! Well done! says the husband, now carry back the pan. (Bernoni, Fiabe pop. veneziane, p. 67, No 13, 'La Scomessa;' Crane, Italian Popular Tales, p. 284.)

John makes terms with his wife that which of the two eats first of a soup which she has brought in, or speaks the first word, shall have a beating. William, of whom the husband is jealous, comes to offer his company to go to a fight which is to come off. Man and wife will neither eat nor speak, and he thinks them possessed. He takes the woman by the hand, and she goes with him. John cries out, Let my wife be! She says, John, you have spoken and lost. (Ayrers Dramen, ed. von Keller, III, 2006–08.)

A man who has been taunting his wife as a cackler is challenged by her to a trial at silence. A tinker comes in asking for kettles

to mend. He can make neither of them open
their mouth, and, as a last resource, offers to
kiss the woman. The husband cannot contain himself; the wife says, You have lost!

and remains mistress of the house, as she had
been before. (Farce d'un Chauldronnier,
Viollet Le Duc, Ancien Théâtre François, II,
109 ff.)*

A

a. Herd, The Ancient and Modern Scots Songs, 1769,
p. 330. b. [Pinkerton], Select Scotish Ballads, 1783, II,
150.

1 It fell about the Martinmas time,
  And a gay time it was then,
  When our goodwife got puddings to make,
  And she 's boild them in the pan.

2 The wind sae cauld blew south and north,
  And blew into the floor;
  Quoth our goodman to our goodwife,
  ' Gae out and bar the door.'

3 ' My hand is in my hussyfskap,
  Goodman, as ye may see ;
  An it shoud nae be barrd this hundred year,
  It 's no be barrd for me.'

4 They made a paction tween them twa,
  They made it firm and sure,
  That the first word whaeer shoud speak,
  Shoud rise and bar the door.

5 Then by there came two gentlemen,
  At twelve o clock at night,
  And they could neither see house nor hall,
  Nor coal nor candle-light.

6 ' Now whether is this a rich man's house,
  Or whether is it a poor ? '
  But neer a word wad ane o them speak,
  For barring of the door.

7 And first they ate the white puddings,
  And then they ate the black ;
  Tho muckle thought the goodwife to hersel,
  Yet neer a word she spake.

8 Then said the one unto the other,
  ' Here, man, tak ye my knife ;
  Do ye tak aff the auld man's beard,
  And I 'll kiss the goodwife.'

9 ' But there 's nae water in the house,
  And what shall we do than ? '
  ' What ails ye at the pudding-broo,
  That boils into the pan ? '

10 O up then started our goodman,
  An angry man was he :
  ' Will ye kiss my wife before my een,
  And scad me wi pudding-bree ? '

11 Then up and started our goodwife,
  Gied three skips on the floor:
  ' Goodman, you 've spoken the foremost word,
  Get up and bar the door.'

B

Macmath MS. p. 74. "From the singing of Miss Jane
Webster, 15th October, 1886, and 26th August, 1887, who
learned it at Airds of Kells, Kirkcudbrightshire, many
years ago, from James McJannet."

1 There leeved a wee man at the fit o yon hill,
  John Blunt it was his name, O
  And he selld liquor and ale o the best,
  And bears a wondrous fame. O
  Tal lara ta lilt, tal lare a lilt,
  Tal lara ta lilt, tal lara

2 The wind it blew frae north to south,
  It blew into the floor;
  Says auld John Blunt to Janet the wife,
  Ye maun rise up and bar the door.

3 ' My hans are in my husseyskep,
  I canna weel get them free,
  And if ye dinna bar it yersel
  It 'll never be barred by me.'

* All the above have been cited by Reinhold Köhler,
Jahrbuch für romanische u. englische Literatur, XII, 348 f.,
or by Clouston, Popular Tales and Fictions, II, 15 ff.

4 They made it up atween them twa,
   They made it unco sure,
   That the ane that spoke the foremost word
   Was to rise and bar the door.

5 There was twa travellers travelling late,
   Was travelling cross the muir,
   And they cam unto wee John Blunt's,
   Just by the light o the door.

6 'O whether is this a rich man's house,
   Or whether is it a puir?'
   But never a word would the auld bodies speak,
   For the barring o the door.

7 First they bad good een to them,
   And syne they bad good morrow;
   But never a word would the auld bodies speak,
   For the barring o the door, O.

8 First they ate the white puddin,
   And syne they ate the black,
   And aye the auld wife said to hersel,
   May the deil slip down wi that!

9 And next they drank o the liquor sae strong,
   And syne they drank o the yill:
   'And since we hae got a house o our ain
   I'm sure we may tak our fill.'

10 It's says the ane unto the ither,
   Here, man, tak ye my knife,
   An ye'll scrape aff the auld man's beard,
   While I kiss the gudewife.

11 'Ye hae eaten my meat, ye hae drucken my
        drink,
   Ye'd make my auld wife a whore!'
   'John Blunt, ye hae spoken the foremost word,
   Ye maun rise up and bar the door.'

————————

C

Johnson's Museum, IV, 376, No 365, 1792. Contributed
by Robert Burns.

1 THERE livd a man in yonder glen,
   And John Blunt was his name; O
   He maks gude maut and he brews gude ale,
   And he bears a wondrous fame. O

2 The wind blew in the hallan ae night,
   Fu snell out oer the moor;
   'Rise up, rise up, auld Luckie,' he says,
   'Rise up, and bar the door.'

3 They made a paction tween them twa,
   They made it firm and sure,
   Whaeer sud speak the foremost word
   Should rise and bar the door.

4 Three travellers that had tint their gate,
   As thro the hills they foor,
   They airted by the line o light
   Fu straught to Johnie Blunt's door.

5 They haurld auld Luckie out o her bed
   And laid her on the floor,
   But never a word auld Luckie wad say,
   For barrin o the door.

6 'Ye've eaten my bread, ye hae druken my ale,
   And ye'll mak my auld wife a whore!'
   'A ha, Johnie Blunt! ye hae spoke the first
        word,
   Get up and bar the door.'

————————

A. a. *Johnson's Museum has these variations:*
   2⁴. Gat up and.
   4³. first who should speak the foremost word.
   b. 1³. That our gudewife had.   1⁴. she boild.
   2¹. wind blew cauld frae east.   2⁴. Get up and.
   3³. hunder.   3⁴. Its neer be barrd by.
   4². word whaever spak.   5¹. come.
   5³. Whan they can see na ither house.

5⁴. And at the door they light.   7². And syne.
7³. Tho *wanting.*
8¹. Then ane unto the ither said.   9³. bree.
11¹. O up then started.
11³. you have spak the first word.
O *is added to the second and fourth lines for*
   singing, in both of the Museum copies and
   in B.

276

THE FRIAR IN THE WELL

A. a. 'The Fryer well fitted,' etc., Rawlinson Ballads, 566, fol. 63, 4°. **b.** 'The Fryer well fitted,' etc., Roxburghe Ballads, II, 172; Ebsworth, Roxburghe Ballads, VII, 222. **c.** 'The Fryer and the Maid,' Wit and Mirth, or, Pills to purge Melancholy, "I, 340, 1707," III, 325, 1719.

B. a. 'The Friar and Fair Maid,' Buchan's MSS, II, 351. **b.** 'The Friar,' Kinloch MSS, VI, 97. **c.** Kinloch MSS, V, 60.

THE broadside, A a, b, is found in many other collections: Pepys, III, 145, No 143; Crawford, No 94, etc. (see Ebsworth). B, the Scottish ballad (an improvement on the English), is without doubt derived from print, but not directly from A a, b. In B the maid feigns to be afraid of her master, as in A c, not of her father. From Halliwell's Notices of Fugitive Tracts, p. 37, No 49, Percy Society, vol. xxix, we learn that The Royal Garland of Protestant Delight, London, 1689, has a ballad with the title 'The witty lass of Somersetshire, or the fryer servd in his kind,' with an "answer," in the last stanza of which 'the inn-keeper, her master,' laughs at the fryer's disaster.

The tune of 'The Friar in the Well' occurs in The Dancing Master, from 1650 to 1686: Chappell's Popular Music, p. 274. Munday, in his 'Downfall of Robert, Earl of Huntington,' Act iv, Scene 2, 1598, refers to the 'merry jest . . . how the friar fell into the well, for love of Jenny, that fair bonny belle.' A reference of Skelton's in his Colyn Cloute* carries the story, and almost certainly the ballad, back to the first quarter of the sixteenth century.

The copy in Kinloch's Ballad Book, p. 25, was compounded by the editor from B b, c.

A maid, solicited by a friar, says that she

fears hell-fire; the friar reminds her that if she were in hell he could sing her out. She stipulates for money in advance; while the friar is gone to fetch some, she hangs (spreads) a cloth before (over) a well. The money in hand, she calls out that her father (master) is coming; the friar runs to hide behind the cloth (a screen), and falls into the well. The friar cries for help; he is left to sing himself out. Extricated after a sufficient cooling, he asks his money back, but is told that he must pay for fouling the water.

This story, one might safely say, is not beyond the "imaginary forces" of any Western people, but an open well inside of an English house is at least of unusual occurrence, and if we find something of the kind to our hand in an Eastern tale of similar character, a borrowing seems more plausible than an invention. There is a considerable class of tales, mostly Oriental, in which a chaste wife discomfits two or three would-be seducers, bringing them to shame and ridicule in the end. In some, she exacts or receives money from her suitors at the outset; in some, an allegation that her husband is coming is the pretext for her concealing them. An example in English is 'The Wright's Chaste Wife,' by Adam of Cobsam, edited for the Early English Text Society, in 1865, by Dr Furnivall. In this, three men successively are tumbled through a trap door into an underground room. But in the Persian Túti Náma, or Book of the Parrot, of Nakhshabí, the wife

* But when the freare fell in the well
He coud not syng himselfe therout
But by the helpe of Christyan Clout.
(vv. 879-91.)

lays a bed over a dry well, her suitors are invited to sit on it, and they fall in; and here, it is not extravagant to suppose, we may have the remote source of the trick in our ballad.*

There is a French ballad of the same general type: 'Le lourdaud moine,' Tarbé, Romancero de Champagne, II, 135; 'Le moine Nicolas,' Bujeaud, II, 284. A monk, enamored of a married woman, is appointed to come to her while her husband is away; he is told to lay off his frock, which she secures, and she takes money which he has brought. He is then sent to the door to see if the husband be coming, and is locked out. He asks to have his frock and money returned; she will keep them for her husband. The convent jeer at him when he comes back: 'Dieu bénisse la commère qui t'a joué ce tour-là!'

'Munken i Vaande,' a rather flat Danish ballad from a MS. of the 16th century, tells of a monk who knocks at the door of a woman whom he has been courting, and calls to her to keep her word; she tells her husband to slip under the bed, and lets the monk in; the monk hands the woman gold rings which he had promised; the goodman comes out and gives him a beating; the monk leaps out of the window and goes to his cloister; his superior asks why he has been away; he has been shriving the farmer's wife, and it has nearly cost him his life.

A

a. Rawlinson, 566, fol. 63, 4°. b. Roxburghe, II, 172; Ebsworth, Roxburghe Ballads, VII, 222. c. D'Urfey's Pills to purge Melancholy, ed. 1719, III, 325.

1 As I lay musing all alone,
    fa, la, la, la, la
A pretty jeast I thought upon;
    fa, la, la, la, la
Then listen a while, and I will you tell
Of a fryer that loved a bonny lass well.
    fa, la, la, la, la
    fa, la, la, lang-tre-down-dilly

2 He came to the maid when she went to bed,
Desiring to have her maidenhead,
But she denyëd his desire,
And told him that she feard hell-fire.

3 'Tush,' quoth the fryer, 'thou needst not doubt
If thou wert in hell I could sing thee out:'
'Then,' quoth the maid, 'thou shalt have thy request;'
The fryer was glad as a fox in his nest.

4 'But one thing,' quoth she, 'I do desire,
Before you have what you require;

Before that you shall do the thing,
An angel of mony thou shalt me bring.'

5 'Tush,' quoth the fryer, 'we shall agree,
No mony shall part my love and me;
Before that I will see thee lack,
I 'le pawn the grey gown from my back.'

6 The maid bethought her of a wile
How she the fryer might beguile;
While he was gone, the truth to tell,
She hung a cloth before the well.

7 The fryer came, as his covenant was,
With money to his bonny lass;
'Good morrow, fair maid!' 'Good morrow!' quoth she.
'Here is the mony I promised thee.'

8 She thankt the man, and she took his mony:
'Now let us go to 't,' quoth he, 'sweet hony:'
'O stay,' quoth she, 'some respite make,
My father comes, he will me take.'

9 'Alas!' quoth the fryer, 'where shall I run,
To hide me till that he be gone?'
'Behinde the cloath run thou,' quoth she,
'And there my father cannot thee see.'

* For the class of tales referred to, see von der Hagen, Gesammtabenteuer, III, xxxv f., lxxxiii f.; Reinhold Köhler, in Jahrbuch für romanische und englische Literatur, VIII, 44–65; Clouston, Popular Tales and Fictions, II, 289–310.

10 Behind the cloath the fryer crept,
   And into the well on the sudden he leapt;
   ' Alas,' quoth he, ' I am in the well ! '
   ' No matter,' quoth she, ' if thou wert in hell.

11 ' Thou sayst thou couldst sing me out of hell,
   Now prithee sing thy self out of the well : '
   The fryer sung with a pittiful sound,
   Oh help me out, or I shall be dround !

12 ' I trow,' quoth she, ' your courage is coold.'
   Quoth the fryer, I was never so foold,
   I never was servëd so before.
   ' Then take heed,' quoth she, ' thou comst there
   no more.'

13 Quoth he, For sweet Saint Francis sake
   On his disciple some pitty take :

Quoth she, Saint Francis never taught
His scholars to tempt young maids to naught.

14 The fryer did entreat her still
   That she should help him out of the well ;
   She heard him make such pittious moan
   She helpd him out, and bid him be gone.

15 Quoth he, Shall I have my mony again,
   Which thou from me hast beforehand tane ?
   ' Good sir,' said she, ' there 's no such matter ;
   I 'le make you pay for fouling my water.'

16 The fryer went all along the street,
   Droping wet, like a new-washd sheep ;
   Both old and young commended the maid
   That such a witty prank had plaid.

B

a. Buchan's MSS, II, 351. b. Kinloch MSS, VI, 97, in
Kinloch's handwriting. c. Kinloch MSS, V, 60, in the
handwriting of James Beattie.

1 O HEARKEN and hear, and I will you tell
      Sing, Faldidae, faldidadi
  Of a friar that loved a fair maiden well.
      Sing, Faldi dadi di di (bis)

2 The friar he came to this maiden's bedside,
  And asking for her maidenhead.

3 ' O I would grant you your desire,
  If 't werena for fear o hell's burning fire.'

4 ' O hell's burning fire ye need have no doubt ;
  Altho you were in, I could whistle you out.'

5 ' O if I grant to you this thing,
  Some money you unto me must bring.'

6 He brought her the money, and did it down
      tell ;
  She had a white cloth spread over the well.

7 Then the fair maid cried out that her master
      was come ;
  ' O,' said the friar, ' then where shall I run ? '

8 ' O ye will go in behind yon screen,
  And then by my master ye winna be seen.'

9 Then in behind the screen she him sent,
  But he fell into the well by accident.

10 Then the friar cried out with a piteous moan,
   O help ! O help me ! or else I am gone.

11 ' Ye said ye wad whistle me out o hell ;
   Now whistle your ain sel out o the well.'

12 She helped him out and bade him be gone ;
   The friar he asked his money again.

13 ' As for your money, there is no much matter
   To make you pay more for jumbling our water.'

14 Then all who hear it commend this fair maid
   For the nimble trick to the friar she played.

15 The friar he walked on the street,
   And shaking his lugs like a well-washen sheep.

A. a, b. The Fryer well fitted, or,
    A pretty jest that once befell,
    How a Maid put a Fryer to cool in the well.
    To a merry tune.

a. London. Printed for F. Coles, T. Vere, and
    J. Wright.
b. Printed for W. Thackeray and T. Passinger.
a. $3^{1,3}$, 7^3, $8^{2,3}$, $9^{1,3}$, 10^4, 12^4, qd. *for* quoth.
    7^3. qd. he. 8^2. too't. 8^3. Oh.
    10^1. did crept. 16^2. Drooping.
b. 5^4. my grey. 7^3. quoth she. 10^1. fryer crept.
    10^2. on a. 11^3. sung on. 12^2. never was.
    14^2. she would. 15^2. Which from me thou.
    16^2. Dropping.
c. *The variations are insignificant until we*
    come to 8^3 ; *from that point this copy*
    (which is abridged) runs as follows :
8^3. ' Nay, stay a while, some respite make ;
    If my master should come he would us
    take.

9. ' Alas,' quoth the maid, ' my master doth
    come ! '
    ' Alas ! ' quoth the fryer, ' where shall I
    run ? '
    ' Behind yon cloth run thou,' quoth she,
    ' For there my master cannot see.'

10. Behind the cloth the fryer went,
    And was in the well incontinent.
    ' Alas,' quoth he, ' I 'm in the well ! '
    ' No matter,' quoth she, ' if thou wert in
    hell.

$11^{1,2}$. ' Thou saidst thou could sing me out of
    hell,
    I prithee sing thy self out of the well.
    Sing out,' quoth she, ' with all thy might,
    Or else thou 'rt like to sing there all
    night.'

$11^{3,4}$. The fryer sang out with a pitiful sound,
    Oh help me out, or I shall be drownd !

$14^{3,4}$. She heard him make such pitiful moan
    She hope [= holp] him out and bid him
    go home.

$12^{3,4}$. Quoth the fryer, I never was servd so
    before :
    ' Away,' quoth the wench, ' come here
    no more.'

$16^{1,2}$. The fryer he walkd along the street
    As if he had been a new-washd sheep.

    Sing, hey down a derry, and let 's be
    merry,
    And from such sin ever keep.

The fa la *burden is not given.*

B. b. *Apparently a revised by Kinloch.*
    4^2. sing *for* whistle. 7^2. then *wanting.*
    10^1. a *wanting.* 15^2. sheet *for* sheep.

c. 1. Listen and I will you tell
    Wi a falaldirry, falaldirry
    How a friar in love wi a lassie fell.
    Wi a falee and latee and a lee-tiddle-
    tiddle-tee

7. The lassie cries, My master comes !
    The friar cries, Where shall I run ?

8. ' O you 'll do you in below this cloth ;
    That you be seen I wad be loth.'

10. The friar cries, I 'm in the well !
    ' I care na tho you were in hell.

11. ' You said you w[a]d sing me out of hell ;
    Sing yoursell out o the well.'

12. ' If you 'll help me out, I will be gone,
    Back to you I 'll neuer come.'

    She helped him out, and he was begone ;
    Back to her he never came.

15. The frier he gaed up the street,
    Hanging his lugs like a washen sheet.

2–6, 9, 13, 14, *wanting.*

277

THE WIFE WRAPT IN WETHER'S SKIN

A. a. 'Sweet Robin,' Jamieson's Popular Ballads, I, 319. **b.** Macmath MS., p. 100, three stanzas.

B. 'Robin he's gane to the wude,' Harris MS., fol. 26 b.

C. 'The Cooper of Fife,' Whitelaw, The Book of Scottish Song, p. 333.

D. Jamieson-Brown MS., Appendix, p. iii.

E. Jamieson's Popular Ballads, I, 324.

———

JAMIESON cites the first two stanzas of **A a** in a letter of inquiry to The Scots Magazine, October, 1803, p. 700, and the first half of **D** (with alterations) in his preface, Popular Ballads, I, 320. The ballad, he says, is very popular all over Scotland.

Robin has married a wife of too high kin to bake or brew, wash or wring. He strips off a wether's skin and lays it on her back, or prins her in it. He dares not beat her, for her proud kin, but he may beat the wether's skin, and does. This makes an ill wife good.

A fragment in Herd's MSS, I, 105, II, 161, belongs, if not to this ballad, at least to one in which an attempt is made to tame a shrew by castigation.

> 'Now tak a cud in ilka hand
> And bace * her up and doun, man,
> And she 'll be an o the best wives
> That ever took the town, man.'

* *Bace* in the second copy, rightly, that is, *bash*, beat; *bare* in the first (probably mistranscribed).

† A merry jeste of a shrewde and curste wyfe lapped in Morrelles skin for her good behauyour. Imprinted at London in Fleetestreete, beneath the Conduite, at the signe of Saint John Euangelist, by H. Jackson; without date, but earlier than 1575, since the book was in Captain Cox's library. Reprinted in Utterson's Select Pieces of Early Popular Poetry, 1825, II, 169; The Old Taming of the Shrew, edited by T. Amyot for the Shakespeare Society, 1844, p. 53; W. C. Hazlitt's Early Popular Poetry, IV, 179.

* * * * * *
> And Jammie 's turnd him round about,
> He 's done a manly feat :
> 'Get up, get up, ye dirty slut,
> And gie to me my meat.'

* * * * * *
> 'Say 't oer again, say 't oer again,
> Ye thief, that I may hear ye ;
> I 'se gar ye dance upon a peat,
> Gin I sall cum but near ye.'

The story of the ballad was in all likelihood traditionally derived from the good old tale of the wife lapped in Morrel's skin.† Here a husband, who has put up with a great deal from an excessively restive wife, flays his old horse Morrell and salts the hide, takes the shrew down cellar, and, after a sharp contest for mastery, beats her with birchen rods till she swoons, then wraps her in the salted hide : by which process the woman is perfectly reformed.‡

‡ These passages are worth noting :

> She can carde, she can spin,
> She can thresh and she can fan.   (v. 419 f.)

> In euery hand a rod he gate
> And layd vpon her a right good pace.   (v. 955 f.)

> Where art thou, wife ? shall I haue any meate ?   (v. 839.)

(Compare Herd's fragments with the last two, and with 903–10.)

A

Jamieson's Popular Ballads, I, 319. "From the recitation of a friend of the editor's in Morayshire."

1 She wadna bake, she wadna brew,
     Hollin, green hollin
  For spoiling o her comely hue.
     Bend your bow, Robin

2 She wadna wash, she wadna wring,
  For spoiling o her gay goud ring.

3 Robin he's gane to the fald
  And catched a weather by the spauld.

4 And he has killed his weather black
  And laid the skin upon her back.

5 'I darena pay you, for your kin,
  But I can pay my weather's skin.

6 'I darena pay my lady's back,
  But I can pay my weather black.'

7 'O Robin, Robin, lat me be,
  And I'll a good wife be to thee.

8 'It's I will wash, and I will wring,
  And never mind my gay goud ring.

9 'It's I will bake, and I will brew,
  And never mind my comely hue.

10 'And gin ye thinkna that eneugh,
  I'se tak the goad and I'se ca the pleugh.

11 'Gin ye ca for mair whan that is doon,
  I'll sit i the neuk and I'll dight your shoon.'

B

Harris MS., fol. 26 b, No 25, from Miss Harris.

1 Robin he's gane to the wast,
     Hollin, green hollin
  He's waled a wife amang the warst.
     Bend your bows, Robin

2 She could neither bake nor brew,
  For spoilin o her bonnie hue.

3 She could neither spin nor caird,
  But fill the cup, an sair the laird.

4 She could neither wash nor wring,
  For spoilin o her gay goud ring.

5 Robin's sworn by the rude
  That he wald mak an ill wife gude.

6 Robin he's gaun to the fauld,
  An taen his blaik [wither] by the spauld.

7 He's taen aff his wither's skin
  An he has preened his ain wife in.

8 'I daurna beat my wife, for a' her kin,
  But I may beat my wither's skin.'

9 'I can baith bake an brew;
  What care I for my bonnie hue?

10 'I can baith wash an wring;
  What care I for my gay gowd ring?

11 'I can baith spin an caird;
  Lat onybodie sair the laird.'

12 Robin's sworn by the rude
  That he has made an ill wife gude.

C

Whitelaw's Book of Scottish Song, p. 333.

1 THERE was a wee cooper who lived in Fife,
   Nickity, nackity, noo, noo, noo
And he has gotten a gentle wife.
   Hey Willie Wallacky, how John Dougall,
   Alane, quo Rushety, roue, roue, roue

2 She wadna bake, nor she wadna brew,
   For the spoiling o her comely hue.

3 She wadna card, nor she wadna spin,
   For the shaming o her gentle kin.

4 She wadna wash, nor she wadna wring,
   For the spoiling o her gouden ring.

5 The cooper 's awa to his woo-pack
   And has laid a sheep-skin on his wife's back.

6 'It 's I 'll no thrash ye, for your proud kin,
   But I will thrash my ain sheep-skin.'

7 'Oh, I will bake, and I will brew,
   And never mair think on my comely hue.

8 'Oh, I will card, and I will spin,
   And never mair think on my gentle kin.

9 'Oh, I will wash, and I will wring,
   And never mair think on my gouden ring.'

10 A' ye wha hae gotten a gentle wife
   Send ye for the wee cooper o Fife.

D

Jamieson-Brown MS., Appendix, p. iii, letter of R. Scott to Jamieson, June 9, 1805.

1 THERE livd a laird down into Fife,
   Riftly, raftly, now, now, now
An he has married a bonny young wife.
   Hey Jock Simpleton, Jenny['s] white petti-
      coat,
   Robin a Rashes, now, now, now

2 He courted her and he brought her hame,
   An thought she would prove a thrifty dame.

3 She could neither spin nor caird,
   But sit in her chair and dawt the laird.

4 She wadna bake and she wadna brew,
   An a' was for spoiling her delicate hue.

5 She wadna wash nor wad she wring,
   For spoiling o her gay goud ring.

6 But he has taen him to his sheep-fauld,
   An taen the best weather by the spauld.

7 Aff o the weather he took the skin,
   An rowt his bonny lady in.

8 'I dare na thump you, for your proud kin,
   But well sall I lay to my ain weather's skin.'
   *   *   *   *   *   *   *

E

Jamieson's Popular Ballads, I, 324.

1 THERE lives a landart laird in Fife,
   And he has married a dandily wife.

2 She wadna shape, nor yet wad she sew,
   But sit wi her cummers and fill hersell fu.

3 She wadna spin, nor yet wad she card,
   But she wad sit and crack wi the laird.

4 He is down to his sheep-fald
   And cleekit a weather by the back-spald.

5 He 's whirpled aff the gude weather's-skin
   And wrappit the dandily lady therein.

6 'I darena pay you, for your gentle kin,
   But weel I may skelp my weather's-skin.'
   *   *   *   *   *   *   *

A. a. *The refrain, altered by Jamieson, has been restored from his preface. Five stanzas added by him at the end have been dropped.*

b. From the recitation of Miss Agnes Macmath, 29th April, 1893; learned by her from her mother, who had it from *her* mother, Janet Spark, Kirkcudbrightshire.

2. She could na wash and she could na wring,
    Hey, Wullie Wyliecot, noo, noo, noo
For the spoiling o her gay gold ring.

Wi my Hey, Wullie Wyliecot, tangie dooble,
That robes in the rassiecot, noo, noo, noo
(*Refrain perhaps corrupt.*)

3. He 's gane oot unto the fauld,
    He 's catched a wather by the spaul.

5. 'I darena thrash ye, for yer kin,
    But I may thrash my ain wather-skin.'

278

THE FARMER'S CURST WIFE

A. 'The Farmer's Old Wife,' Dixon, Ancient Poems, Ballads, and Songs of the Peasantry of England, p. 210, Percy Society, vol. **xvii.** The same in Bell, p. 204.

B. Macmath MS., p. 96.

THE devil comes for a farmer's wife and is made welcome to her by the husband. The woman proves to be no more controllable in hell than she had been at home; she kicks the imps about, and even brains a set of them with her pattens or a maul. For safety's sake, the devil is constrained to take her back to her husband.

B. The ballad of 'Kellyburnbraes,' Johnson's Museum, No 379, p. 392, was composed by Burns, as he has himself informed us, "from the old traditional version." "The original ballad, still preserved by tradition," says David Laing, "was much improved in passing through Burns's hands:" Museum, IV, *389, 1853. Cromek, Remains of Nithsdale and Galloway Song, p. 83, 1810, gives us what he calls the "Original of Burns's Carle of Kelly-Burn Braes," remarking, with some effrontery, that there is reason to believe that Burns had not seen the whole of the verses which constitute this copy. Allan Cunningham, Songs of Scotland, II, 199, undertook

"to make a more complete version than has hitherto appeared" out of Burns, Cromek, and some "fugitive copies." So we get the original from none of them, but are, rather, further from it at each step. Whether B has come down pure, unaffected by Burns and Cromek, it is impossible to say. That it shows resemblances to both copies is not against its genuineness, if there was a fair leaven of the popular ballad in each of these reconstructions; and it is probable that there would be, at least in Burns's.

A curst wife who was a terror to demons is a feature in a widely spread and highly humorous tale, Oriental and European. See Benfey, Pantschatantra, I, 519–34; and, for a variety which is, at the beginning, quite close to our ballad, Ralston, Russian Folk-Tales, p. 39 (Afanasief, I, No 9).

Cromek's ballad is translated by Wolff, Halle der Völker, I, 93, Hausschatz, p. 230.

A

Dixon, Ancient Poems, Ballads, and Songs, p. 210, Percy Society, vol. xvii.

1　THERE was an old farmer in Sussex did dwell,
　　　(*Chorus of whistlers*)
　　There was an old farmer in Sussex did dwell,
　　And he had a bad wife, as many knew well.
　　　(*Chorus of whistlers*)

2　Then Satan came to the old man at the plough:
　　'One of your family I must have now.'

3　'It is not your eldest son that I crave,
　　But it is your old wife, and she I will have.'

4　'O welcome, good Satan, with all my heart!
　　I hope you and she will never more part.'

5　Now Satan has got the old wife on his back,
　　And he lugged her along, like a pedlar's pack.

6　He trudged away till they came to his hall-gate;
　　Says he, Here, take in an old Sussex chap's mate.

7　O then she did kick the young imps about;
　　Says one to the other, Let's try turn her out.

8　She spied thirteen imps all dancing in chains,
　　She up with her pattens and beat out their brains.

9　She knocked the old Satan against the wall:
　　'Let's turn her out, or she'll murder us all.'

10　Now he's bundled her up on his back amain,
　　And to her old husband he took her again.

11　'I have been a tormentor the whole of my life,
　　But I neer was tormented so as with your wife.'

B

Macmath MS., p. 96. Taken down by Mr Macmath from the recitation of his aunt, Miss Jane Webster, Crossmichael, Kirkcudbrightshire, August 27th, 1892; learned many years ago, at Airds of Kells, from the singing of Samuel Galloway.

1　THE auld Deil cam to the man at the pleugh,
　　　Rumchy ae de aidie
　　Saying, I wish ye gude luck at the making o yer sheugh.
　　Mushy toorin an ant tan aira.

2　'It's neither your oxen nor you that I crave;
　　It's that old scolding woman, it's her I must have.'

3　'Ye're welcome to her wi a' my gude heart;
　　I wish you and her it's never may part.'

4　She jumped on to the auld Deil's back,
　　And he carried her awa like a pedlar's pack.

5　He carried her on till he cam to hell's door,
　　He gaed her a kick till she landed in the floor.

6　She saw seven wee deils a sitting in a raw,
　　She took up a mell and she murdered them a'.

7　A wee reekit deil lookit owre the wa:
　　'O tak her awa, or she'll ruin us a'.'

8　'O what to do wi her I canna weel tell;
　　She's no fit for heaven, and she'll no bide in hell.'

＊　＊　＊　＊　＊　＊　＊　＊

9　She jumpit on to the auld Deil's back,
　　And he carried her back like a pedlar's pack.

＊　＊　＊　＊　＊　＊　＊　＊

10　She was seven years gaun, and seven years comin,
　　And she cried for the sowens she left in the pot.

279

THE JOLLY BEGGAR

A. 'Ther was a wife in yon toun,' "Old Lady's Collection," No. 36.

B. a. 'The Jolly Beggar,' Herd, The Ancient and Modern Scots Songs, 1769, p. 46 ; ed. 1776, II, 26.

b. 'The Jolly Beggars,' Curious Tracts, Scotland, British Museum, 1078. m. 24. No 30 (a collection made by James Mitchell at Aberdeen in 1828). **c.** 'The Jolly Beggar-Man,' Macmath MS., p. 103, a fragment. **d.** The same, a fragment.

I HAVE not found this piece in any printed collection older than Herd, 1769, but it is cited in the second edition of Percy's Reliques, 1767, II, 59 (preface to 'The Gaberlunyie-Man'), and was known before that to Horace Walpole, who, as Percy remarks, confounds it with 'The Gaberlunyie-Man,' or gives it that title: Catalogue of Royal and Noble Authors, II, 202 f., second edition, 1759 (not mentioned in the first edition). It was probably in circulation as a flying-sheet.*

We are regularly informed by editors that tradition imputes the authorship of both 'The Jolly Beggar' and 'The Gaberlunyie-Man' to James Fifth of Scotland. 'The Gaberlunyie-Man' was, so far as can be ascertained, first printed in the Tea-Table Miscellany (in 1724), and I am not aware that it is mentioned anywhere before that date. Ramsay speaks of it as an old piece, but says nothing about the authorship. The tradition as to James Fifth is, perhaps, not much older than the publication in either case, and has no more plausibility than it has authority.

The copies in Pinkerton's Select Scotish Ballads, II, 35, 1783, Johnson's Museum, p. 274, No 266, 1790, Ritson's Scotish Songs, I, 168, 1794, etc., are all from Herd's second edition, 1776. In this we have, instead of the Fa la la burden, the following, presumably later (see Herd's MSS, I, 5):

> And we 'll gang nae mair a roving,
> Sae late into the night,
> And we 'll gang nae mair a roving, boys,
> Let the moon shine neer sae bright,
> And we 'll gang nae mair a roving.

Motherwell's MS., p. 124, has a recited copy which seems to be B a as in Herd, 1776, corrupted by oral transmission. It does not seriously differ from the original until we come to the end, where we find an absurd stanza which is derived from B b.

The variations of B b are not the accidents of tradition, but deliberate alterations. 'The Jovial Beggarman,' in The Forsaken Lover's Garland, No 15 of a collection of garlands, British Museum, 11621. e. 1 ("Newcastle? 1750?"), is a *rifacimento*, and a very inferior piece. Of this Rev. S. Baring-Gould took down a copy from the singing of a laborer on Dartmoor, in 1889.†

'The Jovial Tinker and Farmer's Daughter,' British Museum, 1346. m. 7 (31), 'The Tinker and Farmer's Daughter's Garland,' British Museum, 11621. a. 6 (34), is another *rifacimento*, with less of the original in it. The tinker, we are told at the outset, is a noble lord disguised.

---

* And may have been omitted by Ramsay because he "kept out all ribaldry" from the Tea-Table Miscellany. This is not a Tea-Table Miscellany, and I have no discretion.

† I owe my knowledge of all of these three copies to Mr Baring-Gould. He informs me that the ballad which he took down is sung thoughout Cornwall and Devon.

An English broadside ballad of the second half of the seventeenth century, Pepys, III, 73, No 71, has the same story as the Scottish popular ballad, and may have been the foundation of it, but the Scottish ballad is a far superior piece of work. The English broadside is given, substantially, in the notes.

'Der Bettelman,' Hoffmann u. Richter, Schlesische Volkslieder, p. 45, No 24, has a generic resemblance to this ballad.* So, more remotely, a Flemish ballad, ' Ein schöner Krüppel,' Hoffmann, Niederländische Volkslieder, p. 129 and elsewhere. Again, a very pretty and innocent Portuguese ballad, ' O

Cego,' Almeida-Garrett, III, 191, No 35, Braga, Romanceiro Geral, p. 147, No 55, and Cantos pop. do Archipelago Açoriano, p. 372, No 76 (all in Hartung, II, 103 ff.), which Almeida-Garrett, quite extravagantly, supposed might be derived from ' The Gaberlunyie-Man,' brought home from Scotland by Portuguese sailors. There is an accidental similarity in one or two points with the Spanish ballad ' Tiempo es, el caballero,' Duran, I, 163, No 307, Primavera, II, 91, No 158.

' The Gaberlunyie-Man ' is given in an appendix.

A

"Old Lady's Collection," No 36.

1 ' THER is a wife in yone toun-end, an she has dothers three,
    An I wad be a beager for ony of a' the three.'

2 He touk his clouty clok him about, his peak-staff in his hand,
    An he is awa to yon toun-end, leak ony peare man.

3 ' I ha ben about this fish-toun this years tua or three,
    Ha ye ony quarters, deam, that ye coud gie me ? '

4 ' Awa, ye pear carl, ye dinne kean my name ;
    Ye sudd ha caed me mistress fan ye called me bat deam.'

5 He tuke his hat in his hand an gied her juks three :
    ' An ye want manners, misstres, quarters ye 'll gie me.'

6 ' Awa, ye pear carle, in ayont the fire,
    An sing to our Lord Gray's men to their hearts' disire.'

7 Some lowked to his goudie lowks, some to his milk-whit skine,
    Some to his ruffled shirt, the gued read gold hang in.

8 Out spak our madin, an she was ay shay,
    Fatt will the jolly beager gett afore he gaa to lay ?

9 Out spak our goudwife, an she was not sae shay,
    He 'se gett a dish of lang kell, besids a puss pay.

10 Out spak the jolly beager, That dish I dou denay ;
    I canne sup yer lang kell nor yet yer puss pay.

11 Bat ye gett to my supper a capon of the best,
    Tuo or three bottels of yer wine, an bear, an we sall ha a merry feast.

12 ' Ha ye ony siler, carll, to bint the bear an wine ? '
    ' O never a peney, misstress, had I lang sine.'

13 The beager wadne lay in the barn, nor yett in the bayr,
    Bat in ahind the haa-dor, or att the kitchen-fire.

---

* Other copies, which are rather numerous, much less : Norrenberg, Des dülkener Fiedlers Liederbuch, p. 10, No 13 ; Peter I, 182 ; Uhland, No 285, p. 737 ; Haupt u. Schmaler, I, 102, No 67 ; etc. See Hoffmann's notes, pp. 46, 47 ; Barack, Zimmerische Chronik, 2d ed., II, 111, and Liebrecht's note, Germania, XIV, 38 ; Schade, Weimarisches Jahrbuch, III, 259 ff., 465 ff.

14 The beager's bed was well [made] of gued
    clean stray an hay,

.   .   .   .

15 The madin she rose up to bar the dor,
    An ther she spayed a naked man, was rinen
    throu the flour.

16 He tuke her in his arms an to his bed he
    ran ;
    ' Hollie we me, sir,' she says, ' or ye 'll waken
    our pear man.'

17 The begger was a cuning carle, an never a
    word he spake
    Till he got his turn dean, an sayn began to
    crak.

18 ' Is ther ony dogs about this toun? madin, tell
    me nou : '
    ' Fatt wad ye dee we them, my hony an my
    dou ? '

19 ' They wad ravie a' my meall-poks an die me
    mukell wrang : '
    ' O doll for the deaing o it ! are ye the pear
    man ?

20 ' I thought ye had ben some gentelman, just
    leak the leard of Brody !

    I am sorry for the doing o itt ! are ye the
    pore boddie ? '

21 She tuke the meall-poks by the strings an
    thrue them our the waa :
    ' Doll gaa we meall-poks, madinhead an a' ! '

22 She tuke him to her press, gave him a glass of
    wine ;
    He tuke her in his arms, says, Honey, ye 'ss be
    mine.

23 He tuke a horn fra his side an he blue loud
    an shill,
    An four-an-tuenty belted knights came att the
    beager's will.

24 He tuke out a pean-kniff, lute a' his dudes faa,
    An he was the braest gentelman that was
    among them a'.

25 He patt his hand in his poket an gaa her ginnes
    three,
    An four-an-tuenty hunder mark, to pay the
    nires feea.

26 ' Gin ye had ben a gued woman, as I thought
    ye had ben,
    I wad haa made ye lady of castels eaght or
    nine.'

———◆———

B

a. Herd, The Ancient and Modern Scots Songs, 1769, p.
46. b. Curious Tracts, Scotland, British Museum, 1078, m.
24, No 30.

1 THERE was a jolly beggar, and a begging he
    was bound,
    And he took up his quarters into a landart
    town.
    Fa la la, etc.

2 He wad neither ly in barn, nor yet wad he in
    byre,
    But in ahint the ha-door, or else afore the fire.

3 The beggar's bed was made at een wi good
    clean straw and hay,
    And in ahint the ha-door, and there the beggar
    lay.

4 Up raise the goodman's dochter, and for to
    bar the door,
    And there she saw the beggar standin i the
    floor.

5 He took the lassie in his arms and to the bed
    he ran,
    ' O hooly, hooly wi me, sir ! ye 'll waken our
    goodman.'

6 The beggar was a cunnin loon, and neer a word
    he spake
    Until he got his turn done, syne he began to
    crack.

7 ' Is there ony dogs into this town ? maiden, tell
    me true.'
    ' And what wad ye do wi them, my hinny and
    my dow ? '

8 'They 'll rive a' my mealpocks, and do me
       meikle wrang.'
   'O dool for the doing o't! are ye the poor
       man?'

9 Then she took up the mealpocks and flang
       them oer the wa:
   'The d—l gae wi the mealpocks, my maiden-
       head and a'!

10 'I took ye for some gentleman, at least the
        Laird of Brodie;
    O dool for the doing o't! are ye the poor
        bodie?'

11 He took the lassie in his arms and gae her
        kisses three,

And four-and-twenty hunder merk to pay the
       nurice-fee.

12 He took a horn frae his side and blew baith
        loud and shrill,
    And four-and-twenty belted knights came
        skipping oer the hill.

13 And he took out his little knife, loot a' his
        duddies fa,
    And he was the brawest gentleman that was
        amang them a'.

14 The beggar was a cliver loon and he lap shoul-
        der height:
    'O ay for sicken quarters as I gat yester-
        night!'

———————

A. 6². disere.
    9². puss *might be* russ *here, but is unques-
        tionable in the next stanza.*
    24². blaest *for* braest. 26². ninge (nigne *may
        be what was intended).*
B. b. *A slip with no imprint. Dated in the Mu-
        seum catalogue* 1800?

1 There was a jolly beggar, and a begging he had
        been,
       With his fal de diddle de dal dal
    And he took up his quarters in a house in Aber-
        deen.
       With his toran oran ad de odi

2 This beggar would not lye in barn nor yet would
        he in byre,
    But he would lye into the ha, or beyond the kitchen-
        fire.

3 The beggar's bed it was well made, with clean
        straw and hay,
    And beyond the kitchen-fire, there the jolly beggar
        lay.

4 The lassie then she did get up to bar the kitchen-
        door,
    An there she met the jolly beggar, standing naked
        on the floor.

5 He gript the lassie by the middle jimp, laid her
        against the wa,
    'O kind sir,' she said, 'be civil, for ye will wake
        my dadda.'

6 He never minded what she said, but carried on his
        stroke,
    Till he got his job done, then he began to joke.

7 'Have you got any dogs about the house, or any
        cats ava?
    For I 'm feared she 'll cut my mealpocks before I
        gang awa.'

8 The lassie took up the mealpocks, threw them
        against the wa,
    'O deil tak your mealpocks! my maidenhead 's
        awa.'

9 The lassie she got up again the hour before 't was
        day,
    For to gie the beggar hansel before he went
        away.

10 She went into the cellar, to draw a pot of ale,
    The beggar followed after, and did the job again.

11 He laid her on the ringle-tree, and gave her kisses
        three,
    And he gave her twenty guineas, to pay the nurse's
        fee.

12 'Had you been an honest lass, as I took you to be,
    You might have rode in your carriage and gone
        along with me.'

13 The beggar he took a horn and blew it wondrous
        shrill;
    There was four-and-twenty belted knights came
        riding oer the hill.

14 'Now if you are afraid you should miscall your
    child,
    You may call him for the daddy o't, the great
    Duke of Argyle.'

1¹. jelly : *but* 3², 4², jolly.
3¹. hay and straw.
9¹. hours.
13². kinpa *for* knights.
There are many other misprints ; some, per-
haps, which are not corrected, as she 'll
cut, 7².
The copy in Motherwell's MS, p. 124, *ends :*

He louted oure the saddle to her and gave her
    kisses three,
And he gave her fifty guineas, to pay the
    nourice-fee.

' Oh had you been an honest maid, as I thocht
    ye wud hae been,
I would have made you lady of a' the land,
    and then the Scotish queen.'

B. c. From the recitation of Miss Jane Webster,
    Crossmichael, August 8, 1893 ; learned by
    her many years ago from her mother, Janet
    Spark.

1 There was a jolly beggar, as mony a ane
    has been,
    An he 's taen up his lodging in a house near
        Aberdeen.
    Wi his yi yi yanti O, his eerie eerie an
    Wi his fine tan taraira, the jolly beggar-
        man

2 He wadna lie in barn, nor he wadna lie in
    byre,
    But he wad lie at the ha-door or the back
        o the kitchen-fire.

B. d. From the recitation of the same, on the same
    occasion ; learned in youth at Airds of Kells,
    from the singing of Thomas Duffy, joiner,
    Parton.

Refrain :
    Wi his long staff, and ragged coat, and
        breeches to his knee,
    And he was the bauldest beggar-man that
        eer my eyes did see.

a. 4 Up rose the farmer's daughter, for to bar
        the door,
    There she beheld a naked man, was stand-
        ing on the floor.

*   *   *   *   *   *   *

7 ' Hae ye ony cats or dogs, or hae ye eer a
        grew ?
    I 'm feared they rive my meal-pokes, when
        I am kissing you.'

9 She 's taen up his meal-pokes an thrown
        them owre the wa :
    ' O the deil gang wi your meal-pokes ! for
        my maidenhead 's awa.'

*   *   *   *   *   *   *

' It 's fare ye weel, gudewife, an it 's fare
        ye weel, gudeman,
    Ye hae a gude fat doughter, an I rattled on
        her pan.

b. 12 ' If she had been an honest lass, as I took
        her to be,
    She micht hae ridden in her coach-an-four
        this day along wi me.'

a. 12 Then he took oot a whistle, an he 's blawn
        baith loud and shrill,
    There was four-an-twenty foresters cam at
        their master's will.

13 Then he took oot a wee pen-knife, an let
        his duddies fa,
    And he was the brawest gentleman that
        was amang them a'.

The English broadside, Pepys Ballads, III, 73, No
71.

THE POLLITICK BEGGER-MAN.

Who got the love of a pretty maid
And on her cittern sweetly plaid ;
At last she slung her milk-pail over the wall,
And bid the De'l take milk-pail, maidenhead and all.
        Tune is, There was a jovial begger.*

Printed for F. Coles, T. Vere, J. Wright, and J.
Clarke.

* For this older piece, see Ebsworth, Bagford Ballads, I,
216. There is no adventure ; the subject is the beggar's
way of life.

1 There was a jovial begger-man,
    a begging he was bound,
And he did seek his living
    in country and in town.
With a long staff and a patcht coat,
    he prancd along the pad,
And by report of many a one
    he was a proper lad.
        His·cheeks were like the crimson rose,
        his forehead smooth and high,
        And he was the bravest begger-man
        that ever I saw with eye.

2 He came unto a farmer's gate
    and for an alms did crave ;
The maid did like the begger-man
    and good relief she gave.
She took him by the lilly hand
    and set him to the fire,
Which was as well as tongue could tell
    Or heart of man desire.

3 A curious mess of firmaty
    for him she did provide,
With a lovely cup of nut-brown
    and sugar sops beside.
    .   .   .   .
    .   .   .   .
    .   .   .   .

4 ' Sweet-heart, give me some lodging,
    that I all night may stay,
Or else give me my answer,
    that I may go away.'
The maid went to the hay-mow
    and fetcht a bottle of hay,
And laid it behind the parlor-door,
    On which the begger-man lay.

5 ' Resolve me,' said the maiden,
    ' if that you will or can,
For I do verily believe
    thou art a gentleman.'
' In truth then,' said the begger,
    ' my parents they are poor,
And I do seek my living
    each day from door to door.'

6 ' 'T is pity,' said this maiden fair,
    ' that such a lively lad
Should be a begger's only heir,
    a fortune poor and bad.
I wish that my condition
    were of the same degree,
Then hand in hand I 'de quickly wend
    throughout the world with thee.'

7 When he perceivd the maiden's mind,
    and that her heart was his,
He did embrace her in his arms
    And sweetly did her kiss.
    .   .   .   .   .
    .   .   .   .   .
    .   .   .   .   .

8 In lovely sport and merriment
    the night away they spent
In Venus game, for their delight
    and both their hearts content :
    .   .   .   .   .
    .   .   .   .   .
    .   .   .   .   .

9 Betimes in the morning then,
    as soon as it was day,
He left the damosel fast asleep
    and nimbly budgd away.
When he from her an hour was gone
    the damosel she did wake,
And seeing the begger-man not there
    her heart began to ake.

10 Then did she sigh and wring her hands,
    the tears did trickling pour,
For loosing her virginity
    and virgins maiden flower.
When twenty weeks were come and gone
    her heart was something sad,
Because she found herself with barn,
    and does not know the dad.

11 ' There is, I see, no remedy
    for what is past and gone,
And many a one that laughs at me
    may do as I have done.'
Then did she take her milk-pail,
    and flung it over the wall :
' O the Devil go with my milk-pail,
    my maidenhead and all ! '

12 You maidens fair, where ere you are,
    Keep up your store and goods,
For when that some have got their wills
    They 'l leave you in the suds.
Let no man tempt you nor entice,
    be not too fond and coy,
But soon agree to loyalty,
    Your freedom to enjoy.

4^4. go that way.

APPENDIX

THE GABERLUNYIE–MAN

Printed in the first volume of Ramsay's Tea-Table Miscellany, 1724, from which it was repeated in Thomson's Orpheus Caledonius, 1725, fol. 43, and Old Ballads, III, 259, the same year; in the Dublin reprint of the Miscellany, 1729, I, 96, the "fifth edition," London, 1730, and the ninth edition, London, 1733, I. 84. The first edition, 1724, being of extreme rarity, if anywhere now to be found, the piece is given here from Old Ballads, which agrees with Orpheus Caledonius except as to the spelling of a single word.

The Gaberlunyie-Man is one of the pieces which were subjected to revision in the Miscellany; " such old verses as have been done time out of mind, and only wanted to be cleared from the dross of blundering transcribers and printers, such as 'The Gaberlunzie-man,' 'Muirland Willy,'" etc. (Ramsay's preface.)

In recited copies, as the " Old Lady's Collection," No 13 (Skene MS., p. 65), and Motherwell's MS., p. 31, the girl is made to come back again to see her mother (or the gaberlunyie-man brings her) 'wi a bairn in her arms and ane in her wame;' but for all that a fine lady, 'wi men- and maid-servants at her command.'

Translated by Herder, II, 264; Bodmer, I, 68; Fiedler, p. 23; Loeve-Veimars, p. 356.

1   The pauky auld carle came oer the lee,
      Wi many good eens and days to me,
      Saying, Goodwife, for your courtesie,
          Will ye lodge a silly poor man?
      The night was cauld, the carle was wat,
      And down ayont the ingle he sat;
      My daughter's shoulders he gan to clap,
          And cadgily ranted and sang.

2   'O wow!' quo he, 'were I as free
      As first when I saw this country,
      How blyth and merry wad I be!
          And I wad never think lang.'
      He grew canty, and she grew fain,
      But little did her auld minny ken
      What thir slee twa togither were sayn,
          When wooing they were sa[e] thrang.

3   'And O!' quo he, 'ann ye were as black,
      As eer the crown of your dady's hat,
      'T is I wad lay thee by my back,
          And awa wi me thou shoud gang.'

'And O!' quoth she, 'ann I were as white
    As eer the snaw lay on the dike,
    I 'd clead me braw, and lady-like,
        And awa with thee I 'd gang.'

4   Between the twa was made a plot;
      They raise a wee before the cock,
      And wyliely they shot the lock,
          And fast to the bent are they gane.
      Up the morn the auld wife raise,
      And at her leasure pat on her claiths;
      Syne to the servants bed she gaes,
          To speer for the silly poor man.

5   She gaed to the bed where the beggar lay,
      The strae was cauld, he was away;
      She clapt her hands, cry'd, Waladay!
          For some of our gear will be gane.
      Some ran to coffers, and some to kists,
      But nought was stown that coud be mist;
      She danc'd her lane, cry'd, Praise be blest,
          I have lodg'd a leal poor man!

6   'Since nathing 's awa, as we can learn,
      The kirn 's to kirn and milk to earn;
      Gae butt the house, lass, and waken my bairn,
          And bid her come quickly ben.'
      The servant gade where the daughter lay,
      The sheets was cauld, she was away;
      And fast to her goodwife can say,
          She 's aff with the gaberlunyie-man.

7   'O fy, gar ride, and fy, gar rin,
      And hast ye find these traitors again;
      For she 's be burnt, and he 's be slain,
          The wearifu gaberlunyie-man.'
      Some rade upo horse, some ran a-fit,
      The wife was wood and out o 'er wit;
      She coud na gang, nor yet coud she sit,
          But ay she cursd and she band.

8   Mean time far hind outoer the lee,
      Fou snug in a glen, where nane coud see,
      The twa, with kindly sport and glee,
          Cut frae a new cheese a whang.
      The priving was good, it pleasd them baith,
      To loe her for ay he gae her his aith;
      Quo she, To leave thee, I will be laith,
          My winsome gaberlunyie-man.

9   'O kend my minny I were wi you,
      Illfardly wad she crook her mou;
      Sic a poor man she 'd never trow,
          After the gaberlunyie-man.'
      'My dear,' quo he, ' ye 'r yet oer young,
      And ha na learnd the beggar's tongue,
      To follow me frae town to town,
          And carry the gaberlunyie on.'

10 'Wi kauk and keel, I'll win your bread,
   And spindles and whorles for them wha need,
   Whilk is a gentil trade indeed,
      To carry the gaberlunyie, O.
   I 'll bow my leg, and crook my knee,

And draw a black clout oer my eye ;
A criple or blind they will ca me,
   While we shall be merry and sing.'

3². my dady's, Dublin, 1729, London, 1730, 1733.

280

THE BEGGAR–LADDIE

A. 'The Shipherd Boy,' "Old Lady's Collection,"
No 35.

B. 'The Beggar's Dawtie,' Murison MS., p. 85.

C. 'The Beggar-Laddie,' Motherwell's MS., p. 249.

D. 'The Gaberlunzie Laddie, or, The Beggar's Bride,'
Christie, Traditional Ballad Airs, I, 100.

E. 'The Shepherd's Bonny Lassy,' Kinloch MSS, V,
249, II, 17.

THIS is a sort of 'Gaberlunyie-Man' with
a romantic conclusion, resembling that of
'Lizie Lindsay.' A pretended beggar, who
is for the time acting as shepherd's swain,
induces a young lady, or young woman of
good standing, to follow him as his beggar-
lassie. They come to a hall (his father's, **A**,
D, **E**, brother's, **C**), he knocks loudly, four
and twenty gentlemen welcome him in, and

as many ladies the lassie, and she is thence-
forth a knight's or squire's lady.

There is corruption in all the copies,* and
the rhyme is frequently lost. A 2 (B 3, C 3,
D 7, E 5) is taken almost bodily from ' The
Gaberlunyie-Man,' 10. D is not the better
for being a mixture of three copies. D 4 an-
ticipates the conclusion, and it is inconceivable
that any meddler should not have seen this.
D 14 is caught from ' The Jolly Beggar.'

A

The "Old Lady's Collection," No 35 ; north of Scotland.

1 SHIPERD-BOY, what is yer trade?
   Or what way do ye wine yer bread ?
   Or what way do ye wine yer bread,
      Fan the kipeng nout gies over ?

2 'Spindels an forls it is my trade,
   An bits o sticks to them who need,
   Whilk is a gentell trade indeed ;
      Bony lassie, cane ye lea me ? '

* **B** 4³, As Jessie loved the cups o gold,
   C 5¹, As Judas loved a piece of gold,
   D 3³, As Jesse lovd the fields of gold ;

3 'I lea you as I supos
   Rachell loved Jacob of old,
   As Jason loied his flice of gould,
      Sae dearly do I lea ye.

4 'Ye cast off yer clouty coat,
   An ye pitt one my scarlett cloke,
   An I will follou you just att the back,
      Becass ye are a bonny laddie.'

5 He cust off his cloutty coat,
   An he patt on her scarlet cloke,

the original reading being as in
   A 3³, As Jason loied his flice of gould.

An she folloued him just att the back,
   Becaus he was a bonny laddie.

6 They gaed on, an forder on,
   Till they came to yon borrous-toun;
   She bought a loaf an they both satt doun,
      Bat she ate no we her laddie.

7 They gaed on, an forder one,
   Till they came to the nest borrous-toun;
   I wat the lassie louked doun,
      For the following of her laddie.

8 'O if I wer on the head of yon hill,
      Ther I wad greet my fill,
   For the follouing of my laddie.'

9 'O had yer toung, my dearest dear,
   I ill ha ye back as I brought ye hear,
      For I canna bear yer morning.'

10 'O had yer toung, my dearest dear,
   I will gae throu the warld baith far an near,
      Becaus ye 'r a bonny ladie.'

11 They gad on, an forder on,
   Till they came to his father's haa,
      An he knoked ther fue loudly.

12 'O had yer hand, my dear[est] dear,
   An dou not knoke sae loudly,
      For fear they sud be angry.'

13 Four-an-tuenty gentelmen
   They conved the beager ben,
   An as mony gay ladës
      Conved the beager's lassie.

14 His brother lead her throu the haa:
   'I wis, brother, we had beagged a',
      For sick a bonny lassie.'

15 That same night she was bedded,
   An the nist morning she was wedded;
   She came to gued by grait misgiding,
      By the follouing of her laddie.

————◆————

B

Murison MS., p. 85; from Aberdeenshire.

1 'T WAS on a day in the month o June
   .   .   .   .

   .   .   .   .
   When Phoebus shines sae clearly.

2 .   .   .   .

   She says, My dear, what is your trade
      When thiggin ye give over?

3 'Spinls and forls is my trade,
   Wi bits o sticks I win my bread,
   An O it is a winnin trade;
      Bonnie lassie, can ye loo me?'
         An O it is, etc.

4 'O I can love ye manyfold,
   As Jacob loved Rachel of old,
   And as Jessie loved the cups o gold;
      My dear, can ye believe me?'
         As Jessie, etc.

5 'It 's ye 'll tak aff the robes o red,
   An ye 'll pit on the beggin-weed,
   An ye 'll gang wi me an ye 'll beg your bread,
      An ye 'll be the beggar's dawtie.'

6 When they cam to yon borough-toon,
   They bocht a loaf an they baith sat doon,
   They bocht a loaf an they baith sat doon,
      An the lassie ate wi her laddie.

7 When they cam to yon grassy hill,
   Where spotted flocks do feed their fill,
   'I 'll sit me doon an I 'll greet a while,
      For the followin o my laddie.'

8 'It 's ye 'll tak aff yer beggin-weed,
   An ye 'll pit on the goons o red,
   An ye 'll gang ye back the road ye cam,
      For I canna bide yer greetin.'

9 'Betide me weel, betide me woe,
   It 's wi the beggar an I 'll go,
   An I 'll follow him through frost an snow,
      An I 'll be the beggar's dawtie.'

10 When they cam to yonder ha,
   He knockit loud an sair did ca;
   She says, My dear, we'll be foun in fa
      For knockin here sae loudly.

11 Four-an-twenty gentlemen
   Cam a' to welcome the beggar in,
   An as monie fair ladies gay
      To welcome 's bonnie lassie.

12 When at he gied through the ha,
   They a' did laugh, they were like to fa,
   Sayin, Brither, I wish we had beggit a',
      For sic a bonnie lassie.

13 'The streen ye was the beggar's bride,
   An noo this nicht ye'll lie by my side,
   Come weel, come woe, whateer betide,
      An ye'll be aye my dawtie.'

C

Motherwell's MS., p. 249; from the recitation of Miss
Ann Wilson, of the Tontine Inn, Paisley, who learned it
from the cook in her father's house.

1 Down in yonder garden gay,
   Where many a ladie does repair,
   Where many a ladie does repair,
      Puing of flowers sae bonnie.

2 'O do you see yon shepherd's son,
   Feeding his flocks in yonder loan,
   Feeding his flocks in yonder loan?
      Vow but he feeds them bonnie!'

3 'O laddie, laddie, what is your trade?
   Or by what means do you win your bread?
   Or by what means do you win your bread?
      O laddie, tell unto me.'

4 'By making spindles is my trade,
   Or whorles in the time o need,
   And by which ways I do win my bread:
      O lady, do you love me?'

5 'As Judas loved a piece of gold,
   As Jacob loved Rachel of old,
   As Jacob loved Rachel of old,
      O laddie, I do love thee.'

6 'You must put off your robes of silk,
   You must put on my cloutit claes,
   And follow me hard at my back,
      And ye'll be my beggar-lassie.'

7 She's put aff her robes of silk,
   And she's put on his cloutit claes,

And she's followed him hard at his back,
   And she's been his beggar-lassie.

8 O when they cam to [the] borrowstoun,
   Vow but the lassie lookit doun!
   Vow but the lassie lookit doun!
      Following her beggar-laddie.

9 O when they cam to Stirling toun,
   He coft a loaf and they baith sat doun,
   He coft a loaf and they baith sat doun,
      And she's eaten wi her beggar-laddie.

10 'O do you see yon hie, hie hill,
   Where the corn grows baith rank and tall?
   If I was there, I would greet my fill,
      Where naebody wuld see me.'

11 When they came to his brother's hall,
   Vow but he chappit loud and schill!
   'Don't chap sae loud,' the lassie said,
      'For we may be fund faut wi.'

12 Four-and-twenty gentlemen,
   And twice as many gay ladies,
   And twice as many gay ladies,
      Came to welcome in the lassie.

13 His brother led her thro the hall,
   With laughter he was like to fall;
   He said, I think we should beg it all,
      For she is a bonnie lassie.

14 'You must put aff your cloutit claes,
   You must put on your robes of silk,
   You must put on your robes of silk,
      For ye are a young knicht's ladye.'

D

Christie's Traditional Ballad Airs, I, 100; from three copies, two in Banffshire, and one in Aberdeenshire.

1 'T was in the pleasant month of June,
    When woods and valleys a' grow green,
    And valiant ladies walk alane,
        While Phoebus shines soe clearly.
        And valiant ladies, etc.

2 Out-ower yon den I spied a swain,
    Wi a shepherd's club into his han;
    He was driving ewes out-ower yon knowes,
        And said, Lassie, I could love you.
        He was driving ewes, etc.

3 'Oh, I could love you manifold,
    As Jacob lovd Rachel of old,
    As Jesse lovd the fields of gold,
        So dearly could I love you.

4 'In ha's and chambers ye 'se be laid,
    In silks and cambrics ye 'se be clade,
    An wi the finest ye 'se be fed,
        My dear, gin ye would believe me.'

5 'Your ha's and chambers ye'll soon sweep
        clean,
    Wi your flattering tongue now let me alane;
    You are designd to do me wrang,
        Awa, young man, and leave me.

6 'But tell me now what is your trade,
    When you 've given over sheep and club?'
    .   .   .   .
        .   .   .   .

7 'By making besoms I win my bread,
    And spindles and whorles in time o need;
    Is n't that a gentle trade indeed?
        Bonnie lassie, can you loe me?

8 'Will ye cast aff your mantle black
    And put on you a clouty cloak,
    And follow me close at the back,
        The gaberlunyie-laddie?'

9 Then she coost aff her mantle black,
    And she put on a clouty cloak,
    And she followd him close at the back,
        Her gaberlunyie-laddie.

10 As they gaed through yon borough-town,
    For shame the lassie lookit down;
    But they bought a loaf and they both sat down,
        And the lassie ate wi her laddie.

11 When they came to his father's gate,
    Sae loudly as he rappd thereat;
    'My dear,' said she, 'ye 'll be found in faut
        For rapping there sae loudly.'

12 Then four-and-twenty gentlemen
    Convoyd the gentle beggar ben,
    And aye as mony gay ladies
        Convoyd the bonny lassie.

13 When they were come into the ha,
    Wi laughter a' were like to fa:
    'I wish, dear brother, we had beggëd a',
        For sic a bonnie lassie.'

14 Then as he stood amang them a',
    He let his meal-pocks a' down fa,
    And in red gowd he shone oer them a',
        And she was a young knight's lady.

15 Yestreen she was the begger's bride,
    As his wife she now stood by his side,
    And for a' the lassie 's ill misguide,
        She 's now the young knight's lady.

———◆———

E

Kinloch MSS, V, 249. As recited by John Laurie, Abbeygreen.

1 'T was in the merry month of June,
    When woods and gardens were all in bloom,
    When woods and gardens were all in bloom,
        And Phœbus shining clearly.

2 Did you not see your shepherd-swain,
    Feeding his flocks upon the plain,
    Feeding his flocks all one by one,
        And keeping them together?

3 Did you not see yon bonny green,
    Where dukes and lords and my love hath
        been,

Where dukes and lords and my love hath
    been,
  And Phœbus shining clearly ?

4 ' O shepherd, shepherd, tell me indeed
  Which is the way you dou win your bread,
  Which is the way you dou win your bread,
    When feeding you give over ? '

5 ' By making spindles I win my bread,
  By turning whorles in time of need,
  By turning whorles in time of need,
    Say, lassy, can you love me ? '

6 ' I could love you manifold,
  As Jacob loved Rachel of old,
  As Jacob loved Rachel of old,
    So dearly could I love you.'

7 ' You must cast off these robes of silk,
  And put about my shepherd's cloak,
  And you must walk down at my back,
    Like a shepherd's bonny lassie.'

8 She has cast off her robes of silk,
  And put about his shepherd's cloak,
  And she has walkd down at his back,
    Like a shepherd's bonny lassie.

9 O they walked up, and they walked down,
  Till this fair maiden she 's wearyed grown ;
  Says she, My dear, we 'll go to some town,
    And there tak up our lodgings.

10 O whan they cam to his father's gate,
  Sae loudly, loudly as he did rap ;
  Says she, My dear, we 'll be found in fault
    For rapping here sae boldly.

11 But whan they cam to his father's hall,
  O loud, loud laughter they laughed all,
  Saying, Brother, I wish we had herded all,
    Ye 've got sic an a bonny lassie.

12 Now this young couple they were wed,
  And all the way the flowers were spread,
  For in disguise they were married ;
    She 's now the young squire's lady.

———•———

A. 2^2. who wad. *Cf.* 'Gaberlunyie-Man,' 10^2. C,
  D, E, time o need.
  4^1. clouty clok. *Cf.* 5^1.
  4, 5. *In the other copies, the lady casts off her*
  better clothes, and puts on the beggin-weed,
  his cloutit claes, a clouty cloak, his shepherd's cloak, *and this disposition is no doubt*
  the right one.

6^3. She bought. He, C, They, B, D, *either*
  of which is preferable.
15^2. wouded.
C. 8^1, 9^1; 10^1. Oh.
  8^1. Borrowstoun.
D. 6, 7 *are printed together.*

281

THE KEACH I THE CREEL

A. 'The Keach i the Creel,' Alexander Whitelaw, The Book of Scottish Ballads, p. 35, 1845; Dixon, Ancient Poems, Ballads, and Songs, p. 112, Percy Society, vol. xvii, 1846.

B. 'The Creel, or, Bonnie May.' Communicated by Mr David Louden, Morham, Haddington, 1873.

C. 'The Cunning Clerk,' Buchan's Ballads of the North of Scotland, I, 278, 1828.

D. 'The Covering Blue,' Kinloch MSS, I, 276; Kinloch's Ballad Book, p. 61, 1827.

A FEW copies of A were printed about 1845 by a Northumbrian gentleman for private distribution. One of these came into Whitelaw's hands, another into Dixon's. Dixon made some changes in reprinting. Bell, Ancient Poems, etc., p. 75, 1857, and Bruce and Stokoe, Northumbrian Minstrelsy, p. 82, 1882, repeat Dixon. This last remarks that " this old and very humorous ballad has long been a favorite on both sides of the Border."

James Telfer, writing to Sir W. Scott, May 12, 1824 [Letters, XIII, No 73], says: " I have an humorous ballad sung by a few of the old people on this side of the Border. It is entitled The Keach in the Creel. It begins thus :

A bonny may went up the street
  Some whitewish (*sic*) for to buy,
And a bonny clerk 's faen in love with her,
  And he 's followed her by and by, by,
  And he 's followed her by and by."

Buchan notes, I, 319, that Motherwell had sent him a ballad "somewhat similar in incident," taken down from the recitation of an old woman in or near Paisley.

This was perhaps a copy of which the first stanza is entered in Motherwell's Note-Book, p. 55 :

When I gade doun to Colliestoun,
  Some white-fish for to buy, buy,
The cannie clarkie follows me,
  And he follows me spedily, -ly.

Or the ballad called ' Ricadoo' in the Appendix to Motherwell's Minstrelsy, p. xxiii, No 29, where this first stanza is given :

The farmer's daughter gade to the market,
  Some white-fish for to buy ;
The young squire followed after her, .
  As fast as he could hie. Ricadoo,
  Tunaway, ricadoo a doo a day,
  Raddle ricadoo,
  Tunaway

Though occurring only in a late Scottish ballad, the story is somewhat old. In Gasté, Chansons normandes du XV⁰ siècle, MS. de Vire, No 19, p. 15, a gentleman of Orleans causes his servants to let him down a chimney in a basket, and conceals himself under a lady's bed. She, made aware of his presence, sends her husband off to the barn, where, she says, he will find the curé, who has made love to her. On returning, the husband gets his feet into the basket, and the servants without draw the basket up. The man cries out to his wife that the devil is making away with him.

Again, in a fabliau considerably older: ' Du chevalier à la corbeille,' MS. of the end of the fourteenth century, F. Michel, Gautier d'Aupais, Le chevalier à la Corbeille, Fabliaux du XIII⁰ siècle, p. 35 ; Montaiglon et Raynaud, Recueil général des Fabliaux, etc., II, 183. A gentleman makes appointment to visit a lady one night when her husband is away. An old woman, the husband's mother, sleeps in a bed beside the lady's, and keeps strict watch over her. The gentleman's squires hoist him in a basket over the wall of the house, so that he obtains entrance into the hall, whence he passes into the lady's chamber. The old woman observes a disturbance, and gets up, pretending that she is going to the kitchen. In the hall she goes astray and falls into the basket. The squires, noticing a movement of the cords, pull at the basket. The old woman is 'towed' up and down, and knocked about, much as in the ballad. She thinks that devils have carried her off. Finally the squires let the cords go, and the basket comes flat to the ground.

The story is also told in Henri Estienne's Apologie pour Hérodote, 1566 ; here, of a girl and her lover, and it is the girl's father that gets his feet into the basket. Ed. Ristelhuber, 1879, I, 282 f.

No one looks for decorum in pieces of this description, but a passage in this ballad, which need not be particularized, is brutal and shameless almost beyond example.

C is translated by Gerhard, p. 192.

———————

A

Whitelaw's Book of Scottish Ballads, p. 35 ; "taken down from the recitation of a gentleman in Liddesdale."

1 A FAIR young may went up the street,
 Some white-fish for to buy,
And a bonnie clerk 's faen in love wi her,
 And he 's followed her by and by, by,
 And he 's followed her by and by.

2 'O where live ye, my bonnie lass,
 I pray thee tell to me ;
For gin the nicht were ever sae mirk
 I wad come and visit thee.'

3 'O my father he aye locks the door,
 My mither keeps the key ;
And gin ye were ever sic a wily wight
 Ye canna win in to me.'

4 But the clerk he had ae true brother,
 And a wily wight was he ;
And he has made a lang ladder,
 Was thirty steps and three.

5 He has made a cleek but and a creel,
 A creel but and a pin ;
And he 's away to the chimley-top,
 And he 's letten the bonnie clerk in.

6 The auld wife, being not asleep,
 Heard something that was said ;

'I 'll lay my life,' quo the silly auld wife,
 'There 's a man i our dochter's bed.'

7 The auld man he gat owre the bed,
 To see if the thing was true ;
But she 's ta'en the bonny clerk in her arms,
 And coverd him owre wi blue.

8 'O where are ye gaun now, father ?' she says,
 'And where are ye gaun sae late ?
Ye 've disturbd me in my evening prayers,
 And O but they were sweet !'

9 'O ill betide ye, silly auld wife,
 And an ill death may ye die !
She has the muckle buik in her arms,
 And she 's prayin for you and me.'

10 The auld wife being not asleep,
 Then something mair was said ;
'I 'll lay my life,' quo the silly auld wife,
 'There 's a man i our dochter's bed.'

11 The auld wife she got owre the bed,
 To see if the thing was true ;
But what the wrack took the auld wife's fit ?
 For into the creel she flew.

12 The man that was at the chimley-top,
 Finding the creel was fu,
He wrappit the rape round his left shouther,
 And fast to him he drew.

13 'O help! O help! O hinny, now, help!
　　O help, O hinny, now!
　　For him that ye aye wished me to
　　He's carryin me off just now.'

14 'O if the foul thief's gotten ye,
　　I wish he may keep his haud;
　　For a' the lee lang winter nicht
　　Ye'll never lie in your bed.'

15 He's towed her up, he's towed her down,
　　He's towed her through an through;

'O Gude assist!' quo the silly auld wife,
　'For I'm just departin now.'

16 He's towed her up, he's towed her down,
　　He's gien her a richt down-fa,
　　Till every rib i the auld wife's side
　　Playd nick-nack on the wa.

17 O the blue, the bonnie, bonnie blue,
　　And I wish the blue may do weel!
　　And every auld wife that's sae jealous o her dochter,
　　May she get a good keach i the creel!

———◆———

B

Communicated February, 1873, by Mr David Louden, of Morham, Haddington, N. B., as derived from Andrew Hastie, Rentonhall.

1 As bonnie may went up the street,
　　Some sweetmeats for to buy,
　　There was a young clerk followed after her,
　　And followed her by and by, by,
　　And followed her by and by.

2 'It's bonnie may, where do you stay?
　　Or where is't that you be?
　　Oh if the night be neer so dark,
　　Awat I'll come and visit thee.'

3 'My father locks the door at een,
　　My mother keeps the key;
　　Gin ye were neer sic a rovin blade,
　　Ye canna win in to me.'

4 The young clerk has a young brither,
　　And a wily wag was he;
　　He's made to him a long ladder,
　　Wi thirty steps and three.

5 And he's put it to the chimney-top,
　　And the creel he's put on a pin,
　　And he's put it to the chimney-top,
　　And he's let the young clerk in.

6 The auld wife she was standing by,
　　She heard a word was said;
　　'I could lay my life,' said the silly auld wife,
　　'There's a man in oor dochter's bed.'

7 The auld man he cam doun the stairs
　　To see if it were true;
　　The young clerk was lying in bonnie may's arms,
　　And she's covered him oer wi blue.

8 'Where are you going, dear father?' she says,
　　'Where are you going so late?
　　You stopped me of my evening prayers,
　　And oh, but they were sweet!'

9 'The deil tak you, ye silly auld wife,
　　And an ill death may ye dee!
　　For your dochter was lyin wi the book in her arms,
　　And she's prayin for you and me.'

10 The auld wife still standin no far by,
　　Still hearin a word, she said,
　　'Ye may say as ye like, ye silly auld man,
　　There's a man in oor dochter's bed.'

11 I dinna ken what's taen the auld wife's fit,
　　But into the creel she flew;
　　The young clerk['s brither] being at the chimney-top,
　　He found the creel was fu.

12 He's thrown the rope out-owre his shouther,
　　And to him he did draw;
　　He's drawn her up, he's drawn her doun,
　　He's drawn her through and through.

13 Till the auld wife she began to cry,
　　I'm just departin noo!

But aye he drew her up and doun,
　　And drew her through and through.

14 He 's drawn her up, he 's let her doun,
　　He 's gien her evendoun fall,
　　Till every rib on the auld wife's side
　　Played nick-nack on the wall.

————◆————

C

Buchan's Ballads of the North of Scotland, I, 278.

1 As I gaed down to Collistown,
　　Some white-fish for to buy, buy,
　　The cunning clerk he followed me,
　　And he followed me speedily, ly,
　　And he followed me speedily.

2 Says, Faur ye gaun, my dearest dear ?
　　O faur ye gaun, my dow ?
　　There 's naebody comes to my bedside,
　　And naebody wins to you.

3 ' Your brother is a gallant square-wright,
　　A gallant square-wright is he ;
　　Ye 'll gar him make a lang ladder,
　　Wi thirty steps and three.

4 ' And gar him big a deep, deep creel,
　　A deep creel and a string,
　　And ye 'll come up to my bedside,
　　And come bonnily linken in.'

5 The auld gudeman and auld gudewife,
　　To bed they went, to sleep ;
　　But wae mat worth the auld gudewife !
　　A wink she coudna get.

6 ' I dreamd a dreary dream this night,
　　I wish it binna true,
　　That the rottens had come thro the wa,
　　And cutted the coverin blue.'

7 Then up it raise the auld gudeman,
　　To see gin it was true ;
　　And he 's gane to his daughter dear,
　　Says, What are ye doing, my dow ?

15 It 's O the blue, the bonnie, bonnie blue,
　　I wish the blue may do weel !
　　For every auld wife that is jealous o her dochter
　　May be rockit to the d — l in a creel !

8 ' What are ye doing, my daughter dear ?
　　What are ye doing, my dow ? '
　　' The prayer book 's in my hand, father,
　　Praying for my auld minnie and you.'

9 The auld gudeman and auld gudewife,
　　To bed they went, to sleep ;
　　But wae mat worth the auld gudewife !
　　But aye she wakend yet.

10 ' I dreamd a dreary dream this night,
　　I wish it binna true,
　　That the cunning clerk and your ae daughter
　　Were aneath the coverin blue.'

11 ' O rise yoursell, gudewife,' he says,
　　' The diel may had you fast !
　　Atween you and your ae daughter
　　I canno get ae night's rest.'

12 Up then raise the auld gudewife,
　　To see gin it was true,
　　And she fell arselins in the creel,
　　And up the string they drew.

13 ' Win up, win up, gudeman,' she says,
　　' Win up and help me now !
　　For he that ye gae me to last night,
　　I think he 's catchd me now.'

14 ' Gin Auld Nick he has catchd you now,
　　I wish he may had you fast ;
　　As for you and your ae daughter,
　　I never get kindly rest.'

15 They howded her, and they showded her,
　　Till the auld wife gat a fa,
　　And three ribs o the auld wife's side
　　Gaed knip-knap ower in twa.

D

Kinloch MSS, I, 276; from Alexander Kinnear, of Stonehaven.

1 ' My father he locks the doors at nicht,
    My mither the keys carries ben, ben;
    There's naebody dare gae out,' she says,
      ' And as few dare come in, in,
      And as few dare come in.'

2 ' I will mak a lang ladder,
    Wi fifty steps and three,
    I will mak a lang ladder,
    And lichtly come doun to thee.'

3 He has made a lang ladder,
    Wi fifty steps and three,
    He has made a lang ladder,
    And lichtly come doun the lum.

4 They had na kissd nor lang clappit,
    As lovers do whan they meet,
    Till the auld wife says to the auld man,
    I hear somebody speak.

5 ' I dreamed a dreem sin late yestreen,
    And I'm feard my dream be true;
    I dreamd that the rottens cam thro the wa,
    And cuttit the covering blue.

6 ' Ye'll rise, ye'll rise, my auld gudeman,
    And see gin this be true;'
    ' If ye're wanting rising, rise yoursel,
    For I wish the auld chiel had you.'

7 ' I dreamed a dream sin late yestreen,
    And I'm feard my dream be true;
    I dreamd that the clerk and our ae dother
    War rowed in the covering blue.

8 ' Ye'll rise, ye'll rise, my auld gudeman,
    And see gin this be true:'
    ' If ye're wanting rising, rise yoursel,
    * For I wish the auld chiel had you.'

9 But up she raise, and but she gaes,
    And she fell into the gin;
    He gied the tow a clever tit,
    That brought her out at the lum.

10 ' Ye'll rise, ye'll rise, my auld gudeman,
    Ye'll rise and come to me now,
    For him that ye've gien me sae lang till,
    I fear he has gotten me now.'

11 ' The grip that he's gotten, I wish he may haud,
    And never let it gae,
    For atween you and your ae dother
    I rest neither nicht nor day.'

———◆———

A. 1¹. May (*not* may).
    Dixon says: In the present impression some
    trifling typographical mistakes are corrected,
    and the phraseology has been rendered uni-
    form throughout.

In 6², *he prints,* Tho late, late was the hour;
    6⁴, dochter's bower; 10⁴, by our; 13², hinny,
    do; 13⁸, wished me at.

B. 1¹, 2¹, 7⁸. May (*not* may). 1⁴. by and bye.
    15¹. She cries aye, It's oh.

282

JOCK THE LEG AND THE MERRY MERCHANT

Buchan's Ballads of the North of Scotland, II, 165.

———•———

Jock the Leg and a merchant (packman, pedlar) put up at the same tavern. Jock makes free to order a good supper at the merchant's expense; the packman gives notice that he will not pay a penny beyond his own shot. They go to bed in rooms separated by a locked door, but before the merchant is well asleep Jock appears at his feet and rouses him; it is more than time that they were on their road. The merchant will not stir a foot till daylight; he cannot go by Barnisdale or Coventry for fear that Jock the Leg should take his pack. His self-imposed comrade promises to see him safely through these places, but when they come to dangerous ground avows himself as Jock the Leg, and demands the pack. The merchant puts his pack under a tree, and says he will fight for it till daylight; they fight; the robber finds a more than equal match, cries Hold! and begs the boon of a blast on his horn, to which the merchant contemptuously accedes. Four-and-twenty bowmen come to Jock's help. The merchant offers to give up his pack if the six best of these, and Jock, the seventh, can drive him one foot from it. The seven make the attempt and fail. The merchant, holding his pack in one hand, slays five of the six with his broadsword, and knocks over the other.

Jock declares him to be the boldest swordsman he has ever fought with; if he were equally good with the bow, he should have service with Jock's master in the greenwood. The merchant would not join a robber-band. Jock proposes a barter of deerskins for fine linen. The merchant wants no stolen deerskins. 'Take your pack,' says Jock, 'and wherever we meet we shall be good comrades.' 'I'll take my pack,' says the uncompromising merchant, 'and wherever we meet I'll call thee a rank thief.'

This piece, but for names (and Jock the Leg is only a thin shrouding for Little John), might have gone with the Robin Hood ballads. It was composed, probably, in the last half of the eighteenth century, and for hawkers' purposes, but it is a better ballad, imitation as it is, than some of the seventeenth-century broadsides of the same class (which is indeed saying very little). The fight for the pack, 13, 14, 20, we have in 'The Bold Pedlar and Robin Hood' (also a late ballad), No 132, 6, 7, 10; the "asking" of a blast on the horn and the scornful reply, 16, 17, in 'Robin Hood and the Shepherd,' No 135, 15, 16, with verbal similarity in the first case. (17 is all but a repetition of No 123, B 26, and No 140, B 25.)

———•———

1 As Jock the Leg and the merry merchant
    Came from yon borrow's town,
  They took their budgets on their backs,
    And fieldert they were boun.

2 But they came to a tavern-house,
    Where chapmen used to be:
  'Provide, provide,' said Jock the Leg,
    'A good supper for me.

3 'For the merry merchant shall pay it a',
    Tho it were good merks three ; '
'But never a penny,' said the merry merchant,
    'But shot, as it fa's me.

4 'A bed, a bed,' said the merry merchant,
    'It 's time to go to rest ; '
'And that ye shall,' said the good goodwife,
    'And your covrings o the best.'

5 Then Jock the Leg in one chamber was laid,
    The merchant in another,
And lockfast door atween them twa,
    That the one might not see the other.

6 But the merchant was not well lain down,
    Nor yet well fa'en asleep,
Till up it starts him Jock the Leg,
    Just at the merchant's feet.

7 'Win up, win up,' said Jock the Leg,
    'We might hae been miles three ; '
'But never a foot,' said the merry merchant,
    'Till day that I do see.

8 'For I cannot go by Barnisdale,
    Nor yet by Coventry ;
For Jock the Leg, that common thief,
    Would take my pack from me.'

9 'I 'll hae you in by Barnisdale,
    And down by Coventry,
And I 'll guard you frae Jock the Leg
    Till day that ye do see.'

10 When they were in by Barnisdale,
    And in by Coventry,
'Repeat, repeat,' said Jock the Leg,
    'The words ye ance tauld me.'

11 'I never said aught behind your back
    But what I 'll say to thee ;
Are ye that robber, Jock the Leg,
    Will take my pack frae me ? '

12 'O by my sooth,' said Jock the Leg,
    'You 'll find that man I be ;
Surrender that pack that 's on your back,
    Or then be slain by me.'

13 He 's ta'en his pack down frae his back,
    Set it below yon tree ;
Says, I will fight for my good pack
    Till day that I may see.

14 Then they fought there in good greenwood
    Till they were bloody men ;
The robber on his knees did fall,
    Said, Merchant, hold your hand.

15 'An asking, asking,' said Jock the Leg,
    'An asking ye 'll grant me ; '
'Ask on, ask on,' said the merry merchant,
    'For men to asking are free.'

16 'I 've dune little harm to you,' he said,
    'More than you 'd been my brother ;
Give me a blast o my little wee horn,
    And I 'll give you another.'

17 'A blast o your little wee horn,' he said,
    'Of this I take no doubt ;
I hope you will take such a blast
    Ere both your eyes fly out.'

18 He set his horn to his mouth,
    And he blew loud and shrill,
And four-and-twenty bauld bowmen
    Came Jock the Leg until.

19 'Ohon, alas ! ' said the merry merchant,
    'Alas ! and woe is me !
Sae many, a party o common thiefs,
    But nane to party me !

20 'Ye 'll wile out six o your best bowmen,
    Yourself the seventh to be,
And, put me one foot frae my pack,
    My pack ye shall have free.'

21 He wiled six o his best bowmen,
    Himself the seventh to be,
But [him] frae his pack they couldna get,
    For all that they could dee.

22 He 's taen his pack into one hand,
    His broadsword in the other,
And he slew five o the best bowmen,
    And the sixth he has dung over.

23 Then all the rest they gae a shout,
    As they stood by the tree ;
Some said they would this merchant head,
    Some said they 'd let him be.

24 But Jock the Leg he then replied,
    To this I 'll not agree ;
He is the boldest broadsword-man
    That ever I fought wi.

25 'If ye could wield the bow, the bow
       As ye can do the brand,
   I would hae you to good greenwood,
       To be my master's man.'

26 'Tho I could wield the bow, the bow
       As I can do the brand,
   I would not gang to good greenwood,
       To join a robber-band.'

27 'O give me some of your fine linen,
       To cleathe my men and me,
   And ye 'se hae some of my dun deers' skins,
       Below yon greenwood-tree.'

28 'Ye 'se hae nane o my fine linen,
       To cleathe your men and thee,
   And I 'll hae nane o your stown deers' skins,
       Below yon greenwood-tree.'

29 'Ye 'll take your pack upon your back,
       And travel by land or sea ;
   In brough or land, wherever we meet,
       Good billies we shall be.'

30 'I 'll take my pack upon my back,
       And go by land or sea ;
   In brough or land, wherever we meet,
       A rank thief I 'll call thee.'

283

THE CRAFTY FARMER

a. 'The Crafty Farmer,' Logan, A Pedlar's Pack, p. 126, from a chap-book of 1796 ; 'The Crafty Miller,' Maidment, Scotish Ballads and Songs, 1859, p. 208, from a Glasgow stall-copy ; a stall-copy, printed by M. Randall, Stirling.

b. 'The Yorkshire Farmer,' Kidson, Traditional Tunes, p. 140, from The Manchester Songster, 1792.

c. 'Saddle to Rags,' Dixon, Ancient Poems, etc., p. 126, Percy Society, vol. xvii., taken down from the recitation of a Yorkshire yeoman in 1845.

d. 'The Thief Outwitted,' Notes and Queries, Fourth

Series, XI, 112, 1873, taken down by E. McC., Guernsey, "from the recitation of an old woman now in her eighty-second year, who learnt it in her childhood from her father, a laborer from the neighborhood of Yeovil."

e. 'The Silly Old Man,' Baring-Gould and Sheppard, Songs and Ballads of the West, 3d ed., No 18, Part I, p. 38, as sung by the Rev. E. Luscombe, a Devonshire man, about 1850 (Part IV, p. xviii).

f. 'The Silly Old Man,' Miss M. H. Mason's Nursery Rhymes and Country Songs, p. 43, as sung in Devonshire.

An old farmer who is on his way to pay his rent imparts the fact to a gentlemanlike highwayman who overtakes him. The highwayman cautions him not to be too communicative, since there are many thieves on the roads. The old man has no fear ; his money is safe in his saddle-bags. At the right time and place the thief bids him stand and deliver. The farmer throws his saddle over a hedge ; the thief dismounts to fetch it, and gives his horse to the farmer to hold ; the farmer mounts the thief's horse and rides off. The thief hacks the saddle to pieces to get at the bags. Arrived at his landlord's, the farmer opens the thief's portmanteau, and finds in it six hundred pounds. The farmer's wife is made very happy by her husband's report of his performances ; the thief's money will help to enlarge her daughter's marriage portion.

This very ordinary ballad has enjoyed great popularity, and is given for that reason and as a specimen of its class. There is an entirely similar one, in which a Norfolk

(Rygate, Cheshire) farmer's daughter going to market to sell corn is substituted for the farmer going to pay his rent: 'The Norfolk Maiden,' in The Longing Maid's Garland, of the last century, without place or date ;* 'The Maid of Rygate,' Logan's Pedlar's Pack, p. 133; 'The Highwayman Outwitted,' Leigh's Ballads and Legends of Cheshire, p. 267. Another variety is of a Yorkshire boy sent to a fair to sell a cow: 'Yorkshire Bite,' etc., The Turnip-Sack Garland (like The Longing Maid's Garland, one of a collection of Heber's) ;* 'The Yorkshire Bite,' "from a collection of ballads *circa* 1782," Logan's Pedlar's Pack, p. 131; 'The Crafty Ploughboy,'

Ingledew's Ballads and Songs of Yorkshire, p. 209.

For certain ballads in which a country girl, beset by an amorous gentleman, mounts his horse and makes off with his valise or the like, see II, 483, and the page preceding.

'The Politick Squire, or, The Highwaymen catch'd in their own play,' is a ballad of a gentleman who, having been robbed by five highwaymen that then purpose to shoot him, tells them that he is the Pretender, and is taken by them as such to a justice. The squire makes explanations, four of the thieves are hanged, and the fifth, who had shown some mercy, is transported.†

---

1 THE song that I 'm going to sing,
   I hope it will give you content,
Concerning a silly old man,
   That was going to pay his rent.

2 As he was riding along,
   Along all on the highway,
A gentleman-thief overtook him,
   And thus to him did say.

3 'Well overtaken!' said the thief,
   'Well overtaken!' said he;
And 'Well overtaken!' said the old man,
   'If thou be good company.'

4 'How far are you going this way?'
   Which made the old man for to smile;
'By my faith,' said the old man,
   'I 'm just going two mile.

5 'I am a poor farmer,' he said,
   'And I farm a piece of ground,
And my half-year's rent, kind sir,
   Just comes to forty pound.

6 'And my landlord has not been at home,
   I 've not seen him this twelvemonth or more,
Which makes my rent be large;
   I 've to pay him just fourscore.'

7 'Thou shouldst not have told any body,
   For thieves there 's ganging many;
If any should light on thee,
   They 'll rob thee of thy money.'

8 'O never mind,' said the old man,
   'Thieves I fear on no side,
For the money is safe in my bags,
   On the saddle on which I ride.'

9 As they were riding along,
   The old man was thinking no ill,
The thief he pulled out a pistol
   And bid the old man stand still.

10 But the old man provd crafty,
   As in the world there 's many;
He threw his saddle oer the hedge,
   Saying, Fetch it, if thou 'lt have any.

11 The thief got off his horse,
   With courage stout and bold,
To search for the old man's bag,
   And gave him his horse to hold.

12 The old man put 's foot i the stirrup
   And he got on astride;
To its side he clapt his spur up,
   You need not bid the old man ride.

---

* Also among the garlands collected by J. Bell, Newcastle, British Museum: the first, 11621. c. 2 (36), and 4 (13); the other, c. 2 (70). The garlands in 4 were printed, according to Bell, by J. White, †1769, or by T. Saint, †1788.

† Douce Ballads, III, fol. 78 b., London, Printed and sold at Sympson's Warehouse, in Stonecutter-Street, Fleet-Market.

13 'O stay!' said the thief, 'O stay!
    And half the share thou shalt have;'
    'Nay, by my faith,' said the old man,
    'For once I have bitten a knave.'

14 The thief he was not content,
    But he thought there must be bags;
    He out with his rusty old sword
    And chopt the old saddle in rags.

15 When he came to the landlord's house,
    This old man he was almost spent;
    Saying, Come, show me a private room
    And I 'll pay you a whole year's rent.

16 'I 've met a fond fool by the way,
    I swapt horses and gave him no boot;
    But never mind,' said the old man,
    'For I got the fond fool by the foot.'

17 He opend this rogue's portmantle,
    It was glorious to behold;
    There were three hundred pounds in silver,
    And three hundred pounds in gold.

18 And as he was riding home,
    And down a narrow lane,
    He espied his mare tied to a hedge,
    Saying, Prithee, Tib, wilt thou gang hame?

19 When he got home to his wife
    And told her what he had done,
    Up she rose and put on her clothes,
    And about the house did run.

20 She sung, and she sung, and she sung,
    She sung with a merry devotion,
    Saying, If ever our daughter gets wed,
    It will help to enlarge her portion.

----·----

a. *There are some slight verbal differences in
    the three copies, but none worthy of notice.*

b. 1 A song I will sing unto you,
    A song of a merry intent,
    It is of a silly old man
    That went to pay his rent,
    That went to pay his rent.

2 And as he was riding along,
    A riding along the highway,
    A gentleman-thief steps before the old man
    And thus unto him he did say.

3 'My friend, how dare you ride alone?
    For so many thieves there now be;
    If any should but light on you,
    They 'd rob you of all your money.'

4 'If that they should light upon me,
    I 'm sure they 'd be very ill-sped,
    For, to tell you the truth, my kind sir,
    In my saddle my money I 've hid.'

5 So as they were riding along,
    And going down a steep hill,
    The gentleman-thief slipped before the old
        man
    And quickly he bid him stand still.

6 The old man, however, being cunning,
    As in this world there are many,
    He threw the saddle right over the hedge,
    Saying, Fetch it if thou wouldst have any.

7 The thief being so greedy of money —
    He thought that of it there 'd been bags —
    Whipt out a rusty old sword
    And chopped the saddle to rags.

8 The old man put his foot in the stirrup
    And presently he got astride;
    He put the thief's horse to the gallop,
    You need not bid the old man ride.

9 'Nay, stay! nay, stay!' says the thief,
    'And half the money thou shalt have;'
    'Nay, by my troth,' says the old man,
    'For once I have cheated a knave.'

10 And so the old man rode along,
    And went with a merry devotion,
    Saying, If ever I live to get home,
    'T will enlarge my daughter's portion.

11 And having arrived at home,
    And got there with merry intent,
    Says he, Landlord, show me a room,
    And I 'll pay you your half-year's rent.

12 They opened the thief's portmanteau,
    And from it they took out so bold
A hundred pounds in silver
    And a hundred pounds in gold.

c–f, *the traditional copies, were beyond doubt all
derived originally from print.* c *is from* a ;
d–f *are from another edition, not recovered,
resembling* b. *This had variations, especially at the beginning and end, of which
some specimens will suffice.*

d. 1 Oh 't is I that will sing you a song,
    A song of merry intent ;
'T is about a silly old man
    That was going to pay his rent.

2 And as he was riding along,
    Along and alone in a lane,
A gentleman-thief overtook him,
    And said, Well overtaken, old man !

3 ' You 're well overtaken, old man,
    You 're well overtaken by me ; '
' Nay, further go,' said the old man,
    ' I 'm not for thy company.'

4, 6 *are wanting, as also in* e, f, *(and in* b).

8²·⁴ ' He shall but poorly speed,
    For all the money I have
In my old saddle 't is hid.'

19, 20 Oh, when that he came home,
    His daughter she looked like a duchess,
And his old woman capered for joy,
    And danced him a gig on her crutches.

e. 1 Aw come now, I 'll sing you a song,
    'T is a song of right merry intent,
Concerning a silly old man
    Who went for to pay his rent.

2 And as this here silly old man
    Was riding along the lane,
A gentleman-thief overtook him,
    Saying, Well overtaken, old man !

3 ' What, well overtaken, do'y say ? '
    ' Yes, well overtaken,' quoth he ;
' No, no,' said the silly old man,
    ' I don't want thy company.'

8²·⁴ ' Why, badly the thief would be sped,
    For the money I carry about me
In the quilt o my saddle is hid.'

19, 20 Aw, when to his home he were come,
    His daughter he dressd like a duchess,
And his ol woman kicked and she capered
    for joy,
    And at Christmas danced jigs on her
    crutches.

f. *Resembles* d, e *in the passages cited.*

284

JOHN DORY

Ravenscroft's Deuteromelia, London, 1609; No 1 of Freemen's Songs, sig. B.

JOHN DORY goes to Paris and offers King
John, in return for a pardon asked for himself and his men, to bring the French king all
the churls in England in bonds. Nicholl, a
Cornish man, fits out a good bark, has an
encounter with John Dory, and after a smart
fight takes him prisoner.

This ballad had a remarkable popularity
in the seventeenth century, as is evinced by
the numerous cases of its being cited which

Chappell has collected, Popular Music, p. 67 f.*

As to the history of the transactions set forth in the ballad, I am not aware that anything has been added to the account given by Carew in his Survey of Cornwall, 1602, p. 135, which Ritson has quoted in the second edition of his Ancient Songs, II, 57, an account which is likely to have been taken from the ballad, with the specification from tradition that Nicholl was "son to a widow near Foy."

"Moreover, the prowess of one Nicholas, son to a widow near Foy, is descanted upon in an old three-man's song, namely, how he fought bravely at sea with John Dory (a Genowey, as I conjecture), set forth by John, the French king, and, after much bloodshed on both sides, took, and slew him, in revenge of the great ravine and cruelty which he had fore committed upon the Englishmen's goods and bodies." (Page 316 of the edition of 1813.)

The king in the ballad would be John II, the Good, who was taken prisoner at Poitiers, and died in 1364. No John Doria is mentioned as being in his service.

---

1   As it fell on a holy-day,
      And vpon an holy-tide-a,
   Iohn Dory bought him an ambling nag,
      To Paris for to ride-a.

2   And when John Dory to Paris was come,
      A little before the gate-a,
   John Dory was fitted, the porter was witted
      To let him in thereat-a.

3   The first man that John Dory did meet
      Was good king John of France-a ;
   John Dory could well of his courtesie,
      But fell downe in a trance-a.

4   'A pardon, a pardon, my liege and my
         king,
      For my merie men and for me-a,
   And all the churles in merie England,
      I 'le bring them all bound to thee-a.'

5   And Nicholl was then a Cornish man,
      A little beside Bohide-a,

And he mande forth a good blacke barke,
   With fiftie good oares on a side-a.

6   ' Run vp, my boy, vnto the maine top,
      And looke what thou canst spie-a : '
   'Who ho! who ho! a goodly ship I do
         see,
      I trow it be John Dory[-a.']

7   They hoist their sailes, both top and top,
      The meisseine and all was tride-a,
   And euery man stood to his lot,
      What euer should betide-a.

8   The roring cannons then were plide,
      And dub-a-dub went the drumme-a ;
   The braying trumpets lowde they cride
      To courage both all and some-a.

9   The grappling-hooks were brought at length,
      The browne bill and the sword-a,
   John Dory at length, for all his strength,
      Was clapt fast vnder board-a.

---

* The song "I cannot eat but little meat," introduced into Gammer Gurton's Needle, which was acted in 1566, was sung to 'John Dory,' says Mr Chappell, as above ; but there is nothing to show that this was the original tune.

285

THE GEORGE ALOE AND THE SWEEPSTAKE

a. Percy Papers, "from an ancient black-letter copy in Ballard's collection."

b. Rawlinson, 566, fol. 183, 4°.

c. Roxburghe, III, 204, in Ebsworth, Roxburghe Ballads, VI, 408.

MARCH 19, 1611, there were entered to Richard Jones, "Captayne Jenninges his songe, whiche he made in the Marshalsey," etc., and "the second parte of the George Aloo and the Swiftestake, beinge both ballades:" Arber, III, 456. The second part of the George Aloo must needs mean a second ballad, not the printers' second half (which begins in c at the stanza here numbered 14). In 'The Two Noble Kinsmen,' printed in 1634, and perhaps earlier, the Jailer's Daughter sings the two following stanzas (Dyce, XI, 386):

> The George Alow came from the south,
>   From the coast of Barbary-a,
> And there he met with brave gallants of war,
>   By one, by two, by three-a.

> Well haild, well haild, you jolly gallants,
>   And whither now are you bound-a?
> Oh, let me have your company
>   Till [I] come to the sound-a.

These verses, whether accurately reported or not, certainly seem to belong to another ballad. Whether they are from the first part or the second part, we have no means of assuring ourselves. It is to be observed that in the ballad before us the George Aloe and the Sweepstake are sailing *for* Safee, and in the other case the George Aloe is coming *from* the south, from the coast of Barbary, so that the adventure, whatever it was, may have occurred in the homeward voyage; but the circumstance is not decisive.*

The George Aloe and the Sweepstake, merchantmen, are bound for Safee. The George Aloe anchors, the Sweepstake keeps on, is taken by a French rover, and her crew thrown overboard. The George Aloe hears of this, and sets out to take the Frenchman. Her second shot carries away the enemy's mainmast; the Frenchmen cry for mercy. The English ask what they did with the crew of the Sweepstake; the Frenchmen confess that they threw them into the sea. Such mercy as you shewed such mercy shall you have, say the English, and deal with the French accordingly.

'Aboard,' 6^2, 16^2, I suppose to mean alongside. 'Amain,' 7^1, 16^1, is strike (sails) in sign of surrender. The French use the word derived from their own language; the English say, strike. 'Gallant' Englishmen in 7^1, after 'English dogs' in 6^1, is unlikely courtesy, and is not found in 16^1.

'The Swepstacke' is a king's ship in 1545, and 'The Sweepstakes' apparently again in 1666: Historical MSS Commission, 12th Report, Appendix, Part VII, pp. 8, 45.

---

* There is an entry, July 31, 1590, of A Ditty of the fight upon the seas the fourth of June last in the Straits of Gibraltar between the George and the Thomas Bonaventure and eight galleys with three frigates (Arber, II, 557), but it is likely that there were Georges many, and only one George Aloe.

Mr Ebsworth has pointed out that a ballad called The Sailor's Joy, the name of the tune to which 'The George Aloe and the Sweepstake' was to be sung, was entered in the Stationers' Registers, January 14, 1595: Arber, II, 669.

1   THE George Aloe and the Sweepstakes too,
    With hey, with ho, for and a nony no
They were two merchant-men, a sailing for
    Safee.
    And along the course of Barbary

2   [The George Aloe to anchor came,
    But the jolly Sweepstake kept on her way.]

3   They had not sayled leagues two or three
    Before they spyed a sail upon the sea.

4   ' O hail, O hail, you lusty gallants,
    From whence is your good ship, and whither
      is she bound ? '

5   ' O we are some merchant-men, sailing for
      Safee : '
    ' And we be French rebels, a roving on the sea.

6   ' O hail, O hail, you English dogs, [hail !] '
    ' The[n] come aboard, you French dogs, and
      strike down your sail ! '

7   ' Amain, amain, you gallant Englishmen ! '
    ' Come, you French swades, and strike down
      your sails ! '

8   They laid us aboard on the starboard side,
    And they overthrew us into the sea so wide.

9   When tidings to the George Aloe came
    That the jolly Sweepstakes by a Frenchman
      was tane,

10 ' To top, to top, thou little ship-boy,
    And see if this French man-of-war thou canst
      descry.'

11 ' A sail, a sail, under your lee,
    Yea, and another under her bough.'

12 ' Weigh anchor, weigh anchor, O jolly boat-
    swain,
    We will take this Frenchman if we can.'

13 We had not sailed leagues two or three
    But we met the French man-of-war upon the
      sea.

14 ' All hail, all hail, you lusty gallants,
    Of whence is your fair ship, and whither is she
      bound ? '

15 ' O we are merchant-men, and bound for
      Safee ; '
    ' And we are Frenchmen, roving upon the sea.

16 ' Amain, amain, you English dogs ! '
    ' Come aboard, you French rogues, and strike
      your sails ! '

17 The first good shot the George Aloe shot,
    It made the Frenchmen's hearts sore afraid.

18 The second shot the George Aloe did afford,
    He struck the main-mast over the board.

19 ' Have mercy, have mercy, you brave Eng-
    lish[men].'
    ' O what have you done with our brethren on
      [shore] ? '
      As they sail[ed].

20 ' We laid them aboard on the starboard side,
    And we threw them into the sea so wide.'

21 ' Such mercy as you have shewed unto them,
    Even the like mercy shall you have again.'

22 We laid them aboard on the larboard side,
    And we threw them into the sea so wide.

23 Lord, how it grieved our hearts full sore
    To see the drowned Frenchmen float along the
      shore !

24 Now, gallant seamen all, adieu,
    With hey, with ho, for and a nony no
    This is the last news that I can write to you.
    To England's coast from Barbary

———◆———

a. The Seamans only Delight : Shewing the
    brave fight between the George Aloe, the
    Sweepstakes, and certain French Men at sea.

    Tune, The Sailor's Joy, etc.   (*No printers
    given in the transcript.*)
b. The Saylors only Delight : Shewing the brave

fight between the George-Aloe, the Sweep-stake, and certain Frenchmen at sea. To the tune of The Saylors Joy. London, Printed for F. Coles, T. Vere and J. [Wright] (*torn*). 1655-80, Chappell.

c. The Sailors onely Delight: Shewing the brave fight between George-Aloe, the Sweep-stakes, and certain French-men at sea. To the tune of The Saylor's Joy. Printed for F. Coles, J. Wright, Tho. Vere, and W. Gilbertson. The earliest known ballad by the four together is dated 1655, Chappell. (See No 273, Appendix, III, b.)

a. 1, 24. *Burden*[1]. anony.

1. *Burden*[2]. course *should probably be* coast.
2. *Wanting; supplied from* b, c.
4[1]. O hail, oh. 5[1], 6[1], 15[1]. Oh.
10[2]. Frenchman of war.
13[2]. French Men of War.
17[2]. French Mens.
19. *Ends torn away. Percy gives, after* english, A, *which may be the first half of an* M; *after* on, fl, *which may possibly be a wrong reading of* fh. Shore *is not what we should expect. Defects supplied from* b, c.
23[2]. French Men.

b. 1. *Burden*[1]. a nony. *Burden*[2]. alongst the cost.
1[1], 9[2]. Sweepstake.
1[2]. O they were marchant men and bound.
3[2]. But they met with a Frenchman of war upon.
4[1]. All hayl, all hayl.
4[2]. Of whence is your fair ship, whether are you bound.
5[1]. We are Englishmen and bound.
5[2]. Of whence is your fair ship, or whether are you bound.
6. *Wanting.* 7[2]. swads. 10[2]. Frenchman.
11[1]. our lee. 11[2]. under her obey.
13[2]. Frenchman. 14[2]. is it.
15[2]. I, and we are Frenchmen and war.
16[2]. strike down. 17[2]. He made: heart.
18[2]. strook. 19[1]. brave Englishmen.
19[2]. brethen on shore.
Burden[2]. As they sayled into Barbary.
23[1]. greives. 23[2]. swim along.

c. 4[2]. or whither. 7[1]. Englishman. 7[2]. sayle.
14[2]. whither are you. 16[2]. rogue.
17[2]. hearts. 18[2]. struck their.
19[2]. brethren on shore. *Burden*[2]. sayled in.
21[2]. Then the. *Variations otherwise as in* b.

286

THE SWEET TRINITY (THE GOLDEN VANITY)

A. 'Sir Walter Raleigh sailing in the Low-lands,' etc., Pepys Ballads, IV, 196, No 189 (1682-85).

B. a. 'The Goulden Vanitie,' Logan's Pedlar's Pack, p. 42; Mrs Gordon's Memoir of John Wilson, II, 317. **b.** As sung by Mr G. Du Maurier, sent me by J. R. Lowell. **c.** 'The French Galley,' Motherwell's MS., p. 420. **d.** Communicated by Mrs Moncrieff, of London, Ontario. **e.** 'The Lowlands Low,' Findlay MSS, I, 161. **f.** Sharpe's Ballad Book, 1880, p. 160, notes of Sir Walter Scott.

C. a. 'Golden Vanity, or, The Low Lands Low,' Pitts, Seven Dials, in Logan's Pedlar's Pack, p. 45; Ebsworth, Roxburghe Ballads, VI, 419. **b.** 'The Lowlands Low,' Long, Dictionary of the Isle of Wight Dialect, p. 145. **c.** 'Low in the Lowlands Low,' Christie, I, 238. **d.** 'The Golden Vanity,' Baring-Gould and Sheppard, 'Songs of the West,' No 64. **e.** 'The French Gallio,' 'The French Gallolee,' Buchan MSS, II, 390, 414. **f.** 'The Turkish Galley,' Motherwell's MS., p. 392, and Note-Book, p. 50. **g.** 'The Lowlands Low,' Macmath MS., p. 80.

A also in Euing, No 334, Crawford, No 1073, Huth, II, No 134; all by the same printer, 1682-85.

Motherwell enters the first stanza of an-other copy of 'The Turkish Galley' in his Note-Book, p. 10, and refers to three copies more, besides **B d,** at p. 51.

There is a retouched copy of **C** in English

County Songs, Lucy E. Broadwood and J. A. Fuller Maitland, p. 182.

B, C, are probably traditional variations of the broadside A. The conclusion of the broadside is sufficiently inadequate to impel almost any singer to attempt an improvement, and a rather more effective catastrophe is the only signal difference besides names. It is, however, not quite impossible that the ultimate source of the traditional copies may be as old as the broadside.

A. 'The Sweet Trinity,' a ship built by Sir Walter Raleigh, has been taken by a galley of a nationality not specified. The master of some English ship asks what seaman will take the galley and redeem The Sweet Trinity. A ship-boy asks what the reward shall be; the reward shall be gold and fee, and the master's eldest daughter. The ship-boy, who is possessed of an auger which bores fifteen holes at once, swims to the galley, sinks her, and releases The Sweet Trinity; then swims back to his ship and demands his pay. The master will give gold and fee, but not his daughter to wife. The ship-boy says, Farewell, since you are not so good as your word.

B. No ship has been taken by an enemy. The Golden Vanity, Golden Victorie, e, falls in with a French galley, which a cabin-boy undertakes to sink for a reward. The reward is to be, a, b, an estate in the North Country; c, half the captain's lands in the South Country, meat and fee, and the captain's eldest daughter; e, gold and fee, and the captain's daughter. The boy is rolled up in a bull-skin and thrown over the deck-board (a corruption, see C). He takes out an instrument, and bores thirty holes at twice, a; a gimlet,

and bores sixty holes and thrice, b; he struck her with an instrument, bored thirty holes at twice, c; threescore holes he scuttled in a trice, d; struck her wi an auger, thirty three and thrice, e. After sinking the galley he calls to the Golden Vanity to throw him a rope, take him on board, and be as good as their word, all which is refused. He threatens to serve them as he has the galley, a, b, d; they take him up and prove better than their word, a, d, or as good, b. (Of f very little was remembered by Scott, and the ballad was besides confounded with 'The George Aloe.'*)

C. The distinguishing feature is that the boy dies after he is taken up from the water, and is sewed up in a cow's hide and thrown overboard, 'to go down with the tide.' The Golden Vanity, a–d, The Gold Pinnatree, e, The Golden Trinitie, g, is in danger from a Turkish galleon, a, f, g, a Spanish, b, c (pirate Targalley), d, French, e. The captain of the English ship promises the cabin-boy gold, fee, and daughter, if he will sink the enemy. The boy has, and uses, an auger, to bore two holes at twice, a, that bores twenty holes in twice, b, to bore two holes at once, c; a case of instruments, ca's fifty holes and drives them a' at once, e; an instrument, and bores nine holes in her water-sluice, f; an auger fitted for the use, and bores in her bottom a watery sluice, g. The master will not take him on board, will kill him, shoot him, sink him, a–d; will not keep his bargain, 'for as you've done to her, so would you do to me,' e (compare the threat in B 13). The boy is taken up by his mess-mates and dies on the deck, a, c, d; is sewed in a cow-hide and thrown overboard, a, c–g; in b sinks from exhaustion and drowns.

A

Pepys Ballads, IV, 196, No 189.

1 SIR WALTER RAWLEIGH has built a ship,
    In the Neatherlands

Sir Walter Rawleigh has built a ship,
    In the Neather-lands
And it is called The Sweet Trinity,
    And was taken by the false gallaly.
Sailing in the Low-lands

* Scott says at the end, "I will not swear to the accuracy of the above."

2 'Is there never a seaman bold
  In the Neather-lands
Is there never a seaman bold
  In the Neather-lands
That will go take this false gallaly,
And to redeem The Sweet Trinity?'
  Sailing, etc.

3 Then spoke the little ship-boy;
  In the Neather-lands
Then spoke the little ship-boy;
  In the Neather-lands
'Master, master, what will you give me
And I will take this false gallaly,
And release The Sweet Trinity?'
  Sailing, etc.

4 'I 'll give thee gold, and I 'le give thee
  fee,
  In the Neather-lands
I 'll give thee gold and I 'le give thee fee,
  In the Neather-lands
And my eldest daughter thy wife shall be.'
  Sailing, etc.

5 He set his breast, and away he did swim,
Until he came to the false gallaly.

6 He had an augor fit for the [n]once,
The which will bore fifteen good holes at once.

7 Some ware at cards, and some at dice,
Until the salt water flashd in their eyes.

8 Some cut their hats, and some cut their caps,
For to stop the salt-water gaps.

9 He set his breast, and away did swim,
Until he came to his own ship again.

10 'I have done the work I promised to do,
For I have sunk the false gallaly,
And released The Sweet Trinity.

11 'You promised me gold, and you promised me
  fee,
Your eldest daughter my wife she must be.'

12 'You shall have gold, and you shall have fee,
But my eldest daughter your wife shall never
  be.'
  For sailing, etc.

13 'Then fare you well, you cozening lord,
Seeing you are not so good as your word.'
  For sailing, etc.

14 And thus I shall conclude my song,
  Of the sailing in the Low-lands
Wishing all happiness to all seamen both old
  and young.
  In their sailing in the Low-lands

B

a. Logan's Pedlar's Pack, p. 42, as sung about 1840 by
Mr P. S. Fraser, of Edinburgh, and obtained by him orally.
b. As sung by Mr George Du Maurier to Mr J. R. Lowell,
1884. c. Motherwell's MS., p. 420; from Mr John Cle-
land, marble-cutter, Glasgow, who had it of Mr Forrester,
Stirling. d. Communicated by Mrs Moncrieff, as taught
to a relative of hers by an old Scottish lady about 1830.
e. Findlay MSS, I, 161, "from Strang, Divinity Student,
1868." f. Sharpe's Ballad Book, 1880, p. 160, note by Sir
Walter Scott.

1 THERE was a gallant ship, and a gallant ship
  was she
  Eck iddle du, and the Lowlands low
And she was called The Goulden Vanitie.
  As she sailed to the Lowlands low

2 She had not sailed a league, a league but only
  three,
  Eck, etc.
When she came up with a French gallee.
  As she sailed, etc.

3 Out spoke the little cabin-boy, out spoke he;
  'What will you give me if I sink that French
  gallee?'
  As ye sail, etc.

4 Out spoke the captain, out spoke he;
  'We 'll gie ye an estate in the North Countrie.'
  As we sail, etc.

5 'Then row me up ticht in a black bull's skin,
And throw me oer deck-buird, sink I or swim.'
As ye sail, etc.

6 So they've rowed him up ticht in a black bull's
skin,
And have thrown him oer deck-buird, sink he
or soom.
As they sail, etc.

7 About, and about, and about went he,
Until he cam up with the French gallee.
As they sailed, etc.

8 O some were playing cards, and some were
playing dice,
When he took out an instrument, bored thirty
holes at twice.
As they sailed, etc.

9 Then some they ran with cloaks, and some
they ran with caps,
To try if they could stap the saut-water draps.
As they sailed, etc.

10 About, and about, and about went he,
Until he cam back to The Goulden Vanitie.
As they sailed, etc.

11 'Now throw me oer a rope and pu me up on
buird,
And prove unto me as guid as your word.'
As ye sail, etc.

12 'We'll no throw you oer a rope, nor pu you up
on buird,
Nor prove unto you as guid as our word.'
As we sail, etc.

13 Out spoke the little cabin-boy, out spoke he ;
Then hang me, I'll sink ye as I sunk the
French gallee.
As ye sail, etc.

14 But they've thrown him oer a rope, and have
pu'd him up on buird,
And have proved unto him far better than
their word.
As they sailed, etc.

C

a. Stall-copy, Pitts, Seven Dials, Logan's Pedlar's Pack,
p. 45. b. Long's Dictionary of the Isle of Wight Dialect,
p. 145. c. Christie, Traditional Ballad Airs, I, 238, compounded from the recitation of an old woman of Buckie,
Banffshire, and a chap-book copy. d. Baring-Gould and
Sheppard, Songs of the West, No 64, Part III, p. 24, Part
IV, p. xxxi, taken down from James Olver, Launceston (an
improved copy). e. Buchan's MSS, II, 390, 414. f. Motherwell's MS., p. 392, and Note-Book, p. 50, from the recitation
of Agnes Lyle, 24th August, 1825. g. Macmath MS., p. 80,
from the recitation of Miss Agnes Macmath, 1893 ; learned
at Airds of Kells, Kirkcudbrightshire.

1 'I HAVE a ship in the North Countrie,
And she goes by the name of The Golden
Vanity ;
I'm afraid she will be taken by some Turkish
gallee,
As she sails on the Low Lands Low.'

2 Then up starts our little cabin-boy,
Saying, Master, what will you give me if I do
them destroy ?
'I will give you gold, I will give you store,

You shall have my daughter when I return on
shore,
If ye sink them in the Low Lands Low.'

3 The boy bent his breast and away he jumpt in ;
He swam till he came to this Turkish galleon,
As she laid on the Low Lands Low.

4 The boy he had an auger to bore holes two at
twice ;
While some were playing cards, and some
were playing dice,
He let the water in, and it dazzled in their eyes,
And he sunk them in the Low Lands Low.

5 The boy he bent his breast and away he swam
back again,
Saying, Master take me up, or I shall be slain,
For I have sunk them in the Low Lands
Low.

6 'I'll not take you up,' the master he cried ;
'I'll not take you up,' the master replied ;

'I will kill you, I will shoot you, I will send
you with the tide,
I will sink you in the Low Lands Low.'

7 The boy he swam round all by the starboard-
side;

They laid him on the deck, and it's there he
soon died;
Then they sewed him up in an old cow's-hide,
And they threw him overboard, to go down
with the tide,
And they sunk him in the Low Lands Low.

———•———

A. Sir Walter Raleigh sailing in the Low-lands:
Shewing how the famous ship called The
Sweet Trinity was taken by a false gally,
and how it was again restored by the craft
of a little sea-boy, who sunk the galley: as
the following song will declare. To the
tune of The Sailing of the Low-land.
(End.) This may be printed. R. L. S. (Sir R.
L'Estrange was licenser from 1663 to 1685.)
Printed for J. Conyers at the Black-Raven, the
first shop in Fetter-Lane next Holborn. (J.
Conyers, 1682–91. Chappell.)
a. 7¹. at somt dice.
B. a. 8¹. Oh.
b. *The variations are but trifling.*
   7. And awa, and awa, and awa swam he,
      Till he swam up to.
   8². He just took out a gimlet and bored sixty
      holes and thrice.
   9². But they couldna run awa from the salt-
      water drops.
   10. Then awa, and awa, and awa swam he,
      Till he swam back to.
   12¹. I 'll na: rope, I 'll na.
   12². I 'll na: unto thee: my word.
   13. An ye na throw me oer a rope an ye na
      pull me up aboard,
      I 'll just sink ye.
   14². And they proved unto him as good as
      their word.

c. 1 There was an auncient ship, and an auncient
      ship was she,
      Eee eedle ee, in the Lowlands so low
   And the name of the ship was The Golden
      Vanitie.
   As she sailed from the Lowlands so low

   2 She had not sailed a league, no, not a league
      but three,
      Until that shee spied a French galley.

   3 'It 's master, O master, what 'll ye gie me,
      If I go and sink yon French galley?'

4 O then said the master, I will gie till ye
   The half of my lands in the South Countrie.

5 'It 's I 'll gie ye meat, and I 'll gie ye fee,
   And my eldest daughter your bride for to be.'

6 'It 's wrap me up tight in a gude bull's-skin,
   And throw me over deck-board, sink I or
      swim.'

7 So they wrapt him tight in a gude bull's-skin,
   And they 've thrown him over deck-board, sink
      he or swim.

8 And about, and about, and about went he,
   Until that he came to the French galley.

9 It 's some were playing at cards, and some were
      playing at dice,
   But he struck her with an instrument, bored
      thirty holes at twice.

10 Some ran wi hats, and some ran wi caps,
   All for to stop the salt-waters draps.
      As they, etc.

3¹, 4¹. oh, Oh.

d. 1 There was an ancient ship, and an ancient ship
      was she,
      Italy and the Lowlands low
   And her name it was The Golden Vanity.
      As she sailed for the Lowlands low

2 She had not sailed a mile, a mile but barely
      three,
   When she hove in sight of a French galley.

3 Up spak the prentice-boy; What'll ye gie me,
   If I gang and sink yon French galley?
      As she sails, etc.

4 Up spak the captain; What 'll I gie ye,
   • • • • • • • • •
      As she sails, etc.

5 *forgotten.*

6 'It 's row me up in a tough bull's-skin,
   And throw me overboard, let me sink or swim.'
   As we sail, etc.

7 They 've rowed him up tight in a tough bull's-
   skin,
   And they 've thrown him overboard, let him sink
   or swim.
   As they sailed, etc.

8 Then about, and about, and about went he,
   Until that he reached that French galley.
   As she sailed, etc.

9 . . . .
   And three-score holes he scuttled in a trice.
   As she sailed, etc.

10 'Now throw me owre a rope and pull me up on
   board,
   And prove unto me as gude as yere word.'
   As we sail, etc.

11 'I 'll not throw ye owre a rope, nor pull ye up
   on board,
   Nor prove unto ye as guid as my word.'
   As we sail, etc.

12 'Throw me owre a rope and pull me up on
   board,
   Or I 'll do to ye as I did the French galley.'
   As she sailed, etc.

13 Then they threw him owre a rope and pulled
   him up on board,
   And proved unto him far better than their word.
   As they sailed, etc.

e. 1 O she was an English ship, an an English ship
   was she,
   Hey diddie dee for the Lowlands low
   And her name it was The Golden Victorie.
   As she sailed for the Lowlands low.

2 . . . .
   And she fell in wi a French galee.
   As she sailed, etc.

3 'O what 'll ye gie me, captain, what 'll ye gie me,
   If I go an sink yon French galee ?'
   As she sails, etc.

4 'O I 'll gie thee goud, an I 'll gie thee fee,
   An my eldest daughter your wife shall be.'
   As we sail, etc.

5 'Then wrap me up tight in tough bull-hide,
   An to sink or swim ye 'll pitch me ower the side.'
   As we sail, etc.

6 They wrapt him up tight in tough bull-hide,
   An to sink or swim they pitchd him ower the
   side,
   As they sailed, etc.

7 He swam, an he swam, an he better swam,
   Until he to the French galley cam.
   As she sailed, etc.

8 O some were playin cards, an some were playin
   dice,
   But he struck her wi an auger thirty three and
   thrice.
   As she sailed, etc.

9 Aboot, an aboot, an aboot went she,
   Until she cam to the bottom of the sea.
   As she sailed, etc.

f. *Sir Walter Scott's recollections here seem not trustworthy, and of this he was himself aware.*

1 The George-a-Low eame down the strait,
   Hey low and the Lowlands so low
   And she will be lost, both vessel and freight,
   For the chasing of a French galerie O

5 'Row me in a good bull-skin,
   And fling me overboard, for to sink or to
   swim,'
   For the sinking of yon French galerie O

6 They row him, etc.

8 Some were playing at cards and dice,
   When the sea came gushing in a trice.
   For the sinking, etc.

C. b. 1 Our ship she was called The Golden Vanitie ;
   We had sailed from our port about miles fifty-
   three,
   When up came with us a Spanish gallee,
   To sink us in the Lowlands low.

2 Our master wrung his hands, but our little
   cabin-boy
   Said, What will you give me, master, if I do
   them destroy ?
   'Oh I will give you gold, and my daughter too,
   with joy,
   If you sink them,' etc.

3 The boy gave a nod, and then jumped into
   the sea,
   And he swam till he came to the Spanish
   gallee ;
   He climbed up aboard, and below to work
   went he,
   To sink them, etc.

4 For this boy he had an auger that bored
    twenty holes in twice,
And while some were playing cards, and
    some were playing dice,
Through the bottom of the ship he bored it
    in a trice,
    And he sunk them, etc.

5 The galley she went down, but the boy swam
    back again,
Crying, Master, pick me up, or I shall soon
    be slain ;
Pray heave to me a rope, or I shall sink in
    the main ;
    For I 've sunk them, etc.

6 'I will not pick you up,' the master loudly
    cried,
'I will not heave a rope,' the master he replied;
'I will kill you, I will sink you, I will leave
    you in the tide,
    I will sink you,' etc.

7 The boy he swam around the ship from side
    to side,
But he could not get aboard, so he sank, and
    he died,
And they left him where he was, to go down
    with the tide ;
    So they sunk him, etc.

c. 1 There was a good ship from the North Coun-
    trie,
    Sailing low in the Lowlands low
There was, etc.
And that ship's name was The Golden Van-
    ity.
    Sailing low in the Lowlands, low in the sea,
    Sailing low in the Lowlands low

The master said, I fear for my good ship
    Vanity,
Oh, I fear for my good ship, The Golden
    Vanity,
That she will be taken by the pirate Tar-
    galley,
    As she sails in, etc.

2² 'Oh, master, good master, what will you give me
    If I sink yon Targalley low in the sea?'

10 *stanzas.*

d. 1 A ship I have got in the North Country,
    And she goes by the name of The Golden
      Vanity ;
O I fear she 'll be taken by a Spanish Galalie,
    As she sails by the Lowlands low.

8 *stanzas.*

e. Buchan ; MSS, II, 390.

1 Our ship sailed to the North Country,
    Sing, How the Lowlands lo[w]
Our ship sailed on to the North Countrie,
And the name o her was The Gold Pinnatree,
She was as fine a vessel as ever sailed the sea,
    And she sails by the Lowlands lo[w]

2 We hadna sailed leagues but only three,
Till the captain from the maindeck fixed an ee ;
He spied a lofty frigate was sailing closely tee,
    And her name was The French Gallio.

3 Then out it speaks the pilot, by the mainyard
    did stand,
Says, O my pretty boys, we are all undone ;
We must prepare to fight or be sunk to the sand,
    For yonder comes the French gallio.

4 Then spoke the little cabin-boy, [where stood
    he,]
Said, O my loving master, what will ye gie me
And I will sink this proud Gallio in the sea,
    And I will sink the French gallio?

5 'I will gie you gold, boy, and I will gie you fee,
Besides a rarer gift that I will give thee ;
Ye 'se have my eldest daughter your wedded
    wife to be,
    If ye will sink the French gallio.'

6 The boy bent his breast, and away swam he,
And took a bold venture thro the stormy sea,
And cam close by his enemy, as sly as he could
    be,
    It was to sink the French gallio.

7 Some there were at cards, and some there were
    at dice,
But the little cabin-boy was at the best device,
He was sinking the French gallio in the sea,
    He was sinking the French gallio.

8 This boy had a case o fine instruments,
He ca'd fifty holes, and drove them a' at once,
And he soon sank the French gallio in the sea,
    And he soon sank the French gallio.

9 Then the boy bent his breast, and back swam he,
Till that he cam to The Gold Pinnatree ;
Says, Now, my loving master, what will ye gie
    me?
    For I have sunk the French gallio.

10 'Now give to me my gold, master, [give to me
    my fee,]
Or give to me the other rare gifts ye promised
    me ;

It was your eldest daughter, my wedded wife to
be ;
For the sinking o the French gallio.'

11 'Ye shall have no gold, boy, ye shall have no
fee ;
I wadna ware my daughter on ony such as
thee;
For as you've done to her, boy, so wad you do to
me,
By the sinking o the French [gallio].'

12 Then they put out their long-boat and catched
him by the side,
And rowed him into ane auld cow's-hide,
And tossed him overboard, to float on the tide,
For sinking the French gallio.

Gallio *may be surmised to be properly* galley O.

*The other copy in Buchan's MSS, II, 414, is only
the foregoing a little retouched or regulated. It
has throughout* Gallolee *for* Gallio. *The first line
of the burden is,* Sing, Low, the Lowlands low.
4¹. where stood he.   6². could dee.
10¹. give to me my fee.

f. 1 I spied a ship, and a ship was she,
Sing, Oh, the low and the Lowlands low
And she was called the Turkish Galley,
She was sailing in the Lowlands, low, low,
low,
She was sailing in the Lowlands low.

2 'Master, master, what wud ye gie me
Gin I wud sink yon Turkish galley?
She's sailing, etc.'

3 'I'll gie you gold, I'll gie you fee,
Gin ye wud sink yon Turkish galley,
That is sailing,' etc.

4 He bent his breast, and awa swam he,
Till he cam to yon Turkish galley,
That's sailing, etc.

5 He had an instrument, made for the use,
He bored nine holes in her water-sluice,
Left her sinking, etc.

6 Some took their hats, and some took their caps,
All for to stop her watery leaks.
She was sinking, etc.

7 They took him up by their ship-side,
They sewed him in an auld cow's-hide,
Left him sinking, etc.

*Motherwell sent this copy to C. K. Sharpe in a letter
dated October 8, 1825, in which he says :* I also
send rather a curious song, which perchance
you may have seen, entitled ' The Turkish Galley,' the air of which pleased me much.   But as
I learn there are two other different sets of the
words more complete than my copy, and with
different airs, I shall defer sending the musick
till I can send also that which belongs to the
other copies.

g. 1 There was a ship of the North Countrie,
And the name of the ship was The Golden
Trinitie.
She was sailing in the Lowlands low, low,
low,
She was sailing in the Lowlands low.

2 .   .   .   .
And the name of the ship was The Turkish
Gallee,
And she was sailing in the Lowlands low,
low, low,
She was sailing, etc.

3 'O captain, O captain,' said the young cabin-
boy,
'What will you give me if yon ship I do destroy ?
And sink her in,' etc.

4 'I'll give you gold, and I'll give you fee,
And my eldest daughter your wedded wife shall
be,
If you sink her in,' etc.

5 The boy bent his bow, and away swam he,
Until that he came to the Turkish gallee.
She was sailing in, etc.

6 The boy had an auger, right fitted for the use,
And into her bottom he bored a watery sluice.
She is sinking in, etc.

7 The boy bent his bow, and back swam he,
Until that he came to the Golden Trinitie.
She is sailing in, etc.

8 'O captain, O captain, take me on board,
And O be as good, as good as your word,
For I've sunk her in the Lowlands low, low,
low,
I've sunk,' etc.

9 They threw him a rope oer the larboard side,
And sewed him up in an auld cow's-hide,
And threw him out to a fair wind and tide,
And sunk him in, etc.

287

CAPTAIN WARD AND THE RAINBOW

Bagford Ballads, I, 65.

OTHER black-letter copies are Pepys, IV, 202, No 195 ; Roxburghe, III, 56 ; Euing, No 108 ; British Museum, 112. f. 44 (19). This copy is printed in Halliwell's Early Naval Ballads, p. 59, Bell's Early Ballads, p. 167, Ebsworth's Roxburghe Ballads, VI, 426.

There are Aldermary Churchyard copies, as Roxburghe Ballads, III, 652, 861 ; Scottish stall-copies, as Greenock, W. Scott, Stirling, M. Randall ; English, by Pitts, Seven Dials, one of which is printed in Logan's Pedlar's Pack, p. 1.

A copy in Buchan's MSS, II, 245, is nearly the old broadside ; another, II, 417, is the stall-copy. Kinloch, MSS, V, 109, II, 265, has the stall-copy from oral transmission (with Weir for Ward). Rev. S. Baring-Gould has recently taken down this ballad (much changed by tradition) in the west of England.

Captain Ward, a famous rover, wishes to make his peace with the king, and offers thirty ton of gold as "ransom" for himself and his men. The king will not trust a man who has proved false to France and to Spain, and sends the Rainbow, with five hundred men, against Ward. The Rainbow has easy work with Dutch, Spaniards, and French, but her fifty brass pieces have no effect on Ward ; though the Rainbow is brass without, he is steel within, 8^2 (suggested by 'Sir Andrew Barton,' A 27^1, B 25^1, 'He is brass within and steel without).' The Rainbow retires, and reports to the king that Ward is too strong to be taken. The king laments that he has lost three captains, any one of whom would have brought Ward in : George Clifford, Earl of Cumberland, †1605, Charles Blount, Lord Mountjoy, †1606 (both of whom had a part in the defeat of the Armada), and Robert Devereux, Earl of Essex, †1601.

The Rainbow was the name of one of Drake's four ships in his expedition against Cadiz in 1587. The Rainbow is mentioned very often from 1589 ; as in The Manuscripts of the Earl Cowper, vol. i, Hist. MSS Commission, XIIth Report, Appendix, Part I ; Index in Part III of the same, p. 296.

John Ward, an Englishman of Kent, is said to have commenced 'rover' about 1604, by inducing the crew of a king's ship in which he had some place to turn pirates under his command. His race, though eventful, was, naturally enough, not long. He seems not to be heard of after 1609, in which year Ward and his colleague, Dansekar, are spoken of as the "two late famous pirates." See Mr Ebsworth's preface to the ballad, VI, 423 ff., founded on Andrew Barker's book about Ward and Dansekar, published in the year last named.

Two other ballad-histories, 'The Seamen's Song of Captain Ward' and 'The Seamen's Song of Dansekar' (i. e. Dansekar and Ward), entered in the Stationers' Registers July 3, 1609, are given by Mr Ebsworth, VI, 784, 423.

1 STRIKE up, you lusty gallants, with musick
     and sound of drum,
For we have descryed a rover, upon the sea is
     come ;
His name is Captain Ward, right well it doth
     appear,
There has not been such a rover found out this
     thousand year.

2 For he hath sent unto our king, the sixth of
     January,
Desiring that he might come in, with all his
     company :
' And if your king will let me come till I my
     tale have told,
I will bestow for my ransome full thirty tun of
     gold.'

3 ' O nay ! O nay !' then said our king, ' O
     nay ! this may not be,
To yield to such a rover my self will not agree ;
He hath deceivd the French-man, likewise the
     King of Spain,
And how can he be true to me that hath been
     false to twain ? '

4 With that our king provided a ship of worthy
     fame,
Rainbow she is called, if you would know her
     name ;
Now the gallant Rainbow she rowes upon the
     sea,
Five hundred gallant seamen to bear her com-
     pany.

5 The Dutch-man and the Spaniard she made
     them for to flye,
Also the bonny French-man, as she met him on
     the sea :
When as this gallant Rainbow did come where
     Ward did lye,
' Where is the captain of this ship ? ' this gal-
     lant Rainbow did cry.

6 ' O that am I,' says Captain Ward, ' there 's
     no man bids me lye,
And if thou art the king's fair ship, thou art
     welcome unto me :'
' I 'le tell thee what,' says Rainbow, ' our king
     is in great grief
That thou shouldst lye upon the sea and play
     the arrant thief,

7 ' And will not let our merchants ships pass as
     they did before ;
Such tydings to our king is come, which
     grieves his heart full sore.'
With that this gallant Rainbow she shot, out of
     her pride,
Full fifty gallant brass pieces, charged on every
     side.

8 And yet these gallant shooters prevailed not a
     pin,
Though they were brass on the out-side, brave
     Ward was steel within ;
' Shoot on, shoot on,' says Captain Ward,
     ' your sport well pleaseth me,
And he that first gives over shall yield unto
     the sea.

9 ' I never wrongd an English ship, but Turk
     and King of Spain,
For and the jovial Dutch-man as I met on the
     main.
If I had known your king but one two years
     before,
I would have savd brave Essex life, whose
     death did grieve me sore.

10 ' Go tell the King of England, go tell him thus
     from me,
If he reign king of all the land, I will reign
     king at sea.'
With that the gallant Rainbow shot, and shot,
     and shot in vain,
And left the rover's company, and returnd
     home again.

11 ' Our royal king of England, your ship 's re-
     turnd again,
For Ward's ship is so strong it never will be
     tane : '
' O everlasting ! ' says our king, ' I have lost
     jewels three,
Which would have gone unto the seas and
     brought proud Ward to me.

12 ' The first was Lord Clifford, Earl of Cumber-
     land ;
The second was the lord Mountjoy, as you
     shall understand ;
The third was brave Essex, from field would
     never flee ;

Which would a gone unto the seas and brought
   proud Ward to me.'

The Famous Sea-Fight between Captain Ward
   and the Rainbow. To the tune of Captain
   Ward, etc. Licensed and entered.
London, Printed by and for W. Onley, and are

to be sold by the Booksellers of Pye-corner
and London-bridge. *Dated at the British
Museum* 1680 *at the earliest.*

11³. Everlasting shame, *in the Scottish stall-
copies.*

A collation of Roxburghe, III, 56, *shows only
variations too trivial to note.*

288

THE YOUNG EARL OF ESSEX'S VICTORY OVER THE EMPEROR OF GERMANY

A. 'Queen Elizabeth's Champion, or, Great Britain's Glory,' etc. a. Douce Ballads, III, fol. 80 b.

b. Roxburghe, III, 416, in Ebsworth's Roxburghe Ballads, VI, 405.

B. 'Earl of Essex', Kinloch MSS, I, 113.

A is printed also in Evans's Old Ballads, 1777, II, 110, with slight variations from both Douce and Roxburghe.

No printer's name is given in either copy of A. From the use of a peculiar ornament between the columns in a (and perhaps in b), such as occurs in ballads printed at Newcastle-upon-Tyne, by John White, the broadside may plausibly be attributed to him. White died in 1769.

A. Queen Elizabeth fits out a powerful fleet to go in search of a vast navy under command of the emperor of Germany. The fleets sight each other after a week or ten days. The emperor, amazed at the splendid show made by the English, asks his officers who this can be that is sailing toward him, and is told that it is the young Earl (third earl) of Essex, the queen's lieutenant. The emperor has heard enough of the father to make him fear a fight with the son, and proposes to tack and sail away; but the son asks his father to put the ships into his hands and let him fight with Essex. The emperor consents with a

warning; if the young Essex shall prove like his father, farewell to their honor. Young Essex takes the emperor's son prisoner; the emperor offers as a ransom three keys of gold, one of which shall be the key of High Germany. Essex cares not for the three keys; the emperor's son must go to England and be exhibited to the queen. The emperor declares that, if it must be so, his fifty good ships shall go as well for company.

All this is, no doubt, as foolish as it is fictitious, but the ballad-maker's independence, in fact unconsciousness, of history and common sense, beginning with the title, in which young Essex is made Queen Elizabeth's champion, is amusing and not unpleasing. The ballad belongs undoubtedly to the eighteenth century, when High Germany had become familiar to the humble English.

B. The traditional copy begins with a prologue of half a dozen stanzas in the form of a colloquy between Billy, who is to be of the expedition, and Nelly, his sweetheart. This prologue must be derived from some other ballad or song. Nelly reminds her lover of the fate of old Benbow, who lost at least one of his legs in a fight with a French fleet in 1702, and died of the consequences, and of that of "proud Shawfield, that honoured knight," under which name is disguised Sir

Cloudesley Shovell, "who came with his navy to the Spanish shore" in 1705, and whose ship went on the rocks off the Scilly Isles ('Salem'), and sank with all on board, some eight hundred men, in 1707. We then make connection with the broadside.

A

a. Douce Ballads, III, fol. 80 b. b. Roxburghe, III, 416, in Ebsworth's Roxburghe Ballads, VI, 405.

1 COME, sound up your trumpets and beat up
          your drums,
     And let's go to sea with a valiant good
          cheer,
   In search of a mighty vast navy of ships,
     The like has not been for these fifty long
          year.
               Raderer two, tandaro te,
               Raderer, tandorer, tan do re.

2 The queen she provided a navy of ships,
     With sweet flying streamers, so glorious to
          see,
   Rich top and top-gallants, captains and lieu-
          tenants,
     Some forty, some fifty, brass-pieces and
          three.

3 They had not saild past a week on the seas,
     Not passing a week and days two or three,
   But they were aware of the proud emperor,
     Both him and all his proud company.

4 When he beheld our powerful fleet,
     Sailing along in their glory and pride,
   He was amazed at their valour and fame,
     Then to his warlike command[er]s he cry'd.

5 These were the words of the old emperor:
     Pray who is this that is sailing to me?
   If he be king that weareth a crown,
     Yet I am a better man than he.

6 'It is not a king, nor lord of a crown,
     Which now to the seas with his navy is come,
   But the young Earl of Essex, the Queen's
          lieutenant,
     Who fears no foes in Christendom.'

7 'Oh! is that lord then come to the seas?
     Let us tack about and be steering away;
   I have heard so much of his father before
     That I will not fight with young Essex to-
          day.'

8 O then bespoke the emperor's son,
     As they were tacking and steering away,
   'Give me, royal father, this navy of s[h]ips,
     And I will go fight with Essex today.'

9 'Take them with all my heart, loving son,
     Most of them are of a capital size;
   But should he do as his father has done,
     Farewel thine honour and mine likewise.'

10 With cannons hot and thundering shot,
     These two gallants fought on the main,
   And as it was young Essex's lot,
     The emperor's son by him was taen.

11 'Give me my son,' the emperor cry'd,
     'Who you this day have taken from
          me,
   And I'll give to the[e] three keys of gold,
     The one shall be of High Germany.'

12 'I care not for thy three keys of gold,
     Which thou hast profferd to set him
          free,
   But thy son he shall to England sail,
     And go before the queen with me.'

13 'Then have I fifty good ships of the best,
     As good as ever were sent to the sea,
   And eer my son into England sail,
     They shall go all for good company.'

14 They had not fought this famous battle,
     They had not fought it hours three,
   But some lost legs, and some lost arms,
     And some lay tumbling in the sea.

15 Essex he got this battle likewise,
     Tho 't was the hotest that ever was seen ;
   Home he returnd with a wonderful prize,
     And brought the emperor's son to the queen.

16 O then bespoke the prentices all,
     Living in London, both proper and tall,
   In a kind letter, sent straight to the queen,
     For Essex's sake they would fight all.

B

Kinloch MSS, I, 113.   From Mary Barr, June, 1827.

1 ' 'T IS, old England, old England, I bid thee
     adieu,
   The drums and the trumpets command me
     frae shore ;
   And you lusty fellows, both valiant and true,
     Will you venture with me where loud can-
     nons roar ? '

2 ' O Billy, O Billy, talk not of the seas,
     But stay at home with me on the shore ;
   I 'll do my endeavour thy fancy to please,
     And there 's others to go where loud can-
     nons roar.'

3 ' O Nelly, O Nelly, I must to the seas,
     For there is no gold to be had upon shore ;
   There 's honour, and gold, and riches likewise,
     To the man that doth die where loud can-
     nons roar.'

4 ' Remember the winds, love, remember the
     waves,
   Remember the dangers that are upon seas ;
   Remember there is neither coffin nor grave
     To the man that doth die where loud can-
     nons roar.'

5 ' Remember old Benbow, and think on his
     blows ;
   Remember the dangers he felt upon seas ;
   He lost both his legs by one shot of his foes ;
     He lost his sweet life, yet his honour 's the
     more.'

6 ' Remember proud Shawfield, that honoured
     knight,
   Who came with his navy to the Spanish
     shore ;
   At the rock of Salem his life took a flight,
     And with him there died some hundreds
     more.'

7 ' Our queen she has builded a navy of ships,
     And they are arrayed all right gloriously ;
   With top and top-gallant, with captain, lieu-
     tenant,
   Some fifty, some sixty, brass pieces and
     three.'

8 ' Well, since you 'll go, may my blessing ad-
     vance,
     And carry you safely from Flanders to
     Spain ;
   And when you 've conquered that tyrant in
     France,
     Then my blessing return you to old England
     again.'

9 They had not sailed one hour upon sea,
     Not one hour passing days two or three,
   Till up came the bold emperour,
     The bold emperour of High Germanie.

10 ' O who is this ? ' the bold emperour cries,
     ' Who is this that comes sailing to me ?
   I 'm sure he 's a knight, or a king of crown,
     Or I 'm sure I am a far better fellow than
     he.'

11 ' I am neither a knight, nor a king of a
     crown,
     But here, with my navy, on board I am
     come ;
   For I am Lord Essex, the Queen's lieutenant,
     Who never feard foe in all Christendom.'

12 Out and spoke the bold emperour's son,
     All as they were mounting and hyeing
     away ;
   ' O father, lend me your navy of ships,
     And I 'll go fight with Lord Essex today.'

13 ' O son, I 'll lend thee my navy of ships,
     And they are all of a capable size ;
   But if he be as good as his old father was,
     Adieu to your honour, and mine likewise.'

14 O they have fought on at a terrible rate,
　　　Until it drew nigh to the cool of the day,
　　And as it fell in young Essex's lot,
　　　The bold emperour's son he's taen prisoner
　　　　away.

15 'O give me my son,' the bold emperour cried,
　　　'O give me my son thou hast taken from
　　　　me,
　　And you shall have three keys of gold,
　　　And one of them opens High Germanie.'

16 'What value I thy three keys of gold,
　　　Or any proud offer thou canst give to me?
　　For up to old England thy son he must go,
　　　And stand before our queen's high majesty.'

17 ''T is I have fifteen ships of the best,
　　　And other fifteen distant on sea;

Since up to old England my son he must go,
　　　Then we'll all go together for good compa-
　　　nie.'

A. a. Queen Elizabeth's Champion, or, Great
　　　Britain's Glory, Being a victory obtained by
　　　the young Earl of Essex over the old em-
　　　peror of Germany by a fight at sea in which
　　　he took the emperor's son and brought him
　　　a prisoner to Queen Elizabeth.

b *omits* Being *after* Glory *and* a *before* prisoner.

a. *Burden* ran do re *in second line after stanza*
　　　1. tandato *in first line after stanza* 2.
　　　Rederer, *after* 7.   Raderer two *for* Raderer
　　　in second line after 9.
　　　1^4. years. 8^1. Oh.

b. 1^2. gallant good. 1^4. for this.
　　　4^4. commanders. 5^2. Praying. 5^3. be a.
　　　14^2. hours but.

289

THE MERMAID

A. 'The Seamen's Distress,' the second piece in The
Glasgow Lasses Garland, British Museum, 11621. c.
3 (68). "Newcastle, 1765?"

B. a. 'The stormy winds do blow,' Chappell's Popular Music of the Olden Time, p. 742. b. The same,
p. 743. c. Notes and Queries, 6th Series, VII, 276.

C. Communicated by Mr Chappell. Now printed in
Old English Ditties, Oxenford and Macfarren, 'The
Mermaid,' I, 206.

D. 'The Mermaid.' a. Long, Dictionary of the Isle of
Wight Dialect, 1886, p. 42. b. Broadside, H. Such,
177 Union St., Boro'.

E. a. Motherwell's MS., p. 145. b. 'The Bonnie
Mermaid,' Motherwell's Minstrelsy, Appendix, p.
xxiii, No XXX, one stanza.

F. 'Greenland,' Kinloch MSS, VII, 245.

THIS is the ballad referred to under 'Sir
Patrick Spens,' II, 19. It is still common as
a broadside.

E a 6 has taken a burlesque turn. It is
scarcely worth while to attempt to account
for the vagaries of F, in which 'the kemp o
the ship' takes the place of the mermaid, and
the kaim and glass are exchanged for the
bottle and glass. The first stanza of F may
not belong here, or possibly (but not probably)

a voyage to Greenland may have been lost
from the other copies.

In B, C, D, the ship sails on Friday, against
all good rules.

'The Sailor's Caution,' the third piece in
The Sailing Trade, Glasgow, Printed by J.
and M. Robertson, Saltmarket, 1801, begins
like A, has a stanza (the fifth) representing
A 4, 5, and concludes thus, after a stanza (the
sixth) resembling A 3:

The mermaid on the rock doth sit,
  With comb and glass in hand :
' Cheer up, cheer up, bold mariners,
  You are not far from land.

' So now cheer up, bold mariners,
  Or smother in the deep ;

All this I do for a sailor's sake,
  Whilst losing of my sleep.

' Here is a token, bold mariners,
  A token of good will,
And if ever that you come this way,
  ' Tis here you 'll find me still.'
      British Museum, 11621. b. 13 (15).

<hr>

A

The Glasgow Lasses Garland, the second piece, British Museum, 11621. c. 3 (68). " Newcastle, 1765 ? "

1 As we lay musing in our beds,
    So well and so warm at ease,
  I thought upon those lodging-beds
    Poor seamen have at seas.

2 Last Easter day, in the morning fair,
    We was not far from land,
  Where we spied a mermaid on the rock,
    With comb and glass in hand.

3 The first came up the mate of our ship,
    With lead and line in hand,
  To sound and see how deep we was
    From any rock or sand.

4 The next came up the boatswain of our ship,
    With courage stout and bold :
  ' Stand fast, stand fast, my brave lively lads,
    Stand fast, my brave hearts of gold ! '

5 Our gallant ship is gone to wreck,
    Which was so lately trimmd ;
  The raging seas has sprung a leak,
    And the salt water does run in.

6 Our gold and silver, and all our cloths,
    And all that ever we had,
  We forced was to heave them overboard,
    Thinking our lives to save.

7 In all, the number that was on board
    Was five hundred and sixty-four,
  And all that ever came alive on shore
    There was but poor ninety-five.

8 The first bespoke the captain of our ship,
    And a well-spoke man was he ;
  ' I have a wife in fair Plymouth town,
    And a widow I fear she must be.'

9 The next bespoke the mate of our ship,
    And a well-bespoke man was he ;
  ' I have a wife in fair Portsmouth,
    And a widow I fear she must be.'

10 The next bespoke the boatswain of our ship,
    And a well-bespoke man was he ;
  ' I have a wife in fair Exeter,
    And a widow I fear she must be.'

11 The next bespoke the little cabbin-boy,
    And a well-bespoke boy was he ;
  ' I am as sorry for my mother dear
    As you are for your wives all three.

12 ' Last night, when the moon shin'd bright,
    My mother had sons five,
  But now she may look in the salt seas
    And find but one alive.'

13 ' Call a boat, call a boat, you little Plymouth
      boys,
    Don't you hear how the trumpet[s] sound ?
  [For] the want of our boat our gallant ship is
      lost,
    And the most of our merry men is drownd.'

14 Whilst the raging seas do roar,
    And the lofty winds do blow,
  And we poor seamen do lie on the top,
    Whilst the landmen lies below.

B

a. Chappell's Popular Music of the Olden Time, p. 742.
b. The same, p. 743, one stanza and the burden, contributed
by Mr Charles Sloman, in 1840.   c. Notes and Queries, 6th
Series, VII, 276, communicated from memory by Mr Thomas
Bayne, Helensburgh, N. B., stanzas 1, 6.

1 ONE Friday morn when we set sail,
   Not very far from land,
  We there did espy a fair pretty maid
    With a comb and a glass in her hand, her
      hand, her hand,
    With a comb and a glass in her hand.
     While the raging seas did roar,
      And the stormy winds did blow,
     While we jolly sailor-boys were up into
      the top,
      And the land-lubbers lying down below,
       below, below,
      And the land-lubbers lying down below.

2 Then up starts the captain of our gallant ship,
   And a brave young man was he:
  ' I 've a wife and a child in fair Bristol town,
   But a widow I fear she will be.'
    For the raging seas, etc.

3 Then up starts the mate of our gallant ship,
   And a bold young man was he:
  ' Oh! I have a wife in fair Portsmouth town,
   But a widow I fear she will be.'
    For the raging seas, etc.

4 Then up starts the cook of our gallant ship,
   And a gruff old soul was he:
  ' Oh! I have a wife in fair Plymouth town,
   But a widow I fear she will be.'

5 And then up spoke the little cabin-boy,
   And a pretty little boy was he;
  ' Oh! I am more grievd for my daddy and my
    mammy
   Than you for your wives all three.'

6 Then three times round went our gallant
    ship,
   And three times round went she;
  For the want of a life-boat they all went
    down,
   And she sank to the bottom of the sea.

C

Communicated by Mr W. Chappell, as noted down by
him from the singing of men dressed as sailors, on Tower
Hill.   Subsequently printed, with a few variations, in Old
English Ditties, Oxenford and Macfarren, I, 206.

1 ONE Friday morn as we 'd set sail,
   And our ship not far from land,
  We there did espy a fair mermaid,
    With a comb and a glass in her hand, her
      hand, her hand,
    With a comb and a glass in her hand.
     While the raging seas did roar,
      And the stormy winds did blow,
     And we jolly sailor-boys were up, up aloft,
      And the landsmen were lying down be-
      low,
      And the landlubbers all down below,
      below, below,
      And the landlubbers all down below.

2 Then up spoke the captain of our gallant
    ship,
   Who at once did our peril see;
  I have married a wife in fair London town,
   And tonight she a widow will be.'

3 And then up spoke the litel cabin-boy,
   And a fair-haired boy was he;
  ' I 've a father and mother in fair Portsmouth
    town,
   And this night she will weep for me.'

4 Now three times round goes our gallant
    ship,
   And three times round went she;
  For the want of a life-boat they all were
    drownd,
   As she went to the bottom of the sea.

D

a. Long, A Dictionary of the Isle of Wight Dialect, London, 1886, p. 142. b. H. Such, 177 Union St., Boro'.

1 'T WAS a Friday morning when we set sail,
　　And our ship was not far from land,
　　When there we spied a fair pretty maid,
　　　With a comb and a glass in her hand.
　　　　Oh, the raging seas they did roar,
　　　　　And the stormy winds they did blow,
　　　　While we poor sailor-boys were all up aloft,
　　　　And the land-lubbers lying down below,
　　　　　below, below,
　　　　And the land-lubbers lying down below.

2 Then up spoke the captain of our gallant ship,
　　And a mariner good was he ;
　'I have married a wife in fair London town,
　　And this night a widow she will be.'

3 Then up spoke the cabin-boy of our gallant
　　ship,
　　And a brave little boy was he ;
　'I 've a father and a mother in old Portsmouth
　　town,
　　And this night they will both weep for me.'

4 Then up spoke a seaman of our gallant ship,
　　And a well-spoken man was he ;
　'For want of a long-boat we shall all be
　　drowned,
　　And shall sink to the bottom of the sea.'

5 Then three times round went that gallant ship,
　　And down like a stone sank she ;
　　The moon shone bright, and the stars gave
　　　their light,
　　But they were all at the bottom of the sea.

E

a. Motherwell's MS., p. 145. b. Motherwell's Minstrelsy, Appendix, p. xxiii, No XXX, the first stanza.

1 UP and spoke the bonny mermaid,
　　Wi the comb and the glass in her hand ;
　Says, Cheer up your hearts, my mariners all,
　　You are not very far from the land.
　　　And the raging seas do foam, foam,
　　　　And the stormy winds do blow,
　　　While we poor sailors must mount to the
　　　　top,
　　　When the landsmen they lye low.

2 Out and spoke the captain of our ship,
　　And a fine little man was he ;
　'O I 've a wife in fair London town,
　　And a widow this night she shall be.'

3 Out and spoke the mate of our ship,
　　And a tight little man was he ;
　'O I 've a wife in Dublin city,
　　And a widow this night she shall be.'

4 Out and spoke our second mate,
　　And a clever little man was he ;
　'Oh I have a wife in Greenock town,
　　And a widow this night she shall be.'

5 Out and spoke our little prentice boy,
　　And a fine little boy was he ;
　'Oh I am sorry for my mother,' he said,
　　'As you are for your wives all three.'

6 Out and spoke the cook of our ship,
　　And a rusty old dog was he ;
　Says, I am as sorry for my pats and my pans
　　As you are for your wives all three.

Kinloch MSS, VII, 245. From the recitation of a little boy from Glasgow, who sang it in Grove St., Edinburgh, July, 1826.

1 GREENLAND, Greenland, is a bonny, bonny
　　place,
　　Whare there 's neither grief nor flowr,

Whare there 's neither grief nor tier to be seen,
　　But hills and frost and snow.

2 Up starts the kemp o the ship,
　　Wi a psalm-book in his hand :
　'Swoom away, swoom away, my merry old
　　boys,
　　For you 'll never see dry land.'

3 Up starts the gaucy cook,
    And a weil gaucy cook was he;
    ' I wad na gie aw my pans and my kettles
        For aw the lords in the sea.'

4 Up starts the kemp o the ship,
    Wi a bottle and a glass intil his hand;

A. 6^2. *Qy*, that ever we did have?
      $7^{3,4}$. *Qy*, And in all, there was but poor ninety-
          five
          That ever came alive on shore. ?
      14^1. Whilst we in the raging seas do blow.
      14^2. And there lofty minds.
B. b. 2^1. Then up spoke.
      $2^{3,4}$. I have sixty gallant seamen aboard of my
          ship,
          But none half so gallant as he, as he,
            as he,
          But there's none half so gallant as he.
      Burden :
        While the vivid lightnings flash,
        And the stormy winds do blow,
        While we poor seamen are up, up aloft,
        And the landsmen are all down below,
          below, below,
        And the landsmen are all down below.
  c. 1^2. And our ship not far.
     6^3. we all. 6^4. And sank.
C. 1^3. *Var.*, a fair pretty maid.
    In Old English Ditties, *etc.* (*perhaps Oxen-
        ford's changes*) :
    1^1. when we set. 1^3. a fair pretty maid.
    2^4. this night. 3^4. they will.
    4^1. Then three times round went.
    4^3. they both went down. 4^4. As she sunk to.
    Burden :
    4. And the land-lubbers lying down below, be-
        low, below.
    5. And the landsmen were all down below.
    6. *Wanting.*
D. b. 1 On Friday morning as we set sail,
      It was not far from land,
      O there I espy'd a fair pretty girl,
      With the comb and the glass in her hand.
      O the stormy winds they did blow,
        And the raging seas did roar,
      While we poor sailors go up to the top,
        And the land-lubbers lie down below.

'Swoom away, swoom away, my merry old
    sailors,
    For you'll never see dry land.'

5 O the raging seas they row, row, row,
    The stormy winds do blow,
    As sune as he had gane up to the tap,
    As . . . . . low.

2 Then up spoke a boy of our gallant ship,
    And a well-spoken boy was he;
    ' I 've a father and mother in fair Ports-
        mouth town,
      And this night they will weep for me.'

3 Then up spoke a man of our gallant ship,
    And a well-spoken man was he;
    ' I have married a wife in fair London
        town,
      And this night a widow she shall be.'

4 Then up spoke the captain of our gallant
      ship,
    And a valiant man was he;
    ' For want of a long-boat we shall all be
        drowned,'
    So she sunk to the bottom of the sea.

5 The moon shone bright, and the stars gave
      light,
    And my mother is looking for me;
    She might look, she might weep, with
      watery eyes,
    She might look to the bottom of the sea.

*A broadside by Birt, otherwise like Such's,
adds :*

    Three times round went our gallant ship,
    And three times round went she;
    Three times round went our gallant ship,
    Then she sunk to the bottom of the sea.
    British Museum, 11621. k. 5 (167).

E. b. 1. O up and spak the bonnie mermaid,
      Wi the glass and the kaim in her hand;
    ' Reek about, reek about, ye mariners all,
      For ye're not very far from the land.'

F. 3^2. was she.

290

THE WYLIE WIFE OF THE HIE TOUN HIE

A. 'My lady ye shall be,' "Scotch Ballads, Materials for Border Minstrelsy," Thomas Wilkie's MS., p. 74, Abbotsford.

B. John Struthers, The British Minstrel, 1821, I, xxv.

C. 'The Bonnie Lass o the Hie Toun End.' Communicated by Mr David Louden, of Morham, Haddington, 1873.

D. 'The Flowers of Edinburgh,' Gibb MS., No 14, p. 57.

THIS ballad, which Motherwell pronounces to be "of some antiquity and of considerable popularity," is of the same pernicious tenor as 'The Broom o Cowdenknows,' with the aggravation of treachery. The dénoûment is similar in 'The Dainty Downby,' Herd's MSS, I, 45, printed in his Scottish Songs, 1776, II, 232, 'The Laird o the Dainty Downby,' Kinloch MSS, V, 145, and in 'The Laird o Keltie,' Kinloch MSS, I, 363, 'The Young Laird o Keltie,' III, 107, Motherwell MS., p. 21, both of one pattern, and that quite trashy.

A

"Scotch Ballads, Materials for Border Minstrelsy," No 72, Thomas Wilkie's MS., 1813–15, p. 74, Abbotsford; taken down from the recitation of a female friend, who sang it to a lively air.

1 IT fell about the Martinmas,
    When the gentlemen were drinking there wine,
    And a' the discourse that they had
    Was about the ladies they gude fine.

2 It 's up an spake a tall young man,
    The tallest o the companie;
    'The bonniest lass that I ken off
    She lives into the hee toun hee.

3 'O I would give a guinea of gold,
    A guinea and a pint of wine,
    I would give it to the hostler's wife,
    For to wile that bonny lassie in.'

4 The hostler's wife gaed down the stair,
    And she 's looked hersell round near by,
    And there she spied the bonny handsom girl,
    Coming walking down the hee town high.

5 'Come in, come in, my bonny handsom girl,
    Come speak one word with me;
    Come taste a little of our wine,
    For it 's new come out of Italie.'

6 So willillie she wil'd her up,
    And so willillie she wil'd her in,
    And so cunningly she 's locked the door,
    And she 's comd down the stair again.

7 One of them took her by the milk-white hand,
    And he 's laid her body on the ground,
    And aye she sightd, and said, Alass,
    'T is a sin to do me wrong!

8 'But since ye hae done sae muckle to me,
    And brought me to so muckle shame,
    O wad ye be so kind to me
    As to tell to me your name.'

9 'O if I tell to you my name,
    It 's a thing I never did to none;
    But I will tell to the, my dear;
    I am the Earl of Beaton's son.'

10 When two years were past and gone,
     This gentleman came walking by,
   And there he spied the bonny handsome girl,
     Coming walking down the hie town high.

11 'To whom belongs that pretty child,
     That blinks with its pretty eye?'
   'His father 's from home and has left me alone,
     And I have been at the fold milking my ky.'

12 'You lie, you lie, my bonny handsome girl,
     So loudlie I hear you lie;
   O do not you mind that happie day
     When ye was drinking the wine wi me?'

13 He 's lighted off his milk-white steed,
     He 's kissd her both cheeck and chin;
   He 's made a' the servants in Beaton castle
     To welcome this fair lady in.

B

Struthers's British Minstrel, I, xxv., from recitation.

1 It fell about the Martinmas time,
     When the nobles were drinking wine,
   And the matter of their discourse it was,
     'O the ladies they go fine:'

2 Up then spake a brave gentleman,
     The best in the companie;
   'The bonniest lass that eer I saw,
     She dwells in the hie town hie.

3 'I wad give a guinea of red gold,
     Sae wad I a pint of wine,
   To onie of the hostler-wives
     That wad wyle to me the bonnie lassie in.'

4 Up then spake the hostler's wife,
     And an ill death may she die!
   'An ye 'll gie me a guinea of gold,
     I will wyle the bonnie lassie in to thee.'

5 The hostler's wife stood on the stair-head,
     To see what she could see,
   And there she saw this fair creature,
     Coming down frae the hie town hie.

6 'Come in, come in, my bonnie, bonnie lass,
     Come in and speak with me;
   Come in and drink a glass of wine,
     That 's new come aff the raging sea.'

7 'My father 's out upon the plain,
     And I am waiting his incoming;
   And I 'm a girl so neat and trim
     That I 'm afraid of your merry men.'

8 'My merry men are all gone out,
     And they will not be in till nine,
   And, if ye would my favour win,
     Come in and drink a glass of wine.'

9 Sae cunningly she wyld her in,
     And sae cunningly she led her round,
   Till she wyld her to the room where he was,
     And she locked the door the bonnie lass
       behind.

10 First he kissd her cherry cheeks,
     And than he kissd her cherry chin,
   And than he kissd her ruby lips,
     Saying, Indeed ye 're a weel-faurd thing.

* * * * * * * *

11 'O since ye 've got your will o me,
     And brought me unto public shame,
   I pray, kind sir, ye 'll marry me,
     Or that ye 'll tell me what 's your name.'

12 'If I tell my name to you, bonnie lassie,
     It 's mair than ever I telld ane;
   But I will tell to you, bonnie lassie;
     I am an earl's second son.

13 'I am an earl's second son,
     My father has more children than me;
   My eldest brother he heirs the land,
     And my father he sent me to the sea.'

14 He put his hand into his pocket,
     And he gave her sixty guineas and three,
   Saying, Fare thee weel, my lovely young
       creature,
     Ye 'll never get mair of me.

15 As she went down through Edinburgh streets,
     The bonnie bells as they did ring,
   'Farewell, fareweel, my bonnie, bonnie lassie,
     Ye 've got the clod that winna cling.'

* * * * * * * *

16 He hadna been ae week at the sea,
     Not a week but only five,
   Till the king made him a captain sae brave,
     And he made the bonnie lassie his wife.

C

Communicated, February, 1873, by Mr David Louden, of Morham, Haddington, as recited by Mrs Richard Dodds, Morham, Loanhead, " aged over seventy."

1 In Edinburgh, on a summer evening,
   Our gentlemen sat drinking wine,
   And every one to the window went,
     To view the ladies, they went so fine.

2 They drank the wine, and they spilt the beer,
   So merrily as the reel went round,
   And a' the healths that was drucken there
     Was to the bonnie lass o the hie toun end.

3 Up then spoke a young squire's son,
   And as he spoke it all alone ;
   ' Oh, I would give a guinea of gold,
   And so would I a pint of wine,
   And I would make them their licence free
     That would welcome this bonnie lassie in.'

4 The ostler's wife, on hearin this,
   So nimbly down the stairs she ran,
   And the first toun's-body that she met
     Was the bonnie lass o the hie toun end.

5 ' Mistress, ye maun gang wi me
   And get a cup o oor claret wine ;
   It 's new come oer the ragin sea,
     Awat it is baith gude and fine.'

6 ' To gang wi you I daurna stay,
   My mither 's wearyin for me in ;

I am so beautiful and fine
   I am a prey to all young men.'

7 Wi sattin slippers on her feet,
   So nimbly up the stair she ran,
   And wha so ready as this young squire
     To welcome the bonny lassie in.

8 He ['s] taen her by the milk-white hand,
   He 's gently led her through the room,
   And aye she sighed, and aye she said,
     It would be a pity to do me wrong.

9 ' Now, since you 've taken your will o me,
   I pray, kind sir, tell me your name ; '
   ' Oh yes, my dear, indeed,' he said
     ' But it 's more than I ever did to one.

10 ' I am a squire and a squire's son,
   My faither has fifty ploughs o land,
   And I 'm a man in the militrie,
     And I must away and rank up my men.

11 ' And Jamie Lumsdaine is my name,
   From the North Countrie, love, I really came.'

12 About a twelvemonth after that,
   He sent a letter owre the main,
   And muckle writin was therein,
     To the bonnie lass o the hie toun end.

13 About a twelvemonth after that,
   He himsel cam owre the main ;
   He made her Duchess o Douglas Dale,
     And to him she 's had a fine young son.

D

Gibb MS., No 14, p. 57. From the recitation of Eppie Fraser, daughter of a tramp, and unable to read, about 1840.

1 All the soldiers in Edinburgh town
   Were sitting drinking at the wine,
   An all the toasts that were among them
     Was a health to the lassie that goes sae fine.

2 Up then spake an officier,
   The bravest in the company ;
   ' To every one I will give a guinea,
   A guinea and a pint of wine,
   To the ostler's wife I wald double it a',
     If she 'd entice that young lassie in.'

3 The old wife tripped down the stair,
   And aye she said, ' A good morrow, dame ! '
   And aye she said, an the maid replied,
     ' What is your will wi me, madam ? '

4 ' It 's not to do you any harm,
   Or yet your body any ill,
   But, if you would my favour gain,
     Come up an taste one glass of wine.'

5 ' My father stands on the stair-head,
   Just lookin for me to come in ;
   I am so proper and so tall
     I 'm much afraid of your merry men.'

6 'My merry men, they are all gone out,
  An they will not be in till dine ;
So, if you would my favour gain,
  Come up an taste a glass of wine.'

7 The fair maid tripped up the stair,
  The old wife bolted the door behind ;
He 's tane her in his arms twa,
  Says, O but ye are a bonny thing !

8 Twenty times he kissed her cheek,
  An twenty times her bonny chin,
An twenty times her ruby lips :
  ' O but ye are a bonny thing ! '

*   *   *   *   *   *   *

9 ' Noo, since ye 've got your wills o me,
  What is your name, I pray you tell ;
.   .   .   .
    .   .   .   . where you dwell.'

10 .   .   .   .
    ' My eldest brother, he heirs the land ;
I was forced to be a highwayman,
  Or else a soldier, as I am.'

11 An aye the lassie she sat an grat,
  An aye thae words spak them atween,
An aye the lassie she sat an grat,
  And cursed the auld wife that brocht her in.

12 They had na been in Edinburgh
  A month, a month but only nine,

When they have got the royal commission
  For to march to Aberdeen.

13 An aye the lassie she sat an grat,
  An aye thae words spak them atween,
An aye the lassie she sat an grat,
  And cursed the auld wife that brocht her in.

14 They had na been in Aberdeen
  A month, a month but only one,
When he got on the captain's coat,
  An made her lady o his land.

15 An aye the lassie she sat an sang,
  An aye thae words spak them atween,
An aye the lassie she sat an sang,
  An hersed the auld wife that brocht her in.

A. 1⁴. *Qy*, gade ?
   3¹. *Written* and af pint gold, *with* pint *struck
       out (anticipation of the next line).*
   5⁴. now come.
B. *Motherwell, Minstrelsy,* p. xci, *supplies, from
   a recited version, after* 15 :
   Aye she sat, and aye she grat,
     And kaimd her yellow hair,
   And aye she cursd the hostler's wife,
     That wysit her in at the door.
   And after 16 :
   Aye she sat, and aye she sang,
     And kaimd her yellow hair,
   And aye she blessd the hostler's wife,
     That wysit her in at the door.
Compare D 13, 15.

291

CHILD OWLET

' Childe Owlet,' Buchan's Ballads of the North of Scotland, I, 27 ; Motherwell's MS., p. 572.

LADY ERSKINE invites Child Owlet to be her paramour. Child Owlet revolts at the suggestion ; he is sister's son to Lord Ronald. The lady cuts herself with a penknife sufficiently to draw blood ; Lord Ronald hears her moaning, comes in, and asks what blood this is ; his wife gives him to understand that

Child Owlet has offered her violence. A council is held upon the case, and the youth is condemned to be torn by four horses. There was not a twig or a rush on the moor that was not dropping with his blood.

The chain of gold in the first stanza and the penknife below the bed in the fourth have a false ring, and the story is of the tritest. The ballad seems at best to be a late one, and is perhaps mere imitation, but, for an imitation, the last two stanzas are unusually successful.

1 LADY ERSKINE sits in her chamber,
  Sewing at her silken seam,
A chain of gold for Childe Owlet,
  As he goes out and in.

2 But it fell ance upon a day
  She unto him did say,
Ye must cuckold Lord Ronald,
  For a' his lands and ley.

3 'O cease! forbid, madam,' he says,
  'That this shoud eer be done!
How would I cuckold Lord Ronald,
  And me his sister's son?'

4 Then she's ta'en out a little penknife,
  That lay below her bed,
Put it below her green stay's cord,
  Which made her body bleed.

5 Then in it came him Lord Ronald,
  Hearing his lady's moan;
'What blood is this, my dear,' he says,
  'That sparks on the fire-stone?'

6 'Young Childe Owlet, your sister's son,
  Is now gane frae my bower;
If I hadna been a good woman,
  I'd been Childe Owlet's whore.'

7 Then he has taen him Childe Owlet,
  Laid him in prison strong,
And all his men a council held
  How they woud work him wrong.

8 Some said they woud Childe Owlet hang,
  Some said they woud him burn;
Some said they woud have Childe Owlet
  Between wild horses torn.

9 'There are horses in your stables stand
  Can run right speedilie,
And ye will to your stable go,
  And wile out four for me.'

10 They put a foal to ilka foot,
  And ane to ilka hand,
And sent them down to Darling muir,
  As fast as they coud gang.

11 There was not a kow in Darling muir,
  Nor ae piece o a rind,
But drappit o Childe Owlet's blude
  And pieces o his skin.

12 There was not a kow in Darling muir,
  Nor ae piece o a rash,
But drappit o Childe Owlet's blude
  And pieces o his flesh.

292

THE WEST–COUNTRY DAMOSEL'S COMPLAINT

a. Douce Ballads, II, fol. 254 b; Roxburghe Ballads, II, 499, Ebsworth, VI, 635. b. Douce Ballads, II, 245 b.

ALSO, Crawford Ballads, No 1331, Euing, 384. All the five: Printed for P. Brooksby, at the Golden-Ball in West-Smithfield, neer the Hospital-gate. (1672–95.)

A maid entreats her lover, William, to marry her or put an end to her life. He un-feelingly bids her go to the wood and live on hips and haws. She leads this life for three months; then, exhausted with the hardship, goes to her sister's house and begs an alms of food. The sister (who is her rival, st. 18) orders her men to hunt away the wild doe,

and they drive her back to the forest, where
she lies down and dies. Sweet William comes,
stands at her head and her feet, kisses her,
gives vent to his repentance and admiration
in intense and elaborate expressions, then lies
down by her side and dies.

The first eleven stanzas are in a fairly pop-

ular tone. It will be observed that the first
and third verses rhyme in 12–24, but not in
1–11. The whole may be one man's work,
who may have thought that an elegy should
properly be more artificial, both in form and
in style, than a story, but I incline to think
that the lament is a later attachment.

1 'WHEN will you marry me, William,
　　And make me your wedded wife?
　Or take you your keen bright sword
　　And rid me out of my life.'

2 'Say no more so then, lady,
　　Say you no more then so,
　For you shall into the wild forrest,
　　And amongst the buck and doe.

3 'Where thou shalt eat of the hips and haws,
　　And the roots that are so sweet,
　And thou shalt drink of the cold water,
　　That runs underneath [thy] feet.'

4 Now she had not been in the wild forrest
　　Passing three months and a day,
　But with hunger and cold she had her fill,
　　Till she was quite worn away.

5 At last she saw a fair tyl'd-house,
　　And there she swore by the rood
　That she would to that fair tyl'd-house,
　　There for to get her some food.

6 But when she came unto the gates,
　　Aloud, aloud she cry'd,
　An alms, an alms, my own sister!
　　I ask you for no pride.

7 Her sister calld up her merry men all,
　　By one, by two, and by three,
　And bid them hunt away that wild doe,
　　As far as ere they could see.

8 They hunted her ore hill and dale,
　　And they hunted her so sore
　That they hunted her into the forrest,
　　Where her sorrows grew more and more.

9 She laid a stone all at her head,
　　And another all at her feet,

And down she lay between these two,
　　Till death had lulld her asleep.

10 When sweet Will came and stood at her head,
　　And likewise stood at her feet,
　A thousand times he kist he[r] cold lips,
　　Her body being fast asleep.

11 Yea, seaven times he stood at her feet,
　　And seaven times at her head,
　A thousand times he shook her hand,
　　Although her body was dead.

12 'Ah wretched me!' he loudly cry'd,
　　'What is it that I have done?
　O woud to the powers above I 'de dy'd,
　　When thus I left her alone!

13 'Come, come, you gentle red-breast now,
　　And prepare for us a tomb,
　Whilst unto cruel Death I bow,
　　And sing like a swan my doom.

14 'Why could I ever cruel be
　　Unto so fair a creature?
　Alas! she dy'd for love of me,
　　The loveliest she in nature!

15 'For me she left her home so fair
　　To wander in this wild grove,
　And there with sighs and pensive care
　　She ended her life for love.

16 'O constancy, in her thou 'rt lost!
　　Now let women boast no more;
　She 's fled unto the Elizium coast,
　　And with her carryd the store.

17 'O break, my heart, with sorrow filld,
　　Come, swell, you strong tides of grief!
　You that my dear love have killd,
　　Come, yield in death to me relief.

18 'Cruel her sister, was 't for me
　　That to her she was unkind?

Her husband I will never be,
But with this my love be joynd.

19 'Grim Death shall tye the marriage-bands,
Which jealousie shan't divide;
Together shall tye our cold hands,
Whilst here we lye side by side.

20 'Witness, ye groves, and chrystial streams,
How faithless I late have been,
But do repent with dying leaves
Of that my ungrateful sin;

21 'And wish a thousand times that I
Had been but to her more kind,
And not have let a virgin dye
Whose equal there 's none can find.

22 'Now heaps of sorrow press my soul;
Now, now 't is she takes her way ;
I come, my love, without controule,
Nor from thee will longer stay.'

23 With that he fetchd a heavy groan
Which rent his tender breast,
And then by her he laid him down,
When as death did give him rest.

24 Whilst mournful birds, with leavy boughs,
To them a kind burial gave,
And warbled out their love-sick vows,
Whilst they both slept in their grave.

The West-Country Damosels Complaint,
or,
The Faithful Lovers Last Farewel.
Being the relation of a young maid who pined
herself to death for the love of a young man,
who, after he had notice of it, dyed likewise
for grief.
Careless young men, by this a warning take
How you kind virgins, when they love, forsake ;
Least the same fate oretake you, and you dye
For breach of vows and infidelity.
Be kind, but swear not more then what you mean,
Least comick jests become a trajeck scean.

To the tune of Johnny Armstrong.

a. 20⁸. leaves (*so in all*) *seems doubtful, but I
can conjecture nothing better.* gleams *is
just possible.*
b. 2³. thou shalt unto. 3⁴. runs beneath thy.
11². times stood. 20⁴. that *wanting.*
22⁴. will no longer.

293

JOHN OF HAZELGREEN

A. Elizabeth Cochrane's MS., p. 126.

B. 'Jock o Hazelgreen,' Kinloch MSS, VII, 135 ; Kinloch's Ancient Scottish Ballads, p. 206.

C. 'John o Hazelgreen,' Kinloch MSS, I, 319.

D. a. 'John o Hazelgreen,' Buchan's Ballads of the North of Scotland, II, 253. **b.** 'Jock of Hazelgreen,' Chambers, Scottish Ballads, p. 319.

E. a. Fragmentary verses obtained by Mr Pringle, Kinloch MSS, I, 321. **b.** Kinloch MSS, VII, 2, one stanza.

A is found, with the doubtless accidental variation of three words, in a folio volume at Abbotsford labelled Miscellanies, article 43, having been transcribed by C. K. Sharpe for Sir W. Scott " from a 4to MS., in a female hand, written probably about one hundred years ago, sold at one Inglis's roup at the West Port, Edinburgh, now in the possession of David Laing" (that is, Elizabeth Cochrane's MS.). D b was compounded from D a and B, " omitting," says Chambers, " many of the coarser stanzas of both, and improving a few by collation with a third version which I took down from recitation, and another which has been shown to me in manuscript by Mr Kinloch " (C). D b is, after all, mainly D a with omissions ; the improvements from the recited copy (or the variations from Buchan and Kinloch) are not remarkable in amount or quality. E is given on Kinloch's authority. Alexander Campbell, when on a tour on the borders of Scotland to collect Scottish airs, is said to have received the first stanza from Mr Thomas Pringle, who derived it from his mother's singing. (Chappell, Popular Music, p. 575.) Upon this traditional stanza was built Scott's ' Jock of Hazeldean,' first printed in Campbell's Albyn's Anthology, I, 18, 1816.

A. A gentleman overhears a damsel making a moan for Sir John of Hazelgreen. After some compliment on his part, and some slight information on hers, he tells her that Hazelgreen is married ; then there is nothing for her to do, she says, but to hold her peace and die for him. The gentleman proposes that she shall let Hazelgreen go, marry his eldest son, and be made a gay lady ; she is too mean a maid for that, and, anyway, had rather die for the object of her affection. Still she allows the gentleman to take her up behind him on his horse, and to buy clothes for her at Biggar, though all the time dropping tears for Hazelgreen. After the shopping they mount again, and at last they come to the gentleman's place, when the son runs out to welcome his father. The son is young Hazelgreen, who takes the maid in his arms and kisses off the still-falling tears. The father declares that the two shall be married the next day, and the young man have the family lands.

The other versions have the same story, but the clothes are bought at Edinburgh, and the Hazelgreen estate seems to be in the neighborhood.

In a preface to C, Kinloch, following either D 5 or some foolish popular gloss, remarks that the lady is presumed to have seen young Hazelgreen only in a dream, which left so deep an impression on her mind as to cause her to fall in love with his image. To improve upon this, D 15 makes the young man also to have seen the maid in a dream.

A

Elizabeth Cochrane's MS., p. 126.

1 INTO a sweet May morning,
　　As the sun clearly shone,
I heard a propper damsell
　　Making a heavy moan ;
Making a heavy moan,
　　I marvelled what she did mean,
And it was for a gentleman,
　　Sir John of Hasillgreen.

2 ' What aileth thee now, bony maid,
　　To mourn so sore into the tide ?
O happy were the man,' he sayes,
　　' That had thee to his bride,
To ly down by his side ;
　　Then he were not to mean ; '
But still she let the tears down fall
　　For pleasant Hasillgreen.

3 ' Oh what for a man is Hasillgreen ?
　　Sweet heart, pray tell to me.'
' He is a propper gentleman,
　　Dwels in the South Countrie ;
With shoulders broad and arms long,
　　And comely to be seen ;
His hairs are like the threeds of gold,
　　My pleasant Hasilgreen.'

4 ' Now Hasilgreen is married,
　　Let all this talking be.'
' If Hasilgreen be married,
　　This day then woe to me ;
For I may sigh and sob no more,
　　But close my weeping een,
And hold my peace and cry no more,
　　But dy for Hasilgreen.'

5 ' Will you let Hasilgreen alone,
　　And go along with me ?
I 'll marry you on my eldest son,
　　Make you a gay lady.'

'Make me a gay lady?' she sayes,
  'I am a maid too mean;
I 'll rather stay at home,' she cries,
  'And dy for Hasilgreen.'

6 He takes this pretty maid him behind
  And fast he spurred the horse,
And they 're away to Bigger toun,
  Then in to Biggar Cross.
Their lodging was far sought,
  And so was it foreseen;
But still she let the tears doun fall
  For pleasant Hasillgreen.

7 He 's ta'en this pretty maid by the hand,
  And he is doun the toun;
He bought for her a pettycoat,
  Yea, and a trailing goun;
A silken kell fitt for her head,
  Laid oer with silver sheen;
But still she let the tears doun fall
  For pleasant Hasilgreen.

8 He 's taen this bony mey him behind,
  And he is to the Place,

Where there was mirth and merryness,
  And ladyes fair of face;
And ladyes fair of face,
  Right seemly to be seen,
But still she let the tears doun fall
  For pleasant Hasilgreen.

9 Young Hasilgreen ran hastilie
  To welcome his father dear;
He 's ta'en that pretty maid in his arms,
  And kist off her falling tear:
'O bony mey, now for thy sake
  I would be rent and rien;
I would give all my father's lands
  To have thee in Hasilgreen.'

10 'O hold your tongue now, son,' he sayes,
  'Let no more talking be;
This maid has come right far from home
  This day to visit thee.
This day should been your wedding-day,
  It shall be thy bridall-een,
And thou 's get all thy father's lands,
  And dwell in Hasillgreen.'

B

Kinloch's MSS, VII, 135; from the recitation of Jenny Watson, Lanark, 24 April, 1826.

1 It was on a morning early,
  Before day-licht did appear,
I heard a pretty damsel
  Making a heavy bier;
Making a heavy bier,
  I wonderd what she did mean;
But ay the tears they rappit doun,
  Crying, O Jock o Hazelgreen!

2 'O whare is this Hazelgreen, maid?
  That I may him see.'
'He is a ticht and a proper man,
  Lives in the South Cuntree.
His shoulders broad, his arms lang,
  O he 's comely to be seen!' —
But ay the tears they drappit doun
  For Jock o Hazelgreen.

3 'Will ye gang wi me, fair maid?
  . . . .

And I 'll marry ye on my son,'
  . . . .

'Afore I 'd go along wi you,
  To be married on your son,
I 'd rather choose to stay at hame,
  And die for Hazelgreen.'

4 But he has tane her up behind,
  And spurred on his horse,
Till ance he cam to Embro toun,
  And lichted at the corss.
He bought to her a petticoat,
  Besides a handsome goun;
He tied a silver belt about her waist,
  Worth thrice three hunder pund.

5 And whan he cam to Hazelyetts,
  He lichted doun therein;
Monie war the brave ladies there,
  Monie ane to be seen.
She lichted doun amang them aw,
  She seemed to be the queen;
But ay the tears they rappit doun
  For Jock o Hazelgreen.

6 Young Hazelgreen took her by the hand
   And led her out and in:
Said, Bonnie lady, for your sake,
   I could be baith rent and rien;
I wad gie aw my lands and rents,
   Tho I had kingdoms three,
If I could hae the great pleasure
   To enjoy thy fair bodie.

7 'No more of this,' his father said,
   'Of your mourning let abee;
I brought the damsel far frae hame,
   She 's thrice as wae for thee.
The morn is your bridal-day,
   The nicht is your bridal-een,
And I 'll gie you aw my lands and rents,
   My pleasing son, Hazelgreen.'

C

Kinloch MSS, I, 319.

1 As I gaed out in a May morning,
   Afore that I could see,
And there I heard a pretty fair may
   Making sweet melodie.
She was making sic melodie,
   I wonderd what she could mean;
But ay she sang and sang about
   Sweet John o Hazelgreen.

2 'O what na man is Hazelgreen?
   Fair may, pray tell to me.'
' He is a stout and a tall young man
   As in a' the South Countrie.
He is a stout and a tall young man,
   And comely to be seen;
But still O I maun weep and wail
   For John o Hazelgreen.'

3 'Hold your tongue, fair maid,' he says,
   ' And let your weeping alane;
I 'll marry you to my eldest son,
   And you shall be ca'd my dame.'

4 He has tane her on ahint him,
   And fast he spurred the steed;
For Edinbro town he there was bound,
   Where they soon came wi speed.

7 He 's tane her to the Luckenbooths,
   Coft her a braw new gown,
A handsome feather for her hat,
   And a pair o silken shoon.

8 He has tane the fair may up again,
   And fast awa rode he;
For Hazelgreen now he was bound,
   Her lodging there to be.

9 She jumped aff frae ahint him,
   As fair as any queen;
'Come down, come down, Lord John,' he says,
   'And welcome your lady hame.

10 ' It is the tall and comely youth,
   Sweet John o Hazelgreen;
If we canna see it bridal-day,
   It shall be bridal-een.'

D

a. Buchan's Ballads of the North of Scotland, II, 253.
b. Chambers, Scottish Ballads, p. 319.

1 As I went forth to take the air
   Intill an evening clear,
And there I spied a lady fair,
   Making a heavy bier;
Making a heavy bier, I say,
   But and a piteous meen,
And aye she sighd, and said, Alas,
   For John o Hazelgreen!

2 The sun was sinking in the west,
   The stars were shining clear,
When thro the thickets o the wood,
   A gentleman did appear.
Says, Who has done you the wrong, fair maid,
   And left you here alane?
Or who has kissd your lovely lips,
   That ye ca Hazelgreen?

3 'Hold your tongue, kind sir,' she said,
   ' And do not banter so;
How will ye add affliction
   Unto a lover's woe?

For none's done me the wrong,' she said,
   'Nor left me here alane;
Nor none has kissd my lovely lips,
   That I ca Hazelgreen.'

4 'Why weep ye by the tide, lady?
   Why weep ye by the tide?
How blythe and happy might he be
   Gets you to be his bride!
Gets you to be his bride, fair maid,
   And him I'll no bemean;
But when I take my words again,
   Whom call ye Hazelgreen?

5 'What like a man was Hazelgreen?
   Will ye show him to me?'
'He is a comely, proper youth
   I in my sleep did see;
Wi arms tall, and fingers small,
   He's comely to be seen;'
And aye she loot the tears down fall
   For John o Hazelgreen.

6 'If ye'll forsake young Hazelgreen,
   And go along with me,
I'll wed you to my eldest son,
   Make you a lady free.'
'It's for to wed your eldest son
   I am a maid oer mean;
I'll rather stay at home,' she says
   'And die for Hazelgreen.'

7 'If ye'll forsake young Hazelgreen,
   And go along with me,
I'll wed you to my second son,
   And your weight o gowd I'll gie.'
'It's for to wed your second son
   I am a maid oer mean;
I'll rather stay at home,' she says,
   'And die for Hazelgreen.'

8 Then he's taen out a siller comb,
   Combd down her yellow hair;
And lookëd in a diamond bright,
   To see if she were fair.
'My girl, ye do all maids surpass
   That ever I have seen;
Cheer up your heart, my lovely lass,
   And hate young Hazelgreen.'

9 'Young Hazelgreen he is my love,
   And ever mair shall be;
I'll nae forsake young Hazelgreen
   For a' the gowd ye'll gie.'

But aye she sighd, and said, Alas!
   And made a piteous meen,
And aye she loot the tears down fa
   For John o Hazelgreen.

10 He lookëd high, and lighted low,
   Set her upon his horse;
And they rode on to Edinburgh,
   To Edinburgh's own cross.
And when she in that city was,
   She lookd like ony queen:
''Tis a pity such a lovely lass
   Shoud love young Hazelgreen.'

11 'Young Hazelgreen, he is my love,
   And ever mair shall be;
I'll nae forsake young Hazelgreen
   For a' the gowd ye'll gie.'
And aye she sighd, and said, Alas!
   And made a piteous meen,
And aye she loot the tears down fa
   For John o Hazelgreen.

12 'Now hold your tongue, my well-fard maid,
   Lat a' your mourning be,
And a' endeavours I shall try
   To bring that youth to thee,
If ye'll tell me where your love stays,
   His stile and proper name.'
'He's laird o Taperbank,' she says,
   'His stile, Young Hazelgreen.'

13 Then he has coft for that lady
   A fine silk riding-gown,
Likewise he coft for that lady
   A steed, and set her on;
Wi menji feathers in her hat,
   Silk stockings and siller sheen,
And they are on to Taperbank,
   Seeking young Hazelgreen.

14 They nimbly rode along the way,
   And gently spurrd their horse,
Till they rode on to Hazelgreen,
   To Hazelgreen's own close.
Then forth he came, young Hazelgreen,
   To welcome his father free:
'You're welcome here, my father dear,
   And a' your companie.'

15 But when he lookd oer his shoulder,
   A light laugh then gae he;
Says, If I getna this lady,
   It's for her I must die.

I must confess this is the maid
    I ance saw in a dream,
A walking thro a pleasant shade,
    As fair's a cypress queen.

16 ' Now hold your tongue, young Hazelgreen,
    Lat a' your folly be ;
If ye be wae for that lady,
    She's thrice as wae for thee.
She's thrice as wae for thee, my son,
    As bitter doth complain ;

Well is she worthy o the rigs
    That lie on Hazelgreen.'

17 He's taen her in his arms twa,
    Led her thro bower and ha :
' Cheer up your heart, my dearest dear,
    Ye're flower out-oer them a'.
This night shall be our wedding-een,
    The morn we'll say, Amen ;
Ye'se never mair hae cause to mourn,
    Ye're lady o Hazelgreen.'

E

a. "Got in the South County by Mr Pringle : " Kinloch's
MSS, I, 321. b. Kinloch's MSS, VII, 2.

1 ' WHY weep ye by the tide, ladye ?
    Why weep ye by the tide ?
I'll wed ye to my youngest son,
    And ye sall be his bride.
And ye sall be his bride, ladye,
    Sae comely to be seen ; '

But aye she loot the tears down fa
    For John o Hazelgreen.

2 ' O whaten a man is Hazelgreen ?
    I pray thee tell to me.'
' O there's not a handsomer gentleman
    In a' the South Countrie.
His arms are long, his shoulders broad,
    Sae comely to be seen ! '
And aye she loot the tears down fa
    For John o Hazelgreen.

A. 1⁵. she meant.

Sharpe's transcript reads : 1¹. In *for* Into.
    5². come *for* go. 8⁶. Most *for* Right.

B. 5². thereat ; *changed to* therein *in printing.*
    The line is run through in pencil.

    6⁴. raving. *Cf.* A 9⁶.

    Kinloch made some changes in printing.

C. *Written throughout in stanzas of four verses.*

D. b. *Since Chambers in some measure adjusted
    phraseology with a view to " literary "
    effect, it is impossible to make out which
    of the variations in his ballad came from
    the copy which he took down from recita-
    tion. Upon extracting all his variations,
    they have not turned out to be important.
    A few, which seem the most likely to
    have belonged to his recited copy, are sub-
    joined.*
    1³. I spied a lady in a wood.
    2⁴. An auld knicht.
    7³,⁵. youngest *for* second.

10⁵⁻⁸. And he has coft her silken claes
    Garred her look like a queen :
' Ye surely now will sick nae mair
    For Jock o Hazelgreen.'

13⁷. And they have ridden far athort.

After 15. For her sake I did vow a vow
    I neer should wed but she ;
Should this fair lady cruel prove,
    I'll lay me doun and dee.

16³,⁴,⁵. sick *for* wae.

16⁷,⁸. And a' she wants to heal her woe
    Is Jock o Hazelgreen.

17⁴. Ye're lady ower.

E. b. 2. ' What like a man is Haselgreen ?
    Lady, tell to me.'
' He's a handsome, proper youth
    As ever my eyes did see.
With shoulders broad and arms long,
    Most comely to be seen ; '
And still she lout the tears doun fa
    For Jock of Haselgreen.

294

DUGALL QUIN

'Dugall Quin,' The Old Lady's MS. Collection, No 27.

In this little ballad, which has barely story enough to be so called, Dugald Quin, a Highlander, who seems to give himself out as a man in very humble circumstances, induces Lizzie Menzies, a young lady who appears to have nine maids at her command, to follow him, regardless of her father's opposition. She cannot resist his merry winking eyes. After she has cast in her lot with his, he promises her nine mills (to match the nine maids), and to make her lady of Garlogie. The old lady minutes at the end of her copy that "it was the Marquis of Huntly."

One version of 'Rob Roy,' No 225, I, 8, has a stanza like 2.

'What think ye o my coal-black hair,
But and my twinkling een, lady,

A little bonnet on my head,
And cocket up aboon, lady?'

I suppose the Farie of 6^2, 9^2, to stand for a locality on the way north to Boggie (Strathbogie); I cannot, however, identify the place. 'Tempeng chiss of farie,' 6^4, 9^4, 10^4, may be a tempting fairy treasure. 'Chis' is Gaelic for *tribute*, but I am at present unable, making whatever allowance for the capricious spelling of the manuscript, to suggest any satisfying explanation of this important phrase.

Sir Walter Scott makes this note: "How the devil came Dugald Gunn [so he chooses to read Quin] to be identified with the Marquis of Huntly? I never saw the song before; it has some spunk in it." Sharpe's Ballad Book, ed. 1880, p. 154.

---

1 Dugall Quin came to the toun,
   An he's ben lang awaa,
   An he is one to Lissie's bed,
   Tartan, trues, an a'.

2 'Hou wad ye leak me, Lisie,' he says,
   'Gin that I war yer ain,
   We raged cot apon my back,
   An singel-soled sheen,
   A littel we bonnet on my head,
   An tua merry wenking ean?'

3 'Well wad I leak ye, Dugall,' she says,
   'Gin that ye war my ain,
   We ragged coat upon yer back,
   An singel-soled sheen,
   A littel we bonnet on yer head,
   An tua merry wenking eyn.

4 'Hou wad ye leak me, Dugall,' she says,
   'Gin I wer yer ain,
   We silken sneed upon my head,
   An gold fann in my hand,
   An madins ning, a' clead in green,
   To be att my comand?'

5 'Well wad I leak ye, Lisie,' he says,
   'Gin ye wer my ain,
   We silken sneed upon yer head,
   An a goud fan in yer hand,
   An madins nine, a' clad in green,
   To be att yer command.

6 'Follou me nou, Lisie,' he says,
   'Follou me throu Farie,
   An reap the boddoms of my pakets,
   An ye'll gett tempeng chiss of farei.'

7 Outspak her father, says,
    Lissie, I widna wish ye,
For gin ye gay we this young man
    They will say I ha bat lost ye.

8 'O had yer toung, my father dear,
    For a' that winne brake me ;
For I will gaa we this young man,
    Since it 's his will to take me.'

9 'Follou me nou, Lissë,' he says,
    'An follou me throu Farie,
An reap the boddom of my poket,
    An ye 'll gett tempeng chess of farie.'

10 'Wea matt worth yer well-fared face,
    Alas that ever I saa ye !

The first an thing that ever ye gaa to me
    Was the tempen chess of farie.'

11 Dugall Quin read doun the toun,
    Upon Dumfarling's horses,
An Lisie Meanes folloued him,
    For a' her father's forces.

12 'Follou me nou, Lisie,' he says,
    'An follou me our Boggie ;
I ill make ye lady of ning mills,
    An lady of bonny Garlogë.'

13 She has folloued her trou-love
    [An folloued him] our Boggie,
An she has marred Dugall Quin,
    An lives belou Strathbogy.

————•————

2⁵. bomnet. 4⁵, 12³. ning : *a frequent spelling of the old lady's, conceived, perhaps,
as* nign. *We have* nine *in* 5⁵.

12³. ill ; *MS.* aill.
Note at the end : it was the markes of
Huntly.

———————————————

295

THE BROWN GIRL

A. 'The bonny Brown Girl,' 'The Brown Girl,' The
Brown Girl's Garland, British Museum, 11621. c. 3
(10).

B. As lately taken down in Devon by Rev. S. Baring
Gould.

————•————

A YOUNG man who has been attached to a
girl sends her word by letter that he cannot
fancy her because she is so brown (he has left
her for another maid in B). She sends a disdainful reply. He writes again that he is dan-
gerously ill (he is love-sick in B), and begs
her come to him quickly and give him back
his faith. She takes her time in going, and
when she comes to the sick man's bedside,
cannot stand for laughing. She has, however,
brought a white wand with her, which she
strokes on his breast, in sign that she gives
him back the faith which he had given her.
But as to forgetting and forgiving, that she
will never do ; she will dance upon his grave.

This little ballad recalls ' Lord Thomas and
Fair Annet ' (' Lord Thomas and Fair Ellinor,
with the downfall of the Brown Girl '), ' Sweet
William's Ghost,' ' Clerk Saunders,' ' The
Unquiet Grave,' ' Bonny Barbara Allan,' and
has something of all of them. Compare No
73 ; No 77, **A** 4, **B** 2, 9, **C** 6, 14, **D** 4, 13, **E** 6,
14 ; No 84 (for the laughing, **B** 12) ; No 69,
A 20–22, **D** 11, 14, **E** 17–20, **G** 23–25 ; No
78, **B** 2, **E** 2, **F** 2. Still it is not deliberately
and mechanically patched together (as are
some pieces in Part VIII), and in the point
of the proud and unrelenting character of the
Brown Girl it is original.

A

The Brown Girl's Garland, British Museum, 11621. c. 3 (10), n. d., before 1788.

1 'I am as brown as brown can be,
  My eyes as black as a sloe;
  I am as brisk as a nightingale,
  And as wilde as any doe.

2 'My love has sent me a love-letter,
  Not far from yonder town,
  That he could not fancy me,
  Because I was so brown.

3 'I sent him his letter back again,
  For his love I valu'd not,
  Whether that he could fancy me
  Or whether he could not.

4 'He sent me his letter back again,
  That he lay dangerous sick,

That I might then go speedily
  To give him up his faith.'

5 Now you shall hear what love she had
  Then for this love-sick man;
  She was a whole long summer's day
  In a mile a going on.

6 When she came to her love's bed-side,
  Where he lay dangerous sick,
  She could not for laughing stand
  Upright upon her feet.

7 She had a white wand all in her hand,
  And smoothd it all on his breast;
  'In faith and troth come pardon me,
  I hope your soul's at rest.

8 'I'll do as much for my true-love
  As other maidens may;
  I'll dance and sing on my love's grave
  A whole twelvemonth and a day.'

————•————

B

Taken down lately by Rev. S. Baring-Gould from a black-smith, parish of Thrushleton, Devon.

1 'I am as brown as brown can be,
  And my eyes as black as sloe;
  I am as brisk as brisk can be,
  And wild as forest doe.

2 'My love he was so high and proud,
  His fortune too so high,
  He for another fair pretty maid
  Me left and passed me by.

3 'Me did he send a love-letter,
  He sent it from the town,
  Saying no more he loved me,
  For that I was so brown.

4 'I sent his letter back again,
  Saying his love I valued not,
  Whether that he would fancy me,
  Whether that he would not.

5 'When that six months were overpassd,
  Were overpassd and gone,

Then did my lover, once so bold,
  Lie on his bed and groan.

6 'When that six months were overpassd,
  Were gone and overpassd,
  O then my lover, once so bold,
  With love was sick at last.

7 'First sent he for the doctor-man:
  'You, doctor, me must cure;
  The pains that now do torture me
  I can not long endure.'

8 'Next did he send from out the town,
  O next did send for me;
  He sent for me, the brown, brown girl
  Who once his wife should be.

9 'O neer a bit the doctor-man
  His sufferings could relieve;
  O never an one but the brown, brown girl
  Who could his life reprieve.'

10 Now you shall hear what love she had
  For this poor love-sick man,
  How all one day, a summer's day,
  She walked and never ran.

11 When that she came to his bedside,
    Where he lay sick and weak,
O then for laughing she could not stand
    Upright upon her feet.

12 'You flouted me, you scouted me,
    And many another one;
Now the reward is come at last,
    For all that you have done.'

13 The rings she took from off her hands,
    The rings by two and three:
'O take, O take these golden rings,
    By them remember me.'

14 She had a white wand in her hand,
    She strake him on the breast:
'My faith and troth I give back to thee,
    So may thy soul have rest.'

15 'Prithee,' said he, 'forget, forget,
    Prithee forget, forgive;
O grant me yet a little space,
    That I may be well and live.'

16 'O never will I forget, forgive,
    So long as I have breath;
I'll dance above your green, green grave
    Where you do lie beneath.'

A. *Heading.* The Brown Girl; to an excellent tune.
B. *From* A right merry book of Garlands. Collected by J. Bell, on the Quay, Newcastle upon Tyne. *A slip inserted after the 6th Garland bears these words:* The old garlands in these volumes [11621. c. 3, c. 4] are printed by J. White, who died in 1769, and by T. Saint, who died in 1788. . . . Letter of J. Bell.

The Brown Girl's Garland, composed of four extraordinary new songs.

The bonny Brown Girl, etc., etc.

4⁴. his Eilk.

296

WALTER LESLY

'Walter Lesly,' Buchan's Ballads of the North of Scotland, II, 139.

A LATE, but life-like and spirited ballad. Walter Lesly steals a girl, not for her beauty or blood, but for her mother's dollars, of which he has need. She is tied on to a horse, taken to an ale-house, and put to bed. Lesly, weary with hard riding, falls asleep; the girl gets up and runs over moss, moor, hill and dale, barefoot. Lesly's men pursue, but the road is full of pools and tires the men out. The girl effects her escape.

---

1 On the second of October, a Monday at noon,
    In came Walter Lesly, to see his proper one;
    He set a chair down by her side, and gently sat her by,
Says, Will ye go to Conland, this winter-time to lye?

2 He's taen a glass into his hand, inviting her to drink,
    But little knew she his meaning, or what the rogue did think;
    Nor what the rogue did think, to steal the maid away;
'Will ye go to Conland, this winter-time to lye?'

3 When they had taen a glass or two, and all
  were making merry,
  In came Geordy Lesly, and forth he did her
  carry ;
  Then upon high horseback sae hard 's he did
  her tye,
  'Will ye go to Conland, this winter-time to
  lye ? '

4 Her mother she came to the door, the saut tears
  on her cheek,
  She coudna see her daughter, it was for dust
  and reek ;
  It was for dust and reek, the swords they glancd
  sae high ;
  'And will ye go to Conland, this winter-time
  to lye ? '

5 When they came to the ale-house, the people
  there were busy ;
  A bridal-bed it was well made, and supper well
  made ready ;
  When the supper down was set, baith plum-
  pudding and pie,
  'And will ye go to Conland, this winter-time
  to lye ? '

6 When they had eaten and well drunken, and
  a' man bound for bed,
  The laddie and the lassie in ae chamber were
  laid ;
  He quickly stript her to the smock, and gently
  laid her bye,
  Says, Will ye go to Conland, this winter-time
  to lye ?

7 But Walter being weary, he fell fast asleep,
  And then the lassie thought it fit to start up
  till her feet ;
  To start up till her feet, and her petticoats to tye,
  'We 'll go no more to Conland, the winter-time
  to lye.'

8 Then over moss and over muir sae cleverly she
  ran,
  And over hill and over dale, without stockings
  or shoon ;
  The men pursued her full fast, wi mony shout
  and cry,
  Says, Will ye go to Conland, the winter-time
  to lye.

9 'Wae to the dubs o Duffus land, that eer they
  were sae deep ;
  They 've trachled a' our horsemen and gart
  our captain sleep ;
  And gart our captain sleep, and the lassie win
  away,
  And she 'll go no more to Conland, the winter-
  time to lye.'

10 'I 'd rather be in Duffus land, selling at the
  ale,
  Before I was wi Lesly, for a' his auld meal ;
  For a' his auld meal, and sae mony comes to
  buy ;
  I 'll go no more to Conland the winter-time to
  lye.

11 'I 'd rather be in Duffus land, dragging at the
  ware,
  Before I was wi Lesly, for a' his yellow hair ;
  For a' his yellow hair, and sae well 's he can
  it tye ;
  I 'll go no more to Conland, this winter-time to
  lye.'

12 It was not for her beauty, nor yet her gentle
  bluid,
  But for her mither's dollars, of them he had
  great need ;
  Of them he had great need, now he maun do
  them by,
  For she 'll go no more to Conland, this winter-
  time to lye.

Printed in stanzas of eight short lines.

297

EARL ROTHES

'Earl Rothes,' Kinloch MSS, I, 333.

———•———

LADY ANN has an adulterous connection with Earl Rothes, and her youthful brother seeks to sunder it. He offers to pay a tocher for her if she will forsake the earl's company; to keep her in his castle till she is safely brought to bed, and make her a marquis's lady; she rejects all his offers with scorn. The boy declares that when he is old enough to wear a sword he will thrust it through Earl Rothes for using his sister so badly.

———•———

1 'O EARL Rothes, an thou wert mine,
  And I were to be thy ladie,
  I wad drink at the beer, and tipple at the
      wine,
  And be my bottle with any.'

2 'Hold thy tongue, sister Ann,' he says,
  'Thy words they are too many;
  What wad ye do wi sae noble a lord,
  When he has so noble a ladie?

3 'O I'll pay you your tocher, Lady Ann,
  Both in gear and money,
  If ye'll forsake Earl Rothes's companie,
  And mind that he has a ladie.'

4 'I do not value your gold,' she says,
  'Your gear it's no sae readie;
  I'll neer forsake Earl Rothes's companie,
  And I don't gie a fig for his ladie.'

5 'I'll keep ye i the castle, Lady Ann,
  O servants ye shall hae monie;

I'll keep ye till ye're safely brocht to bed,
  And I'll mak you a marquis's ladie.'

6 'I do not value your castle,' she says,
  'Your servants are no sae readie;
  Earl Rothes will keep me till I'm brocht to
      bed,
  And he'll mak me a marquis's ladie.'

7 'Woe be to thee, Earl Rothes,' he says,
  'And the mark o the judge be upon thee,
  For the using o this poor thing sae,
  For the using my sister so badly.

8 'When I'm come to the years of a man,
  And able a sword to carry,
  I'll thrust it thro Earl Rothes' bodie
  For the using my sister sae basely.

9 'Fare thee well, Lady Ann,' he says,
  'No longer will I tarry;
  You and I will never meet again,
  Till we meet at the bonny town o Torry.'

298

YOUNG PEGGY

'Young Peggy,' Kinloch's Ancient Scottish Ballads, p. 153.

PEGGY has been seen in the garden with Jamie late in the night, for which her mother calls her to account. She does not deny the fact; she takes the blame on herself; the thing will happen again. But going to her bower, where Jamie is attending her, she tells him they must meet no more. He makes a tryst with her in the greenwood at midnight, she keeps it and goes off with her lover. Her father pursues them, but they are married before he gets to the top of the hill.

---

1 'O WHARE hae ye been, Peggy?
  O whare hae ye been?'
'I the garden amang the gilly-flowrs,
  Atween twal hours and een.'

2 'Ye've na been there your leen, Peggy,
  Ye've na been there your leen;
Your father saw you in Jamie's arms,
  Atween twal hours and een.'

3 'Tho my father saw me in Jamie's arms,
  He'll see me there again;
For I will sleep in Jamie's arms
  When his grave's growin green.'

4 'Your Jamie is a rogue, Peggy,
  Your Jamie is a loun,
For trysting out our ae dochter,
  And her sae very young.'

5 'Lay no the wyte on Jamie, mither,
  The blame a' lies on me;
For I will sleep in Jamie's arms
  When your een winna see.'

6 Now she has to her ain bouer gane;
  He was waiting there him leen:
'I'm blythe to see ye, Jamie, here,
  For we maunna meet again.'

7 She's tane the wine-glass in her hand,
  Pourd out the wine sae clear;
Says, Here's your health and mine, Jamie,
  And we maun meet na mair.

8 She has tane him in her arms twa,
  And gien him kisses five;
Says, Here's your health and mine, Jamie,
  I wish weel mote ye thrive.

9 'Your father has a bonnie cock,
  Divides the nicht and day,
And at the middle watch o the nicht
  In greenwud ye'll meet me.'

10 Whan bells war rung, and mass was sung,
  And a' men boun for bed,
She's kilted up her green claithing,
  And met Jamie in the wud.

11 Whan bells war rung, and mass was sung,
  About the hour o twa,
It's up bespak her auld father,
  Says, Peggy is awa!

12 'Ga saddle to me the black, the black,
  Ga saddle to me the grey;'
But ere they wan to the tap o the hill
  The wedding was a' bye.

299

TROOPER AND MAID

A. ' The Trooper and Fair Maid,' Buchan's Ballads of the North of Scotland, I, 230.

B. ' The Trooper,' Motherwell's MS., p. 27.

C. Jamieson's Scottish Ballads, II, 158.

A TROOPER comes to the house of his mistress in the evening and is kindly received. They pass the night together and are wakened by the trumpet. He must leave her; she follows him some way, he begging her to turn back. She asks him repeatedly when they are to meet again and marry. He answers, when cockle shells grow siller bells, when fishes fly and seas gang dry, etc.: see I, 168, 437.

There are several other ballads of a trooper and a maid (Peggy). In 'The Bonnie Lass o Fyvie,' Christie, I, 276, Murison MS., p. 50, Kinloch MS., VII, 339, Buchan MS., II, 270, 'Irish Dragoons,' Motherwell's MSS., p. 428, a captain falls in love with a Peggy and dies thereof; but in another copy, ' Pretty Peggy,' Gibb MS., No 13, p. 53, all is made to end well. A dragoon very constant and liberal to Peggy, and she very fond to him, are happily married in 'The Dragoon and Peggy,' Maidment, Scotish Ballads and Songs, 1859, p. 98, from a Glasgow copy of the date 1800. The first half of this ballad is found under the title of 'The Laird of Kellary' in Kinloch MSS, I, 359. In an English broadside which is perhaps of the first half of the seventeenth century, a married Peggy leaves her husband to follow a soldier over sea, but returns and is forgiven: ' The Soldier and Peggy,' Roxburghe collection, I, 370 (also Pepys, Euing, Douce), Chappell, The Roxburghe Ballads, II, 475. ' Peggie is over the sie with the souldier' is the title of a tune (No 95) in the Skene MSS, which date from the first quarter of the seventeenth century. A correspondent of C. K. Sharpe sent him one stanza of a Scottish ballad upon this theme:

Peggie 's gane oer the seas, a' dressed in red,
An Peggie 's come back again, beggin her bread.
The landladie looked wi the tail o her ee:
' O foul fa ye, Peggie, for leaving o me.'

There is also a ballad of a valiant trooper and a pretty Peggy who, at first inconstant, turns out a loving wife, in Pepys, IV, 40, No 37.

A is translated by Gerhard, p. 189.

A

1 One evening as a maid did walk,
  The moon was shining clearly,
    She heard a trooper at the gates,
    She thought it was her dearie.
  She 's taen his horse then by the head,
    And led him to the stable,

And gien to him baith corn and hay,
  To eat what he was able.
    Bonny lass, gin I come near you,
    Bonny lass, gin I come near you,
  I 'll gar a' your ribbons reel,
    Bonny lass, or eer I lea you.

2 She 's taen the trooper by the hand,
    And led him to the table,

And furnishd him wi bread and cheese,
　To eat what he was able.
She 's taen the wine-glass in her hand,
　Poured out the wine sae clearly ;
' Here is your health an mine,' she cried,
　' And ye 're welcome hame, my deary !

3 ' A glass o wine for gentlemen,
　And bonny lads for lasses,
And bread and cheese for cavaliers,
　And corn and hay for asses.'
Then she went but and made his bed,
　She made it like a lady,
And she coost aff her mankie gown,
　Says, Laddie, are you ready ?

4 Then he coost aff his big watch-coat,
　But and his silken beaver,
A pair o pistols frae his side,
　And he lay down beside her.
' Bonny lassie, I am wi you now,
　Bonny lassie I am wi you,
But I 'll gar a' your ribbons reel,
　Bonny lassie, ere I lea you.'

5 The trumpet sounds thro Birldale,
　Says, Men and horse, make ready ;
The drums do beat at Staneman hill,
　' Lads, leave your mam and daddie.'
The fifes did play at Cromley banks,
　' Lads, leave the lewes o Fyvie ; '
And then the trooper he got up,
　Says, Lassie, I must lea you.

6 ' Bonny lassie, I maun lea you now,
　Bonny lassie, I maun lea you ;
But if ever I come this road again,
　I will come in and see you.'

7 She 's taen her gown out-ower her arms,
　And followed him to Stirling,
And aye the trooper he did say,
　O turn ye back, my darling.
' O when will we twa meet again ?
　Or when will you me marry ? '

' When rashin rinds grow gay gowd rings,
　I winna langer tarry.'

8 ' O when will we twa meet again ?
　Or when will you me marry ? '
' When heather-knaps grow siller taps,
　I winna langer tarry.'
' O when will we twa meet again ?
　Or when will you me marry ? '
' When heather-cows grow owsen-bows,
　I winna langer tarry.'

9 ' O when will we twa meet again ?
　Or when will you me marry ? '
' When cockle-shells grow siller bells,
　I winna langer tarry.'
' O when will we twa meet again ?
　Or when will you me marry ? '
' When apple-trees grow in the seas,
　I winna langer tarry.'

10 ' O when will we twa meet again ?
　Or when will you me marry ? '
' When fishes fly, and seas gang dry,
　I winna langer tarry.'
' O when will we twa meet again ?
　Or when will you me marry ? '
' When frost and snaw shall warm us a',
　I winna langer tarry.'

11 ' Yestreen I was my daddie's dow,
　But an my mamy's dawtie ;
This night I gang wi bairn to you,
　Wae 's me that I eer saw thee ! '
' Yestreen ye were your daddie's dow,
　But an your mammie's dawtie ;
But gin ye gang wi bairn to me,
　Ye may rue that eer ye saw me.

12 ' O turn back, my bonny lass,
　And turn back, my dearie ;
For the Highland hills are ill to climb,
　And the bluidy swords woud fear ye.'

———◆———

B

Motherwell's MS., p. 27 ; from the recitation of Widow
Nicol.

1 There cam a trooper frae the West,
　And of riding he was weary ;

He rappit at and clappit at,
　In calling for his dearie.
By chance the maid was in the close,
　The moon was shining clearly,
She opened the gates and let him in,
　Says, Ye 're welcome hame, my dearie.

2 She took the horse by the bridle-reins
  And led him to the stable ;
  She gave him corn and hay to eat,
    As much as he was able.
  She up the stair and made the bed,
    She made it fit for a lady,
  Then she coost aff her petticoat,
    Said, Trooper, are ye ready ?

3 .   .   .   .

    .   .   .   .

    .   .   .   .

  'There 's bread and cheese for musqueteers,
    And corn and hay for hor[s]es,
  Sack and sugar for auld wives,
    And lads for bonnie lasses.'

4 He coost aff his gude buff coat,
    His boots, likewise his beaver,
  He drew his rapier frae his side,
    And streekit him down beside her.
  'Bonnie lass, I trew I 'm near the[e] now,
    Bonnie lass, I trew I 'm near thee,

And I 'll gar a' thy ribbons reel,
  Bonnie lassie, or I lea thee.'

5 They had but spoken little a while
    Till of speaking they were weary ;
  They slept together in each other's arms
    Till the sun was shining clearly.
  The very first sound the trumpet gave
    Was, Troopers, are ye ready ?
  Away you must to London town,
    Or else for Londonderry.

6 She took the bottle in her hand,
    The glass into the other,
  She filled it up with blood-red wine,
    Until it ran quite over.
  She drank a health to her love on the stair,
    Saying, When shall we two marry ?
  Or when shall we two meet again,
    On purpose for to marry ?

7 'O when shall we two meet again ?
    Or when shall we two marry ?'
  'When cockle-shells grow siller bells ;
    No longer must I tarry.'

C

Jamieson, Popular Ballads, II, 158, as often heard by him
in Morayshire.

1 THERE cam a trooper frae the west,
    And he 's ridden till his deary ;
  'It 's open and lat me in,' he says,
    For I am wet and weary.'

  *   *   *   *   *   *   *

2 'O whan sall we be married, love ?
    O whan sall we be married ?'

'Whan heather-cows turn owsen-bows,
    It 's then that we 'll be married.'

3 'O whan sall we be married, love ?
    O when sall we be married ?'
  'When cockle-shells turn siller bells,
    It 's then that we 'll be married.'

4 .   .   .   .

    .   .   .   .

  'Whan the sun and moon dance on the green,
    It 's then that we 'll be married.'

A. 5⁶. Lewas.   5⁸. lea you now.
B. 4³. threw ? *Motherwell*.   4⁷. gard.
C. *The verses are given incidentally in a preface
    to another ballad. Between* 1 *and* 2 : The
    kind fair one puts his horse into the stable

and takes himself to her bower, where she
gives him 'the good white bread and blood-
red wine,' and a part of her bed. In the
morning, when he proposes to depart, she
naturally enough asks [*as in st.* 2].

300

BLANCHEFLOUR AND JELLYFLORICE

'Blancheflour and Jellyflorice,' Buchan's Ballads of the North of Scotland, I, 125 ; Motherwell's MS., p. 588.

A MAID who has been some years in a lady's service aspires to something higher ; she seeks and obtains a place with a queen, 'to sew the seams of silk.' The queen warns her to keep herself from the young prince, but the pair become familiar, and the queen has her mounted on a wild horse without a bridle, expecting to dispose of her summarily in this way. But the prince takes her from the horse and declares that he will marry her within the month.

Buchan suspects that some "poetaster" has remodelled the story of the romance of Florice and Blancheflour, "modernizing it to suit the climate of his time," that is, perhaps, turning a princess into a sempstress. The only thing in the romance that is even remotely like what we find in the ballad is that Florice saves Blancheflour from the death which his father had contrived for her in order to part the lovers, and this passage does not occur in the English versions of the romance.

There is a Flemish ballad, so to call it, composed from the romance: Coussemaker, p. 177, No 51, Baecker, Chansons historiques de la Flandre, p. 121 ; Oude Liedekens in Bladeren, L. van Paemel, Gend, No 17.

1 THERE was a maid, richly arrayd,
    In robes were rare to see,
For seven years and something mair
    She servd a gay ladie.

2 But being fond o a higher place,
    In service she thought lang ;
She took her mantle her about,
    Her coffer by the band.

3 And as she walkd by the shore-side,
    As blythe 's a bird on tree,
Yet still she gaz'd her round about,
    To see what she could see.

4 At last she spied a little castle,
    That stood near by the sea ;
She spied it far and drew it near,
    To that castle went she.

5 And when she came to that castle
    She tirled at the pin,
And ready stood a little wee boy
    To lat this fair maid in.

6 'O who 's the owner of this place,
    O porter-boy, tell me ; '

' This place belongs unto a queen
    O birth and high degree.'

7 She put her hand in her pocket,
    And gae him shillings three :
' O porter, bear my message well
    Unto the queen frae me.'

8 The porter 's gane before the queen,
    Fell low down on his knee :
' Win up, win up, my porter-boy,
    What makes this courtesie ? '

9 ' I hae been porter at your yetts,
    My dame, these years full three,
But see a ladie at your yetts
    The fairest my eyes did see.'

10 ' Cast up my yetts baith wide and braid,
    Lat her come in to me,
And I 'll know by her courtesie
    Lord's daughter if she be.'

11 When she came in before the queen,
    Fell low down on her knee :
' Service frae you, my dame the queen,
    I pray you grant it me.'

12 ' If that service ye now do want,
          What station will ye be?
     Can ye card wool, or spin, fair maid,
          Or milk the cows to me? '

13 ' No, I can neither card nor spin,
          Nor cows I canno milk,
     But sit into a lady's bower
          And sew the seams o silk.'

14 ' What is your name, ye comely dame?
          Pray tell this unto me : '
     ' O Blancheflour, that is my name,
          Born in a strange countrie.'

15 ' O keep ye well frae Jellyflorice —
          My ain dear son is he —
     When other ladies get a gift,
          O that ye shall get three.'

16 It wasna tald into the bower
          Till it went thro the ha,
     That Jellyflorice and Blancheflour
          Were grown ower great witha.

17 When the queen's maids their visits paid,
          Upo the gude Yule-day,

When other ladies got horse to ride,
          She boud take foot and gae.

18 The queen she calld her stable-groom,
          To come to her right seen ;
     Says, Ye 'll take out yon wild waith steed
          And bring him to the green.

19 ' Ye 'll take the bridle frae his head,
          The lighters frae his een ;
     Ere she ride three times roun the cross,
          Her weel-days will be dune."

20 Jellyflorice his true-love spy'd
          As she rade roun the cross,
     And thrice he kissd her lovely lips,
          And took her frae her horse.

21 ' Gang to your bower, my lily-flower,
          For a' my mother's spite ;
     There 's nae other amang her maids,
          In whom I take delight.

22 ' Ye are my jewel, and only ane,
          Nane 's do you injury ;
     For ere this-day-month come and gang
          My wedded wife ye 'se be.'

301

THE QUEEN OF SCOTLAND

' The Queen of Scotland,' Buchan's Ballads of the North of Scotland, I, 46 ; Motherwell's MS., p. 577.

A QUEEN in the king's absence invites young Troy Muir to her bower and bed ; he declines, and the queen resolves to do him an ill turn. She tells him that if he will lift a stone in the garden he will find in a pit under the stone gold enough to buy him a dukedom. The next morning Troy Muir lifts the stone, and a long-starved serpent winds itself round his middle. A maid comes by and allays the serpent's rage by cutting off her pap for him.

Troy Muir is immediately released and the wound in the maid's breast heals in an hour. Troy Muir marries the maid the same day ; she bears him a son, and by heaven's grace recovers her pap thereupon.

The insipid ballad may have been rhymed from some insipid tale. Motherwell conjectured that Troy Muir stands for Triamour, but the story here has no sort of resemblance to the romance.

1 ' O TROY MUIR, my lily-flower,
          An asking I 'll ask thee ;
     Will ye come to my bigley bower
          And drink the wine wi me? '

2 ' My dame, this is too much honour
          You have conferrd on me ;
     I'm sure it 's mair than I 've deservd
          Frae sic a one as thee.'

3 'In Reekie's towers I hae a bower,
  And pictures round it set;
There is a bed that is well made,
  Where you and I shall sleep.'

4 'O God forbid,' this youth then said,
  'That ever I drie sic blame
As ever to touch the queen's bodie,
  Altho the king's frae hame.'

5 When that he had these words spoken,
  She secretly did say,
Some evil I shall work this man,
  Before that it be day.

6 Whan a' her maids were gane to bed,
  And knights were gane frae hame,
She calld upon young Troy Muir,
  To put fire in her room.

7 'An asking, asking, Troy Muir,
  An asking ye'll grant me;'
'O, if it be a lawful thing,
  My dame it's granted be.'

8 'There is a stane in yon garden,
  Nae ane lifts it for me;
But if that ye woud lift the same,
  A brave man I'll ca thee.

9 'Under yon stane there is a pit,
  Most dreary for to see,
And in it there's as much red gowd
  As buy a dukedom to thee.'

10 'O if I had ae sleep in bed,
  And saw the morning sun,
As soon's I rise and see the skies,
  Your will it shall be done.'

11 When birds did sing, and sun did rise,
  And sweetly sang the lark,
Troy Muir to the garden went,
  To work this dreary wark.

12 He's taen the stane then by a ring,
  And lifted manfullie;
A serpent that lang wanted meat
  Round Troy Muir's middle did flee.

13 'How shall I get rid o this foul beast?
  It's by it I must dee;
I never thought the queen, my friend,
  Woud work this mischief to me.'

14 But by there came a weelfaird may,
  As Troy Muir did tauk,
The serpent's furious rage to lay,
  Cut aff her fair white pap.

15 As soon as she the same had done,
  Young Troy Muir was set free,
And in ane hour the wound was heald,
  That nae mair pain had she.

16 Says Troy Muir, My lily-flower,
  Ye hae releasëd me;
But before I see another day,
  My wedded wife ye'se be.

17 He married her on that same day,
  Brought her to his ain hame;
A lovely son to him she bare,
  When full nine months were gane.

18 As heaven was pleasd, in a short time,
  To ease her first sad pain,
Sae was it pleasd, when she'd a son,
  To hae a pap again.

302

YOUNG BEARWELL

'Young Bearwell,' Buchan's Ballads of the North of Scotland, II, 75 ; Motherwell's MS., p. 456, derived from
Buchan ; Motherwell's Minstrelsy, p. 345.

———————————+———————————

THIS is one of half a dozen pieces sent
Buchan by Mr Nicol of Strichen, " who wrote
them from memory as he had learned them in
his earlier years from old people." It is also
one of not a few flimsy and unjointed ballads
found in Buchan's volumes, the like of which
is hardly to be found elsewhere, that require
a respectable voucher, such as Mr Nicol undoubtedly was, for the other five pieces communicated by him were all above suspicion,
and have a considerable value. It will not,
however, help the ballad much that it was
not palmed off on Buchan in jest or otherwise, or even if it was learned from an old
person by Mr Nicol in his youth. The intrinsic character of the ballad remains, and
old people have sometimes burdened their
memory with worthless things.

Young Bearwell and a mayor's daughter
are lovers. Seeing him coming along one day,
the lady tells him that there are such reports
in circulation about him that he will have to
sail the sea beyond Yorkisfauld, which may
be beyond Ultima Thule for aught we know.
Bearwell's life is in danger where he is, and
the lady has had the forethought to build him
a ship, in which she sends him off. By the
process of sailing both east and west and then
meeting wind from the north, he is blown to a
land where the king and court, who pass their
time mostly in playing ball, put a harp into the
hand of every stranger and invite him to stay
and play. Bearwell stays, and perhaps plays,
twelve months. During this time the lady is
so beset with suitors that she feels constrained
to apply to a young skipper named Heyvalin
to fetch her true-love back. To do this he
must sail first east, then west, and then have
a blast of north wind to blow him to the land.
All this comes to pass ; the king and court
are playing ball, but immediately put a harp
into Heyvalin's hand and urge him to stay
and play. Skipper though he be, he falls to
playing, and finds Bearwell the first man in
all the company.

" From circumstances," which do not occur
to me, Motherwell would almost be inclined
to trace this piece to a Danish source, " or it
may be an episode of some forgotten metrical
romance." It may also, and more probably,
be the effort of some amateur ballad-monger
in northern Scotland whose imagination was
unequal to the finishing of the inane story
which he had undertaken.

———————————+———————————

1 WHEN two lovers love each other well,
    Great sin it were them to twinn ;
  And this I speak from Young Bearwell ;
    He loved a lady young,
  The Mayor's daughter of Birktoun-brae,
    That lovely, leesome thing.

2 One day when she was looking out,
    When washing her milk-white hands,

That she beheld him Young Bearwell,
    As he came in the sands.

3 Says, Wae 's me for you, Young Bear-
    well,
    Such tales of you are tauld ;
  They 'll cause you sail the salt sea so
    far
    As beyond Yorkisfauld.

4 . . . .
    . . . . . .
    'O shall I bide in good greenwood,
      Or stay in bower with thee?'

5 'The leaves are thick in good greenwood,
    Would hold you from the rain ;
  And if you stay in bower with me
    You will be taken and slain.

6 'But I caused build a ship for you
    Upon Saint Innocent's day ;
  I 'll bid Saint Innocent be your guide,
    And Our Lady, that meikle may.
  You are a lady's first true-love,
    God carry you well away!'

7 Then he sailed east, and he sailed west,
    By many a comely strand ;
  At length a puff of northern wind
    Did blow him to the land.

8 When he did see the king and court,
    Were playing at the ba ;
  Gave him a harp into his hand,
    Says, Stay, Bearwell, and play.

9 He had not been in the king's court
    A twelvemonth and a day,
  Till there came lairds and lords anew
    To court that lady gay.

10 They wooed her with brooch and ring,
    They nothing could keep back ;

The very charters of their lands
  Into her hands they pat.

11 She 's done her down to Heyvalin,
    With the light of the moon ;
  Says, Will ye do this deed for me,
    And will ye do it soon ?

12 'Will ye go seek him Young Bearwell,
    On seas wherever he be?
  And if I live and bruik my life
    Rewarded ye shall be.'

13 'Alas, I am too young a skipper,
    So far to sail the faem ;
  But if I live and bruik my life
    I 'll strive to bring him hame.'

14 So he has saild east and then saild west,
    By many a comely strand,
  Till there came a blast of northern wind
    And blew him to the land.

15 And there the king and all his court
    Were playing at the ba ;
  Gave him a harp into his hand,
    Says, Stay, Heyvalin, and play.

16 He has tane up the harp in hand,
    And unto play went he,
  And Young Bearwell was the first man
    In all that companie.

*   *   *   *   *   *   *

303

THE HOLY NUNNERY

'The Holy Nunnery,' Buchan's Ballads of the North of Scotland, I, 193.

WILLIE'S father and mother have vowed that he shall never marry Annie. Annie resolves that she will be a nun, asks her father's consent and obtains it readily. At the nunnery-gate there is a maiden porter 'wi gowd upon her hat,' who would not have been quite out of place at the wicket of the garden of the Rose. Porter though she be, she seems to exercise the authority of a mother-superior. Annie asks admission, 'there to live or die,' and is allowed to come in on terms : never to kiss a young man's mouth, and to work hard; conditions not surprising, but there is another which is unusual, never to go to church (or is it Kirk that is meant?) Annie is seven years in the nunnery, all which time Willie lies languishing. His mother asks him if there is nothing that would help him; there is nothing, he says, but his love Annie. They dress him up like a lady, in silk and gold, he goes to the nunnery-gate, and the maiden porter 'wi gowd upon her hat' makes no difficulty about letting him in. Annie knows him, and says, Come up, my sister dear. Willie essays to kiss her lips, but she whispers, This I dare not avow. The rest is wanting, and again we may doubt whether the balladist had not exhausted himself, whether a story so begun could be brought to any conclusion.

———•———

1 FAIR ANNIE had a costly bower,
　　Well built wi lime and stane,
　And Willie came to visit her,
　　Wi the light o the meen.

2 When he came to Annie's bower-door,
　　He tirled at the pin :
　'Ye sleep ye, wake ye, Fair Annie,
　　Ye 'll open, lat me come in.'

3 'O never a fit,' says Fair Annie,
　　'Till I your errand ken ; '
　'My father 's vowd a vow, Annie,
　　I 'll tell you when I 'm in.

4 'My father 's vowed a rash vow,
　　I darena marry thee ;
　My mither 's vowed anither vow,
　　My bride ye 'se never be.'

5 'If ye had tauld me that, Willie,
　　When we began to woo,
　There was naithing in this warld wide
　　Shoud drawn my love to you.

6 'A nun, a nun,' said Fair Annie,
　　'A nun will I be then ; '
　'A priest, a priest,' said Sweet Willie,
　　'A priest will I be syne.'

7 She is gane to her father,
　　For mither she had nane ;
　And she is on to her father,
　　To see if she 'd be a nun.

8 'An asking, asking, father dear,
　　An asking ye 'll grant me ;
　That 's to get to the holy nunnery,
　　And there to live or die.'

9 'Your asking 's nae sae great, daughter,
　　But granted it shall be ;
　For ye 'se won to the holy nunnery,
　　There to live or die.'

10 Then they gaed on, and farther on,
　　Till they came to the yate ;
　And there they spied a maiden porter,
　　Wi gowd upon her hat.

11 'An asking, asking, maiden porter,
　　An asking ye 'll grant me ;
　If I 'll won to the holy nunnery,
　　There to live or die.'

12 'Your asking 's nae sae great, lady,
　　But granted it shall be ;
　For ye 'se won to the holy nunnery,
　　There to live or die.

13 'But ye maun vow a vow, lady,
　　Before that ye seek in ;
　Never to kiss a young man's mouth
　　That goes upon the grun.

14 'And ye must vow anither vow,
　　Severely ye must work ;
　The well-warst vow that ye 're to vow,
　　Is never to gang to kirk.'

15 'I will vow a vow,' she said,
　　'Before that I seek in ;
　I neer shall kiss a young man's mouth
　　That goes upon the grun.

16 'And I will vow anither vow,
　　Severely I will work ;
　The well-warst vow that I 'm to vow
　　Is never to gang to kirk.'

17 For seven years now Fair Annie,
   In the holy nunnery lay she,
  And seven years Sweet Willie lay,
   In languish like to die.

18 'Is there nae duke nor lord's daughter,
   My son, can comfort thee,
  And save thee frae the gates o death?
   Is there nae remedie?'

19 'There is nae duke nor lord's daughter,
   Mother, can comfort me,
  Except it be my love, Annie,
   In the holy nunnery lies she.'

20 They 've dressd Sweet Willie up in silk,
   Wi gowd his gown did shine,
  And nane coud ken by his pale face
   But he was a lady fine.

21 So they gaed on, and farther on,
   Till they came to the yate,

And there they spied a maiden porter,
   Wi gowd upon her hat.

22 'An asking, an asking, maiden porter,
   An asking ye 'll grant me;
  For to win in to the holy nunnery,
   Fair Annie for to see.'

23 'Your asking 's nae sae great, lady,
   But granted it shall be;
  Ye 'se won into the holy nunnery,
   Fair Annie for to see.

24 'Be she duke's or lord's daughter,
   It 's lang sin she came here:'
  Fair Annie kent her true love's face;
   Says, Come up, my sister dear.

25 Sweet Willie went to kiss her lips,
   As he had wont to do;
  But she softly whispered him,
   I darena this avow.

304

YOUNG RONALD

Buchan's Ballads of the North of Scotland, II, 282; Motherwell's MS., p. 601, derived from Buchan.

YOUNG RONALD, a noble squire, but still school-boy (11, 29), lays his love on the daughter of the king of Linne, a locality which, as it occurs several times in ballads, we are glad to learn is not far from Windsor. In the course of an interview with the lady in her garden, she tells him that though she entirely feels the honor he has done her, she must be subject to her father's will. Ronald's father and mother are greatly concerned for their son, seeing that the lady has already rejected many suitors. He pays his love a second visit, and protests that for her sake he would fight long and hard. Be not too hasty, she answers; you must buckle with a more dangerous foe than you wot of, ere you win me by war. She proceeds to explain that her father will have to go to war the next day with a giant who has been very troublesome, and then to make him various offers with the view of enlisting him in the affair; among which are two standard rings, one of which will stanch the blood of any of his men who may be hurt, the other prevent the drawing of his own blood.

Young Ronald reports to his father the encouragement which he has received from his love, the impending contest with the giant, and the gifts which she has made him; and the father, on his part, promises him a company of a hundred well-armed men. Supported by these, and invigorated by a third meeting in the garden, Ronald rides proudly to the field. The giant, who is handicapped with three heads on his neck, and three more on his breast, challenges the king of Linne to combat, and the king offers his daughter and a third of his lands to any champion who will undertake the giant. Ronald is ready, and, according to the rule in such cases, disdains the offer of any reward but the daughter. The thought of her gives him a lion's courage, and such potency to his arm that he cuts off all the six heads of the giant at one sweep.

If any lover of ballads should feel his understanding insulted by the presentation of such a piece as this, I can have no quarrel with him. There is certainly much in it that is exasperating, — the greeters in the school, the lifting of the hat, and, most of all, perhaps, the mint in meadows. These are, however, the writer's own property; the nicking with nay and the giant are borrowed from romances. In this and not a very few other cases, I have suppressed disgust, and admitted an actually worthless and a manifestly — at least in part — spurious ballad, because of a remote possibility that it might contain relics, or be a debased representative, of something genuine and better. Such was the advice of my lamented friend, Grundtvig, in more instances than those in which I have brought myself to defer to his judgment.

———◆———

1 It fell upon the Lammas time,
    When flowers were fresh and green,
  And craig and cleugh was covered ower
    With cloathing that was clean.

2 'T was at that time a noble squire,
    Sprung from an ancient line,
  Laid his love on a lady fair,
    The king's daughter o Linne.

3 When cocks did craw, and day did daw,
    And mint in meadows sprang,
  Young Ronald and his little wee boy
    They rode the way alang.

4 So they rode on, and farther on,
    To yonder pleasant green,
  And there he spied that lady fair,
    In her garden alane.

5 These two together lang they stood,
    And love's tale there they taul;
  The glancing o her fair color
    Did Ronald's own impale.

6 He lifted 's hat, and thus he spake;
    O pity have on me!
  For I could pledge what is my right,
    All for the sake of thee.

7 'Ye 're young amo your mirth, kind sir,
    And fair o your dull hours;

There 's nae a lady in a' London
    But might be your paramour.

8 'But I 'm too young to wed, kind sir,
    You must not take it ill;
  Whate'er my father bids me do,
    I maun be at his will.'

9 He kissd her then and took his leave,
    His heart was all in pride,
  And he is on to Windsor gone,
    And his boy by his side.

10 And when he unto Windsor came,
    And lighted on the green,
  There he spied his mother dear,
    Was walking there alane.

11 'Where have ye been, my son, Ronald,
    From gude school-house, this day?'
  'I hae been at Linne, mother,
    Seeing yon bonny may.'

12 'O wae 's me for you now, Ronald,
    For she will not you hae;
  For mony a knight and bauld baron
    She 's nickd them a' wi nae.'

13 Young Ronald 's done him to his bower,
    And he took bed and lay;
  Nae woman could come in his sight,
    For the thoughts o this well-fard may.

14 Then in it came his father dear,
    Well belted in a brand ;
    The tears ran frae his twa gray eyes,
    All for his lovely son.

15 Then Ronald calld his stable-groom
    To come right speedilie ;
    Says, Ye 'll gang to yon stable, boy,
    And saddle a steed for me.

16 ' His saddle o the guid red gowd,
    His bits be o the steel,
    His bridle o a glittering hue ;
    See that ye saddle him weel.

17 ' For I 've heard greeters at your school-house,
    Near thirty in a day ;
    But for to hear an auld man greet,
    It passes bairns' play.'

18 When cocks did craw, and day did daw,
    And mint in meadows sprang,
    Young Ronald and his little wee boy
    The way they rode alang.

19 So they rode on, and further on,
    To yonder pleasant green,
    And there they saw that lady fair,
    In her garden alane.

20 And twenty times before he ceasd
    He kissd her lips sae clear,
    And said, Dear lady, for your sake,
    I 'll fight fell lang and sair.

21 ' Full haste, nae speed, for me, kind sir,'
    Replied the lady clear ;
    ' Far better bucklings ye maun bide
    Or ye gain my love by weir.

22 ' King Honour is my father's name,
    The morn to war maun fare,
    And that 's to fight a proud giant,
    That 's wrought him muckle care.

23 ' Along wi him he is to take
    Baith noble knights and squires ;
    I woud wish you as well-dressd a knight
    As ony will be there.

24 ' And I 'll gie you a thousand crowns,
    To part amang your men ;
    A robe upon your ain body,
    Weel sewd wi my ain hand.

25 ' Likewise a ring, a royal thing,
    The virtue it is gude ;
    If ony o your men be hurt,
    It soon will stem their blude.

26 ' Another ring, a royal thing,
    Whose virtue is well known ;
    As lang 's this ring your body 's on,
    Your bluid shall neer be drawn.'

27 He kissd her then, and took his leave,
    His heart was all in pride,
    And he is on to Windsor gone,
    And his boy by his side.

28 And when he unto Windsor came,
    And lighted on the green,
    There he saw his auld father,
    Was walking him alane.

29 ' Where hae ye been, my son, Ronald,
    From gude school-house the day ? '
    ' O I hae been at Linne, father,
    Seeking yon bonny may.'

30 ' O wae 's me for you now, Ronald,
    For she will not you hae ;
    Mony a knight and bauld baron
    She 's nickd them a' wi nay.'

31 ' O had your tongue, my father dear,
    Lat a' your folly be ;
    The last words that I wi her spake,
    Her love was granted me.

32 ' King Honour is her father's name,
    The morn to war maun fare,
    And that 's to fight a proud giant,
    That 's wrought him muckle care.

33 ' Alang wi him he means to take
    Baith knights and noble squires ;
    And she wishes me as well drest a knight
    As ony will be there.

34 ' And she 's gaen me a thousand crowns,
    To part amang my men ;
    A robe upon my ain body,
    Weel sewd wi her ain hand.

35 ' Likewise a ring, a royal thing,
    The virtue it is gude ;
    If ony o my men be hurt,
    It soon will stem their blude.

36 'Another ring, a royal thing,
　　Whose virtue is unknown;
　As lang 's this ring my body 's on,
　　My blude will neer be drawn.'

37 'If that be true, my son, Ronald,
　　That ye hae tauld to me,
　I 'll gie to you an hundred men,
　　To bear you companie.

38 'Besides as muckle gude harness
　　As carry them on the lee;
　It is a company gude enough
　　For sic a squire as thee.'

39 When cocks did craw, and day did daw,
　　And mint in meadows spread,
　Young Ronald and his merry young men
　　Were ready for to ride.

40 So they rode on, and farther on,
　　To yonder pleasant green,
　And there they spied that lady fair,
　　In her garden, sair mourning.

41 These twa together lang they stood,
　　And love's tale there they taul,
　Till her father and his merry young men
　　Had ridden seven mile.

42 He kissd her then, and took his leave,
　　His heart was all in pride,
　And then he sprang alang the road
　　As sparks do frae the gleed.

43 Then to his great steed he set spur;
　　He being swift o feet,

They soon arrived on the plain,
　Where all the rest did meet.

44 Then flew the foul thief frae the west,
　　His make was never seen;
　He had three heads upon ae hause,
　　Three heads on ae breast-bane.

45 He bauldly stept up to the king,
　　Seiz'd 's steed in his right hand;
　Says, Here I am, a valiant man,
　　Fight me now if ye can.

46 'Where is the man in a' my train
　　Will take this deed in hand?
　And he shall hae my daughter dear,
　　And third part o my land.'

47 'O here am I,' said young Ronald,
　　'Will take the deed in hand;
　And ye 'll gie me your daughter dear,
　　I 'll seek nane o your land.'

48 'I woudna for my life, Ronald,
　　This day I left you here;
　Remember ye yon lady gay
　　For you shed mony a tear.'

49 Fan he did mind on that lady
　　That he left him behind,
　He hadna mair fear to fight
　　Nor a lion frae a chain.

50 Then he cut aff the giant's heads
　　Wi ae sweep o his hand,
　Gaed hame and married that lady,
　　And heird her father's land.

———◆———

5³. collar.
5⁴. one *for* own.
14². and a.

26³. ring 's: *cf.* 36³.
33¹. I mean: *cf.* 23¹.
36². Which: *cf.* 26².

305

THE OUTLAW MURRAY

A. a. 'The Sang of the Outlaw Murray,' Herd's MSS, II, fol. 76 ; 'The Outlaw Murray,' I, 255. **b.** 'The Sang of the Outlaw Murray,' Scott's Minstrelsy, second edition, 1803, I, 1. **c.** 'The Song of the Outlaw Murray,' Aytoun's Ballads of Scotland, 1859, II, 131, "from an old manuscript in the Philiphaugh charter-chest." **d.** 'The Sang of the Outlaw Murray,' the copy now extant among the Philiphaugh papers.

B. 'An old song called Outlaw Murray,' Glenriddell MSS, XI, 61, 1791.

C. 'Outlaw Murray, an antient historical ballad,' fragments, "Scotch Ballads, Materials for Border Minstrelsy," No 31, Abbotsford, in the handwriting of William Laidlaw.

FIRST printed in Scott's Minstrelsy, 1802, I, 1.

A a, b, c (disregarding Scott's interpolations in b), do not differ more than transcripts of one original may be expected to do, remembering that copyists are apt to indulge in trivial verbal improvements.* a was sent David Herd, with a letter dated January 12, 1795, by Andrew Plummer, Sheriff-Depute of Selkirk, as received by carrier from a lady, who neglected to impart how she came by the copy. In this instance, contrary to what I believe to be the general rule, the second volume of Herd's MSS seems to have the original text.† a was printed, but not with absolute fidelity, by Maidment, Scotish Ballads and Songs, 1868, II, 66. For b, "the copy principally resorted to," says Scott, "is one, apparently of considerable antiquity, which was found among the papers of the late Mrs Cockburn of Edinburgh." Scott made occasional use of Herd's MS. and of Glenrid-

dell's, inserted some stanzas which he had received from Sheriff Plummer, and in the second edition (otherwise slightly altered) two stanzas from the recitation of Mungo Park. Mrs Cockburn's MS. evidently agreed very nearly with the copy in Herd, so far as the latter goes. I much regret that exertions made to secure the Cockburn MS. did not result successfully. c. " From a note appended to the ballad, explanatory of its circumstances, in which reference is made to Lord Philiphaugh (a judge of Session) as being then alive," says Aytoun, "the manuscript must have been written between the years 1689 and 1702." ‡ The original manuscript, unfortunately and inexplicably, is no longer in the Philiphaugh archives, and has not come to light after search. The text, if earlier transcribed, shows no internal evidence of superior age, and exhibits several inferior readings, — two that are highly objectionable.§ d, the copy actually preserved among the

* That the four copies of a are transcripts from writing, and not from oral recitation, will be obvious when we observe their correspondence. The first thirty stanzas of a, b, have the same lines in the same order, and with an approach to verbal agreement. There is not so close a concurrence after 30, but still a virtual concurrence, excepting that b inserts sixteen lines between 52 and 53 which the other copies lack. c has throughout the same lines as a, in the same order (with verbal differences), excepting that c introduces two lines after 50⁴ (which are a repetition, with corruption, of 8¹,²), and that a repeats 43 at 60, which c does not. d has only a few verbal variations from c.

† Plummer's letter follows the ballad in the second volume, but is not given in the first.

‡ Rather 1708. Sir James Murray was appointed an or-

dinary Lord of Session October 28, 1689, and took his seat as Lord Philiphaugh November 1. In 1702 he was appointed Lord Clerk Register, and this place he held, except a short interval, till his death, July 1, 1708. (T. Craig-Brown, History of Selkirkshire, II, 345 f.)

§ I mean Soldan Turk, c 22³, for Soudron, **a, b, d,** and Soldanie, c 33², for Soudronie, Southronie, **a, b.** (Soudan Turk, also **B** 26³, Souden Turk, **C** 3³, 5³.) Nothing is easier than the corruption of Soudron into Soudan, upon which change the addition of Turk would be all but inevitable. The corruption would be likely to be made by one who had heard of an irruption of Saracens (or, if you please, Moors) into Galloway. (See note, p. 190.) The winning of Ettrick Forest by and from the Southron is historical, and this pretends to be an historical poem.

Philiphaugh papers, is evinced by a water-mark to be not older than 1848. It shows variations from Aytoun's printed text which cannot be other than wilful alterations.

B, which is both defective, corrupted, and chargeable with flat repetition, and C, a few fragmentary verses, are all that have been re-trieved from tradition, although Scott says that the ballad " has been for ages a popular song in Selkirkshire."

A manuscript copy was understood to be in possession of the late Mr George Wilson, S. S. C., Edinburgh, but, as in the case of the original of the Philiphaugh MS. and in that of Mrs Cockburn's copy, inquiry and search were fruitless.

The king of Scotland is informed that there is an Outlaw in Ettrick Forest who makes no account of him; the king vows that he will be king of Ettrick Forest, or the Outlaw shall be king of Scotland. Earl Hamilton advises that an envoy be sent to the Outlaw to ascertain whether he is willing to do homage to the king and hold the forest of him; if the Outlaw should refuse, then they will proceed to extremities with him. The king sends Boyd, Earl of Arran, to an-nounce his terms: the Outlaw is to do hom-age; otherwise he and his lands will be sub-jugated, his castle levelled, his wife made a widow, and his men be hanged. The mes-senger demands of the Outlaw, in the king's name, of whom he holds his lands; the Out-law replies that the lands are his own, won by himself from the Southron, and that he recognizes no king in Christendom. The mes-senger intimates that it will nevertheless be necessary for the Outlaw to do homage to the king of Scotland, under the penalties before mentioned. Many of the king's nobles shall lie cold first, he replies. Boyd reports to his master that the Outlaw claims to hold the forest by his own right, which he will maintain against all kings in Christendom; the king prepares to enforce his sovereignty with five thousand men.

The Outlaw vows that the king shall pay dear for his coming, and sends for succor to three of his kinsmen, all of whom promise help. As the king approaches the forest, Hamilton ventures to give further advice: that the Outlaw should be summoned to come with four of his best men to meet the king and five earls; fire, sword, and forfeiture to follow upon refusal. The Outlaw bethinks himself of his children, and complies. He and his company fall on their knees and im-plore the king's mercy; his mercy shall be the gallows, says the king. The Outlaw pro-tests again that he won his lands from the enemy, and as he won them so will he keep them, against all kings in Christendom; but having indulged in this vaunt asks mercy again, and offers to give up the keys of his castle if the king will constitute him and his successors sheriffs of the forest. The king, on his part, is equally ready for a compro-mise. The Outlaw, on surrendering the keys of his castle, shall be made sheriff of Ettrick Forest, and shall never be forfeited as long as he continues loyal, and his men shall have pardon if they amend their lives. After all the strong language on both sides, the Outlaw has only to name his lands (but gives a very imperfect list), and the king (waiving com-plete particulars) renders him whatever he is pleased to claim, and makes him sheriff of Ettrick Forest while upwards grows the tree.

So far all the copies of A concur, as to the story, except that c 22, 33, by an absurd corruption, makes the Outlaw to have won his lands, not from the Soudron, the Sou-dronie, but from Soldan Turk, the Soldanie; in which respect A c is followed by B 26, C 3, 5. Between 52 and 53, b introduces this passage:

> Then spak the kene laird of Buckscleuth,
>   A stalworthye man and sterne was he:
> ' For a king to gang an outlaw till
>   Is beneath his state and his dignitie.

> ' The man that wons yon foreste intill,
>   He lives by reif and felonie;
> Wherefore, brayd on, my sovereign liege,
>   Wi fire and sword we 'll follow thee,
> Or, gif your courtrie lords fa back,
>   Our borderers sall the onset gie.'

Then out and spak the nobil king,
  And round him cast a wilie ee :
' Now haud thy tongue, Sir Walter Scott,
  Nor speik of reif nor felonie,
For had everye honeste man his awin kye,
  A right puir clan thy name wad be.' *

B represents that the king, after appointing a meeting with the Outlaw ' in number not above two or three,' comes with a company of three hundred, which violation of the mutual understanding naturally leads the Outlaw to expect treachery. The king, however, not only proceeds in good faith, but, without any stipulations, at once makes the Outlaw laird of the Forest.

From the note, otherwise of no value, which accompanies the Philiphaugh MS., it is clear that the ballad was known before 1700 ; how much earlier it is to be put we can neither ascertain nor safely conjecture, but we may say that there is nothing in the language of the piece as it stands which obliges us to assign it a much higher antiquity.†

As to James Murray, laird of Traquair, whose lands the king had gifted lang syne, A 45[3], 48[1], Sheriff Plummer remarks in Herd's MS. : " Willielmus de Moravia had forfeited the lands of ' trakware ' ante annum 1464. As of that date I have a charter of these lands, proceeding upon his forfeiture, granted Willielmo Douglas de Cluny." Thomas Boyd was created Earl of Arran after his marriage with the eldest sister of James III, 1467. The Earl of Hamilton is mentioned A 7[1], 50[1]. Sheriff Plummer observes that there was an earl of that surname till 1503.

Scott, in his preface in the Border Minstrelsy, after professing himself unable to ascertain the foundation of the tale, goes on to state the following historical possibilities :

" This ballad . . . commemorates a transaction supposed to have taken place betwixt a Scottish monarch and an ancestor of the ancient family of Murray of Philiphaugh in Selkirkshire. . . . It is certain that during the civil wars betwixt Bruce and Baliol the family of Philiphaugh existed and was powerful, for their ancestor, Archibald de Moravia, subscribes the oath of fealty to Edward I, A. D. 1296. It is therefore not unlikely that, residing in a wild and frontier country, they may have, at one period or other during these commotions, refused allegiance to the feeble monarch of the day, and thus extorted from him some grant of territory or jurisdiction. It is also certain that, by a charter from James IV, dated November 30, 1509, John Murray of Philiphaugh is vested with the dignity of heritable Sheriff of Ettrick Forest, an office held by his descendants till the final abolition of such jurisdictions by 28th George II, cap. 23. But it seems difficult to believe that the circumstances mentioned in the ballad could occur under the reign of so vigorous a monarch as James IV. It is true that the *dramatis personæ* introduced seem to refer to the end of the fifteenth or beginning of the sixteenth century ; but from this it can only be argued that the author himself lived soon after that period. It may therefore be supposed (unless further evidence can be produced tending to invalidate the conclusion) that the bard, willing to pay his court to the family, has connected his grant of the sheriffship by James IV with some former dispute betwixt the Murrays of Philiphaugh and their sovereign, occurring either while they were engaged upon the side of Baliol, or in the subsequent reigns of David II and Robert II and III, when the English possessed great part of the Scot-

---

* " The feud betwixt the Outlaw and the Scots may serve to explain the asperity with which the chieftain of that clan is handled in the ballad." Were it not for these words in Scott's preface, I should have been inclined to think that this humorous episode came from the hand of the editor of ' Kinmont Willie.' It is quite in Scott's way, and also in contrast with the tone of the rest of the narrative. If the author of the ballad was capable of this smartness, he ought to have been aware that the Outlaw (not to say the king), after all his bluster, cuts a ridiculously tame

figure in the conclusion. I now observe that the line ' Wi fire and sword we 'll follow thee ' is in A a, 52[2], and nearly the same in c ; which suggests that something may have been lost in the MS.

† A 22[3,4] might be a reminiscence of ' Johnie Armstrong,' C 27[3,4], III, 371. C 3[3,4] (from recitation) agrees strikingly with the stanza cited III, 363, note * ; but this fact is of not the least importance. Mr Macmath notes that A a 1[3], ' The hart, the hynd, the dae, the rae,' occurs in Alexander Montgomerie's Cherrie and the Slae, Edinburgh, 1597.

tish frontier, and the rest was in so lawless a state as hardly to acknowledge any superior.

"At the same time, this reasoning is not absolutely conclusive. James IV had particular reasons for desiring that Ettrick Forest, which actually formed part of the jointure-lands of Margaret, his queen, should be kept in a state of tranquillity: Rymer, vol. xiii, p. 66. In order to accomplish this object, it was natural for him, according to the policy of his predecessors, to invest one great family with the power of keeping order among the rest. It is even probable that the Philiphaugh family may have had claims upon part of the lordship of Ettrick Forest, which lay intermingled with their own extensive possessions, and in the course of arranging, not, indeed, the feudal superiority, but the property of these lands, a dispute may have arisen of sufficient importance to be the groundwork of a ballad.

"It is farther probable that the Murrays, like other Border clans, were in a very lawless state, and held their lands merely by occupancy, without any feudal right. Indeed, the lands of the various proprietors in Ettrick Forest (being a royal demesne) were held by the possessors, not in property, but as the kindly tenants, or rentallers, of the crown. . . . This state of possession naturally led to a confusion of rights and claims. The kings of Scotland were often reduced to the humiliating necessity of compromising such matters with their rebellious subjects, and James himself even entered into a sort of league with Johnnie Faa, the king of the gypsies. Perhaps, therefore, the tradition handed down in this way may have had more foundation than it would at present be proper positively to assert."

In the way of comment upon these surmises of Scott, which proceed mainly upon what we do not know, it may be alleged that we have a fairly good record of the relations of Selkirkshire to the Scottish crown during the

fourteenth century, when this district was so often changing hands between the English and the Scotch, and that there is no indication of any Murray having been concerned in winning it from the Southron, as is pretended in the ballad, either then or at any time, so that this part of the story may be set down as pure invention.* Hardly less fictitious seems to be the dispute between the Scottish king and a Murray, in relation to the tenure. The Murrays first became connected with Selkirkshire in 1461. John de Moravia then acquired the lands of Philiphaugh, and was afterwards appointed Custos of Newark Castle, and came into possession of Hangingshaw and Lewinshope. All of these are attributed to the Outlaw in the ballad. This John Murray was a contemporary of Boyd, Earl of Arran, and of the forfeited Murray of Traquair, but, with all this, nobody has pitched upon him for the Outlaw; and it would not have been a happy idea, for he was on perfectly good terms, and even in great favor, with the court under James III. His grandson, John Murray, was in equal or greater favor with James IV, and was made hereditary Sheriff of Selkirk in 1509, and for this last reason has been proposed for the Outlaw, though "nothing could be more improbable than that this orderly, 'circumspect,' and law-enforcing officer of the crown should ever take up an attitude of rebellious defiance so diametrically opposed to all we really know of his character and conduct." †

Scott thought that light might be thrown upon the history of the ballad by the Philiphaugh family papers. Mr Craig-Brown gave them the accurate examination which Scott suggested, and came to the same conclusion as Aytoun, that the story told in the ballad is, if not altogether fictitious, at least greatly exaggerated. He is inclined to think that "some clue to the date of the ballad lies in the minstrel's animus against the house of Buccleuch" (shown only in A b). "James

* Mr David MacRitchie, in his very interesting Ancient and Modern Britons, a book full of novel matter and views, accepts the ballad as "partly true," apparently to the extent "that this 'outlaw' was as yet an actual, independent king, and that modern Selkirkshire was not a part of Scot-

land:" and this whether the king of Scotland was James IV or an earlier monarch, II, 136–139. This is pitting the ballad against history.

† Craig-Brown, II, 336–338.

Murray, tenth laird," he says, "is the last mentioned in the family MSS as possessor of Newark, which castle passed into the hands of Buccleuch either in his lifetime or that of his successor, Patrick Murray. After the death of James IV at Flodden, the Queen-Regent complained loudly of Buccleuch's encroachment upon her dowry lands of Ettrick Forest, the Custos of which domain had Newark for a residence. Buccleuch continued to keep his hold, and, as he could only do so by displacing Murray, the ill-will of the latter family was a natural consequence. By way of showing the earlier and superior title of the Murrays, the ballad-writer has either invented the story *in toto*, or has amplified the tradition of an actual visit paid to a former Murray by the king. Both Sir Walter Scott and the compiler of the Family Records are of opinion that John Murray, eighth laird, is the presumptive Outlaw of the song; and, as he was undoubtedly in great favor with King James IV, nothing is more likely than that the young monarch may have ended one of his hunting-expeditions to the Forest by confirming John in his hereditary sheriffship, interrupted for a few years by the appointment of Lord Home. As a matter of fact, John Murray did in 1509 obtain a royal charter from his sovereign, of the sheriffship; but, as the office had been vacant since 1506, there is nothing improbable in the supposition that he had already claimed the family rights and taken possession of the castle. Indeed, in 1503, he acted as sheriff at the queen's infeftment in her dowry-lands of Ettrick Forest. It would have been in thorough keeping with all that is known of James IV if his Majesty had taken the opportunity to give his favorite a half-jesting reproof for his presumption; but that Murray was ever seriously outlawed is out of the question. His king heaped honors on him; and only eighty years after his death his descendant obtained a feudal precept of his lands for gratuitous services rendered to the crown by his family, 'without default at any time in their due obedience as became faithful subjects.' So that, granted a royal progress to Newark, followed by Murray's investiture with the sheriffship, the poet remains chargeable with considerable embellishment. A glorification of the family of Philiphaugh and a sneer at the rapacity of Buccleuch are the evident motives of his rhyme." *

" The tradition of Ettrick Forest," says Scott, Minstrelsy, 2d ed., 1803, I, 4, "bears that the Outlaw was a man of prodigious strength, possessing a batton or club with which he laid lee (*i. e.* waste) the country for many miles round, and that he was at length slain by Buccleuch or some of his clan." † This account is not in keeping with the conception of the Outlaw given by the ballad, but indicates the ferocious robber and murderer, the Cacus of popular story, of whom no doubt the world was actually once very guilty, and of whom there are many specimens in British tradition as elsewhere.‡ As such he seems to turn up again in Galloway, where he haunts a forest of Kirkcudbrightshire, called the Black Morrow wood, from which he sallies out "in the neighboring country at night, committing horrible outrages." Of this personage, Mactaggart, in his Gallovidian Encyclopedia, p. 73, says:

" Tradition has him a Blackimore, . . . but my opinion is that he was no Blackimore; he never saw Africa; his name must have been Murray, and as he must have been, too, an outlaw and a bloody man, gloomy with foul crimes,§ Black prefaced it, as it did Black Douglass, and that of others; so he became Black Murray." And he adds

---

* History of Selkirkshire, II, 355–357 ; see also p. 338.

† An account varying as to the place where the Outlaw was slain specifies Scott of Haining as the author of his death. John Murray, the Sheriff, was killed in 1510, and Andrew Ker and Thomas Scot were charged with the act, traditionally put to the account of Buccleuch and his clan, and, in particular, of Scott of Haining. (Craig-Brown, II, 338.)

‡ See Mr MacRitchie's Ancient and Modern Britons, I, 156 ff., 136 ff., for these monsters, often described as black, in which sense, it is maintained, Murray (Morrow, Moor) is frequently to be understood.

§ More of this Murray in Historical and Traditional Tales, Kirkcudbright, 1843, p. 112.

that this pest was disposed of by the people pouring a barrel of spirits into a spring one night when he was out on his rambles, whereof drinking the next day, he was made drunk and fell asleep, in which condition his foes dirked him ; or according to others, one of the McLellans of Kirkcudbright took to the wood single-handed, found the outlaw sleeping, and drove a dirk through his head, whence the head on the dagger in the McLellans' coat of arms.*

2. The castle, says Scott, is supposed by the common people to have been the castle of Newark ; but " this is highly improbable, because Newark was always a royal fortress." The only important point, however, would seem to be who was the keeper of the castle. The Douglasses are spoken of as holding it from about 1326 to 1455 ; John de Moravia was Custos after 1462. The Outlaw's five hundred men are shooting on Newark lee in A b 18[4], and Newark lee is twice mentioned elsewhere in that copy. Sheriff Plummer in his letter to Herd says : This I take to be the castle of New-wark, on the west end of which are the arms of Scotland supported by two unicorns. But in Scott's preface we are told that Sheriff Plummer has assured the editor that he remembered the *insignia* of the unicorns, etc., so often mentioned in the ballad, in existence upon the old tower at Hangingshaw. Whether the etc. covers the picture of the knight and the lady bright, and Sheriff Plummer had therefore changed his opinion, does not appear.

15[3]. " Birkendale brae, now commonly called Birkendailly [see C 2[1]], is a steep descent at the south side of Minchmoor, which separates Tweed-dale from the Forest, at the top of which you come first in sight of New-wark Castle." Plummer's letter to Herd.

19. Mr MacRitchie, II, 141 ff., considers that the Lincoln green dresses of the Outlaw's men, and perhaps the purple of the Outlaw and his wife, show that they were " gypsies," not perhaps of a swarthy color, but still people " living a certain archaic ' heathen ' life," at any rate a " wild and lawless life," and " refusing to follow the course of civilization." This inference from the costume seems to be not quite necessary, unless, or even if, all outlaws are " gypsies." Robin Hood, in ' Robin Hood and Queen Katherine,' is dressed in scarlet red, and his men in Lincoln green (III, 199, 201). But green is the regular attire for men who shoot with the bow, III, 76 f., 91. Johnie Cock, when going out to ding the dun deer down, puts on Lincoln green, III, 3 ff. Will Stewart, even, when only going to a ball-match, clothes his men in green, and himself in scarlet red, II, 434, 437.

51. " Penman's core, generally called Perman's core [Permanscore in Scott, ed. 1833], is a nick or hollow on the top of a high ridge of hills a little to the east of Minchmoor." Plummer, as before. In B 50, poor man's house ; 52, poor man's score.†

---

* " Sometimes it [the crest] represents some valiant act done by the bearer ; thus McClelland of Bombie did, and now Lord Kirkcudbright does, bear a naked arm supporting on the point of a sword a More's head, because, Bombie being forfeited, his son killed a More who came in with some Sarazens to infest Galloway, to the killer of whom the king had promised the forfeiture of Bombie, and thereupon he was restored to his father's land." Sir George Mackenzie, The Science of Herauldry, 1680, p. 90. (This reference

and those to Mactaggart and the Kirkcudbright Tales were given me by Mr W. Macmath in 1883.)

† That it was not originally intended to insert ' The Outlaw Murray ' in this collection will be apparent from the position which it occupies. I am convinced that it did not begin its existence as a popular ballad, and I am not convinced that (as Scott asserts) " it has been for ages a popular song in Selkirkshire." But the " song " gained a place in oral tradition, as we see from **B, C**, and I prefer to err by including rather than by excluding.

A

a. Herd's MSS, II, fol. 76, I, 255, 1795. b. Minstrelsy of the Scottish Border, 1803, I, 1; principally from a copy found among the papers of the late Mrs Cockburn, of Edinburgh. c. Aytoun's Ballads of Scotland, 1859, II, 131; "from an old manuscript in the Philiphaugh charterchest," now not accessible. d. A copy among the Philiphaugh papers, transcribed not earlier than 1848.

1 ETRICK FOREST is a fair foreste,
  In it grows manie a semelie trie;
The hart, the hynd, the dae, the rae,
  And of a' [wylde] beastis grete plentie.

2 There's a castell biggit with lime and stane,
  O gin it stands not pleasantlie!
In the fore front o that castell fair
  Twa unicorns are bra to see.

3 There's the picture of a knight and a ladye
    bright,
  And the grene hollin aboon their brie;
There an Outlaw keepis five hundred men,
  He keepis a royalle companie.

4 His merrie men are in [ae] liverie clad,
  Of the Lincoln grene so fair to see;
He and his ladie in purple clad,
  O if they live not royallie!

5 Word is gane to our nobell king,
  In Edinburgh where that he lay,
That there was an Outlaw in Etterick forest
  Counted him nought and all his courtrie gay.

6 'I mak a vowe,' then the goode king said,
  'Unto the man that dear bought me,
I 'se either be king of Etrick forest,
  Or king of Scotland that Outlaw 's bee.'

7 Then spak the erle hight Hamilton,
  And to the noble king said he;
My sovereign prince, sum counsell tak,
  First of your nobles, syne of me.

8 'I redd you send yon bra Outlaw till
  And see gif your man cum will he;
Desire him cum and be your man,
  And hald of you yon forest frie.

9 'And gif he refuses to do that,
  We 'll conquess both his lands and he,
Or else we 'll throw his castell down,
  And mak a widowe of his gaye ladie.'

10 The king called on a gentleman,
   James Boyd, Erle of Arran, his brother was
     he;
When James he came before the king
   He fell before him on his knie.

11 'Welcum, James Boyd,' said our nobil king,
   'A message ye maun gang for me;
Ye maun hie to Etrick forrest,
   To yon Outlaw, where dwelleth he.

12 'Ask hym of quhom he haldis his lands,
   Or, man, wha may his master be;
Desyre him come and be my man,
   And hald of me yon forrest frie.

13 'To Edinburgh to cum and gang
   His safe-warrand I sall be;
And, gif he refuses to do that,
   We 'll conquess baith his lands and he.

14 'Thou mayst vow I 'll cast his castell doun,
   And mak a widow of his gay ladie;
I 'll hang his merrie men pair by pair
   In ony frith where I may them see.'

15 James Boyd took his leave of the nobill
     king,
   To Etrick forrest fair came he;
Down Birkendale brae when that he cam,
   He saw the fair forest with his ee.

16 Baith dae and rae and hart and hynd,
   And of all wylde beastis grete plentie;
He heard the bows that bauldly ring,
   And arrows whidderand near him by.

17 Of the fair castell he got a sight,
   The like he nere saw with his ee;
On the fore front of that castell
   Twa unicorns were bra to see.

18 The picture of a knight and a ladie bright,
   And the grene hollin aboon their brie;
Thereat he spy'd five hundred men,
   Shuting with bows upon the lee.

19 They a' were in ae liverie clad,
   Of the Lincoln grene, sae fair to see;
The knight and his ladye in purple clad;
   O gif they lived right royallie!
Therefore he kend he was master-man,
   And served him in his ain degree.

20 'God mot thee save, brave Outlaw Murray,
      Thy ladie and a' thy chivalrie!'
   'Marry, thou 's wellcum, gentleman,
      Sum king's-messenger thou seems to be.'

21 'The King of Scotland sent me hier,
      And, gude Outlaw, I 'm sent to thee;
   I wad wat of whom ye hald your lands,
      Or, man, wha may thy master be.'

22 'Thir landis are mine,' the Outlaw said,
      ' I own na king in Christentie;
   Frae Soudron I this forest wan,
      When the king nor 's knights were not to
         see.'

23 'He desires you 'l come to Edinburgh,
      And hald of him this forest frie;
   And gif you refuse to do this,
      He 'll conquess both thy landis and thee;
   He has vowd to cast thy castell down,
      And make a widow of thy gaye ladie.

24 'He 'll hang thy merrie men pair by pair,
      In ony frith where he may them finde ; '
   'Aye, by my troth,' the Outlaw said,
      'Then wad I think me far behinde.

25 'Eere the king my fair countrie get,
      This land that 's nativest to me,
   Mony of his nobils sall be cauld,
      Their ladies sall be right wearie.'

26 Then spak his ladye fair of face,
      She said, Without consent of me
   That an outlaw shuld come before the king:
      I am right rad of treasonrie.

27 'Bid him be gude to his lordis at hame,
      For Edinburgh my lord sall never see : '
   James tuke his leave of the Outlaw keene,
      To Edinburgh boun is he.

28 And when he came before the king,
      He fell before him on his knie :
   'Wellcum, James Boyd,' said the nobil king,
      ' What foreste is Etrick forest frie ? '

29 'Etrick forest is the fairest forest
      That ever man saw with his ee ;
   There 's the dae, the rae, the hart, the
         hynde,
      And of all wild beastis great plentie.

30 'There 's a prittie castell of lime and stone,
      O gif it stands not pleasauntlie !
   There 's on the fore side of that castell
      Twa unicorns sae bra to see.

31 'There 's the picture of a knight and [a] ladie
         bright,
      And the grene hollin aboon their brie ;
   There the Outlaw keepis five hundred men,
      O gif they live not royallie !

32 'His merry men in [ae] liverie clad,
      O the Lincoln grene, so fair to see ;
   He and his ladye in purple clad,
      O gif they live not royallie !

33 'He says yon forest is his ain,
      He wan it from the Soudronie ;
   Sae as he won it, sae will he keep it,
      Contrair all kings in Christentie.'

34 'Gar ray my horse,' said the nobil king,
      ' To Etrick [forest] hie will I me ; '
   Then he gard graith five thousand men,
      And sent them on for the forest frie.

35 Then word is gane the Outlaw till,
      In Etrick forest where dwelleth he,
   That the king was cumand to his cuntrie,
      To conquess baith his lands and he.

36 'I mak a vow,' the Outlaw said,
      ' I mak a vow, and that trulie,
   Were there but three men to tak my part,
      Yon king's cuming full deir suld be.'

37 Then messengers he called forth,
      And bade them haste them speedilie :
   'Ane of you go to Halliday,
      The laird of the Corehead is he.

38 'He certain is my sister's son,
      Bid him cum quick and succour me ;
   Tell Halliday with thee to cum,
      And shaw him a' the veritie.'

39 'What news ? what news,' said Halliday,
      ' Man, frae thy master unto me ? '
   'Not as ye wad ; seeking your aid ;
      The king 's his mortal enemie.'

40 'Aye, by my troth,' quoth Halliday,
      ' Even for that it repenteth me ;

For, gif he lose fair Ettrick forest,
　　He 'll take fair Moffatdale frae me.

41 'I 'll meet him wi five hundred men,
　　And surely mae, if mae may be : '
[The Outlaw calld a messenger,
　　And bid him hie him speedily.]

42 'To Andrew Murray of Cockpool,
　　That man 's a deir cousin to me ;
Desire him cum and make me aid,
　　With all the power that he may be.

43 'The king has vowd to cast my castell down,
　　And mak a widow of my gay ladye ;
He 'll hang my merry men pair by pair
　　I[n] ony place where he may them see.'

44 'It stands me hard,' quoth Andrew Murray,
　　'Judge if it stands not hard with me,
To enter against a king with crown,
　　And put my lands in jeopardie.

45 'Yet, gif I cum not on the daye,
　　Surelie at night he sall me see : '
To Sir James Murray, laird of Traquair,
　　A message came right speedilie.

46 'What news ? what news,' James Murray said,
　　'Man, frae thy master unto me ? '
'What needs I tell ? for well ye ken
　　The king 's his mortal enemie.

47 'He desires ye 'll cum and make him aid,
　　With all the powers that ye may be : '
'And, by my troth,' James Murray said,
　　'With that Outlaw I 'll live and die.

48 'The king has gifted my lands lang syne,
　　It can not be nae war with me ; '

　·　　·　　·　　·　　·　　·　　·　　·

　　·　　·　　·　　·　　·　　·　　·　　·

49 The king was cumand thro Cadden ford,
　　And fiftene thousand men was he ;
They saw the forest them before,
　　They thought it awsom for to see.

50 Then spak the erle hight Hamilton,
　　And to the nobil king said he,
My sovereign prince, sum counsell take,
　　First at your nobles, syne at me.

51 'Desyre him meet you at Penman's Core,
　　And bring four in his cumpanie ;
Fyve erles sall gang yoursell before,
　　Gude cause that you suld honord be.

52 'And, if he refuses to do that,
　　Wi fire and sword we 'll follow thee ;
There sall never a Murray after him
　　Have land in Etrick forest frie.'

53 The king then called a gentleman,
　　Royal-banner-bearer then was he,
James Hope Pringle of Torsonse by name ;
　　He came and knelit upon his knie.

54 'Welcum, James Pringle of Torsonse ;
　　Ye man a message gae for me ;
Ye man gae to yon Outlaw Murray,
　　Surely where bauldly bideth he.

55 'Bid him meet me at Penman's Core,
　　And bring four of his companie ;
Five erles sall cum wi mysell,
　　Gude reason I suld honord be.

56 'And if he refuses to do that,
　　Bid him look for nae gude o me ;
There sall never a Murray after him
　　Have land in Etric forest frie.'

57 James came before the Outlaw keene,
　　And served him in his ain degree :
'Wellcum, James Pringle of Torsonse,
　　What tidings frae the king to me ? '

58 'He bids you meet him at Penman's Core,
　　And bring four of your companie ;
Five erles will cum with the king,
　　Nae more in number will he be.

59 'And gif you refuse to do that,
　　I freely here upgive with thee,
There will never a Murray after thee
　　Have land in Etrick forest frie.

60 'He 'll cast your bonny castell down,
　　And make a widow of your gay ladie,
He 'll hang your merry men pair by pair
　　In ony place where he may them see.'

61 'It stands me hard,' the Outlaw said,
　　'Judge if it stands not hard with me ;

I reck not of losing of mysell,
    But all my offspring after me.

62 'Auld Haliday, young Haliday,
    Ye sall be twa to gang wi me;
  Andrew Murray and Sir James Murray,
    We'll be nae mae in cumpanie.'

63 When that they came before the king,
    They fell before him on their knee :
  'Grant mercy, mercy, royal king,
    Een for his sake who died on tre!'

64 'Sicken-like mercy sall ye have,
    On gallows ye sall hangit be;'
  'God forbid!' quo the Outlaw then,
    'I hope your Grace will better be.

65 'These lands of Etrick forest fair,
    I wan them frae the enemie;
  Like as I wan them, sae will I keep them,
    Contrair all kings in Christentie.'

66 All the nobilis said, the king about,
    Pitye it were to see him die :
  'Yet graunt me mercye, sovereign prince,
    Extend your favour unto me!

67 'I'll give you the keys of my castell,
    With the blessing of my fair ladie;
  Mak me the sheriff of the forest,
    And all my offspring after me.'

68 'Wilt thou give me the keys of thy castell,
    With the blessing of thy fair ladye?
  I'll mak the[e] shiryff of the forest,
    Surely while upwards grows the trie;

If you be not traytour to the king,
    Forfaulted sall ye never be.'

69 'But, prince, what sall cum o my men?
    When I go back, traitour they'll ca me;
  I had rather lose my life and land,
    Eer my merry men rebukëd me.'

70 'Will your merry men amend their lives
    And all their pardouns I grant thee :
  Now name thy landes whe'ere they be,
    And here I render them to thee.'

71 'Fair Philiphaugh, prince, is my awin,
    I biggit it wi lime and stane;
  The Tinnies and the Hangingshaw,
    My leige, are native steeds of mine.

72 '.   .   .   .   .   .
    .   .   .   .   .   .
  I have mony steeds in the forest shaw,
    But them by name I dinna knaw.'

73 The keys of the castell he gave the king,
    With the blessing of his fair ladye;
  He was made sheryff of Etrick forest,
    Surely while upward grows the trie;
  And, if he was not traytour to the king,
    Forfaulted he suld never be.

74 Wha ever heard, in ony tymes,
    Sicken an outlaw in his degree
  Sic favour get before a king
    As did the Outlaw Murray of the forest
    frie?

B

Glenriddell's MSS, XI, 61, 1791.

1 ETTERICK FOREST's a pleasant land,
    And it grows mony a bonny tree;
  With buck and doe and a' wild beast,
    A castle stands right bonnilie.

2 Yon castle has twa unicorns,
    The like I never saw wi my ee,
  The picture of a knight and lady bright,
    And the green hollin's aboon her [bree].

3 Word is gane to Edinbro town
    .   .   .   .   .   .
  That there's an Outlaw in Etterick forest
    That keeps as fine a court as he.

4 The king has sworn a solemn oath,
    And he has sworn by [the Virgin Mary],
  He would either be king of Etterick forest,
    Or king of Scotland the Outlaw should be.

5 He has ca'd up Mr James Boyd,
    A highland laird I'm sure was he :

'Ye must gae to Etterick forest
    And see of wha he hads his land,
    And wha pays yon men meat and fee.'

6 He 's tane his leave o the king and court,
    Een as hard as he may dree;
When he came in o'er Loudon edge,
    He viewed the forest wi his eee.

7 He thought it was as pleasant a land
    As ever his two eyes did see,
But when he came in oer . . . ,
    They were a' ranked on Newark lee.

8 O waly, but they were bonny to see!
    Five hundred men playing at the ba;
They were a' clad in the Lincoln green,
    And the Outlaw's sell in taffety.

9 'Weel met you save, Outlaw,' he says,
    'You and your brave companie;
The King of Scotland hath sent me here,
    To see whom on you hold your lands,
    Or who pays thir men meat and fee.'

10 The first ae man the answer made,
    It was the Outlaw he:
'The lands they are all mine,
    And I pay thir men meat and fee,
And as I wan them so will I lose them,
    Contrair the kings o Cristendie.

11 'I never was a king's subject,
    And a king's subject I 'll never be;
For I wan them i the fields fighting,
    Where him and his nobles durst not come
    and see.'

12 O out bespeaks the Outlaw's lady,
    I wot she spake right wisely;
'Be good unto your nobles at home,
    For Edinbro mine shall never see;'
But meat and drink o the best I 'm sure got
    he.

13 He has taen his leave o the Outlaw free,
    And een as hard as he may dree,
While he came to the king's court,
    Where he kneeld low down on his knee.

14 'What news? what news, James,' he says,
    'Frae yon Outlaw and his company?'
'Yon forest is as fine a land
    As ever I did see.

15 'Yon Outlaw keeps as fine a court
    As any king in Cristendie;
Yon lands they are here all his own,
    And he pays yon men meat and fee,
And as he wan them so will he lose them,
    Contrair the kings of Cristendie.

16 'He never was a king's subject,
    And a king's subject he 'll never be;
For he wan them in the fields fighting,
    Where the king and his nobles durst not
    come to see.'

17 The king has sworn a solemn oath,
    And he has sworn by the Virgin Mary,
He would either be king of Etterick forest,
    Or king of Scotland the Outlaw should be.

18 The king has ca'd up Mr James Pringle,
    Laird of Torson[s]e at the time was he:
'Ye must gae to Etterick forest,
    And see wha of he hads his land,
    And wha pays yon men meat and fee.'

19–25=6–12.

26 'And as I wan them so will I lose them,
    Contrair the kings o Cristendie;
I wan them frae the Soudan Turk,
    When their cuckold king durst not come to
    see;
For I wan them in the fields fighting,
    Where him and his nobles durst not come
    to see.'

27–32=12–17.

33 'Gar warn me Perthshire and Angus both,
    Fifeshire up and down, and Loudons three,
For I fear of them we hae great need,
    .   .   .   .   ,'

34 Then word is come to the Outlaw then,
    'Our noble king comes on the morn,
    Landless men ye will a' be;'
He 's called up his little foot-page,
    His sister's son I trow was he.

35 'Ye must tak Etterick head
    Een as hard as ye can drie;
Ye must gae to the Corhead and tell
    Andrew Brown this frae me.

36 ' The noble king comes in the morn,
    And landless men we will a' be ;
   .   .   .   .   .   .
    And tell him to send me some supply.'

37 The boy has taen Etterick head,
    And een as hard as he may drie,
    Till he came to the Corhead,
    And he shouted out and cry'd well he.

38 ' What news ? what news, my little boy ?
    What news has thy master to me ? '
  ' The noble king comes in the morn,
    And landless then ye will a' be.

39 ' Ye must meet him on the morn,
    And mak him some supply ; '
  ' For if he get the forest fair frae him,
    He 'll hae Moffat-dale frae me.

40 ' I 'll meet him the morn wi five hundred men,
    And fifty mair, if they may be ;
  And if he get the forest fair
    We 'll a' die on the Newark lee.'

41 Word is gane to the Border then,
    To . . . , the country-keeper I 'm sure
      was he:
  ' The noble king comes in the morn,
    And landless men ye will a' be.'

42 ' I 'll meet him the morn wi five hundred men,
    And fifty mair, if they may be ;
  And if he get the forest fair,
    We 'll a' die on the Newark lee.'

43 Word is gane to Philiphaugh,
    His sister's son I 'm sure was he,
  To meet him the morn wi some supply,
  ' For the noble king comes in the morn,
    And landless men ye will a' be.'

44 ' In the day I daur not be seen,
    For he took a' my lands frae me
  And gifted me them back again ;
    Therefore against him I must not be ;
  For if I be found against him rebel,
    It will be counted great treason[rie].

45 ' In the day I daur not be seen,
    But in the night he shall me find
    With five hundred men and fifty, if they
      may be,

And before he get the forest fair
    We 'll a' die on the Newark lee.'

46 When the king came in oer Loudon edge,
    Wi three thousand weel teld was he,
  And when he came in oer . . .
    He viewd that forest wi his ee.

47 The Outlaw and his men were a'
    Ranked on the Newark lee ;
  They were a' clad in the Lincoln green,
    And he himsell in the taffety.

48 An auld grey-haird knight has taen aff his
    cap,
   .   .   .   .   .
  ' Pardon, pardon, my sovereign liege,
    Two or three words to speak wi you.

49 ' If you please to send for the Outlaw,
    To see if he could with you agree,
  There 's not a man yon Outlaw has
    But of yours he 'll choose to be.'

50 The king he has taen af his cap,
    He held it on his majesty ;
  ' I 'll meet him the morn at the poor man's
    house,
    In number not above two or three ; '
  The Outlaw says, I 'll hae as few as thee.

51 ' There 's Andrew Brown, and Andrew Murray,
    And Mess James Murray shall gang wi me,
  .   .   .   .
    And nae mae shall my number be.'

52 And when they came to the poor man's core
    They waited two lang hours or three,
  And they were aware of the noble king com-
    ing,
    And hundreds three in his company.

53 ' I wonder what the muckle Deel
    He 'll learned kings to lie,
  For to fetch me here frae amang my men
    Even like a dog for to die ;
  But before I gang to Edinbro town
    Monny toom saddles shall there be.'

54 The king he has taen aff his cap ;
   .   .   .   .   .   .
  ' It [were] great offence here,' he says,
    ' And great pity to see thee die.

55 'For thou shalt be laerd o this forest fair
    As lang as upwards grows the tree
And downward the twa rivers run,
    If the steads thou can but rightly name to
        me.'

56 'There's Hangingshaw high and Hanging-
    shaw laigh,

.   .   .   .

    The Tinis and the Tinis-burn,
    The Newark and the Newark lee.'

*   *   *   *   *   *   *

C

"Scotch Ballads, Materials for Border Minstrelsy," No 31, Abbotsford; in the handwriting of William Laidlaw.

1 'GAE fetch to me James Pringle wi hast,
    An see that he come speedilie,
For he maun on to Ettrick forest,
    An see whae pays yon men meat and
        fee.'

2 When James Pringle cam down oer Birken-
    dalee,
The hawks war yellin right loudlie,
The hunds war rinnin oer hill and dale,
    As the bugle-horn soundit bonnilie.

3 'Gae tell yer king this land's my ain,
    An to thir men I pay meat and fee;
I took it thrae the Souden Turk,
    When nae sic cuckold king might be.

4 'Sae as I wan, sae will I lose,
    Spite o the kings in Christendie;
I never was a king's subject,
    Nor a king's subject will I ever be.'

5 'Outlaw Murray says yon land's his ain,
    And to yon men he pays meat and fee;
He took it frae the Souden Turk,
    When you and your men durstna come and
        see.'

6 It was than the king he gat up in hast,
    An wow an angrie man was he!
'I 'se either be king o Ettrick forest,
    Or king o Scotland sal he be.

7 'Gar warn me Fife an a' Lothian land,
    An Perth an Angus, to ride wi me,

For gin we war five thousan strang
    Master and mair I fear he 'll be.'

8 When the king came oer be Birkendalee,
    He spy'd the forest wi his ee;
There war daes an raes an monie wild beast,
    An a castle stannin right bonnilie.

9 An in that castle a unicorn,
    An, waly, but they war fair to see!
A warlike knight and a lady bright,
    An the green halleen aboon her bree.

10 An Outlaw Murray an his merry men
    War a' rankit up i the Newark lee,
Well mountit on a milk-white steed;
    Waly, he rankit them bonnilie!

11 His men war a clad oer wi green,
    An he was clad i the taffatie,
Wi belt an pistle by his side;
    O waly, but they war fair to see!

*   *   *   *   *   *   *

12 'Haliday young an Halliday auld,
    Ye ir the men that man ride wi me;
But gin we war five hunder strang
    Master an mair I fear they 'll be.'

*   *   *   *   *   *   *

13 'Philliphaugh it is my ain,
    An Newark it belangs to me;
Lewinshope an Hanginshaw
    Nae mortal man can claim thrae me.'

*   *   *   *   *   *   *

14 It was than James Boyd got up in hast,
    An to his merry men a' spak he;

.   .   .   .

.   .   .   .   .   .

A. a. *The division of stanzas as made in the MS. has been changed in* 19^5–23^6, 68^5–73^6. *Of course all the stanzas were originally of four verses, but in some cases it is not now possible to determine at what points verses have been lost. Two lines are in the MS. indicated (conjecturally, no doubt) to have dropped out after* 41^2, 48^2, 70^4. $41^{3,4}$ *have been supplied from the copy in Herd's first volume. There are asterisks in Herd I after* 52^4.

1^4. *Cf.* 16^2, 29^4, *and* b.

4^1, 32^1. *Cf.* 19^1 *and* b. *But* c *agrees with* a.

5^1. *Side note in MS.*: James II, 1454.

31^4. lived. 34^2. *Cf.* b, c.

Variations in Herd, I (not regarding spelling). 2^4, 4^1. *are* wanting. 3^2. the brie.

3^3. hundir. 5^4. his country.

6^1. then *wanting.* 11^4. he dwelleth he.

16^4. him near by. 17^3. fair front.

21^3. land. 31^1. and a.

31^3. keeps him : hunder.

35^1. Outlaws (*wrongly*).

$41^{3,4}$. *As supplied in the text.* *Cf.* c.

58^2. bring him four.

58^4. Nae mae. 62^4. nae mair. 63^4. sake that.

65^1. Thir. 68^3. mak thee. 68^4. upward.

b. 1^3. There's hart and hynd and dae and rae.

1^4. wilde beastes. 2^1. a feir. 3^3. keeps.

4^1. are a' in ae. 4^2. sae gaye.

4^4. gin they lived.

5^4. nor a'. 6^4. outlaw sall. 7^1, 50^1. the lord.

7^4. at your : at me. 8^1. ye.

9^1. And *wanting*.

9^2, 12^1, 13^4, 21^3, 35^4, 44^4, 48^1, 65^1, 70^3. landis.

10^1. then called a. 10^2. the erle.

10^4. He knelit. 11^4. where bydeth.

12^3. And desyre. 13^2. sall gie.

16^4. hym neir bi. 17^1. Of that.

17^3. castell feir. 17^4. were gaye.

18^4. on Newark lee. 19^1. were a'.

19^2. sae gaye.

19^4. 1802, gin. 1803, *instead of* $19^{3,4}$:

  His men were a' clad in the grene,
    The knight was armed capapie,
  With a bended bow, on a milk-white steed,
    And I wot they ranked right bonilie.

19^5. Thereby Boyd. 20^4. seemis. 22^2. I ken.

22^4. his knightis. 23^3, 37^3, 58^1. ye.

23^5. hath. 25^3, 50^4. nobilis. 26^3. befor a.

27^3. James Boyd. 28^1. When James he.

28^2. He knelit lowlie on : seyd our.

30^3. in the forefront. 31^1. and a.

31^2. Wi the.

31^4. He keepis a royalle cumpanie.

32^1. in ae. 32^2. sae gaye. 32^4. gin.

33^2. frae the Southronie. 33^4, 65^4. kingis.

34. ' Gar warn me Perthshire and Angus baith,
    Fife up and down and the Louthians
      three, (*cf.* B $33^{1,2}$)
  And graith my horse,' said the nobil king,
    ' For to Ettricke Foreste hie will I me.'

35^3. 1803, cuming. 36^4. 1802, cumand.

37^2. hie them. 37^3, 69^2. gae.

$38^{3,4}$. The king cums on for Ettricke Foreste,
    And landless men we a' will be. (*Cf.*
      B 34.)

40^1. said.

41^2. surely mair.

Between $41^{1,2}$ *and* $41^{3,4}$:

  And before he gets the Foreste feir,
    We a' will die on Newark Lee. (*Cf.* B
      40.)

$41^{3,4}$. The Outlaw calld a messenger,
    And bid him hie him speedilye.

43 *wanting*. 44^1. Andrew Murray said.

44^2, 61^2. gif : na. 44^4. And set. 45^1. if.

45^3. laird *wanting*.

$47^{1,2}$. And now he is cuming (1802, cumand)
    to Ettricke Foreste,
    And landless men ye a' will be. (*Cf.* B
      $41^{3,4}$).

47^4. will I live. 48^2. 1802, canna : warse.

49^1. 1803, cuming. 49^2. full five.

49^3. the derke. 50^3. sovereign liege.

51^1. mete thee. 52^1, 56^1. gif.

52^2. We'll conquess baith his landis and he.

52^4. Hald.

Between 52 *and* 53 :

  Then spak the kene laird of Buckscleuth,
    A stalworthye man and sterne was he ;
  ' For a king to gang an Outlaw till
    Is beneath his state and his dignitie.

  ' The man that wons yon Foreste intill,
    He lives by reif and felonie ;
  Wherefore, brayd on, my sovereign liege,
    Wi fire and sword we'll follow thee ;
      (*see* a 52^2)
  Or, gif your courtrie lords fa back,
    Our borderers sall the onset gie.'

  Then out and spak the nobil king,
    And round him cast a wilie ee ;
  ' Now haud thy tongue, sir Walter Scott,
    Nor speik of reif nor felonie,

For, had everye honeste man his awin kye,
  A right puir clan thy name wad be.'

53². there was. 53⁸. Hop.
54². A message ye maun gang.
55², 58². four in. 57⁴. What message.
58⁸. erles sall gang himsell befor.
59³,⁴. He 'll cast yon bonny castle down,
    And mak a widowe o that gaye ladye.
60. He 'll loose yon bluidhound borderers
    Wi fire and sword to follow thee ;
  There will nevir a Murray after thysell
  Have land in Ettricke Foreste frie.
61⁸. Wha reck not losing.
After 61 :
    My merryemen's lives, my widowe's teirs,
    There lies the pang that pinches me !
    When I am straught in bluidie eard,
    Yon castell will be right dreirie.
63⁸. nobil king. 63⁴. sake that.
64⁸. Over God's forbode, quoth.
After 64⁴ (*added in* 1803) :
    Else ere ye come to Edinburgh port
    I trow thin guarded sall ye be.
65¹. Thir. 65². from.
66¹. said *wanting*.
66². Said pitie. 67¹. give thee.
67², 68². gaye *for* fair.
67⁸. Gin thoult mak me sheriffe of this.
68⁸. I 'se : of Ettricke Foreste. 68⁶. sall thou.
70⁸. they lie.
71. 1802.
    Fair Philiphaugh, prince, is my ain,
    But and a part of the Newark lee,
    The Finnies and the Hangingshaw,
    My liege, are native steads to me.
1803.
    Fair Philiphaugh is mine by right,
    And Lewinshope still mine shall be ;
    Newark, Foulshiells and Tinnies baith
    My bow and arrow purchased me.
72¹,². 1803.
    And I have native steads to me
    The Newark lee and Hangingshaw ;
73⁴. upwards. 73⁵. was na.
c. *This copy agrees closely, as to substance, with*
  a. *After* 50⁴ *it has two lines, partially
    corrupted, which do not occur in* a, *and it
    lacks st.* 60, *which, it is to be observed,
    does not occur in the king's instructions to
    Pringle,* 54–56 (*though found in the instruc-
    tions to Boyd,* 14), *and was therefore not to
    be expected. Verbal differences are numer-*

*ous, but in only a very few cases of the least
importance, and in these for the worse.*
1⁴, 16², 29⁴. wild beasts. 2¹. builded of.
2⁸. There 's in. 2⁴. is braw. 3¹. and lady.
3³,⁴, 31⁸. keeps. 4¹. men 's in livery.
4². is fair. 4⁴. O gin. 5⁴. country.
6¹. then *wanting*. 6⁴. sall be.
7¹, 26¹. spoke. 7⁴. good nobles, and syne.
8², 45¹, 59¹. if. 8². yon man.
8⁸, 12⁸, 42⁸, 51¹, 55¹. him to.
9¹, 13⁸, 19⁴, 23⁸, 30², 31⁴, 32⁴, 40⁸. gin.
9¹, 13⁸. refuse. 9², 13⁴, 23⁴, 35⁴. conqueist.
9⁸. we 'll cast.
9⁴, 14², 23⁶, 43². his (thy, my) fair.
10². and his brother-in-law.
11¹. said the. 11². gae. 11⁸. to fair E.
12¹. holds. 12⁴. yon fair forrest of me.
13¹, 15², 44⁸. Till. 14¹. may : I 'se.
16⁸. There heard he bows did.
16⁴. whithering him near by. 17¹. the great.
17⁸. the castle he saw. 17⁴. unicorns so braw.
19¹. They were all in ane. 19⁴. not royallie.
19⁵. he knew. 19⁶. He served.
20¹. Good mot ye.
20². Thy fair lady and thy.
21¹. he sent. 21⁴. may your. 22¹. lands is.
22². And I ken. 22⁸. From Soldan Turk.
22⁴. king and his men was.
23¹. ye, man, to come. 23⁸. ye. 24⁸. Then.
24⁴. will I. 25². Thir lands.
25⁸. they sall lie. 26². Said she.
26⁸. That any : enter before a. 26⁴. rad for.
27¹. lords. 27⁸. leave at.
27⁴. Unto : bound he.
29¹. is ane of the : forrests. 30⁸. that fair c.
31¹. There 's *wanting :* and a. 31⁸. There an.
31⁴. live. 32¹. is in l. 32². is fair.
33¹. is truely his.
33². He says he : Soldanie.
33⁸. Like as : he loss it. 34². In E. Forrest.
34⁴. And made for. 35¹. to the.
35². where lay. 35⁸. coming to this.
35⁴. And ould. 36⁸. Will : men take.
36⁴. Your : sall. 37². speed them.
38¹. Be certain he.
38². And bid him come and.
38⁸. Till Halliday till that he come.
38⁴. You show. 39⁸. Nought.
40¹, 44¹. said. 40⁸, 69⁸. loss. 41². if I.
41³,⁴ *wanting*. 42¹. Laird of.
42⁴, 47². that *wanting*. 44², 61². O gin it.
45². in the night ye. 45⁴. right hastilie.
46⁸. needs me. 47¹. desired ye to.

48[1]. he 's. 48[2]. no worse for.

49[1]. coming oer Cadron. 49[4]. awfu.

50[2]. Unto. 50[4]. First of : and then of.
After 50[4]:

> Yet I reid you send yon Outlaw till,
> And if you man them, come will he.
> (*Repetition, with corruption, of* 8[1,2].)

51[2]. four of the best of. 51[3], 62[2]. gae.

51[3], 55[3]. aun sell. 51[4]. Good reason you.

52[2]. follow will we.

52[3]. never after him again.

53[1]. king he called. 53[2]. bearer of Scotland.

53[3]. Hoppringle. 53[4]. on.

54[1], 57[3]. Laird of. 54[2,3]. Thou. 55[1]. Desire.

55[2], 58[2]. Bring four of the best of the (your).

55[4]. reason in some part I. 56[2]. good from.

57[4]. What biddings. 58[1]. desires you to.

58[4]. Nae mae. 59[1]. ye. 59[2]. Truelie here I.

60 *wanting.* 61[3]. What rack of the.

62[3]. Sir *wanting.* 63[4]. sake that.

64[1]. Siccan mercie you sal. 64[2]. sal you.

64[3]. said the O. syne. 65[1]. The.

65[2]. from. 65[3]. sae will I loss. 66[1]. noblemen.

66[2]. Pitie, Outlaw : see thee.

66[4]. Let your favour be given to.

67[1]. my fair.

67[3]. Why, ye will make me sheriff : the fair.

68[1]. Will ye : your. 68[2]. of your.

68[3]. of Ettrick Forrest.

68[5]. If ye be not a : to your.

68[6]. Forfeited.

69[1]. But alace, prince : become. 69[3]. lands.

70[1]. thy. 70[2]. grant I frie. 70[3]. where.

71[4]. Prince, they are native lands.

72[4]. But well their names I do not.

73[3]. He made him.

73[5]. a traitor to the crown. 73[6]. should he.

74[1]. any time. 74[2]. Sic ane Outlaw.

74[4]. Outlaw in the Forrest.

d. *The MS. extant in the Philiphaugh archives exhibits, besides many differences of spelling, the following variations in reading from* c *as printed by Aytoun:*

5[1]. *Side note:* Jas the 2d, 1454.

17[4]. is bra *for* so braw.

19[2]. is fair *for* so fair.

21[4]. mak *for* man, *wrongly.*

22[3]. From Soudron *for* From Soldan Turk.

24[2]. see *for* find. 26[2]. said *wanting, wrongly.*

33[2]. Soudonie *for* Soldanie.

33[3], 65[3]. tyne *for* loss. 38[3]. Tell *for* Till.

40[4]. Mosaldale *for* Moffat-dale.

43[2]. ane *for* a. 45[2]. he *for* ye.

48[2]. work *for* worse, *wrongly.*

50[4]. syne *for* then.

51[1], 55[1], 58[1]. Penman score, *wrongly.*

52[1], 56[1]. refuse *for* refuses.

56[2]. frae *for* from.

65[1]. Thir *for* the.

73[2]. With his *for* With the, *wrongly.*

B. *The division of stanzas has been rearranged.*

5[2]. " Reciters," *says Scott,* " sometimes call the messenger the laird of Skene."

21=8. 21[3]. the *wanting.* 21[4]. in the.

22=9. 22[4]. land. 24=11. 24[4]. come to.

35[3]. Carhead.

50, 54. *Passing over the king's taking off his cap to an outlaw, which is monstrously* ' beneath his state and his dignitie,' *I can make nothing of the line which succeeds in each of these stanzas.*

52[1]. score *for* core.

C. 14. *Displaced. James Boyd should of course come in before James Pringle.*

FRAGMENTS

———

" DISPERSED thro Shakspere's plays are innumerable little fragments of ancient ballads, the entire copies of which could not be recovered," says Bishop Percy in his preface to 'The Friar of Orders Gray.' What he says of Shakspere is equally true of Beaumont and Fletcher, but it is not true, in either case, that there are many fragments of popular traditional ballads. Portions of ballads of one kind or another, and still more of songs, are introduced into the plays of these authors, though not so frequently as one would suppose from Percy's words. Ten of the twenty-eight stanzas of ' The Friar of Orders Gray ' are taken, mostly in part only, from Shakspere and Fletcher,* but the original verses are from songs, not properly from ballads. It is not, however, always easy to say whether an isolated stanza belonged to a ballad or a song. Some snatches from familiar ballads, which occur in Beaumont and Fletcher, have already been given at the proper places. A few bits from unknown pieces, which occur in Shakspere, or Beaumont and Fletcher (strictly, perhaps, Fletcher), will be given here. It is surprising that other dramatists have not furnished something.

A very meagre gathering of fragments from other sources follows those which have been gleaned from the dramatists, but it must be once more said that there is not an absolute certainty that all of these belong to ballads.

Some popular tales are interspersed with verses of a ballad character, and one or two cases have been incidentally noted already. Examples are ' The Paddo,' Chambers's Popular Rhymes of Scotland, 1870, p. 87 ; † ' The Red Etin,' *ib.* p. 89 ; ' The Black Bull of Norroway,' *ib.* p. 95 ; ' Child Rowland and Burd Ellen,' Illustrations of Northern Antiquities, p. 397 ; ‡ ' The Golden Ball,' see No 95, **H**, II, 353–55.

SHAKSPERE

From King Lear, Act iii, sc. 4, printed 1608.

> Child Rowland to the darke tower came.
> His word was still, Fy, fo, and fumme !
> I smell the bloud of a British man.

1. *So* 1623 : *both quartos*, darke towne come.

Act iii, sc. 6.

> Sleepest or wakest thou, jolly shepheard ?
> Thy sheepe bee in the corne ;
> And for one blast of thy minikin mouth
> Thy sheepe shall take no harme.

From The Taming of the Shrew, Act iv, sc. 1, printed 1623, I, 221.

> It was the friar of orders gray,
> As he forth walked on his way.

BEAUMONT AND FLETCHER

From The Knight of the Burning Pestle, produced apparently in 1611, Act ii, sc. 8 ; Dyce, II, 173.

> She cares not for her daddy,
>   Nor she cares not for her mammy,

* Stanza 1¹,² of Percy's ballad is from The Taming of the Shrew, iv, 1 ; 3, 5, 7, are, wholly or in part, from Hamlet, iv, 5 ; 12, 13, from Fletcher's Queen of Corinth, iii, 2 ; 15 from Hamlet, as before ; 17, 18, from Much Ado about Nothing, ii, 3 ; one line of 22 from King Lear, iii, 4.

† The verses from this tale are printed separately in Buchan's Ballads of the North of Scotland, I, 117, ' The Maid and Fairy.'

‡ But Jamieson confesses: " Of the verses which have been introduced I cannot answer for the exactness of any,

except the stanza put into the mouth of the king of Elfland, which was indelibly impressed upon my memory [though J. was only seven or eight years old] long before I knew anything of Shakspere." The stanza is : [in came the king of Elfland,]

> ' With fi, fi, fo and fum !
>   I smell the blood of a Christian man ;
> Be he dead, be he living, wi my brand
>   I 'll clash his harns frae his harn-pan.'

For she is, she is, she is, she is
  My lord of Lowgave's lassy.
(*Perhaps only a song.*)

Give him flowers enow, palmer, give him flowers
  enow,
Give him red and white, and blue, green, and
  yellow.

Act v, sc. iii ; Dyce, p. 226.

With that came out his paramour,
She was as white as the lily-flower.
    Hey, troul, troly, loly

With that came out her own dear knight,
He was as true as ever did fight.

From Bonduca, produced before March, 1619 : Act v,
sc. 2, Dyce, V, 88.

It was an old tale, ten thousand times told,
Of a young lady was turnd into mould,
Her life it was lovely, her death it was bold.

From The Two Noble Kinsmen, printed in 1634, Act
iii, sc. 4; Dyce, XI, 383.

For I 'll cut my green coat a foot above my knee,
And I 'll clip my yellow locks an inch below mine ee.
    Hey, nonny, nonny, nonny

He 's buy me a white cut, forth for to ride,
And I 'll go seek him through the world that is so
  wide.
    Hey, nonny, nonny, nonny

———◆———

The Complaynt of Scotland, 1549, gives
two lines of a song on the murder, in 1517, of
the Sieur de la Bastie, a distinguished knight
in the service of the Regent, Duke of Albany.
The song may, or may not, have been a ballad.

God sen the Duc hed byddin in France,
  And Delabauté hed neuyr cum hame.
                    ed. Leyden, p. 100.

———◆———

The History of the Houses of Douglas and Angus, written
by Master David Hume of Godscroft, p. 155, Edinburgh,
1644.

Of the treacherous execution of William,
sixth Earl of Douglas, at the castle of Edinburgh, in 1440, Hume of Godscroft says : " It

is sure the people did abhorre it, execrating
the very place where it was done; in detesta-
tion of the fact of which the memory remain-
eth yet to our dayes in these words." Since
Hume mentions no ballad, it is not likely that
he knew of more than this single stanza, or
that more existed. (Sir Walter Scott, however, confidently assumes that there was a
ballad. Minstrelsy, 1833, I, 221 f.)

    Edinburgh castle, towne, and tower,
      God grant thou sinke for sinne !
    And that even for the black dinner
      Earle Douglas got therein.

———◆———

Written on the fly-leaf of a little volume printed at Edinburgh about 1670 (Quevedo's Novels), Laing MSS, University of Edinburgh, Div. II, 358. (Communicated by Mr
Macmath.)

' He steps full statly on yᵉ stre[et],
  He hads yᵉ charters of him sell,
In to his cloathing he is compl[ete],
  In Craford's mure he bears yᵉ bell.

' I wish I had died my own fai[r] death,
  In tender age, qⁿ I was young ;
I would never have broke my heart
  For yᵉ love of any churl's son.

' Wo be to my parents all,
  Yᵗ lives so farr beyond yᵉ sea !
I might have lived a noble life,
  And wedded in my own countrë.'

———◆———

Finlay's Scottish Ballads, I, xxxii.

A " romantic ballad, of which, unfortunately, one stanza only has been preserved.
The tradition bears that a young lady was
carried away by the fairies, and that, although
invisible to her friends who were in search of
her, she was sometimes heard by them lamenting her destiny in a pathetic song, of
which the stanza just mentioned runs nearly
thus : "

    O Alva hills is bonny,
      Dalycoutry hills is fair,
    But to think on the braes of Menstrie
      It maks my heart fu sair.

———◆———

KING EDELBRODE

Sent by Motherwell to C. K. Sharpe, with a letter dated
October 8, 1825. Also entered in Motherwell's Note-Book,
p. 53 (excepting the second line of the first stanza).

> King Edelbrode cam owre the sea,
>> Fa la lilly
> All for to marry a gay ladye.
>> Fa la lilly.

(Then follows the description of a queen,
jimp and sma, not remembered.)

> Her lilly hands, sae white and sma,
>> Fa la lilly
> Wi gouden rings were buskit braw.
>> Fa la lilly

" I cannot get any precise account of its
subject, but it related somehow to a most
magnificent marriage. The old lady who
sung it died some years ago." (Letter to
Sharpe.)

" It may be the same ballad as the scrap
I have, with something of a similar chorus."
(Note-Book, where the " chorus " is Fa fa
lilly.)

The reference seems to be to ' The Whummil Bore,' No 27, I, 255.

———◆———

C. K. Sharpe's Letters, ed. Allardyce, II, 106 (1813).

> ' O come you from the earth ? ' she said,
> ' Or come you from the skye ? '
> ' Oh, I am from yonder churchyard,
>> Where my crumbling relicks lie.'

Sharpe somewhere asks, Where does this
belong ?

Possibly in some version of ' Proud Lady
Margaret,' No 47, II, 425.

———◆———

MS. of Thomas Wilkie, p. 79, " Scotch Ballads, Materials
for Border Minstrelsy," No 73 a, Abbotsford.

> The great bull of Bendy-law
> Has broken his band and run awa,
> And the king and a' his court
> Canna turn that bull about.

———◆———

" Scotch Ballads, Materials for Border Minstrelsy," No
86 a, Abbotsford, in the handwriting of Thomas Wilkie.

> Red-Cap he was there,
>> And he was there indeed,

> And he was standing by,
>> With a red cap on his head.

———◆———

" Scotch Ballads, Materials for Border Minstrelsy," No
73 a; MS. of Thomas Wilkie, Abbotsford, derived by
Wilkie from his father, " who heard a Lady Brigs sing
this when he was a boy."

> He took a sword in every hand
> And on the house did venture,
> And swore if they wad not gee her up
> He would make all their doors play clatter.

> Her angry father, when he saw this,
> That he would lose his ae daughter,
> He swore if he had not been gude at the sword
> He durst not come to make his doors clatter.

———◆———

> It was far in the night, and the bairnies grat ;
> The mither beneath the mools heard that.

sung in Wuthering Heights, ch. 9, has not
unnaturally been taken for a relic of a traditional Scottish ballad of a dead mother returning to her abused children. It is, in fact,
a stanza (not literally well remembered) from
the Danish ballad ' Moderen under Mulde,'
Grundtvig, II, 470, No 89, B 11, translated
by Jamieson, and given in the notes to the
fourth canto of Scott's Lady of the Lake.

———◆———

The following " fragment," given in Motherwell's MS., p. 184, " from Mr William Steele
of Greenock, advocate," I suppose to have
been the effort of a self-satisfied amateur, and
to have been written as a fragment. The
third and fourth stanzas recall the broadside
ballad ' The Lady Isabella's Tragedy.'

> Lady Margaret has bound her silken snood
>> A little aboon her bree,
> Lady Margaret has kilted her grey mantel
>> A little aboon her knee.

> Lady Margaret has left her bonnie bower,
>> But and her father's ha,
> And with Lord Hugh Montgomerie
>> Lady Margaret has gane awa.

*   *   *   *   *   *   *   *

> ' I have made a bed, Lady Margaret,
>> Beneath the hawthorn-tree ;

It's lang and it's deep, and there thou shalt
     sleep
  Till I come back to thee.'

*   *   *   *   *   *   *   *   *

Then out and spake her father dear,
  As he sat down to dine,
'Gae, page, and tell Lady Margaret to come
  And fill for me the wine.

'Gae, page, and tell Lady Margaret to come
  And glad her father's ee ;

The wine that is poured by her fair, fair hand
  Is sweetest aye to me.'

Then out and spake the fat earth-worm,
  That wons beneath the stane ;
'Yestreen I fed on a rosie cheek
  And on a white hause-bane.

'Yestreen I fed on a rosy cheek
  And on a snaw-white bree ;
But never again Lady Margaret
  Shall fill the wine for thee."

ADDITIONS AND CORRECTIONS

VOL. I.

1. Riddles Wisely Expounded.

P. 1 a, VI, 496 a. Guess or die. Kristensen, Jyske Folkeminder, X, 2, 'Svend Bondes Spørgsmaal,' **B.**
3–5. From Miss M. H. Mason's Nursery Rhymes and Country Songs, p. 31; sung in Northumberland.

E

1 There was a lady in the West,
 Lay the bank with the bonny broom
She had three daughters of the best.
  Fa lang the dillo
  Fa lang the dillo dillo dee

2 There came a stranger to the gate,
 And he three days and nights did wait.

3 The eldest daughter did ope the door,
 The second set him on the floor.

4 The third daughter she brought a chair,
 And placed it that he might sit there.

  (*To first daughter.*)

5 'Now answer me these questions three,
 Or you shall surely go with me.

  (*To second daughter.*)

6 'Now answer me these questions six,
 Or you shall surely be Old Nick's.

  (*To all three.*)

7 'Now answer me these questions nine,
 Or you shall surely all be mine.

8 'What is greener than the grass?
 What is smoother than crystal glass?

9 'What is louder than a horn?
 What is sharper than a thorn?

10 'What is brighter than the light?
 What is darker than the night?

11 'What is keener than an axe?
 What is softer than melting wax?

12 'What is rounder than a ring?'
 'To you we thus our answers bring.

13 'Envy is greener than the grass,
 Flattery smoother than crystal glass.

14 'Rumour is louder than a horn,
 Hunger is sharper than a thorn.

15 'Truth is brighter than the light,
 Falsehood is darker than the night.

16 'Revenge is keener than an axe,
 Love is softer than melting wax.

17 'The world is rounder than a ring,
 To you we thus our answers bring.

18 'Thus you have our answers nine,
 And we never shall be thine.'

Findlay's MSS, I, 151, from J. Milne.

 ' What 's greener than the grass?
 What 's higher than the clouds?
 What is worse than women's tongues?
 What 's deeper than the floods? '

 ' Hollin 's greener than the grass,
 Heaven 's higher than the clouds,
 The devil 's worse than women's tongues,
 Hell 's deeper than the floods.'

2. The Elfin Knight.

P. 7 b, III, 496 a, IV, 439 a. 'Store Fordringer,' Kristensen, Jyske Folkeminder, XI, 175, No 66 (three copies), 294, No 4. 'Umulige Fordringer,' Kristensen, Efterslæt til Skattegraveren, p. 20, No 16.
14 a, II, 495. After the note to 14 a at II, 495, add : C. R. Lanman.
17. Communicated by Mr Walker, of Aberdeen, as sung, 1893, by John Walker, Portlethen ; learned by him from his father, above fifty years before.

1 There was a knight on the head o yon hill
   Blowing his horn lood and shrill.
     Blow, blow, blow the wind, blow

2 ' Ye 'se get to me a camrick sark
   Without ae steek o needlewark.

3 ' An ye will wash it in a wall
   Where rain never fell nor water sprang.

4 ' An ye sall dry it on a thorn
   That never wis sprung sin Adam was born.'

5 ' Ye 'se gie me an acre o red lan
   Atween the see an the watery san.

6 ' An ye will plough it wi yer horn,
   An sa it a' wi ae pick o corn.

7 '.   .   .   .   .   .   .
   An cut it doon wi a sheepshank bone.

8 ' An ye will big it in the sea,
   An bring the foonshief dry to me.

9 ' An when ye have done and finished yer wark,
   Come in, Jock Sheep, an ye 'll get yer sark.'

As delivered, 5–8 precede 2–4.

17, 484 b. **M.** Findlay's MSS, I, 21, from the
recitation of Jeany Meldrum, Framedrum, Forfarshire.
17, II, 495 b. In The Monthly Chronicle of North
Country Lore and Legend, III, 7, ' Whittingham Fair '
is given by Mr Stokoe with a few variations.

   1. *Second line of refrain,*
      For once she was a true lover of mine.
   2, 4. *Second line of refrain,*
      Then she shall be a true lover.
   3. *Second line of refrain,*
      And she shall be a true lover.
   5. *Second line of refrain,*
      Before he shall be a true lover.
   6. *Second line of refrain,*
      Then he shall be a true lover.
   7, 8, 9. *Second line of refrain,*
      And he shall be a true lover.
   6[1]. to buy.   8[1]. to sheer 't.
After 8 : Tell him to thrash it on yonder wall,
      And never let one corn of it fall.
      Then he shall be a true lover of mine.

17, 484 f., II, 495 f., IV, 439 f.
' Scarborough Fair,' taken down by H. M. Bower,
December, 1891, from William Moat, a Whitby fisherman. English County Songs, by Lucy E. Broadwood
and J. A. Fuller Maitland, 1893, p. 12.

1 ' Is any of you going to Scarborough Fair?
   Remember me to a lad as lives there ;
   Remember me to a lad as lives there ;
   For once he was a true lover of mine.

   (*Second line always twice.*)

2 ' Tell him to bring me an acre of land
   Betwixt the wild ocean and yonder sea sand ;
   And then he shall be a true lover of mine.

3 ' Tell him to plough it with one ram's horn,
   And sow it all over with one pepper corn ;
   And then he shall be a true lover of mine.

4 ' Tell him to reap it with sickle of leather,
   And bind it together with one peacock-feather ;
   And then he shall be a true lover of mine.

5 ' And now I have answered your questions three,
   I hope you 'll answer as many for me ;
   And then thou shalt be a true lover of mine.'

6 ' Is any of you going to Scarborough Fair ?
   Remember me to a lass as lives there ;
   For once she was a true lover of mine.

7 ' Tell her to make me a cambric shirt,
   Without any needles or thread, or owt through't ;
   And then she shall be a true lover of mine.

8 ' Tell her to wash it by yonder wall,
   Where water neer sprung, nor a drop o rain fall ;
   And then she shall be a true lover of mine.

9 ' Tell her to dry it on yonder thorn,
   Where blossom neer grew sin Adam was born ;
   And then she shall be a true lover of mine.

10 ' And now I have answered your questions three,
   And I hope you 'll answer as many for me ;
   And then thou shalt be a true lover of mine.'

Rev. S. Baring-Gould gives me these variations, from
the West of England :

   ' O tell her to bleach it on yonder fresh grass,
   Where never a foot or a hoof did pass.'

   ' O tell him to thresh it in yonder barn,
   That hangs to the sky by a thread of yarn.'
             (Dartmoor.)

   ' Pray take it up in a bottomless sack,
     And every leaf grows merry in time
   And bear it to the mill on a butterfly's back.
   O thus you shall be a true lover of mine '
             (Cornwall.)

4. Lady Isabel and the Elf-Knight.

P. 26 b. **Danish.** ' Kvindemorderen,' two fragments ; Kristensen, Folkeminder, XI, 62, No 33.
29–37, 486 a, IV, 441 a. **FF.** ' Schön Hannchen,'
Frischbier und Sembrzycki, Hundert Ostpreussische

Volkslieder, 1893, p. 35, No 22, from Angerburg, 51 vv. The ballad is of the third class. Hannchen walks in the wood, and Ulrich advances to meet her. The birds are all singing, and the maid asks why. 'Every bird has its song,' says Ulrich; 'go you your gait.' He takes her under a briar where there is a pretty damsel (who is quite superfluous). Hannchen lays her head in the damsel's lap and begins to weep. The damsel asks whether her weeping is for her father's gear, or because Ulrich is not good enough for her. It is not for her father's gear, and Ulrich is good enough. 'Is it, then,' says the damsel or Ulrich, 'for the stakes on which the eleven maidens are hanging? Rely upon it, you shall be the twelfth.' She begs for three cries, which are addressed to God, her parents, and her brothers. The brothers hear, hasten to the wood, and encounter Ulrich, who pretends to know nothing of their sister. His shoes are red with blood. 'Why not?' says Ulrich, 'I have shot a dove.' They know who the dove is. Hannchen is borne to the churchyard, Ulrich is strung up on the gallows. No 23 of the same collection is **X**.

'Die schöne Anna,' Böckel, Deutsche Volkslieder aus Oberhessen, p. 86, No 103, 'Als die wunderschöne Anna,' Lewalter, Deutsche V. l. in Niederhessen gesammelt, 1ᵉ Heft, No 24, p. 51, and also No 25, are fragmentary pieces, varieties of **DD**, I, 486 a.

37 b, 3d paragraph. A variety of **A** is printed in Altpreussische Monatschrift, N. F., XXVIII, 632, 1892, without indication of local derivation, 'Der Ritter und die Königstochter.' The knight takes measures (not very summary ones) to drown himself.

43 b (or 44 a), 488 a, III, 497 a, IV, 441 b. **Italian.** Add: Canti popolari Emiliani by Maria Carmi, Archivio, XII, 178, No 2.

44 b, 1st paragraph. Add: 'El Mariner' and 'Giovanina,' Villanis, Canzoni p. Zaratine, in Archivio XI, 33, 34, Nos 2, 3.

58. **E.** A copy of 'The Outlandish Knight,' with unimportant verbal variations, is given in English County Songs, by Lucy E. Broadwood and J. A. Fuller Maitland, p. 164.

III, 497 b. A pair on horseback go a long way without speaking. A trait in Polish, French, and Italian versions of No 4. Add: Munthe, Folkpoesi från Asturien, p. 118 f., VII, **A**, 76 f., **B**, 70 f. ('Don Bueso,' Duran, I, lxv, no hablara la niña.) Dead lover and maid in Bartoš, Nové národne pisně moravské, p. 150. Lagus, Nyländske F. visor, 'Kung Valdemo' (= Ribold), No 1, a, 28, b, 18, 'Kämpen Grimborg,' No 3, a, 21, b, 19.

5. Gil Brenton.

P. 62. In Traditional Stories of Old Families, by Andrew Picken, 1833, I, 289, 'The Three Maids of Loudon,' occur the following stanzas:

Seven pretty sisters dwelt in a bower,
  With a hey-down, and a ho-down

And they twined the silk, and they workd the flower.
  Sing a hey-down and a ho-down

And they began for seven years' wark,
  With a hey-down and a ho-down
All for to make their dear loves a sark.
  With a hey down and a ho-down

O three long years were passd and gone,
And they had not finishd a sleeve but one.

'O we'll to the woods, and we'll pull a rose,'
And up they sprang all at this propose.

(W. Macmath.)

6. Willie's Lady.

P. 82 a. 'Barselkvinden,' three fragments, Kristensen, Folkeminder, XI, 42, No 23.

85 b, 3d paragraph. Say, of the parish of Logierait.

7. Earl Brand.

P. 88, III, 498 b, IV, 443 a. 'Hr. Ribolt.' **Danish.** Add: Skattegraveren, VI, 17, No 257, 'Nævnet til døde,' Kristensen, Efterslæt til Skattegraveren, p. 81, No 76; Folkeminder, XI, 36, No 22, A–D.

91 f. 489 b, III, 498 b, IV, 443 a. **Swedish.** ['Ridborg,'] Thomasson, Visor från Bleking, Nyare Bidrag, etc., VII, No 6, p. 12, No 7.

96 b. **Danish.** 'Hertug Frydenborg,' Danmarks g. Folkeviser, No 305, V, II, 216. **A a, b, h, n, o; B b, c; E, k, l; F b, c, e, f**; with diversities, the plant nearly always lilies. (A few of these, from Kristensen, have been already cited.)

9. The Fair Flower of Northumberland.

P. 116. **D.** In a copy sent by Motherwell to C. K. Sharpe with a letter, October 8, 1825, this version is said to have been obtained from Mrs Nicol, of Paisley.

117, 493 a.

G

'The Heiress of Northumberland,' from C. K. Sharpe's first collection, p. 7.

Sir W. Scott, commenting on this copy (to which he by mistake gives the title of The Stirrup of Northumberland), says: "An edition considerably varied both from Ritson's and the present I have heard sung by the Miss Tytlers of Woodhouselee. The tune is a very pretty lilt." Sharpe's Ballad Book, ed. 1880, p. 142.

At the end of the ballad we are told: Tradition's story is that the hero of this song was one of the Earls of Douglass, who was taken captive and put in prison by Percy, Earl of Northumberland.

1 'Why, fair maid, have pity on me,'
　　Waly 's my love wi the life that she wan
　'For I am bound in prison strong,
　　And under the heir o Northumberland.'

2 'How can I have pity on thee,'
　　Waly 's my love, etc.
　'When thou hast a wife and children three,
　　All dwelling at home in fair Scotland ? '

3 Now he has sworn a solemn oath,
　　And it was by eternity,
　That wife and children he had none,
　　All dwelling at home in fair Scotland.

4 Now she 's gone to her father's bedstock,
　　Waly 's my love, etc.
　And has stolen the key of the dungeon-lock,
　　And she the great heir o Northumberland.

5 And she 's gone to her father's chest,
　　She has stolen away a suit of the best,
　　Altho she was heir o Northumberland.

6 Now she 's gone to her father's coffer,
　　And has taen out gold nane kens how meickle,
　　Altho she, etc.

7 She 's gane to her father's stable,
　　And taen out a steed baith lusty and able,
　　For a' she was heir, etc.

8 The rade till they came to Crafurdmoor,
　　He bade her light down for an English whore,
　　Altho she, etc.

9 The rade till the came to the water o Clyde,
　　He bade her light down, nae farer she should
　　　ride,
　'For now I am at hame in fair Scotland.'

10 'Yonder view my castle,' said he ;
　'There I hae a wife and children three,
　　All dwelling at home,' etc.

11 'O take me by the middle sae sma
　　And thro me oer your castle-wa,
　　For I darena gang hame to Northumber-
　　　land.'

12 When she came to her father's yett,
　　She durst hardly rapp thereat,
　　Altho she was, etc.

13 Out then spoke her stepmother sour,
　　She bad her pack off for an impudent whore,
　'For thou shalt not be heir o Northumber-
　　　land.'

14 Out then spock her bastard brother ;
　'She 'll hae nae mair grace than God has gien
　　　her,
　　And she shall be heir o Northumberland.'

15 Out and spoke her father sae mild,
　'She 's no the first maid a false Scot has be-
　　　guild,
　　And she shall be,' etc.

10. The Twa Sisters.

P. 125, 493 b, II, 498 b, III, 499 a, IV, 447 b. 'Les roseaux qui chantent, Revue des Traditions Populaires, VII, 223 (blue flower) ; 'L'os qui chante,' discussion of the tale by M. Charles Ploix, Rev. des Trad. Pop., VIII, 129 ff.

11. The Cruel Brother.

P. 142 b, 496 a, III, 499 a, IV, 449 a. Add a ballad of Rissiäld, Canti popolari Emiliani, Maria Carmi, Archivio, XII, 185, No 7.

144 a, l. 18. 'Le Testament de Marion.' Another version, 'La belo Marioun,' Laroche, Folklore du Lauraguais, p. 247.

144 b, 2d paragraph. Add at the end : the (she) ass, Testament de l'Âne, Buchon, Noels et Chants pop. de la Franche-Comté, p. 89, No 28 ; and elsewhere.

147. **E.** For this stanza we find, whatever may be the explanation, the following in Findlay MSS, I, 146. "From Miss Butchart, Arbroath."

　　There were three sisters livd in a bouer,
　　　With a hech hey an a lillie gay
　　There cam a knicht to be their wooer.
　　　An the primrose springs sae sweetly
　　　　Sing Annet, an Marrot, an fair Maisrie,
　　　　An the dew hangs in the wood, gay ladie.

12. Lord Randal.

P. 152 b, 498 b, III, 499 b. **Italian.** Three imperfect versions (Sardinian) in Ferraro, C. p. in dialetto logudorese, 1891, pp. 3–5.

156 a, last paragraph, northern ballad. Add : ' Den onde svigermoder,' Kristensen, Jyske Folkeviser, I, 332, No 122; Skattegraveren, V, 84, No 635.

157, 499, IV, 449.

'Lairde Rowlande, or Ronalde,' The Sporting Magazine, XXV, 209, January, 1805; communicated by

Philodice, as recited by a "peasant's girl" at Rand-callas, Perthshire. (Reprinted by Mr Edward Peacock in The Athenæum, August 27, 1892, p. 288.)

1 ' Ah, where have you been, Lairde Rowlande, my son?
Ah, where have you been, Lairde Rowlande, my son?'
' I 've been in the wild woods ; mither, mak my bed soon,
For I 'm weary wi hunting and faine would lie down.'

2 ' Oh, you 've been at your true-love's, Lairde Rowlande, my son,' etc.
' I 've been at my true-love's ; mither,' etc.

3 ' What got you to dinner?' etc.
' I got eels boild in brue ; mither,' etc.

4 ' What 's become of your warden?' etc.
' He died in the muirlands ; mither,' etc.

5 ' What 's become of your stag-hounds ?' etc.
' They swelled and they died; mither,' etc.

' Jacky, my son,' written out by Miss F. J. Adams, a Devonshire lady, and derived by her from her Devonshire nurse, sixty or seventy years ago. (Rev. S. Baring-Gould.)

1 ' Where hast thou been to-day, Jacky, my son?
Where hast thou been to-day, my honey man?'
' Oh, I 've been a courting, mother, make my bed soon,
For I am sick to the heart, fain would lie down.'

2 ' Where shall I make it to?' etc.
' Oh, in the churchyard, mother,' etc.

3 ' What wilt thou leave thy mother?' etc.
' Oh, I 'll leave her my money, mother,' etc.

4 ' What wilt thou leave thy father?' etc.
' Oh, I 'll leave him my 'state, mother,' etc.

5 ' What wilt thou leave thy sweetheart?' etc.
' A rope for to hang her, mother,' etc.

' The Croodin Doo.' Findlay MSS, I, 192.

1 ' Whare did ye get your dinner the day,
My wee, wee croodin doo?'
(Twice.)

2 ' I got it in my step-mither's ha,
Oh, granny, mak my bed noo.'
(Twice.)

3 ' What did ye get to your dinner the day,
My wee, wee croodin doo?'
(Twice.)

4 ' I got a wee fishie wi four wee feeties,
Oh, granny, mak my bed noo.'
(Twice.)

5 'Did ony body eat it but yoursel,
My wee, wee croodin doo?'
(Twice.)

6 ' I gied the banes to my wee, wee dogie,
Oh, granny, mak my bed noo ;
He streekit out his head an died at my feet,
O, granny, een as I do noo.'

Among C. K. Sharpe's papers, and in his handwriting, is a piece in dialogue between Mother and Son headed, Death of Lord Rounal, a Gaelic ballad founded on a tradition of his receiving poison by treachery at the castle of his mistress' father, and dying on his return home. This is the familiar Scottish ballad made over in English and mildly sentimental phraseology. All the Celtic in it is "dark Dungael, the chief of meikle guile," the father.

13. Edward.

P. 167 b, 501 b, III 499 b. **Swedish.** 'Sven i Rosengård' in Thomasson, Visor från Bleking, Nyare Bidrag, etc., VII, No 6, p. 16, No 9.

168 a, second paragraph, 'when stones float,' etc. Compare Sir John Mandeville, as to the Dead Sea, ch. 9 (of the Cotton MS.): "And zif a man caste iren therein, it wole flete aboven, and zif men caste a fedre therein, it wol synke to the botme."

14. Babylon, or, The Bonnie Banks o Fordie.

P. 170, II, 499 a, III, 500. Add to the French ballad, ' C'est trois garçons dépaysés,' Pineau, Le Folk-Lore du Poitou, p. 281 ; ' Les Coumpagnons,' Laroche, Folklore du Lauraguais, p. 245.

171 a. **Danish.** Add : Hr. Tures Døtre, Kristensen, Folkeminder, XI, 145, No 56.

15. Leesome Brand.

P. 178 b. **Danish.** Add : ' Barnefødsel i Lunden,' Kristensen, Folkeminder, XI, 102, No 45, **A-I,** 9 copies.

181 b, II, 499 a. **French, B.** Add : ' La-bas, sus ces grands champs,' Pineau, Le Folk-Lore du Poitou, p. 315.

16. Sheath and Knife.

P. 185, III, 500. In C. K. Sharpe's papers there is the following version, in Motherwell's handwriting, sent by him to Sharpe with a letter dated Paisley, 8th October, 1825.

F

'The Broom blooms bonnie,' from the recitation of Agnes Lyle, Kilbarchan.

1 'There is a feast in your father's house,
    The broom blooms bonnie, and so is it fair
    It becomes you and me to be very douce.'
      And we 'll never gang up to the broom nae mair

2 'Will you go to yon hill so hie,
    Take your bow and your arrow wi thee.'

3 He 's tane his lady on his back,
    And his auld son in his coat-lap.

4 'When ye hear me give a cry,
    Ye 'll shoot your bow and let me ly.

5 'When ye see me lying still,
    Throw awa your bow and come running me till.'

6 When he heard her gie a cry,
    He shot his bow and he let her lye.

7 When he saw she was lying still,
    He threw awa his bow and came running her till.

8 It was nae wonder his heart was sad,
    When he shot his auld son at her head.

9 He howkit a grave lang, large and wide,
    He buried his auld son down by her side.

10 It was nae wonder his heart was sair,
    When he shooled the mools on her yellow hair.

11 'Oh,' said his father, ' son, but thou 'rt sad,
    At our braw meeting you micht be glad.'

12 'Oh,' said he, 'father, I 've lost my knife,
    I loved as dear almost as my own life.

13 'But I have lost a far better thing,
    I lost the sheathe that the knife was in.'

14 'Hold thy tongue and mak nae din,
    I 'll buy thee a sheath and a knife therein.'

15 'A' the ships ere sailed the sea
    Neer 'll bring such a sheathe and knife to me.

16 'A' the smiths that lives on land
    Will neer bring such a sheath and knife to my hand.'

III, 500. **E.** Colonel W. F. Prideaux has printed this piece, from a manuscript of Motherwell's in his possession, in Notes and Queries, Eighth Series, I, 372, with the trifling variations (or confirmations of doubtful readings) here annexed.

    1¹ Ane.   3¹. we 'll hunt
    6¹. let me doun by the rute o the.
    7². And *wanting* : as ony.
    9². faithless.   10¹. The ae.

17. Hind Horn.

P. 196 a (7). Historia: Hertzog Heinrich der löw, XVI, 221, of the edition of the Litt. Verein in Stuttgart, ed. Goetze, 228 vv.

198 a. Tales. Add : Stier, Ungarische Volksmärchen, p. 53.

198 b, 502 b, II, 499 b, IV, 450 b. 'Le retour du mari,' Pineau, Le Folk-Lore du Poitou, p. 385; La Tradition, VI, 207 f.

199 b. **Romaic.** Add : Manousos, II, 73; Ζωγραφεῖος Ἀγών, p. 76, No 26.

205. **G.** Kinloch has made numerous small changes. The ballad will now be given as first written down, Kinloch MSS, VII, 117. It appears to have been derived by Miss Kinnear from Christy Smith.

1 'Hynde Horn 's bound, love, and Hynde Horn 's free;
    Whare was ye born? or frae what cuntrie?'

2 'In gude greenwud whare I was born,
    And all my friends left me forlorn.

3 'I gave my love a gay gowd wand,
    That was to rule oure all Scotland.

4 'My love gave me a silver ring,
    That was to rule abune aw thing.

5 'Whan that ring keeps new in hue,
    Ye may ken that your love loves you.

6 'Whan that ring turns pale and wan,
    Ye may ken that your love loves anither man.'

7 He hoisted up his sails, and away sailed he
  Till he cam to a foreign cuntree.

8 Whan he lookit to his ring, it was turnd pale and
      wan ;
  Says, I wish I war at hame again.

9 He hoisted up his sails, and hame sailed he
  Until he cam till his ain cuntree.

10 The first ane that he met with,
   It was with a puir auld beggar-man.

11 ' What news? what news, my puir auld man?
   What news hae ye got to tell to me?'

12 ' Na news, na news,' the puirman did say,
   ' But this is our queen's wedding-day.'

13 ' Ye 'll lend me your begging-weed,
   And I 'll lend you my riding-steed.'

14 ' My begging-weed is na for thee,
   Your riding-steed is na for me.'

15 He has changed wi the puir auld beggar-man.

16 ' What is the way that ye use to gae?
   And what are the words that ye beg wi?'

17 ' Whan ye come to yon high hill,
   Ye'll draw your bent bow nigh until.

18 ' Whan ye come to yon town-end,
   Ye 'll lat your bent bow low fall doun.

19 ' Ye'll seek meat for St Peter, ask for St Paul,
   And seek for the sake of your Hynde Horn all.

20 ' But tak ye frae nane o them aw
   Till ye get frae the bonnie bride hersel O.'

21 Whan he cam to yon high hill,
   He drew his bent bow nigh until.

22 And when he cam to yon toun-end,
   He loot his bent bow low fall doun.

23 He sought for St Peter, he askd for St Paul,
   And he sought for the sake of his Hynde Horn all.

24 But he took na frae ane o them aw
   Till he got frae the bonnie bride hersel O.

25 The bride cam tripping doun the stair,
   Wi the scales o red gowd on her hair.

26 Wi a glass o red wine in her hand,
   To gie to the puir beggar-man.

27 Out he drank his glass o wine,
   Into it he dropt the ring.

28 ' Got ye 't by sea, or got ye 't by land,
   Or got ye 't aff a drownd man's hand?'

29 ' I got na 't by sea, I got na 't by land,
   Nor gat I it aff a drownd man's hand;

30 ' But I got it at my wooing,
   And I 'll gie it to your wedding.

31 ' I 'll tak the scales o gowd frae my head,
   I 'll follow you, and beg my bread.

32 ' I 'll tak the scales o gowd frae my hair,
   I 'll follow you for evermair.'

33 She has tane the scales o gowd frae her head,
   She 's followed him, to beg her bread.

34 She has tane the scales o gowd frae her hair,
   And she has followd him evermair.

35 Atween the kitchen and the ha,
   There he loot his cloutie cloak fa.

36 The red gowd shined oure them aw,
   And the bride frae the bridegroom was stown awa.

19. King Orfeo.

P. 215. Professor Sophus Bugge maintains that the
Scandinavian ballad ' Harpens Kraft ' shows acquaint-
ance with the English romance, and indeed, like the
English ballad, is derived from it. (Arkiv för nordisk
Filologi, VII, 97 ff., 1891.)

20. The Cruel Mother.

P. 218. Findlay's MSS, I, 58 f., derived from his
mother.

1 I lookëd ower the castle-wa,
    Hey rose, ma lindie, O
  Saw twa bonnie babies playin at the ba.
    Doon in the green wood-sidie, O

2 ' O bonnie babies, an ye were mine,
   I wad feid ye wi flour-breid an wine.'

3 ' O cruel mother, when we were thine,
   You did not prove to us sae kin.'

4 ' O bonnie babies, an ye were mine,
   I wad cleid ye wi scarlet sae fine.'

5 ' O cruel mother, when we were thine,
   You did not prove to us sae fine.

6 ' For wi a penknife ye took our life
  And threw us ower the castle-wa.'

7 ' O bonnie babies, what wad ye hae dune to me
  For my bein sae cruel to thee?'

8 ' Seven yeare a fish in the flood,
  Seven yeare a bird in the wood.

9 ' Seven yeare a tinglin bell,
  Seventeen yeare in the deepest hell.'
  Under the green wood-sidie, O

219 b, 504 a, II, 500 a, III, 502 b, IV, 451 a. Add
S, Deutsche Volksballaden aus Südungarn, Grünn und
Baróti, in Ethnologische Mitteilungen aus Ungarn, II,
201, No 4, 1892.

21. The Maid and the Palmer.

P. 228. M. G. Doncieux has attempted to arrange
"Le cycle de Sainte Marie-Madelaine," in Revue des
Traditions Populaires, VI, 257.

22. St Stephen and Herod.

P. 233 ff. ' Stjærnevisen,' Kristensen, XI, 207, No
76 **A, B**, has nothing about Stephen, but is confined to
the scripture-history, piety, and New Year's wishes.

P. 236 a, IV, 451 b. **French.** An imperfect French
ballad in Mélusine, VI, 24, from a wood-cut "at least
three centuries old."

Add a Piedmontese popular tale communicated by
Count Nigra to the editor of Mélusine, VI, 25 f.

M. Gaidoz, at the same place, 26 f., cites two versions of the resuscitation of the cock, from example-
books. The first, from Erythræus (i. e. Rossi), ch. CLV,
p. 187, is essentially the same as the legend of St Gunther
given from Acta Sanctorum (p. 239 a). The other, from
the Giardino d' Essempi of Razzi, is the story told by
Vincentius (p. 237, note †).

25. Willie's Lyke-Wake.

P. 250, II, 502 a, III, 503 a. **Italian.** Add : Canti
pop. Emiliani, Maria Carmi, Archivio, XII, 187, No 9.
A fragment in Dalmedico, Canti del popolo veneziano,
p. 109, seems, as Maria Carmi suggests, to belong to this
ballad.

26. The Three Ravens.

P. 253. It has already been noted that traditional
copies of ' The Three Ravens' have been far from infre-
quent. When a ballad has been nearly three hundred
years in print, and in a very impressive form, the
chance that traditional copies, differing principally by
what they lack, should be coeval and independent
amounts at most to a bare possibility. Traditional

copies have, however, sometimes been given in this collection on the ground of a very slight chance; and not
unreasonably, I think, considering the scope of the
undertaking.

The copy which follows was communicated by E. L.
K. to Notes and Queries, Eighth Series, II, 437, 1892,
and has been sent me lately in MS. by Mr R. Brimley
Johnson, of Cambridge, England, with this note :

" From E. Peacock, Esq., F. S. A., of Dunstan
House, Kirton-in-Lindsay, Lincolnshire, whose father,
born in 1793, heard it as a boy at harvest-suppers and
sheep-shearings, and took down a copy from the recitation of Harry Richard, a laborer, who could not read,
and had learnt it ' from his fore-elders.' He lived at
Northorpe, where a grass-field joining a little stream,
called Ea, Ee, and Hay, is pointed out as the scene of
the tragedy."

1 There was three ravens in a tree,
  As black as any jet could be.
        A down a derry down

2 Says the middlemost raven to his mate,
  Where shall we go to get ought to eat?

3 ' It 's down in yonder grass-green field
  There lies a squire dead and killd.

4 ' His horse all standing by his side,
  Thinking he 'll get up and ride.

5 ' His hounds all standing at his feet,
  Licking his wounds that run so deep.'

6 Then comes a lady, full of woe,
  As big wi bairn as she can go.

7 She lifted up his bloody head,
  And kissd his lips that were so red.

8 She laid her down all by his side,
  And for the love of him she died.

6². *Var.* child.

27. The Whummil Bore.

P. 255. Serving the king long without sight of his
daughter. Prof. Wollner notes that this trait is rather
frequently found in Slavic. For example, in Karadžič,
II, 617, No 96, Yakšič Mitar serves the vojvode Yanko
nine years and never sees his sister.

29. The Boy and the Mantle.

P. 268 ff., II, 502 a, III, 503, IV, 454 a. Tests of
chastity. On the Herodotean story, I, 271, see E.
Lefébure, Mélusine, IV, 37–39. — St Wilfred's Needle,
in Ripon Minster. ' In ipso templo, avorum memoria
Wilfridi acus celeberrima fuit. Id erat augustum in

cryptoporticu foramen quo mulierum pudicitia explorabatur ; quæ enim castæ erant facile transibant, quæ dubia fama nescio quo miraculo constrictæ detinebantur.' Camden, Britannia, ed. 1607, p. 570; see Folk-Lore Journal, II, 286. (G. L. K.)

31. The Marriage of Sir Gawain.

P. 293. Mr Clouston, Originals and Analogues of some of Chaucer's Canterbury Tales, p. 520 cites a pretty story from a modern Turkish author, in which, as so often happens, parts are reversed. A young king of the fairies of a certain realm is cursed by his mother to appear old and ugly until a fair mortal girl shall love him enough to miss his company. This comes to pass after forty years, and the ugly old man becomes a beautiful youth of seventeen. (Phantasms from the Presence of God, written in 1796–97 by 'Ali 'Aziz Efendi, the Cretan.)

33. Kempy Kay.

P. 301. A was communicated to C. K. Sharpe by Robert Pitcairn with the stanzas in the order printed by Sharpe. The arrangement in A would seem, therefore, to have been an afterthought of Pitcairn's. There is some slight difference of reading, also, in Pitcairn's MS., and one defect is supplied. The variations in the copy sent Sharpe are (besides the order, as aforesaid) as follows :

2^1. I 'm coming. 2^4. o weir.
3^4. three heire *wanting*. 4^4. Shone. 5^2. bruchty.
5^3. the night. 6^3. And in. 7^4. Between.
9^4. a lintseed bow (*with the variant* a bruchtit ewe).
10^1. lauchty. 10^4. A' *wanting*. 12^3. teeth into.
13^2. sheets (*no doubt erroneously*). *A stanza between* 8 *and* 9 *is noted as deficient, and something after* 13.

303. **C.** In a copy of **C** sent Sharpe by Motherwell in a letter of December 6, 1824, the fourth stanza is lacking, the fifth is third.

3^2. span : years. 5^2. stool.

'Knip Knap,' taken down in the summer of 1893 by Mr Walker, of Aberdeen, at Portlethen, from the singing of an old man, as learned more than fifty years before from an old blacksmith at Dyce, near Aberdeen.

1 Knip Knap a hunting went,
    Out-ower the head o yon hill, aye, aye
Wi a lust o pig-staves out-oer his shouther,
    An mony a dulchach forby, aye, aye

2 There he met an old woman,
    Was herdin at her kye;
'I 'm come yer ae dochter to woo,'
    'She 's a very good servant,' said I.

3 The wife gaed hame to her ain hole-house,
    Lookit in at her ain spunk-hole,
An there she saw her ain foul flag,
    Loupin across the coal.

4 'Win up, win up, my ae foul flag,
    An mak yer foul face clean,
For yer wooer is comin here the nicht,
    But yer foul face canna be seen. na, na '

5 She 's taen the sheave-wisps out o her sheen,
    An in behint the door,
An she has faen to the stale strang,
    Seven year auld an more.

6 An aye she scrubbit, an aye she weesh,
    Out-ower the pint o her chin,
Till a knip-knap cam to the door,
    She kent it was her wooer.

7 He 's taen her in his airms twa,
    Kissd her cheek an chin :
'An I hae gotten kisses twa,
    Whaur I never thocht to get ane.'

8 The verra hair was in her head
    Was like the heather-cowe,
An ilka louse at the reet o that
    Was like a brockit ewe.

9 The verra ee was in her head
    Was like a muckle pan,
The hunkers and clunkers that hang frae her sheen
    Wad hae covered an acre o lan.

10 The verra teeth was in her head
    Was like a tether's check,
An the sneeters and snotters that hang frae her nose
    Wad a gart a frozen mill gang.

11 The verra tongue was in her head
    Wad been a guid mill-clap,
    .   .   .   .
    .   .   .   .

12 .   .   .   .
    An ye may know very weel by that
    She was a comely woman.

34. Kemp Owyne.

P. 309. From a manuscript collection of Charles Kirkpatrick Sharpe's, p. 2 ; "Second Collection," see Sharpe's Ballad Book, ed. 1880, p. 144. This copy closely resembles **A.**

1 Her mother died when she was young,
    And was laid in the silent tomb ;

The father weded the weel worst woman
  This day that lives in Christiendom.

2 She served her with hands and feet,
  In every way that well could be,
Yet she did once upon a day
  Throw her in over a craig of sea.

3 Says, Ly you there, you dove Isabeal,
  And let you never borrowed be
Till Kempenwine come ower the sea
  And borrow you with kisses three ;
Whatever any may do or say,
  O borrowed may you never be!

4 Her breath grew strong, and her hair grew long,
  And twisted thrice about a tree,
And so hideous-like she did apear
  That all who saw her from her did flee.

5 Now Kempenwine gat word of this
  Where he was living beyond the sea ;
He hied him straight unto that shoar,
  The monstrous creature for to se.

6 Her breath was strong, and her hair was long,
  And twisted was around the tree,
And with a swing she cried aloud,
  Come to craig of sea and kiss with me.

7 ' Here is a royal ring,' she cried,
  ' That I have found in the green sea,
And while your finger it is on
  Drawn shall your blood never be ;
But if you touch me, tail or fin,
  I vow this brand your death shall be.'

8 He steppëd in, gave her a kiss,
  The royal ring he brought him wi ;
Her breath was strong, and [her] hair was long,
  Yet twisted twice about the tree,
And with a swing she came about,
  ' Come to craig of sea and kiss with me.

9 ' Here is a royal belt,' she cried,
  ' That I have found in the green sea,
And while your body it is on
  Drawn shall your blood never be ;
But if you touch me, tail or fin,
  I vow this brand your death shall be.'

10 He steppëd in, gave her a kiss,
  The royal belt he brought him wee ;
Her breath yet strong, her hair yet long,
  Yet twisted once about the tree,
And with a swing she came about,
  ' Come to craig of sea and kiss with me.

11 ' Here is a royal brand,' she cried,
  ' That I have found in the green sea,

And while your body it is on
  Drawn shall your blood never be ;
But if you touch me, tail or fin,
  I vow my brand your death shall be.'

12 He steppëd in, gave her a kiss,
  The royal brand he brought him wee ;
Her breath now soft, her hair now short,
  And disengagëd from the tree,
She fell into his arms two,
  As fair a woman as ever could be.

Written in long lines, and not divided into stanzas.
8^2. him with. 6^4, 8^6, 10^6. Craig of sea.

35. Allison Gross.

P. 314. Gifts offered by a hill-maid. ' Bjærgjom-
fruens Frieri,' Kristensen, Skattegraveren, II, 100, No
460 ; XII, 22 ff., Nos 16, 17 ; Folkeminder, XI, 20 ff.,
No 18, A–E.

36. The Laily Worm and the Mackrel of the Sea.

P. 315. Though Skene has rendered this ballad
with reasonable fidelity, for an editor, it shall, on account of its interest, be given as it stands in the old
lady's MS., where it is No 2. It proves not absolutely
true, as I have said, that the Skene ballad has " never
been retouched by a pen."

1 ' I was bat seven year alld
  Fan my mider she did dee,
My father marrëd the ae warst woman
  The wardle did ever see.

2 ' For she has made me the lailly worm
  That lays att the fitt of the tree,
An o my sister Meassry
  The machrel of the sea.

3 ' An every Saterday att noon
  The machrl comes ea to me,
An she takes my laylë head,
  An lays it on her knee,
An keames it we a silver kemm,
  An washes it in the sea.

4 ' Seven knights ha I slain
  Sane I lay att the fitt of the tree ;
An ye war na my ain father,
  The eight an ye sud be.'

5 ' Sing on your song, ye l[a]ily worm,
  That ye sung to me ;'
' I never sung that song
  But fatt I wad sing to ye.

6 'I was but seven year aull
  Fan my mider she [did] dee,
My father marrëd the a warst woman
  The wardle did ever see.

7 'She changed me to the layel[y] worm
  That layes att the fitt of the tree,
An my sister Messry
  [To] the makrell of the sea.

8 'And every Saterday att noon
  The machrell comes to me,
An she takes my layly head,
  An layes it on her knee,
An kames it weth a siller kame,
  An washes it in the sea.

9 'Seven knights ha I slain
  San I lay att the fitt of the tree ;
An ye war na my ain father,
  The eight ye sud be.'

10 He sent for his lady
  As fast as sen cod he :
'Far is my son,
  That ye sent fra me,
And my daughter,
  Lady Messry ?'

11 'Yer son is att our king's court,
  Sarving for meatt an fee,
And yer doughter is att our quin's court,
  A mary suit an free.'

12 'Ye lee, ye ill woman,
  Sa loud as I hear ye lea,
For my son is the layelly worm
  That lays att the fitt of the tree,
An my daughter Messry
  The machrell of the sea.'

13 She has tain a silver wan
  An gine him stroks three,
An he started up the bravest knight
  Your eyes did ever see.

14 She has tane a small horn
  An loud an shill blue she,
An a' the came her tell but the proud machrell,
  An she stood by the sea :
'Ye shaped me ance an unshemly shape,
  An ye 's never mare shape me.'

15 He has sent to the wood
  For hathorn an fun,
An he has tane that gay lady,
  An ther he did her burne.

Written without division into stanzas or verses.
3². comes ea (aye); *but, on repetition in* 8², comes
  simply, with better metre.
15¹. hes has.   15³. that that.

316. 'Nattergalen,' in Kristensen, Folkeminder,
XI, 25, No 20, A–C.
In a Kaffir tale a girl marries a crocodile. The crocodile bids her lick his face. Upon her doing so, the
crocodile casts his skin and turns into a strong and
handsome man. He had been transformed by the enemies of his father's house. (Theal, Kaffir Folk-Lore,
1882, p. 37, cited by Mr Clouston.)

39. Tam Lin.

P. 339. Teind to hell. See Isabel Gowdie's case,
in the Scottish Journal, I, 256, and compare Pitcairn's
Criminal Trials.
345. **D a.** This copy occurs in " the second collection " of Charles Kirkpatrick Sharpe, p. 3, with a few
variations, as follows. (See Sharpe's Ballad Book, ed.
1880, p. 145.)

> 1³. Charters wood, *and always.* 3¹. the seam.
> 3³. is gone. 5². ye. 6⁴. ask no. 10⁴. we have.
> 11¹. to me. 12². aft. 12³. the Lord of Forbes.
> 12⁴. all his. 15 *occurs after* 24. 15¹. Tho Elfin.
> 15⁴. the tenth one goes. 15⁵. I am an, *or,* I a man.
> 16⁵. if that. 16⁶. miles Cross.
> 17¹. go unto the Miles cross. 20⁴. next the.
> 23¹, 24¹. int. 25¹. She did her down.
> 27². so green. 27³. Where. 27⁴. ride next.
> 28⁴. he is. 29⁴. He. 32². and cry.
> 34¹. I thought.

40. The Queen of Elfan's Nourice.

P. 358, II, 505 b, III, 505 b, IV, 459 a. Mortal mid-
wife for fairies. 'La Sage-femme et la Fée,' R. Basset,
Contes pop. berbères, 1887, No 26, p. 55 (and see notes,
pp. 162, 163). (G. L. K.)

41. Hind Etin.

P. 361 b, III, 506 a, IV, 459 a. **Danish.** 'Jom-
fruen i Bjærget,' fragment, in Kristensen, Folkeminder, XI, 6, No 12.
364 a, III, 506 a, IV, 459 a. **Danish.** 'Agnete og
Havmanden,' Kristensen, Skattegraveren, III, p. 17,
No 34, XII, 65 ff., Nos 136, 137 ; Efterslæt, p. 2, No 2,
p. 174, No 126 ; Folkeminder, XI, 7, No 13, A–D.

42. Clerk Colvill.

P. 371, No 42, p. 389. **C** in Findlay MSS, I, 141 :
'Clerk Colin,' from Miss Butchart, Arbroath, 1868.
Miss Butchart, who died about 1890, aged above ninety
years, was the daughter of the Mrs Butchart from
whom Kinloch got certain ballads, and niece to the
Mrs Arrot who was one of Jamieson's contributors. In
the MS. there are these readings :

2⁸. To gang.   4³. maun gae.   5². could gang.
6¹. To Clyde's.

374 b, IV, 459 a.   **Danish.**   'Elveskud,' Kristensen,
Skattegraveren, XII, 54, No 125 ; 'Elvedansen,' Folkeminder, XI, 15, No 17, **A–C.**

380, II, 506 a, III, 506 a, IV, 459 a.   **TT,** 'La chanson de Renaud,' Pineau, Le Folk-Lore du Poitou,
p. 399 ; **UU,** 'La Mort de Jean Raynaud, Wallonia,
I, 22.

VV, WW. Versions de la Bresse, one, and a fragment, J. Tiersot, Revue des Traditions Populaires,
VII, 654 ff.

382, II, 506 a, III, 506 a.   **Italian.   N.** 'El conte
Anzolin,' Villanis, Canzoni pop. Zaratine, Archivio, XI,
32.   A burlesque form in Canti pop. Emiliani, Maria
Carmi, Archivio, XII, 186, and a Venetian rispetto of
the same character (noted by Maria Carmi) in Bernoni,
Canti pop. Veneziani, 1873, Puntata 7, p. 12, No 62.

44. The Twa Magicians.

P. 400 a, III, 506 b, IV, 459 b.   **French.   Y.** 'Les
Transformations,' Wallonia, I, 50.

401 b, 3d paragraph.   Say: Cosquin, Contes lorrains, I, 103, No 9, and notes.

402 a, last paragraph, Gwion.   See the mabinogi of
Taliesin in Lady Charlotte Guest's Mabinogion, Part
VII, p. 358 f.

45. King John and the Bishop.

P. 405 b, II, 506, IV, 459 b.   Another Magyar version in Zs. f. vergleichende Literaturgeschichte, N. F.
V, 467.

46. Captain Wedderburn's Courtship.

P. 414.   Rev. J. Baring-Gould informs me that there is
an Irish version of this piece in Ulster Ballads, British
Museum, 1162. k. 6, entitled 'The Lover's Riddle.'   The
lady, who in **B, C** is walking through the wood 'her lane,'
is in the Ulster copy walking 'down a narrow lane,'
and she meets 'with William Dicken, a keeper of the
game.'   The only important difference as to the riddles
and the answers is that the young lady remembers her
Bible to good purpose, and gives Melchisedec as an example of a priest unborn (Hebrews vii, 3).

415, note †.   Miss M. H. Mason gives two copies in
her Nursery Rhymes and Country Songs, pp. 23, 24,
'A Paradox.'

417, note †, II, 507 b, III, 507 a, IV, 459 b.   "They
were told that in front of the king's house there
were twenty-score poles, with a head on each pole with
the exception of three."   'The Lad with the Skin Cov-
erings,' J. G. Campbell, The Fians, p. 261.   (There
are three adventurers in this case.)   (G. L. K.)

421. **B. h.** 'Captian Wederburn,' "The Old Lady's
Collection," No 38.

B. a. 1   The lard of Roslie's doughter was walking on
        the green,
        An by came Captain Wederburn, a servant
        to our king,
        An he said to his livery-man, Wer it no
        agenst our laa,
        I wad take her to my ain bed an lay her neast
        the waa.

   a. 2   'I am in my father's garden, walken among
        my father's trees,
        An ye dou latt me walk a whill nou, kind
        sir, if ye pleas ;
        For the supper-beals they will be rung an I
        will be mised awa,
   a. 4³. An my father will ate nae supper gine I be
        mised awa.'

   a. 6.   He lighted off his hors an sett the lady one,

        .   .   .   .

A. a. 6¹,³. He sett her ahind his livery-man, was leath
        to latt her faa :
A. a. 5⁴.   'We 's baith lay in ae bed, an ye 's lay neast
        the wa.'

B. a. 7   Fan they came to his quarter-house, his land-
        l[ad]y came ben :
        'Ther is mony bonny lady in Edenbrugh toun,
        Bat sick a bonny lady is no in it aa ;'
        Says, 'Lass, mak up a doun-bed, we will lay
        her nist the waa.'

   a. 8   'Hold yer toung, young man,' she says, 'an
        latt yer folly be ;
        I winnë come to my bed till ye gett to me
        · things three.

        .   .   .   .

   a. 9   'Ye gett to my supper a cherrey without a
        ston,
        An ye gett to my suppeer a chiken without a
        bone,
        An ye gett to my super a burd that flayes
        without a gaa,
        Or I winnë lay in your bed, nether att stok
        nor waa.'

   a. 10 'The cherry when it is in the bloum, it is with-
        out a ston ;
        The chiken when it is in the egg is without a
        bon ;
        The dove she is a harmless burd, she flays
        without a gaa ;
        An we 's baith lay in ae bed, an ye 's lay nist
        the waa.'

   a. 15 'Hold off yer hands, young man,' she says,
        'an dou not me perplex ;

I winnë gae to my bed till ye tell me qustens
six ;

. . . .

. . . .

a. 16 'What is greaner nor the grass? what is
hig[h]er the[n] the tree?
What is war nor woman's wish? what is deaper
nor the sea?
What burd sings first? what life buds first, an
what dos on it faa?
I winnë lay in your bed, nether att stok nor
waa.'

a. 17 'Death is greaner nor the grass; heaven is
higher nor the tree ;
The devill is war nor woman's wish ; hell is
deaper nor the sea ;
The coke crous first ; the suderen wood springs
first, the due dos on it faa ;
An we 's baith lay in ae bed, an ye 's lay neast
the waa.'

a. 11 'Hold off yer hands, young man,' she says,
'an yer folly gie our,
I winne come to your bed till ye gett to me
things four ;

. . . .

a. 12 'Ye gett to me a cherry that in December
grou ;
Leguays a fine silk mantell that waft gad
never throu ;
A sparrou's horn, a prist unborn, this night
to join us tua;
Or I winnë lay in your bed, nether att stok
nor waa.'

a. 13 'Ther is a hote-bed in my father's garden
wher winter chirrys grou,
Lequays a fine silk mantell in his closet which
waft never gaid throu;

. . . .

. . . .

a. 14 'Ther is a prist nou att the dore, just ready
to come in,
An never one could say he was born,
For ther was a holl cut out of his mother's
side, an out of it he did faa;
An we 's baith lay in ae bed, an ye 's lay nist
the waa.'

a. 18 Littel kent the lassie in the morning fan she
raise
That wad be the last of a' her maiden days;
For nou she is marrëd to Captian Wederburn,
that afore she never saa,

An they baith lay in ae bed, an she lays nest
the waa.

7⁴. Lays, Lass. 10¹. bloun. 12¹. grous.

49. The Twa Brothers.

P. 436 a, 3d paragraph. It ought to have been remarked that it was a William Somerville that killed
John. The names being the same as in the ballad,
"unusually gratuitous" is not warranted.

438. A was derived by Sharpe from Elizabeth
Kerry. The original copy was not all written at one
time, but may have been written by one person. The
first and the last stanza, and some corrections, are in
the same hand as a letter which accompanied the
ballad. The paper has a watermark of 1817. A few
trifling differences in the MS. may be noted:

1¹. twa.
1². school (*Note.* "I have heard it called the
Chase ") : the githar.
1⁴. a far. 2¹. wrestled. 4⁴. And. 5¹. brother.
6³. both. 7², 8², 9². Should *for* Gin.
8¹. what shall. 10¹. But *wanting.*
10³. in fair Kirkland. (*Letter.* " I remembered a
fair Kirk something, and Kirkland it must have
been.")
10⁴. again *wanting.*

H

'Perthshire Tredgey.' From a copy formerly in the possession of Charles Kirkpatrick Sharpe. This fragment has
some resemblances to **F.** "Copied 1823 " is endorsed on
the sheet (in the hand which made an insertion in st. 11)
and crossed out.

1 Two pretty boys lived in the North,
The went to the school so rare ;
The one unto the other said,
We 'll try some battle of war.

2 The worselaid up, the worselaid down,
Till John lay on the ground ;
A pen-knife out of William's pocket
Gave John a deadly wound.

3 'O is it for my gold ?' he said,
'Or for my rich monie?
Or is it for my land sa broad,
That you have killed me?'

4 'It 's neither for your gold,' he said,
'Or for your rich monie,
But it is for your land sa broad
That I have killed thee.'

5 'You 'll take [me] up upon your back,
     Carry me to Wastlen kirk-yard ;
You 'ill houk a hole large and deep,
     And lay my body there.

6 'You 'll put a good stone ou my head,
     Another at my feet,
A good green turf upon my breast,
     That the sounder I m[a]y sleep.

7 'And if my father chance to ask
     What 's come of your brother John,
.   .   .   .

*   *   *   *   *   *   *

8 'What blood is this upon your coat ?
     I pray come tell to me ; '
'It is the blood of my grey hound,
     It would not run for me.'

9 'The blood of your greyhound was near so red,
     I pray come tell to me ; '
'It is the blood of my black horse,
     It would not hunt for me.'

10 'The blood of your black horse was near so red,
     I pray come tell to me ; '
'It is the blood of my brother John,
     Since better canna be.'

*   *   *   *   *   *   *   *

11 He put his foot upon a ship,
     Saying, I am gane our the sea ;
'O when will you come back again,
     I pray come tell to me.'

12 'When the sun and the moon passes over the
     broom,
     That ['s] the day you 'll never see.'

2¹. worse laid, *misheard for* warseled.
3⁸. lands abroad *for* land sae broad (*misheard*).
4¹. *After* your, la *and half of an* n, lan *caught from* 3⁸.
4⁸. land abroad. *The reciter, or more probably the transcriber, has become confirmed in the error made in* 3⁸.
11⁸. come *inserted in a different hand.*
11³,⁴ *should probably be the first half of stanza* 12.

50. The Bonny Hind.

P. 444 a. Motherwell MS., p. 485, professes to copy the ballad from Herd's MS. by way of supplying the stanzas wanting in Scott. There are, however, in Motherwell's transcript considerable deviations from Herd, a fact which I am unable to understand.

53. Young Beichan.

P. 454. 'Lord Beichim,' Findlay's MSS, I, 1, from Jeanie Meldrum, Framedrum, Forfarshire, has these verses, found in G and in Spanish and Italian ballads.

("She meets a shepherd and addresses him.")

'Whas are a' thae flocks o sheep?
     And whas are a' thae droves o kye?
And whas are a' thae statelie mansions,
     That are in the way that I passd bye? '

'O these are a' Lord Beichim's sheep,
     And these are a' Lord Beichim's kye,
And these are a' Lord Beichim's castles,
     That are in the way that ye passd bye.'

There are three or four stanzas more, but they resemble the English vulgar broadsides. There must have been a printed copy in circulation in Scotland which has not been recovered.

468. D is now given as it stands in "The Old Lady's Collection," from which it was copied by Skene : 'Young Beachen,' No. 14.

1 Young Beachen as born in fair London,
     An foiren lands he langed to see,
An he was tean by the savage Mour,
     An they used him mast cruely.

2 Throu his shoulder they patt a bore,
     An throu the bore they patt a tree,
An they made him tralle ther ousen-carts,
     An they used him most cruely.

3 The savige More had ae doughter,
     I wat her name was Susan Pay,
An she is to the prison-house
     To hear the prisenor's mone.

4 He made na his mone to a stok,
     He made it no to a ston,
But it was to the Quin of Heaven,
     That he made his mone.

5 'Gine a lady wad borrou me,
     Att her foot I wad rune,
An a widdou wad borrou me,
     I wad becom her sone.

6 'Bat an a maid wad borrou me,
    I wad wed her we a ring,
I wad make her lady of haas an bours,
    An of the high tours of Line.'

7 'Sing our yer sang, Young Bichen,' she says,
    'Sing our yer sang to me ;'
'I never sang that sang, lady,
    Bat fat I wad sing to ye.

8 'An a lady wad borrou me,
    Att her foot I wad rune,
An a widdou wad borrou me,
    I wad becom her son.

9 'Bat an a maid wad borrou me,
    I wad wed her we a ring,
I wad mak her lady of haas an bours,
    An of the high tours of Line.'

10 Saftly gaid she but,
    An saftly gaid she ben ;
It was na for want of hose nor shone,
    Nor time to pit them on.

11 .   .   .   .   .   .
    .   .   .   .   .   ,
An she has stoun the kees of the prison,
    An latten Young Beachen gang.

12 She gae him a lofe of her whit bread,
    An a bottel of her wine,
She bad him mind on the leady's love
    That fread him out of pine.

13 She gae him a stead was gued in time of nead,
    A sadle of the bone,
Five hundred poun in his poket,
    Bad him gae speading home.

14 An a lish of gued gray honds,
    .   .   .   .   .   .
    .   .   .   .   .   .

15 Fan seven lang year wer come an gane,
    Shusie Pay thought lang,
An she is on to fair London,
    As fast as she could gang.

16 Fan she came to Young Beachen's gate,
    .   .   .   .   .   .
'Is Young Beachen att home,
    Or is he in this country ?'

17 'He is att home,
    [H]is bearly bride him we ;'
Sighan says her Susë Pay,
    'Was he quit forgotten me ?'

18 On every finger she had a ring,
    An on the middel finger three ;
She gave the porter on of them,
    'Gett a word of your lord to me.'

19 He gaed up the stare,
    Fell lau doun on his knee :
'Win up, my proud porter,
    What is your will we [me] ?'

20 'I ha ben porter att your gate
    This therty year an three ;
The fairest lady is att yer gate
    Mine eays did ever see.'

21 Out spak the brid's mother,
    An a haghty woman was she ;
'If ye had not excepted the bonny brid,
    Ye might well ha excepted me.'

22 'No desparegment to you, madam,
    Nor non to her grace ;
The sol of yon lady's foot
    Is fairer then yer face.'

23 He 's geen the table we his foot,
    An caped it we his knee :
'I wad my head an a' my land
    It 's Susie Pay come over the sea.'

24 The stare was therty steps,
    I wat he made them three ;
He toke her in his arms tua,
    'Susie Pay, y 'er welcom to me !'

25 'Gie me a shive of your whit bread,
    An a bottel of your wine ;
Dinner ye mind on the lady's love
    That freed ye out of pine ?'

26 He took her
    Doun to yon garden green,
An changed her name fra Shusie Pay,
    An called her bonny Lady Jean.

27 'Yer daughter came hear on high hors-back,
    She sall gae hame in coaches three,
An I sall dubel her tocher our,
    She is nean the war of me.'

28 'It 's na the fashon of our country,
    Nor yet of our name,
To wed a may in the morning
    An send her hame att none.'

29 'It 's na the fashon of my country,
    Nor of my name,
Bat I man mind on the lady's love
    That freed me out of pine.'

5². I att her foot I : *cf.* 8². 9². tours : *cf.* 6³.
13⁴. spending. 17³. Sigh an. 18². niddel.
After 29 :

> Courtes kind an generse mind,
>   An winne ye ansur me?
> An fan they hard ther lady's word,
>   Well ansuared was she.

P. 476, II, 508. **L.** For the modern vulgar ballad,
Catnach's is a better copy than that of Pitts. See
Kidson, Traditional Tunes, p. 34, for Catnach.

———◆———

VOL. II.

54. The Cherry-Tree Carol.

P. 1 b. (Apple tree.) Chanson de la Corrèze,
Mélusine, VI, 40.

55. The Carnal and the Crane.

P. 7. The Sower : La Tradition, VII, 312.

56. Dives and Lazarus.

P. 10 b, IV, 462 b. 'Lazare et le mauvais riche,'
L'Abbé Durdy, Anthologie pop. de l'Albret, Poésies
gasconnes, p. 6.
Esthonian, Hurt, Vana Kannel, II, 210, No 296.

57. Brown Robyn's Confession.

P. 13 b, IV, 463 a. **Danish.** 'Sejladsen,' Kristensen, Efterslæt til Skattegraveren, p. 22, No 18, p. 161
ff., Nos 116, 117 ; Folkeminder, XI, 148, No 57.
15 b. For Sadko, see Vesselofsky in Archiv für slavische Philologie, IX, 282.

58. Sir Patrick Spens.

P. 17. Among Charles Kirkpatrick Sharpe's papers
there is a copy of this ballad, which, from its being entirely in Sharpe's hand excepting the first line, we may
suppose to have been intended as a reply to some person who had inquired for a ballad so beginning. This
copy is mainly compounded, with a word altered here
and there, from **D** (which Sharpe gave Motherwell), ten
stanzas of **H**, and two resembling **L** 2, 3. The Sir
Andrew Wood of **D** is changed to Sir Patrick Spens,
and there is this one stanza which I have not observed
to occur elsewhere, following **D** 7, or **H** 21 :

> O laith, laith war our gude Scots lords
>   To weet their silken sarks,

> But lang or a' the play was playd
>   The weet gade to their hearts.

62. Fair Annie.

P. 65 a. **Danish.** 'Skjön Anna,' Kristensen, Folkeminder, XI, 91, No 92.

63. Child Waters.

P. 83. 'Fair Ellen,' from "The Old Lady's Collection," No 30, a version resembling **J.** The first two
stanzas belong to 'Glasgerion ;' compare No 67, **C,** 1,
2, II, 140.

K

1 Willie was a harper guid,
    He was a harper fine ;
He harped the burds out of the tree,
    The fish out of the flood,
The milk out of a woman's brist
    That bab had never nean.

2 He harped out, an he harped in,
    Till he harped them a' aslep,
Unless it was her Fair Elen,
    An she stood on her feett.

3 Willie stod in stabile dor,
    He said he wad ride,

. . . . . .

  . . . . .

4 'Na women mane gae we me, Hellen,
    Na women mane gaie we me
Bat them that will saddle my hors,
    An bridell my steed,
An elky toun that I come to
A lish of hons mane lead.'

5 'I will saddle yer hors, Willie,
    An I will bridel yer steed,
An elky toun att we come tell
A leash of honds will lead.'

6 'The dogs sall eat the gued fite bread,
    An ye the douë pran,
An ye sall bliss, an na curse,
    That ever ye lied a man.'

7 'The dogs sall eat the whit bread,
    An me the douë pran,
An I will bliss, an na curs,
    That ear I loved a man.'

8 She has saddled his hors,
　　An she has bridled his stead,
　　An ealky toun att they came throu
　　A lish of honds did lead.

9 The dogs did eatt the whit bread,
　　An her the douey pran,
　　An she did bliss, an she did na curs,
　　That ever she loyed a man.

10 Fan they came to yon wan water
　　That a' man caas Clayd,
　　He louked over his left shoder,
　　Says, Ellen, will ye ride?

11 'I learned it in my medder's bour,
　　I wiss I had learned it better,
　　Fan I came to wane water
　　To sume as dos the otter.

12 'I learned in my midder's bour,
　　I watt I learned it well,
　　Fan I came to wan water,
　　To sume as dos the ell.'

13 .　　.　　.　　.　　.　　.　　.
　　.　　.　　.　　.　　.　　.
　　Or the knight was in the middell of the water,
　　The lady was in the eather side.

14 She leaned her back to a stane,
　　Gaa a call opon:
　　'O my back is right sore,
　　An I sae farr frae hame!

15 'Hou monny mill ha ye to rid,
　　An hou mony I to rine?'
　　'Fifty mill ha I to rid,
　　Fifty you to rine,
　　An by that time I dou supos
　　Ye will be a dead woman.'

16 Out spak a bonny burd,
　　Sate on yon tree,
　　'Gaa on, fair Ellen,
　　Ye ha scarcly milles three.'

17 Four-an-tuenty bony ladys
　　Mett Willie in the closs,
　　Bat the fairest lady among them a'
　　Took Willie frae his horse.

18 Four-an-tuenty bonny ladys
　　Lead Willie to the table,

Bat the fairest lady among them a'
　　Led his hors to the stable.

19 She leaned betuen the gray folle an the waa,
　　An gae a call opon;
　　'O my back is fue sore,
　　An I sae far fra home!

20 'Fan I was in my father's bour,
　　I ware goud to my hell;
　　Bat nou I am among Willie's hors feet,
　　An the call it will me kell.

21 'Fan I was in my midder's bour
　　I wear goud to my head;
　　Bat nou I am among Willie's hors feet,
　　And the calle will be my dead.'

22 'Fatten a heavey horse-boy, my son Willie,
　　Is this ye ha brought to me?
　　Some times he grous read, read,
　　An some times paill an wane;
　　He louks just leak a woman we bairn,
　　An no weis es leak a man.'

23 'Gett up, my heavey hors-boy,
　　Gie my hors corn an hay;'
　　'By my soth,' says her Fair Ellen,
　　'Bat as fast as I may.'

24 'I dreamed a dream san the straine,
　　Gued read a' dreams to gued!
　　I dreamed my stable-dor was opned
　　An stoun was my best steed.
　　Ye gae, my sister,
　　An see if the dream be gued.'

25 .　　.　　.　　.　　.　　.
　　.　　.　　.　　.　　.　　.
　　She thought she hard a baby greet,
　　Bat an a lady mone.

26 .　　.　　.　　.　　.　　.
　　.　　.　　.　　.　　.　　.
　　'I think I hard a baby greet,
　　Bat an a lady mone.'

27 'A askend, Willie,' she says,
　　'An ye man grant it me;
　　The warst room in a' yer house
　　To your young son an me.'

28 ['Ask on, Fair Ellen,
　　Ye 'r sure yer asken is free;]

The best room in a' my house
  To yer young son an ye.'

29 '[A] asken, Willie,' she sayes,
  'An ye will grant it me ;
  The smallest bear in yer house
  To [yer] young son an me.'

30 'Ask on, Fair Ellen,
  Ye 'r sure your asken is free ;
  The best bear in my house
  [To yer young son an ye.]

31 'The best bear in my house
  Is the black bear an the wine,
  An ye sall haa that, Fair Ellen,
  To you an yer young son.'

32 '[A] askent, Willie,' she says,
  'An ye will grant [it] me ;
  The warst maid in yer house
  To wait on yer young son an me.'

33 'The best maid in my house
  Is my sister Meggie,
  An ye sall ha her, Fair Ellen,
  To wait on yer young son an ye.

34 'Chire up, Fair Ellen,
  Chire up, gin ye may ;
  Yer kirking an yer fair weding
  Sall baith stand in ae day.'

1[6]. bab have.
3[2]. bide. *Cf.* B 3, G 1, I 1, J 1. 20[3]. I an.
20[4]. me gell. 21[2]. my hell *again*.
21[4]. And an. 30[2]. sure yours.

64. Fair Janet.

P. 102. (See III, 497 b, No 5.) Add : ' La Fiancée
du Prince,' Revue des Traditions Populaires, VIII,
406–409, two versions.

65. Lady Maisry.

P. 114. **A.** The variations in the Abbotsford MS.
" Scottish Songs " are of the very slightest value ; but
as the MS. is in Scott's hand, and as Scott says that
they were from his recollection of recitation in the
south of Scotland, they may be given for what they are
worth. (See the note, IV, 387.)
  ' Lady Maiserye,' fol. 34, back.
  1[2]. Are a'. 1[4]. she 'll hae. 2, 3, *wanting*.
  4[1,2]. They woo'd her up, they woo'd her doun,
    They woo'd her in the ha.

5[1]. my lords, she said. 5[2]. on me.
5[4]. And I have na mair to gie.
6[1]. father's wily page.
6[3]. For he has awa to her bauld brother.
7[1]. O are my father and mother. 7[2]. brethren.
8[1]. are weel. 8[2]. Likewise your brethren.
8[4]. But she 's shamed thy name and thee.
9[1]. true, thou little page.
9[2]. A bluidy sight thou 's see. 9[3]. thou tells.
9[4]. High hanged sall thou be.
10[1]. O he has gane to. 10[4]. Kaming.
11. *A stanza with* " modern " *in the margin.*
12[1]. The lady turnd her round about.
12[2]. The kame fell.
12[3,4]. The bluid ran backward to her heart
    And left her cheek sae wan.
13. 'O bend nae sae, my dear brother,
    Your vengefu look on me !
   My love is laid on Lord William,
    And he is married to me.'
14[1]. ye hae gotten knights and lords.
14[2]. Within. 14[3]. drew. 15[1]. your English love.
15[3]. For shouldst think of him an hour langer.
15[4]. Thy. 16[1]. I wad gie up my English love.
16[3]. or an hour.
After 16 this stanza, not marked " modern : "

   ' Ah, faithless woman, trow nae sae
    My just revenge to flee,
   For a' your English lordling's power,
    Our ancient enemy.'

17[1]. where are a' my wight. 17[4]. this strumpet.
18[2]. at my. 19[1]. and spake.
19[2]. Stude weeping by her side.
19[3]. wad rin this. 20 *wanting.*
21[1], 22[1]. And when. 21[3]. to grass growing.
22[1,5]. yate. 22[2]. bade na chap nor. 22[3]. to his.
22[5]. And er. 23[1]. O are. 23[2]. Or are.
23[3]. Or has my lady gien to me.
23[4]. A dear : or a.
24[1]. biggins are na broken, lord. 24[2]. Nor yet.
24[3]. a' Scotlande. 24[4]. This day for you.
25[1]. to me the black horse.
25[2]. O saddle to me. 25[3]. Or saddle to me.
25[4]. ere yet rode. 26[2]. neeze.
26[3]. your fire, my fierce.
26[4]. no yet at. 27[1]. And when : yate.
28[1,2]. And still, Mend up the fire, she cried,
    And pour its rage round me.
28[4]. will mend it soon for. 29[1]. O had my hands.
29[2]. Sae fast. 29[4]. To save thy infant son.
30[1,3]. for thee. 30[2]. Thy sister and thy brother.
30[4]. Thy father and thy mother. 31[1]. for thee.
31[2]. a' thy. 31[3]. that I make. 31[4]. I sall.

115. **B.** Variations of C. K. Sharpe's own MS.
(" second collection ") :

2[4]. on my (*wrongly*). 4[4]. It 's liars.
8[2]. That 's what I 'll. 10[2]. brother.

13³. But when. 20¹, 21¹, 22¹. rode on.

22⁴. Janet's excit (*Motherwell*, exite). 24¹. said.

27⁴. mony one.

66. Lord Ingram and Chiel Wyet.

P. 128. **A**. Collated with Sharpe's MS., p. 17. The MS., which is in the handwriting of Sharpe, contains the same ballads as an Abbotsford MS. called North Country Ballads, but the two copies are independent transcripts. In a note to Sharpe, without date (Sharpe's Ballad Book, ed. 1880, p. 148), Scott says, "I enclose Irvine's manuscripts, which are, I think, curious. They are at your service for copying or publishing, or whatever you will." Hugh Irvine, Drum, communicated to Scott a copy of 'Tam Lin' (see IV, 456), and it is possible that the manuscripts referred to in Scott's note were the originals of the "North Country Ballads."

1⁴. their bonneur. 8². to kill. 11¹. boy says.

11². An will. 14¹,³. line that he. 15¹. (bacon).

16⁴. she *wanting.*

18²,⁴. garl, marl, *are Sharpe's corrections for words struck out, which seem to be* guell, meal.

19¹. and that. 21². saft. 23¹. twice, so did I.

26¹. did stand. 31⁴. he *wanting.*

Only 14¹,³, 16⁴, 23¹, 31⁴, *are wrongly given in Motherwell.*

Scott's MS.— *The name* Maisery *is wanting throughout.*

23³. only *for* one. 28 *wanting.* 30³. had.

31². beg *wrongly copied* by.

68. Young Hunting.

P. 145. **A** 22. Findlay's MSS, I, 146, gives a corresponding stanza, from Miss Butchart, Arbroath :

'Ye 'll gie ower your day's doukin
An douk upon the nicht,
An the place Young Redin he lies in
The torches will brin bricht.'

148. **C** 21, 22. At the same place in Findlay's MSS we find these stanzas, from Miss Bower :

The firsten grasp that she got o him,
It was o his yellow hair ;
O wasna that a dowie grasp,
For her that did him bear !

The nexten grasp that she got o him,
It was o his lillie hand ;
O was na that a dowie grasp,
For her brocht him to land !

69. Clerk Saunders.

P. 156 b, 2d paragraph. Austerities. 'Mijn haer sel onghevlochten staen,' etc. 'Brennenberg,' Hoffmann, Niederländische Volkslieder, p. 33, No 6, st. 17.

IV, 468 a, 3d line. Add : also four versions of Karl Hittebarn, No 294.

71. The Bent sae Brown.

P. 170. **Danish**. 'Jomfruens Brødre,' Kristensen, Skattegraveren, II, 145 ff., Nos 717–23 V, 81 ff., Nos 632–34; Efterslæt til Sk., p. 15, No 13, p. 84, No 79, 'Den ulige Kamp;' Folkeminder, XI, 139, No 53, A-C, p. 307, No 53.

73. Lord Thomas and Fair Annet.

P. 181, III, 510 b, IV, 469 a. Add another version of 'Le Rossignolet,' Rev. des Trad. pop., VIII, 418.

192. **G** as it stands in "The Old Lady's Collection," No 24.

1 Suit Willie an Fair Annë,
   They satt on yon hill,
An fra the morning till night this tua
   Never ta'ked ther fill.

2 Willie spak a word in jeast,
   An Anny toke it ill :
'We 's court ne mare mean madens,
   Agenst our parents' will.'

3 'It 's na agenst our parents' will,'
   Fair Annie she did say ;

. . . .

. . . .

4 Willie is hame to his bour,
   To his book alean,
An Fair Anni is to her bour,
   To her book an her seam.

5 Suit Willie is to his mider dear,
   Fell lou doun on his knee :
'A asking, my mider dear,
   An ye grant it me ;
O will I marry the nut-broun may,
   An latt Faire Anny be ? '

6 'The nut-broun may has ousen, Willie,
   The nut-broun may has kay ;
An ye will wine my blissing, Willie,
   An latt Fair Anny be.'

7 He did him to his father dear,
   Fell lou doun on his knee :
'A asken, my father,
   An ye man grant it me.'

8 'Ask on, my ae sin Willie,
   Ye 'r sear yer asking is frea ;
Except it be to marry her Fair Anny,
   An that ye manna deei.'

9 Out spak his littel sister,
     As she sat by the fire ;
The oxe-lig will brak in the plough,
     An the cou will droun in the mire.

10 'An Willie will hae nathing
     Bat the dam to sitt by the fire,
An Faire Annie will sit in her beagly bour,
     An wine a eearl's hire.'

11 'Fair faa ye, my littel sister,
     A gued dead matt ye dee !
An ever I hae goud,
     Well touchered sall ye be.'

12 Hi 'se away to Fair Annie,
     As fast as gang coud he :
'O will ye come to my marrag?
     The morn it 's to be.'
'O I will come to yer marrag the morn,
     Gin I can wine,' said she.

13 Annie did her to her father d[ea]r,
     Fell lou doun on her knee :
'An askin, my father,
     An ye mane grant it me ;
Latt me to Suit Willie's marrage,
     The morn it is to be.'

14 'Your hors sall be siler-shod afor,
     An guid read goud ahind,
An bells in his main,
     To ring agenst the wind.'

15 She did her to her mother dear,
     Fell lou on her knee :
'Will ye latt me to Willie's marrage?
     To-morraa it is to be.'
'I ill latt ye to Willie's marrage,
     To-morray it is to be.'

16 Fan Annë was in her sadel sett,
     She flamd agenst the fire ;
The girdell about her sma middell
     Wad a wone a eearl's hire.

17 Fan they came to Mary kirk,
     An on to Mary quir,
'O far gat ye that water, Annë,
     That washes ye sae clean?'
'I gat it in my fa(t)hers garden,
     Aneth a marbell stane.'

18 'O fare gatt ye that water, Annë,
     That washes ye sae fett?'
'I gat it in my mider's womb,
     Far ye never gat the leak.

19 'For ye ha ben cirsned we mose-water,
     An roked in the reak,

An sin-brunt in yer midder's womb,
     For I think ye 'll never be faitt.'

20 The broun bride pat her hand in
     Att Annë's left gare,
An gen her . . . .
     A deap wound an a sare.

21 O Annë gid on her hors back,
     An fast away did ride,
Batt lang or kok's crawang
     Fair Annë was dead.

22 Fan bells was rung, an messe was sung,
     An a' man boun to bed,
Suit Willie an the nut-broun bride
     In a chamber was lead.

23 But up an wakned him Suit Willie,
     Out of his dreary dream :
'I dreamed a dream this night,
     God read a' dreams to gued !

24 'That Fair Annë's bour was full of gentelmen,
     An her nen sellf was dead ;
Bat I will on to Fair Annie,
     An see if it be gued.'

25 Seven lang mille or he came near,
     He hard a dulfull chear,
Her father an her seven bretheren
     Making to her a bear,
The half of it guid read goud,
     The eather silver clear.

26 'Ye.berl att my love's leak
     The whit bread an the wine,
Bat or the morn att this time
     Ye 's de the leak att mine.'

27 The tean was beared att Mary kirk,
     The eather att Mary quir ;
Out of the an grue a birk,
     Out of the eather a brear.

28 An ay the langer att they grue
     They came the eather near,
An by that ye might a well kent
     They war tua lovers dear.

4². *There may have been a word between* book *and* alean.
5⁶. bay : *cf.* 6⁴. 16². flamd *is doubtful.* 21⁴. farie.
23³. might.

74. Fair Margaret and Sweet William.

P. 199. The Roxburghe copy, III, 338, Ebsworth, VI, 640, is a late one, of Aldermary Church-Yard.

200 b.   **A c** is translated by Pröhle, G. A. Bürger, Sein Leben u. seine Dichtungen, p. 109.

75. Lord Lovel.

P. 204 f., note †, 512 b, IV 471 a.   Add 'Der Graf und das Mädchen,' Böckel, Deutsche V.-l. aus Oberhessen, p. 5, No 6; 'Es schlief ein Graf bei seiner Magd,' Lewalter, Deutsche V.-l. in Niederhessen gesammelt, 2ᵃ Heft, p. 3, No 2: 'Der Graf und sein Liebchen,' Frischbier u. Sembrzycki, Hundert Ostpreussische Volkslieder, p. 34, No 21.

205 a, note, III, 510 b, IV, 471 b.   **Scandinavian**, Other copies of 'Lille Lise,' 'Greven og lille Lise,' Kristensen, Efterslæt til Skattegraveren, p. 18, No 15, Folkeminder, XI, 159, No 62, A–D.

205.   'Den elskedes Død,' Berggreen, Danske Folkesange, 3d ed., p. 162, No 80 b; Svenske Fs., 2d ed., p. 84, No 66 b.

The ballad exists in Esthonian: Kaarle Krohn, Die geographische Verbreitung estnischer Lieder, p. 23.

76. The Lass of Roch Royal.

P. 213.   **B** was received by Herd, with several other ballads, "by post, from a lady in Ayrshire (?), name unknown:" Herd's MSS, I, 143.

215 b, 2d paragraph, tokens.   Add: Ζωγραφεῖος 'Αγών, p. 90, No 67, p. 91, No 69, p. 95, No 81.

The lady demands love-tokens of Clerk Saunders' ghost, No 69, **G**, 33, II, 166.

219.   **C** occurs in C. K. Sharpe's small MS. volume "Songs," p. 40, and must have been communicated to Sharpe by Pitcairn.   Collation:

2. It 's open, etc.: *not written in full.*
3³, 4³. Ruchley hill.   5³. give me.
6. Do not you mind, etc.: *not written in full.*
7 *wanting.*   8¹. turned round.
10¹. It 's awa.   10³. have got the.   13¹. that he.
14¹. Let down, let down.   14³. late *wanting.*
15³. morrow.   15⁴. of mine.   16, 17, *wanting.*

77. Sweet William's Ghost.

P. 228, note †.   Add: Zingerle, in Zeitschrift für Volkskunde, II, 147.

229.   **C** is translated by Pröhle, G. A. Bürger, Sein Leben u. seine Dichtungen, p. 106.

78. The Unquiet Grave.

P. 236 b, last paragraph.   See the preface to 'The Suffolk Miracle' in this volume, p. 58 ff.

This "fragment," in a small MS. volume entirely in C. K. Sharpe's handwriting ("Songs"), p. 21, "from the recitation of Miss Oliphant of Gask, now Mrs Nairn" (later Lady Nairne), evidently belongs here.

O wet and weary is the night,
  And evendown pours the rain, O,
And he that was sae true to me
  Lies in the greenwood slain, O.   P. 21.

80. Old Robin of Portingale.

P. 240.   'Sleep you, wake you.' So, 'Soldatenlohn,' Zeitschrift für Volkskunde, II, 426, sts. 6, 7; Hruschka u. Toischer, Deutsche Volkslieder aus Böhmen, p. 183, No 147 a, 4⁵, b 3⁵, p. 195, No 171, 2¹, No 172, 4.

240, 513 a, III, 514, IV, 476.   Two religious persons from India display to the Pope a cross burned on the breast in token of Christian faith, and also a baptismal mark on the right ear, "non flumine sed flamine:" Chronicon Adae de Usk ad ann. 1404, ed. E. M. Thompson, p. 90.   See also the reference to York's Marco Polo, 1875, II, 421, in Mr Thompson's note, p. 219.   (G. L. K.)

81. Little Musgrave and Lady Barnard.

P. 242.   'Little Musgrave' is entered to Francis Coules in the Stationers' Registers, 24 June, 1630: Arber, IV, 236.

85. Lady Alice.

P. 279.

C

Miss M. H. Mason's Nursery Rhymes and Country Songs, p. 46, 'Giles Collin.'

1 Giles Collin he said to his mother one day,
    Oh, mother, come bind up my head!
  For tomorrow morning before it is day
    I 'm sure I shall be dead.

2 'Oh, mother, oh, mother, if I should die,
    And I am sure I shall,
  I will not be buried in our churchyard,
    But under Lady Alice's wall.'

3 His mother she made him some water-gruel,
    And stirred it up with a spoon;
  Giles Collin he ate but one spoonful,
    And died before it was noon.

4 Lady Alice was sitting in her window,
    All dressed in her night-coif;
  She saw as pretty a corpse go by
    As ever she 'd seen in her life.

5 'What bear ye there, ye six tall men?
    What bear ye on your shourn?'

'We bear the body of Giles Collin,
  Who was a true lover of yourn.'

6 'Down with him, down with him, upon the
    grass,
  The grass that grows so green;
For tomorrow morning before it is day
  My body shall lie by him.'

7 Her mother she made her some plum-gruel,
  With spices all of the best;
Lady Alice she ate but one spoonful,
  And the doctor he ate up the rest.

8 Giles Collin was laid in the lower chancel,
  Lady Alice all in the higher;
There grew up a rose from Lady Alice's breast,
  And from Giles Collin's a briar.

9 And they grew, and they grew, to the very
    church-top,
  Until they could grow no higher,
And twisted and twined in a true-lover's knot,
  Which made all the parish admire.

90. Jellon Grame.

P. 303 b, 513 b, III, 515 b, IV, 479 b. Precocious
growth.

The French romance of Alexander. Albéric de
Besançon : Alexander had more strength when three
days old than other children of four months; he walked
and ran better from his first year than any other child
from its seventh. (The same, nearly, in Lamprecht, vv.
142–4 : he throve better in three days than any other
child of three months; 178–80, in his first year his
strength and body waxed more than another's in three.)
MS. de l'Arsenal : the child grew in vitality and knowledge more in seven years than others do in a hundred.
MS. de Venise : he grew more in body and knowledge
in eight years than others in a hundred. P. Meyer,
Alexandre le Grand, I, 5, v. 56 f., 6, v. 74 f., 27, v. 39
f., 240, v. 53 f. 'Plus sot en x jors que i. autres en c:'
Michelant, p. 8, v. 20. A similar precocity is recorded
of the Chinese Emperor Schimong: Gützlaff, Geschichte
der Chinesen, hrsgg. v. Neumann, S. 19, cited by Weismann, Lamprecht's Alexander, I, 432.

In the romance of Mélusine it is related how, after
her disappearance in serpent-form, she was seen by the
nurses to return at night and care for her two infant
sons, who, according to the earliest version, the prose
of Jehan d'Arras, grew more in a week than other children in a month: ed. Brunet, 1854, p. 361. The same
in the French romance, l. 4347 f., the English metrical
version, l. 4035–37, and in the German Volksbuch.
(H. L. Koopman.)

Tom Hickathrift "was in length, when he was but
ten years of age, about eight foot, and in thickness five
foot, and his hand was like unto a shoulder of mutton,
and in all parts from top to toe he was like a monster."
The History of Thomas Hickathrift, ed. by G. L.
Gomme, Villon Society, 1885, p. 2. (G. L. K.)

305. **B.** The following, a variety of **B**, is from the
papers of Charles Kirkpatrick Sharpe, "second collection," p. 6.

1 Word has come to May Young Ro,
  In her bower where she sat,
  'You 'r bidden come to good green wood
  And sew your love a shirt.'

2 'I wonder much,' said May Young Roe,
  'Such word is come to me;
Ther 's not a month throwout this year
  But I have sewed him three.'

3 Then out it spake her mother,
  And a wise word spoke she ;
Said, Stay at home, my daughter,
  They want to murder thee.

4 'I will cast off my gloves, mother,
  And hing them on a pin ;
If I come never back again,
  You 'l mind on your daugh[t]er young.

5 'Come here, my boy,' she cried,
  'And bring my horse to me,
That I may ride to good green wood,
  The flowers in it to see.'

6 When she was got to good green wood,
  No further did she ride
Till up did start him Hind Henry,
  Just at the ladie's side.

7 'O stop, O stop there, May,' he cried,
  'O stop, I say to thee ;
The boy who holds your bridle-reins
  Shall see your body wea.'

8 Then out he drew a large long brand,
  And struck it ower a str[ow],
And throw and throw that ladie's side
  He made the cold steel go.

9 Said, Take you that now, May Young Roe,
  Just take you that from me,
Because you loved Brown Robin,
  And never would love me.

10 The boy was in a dreadful fright,
  And in great haste rode home,
Lamenting sadly all the way,
  And made a piteous moan.

11 And when her mother heard his tale
    She took the bed of care ;
    Her sister ran to good green wood,
    A tearing of her hair.

12 There was small pity for that lady,
    Where she was lying dead,
    Compared with for the pretty babe,
    Weltring among the blood.

13 'I will take up this babe,' she said,
    'And lull him on my sleeve ;
    Altho his father should wish me woe,
    His mother was to me live.'

14 Now she has taken the boy up,
    And she has brought him hame,
    And she has called him Brown Robin,
    It was his father's name.

15 And she has nursed him carefuly,
    And put him to the school,
    And any who affronted him
    He soon did make cry dule.

16 And it fell ance upon a time
    It was a haly day,
    And all the boys at that school
    On it they got the play.

17 He hied him unto good green wood,
    And leap from tree to tree,
    And there did pull some hollin wands,
    To play his own self we.

18 And aft he looked on a spot,
    And at it marvelled sair,
    That all the wood was clad with leaves,
    And that one spot was bare.

19 And he said unto Hind Henry,
    'I wonder very sair
    That all the wood is clad with leaves,
    And this one spot is bare.'

20 'You need not wonder, boy,' he said,
    'You need not wonder none,
    For it is just the very spot
    I killed your mother on.'

21 The boy 's pulled out his daggar then,
    And struck it ower a strow,
    And even to Hind Henry's heart
    He made the cold steel go.

22 Says, Take you that, you vile Henry,
    Just take you that from me,
    For killing of my mother dear,
    And she not harming thee.

91. Fair Mary of Wallington.

P. 314, IV, 480 a. **D.** 10³ in Kinloch MSS, V, 363, reads, I hear this babe now from her side ; but in Mr Macmath's transcript of Burton's MS., No 2, I bear . . . my side.

316. 'The Lady of Livenston,' from " The Old Lady's Collection," No 32.

G

1 'We was sisters, we was seven,
    Five of us dayed we child,
    An you an me, Burd Ellen,
    Sall live maidens mild.'

2 Ther came leards, an ther came lords,
    An knights of high degree,
    A' courting Lady Messry,
    Bat it widne deei.

3 Bat the bonny lord of Livenston,
    He was flour of them a',
    The bonny lord of Livenston,
    He stole the lady awaa.

4 Broad was the horses hoves
    That dumped the water of Clide,
    An a' was for honor of that gay lady
    That day she was Livenston's bride.

5 Fan she came to Livenston
    Mukell mirth was ther ;
    The knights knaked ther whit fingers
    The ladys curled ther hear.

6 She had no ben in Livenston
    A tuall-month an a day,
    Till she was as big we bearn
    As a lady coud gaa.

7 She had ne ben in Livenston
    A tuall-month an a hour,
    Till for the morning of the may
    The couldne ane come near her bour.

8 'Far will I gett a bonny boy
    That will rean my earend shoun,
    That will goo to leve London,
    To my mother, the quin ? '

9 'Hear am I, a bonny boy
    Will rin yer earend sune,

That will rin on to fair London,
　　To yer mother, the quin.'

10 'Hear is the bruch fra my breast-bane,
　　The garlands fra my hear;
　Ye ge that to my mider,
　　Fra me she 'll never gett mare.

11 'Hear is the rosses fra my shoun,
　　The ribbons fra my hear;
　Ye gee that to my mider,
　　Fra me she 'll never gett mare.

12 'Hear is my briddel-stand,
　　It is a' goud to the heam;
　Ye gie that to Burd Ellen,
　　Forbed her to marry men.

13 'Ye bid them and ye pray them bath,
　　If they will dou it for my sake,
　If they be not att my death,
　　To be att my leak-wake.

14 'Ye bid them and ye pray them baith,
　　If they will dou it for my name,
　If they be not att my leak-wake,
　　To be att my birrien.'

15 Fan he came to grass grouen,
　　He strated his bou an rane,
　An fan he came to brigs broken
　　He slaked his bou an swam.

16 An fan he came to yon castell,
　　He bad nether to chap nor caa,
　But sait his bent bou to his breast
　　An lightly lap the waa;
　Or the porter was att the gate,
　　The boy was in the haa.

17 'Mukell meatt is on yer table, lady,
　　An littil of it is eaten,
　Bat the bonny lady of Livenston
　　Ye have her clean forgotten.'

18 'Ye lie, ye lie, ye bonny boy,
　　Sae loud as I hear ye lie;
　Mukell ha I sold the [meatt],
　　An littel hae I bought,
　Batt the bonny lady of Livenston
　　Gaas never out of my thought.

19 'Mukell have I bought, bonny boy,
　　An littel haa I sale,

Bat the bonny lady of Livenston
　　She couls my heart fue cale.'

20 'Hear is the ribbings fra her hear,
　　The roses fra her shoun;
　I was bidden gie that to her midder,
　　To her midder, the quin.

21 'Hear is the bruch fra her breast-bean,
　　The garlands frae her hear;
　I was bidden gee that to her mother,
　　Fra her she 'll never gett mare.

22 'Hear is her bridell-stand,
　　The' r a' goud to the heam;
　I was bidden ga that to Burd Ellen,
　　Forbid her to marry man.

23 'She bids ye an she prays ye bath,
　　Gin yee 'll di et for her sake,
　If ye be not att her death,
　　To be att her leak-wake.

24 'She bidds yee an she prays ye bath,
　　Gine ye 'll dou et for her name,
　If ye be not att her leak-wake,
　　To be at her burrien.'

25 'Garr saddell to me the blak,
　　Saddle to me the broun,
　Gar saddel to me the suiftest stead
　　That ever read fraa a toun,
　Till I gaa to Livenston
　　An see hou Measry fairs.'

26 The first stead was saddled to her,
　　It was the bonny black;
　She spured him aftt and she spared him na,
　　An she tayened him at a slap.

27 The neast stead that was saddled to her
　　Was the berrey-broun;
　She spured him aftt an she spared him not,
　　An she tayned him att a toun.

28 The neast an steed that was saddled to her,
　　It was the milk-white:
　'Fair faa the mear that folled the foll
　　Had me to Meassry's leak!'

29 Fan she came to Livenston,
　　Mukel dolle was ther;
　The knights wrang ther whit fingers,
　　The ladys tore ther hear.

30 The knights they wrang ther whit fingers,
　　The rings they flue in four :
　'Latt haas an tours an a' doun fau !
　　My dear thing has gine it our.'

31 Out spak him Livenston,
　　An a sorry man was he ;
　'I had rader lost the lands of Livenston,
　　Afor my gay lady.'

32 'Had yer toung nou, Livenston,
　　An latt yer folly be ;
　I bare the burd in my bosom,
　　I man thole to see her diee.'

33 Fan she came to her doughter's boure,
　　Ther was littel pride ;
　The scoups was in her doughter's mouth,
　　An the sharp shirrs in her side.

34 Out spake her Burd Ellen,
　　An she spake ay threu pride ;
　The wife sall never bear the sin
　　Sall lay doun by my side.

35 'Had your toung nou, Burd Ellen,
　　Ye latt yer folly a be ;
　Dinnë ye mind that ye promised yer love
　　To him that is ayond the seaa ? '

36 'Hold yer toung, my mother,
　　Ye speak just leak a fooll ;
　Tho I wer marred att Martimes,
　　I wad be dead or Yeull.'

37 'I have five bonny oyes att heam,
　　Ther was never ane of them born,
　Bat every ane of them
　　Out of ther midder's sides shorn.'

　5². The knights knaked ther whit fingers *is
　certainly an anticipation. This is always
　done for anguish : see* 29³·⁴, 30¹·².
　7³·⁴. Till ther couldne ane come near her bour
　　　For the morning of they may. *Per-
　　　haps* moaning.
　16². he had.
　18³. *Perhaps* the meat.
　19²·⁴. sale, cale (*for* sold, cold).
　22². hean.　22³. bidden ga.
　35³. Didde.

92. Bonny Bee Horn.

P. 317. 'The Lowlands of Holland.' In 'The Sorrowful Lover's Regrate, or, The Low-Lands of Holland,' British Museum 1346. m. 7(40), dated May the
5th, 1776, a threnody in eleven double stanzas. 1, 2
of the copy in Johnson's Museum are 1, 2 ; Johnson,
3 = 7, 4 = 4, 5 = 6, 6 = 3, and the stanza added by
Stenhouse is 9 (with verbal divergences). 'The Maid's
Lamentation for the loss of her true love,' Museum
11621. c. 3(39), "Newcastle, 1768 ?," the fifth piece
in The Complaining Lover's Garland, has five stanzas :
1 corresponding to 2 of Johnson, 2 to 5, 5 to 6, 3 to 5
of the Regrate, and 4 to 9, with considerable differences. 'The Seaman's Sorrowful Bride,' Roxburghe,
IV, 73, Ebsworth, VI, 444, begins with two stanzas
which resemble Johnson, 2, 1. This last was printed
for J. Deacon, in Guilt-spur-street, and the date, according to Chappell, would be 1684-95.

93. Lamkin.

P. 331, **I,** as it stands in " The Old Lady's Collection," No 15.

1 Lamken was as gued a masson
　　as ever did hue ston ;
　He bigged Lord Weary's house,
　　an pament never got non.

2 It fell ance on a day
　　Lord Weary went from home,
　An Lamkin came to the fause nirice,
　　.　.　.　.　.　.

　　*　　*　　*　　*　　*　　*　　*　　*

3 'O still my bairn, nirice,
　　still him we the kniff :'
　'He winnë still, lady,
　　tho I sud lay doun my life.'

4 'O still my bairn, nirice,
　　still him we the bell :'
　'He winnë still, lady,
　　till ye come doun yersell.'

5 The first step she came on,
　　it was the stane ;
　The nest step
　　she mett him Lamkin.

6 'O spare my life, Lamkin,
　　an I ell gee ye a peak of goud well laid on ;
　An that dinnë pleas ye,
　　I ell heap it we my hand.'

7 'O will I kill the lady, nirice,
    or will I lat her gang ?'
'O kill her, Lanken,
    she was never gued to me.'

8 'O wanted ye yer meatt, nirice ?
    or wanted ye yer fiee ?
Or wanted ye the other bountys
    lady's are wont to gee ?'

9 .   .   .   .   .
    .   .   .   .   .
'Kill her, Lanken,
    she was never gued to me.'

10 'Ye wash a bason, nirice,
    an ye wash it clean,
To cape this lady's blode ;
    she is come of high kine.'

11 'I winnë wash a bason,
    nor wash it clean,
To cap this lady's blod,
    tho she be come of high kine.'

12 Bonny sang yon burd
    as he satt on the tree,
Bat sare grat Lamkin
    fan he was hanged hie.

13 Bonny sang the burd
    that satt on the hill,
Bat sare grat the nirice
    fan the caldron began to boill.

14 Lankin was hanged,
    .   .   .   . high,
An the faus nirice
    was burnt in the cadron was she.

339 ff., 513, IV, 480.

Y

'Lammikin,' Findlay's MSS, I, 173, "from J. Milne, who
wrote it down from recitation by John Duncan."

1 Lie in your room, my wife,
    .   .   .   .   .   .
    .   .   .   .   .   .
    .   .   .   .   .   .

2 'You 'll fasten doors and windows,
    you 'll fasten them out an in,
For if you leave ae window open
    Lammikin will come in.'

3 They 've fastened doors an windows,
    they 've fastened them out an in,
But they have left ae window open,
    an Lammikin cam in.

4 'O where are a' the women
    that dwell here within ?'
'They 're at the well washin,
    and they will not come in.'

5 'O where are a' the men
    that dwell here within ?'
'They 're at the .   .   .   . ,
    and they will not come in.'

6 'O where is the lady
    that dwells here within ?'
'She 's up the stair dressin,
    an she will not come doun.'

7 'It 's what will we do
    to mak her come doun ?
We 'll rock the cradle, nourrice,
    an mak her come doun.'

8 They [hae] rocked the cradle
    to mak her come doun,
    .   .   .   .   .   .
    the red bluid out sprung.

9 'O still the bairn, nourrice,
    O still him wi the bell :'
'He winna still, my lady,
    till ye come doun yersel.'

10 The first step she steppit,
    it was upon a stane ;
The next step she steppit,
    she keppit Lammikin.

11 'O mercy, mercy, Lammikin,
    hae mercy upo me !
Tho ye hae killed my young son,
    ye may lat mysel abee.'

12 'O it 's will I kill her, nourrice,
    or will I lat her be ?'
'O kill her, kill her, Lammikin,
    she neer was gude to me.'

13 'O it 's wanted ye your meat ?
    or wanted ye your fee ?'
    .   .   .   .   .   .
    .   .   .   .   .   .

14 ' I wanted not my meat,
    I wanted not my fee,
    But I wanted some bounties
      that ladies can gie.'

95. The Maid freed from the Gallows.

P. 346, III, 516 a, IV, 481 b. **Italian.** Maria Carmi, Canti pop. Emiliani, Archivio, XII, 189. Brunetina, after she has been rescued by her lover, is informed, while she is dancing at a ball, that her mother is dead. Bury her, she replies, I will dress in complete red, and she goes on dancing. So of her father. But when told that her lover is dead, she says she will dress in complete black, and bids the music stop, for she wishes to dance no more. 'La Ballerina,' Nigra, No 107, p. 469, is no doubt the last half of this ballad corrupted at the conclusion. The woman will not stop dancing for the reported death of father, mother, brother, sister, husband, but when told that her boy is dead asks the players to cease, her legs are broken, she can dance no more.

In ' Leggenda Marinesca' (di Catanzaro), La Calabria, October, 1893, VI, 16, a wife (or perhaps an affianced young woman) is ransomed from pirates by her husband (or betrothed), after father, mother, and brother have refused. If her father, mother, brother, should die, she would deck her hair, dress in red, yellow, or white, bid the guitar strike up, and dance ; but if her true-love died, she would put on black, cut her hair, and throw the guitar into the sea.

349. Mr Kaarle Krohn, of the University of Helsingfors, has favored me with the following study of the very numerous Finnish and Esthonian versions of this ballad, incorporating therein the researches of his father, Julius Krohn, already referred to at IV, 482 a. (Estlander's discussion, which I had not seen, " Sången om den friköpta," occupies pp. 331–356 of the tenth volume of Finsk Tidskrift.)

I. The West Finnish versions, dispersed over West and East Finland and Ingria. These are in the modern metre, which came into use hardly before the end of the seventeenth century, and it is in the highest degree probable that they were learned from the Swedes. About thirty copies known. Specimen, Reinholm's collection, H 12, No 76, from the Nystad district northward from Åbo, in Southwest Finland ; J. K., p. 11*.

Prevailing traits : 1. The maid is sitting in a little room, less frequently in a ship's cabin or a boat. 2. The father has three horses. 3. The mother has three cows. 4. The brother has three swords. 5. The sister has three crowns, or, in copies from further east, where crowns are not used for head-gear, three silk kerchiefs. 6. The lover has three ships, or almost as often three castles (mansions). There are variations, but rarely,

* This reference is to the article by Julius Krohn mentioned at IV, 482 a.

as to the objects possessed, and sometimes exchanges, but only two cases are of importance. In one copy from the extreme of Southeast Finland, the father has three oxen, which seems to be the original disposition, the change to horses coming about from the circumstance that oxen are seldom employed for ploughing in Finland. In four copies from the most eastern part of Finland the sister has three sheep, perhaps owing to the influence of the East Finnish versions. 7. The imprecations and benedictions at the end occur regularly. May the horses be knocked up or die at ploughing-time ; may the cows die, dry up, etc., at milking-time ; the swords shiver in war-time ; the crowns fall off or melt at wedding or dance (the silk kerchiefs tear, fade, spoil with wet) ; and on the other hand, may the ships sail well, do well, make money at trading-time ; the castles rise, flourish in time of destitution, of bad crops. Etc.

II. The later Esthonian versions, Esthonia and Livonia, in modern metre, of more recent origin, probably, than in Finland. About twenty copies known. Specimen, J. Hurt, Vana Kannel, II, 365, No 367. Lilla is sitting in the little room in weary expectation. She sees her father walking on the sea-beach. 'Dear father, beloved father, ransom me !' 'Wherewith ransom you, when I have no money ?' 'You have three horses at home, and can pawn one.' 'I can do better without my Lilla than without my three horses ; the horses are mine for all my life, Lilla for a short time.' In like fashion, the mother is not willing to sacrifice one of her three cows, the brother one of his three swords, the sister one of her three rings. But the lover, who has three ships, says, I can better give up a ship than give up my dear Lilla ; my ships are mine for a short time, but Lilla for all my life. Lilla breaks out in execrations : may her father's horses fall dead when they are ploughing in summer, may her mother's cows dry up in milking, her brother's swords shiver in war, her sister's rings break in the very act of marrying ; but may her true-love's ships long bring home precious wares.

Prevailing traits : 1. Lilla ; in some copies from East Livonia, Roosi. 2. Little room ; quite as often prison-tower. 3. The father has horses, the mother cows, the brother swords, as in the West Finnish versions. The independency of the Esthonian ballad is exhibited in the sister's three rings. It must, as far as I can at present see, have been borrowed directly from the Swedish, not through the medium of the Finnish. The lover has always three ships, and it is often wished that these ships may sail well in storm and in winter. The maledictions occur regularly, as in the example cited. There are some divergences as to the items of property, mostly occasioned by the older Esthonian version : thus, the father has sometimes oxen or corn-lofts, the brother horses, the sister brooches.

III. The older Esthonian versions, disseminated in Esthonia and Livonia, and also among the orthodox Esthonians beyond Pskov. These are in the old eight-syllable measure of the runes (and of Kalevala). More than a hundred copies have been obtained.

a. Best preserved and of most frequent occurrence in the island of Ösel. Twenty copies. Specimen from J. Hurt's manuscript collections. Anne goes into the cow-house and soils her cap. She proceeds to the sea-beach to wash her cap. Ships come from Russia, from Courland. Anne is made captive. She weeps, and begs that the ship may be stopped ; she wishes to take a look homewards. Her father has three oxen, one of which has silver horns, another copper, the third golden, but he will give none of them for her. Her mother has three cows, with silver, copper, golden udders ; her brother, three horses, with the same variety of manes ; her sister, three sheep, with wool of the three sorts ; a neighbor's son, three lofts full of wheat, rye, barley. She wishes that the oxen may die in plough-ing-time, the cows in milk-time, the horses at wooing-time, the sheep at wool-time; but may the corn-lofts of the neighbor's son grow fuller in the direst famine-time.

Prevailing traits : 1. The maid's name is Anne. 2. The pirates are Russians (10 times), Poles (6), Cour-landers (2), Swedes (1), Germans (1), English (1). 3. The father has commonly oxen ; the mother, cows always ; the brother, almost always horses ; the sister, sheep, six times, oftener than anything else ; the lover, ordinarily corn-lofts. 4. The cursing occurs ten times. There are in a few cases exchanges of the sorts of property (thus, the father has corn-lofts, the sister has brooches, each four times), and in two instances the lover is omitted. The ballad has perhaps been affected by another (see II, 347 f.) in which a girl receives in-formation that she has been sold by her relations : by her father for a pair of oxen (25 cases) or for a horse (18), by her mother for a cow, by her brother for a horse (24) or for a pair of oxen (14), by her sister for a brooch ; and she curses all that they have got by the sale.

b. Less perfect and not so well preserved on the Es-thonian mainland. About 100 copies, more or fewer. Specimens, Neus, p. 109, No 34, Hurt, Vana Kannel, I, 166, No 103, II, 310, No 442.

Prevailing traits : 1. The name of the maid, Anne, and the introduction linked to it, are often dropped, especially in the southeast of the Esthonian district, and a passage about a young conscript who wishes to be bought off from serving is substituted. The maid, whose brothers have hidden away, is pressed instead of them, and sent into service. As she is driven by the house of her parents in the military wagon she entreats her guards not to make sail ! 2. The kidnapper is most frequently a Russian, then Pole, Swede, less commonly German, Courlander. In the northeast of the Estho-nian district, on the border of Ingria, Karelian, four times. 3. The father often keeps the oxen, but almost as often has horses ; the brother, in these last cases, has seldom oxen, generally horses as well as the father. The alteration is in part owing to the same material

occasion as in the West Finnish versions ; sometimes an influence from the ballad of the maiden who has been sold by her relatives may be suspected (in which ballad it is not easy to say whether the oxen belong originally to father or brother). Frequently the father has corn-lofts, the lover, to whom these would belong, having dropped out. The mother has almost always cows ; in the northeast, on the Ingrian border, three times, aprons. The brother has generally horses, five times oxen, with other individual variations. The sister has preserved the sheep only four times; eight times she has brooches, and in one of these cases the ballad of the maid sold by her relatives is blended with ours, while in the remainder the influence of that ballad is observable. In six cases she has rings, perhaps under the influence of the later Esthonian versions. In the southeast she has chests seven times, and in most of these cases the lover has the rings. Other variations occur from one to four times. The lover has his corn-lofts nine times. Eight times he has horses, and in half of these instances he has exchanged with the brother, or both have horses. Twice he has ships, through the influence of the later Esthonian versions ; or rings, in which cases the father ordinarily has the corn-lofts. 4. The imprecation in the conclusion is but rarely preserved.

IV. The East Finnish versions. Diffused in Ingria, East Finland, and Russian Karelia. In the old rune-measure, about forty copies. Specimen, Ahlqvist's collection, from East Finland, No 351: see J. K., p. 11.

Prevailing traits : 1. The maid is in a boat on the Neva. 2. The kidnapper is a Russian. 3. The father has a horse, the mother a cow, the brother a horse, the sister a sheep (each with an epithet). 4. The impreca-tion is almost without exception preserved. This ver-sion arose from a blending of the West Finnish, I, the older Esthonian, III, and the ballad of the maid sold by her relatives. This latter occurs in West Ingria in the following shape : The maid gets tidings that she has been sold. The father has received for her a gold-horse (may it founder when on the way to earn gold !), the mother a portly cow (may it spill its milk on the ground !), the brother a war-horse (may the horse founder on the war-path !), the sister a bluish sheep (may wolf and bear rend it !). In some copies the father or the brother has oxen (may they fall dead in ploughing !), as in the Esthonian ballad, from which the Ingrian is borrowed. The sister's sheep instead of brooch shows perhaps the influence of the older Esthonian ballad of the maid begging to be ransomed, or it may be an innovation.

The ballad of the maid sold by her family occurs in West Ingria independently, and also as an introduction to the other, and has been the occasion for the changes in the possessions of the relatives. North of St Peters-burg the combination is not found, though it has left its traces in the course of the spreading of the ballad from Narva to St Petersburg.

The maid's sitting in a boat may come as well from the older Esthonian as from the West Finnish version, although it is more common in the latter for her to be sitting in the "little room." The Russian as the kidnapper is a constant feature in the older Esthonian version, but occurs also three times in the West Finnish (once it is the red-headed Dane, in the copy in which the oxen are preserved). Besides Russian, the kidnapper is once called Karelian in West Ingria, often in East Finland, and this denomination also occurs in Northeast Esthonia. The influence of the older Esthonian versions is shown again in some copies preserved in West Ingria which are not mixed up with the ballad of the maid that has been sold ; the mother having three aprons in two instances, as in some Northeast Esthonian copies.

The river Neva as a local designation is preserved in East Finland, and shows that the version in which it occurs migrated from Ingria northwards. In the course of its migration (which ends in Russian Karelia) this version has become mixed with the West Finnish in multiform ways. The prelude of the East Finnish has attached itself to the West Finnish, notwithstanding the different metre. The trilogy of the latter has made its way into the former, and has spoiled the measure. It is no doubt owing to the influence of the Western version that, in North Ingria and Karelia, the brother, more frequently the lover, has a war-sword, the lover once a sea-ship, or the brother a red boat or war-boat.

Finally it may be noted that in those West Ingrian copies in which the ballads of the maid sold and the maid ransomed are blended the ransomer is a son-in-law, and possesses "a willow castle" (wooden stronghouse?), the relation of which to the castle in the West Finnish version is not clear.

If we denote the West Finnish versions by **a**, the older Esthonian by **b**, the ballad of the maid sold by her family by **c**, the status of the East-Finnish versions may be exhibited thus :

In West Ingria, **b** + **c** + **a**.
In North Ingria, **b** + **c** + **a** + **a**.
In Karelia, **b** + **c** + **a** + **a** + **a**.

That is to say, there has been a constantly increasing influence exerted by the West Finnish versions upon the East Finnish Ingrian versions, and reciprocally. This circumstance has caused it to be maintained that the East Finnish versions were derived from the West Finnish, in spite of the difference of the metre.

353 a. **F** was communicated by Rev. W. Findlay : Findlay MSS, I, 100.

353. **H. c.** Mrs Bacheller, of Jacobstown, North Cornwall (sister of Mrs Gibbons, from whom 78 **H** was derived, see IV, 474 b), gave Rev. S. Baring-Gould the following version of the tale, taught her by a Cornish nursery maid, probably the same mentioned at the place last cited.

"A king had three daughters. He gave each a golden ball to play with, which they were never to lose. The youngest lost hers, and was to be hung on the gallows-tree if it were not found by a day named. Gallows ready, all waiting to see the girl hung. She sees her father coming, and cries :

'Father, father, have you found my golden ball,
     And will you set me free?'

'I've not found your golden ball,
     And I can't set you free ;
But I am come to see you hanged
     Upon the gallows-tree.'

The same repeated with every relationship, brother, sister, etc.; then comes the lover :

'Lover, lover, have you found the golden ball,' etc.

'Yes, I have found your golden ball,
     And I can set you free ;
I'm not come to see you hung
     Upon the gallows-tree.'"

354, IV, 481 f.

K

'The Prickly Bush,' Mr Heywood Sumner, in English County Songs, by Lucy E. Broadwood and J. A. Fuller Maitland, p. 112. From Somersetshire.

1 'O hangman, hold thy hand,' he cried,
     'O hold thy hand awhile,
For I can see my own dear father
     Coming over yonder stile.

2 'O father, have you brought me gold?
     Or will you set me free ?
Or be you come to see me hung,
     All on this high gallows-tree ?'

3 'No, I have not brought thee gold,
     And I will not set thee free,
But I am come to see thee hung,
     All on this high gallows-tree.'

4 'Oh, the prickly bush, the prickly bush,
     It pricked my heart full sore ;
If ever I get out of the prickly bush,
     I'll never get in any more.'

The above is repeated three times more, with the successive substitution of 'mother,' 'brother,' 'sister,' for 'father.' Then the first two stanzas are repeated, with 'sweetheart' for 'father,' and instead of 3 is sung :

5 'Yes, I have brought thee gold,' she cried,
   'And I will set thee free,
And I am come, but not to see thee hung
   All on this high gallous-tree.'
'Oh, the prickly bush,' etc.

In this version, a man is expressly delivered by a maid, contrary to the general course of tradition. So apparently in J, IV, 481, as understood by Dr. Birkbeck Hill.

96. The Gay Goshawk.

P. 355. M. G. Lewis, in a letter of May 29, 1800 (Letters at Abbotsford, I, No 30), refers to a copy of this ballad (and one of ' Brown Adam ') which he had furnished Scott. This might perhaps be the " MS. of some antiquity " (printed, IV, 482).

As to the bird's part in this ballad, compare the following passage. A son, in prison, sending a letter to his mother by a bird, gives this charge :

   Quando giugnerete alla porta mia,
   Là sta un ulivo.
   Posati su quell' ulivo,
   V' agita e dibatti l' ali,
   Ché di te caderà il foglio di carta.

De Rada, Rapsodie d' un poema Albanese, I, canto xvi, p. 29.

P. 356 a, III, 517 a, IV, 482 a. **French.** Add : ' La belle qui fait la morte,' ' La fille du duc de Montbrison,' Pineau, Le Folk-Lore du Poitou, p. 311, p. 389 (each, six stanzas) ; ' La belle dans la tour,' six copies (besides Belle Idoine repeated), M. Wilmotte in Bulletin de Folklore, Société du Folklore Wallon, 1893, p. 35.

356 b, 3d paragraph, III, 517 a. Add : A copy of ' Les trois capitaines,' in Mélusine, VI, 52, 183 ; Wallonia, I, 38 ; " Fréd. Thomas, La Mosäique du Midi, V, 1841 ; C. Beauquier, Mém. de la Soc. d'Émulation du Doubs, 1890," Mélusine, VI, 220, where also a Catalan version, which had escaped my notice, Milà y Fontanals, Romancerillo, p. 259, No 264, is registered by M. Doncieux. A Breton version, Mélusine, VI, 182.

99. Johnie Scot.

P. 379. **A.** Considering that Sir Walter Scott professes to have derived some variations from recitation in the south of Scotland (see the note, IV, 387), the copy in " Scottish Songs " may be fully collated, small as will be the value of the result.

' John the Little Scott,' fol. 24.

1 John the Scot was as brave a knight
   As ever shook a speir,
And he is up to fair England,
   The king's braid banner to bear.

2 And while he was in fair England,
   Sae fair his hap did prove
That of the king's ae daughter dear
   He wan the heart and love.

3 But word is gane to the English king,
   And an angry man was he,
And he has sworn by salt and bread
   They should it dear abye.

4 *wanting.* 5^1. Then Johny 's gane. $5^{2,4}$. I wot.
5^3. the English.
$6^{3,4}$. To hear some news from his true love,
   Least she had sufferd wrang.
7^2. That will win hose and shoon.
7^3. will gang into. 8^1. Then up there.
9 *wanting.* 10^3. to grass growing.
11^1. And when : to the king's castle.
11^3. saw that fair ladye. 12^2, 13^2. ain sel.
12^4. And speer na your father's. 13^1. Here take.
13^3. to feir Scotland. 13^4. Your true love waits.
14^1. The ladie turned her round about.
14^4. Unless. 15^2. In prison pinching cold.
15^3. My garters are of. 15^4. the silk and gold.
16^3. And hie thee back to yon Scottish knight.
17^1. quickly sped.
18^1. He told him then that ladie's words.
18^2. He told him.
$18^{3,4}$. But ere the tale was half said out
   Sae loudly to horse he did ca.
19^4. That should have been my bride.
20^1. And spak his mither dear.
20^3. For gin you 're taen. 20^4. ye 'll.
21^1. and spak. 21^2. And Johny 's true.
21^4. And his surety I will.
22. Then when they cam to English ground
   They gard the mass be sung,
  And the firsten town that they cam to
   They gard the bells be rung
23^1. And the nextin : cam to. $23^⁹$. Were.
24^1. And when : the high castle. 24^2. rode.
25^3. Or is it. 26^1. I 'm not. 26^2. James our.
26^3. But Johny Scot, the little Scot.
27^1. is thy name. 27^3. eer.
28^1. and spak the gallant. 28^3. hundred.
28^4. That will die or. 29^1. and spak.
29^2. And sae scornfully leugh he. 29^3. my bower.
30^1. boon, said the little Scot.
30^2. Bring forth your. 30^3. falls. 30^4. I hae.

31 Out then cam that Italian knight,
   A griesly sight to see ;
Between his een there was a span,
   Between his shoulders three and three.

And forth then came brave John the Scot,
   He scarcely reachd his knee,
Yet on the point of Johny's brand
   The Italian knight did die.

32 And syne has he waved his bludie glaive,
  And slait it on the plain ;
 ' Are there any more Italian dogs
  That you wish to be slain ? '

33 ' A clerk, a clerk,' the king he cried,
  ' To register this deed ; '
 ' A priest, a priest,' Pitnochtan cried,
  ' To marry us wi speed.'

34 *wanting.*

384. A copy of **D** was sent by Motherwell to C. K. Sharpe with a letter of December 6, 1824, in which many of the variations of **b** were introduced into **a**.

101. Willie o Douglas Dale.

P. 407. **A.** Collated with the copy in the Abbotsford MS. " Scottish Songs,' as to which see the note at IV, 387.
' Willie of Douglas-dale,' fol. 16.
 1¹. was a gallant squire. 2¹. the English court.
 2³. When. 2⁴. But her he neer could. 3¹. once.
 3². the *wanting.* 3⁴. By the ae. 4¹. louted low.
 4². His cap low in his.
 4³. I greet ye well, ye gentle knight.
 4⁴. your cap. 5¹. knight, fair dame.
 5². Nor eer can hope. 5³. am but a humble squire.
 5⁴. That serves. 6¹. Gae. 6². baith night.
 6³. tempting *written before* face *and* struck out.
 6⁴. ever I. 7 *wanting.*
 8². He watchd that ladye's.
 8³. passd the twa between.
 9¹. O narrow is my gown, Willy.
 9³. And short are my petticoats. 9⁴. sae wide.
 9⁶. is laid. 10¹. gin my father get wit.
 10². never eat. 10³,⁵. get wit. 10⁴. gae.
 10⁶. Ah, Willy, you 'll. 11¹. O gin ye 'll.
 11². gang. 11³. into. 12 *wanting.*
 14¹. day was come. 14². den.
 14³. That gentle ladye. 14⁴. While the.
 15³,⁴. Or lack ye ony tender love
   That may assuage your pain.
 16¹. wan na. 16². for my. 16³. And alas, alas.
 17¹. He 's felld the thorn in.
 17². And blawn it to a flame.
 17³. He 's strewd it.
 17⁴. To cheer that lovely dame.
 18¹. He 's : in gude.
 18². And laid the fair ladye.
 18³. he 's happed her oer wi withered.
 18⁴. his coat and goun. 19 *wanting.*
 20¹. branch red. 20². grew in gude grene wood.
 20³. And brought her a draught.
 20⁴. I wot they did her good.
 21–23 *wanting.* 24¹. to shoot.
 24². has he *wanting.* 25 (*after* 30).

26¹,². Syne has he sought the forest through,
  Sum woman's help to gain.
26³. he came to a bonny.
27¹. O will ye leave the sheep, he says.
27². And come. 27³. ye. 27⁴. give.
28². She fell down. 28³. fair dame. 28⁴. **For a.**
29². but *wanting.* 29³. ye : flocks.
29⁴. And gang to fair. 30³. for you.
30⁴. marry *wanting :* Scottish man.
After 30 (see 25) :
  O taen has she the bonny knave-boy
  And washd him in the milke,
  And she has tended the sick lady,
  And rowd her in the silk.
31¹. maid. 31³. took to fair. 32¹. an *wanting.*
32³. they gat safe. 32⁴. Himself was lord therein.

411. From " The Old Lady's Collection," No 33, ' Willie of Duglass Daill.' The Dame Oliphant of the other versions is somewhat disguised in the old lady's writing as Demelefond, Demelofen, etc.

D

1 Willie was a rich man's son,
  A rich man's son was he ;
 Hee thought his father lake to sair,
  An his mother of mine digree,
 An he is on to our English court,
  To serve for meatt an fee.

2 He hadno ben in our king's court
  A tuall-month an a day,
 Till he fell in love we Mary, Dem [Ele]fon,
  An a great buity was she.

3 He hadno ben in our king's court
  A tuall-month an a houre,
 Till he dreamed a lady of buty bright
  Gave him a rosey flour.

4 The lady touk her mantell her about,
  Her gooun-teall in her hand,
 An she is on to gued grean woud,
  As fast as she could gang.

5 . . . .

 . . . .
 An ther she spayed a gellant knight,
  Kamen his yallou hear.

6 ' What is yer name, sir knight ?
  For a knight I am sure ye be ; '
 ' I am called Willie of Duglas Dall,
  Did ye never hear of me ? '

'If ye be Willie of Duglass Daill,
  I afft have heard of thee.'

7 'What is yer name, ye lovely dame?
  For a lady I trou ye be;'
'I am called Mary, Dem Elefond,
  Did ye never hear of me?'

8 'In ye be Mary, Dem Elefon,
  As I trust well ye be,
.   .   .   .   .   .
  My heart ye haa ye we.'

9 The lady was fair an rear,
  The knight's heart had she;
The knight was tall an straght withall,
  The lady's hart had he.

10 It fell ance upon a day
  Dem Elofen thought lang,
An she is on to Willie's bour,
  As fast as she could gang.

11 'Narrou is my pettecot, Willie,
  It ance was saa wide,
An narrou is my stays, Willie,
  Att ance wer saa wide,
An paill is my chikes, Willie,
  An laigh, laigh is my pride.

12 '.   .   .   .   .   .
.   .   .   .   .   .
An the knights of my father's court gat word
  of this,
  I feer they wad gare ye diee.'

13 He touke .   .   .   .   .   .
  The lady by the hand,
An they are one to gued green woud,
  As fast as they coud gang.

14 It fell ance upon a day
  Strong travileng came her tell,
.   .   .   .   .   .
  .   .   .   .   .   .

15 'Ye take your boue on yer shoulder,
  Yer arrous in yer hand,
An ye gaa farr throu green woud,
  An shout some veneson.

16 'Fan ye hear me loud cray,
  Bide far awaa fra me,

Bat fan ye hear me laying still
  Ye may come back an see.'

17 Fan he hard her loud cray,
  He bad far awaa,
Bat fan he heard her laying still
  He did come an see,
An he got her
  An her young son her wee.

18 He milked the goats,
  An feed his young son wee,
And he made a fire of the oken speals,
  An warmed his lady wee.

19 It fell ance upon a day
  The lady though[t] lang:
'An ye haa any place in fair Scotland, Willie,
  I wiss ye wad haa me hame.'

20 '.   .   .   .   .   .
  I ha lands an reants saa friee,
The bonny lands of Duglass Daill,
  They a' lay bread an friee.'

21 He's taen the knight-bairn in his arms,
  His lady by the hand,
An he is out throu gued green woud,
  As fast as they coud gang.

22 .   .   .   .   .   .
  .   .   .   .   .   .
Till they came to a maid kepping her goats,
  .   .   .   .   .   .

23 'Hallë, ye maid,
  For a maid ye seem to be;
Will ye live your goats kepping
  An goo we me?

24 'I cannot live my father, I canno live my
  midder,
  Nor yet my brethren three;
I cannot live my goats kepping,
  An goo along we the.

25 'Fatt is your name, ye lovely dame?
  For a lady I am shour ye be;'
'I am called Mary, Dem Elifond,
  Did ye never hear of me?'

26 'If ye be Mary, Dem Elifond,
  As I trust well ye be,

I will live my goats kepping
  An goo along we the.

27 'For I will live my father, an I ill live my
    mother,
  An my brothers three,
An I will live my goats,
  An go along we thee.'

28 The maid touke the knight-bairn in her ar[m]s,
  An his lady took he,
An they are to gued ship-bourd,
  And took God to be ther foresteed, an didne
    fear to droun.

29 An they landed att Duglas Dalle,
  Far the lands was braid an frie,
An the knight-bairn was Black Sir James of
    Duglas Dall,
  An a gallant knight was hee.

*Written, like all the other pieces in the col-
lection, without division into stanzas or
verses.*

2³. Demefon; *contracted at the edge.*
9³. was tell. 11². *Read* side ?
14². *Perhaps* her tee.

105. The Bailiff's Daughter of Islington.

P. 426 f. Of the Italian ballad there are many more
versions, but it is needless to cite them. Add for
Spanish: 'La Ausencia,' Pidal, Asturian Romances,
Nos 31, 32, p. 152 f.

107. Will Stewart and John.

P. 433 b, 2d paragraph. Beating of daughters.
Elizabeth Paston, a marriageable woman, was
"betyn onys in the weke, or twyes, and som tyme
twyes on a day, and hir hed broken in to or thre
places." (1449.) Paston Letters, ed. Gairdner, I, 90.

110. The Knight and the Shepherd's Daughter.

P. 457, IV, 492. From "The Old Lady's Collection," No 34, 'Earl Richerd,' = Skene, **M**.

N

1 Ther was a sheperd's daughter
  Keeped hogs upon yon hill,

An by came [t]her a gentell knight,
  An he wad haa his will.

2 Fan his will
  Of her he had taiin,
'Kind sir, for your curtisy,
  Will ye tell me yer name?'

3 'Some they caa me Joke,
  An some caa me John,
Bat fan I am in our king's court
  Hichkoke is my name.'

4 The lady bieng well book-read
  She spealled it our agen:
'Hichkoke in Latin
  Is Earl Richerd att heam.'

5 He patt his liag out-our his stead
  An to the gate has gain;
She kilted up her green clathing
  An fast folloued she.

6 'Turn back, ye carl's dother,
  An dinnë follou me;
It setts no carl's dothers
  King's courts to see.'

7 'Perhaps I am a carle's dother,
  Perhaps I am nean,
Bat fan ye gat me in free forest
  Ye sud haa latten alean.'

8 Fan they came to yon wan water
  That a' man cas Clide,
He luked our his left shoulder,
  Says, Fair maid, will ye ride?

9 'I learned it in my mother's bour,
  I watt I learned it well,
Fan I came to wan water
  To soum as dos the eall.

10 'I learned it in my mother's bour,
  I wiss I had learned it better,
Fan I came to wan watter
  To sume as dos the otter.'

11 She touk a golden comb,
  Combed out her yallou hear,

.   .   .   .   .   .

.   .   .   .   .   .

12 'Far gatt ye that, ye carl's dother,
   I pray ye tell to me;'
'I gatt it fra my mither,' she says,
   'To begulle sick sparks as ye.'

13 'Gin ye be a carl's gett,
   As I trou well ye be,
Far gatt ye a' that fine clothing,
   To cloath yer body we?'

14 'My mother was an ill woman,
   An ill woman was she,
An she gatt a' that fine clathing,
   Frae sick chaps as ye.'

15 Fan they came to our king's court,
   She fell lou doun on her knee:
'Win up, ye fair may,
   What may ye want we me?'
'Ther is a knight in your court
   This day has robbed me.'

16 'Has he robbed you of your goud?
   Or of your whit monie?
Or of your meadnhead,
   The flour of your body?'

17 'He has no robbed me of my goud,
   Nor yet of my fiee,
Bat he has robed me of my madinhead,
   The flour of my body.'

18 'Wad ye keen the knight,
   If ye did him see?'
'I wad keen him well by his well-fared face
   An the blieth blink of his eay.'
An sighan says the king,
   I wiss it binë my brother Richie!

19 The king called on his merry men a',
   By an, by tua, by three;
Earl Richerd had ay ben the first,
   Bat the last man was he.

20 By that ye might a well kent
   The gulty man was he;
She took him by the hand,
   Says, That same is hee.

21 Ther was a brand laid doun to her,
   A brand batt an a ring,
Three times she minted to the brand,
   Bat she took up the ring;

A' that was in the court
   'S counted her a wise woman.

22 'I will gee ye five hundred pound,
   To make yer marrage we,
An ye gie hame, ye carl's dother,
   An fash na mare we me.'

23 'Ye keep yer five hundred pound,
   To make yer marreg we,
For I will ha nathing bat yer sell,
   The king he promised me.'

24 'I ill gee ye a thousand poun,
   To make yer marrage we,
An ye gae hame, ye carl's gett,
   An fash na mare we me.'

25 'Ye keep yer thousand pound,
   To make yer marreg we,
For I ill ha nathing batt yer sell,
   The king he promised me.'

26 He toke her doun
   An clothed her in green;
Fan she cam up,
   She was fairer then the quin.

27 Fan they gaid to Mary Kirk,
   The nettels grue by dike:
'O gin my midder war hear,
   Sai clean as she wad them peak!'

28 He drue his hat out-our his eayn,
   The tear blinded his eay;
She drue back her yallou loaks,
   An a light laughter luke she.

29 Fan she came by yon mill-toun,
   .   .   .   .   .   .
'O well may the mill goo,
   An well matt she be!
For aften ha ye filled my poke
   We the whit meall an the gray.'

30 'I wiss I had druken the water
   Fan I drank the aill,
Or any carl's dother
   Suld ha tald me siken a teall.'

31 'Perhaps I am a carl's dother,
   Perhaps I am nean;

Fan ye gatt me in frie forest,
Ye sud ha latten alean.

*   *   *   *   *   *

32 'Take awa yer silver spons,
    Far awa fra me,
An ye gee me t[he] ram-horn [s]pons,
    Them I am best used we.

33 'Ye take awa yer tabel-cloths,
    Far awa fra me,
An ye gee me a mukell dish
    I am best used we.

34 'For if I had my mukel dish hear,
    An sayn an it war fou,
I wad sup till I war sared,
    An sayn lay doun my head an slep like ony
      sou.

35 'Ye take away yer hollan shits,
    Far awa fra me,
An ye bring me a cannas,
    It's the thing I ben eased we.'

36 Fan bells wer rung, an mess was sung,
    An a' man boun to bed,
Earl Richerd an the carl's dother
    In a bed [were laid].

37 'Lay yond, lay yond, ye carl's dother,
    Your hot skin . . me ;
It setts na carl's dothers
    In earls' beds to be.'

38 'Perhaps I am a carl's dother,
    Perhaps I am nean ;
Bat fan ye gat me in free forest
    Ye might a latten alean.'

39 Up starts the Bellie Blind,
    Att ther bed-head :
'I think it is a meatt marrage
    Betuen the ane an the eather,
The Earl of Heartfourds ae daughter
    An the Quien of England's brother.'

40 'If this be the Earl of Heartfourd's ae
    doughter,
    As I trust well it be,
Mony a gued hors have I redden
    For the love of the.'

2². ha had.
8². cas es : *perhaps* caes *was meant.*
9⁴. to eull. 18⁵. sigh an. 21⁸. courts.
32⁸. t *with an imperfect letter, for* the.
37². *Perhaps* we.
39⁵, 40¹. *The* t *is not crossed in* Heartfourd,
    and Hearlfourd *may be meant.*

O

Kidson's Traditional Tunes, p. 20, from Mr Benjamin
Holgate, Leeds.

1 There was a shepherd's daughter
    Who kept sheep on yon hill ;
There came a young man riding by,
    Who swore he'd have his will.
    Fol lol lay
    Fol lol di diddle lol di day

2¹,². He took her by the lilly-white hand
    And by her silken sleeve,

3⁴. Or tell to me your name.

4 'Oh, some they call me Jack, sweetheart,
    And some they call me Will,
But when I ride the king's high-gate
    My name is Sweet William.'

4⁴. But name.

P

Findlay's MSS, I, 208, from Mr McKenzie, Advie, Morayshire.

1 'T is said a shepherd's ae daughter
    Kept sheep upon a hill,
An by there cam a courteous knight,
    An he wad hae his will.

2 He's taen her by the milk-white hand
    An by the grass-green sleeve,
He's laid her doon at the fit o a bush,
    An neer ance speired her leave.

112. The Baffled Knight.

P. 480 a, 4th paragraph. 'The Politick Maid' was
entered to Thomas Lambert, 16th May, 1637 : Arber,
Stationers' Registers, IV, 385.

    481 b, III, 518 a, IV, 495 a. Tears. 'Chasseur,
mon beau chasseur,' Pineau, Le Folk-Lore du Poitou,
p. 251.

Varieties. 'La jolie Couturière,' Pineau, p. 285.
483 b. 'La jolie Batelière,' Romania, XIII, 410 ;
La Tradition, VII, 110.

VOL. III.

117. A Gest of Robyn Hode.

P. 40 b. References to Robin Hood in the 15th century.

And many men speken of Robyn Hood
And shotte nevere in his bowe.

Reply of Friar Dow Topias, in Wright's Poetical Poems and Songs relating to English History, II, 59, dated by Wright 1401, which may be rather too early. The proverbial phrase shows that Robin Hood had long been familiar to the English People.

120. Robin Hood's Death.

P. 103 a, note *. 'Give me my God' is not perhaps too bold a suggestion. We have 'yeve me my savyour' in the Romance of the Rose, Morris, v. 6436, translating 'le cors nostre seigneur.'

132. The Bold Pedlar and Robin Hood.

P. 155. The following copy, entitled 'Robin Hood and the Proud Pedlar,' is from a garland in a collection of folio sheet-ballads mostly dated 1775, in the British Museum, 1346. m. 7(9). The Museum catalogue assigns the ballads to Edinburgh. I owe my knowledge of this piece to Mr P. Z. Round.

1 There was a proud pedlar, a fine pedlar,
    a proud pedlar he seemd to be,
And he 's taen his pack upon his back,
    and went linking over the lee.

2 Where he met two troublesome men,
    troublesome men they seemd to be,
The one of them was Robin Hood,
    the other Little John so free.

3 ' O what is that into thy pack?
    thou pedlar proud now tell to me ; '
' There 's seven suits of good green silk,
    and bow-strings either two or three.'

4 ' If there 's seven suits of good green silk,
    and silken bow-strings two or three,
Then be my sooth,' says Little John,
    ' there 's some of them must fall to me.'

5 Then he 's taen his pack off his back,
    and laid it low down by his knee :
' Where 's the man fit to drive me frae 't?
    then pack and all to him I 'll gie.'

6 Then Little John pulld out his sword,
    the pedler he pulld out his brand,
They swapped swords till they did sweat ;
    ' O pedlar fine, now hold thy hand !'

7 ' O fy ! O fy !' said Robin Hood,
    ' O fy ! O fy ! that must not be,
For I 've seen a man in greater strait
    than to pay him and pedlars three.'

8 ' Then try him, try him, master,' he said,
    ' O try him now, master,' said he,
' For by me sooth,' said Little John,
    'master, 't is neither you nor me.'

9 Bold Robin pulld out his sword,
    the pedlar he pulld out his brand,
They swapped swords till they did sweat ;
    ' O pedlar fine, now hold thy hand!

10 ' O what 's thy name,' says Robin Hood,
    ' now, pedlar fine, come tell to me ; '
' No, be my sooth, that will I not,
    till I know what your names may be.'

11 ' The one of us ['s] calld Robin Hood,
    the other Little John so free,
And now it lies into thy breast
    whether thou 'lt tell thy name to me.'

12 ' I 'm Gamwell gay, of good green wood,
    my fame is far beyond the sea ;
For killing a man in my father's land
    my native land I was forcd to flee.'

13 ' If thou be Gamwell of the green wood,
    thy fame is far beyond the sea ;
And be my sooth,' said Little John,
    ' my sister's son thou needs must be.

14 ' But what was that was on thy back?
    O, cousin Gamwell, tell unto me ; '
' It is seven sarks and three gravats,
    is all the kitt that I carry.'

15 They smoothd their words and sheathd their swords,
    and kissd and clapt most tenderly;
To a tavern then they went to dine,
    and drank about most heartily.

July, 1775.

Captain Delany's Garland, containing five new songs, . . . II, Robin Hood and the Proud Pedlar.
6², 6⁴, 9⁴. padler.

152. Robin Hood and the Golden Arrow.

P. 223. Letter shot to its address on an arrow. Afanasief, Russian Popular Tales, V, 183.

155. Sir Hugh, or, The Jew's Daughter.

P. 233, IV, 497.

T

'Little Sir William,' Miss M. H. Mason's Nursery Rhymes and Country Songs, p. 46.

1 Easter Day was a holiday,
   Of all days in the year,
And all the little schoolfellows went out to
     play,
   Bat Sir William was not there.

2 Mamma went to the Jew's wife's house,
   And knockèd at the ring,
Saying, Little Sir William, if you are there,
   Oh, let your mother in!

3 The Jew's wife opened the door and said,
   He is not here to-day;
He is with the little schoolfellows out on the
     green,
   Playing some pretty play.

4 Mamma went to the Boyne water,
   That is so wide and deep,
Saying, Little Sir William, if you are there,
   Oh, pity your mother's weep!

5 'How can I pity your weep, mother,
   And I so long in pain?
For the little penknife sticks close in my heart,
   And the Jew's wife has me slain.

6 'Go home, go home, my mother dear,
   And prepare my winding sheet,
For tomorrow morning before eight o'clock
   You with my body shall meet.

7 'And lay my Prayer-Book at my head,
   And my grammar at my feet,
That all the little schoolfellows as they pass
     by
   May read them for my sake.'

U

Notes and Queries, Eighth Series, II, 43, July, 1842. 'The Jew's Daughter,' communicated by Mr C. W. Penny, as repeated to his brother, the vicar of Stixwould, Lincolnshire, by one of the oldest women in the parish. "A song sung by his nurse to a Lincolnshire gentleman, now over sixty years of age."

1 You toss your ball so high,
   You toss your ball so low,
You toss your ball into the Jew's garden,
   Where the pretty flowers grow.

2 Out came one of the Jew's daughters,
   Dressed all in green:
'Come hither, pretty little dear,
   And fetch your ball again.'

3 She showed him a rosy-cheeked apple,
   She showed him a gay gold ring,
She showed him a cherry as red as blood,
   And that enticed him in.

4 She set him in a golden chair,
   She gave him kisses sweet,
She threw him down a darksome well,
   More than fifty feet deep.

156. Queen Eleanor's Confession.

P. 259. B. Here given as it stands in "The Old Lady's Collection," No 6.

1 Our quin 's seek, an very seek,
   She 's seek an leak to dee,
An she has sent for the friears of France,
   To speak we her spedely.

2 'Ye 'll pit on a frier's robe,
   An I 'll put one anether,
An we 'll goo to madam the Quin,
   Leak frayers bath together.'

3 'God forbid,' sayes Earl Marchell,
   'That ever the leak sud be,
That I sud begule madam the Quin;
   I wad be hangèd hei.'

4 .   .   .   .   .   .
   .   .   .   .   .
The King suar by the croun an the septer roun
   Eearl Marchell sudne dei.

5 The king pat on a frier's rob,
   Eearl Marchell on anether,
The 'r on to the Quin,
   Like frayers bath together.

6 'Gin ye be the frayers of France,' she says,
   'As I trust wiell ye be,
Bat an ye be ony eather men
   Ye sall be hangèd he.'

7 The king he turned him roun,
　　An by his troth suare he,
' We ha na sung masse
　　San we came fra the sea.'

8 ' The first sin ever I did,
　　An a very grat sin it was tee,
I gaa my medenhead to Earl Marchell,
　　Below a green-wood tree.'

9 ' That was a sin, an a very grate sin,
　　Bat pardoned it man be ; '
' We menement,' said Earl Marchell,
　　Bat a heavë, heavë heart had he.

10 ' The nist sin ever I did,
　　An a grat sin it was tee,
I pusned Lady Rosomon,
　　An the King's darling was she.'

11 ' That was a sin, an a grat sin,
　　Bat pardoned it may be ; '
' We menement,' said King Henry,
　　Bat a heavë, heavë heart had he.

12 ' The nist sin I ever did,
　　An a grat sin it was tee,
I keepet pusin in my bosom seven year
　　To pusin him King Henre.'

13 ' That was a sin, an a grat sin,
　　Bat pardoned it may be ; '
' We menement,' sa[i]d King Henrie,
　　Bat a heavë, heavë heart had he.

14 ' O see ye na yon bony boys,
　　As they play att the baa?
An see ye na Earl Merchal's son?
　　I lee him best of all.

15 ' But see ye na King Henry's son?
He is headed leak a bull an baked like a bore,
　　I leak him warst of a' : '
' An, by my soth,' says him King Henry,
　　' I leak him best of the twa.'

16 The king he turned him roun,
　　Pat on the coat of goud,
The Quin turned her roun,
　　The king to behald.

17 '.　　.　　.　　.　　.　　.
　　.　　.　　.　　.　　.
Gin I had na sworn by the croun an the septer roun,
　　Eearl Marchell sud ben gared dee.'

Written without division into stanzas or verses.
2². An ye 'll.

157. Gude Wallace.

P. 265. From C. K. Sharpe's "first collection,"
p. 18.

I

" An old song shewing how Sir Wm Wallace killed thirty
Englishmen." This copy resembles **C**.
' Decencey ' in 8² is the reciter's rendering of the bencite
(benedicite) of **C** 6².

1 ' I wish I had a king,' brave Wallace he said,
　　' That every brave Scotsman might leave by
　　　　his oun,
For between me and my sovreign leige
　　I think I see some ill [seed] sowen.'

2 Brave Wallace out-oer yon river he lap,
　　And he lighted low down on the plain,
And he came to a gay lady,
　　As she was at the well washing.

3 ' Some tidings, some tidings,' brave Wallace he
　　　　said,
　　' Some tidings ye most tell unto me ;
Now since we are met here togither on the
　　plain,
　　Some tidings ye most tell unto me.'

4 ' O go ye down to yon wee ale-house,
　　And there is fifteen Englishmen,
And they are seeking for good Wallace,
　　And him to take and him for to hang.'

5 ' I wish I had a penny in my pocket,' he says,
　　' Or although it were but a bare baubee,
And I wad away to the wee ale-house,
　　The fifeteen Englishmen to see.'

6 She 's put hir hand in hir left pocket,
　　And fifteen shillings to him she told down :
' If ever I live to come back this way,
　　The money 's be well paid agein.'

7 He louted twafauld oer a stick,
　　And he louted threefauld oer a tree,
And he 'es gane awa to the wee ale-house,
　　The fifeteen Englishmen to see.

8 When he came to the wee ale-house,
　　He walked ben, says, Decencey be there !
The Engilish proud captain he awnsered him,
　　And he awnsered him with a graid domi-
　　　　neer.

9 'Why, where wast thou born, thou old crooked
    carle?
    Where and of what country?'
'I am a true Scotsman bred and born,
    And an auld crooked carle, just sic as ye
    may see.'

10 'I wad gee fifteen shillings,' the captain he
    said,
    'To an auld crooked carle, just sic a ane as
    thee,
    If ye wad tell me of Willie Wallace,
    For he 's the man I wad fain see.'

11 'O hold your hand,' brave Wallace he said,
    'And let me see if yeer coin be good;
    If ye wad give fifteen shillings more,
    Ye never bade a better boad.'

12 He 's tean the captain out-oer the chaft-blade,
    Till a bitt of meat he never did eat mair;
    He stickit a' the reste as the saroun the table,
    And he left them all a spraulling there.

13 'Get up, get up, goodwife,' he says,
    'Get up and get me some denner in haste,
    For it is now three days and nights
    Since a bit of meat my mouth did taste.'

14 The denner was not well made ready,
    Nor was it on the table sett,
    Till other fifeteen English men
    Were a' perading about the yett.

15 'Come out, come out now, Wallace,' they crys,
    'For this is the place ye 'es sure for [to] die;'
    'I lippen not sae little to good,' he says,
    'Although I be but ill-wordie.'

16 The goodman ran butt, the goodwife ran ben,
    They put the house in such a fever!
    Five of them he sticket where they stood,
    And other five he smoddered in the gitter.

17 Five of them he folowd to the merry green-
    wood,
    And these five he hangt on a grain,
    And gin the morn at ten o'clock
    He was wi his mirry men at Lochmaben.

6^2. 15.
8^2. *Perhaps we should read* be here, *as in* A
10^2, *but other copies have* bad . . . there,

*and it is likely enough that there is a con-
fusion of the oblique and the direct form.*
14^4. a.

265 b, note †. 'Let me see if your money be good,
and if it be true and right, you'll maybe get the downcome of Robinhood,' from a recited copy, in the preface to Finlay's Scottish Ballads, I, xv.

158. Hugh Spencer's Feats in France.

P. 276. What is narrated of Walter in the Chronicon Novalese is likewise told of Ogier by Alexander
Neckam, De Naturis Rerum, ed. T. Wright, p. 261 ff.
(see also the note at p. lvi), in a copy of Turpin's
Chronicle, Ward, Catalogue of Romances, I, 579 f.,
and (excepting the monastery) in La Chevalerie Ogier,
ed. Barrois, v. 10390 ff.; of Heimir, Saga Ðiðriks af
Bern, c. 429 ff., Unger, p. 361 ff.; and in part in the
ballad of 'Svend Felding,' Grundtvig, No 31, I, 398.
See Grundtvig's preface to No 15, I, 216 ff.; Ward, as
above; Voretzsch, Ueber die Sage von Ogier dem
Dänen, p. 113 ff.

161. The Battle of Otterburn.

P. 289, IV, 499. From C. K. Sharpe's "first collection," p. 21. Tradition in this copy, as in Herd's, **B**,
ascribes the death of Douglas to an offended and treacherous page.

1 It was about the Lammes time,
    When moorland men do win their hay,
    Brave Earl Douglass, in armer bright,
    Marchd to the Border without delay.

2 He hes tean wi him the Lindseys light,
    And sae hes he the Gordons gay,
    And the Earl of Fife, without all strife,
    And Sir Heugh Montgomery upon a day.

3 The hae brunt Northumberland,
    And sae have [the] Northumbershire,
    And fair Cluddendale they hae brunt it hale,
    And he 's left it all in fire fair.

4 Ay till the came to Earl Percy's castle,
    Earl Percey's castle that stands sae high:
    'Come dowen, come dowen, thou proud Percey,
    Come down and talk one hour with me.

5 'Come down, come down, thou proud Percey,
    Come down and talk one hour with me;
    For I hae burnt thy heritage,
    And sae will I thy building high.'

6 'If ye hae brunt my heritage,
    O dule, O dule, and woe is me!

But will ye stay at the Otter burn
　Untill I gather my men to me?'

7 'O I will stay at the Otter burn
　The space of days two or three,
And if ye do not meet me there,
　I will talk of thy coardie.'

8 O he hes staid at the Otter burn
　The space of days two or three;
He sent his page unto his tent-door,
　For to see what ferleys he could see.

9 'O yonder comes yon gallent knight,
　With all bonny banners high;
It wad do ony living good
　For to see the bonny coulers fly.'

10 'If the tale be true,' Earl Douglass says,
　'The tidings ye have told to me,
The fairest maid in Otterburn
　Thy bedfellow sure shall she be.

11 'If the tale be false,' Earl Douglass says,
　'The tidings that ye tell to me,
The highest tree in Otterburn,
　On it high hangëd shall ye be.'

12 Earl Douglass went to his tent-door,
　To see what ferleys he could see;
His little page came him behind,
　And ran him through the fair body.

13 'If I had a little time,' he says,
　'To set in order my matters high,
Ye Gordons gay, to you I say,
　See that ye let not my men away.

14 'Ye Linseys light, both wise and wight,
　Be sure ye carry my coulers high;
Ye Gordons gay, again I say,
　See that ye let not my men away.

15 'Sir Heugh Montgomery, my sistir's son,
　I give you the vangaurd over all;
Let it neer be said into old England
　That so little made a true Scot fall.

16 'O lay me dowen by yon brecken-bush,
　That grows upon yon liley lea;
Let it neer be said into old England
　That so little made a true Scot die.'

17 At last those two stout knights did meet,
　And O but they were wonderous keen!
The foght with sowards of the temperd steel,
　Till the drops of blood ran them betwen.

18 'O yeald thee, Percie,' Montgomery crys,
　'O yeald ye, or I 'll lay the low;'
'To whome should I yeald? to whom should I
　yeald?
To whom should I yeald, since it most be so?'

19 'O yeald ye to yon breckan-bush,
　That grows upon yon lilley lea;
And if ye will not yeald to this,
　In truth, Earl Percey, I 'll gar ye die.'

20 'I will not yeald to a breckan-bush,
　Nor yet will I yeald to a brier;
But fain wad I yeald to Earl Douglass,
　Or Sir Heugh Montgomery, if he were here.'

21 O then this lord begun to faint,
　And let his soward drop to the ground;
Sir Heugh Montgomery, a courtious knight,
　He bravely took him by the hand.

22 This deed was done at the Otter burn,
　Betwen the sunshine and the day;
Brave Earl Douglass there was slain,
　And they carried Percie captive away.

6[8], 7[1], 8[1], 22[1]. Otterburn.

292 b, 2d paragraph, 9th line. **C** 20[3,4] may have
been supplied by Scott; not in Hogg's copy. See IV,
500, st. 21.

294, 520 a, IV, 499. St George, Our Lady's Knight.

O seynt George, oure lady knyght,
　To that lady thow pray for me!

Lydgate, Kalendare, vv. 113, 114, ed. Horstmann, in
Herrig's Archiv, LXXX, 121.

O blessyd Lady, Cristes moder dere,
　And thou Seynt George, that called art her
　knyght!

Fabyan's Chronicles, ed. Ellis, 1811, p. 601.
(G. L. K.)

162. The Hunting of the Cheviot.

P. 306, IV, 502. Fighting on stumps. Agolafre,
fighting on his knees after his legs were broken, 'had
wyþ ys axe a-slawe an hep of frenschemen:' Sir Ferumbras, v. 4603 ff., ed. Herrtage, The English Charlemagne Romances, I, 143. (The French text does not
represent him as fighting on his knees: Fierabras,
ed. Kroeber and Servois, 1860, v. 4878 ff., p. 147.)
(G. L. K.)

163. The Battle of Harlaw.

P. 317 a, 2d paragraph. Of course Sir James the Rose and Sir John the Gryme came in from the ballad of 'Sir James the Rose.'

164. King Henry Fifth's Conquest of France.

P. 323. There is a copy ('The Battle of Agincourt') in C. K. Sharpe's "first collection," p. 29, from which some variations may be given.

n. 2[4]. And bring home the tribute that's due to me.

4[1-3]. My master the king salutes thee well,
    Salutes thee well, most graciously;
    You must go send, etc.

5[2-4]. And darna come to my degree;
    Go bid him play with his tenish balls,
    For in French lands he dare no me see.

7[8,4]. Such tidings from the king of France
    As I'm sure with him you can ner agree.

8[3]. He bids you play with these tenish balls.

10[4]. They were a jovial good company.

After 10:
    He counted oer his merry men,
    Told them by thirty and by three,
    And when the were all numberd oer
    He had thirty thousand brave and three.

12 The first that fird, it was the French,
    Upon our English men so free,
    But we made ten thousand of them fall,
    And the rest were forc'd for there lives to flee.

13[1]. Soon we entered Paris gates.

13[2]. trumpets sounding high.

13[4]. Have mercy on [my] men and me.

14[1,2]. Take home your tribute, the king he says,
    And three tons of gold I will give to thee.

There is also a copy in "The Old Lady's Collection," No 7, but it is not worth collating.

167. Sir Andrew Barton.

P. 338 b, IV, 502 b. Gold to bury body. Apollonius of Tyre. So in Gower, Confessio Amantis, bk. viii, ed. Pauli, III, 312; in the English prose Kynge Apollyn of Thyre, Wynkyn de Worde, 1510, c. 19, fol. 48, of Ashbee's fac-simile, 1870; in the German prose Appollonius Tyrus and Appolonius von Tiria, C. Schröder, Griseldis, Apollonius von Tyrus, aus Handschriften herausg., pp. 46, 110, Leipzig, 1873. (G. L. K.)

170. The Death of Queen Jane.

P. 372. Communicated by Rev. S. Baring-Gould, as recited by Samuel Force.

H

1 Queen Jane, O! Queen Jane, O! what a lady
    was she!
    And six weeks and a day in labour was she;
    Queen Jane was in labour for six weeks and
    more,
    Till the women grew weary and fain would
    give oer.

2 'O women, O women, good wives as ye be,
    Go send for King Henry and bring him to me.'
    King Henry was sent for, and to her he came:
    'Dear lady, fair lady, your eyes they look dim.'

3 King Henry came to her, he came in all speed,
    In a gown of red velvet, from the heel to the
    head:
    'King Henry, King Henry, if kind you will be,
    Send for a good doctor, and let him come to
    me.'

4 The doctor was sent for, he came with all
    speed,
    In a gown of black velvet from the heel to the
    head;
    The doctor was sent for and to her he came:
    'Dear lady, fair lady, your labour's in vain.'

5 'Dear doctor, dear doctor, will you do this
    for me?
    O open my right side, and save my baby:'
    Then out spake King Henry, That never can
    be,
    I'd rather lose the branches than the top of
    the tree.

6 The doctor gave a caudle, the death-sleep slept
    she,
    Then her right side was opened and the babe
    was set free;
    The babe it was christened, and put out and
    nursd,
    But the royal Queen Jane lay cold in the dust.

I

Macmath MS., p. 99. Received November, 1892, from the recitation of Mary Cochrane (Mrs Joseph Garmory), Abbey-yard, Crossmichael, Kirkcudbrightshire. Written down by her husband.

1 Queen Jeanie was in labor for seven weeks in
    summer,
  The women all being tired and quite gave her
    over :
  'O women, dear women, if women you be,
  Send for my mother to come and see me.'

2 Her mother was sent for and instantly came,
  Knelt down at the bedside where Queen Jeanie
    lay on :
  'O mother, dear mother, if mother you be,
  Send for my father to come and see me.'

3 The father was sent for and instantly came,
  Knelt down by the bedside where Queen Jeanie
    lay on :
  'O father, dear father, if father you be,
  Send for King Henry to come and see me.'

4 King Henry was sent for and instantly came,
  Knelt down by the bedside where Queen Jeanie
    lay on :
  'O Henry, King Henry, if Henry you be,
  Send for the doctor to come and see me.'

5 The doctor was sent for and instantly came,
  Knelt down by the bedside where Queen Jeanie
    lay on :
  'O doctor, dear doctor, if doctor you be,
  Open my left side and let the babe free.'

6 Her left side was opened, the young prince was
    found :
  'O doctor, dear doctor, lay me down on the
    ground.'

7 Her bones were all broken and laid at her feet,
  And they anointed her body with the ointment
    so sweet,
  And ay as they weeped they wrung their hands
    sore,
  For the fair flower of England will flourish no
    more.

173. Mary Hamilton.

P. 379. Stanzas 1, 2, 10 of **C** are printed in Mother-well's Minstrelsy, p. 315, and 4, 9 of **L** at p. 316.

380 a, line 13. Say Stewart, or stewart.

384. **A a.** Found in a small MS. volume, with the title " Songs " on the cover, entirely in Sharpe's handwriting, p. 29. The only variations, besides a few in spelling, are these :

    9^1. stairs. 17^8. the night's. 18^2. they 'l.

389. **F.** This version was rendered by Skene with comparative fidelity. Still, the original, ' Quin Mary's Marreys,' No 12 of " The Old Lady's Collection," would of course have been given if it had been in hand, and should be substituted, opportunity occurring. It is therefore printed here.

1 ' My father was the Duck of York,
    My mother a lady frie,
  My sell a dainnty damisall,
    Quin Mary sent for me.

2 ' The quin's meat it was so suit,
    An her clething was sae rair,
  It made me lang for Suit Willie's bed,
    An I ill rue it ever mare.

3 ' Mary Beeten, an Mary Sitton,
    An Lady Livenston, a' three,
  We 'll never mett in Quin Mary's bour nou,
    Marrys tho we be.'

4 Quin Mary satt in her bour,
    Suing her selver seam ;
  She thought she hard a baby greet
    Bat an a lady mean.

5 She throu her neddel frae her,
    Her seam out of her han,
  An she is on to Lady Marry's bour,
    As fast as she could gang.

6 ' Open yer dor, Lady Mary,' she says,
    ' An lat me come in ;
  For I hear a baby greet,
    Bat an a lady meen.'

7 ' Ther is nae bab in my bour, madam the Quin,
    Nor never thinks to be,
  Bat the strong pains of gravell
    This night has sesed me.'

8 She paat her fitt to the dor,
    Bat an her knee,
  Bolts of brass an irn bands
    In flinders she gart flee.

9 She pat a han to her bed-head
    A nether to her bed-feet,
  An bonny was the bab
    Was blabring in its bleed.

10 'Wae worth ye, Lady Mary,
    An ill dead sall ye die!
  For in ye widne keepet the bonny bab
    Ye might ha gen 't to me.'

11 'Lay na the witt on me, madam,
    Lay na the witt on me,
  For my fals love bare the v[e]pan att his side
    That gared my bern dee.'

12 'Gett up, Lady Betton, get up, Lady Setton,
    An Lady Livenston, three,
  An we will on to Edenbrugh
    An tray this gay lady.'

13 As she cam in the Cannogate,
    The burgers' wives they crayed hon, ochon,
      ochree!

14 'O had yer still, ye burgers' wives,
    An make na mane for me ;
  Seek never grace out of a graslass face,
    For they ha nan to gee.

15 'Ye merchants an ye mareners,
    That trad on the sea,
  Ye dinnë tell in my country
    The dead I am gaine to dee.

16 'Ye merchants an ye mareners,
    That traid on the fame,
  Dinnë tell in my countray
    Bat fatt I am coming hame.

17 'Littel did my father think,
    Fan he brouch[t] me our the sea,
  That he woud see my yallou lokes
    Hang on a gallou-tree.

18 'Littel did my midder think,
    Fan she brought me fra hame,
  That she maugt see my yallou lokes
    Hang on a gallou-pine.

19 '.   .   .   .   .
    O had yer han a wee !
  For yonder comes my father,
    I am sure he 'll borrou me.

20 'O some of yer goud, father,
    An of yer well won fee,
  To safe me [fra the high hill],
    [An] fra the gallage-tree.'

21 'Ye 's gett nane of my goud,
    Ner of my well wone fee,
  For I wead gee five hundred poun
    To see ye hanged hee.'

22 '.   .   .   .   .
    O had yer han a wee !
  Yonder is my love Willie,
    He will borrou me.

23 'O some of yer goud, my love Wille,
    An some of yer well wone fee,
  To save me fraa the high hill,
    An fraie the gallou-tree.'

24 'Ye 's gett a' my goud,
    An a' my well won fee,
  To save ye fra the heading-hill,
    An fra the galla-tree.'

4². *Perhaps* silver. 6³. lady greet : *cf.* 4⁸.
7¹. næ. 11². watt. 11³. vpan ? 23¹. son Willë.

392 a, **H** 8⁴. The nine. "Anciently the supreme
criminal court of Scotland was composed of nine
members." Kinloch's note, Ancient Scottish Ballads,
p. 259. This may afford a date.

I. b. The three stanzas were given as written down
from memory by Finlay : see VIII, 507 b.

174. Earl Bothwell.

The following entry in the Stationers' Registers may
refer to this ballad: "24 March, 1579, Thomas Gosson.
Receaved of him for a ballad concerninge the murder
of the late Kinge of Scottes." Arber, II, 349.

178. Captain Car, or, Edom o Gordon.

P. 423, IV, 513.

I

From "The Old Lady's Collection," No 28, 'Edom of
Achendoon.'

1 It fell about the Martimas time,
    Fan the wind blue loud an calld,
  Said Edom of Gordon to his men,
    We man dra till a hall.

2 'An fatten a hall will we dra tell,
    My merry men a' an me ?
  We will to the house of Rothes,
    An see that gay lady.'

3 The lady louked our castell-wa,
    Beheld the day ga doun,

An she saa Edun of Gordon,
Fase Edom of Ach[en]doun.

4 'Gee our yer house, ye gay lady,
Gee our yer house to me;
The night ye 's be my leall leman,
The morn my lady free.'

5 'I winnĕ gee our my bonny house,
To leard nor yet to loun,
Nor will I gee our my bonny house
To fase Edom of Achendoun.

6 'Bat ye gett me Cluny, Gight, or Glack,
Or get him young Lesmore,
An I ell gee our my bonny house
To ony of a' the four.'

7 'Ye 's nether gett Cluny, Gight, nor Glack,
Nor yet him young Lesmore,
An ye man gee our yer bonny house,
Winten ony of a' the four.'

8 The ladie shot out of a shot-windou,
It didne hurt his head,
It only grased his knee

.   .   .   .

9 'Ye hast, my merry men a',
Gather hathorn an fune,

.   .   .   .

To see gin this lady will burn.'

10 'Wai worth ye, Joke, my man!
I paid ye well yer fee,
An ye tane out the quinĕ-stane,
Laten in the fire to me.

11 'Wae worth ye, Joke, my man!
I paid ye well yer hair,
An ye t[a]en out the qunie-stane,
To me laten in the fire.'

12 'Ye paid me well my meatt, lady,
Ye paid me well my fee,
Bat nou I am Edom of Gordon's man,
Mane eather dee 'd or dree.

13 'Ye paid me well my meatt, lady,
Ye paid me well my hire,
But nou I am Edom of Gordon's man,
To ye mane lat the fire.'

14 Out spak her doughter,
She was bath jimp an smaa;
'Ye take me in a pair of shets,
Lat me our the castell-waa.'

15 The pat her in a pair of shets,
Lute her oure the castell-waa;
On the point of Edom of Gordon's lance
She got a deadly faa.

16 Cherry, cherry was her cheeks,
An bonny was her eyen;

.   .   .   .

.   .   .   .

17 He turned her about,

.   .   .   .

'I might haa spared that bonny face
To ha ben some man's delight.

18 'Chirry is yer chik,
An bonny is yer eayn;
Ye 'r the first face I ever saa dead
I wist liveng agen.'

19 Out spak one of his men,
As he stad by a stane;
'Lat it never be sade brave Edom of Gordon
Was dantoned by a dame.'

20 Out spake the bonny barn,
It̨ sat on the nurce's knee;
'Gee our yer house, my mider dear,
The reak it smothers me.'

21 'I wad gee a' my silks,' she says,
'That lays in mony a fall,
To haa ye on the head of Mont Ganell,
To gett three gasps of the call.

22 'I wad gee a' my goud,' she says,
'Far it lays out an in,
To haa ye on the head of Mount Ganill,
To get three gasps of the wind.'

23 .   .   .   .   that gued lord,
As he came fraa the sea,
'I see the house of Rothes in fire,
God safe my gay ladie!'

15³. land.

VOL. IV.

190. Jamie Telfer of the Fair Dodhead.

P. 4. I am now able to give the unprinted copy, referred to in the Border Minstrelsy, in which the Elliots take the place assigned in the other version to the Scotts. This I do by the assistance of Mr Macmath, the present possessor of the manuscript, which was formerly among the papers of Charles Kirkpatrick Sharpe. The hand "is a good and careful one of about the beginning of this century, with a slight shake in it, and probably that of a person advanced in life." Be it observed that the title, in this case, is 'Jamie Telfer in the Fair Dodhead,' signifying, according to Scottish usage, that Telfer was tenant simply, whereas 'of' would make him proprietor.

Hogg, writing to Sir W. Scott (Letters, vol. i, No 44), says that 'Jamie Telfer,' as printed in the Minstrelsy, differs in many particulars from his mother's way of giving it. Mrs Hogg's version may very likely have been a third copy.

In this version, Telfer, after the loosing of his nolt and the ranshakling of his house, runs eight miles to Branxholm, to seek aid of Buccleugh, who refers him to Martin Elliot, to whom, and not to himself, Buccleugh affirms, Telfer has paid blackmail. Telfer, as in the other version, runs up the water-gate to Coultart Cleugh, and invokes the help of Jock Grieve, who sets him on a bonny black to take the fray to Catlock Hill, as in the other version again. Catlock Hill Mr R. B. Armstrong considers to be probably Catlie Hill, marked in Blaeu's map as near Braidlie. It was occupied by an Elliot in 1541. At Catlock Hill Martin's Hab sets Telfer on a bonny black to take the fray to Prickenhaugh, a place which, Mr Armstrong observes, is put in Blaeu's map near Larriston. Auld Martin Elliot is at Prickenhaugh, and he orders Simmy, his son, to be summoned, and the water-side to be warned (including the Currers and Willie o Gorrenberry, who in the other version, st. 27, are warned as owing fealty to Scott; but an Archibald Ellot is described as "in Gorrenberrie" in 1541,[*] and Will Elliot of Gorrombye was concerned in the rescue of Kinmont Willie in 1596, Sim Elliot takes the lead in the pursuit of the marauders which Willie Scott has in the other version, and like him is killed. Martin Elliot of Braidley had among his sons, in 1580, a Sym, an Arche, and a Hob,[*] and was, during a portion of the second half of the sixteenth century, says Mr Armstrong, perhaps the most important person of his name.[†] This Martin Elliot would fit very well into our ballad, but that he should be described as of Prickenhaugh, not of Braidley, raises a difficulty.

Braidley, at the junction of the Braidley burn with the Hermitage water, is well placed for our purposes; Prickenhaugh, down by the Liddel water, seems rather remote.

5, 582. See more as to Dodhead in The Saturday Review, May 20, 1893, p. 543.

JAMIE TELFER IN THE FAIR DODHEAD.

1 It fell about the Martinmas,
   When steads were fed wi corn and hay,
The Captain of Bewcastle said to his lads,
   We 'll into Tiviotdale and seek a prey.

2 The first ae guide that they met with
   Was high up in Hardhaugh swire,
The second guide that they met with
   Was laigh down in Borthick water.

3 'What tidings, what tidings, my bonny guide?'
   'Nae tidings, nae tidings I hae to thee;
But if ye 'll gae to the Fair Dodhead
   Mony a cow's calf I 'll let ye see.'

4 When they came to the Fair Dodhead,
   Right hastily they clam the peel,
They loosd the nolt out, ane and a',
   And ranshakled the house right weel.

5 Now Jamie's heart it was right sair,
   The tear ay rowing in his eye;
He pled wi the Captain to hae his gear,
   Or else revengèd he would be.

6 Bat the Captain turnd himsel about,
   Said, Man, there 's naething in thy house
But an auld sword without a scabbard,
   That scarcely now would fell a mouse.

7 The moon was up and the sun was down,
   'T was the gryming of a new-fa'n snaw;
Jamie Telfer has run eight miles barefoot
   Between Dodhead and Branxholm Ha.

8 And when he came to Branxholm Ha
   He shouted loud and cry'd well he,
Till up bespake then auld Buccleugh,
   'Whae 's this that brings the fray to me?'

---

[*] R. H. Stodart, Scottish Arms, 1881, II, 277, 276. What is there said of Elliot of Braidley was mostly communicated by Mr. R. B. Armstrong.

[†] Proceedings of the Society of Antiquaries of Scotland, 1880–81, p. 93. At several places above I have used a letter from Mr. Armstrong to Mr. Macmath.

9 'It 's I, Jamie Telfer i the Fair Dodhead,
    And a harried man I think I be;
There 's naething left i the Fair Dodhead
    But only wife and children three.'

10 'Gae seek your succour frae Martin Elliot,
    For succour ye 's get nane frae me;
Gae seek your succour where ye paid black-
        mail,
    For, man, ye never paid money to me.'

11 Jamie he 's turnd him round about,
    And ay the tear blinded his eye :
'I 'se never pay mail to Scott again,
    Nor the Fair Dodhead I 'll ever see.'

12 Now Jamie is up the water-gate,
    Een as fast as he can drie,
Till he came to the Coultart Cleugh,
    And there he shouted and cry'd weel he.

13 Then up bespake him auld Jock Grieve,
    'Whae 's this that bring[s] the fray to me ? '
'It 's I, Jamie Telfer i the Fair Dodhead,
    And a harried man I think I be.

14 'There 's naething left i the Fair Dodhead
    But only wife and children three,
And sax poor calves stand i the sta,
    A' routing loud for their minnie.'

15 'Alack, wae 's me ! ' co auld Jock Grieve,
    'Alack, alack, and wae is me !
For ye was married t' the auld sister,
    And I t' the younges[t] o the three.'

16 Then he 's taen out a bonny black,
    It was weel fed wi corn and hay,
And set Jamie Telfer on his back,
    To the Catlock hill to take the fray.

17 When he came to the Catlock hill,
    He shouted loud and cry'd weel he;
'Whae 's that, whae 's that ? ' co Martin's Hab,
    'Whae 's this that brings the fray to me ? '

18 'It 's I, Jamie Telfer i the Fair Dodhead,
    And a harried man I think I be;
There 's neathing left i the Fair Dodhead
    But only wife and children three.'

19 'Alack, wae 's me ! ' co Martin's Hab,
    'Alack, awae, my heart is sair !

I never came bye the Fair Dodhead
    That ever I faund thy basket bare.'

20 Then he 's taen out a bonny black,
    It was weel fed wi corn and hay,
And set Jamie Telfer on his back
    To the Pricken haugh to take the fray.

21 When he came to the Pricken haugh,
    He shouted loud and cry'd weel he;
Up then bespake auld Martin Elliot,
    'Whae 's this that brings the fray to me ? '

22 'It 's I, Jamie Telfer i the Fair Dodhead,
    And a harried man I think I be ;
There 's naething left i the Fair Dodhead
    But only wife and children three.'

23 'Ever alack ! ' can Martin say,
    'And ay my heart is sair for thee !
But fy, gar ca on Simmy my son,
    And see that he come hastily.

24 'Fy, gar warn the water-side,
    Gar warn it soon and hastily ;
Them that winna ride for Telfer's kye,
    Let them never look i the face o me.

25 'Gar warn the water, braid and wide,
    And warn the Currers i the shaw ;
When ye come in at the Hermitage slack,
    Warn doughty Willie o Gorrenberry.'

26 The gear was driven the Frostily up,
    From the Frostily into the plain ;
When Simmie lookëd him afore,
    He saw the kye right fast driving.

27 'Whae drives the kye,' then Simmy can
        say,
    'To make an outspeckle o me ? '
'It 's I, the Captain o Bewcastle, Simmy,
    I winna lain my name frae thee.'

28 'O will ye let the gear gae back?
    Or will ye do ony thing for me ? '
'I winna let the gear gae back,
    Nor naething, Simmy, I 'll do for the[e].

29 'But I 'll drive Jamie Telfer's kye
    In spite o Jamie Telfer's teeth and thee ; '
'Then by my sooth,' can Simmy say,
    'I 'll ware my dame's calfskin on thee.

30 'Fa on them, lads!' can Simmy say,
  'Fy, fa on them cruelly!
For or they win to the Ritter ford
  Mony toom saddle there shall be.'

31 But Simmy was striken oer the head,
  And thro the napskape it is gane,
And Moscrop made a dolefull rage
  When Simmy on the ground lay slain.

32 'Fy, lay on them!' co Martin Elliot,
  'Fy, lay on them cruelly!
For ere they win to the Kershop ford
  Mony toom saddle there shall be.'

33 John o Biggam he was slain,
  And John o Barlow, as I heard say,
And fifteen o the Captain's men
  Lay bleeding on the ground that day.

34 The Captain was shot through the head,
  And also through the left ba-stane;
Tho he had livd this hundred years,
  He'd neer been loed by woman again.

35 The word is gane unto his bride,
  Een in the bower where she lay,
That her good lord was in's enemy's land
  Since into Tiviotdale he led the way.

36 'I loord a had a winding sheed
  And helpd to put it oer his head,
Or he'd been taen in's enemy's lands,
  Since he oer Liddle his men did lead.'

37 There was a man in our company,
  And his name was Willie Wudëspurs:
'There is a house in the Stanegarside,
  If any man will ride with us.'

38 When they came to the Stanegarside,
  They bangd wi trees and brake the door,
They loosd the kye out, ane and a',
  And set them furth our lads before.

39 There was an auld wif ayont the fire,
  A wee bit o the Captain's kin:
'Whae loo[s]es out the Captain's kye,
  And sae mony o the Captain's men wi[t]hin?'

40 'I, Willie Wudëspurs, let out the kye,
  I winna lain my name frae thee,
And I'll loose out the Captain's kye
  In spite o the Captain's teeth and thee.'

41 Now on they came to the Fair Dodhead,
  They were a welcome sight to see,
And instead of his ain ten milk-kye
  Jamie Telfer's gotten thirty and three.

16². feel fed: *cf.* 20².

195. Lord Maxwell's Last Goodnight.

P. 34 b, 525 a. **B.** The ballad has no title in the Glenriddell MS. The table of contents was the work of a copyist.

196. The Fire of Frendraught.

P. 39 b. Thirteen stanzas of **C** are given, in the course of an article on The Burning of the House of Frendraucht, in the Aberdeen Magazine, 1832, II, 561.

P. 44. **A a.** Collation with Sharpe's MS. and with another copy of the same pieces in "North Country Ballads," Miscellanea Curiosa, Abbotsford Library.

4¹. Well, turn. 12⁵. were.

15⁴. Let Rothiemay may ly, may ly. But Rothiemay lie, *written under, probably as an emendation by Sharpe (not in Scott).*

16⁴. Turn *in Scott, an easy misreading of* Twin.

26¹. Ahon. *With a few slight differences of spelling.*

we *in* 9² *is a misprint for* he.

IV, 522 a. The Satyr begins:

  O world of woes, O greif of griefs, to see
  This damned den wher sure brave sp'rits did dye.

197. James Grant.

These verses occur in a manuscript collection of C. K. Sharpe's ("second collection"), with slight verbal differences. They are written in long lines not divided into stanzas. Sir W. Scott remarks, Sharpe's Ballad Book, 1880, p. 145, "I conceive Ballindalloch, being admitted by Grant, set upon him, and that there should be asterisks between the fourth line [the second stanza] and those which follow."

1¹. Away, away now, James the Grant. 1². You'll. 1³. For Ballendalloch is at your gate. 2¹,⁴. Badendalloch. 2². Nor I. 2³. Set up my gat both. 2⁴. And let. 3¹. James the. 3⁴. no get so. 4³. he get but one mile in the highland hill. 4⁴. defy the.

198. Bonny John Seton.

P. 52. **A.** Found in a MS. of Charles Kirkpatrick Sharpe, and in "North Country Ballads," Miscellanea

Curiosa, Abbotsford Library (another copy of the same pieces), with the following variations.

Sharpe. 1³. The Southeron lords to.

2¹. And bonny : Pitmedden, *and always.* 2². bald. 2⁴. And the. 3⁴. Sat on. 5². Cried, Brave soldiers. 5⁵. my steed back. 5⁶. But let me never see thee. 6³. And his. 7⁴. That dang Pitmedden's middle in three. 8¹,². rade. 8⁸. But bonny John Seton of Pitmedden. 9¹. Then up it came a. 9². from Drimmorow. 9⁸. Says, There thou lies. 9⁴. ride thee thorow. 10¹. Craigyvar (*always*) : man. 10². your fiddle. 10⁸. land. 12¹. They 've taken. 14⁴. ring. 15¹. For cannons roars : summer's. 15². Like thunder. 15⁴. cannons fair.

Scott (*also*). — 3¹. lands.

None of the readings in Aytoun given in the notes at p. 53 were derived from Sharpe's copy except **A** 8⁸, *and all of them may now be dropped.*

199. The Bonnie House o Airlie.

P. 56. In a small MS. volume with the title " Songs " on the cover, entirely in Sharpe's handwriting. **A a** is found at p. 24 (with some variations, undoubtedly arbitrary) prefaced with these words : " This song [referring to a copy presently to be given], like most others, would suffer amendment : here follows a copy somewhat improved. I have availed myself of a fragment in a former page of this work, and introduced a stanza [9] marked *, picked up in Perthshire." Had **A a** been known to be an " improved " copy, it would not have been made so prominent.

The fragment (of slight value) was " from the recitation of Miss Oliphant of Gask, now Mrs Nairn " (afterwards Lady Nairne). It is (p. 21) — disregarding things misunderstood or avowedly added :

' Come down, come down, my lady Ogilvie,
　Come down, and tell us your dower : '
' It 's east and west yon wan water side,
　And it 's down by the banks of the Airly.

' Had my lord Ogilvie been at hame,
　As he was wi King Charlie,
There durst nae a Campbel in a' Argyle
　Avowd to the plundering o Airly.'

' Come down, come down, ye lady fair,
　Come down, and kiss me fairly : '
' I wunna come down, ye fause Argyle,
　If ye sudna leave a standing stane in Airly.

The unimproved copy, p. 22, is as follows.

1 It fell on a day, and a bonny summer day,
　　When corn grew green and yellow,
　That there fell out a great dispute
　　Between Argyll and Airly.

2 Argyll has raisd an hundred men,
　　An hundred men, and so many,
　And he is away by the back of Dunkeld
　　For to plunder the bonny house of Airly.

3 Lady Margaret looks oer her bower-window,
　　And O but she looks weary !
　And there she spied the great Argyll,
　　Coming to plunder the bonny house of Airly.

4 ' Come down, come down, Lady Margret,' he said,
　　' Come down, and kiss me fairly : '
　' O I will not kiss the great Argyll,
　　If he should not leave a standing stone in Airly.'

5 He hath taken her by the left shoulder,
　　Says, Lady, where lyes thy dowry ?
　' It 's up and it 's down by the bonny bank-side,
　　Amongst the planting of Airly.'

6 They have sought it up, they have sought it down,
　　They have sought it both late and early,
　And they have found it in the bonny plumb-tree
　　That shines on the bowling-green of Airly.

7 He hath taken her by the middle so small,
　　And O but she lookd weary !
　He hath laid her down by the bonny burn-side
　　Till he hath plunderd the bonny house of Airly.

8 ' If my good lord were at home this night,
　　As he is with Prince Charly,
　Nouther you nor no Scottish lord
　　Durst have set a foot on the bowling-green of
　　　Airly.

9 ' Ten bonny sons I have born unto him,
　　And the eleventh neer saw his daddy ;
　Although I had an hundred more,
　　I would give them all to Prince Charly.'

58 c.　This is one of the pieces contained in " The Old Lady's Collection," No 1. The differences from Skene (save spelling) are as follows :

3¹. ore castell-waa. 3⁸. an his three hunded men. 4¹,². Come doun the stare, Lady Airly, he says, an kiss me fairly. 4⁴. Altho ye live no. 5². An tell fare layes yer. 7². An he leed. 10² (7²). his. 10⁸ (7⁸). An tho. 10⁴ (7⁴). I wad gie them a'.

200. The Gypsy Laddie.

P. 66.　**B a.** A copy of this version in C. K. Sharpe's papers, " written from recitation in Nithisdale, November, 1814," shows that improvements had been introduced by two hands, one of them Sharpe's, neither of them the writer's. The changes are of no radical importance ; simply of the familiar kind which almost every editor has, for some reason, felt himself called upon to make. It may be thought that they are no more worth indicating than they were worth making, but it has been an object in this book to give things exactly as they were delivered. The original readings are as follows.

1[1]. C *for* Cassilis *throughout.* 1[3]. so. 1[4]. Till. 2[4]. cast. 3[1]. to *wanting.* 3[2,3]. give. 3[4]. rings of her fingers. 4[1,2]. you. 4[3]. hilt of. 4[4], 9[4], 16[4]. no more. 6[1,3]. Jackie. 7[3], 8[3]. farmer's barn. 8[3], 11[3]. most. 8[4]. crae. 9[1,2]. O *wanting.* 10[3], 11[1], 14[3]. on water. 11[1]. Many a time have. 17[4]. mother bore me. 18[3]. And *wanting.*

73.

L

Communicated to the Journal of The Gypsy Society, II, 85, by Mr John Sampson, from the dictation of Lias Robinson, a Gypsy. A translation into Gypsy, by Robinson and his brothers, is given at p. 84 of the same.

1 A band of gypsies, all in a road,
　　All so black and brawny, oh
　Away come a lady all dressed in silk,
　　To follow the roving gypsies. oh
　　　The gypsies, oh !
　　　The gypsies, oh !
　　To follow the roving gypsies, oh !

2 Her husband came home at ten o'clock of night,
　　And asked for his lady fair ;
　The servant informed him very soon
　　She had gone with the roving gypsies.

3 ' Saddle to me my bonny gray mare,
　　Saddle to me my pony ;
　I will go where the green grass grow,
　　To find out the roving gypsies.

4 ' Last night she slept in a fair feather-bed,
　　And blankets by bonins ;
　Tonight she sleeps in a cold shed-barn,
　　Through following the roving gypsies.

5 ' Why did you leave your houses and your
　　　lands ?
　Why did you leave your babies ?
　Why did you leave your decent married man,
　　To follow the roving gypsies ? '

6 ' What cares I for my houses and my lands ?
　　What cares I for my babies ?
　What cares I for my decent married man ?
　　I will go with the roving gypsies.'

1[2]. *Var.* and bonny.

From a small MS. volume, " Songs," entirely in C. K. Sharpe's handwriting, p. 32 (corresponding to **B** 11, **D** 6, **E** 7.)

Yestreen I rade yon wan water,
　Wi my gude lord before me ;
The day I maun pit down my bonnie fit and wade,
　What ever may come oer me.

201. Bessy Bell and Mary Gray.

P. 76 a, 4th paragraph, 1st line. The date 1666 is corrected to 1645 by Cant in his Errata.

77. In the small MS. volume, " Songs," entirely in C. K. Sharpe's handwriting, p. 26, **a** 3 is given " from the Catalogue of the Edinburgh Exhibition of Pictures, 1810 " as here, excepting that in the second line the reading is (absurdly) " royal kin."

203. The Baron of Brackley.

P. 79. Fragment from Findlay MSS, I, 209, derived from Mrs McKenzie, Advie, Morayshire.

1 ' O are ye sleepin, baul B[r]achlie, or are ye at
　　　hame ?
　For the caterans are at ye, an a' your kye's taen.'

2 . 　.　 .　 .　 .　 .　 .　 .
　' Ye'll fling your rocks, lasses, we'll fecht them
　　　our lane.

3 ' We'll fecht them an fleg them, an gar them rin
　　　hame,
　We'll stand them in battle, as gin we were men.

4 ' There's four-an-twenty milk-white kine in Glen-
　　　tanner free,
　In the parks o Glentanner sae fain's I wad be ! '

5 He's called on his lady to give him his gun :
　' I'm gaun oot, Katie, but I'll never come home.'

6 She's a' her gates wide open flung, an she's wel-
　　　comed them in,
　An she sleeps wi the villain that slew her baron.

1[1]. Baulbachlie. 5[2]. home *originally; altered to* in. *The stanzas have been arranged by the light of* **A**.

87. **D**, as it stands in " The Old Lady's Collection," No 25, ' The Barron of Breachell.'

1 ' Barron of Breachell, are ye withen ?
　The sharp sourd is att yer gate, Breachell, will
　　gar yer blod spine.'

2 ' The 'r at yer gate, Brichell, the 'r nether men
　　nor lads,
　Bat silly heard widifaus, we belted plaids.

3 'O if I had a man,' she says, 'as it louks I haa
        nean,
    He widne sit in the house an see my kay tean.

4 'Bat, lasses, tak doun yer rokes, an we will defend,'
    .   .   .   .

5 'O kiss me, d[ea]r Peggey, an gee me doun my
        gun,
    I may well gaa out, bat I ill never come in.'

6 Out spak his brother, says, Gee me your hand,
    I [ill] fight in your caus as lang as I may stan.

7 Fan the Barron of Brechell came to the closs,
    A braver barron never read upon horse.

8 .   .   .   .
    'I think the silly heard widdefus are groun fighten
        men.'

9 First they killed an, and sayn they killed tua,
    An the Barron of Brichell is dead an awa.

10 They killed Sandy Gordon, Sandy Gordon of the
        Knok,
    The miller an his three sons, that lived att Glen-
        muke.

11 First they killed ane, an sayn they killed tua,
    An the Barron of Brichell is dead an awaa.

12 Up came Crigevar an a' his fighten men :
    'Had I come an houre sinner, he sudna ben slain.'

13 For first they killed an, an sayn they killed tua,
    An the Barron of Breachell is dead an awa.

14 'O came ye by Brechell, lads? was ye in ther?
    Saw ye Peggie Doun, raving her hear?'

15 'We came by Breache[l], lads, we was in ther ;
    We saa Peggie Doun, curling her hear.

16 'She ate we them, drank we them, bad them come
        in
    To her haas an her bours that had slain her barron.'

17 'Come in, gentelmen, ate an drink we me ;
    Tho ye have slain my barron, I ha na ill well att
        thee.'

18 'O was ye att Glenmuck, lads? was ye in ther?
    Saa ye Catren Gordon, raving her hear?'

19 'We was att Gleanmuck, lads, we was in ther,
    We saa Catren Gordon, ravi[n]g her hear.

20 'We the tear in her eay, ...
    Seven bearns att her foot, the eaght on her knee.

21 They killed Peater Gordon, Peater Gordon of the
        Knok.
    The miller an his three sons, that lives att Glen-
        muck.

22 First they killed an, an sayn they killed twa,
    An the Barron of Breachell is dead an awaa.

208. Lord Derwentwater.

P. 116 b. Add at the end of the first paragraph :
Robert Patten, The History of the Rebellion in the
Year 1715, 4th ed., 1745, p. 47.
    123. From "The Old Lady's Collection," second
part, p. 6.

J

1 The king has written a brod letter,
        An sealled it our with gould,
    An sent it to Lord Darnwater,
        To read it if he could.

2 Whan Lord Darnwater saa the letter,
        A light laughter lough he ;
    Bat or he read it to an end
        The tear blinded his eye,
    An sighan said him good Lord Darnwater,
        I am near the day to dei.

3 Out spak his lady,
        In child-bed wher she lay ;
    'My d[ea]r Lord Darnweter, what is to be-
        com of me,
        An my young famely?'

4 'I will leave my young famely
        As well as I cane ;
    For I will leave to my lady
        The third part of my land,
    An I will live to my e[l]dest son,
        The tua part of my land.

5 'An I will live to my eldest daught[er]
        Five thousand pound of gold,
    An I will live to my second daughter
        Three thousand pound of gold.

6 'Ye saddel to me my littel gray horse,
        That I had wont to ried ;
    .   .   .   .
    .   .   .   .

7 The first stape Lord Darnwater staped,
        He stumbled on a ston ;
    Said Lord Darnwater,
        I feer I ill never come home.

8 When he came to fair London city,
    An near unt[o] the toun,
  'A trater! a trater!' said they,
    'A trator we see!'

9 'A trater?' said good Lord Darnwater,
    'A trator I nier could be,
  Unless it was bringen three hundred men
    To fight for young Jamie.'

10 But when he came to Tour Hill
    Befor him came a bold man,

  .   .   .   .   .   .

    With a broad aix in his hand.

11 .   .   .   .   .   .

  .   .   .   .   .   .

  'Hear is five ginies of gold an my green velvet
    coat,
    For to be your fee.'

12 'Ye nobels all,
    Come hear to see me die,
  An ye peopell of fair Sco[t]land,
    Be kind to my family.'

13 Lord Darnuater was dumed to die, to die,
    Good Lord Darnwater was dumed to die.

  2⁵. *sigh an.* 2⁶. *am* doubtful.
  4⁴, 5⁴, 9³. 3. 4⁵. *will live* twice. 4⁶, 5³. 2.
  5², 11³. 5. 7³, 9¹. L. D. 13². Daruan Water.

314. The Braes o Yarrow.

P. 160 ff., 522 ff.

S

Findlay's MSS, I, 181; The Dowie Dens o Yarrow, "from
Banffshire, through James Milne, Arbroath."

1 There lived a lady in the South,
    Ye would scarcely find her marrow;
  She was courted by nine gentlemen
    An a ploughman-lad frae Yarrow.

2 Ae nicht the nine sat drinkin wine
    To the lass wha had nae marrow,
  When the ploughman swore, tho they were
    a score
  He wad fecht them a' in Yarrow.

3 It's he's gane ower yon high, high hill,
    And doon yon glen sae narrow,

An there he saw nine armëd men,
    To fecht wi him in Yarrow.

4 'There's nine o you an I'm but ane,
    An that's an unequal marrow,
  But wi this gude blade and powerfu arm
    I'll lay you low on Yarrow.'

5 It's three he slew, and three withdrew,
    And three lay dead on Yarrow,
  But in behind cam her brother John,
    An pierced his body thorough.

6 'Gae hame, gae hame, you fause young man,
    An tell your sister sorrow,
  That her true-love John lies dead and gone
    In the dowie dens o Yarrow.'

7 'O father dear, I've dreamed a dream,
    I'm feared it will prove sorrow;
  I dreamed I was puin the heather-bells
    sweet
    On the bonny braes o Yarrow.'

8 'O daughter dear, your dream is read,
    I'm feared it will prove sorrow;
  Your true-love John lies dead and gone
    In the dowie dens o Yarrow.'

9 It's she's gane ower yon high, high hill,
    An doon yon glen sae narrow,
  An there she saw her true-love John
    Lyin cauld an dead on Yarrow.

10 She washed his face an combed his hair,
    Wi muckle grief an sorrow,
  She rowed him i the plaid she wore,
    In the dowie dens o Yarrow.

11 Her hair it was three quarters lang,
    The colour being yellow;
  She tied it round his middle sma,
    An carried him hame frae Yarrow.

12 'O daughter dear, I pray forbear,
    I'll wed you to another marrow;
  I'll wed you to some fitter match
    Than the lad that died on Yarrow.'

13 'O father dear, you hae seven sons,
    Should you wed them a' to-morrow,
  A fairer flower never grew in June
    Than the lad that died on Yarrow.'

14 This lady, being six months with child
     To the ploughman lad of Yarrow,
     She fell into her father's arms
     An died wi grief on Yarrow.

5[1]. slew *should of course be* wounded, *or* hurt,
     as in A 9[1], B 9[1], D 7[1], E 8[1], I 7[1], K 7[1],
     Q 6[1,2].

215. Rare Willie drowned in Yarrow, or, The Water o Gamrie.

P. 180. **D** stands as follows in "The Old Lady's Collection," No 10, 'The Water of Gamry.'

1 ' Willie is fair, an Willë 's rair,
     An Willë 's wondres bonny,
     An Willë has promised to marey me,
     Gin ever he marred ony.'

2 ' Ye 's gett Jeamie, or ye 's gett Jonny,
     Or ye 's gett bonny Piter ;
     Ye 's gett the walle of a' my sins,
     Bat live to me Willë the writter.'

3 ' I winnë ha Jamie, I winnë ha Jonny,
     Nor will I ha bonny Peter ;
     I winnë ha ony of yer sins,
     In I gett na Willie the writter.'

4 Ther was three score an ten brisk young men
     Was boun to brid-stell we him.

5 ' Ride on, ride on, my merry men a',
     I forget some thing behine me ;
     I [ha] forgetten my mider's blissing,
     To boun to bridstell we me.'

6 ' God's blissing an mine gae we ye, my son Willie,
     A' the blissings of God ga we ye ;
     For y 'er na an hour but bare ninten,
     Fan y 'er gain to meet yer Meggey.'

7 They road on, an ferder on,
     Till they came to the water of Gamry ;
     An they all wen safe throu,
     Unless it was Suet Willie.

8 For the first an step att Willie's hors steped,
     He steped to the bridel ;
     The nixt an step att Wellie's hors steped,
     Toom grue Willë's sadle.

9 They rod on, an forder on,
     Till they came to the kirk of Gamry,
     .   .   .   .
     .   .   .   .

10 .   .   .   .
     .   .   .   .
     ' A rounin, a rouning,' she says,
     ' An fat means a' this rouning ? '

11 Out spak the bonny bried,
     Just att the kirk of Gamrie ;
     ' Far is the man that was to gee me his han
     This day att the kirk of Gamry ? '

12 Out spak his breder John,
     An O bat he was sorry !
     ' It fears me sair, my bonny brid,
     He slipes our sune in Gaamry.'

13 The ribbons they wer on her hare,
     They wer thik an mony ;
     She rive them a', late them doun faa,
     An she is on to the water of Gamry.

14 She sought it up, she sought it doun,
     She sought it braid an narrow,
     An the depest pot in a' Gamry,
     Ther she got Suit Willie.

15 She has kissed his comly mouth,
     As she had don befor, O :
     ' Baith our miders sall be alike sory,
     For we 's baith slep soun in Gamry.'

216. The Mother's Malison, or, Clyde's Water.

P. 187. **A** is now given as it stands in "The Old Lady's Collection," 'Clide's Water,' No 11. It will be observed that 19, 20 repeat No 215, **D**, 13, 14 (14, 15, of the copy just given).

1 ' Ye gie corn to my hors,
     An meatt to my man,
     For I will gai to my true-love's gates
     This night, gin I can wine.'

2 ' O stay att home, my son Willie,
     This a bare night we me ;
     The best bed in a' my house
     Sall be well made to the.'

3 ' I care na for your beds, mider,
     I care na a pin ;
     For I ill gae to my love's gates
     This night, gin I can wine.'

4 ' O stay, my son Willie,
     This night we me ;
     The best hen in a' mey reast
     Sall be well made ready for the.'

5 'I care na for your heans, midder,
    I care na a pin ;
For I ull gae to my love's gates
    This night, gin I can wine.'

6 'Gin ye winnë stay, my son Willie,
    This a bare night we me,
Gin Claid's water be dip an fue of flud,
    My malicen droun ye in.'

7 He road up yon high hill,
    An doun yon douë den ;
The roring of Clid's water
    Wod ha flied ten thousand men.

8 'O spair me, Claid's water,
    Spare me as I gaa !
Make me yer wrak as I come back,
    Bat spare me as I gaa !'

9 He raid in, an forder in,
    Till he came to the chin ;
An he raid in, an forder in,
    Till he came to dray lan.

10 An fan he came to his love's gates
    He tirled att the pin :
' Open yer gates, May Meggie,
    Open yer gates to me,
For my bets is fue of Claid's water,
    An the rain rins on a' my chine.'

11 'I ha ne loves therout,' she says,
    'I haa ne love theren;
My true-love is in my arms tua,
    An nean will I latt in.'

12 ' Open yer gates, Meggie,
    This night to me,
For Clide's water is full of flood,
    An my mider's mallison will droun me in.'

13 ' An of my chambers is full of corn,' she says,
    ' Anether is full of hay,
The other is full of gentelmen,
    An they winnë remove till day.'

14 Out waked her May Meggie,
    Out of her drussie dream :
'I dreamed a dream nou san the streen,
    God read a' dreams to gued !
That my true-love Willie
    Was staning att my bed-feet.'

15 'Nou lay still, my a dather,
    An keep my back fraa the call ;
It 's na the space of haf an hour
    Sayn he gade fra your hall.'

16 'Hey, Willie ! an hou, Willie !
    An Willie, winnë ye turn agen?'
But ay the louder that she crayed
    He read agenst the wind.

17 He raid up yon high hill,
    An doun yon douë den,
An the roring that was in Clid's water
    Wad ha fleed ten thousand men.

18 He raid in
    Tell he came to the chine,
An he raid forder in,
    Bat never mare came out agen.

19 She sought him up, she sought him doun,
    She sought him braid an narrou;
In the depest pot in a' Claid's water,
    Ther she gat Suit Willie.

20 She has kissed his comly mouth,
    As she had den afore :
' Baith our midders sall be alike sorry,
    For we 's bath slipe soun in Clide's water.'

21 Ther was na mare seen of that gued lord
    Bat his hat frae his head ;
There was na mare seen of that gued lady
    Bat her keem an her sneed.

22 Ther mideers went up an doun the water,
    Saying, Clayd's water din us wrong !

10⁶. on a.
18⁴. ther *follows* agen, *intended perhaps as a beginning of* 21.

217. The Broom of Cowdenknows.

P. 195. **D b.** Macmath MS., p. 105 ; from the
recitation of Mary Cochrane (Mrs Garmory), Abbey-
yard, Crossmichael, August 12, 1893.

1 Bonny May to the ewe-buchts is gane,
    To milk her daddie's yowes,
And aye as she sang, her bonny voice it rang
    Outoer the taps o the knowes, knowes,
    Outoer the taps o the knowes.

2 .   .   .   .
    .   .   .   .
A troop o noble gentlemen
    Came riding merrily by.

5 He took her by the middle sae sma,
    And by the green gown sleeve,
And he 's laid her down on the dewy, dewy ground,
    And he 's askëd no man's leave.

9 He 's mounted on his milk-white steed,
    And he 's rode after his men,
    And all that his merry men said to him
      Was, Dear master ye 've tarried long.

10 'I have ridden east and I have ridden west,
    And I 've ridden among the knowes,
    But the bonniest lass that eer I saw
      Was milking her daddie's yowes.'

11 She 's taen the milk-pail on her head,
    And she 's gane singing hame,
    And all that her father said to her
      Was, Dear daughter, ye 've tarried long.

13 'O there cam a tod amang my yowes,
    An a waefu tod was he ;
    Afore he had taen my wee yowe-lamb,
      I wad rather he had taen ither three.'

15 It happened on a day, and a bonny summer day,
    As she was ca'in in her father's kye,
    The same troop o noble gentlemen
      Came riding merrily by.

16 One of them calls out
    Lassie, have ye got a man?
    She turned her head right saucy about,
      Saying, I 've got ane at hame.

17 'Hold your tongue, my bonny lass,
    How loud I hear ye lee !
    Do you no remember the caul mirky nicht
      When ye were in the yowe-buchts wi me?'

18 He 's ordered one of his merry men
    To licht and set her on behind him,
    Saying, Your father may ca in his kye when he likes,
      For they 'll neer be ca'ed in by thee.

19 'For I am the laird o the Ochiltree walls,
    I have fifty ploughs and three,
    And I have got the bonniest lass
      In a' the North Countrie.'

219. The Gardener.

P. 212. Rev. S. Baring-Gould has pointed me to a printed copy of this ballad, considerably corrupted, to be sure, but also considerably older than the traditional versions. It is blended at the beginning with a "Thyme" song, which itself is apt to be mixed up with ' I sowed the seeds of love.' The second stanza is from the "Thyme" song ; the third is a traditional variation of a stanza in ' I sowed the seeds of love.' (See the piece which follows this.) The ballad begins with the fourth stanza, and the fifth is corrupted by being transferred from the gardener to the maid. Mr Baring-Gould has lately taken down copies of the "Thyme" song in the west of England. See one in Songs and Ballads of the West, No 7, and the note thereto in the preface to Part IV of that work, p. xv ; also Campbell's Albyn's Anthology, I, 40, Bruce and Stokoe, Northumbrian Minstrelsy, p. 90, and Chappell's Popular Music, p. 521 f. Rev. S. Baring-Gould has given me two copies, one from recitation, the other from " a broadside published by Bebbington, Manchester, Brit. Mus., 1876. d., A Collection of Songs and Broadsides, I, 264."

Five Excellent New Songs. Edinburgh. Printed and sold by William Forrest, at the head of the Cowgate, 1766. British Museum, 11621. b. 6 (8).

1 The wakeing all the winter night,
    And the tippling at the wine,
    And the courting of a bonny lass,
      Will break this heart of mine.
    Brave sailing here, my dear,
      And better sailing there,
    Brave sailing in my love's arms,
      O give I were there !

2 I had a bed of thyme,
    And it flourishd night and day,
    There came by a squire's son
      That stole my heart away.
    Brave sailing, etc.

3 Then up comes the gardener-lad,
    And he gave me profers free,
    He gave to me the jully-flowers,
      To clothe my gay bodie.

4 The gardener stood in his garden,
    And the prim-rose in his hand,
    And there he spi'd his own true love,
      As tight 's a willy wand.

5 'If he 'll be a lover true,' she said,
    ' A lover true indeed,
    And buy all the flowers of my garden,
      I 'll shape to thee a weed.'
    Brave sailing, etc.

6 ' The prim-rose shall be on thy head,
    And the red rose on thy breast,
    And the white-rose shall be for a smock,
      To cover thy body next.
    Brave sailing, etc.

7 ' Thy glove shall be the jully-flower,
    Comes lockren to thy hand,
   .   .   .   .
     .   .   .   .

8 'Thy stockings shall be of the thyme,
    Fair maid, it is a pleasant view;
Put on, fair maid, whenever you please,
    And your shoes shall be of the rue.'
      Brave sailing here, my dear,
        And better sailing there,
      And brave sailing in my love's arms,
        O if I were there!

9 'You shape to me, young man,' she says,
    'A weed amongst the flowers,
But I will shape to you, young man,
    A weed amongst the flowers.

10 'The hail-stones shall be on thy head,
    And the snow upon thy breast,
And the east-wind shall be for a shirt,
    To cover thy body next.

11 'Thy boots shall be of the tangle,
    That nothing can betide,
Thy steed shall be of the wan water,
    Loup on, young man, and ride.'
      Brave sailing there, my dear,
        And better sailing here,
      And 't is brave sailing twixt my love's arms,
        O if I were there!

Five Excellent New Songs. II. The New Lover's
Garland. III. The Young Maid's Answer.

    5[1] *should read*, If thou 'lt . . he said.
    5[2] *should read nearly as in* **B** 8[8], Among all.
    6[4], 10[4]. next *should be* neist.
    7[1]. grove. 7[1,2], 8[1,2], *make a stanza*.
    After 8: The Young Maid's Answer, *printed as*
    No 3 of the five songs.
    9[1]. to be a.
    9[3,4] *could be easily corrected* from **A**7[5,6], **B** 15[3,4].
    11[1]. stangle.
    11[2] *should read to the effect*, That's brought in by
    the tide.

The piece which follows is little more than a variation of 'I sow'd the seeds of love' (one of "three of
the most popular songs among the servant-maids of the
present generation," says Mr Chappell : see a traditional version of the song, which was originally composed by Mrs Habergham towards the end of the seventeenth century, in Popular Music, p. 522 f.). But the
choosing of a weed for a maid from garden-flowers is
here, and is not in the song. It will be observed that
the maid chooses no weed for the gardener, but dies
of a thorn-prick, a trait which is found in neither the
song nor the ballad.

Taken down by Rev. S. Baring-Gould from the singing of Joseph Paddon, Holcombe Burnell. Printed,
with changes, in Baring-Gould and Sheppard's Songs

and Ballads of the West, No 107, Part IV, p. 50, 1891
here as sung.

DEAD MAID'S LAND.

1 A garden was planted around
    With flowers of every kind,
I chose of the best to wear in my breast,
    The flowers best pleased my mind.

2 A gardener standing by
    I asked to choose for me ;
He chose me the lily, the violet, the pink,
    But I liked none of the three.

3 A violet I don't like,
    A lily it fades so soon,
But as for the pink I cared not a flink,
    I said I would stop till June.

4 'The lily it shall be thy smock,
    The jonquil shoe thy feet,
Thy gown shall be of the ten-week stock,
    Thy gloves the violet sweet.

5 'The gilly shall deck thy head,
    Thy way with herbs I'll strew,
Thy stockings shall be the marigold,
    Thy gloves the violet blue.'

6 'I like not the gilly-flower,
    Nor herbs my way to strew,
Nor stockings of the marigold,
    Nor gloves of violet blue.

7 'I will not have the ten-week stock,
    Nor jonquils to my shoon,
But I will have the red, red rose
    That flowereth in June.'

8 'The rose it doth bear a thorn
    That pricketh to the bone ; '
'I little heed what thou dost say,
    I will have that or none.'

9 'The rose it doth bear a thorn
    That pricketh to the heart ;'
'O but I will have the red, red rose,
    For I little heed its smart.'

10 She stoopëd to the ground
    To pluck the rose so red,
The thorn it pierced her to the heart,
    And this fair maid was dead.

11 A gardener stood at the gate,
    With cypress in his hand,
And he did say, Let no fair may
    Come into Dead Maid's Land.

A fragment in Motherwell's MS., obtained from
Widow Nicol, 'It's braw sailing here,' p. 110, has
something of both pieces without any suggestion of the
flower-dress.

1 It's braw sailing here,
   And it's braw sailing there,
   And it's braw sailing on the seas
   When wind and tide are fair.

2 It's braw drinking beer,
   And it's braw drinking wine,
   And it's braw courting a bonnie lass
   When she is in her prime.

3 O the gardener sent me word,
   He that pued the rose for me,
   The willow, primrose, the red rose,
   But I denied all three.

4 The willow I'll deny,
   The primrose it buds soon,
   But I'll chuse for me the red rose,
   And I vow it'll stand till June.

5 In June my red rose sprung,
   It was not a rose for me,
   So I'll pull the top of my red rose,
   And I'll plant the willow-tree.

6 For the willow I must wear,
   With sorrows mixed amang,
   And all the neighbours far and near
   Say I luved a false luve lang.

2². braw *altered to* better.

221. Katharine Jaffray.

P. 222. **E**, as it stands in "The Old Lady's Collection," No 17, 'Bony Catrain Jaffry.'

1 Bonny Catrain Jaffrie,
   That proper maid sae fare,
   She has loved yong Lochinwar,
   She made him no compare.

2 He courted her the live-lang winter night,
   Sa has he the simmer's day;
   He has courted her sae lang
   Till he sta her heart away.

3 Bat the lusty lard of Lamerdall
   Came fra the South Countrey,
   An for to ga[i]n this lady's love
   In intred he.

4 .   .   .   .
   .   .   .   .
   An he has gained her friends' consent,
   An sett the weding-day.

5 The weding-day it being sett,
   An a' man to it boun,
   She sent for her first fair love,
   Her wedding to come to.

6 His father an his mother came,
   .   .   .   .
   They came a', but he came no,
   It was a foull play.

7 Lochenwar an his comrads
   Sat drinken att the wine;
   'Faue on you!' sad his comrads,
   'Tak yer bride for shame.

8 'Had she ben mine, as she was yours,
   An den as she has don to you,
   I wad tak her on her bridell-day
   Fra a' her compinay.

9 'Fra a' her compinay,
   Without any other stay;
   I wad gee them frogs insted of fish,
   An take ther bride away.'

10 He got fifty young men,
   They were gallant an gay,
   An fifty madens,
   An left them on a lay.

11 Fan he came in by Callien bank,
   An in by Calline bray,
   He left his company
   Dancing on a lay.

12 He came to the bridel-house,
   An in entred he;
   .   .   .   .
   .   .   .   .

13 'Ther was a young man in this place
   Loyed well a comly may,
   Bat the day she gaes anether man's bride,
   An has plaed him foull play.

14 'Had it ben me, as it was him,
   An don as she has dien him tee,
   I wad ha geen them froges insteed of fish,
   An tane ther bride away.'

15 The Englesh speared gin he wad fight,
   It spak well in his mind;
   .   .   .   .
   .   .   .   .

16 'It was na for fighten I cam hear,
   But to bear gud fileshap gay;
   Wan glass we yer bridgrom,
   An so I goe my way.'

17 The glass was filled of gued read wine
    Betuen them tua :
    ' Wan word we yer brid,
      An so I goo my waa.'

18 He was on gued horse back,
    An whipt the bride him we;
  She grat an wrang her hands,
    An said, It 's foull play !

19 . . . .
    ' An this I dar well say,
  For this day I gade anether man's bride,
    An it 's ben foull play.'

20 Bat nou she is Lochenw[ar]'s wife,
  . . . .
  An he gaed them froges insted of fish,
    An tain ther bried away.

      1. him *imperfect; might be* hir. 5^2. boung.

    225. G. Collated with a MS. of Charles Kirkpatrick Sharpe's and with another copy of the same pieces in " North Country Ballads," Miscellanea Curiosa, Abbotsford Library.
    Sharpe, p. 13. 1^1. O *wanting.* Jaffray.
    1^3. For she has lovd young L.
    $3^{1,2}$. Lauderdale 's come. 3^3. That pretty.
    4^3. He agreed with. 5^3. lossing of the.
    6^1. were you, L. 7^1. Ye get.
    7^2. And send through. 7^3. Get 150. 7^4. be all.
    8^3. And still : trumpets. 9^2. And sent.
    9^3. Gat full. 9^4. To be all. 10^1. To be.
    10^2. to obey. 10^3. And still : trumpets.
    11^3. When he went in upon. 12^2. who was.
    12^3. Come never. 13^1. They 'll.
    14^3. Askd if he had. 15^1. ever. 15^2. As was.
    15^4. Was. 16^3. I did.
    16^4. Was leaping on the hays.
    17^3. with you, b.
    17^4, 18^4. bound. 18^2. drank. 19^1. taken.
    19^4, 20^4. no. 20^1. so great. 20^2. And so.
    20^3. That. 21^1. take their. 21^3. trumpets.
    22^1. There was. 22^2. Was walking on a hay.
    22^3. Gave them the bonny bride by the hand.
    22^4. bad them bound. 23^1. pieces nine.
  Scott. 15^2. array *miscopied* away.

222. Bonny Baby Livington.

    P. 231. ' Bonnie Annie Livieston ' in C. K. Sharpe's first MS. collection, p. 24, resembles **D** and **B**, and has as many commonplaces as **B**, ending with the last three stanzas of several versions of ' Lord Thomas and Fair Annet ' or of ' Lord Lovel,' **I**.

1 Bonny Anny Livieston
    Went out to see the play,
  By came the laird of Glenlion,
    And [he 's] taen hir quite away.

2 He set hir on a milk-white steed,
    Himself upon a gray,
  He 's teen hir oer the Highland hills,
    And taen hir quite away.

3 When they came to Glenlion's gate,
    The lighted on the green ;
  There was mony a bonny lad and lass
    To wolcome the lady hame.

4 They led hir through high towers and bowers,
    And through the buling-green,
  And ay when they spake Erse to hir
    The tears blinded hir een.

5 Says, The Highlands is no for me, kind sir,
    The Highlands is no for me ;
  If that ye would my favour win,
    Take me unto Dundee.

6 ' Dundee !' he says, ' Dundee, lady !
    Dundee you shall never see ;
  Upon the laird of Glenlion
    Soon wadded shall ye be.'

7 When bells were rung, and mas was sung,
    And all were bound for bed,
  And bonny Annie Livieston
    By hir bridegroom was laid.

8 ' It 's O gin it were day !' she says,
    ' It 's O gin it were day !
  O if that it were day,' she says,
    ' Nae langer wad I stay.'

9 ' Your horse stands in a good stable,
    Eating both corn and hay,
  And you are in Glenlion's arms,
    Why should ye weary for day ? '

10 ' Glenlion's arms are good enough,
    But alais ! the 'r no for me ;
  If that you would my fevour win,
    Taike me unto Dundee.

11 ' Bat fetch me paper, pen and ink,
    And candle that I may see,
  And I 'll go write a long letter
    To Geordie in Dundee.

12 ' Where will I get a bonny boy,
    That will win hose and shoon,
  That will gang to my ain true-luve,
    And tell him what is done ? '

13 Then up then spake a bonny boy,
    Near to Glenlion's kin,
  Says, Many time I hae gane his erand,
    But the lady's I will rin.

14 O when he came to broken brigs
    He bent his bow and swame,
  And when he came to grass growing
    Set down his feet and ran.

15 And when he came to Dundee gate
    Lap clean outoer the wa ;
  Before the porter was thereat,
    The boy was in the haa.

16 'What news? what news, bonny boy?
    What news hes thou to me?'
  'No news, no news,' said bonny boy,
    'But a letter unto thee.'

17 The first three lines he looked on,
    A loud laughter gied he,
  But or he wan to the hinder en
    The tears blinded his eie.

18 'Gae saddle to me the black,' he says,
    'Gae saddle to me the broun,
  Gae saddle to me the swiftest steed
    That eer took man to towen.'

19 He burst the black unto the slack,
    The browen unto the brae,
  But fair fa on the siller-gray
    That carried him ay away !

20 When he came to Glenlion's yett,
    He tirled at the pin,
  But before that he wan up the stair
    The lady she was gone.

21 'O I can kiss thy cheeks, Annie,
    O I can kiss thy chin,
  O I can kiss thy clay-cold lips,
    Though there be no breath within.

22 'Deal large at my love's buriell
    The short bread and the wine,
  And gin the morn at ten o clock
    Ye may deal as mukle at mine.'

23 The taen was biried in Mary's kirk,
    The tither in St Mary's quire,
  And out of the taen there grew a birk,
    And the ither a bonny brier.

24 And ay they grew, and ay they threw,
    Till they did meet aboon,
  And a' that ere the same did see
    Knew they had true lovers been.

17[3]. hinderen.   21[1]. thy thy.

223. Eppie Morrie.

P. 239.   Collated with a MS. of Charles Kirkpatrick Sharpe's, and with another copy of the same pieces, "North Country Ballads," in Miscellanea Curiosa, Abbotsford Library.

    Sharpe, p. 21.   1[2]. all.   1[3]. away.   1[4]. Because.
      2[1]. Out it.   2[2]. moonlighty.   3[1,2]. Hald.
      3[4]. That shall be wedded.   5[1]. He has.
      5[2]. it *wanting*.   5[3]. Says, Marry.
      6[1,2], 7[1,2], 10[1,2], 15[1,2]. Hold.   6[4]. be married.
      7[3]. dare not avow to marrying.   7[4]. she were.
      8[2]. could not.   8[3]. are away.   9[1]. bells was.
      9[2]. all men bound.   10[1,2], 15[1,2]. away from.
      10[3]. I loss.   12[3]. Scallater.   13[1]. Says, Get.
      13[4]. sure I am : as ye.   14[1]. fall.
      14[2]. you could not.   14[3]. taken.
      14[4]. kis[s]ed your hand.   15[3]. For there 's.
      15[4]. that 's be wedded to me.
      16[1]. in it came Belbardlane.
      16[3]. Says, come away home.   17[2]. And get to me.
      17[4]. came.   18[2]. and hey the light.
      Written in long lines, without division into stanzas.
    Scott.   Norrie *throughout*.   2[2]. moonlight.
      16[3]. home *wanting*.

225. Rob Roy.

P. 245. **A.** This version is No 9 of "The Old Lady's Collection," and was copied by Skene without much variation. The following original readings may be noted.

      2[3]. Or she.   3[1]. serundad.   3[4]. fra each other.
      6[4]. to me has.   7[4]. Him sell beside her.
      8[1]. came by Black.   8[4]. not be.
      10[1,2]. Be content *twice only*.
      11[2], 12[2]. lady *wanting*.   12[1]. land.   12[2]. for his.
      12[3]. An *wanting*.   12[4]. took them.
      13[1]. he *wanting*.   13[3]. pound.   14[1]. Y 'er.

    249. **E.** In Sharpe's small MS. volume, "Songs," p. 42.

      1[2]. Cam to.   2[1]. It's when.   2[4]. her to.   5[3]. hasted.
      7[3]. cries *for* sighs.   7[4]. was laid behind.
      8[1]. He says to her, etc., Oh, be.
      Readings from **A** 1, 2, *are added, in a later hand, in the margin of* 1, 3.

    254.

L

From a copy formerly in the possession of Charles Kirkpatrick Sharpe, now belonging to Mr Macmath. The paper on which it is written has the water-mark 1822. This version closely resembles **C** and **K**.

1 Rob Roy 's from the Highlands come
    Down to the Lowland border,

And there he's stole a fair lady away,
  To keep his house in order.

2 As he came in by Blackhill gate,
  Twenty men his arms did carry,
  And he has stole a fair lady away,
  On purpose hir to marry.

3 No tidings came unto the house,
  Nor none went in before him,
  Or else she had been run away,
  For she did still abhor him.

4 But with his men he surunded the house,
  Himself went in unto hir,
  And when that he had found her out
  He profest how much he lovt hir.

5 'O wilt thou be my dear?' he says,
  'O wilt thou be my hony?
  O wilt thou be my wedded wife?
  For I love you far better than ony.'

6 'I will not be your dear,' she says,
  'I will not be your honey,
  I will not be your wedded wife;
  You love me for my money.'

7 But he hir drew amongst his crew,
  She holding by hir mother;
  With doleful cries and watry eyes
  The parted from each other.

8 He gave hir no time for to dress
  As brides do when the marry,
  But fast he hurried hir away,
  And rowd hir in his plaidy.

9 He set hir on a milk-white steed,
  Himself lept on behind hir,
  And he has carried hir away,
  Hir friends the could not find hir.

10 The lady's cries were oftimes heard,
  But none durst venture to hir;
  She gaurded was on every side,
  Hir friends could not rescue hir.

11 As the went over hills and rocks,
  The lady oftimes fainted;
  Cries, Wo be to my curst mony,
  These roads to me invented.

12 As the came in by Drummond town
  And at Bachannan tarried,
  He bought to her a cloak and gown,
  Yet wad she not be married.

13 And when she came the priest before
  He askd if she would marry,
  But the parson's zeal it was so hot
  For her will he did not tarry.

14 Four held hir up before the priest,
  Tow laid hir in hir bed, O,
  But still she cried, with watry eyes,
  When she was by him laid O.

15 'Now you'r to the Highlands come,
  Out of your native clime, lady,
  Never think of going back,
  But tak it for your hame, lady.

16 'Be content, be content,
  Be content to stay, lady,
  Now you are my wedded wife,
  Until your dying day, lady.

17 'Rob Roy was my father calld,
  McGregor was his name, lady,
  And all the country where he dwelt
  None could exceed his fame, lady.

18 'I'll be kind, I'll be kind,
  I'll be kind to thee, lady,
  A' thy kindred for thy sake
  Shall truly favoured be, lady.

19 'My father reignd as Highland king,
  And ruled at his will, lady,
  There was nether lord nor duke
  Durst do him ony ill, lady.

20 'Ay through time, ay through time,
  Ay through time was he, lady,
  Filled was w[ith] sweet revenge
  On a' his enemys, lady.

21 'He was a hedge about his friends,
  A heckle till his foes, lady,
  And every ane that did him rang,
  He took them oer the nose, lady.

22 'I'm as bold, I'm as bold,
  [As bold] as forest boar, lady,

Every ane that does thee rang
  Shall feell my stell claymore, lady.

23 'Neer a man from Highlands came
  That ever did him dare, lady,
But if those persons did escape
  He sized upon there gear, lady.
    Ay through time, etc.

24 'My father dealt in horse and cows,
  But thou in goats and sheep, lady,
Thre and twenty thousand merk
  Makes me a man complete, lady.
    Be content, etc.

25 'Of all the exploits my father did
  I do him now outshine, lady ;
He never took a prize in 's life
  With sic a face as thine, lady.'

Title : Old Song, Rob Roy. Tune, Jonny Fa,
the Gipsy Laddy.

After 14. Tune, Had away frae me, Donald.

Here may be added, as an appendix, a fragment of a
ballad on the "Abduction of Nelly Symon." "The
chorus is in Gaelic and the song is sung to one of the
finest native airs." From The Aberdeen Herald and
Weekly Free Press, February 3, 1883.

1 They hoised her up upon a mare ;
It was not for her gowd nor gear ;
'T was for her beauty, keen and rare,
  That they stealt Ellen Symon.
Se ho or so gur tallum tallum,
Se ho or so gur e so hallum ;
Bheir mis ma chinteach ghuds gur tallum,
  Chaileig, Eilie Symon.

2 Her father made a bow o bere,
Her uncle he gae twa pound mair,
To hang the rogue he vowed and sware
  That stealt his Ellen Symon.

3 When they came on till Allanqooich,
They drank the whisky oot o a quaich,
And ilka ane was blythe eneuch,
  But wae was Ellen Symon.

4 When they came to the brig o Don,
Peter swore he would move on ;
Says Charlie, Lad, ye sanna win,
  For my brave Ellen Symon.

226. Lizie Lindsay.

P. 255.

H

From "The Old Lady's Collection," No 39.

1 Ther lives a maid in Edinbrugh citty,
  Elisa Lindsy they call her by name ;
Monye an came to court her,
  But a' ther suit was in vain.

2 Out spak the hear of Carnussë,
  An out spak he ;
'Fat wad ye think of me if I wad gae to
    Edinbrugh citty
  An bring this fair creatur we me?'

3 'If ye gae to Edinbrugh city
  An bring this fair creatur we the,
Bring her home we ne flatry,
  But by grait policy.'

4 Fan he came to the Netherbou,
  Elisa Lindsy for to see,
She drank we him a bottel of cherry,
  And bare him gued company.

5 'Will ye goo to the Hillands we me, Lisee ?
  Will ye go to [the] Hillands we me ?

  .   .   .   .   .   .

  Ye 's gett cruds an grean why.'

6 Out spak Lissy's mother,
  An out spak she ;
'If ye say so to my daughter,
  [I] swaer I ell gar ye die.'

7 'Keep well yer dother, old lady,
  Keep well yer dother fra me,
For I care as littel for yer dother
  As she dos for me.'

8 Out spak Lissie Lindsy,
  We the tear in her eay ;
'I will gie ye ten gunies,
  If ye wad bat sitt in my roum bat a whill
Till I dra you[r] picter,
  To mind me on your swit smill.'

9 'I care as littel for your ten gunies
  As ye dou for mine,
But if ye love my person,
  Goo we me if ye inclayn.'

10 Fan they came to Carnusie, an even to the
    glen,
    Out came the old day:
  'Ye 'r welcom home, Sir Donall, ye 'r welcom
    home,
    An that fair creatur ye we.'

11 'Caa na me mare Sir Donald,
    Bat caa me Donall, yer son,
    An I 'll caa ye my mother,
    An caa me Donall, yer son:'
    The words wer spoken in Ears,
    Lissie she had nean.

12 'Gett us a supper of cruds,
    [A supper of cruds] an green whay,
    An a bed of the best of yeer rushes,
    Besids a covering of gray.'

13 Lissy Lindsy bieng weary,
    She lay over long in they day:
  'Win up, Lissy Lindsy,
    Ye haa layen our lang in the day;
    Ye might haa ben out we my mider,
    Milken the eus an the kay.'

14 Out spak Lissie Lindsy,
    The tear in her eay;
  'I wiss I wer in Edenbrugh citty,
    I cannë milk eus nor kay.'

15 'Hold your toung, Lissie Lindsy,
    An dou not freat on me,
    For I will haa ye back to Edenbrugh citty,
    Nou we grait safity.'

16 Out spak Lissie Lindsy,
    The tear in her eay;
  'If I wer in Edenbrugh citty,
    They woud think littel of me.'

17 He touk her by the milk-white hand,
    Some other forest to vue;

  .   .   .   .
    .   .   .   .   .   .

18 Fan they came to Carnusy, out came Donal's
    father,
    A gay old knight was he;
    Out cam Donald's father,
    An four-an-tuenty him we.

19 'Ye 'r welcom, Lissie Lends[y],
    Dear welcom to me;

    Ye 's be Lady Carnusie,
    An gett Donal, my son.'

20 Out came Donald's mother,
    An four-an-tuenty her we:
  'Ye 'r welcom, my son,
    An that fair creatur ye we.'

17². Forest: *doubtful.*

227. Bonny Lizie Baillie.

P. 266. **h.** 'Elisa Bailly,' "The Old Lady's Collection," No 37.

3 As I came in by Carron sid,
    An in nou by Dumblain,
    Ther I mett we Dugall Grame:
    He said he wad see me hame.

4 'My bonny Lisey Ballie,
    I ill rou ye in my plady,
    An ye wad gaa along we me,
    I wad make ye a Heallend lady.'

5 'If I wad gaa along we ye,
    They wad say I wer na wise;
    For I cane nether milk cou nor ewe,
    Nor can I speak Ears.'

6 'My bonny Lisie Bailly,
    For that ye nead na fear;
    For onye that I cane dou,
    I ill learn to you, my dear.'

19, 21 'Then I ill cast off my bra nou goun,
    Made of the silk an saten,
    An I ell pitt on the hame-made grays,
    To skip among the breachan.'

  'My bonny Lisie Bailly,
    I ill rou ye in my plaidy,
    An ye will go along we me,
    I ill make ye a Healend lady.'

20 'Then I ell cast aff my bra nou shous,
    Made of the Turky lader,
    An I ell pit on the hame-made broges,
    To skip among the header.'

  'My bonny Lisie Bailly,
    I ell rou ye in my plady;
    Since ye 'r to goo along we me,
    I ell make ye a Healend lady.'

16 Foull faa the logarheaded Loland lads
    That lives near Castell Carey,
    Has latten the bonny lass away
    The Heallend lad to marry.

16². Carey *written so as to look like* Carly.

228. Glasgow Peggie.

P. 271. A is extant among Sharpe's relics, written on paper having 1819 in the water-mark, in two hands : stanzas 1–6, 8, 9[1], in one, 7 (inserted in the margin) and the rest in another.   Sharpe has made a few slight changes in the text, besides regulating the spelling. The ballad is now given as it stands in the original copy.

1 ' As I cam in by boney Glassgow town,
    The Highland troops were a' before me,
  And the bon[ey]est lass that ere I saw,
    She lives in Glassgow, tha ca her Peggy.

2 ' I wad gie my boney black horse,
    So wad I my good gray nagie,
  If I were a hundred miles in the North,
    And nan wee me but my boney Peggy.'

3 Up then spoke her father dear,
    Dear vow ! but he was wondrous sorey ;
  ' Weel may yea steel a cow or a ewe,
    But ye darna steel my boney Peggy.'

4 Up then spoke her mother dear,
    Dear vow ! but she spoke wondrious sorey ;
  ' Now, since I 've brought ye up this length,
    Wod ye gang awa wee a Highland fellow ? '

5 He set her on his boney black horse,
    He set himsel on his good gray nagy ;
  They have riden over hill[s] and dales,
    Now he is awa wee his boney Peggy.

6 They are riden or hills and dales,
    They have riden or mountains maney,
  Untill that thay com to a low, low glen,
    And there he 's lain down wee his boney Peggy.

7 Up then spoke the Earll o Argyle,
    Dear vow ! bet he spoke wondrous sorry ;
  ' The bonniest lass in a' Scotland
    Is af an awa wi [a] Highland fellow ! '

8 There bed was of the boney green grass,
    There blankets was o the hay sa boney ;
  He falded his philabeg below her head,
    Now he 's lawing down wee his boney Peggy.

9 Up then spoke the boney Lawland lass,
    And oh, but she spoke wondrous sorry ;
  ' A 's warruant my mother would hae a gae soir
      heart
    To see me lian here wi you, my Willie ! '

10 ' In my father's house there 's feather-beds,
     Feather-beds an blankets many ;
   The 're a' mine, an the 'll shoon be thine,
     An what needs your mother be sae sorry, Peggie ?

11 ' Dinna you see yon nine score o kye,
     Feding on yon hill sae boney ?
   The 're a' mine, an the 'll shoon be thine,
     An what needs your mother be sorry, Peggie ?

12 ' Dinna you see yon nine score o sheep,
     Feeding on yon brae sae bonny ?
   The 're a' mine, an the 'll shoon be thine,
     An what needs your mother be sorry for you ?

13 ' Dinna you see yon bonny white house,
     Shining on yon brae sae bonny ?
   An I am the earl o the Isle o Sky,
     And surely my Peggie will be calle[d] a lady.'

1[2], 2[8]. where.   2[8]. a : *not unlike* 2, *but really* a.
9[2]. she sape.   9[8]. soir : i *not dotted.*
10[8]. be the thene.

275.

G

Macmath MS., p. 93.   Taken down at Crossmichael, Kirkcudbrightshire, 24th August, 1892, from the recitation of Miss Jane Webster, who had learned it more than fifty years before, at Airds of Kells, from the singing of Rosanna McGinnies.

1 It was on a day, and a fine summer's day,
    When the Lowlands they were making ready,
  There I espied a weel-far'd lass,
    She was gaun to Glasgow, and they ca her
      Peggy.

2 It 's up then spak a silly auld man,
    And O but he spak wondrous poorly !
  Sayin, Ye may steal awa my cows and my ewes,
    But ye 'll never steal awa my bonny Peggy.

3 ' O haud yer tongue, ye silly auld man,
    For ye hae said eneugh already,
  For I 'll never steal awa yer cows and yer ewes,
    But I 'll steal awa yer bonny Peggy.'

4 So he mounted her on a milk-white steed,
    Himsel upon a wee grey naigie,
  And they hae ridden ower hill and dale,
    And over moors and mosses many.

5 They rade till they cam to the head o yon glen,
    It might hae frightened anybody ;
  He said, Whether will ye go alongst with me,
    Or will ye return back again to your mam-
      mie ?

*   *   *   *   *   *   *   *

6 Their bed was o the green, green grass,
  And their blankets o the bracken sae bonnie,
And he 's laid his trews beneath their head,
  And Peggy 's lain doun wi her Heilan laddie.

7 They lay till it cam to the break o day,
  Then up they rose and made them ready ;
He said, Whether will ye go alongst with me,
  Or will ye return back again to your mam-
    mie ?

8 'I 'll follow you through frost and snow,
    I 'll follow you through dangers many,
And wherever ye go I will go alongst with you,
  For I 'll never return back again to my
    mammie.'

9 'I hae four-and-twenty gude milk-kye,
    They 're a' bun in yon byre sae bonny,
And I am the earl o the Isle o Skye,
  And why should not Peggy be called a lady ?

10 'I hae fifty acres o gude land,
    A' ploughed ower and sawn sae bonny,
And I am young Donald o the Isle o Skye,
  And wherever I 'm laird I 'll make ye lady.'

231. The Earl of Errol.

P. 284. **B** as it stands in " The Old Lady's Collection," No 26.

1 Earell is a bonny place,
    Itt stands upon yon plain ;
The gratest faut about the toun,
  Earell 's na a man.
      For fat ye caa the danton o'tt,
        According as ye ken,
      For the pearting . . . . ,
        Lady Earel lays her lean.

2 Eearel is a bonny place,
    It stans upon yon plain ;
The rosses they grou read an whit,
  An the apples they grou green.

3 'Fatt nead I my apron wash
    An hing upon yon pinn?
For lang will I gaa out an in
  Or I hear my barn's dinn.

4 'Fatt nead I my apron wash,
    Or hang upon yon dor?
For side an wid is my petecot,
  An eaen doun afore.

5 'Bat I will laice my stays agean,
    My middel jump an smaa ;
I ull gaa a' my days a meaden,
  Awaa, Earell, awaa !'

6 It fell ance upon a day Lord Earell
    Went to hunt him lean,

    .   .   .   .

    .   .   .   .

7 He was na a mill fra the toun,
    Nor yett sae far awaa,
Till his lady is on to Edinbrugh,
  To tray him att the laa.

8 Littel did Lord Earell think,
    Fan he satt doun to dine,
That his lady was one to Edinbrugh,
  Nor fatt was in her mind.

9 Till his best servant came
    For to latt him kenn,

    .   .   .   .

    .   .   .   .   .   .

10 She was na in att the toun-end,
    Nor yett sa far awa,
Till Earell he was att her back,
  His goudy lokes to sha.

11 She was na in att the toun-head,
    Nor just att the eand,
Till Earell he was att her back,
  Her earent for to ken.

12 'As lang as they caa ye Kett Carnegë,
    An me Sir Gilbert Hay,
I us gar yer father sell Kinnerd,
  Yer tougher for to pay.'

13 'For to gar my father sell Kennerd,
    It wad be a sin,
To gee 't to ony naughty knight
  That a toucher canna wine.'

14 Out spak the first lord,
    The best among them a' ;
'I never seed a lady come to Edinbrugh
  We sick matters to the laue.'

15 Out spak the nixt lord,
    The best of the toun ;
'Ye gett fiften weell-fared maids,
    An pitt them in a roun,
An Earl in the midst of them,
  An latt him chouss out ane.'

16 They ha gotten fiften well-fared maids,
    An pat them in a roun,

An Earel in the mids of them,
An bad him chuse out ane.

17 He voued them a' intell a rau,
Even up an doun,
An he has chossen a well-fared may,
An Meggie was her name.

18 He touk her by the hand,
Afore the nobles a',
An tuenty times he kissed her moue,
An lead her throu the haa.

19 'Louk up, Meggie, luke up, Meggie,
An thinkne sham[e] ;
As lang as ye see my goudy loks,
Lady Earel's be yer name.'

20 Thir was fifteen nobelmen,
An as mony ladys gay,
To see Earel proven a man
.   .   .   .   .   .

21 'Ye tak this well-fared may,
An keep her three roun reaths of a year,
An even att the three raiths' end
I ull draue near.'

22 They ha tane that well-fared may,
An kepeed her three roun reaths of a year,
An even att the three raiths' end
Earel's son she bare.

23 The gentelmen they ga a shout,
The ladys gaa a caa,
Fair mat faa him Errel,
But vou to his lady !

24 He was na in at the toun-head,
Nor just att the end,
Till the letters they wer metting him
That Errol had a son.

25 ' Luke up, Megie, luk up, Meggie,
An think na shame;
As lang as ye see my bra blak hat,
Lady Earrol 's be yer name.

26 'I will gie my Meggie a mill,
Bat an a pice of land,
.   .   .   .   .   .
To foster my young son.

27 'Fare is a' my merry men a',
That I pay meat an gair,
For to convë my Meggie hame,
.   .   .   .   .   ?'

28 .   .   .   .   .   .
.   .   .   .   .   .
Even in Lord Earrel's coach
They conved the lassie hame.

29 'Tak hame yer dother, Lord Kennard,
An take her to the glen,
For Earell canno pleas her,
Earell nor a' his men.'

30 'Had I ben lady of Earrol,
Of sick a boony place,
I wadne gain to Edinbrugh
My husband to disgrace.'

Refrain.   Given only at the end.
15⁴, 16². roum.   20². gay ladys.   24⁴. that that.

288.   **E** is also in the small MS. volume of C. K. Sharpe's, " Songs," p. 17.   The reading in 3⁴ is " toss," " top " being a mis-copy.

289.   Findlay MSS, I, 135 ; ' Airlie,' from Miss Butchart, Arbroath.

1 Lord Airlie 's courted mony a lady,
He 's courted mony a ane, O
An he 's awa to bonny Kinnaird,
Lady Katrine's love to win. O

2 An when he cam to bonny Kinnaird,
An on the bowlin-green,
There he saw his ain Katrine,
Was walking there alane.

3 'O will ye go to bonnie Airlie,
Alang wi me to dine ?·
Or will ye go to bonny Airlie,
To be my lady fine ? '

4 ' I winna go to bonny Airlie
Alang wi you to dine,
But I will go to bonny Airlie
To be your lady fine.'

*   *   *   *   *   *

5 He would not hae the lady gay,
That rustled in her silk,
But he would hae the country-girl,
Goin to sell her milk.

6 He took his Peggie by the hand
An led her through the ha,
An twenty times he kissëd her,
Before the nobles a'.

7 He took his Peggie by the hand
An led her through the trance,
An twenty times he kissëd her
Before he bade her dance.

Findlay MSS, I, 153, from Bell Harris, Muirside of Kinnell, Forfarshire, "once a servant of the family of Carnegie, and now upwards of eighty years of age (1868)."

1 They hae made a marriage o 't,
　An they hae made it sune, O
　An they hae made a marrige o 't,
　It stood at Earlstoon. O

2 When een was come, an bells were rung,
　An a' men boond for bed,
　The earl and his gay ladie
　In ae chamber were laid.

3 It 's up i the mornin the earl rose,
　Went to anither room ;
　Up she rose an away she goes,
　An to Kinnaird she came.

4 They socht her up, they socht her doon,
　They socht her through a' the toon,
　An she was seen walkin her lane,
　An her bed-goon it was on.

5 He wissd his horse had broken 's neck
　When first he to Kinnaird did come.

6 There was na ane bade him come in
　But John Lindsay him lane.

7 When he was at bonny Kinnaird,
　An on the bowlin-green,
　His hair was like the threeds o gold,
　An his eyes like diamonds sheen ;
　He micht 'll ae served the best Carnegie,
　That ever bore the name.

8 He said, Tho ye be Kate Carnegie,
　I am Sir Gilbert Hay ;
　I 'll gar your father sell Kinnaird,
　Your tocher-gude he maun pay.

9 ' To gar my father sell his land
　I think it were a sin,
　For ony silly brat like you ;
　Ye couldna tocher win.

10 ' I may wash my apron
　An hing it on the tower,
　An I may kilt my petticoats,
　They 're even doon afore.'

11 But the earl he 's awa to Edinbro,
　To prove himself a man ;
　The lady she fast followd him,
　To swear that he was none.

12 An when they cam to Edinbro,
　And into the ha,

There she saw her ain gude lord,
　Amang the nobles a'.

13 He took the tapster-lass
　An led her through the room,
　An twenty times he kissed her mou,
　Afore his lady's een.

14 She took the cocks all frae her head
　An dashed them at the wa ;
　' Awa ! awa, Lord Earl !' she says,
　' Awa, Lord Earl, awa !'

15 But the earl he hae gotten leave
　To choise a maid unto himsel,
　An he hae choised a country-lass,
　Cam butter an eggs to sell.

16 He took the lassie by the hand
　An led her through the room :
　' I'd gie thee three times three hundred pound,
　If you 'd bear to me a son.'

17 ' Haud aff your hands, Lord Earl,' she said,
　' Haud aff your hands frae me ;
　For I wad think it a great disgrate
　For a' my kin an me.'

18 But he has called for a private room,
　An there he laid her doun,
　An there he took his will o her,
　Upon a bed o down.

19 She was three quarters of a year
　Confined to a room,
　And bonny was the babe she bore,
　Sir John Hay was his name.

20 ' Wae be to you, Peggie Stuart,
　That ae sister o mine !
　Ye 've pairted me an my gude lord,
　We 'll never meet again.'

21 Up spak her sister, Lady Jean,
　. . . . . . .
　An I could gain sick an estate,
　I wad gien my husband up to disdain.

6². John Lindsay *is explained to be* the gardener.
11⁸. They lady.
13⁴. *Followed by* Wi twenty lookin on, *perhaps an alternative verse.*
14¹. She *is explained as the tapster-lass.*
20¹. *Query by Mr Findlay:* Lady Jean?

290. **D b.** Now collated with a MS. of Charles Kirkpatrick Sharpe, and with another copy of the same pieces in " North Country Ballads," Miscellanea Curiosa, Abbotsford Library.
Sharpe, p. 15. *Burden* ¹,³. of it.

Burden ⁸. you call : of it.   ⁴. lies alone O.
1⁸. at it grows.   2². upon a.   2⁴. He 's not.
4¹. It 's sure.   6⁸. good witness.
7⁸. Said, Had I been the lady of Errol.
7⁴. of such.   8⁸. And he gave her an.
10¹. lien down.   10². And a.   12¹. Take home.
12². take.   12⁸. cannot please her.
Scott.   7⁴. O come.   12⁴. No can.

232. Richie Story.

P. 292 b, 2d paragraph, first line. Say : L. F., a
daughter of John, third Earl.
3d paragraph.   Say : Lord John Fleming was created Earl of Wigton, Lord Fleming of Biggar and
Cumbernauld, by letters patent dated 19th March, 1606.
Hunter (2d ed.), p. 547.
293.   **B**, as it stands in " The Old Lady's Collection," No 21.

1 Comarnad it is a very bonny place,
   An ther is ladys three, madam,
Bat the farest an rarest of them a'
   Has marred Richerd Storry.

2 ' O hear is a letter to ye, madam,
   Hear is a letter to ye, madam ;
The Earl of Hume, that galant knight,
   Is faln in love we you, madam.

3 ' Ther is a letter to you, madam,
   [Ther is a letter to you, madam ;]
The Eearl of Hume, that galant knight,
   Disers to be yer servant trou, madam.'

4 ' I ill haa nan of his letters, Richerd,
   I ill hae nane of his letters, [Richerd,]
I have voued, an I ill keep it trou,
   I ill marry nane bat ye, Richie.'

5 ' Say na saa to me, lady,
   Sai na saie to me, lady,
For I ha nether lands nor rents
   For to manten ye on, lady.'

6 ' Hunten Tour an Tillebarn,
   The house of Athell is mine, Richë,
An ye sall haa them a',
   Fan ever ye inclen, Richë.

7 ' For we will gaa to sea, Richë,
   I ill sitt on the deak, Richë,
I ill be yer servant air an lait,
   Att any houre ye laek, [Richë.] '

8 ' O manie ye be sad, sister,
   An mennie ye be sorry, Nelly,
To live the has of bony Comernid,
   An follou Richert Storry ? '

9 ' O fatt neads I be sad, sister,
   Or fou cane I be sorry, Anna ?
A bony lad is my delit,
   An my lot has been laid afore me.'

10 As she wen[t] up the Parliment Closs,
   We her lassed shene so fine,
Monny an bad the lady good day,
   But fue thought she was Richert's lady.

11 As she went up the Parliment Closs,
   We her laised shon so fine,
Monny an halled that gay lady,
   But fue halled Richerd Storry.

*The first, second, and fourth verse, perhaps, certainly
the second and fourth, should have the trochaic ending
which we find in stanzas 2, 5. It may have been supplied
ad libitum.*
296.   **F a.** Preserved in a small MS. volume with the
title " Songs " on the cover, entirely in Sharpe's handwriting, p. 27.
297.   **I.** A stanza from the authority of Nannie
Blake, an old servant at Peebles : Robert Chambers, in
Sharpe's Ballad Book, 1880, p. 131.

' Fair Rosewoodie is a' my ain,
   My father left it to me so lately ;
Gin ye 'll consent to be my ain,
   I 'll gie ye 't a', my Ritchie Storie.'

235. The Earl of Aboyne.

P. 314.   **C**. Here given as it stands in " The Old
Lady's Collection," No 8.

1 The Earl of Aboyn he 's carrlis an kind,
   An he is nou come frae Lonon ;
He sent his man him befor,
   To tell of his hame-coming.

2 First she called on her chambermad,
   Sayn on Jeanie, her gentelwoman :
' Bring me a glass of the best claret wine,
   To drink my good lord's well-hame-coming.

3 ' My sarvants all, be ready att a call,
   . . . . . .
   . . . . . .
   For the Lord of Aboy[n] is coming.

4 ' My cooks all, be ready at a [c]all,
   . . . . . .
We the very best of meatt,
   For the Lord of Aboyn is coming.

5 ' My maids all, be ready at a call,
   . . . . . .
The rooms we the best all to be drest,
   For the Lord of Aboyn is coming.'

6 She did her to the closs to take him from his hors,
  An she welcomed him fra London :

  . . . .
  ' Yer welcome, my gued lord, fra London ! '

7 ' An I be saie welcom,' he says,
  ' Ye 'll kiss me for my coming,
  For the morn sud ha ben my weding-day
  Gif I had stayed att London.'

8 She turned her about we a disdanfull look,
  O dear, she was a pritty woman !
  ' Gin the morn sud ha ben yer weding-day,
  Ye may kiss yer houers at London.'

9 . . . .
  ' So I shall, madam, an ye 's ha na mare to say,
  For I ill dine we the markes of Huntly.'

10 She did her to his servant-man,
   I wat they caed him Peater Gordon :
   ' Ye will ask my good lord if he will late me
   We him a singel mille to ride [to London].'

11 ' You ned not, madam, ...
   I haae asked him already ;
   He will not lett you a singel mille ride,
   For he is to dine we the markes of Huntly.'

12 She called on her chamber-maid,
   Sine on Jean, her gentelwoman :
   ' Ye make my bed an tay up my head,
   Vou 's me for his hear coming ! '

13 She lived a year an day, we mucell grife an wae,
   The docters were we her dealing ;
   Withen a crak, her heart it brack,
   An the letters they went to London.

14 He gae the table we his foot,
   An caped it we his knee,
   Gared silver cup an easer dish
   In flinders flie.

15 . . . .
   ' I rader I had lost a' the lans of Aboyne
   Or I had lost bonny Margrat Irven.'

16 He called on his best servang-man,
   I wat they [caed] him Piter Gordon :
   ' Ye gett our hosses sadled we speed,
   Vou 's me for our hear coming !

17 ' . . . .
   For we 'll a' be in black, fra the hose to the hat,
   Vou 's me for bonny Margrat Irvieen !

18 ' We must to the North, to burry her corps,
   Aless for our hear coming !
   I rather I had lost a' the lands of Aboyn
   Or I had lost bonny Marg[ra]t Irvien ! '

1¹. carliss : *perhaps* courtis.   8². pritty : *doubtful.*

318–20.   Copies of **G**, **I**, **J**, were sent by Motherwell to C. K. Sharpe, in a letter dated December 6, 1824. In all the transcripts there are some slight changes of the MS. text, such as Motherwell was quite in the way of making.   To **I** he added the following lines, which are found substantially in **J**.   They may have been subsequently recollected by the reciter of **I**.

10 She has called her servant-maid,
   And Jean, her gentlewoman :
   ' Go make me a bed and lay me down,
   I 'm as sick as any woman.'

11 Word has to new London gane,
   To the tavern where he was dining ;
   He gave such a rap on the table where he sat
   Made all the house to wonder.

12 . . . .
   ' I would rather hae lost a' the lands o Aboyne
   Or I 'd lost my Peggy Irvine ! '

11¹. *Motherwell suggests :* Word has now to.

321.   Findlay MSS, I, 120.   ' The Yerle o Aboyne,' from Mrs Main, Inchmarlo, Kincardineshire.

1 The Yerle o Aboyne 's to London gane,
  He met in wi a temptin woman ;
  For she sat an sang an birld at the wine,
  An she wadna lat him hame fae Lunon.

  * * * * * * * *

2 ' My cook-maids a', be well in ca,
  Had pots an pans a boilin,
  Wi the roast an the boil,
  To attend my guid lord's comin.'

3 She steppit sae neatly oot the way,
  She gaed, she went an met him :
  ' Ye 're welcome home, my ain guid lord,
  You 'r thrice weelcome fae Lunon.'

4 ' An I be welcome home,' he says,
  ' Ye 'll kiss me for my comin,
  For this very day I 'd been wedded to a maid
  Gin I 'd staid langer in Lunon.'

5 She turnd her about wi a sorrowfu look,
  Such a sorry an angry woman !
  ' An the letters be true I receivd last frae you,
  Gae kiss your whores in Lunon.'

6 Haem she gaed frae . . . .

   .   .   .   .   .

   But wi a crack her heart did brak,

7 Fifty letters seald wi black,
   An they are on to Lunon,
   An when he lookd the letters upon
   He says, O wae 's me for my pairtin !

*   *   *   *   *   *

8 When he cam to bonny Aboyne,
   He thocht that she was sleepin,
   But when he drew the sma curtain by
   Then he fell oot a weepin.

9 ' O dear ! is she dead ? and a wow ! is she dead ?
   Ah, woe 's me for our pairtin !
   I rather had lost a' the lands o Aboyne
   Or I 'd pairted wi Peggie Irvine.

*   *   *   *   *   *

10 ' A' my friends did me disdain
   For marryin the name o Irvine.'

The first stanza is also given thus (p. 121):

   The Earl of Aboyne he 's courtous an kin,
   He 's kin to every woman ;
   He 's kind when he comes, an he 's kind when he
      gangs,
   But he never brings his lady to London.

From Miss Butchart, Arbroath, p. 146.

1 The Earl o Aboyne 's to London gane,
   An taen Duke Huntly wi him,

*   *   *   *   *   *

2 She called on Jack, her gentleman,
   An Jean, her gentlewoman :
   ' Gae dress my fair body in some finer dress,
   For the Earl o Aboyne is comin.'

*   *   *   *   *   *

3 She 's gaen doun by yon burnside,
   An there she saw him comin :
   ' Ye 're welcome, welcome, Earl o Aboyne,
   Ye 're welcome hame frae Lunon.

*   *   *   *   *   *

4 ' Gae back, gae back then, Earl o Aboyne,
   Nae thanks to you for comin ;
   Gin tomorrow wad hae been your fair weddin-day,
   Gae kiss your dames in Lunon.'

236. The Laird o Drum.

P. 324. **B**, as it stands in " The Old Lady's Collection," No 16, ' The Lard of Drum.'

1 Ther was a knigh[t],
   An a gillan knight was he,
   An he 's faein in love we his shiperd's daughter,

   .   .   .   .   .

2 .   .   .   .   .
   He could nether gang nor ride;
   He fell so deap in her fancy
   Till his nose began to blead.

3 ' Bonny may, an bra may,
   Canno ye on me rue?
   By a' the meads I ever saa,
   Ther is nane I lou by you.

4 ' Ye 'r a shepherd's ae dother,
   An I am a barron's son,
   An gratt is the pleasur I wad haa
   To see you gaa out an in, may.'

5 ' I am a shiperd's ae dother,
   An ye 'r a barron's son,
   An ther is ne pleasur I could ha
   To see you gae out nor in.

6 ' .   .   .   .   .

   .   .   .   .   .
   For I widne gee the fancey of my bonny love
   For ne love nor favour of you, sir.'

7 ' Bonny may, an bra may,
   Canna ye on me rue?
   By a' the maids I ever saa,
   Ther is nane I loie but you.'

8 ' Lay not your love on me,' she says,
   ' Lay not your love on me,
   For I am our lake to be yer bride,
   An you[r] quen I ell never be.

9 ' For I will wear nane of your silks,
   Nor nean of yer scarlet clase ;
   For the hue of the eue sall be my goun,
   An I will goo as I pleas.'

10 ' .   .   .   .   .

   .   .   .   .   .
   Ye 'r na our lake to be my bride,
   An my quien ye 's never be.

11 ' Bonney may, an bra may,
   Winnë ye on me rue?
   By a' the may[s] I see,
   Ther is nane I loe but you, may.'

12 ' If ye ha faen sae deap in my fancy
　　Ye cane nether gang nor rid,
　　Ye take me to the middel of the ring,
　　An bear me guid comp[a]ny.'

13 He has tane her by the milk-whit hand
　　An led her thro hase an bours :
　　' Ye 'r the jule of my heart,
　　An a' I have is yours.'

14 He tuke her by the milk-whit hand
　　An led her out an in :
　　' Ye 'r the jule of my heart,
　　My d[ea]r, ye 'r welcom in.'

15 Out spak his brother John,
　　' Brother, ye haa don grate wrong ;
　　Ye ha marred a wife this night
　　Discredet to all yer kin.'

16 ' Hold yer toung, my brother John,
　　For I hae don ne wrang,
　　For I ha marred a wife to wine,
　　An ye ha ane to spend.'

　　May, 4⁴, 11⁴, sir, 6⁴, *are added for singing as* O *is
　　in other copies, and either one of these, or* O,
　　would naturally be appended in the other stanzas.
　　8¹. Lay not fancyour love on me. *The next line
　　shows that* fanc *was written by mistake.*

325. Findlay's MS., p. 13, has five stanzas of the
ballad, from the recitation of a woman in Kincardineshire. The five stanzas are very nearly the same as
D 1, 2, 4, 5, 6¹,², with the matter-of-fact conclusion,
6³,⁴,

　　An a' body seemed to be content,
　　And she was at his will.

A stanza from another version is given at the same
place which resembles **E** 8 :

　　She canna wash your china cups,
　　Nor dress you a dish o tea, O
　　But weel can she milk baith cow and ewe,
　　Wi her cogie at her knee. O

I have received nearly the same from Mr Walker of
Aberdeen as sung by John Walker, crofter, Portlethen,
1893.

　　Yer china cups I canna wash,
　　Nor cook a cup o tea, O
　　But weel can I milk the cowes and the ewes,
　　Wi the cogie on my knee. O

237. The Duke of Gordon's Daughter.

P. 332. There is a copy in a collection of folio
sheet ballads, British Museum, 1346. m. 8, with the
date September 8th, 1775, at the end ; earlier, therefore, than any of those I had before me excepting **a,**
and worth collating.

　　1⁴. they *wanting.*　2⁴, 3⁴. she did.　3². the *wanting.*
　　3³. Jean 's fallen in.　4⁴. mony.　5³. with *wanting.*
　　5⁴. Jeanny.　6⁴. she 's no.
　　7³. Lady Jean 's fallen in love with.
　　7⁴. she would.　8². upon yon.　8³. he did.
　　8⁴. a training of.　9¹. O woe be.
　　9². And *wanting :* death shall you.　9⁴. shalt thou.
　　10¹. Duke of.　10⁴. he did such a thing.
　　11³. him put off his gold lace.　11⁴. the *wanting.*
　　13⁴. will I.　14². a yer but only three.
　　14³. babe on.　15¹. O I 'm weary with.
　　16 *comes before* 15.
　　16¹. O I am weary wandering.　16². think it lang.
　　17³. sheen : all *wanting.*　17⁴. she could.
　　18, 19, *wanting.*　20¹. I was : glen of Foudland.
　　20⁴. either house or sheen.
　　21¹. When they : to bonny C. G.　21³. out *wanting.*
　　22¹. O *wanting :* dear Jeannie G.
　　22². welcome dear.　22⁴. Captain *wanting.*
　　23¹. over the.　23². As *wanting.*　24¹. ye.
　　25¹. what means this.　25³. are all dead.
　　26². drink, be jovial.　27³. out with *wanting.*
　　28¹. pretty *wanting.*　28³. can enter my.
　　30–32 *wanting.*　33². you 're welcome dear to me.
　　33³. You 're welcome, bonny Jeanny Gordon.
　　33⁴. With my young family.

238. Glenlogie, or, Jean o Bethelnie.

P. 346. **I b.** A copy of this version has been
found at Abbotsford, in a portfolio labelled ' The
Rever's Wedding and other important papers.' There
are a few differences of reading.

　　In the stanza after 1, *line* 3, be richer, *line* 4, maun
　　hae.
　　2¹. Oh whare.　2²,⁴. gang : again soon.
　　3¹. he cam : gae.　3². gae.　3³. my maister's.
　　3⁴. stop till.　5¹. Gae : gar.　5³. lang or ere.
　　5⁴. O *wanting.*　6³. quo she.　7². But *wanting.*

239. Lord Saltoun and Auchanachie.

P. 349. **A b.** Now collated with a MS. of Charles
Kirkpatrick Sharpe's and another copy of the same
pieces in " North Country Ballads," Miscellanea Curiosa, Abbotsford Library. Stanzas mostly of four lines.

　　Sharpe, p. 10.　1¹. stepping on.　1². ye 're.
　　2¹. caren.　2². Achanachie (*and always*).
　　3¹. not take ; it *wanting.*　3². and he 's thrawn.
　　4¹. I 'm bown : you.　4². not.
　　5². out *wanting :* and they cutit.　7¹. came.
　　8¹. fleed.　8². Jeanie is.

350. **B c.** From "The Old Lady's Collection,"
No 29. We have here Gordon of Auchanachie, though
the scene is in Buchan.

1 Buchan is bonny an ther lays my love,
  My fancë is fixed on him, it winnë remove;
  [It winnë remove] for a' I cane dee,
  Achanacë Gordon is my love an sall be.

2 Ben came her father, steps on the floor,
  Says, Jeanie, ye 'r acting the part of a hour;
  Ye 'r leaking ane that cares na for ye;
  Wed Salton, an latt Achenecy be.

3 'Achainace Gordon is a pritty man,
  Bat Acchanace Gordon has na free land;
  For his land is laying wast, an his castell faaen
    doun,
  So ye man take Salton, latt Achennecy be.'

4 'My friends may case me we Salton to wed,
  Bat my friends sall na case me we him to bed;
  I ill never bear to him dother nor sin till the day
    I sall deei,
  For Achannace Gordon is my love an sall be.'

5 Her friends they have cassed her we Salton to wed,
  Bat they never got her we him to bed;
  She never bare dother nor sin till the day that she
    dead deei,
  For Achainace Gordon was her love and sud be.

6 'Ye that are her madins, ye take aff her goun,
  An I will infeft her in five thousand pound;
  She sall werr silk till her heel and goud till her
    kneee,
  An she man forget him young Achanice.'

7 'Ye that are my madins sanna take aff my goon,
  Nor will I be infefted in five thousand pound;
  I winnë wer goud on my head nor silk to my knee,
  Nor will I forsake young Achanice.'

8 'Ye that are her madins bring her to my bed,
  The bed is made ready an the shits doun spread;
  She sall lay in her bed till tuall in the day,
  An sin forget him young Achanace.'

9 'Ye that are my madins sanna ha me to his bed,
  Tho the bed be made ready an the shits doun
    spread;
  Nor will I lay in his bed till tuall of the day,
  Nor forsake him young Achanicy.

10 'For rather then have wedded Salton to wear goud
    to my knee,
  I rather wedded Achanicy tralled fait fish fraa the
    sea;
  Or I had weded Salton an wore robes of read,
  I rader wead Achanace, we him begg my b[r]ead.'

11 Achanicy Gordon came fra the sea,
  We a gallant regment an brave companie;
  He sought out his Jeanie we doll an we care,
  An Achanice Gordon is leak to dispear.

12 Doun came her handmaid, wringen her hands:
  'Alass for your staying sa lang in strang lands!
  For Jeanie is marred, an nou she is dead.
  Alass for your staying sae lang on the flood!'

13 . . . .
  'Take me to the room far my love lays in;'
  He has kessed her comly lips, they wer paill an
    wan,
  An he dyed for his Jeanie that very same night.

1^3. came. 5^3. she deaded. 12^2. strying.
12^4. on *doubtful*.

240. The Rantin Laddie.

P. 352. **B** as it stands in "The Old Lady's Collection," No 3, 'The Rantan Laddy.'

1 'Aft have I played att the cards an the dice,
  They wer so very entisen,
  But this is a sad an a sorofull seat,
  To see my apron riseng.

2 'Aft ha I plad att the cards an the dice,
  For love of my laddy,
  Bat nou I man sitt in my father's kittchë-nouk,
  An roke my baby.

3 'Bat gin I had an of my father's servens,
  For he has so mony,
  That wad gaa to the woods of Glentaner
  We a letter to the ranten laddy!'

4 'Hear am I, an of your father's servants,
  For he has so many,
  That will gaa to the woods of Glentaner
  We a letter to the ranten laddy.'

5 'Fan ye gee to Aboyn,
  To the woods of Glentaner sie bonny,
  We yer hat in yer hand, gee a bou to the grond,
  In the presenc[e] of the ranten laddy.'

6 Fan he gad to Aboyn,
  To the woods of Glentaner saae bonny,
  We his hat in his han, he gied a bou to the grond,
  In the preasence of the ranten laddy.

7 Fan he louked the letter on,
  Saa loud as he was laughing;
  Bat or he read it to an end
  The tears they came doun raping.

8 'O faa is this, or faa is that,
　　Has ben so ill to my Meggie?

. 　 . 　 . 　 . 　 . 　 . 　 .

　　. 　 . 　 . 　 . 　 . 　 .

9 'Bat ye gett four-an-tuinty milk-whit steads,
　　We an E an O me!
An as monny gay ladys to ride them on,
　　To gaa an bring hame my Meggie.

10 'Ye gett four-an-tuinty berrie-broun steeds,
　　We an E an O an O me!
An as mony knights to ride them one,
　　To gaa an bring hame my Meggie.'

11 Ye lasses a', war ever ye be,
　　An ye match we ony of our Deesid ladds,
Ye 'll happy be, ye 'll happy be,
　　For they ar frank an kin.

12 The 'r frank an kin
　　The 'r free,
An ye match we ony of our Deesid ladds,
　　Ye 'll happy be.

9², 10². ome. 9³. laddys.

In Findlay's MSS, I, 84 is this stanza, = B 5, C 12,
D 4 :

　　' When ye come to Aboyne's yetts,
　　　Aboyne's yetts they shine clearly,
　　Ye 'll tak aff your hat, gie a bow wi your knee,
　　　Gie the letter to my rantin laddie.'

241. The Baron o Leys.

P. 355. Findlay's MSS, I, 85, gives the first stanza
thus (from Mrs Main, Inchmarlo, Kincardineshire).

　　The baron o Leys is to London gane,
　　　All in a mornin early ;
　　He 's shod his horse wi siller sheen,
　　　An shown them a' his folly.

245. Young Allan.

376 b, last paragraph. Talking Ships. See Liebrecht, Zur Volkskunde, p. 365 f., apropos of Árnason's Skipamál, Þjoðsögur, II, 8. Árnason notes two
talking ships in Flóamanna Saga, c. 36, and Liebrecht
the Argo.
377. A. The original, altered in places by Skeat,
stands as follows in "The Old Lady's Collection,"
where it is No 4.

1 Aa the skippers of merry Lothen,
　　As they sat att the wine,

Ther fell a rosin them among,
　　An it was in an unhappy time.

2 Some of them roused ther haks,
　　An some of them ther hounds,
An some of them ther gay ladys,
　　Trood neat on the plain :
Young Allan he roused his comely coug,
　　That lay upon the strand.

3 'I haa as good a ship this day
　　As ever sailled our seas,
Except it be the Burges Black,
　　Bat an the Small Cordvine,
The comly coug of Dornisdall ;
　　We sall lay that three bay in time.'

4 Out spak a littel boy,
　　Just att Young Allan's knee,
'Ye lie, ye lie, ye Young Allan,
　　Sae loud as I hear ye lie.

5 'For my master has a littel boat
　　Will sail thris as well as thin ;
For she 'll come in att your formast
　　An gee out att yer forlee,
An nine times in a winter night
　　She 'll take the wine fra the.

6 'O fatt will ye wade, ye Young Allan,
　　Or fatt will ye wad we me ? '
'I ill wad my head agenst yer land,
　　Till I gett more monie.'

7 They hed na sailed a legg, [a legg,]
　　A legg bat bairiy three,
Till throug an throu ther bonny ship
　　They saa the green wall sea.

8 They had na sailled a leag, [a leag,]
　　A leag bat barly fave,
Till through en throu ther bonny ship
　　They saa the green wall wave.

9 He gied up to the tapmast,
　　To see fat he coud see,
An ther he saa the Burges Black,
　　Bat an the Small Cordvine,
The comly coug of Dornasdell ;
　　The three was rent in nine.

10 Young Allan he grat, an he wrang his hans,
　　An he kent na fat till dee :
'The win is loud, an the waves is prood,
　　An we will a' sink in the sea.

11 'Bat gin I cod gett a bonny boy
　　To tak my healm in han,
. 　 . 　 . 　 . 　 that wad bring
　　My bonny ship safe to lan,

12 'He sud gett the tua part of my goud,
 An the therd part of my lan,
 An gin me wine safe to shor
  He sud gett my daughter Ann.'

13 'Hear am I, a bonny boy
 That will take yer helm in han,
 . . . . an will bring
  Your bonny ship safe to land.

14 'Ye take four-an-twenty fether-beds,
 An ye lay the bonny ship roun,
 An as much of the good cannis
  As make her hell an soun.'

15 They took four-an-twenty fether-beds,
 An laid the bonny ship roun,
 An as much of the good canies
  As made her hell an soun.

16 'Spring up, my bony ship,
 An goud sall be yer hair!'
 Fan the bonny ship hard of that,
 Att goud sud be her hire,
 She sprang as fast fra the sate water
  As the spark dis frae the fire.

17 'Spring up, my bonny ship,
 An goud sall be yer fee!'
 An fan the bonny ship hard of that,
 Goud was to be her fee,
 She sprang as fast fra the sat water
  As the life dos fra the tree.

18 The salors stans on the shore-sid,
 We ther ill-bukled shen :
 'Thanks to God an our gued master
  That ever we came to land!'

19 'Far is the bonny boy
 That took my healm in hand?
 . . . . that brought
  My bonny ship safe to land?

20 'He 's gett the twa part of my goud,
 The therd part of my lan,
 An since we ha wone safe to shore
  He 's gett my doughter Ann.'

21 'Hear am I, the bonny boy
 That took yer healm in han,
 That brought yer bonny ship,
  An brought her safe to lan.

22 'I winnë ha the tua part of yer goud,
 Nor the therd part of yer lan,
 Bat since we ha wine safe to shor
  I will wed yer daugter Ann.'

23 Fortey ships went to the sea,
 Forty ships an five,
 An ther came never on back
  Bat Young Allan alive.

9⁵. comly cord. 12⁴, 20⁴, 22⁴. Anna.
17²,⁴. hire *for* fee (*caught from* 16).
23². ane *changed to* Five.
Written without division into stanzas or verses.

246. Redesdale and Wise William.

P. 383. There is a copy in C. K. Sharpe's "second collection" which is substantially the same as **A**. The variations here follow:

A b. 1². Was. 1³. There was a praising.
 1⁴. In an unhappy.
 2¹. For some ones they did praise.
 2⁴. And *wanting*. 3¹. That out did speak.
 3³. Says, I saw never a.
 3⁵. But what I would her favour gain.
 3⁶. With one blink of. 3⁶, 4⁶. eye.
 4¹. out did speak. 4². spoke.
 4⁵. Whose favour you would never gain. 5¹. you.
 After 5 : 'That is too good a wager, William,
   Upon a woman's mind,
    It is to[o] good a wager Wil[lia]m,
   I 'm very sure you 'l tyne.'
 6¹. So. 6³. he could neither go. 6⁴. Nor no.
 7¹. has wrote a broad. 7³. his only.
 8¹. read the letter over. 8². She lookëd.
 8⁴. enough. 9³. she saw. 9⁴. riding throw.
 10¹. Says *wanting :* Come hitherward.
 10³. here does come. 10⁴. For injury to me.
 11¹. ˙Come down, come down, said Reedesdale.
 11². One sight of you I 'll see. 11³. my gate.
 12, 13, *wanting.*

14 'Come down, come down, O lady fair,
 One sight of you I 'll see,
 And bony is the rings of gold
  That I will give to thee.'

15 'If you have boney rings of gold,
 O mine is bony tee ;
 Go from my gate now, Reedesdale,
  For me you will not see.'

16 'Come down, come down, O lady fair,
 One sight of you I 'll see,
 And boney is the bowers and halls
  That I will give to the.'

17 'If you have boney bowers and halls,
 I have bowers and halls the same;
 Go from my gate now, Reedesdale,
  For down I will not come.'

18–21 *wanting.* 22[1]. O lady. 22[3]. Or then.
22[4]. Since. 23[1]. So he has set that bower.
23[2]. the house it took. 24 *wanting.*

25 'Come hitherward,' the lady cried,
'My maidens all, to me;
For throw the smoak and throw the heat,
All throw it we must be.'

26[1]. their mantles.
26[3]. And throw the smoak and throw the heat.
26[4]. They throw it all did win.
27[1]. had all got safely out. 27[2]. able for.
27[3]. Sent some of them to.
28[2]. Have not I gaind.

The Danish ballad Væddemaalet,' Grundtvig, No
224, spoken of under 'The Twa Knights,' ought to
have been noticed here also.

252. The Kitchie Boy.

P. 401. **A** as it stands in "The Old Lady's Collection," No 20.

1 Ther was a lady fair an rear,
A lady of birth an fame,
She loyed her father's kittchen-boy,
The greater was her shame.

2 She coud never her love revell,
Nor to him take,
Bat in the forests weed an brade,
Far they wer wont to wake.

3 It fell ance apon a day
Her father went fra home,
An she sent for the kitchë-boy
Into her room.

4 'Canna ye fancë me, Willie?
Cannie ye fancë me?
By a' the lords I ever seed,
Ther is nane I cane loie bat ye.'

5 'O latt ne this be kent, lady,
O lat ne this be knouen,
For in yer father got word of this,
I vou he wad gare me die.'

6 'Yer life sall na be tane, Willie,
Yer life sall na be tean;
I rader loss my ain heart-blead
Or thy body gat wrang.'

7 We her mery fair spiches
She made the boy bold,
Till he began to kiss an clap,
An on his love lay hold.

8 They hadne kissed an love-claped,
As lovers fan they meatt,
. . . .
. . . . . .

9 'The master-cook he will on me call,
An ansured he man be;
In it war kent I war in bour we the,
I fear they woud gar me diei.'

10 'The master-cook may on ye call,
But ansured he will never be,
For I haa thrie coffers fue of goud,
Yer eyen did never see.

11 'An I will buld a bony ship for my love,
An sett her to the seea,
An saill she east, or saill she west,
The ship sall be fair to see.'

12 She has buld a bonny ship,
An sett her to the sea;
The top-masts was of the read goud,
The saill of taffety.

13 She gaie him a gay gold ring,
. . . .
To mind him on a gay lady
That ance bair love to him.

14 The day was fair, the ship was rair,
Fan that suan sett to sea;
Fan that day tuall-month came an gade,
Att London landed he.

15 A lady louked our castell-wa,
Beheld the day gaa doun,
An she beheld that bonny ship,
Came halling to the toun.

16 'Come hear, come hear, my mairës a',
Ye see na fat I see;
The bonnest ship is coming to land
Yer eyen did ever see.

17 'Ye busk ye, busk ye, my marrës a',
Ye busk ye unco fine,
Till I gaa doun to yon shore-side
To invite yon squar to dine.

18 'O ye come up, ye gay young squar,
An take we me a dine;
Ye sall eatt of the gued white lofe,
An drink the claret wine.'

19 'I thank ye for yer bread,
I thank ye for yer wine,
I thank ye for yer courticë,
Bat indeed I hanna time.'

20 ‘ Canna ye fancë me ? ’ she says,
   ‘ Cannie ye fancë me ?
Bay a’ the lords an lairds I see,
   Ther is nane I fancë bat ye.’

21 ‘ They are farr awa fra me,’ he says,
   ‘ The ’r farr ayont the sea,
That has my heart an hand,
   An my love ay sall be.’

22 ‘ Hear is a gued gould ring,
   .   .   .   .   .
It will mind ye on a gay lady
   That ance bare love to ye.’

23 ‘ I haa a ring on my finger
   I lee thrice as well as thine,
Tho yours war of the gued read goud,
   An mine bat simpell tin.’

24 The day was fair, the ship was rair,
   Fan that squar sett to sea ;
Fan that day tuall-month came an gaid,
   Att hame again landed he.

25 The lady’s father louked over castell-wa,
   Beheld the day gaa doun,
An he beheld that bonny ship
   Come halling to the toun.

26 ‘ Come hear, my a dother,
   Ye see na fat I see ;
The bonnest ship is coming to land
   My eyen did ever see.

27 ‘ Ye busk ye, my dother,
   Ye busk ye unco fine,
An I ill gai doun to yon shore-side
   An invite yon squer to dine :
I wad gie a’ my reants
   To haa ye marrëd to him.’

28 ‘ They ar farr awa fra me,’ she says,
   ‘ The ’r far ayont the sea,
That has my heart an han,
   An my love ay sall be.’

29 ‘ O will ye come, ye gay hine squar,
   An take we me a dine ?
Ye sall eat of the gued fait bread
   An drink the claret wine.’

30 ‘ I thank ye for yer bread,
   I thank ye for your wine,
I thank ye for your courtisy,
   For indeed I haa na grait time.’

31 ‘ O cannie ye fancë me ? ’ [he says,
   ‘ Cannie ye fancë me ?]

By a’ the ladys I ever did see,
   Ther is nain I lue bat ye.’

32 ‘ They are farr awa fra me,’ she says,
   They are farr ayont the sea,
That has my heart an han,
   An my love ay sall be.’

33 ‘ Hear it is, a gay goud ring,
   .   .   .   .   .
It will mind ye on a gay hin chill
   That ance bare love to ye.’

34 ‘ O gatt ye that ring on the sea saling ?
   Or gat ye it on the sand ?
Or gat ye it on the shore laying,
   On a drouned man’s hand ? ’

35 ‘ I got na it on the sea saling,
   I got na it on the sand,
Bat I gat it on the shore laying,
   On a drouned man’s hand.

36 ‘ O bonny was his chike,
   And lovely was his face ! ’
‘ Alass,’ says she, ‘ it is my true-love Willie,
   .   .   .   .’

37 He turned him rond about,
   An suitly could he smill ;
She turned her round, says, My love Willie,
   Hou could ye me biggeall ?

38 ‘ A prist, a prist,’ the old man crayed,
   ‘ Latt this tua marrëd be : ’
Bat lettel did the old man keen
   It was his ain kittchen-boy.

4⁴. I came. 7⁴. her love. 28². seas. 35³. laiying.

257. Burd Isabel and Earl Patrick.

P. 418 b, 3d paragraph. Say : **A** 7 (nearly) occurs in No 91, **B** 7, II, 313, and something similar in other places (as No 91, **A** 5, 6, **D** 7, No 92, **B** 17).

422. **C.** There is another copy of this version in C. K. Sharpe’s “ second collection,” with the following variations.

b. 1¹. Take warning, all ye maidens fair.
   2². father’s heir. 2⁴. she did rue full sair.
   3¹. Says, We. 3². Which. 3³. Go ye.
   4¹. He hied him to the.
   4². As fast as he could gang. 4³. And he brought.
   4⁴. sign with.

5. And long before the sun went down
   Bird Isabeal bore his son,

And she has called him Patrick,
As it was his father's name.

6², 7². Right far. 6³. parents was.
6⁴. Had little gear. 7⁴. And dowrey.

8. Now it fell out up on a time
His wedding day was come,
And all his friends invited were,
His bride to welcome home.

While every one engaged was
That all should ready be,
He hied him to his great-grand aunt,
She was a lady free.

9¹. Says, Go for me this. 9². O do go it for me.
9⁴. I 'll do as much. 10¹. Go bring to.
10². Dress him in silk.
10³. For if he lives and bruiks his life.
10⁴. He is to heir my.
11¹. hailing through the closs. 12¹. I am come.
12². Dress him in silk. 12³. lives.
13¹, 14¹. O was. 13³. that bairn from my foot.
14². Altho in station high.
14³. Durst take that bairn from.
15¹,². Now she got frowning throw the closs,
And frowning on the floor.
15⁴. And he.
16¹,². O this was the worst errand, Patrick,
That ever I went for the.
16³. Bird Isabeal.
17¹,². He looked right surprised like,
Amazed like looked he.
17⁴. She was never.
18¹. And he went hailing throw the closs.
20¹, 21¹. I say.
20³. Dare take that bairn from my foot.
21². Altho in station high. 21³. Dare take that.
22⁴. You wont get.

259. Lord Thomas Stuart.

P. 425. Found in a MS. of Charles Kirkpatrick
Sharpe, and in "North Country Ballads," Miscellanea
Curiosa, Abbotsford Library, which is another copy of
the same pieces.

Sharpe, p. 5. 1¹. Thomas Steuart he.
1². mukle mean (an erasure before mean).
1³. the coat. 3¹. wemen's wits is. 4¹. steeds was.
5³. so sick. 6¹. no leech.
7¹. leeches is come and leeches is gone. 7². I am.
9³. lands and. 10³. got all my lands.
11¹. in their. 11². could not. 11³. leesh.
13³. And as.
14³. I fear it may be mony unco lord.
14⁴. from the. 15³. I fear it is mony unco lord.
With variations of spelling not noted.

Scott (*as above, except*) 1². mickle land : land *was
perhaps the word which is blotted out in Sharpe.*
3¹. women's.

263. The New-Slain Knight.

P. 434 b. Translated also by Gerhard, p. 168.

———◆———

VOL. V.

266. John Thomson and the Turk.

P. 3 b. There may be added another Little-Russian
story communicated to me in translation by Professor
Wollner : Ethnographic Survey, etc. (Etnografičeskoe
Obozrěnie, etc.) Moscow, 1893, V, 104.

A tsar and a tsarina, when dying, charged their son
Soliman not to marry a woman older than himself.
This, however, he did, and his wife hated him, and one
day, when he was hunting, went off to her brother,
ordering the servants to say that she had died. This
report the servants duly made, but Soliman knew that
his wife had gone to her brother, and he felt the loss
so much that he could not keep away from her. Meeting a boy in tattered clothes, he changed with him,
gave the boy everything he had on except his ring, and
put on rags, to play the beggar. He proceeded to the
brother's house, and seeing his wife sitting at a window, held out his hand, on which his ring was sparkling, and asked an alms. His wife knew him at once
by the ring, and bade him come in. 'Who are you?'
she asked. 'Once I was a tsar,' he said, 'but my wife
died, and I became a beggar.' At this point the
brother arrived on the scene. The woman told Soliman to lie down on the threshold; he did so, and she
sat down on him. When her brother came in she said,
'Guess what I am sitting on.' He answered, 'On the
threshold.' 'Wrong,' said she; 'on Tsar Soliman.' 'If
it is he,' said her brother, 'I will cut his head off.'
But here Soliman suggested that if the brother should
take his head off on the spot, nobody would know that
he had killed a tsar ; whereas if he would build a
three-story gallows and hang Soliman on it, all the
world would see that he had been the death of a tsar
and not of a beggar. So a three-story gallows was
built, and as they were taking Soliman up to the first
stage, he said, Give me a horn, to cheer my heart for
the last time. They gave him a horn and he began to
blow, Quick, quick, dear soldiers, for my death and
end is nigh. A black regiment set out for the place.
Bystanders said, Tsar Soliman, you are up high and
see far : what is the black thing coming along the hill?
'My death, which gleams black in the distance.' Soliman mounted to the second stage and blew his horn

again : Quick, quick, dear soldiers, my death and end
is nigh. He saw a white regiment coming. The
people said, Tsar Soliman, you are high up and see
far: what is that white thing which is coming? My
death, which gleams white in the distance. Then
Soliman mounted to the third stage and blew Quick,
quick, dear soldiers, my death and end is nigh, and he
saw a red regiment coming. The people asked, what
red thing was coming. My death, which gleams red
in the distance.* Then the black regiment came up,
after it the white, and finally the red ; they slew Soliman's wife and her brother, took Soliman down from
the gallows, and rode home.

8. **Danish.** Through the friendly help of Dr. Axel
Olrik I am now in a position to say that there is one
fundamental text **A**, in MSS of 1600 and 1615, from
which all the others are derived. In the seventeenth
century **A** was expanded from forty to eighty-two
couplets. **B**, the original of the expanded copy, is
found in a MS. of 1635; from **B** come the other five
later MS. texts, the flying-sheet of 1719, Kristensen's
fragment, and some recent copies.

A. King David, after betrothing the incomparable
Suol-far, has to go on a cruise. He proposes that the
lady stay with his mother while he is away, but Suol-
far does not like this arrangement. Then, says the
king, I shall bind your finger with gold, so that I can
find you wherever you may be. Hardly is King David
gone, when King Adell rides up. Suol-far is out of
doors, brushing her hair ; Adell asks if he may put a
gold crown on it. If God grants King David to come
home with honor, she will soon have a gold crown to
wear, she says. Adell wishes to hear no more of
David, and asks Suol-far to plight herself to him ; she
will not, she has given her troth to King David. Adell
gives her sleeping potions five, sleeping potions nine ;
she swoons, is taken to be dead, and is buried in the
church. Late in the evening Adell goes to the tomb ;
the effect of the potions having passed off, Suol-far
rises. Adell asks her to go off with him, and after some
tears Suol-far permits him to take her away. It had
been supposed that there was no witness, but a little
page was listening, and when King David came home
the page gave him the bad tidings that King Adell
had carried Suol-far out of the country. David goes
in quest, disguised as a pilgrim. He finds the pair
sitting on a stone, resting their weary legs, and asks an
alms. Adell gives something, and Suol-far is at least
about so to do, for David asks, Is it not the way in this
country to give money with bare hand? whereupon she
pulls off her glove and gives. David (seeing of course
the token on her finger) draws his sword and kills
Adell. He then asks Suol-far how she came to break
her troth. Adell gave her nine drinks, which made
her fall dead to the earth, but, thank God, she had
been kept from sin. David loves her so dearly that he

* In the original, apparently by exchange of like sounding words, My death which is cut short ; that is, I suppose,
prevented or postponed.

is easily satisfied; he orders his wedding, and their
troubles are over.

The flying-sheet of 1719 (in seventy-three couplets)
exhibits some differences. King David marries Sølfehr
before he goes on his expedition, and gives the land
into Adel's care during his absence. After the queen
has fallen aswoon in consequence of the nine drinks,
King Adel sends word to King David that she is dead.
After the interment, Adel remains in the church and
digs up Sølfehr. He addresses her as his dearest; she
refuses to be so called. Adel tells her that David is
dead, and asks her if she will follow him out of the
land. She will follow him very willingly if she may
hear of no grief to King David (whatever that may
mean), and Adel wraps her in a cloak and lifts her on
his gray. There had been watchmen in the church,
and they tell David that Adel is off with Sølfehr.
David has pilgrim's clothes made for himself and many
of his men. While asking alms, David gives the queen
to understand that he is her husband ; then turning to
Adel says, I entrusted my kingdom to you, and did not
look to be deceived. Upon this he orders his troop to
spare none of Adel's men, and himself hews Adel in
pieces. The queen falls at his feet and begs forgiveness. The easy king says, I know the fault was not
thine, lifts her on his horse, and goes home.

The two **Swedish** copies in Stephen's collection
are fragments of eight and of fifteen stanzas. In the
first (from Södermanland), King David having dug up
the coffin and found it empty, disguises himself as a
pilgrim, and when asking an alms of Solfager says,

> Travelled have I by water and land,
> But never took alms from a gloved hand.

' Who are you for a vagabond, that never took alms
from a gloved hand?' says Solfager. ' Never was I a
vagabond, but often have I kissed Solfager's hand,' he
replies. Solfager jumps into his arms, exclaiming, I
never can believe you are my former true-love.

In the other (from Småland), after the abduction of
Solfager, David takes staff in hand and goes to a
strange land. He presents himself where the pair are
sitting at table, and asks an alms. Solfager gives him
alms once and twice, but the beggar is not satisfied.
Needy vagrant, she says, take alms where you can ;
insatiable vagrant, take alms where you get most. I
was no vagrant, he answers, when I put gold rings on
Solfager's arm; I was no vagrant when I slept by Solfager. Her tears come ; she can never believe that he
is David, her true-love. She takes David in her arms.
Praise to God, he cries, that I am still her husband !

271. The Lord of Lorn and the False Steward.

P. 45. Other Russian popular tales in which the
characteristic traits of the group spoken of are well
preserved: Afanasief, V, 178, No 37, ed. 1861, I, 239,

No 67 b, ed. 1873, ' Tsarevitch i yevo Sluga ; ' ' Koro-levitch i yevo Djadka,' the same, VIII, 170, No 18, ed. 1863, I, 233, No 67 a, ed. 1873; Khudyakof, II, 33, No 44, 'Udivitelny Muzhitchek;' the same, III, 143, No 115, ' Muzhitchenko s Kulatchenko.' A tsar's son delivers a prisoner; is condemned to leave the country with a servant (tutor, warden); having been let down into a well to drink, is forced to change positions and clothes with his attendant; serves as herdsman, horse-boy, cook, the attendant aspiring to marry a king's daughter ; destroys three dragons (a seven-headed mon-ster in the second, the fourth defective here) ; marries the princess, the servant or tutor being put to death (baited with dogs in the third, set to work in the stable in the fourth).*

Afanasief, IV, 72, ed. 1873, refers to other Russian versions, and gives, p. 73 f., the Russian form of ' The Goose-Girl.'

46 b. Add: (F.) Ivan Tsarevitch i Martha-Tsar-evna, Afanasief, I, 227, No 21, 1863, I, 246, No 68, 1873. (G.) 'Masenzhni Dzjadok,' the same, V, 185, No 38, 1861, I, 254, No 69, 1873. (H.) 'Kiósut,' Sbornik of the Bulgarian Ministry of Education, III, II, 222. (I.) ' Der Königssohn und der Bartlose,' Hahn, Griechische u. Albanesische Märchen, I, 233, No 37. (1.) The son of a king liberates a prisoner (man of iron and copper, bird with human voice), F, G (stealing the key from his mother, G). (2.) The prince is under the necessity of leaving the country, F-I (is attended by a beardless man, H, I). (3.) To get out of a well has to consent to change clothes and position (with the beardless man, whom he had allowed to join him, or who had been hired as horse-driver), H, I. (4.) King's daughter (fair maid with golden locks, I) aspired to by a low fellow, F, H, I. (5.) Prince figures as stable-boy or scullion, F, G, I, kills three dragons, F, defeats an army, G, accomplishes three tasks, H, I. (6.) Prince marries princess, F, G, H (marries Golden Locks, I), treacherous competitor ban-ished, F, hanged, H, thrown into boiling oil, I.*

274. Our Goodman.

P. 89 f. **French.** Add: La Tradition, VII, 145, Le Quercy.

275. Get up and bar the Door.

P. 95. Add two other Eastern stories : ' The Farmer, his Wife and the Open Door,' in Swynnerton's Indian Nights Entertainment, 1892, p. 14, No 11; ' The Beg-gar and the Five Muffins' (of the second set), Folk-lore in Southern India by Pandet Natêsá Sástrî, p. 277,

---

* I have to thank Professor Wollner for giving me in translation the two tales from Afanasief and a Bulgarian tale presently to be mentioned.

† In the Greek tale, **I**, the prince confides his trouble to

---

No 22, and Tales of the Sun, by Mrs Howard Kings-cote and the same, p. 280, No 25. (Both cited by Mr Clouston, in The Athenæum, March 18, 1893.)

To be Corrected in the Print.

I, 62, 68. **A.** The Jamieson-Brown MS. should be cited by pages, not by folios. This correction applies also to Nos 6 b, 10 **B**, a, 32 a, 34 **B**, a, 35, 53, **A**, **C**, a, 62 **E**, 63 **B**, a, 65 **A**, 76 **D**, 82, 96 **A**, 97 **A**, a, 98 **A**, 99 **A**, 101 **A**, 103 **A**.

69 b, 61[1]. *Read* rauked.

138 a, **B** c, 11[2]. I 'll. b, 26[1], 27[1], 28[1]. *MS.* tune (*copy wrong*).

305 b, notes, 10[1]. tauchty, etc. *Drop.*

342, 39[1]. *Read* what.

482 a, **D.** *Insert* 13[2]. bone.

II, 32 b, 6th line from below. *For* **H** *read* **J.**

101 b, 5th line of last paragraph. *Read* II, 246.

101 b, last line but four. *Read* II, 245.

128 b, 2d line of 2d paragraph. *Read* **B** 18.

169 a, last line but two. *Supply* **A** *before* 2[4].

234 a, 5th line. larf *is dropped in Herd 11.*

316 a, notes, 6[2]. *Read* bowers.

367 a, **C** 34[6]. *The MS. reading is* dead syne.

373 b, 21[2]. *Read* grey.

429 a, last line but three of text. *Read* 80 *for* 83.

477 a, **D.** *All the variations except* 11[1], 14[4], *apply to* **C,** *not to* **D.**

III, 11 b, last line but two. *Supply* **C** *before* 4[8].

49 a, 12th line. *Read* alcaldes.

51 b, last two lines. *Read* (extracted from His-toire Litt. de la France, XXX), p. 49.

122 b, 6th line. *Read* No 135.

146 a, 14[3]. *Read* delt *for* felt (felt, *all copies*).

179 b, 5[2]. *Read* clutt *for* cliitt.

183 a, notes, **A** 5[2]. *Add:* clutt was no doubt in-tended.

230, 59[8]. *Read* kickle.

230, 70[2]. *Read* For which.

232, 108[1]. *Read* unpossible.

232, 116[8]. *Read* leave out.

477 a, line 6. *Read* Laird's.

516 a, 95, line 7. *Read* Birkbeck.

517 b, last paragraph of 96, last line but one. *Read* des.

518 b. The notes to III, 44 belong under No 117.

IV, 33 a, last line but one. *Read* 10[8].

44 b, 9[2]. *Read* as he.

254 b, notes. *For* **J** *read* **K.**

275 a, **B** b, 6[1]. *Read* white-milk.

281 a, 2[2]. *Read* and bane.

282 a, 3[2]. *Read* behind my.

---

an old lame horse. The coincidence here with the ballad does not go very far, and may be an accident, but may be more than that.

288 a, **E**, 3[4]. *Read* toss. **F** is in the handwriting of John Hill Burton.

290 b, line 6. *Read* 7[3].

291 b, notes, **E**, 3[4]. *Drop.*

331 b, 8[1]. *Read* out *for* not.

339 b, lines 5, 6. *Read* Belhelvie, the name of an Aberdeenshire parish.

387 b, last line but one of note. *Read* owes its.

392, 21[1]. *Read* you *for* yon.

408 a, notes, **A**, 2d line. *Read* 22[4], 33[4]. *Cf.* 13[4].

437 b, 25[1]. *Read* Well fells.

440 b, 4, 3d paragraph, line 3. *Read* Coussemaker.

447 b, note to 5, after st. 17. *Read* in **a**.

455 a, 3[4]. *Read* wi gowd.

470 a, 20[2], 21[2]. *Read* A'.

471 a, 37[2], 38[4]. *Read* A'.

481 a, **I**, 1[1]. *Read* your hand.

499 b, line 8 from below. *Insert the title,* ' The Battle of Otterburn.'

513 b, **AA**, line 4. *Read* my heir.

514 b, 18[1]. *Read* Out then.

516 a, **B b**, 4[2]. *Read* that *for* thus.

524 a, 3d line. *Read* George Mitchell.

525 a, IV, 34 b, **B**. *Omit the second sentence.*

Trivial Corrections of Spelling.

I, 138 a, **B c**, 5[2]. *Read* brest.

II, 129 b, 21[2]. *Read* saft.

191 a, 18[3]. *Read* of.

191 a, 19[1]. *Read* on.

191 a, 25[3]. *Read* our.

314 a, **D** 1[2]. *Read* wi.

315 a, **D** 8[4]. *Read* mak.

372 b, notes, 7[5,6], lines 1, 3, 4. *Read* her.

373 a, 14[1]. *Read* spak.

373 b, 16[3,4], 1st line. *Read* her.

III, 183 a, **A** 5[2]. *Read* cliitt.

IV, 260 a, 7[3]. *Read* Hielands.

275 a, **B b**, 6[2]. *Read* over : over.

275 a, **B b**, 7[4]. *Read* son, were.

297 a, 11[1]. *Read* ladie.

312 b, 9[1]. *Read* o gold.

312 b, 10[1,2]. *Read* steppet, walket.

371 a, 7[3]. *Read* hale.

372 b, 17[2]. *Read* hame.

387 a, 1[1]. *Read* brent is.

444 b, 1[3]. *Read* bringin.

454 a, line 8. *Read* ravns.

456 a, 8[2]. *Read* bleam.

461 b, 22[1]. *Read* But.

464 a, 6[1]. *Read* when.

468 b, 5[3]. *Read* yow.

470 a, 20[1]. *Read* four-a-twontie.

470 a, 21[1]. *Read* four-an-twontie.

473 b, 42[1]. *Read* cri'd.

479, 7[2]. *Read* we.

493, 17[4], 20[3]. *Read* weddet, mintet.

516 a, **B**, between 5[2] and 5[3]. *Read* yow took, Yow promisd.

Supplementary.

I, 303, **D** 5, taipy-tapples. The MS. has saipy-sapples.

V, 18 a. *For* **C** *read* **c**.

79 b, 2d st. *Read* 26.

81 b, 11. *Read* play thee, great.

151 a. *Insert* **F** *before the last version.*

ADDITIONS AND CORRECTIONS*

VOL. I.

1. Riddles Wisely Expounded.

P. 1. Rawlinson MS. D. 328, fol. 174 b., Bodleian Library.

I was unaware of the existence of this very important copy until it was pointed out to me by my friend Professor Theodor Vetter, of Zürich, to whom I have been in other ways greatly indebted. It is from a book acquired by Walter Pollard, of Plymouth, in the 23d year of Henry VI, 1444–5, and the handwriting is thought to authorize the conclusion that the verses were copied into the book not long after. The parties are the fiend and a maid, as in **C, D**, which are hereby evinced to be earlier than **A, B**. The "good ending" of **A, B**, is manifestly a modern perversion, and the reply to the last question in **A, D**, 'The Devil is worse than eer woman was,' gains greatly in point when we understand who the so-called knight really is. We observe that in the fifteenth century version, 12, the fiend threatens rather than promises that the maid shall be his: and so in **E, V**, 205.

Inter diabolus et virgo.

1 Wol ȝe here a wonder thynge
 Betwyxt a mayd _and_ þe fovle fende?

2 Thys spake þe fend to þe mayd :
 'Beleue on me, mayd, to day.

3 'Mayd, mote y thi leman be,
 Wyssedom y wolle teche the :

4 'All þe wyssedom off the world,
 Hyf þou wolt be true _and_ forward holde.

5 'What ys hyer þan ys [þe] tre?
 What ys dypper þan ys the see?

* All the ballads in Scott's Minstrelsy, excepting a few pieces, of which only 'Cospatrick' and 'The Bonny Hind' require mention, were translated in Historische und romantische Balladen der Schottischen Grenzlande, Zwickau, 1826–7, 7 small vols, by Elise von Hohenhausen, Willibald Alexis, and Wilhelm von Lüdemann, a work now rare, which has just come to hand. Registering these translations here, in 53 entries, would require an unwarrantable space.

6 'What ys scharpper þan ys þe þorne?
 What ys loder þan ys þe horne?

7 'What [ys] longger þan ys þe way?
 What is rader þan ys þe day?

8 'What [ys] bether than is þe bred?
 What ys scharpper than ys þe dede?

9 'What ys grenner þan ys þe wode?
 What ys swetter þan ys þe note?

10 'What ys swifter þan ys the wynd?
 What ys recher þan ys þe kynge?

11 'What ys ȝeluer þan ys þe wex?
 What [ys] softer þan ys þe flex?

12 'But þou now answery me,
 Thu schalt for soþe my leman be.'

13 'Ihesu, for þy myld myȝth,
 As thu art kynge and knyȝt,

14 'Lene me wisdome to answere here ryȝth,
 And schylde me fram the fovle wyȝth !

15 'Hewene ys heyer than ys the tre,
 Helle ys dypper þan ys the see.

16 'Hongyr ys scharpper than [ys] þe thorne,
 Þonder ys lodder than ys þe horne.

17 'Loukynge ys longer than ys þe way,
 Syn ys rader þan ys the day.

18 'Godys flesse ys betur þan ys the brede,
 Payne ys strenger þan ys þe dede.

19 'Gras ys grenner þan ys þe wode.
 Loue ys swetter þan ys the notte.

20 'Þowt ys swifter þan ys the wynde,
 Ihesus ys recher þan ys the kynge.

21 'Safer is ȝeluer than ys the wexs,
 Selke ys softer þan ys the flex.

22 'Now, thu fende, styl thu be ;
   Nelle ich speke no more *with* the !

2². Be leue. 3¹. the leman. 3². theche. 13². kny3t
seems to be altered to knyt. 14². fold : cf. 1². 19². lowe.
Pollarde *is written in the left margin of* 22¹. *and*
WALTERVS POLLARD *below the last line of the
piece.*

['Inter Diabolus et Virgo' is printed by Dr Furnivall in Englische Studien, XXIII, 444, 445, March,
1897.]

P. 2 f., 484 a, II, 495 a, IV, 439 a. Slavic riddle-
ballads. Add : Romanov, I, 420, No 163 (White Russian).

2. The Elfin Knight.

P. 7. Of the custom of a maid's making a shirt for
her betrothed, see L. Pineau in Revue des Traditions
Populaires, XI, 68. A man's asking a maid to sew him
a shirt is equivalent to asking for her love, and her consent to sew the shirt to an acceptance of the suitor. See,
for examples, Grundtvig, III, 918. When the Elf in
'Elveskud,' D 9, Grundtvig, II, 116, offers to give
Ole a shirt of silk, it is meant as a love-token ; Ole replies that his true love had already given him one. The
shirt demanded by the Elfin Knight may be fairly understood to have this significance, as Grundtvig has suggested. So, possibly, in 'Clerk Colvill,' No 42, A 5, I,
387, considering the relation of 'Clerk Colvill' and
'Elveskud.' We have silken sarks sewn by a lady's
hand in several other ballads which pass as simple credentials ; as in 'Johnie Scot,' No 99, A 12, 13, D 6,
E 2, H 4, 5, II, 379, 385, 389; etc. Here they may
have been given originally in troth-plight : but not in
'Child Maurice,' No 83, D 7, F 9, II, 269, 272.

7, 8, 484 a, II, 495 a, III, 496 a, IV, 439 a, V, 205 b.
Add : ' Les Conditions impossibles,' Beauquier, Chansons p. recueillies en Franche-Comté, p. 133.

White Russian. Šejn, Materialy, I, ɪ, 494, No 608
(shirt, etc.). **Croatian**, Marjanović, ' Dar i uzdarje,'
p. 200, No 46.

8 ff. Questions and tasks offset by other questions
and requisitions in the Babylonian Talmud. See Singer,
Sagengeschichtliche Parallelen aus dem babylonischen
Talmud, Zeitschrift des Vereins für Volkskunde, II,
296.

11, note *, 12. The story of the two mares is No 48
of R. Schmidt's translation of the Çukasaptati, p. 68 ff.;
that of the staff of which the two ends were to be distinguished, No 49, p. 70 f. The Clever Wench (daughter of a minister) appears in No 52, p. 73 ff., with
some diversities from the tale noted at p. 12 b, 2d paragraph. More as to the Clever Wench in R. Köhler's
notes to L. Gonzenbach's Sicilianische Märchen, now
published by J. Bolte in Zeitschrift des Vereins für

Volkskunde, VI, 59. [See also Radloff, Proben der
Volkslitteratur der nördlichen türkischen Stämme, VI,
191–202.]

17 f., 484 f., II, 495 f., IV, 439 f., V, 206. The Journal of American Folk-Lore, VII, 228 f., gives the following version, contributed by Miss Gertrude Decrow
of Boston, in whose family the song has been traditional.

1 As I walked out in yonder dell,
   Let ev'ry rose grow merry in time
I met a fair damsel, her name it was Nell,
   I said, ' Will you be a true lover of mine?

2 ' I want you to make me a cambric shirt
   Without any seam or needlework,
   And then you shall be, etc.

3 ' I want you to wash it on yonder hill,
   Where dew never was nor rain never fell.

4 ' I want you to dry it on yonder thorn,
   Where tree never blossomed since Adam was
   born.'

5 ' And since you have asked three questions of me,
   Let ev'ry rose grow merry in time
Now and I will ask as many of thee,
   And then I will be a true lover of thine.

6 ' I want you to buy me an acre of land
   Between the salt sea and the sea-sand,
   And then, etc.

7 ' I want you to plough it with an ox's horn,
   And plant it all over with one kernel of corn.

8 ' I want you to hoe it with a peacock's feather,
   And thrash it all out with the sting of an adder,
   And then,' etc.

19 **J.** At p. 229 of the same are these stanzas from
a version contributed by Mrs. Sarah Bridge Farmer,
as learned from an elderly lady born in Beverly, Massachusetts.

Can't you show me the way to Cape Ann?
   Parsley and sage, rosemary and thyme
Remember me to a young woman that's there,
   In token she's been a true lover of mine.

(" The requirements which follow are identical with
those of the previous version. There is an additional
stanza: " —)

And when he has done, and finished his work,
   If he'll come unto me, he shall have his shirt,
   And then he shall be, etc.

The copy in The Denham Tracts, II, 358, from D. D. Dixon's tractate on The Vale of Whittingham, Newcastle-upon-Tyne, 1887, has been given from elsewhere at II, 495.

4. Lady Isabel and the Elf-Knight.

P. 25, **B.** Een Liedeken van den Heere van Haelewyn, with trifling verbal differences from Hoffmann's text, in Oude Liedekens in Bladeren, L. van Paemel, No 25. The copy in Nederlandsch Liederboek, Gent, 1892, II, 1, No 44, 'Van Heer Halewijn,' is Willems's.

27 a, 32 a, 37 b, 487 b. Lausen des Kopfes durch das Mädchen : notes by R. Köhler to L. Gonzenbach's Sicilianische Märchen, now published by J. Bolte, Zeitschrift des Vereins für Volkskunde, VI, 62. [Cf. Georgeakis et Pineau, Folk-lore de Lesbos, p. 257.]

29–37, 486 a, III, 497 a, IV, 441 a, V, 206 f. **GG, HH,** 'Der Ritter im Walde,' Herrmann u. Pogatschnigg, Deutsche V.-L. aus Kärnten, Salon-Ausgabe, p. 33 ; ' Es ritt ein Räuber wohl über den Rhein,' Wolfram, Nassauische Volkslieder, p. 61, No 33, resemble **N-R** : Liedlein von dreierlei Stimmen ; eleven (two) warning doves, three cries, to father, mother, brother ; huntsman-brother rescues sister and disposes of the knight or robber.

Böhme, in his edition of Erk's Deutscher Liederhort, I, 118–146, 1893, prints twenty German versions under numbers 41, 42. Of these 41^i, 42^k, 42^l are of oral derivation, and 42^h is from Erk's papers. Böhme notes two other copies taken down from singing, and one in MS., which he does not give. Judging by what has been given, what has been withheld must be of trifling value.

486 a, V, 207 a, **DD.** So 'Als die wunderschöne Anna auf dem Brautstuhle sass,' Wolfram, p. 66 f., No 39 a ; and No 39 b, which is even worse preserved. Again, ' Die wunderschöne Anna auf dem Rheinsteine,' K. Becker, Rheinischer Volksliederborn, p. 20, No 17.

37 f., **A.** Add : ' Der Reiter u. die Kaiserstochter,' K. Becker, Rheinischer Volksliederborn, p. 15, No 12.

41–44, III, 497 b, V, 207 a. Pair (or one of a pair) riding a long way without speaking. Add : ' Los dos hermanos,' Milá, Romancerillo catalan, 2d ed., p. 234, No 250: " Siete leguas caminaron, palabra no se decian." Add also : Afzelius (1880), I, 21, st. 22.

42 a, 488 a. Six **Ruthenian** copies (in two of which the girl is a Jewess), Kolberg, Pokucie, II, 20–25, Nos 21–26. **White Russian** versions of the ballad of the Jewess in Šejn, I, ɪ, 490 f., Nos 604, 605 ; Romanov, I, ɪɪ, 199, No 46.

P. 50, note ‖ ; IV, 441 b. Leprosy cured by (children's) blood. See G. Rua, Novelle del " Mambriano," pp. 84, 88 ff. The story about Constantine's leprosy (Reali di Francia, lib. 1, c. 1) occurs also in Higden's Polychronicon, Lumby, V, 122 ff., and in Gower, Confessio Amantis, bk. ɪɪ, Pauli, I, 266 ff. See also Ben Jonson, Discoveries, ed. Schelling, p. 35 (G. L. K. and W. P. Few). [See Prym u. Socin, Kurdische Samm-

lungen, pp. 35, 36. H. von Wlislocki, M. u. S. der Bukowinaer u. Siebenbürger Armenier, pp. 60, 61. The latter gives a number of references for the story about Constantine. Cf. also Dames, Balochi Tales, No 2, in Folk-Lore, III, 518.]

IV, 441 b, 3d paragraph. Another ballad (White Russian) in which the girl is burned, Šejn, Materialy, I, ɪ, 492, No 606.

57. **D a** was derived " from the housekeeper at Methven." Sharpe's Ballad Book, ed. 1880, p. 130.

IV, 442 a, 1st paragraph. Both hands are of the 18th century.

5. Gil Brenton.

P. 67. What is said of the *bilwiz* must be understood of the original conception. Grimm notes that this sprite, and others, lose their friendly character in later days and come to be regarded as purely malicious. See also E. Mogk in Paul's Grundriss der germ. Philologie, I, 1019.

72. Splendid ships. See also Richard Coer de Lion, 60–72, Weber's Metrical Romances, II, 5 f. ; Mélusine, II, 438 f.

Some of the French ships prepared for the invasion of England in 1386 had the masts from foot to cap covered with leaves of fine gold : Froissart, ed. Buchon, X, 169. King Henry the Eighth in 1544 passed the seas in a ship with sails of cloth of gold : Lord Herbert of Cherbury, Life and Raigne of King Henry the Eighth, 1649, p. 513. When Thomas Cavendish went up the Thames in 1589, his seamen and soldiers were clothed in silk, his sails were of damask, "his top-masts cloth of gold." Birch, Memoirs of the Reign of Q. Elizabeth, 1754, I, 57.

6. Willie's Lady.

P. 82 ff. Hindering childbirth. Notes by R. Köhler to Laura Gonzenbach's Sicilianische Märchen, now published by J. Bolte, Zeitschrift des Vereins für Volkskunde, VI, 63.

7. Earl Brand.

[P. 95 f, 489 b, III, 498 a, IV, 443 a. Death-naming, etc. See also W. R. Paton, Holy Names of the Eleusinian Priests, International Folk-lore Congress, 1891, Papers and Transactions, p. 202 ff.]

96 f., 489 f, II, 498, III, 498, IV, 443, V, 207.

Swedish. Cf. Kristensen, Jyske Folkeminder, **XI,** 293.

Romaic. See Ζωγραφεῖος Ἀγών, p. 170, **No 321.** [Georgeakis et Pineau, Folk-lore de Lesbos, pp. 208, 221.]

Italo-Albanian. De Grazia, Canti pop. albanesi, p. 102, No 11.

[**Turkish.** Sora Chenim went down into the grave

of Täji Pascha, which opened to receive her. The "black heathen" ordered one of his slaves to slay him and bury him between the two. "Da wuchs Täji Pascha als eine Pappel aus dem Boden hervor, Sora Chenim wuchs als ein Rosenstrauch hervor. Zwischen diesen Beiden wuchs der schwarze Heide als ein Dornbusch hervor," etc. Radloff, Proben der Volkslitteratur der nördlichen türkischen Stämme, VI, 246.]

100. Looking over the left shoulder. I, 100 f., **A** 21, **B** 4; 103, **E** 1; 464, 21; 490, 14 (left collar-bane); 492, 3; III, 259, 20; 263, 20; 264, 24; 339, 7; 368, 11; 369, 13; 413, 37; 465, 35; 488, 32; 13, 13; 15, 18; 17, 8; 18, 4; 20, 6; 52, 5; 135, 24; 445, 11; 518, 9; 519, 10; 520, 9. [In IV, 11, 21, it is the right shoulder.]

At I, 464, III, 259, 263 f., 339, 368 f, 413, IV, 135, the person looking over the left shoulder is angry, vexed, or grieved; in the other cases, no particular state of feeling is to be remarked. Undoubtedly the look over the left shoulder had originally more significance, since, under certain conditions, it gave the power of seeing spectres, or future events (but looking over the right shoulder had much the same effect). See A. Kuhn, Sagen, u. s. w., aus Westfalen, I, 187, No 206, and his references; and especially Bolte, in Zeitschrift des Vereins für Volkskunde, VI, 205-07 (using R. Köhler's notes). After sowing hemp-seed in the Hallowe'en rite, you look over your left shoulder to see your destined lass or lad. See note to Burns's Hallowe'en, st. 16.

10. The Twa Sisters.

P. 124 a, 4th paragraph. The ballad in Schlegel's Reisen is simply a threnody in Esthonian marriage ceremonies over the carrying away of the bride to her husband's house, and is not to the point.

125, 493 b, II, 498 b, III, 499 a, IV, 447 b, V, 208 b. 'L'os qui chante :' M. Eugène Monseur has continued his study of this tale in Bulletin de Folklore, I, 39-51, 89-149, II, 219-41, 245-51. See also Bugiel in Wisła, VII, 339-61, 557-80, 665-85.

[See also 'Die Geschichte von zwei Freunden,' Socin u. Stumme, Dialekt der Houwāra des Wād Sūs in Marokko, pp. 53, 115, Abhandlungen der Phil.-hist. Classe der K. Sächs. Gesellschaft der Wissenschaften, XV.]

[On disclosure by musical instruments see Revue Celtique, II, 199; Hartland, Legend of Perseus, I, 193. F. N. Robinson.]

126 a. [For a parallel to the South African tale see Jacottet, Contes pop. des Bassoutos, p. 52.]

126 b. **C** is also translated by H. Schubart in Arnim's Tröst Einsamkeit, 1808, p. 146.

11. The Cruel Brother.

P. 144 a. For 'Frau von Weissenburg,' 'Frau von der Löwenburg,' 'Junker Hans Steutlinger,' see Erk, ed. Böhme, Nos. 102, 103, I, 360 ff.

144 b, 2d paragraph, V, 208 b. Add : 'Le Testament du Chien,' Bédier, Les Fabliaux, 2d ed., p. 473 ; 'Testament de la vieille Jument,' 'de la vieille Truie,' 'de la Chèvre,' Luzel, Chansons pop. de la Basse-Bretagne, II, 88-97. 'The Robin's Last Will,' Miss M. H. Mason's Nursery Rhymes and Country Songs, p. 41.

12. Lord Randal.

P. 153 a. **German.** Two other copies in Böhme's Erk, No 190 b, I, 582.

[154 a ; IV, 449 b. **Danish.** 'Den forgivne Datter,' Grundtvig-Olrik, No 341, Ridderviser, I, 146 ff., two versions: **A**=Kristensen, Jyske Folkeminder, No 92, X, 358; **B**, that communicated to Professor Child by Professor Grundtvig and mentioned in I, 154. Olrik mentions 7 **Swedish** copies, 5 of them unprinted.]

156 a, III, 499 b, V, 208 b. 'Donna Lombarda.' See Archivio, X, 380. [See also 'Utro Fæstemø vil forgive sin Fæstemand,' in the Grundtvig-Olrik collection, No 345, Ridderviser I, 165 ff., 3 versions **A-C** (**A**, **B**, from MS. sources going back in part to the 16th century ; **C**, from oral tradition, printed by Kristensen, Jyske Folkeminder, No 19, I, 49, No 56, X, 234). Olrik, in an elaborate introduction, studies the relations of the Danish ballad (which is found also in Norse, Bugge's MS. collections, No. 221) to 'Donna Lombarda' and to the history of the sixth century Lombard queen Rosemunda. He opposes the views of Gaston Paris, Journal des Savants, 1889, pp. 616 ff., and holds that 'Donna Lombarda,' 'Utro Fæstemø,' (his No 345), 'Giftblandersken' (his No 344), 'Fru Gundela' (see above I, 156 b), and the Slavic ballads of the sister who poisons her brother at the instigation of her lover, are all derived from the saga of Rosemunda. He even regards 'Old Robin of Portingale,' No 80, II, 240, as related to the 'Utro Fæstemø.' See below, p. 295.]

156 b, 499 a, II, 499 a, III, 499. The ballad of the maid who poisons her brother and is rejected by the man she expects to win in Lithuanian, Bartsch, Dainu Balsai, I, 172 ff., No 123 a, b. More ballads of poisoning, sister poisoning brother at the instance of her lover, girl poisoning her lover, and at col. 306 one resembling Lord Randal, Herrmann, Ethnologische Mitteilungen aus Ungarn, I, cols 292-308 (with an extensive bibliography). Herrmann's collections upon this theme are continued from cols 89-95, 203-11. [Cf. the Danish ballad 'Tule Slet, Ove Knar og Fru Magnild,' Grundtvig-Olrik, No. 350, Ridderviser, I, 186, where, however, the murderess uses a knife.]

157. Compare, for dialogue and repetition, the Catalan ballad 'El Conde Arnau,' Milá, Romancerillo, No 78, p. 67 ; where, however, the first half of the third line is also regularly repeated in the fourth.

'¿Tota sola feu la vetlla, muller lleyal?
¿Tota sola feu la vetlla, viudeta igual?'

'No la faig yo tota sola, Comte l'Arnau,
No la faig yo tota sola, valga 'm Deu, val!'

157 b. A is translated by Professor Emilio Teza. 'L'Avvelenatrice, Canzone Boema,' Padova, 1891, p. 12. [Atti e Memorie della R. Accademia di Scienze, Lettere ed Arti in Padova, Nuova Serie, VII, 234.]

13. Edward.

P. 167, 501 b, III, 499 b, V, 209 b. 'Svend i Rosensgaard' is No 340 in the Grundtvig-Olrik collection of Danish ballads, Ridderviser, I, 142. Danish versions are limited to three, of which the second is a fragment and the third a copy from Norway in all but pure Danish. Of Swedish versions eleven are enumerated, besides a half-comic copy from a manuscript of 1640, or older, which is spun out to 33 stanzas. As before remarked, a palpable tendency to parody is visible in some of the Scandinavian specimens.

14. Babylon, or, The Bonnie Banks o Fordie.

P. 170, 501 b, II, 499 a, III, 499 f., IV, 450 a, V, 209 b. 'Hr. Truelses Døtre' is No 338 of the Danish ballads in the continuation of Grundtvig's collection by Dr. Axel Olrik, Danske Ridderviser, 1895, I, 114, where the ballad is subjected to a minute study. The existence of a ballad is mentioned in 1624, and indicated as early as 1598. There are Danish, Swedish, and Icelandic versions of the 17th century, and numerous later copies, Danish, Swedish, Norwegian, and Färöe: Danish, in all, 10, one of the 17th century; Swedish 12, 4 of the 17th century ; Norwegian 6; Färöe 4. Five of the Norwegian copies take the direction of the Icelandic and Färöe in the treatment of the story. Two varieties of the ballad may be specially distinguished : one in which we have the miracle of a light burning or a fountain (fountains) springing over the place where the maids were murdered (called by Olrik the legendary form), the other in which the career and fate of the sons are made prominent. The "legendary" versions are the older. In these the maids are regarded as martyrs, and popular religious observances in connection with the miraculous fountains and in commemoration of the murdered maids have been kept up into the present century. The story is localized in not less than thirteen Danish accounts and others in Sweden.

II, 499 a, III, 500, V, 209 b. Add to the French ballads a copy, which has lost still more of the characteristic traits, obtained by M. Couraye du Parc in Basse-Normandie : Études romanes dédiées à Gaston Paris, 1891, p. 47, No 10.

II, 499 a. A Ruthenian story like that of the Great Russian ballad in Kolberg, Pokucie, II, 30, No 33.

15. Leesome Brand.

Pp. 181, 502 a. **German.** Add : Böhme, Erk's Liederhort, I, 592 f., 'Der Reiter und seine Geliebte,' No 194 b, from Erk's papers, c, from oral tradition (fragments). Böckel, 'Das Begräbniss im Walde,' p. 33, No 47. 'Es gingen zwei Liebchen durch einen grünen Wald,' Wolfram, p. 89, No 63.

17. Hind Horn.

[P. 188 b. 'Horn Child.' See the edition by J. Caro, in Englische Studien, XII, 323 ff.]

190 a. Hereward will not drink unless the princess presents the cup : very like Horn here. Michel, Chroniques Anglo-Normandes, II, 18 f.

191, note *. Blonde of Oxford (Jehan et Blonde). See Suchier's edition, Œuvres poétiques de Philippe de Remi, Sire de Beaumanoir, II, 89, 99, 103.

193 a. That Horn Child, though much more modern in its present form than the Gest, "would seem to have been formed on a still older model" was suggested by T. Wright in 1835, and was the opinion of J. Grimm and of Ferdinand Wolf. Wolf maintains that Horn Child was the work of a popular jongleur, or vagrant minstrel, and that for this reason Chaucer put it among the "romances of prys," which are mentioned in Sir Thopas. Anyway, this must have been the form of the story which was known to Chaucer. Wolf, Ueber die Lais, p. 217 f.

195 a (3). Oude Liedekens in Bladeren, L. van Paemel, No 28 = Hoffmann, No 2.

199 a. Albanian. De Grazie, Canti p. albanesi, p. 118.

199 a, note *. Ring in betrothal. So in Twelfth Night, IV, 3, as Prior remarks, II, 277, apropos of 'Axel and Walborg', st. 44.

201, note. These talismans also in India : Tawney's Kathá-Sarit-Ságara, II, 161.

502 b, 5th paragraph, III, 501 b, IV, 450 b. Add: Kolberg, Lud, IV, 23, No 146; VI, 166 f., No 332; XII, 115–118, Nos 221–224 (jumps seven tables and touches the eighth); XVI, 271, No 438 ; XVI, 272, No 440; Valjavec, p. 300, No 17; Kolberg, Mazowsze, II, 109, No 251. A soldier comes back after seven years' absence to his "widow ;" drops ring into cup, and is recognized as her husband. Lud, XXI, 61, No 123.

20. The Cruel Mother.

P. 219 b, 504 a, II, 500 a, IV, 451 a, V, 212 a. Add : **T**, Wolfram, p. 90, No 64, 'Es hütet ein Schäfer an jenem Rain,' 'Die Rabenmutter ;' Böhme's edition of Erk's Liederhort, I, 636, No 212 e; and to the literature several items at p. 637.

219 b, III, 502 b. Similar Slavic ballads : Polish, Kolberg, Lud, IV, 52, No 220 ; XII, 308 f., Nos 611, 612 ; XVII, 9, No 17; XVIII, 188, No 346 ; XXI,

85, No 179; XXII, 160, No 284; Kolberg, Mazowsze, II, 160, No 352; IV, 366, No 436.

P. 220. **C**, sts 9, 10, 11 are in Motherwell's MS., p. 183, written in pencil.

21. The Maid and the Palmer.

P. 228 b, 2d paragraph. The Finnish ballad was first printed by C. A. Gottlund, Otava, 1832, II, 9 (Rolland, Chansons Populaires, VI, 47–50, with a translation).

230 f., III, 502 b, IV, 451 b. White Russian versions, Šejn, II, 607 ff., Nos 12–16, ' Pesn' o grěšnoj děvě, Song of the sinful girl,' five copies, the third imperfect. Jesus sends the girl to church, in the first the earth comes up seven cubits, the lights go out, etc.; she shrives herself, and things are as before. In the other copies she crumbles to dust. Polish (with variations), Kolberg, Lud; XII, 309, No 613; XIX, 187, No 658; XX, 101, No 37; XXI, 86, No 180; XXII, 161 f., Nos 285, 286; Kolberg, Mazowsze, I, 142, No 46; IV, 367, No 437; Siarkowski, in Zbiór wiadomości, IV, 94, No 18.

231 a. Legend of the Magdalen unmixed. **Italian**, Archivio, XIV, 211 f., ' Maria Maddalena,' two copies, fragmentary. In the second, Maria asks the master of a vessel to take her in; a tempest arises; the dona pecatrice, lest the vessel should founder on her account, with many people aboard, throws herself into the sea, is swallowed by a whale, and not disgorged for three-and-thirty years.

22. St. Stephen and Herod.

P. 236 a, last paragraph. Here, and in other places in volumes I, II, Catalan is treated as if it were a dialect of Spanish. The corrections required are as follows : I, 236 a, last paragraph, 384 a, 2d par., 505 a, 2d par.; II, 174 a, 2d par., 347 a, 2d par., 512 a, No 72, read *Catalan* for *Spanish*, and I, 384 a, 2d par., drop **K.** I, 462 a, 3d par., read *Catalan* for **C.** II, 69 a, 7th line, 113 b, 11th line, 158, 2d par., read *Spanish and Catalan*, and at the last place insert *Catalan* before the 3d and 4th citations and transfer them to the end.

237, III, 502 b. The Breton story with the miraculous sustentation of the maid (but without the marvel of the capon): Böhme's Erk, I, 637 ff., No 213 a, ' Die Weismutter,' b, ' Die unschuldig gehangene und gerettete Dienstmagd,' and note to b; Wolfram, p. 38, No 10, ' Zu Frankfurt steht ein Wirtshaus.'

240 f., 505 f., II, 501 b, IV, 451 f. Joie des Bestes. Add : Marin, Cantos Populares, I, 61, No 124; Iglesia, El Idioma Gallego (' a maldicion d' a ovella '), cf. II, 8, note †, III, 174, both cited by Munthe.

240, 241, 505 b, II, 501 b, III, 502 b, IV, 452 a, V, 212 a. A roast pheasant gets feathers and flies away in attestation of a tale: M. Wardrop, Georgian Folk-tales, p. 10 f., No 2. G. L. K.

Fish flying out of the pan. See Wesselofsky, Archiv f. slavische Philologie, VI, 574.

241 b. Herod's questions. Compare Bergström and Nordlander, 98, 3; Pidal, p. 128.

23. Judas.

[P. 243 b. Trinity College MS. B, 14, 39, has been recovered, and Professor Skeat has had the kindness to furnish a copy of the ballad. Wright's text proves to be in all essentials accurate; but, on account of the age and great interest of the poem, Professor Skeat's copy is here reproduced. The ballad has no title in the MS.

Hit wes upon a screþorsday þat vre louerd aros.
  ful milde were þe wordes he spec to iudas.
iudas þou most to iurselem oure mete for to bugge.
  þritti platen of seluer þou bere up oþi rugge.
þou comest fer iþe brode stret fer iþe brode strete.   5
  summe of þine tunesmen þer þou meist i mete.
imette wid is soster þe swikele wimon.
  iudas þou were wrþe me stende the wid ston. .íí.
for the false prophete þat tou bileuest upon.
Be stille leue soster þin herte þe to breke.   10
  wiste min louerd crist ful wel he wolde be wreke.
Iudas go þou on þe roc heie up on þe ston.
  lei þin heued i my barm slep þou þe anon.
Sone so iudas of slepe was awake.
  þritti platen of seluer from hym weren itake.   15
He drou hym selue bi þe cop þat al it lauede ablode.
  þe iewes out of iurselem awenden he were wode.
Foret hym com þe riche ieu þat heiste pilatus.
  wolte sulle þi louerd þat hette iesus.
I nul sulle my louerd for nones cunnes eiste.   20
  bote hit be for þe þritti platen. þat he me bi taiste.
Wolte sulle þi lord crist for enes cunnes golde.
  Nay bote hit be for þe platen. þat he habben wolde.
In him com ur lord * gon as is postles seten at mete.
  Wou sitte ye postles ant wi nule ye ete. .íí.   25
ic am iboust ant isold to day for oure mete.
Vp stod him iudas lord am i þat
  I nas neuer oþe stude þer me þe euel spec.
Vp him stod peter ant spec wid al is miste.
  þau pilatus him come wid ten hundred cnistes. .íí.   30
  yet ic wolde louerd for þi loue fiste.
Still þou be peter. wel i þe i cnowe.
  þou wolt fur sake me þrien. ar þe coc him crowe.   33

V. 24, *. The word *c'st* has here been erased, and should *not* be inserted. Skeat.

V. 27. Blank space. Read ' frek ' (=man). Skeat. The MS. has íí at end of ll. 8, 25, 30. This means that there are here *two* second lines, i. e., that three lines rime together. Skeat. The long ſ's of the MS. are printed s.]

25. Willie's Lyke-Wake.

P. 250, 506 a, II, 502 a, III, 503 a. Add the Croatian ballad, 'Ive umira za Marom,' Hrvatske Narodne Pjesme iz "Naše Sloge," II. Diel, 15, No 11.

29. The Boy and the Mantle.

[P. 261 f. On the Gaelic ballad in the Dean of Lismore's Book see the elaborate article by Professor Ludw. Chr. Stern, Die gälische Ballade vom Mantel in Macgregors Liederbuche, Zeitschrift für celtische Philologie, I, 294 ff. The text is given according to the edition of Alexander Cameron, Reliquiae Celticae, I, 76, with another copy from a 1628 MS. in the Franciscan Convent at Dublin. Stern's translation clears up some points, and brings out one striking similarity between the Gaelic and the English ballad. When MacReith's wife tried on the mantle, " er passte ihr, beides an Fuss und Hand, bis auf die Gabel ihrer kleinen Finger und Zehen." She explains this failure of the mantel to cover her completely : "' Einen Kuss bekam ich verstohlen von O'Duibhnes Sohne Diarmaid ; der Mantel würde bis auf den Boden reichen, wenn es nicht der allein wäre.'" Compare sts 28–30 of ' The Boy and the Mantle.' This similarity, in a feature unknown to other versions of the story, coupled with the form 'Craddocke' in the English ballad (a form which "nur aus dem welschen Caradawc entstanden sein kann ") convinces Stern that ' The Boy and the Mantle,' and probably also the Gaelic ballad, are derived directly from Welsh tradition, independently of the Old French versions, which, however, he thinks also go back ultimately to Wales (p. 310). I am indebted to Dr F. N. Robinson for calling my attention to Stern's article. G. L. K.]

268 ff., 507 a, II, 502 a, III, 503, IV, 454 a, V, 212 f. Tests of chastity. " The jacinth stone will not be worne on the finger of an adulterer, nor the olive grow if planted by one that leadeth his life in unlawful lusts." Greene, Never too late, Pt. II, 1590, Works, ed. Grosart, VIII, 141. A note on the general subject in G. Rua, Novelle del " Mambriano," pp. 66 f., 73–83. G. L. K. [See also Zupitza, Herrig's Archiv f. das Studium der neueren Sprachen, LXXXII, 201 ; Nyrop, Dania, I, 13, n. 2 ; Feilberg, Dania, I, 154; ' La Mensuration du Cou,' Perdrizet and Gaidoz, Mélusine, VI, 225 ff.]

270 a, 1st paragraph. The Shukasaptati story at p. 29 f. of R. Schmidt's translation.

30. King Arthur and King Cornwall.

P. 284. Sts 17, 18. Compare Carle of Carlile, vv. 143 ff., Percy MS., Hales and Furnivall, III, 282.

31. The Marriage of Sir Gawain.

P. 288 ff., II, 289 b, III, 454 a. Mr. Whitley Stokes has pointed out that the incident of a hag turning into a beautiful woman after a man has bedded with her occurs in the Book of Ballymote, an Irish MS. of about 1400, and elsewhere and earlier in Irish story, as in the Book of Leinster, a MS. of the middle of the twelfth century. The Academy, XLI, 399 (1892). It is singular that the sovereignty in the first tale is the sovereignty of Erin, with which the disenchanted hag rewards her deliverer, and not the sovereignty over woman's will which is the solution of the riddle in the ballad. See also the remarks of Mr. Alfred Nutt in the same volume, p. 425 (and, again, Academy, October 19, 1889, p. 255), who, while denying the necessity for any continental derivation of the hideous woman, suggests that Rosette in Gautier's Conte du Graal, vv. 25380–744, furnishes a more likely origin for her than Chrétien's damoisele, since it does not appear that the latter is under spells, and spells which are loosed by the action of a hero. [See also O'Grady, Silva Gadelica, p. 328 ff.; translation, p. 370 ff. F. N. Robinson.]

289 b. Gromere Gromorson (Grummore Gummursum) and Gromore somyr Ioure, in Malory's Morte Darthur, ed. Sommer, 256, 258, 799.

32. King Henry.

P. 290, note †, IV, 454 a. " La nuit si jolie fille, le jour si jolie biche:" Pineau, Le Folk-lore du Poitou, p. 391. [A raven by day, a woman by night: von Wlislocki, M. u. S. der Bukowinaer u. Siebenbürger Armenier, p. 75. On transformations of all kinds, see S. Prato, Bulletin de Folklore, 1892, p. 316 ff.]

298, II, 502 b, IV, 454 a. A man marries a snake. At midnight it becomes a woman, and it keeps that form thereafter : J. Krainz, Mythen u. Sagen aus dem steirischen Hochlande. No. 147, p. 194. A snake (enchanted man) marries a girl, and is thereby freed: Brüder Zingerle, Tirols Volksdichtungen, II, 173 ff.; cf. II, 317. G. L. K.

33. Kempy Kay.

P. 300. I have serious doubts whether this offensive ballad has not been made too important; whether, notwithstanding the points noted at p. 301, it is anything more than a variety of ' The Queen of all Sluts.'

305 b. A 10¹. _lauchty_ in Sharpe with a line drawn in ink through l (probably by the editor, as this is a presentation copy).

V, 213 a. Since we have Pitcairn's copy only in Sharpe's handwriting, we cannot determine which of the two made the changes.

34. Kemp Owyne.

P. 307 f, II, 502 b, III, 504 a. Disenchantment; kissing a serpent. A remarkable case alleged to have occurred at Cesena in 1464 : [Angelo de Tummulillis, Notabilia Temporum, ed. Corvisieri, 1890, p. 124 ff. ;] Giornale Storico della Letteratura Italiana, XVII, 161. G. L. K. On the whole subject see R. Köhler's notes in Mennung, Der Bel Inconnu, p. 20 ; S. Prato's notes, Bulletin de Folklore, 1892, p. 333 f. [W. H. Schofield, Studies on the Libeaus Desconus, in Studies and Notes in Philology and Literature published under the direction of the Modern Language Departments of Harvard University, IV, 199 ff.]

36. The Laily Worm and the Mackrel of the Sea.

P. 316 a. Näktergalsvisan, Bohlin, in Nyare Bidrag till Kännedom om de Svenska Landsmålen, II, 10, Folktoner från Jämtland, pp. 5, 6.

37. Thomas Rymer.

P. 319, note ‡. Dr. W. H. Schofield has furnished me with an abstract of the Visions d'Oger le Dannoys au royaulme de Fairie (which book after all is in the Paris library). There is nothing in the Visions which throws further light on the relation of the stories of Thomas Rhymer and of Ogier.

320, note ‡. Bells. See R. Köhler, Zeitschr. des Vereins f. Volkskunde, VI, 60.

321, note ‡. The duration of paradisiac bliss exceeds three hundred years in some accounts. Three hundred years seem but three days in the Italian legend of three monks, Graf, Miti, Leggende, etc., 1892, I, 87 f., and in that of the young prince who invites an angel to his wedding, Graf, 90 ff., after the Latin text published by Schwarzer, Zeitschrift für deutsche Philologie, XIII, 338–51, 1881. (R. Köhler pointed out in the same journal, XIV, 96 ff., that an abstract of the story had been given in Vulpius's Curiositäten, I, 179 ff., as early as 1811.) In the lai of Guingamor, printed by M. Gaston Paris in Romania, VIII, 50 ff., 1879, three hundred years pass as three days. In both the last, the eating of earthly food brings an immediate decrepitude, followed by speedy death in the case of the prince. [See also W. Hertz, Spielmannsbuch, p. 318 f.]

39. Tam Lin.

[P. 339 b, II, 505 b, III, 505 b. Fairy salve. Kirk's Invisible Commonwealth, ed. Lang, pp. 13, 34 ; Denham Tracts, II, 138 f.]

340 a, II, 505 b, III, 505 b, IV, 455 b. Sleeping under trees: ympe tree. Bugge, Arkiv för nordisk

Filologi, VII, 104, refers to Liebrecht, Gervasius von Tilbury, p. 117, and to W. Hertz, Spielmannsbuch, p. 322.

40. The Queen of Elfan's Nourice.

P. 358 b, II, 505 f., III, 505 f., IV, 459 a, V, 215 b. Mortal midwives for fairies, etc. : Wucke, Sagen der mittleren Werra, II, 25 ; Gebhart, Oesterreichisches Sagenbuch, p. 208 ; Baader, Neugesammelte Volkssagen, No 95, p. 68. G. L. K.

[Kirk's Secret Commonwealth, ed. Lang, p. 13 ; Denham Tracts, II, 138.]

42. Clerk Colville.

[P. 372 b. Der Ritter von Staufenberg. See the edition by Edward Schröder : Zwei altdeutsche Rittermären, Moriz von Craon, Peter von Staufenberg. Berlin, 1894. Schröder dates the composition of the poem about 1310 (p. LI). He shows that Schott's edition, which Culemann followed, was a reprint of one printed by Prüss in 1483 at the earliest, but thinks that it followed that of Prüss at no long interval (p. XXXIV). Cf. also Schorbach, Zeitschr. f. deutsches Altertum, XL, 123 ff.]

374–78. The mother's attempt to conceal the death of her son from his wife occurs also in 'Ebbe Tygesøns Dødsridt' and 'Hr. Magnuses Dødsridt,' Olrik, Danske Ridderviser, Nos 320, 321, and Swedish copies of the former ; borrowed no doubt from 'Elveskud.'

380, II, 506 a, III, 506 a, IV, 459 a, V, 216 a. Add : **XX**, 'La Mort de Jean Renaud,' Beauquier, Chansons p. recueillies en Franche-comté, p. 152.

43. The Broomfield Hill.

[P. 393 a, III, 506 b, IV, 459 b. With the Italian ballad cf. ' Quarante ans j'ai travaillé,' Georgeakis et Pineau, Folk-lore de Lesbos, p. 246.]

393 f., 506. Jäger-Romanze in Böhme, Altdeutsches Liederbuch, No 437, from Melchior Franck, Fasciculus Quodlibeticus, Nürnberg, 1611, No 6: slightly different, no disposition to kill the maid. Three copies of this all but inevitable ballad in Blätter für Pommersche Volkskunde, II. Jahrgang, p. 77 f., 'Jägerslied ;' and more might be added.

44. The Twa Magicians.

[P. 400. **Greek**. Cf. ' Les Transformations,' Georgeakis et Pineau, Folk-lore de Lesbos, p. 210 ff. (no mention of the Turk's transforming himself).]

401. **Polish**. Add : Kolberg, Lud, XXI, 27, No 50; XXII, 102, No 157; Kolberg, Mazowsze, II, 54 f., Nos 131, 132 ; III, 247, 321; IV, 274, No 240.

401 b, II, 506 b, III, 506 f., IV, 459 b, V, 216 a. Trans-

formations during flight. Add R. Köhler's notes to
L. Gonzenbach's Sicilianische Märchen, now published
by J. Bolte, Zeitschrift des Vereins für Volkskunde,
VI, 65.

The incidents of the flight of the girl and her lover,
the pursuit and the transformations, and of the Devil
outwitted by his pupil are discussed by G. Rua, Novelle del "Mambriano" del Cieco da Ferrara, p. 95.
See also M. Wardrop, Georgian Tales, p. 4, No. 1.
G. L. K.

45. King John and the Bishop.

[P. 405 ff., II, 506 f., IV, 459 b, V, 216 a. A Christian ascetic has taken up his abode in a hogshead, on
which he has written, "If thou art wise, live as I live!"
The sultan puts three questions to him : How far is it to
heaven? At how much do you value me? Which is
the best religion? The penalty for failure to solve
them is to be dragged at the tail of the sultan's horse.
The answers are : A day's journey; twenty-nine silver
pieces ; neither of the two religions is the better, for
the two are God's eyes, one of which is as dear to him
as the other. Von Wlislocki, M. u. S. der Bukowinaer
u. Siebenbürger Armenier, ' Der weise Mann,' No 30,
p. 83 ff.]

46. Captain Wedderburn's Courtship.

[P. 417 a, II, 507 b, III, 507 a, IV, 459 b, V, 216 a.
Heads on stakes. See W. H. Schofield, in the (Harvard) Studies and Notes in Philology and Literature,
IV, 175 ff.]
418 a, II, 507 b. See Stiefel, Ueber die Quelle der
Turandot-Dichtung Heinz des Kellners, in Zeitschr. f.
vergleichende Litteraturgeschichte, N. F., VIII, 257 ff.

47. Proud Lady Margaret.

P. 426. Add : ' La fille damnée,' Daymard, p. 178;
' La sposa morta,' Archivio, VIII, 274; the "romance"
in Ballesteros, Cancionero popular gallego, III, 256;
see also the "romance" ' Bernal Francez' from Algarve in Encyclopedia Republicana, Lisbon, 1882,
p. 156.

49. The Twa Brothers.

I.

P. 435, V, 217. Communicated by Mr J. K. Hudson
of Manchester. Sung after a St George play regularly
acted on All Souls' Day at a village a few miles from
Chester, and written down for Mr Hudson by one
of the performers, a lad of sixteen. The play was introduced by a song called Souling (similar to a Ste-

phening, see I, 234), and followed by two songs, of
which this is the last, the whole dramatic company
singing.

1 ' And it's where hast thou been all this night long,
    my son?
    Come tell it unto me.'
 'I have been lying on yonder bull-rushes,
    Which lies beneath yond tree.'

2 ' And it's what are the spots on this thy coat, my
    son?
    Come tell it unto me.'
 'They are the spots of my poor brother's blood,
    Which lies beneath yonder tree.'

3 ' And it's what didst thou kill thy poor brother for,
    my son?
    Come tell it unto me.'
 'Because he killed two pretty little birds,
    Which flew from tree to tree.'

4 ' And it's what will the father say when he comes,
    my son?
    Come tell it unto me.'
 'I will dress me up in sailor's clothes,
    And my face he will never see.'

5 ' And it's what wilt thou do with thy pretty little
    wife, my son?
    Come tell it unto me.'
 'I will dress her up in lad[d]ie's clothes,
    And she will sail along with me.'

6 ' And it's what wilt thou do with thy children three,
    my son?
    Come tell it unto me.'
 'I will leave them to my poor grandfather to rear,
    And comfort [to] him [to be].'

7 ' And it's when shall we see thy face again, my son?
    Come tell it unto me.'
 'When the sun and moon shines both at once,
    And that shall never be.'

53. Young Beichan.

P. 459 a. For a late German ballad on the Moringer
story ('von dem Markgrafen Backenweil ') see Bolte,
Zeitschrift des Vereins für Volkskunde, III, 65–7, and
for notes of dramas upon the theme, pp. 62–4. I do
not observe that I have anywhere referred to the ad-
mirably comprehensive treatment of the subject by von
Tettau, Ueber einige bis jetzt unbekannte Erfurter
Drucke des 15. Jahrhunderts, Ritter Morgeners Wall-
fahrt, pp. 75–123. The book did not come into my
hands till two years after my preface was written.

VOL. II.

56. Dives and Lazarus.

P. 10 b, III, 507 b, 508 a, IV, 462 b, V, 220 a. Add :
Ruthenian ballad, Kolberg, Pokucie, II, 280, No 505.
Legends not in stanzas, **White Russian**, 'Lazar,' Šejn,
II, 578–90, 3 copies ; Romanov, Part V, pp. 341–56, Nos
22–26, 5 copies and variants; **Great Russian**, Jakuškin, p. 44, No 13, 2 copies. Lazarus and the rich man
are brothers.

'Il ricco Epulone,' the Madonna begging, Archivio,
XIV, 209 f.

57. Brown Robyn's Confession.

P. 13, 510 a, IV, 463 a, V, 220 a. A serpent stops a
ship and demands a passenger : Larminie, West-Irish
Folk-Tales, p. 131. On the detention of ships by sub-
marine folk, see Whitley Stokes, Revue Celtique, XV,
294 f. G. L. K. (The article attributed to R. Köhler,
II, 510 a, is by L. Laistner.) [Add Jātaka, Bk. ɪ, No
41, Cowell, I, 110. A ship mysteriously detained because the owner has neglected a promise : Yacoub Artin Pacha, Contes pop. de la vallée du Nil, p. 74.]

59. Sir Aldingar.

[P. 33, 511 b, III, 508 a, IV, 462 a. For parallels,
including the child champion, see R. Köhler's account
of the Breton mystery of Sainte Tryphine, Revue Celtique, I, 222 ff. F. N. Robinson.]

64. Fair Janet.

P. 102 f. (Breton ballad), III (497 b, No 5), 508 b,
IV, 464 a, V, 222 a. Add to the French ballads a copy
from Basse-Normandie obtained by M. Couraye du Parc,
Études romanes dédiées à Gaston Paris, 1891, p. 49;
'L'infidèle punie,' Beauquier, Chansons p. recueillies
en Franche-Comté, p. 254. [On the similarity of the
beginning of ' La Fidanzata Infedele' to that of the
Danish ballad ' Hyrde og Ridderfrue,' see Olrik, Ridderviser, I, 181, No 349.]

P. 109. Something similar to what is narrated in **F**
7–10 is, I am assured by high authorities, familiar to
practising physicians. An eminent professor in the
Harvard Medical School informs me that in the case of
two families under his care the husband has been regularly troubled with "morning sickness" during the first
three or four months of the wife's pregnancy (the husband in neither case being of a nervous or hysterical
disposition). Mr. E. E. Griffith, late of Harvard College, tells me that a respectable and intelligent man of
his acquaintance in Indiana maintained that he always
shared the pains of his wife during parturition, and that
his labors were as intense in degree and as long in time
as hers. A distinguished physician of Indiana, while
testifying to the frequency of cases of the like sympa-
thy, insists that such experiences occur only to husbands who have witnessed the pains in question, or
who have learned about them by reading or conversation on the matter, and that "suggestion" affords an
explanation of the phenomenon.

65. Lady Maisry.

P. 112 f. In a Polish ballad a girl who has had a
child irregularly is burned by her two brothers. Her
paramour comes by when she is half burned, and she
begs him to save her. (How can I? he says ; your
brothers are here. The brothers say, we have done
wrong to burn her ; we have left her child an orphan.)
Kolberg, Lud, XVI, 291, No 476.

P. 114, st. 17.

> O whare is a' my merry young men,
>   Whom I gi meat and fee?

With this common-place compare :

> Hvor ere nu de Kæmper, min Fader giver Brød
> (Løn), Grundtvig, D. g. F., No 184, **G**, 8, 9.

>   Aquí, aquí, los mis doscientos,
>   Los que comeis el mi pan.

Wolf and Hofmann, Primavera, I, 39, 41 f., and Conde
Claros, the same, II, 374.

66. Lord Ingram and Child Wyet.

Pp. 127, 511, III, 509 a. Naked sword as emblem
of chastity. More notes by R. Köhler to Laura Gonzenbach's Sicilianische Märchen, Nos 39, 40, now published by J. Bolte in Zeitschrift des Vereins für Volkskunde, VI, 76.

[Mame Ala, in the Kurdish story 'Mâm and Sîn,'
lays a dagger (*Dolchmesser*) between himself and Sine,
"so dass der Griff desselben gegen ihre, die Spitze gegen
seine eigene Brust gerichtet war." Prym u. Socin,
Kurdische Sammlungen, Petersburg Academy, translation, p. 101.]

127, note *, III, 509 a. Italian ballad (sword reduced
to a straw). Bernoni, Trad. pop. veneziane, p. 36 ;
Ferraro, Canti pop. di Ferrara, pp. 56, 103; Villario,
in Archivio, XI, 35; Menghini, Canzoni pop. romane,
in Sabatini, Il Volgo di Roma, I, 75 ff.

[127 f., 511 b, III, 509 a. Table-jumping.

> Et chil Robert d'Artois n'i fist arestement,
>   La table tressali tost et apertement;
>   Au conte Salebrin ala premierement.

The Vows of the Heron (about 1340), Wright, Political Poems, I, 9 f.]

[128. 'Ebbe Skammelsøn' is now No 354 in the

Grundtvig-Olrik collection of Danish ballads, Ridderviser, I, 197 ff. 8 Danish versions are printed (some of which go back to MSS of the 17th century), with a very elaborate introduction and critical apparatus. Dr. Olrik regards the extant Norwegian texts as derived from print. He enumerates 8 Swedish versions.]

67. Glasgerion.

P. 137, II, 511 f. Soporific effect of harping : cf. Revue celtique, XII, 81, 109, XV, 438. G. L. K.

69. Clerk Saunders.

P. 166. Stanzas 30–37 are inserted in Buchan's first MS. on a separate slip of paper, and at 29, where the ballad originally ended, there is this note : " See the additional stanzas on the annexed leaf." W. Walker.

72. The Clerk's Twa Sons o Owsenford.

P. 174, note *. ' Dass Schloss in Oesterreich,' etc.: see Böhme's Erk, No 61ᵃ⁻ᵍ; Frischbier u. Sembrzychi, Hundert Ostpreussiche Volkslieder, No 16, p. 26 ; Becker, Rheinischer Volksliederborn, No 2, a, b, c, p. 2 ff.; Wolfram, No 44, p. 71; Kristensen, Jyske Folkeminder, XI, 218, No 81.

73. Lord Thomas and Fair Annet.

P. 181, III, 510 b, IV, 469 a, V, 223 b. Add to the Southern ballads ' Le mariage tragique,' Beauquier, Chansons p. recueillies en Franche-comté, p. 81 ; ' Las bodas,' Milá, Romancerillo Catalan, p. 257, No 262. (In this last, ' vert marca esperansa.')

74. Fair Margaret and Sweet William.

P. 199. Communicated by Miss Mary E. Burleigh, of Worcester, Massachusetts, and derived, through a relative, from her great-grandmother, who had heard the ballad sung at gatherings of young people in Webster, Massachusetts, not long after 1820.

1 There was such a man as King William, there was,
  And he courted a lady fair,
  He courted such a lady as Lady Margaret,
  For a whole long twelve-month year.

2 Said he, ' I 'm not the man for you,
  Nor you the maid for me,
  But before many, many long months
  My wedding you shall see.'

3 Said she, ' If I 'm not the maid for you,
  Nor you the man for me,
  Before many, many long days
  My funeral you shall see.'

4 Lady Margaret sat in a green shady bower,
  A combing her yellow, yellow hair,
  When who should she see but King William and his bride,
  And to church they did repair.

5 She threw all down her ivory comb,
  Threw back her yellow hair,
  And to the long chamber she did go,
  And for dying she did prepare.

6 King William had a dream that night,
  Such dreams as scarce prove true :
  He dreamed that Lady Margaret was dead,
  And her ghost appeared to view.

7 ' How do you like your bed ? ' said she,
  ' And how do you like your sheets ?
  And how do you like the fair lady
  That 's in your arms and sleeps ? '

8 ' Well do I like my bed,' said he,
  ' And well do I like my sheets,
  But better do I like the fair lady
  That 's in my arms and sleeps.'

9 King William rose early the next morn,
  Before the break of day,
  Saying, ' Lady Margaret I will go see,
  Without any more delay.'

10 He rode till he came to Lady Margaret's hall,
   And rapped long and loud on the ring,
   But there was no one there but Lady Margaret's brother
   To let King William in.

11 ' Where, O where is Lady Margaret ?
   Pray tell me how does she do.'
   ' Lady Margaret is dead in the long chamber,
   She died for the love of you.'

12 ' Fold back, fold back that winding sheet,
   That I may look on the dead,
   That I may kiss those clay-cold lips
   That once were the cherry-red.'

13 Lady Margaret died in the middle of the night,
   King William died on the morrow,
   Lady Margaret died of pure true love,
   King William died of sorrow.

14 Lady Margaret was buried in King William's churchyard,
   All by his own desire,
   And out of her grave grew a double red rose
   And out of hisn a briar.

15 They grew so high, they grew so tall,
　　That they could grow no higher ;
　　They tied themselves in a true-lover's knot,
　　And both fell down together.

16 Now all ye young that pass this way,
　　And see these two lovers asleep,
　　'T is enough to break the hardest heart,
　　And bring them here to weep.

199 f. Mallet and ' Sweet William.' Full particulars in W. L. Phelps, The Beginnings of the English Romantic Movement, 1893, p. 177 ff.

75. Lord Lovel.

P. 204 f., note †, 512 b, IV, 471 a, V, 225 a. Add : Wolfram, p. 87, No 61, ' Es spielte ein Ritter mit einer Madam.'

205 b, note *. The Swedish ballad (p. 71 f. of the publication mentioned) is defective at the end, and altogether amounts to very little.

[206. **Romaic.** Add : 'La belle Augiranouda,' Georgeakis et Pineau, Folk-lore de Lesbos, p. 223 f.]

206 a, and note *. Add : Wolfram, No 28, p. 55, ' Es war ein Jäger wohlgemut,' and ' Jungfer Dörtchen,' Blätter für Pommersche Volkskunde, II. Jahrgang, p. 12.

211, **H.** I have received a copy recited by a lady in Cambridge, Massachusetts, which was evidently derived from print, and differs but slightly from **a**, omitting 8 ³, ⁴, 9 ¹, ².

76. The Lass of Roch Royal.

P. 215. ' Germaine ' : see Daymard, p. 170 ; Revue des Traditions populaires, III, 364 ; Beauquier, Chansons pop. recueillies en Franche-Comté, p. 259.

77. Sweet William's Ghost.

P. 228 f., 233, 239, III, 514, IV, 474. Of the succession of three cocks, white, red, black (reduced to two in English ballads), see R. Köhler, Der weisse, der rothe und der schwarze Hahn, Germania, XI, 85–92. [So in the tale ' L'Andromède et les Démons,' Georgeakis et Pineau, Folk-lore de Lesbos, p. 82 f.]

228, note †. Two or three additions in Böhme's Erk, I, 598 ff., No 197, c, d, g.

78. The Unquiet Grave.

P. 235 a, last paragraph. Servian ballad in which a child's shirt is wet with its mother's tears, Rajković, p. 143, No 186, ' Dete Lovzar i majka mu ' (' The child and his mother ').

[235. Tears burning the dead. Professor Lanman furnishes the following interesting parallel from the

Mahābhārata, XI, 43 ff. : Dhṛtarāṣṭra is lamenting for his fallen sons. His charioteer says ; — The face that thou wearest, covered with falling tears, is not approved by the sacred books ; nor do wise men praise it. For they [the tears], like sparks, 'tis said, do burn those men (for whom they're shed).]

79. The Wife of Usher's Well.

[P. 238, III, 513. Communicated, 1896, by Miss Emma M. Backus, of North Carolina, who notes that it has long been sung by the " poor whites " in the mountains of Polk County in that State. It has the mother's prayer for the return of her children, as in **C**, III, 513, but is in other respects much nearer to **A**. In the last stanza we should doubtless read " They wet our winding sheet," or the like. In 4⁸ the MS. has *louely* or *lonely*, perhaps meant for *lovely*.

1 There was a lady fair and gay,
　　And children she had three :
　　She sent them away to some northern land,
　　For to learn their grammeree.

2 They hadn't been gone but a very short time,
　　About three months to a day,
　　When sickness came to that land
　　And swept those babes away.

3 There is a king in the heavens above
　　That wears a golden crown :
　　She prayed that he would send her babies home
　　To-night or in the morning soon.

4 It was about one Christmas time,
　　When the nights was long and cool,
　　She dreamed of her three little lonely babes
　　Come running in their mother's room.

5 The table was fixed and the cloth was spread,
　　And on it put bread and wine :
　　' Come sit you down, my three little babes,
　　And eat and drink of mine.'

6 ' We will neither eat your bread, dear mother,
　　Nor we'll neither drink your wine ;
　　For to our Saviour we must return
　　To-night or in the morning soon.'

7 The bed was fixed in the back room ;
　　On it was some clean white sheet,
　　And on the top was a golden cloth,
　　To make those little babies sleep.

8 ' Wake up ! wake up ! ' says the oldest one,
　　' Wake up ! it's almost day.
　　And to our Saviour we must return
　　To-night or in the morning soon.'

9 'Green grass grows at our head, dear mother,
    Green moss grows at our feet ;
The tears that you shed for us three babes
    Won't wet our winding sheet.']

80. Old Robin of Portingale.

[P. 240. Dr. Axel Olrik thinks that this ballad is related to the Danish ballad 'Utro Fæstemø vil forgive sin Fæstemand,' No 345 in the Grundtvig-Olrik collection (Ridderviser, I, 167, note *), which he refers for its origin to the story of the Lombard queen Rosemunda (see note on 'Lord Randal,' No 12, p. 286, above). The drink promised to Old Robin by his wife Dr Olrik thinks may indicate that the English ballad was once more similar to the Danish than it is in the version which we possess.]

87. Prince Robert.

P. 284. A mother prepares wholesome drink for her son, poison for his wife; both son and wife are poisoned. They are buried separately, one in the church, one in the graveyard. Trees from their graves join their tops. White Russian, Šejn, I, i, 444, No 544, 447–51, Nos 546–9 ; Hiltebrandt, p. 64, No 65 ; Kupčanko, 'Vdova otravljaet nevĕstu,' p. 255, No 300. Ruthenian, Kolberg, Pokucie, II, 41, No 48.

90. Jellon Grame.

P. 303 b, 513 b, III, 515 b, IV, 479 b, V, 226 a.
Vol'ga, Volch, of the Russian *bylinas*, must have a high place among the precocious heroes. When he was an hour and a half old his voice was like thunder, and at five years of age he made the earth tremble under his tread. At seven he had learned all cunning and wisdom, and all the languages. Dobrynya is also to be mentioned. See Wollner, Volksepik der Grossrussen, pp. 47 f., 91.
Simon the Foundling in the fine Servian heroic song of that name, Karadžić, II, 63, No 14, Talvj, I, 71, when he is a year old is like other children of three ; when he is twelve like others of twenty, and wonderfully learned, with no occasion to be afraid of any scholar, not even the abbot. (Cf. 'The Lord of Lorne,' V, 54, 9, 10.)
Other cases, Revue Celtique, XII, 63 ; Wardrop, Georgian Folk Tales, No 6, p. 26. G. L. K. [Lady Guest's Mabinogion, III, 32, 65 ; 201, 232 ; Firdusi, Livre des Rois, Mohl, 1838, I, 353 ff. A. and A. Schott, Walachische Märchen, p. 265 (cf. A. Wirth, Danae in christlichen Legenden, p. 34). F. N. Robinson. See also von Wlislocki, M. u. S. der Bukowinaer u. Siebenbürger Armenier, No 24, p. 65 ; Jacottet, Contes pop. des Bassoutos, p. 196 f. ; Georgeakis et Pineau, Folklore de Lesbos, p. 168.]

93. Lamkin.

Pp. 320–42, III, 515, IV, 480 f., V, 229 f.
Denham, Tracts, II, 190, refers to a Northumbrian version of the ballad which associated Long Lonkin with Nafferton Castle in the parish of Ovingham. He also gives a story, obtained from an old man in Newcastle, according to which Long Lonkin is no mason but a gentleman, who kills the lady and her one child because the lord of Nafferton had been preferred to him. The husband, abandoning his journey to London on account of a misgiving that all was not right at home, after finding his wife and child dead, hunts down the murderer, who drops from a tree in which he had concealed himself into a pool, thence called Long Lonkin's pool, and is drowned.

Communicated by Mr. W. W. Newell, with the superscription (by the original transcriber, Miss Emma M. Backus) "as sung in Newbern, North Carolina, seventy-five years ago" (1895).

1 John Lankin was a good mason
    As ever laid a stone ;
He built Lord Arnold's castle
    And the lord he paid him none.

2 John Lankin then swore,
    If the lord did not pay him,
He would break into his castle
    And murder all his kinsmen.

3 Lord Arnold soon did hear
    Of John Lankin's threat so dour;
He did guard all his castle
    With soldiers every hour.

4 He said to his lady,
    'I am going away from home,
And what should you do
    If John Lankin should come?'

5 'I care not for John Lankin,
    Or any of his kin ;
I will bar all my doors
    And I 'll pin my windows in.'

6 The doors were all barrd
    And the windows pinned in,
And out of the kitchen-window
    The nurse she let him in.

7 He killed the good lady
    With a cowardly cruel blow,
And threw her pretty baby
    To the dank moat below.

8 John Lankin was hung
    On the gallows so high,

And the nurse she was chained
In a dungeon to die.

95. The Maid freed from the Gallows.

P. 346 f., III, 516 a, IV, 481 a, V, 231 a. Michele
Barbi, Poesia popolare pistoiese, p. 9, found a fragment
of Scibilia Nobili at Pian dagli Ontani under the
name of Violina, and Giannini's 'Prigioniera' (III,
516 a), otherwise 'Mosettina,' under the name 'Violina,' 'Brunetta,' etc.

The following copy was communicated by Mr W.
W. Newell, as derived from Miss Emma M. Backus,
North Carolina, who says: "This is an old English song,
in the Yorkshire dialect, which was brought over to
Virginia before the Revolution. It has not been written for generations, for none of the family have been
able to read or write." Miss Backus adds that the pronunciation indicated is by no means that which is ordinarily used by the people who sing this ballad. It will,
however, be noted that the Yorkshire dialect is not
well preserved.

THE HANGMAN'S TREE.

1 'Hangman, hangman, howd yo hand,
    O howd it wide and far!
  For theer I see my feyther coomin,
    Riding through the air.

2 'Feyther, feyther, ha yo brot me goold?
    Ha yo paid my fee?
  Or ha yo coom to see me hung,
    Beneath tha hangman's tree?'

3 'I ha naw brot yo goold,
    I ha naw paid yo fee,
  But I ha coom to see yo hung
    Beneath tha hangman's tree.'

4, 5 ⎫
7, 8 ⎬ *as in* 1, 2, *substituting*   meyther ⎫
10, 11 ⎭   sister ⎬ *for* feyther.
  6, 9, *as in* 3.   sweetheart ⎭

12 'Oh I ha brot yo goold,
    And I ha paid yo fee,
  And I ha coom to take yo froom
    Beneath tha hangman's tree.'

3⁴. hangmens. 4⁸. mither. 5². Or ha. 5⁸. hang.
5⁴, 8⁴, 11⁴. gallows tree. 12³. An. 12⁴. the.

348 b. **German.** Böhme, in his edition of Erk's
Liederhort, I, 277, adds a copy, from singing, dated
1878, 'Die Losgekaufte,' No 78 e.

349 f., 514 a, III, 516 b. A young man in prison
bought out by his sweetheart, father, mother, etc., refusing help: Little Russian, Romanov, I, 63, No 2;
Croatian, Valjavec, p. 303, No 19, 'Junak vu Madjarski

vuzi;' Great Russian, Jakuškin, p. 147 f.; Ruthenian,
Kolberg, Pokucie, II, 226 f., Nos 418, 420. Woman
rescued by lover from Tatar who was about to kill her,
the blood-relations declining: Romanov, I, 53, No 105.

514 a. In Nesselmann's Littauische Volkslieder, No
119, p. 96, and Bartsch's Dainu Balsai, I, 147, No 107,
II, 202, No 321 (from Bezzenberger, Litauische Forschungen, p. 17, No 27), we have a ballad of a youth
who does not get release from confinement though his
blood relations lay down handsomely for him, but in the
end is freed by his sweetheart with a trifle of a ring or
a garland. In Bartsch, I, 63, No 53, a girl who has
been shut up nine years is let alone by her father and
her brother, but liberated by her lover; II, 296, Ulmann,
Lettische Volkslieder, p. 168, relations make an attempt
to buy off a conscript, without success, but his sweetheart effects his release by selling her garland. Silly
stories all.

96. The Gay Goshawk.

P. 356, III, 517 a, IV, 482 a, V, 234 a. Chanson du
Roi Loys, ou de la Belle dans la Tour. Add 'Le Prince
qui torture sa Fille,' Beauquier, Chansons p. recueillies
en Franche-Comté, p. 147; copy from Normandy, copy
from Savoy, Revue des Traditions populaires, X, 641 f.

356 b, III, 517 a, IV, 482, V, 234 a. 'Les trois capitaines.' Add: 'Au château de Belfort,' Beauquier, pp.
59 f., 369 f.

III, 517 b. Girl feigns death to avoid a disagreeable suitor; test of water, fire, and hand in bosom, which
last is the hardest to bear: 'Vojvoda Janko i mlada
Andjelija,' Hrvatske Pjesme iz "Naše Sloge," II, 65,
No 68.

100. Willie o Winsbury.

P. 399, note. The ballad need not be older than the
16th century. Drop "but it was hardly," etc.

104. Prince Heathen.

P. 424 b. It is more commonly the lady that is rolled
in silk; the son is laid, dressed, rolled in silk, No 5,
C, 82, No 20, **C**, 8 of the places cited (**C**, 83, **E**, 32, are
to be dropped), and No 104, **B**, 14.

112. The Baffled Knight.

II, 479 a. The Complete Collection of Old and New
English and Scotch Songs, 1735, a rare book, is in the
library of the British Museum, and Mr Round, who
has kindly examined it for me, informs me that all the
ballads in it are repetitions from earlier publications;
in the present case of **B**, from Pills to purge Melancholy.

481 b, IV, 495 a. Add 'Il fallait plumer la perdrix,'
Beauquier, Chansons p. recueillies en Franche-Comté,
p. 303.

481 b, III, 518 a, IV, 495 a, V, 239 b. Tears : add 'L'Amant timide,' Beauquier, Chansons p. recueillies en Franche-Comté, p. 180 ; La Tradition, 1895, p. 69.

483 b, V, 240 a. La Batelière rusée in Beauquier, Chansons populaires recueillies en Franche-Comté, p. 40.

Slavic ballads of similar tenor (Servian), Rajković, 'Mudra devojka,' p. 16, No 23, 'Lukava čobanka,' p. 129, No 173.

VOL. III.

116. Adam Bell, etc.

P. 22. Translated after the original text by Professor Emilio Teza : 'I tre Banditi,' Padova, 1894.

26, 87[1]. I regret having changed 'an oute-horne,' which is the reading in all the texts which have the stanza (b-f), to 'a noute-horne.' Oute horne was originally given, and therefore this reading was not entered in the variations of c-f, as should have been done later, when the reading 'a noute-horne' was adopted.

117. A Gest of Robyn Hode.

P. 43, note §. Right-hitting Brand is one of the attendants of Robin in A. Munday's Metropolis Coronata (1615), Fairholt, Pageants, I, 40. J. M. Manly.

52 and note. See further on Le prêt miraculeusement remboursé, M. René Basset, in Revue des Traditions populaires, IX, 14–31.

54. Mr Macmath has sent me a transcript of another copy of the song in Deuteromelia which exhibits some variations. It was found April 5, 1895, in a bundle of papers that had belonged to John, Duke of Roxburghe. This copy is in a 17th century hand, and at the end is written : " This song was esteemed an old song before the rebellion broke out in 1641."

76, st. 412. The first two verses should be corrected according to f, g, thus :

'Mercy,' then said Robyn to our kynge,
'Vnder this.'

120. Robin Hood's Death.

P. 103, note *, V, 240. Communion-bread called God (Lord). " For it was about Easter, at what times maidens gadded abroade, after they had taken their Maker, as they call it." Wilson, Arte of Logike, fol. 84 b. J. M. Manly.

" In oure louerd þat he had ynome wel ioyful he was þo." St Edmund the Confessor, v. 573, Furnivall, Early English Poems, Philol. Soc., p. 86. " Preostes . . . fette to þis holi maide godes flesch and his blod." St Lucy, v. 168, ib. p. 106. G. L. K.

103, note †. The met-yard, being a necessary part of an archer's equipment for such occasions as p. 29, 148, 158; p. 75, 397 ; p. 93, 28 ; p. 201, 18, 21, may well enough be buried with him.

104. Russian. Similar directions as to the grave in Jakuškin, p. 99.

123. Robin Hood and The Curtal Friar.

P. 128 a, v. 80. The reading should be

Now am I, frere, without, and thou, Robyn, within :

otherwise there is no change in their relative plight.

125. Robin Hood and Little John.

P. 133 a. There is a black-letter copy, printed by and for W. Onley, in Lord Crawford's collection, No 1320 ; the date put at 1680–85. A white-letter copy in Roxburghe, III, 728. See Ebsworth's Roxburghe Ballads, VIII, 504.

155. Sir Hugh or the Jew's Daughter.

[241 a. The Life and Miracles of St William of Norwich have been edited by Drs Jessopp and James.]

156. Queen Eleanor's Confession.

P. 258 b, 3d paragraph. The Danish ballad is printed in Dania, II, 275, 1893 : ' Vise om Caroline Mathilde,' derived from an old lady who in childhood had heard it sung by a peasant girl, about 50 years before the publication.

159. Durham Field.

P. 283 a. Knights wearing the king's armor in battle. This was naturally frequently done. So John at Poitiers had twenty in his " parements," Froissart (Buchon), III, 186, and Charles VIII a good number at Fornovo, Daniel, Histoire de France, VIII, 222.

161. The Battle of Otterburn.

Pp. 294, 520 a, IV, 499, V, 244 b. St George Our Lady's Knight. Add : Torrent of Portyngale, v. 1677 : E. Flügel, Neuenglisches Lesebuch, I, 441.

162. The Hunting of the Cheviot.

P. 306 a, 38 f. Motherwell has cited an apt passage from the romance of Alisaunder which may well be repeated.

Ac theo deol that Alisaunder made
No may Y nought fully rede.
Darie starf in his armes two :
Lord that Alisaunder was wo !
He wrong his hondes saun faile,

Ofte he cried and ofte he uaile :
Y wolde Y hadde al Perce y-geve,
With that Y myghte have thy lif !
                              Weber, Kyng Alisaunder
                                     vv. 4648–55.

P. 306, st. 54, IV, 502, V, 244. Hrafn fights after
Gunnlaugr has hewn off his feet: Gunnlaugs saga Ormstungu, ed. Mogk, p. 27. W. H. Schofield.
Note †. The Highlander is paralleled by an Indian
in The Observations of Sir Richard Hawkins, Markham, The Hawkins' Voyages, Hakluyt Society, p. 243,
and by Mordred in Malory's Morte Darthur, ed. Sommer, Bk 21, ch. 4. G. L. K.

168. Flodden Field.

P. 351 b (12, lapt all in leather), IV, 507 a. The
dying witch of Berkeley says to her children : Insuite
me corio cervino, deinde in sarcophago lapideo supinate,
operculum plumbo et ferro constringite. William of
Malmesbury, Gesta Regum Anglorum, ed. Stubbs, Bk
2, I, 254, § 204.

169. Johnie Armstrong.

[P. 367. Johnie's plain speech to the king. So in Li
Charrois de Nymes, v. 283, in Jonkbloet, Guillaume
d' Orange, I, 80 : "Et dit Guillaumes, 'Dans rois, vos i
mentez.' "]
367, and note. The Baron of Brackley's son (No
203), set on the nurse's knee, uses nearly the same words
as Johnie Armstrong's in B, 24. M. Gaidoz, Mélusine,
VII, 70, cites from Hone the passage in No 54 (B, 5, 6,
see also A, 5, 6, D, 4, 5), in which Jesus speaks from
his mother's womb. See further Mélusine, IV, 447,
V, 36, 257, VI, 92.

170. The Death of Queen Jane.

P. 372–6. Appendix. 'The Duke of Bedford,'
Longman's Magazine, XVII, 217, 1890, " sent from Suffolk," is one half (sts 5–8) a plagiarism from ' The
Death of Queen Jane.' Compare A, 5, 6, B, 8, C, 5, 6,
D 6 of Queen Jane with what follows. The remainder
of ' The Duke of Bedford' is so trivial that it is not
worth the while at present to assign that piece its own
place. I have not attempted to identify this duke of
Bedford ; any other duke would probably answer as
well.

THE DUKE OF BEDFORD.

1 Six lords went a-hunting down by the seaside,
  And they spied a dead body washed away by the
      tide.

2 Said one to the other, ' As I 've heard them say,
  'T is the famous Duke of Bedford, by the tide washed
      away.'

3 They took him up to Portsmouth, to the place where
      he was born,
  From Portsmouth up to London, to the place where
      he was known.

4 They took out his bowels and laid down his feet,
  And they garnished his body with roses so sweet.

5 Six lords went before him, six bare him from the
      ground,
  Eight dukes followed after, in their black velvet
      gowns.

6 .   .   .   .
  And the Royal Princess Mary went weeping away.

7 So black was the funeral and so white were their
      fans,
  And so pretty were the flamboys that they carried in
      their hands.

8 The drums they did beat and the trumpets they did
      sound,
  And the great guns they did rattle as they put him
      in the ground.

173. Mary Hamilton.

P. 382. The passages following relate to the affair
of the Frenchwoman and the apothecary. Calendar of
State Papers, Foreign Series, of the Reign of Elizabeth,
1563. (Indicated to me by Mr Andrew Lang.)
The Queen's apothecary got one of her maidens, a
Frenchwoman, with child. Thinking to have covered
his fault with medicine, the child was slain. They are
both in prison, and she is so much offended that it is
thought they shall both die. Randolph to Cecil, Edinburgh, 21 Dec., 1563, p. 637. The apothecary and the
woman he got with child were both hanged this Friday.
Randolph to Cecil, Dec. 31, 1563, p. 650.
The heroine of this ballad is Mary Hamilton in all
copies in which she has a full name, that is, twelve out
of the twenty-four which have any name ; Mary simply,
or Mary mild,* is found in eleven copies, and Maisry in
one. Finding in the history of the court of Peter the
Great an exact counterpart of the story of the ballad
with a maid of honor named Mary Hamilton filling the
tragic rôle, and " no trace of an admixture of the Russian story with that of the Frenchwoman and the queen's
apothecary," I felt compelled to admit that Sharpe's

* Mild Mary is an appellation which occurs elsewhere (as
in No 91 E), and Mary Hamilton and Mary mild are inter-
changeable in X. It is barely worth remarking that Myle,
Moil, in C, S, are merely varieties of pronunciation, and
Miles in W, an ordinary kind of corruption.

suggestion of the Russian origin of the ballad was, however surprising, the only tenable opinion (III, 382 f.). Somewhat later a version of the ballad (**U**) was found at Abbotsford in which there is mention of the apothecary and of the practices for which he suffered in 1563, and this fact furnished ground for reopening the question (which, nevertheless, was deferred).

Mr Andrew Lang has recently subjected the matter of the origin of the ballad to a searching review (in Blackwood's Magazine, September, 1895, p. 381 ff.). Against the improbability that an historical event of 1718–9 should by simple chance coincide, very minutely and even to the inclusion of the name of the principal actor, with what is related in a ballad ostensibly recounting an event in the reign of Mary Stuart, he sets the improbability that a ballad, older and superior in style to anything which we can show to have been produced in the 18th, or even the 17th century,* should have been composed after 1719, a ballad in which a contemporary occurrence in a foreign and remote country would be transferred to Scotland and Queen Mary's day, and so treated as to fit perfectly into the circumstances of the time: and this while the ballad might entirely well have been evolved from a notorious domestic occurrence of the date 1563, the adventure of Queen Mary's French maid and the apothecary — which has now turned out to be introduced into one version of the ballad.†

I wish to avow that the latter improbability, as put by Mr Lang, has come to seem to me considerably greater than the former.

The coincidence of the name of the heroine is indeed at first staggering; but it will be granted that of all the "honorable houses" no one might more plausibly supply a forgotten maid of honor than the house of Hamilton. The Christian name is a matter of course for a Queen's Mary.

384 ff., IV, 507 ff., V, 246 f.

BB.

THE QUEEN'S MARIES.

Communicated by Mr Andrew Lang as received from Mrs Arthur Smith; sung by a nurse. 4 is clearly modern.

1 Yestreen the queen had four Maries,
  But the nicht she 'll hae but three ;
There was Mary Beaton, and Mary Seaton,
  And Mary Carmichell, and me.

* In the 18th century we have 'Derwentwater' and 'Rob Roy,' both of slight value; in the 17th 'The Fire of Frendraught' and 'The Baron of Brackley,' both fairly good ballads, and others of some merit; but nothing in either to be compared with 'Mary Hamilton.'
† As to the "ballads" about the Maries mentioned by Knox, I conceive that these may mean nothing more than verses of any sort to the discredit of these ladies.

2 Oh little did my mither think,
  At nicht when she cradled me,
That I wad sleep in a nameless grave
  And hang on the gallows-tree.
    Yestreen, etc.

3 They 'll tie a kerchief round my een,
  And they 'll na let me see t' dee,
And they 'll spread my story thro a' the land,
  Till it reaches my ain countrie.

4 I wish I micht sleep in the auld kirkyard,
  Beneath the hazel tree,
Where aft we played in the long simmer nichts,
  My brithers and sisters and me.

176. Northumberland betrayed by Douglas.

P. 411 a. Looking through a ring. "The Dul Dauna put a ring to his eye, and he saw his grandfather on the deck walking." Larminie, West Irish Folk-Tales, p. 9. G. L. K.

177. The Earl of Westmoreland.

P. 417. Dr W. H. Schofield suggests that the romance imitated in the second part of this ballad is, Libeaus Desconus. There the hero, who is but a child in years (in the ballad he has a child's voice), comes to a fair city by a river side, the lady of which is besieged by a giant, black as pitch. Libeaus undertakes to fight the giant, and is received by him with disdainful language. The fight is "beside the water brim." They break their spears at the first encounter ; then fight on foot with swords. Libeaus strikes off the giant's head and carries it into the town ; the people come out to meet him "with a fair procession," and the lady invites him to be her lord in city and castle. Compare the ballad, etc., 54–78, and Libeaus Desconus, v. 1321 ff. [See Dr Schofield's Studies on the Libeaus Desconus, p. 242, in Studies and Notes in Philology and Literature published under the direction of the Modern Language Departments of Harvard University, Vol. IV.]

178. Captain Car, or, Edom o Gordon.

IV, 513 b, **H** 2⁴. Mr Macmath is convinced that the missing (illegible) word is *orghie* (orgeis = a fish, a large kind of ling).

182. The Laird o Logie.

P. 456. Buchan's original MS. p. 216 ff., 'The Laird o Logie.'

1 Lady Margaret carries the keys o the cellar,
  I wyte she carries them carefullie ;

Nae other ane her favour coud gain
But the winsome laird o young Logie.

2 When the king gat word o that,
    I wat an angry man was he;
He 's casten him into prison strong,
    And sware high hanged he shoud be.

3 Lady Margaret tore her yellow hair,
    She 's torn it out locks three by three ;
Says, 'Wae to the day I eer was born,
    Or knew the young laird o Logie.'

4 'Now hold your tongue,' the queen she said,
    'And ye 'll let a' your folly be ;
I hae minded me on a wyle
    Will gain the life o young Logie.'

5 Then she has done her up the stairs,
    And she fell low down on her knee ;
'Win up, win up, my dame the queen,
    What makes ye bow sae low to me? '

6 'O do you mind when we were wed,
    Ye promisd askings three by three?
And a' the boun that I now crave
    Is, Save the life o young Logie.

7 'If ye had asked lands, my dame,
    Ye might had askings three by three ;
But a' the lands in fair Scotland
    Winna save the life o young Logie.'

8 Then she has done her down the stairs,
    But nae gude tidings brought her wi ;
The king has sworn a solemn oath,
    And broken it can never be.

9 'Hold your tongue, Margaret,' said the queen,
    'And ye 'll lat a' your folly be ;
I 'll mind me on another wyle
    To gain the life o young Logie.'

10 She 's counterfeit the king's hand write,
    And she has stole his right glove tee ;
And sent the jailors strict command
    To loose and set young Logie free.

11 She sent him a bag o gude red gowd,
    Another bag o white monie ;
Likewise a pistol by his side,
    And bade him shoot when he wan free.

12 As he passd by the queen's window,
    He fell low down upon his knee ;
Says, 'Peace be wi the queen hersell,
    And joy be in her companie.'

13 As he passd by the king's window,
    There a proud volley then gae he ;
Says, 'Hang your dogs when ye think time,
    For ye 'se neer hang him, young Logie.'

14 Out then speaks the king himsell,
    I wyte a solemn oath sware he ;
'I 'll wad my head an my crown baith,
    I hear the voice o young Logie.'

15 The king he calld his jailors all,
    He called them then three by three ;
Says, 'How are the prisoners ane and a' ?
    Where is the laird o young Logie? '

16 'Did you not send your ain hand write?
    Did you not send your right glove tee?
We took the keys o the jail-house door,
    And loosd and set young Logie free.'

17 Then out it speaks the king again,
    I wyte an angry man was he ;
'The morn, before I eat or drink,
    High hanged shall you jailors be.'

18 Then out it speaks the queen hersell,
    I wyte a light laugh then gae she ;
'If ye 're to hang them ane and a',
    I fear ye will begin wi me.

19 'Did I not steal your ain hand write?
    Did I not steal your right glove tee?
Then sent the jailors strict command
    To loose an' set young Logie free.'

190. Jamie Telfer.

P. 5 a first paragraph. However, "in the list of Border thieves made in the year 1552, William Patrick, the priest, and John Nelson, the curate of Bewcastle, are both included": Denham Tracts, I, 150. This shows that the society was homogeneous.

191. Hughie Grame.

P. 14, **E**. Between 12 and 13 follows in Buchan's original MS. :

Ye 'll tell this news to Maggy my wife,
    The first time ye gang oer the muir,
She is the cause I loose my life :
    She bade me steal the bishop's mare.

192. The Lochmaben Harper.

P. 21. **E** has in Buchan's original MS. this refrain at the end of the verse :

Hey, didentie, didentie, didentie (*bis*).

196. The Fire of Frendraught.

P. 41, note ‡. Read : The peerage of Aboyne was first created in 1626, in favor of John Gordon, fifth son of the first Marquis of Huntly (Viscount of Aboyne and Melgum in 1627). He married Sophia Hay, a daughter of Francis, Earl of Errol, The Records of Aboyne, edited by the Marquis of Huntly, New Spalding Club; 1894, pp. 325, 526.

V, 251 b, P. 44. In " But Rothiemay lie," *may* seems to have been accidentally omitted. The " Turn " in Scott was probably meant for Twin, the dot of i being omitted.

200. The Gypsy Laddie.

P. 61 ff., V, 252. The three stanzas which follow are given in H. A. Kennedy's " Professor Blackie : his Sayings and Doings, London, 1895 " as they were sung by Marion Stodart, Professor Blackie's aunt, to her sister's children. P. 12 f. (Communicated by Mr David MacRitchie, of Edinburgh.)

There were seven gypsies all in a row,
  And they were brisk and bonny ; O
They sang till they came to the Earl o Cassilis' gate,
  And there they sang sae sweetly. O

They sang sae sweet and sae complete
  That doun came the fair leddy ;
And when they saw her weel-faured face
  They cast the glamour ower her.

So she's taen off her high-heeled shoes,
  That are made o the Spanish leather,
And she's put on her Highland brogues,
  To skip amang the heather.

" On the discovery of which the earl ' saddled to him his milk-white steed,' and rested not till he had hanged the seven gypsies on a tree."

O *at the end of the second and the fourth verse of each stanza.*

216. The Mother's Malison, etc.

P. 186 f. In 'Majčina kletva,' Hrvatske Pjesme iz " Naše Sloge," II, 22, No 18, two lovers go off in a boat, under a mother's curse, and are both drowned.

229. Earl Crawford.

P. 280 a, **A**, b. b was written down March 25, 1890.

234. Charlie MacPherson.

P. 310. Mr Walker of Aberdeen suggests that Billy Beg in 3 should be Bellabeg, a small property in Strath-don. It will be observed that two other men in the same stanza are named by their estates.

235. The Earl of Aboyne.

P. 311 b, omit the paragraph beginning J, and say :
Charles, first Earl of Aboyne, married for his first wife Margaret Irvine of Drum, who died in December, 1662. (The Records of Aboyne, edited by the Marquis of Huntly, New Spalding Club, 1894, p. 552.) The story of the ballad, so far as is known, is an absolute fiction.

In vol. ii of *Retours* or Services of Heirs, No 4906 (Aberdeen), 17 June, 1665, there is the entry : Domina Anna Gordoun, hæres Dominæ Margaretæ Irving, sponsæ Comitis de Aboyne matris. (Mr Walker of Aberdeen.)

311, V, 270. Mr Macmath has sent me this stall-copy, printed by J. Morren, Cowgate, Edinburgh.

PEGGY IRVINE.

1 Our lady stands in her chamber-door,
  viewing the Grahams are a coming ;
She knew by the light of their livery so red
  they were new come down from London.

2 She called on her chambermaid,
  and Jeany her gentlewoman :
You 'll dress my body in some fine dress,
  for yon is my good lord a coming.

3 Her smock was of the holland so fine,
  her body round with busting ;
Her shoes were of the small corded twine,
  and her stockings silk and twisting.

4 Her petticoats was of the silk so fine,
  set out with the silver and scolloping ;
Her gown was of the red damask silk so fine,
  trimmed with the red gold gold mounting.

5 'You guildery maids, come trim up my gauze,
  and make them silver shining ;
With strawberry flowers cover all my bowers,
  and hang them round with the linen.

6 'Ye minstrels all, be on our call
  when you see his horses coming ;
With music spring, spare not your string
  when you hear his bridles ringing.'

7 She called on Meg her chamber-maid,
  and Jeanny her gentlewoman :
'Go bring me a bottle of the good Spanish wine,
  for to drink his health that 's coming.'

8 She gently tripped down the stair,
  and away to the gate to meet him :

'You are welcome, you lord of the Boyne,
　　you are welcome home from London.'

9 'If this be so, come let me know,
　　come kiss me for my coming ;
　For tomorrow should have been my wedding-day
　　if I had staid in London.'

10 She gave the glass out of her hand,
　　she was a woeful woman :
　'If the morrow should be your wedding-day,
　　Go back to your whores in London.'

11 He looked oer his right shoulder,
　　his comely court behind him :
　'This is a merry welcome' he says,
　　'that we have got from London.

12 'To your horse, to your horse, my nobles all,
　　to your horse, let us be going ;
　This night we'll lodge in Drummond castle,
　　and tomorrow we'll march to London.'

13 Now this lady has fallen sick,
　　and doctors we her dealing,
　But at length her heart did break,
　　and letters sent to London.

14 He took the letter in his hand,
　　and loud, loud was he laughing,
　But before he read it to an end,
　　the tears did come down rapping.

15 'To your horse, to your horse, my nobles all,
　　to your horse, let's be going ;
　To your horse, let us all go in black,
　　and mourn for Peggy Irvine.'

16 When he came to his own castle-gate,
　　the knight was weary weeping :
　'Cheer up your heart, you lord of Boyne,
　　your lady is but sleeping.'

17 'Sleeping deary, sleeping dow,
　　I'm afraid she's oer sound sleeping ;
　It's I had rather lost all the lands of the Boyne
　　before I would have lost Peggy Irvine.'

4². set out out.　10³. If he.

238. Glenlogie, or, Jean o Bethelnie.

P. 338 b, 2d paragraph. As to the name Melville,
Mr Walker of Aberdeen remarks : If Buchan's story
(given in his notes) of the Glenlogie incident were correct, the maiden's name must have been Seaton, and
not Melville, the Seatons and Urquharts being the only
two names which in historical times could be called
lairds of Meldrum or Bethelnie.

248. The Grey Cock, or, Saw you my Father?

P. 390. Add to the French ballads 'Le voltigeur
fidèle,' Beauquier, Chansons p. recueillies en Franche-
Comté, p. 338.

250. Henry Martyn.

E

P. 393. 'Andrew Bartin,' communicated by Miss
Louise Porter Haskell as derived from Gen. E. P. Alexander of South Carolina, and derived by him from the
singing of a cadet at West Point Military Academy in
the winter of 1856–7. Two or three slight corrections
have been made by Mrs A. C. Haskell, sister of Gen.
Alexander. This copy comes nearer than the others
to the original Andrew Barton ; but sts 11–13 are derived from Captain Ward, No 287, 8, 10.

1 Three bold brothers of merrie Scotland,
　　And three bold brothers were they,
　And they cast lots the one with the other,
　　To see who should go robbing all oer the salt sea;
　And they cast lots the one with the other,
　　To see who should go robbing all oer the salt sea.

2 The lot it fell on Andrew Bartin,
　　The youngest of the three,
　That he should go robbing all oer the salt sea,
　　To maintain his two brothers and he.

3 He had not sailed but one long summer night,
　　When daylight did appear ;
　He saw a ship sailing far off and far round,
　　At last she came sailing quite near.

4 'Who art? who art?' says Andrew Bartin,
　　'Who art thee comes sailing so nigh?'
　'We are the rich merchants of merrie England,
　　Just please for to let us pass by.'

5 'Pass by? pass by?' says Andrew Bartin,
　　'No, no, that never can be ;
　Your ship and your cargo I will take away,
　　And your brave men drown in the sea.'

6 Now when this news reached merrie England —
　　King George he wore the crown —
　That his ship and his cargo were taken away,
　　And his brave men they were all drowned.

7 'Go build me a ship,' says Captain Charles Stewart,
　　'A ship both stout and sure,
　And if I dont fetch this Andrew Bartin,
　　My life shall no longer endure.'

8 He had not sailed but one long summer night,
   When daylight did appear,
He saw a ship sailing far off and far round,
   And then she came sailing quite near.

9 'Who art? who art?' says Captain Charles Stewart,
   'Who art comes sailing so nigh?'
'We are the bold brothers of merrie Scotland,
   Just please for to let us pass by.'

10 'Pass by? pass by?' says Captain Charles Stewart,
   'No, no, that never can be;
Your ship and your cargo I will take away,
   And your brave men carry with me.'

11 'Come on! come on!' says Andrew Bartin,
   'I value you not one pin;
And though you are lined with good brass without,
   I'll show you I've fine steel within.'

12 Then they drew up a full broadside
   And at each other let pour;
They had not fought for four hours or more,
   When Captain Charles Stewart gave oer.

13 'Go home! go home!' says Andrew Bartin,
   'And tell your king for me,
That he may reign king of the merry dry land,
   But that I will be king of the sea.'

2[1], etc. Bartyn. *Gen. Alexander remarks that* "the accent was on the last syllable."

———————

'Row tu me, row tu me,' says He-ne-ry Burgin,
   'Row tu me, row tu me, I prah;
For I ha tarnd a Scotch robber across the salt seas,
   Tu ma-i-ntn my tew brothers and me.'

Fragment of a Suffolk Harvest Home song, remembered by an old Suffolk divine. Contributed by Edward Fitzgerald to Suffolk Notes and Queries in the 'Ipswich Journal,' 1877–78; where another stanza follows which has no connection with the above. See 'Two Suffolk Friends,' by Francis Hindes Groome, Edinburgh and London, 1895, p. 79 f.

269. Lady Diamond.

[P. 29 a. Zupitza, Die mittelenglischen Bearbeitungen der Erzählung Boccaccio's von Ghismonda u. Guiscardo, in Geiger's Vierteljahrsschrift f. Kultur u. Litteratur der Renaissance, 1886, I, 63 ff.]

29. **Italian. D.** 'Ricardo e Germonda,' communicated by P. Mazzucchi, Castelguglielmo, July, 1894, to Rivista delle Tradizioni pop. italiane, I, 691.

[32 ff. On these stories of the husband who gives his

wife her lover's heart to eat, see H. Patzig, Zur Geschichte der Herzmäre, Berlin, 1891.]

34. **A** is translated by Professor Emilio Teza, 'Donna Brigida,' in Rassegna Napolitana, II, 63, 1895.

272. The Suffolk Miracle.

P. 60 ff. See Professor Schischmánov in Indogermanische Forschungen, IV, 412–48, 1894, Der Lenorenstoff in der bulgarischen Volkspoesie. Professor Schischmánov counts more than 140 versions of The Dead Brother, ballad and tale, in Albanian, Bulgarian, Greek, Roumanian, and Servian, 60 of these Bulgarian. Dozon 7 is affirmed to be a mere plagiarism. The versions of the Romaic ballad run up to 41. A very strong probability is made out of the derivation of all of the ballads of 'The Dead Brother' from the Greek.

62. Compare La Jeune Fille et l'âme de sa mère, Luzel, I, 60, 61 ff. A girl who grieves for her dead mother, and wishes to see her again, is directed by the curé to go three nights to the church, taking each time an apron for her mother. The mother tears the apron into 9, 6, 3 pieces successively.

La mère va alors trouver sa fille
Et lui parle de la sorte :

'Tu as eu du bonheur
Que je ne t'aie mise toi-même en morceaux !

'Que je ne t'aie mise en pièces, toute vivante,
Comme je le faisais à mes tabliers !

'Tu augmentais mes peines, chaque jour,
Par la douleur que tu me témoignais !'

64. A dead lover takes his mistress on his horse at midnight and carries her to the grave in which he is to be buried the following day. Her corpse is found there, flattened out and disfigured. 'La fiancée du mort,' Le Braz, La Légende de la mort en Basse-Bretagne, pp. 359–67.

[65 a. **Romaic.** Add: Georgeakis et Pineau, Le Folk-lore de Lesbos, p. 253 (in translation).]

273. King Edward the Fourth and a Tanner of Tamworth.

P. 74 f. Similar tales: Sébillot, Contes pop. de la Haute-Bretagne, II, 149 f. ; Luzel, Contes pop. de la Basse-Bretagne, I, 259.

274. Our Goodman.

P. 88 a. [A version similar to that in Smith's Scotish Minstrel, but not absolutely identical, is mentioned in Blätter f. literarische Unterhaltung, 1855, p. 236, as contained, with a German translation, in "Ten Scottish

Songs rendered into German. By W. B. Macdonald of
Rammerscales. Scottish and German. Edinburgh,
1854." Professor Child refers to this version in a MS.
note. A specimen of the translation is given in the
journal just cited, as well as enough of the Scotch to
show that the copy is not exactly like Smith's. "Vetter Macintosh" and "der Fürst Karl" are mentioned.
Macdonald's book is not at this moment accessible.
G. L. K.]

89 f., 281 a. 'Le Jaloux, ou Les Répliques de Marion;'
add version from Normandy (prose), Revue des Traditions populaires, X, 136 ; Hautes-Pyrénées, p. 515.

The copy in Le chroniqueur du Périgord et de Limousin is 'La rusade,' Poésies pop. de la France, MSS, III,
fol. 84. The copy in Le Pèlerinage de Mireille (A.
Lexandre), is from Provence, and closely resembles that
in Daudet's Numa Roumestan.

Italian. Add 'Marion,' Rivista delle Tradizioni pop.
italiane, II, 34–37. 'O Violina' is repeated, very nearly,
in a Tuscan *Filastrocca*, Rivista delle Tradizioni pop.
italiane, II, 474 f. ; see also Archivio, III, 43, No 18.
A Polish ballad has some little similarity : Kolberg,
Lud, XXI, 54, No 112.

275. Get up and bar the Door.

P. 96 ff., 281. Add : 'Le fumeur de hachich et sa
femme,' cited by R. Basset, Revue des Traditions Populaires, VII, 189. G. L. K. [Also ' The First Fool's
Story,' M. Longworth Dames, Balochi Tales, Folk-
Lore, IV, 195.]

277. The Wife Wrapt in Wether's Skin.

P. 104. From the recitation of Miss Lydia R. Nichols, Salem, Massachusetts, as heard in the early years
of this century. Sung by a New England country fellow on ship-board : Journal of American Folk-Lore,
VII, 253 ff., 1894.

As to "drew her table," 13, the following information is given : "I have often heard a mother tell her
daughter to 'draw the table.' Forty years ago it was
not uncommon to see in farmhouses a large round table,
the body of which was made to serve as an armchair.
When the table was not in use the top was tipped back
against the wall. Under the chair-seat was a drawer
in which the table linen was kept. When meal-time
came the table was drawn away from the wall, the top
brought down on the arms of the chair, and the cloth,
which had been fished out of the drawer, spread over
it."

1 Sweet William he married a wife,
    Gentle Jenny cried rosemaree
To be the sweet comfort of his life.
    As the dew flies over the mulberry tree.

2 Jenny couldnt in the kitchen to go,
  For fear of dirting her white-heeled shoes.

3 Jenny couldnt wash, and Jenny couldnt bake,
  For fear of dirting her white apurn tape.

4 Jenny couldnt card, and Jenny couldnt spin,
  For fear of hurting her gay gold ring.

5 Sweet William came whistling in from plaow,
  Says, 'O my dear wife, is my dinner ready naow?'

6 She called him a dirty paltry whelp :
  'If you want any dinner, go get it yourself.'

7 Sweet William went aout unto the sheep-fold,
  And aout a fat wether he did pull.

8 And daown on his knees he began for to stick,
  And quicklie its skin he thereof did strip.

9 He took the skin and laid on his wife's back,
  And with a good stick went whikety whack.

10 'I'll tell my father and all my kin
  How still a quarrel you've begun.'

11 'You may tell your father and all your kin
  How I have thrashed my fat wether's skin.'

12 Sweet William came whistling in from plaow,
  Says, 'Oh my dear wife, is my dinner ready naow?'

13 She drew her table and spread her board,
  And, ' Oh my dear husband,' was every word.

14 And naow they live free from all care and strife,
  And naow she makes William a very good wife.

Folk-Lore Society, County Folk-Lore, Printed Extracts : No 2, Suffolk, 1893, collected and edited by the
Lady Eveline Camilla Gurdon, p. 139 f. Contributed
by "a Suffolk man" to the Suffolk Notes and Queries
column of The Ipswich Journal, 1877.

1 There wus a man lived in the West,
    Limbo clashmo !
There wus a man lived in the West,
He married the wuman that he liked best.
    With a ricararo, ricararo, milk in the morn,
    O dary mingo.

2 He married this wuman and browt her hom,
  And set her in his best parlour rom.

3 My man and I went to the fowd,
  And ketcht the finest wuther that we could howd.

4 We fleed this wuther and browt him hom,
  Sez I, 'Wife, now youar begun yar doon.

5 I laid this skin on my wife's back,
  And on to it I then did swack.

6 I 'inted har with ashen ile,
    Limbo clashmo !
  I 'inted har with ashen ile,
  Till she could both brew, bake, wash and bile.
    O dary mingo — mingo.

278. The Farmer's Curst Wife.

P. 107 a. This has no connection with the story in
Wendenmuth, Œsterley, I, 366, p. 402; see Œsterley's
note, V, 60.

Compare the broadside ballad 'The Devil and the
Scold,' Roxburghe Collection, I, 340, 341 ; Chappell,
Roxburghe Ballads, II, i, 367 ff. ; Collier, Book of Rox-
burghe Ballads, 1847, p. 35 ff.

280. The Beggar-Laddie.

P. 116. Motherwell sent a copy of **C** to Sharpe with
a letter from Paisley, 8th October, 1825, and printed **C**
in an article on " Scottish Song " in the Paisley Magazine, 1828, p. 621, in both cases with two or three insignificant variations. He mentions in the latter another
version in which the hero is called King James, in
accordance with the vulgar traditions concerning the
Gudeman o Ballengoich.

In Findlay's MSS, I, 144, there are five unimportant
stanzas, nearer to **D** than to the other versions, and
having, like **D**, the title 'The Gaberlunzie Laddie.'

286. The Sweet Trinity (The Golden Vanity).

P. 137. **B.** Mr Macmath has a copy of ' The Goulden Vanitee ' in the handwriting of Peter Scott Fraser
which is identical with that printed by Logan except
that it has *Vanitee* for *Vanitie* in 1³ and 9², *Countree* in
4², *they row'd* in 6¹, *Oh!* in 8¹, and *Eck iddle dee* (not
du) in the burden. Mr. Macmath notes that **B** was
printed by Mrs. Gordon, in Christopher North, a Memoir of John Wilson, Edinburgh, 1862, II, 317 ff., in
a form identical with that in Mr. Fraser's MS. copy
[except for one variation (*they 've row'd* for *they row'd*
in 6¹)].

287. Captain Ward and the Rainbow.

P. 135. A copy taken down from the lips of an old
Suffolk (Monk Soham) laborer was contributed by
Archdeacon Robert Hindes Groome to Suffolk Notes
and Queries in the Ipswich Journal [1877–78], and
is repeated in Two Suffolk Friends, 1895, p. 46.
W. Macmath.

291. Child Owlet.

P. 156. Mr Macmath has called my attention to a
ballad on the story of Child Owlet by William Bennet
in The Dumfries Monthly Magazine, II, 402, 1826.
This piece, called ' Young Edward,' "is founded upon
a tradition still current in the district in which Morton
Castle is situated." Its quality is that of the old-mag-
azine ballad.

294. Dugall Quin.

P. 165. Dugald Gunn, Mr Macmath suggests, may
have been a mistaken reading of Scott's difficult handwriting on the part of the editor of the Ballad Book ;
as is certainly the case with regard to The Stirrup of
Northumberland, V, 207 b, No 9, **G**.

I unhappily forgot Buchan's 'Donald M'Queen's
Flight wi Lizie Menzie,' Ballads of the North of Scotland, II, 117, which, though I think it corrupted at the
end, removes the principal verbal difficulties in the Old
Lady's copy. Mr Walker of Aberdeen has reminded
me of Buchan's ballad, and he had previously suggested
to me that Dunfermline was proprietor of Fyvie, and
this fact had disposed me to read Fyvie where the text
already given has farei, farie. Of the rightfulness of
this reading there can now be no doubt, though information is desirable as to the tempting cheese of Fyvie,
of which I have not found mention elsewhere.

Buchan, II, 319, makes the following note on his
copy : —

"Donald M'Queen, the hero of this ballad, was one of the
servants of Baron Seaton of Fyvie, who, with his master,
had fled to France after the rebellion in 1715. Baron Seaton having died in France, Donald, his man, returned to
Fyvie with one of his master's best horses, and procured a
love potion, *alias* 'the tempting cheese of Fyvie,' which had
the effect of bewitching, or, in other words, casting the glamour oer his mistress, Lizie Menzie, the Lady of Fyvie. Some
years afterwards this lady went through the country as a
common pauper, when, being much fatigued, and in a forlorn condition, she fell fast asleep in the mill of Fyvie,
whither she had gone to solicit an alms (charity): on her
awakening, she declared that she had just now slept as soun
a sleep with the meal-pock beneath her head, as ever she had
done on the best down-bed of Fyvie. This information I
had from James Rankin, an old blind man, who is well acquainted with the traditions of the country."

Alexander Seaton acquired Fyvie, it is said, in 1596,
and in 1606 was created Earl of Dunfermline. Castle
and title were forfeited in 1689, and the property was
purchased of the crown in 1726 by the Earl of Aberdeen. Dunfermline had no horses for Dugald or Donald to take after 1689. The whole story of Lizie Menzie, Baroness of Seaton, seems to be a fiction as sheer
as it is vulgar. Lizie Menzie's forsaking her husband
for a footman is refuted by the well-informed Rankin
himself, who tells us that the husband had died in
France before his man " returned to Fyvie with one of

his master's best horses." The conclusion is borrowed mostly from 'The Gypsy Laddie,' where even the drinking of one's own brewage is to be found; but 'The Gypsy Laddie' is not to be reproached with the foolish last stanza.

1 Donald, he's come to this town,
   And he's been lang awa,
And he is on to Lizie's bedside,
   Wi his tartan trews and a'.

2 'How woud you like me, Lizie,' he said,
   'An I ware a' your ain,
Wi tartan coat upo my back,
   And single-soled sheen,
A blue bonnetie on my head,
   And my twa winking een?'

3 'Weel woud I like you, Donald,' she said,
   'An ye ware a' my ain,
Wi tartan coat upo your back,
   And single-soled sheen,
And little blue bonnetie on your head,
   And blessings on your een.

4 'But how woud ye like me, Donald,' she said,
   'An I ware a' your ain,
Wi a siller snood into my head,
   A gowd fan in my hand,
And maidens clad in green satins,
   To be at my command?'

5 'Weel woud I like you, Lizie,' he said,
   'And ye ware a' my ain,
Wi a siller snood into your head,
   A gowd fan in your hand,
But nane o your maidens clad in green,
   To be at your command.'

6 Then but it speaks her mither dear,
   Says, 'Lizie, I maun cross you ;
To gang alang wi this young man,
   We'd think we had but lost you.'

7 'O had your tongue, my mither dear,
   And dinna think to break me ;
For I will gang wi this young man,
   If it is his will to take me.'

8 Donald M'Queen rade up the green,
   On ane o Dumfermline's horses,
And Lizie Menzie followed him,
   Thro a' her father's forces.

9 'O follow me, Lizie, my heart's delight,
   And follow me for you please ;
Rype well the grounds o my pouches,
   And ye'll get tempting cheese.'

10 'O wae mat worth you, Donald M'Queen!
   Alas, that ever I saw thee !
The first love-token ye gae me
   Was the tempting cheese o Fyvie.

11 'O wae be to the tempting cheese,
   The tempting cheese o Fyvie,
Gart me forsake my ain gudeman
   And follow a footman-laddie !

12 'But lat me drink a hearty browst,
   Just sic as I did brew !
On Seton brave I turnd my back,
   A' for the sake o you.'

13 She didna wear the silken gowns
   Were made into Dumbarton,
But she is to the Highlands gane,
   To wear the weeds o tartan.

14 She's casten aff the high-heeld sheen,
   Made o the Turkey leather,
And she's put on the single brogues,
   To skip amo the heather.

15 Well can Donald hunt the buck,
   And well can Lizie sew ;
Whan ither trades begin to fail,
   They can take their bowies and brew.

299. Trooper and Maid.

P. 174.

D.

'The Trooper Lad.' Communicated by Mr Macmath, with this note : "Received, 21st August, 1895, at Crossmichael, from my aunt, Miss Jane Webster. Learned by her many years ago, at Airds of Kells, from the singing of John Coltart."

1 The trooper lad cam to oor gate,
   And oh ! but he was weary,
He rapped at and chapped at,
   Syne called for his kind deary.

2 The bonnie lass being in the close,
   The moon was shining clearly, —
'Ye'r welcome here, my trooper lad,
   Ye'r welcome, my kind deary.'

3 She's taen his horse by the bridle-reins,
   And led him to the stable,
She's gien him corn and hay to eat,
   As much as he was able.

4 She's taen the knight by the milk-white hand,
   And led him to her chamber,
   And gied him bread and cheese to eat,
   And wine to drink his pleasure.

5 'Bonnie lassie, I'll lie near ye noo,
   Bonnie lassie, I'll lie near ye,
   An I'll gar a' your ribbons reel
   In the morning or I leave ye.'

6 .   .   .   .   .   .
       .   .   .   .   .   .
   And she put off her wee white smock,
   Crying, 'Laddie, are ye ready?'

   *   *   *   *   *   *   *   *

7 The first time that the trumpet played
   Was, Up, up and awa, man!
   The next time that the trumpet played
   Was, The morn's the battle-day, man!

8 'Bonnie lassie, I maun leave ye noo,
   Bonnie lassie, I maun leave ye;
   But, if e'er I come this way again
   I will ca in an see ye.'

9 Bread and cheese for gentlemen,
   An corn and hay for horses;
   Pipes and tobacco for auld wives,
   And bonnie lads for lasses.

10 'When will us twa meet again?
   When will we meet and marry?'
   'When cockle-shells turn silver bells,
   Nae langer, love, we 'll tarry.'

11 So he's taen his auld grey cloak about him noo,
   An he's ower the mountains fairly,
   Crying, 'Fare ye weel, my bonnie lass,
   Fareweel, my ain kind deary.'

Mr Macmath adds the following stanza, "remembered by Miss Agnes Macmath, 2nd January, 1896, from the singing of her mother.''

   'When will we twa meet again?
      When will we meet and marry?'
   'When peace and truth come to this land,
      Nae langer, love, we'll tarry.'

305. The Outlaw Murray.

P. 186 a. Mr Macmath writes (Dec. 24, 1895) that he has examined two boxes of MSS belonging to the late Mr George Wilson and found *not* 'The Song of the Outlaw Murray,' but 'The Song of the Rid Square,' in a transcript (perhaps early rather than late) of the 17th century. He thinks that by a slip of memory on Mr Wilson's part 'The Outlaw Murray' was mentioned instead of this.

Fragments.

P. 202 b, last stanza. Mr Macmath has given me the following variation, communicated (with a story of a wife carried off by fairies) by J. C. to The Scottish Journal, II, 275, 1848.

   O Alva woods are bonnie,
      Tillycoultry hills are fair,
   But when I think on the braes o Menstrie
      It maks my heart aye sair.

———

P. 210 b, to III, 500. Mr Macmath informs me that the manuscript of Motherwell here referred to is the same as that already printed, and correctly printed, at III, 500 f.

GLOSSARY

Notwithstanding every effort to make this glossary as complete as possible, there remain not a few words and phrases with which I can do nothing satisfactory. This is the case not only with ballads from recent tradition, but with some that were taken down in writing three hundred years ago or more.

At every stage of oral transmission we must suppose that some accidental variations from what was delivered would be introduced, and occasionally some wilful variations. Memory will fail at times; at times the listener will hear amiss, or will not understand, and a perversion of sense will ensue, or absolute nonsense, — nonsense which will be servilely repeated, and which repetition may make more gross. Dr Davidson informs me that one of his female relatives rendered 'an echo shrill did make' (in Chevy Chace, 10) 'an achish yirl did make,' and that he took 'aching or frightened earl' to be the meaning until he read the piece. Happy are we when we are sure of the nonsense; as when, in The Gypsy Laddie, 'they cast their glamourie owre her' is turned into 'they called their grandmother over.' "The combination of two words into one," says Dr Davidson, "is not rare in Scotch, nor is the reverse process. For example, the word 'hypochondriac' is turned into 'keepach and dreeach,' and the two parts often used separately. 'I'm unco keepach' and 'I'm unco dreeach' are common expressions among old people. Imagine an etymologist, ignorant of the facts, trying to discover the etymology of 'keepach' or of 'dreeach.'" Words of one or two syllables are long enough for the simple; a laboring man of my acquaintance calls rheumatism 'the tism': what are the other syllables to such, who understand no one of the three? Learned words do not occur in ballads; still an old native word will be in the same danger of metamorphosis. But, though unfamiliarity naturally ends in corruption, mishearing may have the like effect where the original phrase is in no way in fault; hence, perhaps, 'with a bretther a degs ye'll clear up my nags,' 'a tabean briben kame,' 'I'll have that head of thine, to enter plea att my iollye,' etc.

It must be borne in mind, however, that as to nonsense the burden of proof rests always upon the expositor. His personal inability to dispose of a reading is not conclusive; his convictions may be strong, but patience and caution are his part and self-restraint as to conjectures.

It is with a strong feeling of what 'a kindly Scot' signifies that I offer my thanks to many gentlemen who have favored me with comments on lists of words submitted to them. Especial acknowledgment is due to Dr Thomas Davidson, a native of Old Deer, who has made his home in the United States, and to Mr William Walker, of Aberdeen. Besides these, I have to mention with gratitude the Rev. Robert Lippe, Rev. Dr Walter Gregor, the late Dr William Alexander, Principal Sir W. D. Geddes, Dr James Mori, Messrs William Forbes, James Aiken, David Scott, W. Carnie, W. Cadenhead, and William Murison, all of Aberdeenshire; Dr James Burgess, Messrs J. Logie Robertson and William Macmath, of Edinburgh; Professor A. F. Murison, of London, and Dr Robert Wallace, M. P.; Professor James Cappen, Queen's University, Kingston, Ontario; Rev. Professor J. Clarke Murray and Principal Dr W. M. Barbour, of Montreal; Rev. Dr Alexander McDonald, St Francis Xavier's College, Antigonish, N. S.; Rev. Dr Waters, of Newark, N. J. For some difficult English words help has been given by Dr W. Hand Browne of Johns Hopkins University, Professor Manly of Brown University, and Professor Kittredge of Harvard College.

It will be observed that ballads in the Skene MS which were derived from the "Old Lady's Collection" are not glossed, but the originals, which should be substituted for Skene's more or less incorrect copies.

[References are usually to volume, page, and stanza.]

A

a', aa, aw, all.

a'=every. a' man, I, 68, 27; II, 71, 16; 75, 13; 193, 24; IV, 46, 5, 6; 235, 10; V, 169, 6; 221, 10; 224, 22; 237, 8; 239, 36; 260 b, 5. a' body, V, 273 a.

a, abridgment of *have*, I, 315, 11; III, 215, 10; 440, 13; 441, 26; V, 55, 26; 79, 33; 213, 10; 224, 28; 251, 36.

a=he, III, 54, 3, 7.

a=I, in the phrase *a wat* (a wait, a wite, etc.), II, 159, 11, 16, 19; 160, 10–16, 19; III, 299, 9: I know, verily, assuredly. II, 230, 6: used by a mere trick, with hardly a meaning. a's, V, 266, 9: I's, I shall, will.

a=of: III, 91, 2; 93, 36; 298, 59; 307, 10; 308, 12, 24; 309, 40 (a trusti tre ?); 349, 37, 39; 464, 11; IV, 504, 27.

a=on. a grefe, III, 69, 268. a blode (ablode), I, 244, 9; V, 288 b, v. 16. a row, III, 117, 24.

a=one: I, 126, 4; 326, 7; 327, 24.

a=ae, one single: V, 256 b, 2; 257, 6, 15; 278, 26. a warst, V, 215, 6. V, 239, 36: one and the same. See **ae**.

a=to. abound, II, 109, 20: to go. a dee, 110, 25: to do. So, perhaps, *abee*.

a be, abe, a bee, abee, a beene (with *let*), I, 356, **D b** 4; II, 29, 5; 108, 5; 159, 25; 185, 27; III, 455, 4, 8; V, 229, 35: be.

let abee with, IV, 96 f., **D** 9, 13.

let abee of, IV, 97, **E** 4, 5; 98, 15; 99, 14, 15.

abeen, abeene, aboon, abone, etc., I, 315, 8; II, 468, 7; IV, 326, 16, 19: above. his hose abeen his sheen, V, 17, 35; 18, 14: his stockings ungartered, falling above, over his shoes.

abide, abyde, III, 67, 219; 73, 345; V, 82, 24, 40: stop, wait. III, 97, 8; 279, 13: withstand.

pret. abode, III, 63, 143: waited.

p. p. abiden, abyden, III, 57 f., 25, 30: awaited.

able, II, 51, 4: suitable.

ablins, aiblins, III, 467, b 2: perhaps.

aboard, V, 134, 16: alongside; and so 8, 20, 22, or, *laid us aboard* may be *boarded us.*

abode, III, 335 a: waiting, delay.

abode, III, 430, 1, *burden:* endured.

aboone, aboun, abown. See abune.

abound. ill a bound, II, 109, 20: ill (prepared) to go.

about, been, V, 52, 77: been engaged.

abowthe, III, 112, 52: about.

abune, aboone, aboon, abon, abone, abown, aboun, abeen, II, 20, 8; 22, 16; 23, **D** 7, **E** 8; 24, **F** 10; 25, **G** 13; 27, 21; 28, 25; 29, 19; 30, 12; 145, 20: above (above them).

abyde. See abide.

abyden. See abide.

abye, III, 128, 84; V, 234 b, 3: pay, suffer consequences.

Acaron, III, 149, 32: being the oath of a Turk (36), this may be taken as *Alcoran.*

acward, ackward stroke, III, 110, 17; IV, 148, 43: described as a backhanded stroke. See aukeward.

advance, V, 147, 8: help on (?).

aduenture, III, 359, 90: hazard.

aduise, II, 436, 63: observe.

ae=one, single: I, 310, 6; 467, 33; 478, 1; II, 77, 29; IV, 257, 10; 260, 10; 261, 9; 262, 24; 445, 1; 476, 3. ae best, I, 465, 13, 17; IV, 479, 13. ae first, I, 426, 7, 8; 494, 22. ae warst (a warst), V, 214 f., 1, 6. the ae . . . the ither, III, 500 b, 7: the one . . . the other.

ae=mere, sole. ae licht o the moon, IV, 469, 4; 470, 35.

ae=aye, always: I, 245, 7; II, 185, 40; 208, 12; IV, 247, **B** 11; 265, 13.

aer, I, 16, **C** 12: ear, plough.

aevery, III, 465, 25: voracious, very hungry. (A. S. gífre.)

afar, afore, affore, I, 438, **A** 1; II, 21, 15, 16; 138, 8; III, 405, 15; IV, 128 f., 19, 21, 23, 24: before.

aff, I, 346, 12: oft.

affronted, II, 367, 45; IV, 242 b: put to shame, mortified. III, 152, 6: confronted, opposed.

a-fit, V, 115, 7: on foot.

aft, III, 491, 8; V, 299 b, 4: oft.

after, after the way, III, 99, 57: along, on. aftere brade waye, I, 333, 1: along, over. after me, III, 74, 367: according to me, my advice.

against, III, 344, 36: by way of preparation for the case.

agast of him, III, 99, 49: alarmed about him (the consequences to him).

agaste, V, 71, note †: terrified.

agayn(e), ageyn, III, 98, 29; 297, 46: against. a-geyn euyn, III, 13, 3: towards.

agoe, V, 83, 44: gone.

agree, IV, 147, 32: bring to agreement.

a-ʒon, comyn a-ʒon, III, 13, 4: came upon, encountered.

ahind, ahint, ahin, I, 299, 14; II, 105, 11; 315, 5; III, 480, 14; 481, 30; IV, 246, 6: behind. V, 17, 32: over and above.

aiblins, ablins, I, 439, 4: perhaps.

aileth at. See at.

air, in a drowsy air, IV, 20, 11: *air* seems to mean *atmosphere* simply; possibly *disposition, condition.*

air, aire, ayre, by air, by ayre, II, 106, 1; 270, 30; III, 162, 58; 164, b 58; V, 270, 7: early, betimes.

airn, ern, I, 342, 33; 348, 13, 19; 355, 42; III, 474, 39; 481, 35; 505, 21: iron.

airt, art, II, 23, **E** 5: quarter of the heavens, point of the compass. west-airt lands, II, 73, 30: western. rade the airt o, IV, 27, 31: in the direction of. a' airts o wind, II, 341, **Q**. been at that art, III, 163, 87.

airted, V, 99, **C** 4: laid their course.

aith, oath.

a' kin, a' kin kind, II, 114, 2: all kind, every.

'al, that 'al, IV, 17, 3: 'ull, wull, will.

al, I, al so mote I the, III, 68, 243: absolutely.

al, will.

alaffe, III, 34, 11: aloof.

alane, I, 347, 2. mine alane, I, 332, **E** 1, **F** 1. See lane.

alang, along.

albergs, II, 340 b: houses, dwells.

alean, alone.

alee, IV, 516 b, 3: on the lea, a-field, but for the purpose of keeping guard; cf. III, 487, **A** 15; 492, **D** 5; 495, **B b** 4.

aleene, I, 346, 4: alone.

alelladay, I, 220, **A** 1: exclamation of grief.

algate, IV, 93, note *: anyway.

aliment, IV, 91, a: provision for maintenance; here, apparently, alimony.

alive, I loved ye best ye were born alive, IV, 521, 19: corrupted; the sense appears in IV, 26, **A** 16, *I love best that's born alive*, best of all living things.

all. all and, I, 56, 6, 7; III, 432, 16, 17; all as she stood, I, 117, 16; all in my hand, III, 186, 20; all by the roode, III, 188, 2; all by his side, V, 212 b, 8; all on, IV, 393, 5; 394, **B** 2, 5; 395 f., **B b** 2, 3, 5; V, 233 f., 2, 3, 5; all at her head, feet, V, 158, 9; all down, V, 293 b, 5; all oer, 302 b, 2.

allacing, IV, 18, 21: repeating of alace (alas).

allther, III, 57, 9; 70, 283, 284, representing the ancient genitive plural of *all*, allther moste, allther best: best of all, etc.

along of, III, 279, 8: owing to.

alongst, V, 267 a, 7, 8: along.

alow, III, 4, 1: below.

alow, aloe, George Aloe, V, 133.

als, alsua, I, 327, 27; IV, 366 **D** 5: also.

also, I, 328, 46: all so, just as.

althocht, III, 370, 19: although.

amain(e), III, 345, 48; 350, 51: with vigor, strength, force. blew, sound, cald, amain, III, 181, 27; 341, 46; 343, 17; 344, 36: with strength, loudly. II, 385, 24; IV, 13, 2: in force, in numbers. I, 398, 4; III, 176 f., 11, 16; 209, 9: at once, quickly.

amain, V, 134, 7, 16: (Fr. amener) lower, strike.

a-married, IV, 236, 4: married.

a-marvel, II, 386, 12: marvel (Fr. émerveiller).

amense, III, 465, 23: amends. (Should be printed as one word, not a mense as in the MS.)

American leather, I, 494, 14; III, 3, 13; 5, **C** 2: has been explained as morocco made from American horsehides, for which a patent was obtained c. 1799. See The Scots Magazine, 1799, LXI, 286. But the date of the text at III, 3, is 1780.

amo, V, 306 b, 14: among.

among, II, 451, 89: between.

amoued, II, 442, 9: excited, agitated.

an, II, 75, 20; V, 214 b, 4: one.

-an, -ane, -and, -en, etc., annexed to the definite form of the superlative of the adjective (preceded by *the, her*, etc.) or to numerals, or following separately, seems to be *an=one*. (The history of this usage has not been made out.) The firstan, nextan, firsten, nexten, *passim* (*the seconden* only at I, 507, 3); the firstand, I, 135, **O** 18; the nextand, II, 94, 6; her firsten, thirden, etc., II, 161, 9–12; her nexten, II, 164, 19; the firstin, the nextin, II, 380, 22; the first an, the niest an, I, 351, 45; the warst in, the best in, II, 98, 43, 44; the third ane, the fourth ane, etc., II, 71, 5, 6; 78, 8–11; the third one, fourth one, etc., II, 72, 5–7; the first ae, IV, 490, 20; the first y, III, 3, 15; the firsten ane, II, 370, 16. So, that samen, II, 475, 17.

an, I, 295, 30; 468, 6, 9; 480, 6, 7; II, 21, **B** 11: and, if.

ance, anse, I, 341, 9; 342, 23; 344, 21, 22; V, 9, 2, 4: once.

anchor, did on anchor rise so high, III, 344, 34 (c, g, have *ride*): the ship is in full sail; no apparent sense.

ancient, ancyent, III, 286, 40; 340, 37; 341, 46; 406, 30, 31, 39; 420, 20; 422, 65, 66: ensign.

and, *superfluous* (as in "when that I was and a tiny little boy," and two other songs in Shakspere), see II, 57 b; II, 58, 7, 8; 59, 22, 27; 60, 39; 87, 31; III, 145, 6; 277, 16; 419, 8; IV, 448 a, 1, 2. The same usage in German, Swedish, and especially Dutch ballads.

and, if.

-and, -end, termination of the present participle: whissland, singand, cumand, seekand, etc., I, 326–329; II, 268, 17; IV, 195 f., **D** 2, 7, 10, 14; V, 192 f., 35, 49.

ane = a, I, 327, 11.

ane = alone. me ane, I, 333, 1.

ane, II, 191, 37 = en, end.

aneath, aneth, II, 185, 29; 191, 23; V, 224, 17: beneath. aneath the sun, III, 5, **D** 7: sheltering the eyes with the hand. So, below the sun, III, 6, 6; 8, 6.

anent, I, 222, 8; II, 166, 21; 191, 24; 391, 20: over against, in the face of.

anew, I, 305, 1; III, 495, **B b** 3–5; IV, 249, 10; 271, **B** 4: enough, enow.

angel(1), II, 444, 55; 449, 61; 453, 32; III, 156, 4; V, 101, 4: a gold coin, of value varying from 6s. 8d. to 10s.

angerly, III, 286, 55; 361, b 21: angrily.

ankir, III, 66, 198: recluse, hermit.

another, III, 138, 8, 12, 13: *corrupt, or verbiage*.

anse, IV, 518, 3: once.

answere your quarrel, I, 411, 18: be responsible for, take on me to settle, your difference.

answery, *v.*, V, 283, 12: answer.

ant, I, 244; V, 288 b: and.

antine (Fr. antienne), IV, 439 b, 6: anthem.

anunder, I, 302, **A** 9: under.

aout, V, 304 b, 7: out.

apayd, euelle apayd, III, 322 a: ill satisfied, displeased.

ape, lead an ape in hell, penance for old maids : I, 232, 14.

apparent, III, 451, note *: heir apparent. (parand, II, 447, 2, 4.)

applyed, *p. p.*, V, 51, 67: plied.

appone, I, 327, 14, 28: upon.

apurn, V, 304 b, 3: apron.

ar, I, 244, 18; III, 110, 18: or, before.

arblast, I, 311 a: cross-bow.

archborde, III, 340, 23, 29 (in 29, MS. charke-bord): may be a misspelling of *hachebord*, st. 36 (*hatch-bord*, p. 342, 70). Barton grappled the ship to his archborde, from which we should infer that the word meant the side of the ship, as *hatch-bord* would naturally signify at p. 342, 70. But *archborde* might of itself mean the stern of the ship, a timber at the stern being still so called, and German *hack-bord* meaning the upper part of the stern of a ship. (It is singular that none of the difficult words *archborde, hacheberd, hall* (III, 340, 29) occur in the York copy, IV, 503, which, however, has difficulties of its own.)

archery, III, 309, 41: collected archers.

arches, II, 307, 29: aims, shoots.

are, I, 327, 23: before.

armorie, I, 285, 34, seems to be employed in the sense of *armament, men at arms*.

armorye, III, 286, 56: armor.

arselins, V, 124, 12: backwards.

art, airt, quarter of the heavens. been at that art, III, 163, 87: in that quarter, at that place. See **airt**.

as, *pron.*, I, 477, 6, 7, 13, 15; II, 4, **D** 4; 452, 14; V, 206 a, 1; b, 6: that, who.

as, *conj.*, I, 477, 5, 18, 19; II, 453, 28: that.

as, V, 218 b, **D** 1: was.

as ever, III, 281, 10: as long as.

asay, *p. p.*, III, 112, 48: tried. [Read *asayed*?]

asembled, III, 164, b 15: met (encountered).

ask, I, 353, **H** 11; 355, 41; II, 504, 32: newt, lizard. (A. S. áðexe.) Cf. **ass**.

askd, my father he askd me an acre o land, I, 17, **D** 9: *askd* seems to be an erroneous repetition from 8; *aucht*, owned, would be expected ; or *left*, *gave*, as in **K, L.**

asking, asken, askend, askent, II, 91, **D** 27, 28; 92, 22–25; 192, 7, 14; 194, 23; 359, 7–10; V, 221 f., 27, 29, 30, 32; 223, 5, 7; 418, 8: boon, request.

askryede, I, 326, 4: described.

ass, I, 349, 11, 15: ask, newt.

assoyled, absolved.

aste, I, 217, 1: east.

astoned, astonied, V, 76, 24; 82, 35: astonished, amazed.

asurd, I, 334, 5: of azure; should probably be *asur.*

at. reade must rise at, II, 53, 34, 35; take councell at, III, 405, 17, 23; take leaue att, III, 357, 42: from. ask at, beg at, spear at, I, 497, **L** 5–8, **M** 2–5; III, 161, 32; 330, 15; IV, 331, 10: of, from. ails ye at, aileth thee at, II, 72, 3; 78, 7; 80, 3; IV, 95, 12; 96, 4; 99, **H** 7: with (what ail comes to you from me ?). see at me, IV, 345, 8: in. come atte, IV, 507, 81: to, to the presence of. I was at thee, IV, 436, 1: (apud) with.

at, IV, 331 b, 8: out (?).

at, jobbing at, I, 104, **A b** 10: jogging off, away (?).

at, with ellipsis of *the door*, rappit at, clappit at, I, 105 a, 29; IV, 444, 16, 35; V, 173, 1; 306 b, 1.

at, att, *pron.* and *conj.*, II, 472, 24; III, 488, 19; IV, 348, 1; 446, 6; 469 b, 10, 12; V, 79, 31; 118, **B** 12; 220 b, 5; 224, 28; 236, 11⁴; 256, 8: that. (*it*, V, 236, 11², may be for this *at*.)

a ta, III, 464, 1: at all.

athort, I, 305, 3: across (upon). far athort, V, 164, **D b** 13: a long way.

attempt, III, 39, 110: tempt.

attemptattis, III, 451 b: enterprises.

atteynt, I, 328, 34: (here) lay hands on.

attoure, III, 458 b: outowr, over and above.

atweel, I, 22, 2, 3: I wot well, assuredly.

atween, I, 466, 11; II, 315, 6; V, 156, 11, 13: between. atween hands, II, 139, 6: meanwhile.

atwyn, V, 80, 57: from one another.

aucht, aught. wha's aucht ?= who is it owned (owns) ? whose is (are) ? I, 22, 4; 472, 1; II, 114, 11; 164, 8, 11; IV, 32, **C** 6; 194, 8; 199, 21; 202, 9; 203, 17. aught a bairn, II, 494, 4: had. where is the knight aught me for wedding, IV, 182, **F** 6: who was (is) under obligation to marry me ? (This is my ransome I ought to him to pay, I, 294, 12.) It is not unlikely that *aucht* in the phrase *wha's aucht* is present in sense. Indeed we have *aughts*, II, 336, **Q** 5. Cf. *who owes ?* whose is ? IV, 205, 27.

aught, *v.*, suld hae come and aught a bairn to me, II, 494, 4: had (a child by).

aukeward, awkwarde stroke, II, 59, 23; III, 93, 40: backhanded. See **acward.**

auld son, without regard to absolute age: I, 79, 58; 184, 8, 9; IV, 94, **A** 4; 97, **F** 4. So old sister for elder sister, eldest of three: I, 175, 8; auld dochter, II, 462, 33. auld son, of child just born and the only one, II, 105, 7; 107, 3–6, 17; IV, 206, 15. So at II, 95, 11,

called young son immediately after. Of babe in the cradle, II, 325, 10. See **old.**

aull, auld, old. I, 359, 6, 9, in four nights auld: at the age of four days. II, 80, 9, in twall years auld.

aussy pan, I, 301, 6: ash pan.

austerne, I, 134, **N** 3: austere, harsh. See **osterne.**

ava, II, 189, 33; 323, 25; III, 7, 13, 14; IV, 257, 12; 300, 3: of all. II, 360, 10; V, 112, **B b** 7: at all.

avayle, II, 436, 70: put down, doff.

avow, IV, 240, 7: seems to be used as *consent* rather than *own*, *confess* ; but cf. IV, 56, **A** 8; V, 252 a.

avowe, *n.*, III, 65, 180, 187, 190; 68, 240; 73, 346; 297, 44; 307, 1: vow.

avowë, avower, III, 67, 232; 520 a, No 161: patron, protector.

avoyd, V, 53, 102: begone.

aw, all.

await, lie at await, III, 409, note *: in wait.

awaite, awayte, III, 72, 330; 84, 330; 88, 331: lie in wait for. awayte me scathe, III, 66, 202: lie in wait to do me harm.

awende, I, 244, 9: weened, imagined.

awet, III, 112, 64: know. Perhaps, await, descry.

awkwarde stroke, III, 93, 40: a backhanded stroke. See **aukeward.**

awsom, V, 193, 49: awful.

ay, I, 333, 1, 2, 3: a.

ayenst, III, 76, 420: against, towards, about.

ayon, ayone, ayont, I, 301, 1; 302, 1; 428, 20; II, 133, **D** 4, 6; IV, 412, 6: beyond. IV, 330 a, appendix, 1: and oddly of the man, as farther from the wall. III, 392, 20, 21: beyond, across. I, 220, **A** 2; IV, 8, 46: over against, in the face of.

ayre, eare, ere: heir.

B

ba, IV, 354, 1: a lullaby.

baas, balls.

baba, II, 339, 19: baby.

bace, V, 104 a=bash (Swed. basa): beat; *pret.* baist, III, 164, b 26(?). See **baist.**

bacheeleere, II, 58, 13: young knight devoted to the service of a lady.

back-spald, V, 106, **E** 4: hinder part of the shoulder.

bad, bade, V, 18, 9; 27, 41; 243, 11: ordered, offered. (A. S. beódan.)

bad, bade, baed, III, 267, 15: abode, stopped, waited for. II, 115, 22; III, 312, 28; V, 236, 17: remained, staid. (A. S. bídan.)

badgers, III, 477, 8: pedlars.

baed, II, 115, 22: abode, stopped. See **bad.**

baffled, II, 479 : thwarted (perhaps, made a fool of). IV, 146 f., 11, 31: affronted, insulted, or disgraced.

bail, life in, III, 10, 19: in power, at disposal.

bailie, III, 385, 12: municipal officer, alderman. IV, 326, 12: bailiff, steward, manager of an estate. See **baylye.**

bairn, barn, bern, III, 437, 28, 36; 453, 17; IV, 309, 5; 310, 12: child.

baist, *pret.*, III, 164, b 26: beat. baste, *p. p.*, III, 165, 92: beaten. (Icel. beysta?) See bace.

baked, II, 403, 2: becked, curtsied, made obeisance.

bale, II, 45, 30, 44; 58, 11; 419, 51; 466, 34; III, 92, 11, 16; 99, 51: ill, trouble, mischief, harm, calamity, destruction. See balys.

bale, I, 355, 41: fire.

bale-fire, II, 118, 9; 119, 19; 155, 36; IV, 467, 12, 14: bonfire, large fire.

ballants, IV, 129, 30: ballads.

ballup, III, 181, 15 (ballock): front or flap of breeches.

balow, IV, 351, 1; 352, C 1: lullaby, sing a lullaby to.

balys, III, 310, 68: misfortunes, troubles. See bale.

ban, band, I, 69, 38; 73, 53; II, 376, 36; III, 491, 12: hinge.

ban, bann, *v.*, I, 304, E 5; 305, 6; III, 104, 8; IV, 87, 14; V, 115, 7: curse.

ban, band, bande, bond, IV, 388, 7: band. IV, 388, 11: bond.

ban, I, 55, 12: bound (*pret.*).

band(e), III, 430, 8; 431, 7: bond, compact.

band-dogs, bandoggs, III, 123, 16; 125, 31; 126, B b 31; c 31: dogs that are kept chained (on account of their fierceness).

banded, IV, 388, 7: bound, secured with bands.

bane, I, 285, 33; III, 92, 7: destruction, death.

bane. saddle of the bane (MS. bone), I, 468, 13; bouer o bane, II, 185, 31: meaning probably the *royal bone* of I, 466, 10. See roelle bone.

bane-fire, II, 146, 23; 331, 17: bonfire.

bang, II, 438, 4: may be any implement for banging; it is sometimes stick, here strap (*in* should be *wi*).

bang, IV, 85, 5: emend to *hang*.

bangisters, IV, 37, 7; 38, 9: people violent and regardless of law.

banis, III, 78, 453: slayers, murderers.

banished, III, 401, 15: possibly with the meaning banned, but the ordinary sense does well enough.

bank, sea-bank, IV, 229, 3, 7: shore (?).

bankers, I, 334, 9: carpets, tapestries for benches.

banket, III, 446 b: banquet.

banneret, II, 395, N 1: banner-bearer (see B 1; E 1; I 1; K 1; M 1; P 1).

barck, bark, II, 239, 1: birk, birch.

barelins, II, 212, 12: barely.

bargain, III, 181, 13: brawl, fight.

barker, V, 78, 11; 80, 43, 49, etc.; 82, 20: tanner.

barking, I, 109, C 10: who uses bark, as a tanner.

barm, I, 243, 7: lap.

barn-well thrashing, II, 322, 8: the well has no sense, and has probably been caught from 9, at the far well washing. To be dropped.

barn, barne, II, 437, 85; IV, 141, 17; V, 114, 10; 267, 3: (A. S. bearn) child. III, 308, 14: (A. S. beorn) man, fighting man.

baron, I, 293, 2; 294 f., 5, 9, 23, 28: simply knight, and that, in all cases but the first, vaguely.

barras, oer the, IV, 372, 6: beyond the barriers (as 374, A b, after 5).

barrine, bairn.

base-court, III, 470 b: lower or outer court.

bassonet, basnet, basnit, III, 298, 51, 52; 308 f., 29, 32: a light helmet, shaped like a skull-cap.

bat, but.

batit, baited.

batts, blows, burden of, III, 465, 20: all the blows (beating) he can bear.

baubee, bawbee, III, 268, 6; 269, D 6; 270, 4, 5; V, 242 b, 5: halfpenny.

baube, II, 132,. 30: babe.

baucheld sheen, IV, 380, 26: shoes down at the heels (ill-bukled, wrongly, V, 276, 18).

bay, by.

bayberry kame, IV, 471 f., 2, 4: a corrupt passage, yielding no sense (so of other readings here).

bay dogs, III, 126 f., e, f 31: dogs that bring to bay, or that bay (?).

baylleful, III, 298, 58: destructive, deadly.

baylye, III, 28, 140: bailiff, sheriff's officer (to execute writs, etc.). III, 332, 15: chief magistrate, mayor. See bailie.

bayne, perdition.

bayr, V, 110, 13: byre, cowhouse.

be=by. be to and al be on, I, 242, 11: by two[s] and all by one[s]. be, be that, III, 100, 73; 482, 26: by the time that. sey be, V, 79, 26: about. See by.

be 's, it be 's, III, 160, 9: shall be=it s' be.

be wi, IV, 261, 23: tolerate, bear with.

beager, beggar.

beagly, V, 224, 10. See bigly.

beam, beam gold, II, 402, 10: for *beaming?* Probably corrupt.

beame, of the utuer beame, IV, 506, 59: utuer is perhaps utter, outer; but what outer beam would Horsley come to in climbing the mast? Probably corrupt. If we read of, (=on) the utter (outer) bane (bone), which rhymes, we have to explain the outer bone of the buttocke.

bean, bone.

bear, I, 149, 6: move on, proceed.

bear, bier.

bear, beer.

bear, IV, 324, C 1: barley.

bear-seed, IV, 323, 6: barley; bear-seed time seems to refer to barley-harvest.

beare mercy, as the lawes will thee beare, V, 53, 98: have for (as in, bear malice, etc.).

beare, *pret.*, II, 266, 30: bare.

beared, buried.

bearing arrow, III, 29, 150; 202, 33; 341, 53: "an arrow that carries well," Percy; "an arrow made to carry especially straight," Nares; but on the first occasion a broad arrow is used when "an arrow that carries well" (straight) is equally, or even more, necessary, and on the third a bearing and a broad arrow are used indifferently, III, 29, 153, 159; 341, 56. Perhaps a very long arrow, such as required to be carried in the hand. "Longe arrowes like standarts with socetts of stell for my Lord's foutemen to bere in their hands, when they ryn with my Lorde" are noted as *berrying* arrows in the preparations for the Earl of Northumberland's expedition to Terouenne, 5 Henry VIII. Dillon's Fairholt's Costume in England, II, 8, 1885. Mr C. J. Longman, himself an archer, remarking that a bearing arrow is used for a range of 20 score paces, III, 29, 148, 150, and a broad arrow for 6 score, 153, suggests that a bearing arrow was probably what is now called a flight-arrow, — a thin, light arrow with a tapering point for long shooting.

bearly, V, 219, 17: buirdly.

beat, IV, 379, 15: boot, recompense.

became, II, 422, 2: came.

became his courtisie, III, 464, 18: that is, his courtesy became him (as in Shakspere's "youth becomes the livery that it wears"). See **become.**

because, III, 29, 157: in order that.

beck, made a beck on her knee, II, 359, 7, 9: curtsy.

becke (A. S. bec), I, 334, 8: stream, brook.

become them well, IV, 147, 22: look well in them (i. e., they became him well); so III, 464, 18; cf. set, IV, 331, 18. place, part, does well become me, IV, 152, **D** 2; 153, 1: suit. See **became.**

becomed, *pret.* of become, IV, 505, 53.

bed, I, 272, 9: offered. See **bede.**

bed-head, I, 184, 44, 46: the top of the box or case of a Scottish bed. I, 116, **C** 5: should be bed-stock, as the rhyme shows.

bed-stock, I, 115, 3; IV, 94, 7; V, 208, 4: the outer side of a bed, that farther from the wall.

bede, *v.,* II, 499 b: offer. See **bed.**

bedone, I, 271, 2; II, 183, 20: worked, ornamented.

bedyls, III, 28, 140: under-bailiffs, summoners.

bee-ba, II, 330, 11, 12: sounds to lull a child.

beeds. that beeds, I, 69, 67: string of beads.

beek, biek, IV, 69, 22; 77, 3, c 3: bask.

beenits, IV, 381, 12: bayonets.

beere, II, 445, 73: bare, bore.

beerly (bride), II, 132, 24: large and well made; stately. See **bierly.** beerly, burly cheer, I, 298, 4; 300, 1: great, huge.

beet, bete, beik, III, 495 a; IV, 517, 15: better, help. Of fire, II, 120, 16, 17; IV, 467, 13: kindle, keep up. *p. p.* bett, II, 44, 14. See **bete.**

beet, II, 475, 7; III, 281, 2: behooved.

beet, *v., inf.,* II, 151, **H** 2: boot, furnish with boots. *pret.* bet, 4.

beets, *n. pl.,* IV, 187, 10: boots.

beette, III, 298, 54: *pret.* of beat.

befa, IV, 357, **C** 4: may befall (he does not care what name he gets). IV, 357 f., 6, 8, 12, 14: belong to, suit.

befalle, I, 241, 2: may it befall!

before, taen your God before, II, 62 b, 15, representing 'minged not Christ before,' II, 59, 21: an artificial-sounding expression, which may mean, previously taken God for your helper.

beforne, II, 58, 15; III, 13, 12, 14: before. II, 58, 15, before (morning).

beft, III, 161, 26: beat. 164, 92: beaten.

begane, bigane, IV, 366, **D** 4: overlaid, covered.

begeck, begack, give a, III, 162, 63; 164, b 63: play a trick on, make a fool of. (A. S. geác, cuckoo, simpleton.)

begoud, begood, begud, I, 473, 11; II, 99, **B b** 9; IV, 167, **C** 10; 194, **B** 5; 195, 14; 201, 21; 203, 15; 224, 13: began.

beguile, *p. p.,* III, 36, 41: beguiled.

begule, beguile.

behad, II, 160, 3: behold.

behear, II, 240 f., 7, 9; III, 93, 46; 131, 3: hear. beheard him, III, 421, 58: heard.

beheld, II, 61, 12: tarried.

behestë, III, 90 b: promise.

behind his hand, a stroke behind his hand, II, 63, 24: seems = backhanded stroke.

behote, III, 71, 315; *pres.,* promise. thou behotë, III, 71, 297: didst promise.

beik, beet, bete, on, II, 121, 20: put on fuel.

being, II, 410, 26: means of living.

belinger, IV, 74, **G b** 3: corruption or misprint for (best ?) ginger.

beliue, belyfe, b(e)lyue, III, 4, 18; 28, 125; 29, 144; 35, 18; 84, 87, 300; 94, 53; 117, 13: soon, immediately.

bell, silken, III, 261, **D** 7: conical canopy? corrupted from beild, shelter (screen)? Aytoun, with great probability, conjectures pall. Cf. **A** 10; **E** 10; **F** 14, which support the emendation.

Bell (Archie), III, 491, 3, 7: billie (comrade, brother), as in **D**, III, 492, 2.

belle, bere the, I, 328, 42; II, 58, 1; V, 202 b: stand foremost, take the lead.

bell-groat, I, 251, **A** 3, 5. Same as next word.

belling-great, I, 252, 3, 5: groat for ringing bell.

belly-, billie-blind. See **Billie Blin.**

below the sun, lookit below the sun, II, 78, 15; III, 6, 6; in below the sun, 8, 6. See **aneath the sun.**

belted plaids, IV, 84, 11; 85, 3: 87, 2; V, 253, No 203, **D** 2: "properly twelve yards of tartan cloth worn round the waist, obliquely across the breast and left shoulder, and partly depending backwards, ut in bello gestatur."

belyfe, straightway. See **beliue.**

belyue. See **beliue.**

bemean, V, 163, 4: bemoan, compassionate.

ben. Good ben be here, III, 267, 10: God's (or good) benison? Probably corrupt.

ben (shoes o, sheen o), IV, 378, 7; 380, 14: bend, bend-leather, strong ox-leather, thickened by tanning.

ben, I, 56 f., **C** 2, 14; III, 267, 20; 268, 17; 270, 16; 272, 20; 274, 33: towards the inner apartment of the house, or parlor, in, within. come farer ben, I, 369, 51; he was ben, II, 313, 16; he wood her butt, he wood her ben, I, 56, 2. V, 216, **B a** 7; 219, 10; 242 b, 8.

ben, royal ben, I, 478 f., 12, 46: (emended from *bend*) bone. See **roelle-bone.**

benbow, III, 54, 6; 104, 5; 132, 5; bend bow, III, 7, 4; 8, 25; 11, 6; bende bowe, III, 309, 44; bent bow, III, 8 **G** 2; 106, 16, 17: bow, simply, the bow being in actual use only in III, 11, 54, 104 (?), 106, 16, 309.

bend, III, 145, 5: where the way turned (?).

bend, III, 362, 71: *pret.* of bend. So II, 125, **G** 6: *pret.* of bend (should not have been changed to bent, p. 122).

bended, IV, 78, 1: bounded.

benjed, II, 403, 2; beenged, bynged, made humble obeisance, cringed.

bent the way, IV, 442, 13: took her course over.

bent, sword bent in the middle clear, middle brown, IV, 12, 11, 12: nonsense, or close upon nonsense.

bent, I, 3, 1; 5, **D** 1: a coarse, reedy grass.

bent, bents, II, 58, 16, 18; 62, 11; 172, 24, 25, 27, 35, 43; III, 295, 5; 296, 20; 297, 40; 307, 5, 8; 308, 26; 312, 28; IV, 86, 3: field, fields covered with bent grass.

benty ground, atween the brown and benty ground, IV, 27, 12: between heather and bent ground.

benty line, III, 7, 5: line of bent grass.

ber, *pret.* of bear.

berafrynd, V, 71 b: a drinking word, in response to passilodion.

bere, V, 264 a, 2: bigg, a sort of coarser barley (*Hordeum hexastichum*, not *H. vulgare* or *distichum*).

berl, V, 224, 26: birl, dispense.

bern, barn, bairn, IV, 456, 7–9, 12; V, 247, 11: (A. S. bearn) child.

berne, III, 295, 5: (A. S. beorn, fighting man, brave, etc.) man.

berry, brown berry comb, II, 224, 1: the material of this comb is elsewhere said to be haw bayberry; all the passages describing it are corrupt.

beryde, I, 326, 2: made a bere, noise.

bescro, III, 110, 26; V, 80, 49: beshrew, curse.

bese, I, 329, 58: shalt be.

beside, besids, III, 357, 38, 41, 43, 45–7: aside from, away from.

beside, in addition to, four and thirty stripes comen beside the rood, II, 59, 29: referring to the scourging before the crucifixion.

besom, hid herself in the besom of the broom, I, 398, 9: besom seems to be twigs (as *scopae* is both twigs and broom). Wedgwood cites from a Dutch dictionary of 1654, brem-bessen, broom-twigs, scopae spartiae.

bespeak: *pret.* bespa(c)ke, III, 420, 26, 30, 35; 430, 9; 431, 19, 23; bespoke, V, 149, 8–11; bespake him, I, 286, 52–5; III, 419 f., 6, 13, 22, 24: spake.

bespeek, IV, 498, 1, 3, 9: speak with.

bespoke, V, 149, 10, well-bespoke: well-spoken.

bestand, III, 105, 23: help, avail.

bested, bestead, circumstanced. ferre and frembde bested, III, 63, 138: in the position of one from a distance and a stranger. hard bestead, III, 161, 36.

bestial, IV, 41, note *: all the animals of a farm.

best man, IV, 342, 4: principal servant.

bet, II, 151, **H** 4: booted.

betaken, II, 59, 38: made over.

bete, beet, III, 310, 68: better, second, relieve. See beet.

beth, both, III, 59, 53, 54; 79, 54: be, old plural.

bether, V, 283, 8: better.

Bethine, II, 4, 12, for rhyme: if meant for anything, Bethany is meant, however inappropriate.

betide, II, 411 a, last line but two: nearest that ever fall to one, an unlikely phrase. Motherwell reads whateer betide.

betide, I, 503 b, 4, what news do ye betide? i. e. what do you (does your coming) signify? or, as at I, 205, **F** 10 (doth thee betide), what news has befallen you, come to your knowledge?

betide, boots of the tangle (sea-weed) that nothing can betide, V, 259 a, 11: should read to the effect, That's brought in by the tide.

betook, I, 126, 6: took (simply).

bets, *pl.*, V, 257, 10: boots.

bett, II, 44, 14, *pret.* of bete, beet: kindled.

better. she stood, and better she stood (printed bitter), I, 492, 5; they rode, and better they rode, I, 102, 10; 492, 10, 14; he rade and better rade, II, 209, **D** 5: longer, farther still. better swam, V, 140, e 7. better be, I, 128, 13: still more.

beuk, book.

bewch, III, 91 b: bough.

bewrailed, V, 55, 38: berailed.

bewray, V, 86, 35: reveal.

beyt, V, 79, 25: beeth, be.

bickering, IV, 7, 34: (hail) pattering.

bide, byde, I, 430, 4, 5, 8, 9; II, 177, 14; 289, **A** 2; 313, 14; III, 465, 30; V, 108, **B** 8: stay. *p. p.* bidden, IV, 262 f., 32, 33; 524, 9. bide (a doulfou day), II, 159, 23: await, look for. bide anither bode, III, 268, 12; 270, 12: wait for another offer. I never bade a better bode, III, 267, 15. your wedding to bide, III, 387, 11: await. bide it whoso may, IV, 433, 21: await the result? (obscure passage). bide frae me, V, 236, 16: stay away. In: she bade the bride gae in, II, 195, 30, it is not likely that a rival would bid a bride; interpret rather, she waited for the bride to go.

bidene, bydene, bydeene, I, 105 a, 20: immediately (or, all together). I, 273, 34: successively, one after another. III, 65, 185: together. III, 73, 350: simultaneously, or *en masse*.

biek, beek, IV, 77, 3: bask. See beek.

bier, III, 161, 32; V, 161, 1; 162, **D** 1: cry, lamentation.

bierly, beerly (bride), I, 467, 29; II, 75, 19; 132, 24; the same as buirdly bride, II, 82, 51: portly, stately (large and well made). See buirdly.

big, bigg, I, 15, 13; 17, 16; 108, 1; II, 330, 1; 331, 1; 332, 1: build. *pret.* and *p. p.* biggit, bigget, IV, 202, **K** 5; 203, 13. *pret.* bug, IV, 199, 17. *p. p.* buggin, bugn, IV, 445, 1; 446, 1. build a stack for corn, I, 17, 12; 428, 11; V, 206 a, 8.

bigane, I, 334, 5: covered, wrought.

biggeall, beguile.

bigging, biggin, II, 115, 23, 24; 117, 10, 11; 123, 25, 26; 255, 11, 12; 257, 19, 20; IV, 128, 2-4: building, house, "properly of a large size, as opposed to a cottage."

bigly (Icelandic, byggiligr, habitable), commodious, pleasant to live in, I, 68, 32; 107, 1, 3; II, 98, 30-32, 35, 36; 172 f., 40, 42, 45; 294, 4, 5; 370, 6; 417, 3; 419, 45: frequent epithet of bower. II, 358, 26, of a bier: handsomely wrought.

bile, *v.,* V, 305 a, 6: boil.

bill, V, 15, 16, 18: a paper. bills, IV, 422, 45, 46: (the necessary legal) papers. sworne into my bill, III, 411, 5: sworn in writing.

bill, I, 302, **B** 12; 303, 10; IV, 331 b, 2: bull.

billaments, I, 433, 17: habiliments, of head-gear.

billie, billy, comrade, brother; "a term expressive of affection and familiarity : " I, 448, **A** 2, 4; III, 464, 2, 5, 6, 19; 467, 56; 489, 11; V, 128, 29. born billy, III, 495 b, 23, 24. See **bully.**

Billie Blin, Bellie Blind, I, 73, 35, 44; 86, 29; 466 f., 14, 23; II, 464, 15, 16; 470, 60-63; 472, 31; V, 239, 39: see I, 67; V, 285 b.

belly-blind, II, 464, 15, 16: may mean here nothing more than an innocent warlock or wizard.

billy-pot, I, 164, **L** 6: pot with a semicircular handle (bail) ?

binë, be not: V, 238, 18.

binge, IV, 462, 30: bend.

binkes, I, 334, 9: benches.

binna, be not.

bint, V, 110, 12: bind, pay for.

bird (burd), I, 76, 50, 51; II, 314, 29, 30; **C** 10; 316, 12; IV, 422, 2, 5, 10: maid, lady. bird her lane, II, 313, 12, 19: maid by herself, solitary. II, 272, 5: child, boy.

birk. he was standing on the birk, II, 165, 13, seems to be nonsense. There is no birk to stand on unless the floor is birken, and nothing could be more inept than a reference to that matter.

birlin, II, 28, 1: drinking. See **birl.**

birl, berl, II, 28, 1; 92, 17; 219, 6; IV, 154, 9; 166, 1; 234, 35; 385, 1: drink. II, 152, **J** 3; 299, 16; 368, 7: ply with drink. birled in him, II, 144, 3, 4: poured into. Of dispensing both bread and wine: II, 191, 34, 35; V, 224, 26. birled wi them, IV, 438, 8: should apparently be birled them wi. *ptc.,* birlin, II, 28, 1.

birnande, burning.

birtled, I, 273, 42: cut up.

bisette, I, 334, 8: devote (to the matter a space greater by two miles).

bit (used with a noun instead of a diminutive), wee bit banes, I, 225, **L** 7: bits of.

bit, but. bit an(d), II, 30, 4; 132, 26: and also.

bitaihte, I, 244, 11: committed to.

bitten, V, 130, 13: taken in, cheated.

bla, III, 350, 53, 54: blow.

blabring, V, 247, 9: babbling. See **blobberin.**

bla 'd, II, 21, 6: bla it, blow it.

blaewort, IV, 212, 6: corn bluebottle, round-leaved bell-flower, bluebell of Scotland.

blaise, blaisse, IV, 503, 19; 505, 49: display, show forth, display itself.

blan, blane, blanne, II, 53, 29; 140, 23; 265, 9; III, 309, 41; 405, 13; 406, 38; 466, 40: *pret.* of blin, stop, cease.

blast, V, 82, 39: puff, breathe hard.

blate, II, 260, 2; III, 160, 10; 163, 85: dumfoundered, abashed, silly. spake blate, II, 470, 47, 50: bashfully, diffidently.

blavers, V, 213, 14: corn bluebottle (blaewort).

blaw, I, 15, **B** 2; 16 **C** 2: blow. *pret.* blow, III, 112, 65. *p. p.* blawin, I, 17, **D** 1; blawn, I, 15, **B** 1; 16, **C** 1, 2. *pres. p.* blawn (blawing), II, 114, 20.

blee, I, 272, 13, 20, 24; 293, 1; II, 364, 26; 442, 1, 2: color, complexion.

bleed, blood.

bleed, I, 441, 5, 7, *pret.* of bleed : bled.

bleeze, III, 457, **B** 4: blaze.

blewe, I, 326, 7: blew on a horn (see st. 10).

blin, blind.

blin, blyn, blinne, II, 138, 3; V, 14 f., 2, 20: (belin) cease, stop. *pret.* blan. See **blan.**

blind, blint, II, 345, 26; 382, 6; IV, 265, **A b** 8; 486, 10: blinded.

blink, *n.,* IV, 136, 17; 360, 15; 384, 3, 4; look, glance. IV, 390, 7, of the moon : gleam. IV, 389 b: (of time) moment.

blink, to look: II, 433, 6; IV, 127, 14; 351, 7; 353, 18; 416, 2; V, 53, 107; 54, 3; 154, **A** 11: glance, emit, throw a glance. III, 371, 27; IV, 256 f., 1, 10: shine, glitter. blinkin ee, IV, 194, (4,) 5; 201, 25; 203, 5; 211, 9: shining, twinkling. wha is this that blinks in Willie's ee ? II, 189, 25: sends brightness into, whose brightness is reflected from. nor ever did he blink his ee (at the gallows), IV, 12, **B** 8: wink, shut, blench, his look was steadfast. cam blinkin on an ee, II, 475, 17: winking as if blind, playing the blind.

blint, II, 17 b; IV, 515, 12: blinded. See **blind.**

bliss : bless.

blobberin, II, 256, 13: perhaps, blubbering, crying ; perhaps=blabring. V, 247, 9: babbling.

block, II, 216, 16: exchange. IV, 148, 54: bargain ; lost the better block, had the worse in a bargain or dealing.

blood, blude, II, 114, 16; 123, 13: man (disrespectfully), fellow.

blow, *pret.,* blew.

blowe, II, 478, 8: blossom.

blowe (wynde), II, 478, 12: give vent to.

blowe (boste), III, 59, 59: give breath to, utter.

blude, bluid, blood. See **blood.**

bluid is gude, IV, 433, 21: good to dream of.

bluntest, III, 492, 25: stupidest.

blutter, III, 161, 43: dirty.

blyue, belyfe, beliue, III, 29, 144 ; 71, 300 ; 74, 371: quickly, immediately.

boad, *n.,* V, 243, 11: offer.

boams, fire-boams (not beams), IV, 96, **D** 3: bombs.

board-floor, II, 160, 5, 6: should probably be bower-floor, as in 159, 6, 9; 161, 6, 8.

bocht: bought.

bocking, III, 161, 33: vomiting, belching.

boddom, bottom.

bode, n., offer: III, 267, 15; 268, 12; 270, 12; 272, 14.

bodë, p. p., III, 67, 222: bidden, invited.

bodes, wild fowl bodes on hill, II, 410, 7: announces day. Cf. II, 230, 5, the wild fule boded day.

bode-words, III, 4, 19: messages.

body: faith, faikine, of my body, III, 180, 17; 199, 24; 216, 33; 296, 16; 472, 7; truth of my body, III, 180, B, 7; 181, 15, 16, 21; IV, 7, 31: either by my personal faith, or, by my body. faith in my body, III, 411, 6.

body-clothes; IV, 152, 7: clothes of my body.

bold, bauld (of fire), II, 116, 18; 117, 12; 119, 5, 6; 123, 18, 27: sharp, brisk.

boldly (understand), IV, 146, 19: freely, confidently, fully (verbiage).

bokin, bodkin.

bolts, IV, 409, 1: rods, bars (to make a petticoat stand out).

bon, bone, boune, on the way, going. See boun.

bone, boon.

bone, sadle of the bone, V, 219, 13. See bane, roelle-bone.

bonins, by, V, 253 a, 4: in plenty (Gypsy cant).

bonnetie, V, 306, 2, 3: dimin. of bonnet.

booting, III, 159, 1: making of boot or booty.

boot, v., IV, 501, 26: matter. See bote.

bord, borde, bowrd, V, 78, 1; 80, 48, 49: jest, sport, amusement, comic tale.

bord, II, 450, 80; 451, 84: should perhaps be bore, as in 445, 77. Still, carried him out of the saddle by the impact of the spear which bored him through is not unlikely, and we have, p. 454, 55, out of his saddle bore him he did.

borden, adj., IV, 506, 73: of plank; borden tree, wooden plank.

born alive, ye were, IV, 521, 19; A, IV, 26, 16, has 'That I love best that 's born alive,' i. e. of all that are born. The ye should be yᵗ, that, and probably was so meant.

borough-town, borrow's toun, borrous-toun, etc. See borrows-town, burrow-town.

borowe, borrow, n. III, 59, 62-64, 66; 68, 237, 250: security. III, 405, 9: sponsor, vindicator.

borowe, borrow, v., I, 309, A 3; II, 177, 27; III, 25, 50; 298, 69; 329, 6; IV, 33, 15-18, 20, 21: set free, deliver, ransom.

borowehode, III, 68, 239: securityship.

borrows-town, borrous-toun, IV, 229, 1; V, 117, A 6, 7; 126, 1: borough-town, borough, corporate town. See borough (burrow)-town.

boskyd, III, 112, 60: busked, made ready. See busk.

bot, but. bot and: see but and.

bot, without. See but.

bot, II, 94, 3: behoved.

bote, boote, boot, II, 45, 30, 34; III, 27, 104; 94, 55; 187, 33: help, use, advantage. (boot, v., IV, 501, 26: matter.)

both, beth, III, 59, 53, 54; 79, 54: be (old plural).

bottle (of hay), V, 114, 4: bundle.

bottle. be my bottle, V, 170, 1: hold my own, bear my full part, in drinking? Corrupt?

bottys, butts.

boud, V, 176, 17: behoved, were obliged.

bouerie, II, 232, 1: diminutive of bower, chamber.

bought = bucht, IV, 198, 1; 199, 17, 23: fold, pen.

bouk, buik, buke, II, 149, 14; IV, 127, 14; 484 a: trunk, body.

boun, bowne, bune, bound, bownd, bowynd, v., make ready, go. buske yee, bowne yee, III, 91, 5; 431, 25: make ready. boun, bound, I, 369, 44; IV, 183, 2; V, 256, 5: go. make ye boun, I, 75, 18: go. must bound home, V, 9, 4. get up and bound your way, II, 405, 9: go, come. bownd away, III, 161, 30; bowynd hym to ryde, III, 295, 1; bounded for to ride, II, 118, 7: set out, went. bound him to his brand, III, 160, 23: went, betook himself. was boon, boun, bound, II, 298, 5; IV, 432, 2; V, 256 a, 4: going, on the way. how she is bune, II, 191, 30: going on. go boun away, IV, 224, 15, 16 (tautology): go, depart.

boun, bon, bowne, bowen, bowyn, bun, adj. (búinn, p.p. of Icelandic búa, to make ready): bound, ready. made him boun, III, 163, 76. to batell were not bowyn, III, 295, 4. make ye bowne, I, 75, 18, 22; III, 296, 28. bun to bed, bon to rest, II, 191, 26; V, 35, B 3. made him boun, bound, III, 163, 76; V, 81, 2: equipped himself. your friends beene bowne, I, 210, 14: ready to come. ready boun (tautology), IV, 432, 5. See boun, v.

boun, V, 300, 6: boon.

bounties, V, 231, 14: presents, in addition to wages.

bountieth, V, 9, 12: bounty, alms.

bourde, v., III, 179 b: jest.

bourden, III, 179 b: staff.

bourn, III, 470 a: brook.

boustouslie, bousterously, boustresslie, boustrouslie : I, 108, 13; IV, 446, 13; 447, 13; 465, 19, 35: boisterously, roughly.

bout, II, 27, 18: bolt.

bouted, I, 68, 4; 70, 4: bolted.

bow, bough.

bow, lintseed bow, I, 305, 14: the boll or pod containing the seeds of flax.

bow, II, 28, 16: boll, a dry measure; of salt, two bushels; "for wheat and beans, four Winchester bushels; for oats, etc., six bushels." Scottish, four firlots (see firlot). bow o bere, V, 264 a: boll of barley.

bower, chamber: I, 55, A 1; 68, 25, 32; 73, 47; etc., etc. bouerie, II, 232, 1: diminutive of the same.

bower, house, home : I, 56, 3; 79, 3; 80, 1; 107, 1; etc., etc. Often indistinguishable from the above.

bower-head, II, 76, 11: top of the house. (Unless the reading should be tower-head; cf. II, 74, D 5; 78, I 14, but we have an upmost ha, highest room, II, 72, C 14.)

bower-yett, house-gate.

bowie, V, 306, 15: a kind of tub.

bown, V, 273, No 239, 4: bowed, bent.

bowne, bownd, bowyn. See **boun.**

bowrd, I, 264: comic tale. See **bord.**

bows (o London), I, 131, **H** 1: arches of a bridge? windings of the river?

box, V, 19, 18: a compartment partitioned off in a drinking-room.

boyt, III, 109, 3: both.

bra, braw, I, 128, 19; V, 268, 25; 272, 3, 7, 11: brave, fine, handsome. See **braw.**

bracken, braken, brachan, breckin, breaken, breckan, brecken, breachan, IV, 257, **B** 7; 268, 21; 269, d 19, f 19; 272, 11, 3; 501, 28, 31, 37; V, 244, 16, 19, 20; 265 b, 19: fern, brake.

brae, bra, bray, hillside, hill : I, 324, 14; IV, 92, 1; 264, 15; 274, 8; 448 a, 3d st. braes o Yarrow, IV, 164 f., 1-9, **B** 3-5: the equivalent word is sometimes, banks, pp. 168, 169, 170, 178; otherwise houms, p. 168, but downs, p. 166 f., and the topography seems to indicate hills. "Conjoined with a name, it denotes the upper part of a country, as the Braes of Angus." Jamieson.

brae, river-bank : III, 484 a, 32; burn-brae, IV, 275, **C** b 8. Cholar foord brae-head, III, 482, 21?

brae, brow : III, 4, 17.

braid, IV, 399, 28: breadth. See **breed.** *Adj.,* broad.

braid (broad) letter, II, 20, 3; 25, 3; 26, 3; 27, 3; 251, 2; 393, 4; IV, 118, **C** 1; 119, **D** 1; 120, 1; 373, 2; 382, 3: either a letter on a broad sheet or a long letter. The king's letter, II, 21, 3; 23, **E** 3; 24, 3, is lang, and at 22, 3, is large. A braid letter has been interpreted to be an open one, a patent, but in almost every case here cited the letter is said to be sealed. The letter at II, 251, 2, is private and confidential, written by a lady. Private folk write broad letters, IV, 320, 1; 339, 13; 342, 17; 343, 7; a lady again, II, 382, 5; 395, 18; IV, 233, 20; 342, 6; 343, 2.

brain, II, 124, 39; 130, 28; 131, 20; 133, 9; 169, 25; 407, 10; III, 274, 33: mad.

brake, break, V, 166, 8; 306, 7: cause to break off, correct, cure.

braken, III, 299, 12, 14; 300, 25, 26: fern. See **bracken.**

braken, I, 350, 17: *p. p.* of break.

bramly, III, 9, 13: brambly, thorny.

branded (bull), III, 459, 7: of a reddish brown color.

brank, *n.,* III, 440, 10: caper, prance, gallop.

branken, branking, III, 299, 4; 301, **D** 1: galloping.

branks, III, 480, 9: a sort of bridle; a halter with two pieces of wood, instead of a leathern strap or a cord, over the nose, the whole resembling a muzzle.

brash, sickness: II, 364, 20; IV, 483, 16.

brast, I, 370, 14, 18; V, 76, 26; 80, 45; 82, 40: burst, broke, broken.

brauches, I, 271, 2: brooches. But perhaps *branches,* the clothes embroidered with rings and sprigs.

braw, I, 491, 1, 2, etc.; II, 80, 3-7: comely. I, 127, 21; 467, 29; II, 23, **E** 5: fine, handsome, finely dressed. I,

184, 11; V, 210, 11: (of a meeting) pleasant. See **bra** and **braws.** braw wallie, IV, 296, **F** 1: exclamation of admiration.

brawn, IV, 212, 5: calf of the leg.

braws, IV, 269, f, 19: fine things, finery.

bray, brae, hillside, hill.

brayd on, V, 198 b, after 52: move on, fall on.

brayde, breyde, at a brayde, III, 26, 91; of a, III, 32, 91: in a moment, of a sudden.

breachan. See **bracken.**

bread, breed, bred, III, 339, 13, 16; 341, 42: breadth.

bread, broad.

breaden, I, 433, 9: braided (here, perhaps, woven).

break, brake, V, 166, 8; 306, 7: cause to break off, correct, cure.

break, till five minutes break, II, 325, 19, 20: expire.

breaken. See **bracken.**

breast. smoothd his breist and swam, II, 248, 9, 15: made it even, level with the water. set her, his brest and swom, II, 459, 8; V, 137, 5, 9. bent his breast and swam, V, 138, **C** 3, 5; 141 b, 6, 9; 142 a, 4. lay on his brest and swumme, II, 247, 14.

breast, in a, IV, 11, 12, 13: in one voice (all at once, p. 13, 4). in a breast, Scottish, sometimes=abreast, side by side.

breast, *v.,* II, 299, 22, breast a steed : mount, by bringing the breast to it.

breast-mills, II, 403, 15: mills operated by a breast-wheel.

breastplate, II, 380, 15; 383, 14; 385, 4, etc.; IV, 486, 6, etc.: some part of a woman's attire, said here to be of steel instead of gold. Possibly a stomacher. "Curet, breastplate, or stomager." Huloet, 1552. "Torace, also a placket, a stomacher, or brest plate for the body." Florio. At II, 381, 10, we have *bracelets,* which would be a plausible emendation for *breastplate,* did not the latter occur quite a dozen times.

breast-wine, II, 338, **T** 7: milk (Irish ballad).

breathed, II, 47, unto, 21, on, 22: does not seem to be the right word. Possibly *breved,* gave information to (but the word is antique for the text, and *on* in 22 would not suit).

brecham, III, 480, 9: 492, 4; **brechen,** III, 491, 6: a straw collar for a horse, also a pack-saddle made of straw, so more probably here, carts not being used.

brechan, brichan, IV, 157, 7, 12, 14, 18, 19 : (Gael. breacan) plaid.

brechen. See **brecham.**

breckan, -en, -in. See **bracken.**

bred, brede, V, 283, 8, 18: bread.

bred, bread, breed, III, 347, c 44, g 38: breadth.

brede, I, 242, 7: to have the whims attributed to breeding women ? (Not satisfactory, as not being sufficiently simple. Prof. Kittredge has suggested to me gynnyst to wede, to go mad; which seems to me quite worth considering. The rhyme with the same sound in a different sense, is entirely allowable.)

bree, brie, I, 129, 14; 341, 3, 8, 17; 417, 13; III, 11, **K**; V, 191 f., 3, 18, 31: brow, eyebrow.

bree, broth. See broo.

breed, bread, bred, braid, III, 349, 38; IV, 503, 13, 16; 505, 45: breadth.

breek-thigh, III, 464, 15: thigh of his breeches.

breeme, III, 285, 19: fierce.

breist. See breast.

bren, brene, brenne, brin, II, 45, 24; 59, 32; III, 24, 29, 35; 361, b, c, 28: burn. *p. p.* brent, II, 44, 3, 14; 46, 47.

brent (brow), II, 191, 25; IV, 272, 2; 387, 1: high and straight. Also, smooth, unwrinkled.

brents, I, 74, 76, 78: door-posts, or doors. (Icelandic brandar, postes, Egilsson; ships' beaks used as ornaments over the chief door of dwellings, Vigfusson.)

brest. See breast.

brest, burst.

brether, brothers, brethren, I, 104, 10; III, 478, 15. bretheren, III, 26, 74; 478, 14. brethern, bretherne, II, 73, 17; 160, 3, 9; III, 57, 27; 67, 217. brothren, III, 29, 148. brethen, III, 22, 4, 6; 23, 10; V, 135 b, 19.

bretther o degs, with a b. of d. ye 'll clear up my nags, IV, 312, 3 (the reading may be *bretlher . . . clean*): corrupt. "brathay an degs would mean with old cloth and torn rags : brathay (obsolete) worn out brats or clothes." W. Forbes.

breyde, *n.*, with a breyde, III, 110, 20: with a rush, in haste.

breyde, *v.*, III, 110, 9: rushed, bounded.

bride-steel, brid-stell, bride-stool, bride-styl, IV, 181, 7, 8; 182, F 2, 3; 183, 2; V, 256 a, 4, 5: seat in church where the bridegroom and bride sat before the beginning of the service.

brie, brow. See bree.

brig, brigue, I, 118, D 2; II, 24, 14; 177, 13, 15; 272, 13: bridge.

bright, bryghte, I, 285, 25; 293, 2; 296, 51, 56; 327, 12, 21: sheen, beautiful.

brim, II, 274, 3: sea. In, fa oure the brim, IV, 419, 16, 26, the brim of a precipice may be meant.

brin, II, 146, 23; V, 223 a, No 68, A 22: burn.

bring hame, I, 76, 53; 367, 9; II, 97, 24; 425, 9, 10; V, 41, 17; give birth to. brought King James hame, II, 345, 29: brought into the world. (come hame, be born, see hame.)

brirben, II, 217, 2, 4. tabean brirben (printed by Herd birben) is corrupt. A copy mentioned by Finlay had birchen; see IV, 471, 221.

brither, II, 163, 7, 11, 16; 164, 17; 165, 3; V, 123, 4; 299, 4: brother.

Brittaine, Litle, I, 285, 24, 33, 37.

brittled, bryttled, brittened, I, 328, 51; III, 7, 7: cut up.

broad (brode) arrow, brod arwe (aro), III, 13, 9; 29, 153, 159; 106, 16; 307, 5; 341, 56; "catapulta." Prompt. Parv. The Catholicon explains catapulta to be "sagitta cum ferro bipenni, quam sagittam barbatam vocant." Way. Cotgrave: "Rallion. An arrow with a forked, or barbed head; a broad arrow." broode-headed arrowe, IV, 505, 56; 506, 64; broode-arrowe-head, 506, 59.

broad letter. See braid letter.

broad-mouthd axe, IV, 123, 14: broad axe.

broad sow, V, 91, 3: a sow that has a litter (brod= breed).

brockit, brookit, bruckit, I, 303, 8; 304, E 8, F 8; V, 213, 8: streaked or speckled in the face, streaked with dirt. See broked, bruchty.

brodinge, II, 58, 14: shooting up, sprouting. (Old Eng. brodden.)

brogues, IV, 70, G 4; 72, I 7; 269 a, d 20; V, 265, No 227, 20; 301, No 200: coarse light shoes of horse-hide, worn especially by Highlanders.

broke, brook, III, 69 f., 271, 274, 279; 310, 62: enjoy.

broked cow, III, 459, 7: a cow that has black spots or streaks mixed with white in her face. See brockit.

broken, IV, 356, 12: bankrupt, ruined.

broken men, III, 473, 19, 24; IV, 41, note *: men under sentence of outlawry, or who lived as vagabonds and public depredators, or were separated from their clans in consequence of crimes. Jamieson.

broo, brue, bree, brie, II, 30, 11: brow.

broo, brue, bree, I, 160, C 2, D 3; 161, E 3; IV, 449, 2, 3: broth. I, 499, 4; V, 98, 9, 10: water in which something has been boiled.

brook, broke, bruik, II, 189, 33, 34; 420, 7; III, 212, 8; IV, 435, 14: enjoy.

broom-cow, I, 394, 5: twig of broom.

brose-cap, II, 463, 25: pottage-, porridge-bowl.

brot, *p. p.*, V, 296, 2, 3, etc.: brought.

brothered, IV, 373, 17: broidered? (He is to have a change of clothes every month, and those embroidered?)

brough, V, 128, 29, 30: borough, town.

brought hame. See bring hame.

broun, brown, IV, 169, F 2; G 1 (browns, brouns, in the MSS.). Might be thought a corruption of *brand*, but *brand* occurs in each case immediately after. *Brown* for *brown blade* would be extraordinary.

browen, III, 9, 4: brewed. (*brown* corrected from earlier MS.)

browȝt, browt, browthe, brought.

brown ground, IV, 27, 12: brown with heather.

brown sword, I, 70, 22; 294, 24; III, 71, 305. Brún as an epithet of sword in Anglo-Saxon has been interpreted literally, as denoting that the weapon was wholly or in part of bronze; also as gleaming, which may at first seem forced. Gleaming is the meaning given to brown sword by Mätzner, who cites three cases from romances. We have bright brown sword, II, 139, 22; 241, 24; 266, 26, 27; and, blades both browne and bright, III, 93, 36. The late Mr. Edward Bangs, remarking upon these passages, suggests that the blades may have been artificially browned with acid and then polished, as gun-barrels still are, and he refers to P. Lacombe's description of the magnificent sword of Charles V, Armes et Armures, p. 221 : "la lame est d'acier bruni presque noir." We have browne tempered blade, III, 35, 13, meaning, probably, a blade tempered to that color.

browt, browthe, brought.

browst, V, 306, 12: brewage.

bruchty, brucket, brockit, I, 301 f., A 5, 9; V, 213 a,
No 33, 5: spotted or streaked with dirt ; of a sheep,
streaked or speckled in the face. See **brockit**.

brue, V, 209 a: broo, broth, soup.

brue, I, 334, 3: brow.

bruik, II, 422, 2; IV, 385, 27; V, 179, 12, 13: enjoy,
possess. See **brook**.

brune, III, 9, H 8: error for *brume* (which is the reading in an earlier MS.).

brung, *pret.*, *p. p.* of bring, IV, 191, B, after 7; 466, 11.

brunt, IV, 211, 2; 392, 17; 468, 17: burnt.

brusted, brusten, II, 186, 15; IV, 2, 6: burst.

bryde, II, 442, 3; 478, 1: young woman.

bryk, III, 13, 13: breeches, hose.

bryn, I, 136, R 4: should probably be *brim*, as in R,
b, c. *brin*, brow, from the Icelandic, is unlikely.

bryng yow on your way, III, 99, 45: take, accompany.

bryste, I, 327, 12: burst.

brytlyng, bryttlynge, III, 307, 8; 308, 13: (breaking)
cutting up. See **brittled**.

bucht, bught, bought, *n.*, IV, 193, 1, 2, 5; 194, 6, 9;
195 f., 1, 3, 4; 198 f., 1, 3, 6; etc.: a small pen, usually
put up in the corner of the field, into which it was
customary to drive the ewes when they were to be
milked. Jamieson.

bucht, bught, *v.*, IV, 200, 1, 18; 201, 10; 205, 22: go
into the bucht, or pen. *pret.* buchted, IV, 201, 24:
drove into the pen; *p. p.*, 201, 11: built a pen for (cf.
198, 8; 200, 19).

buckle, crisp, curl (of hair). Curling Buckle, IV, 357,
C 6, 7: one with hair crisped or curled.

buckled up our lap, II, 473, 17: fastened up apron or
gown so as to make a bag for carrying away meal.

bucklings, V, 183, 21: encounters ?

bud, I, 72 f., 7, 62: behooved. See **buse**.

bug, IV, 199, 17, *pret.* of big : built.

bugge, I, 243, 1: buy.

buggin, bugn, *p.p.* of big, IV, 445 b, 1; 446 b, 1: built.

buik, bouk, IV, 485, 12, 14: body.

buik, buke, IV, 411, 2; V, 122, 9: book.

buik, II, 71, 10: *pret.* of bake (A. S. bóc).

builded, *pret.*, III, 123, 4 ; sheltered, hid. (A. S. byl-
dan, Scot. bield.)

buird, V, 138, 11, 12, 14: board.

buirdly, buirlie (bride), II, 82, 51 ; 130, 8 : portly,
stately, large and well made. buirdlie men, II, 315,
E 6. See **bierly**.

buke, II, 165, 14: bouk, body. The verse is suspicious;
more sense could be had by reading Maist fair, etc.,
and making the line the beginning of the speech of
the fourth brother. See **bouk, buik**.

buke, buik, book.

bukeld, V, 276, 18. See **baucheld**.

buld, build, built.

bull-baits, I, 103, E 4: represents strokes, blows (cf.
other versions), and must have some such sense. Possibly a corruption of buffets, though I see not how.

A compounding of Old English *bollen*, to strike, and
of *beat* would be unlikely. *Bull-baits*, for violent
assaults, no doubt seemed good enough to the reciter.

bully, billy, IV, 146 f., 5, 12, 18–21, etc.: brother, fellow,
mate. See **billie**.

bullyship, IV, 147, 29, 33: comradeship.

bun, II, 191, 26; IV, 45, 6: boun(d), ready to go.

bun, V, 267 a, 9: bound, tied up.

bune (how she is), II, 191, 30: going on, faring.

burd, bird, I, 69 f., 70, 72; 71, 57; II, 282, 6; III, 393,
14; 394, K 3; IV, 418, 2, 3, 5, etc.; 420, 2, 4, 5, etc.;
424, 1, 2, 4; V, 228 f., 12, 22, 34, 35: damsel, maid, lady.
V, 229, 32: perhaps offspring.

burd-alone, he lay burd-alone, I, 298, 2: solitary, by
himself ; cf. maid alone, II, 149, 2.

Burd Alone, II, 95, 1, 3, 4, 5: desolate, forlorn one;
corruption of Burd Helen, 96, J 2 : cf. bird her lane.

bure, I, 108, 8: bore (*pret.*).

Burgesse (?), IV, 503, 4; 504, 24: Bordeaux. Should
probably be Burdesse.

burgh, IV, 53, 15–17: town.

burken, II, 133, 8: birken, birchen.

Burlow-beanie, I, 287, 60, 65, 70, 74: =Billy Blin, which
see (I, 67).

burly, I, 300, 4. See **beerly**.

burn, bourn, I, 438, A 3, 4; III, 440, 16; 460, 27: brook.

burn-brae, IV, 76, 1: hillside with a brook at the bottom.

burnyssht, III, 63, 136: shining, made bright.

burrow-town, burrows-town, IV, 288, E 3; 299, d
13: properly, chartered town, corporate town ; perhaps
nothing more than a town of some size, larger than a
village. See **borrows-town**.

bursen, IV, 4 b 6 : burst. bursen day, IV, 481, 20:
overpoweringly fatiguing.

buse, þe buse agayne, I, 328, 54: it behoves thee (other
texts, thou most). *pret.* (personal) bot, II, 94, 3;
beet, III, 281, 2; bud, boud, I, 73, 62; V, 176, 17.

busk, buss (Icel. búask, old reflexive of búa, make
ready, from the participle of which comes boun, so
that busk and boun are of the same origin and equivalent). **1.** make ready. buske you, III, 73, 340. busk
and boune, II, 24, 5; III, 434, 22. buske yee, bowne
yee, III, 91, 5. the[y] buske them bowne, he buskes
him bowne, III, 285, 26, 38. they busked and made
them bowne, III, 284, 2. **2.** dress, deck. busk and
mak yow braw, II, 23, E 5. busk the bride, II, 104,
16, 18; 105, 10, 11; 106, 11. *p. p.* busket, III, 433, 3.
weel-busked hat, IV, 199, 9: decorated. buskit wi
rings, V, 203 a. busk on you the flowers, II, 465, 3:
put on as ornaments. buskit fire wi leaves, II, 411,
10: set about. busk your ship roon (with feather
beds), IV, 381, 8, cf. 10: wrap, sheathe. **3.** betake
oneself, go. I wol me buske ouer the salte see: III,
59, 56. See **buskit**.

buske, III, 97, 12: bush.

busker, III, 252, 16 : corrupt; *testament* in other copies.

buskit, -et, III, 433, 3: dressed. buskit his bow in her
hair, I, 131, 15: furnished, strung. See **busk**.

buss, I, 130, 16; II, 133, 8; III, 3, 6; 5, **D** 7; 6, 6: bush.

buss, IV, 510, 4; 513 a, 1: busk, make ready, dress. See **busk.**

busshement, III, 71, 301: ambuscade.

busting, *n.,* V, 301 b, 3: padding or the like used to improve the figure.

but, *prep.,* without: I, 16, 6; 420, 9, 10; 430, 3; III, 161, 30; IV, 41 b; 326, 16; 329, **A,** b after 12.

but, III, 267, 20; 268, 17; 270, 16; 272, 20; 274, 33: towards the outer apartment or kitchen, without, out. gae butt the house and bid her come ben, V, 115, 6. he wood her butt, he wood her ben, I, 56 f., **C** 2, 14; cf. V, 219, 10. but it speaks, V, 306, 6: out speaks.

but, if ye be a maiden but, I, 72, 25: corrupt; read, binna maiden yet?

but and, bot and, but an, bat an=and also: I, 18, **F** 7; 69, 49; 72, 5; 345, **C** 8, 9, 10; 464, 8; 474, 36; IV, 418, 5; V, 246 b, 4, 6, 8.

but nor hed, II, 191, 27: but and had not.

but than=but and, IV, 465, 23.

by (cf. also **be),** II, 56 a; 433, 2; III, 22, 2; 91, 2; IV, 420, 2, 4; 422, 2: about, concerning (as, by a knight I say my song). V, 272 b, 3, 7, 11; 277, 4; 278, 20 (spelled *bay),* 31: in comparison with, on comparing (*by* 272 b, 3⁴, should perhaps be *but*; cf. 11⁴). kend thy freind by thy foe, III, 420, 18: in distinction from. by than, III, 77, 435: by the time that. by weeke, spend forty pounds by weeke, II, 442, 7: distributively, a week. So, by yere, III, 61, 92. he maun do them by, V, 169, 12: do without. no far by, V, 123, 10: not far off. called young Brichen by, I, 465, 5: called on, to. ca'd by Andrew Lammie, IV, 302, 1: called by the name of.

by and bye, the keys hang at that lady by and bye, I, 471, 4: one next to the other (?).

by and by, IV, 196 f., 1, 14: nigh.

by and by, I, 287 f., 60, 71, 75, 77; V, 122, 1; 123, 1: directly, immediately.

by=aby, pay for, atone for: III, 97, 15.

byckarte, *pret.* of bicker, III, 307, 5: (fought) attacked (the deer).

byd, must, am under necessity.

byddys, III, 308, 26: abides.

byde, III, 297, 37: wait. *p. p.* byddin, V, 202 a: staid. *pret.* byde, there was naething byde him wi, IV, 428, 11: nothing which did remain.

bydene. See **bidene.**

bye fell, III, 440, 8: a rocky hill or piece of high land lying off or aside of the way.

bye-yett, IV, 21, 10: side-gate (subsidiary, not principal).

bygane, gone by.

byggande, *ptc.,* I, 327, 33: building.

byrde, I, 327, 22: woman (wife or maid). See **burd.**

byre, II, 182, 8; 184, 13; 188, 13; IV, 293, 9; 297, 9: cow-house.

bystode, hard bystode, III, 98, 33: hard pressed.

bytecke, commit to: I, 327, 29.

C

ca, caw, call=drive, strike. ca a nail, I, 403, 13; III, 495, **B** b, after 7. ca a pin, IV, 381, 9, 11. ca in the stake, II, 123, 14, 27. caw shoon on a steed, IV, 470, 18. ca up a gallows, II, 253, 8. ca'd holes, V, 141 b, 8. ca hogs, II, 258, 32. ca the mare, IV, 17 f., 5, 13. ca horse, IV, 109, 1. call sheep, II, 255, 17. caw ky, IV, 193, 13; 194, 17. ca the pleugh, V, 105, **A** 10. waft (emend from *wraft*) was neer ca'd throw, I, 424 a, 12, 13; 425, 12, 13. ca'd the table wi her foot, II, 313, 20. ca'd out the sheriff's een, IV, 392, 19.

ca'd by, ca'd by Andrew Lammie, IV, 302, 1: called by the name of.

caddie. See **cadie.**

cadger, cauger, an itinerant huckster. corn-caugers, III, 479, 8 (=corn-buyers, 491, 6; corn-dealers, 492, 4).

cadgily, V, 115, 1: merrily.

cadie, caddie, IV, 351, 4, 5; 353, 6, 7, 9, 10, etc.: a young fellow who does errands, or any inferior kind of work.

caft, IV, 330 a, appendix, 2: calved.

cairdman, II, 474, 9, 10: tinker, beggar.

cald, III, 455, 10: could.

cale, call, calle, V, 221, 20; 228, 19; 247, 1 (MS. calld); 248, 21; 257, 15: cold.

call, a call opon, V, 221, 14, 19: a call out, (simply) call.

call, *v.,* III, 62, 113; 111, 38: address.

calland, II, 267, 9: lad.

called their grandmother over, IV, 70, **G** 2: corrupted from cast their glamour oer her.

caller, cauler, IV, 484, after 23; 485, 19: (of air), fresh.

cam, *pret.* of come: III, 61, 91; 69, 259.

came home, hame, of child-birth, IV, 405, 54; 420, 5. See **bring hame.**

cammer, II, 131, 6: (conjecture for *cannell)* cambric (Scottish cammeraige, camroche).

camovine, IV, 212, 4; 213, 12: camomile.

campioun, II, 386, 18: champion.

campy, I, 304, 1: having the quality or make of a champion, or (name) champion (like *kempy).*

camric, cambric.

can, II, 445, 62; 450, 67; III, 66, 210; 67, 227; 162, 55: knows.

can, *inf.,* will never can steer ye, IV, 69, 15.

can, cann, an auxiliary of the present tense, can bee= is: II, 442, 14; 443, 30; 444, 51; 446, 93. Cf. do be (are), I, 184, 47. (may be, II, 448, 33; 451, 100; might be, III, 452, 10, show a misunderstanding of this.) auxiliary of the past tense,=did: II, 446, 81, 84; III, 65, 184; 67, 223; 298, 56. (Probably a corruption of gan.) cold, colde, could, cowde,=did: I, 294, 23, 24; III, 298, 56, 59; 440, 10; IV, 3, 19; V, 278, 37. cold be, II, 443, 34; III, 413, 34: were, was. cold see, III, 413, 32: saw, have seen. (An extension of the use of can=gan.)

cankerdly, III, 160, 13; 267, 10: crossly.

cankred, III, 189, **A** 9: ill-humored, complaining, crabbed (Scottish canker, to fret), with reference to the behavior in 6. But as John shows no crooked temper to the palmers, possibly cankred is to be taken literally as crooked (see **B** 10), having in mind Icel. kengr, a crook of metal, English kink, etc.

cannas, cannis, canies, V, 239, 35; 276, 14, 15: canvas, coarse cloth.

cannel, II, 147, 3, 4: candle.

canny, *adj.*, IV, 303, 16; 304, 4: gentle. IV, 305, 25: cautious. IV, 306, 17: clever, expert. V, 121 a: wily. IV, 132, **G** 4: canny (Cannygate) seems to be for jingle, but may be a term of general commendation.

canny, cannie, cannilie, *adv.*, IV, 154, 4; 304, 14; 306, 29: cautiously. IV, 133, 3, 4; 306, 18; 354, 2, 3: attentively. I, 245 f., 11–14: carefully, expertly. I, 245, 8, 9: expertly, or gently. II, 161, 18: slowly, or softly.

cantie, canty, IV, 261, 3; 317, **F** 6; V, 115, 2: merry.

cap, caup, II, 344, 1: cup.

cap, cape, V, 230 a, 10, 11: catch. *pret., p. p.* caped, II, 317, **B b** 20; V, 219, 23; 271, 14: struck. See **kep.**

cape, V, 79, 32: cloak.

capull-hyde, III, 92, 7; 93, 44; 94, 48: horse-hide.

care, car, cart.

care, *v.*, II, 370, 16: mind, object.

care-bed, II, 58, 4; 433, 3; 434, 28; 435, 47; 436 f., 58, 79 (of a hopeless lover): almost, or quite, sick-bed; (of a mother) III, 3, 2; so, bed of care, V, 227, 11. "care-bed lair, a disconsolate situation; a sick-bed." Jamieson.

carefull, III, 57, 28; 343, 18: full of care, sorrowful.

carket, carknet, I, 69, 56; 71, 46: necklace.

carl, carle, carel, carril, cerl, II, 466 f., 35, 36, 45, 46; III, 189, **B** 10, 11; IV, 493 f., 7, 11, 30; V, 237, 6, 7; 238, 12, 13, etc.: fellow, man of low condition, peasant.

carlin, carline, old woman, V, 26, 24; of a gentleman's mother, I, 71, 31; of a wealthy woman, II, 238, 1, 2. low-born woman, peasant woman: II, 467, 40, 47; 469 f., 42, 51, 56–58; V, 26, 24.

carlish, churlish, uncivilized.

carrlis, careless.

carnal, II, 8, 1, 2, 4: (cornicula, corneille) crow.

carp, carpe, III, 127, play, 31; 310, 58: talk. In, harp and (or) carp, I, 324, 5; 325, 5; 329, 2; IV, 18, 9, 10; 19, **B** 5, 6, 12; 20 f., **C** 7, **D** 7, 8; 21, **E** 8; 23, **A** c 22; 454 b; 455, 8, carp seems to mean tell tales, probably sing or chant tales (ballads) to the harp. See I, 329, 2, 3.

carping, III, 13, 1; IV, 21, 17: talk, tale.

carry, IV, 247, **C** 11; 253, 15: pass, allow to pass, make effective, hold good.

case, in case that, I, 351, 38; II, 103, 1, 8; 171, 22; IV, 205, 17: against the chance that, lest.

case, cassed, V, 274, 4, 5: cause, caused.

casey, cassie, IV, 354, 4; V, 16, 2, 3, 5, 6: causeway.

cast, *n.*, III, 68, 248: venture. (Possibly cost, outlay.)

cast : *pret.,* coost, koost, cust, cuist, keist, kiest, kyst, kest. *p. p.* casten, castin, coosten, custan, cuisten.

cast, III, 308, 17: project, intend. cast on sleepe, III, 401, 10: thrown into a sleep, fallen asleep.

cast, *pret.*, III, 344, 34: struck. (upcast, III, 349, 34.)

casten, castin, *p. p.* of cast, I, 245, 7; 463, 3; II, 115, 29; V, 300, 2; 306, 14.

cat o clay, III, 11, **L**: a roll of straw and clay wrought together, used in building mud walls. Perhaps only a bit of clay.

caterans, V, 253 b, 1: robbers, Highland or Irish irregular soldiers. (Gaelic ceatharnach, soldier.)

cauger. See **cadger.**

caul, kell, IV, 483, 20: a woman's cap.

cauler, IV, 26, 6; 485, 19: cool, fresh. See **caller.**

caup, IV, 472, 27: cup. See **cap.**

cause, in that cause to flee, II, 421, 34: exigency (such exigency that you had to flee).

caution, III, 447 b; 451, note *: surety.

cavil, kavil, kaivle, kevel (Dutch kavel), I, 69, 46, 48: lot.

caw, cawd. See **ca'.**

cawte, III, 296, 26: wary.

ceppet, kepit, II, 410, 6; 407, 13: received, caught, when falling. See **cap, cape.**

cerl. See **carl.**

cerstyn, III, 111, 44: Christian.

certyl, III, 14, 15: kirtle (man's garment).

césererá, sassaray, II, 207, **A** 5; 209, **E** 5: intended for an imitation of the sound of bells.

chaffare, III, 111, 33; 113, 68; V, 79, 21, 25: ware, merchandise.

chaffe, III, 34, 11: chuff, clown, loon, simpleton.

chaft-blade, III, 269, 9; V, 243, 12: jaw-bone.

chafts, III, 267, 16: chaps, jaws.

chalmer, chamer, chaumer, chamber.

chamber thy words, II, 435, 45: restrain, suppress, be chary of.

changehouse, IV, 153, **E** 3: tavern, ale-house.

channerin, II, 239, 11: fretting, petulant.

chap, knock, rap; tap: I, 107, 3, 4; 465, 11; 481, 29; II, 140, 15; 177, 14, 16; 272, 14; 313, 14; IV, 445 f., 3, 4; V, 228, 16; 306 b, 1. of the striking of the hour, II, 371, 7.

chaperine, III, 514, 10, would make some sense as chapel, but the form is unaccountable except as a popular diminutive.

chare, III, 250, **J** 7, 8: turn.

charge, IV, 457, 1, must be understood as *charge not*, forbid.

charter (simply): III, 358, 82. See next word.

chartre of peace, III, 27, 108: grant of pardon, paper condoning past offences.

chase, III, 26, 74: follow up, hunt down. chase the wine, III, 169, 24: follow, keep up, like *follow strong drink.* (But a rhyme-end.)

chaunler-chaftit, I, 303, 6: having chafts (chops) like a chandler (candlestick, lantern), lantern-jawed, with a long, thin face.

chaunter, I, 438, **B** 6: usually, tube of the bagpipe, which would not be expected here. A book of chants would suit. Cf. Sir Hugh, III, 247, 20; 248, 14; 249, **H** 7, **I** 5, etc.

chays, hunting-ground.

che, I, 415 b: she.

chear, II, 193, 27: sounds expressing a state of feeling (here sad). IV, 18, 19: referring to the evening's entertainment, or, simply doing and saying. See chere.

chear well to, III, 160, 11: have good cheer at.

check, tether's check, V, 213, 10: spike of a tether.

cheel, IV, 69, 12: child, fellow.

cheepe, better cheepe, V, 15, 26: (price) cheaper.

cheeped, IV, 516, 15: chipped, broken.

cheik, II, 336, P 2, close to the cheik and chin: cheik is door-post, chin often=gin, the contrivance for fastening, but gin would not come in well here, and it is likely that chin is meaningless, coming in because of its frequent association with cheek (kissed her cheek and chin, etc.), see door-cheik.

chelvellrye, IV, 503, 1: corrupt. Read, chevauchie, excursion on horseback? (would a progress ride, III, 343, 2.)

chepe, cheepe, n., bargain. better chepe, III, 69, 259: more cheaply. gret chepe! III, 111, 34: great bargain!

chepe, v., III, 110, 26; 111, 33: cheapen, bargain for, or buy.

chere, cheer, cheir, chier, chear. carefull, sorry chere, III, 57, 28; 68, 239: face, countenance. I, 109, 14; 117, 6; 330, B 7; II, 189, 37; III, 441, 37; IV, 20, 15: of state of mind, bearing, or behavior. III, 66, 197; 67, 215; 75, 394; IV, 18, 19: entertainment, merrymaking. here is a symple chere, III, 59, 61. made gode chere, III, 100, 67: repast.

cherish, v., I, 76, 19; IV, 96, C 11; 437, 25: cheer.

cherry, V, 264, 4: sherry.

chess, I, 86, 15: jess, strap; properly, leather strap for a hawk's leg (explained by R. Jamieson, hawk's bell).

chess, IV, 457, L 8, dancin in a chess: chace? forest? Probably corrupt, since A 10, B 10, I, 341, 343, have playing at the chess.

chess, chiss of farie, V, 165 f., 6, 9, 10: corrupt; read, cheese o Fyvie (see V, 305 f.).

chest, kist, IV, 342, 12: coffin.

cheue, v., III, 73, 349: end. See chewys.

cheverons, III, 374, 8: gloves.

chewys, I, 327, 20: endest, comest off. (French chevir.) See cheue.

cheys, III, 112, 48: choose.

child, chiel, chil, cheel, child, young fellow: I, 72, 8; 367, 3; IV, 69, 12; 432, 15; V, 278, 33. as an appellation, II, 85 f., 1, 2, 6, etc.; 128 f., 1, 5, 8, etc.; 264 f., 1, 7, etc.; V, 157, 1, 6, etc. auld chiel, V, 125, 6, 8: devil. pl. chylderin, III, 13, 2, 3.

childer, III, 478, 24; IV, 99, 11: children.

chill, V, 287, 16: child.

chimly, II, 71, 9; IV, 481, 22; V, 122, 5: chimney.

chin, chappit at the chin, II, 140, 15, 24; stecked doors close to the chin, II, 336, P 2: gin, that is, pin. See gin, pin.

chine, IV, 188, 18: chin.

chip-hole, I, 305, 3: a hole chipped or cracked, a chink.

chiss, chess, V, 165 f., 6, 9, 10: cheese. See V, 305 f.

chive, II, 362, 34=schive, slice.

chiven, play the, III, 145, 8: "run away precipitately," Nares; chiven, chivin=chub, or any shy fish. chivie =fearful.

choice, choise, II, 463, 17; 469, 34; 473, 12; V, 269, 15: choose.

choised, chosen.

choose, chose, I, 103, 7; 329, 2; IV, 211, notes, 6: choice.

choosed, p. p., III, 440, 23.

chossen, p. p., chosen.

christendom, christendame, christendoun, -doom, I, 341, 21; 344, 20; 346, 11; 350, 24; 369, 48; 370, 15, 19: christening (as in Old English).

christentie, cristendie, I, 286, 46; II, 53, 41; V, 192, 22, 33; 194, 65: christendom.

chrystall, II, 52, 17: rock-crystal, a variety of quartz.

church-style, IV, 412, 14: the gate of the enclosure round a church.

churlish, I, 102, 2: of vulgar derivation.

chylderin. See child.

cirsned, p. p., V, 224, 19: christened.

clade, clead, cleed, clad.

claes, claise, I, 488, 17; II, 90, 25; IV, 18, 16; 262, 22; V, 118, 6, 7, 14: clothes.

claiding, cleadin, etc., IV, 424, 12: clothing.

claith, II, 131, 8: garment.

clam, pret. of climb, II, 166, 35; V, 249, 4.

clap, in a clap, IV, 41 b: moment.

clap, II, 269, 25; IV, 278, 4; 303, 18; 403, 12; 414, 25, 14; V, 125, 4; 277, 7: pat, fondle, embrace.

clappit at, V, 173, 1: knocked at (with ellipsis of the door).

clarry, claret.

clatter, IV, 21, 14: to be loquacious.

clead, cleed, cleid, clied, I, 220, B 6; 224, J 6, 7; 225, L 2, 4; 504 b, 2; IV, 451 a, 2; V, 211 b, 4: clothe. pret. cled, IV, 492 a, 1. p. p. clead, IV, 456, 1.

cleadin, cleeding, cleiding, clieden, cliding, n., II, 92, 7; 108, 6; 183, 19; 273, 24; IV, 445, 12; 457, 2, 7; 515, 4: clothing. one of thy cleeding, II, 271, 18: dresses.

cleare, III, 307, 5; IV, 166, C 7; 477, 21; 506, 22: bright.

cleathe, I, 222, F 11, 12; V, 128, 27, 28: clothe.

clecked, clekit, pret., p. p., I, 254 a; II, 261, 7: hatched.

cleek, n. and v., I, 494, 13; V, 106 E 4; 122, 5: hook.

clef, pret. of cleave, III, 13 f., 5, 15.

cleffe, III, 109, 6; 112, 52: cleave.

cleiding, clieden, clothing. See cleadin.

clekit, clecked, I, 254 a: hatched.

cleugh, clough, III, 22, 1; IV, 6, 13; 7, 26; V, 182, 1; 250, 12: a hollow between steep banks, narrow glen or valley, high rocky bank.

cleynt, pret., V, 80, 43: clung.

clied. See clead.

clift, I, 137, A c 6: cliff.

clifting, IV, 179, 4: clift, cleft, fissure.

cliitt, III, 179, 5: read *clutt*, clouted, patched.

cling, V, 154, 15: shrink.

clintin, IV, 179, **B** 1: crevice, fissure,=clifting, **A** 4.

cloathe, III, 93, 43; 174, 24: garment.

clock, IV, 3, 20, 22: limper, hobbler (Fr. clocher, Picard cloquer).

clocken-hen, V, 92, 15, 16: sitting hen.

clod, got the clod that winna cling, V, 154, 15: the loaf of bread (?) that will not shrink (but will rise ?), referring to the impending increase of her size.

cloks, II, 166, 36: beetles.

Clootie, I, 5, 18: a name for the Devil, from cloot, the half-hoof of a cloven-footed beast.

close, closs, enclosure, yard, and, before a house, court-yard: I, 145, 15; 146, 10, 19, 21; 147, 14; 148, **G** 10; 149, **I** 7; V, 173, 1; 279, No 257, 11; 306 b, 2. castle-yard: IV, 84, 22; 86, **C** 10; 87, 7; 89, 10. lady standing in the close pinning her gown, III, 436, 3. close parler, III, 431, 22: securely enclosed, or fastened ? 23, you are in close : one (not trustworthy) transcript has *to chose*, which would make easier sense. Saint Evron's closs, I, 146, 19, 21: cloister ?

closely, III, 470 a: covertly, without attracting observation.

closs. See close.

cloth and fee, III, 433, 7: clothing and wage. holde with cloth and fee, III, 61, 107: retained by presents of clothes and money.

clot-, clout-lether, V, 79, 27: mending-leather.

cloudy, II, 31, **N** 1, cloudy stone: (A. S. clúdig) rocky. (Read, cloud and stone=reef and rock ?)

clout, *n.*, V, 116, 10: patch. See clouts.

clout-leather, clouting-leather, V, 77, 39; b 39; 83, 55: leather for mending, patching.

clouts, II, 463, 24, 470, 54 : pieces of cloth for bed-coverings, or sheets (linsey clouts, canvas clouts). II, 470, 53: duds, clothes. See clout.

clouty, I, 206, 35; 207, 33; V, 110, 2; 116, 4, 5: patched.

clud, IV, 174, 12, clud o night: cloud.

clunkers, clunkerts, I, 305, 13; V, 213, 9: clots of dirt.

clutt, III, 179, 5: clouted (given wrongly cliitt).

clyffe, III, 91 a (play): rive, sunder, be split.

co, V, 250, 17, 19: quo, quoth.

coad, II, 132, 27. See cod.

coardie, V, 244, 7: cowardice.

coat-neuk, II, 107, 3, 5: corner of his coat.

coate-armor, III, 284, 11, 13: surcoat or tabard, embroidered with armorial bearings, worn over the armor as a personal distinction, and for identification, the face being concealed.

coble, IV, 128, 7; 359, 2, 5, etc.: boat (yawl, flat-bottomed boat).

cock, II, 472, 20, 28; V, 269, 14: knots, or other arrangements, of ribbon for the hair. (French coque.)

cockward, I, 285, 24, 26: old cock, fool (French co-quard).

cod, coad, I, 68, 29; II, 132, 27; 270, 27: pillow.

coffer, trunk or box, for clothes and valuables: I, 69,

60; 71, 49; II, 375 f., 23, 26, 29; IV, 258, 19. In a commonplace with mantle: I, 350, 16; III, 244, 11; IV, 385, 26; V, 175, 2; absurdly introduced in the first two instances; ridiculously corrupted, I, 348 f., **F** 1, 3, 13; II, 475, 5.

coft, I, 356, 56; 394, 9; 397, **D** 8, 10, 12; III, 11, 6; V, 118, 9; 162, **C** 7; 163, 13: bought.

cog, coug, II, 30, 6; IV, 378 f., 2, 3, 20; 379 f., 2, 4, 17-19; V, 275, 2, 3, 9: boat, vessel.

cog, cogie, II, 273 a; IV, 199, 15; 200, 17; 206, 9; V, 273 a: milk-pail.

coif, quoif, II, 280, **B** 3; III, 514 b, 3; 515 a, 1, 4: cap.

coil (of hay), II, 233, 7: cock.

coilyear, V, 70 b: collier, charcoal-burner.

cold, could, coud, understood. cold of wisdome, of curtesye, I, 271, 1, 3. cold of his curtesie, I, 286, 49; V, 132, 3. cold, could, coud his curtesye, II, 433, 10; 435, 35; III, 75, 385; V, 132, 3.

cold, could, coud, did. See can.

cole, III, 74, 372; 76, 421: cowl, monk's hood, also frock, which last is intended here, for the king wears a broad hat and puts on a green garment when he casts off his cowl.

coled (high coled). See colld.

coll, *v.* See cow.

coll, cold.

collaine, collayne, collen, swords of, III, 298, 50: of Cologne steel. collaine, collen brand, I, 286, 45, 42, 43.

colld, coled, cut, shaped, fashioned. high-colld hose, I, 69, 52; 71, 42. high coled stockings, I, 72, 9: made to go to the knee or above (perhaps in contradistinction to short hose, worn by common people). high-coled shoon, I, 73, 64. laigh-colld shoon, I, 69, 52; 71, 42; 72, 9: low-cut shoes. high-colld hat, IV, 204, 12: hat peaked before and behind.

colleen, II, 497 f., 4, 13, 16: (Ir. and Sc. Gaelic cailin, diminutive of caile, simple country maid) girl.

collen, of Cologne. See collaine.

com, come, *pret.* of come, I, 244, 10, 13; 328, 46.

comand, V, 80, 56: commanded. (Read, comanded ?)

comd, *pret.* of come, III, 430, 6; 467, 61. *p. p.*, I, 324, 4; III, 464, 3, 7.

come, *pret.* cam, com, come, coom, comd. *pret. pl.* come. *ptc. pres.* coomin. *p. p.* comen, commen, coom, comd.

come, *pret. pl.* of come, III, 216, 34.

come by (life), IV, 515, 7: get, obtain, gain.

comen, commen, *p. p.* of come, II, 52, 19; 54, 46; III, 35, 32.

comentye, comyntie, III, 361, b, c 58: commonalty.

comfort, *p. p.* of comfort, II, 370, 22.

commant, *p. p.* of command, III, 9, 1.

commaunded theym agayne, III, 77, 430: *come* has perhaps dropped out; later editions, them to come.

compare, made him no compare, V, 260, No 221, 1: made no comparison (of others) with him.

compass, I, 346 f., 17, 25; 351, 32, 44: circle.

compear, compeir, III, 364 b; IV, 81 b; 164 a: appear.

comt, count.

complete, sang sae sweet and sae complete, V, 301, No 200: excellently, skilfully.

compted, III, 77, 437: emendation for *commytted* of 80 and 81, 437. (85, 88, commended for.)

comunye, I, 285, 31: communing.

comyn-bell, III, 100, 73: town bell. a clerc the commun belle rong. Robert of Gloucester, p. 541, Hearne.

condescend upon, IV, 41 b, note §: particularize.

conduction, III, 403 a: direction, charge.

cone, liftet up the cone, IV, 484, a, last stanza: apparently the face-cloth, which may have been gathered into a conical form the better to fit the face. J. Aiken.

conferred, III, 336, note †: made the subject of conference.

conform, IV, 63 b: conformably.

confound, II, 443, 38; 449, 44: be the destruction of.

conquess, V, 191 f., 9, 13, 23, 35: conquer.

convay. See convoy.

convë, V, 117, 13; 268, 27, 28: convoy, escort.

convened, III, 409 a, note: agreed.

convenient, IV, 78, 4: suitable.

convention, made a, III, 364 a: had a meeting.

convey. See convoy.

convoy, convay, n., I, 252, 16; IV, 37, 15; 38, 15; 267, 14: escort. IV, 453, 6: of attendance upon the dead.

convoy, convey, v., II, 27, 4: convey. IV, 267, 3, 10; 269 f., f 2, 3, g 3; 317, 7; 318, 12; V, 119, 12: escort, accompany part of the way homeward, or on a journey, see a friend off, a young woman home.

coom, p. p., V, 296 a: come.

coomin, ptc., V, 296 a: coming.

coops, IV, 461, 4: carts (tip-carts).

coost, koost, pret. of cast, I, 73, 59; 102, 18; IV, 477, 6; V, 173, 3, 4. I, 74, 70; 78, 48: threw things about. p. p. coosten, I, 77, 5; 324, B 6; 371, 3.

coot, queet, IV, 212, 5: ankle.

cop, coppe, I, 244, 9; III, 123, 6: head.

coped, overset. See couped.

cor, Corehead, Corhead, V, 192, 37; 195 f., 35 (MS., Carhead); 196, 52: (Gaelic coire, cauldron, dell) corrie, a hollow in a hill. Jamieson. Penman's Core, 193, 51, 55, 58, described as a hollow on the top of a high ridge of hills, might possibly be Penman score (score, a deep, narrow, ragged indentation on the side of a hill, South of Scotland. Jamieson). poor man's core, V, 196, 52, corruption.

corbie, I, 253, 1; 254, b 1, c 1; III, 473, 23: raven.

cordain, cordan, cordevine, II, 435, 50; IV, 312, 7; 317, F 3: Cordovan leather.

cordin, shoon laced with cordin, IV, 435, 8: cording, cord (and not with whangs of leather).

cordiuant, adj., V, 49, 23: of Spanish, Cordovan leather.

cored, II, 217 f., 5, 10: covered.

coresed (hors), III, 61, 100: bodied (?) (later texts, corese, corse).

corn, II, 88, 17, 18, etc.: in Scotland, unground oats. (Here distinguished from white meal, which is usually oat-meal.)

corn-caugers, III, 479, 8: cadgers, hucksters, in corn.

corp, II, 218, 25; 229, 11: a vulgar singular of a supposed plural; corps, II, 217, 30; these corps, 31; cf. IV, 483, 23; 484 a, after 31. corpes, III, 231, 97, may be corpse.

cors, curse.

corse, corss, I, 117, 7; 351, 31, 32, 44; IV, 53, 8; 512 a, 9; V, 161, 4: cross.

corser, III, 68, 256: should probably be forser = coffer (text g has coffer).

cosh, coush, II, 363, 13: quiet (snug).

cote a pye, coate a pie, cote of pie, III, 65, 194; 80, 194; 86, 194: corruption of courtepi, short cloak or gown. (Dutch kort, short, and pij, coat of warm woolen stuff.)

cots, coats, III, 481, 2, 6: petticoats.

couchd, V, 9, 12: lay, leaned.

coug, cog, V, 275 b, 2, 3, 9: boat.

could, did. See can.

couls, V, 228, 19: cools, chills.

councell, counsell, II, 58, 3; III, 58, 45; V, 52, 78: secret.

cound, IV, 467, 13: count.

counsell, II, 246, C 9-11; III, 217, 53: secret. See councell.

counterfeit, p. p., V, 300, 10: counterfeited.

country-keeper, V, 196, 41: "one employed in a particular district to apprehend delinquents." Jamieson.

coup, cupe, cup.

couped, koupd, coped, I, 469, 23; II, 313, 20; IV, 315, 14: overturned.

couper, cowper, IV, 259, 7; 260, 7: buyer and seller, dealer.

couple-root, I, 302, 13: rafter-end (the end resting on the wall).

courting, III, 146, 20: demonstration of affection, embracing.

courtnolls, V, 85, 14: courtiers.

courtrie, V, 191, 5; 198 b, after 52: belonging to a court, courtiers.

coush, cosh, IV, 483 b: quiet.

coustome, IV, 507, 78: duty (the king will remit).

cout, cowte, IV, 18, 20, 21; 21, 16: colt.

couth, II, 357, 2: sound, word, Jamieson (the sense required, but the suggested derivation from Icel. kviðr, A. S. cwide, is not easy).

couent, III, 60, 86; 357, 55: convent.

coving-tree, II, 193, H 4: meeting-tree. "A large tree in the front of an old Scottish mansion-house, where the laird met his visitors." Similar to trysting-tree. Jamieson. In Roxburghshire, covin; in the north of England, covan, coban, and even capon. Denham Tracts, II, 226 ff.

cow, twig. See broom-cow, heather-cow, kow.

cow, coll (locks), II, 423, 4, 7: clip. (brume), III, 9,

H 8: browse. (Norwegian kolla (Aasen), dock, take off the top.)

cowing, eating.

cowper. See **couper.**

cowte, colt. See **cout.**

coxcomb, III, 35, 19: pate.

crabby (crabbed), III, 488, 23: provoking.

crack, crak, II, 271, 18; 488, 6, 10; III, 161, 28; IV, 261, 3; V, 106, **E** 3: talk. III, 487, 6, 14, 16: brag. **crackd** (the Border-side), IV, 146, 4: defied, challenged. (In Scott's printed copy, *bragged*, defied.)

crack, crak, a moment of time. in a crack, within a crack, IV, 314, 16; 315, 13; 317, **E** 6; V, 271, 13: instantly.

crack fingers, in grief or perplexity, II, 26, **G** 16. See **knack.**

crae, *pret.*, V, 253 a, No 200, **B a** 8: crew.

crak. See **crack.**

cramoisie, cramasie, IV, 93, 8, 2, 3; 410, 17, 20; 472, 9: crimson.

crap, II, 261, 10; 286, 16: crop, top.

crap, *pret.* of creep, II, 323, 3; 330, **H** 3; 336, **P** 2; 337, 3.

crapotee, I, 326, 6: toad-stone, supposed to be generated in the head of toads; "in fact, a petrifaction of the teeth of extinct fishes." Mätzner. Sometimes defined, smaragdus, emerald.

cravin, II, 335, **N** 2: asking for, demanding.

crawen, crawn, *p. p.* of craw, crow, II, 139 f., 7, 12, 22; 222, 17; IV, 473, 36.

cray, cry.

credence, III, 449 b: credit.

creed, *n.*, IV, 262, 13, 14: blame.

creel, V, 122, 5, 11, 12; 123, 5, 11; 124, 4, 12: basket.

creep, *pret.* crap. See **crap.**

cries, *n.*, II, 73, 22: calls, demands.

Cristianté, Cristinty, Cristendie : Christendom.

croche, I, 413, 36: crouch.

croft, IV, 142 a: a piece of land adjoining a house.

crooden, croodin, croodlin, croudlin, I, 163 f., **J** 1, 2, etc.; 165, **M** 1, **N** 1, etc.; 166, **K** c 1: cooing.

cropped (knee), III, 280, 26: crooked (Icel. kroppinn).

cross, *v.*, V, 306, 6 (correct V, 166, 7², in accordance with this reading): oppose. *p. p.*, the sheriff was crost, III, 157, 30: balked.

croudlin. See **crooden.**

crouds, cruds, IV, 260, 5: curds.

crouse, crouselie, crously, II, 169, 9; III, 161, 28; IV, 261, 3; V, 17, 33: briskly, merrily, jubilantly. III, 493, 16: (perhaps) bumptiously. See **crowse.**

crow, craw, crow. ar the coc him crowe, I, 244, 18; V, 288 b, v. 33. *p. p.* crowen, crawen, crawn.

crowen, *p. p.* of crow, II, 138, 7.

crowner, I, 141 b: coroner.

crowse, III, 457, **B** 5: audacious. See **crouse.**

crowt, I, 273, 28: draw together, pucker up.

cruds, *n.*, IV, 260, 7, 18, 19; 262, 30; 265, **A b** 1, 11: curds.

cry, crye, proclaim, proclamation. cry in, III, 320,

A b 7: call in. cry on, upo, I, 127, 6; II, 150, 13; III, 318, 7; IV, 7, 24: call upon, summon. cryed out on Robyn Hode, III, 70, 296: cried out against, or, simply, cried out "R. H."

cryance, II, 58 f., 18, 20, 21: cowardice, faintheartedness (disposition to succumb).

cud, V, 104 a: cudgel.

cuddy, IV, 69, 6: ass.

cuirt, *pret.*, I, 439, **C** 11: covered.

cuist, cust, *pret.* of cast, II, 248, 1, 2; IV, 68, **E** 2; 182, **G** 5; 394, **C** 1; V, 116, 5. keist, kiest, I, 69, 46; 75, 36; 80, 4.

cuisten, *p. p.* of cast, I, 495, 11. See **custan.**

cum, V, 191, 8: become.

cum, *pret.* of come, III, 386, 22.

cumand, *ptc.*, V, 192 f., 35, 49: coming.

cumber, V, 53, 104: oppress, torment. See **cumre.**

cumbruk, cambric.

cummers, V, 106, **E** 2: gossips (commères).

cumre, *n.*, IV, 316, 19: cumber, trouble. See **cumber.**

cun thanke, III, 68, 242: am, feel, grateful.

cunnes. nones cunnes, I, 244, 11: of no kind. enes cunnes, I, 244, 12: of any kind.

cunning, V, 82, 21: craft (mystery, trade).

curch, curche, II, 131, 6; III, 472, 10: kerchief, woman's head covering.

cure, III, 262, 7: pains. McNaughtoun's cure, II, 386, 25: "McNaughtoun's cure to ye is, Devil relieve ye." Motherwell.

curn, III, 160, 19; IV, 85, 3: quantity, parcel, pack.

curst turne, III, 93, 34: malignant, spiteful, ferocious job, piece of work, feat.

curstlye, V, 53, 104: fiercely, savagely.

curtal (frier), III, 124 ff., 6, 7, 11, 13, etc.: (Lat. curtilarius) having charge of, attached to, the vegetable garden of a monastery. curtal dogs, 125, 34.

cust, *pret.* of cast, V, 116, 5. See **cuist.**

custan, *p. p.* of cast, III, 4, 2.

cut, V, 202 a: horse.

cut, V, 112, 7; 124, 6; 125, 5: bite, gnaw.

cutted (friar), III, 123, 3, 11, 13, 15, 17: short-frocked (but apparently a corruption of curtal, see III, 121 f.).

cutters, III, 228, 10: bravos, robbers.

cuttie, I, 72, 13; 74, 74: short.

cutties, II, 470, 49: spoons.

cweet, queet, II, 96, **I** 3: ankle.

cypress queen, as fair as a cypress queen, V, 164, 15: Cyprus, Cypris (Venus).

D

'd, for 't (it). bla'd wind, bla'd weet, II, 21, 6; doo'd, IV, 464, 16; born'd, deal'd, 465, 22, 37; 471, 41; lai'd, 520, 10; dee'd, V, 248, 12.

dabs, II, 167 b, **F**: pricks.

dada, dadda, II, 339, 16, 18; V, 112, **B b** 5: daddie.

daft (love), II, 410, 8: foolishly fond.

dag-durk, I, 55, 12: dagger.

daggie, IV, 258, 25: drizzling (dag, a slight rain).

daghter, dather, daughter.

daghterie, IV, 324, 1: a word of no meaning, the original being simply *daughter*: see V, 272 b, 1.

daigh, daighe, I, 302, **A** 10; II, 467, 42: dough.

dail, IV, 430, 5: (dool) the grief, the ill consequences.

daily, dayly, daily flower, I, 76, 9, 15, 18; II, 393, 2; IV, 19, 8: (Icelandic dælligr, Danish deilig) beautiful, charming.

daily dight, IV, 432, 6: beautifully adorned.

dairgie, II, 195, 41: refection given after a funeral.

dale, been at a, III, 161, 28, 30: dole (to mendicants), satirically.

dam, II, 192, 10: dame.

damasee, II, 327, 32: damson plum.

dame, addressed to an unmarried girl by her father, IV, 195, 7.

dandily, V, 106, **E** 5: over nice or dainty.

dandoo, III, 5, **C** 7, 8: dun doe?

dane, done, I, 68, 20, 24; 69, 45, 53; II, 81 f., 41, 56: done. dane him to, III, 273, 15, 27: betaken himself. See do.

dang, *pret.* of ding, I, 55, 12; 129, **D** 6; 130, **F** 5; 133, **M** 7, 10; II, 253, 19; 261, 9; IV, 305, 18: beat, struck, knocked, thrust, shoved. dang down, III, 460, 32. *p. p.*, II, 282, 10: overpowered.

danger, do danger, III, 163, 67: exercise of the power of a superior? violence?

dank (moat), V, 295, 7: damp, wet.

danting, danton, IV, 287, 1 (burden); V, 267, 1 (burden): (Fr. dompter) sexual conquest.

danton, V, 248, 19: subdue, intimidate. See daunton.

daown, *adv.*, V, 304, 8: down.

dapperpy, IV, 185, 11: diapered, of variegated cloth.

dather, dother, V, 257, 15: daughter.

datit, IV, 467, 15: dawtit, caressed.

dative of pronoun: III, 58, 37, 44; 60, 82; 61, 100; 65, 184; 75, 381, 391. after verbs of motion (dative of the subject): I, 244, 10, 13; 326, 1; III, 70, 281.

daunton, danton, I, 325, 6; III, 364 b: daunt, subdue, put down.

daut, dawt, IV, 104, **O**; 277, 4; 302, 2: fondle, caress, make much of, pet.

daw, *v.*, II, 146, 7: dawn. *p. p.* dawen, II, 139, 7, 12.

dawdy, II, 308, 5: the unborn young of an animal.

dawt, daut, IV, 304, 3; V, 106, **D** 3: caress.

dawtie, V, 117 f., **B** 5, 9, 13; 173, 11: darling.

day, dey, die, dye, IV, 257, **B** 9; 259, 7, 17; 260, 7, 16; 262, 16; V, 265 a, 10: dairy-woman.

day, dayed, die, died.

dayly. See daily.

de, dee, dea, deei, die, = do: I, 165, **N** 8; 183, 24; II, 175 f., 1, 8. a dee, II, 110, 25: to do. dee'd, V, 248, 12: do it. *p. p.* deen. See dee.

dea, die.

dead, deed, deid, dede, died, *n.*, I, 104, 14; 353, 13; 388, **A** 11; 465, 19; II, 385, 25; 505, 92; III, 387, 16, 10; IV, 36, 3; 505, 57: death.

dead. be dead, II, 58, 5, 7; III, 23, 25; 28, 120; 99, 50: die.

deak, V, 270, 7: deck.

dean, den, IV, 167, **D** 5, 6, 11: hollow where the ground slopes on both sides, valley.

dean, done.

dear, deare, dere, I, 411, 5; III, 164, **b** 67: injury.

Dear-Coft, II, 62, 18: Dear-Bought.

dearly, IV, 98, **F** 6: costly.

dearsome, III, 488 f., 38, 44: costly.

dear vow, interjection of surprise or commiseration.

deas, II, 189, 24: pew (stone seat at the door of the church. Chambers). Same word as dais. See dice.

deave, I, 389, **C** 3; IV, 69, 17: deafen.

debate, III, 314, 64: quarrel.

deceivin (tree), III, 396, **N** 3: corruption of savin (see 380 a).

decencey, V, 242 b, 8: corruption of bencite, benedicite.

deck-board, deck-buird, oer (over), V, 138, **B** 5, 6; 139, c 6, 7: overboard.

dede, V, 283, 8: death. See dead.

dee, deei, do. how can this dee, I, 453, 6: be allowed, borne; and so, perhaps, a' this winna dee (wont do), II, 97, 14. a' this winna dee, gif ony prayer can dee, II, 132, 16; 176, 10; it wad na do, IV, 509 b, 13; it widne deei, V, 227, 2: avail.

dee, deei, do. See de.

dee, deei, die.

deed, death. See dead.

deed, *v.*, I, 164, **K** 6; 165, **O** 5: died.

deed, indeed. by my deed, III, 262, 12: on my word.

deed-thraw, III, 501, 10: death-throe.

deei, do, avail; die. See de, dee.

deemed, demed, III, 61, 95: judged. III, 356, 35: condemned.

deen, I, 16, **C** 18; II, 182 a; 409, 18, 19 done (with no sense in 19).

deerlye (dight), III, 340, 28, 36: expensively (ornamented). III, 356, 16, 31, 35: perhaps, with great cost to the sufferer, possibly, to his hurt; lovingly, out of love, would answer in the first two cases, but not in the third.

deft, III, 145, 3: neat, nice-looking.

degree, III, 323, 58; IV, 258, 20: rank, sort. served him in his ain degree, V, 191, 19; 193, 57: rendered him respect accordant with his rank. wee shall beare no degree, III, 333, 19: shall have no position, standing. (requite, thank, show) in euerye degree, V, 84 f., 9, 14, 27: to the full extent demanded by the occasion.

deid, I, 105, 26; 353, 13: death. See dead.

deighte, IV, 504, 29: dight, furnished, adorned, equipped.

delated, III, 449 a, b; IV, 63 b: accused.

dell, V, 79, 32: deal, bit, whit.

dell, II, 345, 29: we are apparently to understand that it was a dismal dell that brought James into the world (not in itself, but from the melancholy fact of his being born there). Possibly we may understand dell

=dule, affliction. But the piece is spurious, and we need not be nice.

delle, I, 327, 22: perhaps, dally, talk, disport; perhaps, deal.

demean, IV, 41, note *; 107, 3: treat, maltreat. (in 107, 3, treat as he deserves, damage, do harm to.)

demed. See **deemed.**

den, dean, IV, 166, **B** 8; 168, 5, 11; 169, 3, 9, **G** 2; 174 f., 2, 7; 306 f., 12, 20, 48; V, 119, **D** 2: small valley, glen, dingle.

den, dien, V, 260, 8, 14: done.

denay, deny, V, 110, 10; 260, 3, 4: refuse.

deol, V, 297 b: sorrow.

dep, gave him a dep unto the heart, III, 281, 14: perhaps dab, Old Eng. dabbe, stroke. But Dr Davidson suggests that the line was misheard, and that what was said was, a dep 'oon (wound), which seems to me very likely.

depart, III, 139, 27: part company.

deputed, III, 414, 52: consigned, handed or delivered over (used of a fugitive carried back for trial).

dere, dear(e), III, 99, 59: injury.

dere-worthy, III, 58, 36, 37; 59, 60; 61, 111; 67, 219; 68, 250; 73, 346: precious, dear.

derf, derf blowes, III, 422, 73: powerful.

dernë, I, 327, 30; III, 57, 21: secret, hidden, privy, obscure.

descryvd, IV, 405, 50: described.

desse, I, 328, 45: dais, the elevated part of the hall, on which was the table for the chief personages.

deuylkyns, III, 79, 73: devilish sort of.

develling, come, I, 302, 5: moving like the devil, whether hieing, scouring, bouncing, or what not; or, possibly, O. Fr. devalant, descending; an equivalence to daundering, sauntering, has been suggested.

devyse, I, 327, 16: will, pleasure.

dey, die, dye, IV, 257, 9; 259, 7, 17; 260, 7; 262, 16: dairy-woman. See day.

deythe, dyth, III, 112, 59: dight, prepared.

di, die, II, 132, 24; V, 35, **B** 5: do. dinna, I, 146, 6, and *passim:* do not. See **dinnë.**

dice, IV, 416, 17=deis: pew in a church.

did, I, 104, 3, 4: used for *should.*

did (be wrought), II, 506 a: caused.

did him to. See **do to.**

did of. See **do.**

die, IV, 264, 5: dey, dairy-woman. See **day.**

die. See **de.**

die, do, din, dien, done.

died, IV, 386, 19: death. See **dead.**

died, IV, 407, 7, 8: dead.

dien. See **den, die.**

dight, dicht, dycht, deight, dyght, III, 57, 19: prepared. dedys that here be dyght, III, 72, 320: done. of grain, I, 16, **B** 16; IV, 242 a: winnow. dight shoon, V, 105, **A** 11: clean. had not men to dight my men, III, 300, 18; IV, 500, 19: serve, handle. she dighted her father's wounds, I, 101, 8; 103, **D** 6: dressed. pinnace, hachebord deerlye dight, III, 340,

28, 36; IV, 504, 29: fitted out. dill (grief) to him was dight, II, 58, 4: ordained.

dight, *adv.,* bird sang fu dight, II, 261, 10: readily, freely (strange use of the word). Cf. **complete.**

dild, God, III, 35, 31: God ild, yield, reward (*d* carried on from the subject).

dill, II, 58, 4, 11: dule, grief.

dimitted, III, 447 b: discharged, released.

din, dien, done.

din, I, 133, 10; II, 186, 16: dun.

dine, I, 127, 23; II, 94, 12; 194, 13, 17; 313, 17; III, 267, 18; V, 277 f., 18, 29: dinner, meal.

ding, II, 62 a, 17; 261, 8; IV, 97, **F** 2; 304, 16, 17: beat, knock. ding down, II, 240, 6; III, 5, **D** 2, 6; 6, 2, 5; 8, 5; 9, 2, 7: lay low, overthrow. *pret.* dang, dung. *p. p.* dung, dang. my ain wand dings me now, IV, 97, **F** 2: I am suffering the consequences of my own folly.

dink, I, 74, 72: neat, trim.

dinna, do not.

dinnë, V, 229 a, 35: do (you) not. V, 229 **b, 6**: (disne) does not. dinner=dinna, dinnë.

dinne, I, 272, 25: (noise) ado, trouble.

dint (of arrow), III, 345, 48; 350, 48: stroke, impact.

dirt, *v.,* V, 304, 2, 3: soil.

dis, does.

Disaware, V, 49, 29; 51, 51, 62: O. E. aver (O. Fr. aver, avoir) seems to be the basis of the word, which would mean stripped of wealth, sans aver (avoir); a Galterius Sine Avero is noted by Ducange.

discared, III, 38, 85: revoked, withdrawn (apparently for discarded).

discharged, IV, 63 b: revoked.

discreene, II, 439, 2: descry, spy out, discover.

discreeue, II, 58, 3, should be *disceuere,* diskevere, discover, reveal.

disgrate, V, 269, 17: disgrace.

disgrate, III, 58, 48: unfortunate, out of fortune's favor. (Ital. disgraziato.)

disna, does not.

distan, IV, 329 a, after 16: (distance) distinguish.

dittay, IV, 245 a: indictment.

dive, II, 132, 25: do.

diuel's mouth. He could not finde a priuy place, for all lay in the dieul's mouth, II, 483, 4: as the devil's mouth is depicted wide open in painted windows, etc., Professor Skeat has suggested that meaning for the phrase.

do, it wad na do, IV, 509 b, 13: avail. See **dee.**

do. See **doo.**

do, doe, doe my thy hawkes, I, 211, 20: give, deliver.

do adowne, III, 67, 226; 69, 263: put down.

do away, III, 59, 63: have done with, stop.

do be, I, 184, 47: are.

do down. See **do to.**

do gladly, III, 58, 34; 61, 103; 67, 232: make yourself happy (=make glad chere, 67, 215).

do (doe) of, off, II, 138, 13; III, 78, 449; V, 49, 23–25: put off. *pret.* doft, II, 490 b.

do on, III, 23, 27; 76, 421: put on, don.

do to, do till, with reflexive pronoun, I, 86, 30; 87 b; 115, **B** 3, 4; 182 f., 7, 11, 13, 17; 352, 32, 44; III, 72, 328: betake. So with *up, down,* V, 300, 5, 8.

do up. See **do to,** and **dop.**

doited, IV, 427, 10: stupid, doting.

doll, dolle, döl, dule, I, 217, 3; V, 111, 19, 21: grief.

domineer, in, wi, III, 268, 9; 270, 9; V, 242 b, 8: with haughtiness, superciliously. (Perhaps a corruption of III, 270, **E** 7, since the captain is said to be buke-learned in 268, 9.)

doo (ynnë gon), III, 91 a : cause, make.

doo, dou, dow, I, 163–165; 497, **L** 2; V, 40 f., 3, 9, 15, etc.: dove.

don, down.

done, how done you? III, 35, 31: old plural, how do you do ?

done upon, V, 48, 6: put on.

doo'd, IV, 464, 16: do it.

dool, doll, dule, II, 175, 17; IV, 85, 42; V, 17, 31; 111, 19, 21: grief. See **dail.**

dool, dool and down, II, 271, 26: corruption of dale and down ; cf. II, 175, 14; 273, 33; IV, 219, **B** 5: and elsewhere.

doon, II, 198 b, 2d line : a corruption, or possibly an Irish word, of which I can make nothing.

doon, youar begun yar doon, V, 304 b, 4.

doorcheeks, II, 99 b, 33: door-posts.

dop, III, 34 f., 6, 21: do up, open.

dorn, II, 300, 5: (sheets of) dornic, table-linen, ordinarily, from Dornick, the Dutch name for Tournay.

dorty, IV, 288, 10: pettish, peevish, saucy.

dother, IV, 327, 15; V, 110, 1; 237 f., 6, 7, 12, 22, etc.; 264, 7: daughter.

dottled, V, 94, **A** 3: in a state of dotage.

dou, dove. See **doo, dow.**

dou, dow (A. S. déah, dugon), III, 245, **B** 12; 247, 18; 370, 10, 13; IV, 472, 22: can (of physical ability). II, 78, 4; 104, 24; 105, 16; 168, 12; III, 386, 21; IV, 31, 9; 512, 12: (with negative) am unable from aversion, want of resolution, etc. dought (A. S. dohte, *pret.* of dugan), *pret.,* I, 146, 20; II, 401, **C** 7; III, 465, 22; IV, 23, **A** c 18: was able, could. *Subjunctive,* I, 326, 18, 19 (be at liberty); I, 330, **B** 3: should be able. dought, he neere dought good day, I, 434, 32: he never was good for anything a good day. But we should expect *him :* never a good day profited him.

double - horsed, III, 489, 42: with horse carrying double.

doubt, doute, dout, *n.* and *v.,* I, 295, 35; 478 f., 19, 28; II, 52, 22; III, 57, 10; 76, 406; 125, 26; 188, 4: fear.

doubt, if tho[u], II, 449, 58: corrupt. **A** 53, without all doubt.

doubtit, III, 364 b: redoubted, held in awe. See **doubt.**

douce, I, 184, 1; V, 210 a, 1: staid and sober. violence douce, II, 271, 19: corrupt; read *done ?*

douë, douey=dowie, V, 257, 7, 17: dreary, melancholy. V, 220 f., 6, 7, 9 (of bran): wretched.

doughetë, III, 308, 28: doughty man.

dought. See **dou.**

douk, duck, II, 151, **H** 6; 153, 16, 17, 19, 21: dive.

doukers, duckers, II, 151, **H** 6, 8: divers.

doulfou, II, 159, 23: doleful.

dounae. See **dou.**

doup (dish-doup), II, 463, 23: bottom.

dour(e), I, 117, 17: hard, severe. V, 295, 3: savage. knocks bauldly and dowr, II, 341, **R** after 3: hard, or pertinaciously.

dout, doute. See **doubt.**

dow, dou, doo, I, 163 f., **J** 1–6, etc.; II, 299, 22–24; 301, 14; V, 111, 18; 302, 17: dove.

dow, do.

dow, downa, *v.* See **dou.**

dowie, dowy, I, 56, **B** 11; II, 146, 19; 148, 21, 22; 189, 36, 37; IV, 33, 24; 165, 12; 166, **C** 4, 5, 6; etc.: sad, doleful, melancholy, wretched. See **douë.**

dowilie, I, 439, 11: sadly.

down, wi meikle dool and down, II, 271, 26: nonsense; corruption of, beheld baith dale and doun, **F** 33.

down-browed, scowling; I, 302, **A** 11.

downfall, downcome of Robin Hood, with the, III, 271, 10; 274, 30: knocked down in R. Hood's fashion ?

dowr. See **doure.**

doyn, III, 111, 39: done.

doyt, III, 109, 1: doth (plural).

draff, refuse, dirt.

drank, II, 30, 7: gave to drink, drenched.

drap, III, 281, 10, drap down: perhaps, drap[d] down; otherwise, should drop.

draps, drops.

draught, I, 432, 1: sketch, picture.

draw, drew her table, V, 304, 13: see explanation, 304 a.

draw, III, 6, 14, 15: move (cf. Germ. ziehen).

draw to, ti, till, draw to hose and sheen, II, 249, 15; 256, 9; IV, 464, 10: draw on. drew till him his hose, II, 189, 35. drew to him his sheen, II, 257, 30.

draw up wi, II, 114, 14: take up with, enter into intimacy, relations of love, with.

drawght that thowe dost drawe, IV, 503, 16: of the drawing of a bow. (So "Chaucer's Dream," v. 788, Morris.)

drawn, ere the horse was drawn and brought, IV, 346 b, **I** b 5: chosen.

drawn a stroke behind his hand, II, 63, 24: evidently means give a back-handed stroke, but the phrase sounds factitious.

dreaded, II, 169, 14: suspected.

dreads, IV, 32, **C** 7: suspicions.

dreamed, I was, I, 432, 1: dreamed, had a dream.

drede, *n.,* III, 296, 8: doubt.

dreder, II, 403, 3, 4: dread, apprehension.

dre(e), dri, drie, drye, suffer, undergo, hold out, stand, be able. dree pine, II, 466, 35; 467, 45. doom, III, 391, 9. death, III, 391, 1. dill I drye, II, 58, 11. dreeing trying hour, I, 73, 47. as fast as they might dree, III, 286, 49: could do it; so, II, 149, 7; 255, 10; III, 106, 12; 267, 9; IV, 2, 6; 6, 13; V, 195, 13, 35; 196,

37. whylle the myghte dre, III, 298, 58; 309, 47: as long as they could hold out. draw carts, which horse were wont to drie, I, 465, 2: do, perform. drie to feel, III, 479, 5: be compelled, come to feel.

dreel, gie a, I, 403, 9: stir up, put into a flurry, make scud. (Old Dutch drillen, ultro citroque cursitare gyrosque agere, etc. Scottish dreel, to move quickly.)

dreigh, IV, 47, 4: seems to mean here, far to jump from.

dress, III, 336 b: redress.

dressen, v. the dressede into the countrey, V, 71, note †: betaken.

drew (her table). See draw.

dri. See dree.

drie, n., III, 415, 22: an unauthorized word of Percy's, to mean suffering.

drie, dri. See dree.

driep, drop.

drifts, IV, 2, 10: droves.

drive, IV, 6, 19; 7, 30, 32: drive off.

droonet, I, 133, 13: drowned.

droop, droop and drowsie (of blood), IV, 220, 13: droop might be the Old English drup, sad, piteous, but a word indicating the quality or condition of the blood would be expected (as in German trübe, thick, muddy). The nearest is drubly, turbid, muddy. Cf. wan and drousie, IV, 224, 23. her lothely lere is droupy and drowsy, Skelton, Elynour Rummynge, 15: downcast and drowsy. See drousie.

droped, III, 164, 88: drooped.

drouflye, III, 85, 22: sad. See drousli.

drousie, wan and drousie, IV, 224, 23. droop and drowsie, IV, 220, 13 (of blood): sluggish, perhaps slowly dripping. The combination occurs in Skelton's Elynour Rummynge, 15, droupy and drowsy, with sense. See droop.

drousli, III, 82, 22, should be droufli (drouflye, or drouslye, 85, 22): (Old Eng. drof, droflie) sad.

drowryis, I, 415 b: love-tokens. See drury.

drowsie. See drousie.

drucken, II, 155, A b 3: drunken (and in A a 3, where there is a misprint).

druken, drucken, p. p., II, 285, 9; V, 99, 11, C 6; 155, C 2: drunk, imbibed.

drumlie, -ly (stream), IV, 185, 8, 14; (eye), IV, 368, 10; 369 b: perturbed, turbulent, turbid, gloomy.

drunken, p. p. of drink, II, 110, 24; 134, 26. drunken was = had drunken, IV, 46, 5, 6.

drunkilie, III, 490, 25: merrily (as being tipsy with pleasure?).

drury, IV, 58, A b 5: dowry. Drowry is used as synonymous with morning-gift in the Acts of James VI. Jamieson. See drowryis.

drussie, V, 257, 14: drowsy.

drye. See dree.

drywyng, driving.

dub, I, 164, J 3; III, 162, 49; IV, 470, 25, 26; V, 169, 9: pool.

dubby, IV, 257, A 6: dirty, having many small pools.

ducatdowns, dukedoons, IV, 128, 8; 139, I b 21: ducatoons. corrupted ridiculously, IV, 137, 2, to ducks.

duck, douk, II, 145, 18, 19, 22, 23: dive.

duckers, doukers, II, 145, 18: divers.

ducks. See ducatdowns.

duddie, I, 208, G 15: ragged.

duddies, dudes, V, 111, 24; 112, B 13; 113 b, 13: duds, poor clothes.

duȝty, III, 98, 32: doughty, valiant.

duke, IV, 295, D 5: dyke, wall.

dukedoons. See ducatdowns.

dulchach, dulget, I, 305, 1; V, 213, 1: bundle, always applied in Aberdeenshire to ill-shaped, untidy bundles of clothes carried on the person (also, bulshach).

dule, dool, I, 169, B 3; 442, E 15; II, 290, 8, 12; IV, 86, 20; 303, 14: grief.

dulget, I, 305, 1. See dulchach.

dumped, V, 227, 4: struck with the feet.

dumpes, III, 313, 50: in the modern sense, but not inelegant.

dune, I, 302, 2; IV, 326, 15: done.

dune out, V, 27, 28: worn out, used up.

dung, pret. of ding, beat, knock, strike, II, 132, 17. p. p., II, 62 a, 17; 392, J 9; 472, 20, 28; III, 161, 43; IV, 479, 4: beaten, worsted, overpowered, put down. IV, 183, 8: overwhelmed, disconsolate. dung over, V, 127, 22: knocked over, struck down. dung down, I, 345, 5: thrust down.

Dunny's well, Dunny's dyke, II, 189, 28: an impersonation, signifying that the washing and drying have been done in dark-colored water and on a dark-colored (dirty) wall.

dunts, III, 491, 13: dints, blows. See dynt.

dwine, IV, 303 f., 12, 21, 27; 304, 10: pine, waste.

dwrf, IV, 290, D c 5: dowf seems to be intended, lethargic, inert, impotent; rather than dwarf, as being puny or incomplete.

dyd him to, III, 72, 328: betook himself. See do to.

dyde adowne, III, 67, 226: put down.

dye, IV, 260, 16: dey, dairy-woman. See day.

dyght, III, 72, 320, dedes that here be dyght: prepared, concerted.

dyght (to the deth), III, 309, 40: done, brought.

dyghtande, III, 75, 388: making ready (but seems to be intended for a past participle).

dyke = wall, IV, 295, E 6; 296, F 6. castle-dyke, II, 410, 4. garden-dyke, II, 370, 5; 371, 5. fail dyke, I, 253, 2: turf wall. hollan dyke, II, 195, 32; nettle-dyke, II, 463, 22: wall on which hollies, nettles, are growing.

dyke, III, 441, 36: ditch.

dyne, garre me ones to dyne, III, 296, 24: give me my dinner, my fill, beat thoroughly. (Able to give the greatest prince in Christendome a mortall breakfast, if he had been the king's enemie. Holinshed's Chronicle, III, 512, ed. 1807-8. G. L. Kittredge.)

dynt(e), dint, III, 309, 42, 45, 46: stroke, hit, lunge, shot (of spear, arrow). See dunts.

dypper, V, 283, 5, 15: deeper.

dysheryte, III, 60 f., 87, 95: dispossessed.

dyspyse, II, 478, 6: cause to be despised.

dyth, deythe, I, 334, 7: dight, furnished or built.

E

E an O me, E an O an O me, V, 275 a, 9, 10: simple exclamations, having here the character of a refrain.

é, II, 217, 24: ae, only.

ea, V, 214 b, 3: to be dropped ; remnant of a corrected reading.

eaen, V, 267, 4: even.

eaght, the, the eighth.

ealky, elky, eke a, ylk a, ilka, V, 220 f., 4, 5, 8: each (one).

ean, V, 165, 2: eyes. See ee.

ear, I, 395, 1; 480, 54: early.

ear, eer, ever.

eare, ere, ayre, heir.

eare, v., I, 15, 12: plough.

earn, V, 115, 6: curdle.

eartly, II, 494, 1: earthly.

eased, III, 61, 101 (of horses): cared for, attended to.

eased we, V, 239, 35: used (as in 33), familiar with.

easer, IV, 315, 14; V, 271, 14: maple (mazer). See ezar.

easterling (born), V, 54, 3, 4 (in A, 48, 3, 4, stranger borne). The boy learned too fast for a native. Easterling, a native of the Hanse towns, or of the East of Germany. Halliwell.

eathe, III, 408, 33: easy.

eather, V, 224, 25; 241, No 156, 6: other.

eay, eayn, V, 238, 18, 28; 248, 18: eye(s). See ee.

edder-flowe, IV, 450 a, 2: adder-morass.

ee, III, 4, 9; 11, K : eye. Pl. een, eeen, II, 158 f., 5, 8, 18; 160, 4, 7, 17. See ean, eay, eghne, eyen.

ee (of a cup), IV, 221, 9: may be eye, top, brim.

ee, the table ee, II, 409, 20 (Motherwell, table eye): seems to be nonsense; edge does not suit. b, the printed copy, has play.

ee (A. S. ege, O. Eng. eȝe, eie, etc.), IV, 3, 15: awe; an unsatisfying emendation of lee, lye (eie would be better ; I have not found ee). The Campbell MS. has fee, meant, I suppose, for value.

ee-bree, III, 11, K; IV, 257, 5: eye-brow.

een, IV, 257, 13: one.

een, v., III, 495, 23, 24; IV, 517, 21: even, make of the same value.

eenin, IV, 169, F 1: evening.

eerie, eiry, I, 342, 24, 36; 355, 46; II, 466, 39; IV, 175, N 5; 368, G 8: dreary, gloomy, weird, exciting super-stitious dread.

eft, eft agayne=eftsones, III, 83, 238; 87, 238.

eftsones, III, 68, 238: hereafter, another time.

eghne, I, 327, 23: eyn, eyes.

eh, IV, 512, 11: exclamation of grief.

eight, the eight, I, 55, 9; 56, B 10; C 5, 11: eighth.

eihte, I, 244, 11: possession, valuable thing.

eild, III, 162, 46: age.

ein, I, 134, 13: een, evening.

eiry. See eerie.

eisin, IV, 331 b, 2: serve.

eke, also. At I, 133, L 1, eke . . . eke seems to be wrongly used for either . . . or.

eke a, III, 298, 57: each (one). See ealky.

elbouthe, I, 334, 5: elbow (the th for g or ȝ).

eldelike, I, 334, 5: elderly.

eldern, eldren, eldrin, I, 350, 12, 13; II, 20, 2; 26, 2; 27, 2; 61, 2; IV, 485, 28: old.

eldrige, elridge (hill, king), II, 58 f., 14, 15, 23, 25-7, 36= Scottish elric, elvish. The eldrige king has something of the character of the ellor-gást family in Beówulf (spirits who belong outside of mankind), haunts a hill, is a pagan, no one that has coped with him has come off alive. The lady who attends him, however, seems in no way extra-human. elric hour, I, 140, N (Pinkerton): hour when elves, or bad spirits, are ac-tive. In Elrick's hill, II, 62, 8, 10, etc., the adjective is improperly turned into a noun. See elrick.

element, I, 286, 44: air, sky.

elephant, III, 211, 2: a species of scabious is so called, according to Halliwell.

elfin, elphin, elphan, n. and adj., I, 15 ff.; 341, 15; IV, 456, 13: elf, elvish. I, 346, 15 (the Elfins); 350, 28; IV, 456 f., 14, 15, 19, 24: fairy-land.

Elfins, the, I, 346, 15: fairy-land. See elfin.

elfish, n., I, 343, 15: elf.

elflyn, of the elves.

Elizium, V, 158, 16: Elysian.

elky. See ealky.

ell, ill, ull, v., will.

ellish, III, 481, 9: ellis, ells. (h may well be dropped.)

elphan, elphin, n. and adj. See elfin.

elrick, elritch, adj., II, 63, 18; I, 357, 53: elvish. El-rick's, 62 f., 8, 10, 16, 21: as a substantive. See eldrige.

embowered, pret., II, 503, 13: used as bower.

eme, III, 296, 26: uncle. emys, III, 98, 38: uncle's.

-en, -n, -yn, sign of plural of verb, I, 244, 9; II, 5 b, 3; 54, 61; 445, 62; III, 13, 2, 3, 4, 8; 35, 31; 63, 134; 92, 11; 104, 7; 105, 9, 11; 277, 15; 284, 3, 8, 17; 285, 30, 32, 33; 286, 48, 49; 404, 3; 406, 28; etc.

end, en, end. hous(e)-end, -en, I, 254, variations of Twa Corbies, b, 1, c, 1; toun-end, V, 267 f., 10, 11, 24. on end, IV, 353, 18: to an end.

-end, termination of the present participle. sighend, I, 55 f., B 7, 9.

endres daye, þis, I, 326, 1: the other day.

eneuch, enew, I, 102, 5; III, 318, 6; 440, 10; IV, 117, 8; 384, 8: enough.

enlured, III, 36, 45: allured (which is the word in b).

enter plea att my iollye, III, 278, 32: unintelligible to me. iollye should probably be iollytë. The king will have the head to serve some inscrutable purpose when he is making merry.

enterprise, v., I, 411, 9; III, 230, 70: undertake.

entertain, III, 153, 18: take into service.

envye, III, 296 f., 12, 30: ill-will, hostility, spite.

ere, V, 300, 3: eer, ever.

ere, eare, ayre, n., heir.

ere, v., heir.

ere, II, 216, 19; 470, 44; IV, 242 a; 378, 6; 433, 31: till.

ere syne, II, 362, 34: ere then, before that.

erlis, I, 329, 60: should probably be ernis, eagle's (herons, yrons in other texts).

erlish, I, 355, 49: elrish, elvish.

ermeline, ermine.

ern, IV, 490, 12: iron.

-ës, -is, -ys, -us, preserved in gen. sing., I, 69, 52; II, 25, 7; III, 40, n.; 98, 21, 35; 99, 47 f., 52; 100, 64 f.; 111, 33, 36, 42, etc. In the plural, I, 72, 15; III, 40, n.; 97, 2, 3, 20; 98, 25, 33, 37, 40–2; 100, 63, 82; 109, 1; 111, 29, 31–37, 45 f., etc.

esk, I, 355, 50: newt. See ask.

ettled, IV, 47, 2: purposed.

even cloth, I, 324, 16: smooth, with the nap well shorn.

even down, IV, 110, 10, 11: flat to the ground. V, 124, B 14: perpendicular. 225 b, No 78: straight down (of heavy rain).

even forward, I, 324, 3: straight forward.

even up, I, 305, 7: straight up.

evening-mass, II, 168, A, 4: a religious service at the end of the day (as in Romeo and Juliet, IV, 1).

euery syde, III, 75, 398: each side of.

euerych, euerichone, euerechone, euerilkon, everlke ane, I, 334, 5; III, 22, 4; 65, 174; 67, 230; 98, 30: each, each one.

evidents, IV, 40 b: title-deeds.

evyll, adv., III, 26, 93: ill. euyll go, III, 77, 429: ill walk.

ew-bught. See bucht.

ewer, IV, 19, 8: dug, udder.

exaltre, III, 90 b: axletree.

examine, II, 58, 15: put you to test.

exite, II, 125, B 22; excit, V, 223 a, No 65, B 22: amended to sight under the supposition that exit must be impossible.

exoner, IV, 307, 42: exonerate.

ey, I, 415 b: egg.

eye (cote with one eye), III, 360, 117: window?

eyen, eyne, I, 472, 29; III, 74, 359: eyes. See ee.

eylde het the, III, 112, 62: yield, requite thee for it.

eylyt, I, 241 f., 5, 7: aileth.

eyre, pl., III, 113, 70: years.

ezar, II, 271, 17; 273, 23: maple. See easer, masar.

F

f, in Northern Scotch, often for wh; as, fa, faa, who; fan, when; far, faer, where.

fa, IV, 260, 6; 261, 6: who.

fa, V, 118, B 10: fault.

fa, my lady cannot fa sic servants, I, 116, 11: have such fall to her, put up with. fa frae her, II, 133, D 1: break off, give up.

fa, fae, IV, 256, 5; 337, f 2, 3, 7: from.

faa, V, 275 a, 8: who.

face, with a, III, 180, 12: with effrontery, boldness.

fache, fetch.

fact, III, 229, 32; IV, 11, 11: offence, crime.

fadge. fat fadge, II, 182, 8: "a lusty and clumsy woman." Jamieson. "fadgy, corpulent, unwieldy. fudge, a little, fat person. North." Halliwell. "fodge, a fat person; evidently the same with fadge." Jamieson. A dirty drab is the phrase corresponding to fat fadge, II, 194, 10 (fusom fag, IV, 469, I 10, 12). See fag, fug.

fadther, IV, 260, 7: father.

fae, fay, fey, fee, fie, I, 245, 6; III, 481 f., 30, 24; 489, 39; 490, 24; 492, 26; IV, 430, 2: (A. S. fǽge) destined to die.

fae, II, 184, 19; 196, 9: foe.

fae, IV, 165 f., 2, 10; 337 f, 2, 3, 7: frae, from. See fa.

faein, faen, fawn, fallen.

faem, fame, I, 68, 1; 70, 1; 86, 1; II, 24, 12; 25, G 14: foam, sea.

faer, IV, 262, 15; 378 f., 6, 19: where.

fag, I, 304, F 2, 3; IV, 469, I 10, 12: a dirty drab. Cf. fusome fug, described as a dirty drab, B 3–6; dirty slut, C 4; dirty bitch, E 4; filthy foul flag, G 4. See fadge, fug.

faikine, III, 199, 24: faith.

fail, feall, fell, I, 304, F 6: turf.

fail-dyke, I, 253, 2: turf-wall.

fails, II, 365 f., 2, 3, 23: falls, befalls.

fain(e), fayn(e), II, 444, 48, 57; 453, 28; III, 100, 66; 298, 50; 309, 32: glad, pleased, eager. IV, 211, 13; V, 115, 2: fond. for faine, III, 479, 40: for glad, for gladness.

fainly, joyfully, blithely.

fair, V, 26 f., 13, 39: far.

fairlie, farlie, ferlie, I, 324, 11; 325, B 9: wonder. gars me fairlie, IV, 357, 2: causes me astonishment.

fairly (fields), IV, 57, D 1: fair, looking well.

fait, faitt, fett, V, 224, 18, 19; 274, 10; 278, 29: white.

faith and troth, to be, IV, 147, 34: to be in the relation of men who have taken the engagement of mutual fidelity, sworn-brethren.

fald, fall, fauld, n., V, 105, A 3; 248, 21: fold.

fall, III, 76, 406: suit, become. well falls me, V, 25, 5: my luck is good.

fall, V, 206 b, 8: pret. of fall, unless there is ellipsis of did.

falling, III, 470 a: sunset.

fallow's deed, I, 448, 7–10: deed of a bad fellow seems unlikely. felloun's? farlie, strange?

falsh, IV, 442, 1, 10, 12: false.

falyf, III, 13, 4: fallow.

fame, faem, I, 68, 1; 86, 1: foam, sea.

fa'n, IV, 6, 7; V, 249, 7: fallen.

fan, fand, found.

fan, IV, 262, 19; V, 110, 4; 116, 1; 184, 49: when.

fancy, fell in her, V, 272 b, 2: fell in love with her. faen deap in my fancy, 273, 12.

fand, found.

fang, III, 160, 5: fastening. (164, b 5, whang.) Perhaps North Scotch for whang.

fankit, IV, 27, 28: entangled, obstructed.

far, III, 513 b, 1–4: fair.

far, fare, faur, I, 165, N 1; II, 191, 23; 335, N 3–5; V, 224, 17, 18; 227, 8; 248, 22: where.

fare, go, I, 170, 4; II, 222, 21; III, 22, 6; 98, 24; 340, 23, 24; 421, 43; V, 183, 22, 32. I fare you well, II, 207, A 1: I bid you fare well. pret. foor. p. p. forn.

fare, go on, comport oneself: III, 188, 6; 357, 59.

fare, n., II, 160, 11, 20: going on, procedure. III, 76, 403: (in the modern sense) fortune, experience.

fared, favored. well-fared, well-(weel-)fard, well-(weel-)faird, weil-faurit, weill-(weel-)faurd, well-fard, II, 268, 21; 317, B a 21; 408, 26; 462, 7, 8; IV, 220, 8, 1, 4; 223, 3; 274, 2; 434, 2, 3; V, 16, 1; 154, 10; 163, 12; 177, 14: well-favored, handsome.

farei, farie, Farie (MS. farie), V, 165 f., 6, 9, 10: should be emended to Fyvie. See V, 305 f.

farer, I, 369, 51; V, 91 f., 4, 8, 12, etc.; 208, 9: further.

ffarley, adj., ffarley thinge, III, 92, 9: strange.

farlies, farleys, ferlies, I, 325, B 9; IV, 147, 26: wonders, novelties. See fairlie.

far sought, was, V, 161, 6: required long to reach.

fart, weel-fart, IV, 223, 3: fared, favored. See fared.

fas, fase, III, 299, 6; V, 248, 5: false.

fa's, IV, 399, 46: fall, 1st per. sing. pres.

fash, IV, 493, 21, 23; V, 238, 22: meddle, make trouble, or, perhaps, trouble yourself. fashed himself, IV, 69, 18, 19: got himself into trouble by meddling.

fashes, II, 238, 4: troubles (emendation for fishes; possibly we should read freshes).

fast, fast they bad, III, 26, 90: strenuously. stare, look, III, 62, 122; V, 82, 35: intently. weep, II, 240, 3: copiously. fast unto, III, 131, 6: close down to.

Fastness, IV, 103, 15: originally meant for faustness, falseness.

fat, fatt, III, 281, 4; IV, 260, 2; 357, C 5, 7, 9, etc.; V, 111, 18; 214 b, 5: what.

fate they coud na fa, II, 130 1: from it (fae it, frae it) they could not desist.

fatten a, V, 221, 22; 247, 2: what, what sort of.

faue, V, 260, 7: fie!

fauld-dyke, IV, 199, 11: fold-wall.

faun, fallen.

faur, V, 124, 2: where. See far.

faurit, faurd. See fared.

fause, false.

fause fa thee, III, 435, F 5: may treachery befall thee, be thy lot!

fave, V, 275 b, 8: five.

fawe, IV, 505, 54: fall.

fawn, IV, 277, 13: fallen.

fay, adj. See fae.

fay, III, 74, 362; 110, 13; V, 85, 16: faith.

ffayne, III, 297 f., 48, 50: glad. III, 100, 66: fond of, pleased with. See fain.

fe, feea, wage, etc. See fee.

feall, feale, fail, fell, IV, 262, 29: turf.

Feansell, feanser, V, 55, 30: emended to le and fell.

fear, II, 470, 51: frighten (us from dancing).

fearder, feardest. See feart.

feare, in, V, 15, 18: together. See fere.

fearsome, II, 394, 18: fearful.

feart, feert, III, 262 f., 11, 13, 15, 17; IV, 456, 15; 498, 12, 14, 16: frightened. fearder, III, 267, 13: more frightened. feardest, III, 162, 55: most frightened.

feather, IV, 512 b, 2, 9: father.

feathern, IV, 482 f., 4, 9, 13: feathers.

fecht, feght, v., II, 319, 16; 391, 16, 17; III, 370, 15; IV, 224, 14, 15: fight. See ficht.

feckless, I, 429, 28 (dress): weak, feeble, effectless, miserable, silly. (here=inefficacious, of no account.)

fedred, ifedred fre, III, 69, 275; 70, 288: feathered liberally, handsomely.

fee (A. S. feoh), I, 327, 16 (wylde fee): animals. I, 58, 2; 434, 31; II, 25, 7; 172 f., 40, 42, 45; 442, 8; 447, 8; III, 94, 51; IV, 18, 17: wealth, possessions, property, having. I, 182, 2; II, 31, N 4; 114, 17; 123, 15; 379, 1; 403, 9; III, 433, 12; 435, F 6; 436, 14; IV, 514, 21: pay, wages. II, 117, 5, 6; III, 163, 72; 299, 5: reward. I, 328, 57: tribute. gentylman of clothynge and of fee, III, 30, 165: entitled to a regular stipend. knights fee, III, 94, 51: land of the value of £20 per annum (under Edward I., II.). See foster of the fe, III, 28, 140. penny-fee(-fie), I, 491, 10; IV, 444, 10: gift.

fee, v., I, 211, 3, 4: hire. (gae fee, go hire yourself.) See feet, pret.

fee, fey, doomed. See fae.

feed, feid, III, 436, 2; 464, 2; 468, c 2; IV, 2, 9; 36, 3; 37 f., 3, 10: feud.

feed, fode, food, I, 309, B 1: child, man.

feed about your fire, II, 184, 13: the sense eat seems unlikely. Possibly, to move about, to sit or move restlessly (like feik).

feed, pret. of feed, V, 236, 18: fed.

feel, fiel, II, 175, 1; 176, C 3; IV, 262, 29: fool.

feel daft, II, 410, 8: foolishly fond.

feel=fell: very.

feere, fere, feire, feer, mate, consort (fere): I, 295, 43; II, 58, 2. V, 15, 13: fellow (contemptuously). See feires.

feert. See feart.

feet, pret., IV, 355 b, D: hired. See fee.

feeties, V, 209 b, 4: feet.

feght, fight. See fecht.

feid: feud. See feed.

feires, feiries, I, 295, 43; IV, 2 f., 7, 20, 22: comrades, consorts. See feere.

felaushyp, III, 67, 229: abstract for concrete, our fellows.

felischepe, fellowship.

fell, fail, feale, feall, IV, 266, E 29: turf.

fell, III, 300, 9; IV, 500, 10: skin, hide.

fell, III, 439 f., 4, 8, 11; IV, 455, 15; V, 55, 30: high land, fit only for pastures, a wild hill. fells, III, 299 f., C 3, 6; IV, 26, 6; 500, 3: chain of hills.

fell (yard), I, 287, 63: severe, cutting. (spice), III,

388, 3: hot, biting. IV, 258, 20: strange, prodigious.
fell thing to see, II, 132, 27: strange. freezes fell,
IV, 93, 7; 105, 7; 514, 17: sharply, severely.

fell, *v.*, II, 419, 46: kill.

fell, feel, I, 478, 14; II, 344, 15; V, 183, 20: very.

fellen, *p. p.* of fell, III, 483, 7: felled (a tree).

fells, befalls. well fells me, IV, 437, 25: good for me !

felon (the kynggis), III, 98, 21, 22: traitor, rebel.

felt, III, 146, 14: should be emended *delt*.

fences, cock shall crow fences three, II, 8, 10, 11: evidently bouts, *coups;* but I have not found this usage elsewhere.

fend, fende, V, 283, 2; 284, 22: fiend.

fend, *v.*, III, 300, 12; IV, 500, 13: provision.

fend, III, 440, 12: defence.

ffend. that ffend I Godys fforbod, III, 113, 72: seems to be a double expression for deprecation, — I inhibit, protest, God forbid (see **forbode**). "I fende to Goddes forbode it should be so : a Dieu ne playse qu'aynsi il aduiengne. Palsgrave, p. 548, col. 1." Hales and Furnivall, Percy MS., III, 554.

fende, III, 61, 106; 117, 8: defend.

fer dayes, III, 57, 16: far on in the day.

ferd, III, 99, 52: fear.

fere, fere love, IV, 219, **B** 3, 5: fair. (fair love, V, 260, **E** 5.)

fere, feere, II, 58, 2; III, 22, 5: mate, consort.

fere, in, on, III, 57, 27; 59, 61; 67, 231; 77, 423; 98, 38: in company, together. See **feare**.

fferli, I, 334, 7: fairly, civilly.

ferlicke, I, 334, 8: strange. See **ferly**.

ferly, ferlie, ferley, farlie, I, 325, **C** 1, 10; 329, 4; 333, 2; 424, **d** 11; III, 440, 20; IV, 455, 1, 13; 524, 10; V, 244, 8, 12: marvel, wonder, news.

ferly, *adj.*, ferly strife, III, 97, 13: strange, extraordinary. See **ffarley**.

ferra-cow, farrow-cow, I, 224, **I** 9, 11; II, 261, 8: a cow not producing a calf for the current year.

fesh, fess, III, 319, 15; IV, 94, 14; 257, 1, 2: fetch.

fet. See **fett**.

fetchie, III, 520 b (note to II, 272, 22): tricky, practising fetches ? Cf. wylie, st. 21.

fetcht a race, II, 454 f., 54, 58: took a swift preliminary run.

fett, I, 432, 5: fetch. *pret.* fet, fette, III, 31, 14; 63, 145; 64, 172; 298, 67.

fett, V, 224, 18: white.

ffettle, III, 92 ff., 15, 37, 56: make ready.

feud, II, 279 a, 16: contest of feeling ?

feughten, *p. p.* of fecht, ficht, fight, I, 109, 15.

feume, IV, 473, 44: foam.

fey, I, 245, 6; IV, 44, 4; 430, 2: destined to death. See **fae**.

ffeyt, faith.

feyther, V, 296 a : father.

ficht, fecht, feght, *v.*, IV, 84 f., 16, 26, 27, etc.: fight. *pret.* focht, foucht. *p. p.* foughten, feughten.

fie. See **fee**.

fie, doomed. See **fae**.

fiel, feel, II, 176, **C** 3: fool.

fieldert, V, 126, 1: fieldward, away (from where they were).

fiend thing, IV, 23, **A** c 18: devil of a thing.

fift, II, 75, 6: fifth.

file, *v.*, I, 135, 4: defile.

file, IV, 494, 33: while, till.

fileshap, V, 260, 16: fellowship.

fill, full.

fill, I, 403, 10: follow, pursue.

filtt, *p. p.*, III, 490, 20: filed.

fin, find.

fin, craig and fin, II, 28, 27: whin, whin-stone, synonymous with greenstone, but applied to any hard rock.

finikin, III, 174, 18: fine, handsomely dressed.

fire-beams, IV, 96, 3: should be fire-boams (bombs), as at 99, **G** 8, **H** 6.

fire-boams, bombs. See **fire-beams**.

firlot, IV, 46, 3; 379, 13: the fourth part of a fou, which is a dry measure varying from two to six Winchester bushels (a Winchester bushel being of a slightly less capacity than the present imperial bushel).

firmaty, V, 114, 3: frumenty; in old cookery, wheat pottage, with flesh in it; hulled wheat boiled in milk and seasoned with cinnamon, sugar, etc.

fit, fitt, fyt, fytte, II, 54, 60: song. I, 329, 62; III, 25, 51; 27, 97; 308, 24: division of a song. (A. S. fitt.)

fit, I, 131, **G** 4, 5; 164, **J** 6; 302, **A** 7; 472, 28; 491, 26; IV, 119, 6: foot, feet.

fit, III, 142, 32; V, 240, 5: ready.

fitches (of deer), II, 132, 19: flitches, sides.

fite (bread), V, 220, 6: (probably) wheat. See **white bread**.

fitt, III, 465, 21: it is better to read sitt, as in Caw's text.

fitted, IV, 18, 9: footed.

fitted, II, 485, 18, 31; V, 103 a: suitably treated or served. V, 132, 2: ready, disposed.

fittie, IV, 450 a, 4: foot.

fivesome, III, 472, 3: five together.

flaff, IV, 470, 20: flap, fan.

flag, I, 305, 3, 4; V, 213, 3, 4: corruption of *fag*, drab, slut. See **fag**.

flain in, IV, 224, 23: correct to *fla* or *flai* (flew) *in ?*

flamboy, V, 298, 7: flambeau, torch.

flat, II, 258, 45, 46: highest and lowest layer of a grave.

flatte, IV, 504, 32: positively determined on.

flattered, flottered (on the faem), II, 25 **G** 14; 27, 22: flitted, floated (O. Eng. floteren, Germ. flattern).

flattering (toung), II, 144, 8 : fluttering, waggling. flattering tongue that flutters, II, 154, 21.

flaugh, flaw, *pret.* of fly, I, 286, 56; 397, **E** 8; II, 314, 9.

flaw, tell me without a flaw, V, 41, 28: lie.

flay, frighten. See **fley**.

flay (A. S. fléon), fly. *pret.* flaw, flaugh.

fleachy, II, 470, 53: infested with fleas.

flear, fleer, I, 454, 11; IV, 392, 7; 410, 26: floor.

flee, *v.*, V, 304 b, 4: flay. *pret.* fleed.

flee, not a, IV, 53, 12 : not a whit (fly, for a small

thing). I count him lighter than a flee, etc., III, 480, 23; 482, 19; 488, 26 (flea); 490, 15. left him not a flee, IV, 53, 12.

fleechin, I, 424, d 11; II, 32, **Q** 2: wheedling, cajoling.

fleed, *pret.*, V, 304 b, 4: flayed.

fleed, flied, V, 257, 7, 17: frightened. See **fleg.**

fleed, IV, 348, 14; 349, 9: flood.

fleer, I, 69, 39; 298, 4; 452, 14: floor. See **flear.**

fleet, flute.

fleg, fley, flay (A. S. flégan, Old Eng. fleyen), V, 253 b, No 203, 3: frighten.

flesse, V, 283, 18: flesh.

flex, V, 283, 11, 21: flax.

fley, flay, III, 457, **A** 2; 474, 36: frighten. *pret.* fleed, flied. See **fleg.**

flight, I, 21, note *: dispute and scold.

flink, care a flink, V, 259, 3: care a whit.

flirry, I, 424, d 10: blossom.

flo, flon(e) (A. S. flá, flán), I, 327, 10; III, 13, 5, 15: arrow.

flotterd. See **flattered.**

flourishd, I, 398, 13: adorned.

flow, IV, 79, 14: moss with a spring in it, morass.

flower, I, 352, 3, 4: get flowers for, or deck with flowers.

flutters, II, 154, 21: waggles.

flyte, flight, III, 414 b: dispute, debate, scold (here Percy's word, replacing *flout* and *mock*).

forward, V, 283, 4: compact.

focht, *pret.* of fecht, ficht, fight, IV, 167, **C** 10. *p. p.* feughten, foughten.

fode. See **feed.**

folde, *pret.*, III, 76, 407: folded.

folle, foal.

folye, I, 327, 17: a very unlikely word (unless we may understand it to have the meaning of Old Fr. foler, errer çà et là). Another text has balye (Fr. baillie), which gives a good sense, under thine own control, in thine own custody. (folye, in 17, may be caught from 18.)

fone, II, 196 b, 2, 8: foes.

fond, fond to see him sleep, II, 269, 26: doted, was foolishly happy? (But probably corrupt: cf. fondly seen thee sleep, 271, 30.)

food, III, 287, 61: man. See **feed.**

ffooder, II, 46, 41: (cf. Ger. fuder, cart-load, the largest or one of the largest measures for corn, liquids, and other things), here, tun, as is clear from *auger*, 41.

foonshief, V, 206 a, 8: foundation, bottom sheaf of a stack.

foor, V, 99, **C** 4: fared, went.

foote, goe two foote, III, 188, 6: corrupt for fold; cf. 267, 9.

for, ffor. ye (yes), for God, nay, for God, III, 61, 105, 107; 69, 259, 267, 269, 271; 76, 413, 414: by.

for, II, 124, 38: before.

for, IV, 21, 6; 438, 9; V, 16 f., 2, 5, 29: where.

for *when* but *would be expected*, II, 58, 11, 13; 59, 22 (see II, 57 b). for and, V, 76, 25; 144, 9.

for no, I, 183, 25; II, 256, **K** 3: phrase of refusal,

obscurely elliptical, after the manner of *why, no;* or corruptly for *fye, no* (cf. II, 158, 2).

forbears, I, 206, 2; II, 63, 19: forefathers.

forbode, forbott, ouer Goddes, III, 29, 162; 123, 18; V, 199 a, 64: God forbid, against God's prohibition; so A. S. ofer cinges bebod, against the king's order; ofer dryhtnes word, against the word of the Lord, etc. Elliptically, God's forbod, as III, 37, 79; 180, 16. III, 113, 72: see **ffend.**

forbye, forebye, I, 402, 1; II, 154, 8, 9; IV, 224, 17; 433, 16: near by. I, 86, 33; II, 70, 22: apart, aside. IV, 203, 2: further.

forbye, forebye, forby, I, 305, 1; IV, 203, 2; V, 17, 32; 213 a, 1: besides.

force, no, III, 57, 13; 67, 227: no matter.

forces. for (thro, V, 306, 8) a' her father's forces, V, 166, 11: in spite of all her father could do?

fordoo, destroy.

fore, first fore love, II, 191, 22, 25, 28, 29: earlier.

forebye. See **forbye.**

fforefend, III, 340, 26; 407, 5: avert, forbid.

forehammer, I, 21 b, 12; III, 474, 34: sledge-hammer, the large hammer, which strikes before the smaller.

foremost man, 1, 146, 12; IV, 412, 19: apparently the bridegroom's "best man."

forenent, fornent, I, 221 f., **E** 7, 17; 504, 7; IV, 77, 3; 288, **F** 2; 451 a, 3, 5: over against, in the face of.

foresteed, V, 237, 28: protection, protector.

foret, I, 244, 10: forth.

forfaulted, V, 194, 68, 73: forfeited.

forfouchald, IV, 4 b, 28: very much tired. (Scottish wauchle, forwauchld, forfaughlit.)

forfoughen, IV, 3, 28: tired out with fighting.

forgone, forgo.

foriete, forgotten.

forked, I, 492, 7; IV, 445, p. 100, **B** 7: of blood from a wound, issued in divided jets.

forl, V, 116, 2; 117, 3: whorl, fly of a spinning-rock.

for-lee, she 'll come in att your formast an gee out att yer forlee, IV, 377, 5; V, 275 b, 5: she 'll cross your bows and sail round you, coming out at your fore-lee or lee-bow.

forlorn, I, 450, 8; II, 114, 15, 16; III, 124, 13; 212, 16: lost. has him forlorn, II, 147, 17: causatively. II, 123, 13; V, 41, 23: destroyed, killed. I, 183, 42; III, 145, 9; V, 210 b, 2: destitute, deserted.

forn, *p. p.* of fare, II, 29, 6, 9. be weel forn: see that ye have fared well, eat and drink heartily.

fornents, forenent, fornent, II, 197 a, 15: opposite to, directly against.

forren, foreign.

forsake, forsake a ring, I, 192 a: let go, part with. forsake that I haue promised, III, 29, 156: withdraw from. forsake this sorowe, III, 73, 341: decline to have to do with this sad matter. II, 454, 52: decline as adversary in a combat. III, 360, 106: refuse an appointment. IV, 172, 1; 173, **K** 2: refuse suitors. III, 149, 33; IV, 181, 2: give up, renounce.

forth. find forth, III, 148, 17; choose forth, III, 440, 9:

out. thou maye well fforth for to pay mee, II, 444, 58; thou mayst well forth, thou shalt pay me, 449, 63; (b, mayst forthwith): go on, or, make out ?

fforthi, I, 329, 60: therefore.

forth withall, III, 127, 16 (play): forthwith.

forthynketh, III, 28, 137: repenteth.

fortune be my chance, III, 308, 21 = my hap it were, 311, 16.

forward, III, 284, 11: van.

forward, V, 283, 4: compact.

foster of the fe, III, 28, 140: "A person who had for some service to the crown a perpetual right of hunting in a forest on paying to the crown a certain rent for the same." Halliwell.

fot, I, 141 b, 10: fetched.

fothe, III, 112, 51: foot.

fou, II, 25, 8; 26, 11: a firlot, which see.

fou, V, 270, 9: how.

fou, fow, full. fou drunken, II, 144, 4.

foucht, *pret.,* II, 391, 21: fought. IV, 200, 1: toiled. *p. p.* foughten, II, 418, 32; III, 277, 22; 281, 14; 333, 30.

fouie, IV, 20, 10: well off, "possessing a comfortable independence." Jamieson.

fouled, a bill was fouled against him, III, 463 a: (equivalent to) found; he was indicted as guilty.

foumart, IV, 389 b: polecat.

found, III, 23, 15: provided for.

foure-eard foole, II, 483, 7: as denoting a double ass ?

fousome, fusom(e), I, 302, **B** 3, 5, 6; 304, 2, 3: (fulsome) disgustingly filthy.

fow, fou, II, 273, 35; III, 490, 13; IV, 168, **D** 14, 15: full.

fowd, V, 304 b: sheep-fold.

fowk, I, 245, 6: folk.

frae, fray, from. be frae, IV, 433, 21: remain away from.

fraine, *v.,* I, 334, 6, 7, 10: question.

frame, IV, 78, 4: succeed. sae weel we frame: we are doing, or beginning so well.

frank, of horses kept in a close, you keep them all both frank and free, II, 450, 64: apparently, fat. Free is a much abused word, and the only apt meaning here would be, liberally treated. In **A** 444, 59, you keepe them ranke and royallye.

ffrankely, II, 440, 13: freely.

free, *n.,* I, 334, 8: (complimentary term for man) noble, etc.

free, *adj.,* is used in a great variety of senses, and is often indefinite and hardly more than a rhyme word: bounteous, gracious, of noble birth or rank, independent, unrestricted, exempt, spirited, valorous, beautiful, precious, excellent in any way. The danger will be in assigning too positive a meaning to the word. of Mary, III, 420 f., 29, 44. lady, ladies free, I, 324, **A** 8; 328, 52; 464, 5; V, 87, 39; 279 a. a true-love free, IV, 461, 22. God make you safe and free (your own master ?), I, 427, 2; II, 177, 28; 421, 22. castles free, I, 465, 6; 474, 21. lands sae free, I, 474, 25. tocher free, II, 380, 33; 383, 26; 385, 27. Clymme of the Clowgh so fre, Little John so free, III, 26, 96;

154, 2. freyke fulle fre, III, 308, 30. of courage free, V, 86, 31. chrystall free, II, 52, 17. gold soe free, V, 49, 23. gowd and jewels free, I, 474, 23. silver free, II, 69, 9; 445, 64; 450, 70. money ffeyre and ffre, III, 113, 82. metal free, III, 300, 7; 368 f., 12, 14; IV, 372, 7; (nonsense in IV, 404, 29). staff of oke so free, III, 138, 15. Less definite are the following: Couentrye faire and free, Derby Hills so free, Cannongate-side so free, III, 284, 17; 323, 10; 386, 10; seas so free, IV, 498, 6; water soe free, V, 51, 68; forest frie, V, 191 f., 8, 12, 23, 28, 34; learning my lesson free, I, 438, **B** 7; chariot, coach, free, I, 475, 44; IV, 410, 29; 462, 35. horses kept free, II, 450, 64: liberally. going free, IV, 289, 7: not under control, running off. free of grace, V, 20, 24: void of grace, cf. 43.

free, *adv.,* arowes ifedred fre, III, 69, 275; 70, 288: in handsome style. ring she brake so free, I, 470, 26: generously (cf. II, 450, 64).

freely, *adj.,* freely feed, I, 309, **B** 1: of noble birth, or beautiful.

freely (naked), I, 508, 10: entirely.

freits, III, 434, 23: superstitious notions concerning omens.

freke, freck, freake, freyke, III, 298, 58; 308, 30; 309, 32, 47: bold man, man. (A. S. freca.)

frem, foreign.

frembde, *adv.,* frembde bested, III, 63, 138: in the position of a stranger (other readings, frend, friend).

frese, frese your, our, bowes of ewe, III, 67, 215; 80, 215: seems to be corrupt. The interpretation in Donaldson's Supplement to Jamieson, where "to frese a bow" (cited as if a phrase in full use) is said to mean unbend, slack, would be entirely inappropriate here, since three men are to make a desperate attack on two hundred and fifty (bende your bowes, st. 218). f, g have, bend we, the required sense. Chese will not do; they have but one bow each. leese = loose is possible, or dress, or even, free.

frichtit, frighted.

frienged, fringed, gray, III, 481, 7; IV, 2, 5: referring to mane and fetlocks, or perhaps to long fetlocks only.

frightened the boar will, I, 214, 3: afraid, etc.

frith, frythe, firthe, V, 191 f., 14, 24: enclosed land, wood.

froom, V, 296 a: from.

froth-mill, I, 305, 13: "wauk-mill, or fulling-mill, from the froth of the soap." But the expression seems not to have been heard of, and froth-mill is more probably corrupt for frozen mill. See next word.

frozen mill, V, 213, 10: mill of which the lade, or canal conveying the water, is frozen.

frush, IV, 185, 13: brittle.

frythe, I, 329, 3: enclosed land, preserve, deer-park, wood. See **frith.**

fue, few.

fug, I, 302, 3, 5: slut, filthy woman. See **fag, flag.**

fuird, II, 471, 6: ford.

fule, fowl.

full, IV, 356, **B** 1: proud.

fun, fune, V, 215, 15; 248, 9: whun, whin, furze.

fundid, I, 334, 8: went. (A. S. fundian.)

fur, II, 188, 12; III, 474, 41: furrow.

fusom, fusome, fousome, I, 302, **B** 3, 5, 6; 304, **F** 2, 3; IV, 469, 10, 12: offensive, disgusting (fulsome).

fusty bandyas, V, 72 b: a drinking-formula.

fute, whute, v., III, 123, 15: whistle.

fynde, III, 308, 24: Professor Skeat would read fyne, end.

fynly, III, 70, 284: goodly.

fyt, fytt, fytte. See fit.

G

ga, gaa, gaw, I, 420, 9, 10; 421, 9, 10; 423, 6, 7; V, 216, 9, 10: gall.

ga, gaa, I, 146, 5; V, 166, 8; 221, 16; 227, 6; 247, 3; 278, 25: go. See gang, gae.

ga, gaa, IV, 513 a, 4; V, 221, 14; 242 a, 8; 268, 23: gave.

gab, n., I, 302, **B** 12: 422, 13: mouth.

gab, v., II, 149, 17: prate.

gab, n., I, 277 f.: joke, sportive brag.

gabber reel, I, 217, 8, 13: evidently a sprightly air. The root may be Icelandic gabb, mockery. Perhaps simply gabber, jabber.

gaberlunyie, V, 115 f., 6-10; 119, 8, 9: beggar's wallet.

gad, gaud, I, 342, 33; 344, 32; 348, 13, 19; 355, 42; III, 505, 21: bar.

gad, gade, IV, 493 f., 13, 26: went.

gaddie, IV, 273, 1=gaudie: showy, dashing.

gae, gai, gay, ga, gaa, gee, gie, I, 69, 49, 62; 71, 39, 50; II, 304, 17; 468, 14; V, 166, 7; 278, 24: go. pret. gaed, gade, gad, gaid, gied, gid, ged, good, gude. p. p. gaen, gain, gane, gaed. pres. p. gain, gan, gaen, gane, gaun, gawen, etc. See gang.

gae, gang, go down, IV, 12, **C** 6, 7; 518, 2: be hanged.

gae, IV, 493 f., 23, 32: give.

gae, pret. of gie, I, 69, 55-58, 68; 71, 45-47; 75, 42; 108, 15: gave.

gae, gay, gey, adv., V, 266, 9: (gay) pretty, rather.

gaed, gade, gad, gaid, pret. of gae, go, I, 102, **D** 4; 103, **E** 3; 131, **G** 10; 439, 14, 15; II, 140, 17, 18; III, 453, 10; IV, 395, 6; 494, 26; V, 117, 11; 238, 27; 274 b, 6; 278, 24.

gaed, p. p., II, 70, 21; III, 473, 30: gone.

gaen, gain, gane, p. p. of gae, I, 70, 19; 108, 12; II, 468 f., 15, 18, 22; IV, 507, 2; V, 237, 5: gone.

gaen, gain, p. p. of gie, gae, give, I, 469, 23 (gaen the table, given a knock); III, 271, 13; V, 183, 34. So perhaps II, 212, 15; cf. gain, fifth word below.

gaeng. See gang.

gae-through-land, IV, 428, 13: vagrant.

gai. See gae.

gaid. See gaed.

gain. See gaen.

gain, gaine, gaing, gan, gaen, gane, gaun, gawn, gawen, pres. p. of gae, ga, go. gain, etc., I, 466, 15;

II, 151, **H** 2, 4; IV, 257, 8; V, 247, 15; 256, 6. gan, etc., II, 144, 12; IV, 210, 3; 507, 2.

gain, II, 212, 15, ye's gain as much at mine : will get, receive. (But will (have) given, dealt, is perhaps possible.)

gain (him at the law), IV, 286, 3: Icel. gegna, to proceed against ?

gain, gane (Icel. gegna, to suit, be meet), II, 25, 8; 26, 11 (with ellipsis of will): serve, suffice. II, 369, 15: suit my case.

gaing. See gain, pres. p.

gair, pay meat and gair, V, 268, 27: gear, clothes an arms ? or money (a variation of pay meat and fee) ?

gair (of clothes). See gare.

gait, III, 266 b ; 272, 5; IV, 265, **A** b 10: way, road. See gate.

galerie, V, 140, **f** 1, 5: for gallaly, galley (doubtful form).

Galiard, III, 459 f., 1, 4, etc.: sobriquet of a freebooter of a gay (perhaps dissipated) character.

galla. See gallowe-tree.

gallage, V, 247, 20: gallows.

gallaly, galalie, V, 136 f., 1-3, etc.; 141, **d** 1: galley, prolonged for metrical convenience.

gallan, gellant, gillan, IV, 260, 4; 315 f., 1, 4-7, 18: gallant, gayly or finely dressed.

gallio, V, 141, 2, 3, etc.=galley O.

gallowe, sing. (like A. S. galga), a gallowe, III, 92, 18. Cf. next word.

gallows, the highest, I, 150, 13: one elevated above a triangular framework, for special offenders ; der höchste Galgen ; see Grimm's Deutsches Wörterbuch, Galgen, column 1168 (?). Perhaps simply the highest that is to be had.

gallows-pin. See pin.

gallow-tree (A. S. galgtréow; O. Eng. galwetre), III, 24, 43; 180, 17; 358, 71; 368, 10. gallou-, gallage-, galla-tree, gallow-pine, V, 247, 17, 18, 20, 23, 24.

gam, game.

game, had god game, V, 80, 46, 47: sport, amusement.

gamene, I, 328, 52: game, sport.

gamon, II, 59, 25: gamen, amuse himself.

gan, gane. See gain, pres. p.

gan, gon, with infinitive : began, did.

gane, II, 26, 11: serve, suffice. See gain.

gane, p. p. of gae, go. See gaen.

gane, III, 281, 14: p. p. of gae, give. See gaen.

gane frae, IV, 378, 3: gone ahead of, left behind.

gang, gange, gaeng, gieng, I, 55, **A** 5; 57, 4; 68 f., 21, 37, 46; 75, 36, 39; 217, 16; II, 175, 13; 468 f., 13, 14, 38, 39; III, 75, 397; V, 16, 2, 5: go, walk. pret. yede, yeede, yeed, yed, зede, yode, yod, youd. p. p. gaen, gain, gane, gaed, gade, gad, gaid, gude, good. inf. also, gon, gone. p. p. ganged : III, 362, 102. See gae.

gang, gae, go down : IV, 11, 9, 12; 12, **C** 6, 7; 518, 2: like the Scottish be put down, be hanged.

gantrees, II, 369, 11; 370, 11: barrel-stands.

gar, gaur, I, 100, 8; 127, 15; 130, 8; 397, **D** 9, 11, 13; II,

115, 30, 31; 153, 16; 358, 17, 22-24: (Icel. göra) make do, cause. as auxiliary, gar lay, I, 5, **D** 1: do lay, lay. So II, 106, 11; 107, 19; 216, 3, 4.

garded, III, 117, 16: looked at.

gare, gair, gore, properly, a triangular piece of cloth inserted in a garment to give width at that part; in Old English often coat or gown. low down by his (her) gare is a frequently recurring expression which may be taken literally, down by that part of a garment where the gore would be=low by his knee, II, 197, 18. In, your ain hand sewed the gare (of a shirt), II, 379, 13; 389, 5; 395, 12 (following ain hand sewed the sleeve), gare in the limited sense seems hardly important enough, and perhaps is to be understood side: cf. rive it (sark) frae gore to gore, gair by gair, I, 439, 4; 440, 5, 7; 441, 6, 7; 442, 5, 6; II, 294, 31, 32. So also in, frae breast to gare, I, 438, **B** 4, probably, though the limited sense would answer. So, riven him frae gair to gair, IV, 416, 17; the brown bride pat her hand in att Annë's left gare, V, 224, 20. penknife, sword, brand, down by (below) his (her) gare, I, 451, 9; II, 98, 40; 144, 6; 154, 11; 172, 34; IV, 465, 38. keys hung leugh down by her gair, IV, 465, 34. she hung 't (cup of wine) low down by her gare, II, 369, 10 (recklessly and absurdly ; the cup is in her hand in the next stanza). In, frae my sark ye shear a gare, I, 388, **A** 8, 9, **B** 6, gare must be a strip large enough to make a bandage for the head.

ʒare, III, 98, 24: ready.

garl, II, 129, 18; V, 223 a, No 66, 18: gravel (suspicious word).

garlande, III, 93, 31; rose-garlonde, III, 75, 398: a circular wreath, apparently hung upon a wand or rod. In III, 93, 31, this can be nothing more than an extemporized circlet of twigs.

garlings, II, 366, 24: garlands.

garmarcie, garmercy, III, 33, 130; 81, 34: gramercy.

garned. the bride she garned round about, IV, 410, 23, is a misprint of Buchan's for gazed, which stands in the original MS.

garrett, III, 332, 16: watch-tower, look-out.

gars, garse, IV, 221, 11; 467, 7: grass.

gartan, garten, gartin, IV, 169, 10; 170, **H** 6; 175, **M** 8; 176, **N** 14, **P** 2; 490, 12: garter. (Gael. gairtein.)

garthes, girths.

gast, guest.

gate, gait, get, I, 225, 8; II, 311 f., 2, 15, 21; 402, 10; III, 92, 11; 477 f., 11, 15 (ford); 480, 24; IV, 3, 21; V, 99, **C** 4: way, road. water-gate, V, 250, 12: round by the water. in this gate, II, 73, 26: in such a way or condition. to the gate (get) has gain, IV, 493, 5; V, 237, 5: has gone away. tuke the gate, II, 30, 7; IV, 392, 9: started, departed.

gaucy, IV, 271, **B** 1; V, 152, 3: lusty, jolly.

gaud. See gad.

gaudie, gaudy, gawdie, IV, 273, 12, 13, of speech: with a stately or pompous air. 274, **D** 19; 297, 13: showy, conspicuous. 274, **E** 1: dashing. gaudy locks, 285, 10, 19: bright-colored. 356, **B** 1: ostentatious.

gaule, I, 272, 11: of the color of gall; or gules, red.

gaun, gawn, gawen, I, 22, **A** 1, **B** 1; III, 473, 21-24; 479, 8; IV, 261, 8; 511 a, 6; 513 a, 3: going.

gaunt, IV, 20, 12: yawn.

gaur, gar, I, 73, 36; IV, 226, 11: make.

gavellock, gavlock, III, 470 b; 493, 10: iron lever.

gavil-post, II, 227 a: gable-post.

gaw. See ga.

gawdie. See gaudie.

gawen, gawn. See ga, and gaun.

gay. See gae.

gay, gae, gey, adv., II, 184, 16; IV, 271, 9; 329, **c** 20; V, 266, 9: pretty, rather.

gaze, IV, 313, 10: gauze.

ge, ye.

ge, give. See gie.

gear, geare, geere, geir, gier, I, 411, 5; II, 182, 5; 184, 9; 185, 38; III, 440, 12; 459, 3; IV, 6 f., 5, 19, 29; 469, 10; V, 170, 3, 4: goods, property, often cattle. silken gear, I, 145, 22: clothes. III, 440, 7, 18, 19; 446 b: fighting equipments. the less gear and the mair, III, 8, 23: smaller game and greater. pay meat an gair, V, 268, 27: clothes and arms? or money? III, 341, 47; 404, 1; IV, 505, 51; 506, 66: business, affair.

geat. See get.

gecks, gien the, II, 105 f., 20, 21: made a fool of. Geck in German, the northern languages and English, fool; in Scottish, according to Jamieson, "sign of derision, gibe, cheat." See gowk.

gee, give. See gie.

gee, gie, IV, 508, 2; V, 238, 22: go. pret. gied, gid, ged. See gae.

geere. See gear.

geet, IV, 494, 37: get, progeny, child.

geid, pret. of gie, give, II, 277, **A** 8. See gied.

gein, p. p. of gie, IV, 316, 18.

geir. See gear.

gell, V, 221, 20 (unnecessarily changed to kell): congeal, freeze. (Aberdonian.)

gellant, gallant. See gallan.

gen, V, 247, 10: given.

gen, gen Pasche, II, 146, 9: against, for, Easter.

general, with the, III, 176, 2: people in general (in public).

genty, I, 421, 10: elegant of form or dress, but here refers to gentleness of disposition.

gep, gip, III, 138, 11; 140, **d** 11=gup, go up, get up (properly, a call to a horse). marry gep, interjection of contempt=marry, come up.

gereamarsey, III, 111, 37: gramercy.

gerss, I, 450, 5; II, 248, 9, 15; 464, 8, 10: grass.

get, IV, 493, 5: gate, road (to the get he 's gane, has gone away). See gate.

get, gett, geat, II, 470, 56-8; V, 238, 13, 24: progeny, brat.

getterne, I, 328, 49: a stringed instrument.

geve, give. See gie.

gey, adv. gey sad, II, 184, 15, 16: pretty, rather. See gay.

ghesting, I, 284, 17, 18: guesting, lodging.

gie, go. See gae.

gie, gi, ge, gee, gae, geve, give. gie, I, 71, 55, 56; 74, 76, 77; 206, 26, 30; 207, 30. gi, I, 68 f., 26, 69, 70; IV, 493, 21. ge, gee, IV, 222, 19; 493, 15; V, 228, 10; 248, 4, 5, 21, 22. *pret.* gae, ga, gaa, gaed, geed, geid, gied. *p. p.* gin, gine, geen, gein, gien, gen, gane, gaen. geve on (like take)=strike, III, 127, 53. gien, II, 232, 13: struck.

gied, gid, ged, *pret.* of gae, gie, go, I, 74, 3; 80, 5; 310, 10, 12, 14; II, 75, 11; 357, 7; III, 434, 27.

gied, geed, geid, *pret.* of gie, give, I, 79 f., 24, 28; 439, 3; II, 408 f., 3, 4; IV, 512 b, 8.

gien, gine, gin, gein, geen, gen, *p. p.* of gie, give: I, 100, 25; 467, 25; IV, 316, 18; 509 a, 13; 510, 16; 513, 12; V, 215, 13; 219, 23; 224, 20; 229, 30; 247, 10; 306 b, 3. V, 219, 23: given (a blow) to.

gieng, II, 61, 3: gang, go.

gier. See gear.

gif, giff=if, I, 70, 16; II, 21 B 10; 28, 3; III, 285, 22.

giff-gaff, I, 21 b, 14: give and take, tit for tat.

gile, III, 482 11: jail.

gill, a steep, narrow glen.

gillan, V, 272 b, 1: gallant. See gallan.

Gilliecrankie, be a, IV, 268, 22: a Gilliecrankie woman, live in Gillecrankie (see 20), be a Highlander. g reads, hae a Killycrankie, that is, a domestic battle, or row.

gillore, III, 136, 34: galore, in plenty.

gilt, III, 370, 10: money.

gimp, I, 387, 1; II, 220, 1, 3: jimp, slender.

gin, gine, ginne, V, 125, 9: a contrivance. specially, the apparatus for fastening a door, I, 107, 4; II, 241, 23; III, 492, 6; IV, 445 f., 3, 4; 446, b 3, 4 ; door and window, IV, 480, 4, 5. chappit (knocked) at the gin, I, 465, 11; IV, 445 f., 3, 4. lift the gin (that is the lever for raising the latch), II, 158, 4; 165, 4, 7, altered to pin, II, 158, 4, in the margin of the MS., and pin stands in 7 of the same piece. Otherwise, chin.

gin, I, 108, B 3, like the gin: corrupt, compare A 4.

gin, II, 23, E 8; 271, 34; 286, 3; IV, 412, 11; 485, 15; V, 243, 17: (of time) against, towards. II, 313, 14; IV, 138, M 1; 166, C 6; 392, 12: by the time that.

gin, *conj.*, I, 5, C 8; 68, 21, 22; 70, 15; 72, 24; 310, 4, 5; 466, 4, 5; 468, 5, 8; 478, 4, 5, 8–10: if.

gin, gine, given.

gine, ginne, *n.* See gin.

gip. See gep.

gird, III, 35, 19: blow, stroke.

girded out, guirded, V, 76, 23; 82, 37: cracked, let.

girdle, I, 403, 12: griddle.

girds, II, 70, 27; IV, 481, 6: hoops.

girn, I, 344, 31: (of a hound) snarl. IV, 69, 18: (of men hanged) grin.

girth was the gold-twist to be, III, 490, 16, see 486 b. girth should probably be graith, but admitting this, the sense is not clear, and further corruption may be suspected. We may understand, perhaps, that after the rescue the mare was to have a caparison of gilded chains. Or we may read, her graith was used the gold-twist to be.

gitter, V, 243, 16: gutter.

giue, II, 442, 7, 10:= gif, if.

gives, II, 448, 26: misgives.

gladdynge, III, 70, 297: gladdening (*cheering* in later texts).

glaive, glaue, IV, 491, 11; V, 235, 32: sword. See **glaue**.

glamer, glamour, glamourie, glaumry, IV, 65, 2; 66, 2; 67, 2; 68, D 2, E 2; 70, F 2, etc.; 367, 8; V, 301, No 200: a charm deluding the eye. IV, 310, 14: glitter, gleam.

glance, III, 394, K 6; 397, 5; IV, 508 a, 8: shine.

glaned, IV, 406, 14: (glant, from glent) glanced, shone.

glar, I, 494, 18: mire.

glashet, I, 434, 36: (O. French, glacer, glachier) darted, flashed.

glasse, III, 340, 32; 344, 30, 31; 349, 31; IV, 504, 36: lantern, ship-light.

glaue, glaive, III, 105, 20: (in this place) a cutting weapon fixed to the end of a pole. See **glaive**.

glaumry. See **glamer**.

glazen, of glass.

gleat (Icelandic glit), I, 100, 28: glitter.

glede, gleed(e), I, 285, 28; 287, 67; 342, 34; III, 308, 14; IV, 379, 14; V, 184, 42: glowing coal. II, 115, 29; 140, 18; V, 27, 46: fire. See **glyde**.

glee (=glue), I, 68, 9, 12: glove.

gleid, gley(e)d, IV, 56, B 3; 58, 3, 4, 9, 10; 135, 23, 24: squint-eyed.

glen, set her on the glen, IV, 284, 25; take her to the glen, 286, 29; set her to the glen, 287, 18: because, the roadways running usually through glens, this amounts to a public exposure.

glent, I, 105 a, 28: glitter, glancing. wi a glent, II, 119, 19; IV, 467, 14: in a flash, a moment (otherwise, in a glent).

glent, III, 307, 6: glanced, went (perhaps, darted).

gley(e)d. See **gleid**.

glided, I, 333, 3: glittered, glinted.

glintin, IV, 450 b, 6: gleaming, flashing.

glister, IV, 510, 5: shine.

gloamin, III, 319, 23: twilight, evening.

gloe, III, 455, 8, 9, 11: glove. See **glee**.

gloom, IV, 94, 9: frown, morose look.

gloom, I, 302, A 11, B 9; 303, C 6; IV, 337, g before 20: frown, look sullen.

glore, II, 319, 13: glory.

glove, cut my glove, etc., II, 105, 18: lovers were wont to cut a glove and each take a part. S. W. will take in his hand the half of his glove which represents Janet and dance for two. T. Davidson. played at the glove, III, 448, 5: some game for braw gallants, unexplained ; possibly, spearing a glove when riding rapidly.

glove tee. See tee.

glowd, glowde, II, 454 f., 54, 58: glided.

glowred, IV, 429, a 15: stared.

glue, II, 147, 12: glove. See **glee, gloe**.

glyde, II, 375, 19: spark. See **glede**.

go, goe, goo, gone, III, 64, 160; 71, 302; 77, 429; 105, 22; 432, 19: walk. go boun away, IV, 224, 15, 16: go, depart. go down, IV, 13, 2, 3; 14, 2: be hanged (cf. **gae down**). goe vppon his death, V, 53, 99: pass upon the question of.

gockies, II, 470, 48: deep wooden dishes.

god, godde, III, 113, 72, 78, 80: property, goods.

God, *omitted*, O save and you may see, III, 181, 19; 184, 16.

God, II, 46, 51; III, 29, 146; 59, 62, 63; 61, 92; 68, 240; 75, 391; 101, 90; 105, 23 (*mood*, wrongly for *my God?*); 359, 103; 444, 16, 17: the second person in the Trinity.

God a marsey, God amercy, God have mercy, III, 111, 39; 138, 22; 149, 41; 445, 30; V, 76, 10; 77, 39; 80, 51, 53; 81, 13; 83, 55: gramercy (not Dieu merci, thank God, which meaning, unlikely in all, is impossible in most of the cases).

God beffore, V, 79, 19: before God (attestation). Cf. *for God*. But perhaps *God before* (*and God before*) is always to be distinguished from *before God*, and to be understood as, God my guide or helper; which sense seems to be required in Shakspere's Henry V, I, II, 307, III, VI, 165; Percy MS., Hales & Furnivall, III, 30, v. 304, 528, v. 57. [So, and God to-forn, in Chaucer, Troilus, I, 1049; II, 431. Cf. also King Edw. and the Shepherd, Hartshorne, Ancient Metrical Tales, p. 47; Peniworth of Witte, Englische Studien, VII, 116, v. 287; Weddynge of Syr Gawen, v. 640, Madden, p. 298ᵉ; etc.]

God's peny, V, 14, 5; 15, 27: an earnest-penny, to bind a bargain.

Godzounds, V, 93, 4, 8, 12, etc.: God's wounds.

gogled, III, 179, 7: joggled, waggled.

golden-knobbed (gloves), II, 133, 6: ornamented with golden balls or tassels. (siller-knapped, 134, 8, 13.)

golett of þe hode, III, 99, 49: throat, part covering the throat.

gon, gone, *infin.* of go, III, 24, 45; 35, 32; 66, 204; 67, 223; 71, 316; 74, 363; 77, 435; 111, 28.

gon, gon gae, I, 333, 3: did go.

gone, *subj.* of gon, go, III, 67, 219.

good, gude, *pret.* of go, III, 464, 4; V, 153, 1.

Good, V, 199 b, 20: **God**.

Good-ben, III, 267, **A** 10. If *ben* is to stand, it must be *benison* abridged. Good benison be here, quoth he, makes a satisfactory line. Compare **B** 9, **D** 9.

good-brother, IV, 168, 9: brother-in-law.

good b'w'ye, III, 134, 6: God be wi you, good-bye.

goodman, III, 274, 33, 35; V, 91, 1, 5, etc.; 98, 2, 3: master of a house.

good-mother, IV, 412, 19: mother-in-law.

good-son, IV, 283, 10: son-in-law.

goodwife, III, 274, 33, 35; V, 91, 2, 6, etc.; **98, 1, 2**: mistress of a house, housewife.

goold, V, 296 a: gold.

gorgett, III, 422, 75: defense for the neck, here a part of a jack.

gorgett, II, 45, 32: a neckerchief. ("Nearly=wimple in Edward I.'s time; in 15th century, neckerchief.")

gorney, journey.

goud = gan, did, IV, 20, 12, 13. (Cf. begoud = began.)

goud, gowd, *n.* and *adj.*, I, 127, 12; 135, 9-12; 351, 35; 429, 28: gold.

gouden, gowden, I, 127, 21, 22; 145, 23: golden.

goudie, goudy, V, 110, 7; 267 b, 10; 268, 19: golden, yellow (locks).

goun-teall. See **gown-tail**.

goupen, I, 356, **D** b after 23: hollow of the hand.

gouernor, I, 286, 40: director, guardian.

gowans, I, 55, **A** 1: daisies.

gowany, I, 315, 12: covered with daisies.

gowd. See **goud**.

gowk, II, 111, 12: (cuckoo), fool. gien me the gowk, made a fool of me. See **gecks**.

gown of green, gien her a, II, 472, 2: defloured. got on the, I, 350, 11: strangely used for to be with child; properly, she got a gown of green eight months before: it can hardly mean, put on a green gown, literally, as at I, 358, 40.

gown-tail, gooun-teall, II, 31, **M** 4; 472, 19; V, 235, 4: lower part of the skirt of a gown.

goy, joy.

graid, great.

graie dogs, III, 7, 1: Scottish hunting dogs, deer dogs, rough greyhounds.

grain, sitt in a graine, I, 210, 5: fork of a tree. III, 267, 21; 269, 14; V, 243, 17: branch of a tree.

graith, *n.*, IV, 86, 8: equipment (horse and arms).

graith, *v.*, V, 192, 34; 198 b, 34: make ready. *p. p.* graithed, IV, 2, 5; 27, 26: equipped in defensive armor. golden graithed behin, II, 191, 18; gowdengraithd before and siller-shod behind, II, 343, 4; shod wi silver afore an gold graithed behind, II, 194, 16, 20: properly, harnessed, but as the horse is silver-shod before and gold behind, 183, 16; 185, 23; V, 224, 14, shod seems to be meant here. So in the patched-up ballad IV, 410, 18. The horse silver-shod before and gold-shod behind is a commonplace; see II, 266, 1; 267, 1.

graithing (gowd), IV, 410, 18: harness or caparison, behind horse. But see **graith**, *v.*

grammarye, grammeree, V, 294 b, 2: grammar, learning. II, 53, 36, 41; 54, 55; 55, 68: magic. Gramery= grammar, learning, occurs three times in the Towneley Mysteries, but strangely enough seems not to have been heard of in the sense of magic till we come to Percy's Reliques. Percy suggests that the word is probably a corruption of the French *grimoire*, a conjuring book. Grimoire, however, does not appear until the 16th century and was preceded by gramoire (Littré). Gramaire in the 13th–15th centuries has the sense of magic: see the history of grimoire in Littré. Godefroi interprets gramaire savant, magicien.

grandmother over, IV, 70, **G** 2: corruption of, glamer, oer her.

grange-house, III, 360, 116: farm-house.

grat, II, 70, 25; 323, 26, 27; IV, 7, 35; V, 156, 11, 13, *pret.* of greet, weep.

gravat, II, 283, 21; V, 240, 14: cravat.

graveld green, II, 158, 1: a green with gravel walks ? Probably corrupt: in yonder green, **B**, garden green **G**.

gravil, I, 350, 18, 19 (pile o the gravil): expounded by Donaldson, Supplement to Jamieson, p. 304, as " the plant graymill or gromwell, of the genus *Lithospermum*, anciently used in the cure of gravel, hence its name. Said to be used also in producing abortion." I fear this is somewhat conjectural or even arbitrary. The pile seems to be simply some downy plant (velvety moss) which grows on stones; indeed we are expressly told this, IV, 456, 9, 12 : ' a flower, it grows on gravel greay,' ' the pile that grows on gravel green.' (We have gravel green and gravel grey in the ordinary sense again, I, 347, 1.)

greaf, grave.

greahondes, grehoundis, greyhounds.

great, I, 252, 3, 5: groat.

great, IV, 373, 15; V, 176, 16: intimate, high in favor.

grece, harte of, III, 27, 105: a fat hart.

gree, III, 61, 108 (made the gree) : paid my dues. (make gre in Old English, to discharge obligation; Old Fr. gre, gret, from gratum.)

gree, from them take the gree, IV, 248, 16: prize, superiority. (Lat. gradus.)

greecy (ghost), II, 390, 27: frightful (grisly).

greeme, I, 69, 51 : (groom) young fellow. See grome.

greet, greit, I, 186, **B** 3; 359, 1, 2; 448 f., **B** 1, 5; II, 77, 30; III, 384, 4; 387, 6; 391, 5; V, 36, **C** 3: weep, cry. *pret.* grat.

greete, III, 105, 26: grit, gravel, sand.

greeter, V, 183, 17: weeper.

greeting, weeping.

grefe, III, 69, 268; 83, 268: 87, 268: offence, displeasure. a-grefe, III, 69, 268: in displeasure.

grehoundis, greyhounds.

greit, greet, weep, cry.

grenner, *compar.*, V, 283, 9, 19: greener.

gret, *pret.* of greet, address, III, 111, 40.

grett wurdes, III, 297, 31: high, haughty words.

grevis, III, 307, 6: groves. See grief.

grew, grow.

grew, V, 113 b, 7: greyhound. See next word.

grew hound, grew(e)hund, I, 328, 47; II, 70, 24; 79, 37: Dr. J. A. H. Murray says Greek hound; " still called in Scotland a grewe, which was the older Scotch for Greek." Grew=Greek is well known in Middle English, and *greyhound* (Icelandic greyhundr) may have been changed to *grewhound* under its influence.

grey (meal), oat-meal and grey, II, 462, 30: barley-(bere-) meal, as distinguished from oat-meal (=white meal).

grief, V, 151, **F** 1: grove. (tier *should be* tree.) See grevis.

grien, III, 397, **Q** 2: yearn, long.

griesly, grisly, grizly, I, 298, 4: 300 a; V, 234 b, 31: frightful.

grievd, *pret.*, III, 162, 58: injured.

grimlie, grimly, II, 45, 19, 31; 199 a; 201, 7: grim, terrible.

grind, II, 216 f., 4, 27, 29: an apparent corruption for *graith, graithed*, accoutre, adorn. Cf. II, 191, 18; 194, 16, and many other places.

grinding, I, 130, 1; 134, **O** 1: this word of the refrain may be suggested by the mill.

grips, IV, 53, 13: clutches, fastenings. See signots.

grisel, grissell, III, 369, 20, 23: gray horse.

grisly, II, 397, **A** 30: terrible. See griesly.

grit, grite, gryte, IV, 312, 9; 445, b 1: great.

grit oats, IV, 20, 14: great, or improved oats as distinguished from the sma corn or oats of the early part of the century.

grith, III, 101, 86, 87: (peace) remission of hostility, " charter of peace." neither grith nor grace, 358, 65.

grizly, IV, 398, 21: frightful. See griesly.

grome, groom, greem, I, 75, 40; 77, 20; 342, 40; 345, 38; 355, 52; 371, 3; III, 56, 4; 67, 224: man, young fellow.

gross, II, 267, 13; 268, 18: big, burly.

ground, the grounds o my pouches, V, 306, 9: bottoms (V, 165, 6 has, the boddoms of my pakets).

ground-wa-stane, III, 433, 12, 13 : foundation-stone. (A. S. grundweall, fundamentum.)

growende, ground.

grumly (A. S. gramlíc, gromlíc), (of the sea) II, 22, 10: furious. (of a seal) II, 494, 2 : fierce-looking. (Jamieson: muddy, turbid.)

grun, ground.

gryming, IV, 6, 7; V, 249, 7: sprinkling, thin covering.

grype, II, 45, 19, 31: griffon (also vulture).

grysely, III, 298, 60: frightfully.

gryte, great: I, 127, 22. See grit.

gude, gued=God, II, 94, 17; V, 221, 24.

gude, guid, gueed, good.

gude, good, *pret.* of go, III, 464, 4; V, 153, 1.

gude father, gude faythir, I, 301, 1; 302, 1; 303, **C** 1: father-in-law.

gudemother, II, 284, 10: mother-in-law.

gude neighbours, I, 352, 8: euphemism for fairies.

gudeson, guidson, II, 463, 20; IV, 309, 3; 310, 6: stepson, son-in-law. wrongly used of an own son, II, 219, 9.

gued, gueed(e), I, 68, 10, 14; V, 221, 24: good.

gued, God. See gude.

guid, good.

guide, gyde, n., I, 101, 9; 102, 7; IV, 174, 19; 425, 5: one who has charge, etc., custodian. I shal be þe munkis gyde: III, 98, 35: take charge of him. death is her guide, II, 191, 29: has her in hand. this sword shall be thy guide, V, 49, 28: shall settle thy case. IV, 309, 2: escort, convoy.

guide, v., I, 481, 44; II, 152, **I** 2; III, 459, 21: treat, use.

guiding, gude, I, 303, **C** 3: thrifty management.

guidson. See **gudeson.**

guildery, guildery maids, V, 301 b, 5 : guildry is Scottish for guild, but this makes small sense here.

guilt, all of guilt, II, 46, 43: of gilding or gilt metal, all begilt.

guirded, V, 77, a b 23. See **girded.**

gull, III, 217, 44: a fool.

gunies, guineas.

gurious, II, 380, 31: (same as gruous, grugous) grim, grisly (or, ugly).

gurly, (sea) II, 26, 14; IV, 366, 7: grim, surly, growling. gurrl(e)y fellow, IV, 489, 24, 25: gruff, surly.

gutter-hole, I, 164, **K** 3: the place where filth from the kitchen is thrown.

gyde, be þe munkis, III, 98, 35: take charge of the monk. See **guide.**

gyff, gif, if.

gyll, II, 478, 4: opprobrious term for woman, here referring to levity.

gyrde, *pret.,* III, 66, 211: girt.

gyst, III, 13, 10: gettest.

ȝare, III, 98, 24: ready. See **yare.**

ȝates, ȝatis, III, 99, 61, 62: gates. See **yate.**

ȝe, V, 283, 1: ye.

ȝe, III, 97, 6: yea.

ȝede, III, 99, 60: went. See **yede.**

ȝelpe, III, 14, 16, 17: brag.

ȝeluer, *compar.,* V, 283, 11, 21: yellower.

ȝeman, ȝoman, III, 99, 58; 100, 74; 101, 86, 87: yeoman.

ȝete, III, 100, 82: ate.

ȝeue, III, 13, 12, 14: give. ȝouyn, 14: given.

ȝone, I, 327, 11, 12; 328, 38–44; III, 13, 1: yon.

ȝowe, I, 328, 53: you.

H

ha, hae, hay, I, 299, 7, 9, 11; 330, **A** 6, **B** 6; 331, **C** 3, 6; **D** 6; 332, **F** 5; II, 74, **E** 6; 145, 27; V, 215, 9; 219, 20, 21; 221, 16, 22: have. See **haed, haet.**

ha, hall, I, 101, 14; 133, **M** 1; II, 371, 8; 387, 13; IV, 84, 5; V, 209 a, the last 2: house, manor-house. hall, IV, 513 b, 1, 2; V, 247, 1, 2, must be hold, as in other versions; but in IV, 514, 15, 16, would be house, unless an error for *hale,* whole.

haad, *v.,* II, 338, **R** 11: hold. See **haud.**

hachebord, hatchbord, III, 340, 36; 342, 70: would most naturally be interpreted gunwale, or side of the ship, and so archborde, 340, 23. But in 36 Sir Andrew lies at the hache-bord (which is hached with gold), and stern would be a better meaning for hachebord in that place, the high stern of the old ship being a conspicuous place for a captain to lie. See **archborde.** Barton lies a larborde in the York copy, IV, 504, 38, which is quite loose.

hached, the hache-bord is hached with gold, III, 340, 36: gilt (possibly inlaid).

haches, hatches, III, 341, 54, 57: deck, properly a frame of crossbars laid over an opening in a ship's deck. (Skeat.)

had, *ellipsis of,* V, 274, 10, [had] rather [have] wedded, and [have] tralled, I [had] rader.

had, haad=hold. See **haud.**

hadden, *p. p.,* I, 402, 4, 6: held.

hadno, had not.

hads, hads slaine, III, 358, 61: the s in hads is perhaps caught from slaine. Other readings are had, hadeste.

hae, have. See **ha.**

hae, II, 97, 18: correct to *has;* cf. drees, 17.

haed, II, 110, 33: had.

haely. See **haly.**

haet, hayt, haȝt, I, 415 b; III, 109, 5; 110, 20; 111, 41; 113, 78: hath.

hafe-gate. See **half-gate.**

hagg-worm, II, 503 : a monstrous snake.

haghty, V, 219, 21: haughty.

ha-house, manor-house.

haik ye up, IV, 219, 13: keep you in suspense (from hake, a frame on which fish are hung to be dried (?), or, haik, to drag up and down to little purpose (Jamieson), "bear in hand," delude with false hopes?

hail, III, 163, 77: whole, wholly. See **hale.**

hail, II, 151, **H** 1; 256, **K** 5: conceal. See **heal.**

hailing (Old Eng. halen=Germ. ziehen, draw, move), denoting rapid motion, driving, rushing. wind come hailing, II, 22, 9. ship come hailing, IV, 402, 15, 25. went hailing to the door, hailing ben the floor, hailing through the closs, IV, 422 f, 11, 15, 18; V, 279 a, No 257, 11. Of tears and blood falling fast, tears came hailing down, II, 407, 14; drops o blude came hailing to the groun, II, 418, 31. See **halling.**

hailing at the ba', II, 269, 8: playing foot-ball. Hail the ba is specifically drive the ball to or beyond goal.

haill. See **hale.**

hailsed, I, 333, 2: greeted.

hain, II, 92, 17, strong participle of have (haven), wald hain=would (have) had.

haind grass, II, 465, 7 (spared, preserved): grass kept from cutting or pasturing.

hair, hire.

haisling, IV, 46, **B** 9, come haisling to the town; cf. hailing, proceeding. (Perhaps miswritten; Hill Burton's hand is not always careful.)

halch, halch vpon, I, 294, 18, 20; III, 419 f., 7, 37: salute, bestow a salutation on.

hald. See **hauld,** hold.

hale, haill, hail, haylle, hell, II, 28, 23; 80, 15; III, 296, 23; IV, 379, 11; 380, 20; 381, 8; 382, 13; V, 276, 14, 15: whole, in sound condition. III, 163, 77; 299, 3: wholly.

Haleigh, as he was walking the Haleigh throw, I, 76, **E** 6: ha-lee, the lea of the hall ?

halfendell, III, 75, 382: the half part.

half-gate, hafe-gate, II, 313, 14, 16: half-way.

halke, III, 74, 366: corner, hiding-place.

hall, house, manor-house. See **ha.**

hall, either in archbord or in hall, he wold ouercome you, III, 340, 29: hull?

hall, hold. See hauld.

hall, IV, 514, 15, 16: perhaps written for hale; in any case meaning whole.

hallan, V, 99, 2: in cottages a wall between the fire-place and the door, to shelter from the air (extending only as far as is thought requisite for that purpose).

halld. See hauld.

hallë, V, 236, 23: hollo! or, perhaps, simply halle= hail.

halled, V, 270, 11: hailed, saluted.

halleen, V, 197, 9: holly. See hollen.

halling, come halling to the town, V, 277 f., 15, 25. See hailing.

hallow, haly, II, 175, 16; 239, 1: holy.

hallow, good hallow, II, 270, 10: a form of salutation; perhaps, God hallow, sanctify, cleanse us from sin! perhaps simply an elliptical Good saint! I have not met the phrase elsewhere, and it seems no longer to be familiar in Scotland.

Hallowday, I, 342, 25; 507, 1; III, 246, E 1: saints' day, All Saints.

hallow seat, I, 367, 7: a saint's place.

hals-bane, hass-bane, hause-bane, hase-bane, I, 394, 8: neck-bone.

halse, I, 327, 10: neck. See hause.

haly, haely, hallow, II, 104, 22; 175, 16; 179, 13; 239, 1; 417, 13; III, 262, 5: holy.

halycon, come halycon to the town, III, 434, E 3: in a rollicking, or a boisterous, turbulent way. North Eng. hallacking, making merry; Scottish hallach, hallokit, crazy.

halyde, hauled.

hame, bring hame, bear a child. See bring.

hame, home, came, IV, 405, 54; 420, 5: was born.

hame, gae hame, III, 398, A c after 3: that is, to the heaven where you belong. seek your lover hame, IV, 174, 11: go for and bring.

hame-gaun, I, 72 f., 11, 66: home-going (to go home).

hamesucken, IV, 244 b: invasion of a private house.

hand, att hand of, III, 278, 30: nearly, about; cf. Old Eng. nearhand. (stroke) behind his hand, II, 63, 24: seems to be intended for backhanded.

hand for hand, III, 465, 34; 466, 48: in a fair match? (hand to hand, 468, 48.)

hand, lokyde at his hand, III, 307, 10: probably, shading his eyes with his hand; possibly, looked aside. Cf. lookit aneath (below) the sun, III, 5, D 7; 6, 6; 8, 6.

hand, on the upper, II, 245, 29: side, uppermost (see II, 247, 32; 254, 22).

hand, out of, III, 440, 25: forthwith? (The line seems to be corrupted; without resource, unable to help themselves, hors de combat, would give an easier sense if allowable.) Should we read: as many as was, out of hand?

hand-write, III, 455, 8, 9, 11; V, 300, 10, 16, 19: hand-writing.

hang, pret. of hing, to hang, I, 327, 23 (hange); 448, 5; 451, 9; II, 154, 11; 172, 34; IV, 465, 38.

hang down, III, 483, D 9: unintelligible to me, whether hang or gang. ding down? (drown my mare and thee, III, 492, 26; 493, 15.)

hanging well, III, 440, 17: draw-well of which the bucket is raised and lowered by a pole or beam turning on an upright post? By some understood as, a well near the place of execution.

hankit, I, 224, J 2, 8: tied tight.

hansell, haffe hansell for the mare, III, 111, 32: have a present, the more you buy? have the first purchase (which was thought lucky) for the larger part (of the ware)? (Doubtful.) III, 284, 10: reward. V, 112, B b 9: used in Galloway of a piece of bread given before breakfast (Jamieson); here apparently of a draught of ale given early in the morning.

hantle, II, 337, 11: a large number.

hap, happing, cover, coverlet: IV, 65, 7; 258 f., 5, 20.

hap, v., I, 15, 18; 299, 5; IV, 233, 2: cover, wrap.

hap, v., IV, 483 b, after 12: hop.

happer, hopper.

happing. See hap.

harbengers, III, 198, 2: harbingers, officers who preceded the king in a progress to provide accommodation for the court.

harl, harl her thro the lin, I, 303, D 4: drag. See haurld.

harme, III, 357, 50: sorrow.

harnessed (men), III, 62, 133: equipped.

harns, V, 201, note ‡: brains. harn-pan, brain-pan, skull.

harried, haryed, pret. and p. p., III, 295, 4, 6; 296, 12; IV, 6, 9, 14, etc.; V, 250, 9, 13: plundered. See herry.

harte of gre(e)ce, III, 27, 105; 124, 3, 4: a fat hart.

hartinge, IV, 504, 31: encouragement.

hart-roote, II, 241, 27: (Icel. hjarta-rœtr, pl., Old Eng. heorte rotes, heart-roots, -strings) term of affection.

has be, I, 86, 24: as if for future (see s, us, etc.); but shall in 7, 16, and sall in b.

hase, halls.

hase, hass, neck, throat. See hause.

hase-bane, hass-bane. See hause-bane.

hast, V, 78, 12: am in haste (as well as þow hast, hastest).

hastëly, hastilye, III, 74, 376; 75, 392; 405, 20: immediately, soon, promptly.

hat, pret. of hit, I, 299, 5; III, 350, 50.

hatches=deck: III, 335 b; IV, 505, 57. See haches.

hather, III, 424 b; 425 a: heather.

haud, had, hawd, haad, howd, I, 21 b, 3, 4; 74, 75; 341, 12; 354, 17; 421, 4, 8, 11; II, 70, 17; 74, D 7; 463, 24, 25; III, 491, 9; V, 296, 1, etc.; 304 b, 3: hold, keep. pret. had, II, 371, 7. p. p. hadden, I, 402, 6; hauden, II, 161, 7.

haud me unthought lang, IV, 260, 10: keep me without the time seeming long, interested, entertained.

haugh, low ground, properly on the border of a river:

III, 9, **G** 10; 483, 5; IV, 3, 17; 77, 3; 273, **C** 7; V, 250, 20, 21.

hauld, hald, halld, hall, hold, III, 281, 1; 371, 33; 433, 1, 2; 434, 1, 2; 436, 1; IV, 513 b, 1, 2; V, 247, 1, 2: place of shelter, stronghold, quarters. See **hold.**

hauld, I, 359, 9, gang by the: walk by taking hold of things. gang by haulds, III, 162, 46.

hauping, II, 463, 16: hopping, hobbling.

haurld=harld, V, 99, **C** 5: dragged.

hause, hase, hass, halse, I, 149, **H** 1; 327, 10; II, 165, 22; 319, 3; 366, 38; III, 163, 75; V, 184, 44: neck, throat.

hause-bane, hase-bane, hass-bane, hals-bane, I, 394, 8; 395, **B** 3; II, 146, 14; 147, 15; IV, 165, 15; 447 b, after 13; 448 a, 2d stanza; V, 204 b: neck-bone.

have, *ellipsis of.* would been, I, 169, 7. I wad taen, I, 356, 54, 55. shuld I slain, II, 169, 7. ye widna kept, III, 390, 10. I woud not swum, III, 489, 42. I should, might, enjoyd, IV, 135, 23; 137, 32. he woud guarded me, IV, 148, 55. they taen, IV, 221, **D** 7. as muckle as wald bocht, IV, 386, 18. I seen 't, IV, 465, 31. euer I seene, V, 53, 105. seem[d] to worn, V, 55, 26. he 'll learned, V, 196, 53. had rather lost, V, 302, 17.

have=proceed, go. have in (to water), have over, III, 128, 76, 77.

have=provide or procure that a thing is done. hae me hame, II, 82, 54; hae me to the town, II, 122 f., 4, 28: take.

have in, had him in, II, 216, 8: had him in my possession (Germ. innehaben)?

have (on the skynne), III, 127, 60: get a blow.

haw, green haw sea, II, 28, 21; IV, 379, 10, 14; 380, 19: bluish. "azure; pale, wan;" Jamieson. (A. S. hæwen, glaucus, caeruleus. Old Eng. hawe, haa.) green raw sea, II, 30, 6, is a corruption; I have been lately informed that the singer ordinarily gave haw. In haw bayberry kame, IV, 471 f., 2, 4, there is again corruption; as in the same passage of other versions.

hawd. See **haud.**

hay, II, 160, 18: for hae, has.

hay, went forth to view the hay, IV, 233, 1; 238, 1: to see how the hay was coming on, as a way of taking the air.

hay, IV, 225, 15; V, 261 a, No 221, **G** 22; hays, 16: in Maidment's text, *lea, leas,* probably right, hays making no reasonable sense.

haylle, III, 296, 23: whole, entire. See **hale.**

hayt, ha3t, I, 415 b; III, 109, 5; 111, 41; 113, 78: hath. See **haet.**

he, him, she, her, with proper names (almost always him, her): like Icelandic hann, hón (hún) ("so frequent in modern conversational usage that a person is scarcely ever named without the pronoun," Vigfusson.) out and spak he Sweet Willie, II, 108, 19; 185, 33. sighing said he Love Robbie, 370, 8. up and raise he Sweet Willie, 108, 15. up and raise he the bridegroom, 108, 13. up and stands she Fair Annie, 189, 32. whare it is him Sir Colin, 61, 1; so

147, 16. out it speaks him Young Bondwell, I, 479, 41; so II, 418, 25; 419, 37, 53. sighing says him Brown Robyn, II, 371, 8, 9. leugh him Childe Vyet, 134, 21. out it spake her Dow Isbel, II, 97, 21; so 418, 34. out spoke her Lady Frendraught, IV, 44, 12. out waked her May Meggie, 188, 14. it was her May Catheren, II, 145, 25. sighan says her Susë Pay, V, 219, 17. Etc., etc. Cf. Chaucer in, he Iakke Straw, he Theodomar, he Pluto,=perhaps, ille; but not, him Arcite, Knight's Tale, 352, 475.) with the objective case: as, sought her Lady Maisry, II, 114, 3, 4, 10; 154, 11, 24, 26, 27; 370, 18; etc. (Him, her, with verbs of motion may possibly be a relic of the old use of a dative, and such cases are not included.)

he, I, 242, 12; III, 13, 4, 8: they.

he, hee, III, 307, 4: high.

header, heather.

heal, healle, hail, I, 453, 9; II, 145, 26; 146, 9, 10; 154, 13, 14; 155, 37: conceal.

healy, hooly, *adj.,* gentle.

healy, heely, hooly, slowly, gently: II, 94, 15; 110, 22, 23.

heans, hens.

heard, V, 253 f., No 203, **D** 2, 8: hired.

hearten, IV, 444, 32: encourage.

heathen (child), II, 246, 13: unbaptized.

heathennest, I, 284, 15: heathendom.

heather-cow(e), I, 302, **A** 9; 304, **E** 8, **F** 8; 305, 14; V, 173, 8; 174, **C** 2; 213, 8; heather-crow, I, 301, note *: tuft or twig of heather.

heather-knaps, V, 173, 8: heather hillocks, knolls.

hech and how, III, 392, 13: to utter these interjections of grief.

heckle, IV, 247, 12; 248, 17: hackle, flax-comb (board set with sharp steel spikes).

hecks, IV, 319, **I,** 5: racks.

hee. See **he.**

heely, II, 220, 21: slowly. See **healy.**

heer, heir, heire, I, 301, 3; 303, **C** 3; 304, **E** 2: the sixth part of a hank of yarn, 240 threads.

hegehen, I, 333, 3: eyen, eyes.

heght, IV, 179, **A** 1: promised.

heigh a ween, and Oh a ween! interjections of grief, II, 504, 27. a ween is probably I ween.

height, heihte, hight, hith, heiste, hette, I, 244, 10; IV, 503, 11, 14; V, 288, 18: was, is, called.

heir, heire. See **heer.**

heiste. See **height.**

hele=heal, conceal.

hell=whole, staunch, tight, V, 276, 14, 15. See **hale.**

hell, heel.

helt, IV, 457, 22: *pret.* of hile: hailed.

heme, III, 434, 27, 28: home.

hempten, V, 87, 11: hempen.

hend, hendë, heynd, hind, hindy, III, 57, 25: noble, gracious. lady hende, of the Virgin, III, 68, 251. hend soldan, II, 59, 36, 37: noble, of rank. III, 110, 27; V, 49, 12: friendly, kindly. I, 71, 41 (?); 329, 57: fine-looking. III, 98, 41: civil. See **hind.**

hende, I, 71, 41 (gallant hende): hind, young fellow ? The adjective, of noble rank, courteous, kindly, is less likely.

hent, III, 110, 14; 123, 8, 10: caught, took.

hepe, III, 66, 204: hip (as II, 273, 35), berry of the wild rose.

herbere, I, 327, 32: garden.

herkeneth, herkens, *imperative plural,* III, 81, 317; 109, 2.

herowed, herowed hell, III, 25, 63: harried, despoiled. See **harried, herry.**

herry, II, 261, 7; III, 473, 23; IV, 26, 2: harry, pillage, rob. See **harried.**

hersed, V, 156, 15: rehearsed, repeated praise of ?

hership, IV, 41, note *: plundering.

he se. See **-s** as sign of future.

het, eat.

het, hot.

hethyne, I, 329, 58: hence.

hett, I, 271, 5: bid.

hette, I, 224, 10: is called. See **height.**

heuch, heugh, I, 312, 13; II, 503 f., 11, 15, 28; IV, 231, I 15: steep hill or bank, glen with steep overhanging sides.

heved, I, 243, 7; III, 70, 290 (?): head.

hewene, V, 283, 15: heaven.

hey, I, 438, B 1: interjection of pleasure, displeasure, pain, excitation. (Not the dance which is called the hay.)

heye, III, 482, 21: hie.

heyer, hyer, *compar.,* V, 283, 5, 15: higher.

heynd, III, 110, 27: friendly, kindly. See **hend, hind.**

heyng, *pret.* of hang, V, 78, 4.

heyt war howte! III, 111, 28: heyt! is a well-known call to horses, as in Chaucer (get up!), and war-oute is a term used in driving, according to Halliwell's Dictionary.

hi, I hi, III, 349, 46: have. I hinna, II, 469, 28: have not.

hich, high.

hide, II, 467, 44, 50: should probably be heed, as written by Motherwell.

hie, hye, *n.,* I, 328, 37; II, 164, 9, 12; III, 99, 50: haste.

hie, she smiled hie, V, 51, 55: with a smile not confined to her mouth, but mounting higher.

hiean, II, 147, 2: hying.

hiesed, IV, 424, b 7, 8: hoised, lifted, dragged.

high-gate, V, 239, O 4: high-road.

highman, I, 203, C 16, 17. In a 16, the reading is hymen, which is in itself plausible, but not balladlike. If highman is right, the meaning would seem to be, the chief man of the occasion, the bridegroom.

hight, III, 441, 30: is, was, called. See **height.**

hight, III, 309, 34: I promise. *pret.* heght, hight, III, 407, 17.

hile, *v.,* IV, 456, 17: hail. *pret.* helt, 457, 22.

hill-gate, IV, 249, F 4: hill-road.

hilt, V, 76, 21: flayed.

him. him, hym come, I, 244, 10, 13, 17; up stod him, 15, 16: dative of subject after verb of motion. stert hym, III, 62, 120. wente hym, III, 62, 126. rade him, IV, 2, 5. ar the coc him crowe, I, 244, 18.

hin-chill, V, 278, 33. See **hind-chiel.**

hinchman, III, 320, A b 16: henchman, servant (man who stands at the hinch, haunch).

hind, hinde, hindy, hynde, *adj.,* courteous, gracious, gentle, kindly: I, 430, 5, 9; II, 177 f., 20, 35; III, 310, 52; 358, 69. See **hend.**

hind, hynde, *n.* (A. S. hína, O. Eng. hine, servant), youth, chiel, callant, seems often to be used as an epithet = young (but this may possibly be hind = kindly courteous, etc., in some cases). Hynde Etin, I, 369 f., 3, 5, etc. (called Young Akin in A 367, 6, etc., Young Hastings the groom in C, 371, 3). Hind Henry, II, 305 f., 6, 18, etc.; Hynde Henry, II, 306 f., 6, 8, etc. hind-chiel, hin-chill, hynd-chiel, I, 367, 3; II, 83, after 38; IV, 432, 15; V, 278, 33. hind-greeme, I, 69, 51. hind-squire, I, 452, C 10; 453, 7; hynde squire, V, 25 f., 2, 13, 19, etc. hine-squar, V, 278, 29 (called young squar in 18). In all three, both parts signify young fellow.

hind, gane hind away, II, 248, 5 = hyne away, far away.

hindy. See **hind.**

hing, II, 194, 22, 27; 239, 6; III, 299, 6; V, 226, 4: hang. *pret.* hang, hanget. *p. p.* hanged, hangit.

hingers, V, 40, 4: hangings.

hinna, I hinna will, II, 469, 28: I have not will, I wish it may not.

hinnie, hinny, honey, IV, 66, 15; 69, 15; 70, 12; 72, I 5: term of affection.

hinnie-mark, honey-mark, IV, 479, 7: mole ? (cf. Germ. honigflecken, yellow spot.)

hinny-drap, II, 283, 5: mole ? = hinnie-mark.

hire, a year's hire, II, 191, 20: rent, revenue.

hirewoman, IV, 202, J 3: female servant. hired your han, IV, 240, 14, if right, must mean, she would have paid you to do it. Other copies, kissed.

hirn, I, 334, 9: corner.

hirpling, II, 474, 8; 476, 3: halting.

hisn, V, 293, 14: his.

hith, I, 334, 7: hight, am called. See **height.**

ho, who.

hochis, III, 306 b, note *: hocks.

hoe, IV, 19, 7: (as a singular of hose) stocking.

hoes, IV, 486, 7, 8: as plural of hoe (?).

hog, II, 258, 32; IV, 325, 6, 7; 328, 3, 4; 332, 13; 469, 10, 12: young sheep that has not yet lost a fleece.

hog-rubber, IV, 208 a : (seemingly) a fellow employed to rub down hogs, or fit for such business.

hoised, hoisd, hoist, I, 206 f., 9, 11; IV, 248, 2, 5; V, 132, 7, *pret.* of hoise, heave, lift, drag.

hoky-gren (burnt like), II, 145, A 27: hoakie, "a fire that has been covered up with cinders, when all the fuel has become red." Jamieson. A branch or stem in such a fire ? or good to make such a fire with ? Scott has, hollins grene.

hold, holde, hauld, II, 216 f., 4, 27, 29; III, 358, 74; 430, 1; 435, 1: housing, quarters, place of shelter, lodging. thirty horsses in one hold, II, 444, 59: perhaps place of keeping (450, 64, in one close). See hauld.

hold, holde, v., III, 97, 11; 176, 5, 6: wager.

holde, III, 61, 93, 107: retain (legally).

hole-house, I, 305, 3; V, 213, 3: said in depreciation of an humble sort of house (hole of a house), as a divot-house, a turf-cottage. (Still in use. W. Walker.)

hollan, hollin, holland, linen.

Hollan, Hollans, boats, I, 467, 18, 22: Dutch boats. Dutch fishing-luggers are to be seen in great numbers on the Scottish coast in summer.

hollan, holland, of holly. hollan dyke, II, 195, 32: wall planted on the top with holly.

hollen, hollin, I, 294 f., 15, 27; II, 153, 29; V, 191 f., 3, 18: holly. (Perhaps hollin's, V, 194, 2, should be hollins.)

hollie, V, 111, 16: (slowly) softly. See hooly.

hollin, holland.

holm, holme, houm, howm, III, 460, 38; 488 f., 31, 34, 41; IV, 522, 4, 10: low ground on a river-bank.

holpe, pret. of help, III, 342, 76. See hope.

holtes, III, 296, 14; 357, 53: woods.

holydame, by my, III, 209, 7: halidom. Originally halidom in oaths meant reliques of saints ; my halidom seems to be used in the sense of sacred oath. (Printed holy dame in three copies, and very likely often so understood.)

hom, V, 304 b, 2, 4: home.

hom, III, 308, 26: them.

home, hame, came, IV, 405, 54; 420, 5; was born. See bring hame.

hondert, hondreth, hondrith, hundred.

honey, term of endearment. See hinny.

honey-mark, II, 282, 12: mole ? See hinnie-mark, hinny-drap.

honey month, she has turned the honey month about, to see if he was coming, IV, 320, J 2: inexplicable.

hongyr, V, 283, 16: hunger.

honour's gate, II, 163, 21: (honour, a manor, the mansion-house of a manor) an imposing gate, such as would be put at the principal entrance to a mansion-house. W. Macmath.

hooding. See huddin.

hook, IV, 19 f., C 3, 8: loop.

hook-tooth, I, 18, F 9: tooth of a sickle with serrated edge.

hooly, adj., II, 107, 9: slow, gentle.

hooly, hoolie, hollie, huly, adv., slowly, softly: I, 451, 12; II, 108, 10; 111, 10; III, 393, 14. See healy.

hope, houp, IV, 25, 4; 27, 12; 184, 2, 3: "a deep and pretty wide glen among hills." Jamieson.

hope, pret., V, 103, A c 14: holp, helped. See holpe.

hope, I, 327, 12; 449, 17; II, 311, 6; V, 54, 3: expect, think.

hore, hoar, gray. grenë wode hore, holtes hore, III, 65, 176; 357, 53: gray as to trunks.

horne and lease, III, 360, 113. See Pegge, Archæologia, III, 1, 1775, "Of the horn as a charter or instrument of conveyance." Professor Gross, of Harvard College, has favored me with the following case: "Pro quo officio [i. e. coroner and escheator of the Honor of Tutbury] nullas evidentias, carta vel alia scripta, proferre possit nisi tantum cornu venatorium." The possession of this horn still conveys the right to hold the office. Cf. J. C. Cox, Three Centuries of Derbyshire Annals, London, 1890, I, 73–79.

horse-brat, I, 302, B 10: horse-cloth (horse's sheet, horse-sheet, of A 13, F 4).

hose, I, 285, 38: embrace, hug (halse, Scottish hawse).

hosen, hose, III, 65, 193: stockings (not breeches; see 196).

hosens, IV, 257, 3: stockings without feet.

hostage, III, 271, F 10; hostage-house, 4, 5, 8, 9: inn.

hosteler-ha, III, 270, E 3, 4, 5, 7: inn.

hostess-house (=hostage-house), IV, 175, N 4: inn.

hostler, III, 266 f., 4, 6, 9, 10; V, 153 f., A 3, 4, B 3–5; 156 b, B: innkeeper.

hostler-wife, IV, 508 1; V, 154, 3: woman keeping an inn.

houk, V, 218, 5: dig. Pret. and p. p. houked, houket, houkit, howket, etc., I, 184, 9; 220, A 2, B 4, C 4; 221 f., E 7, 17; III, 500 b, 8; IV, 451 a, 3, 5; V, 210, 9.

houl, III, 247, 5: hold.

houm, howm, holm, I, 394, 14; III, 370, 5; IV, 168, E 2, 5, 7, 8, 11, 12; 523, 3, 5: level low ground on a river-bank.

hound, IV, 19, 4; 20, 9: chase, drive.

houp, hope, IV, 2, 13: (A. S. hóp) sloping hollow between two hills.

hour, whore.

house, V, 273, No 237, 20: hose.

housen, II, 3, 10; 5 b, 2: house (sing.).

house-end, -en, I, 254, b 1, c 1: gable.

housle, houzle, II, 46, 46; III, 330, 13: give the sacrament.

houzle, III, 105, 22, 23: communion.

hove, hove hole, I, 304, F 2: a hole which one haunts or lives in.

hoved, III, 296, 20: hung about, tarried.

hoved on, III, 358, 69: moved on (hied, 362, 69).

hoves, V, 227, 4: hoofs.

how, how soon, III, 450 a: so soon as.

how, howe, n., III, 164, b 49; 316 a, last line; IV, 110, 10; 303, 7: hollow, sometimes, plain.

how, adj., IV, 476 a, 4: hollow.

how, III, 392, 11, 13 (as verb): exclamation of grief.

howbeit, III, 450 a: although.

howd, hold. See haud.

howded, V, 124, C 15: swung.

howk, howked, etc. See houk.

howm. See houm.

howre, V, 78, 5, 6; 79, 28, 33, 35; 80, 37: our.

howther o dirt, II, 184, 13: a mass of dirt.

howyn, own.

hoyse, hoise, II, 26, 8: hoist.

huddin, hooding (hud, hod, to hide), IV, 262, 30; 266, 15: covering, coverlet.

huddle, II, 246, **B** 7: (hide) cover, protect (Scot. hiddle, hide).

huggar, I, 303, **D** 5: stocking without a foot.

huggell, II, 244, 16: hug, or, perhaps, a variety of huddle.

huly, hooly, healy, II, 168, **B** 4; 169, 12; 216, 2; IV, 413, 18; 436, 8: slowly, softly.

humming, III, 136, 30: heady, strong, as causing a hum in the head.

hunder, hundre, hunner, huner, hundredth, hundred.

hunger, hungre, v., II, 382, 4; 386, 4; 387, 2; 391, 2: starve.

hunkers, V, 213, 9=clunkers, clots of dirt.

hunt's ha, I, 298, 2: hunting-house or lodge.

husbande, husbonde, III, 57, 13; 295, 1: farmer, husbandman. III, 58, 46: economist, manager.

hussyfskap, husseyskep, V, 98, **A** 3, **B** 3: housewifery (she was making puddings). But perhaps, specifically, hussyskep, a sort of basket or bin of straw, formerly used, especially in ruder districts, for holding corn or meal. In like manner, a "platted hive of straw" is called a bee-skep. G. F. Graham's Songs of Scotland, III, 181.

hy, hye, hyght, on, vpon, III, 296, 9; 297, 31, 47, 48; 359, 91: in a loud voice. on hy, hye, III, 309, 51; 297, 45: on high, up, erect. on hyght, III, 297, 34: on high.

hye, hie, n., I, 328, 37; III, 99, 50: haste.

hyer, heyer, compar., V, 283, 5, 15: higher.

hyf, V, 283, 4: if.

hyghte, I, 328, 36: promise. hyght, p. p., III, 297, 29: promised; III, 77, 442: vowed.

hym, wente hym, stert hym, III, 62, 120, 126: dative of subject after verb of motion. See him.

hyndberry, I, 177, **A** c: raspberry or brambleberry.

hynd-chiel. See hind.

hynde, n., III, 64, 164: fellow. hynde Henry, II, 306 f., 6, 8, etc.; hynde squire, V, 25 f., 2, 13, 19, etc. See hind, n.

hynde, adj., II, 177 f., 20, 35: gentle, or the like. See hind, adj.

hyne, II, 314, **C** 3: (up) behind.

hyne, II, 314, **C** 3: hence, away.

hypped, III, 77, 429: hopped.

I

(See also under **J, Y**.)

I, II, 59, 34; 160, 10–16; 264 f., 4, 18; III, 185 f., 3, 4, 15, 23; 203, 18; 287, 59; 356, 28: ay.

i, abridgment of in, passim.

i, abridgment of with: IV, 465, 23.

i-bouht, bought.

ickles of ice, III, 154 f 1: icicles.

i-dyght, y-dyght, III, 62, 131, 132: furnished, adjusted. III, 75, 392: made ready.

if, apparent ellipsis of, II, 62, 9, with honour that ye do return.

i-fedred, feathered.

i-flawe, III, 13, 6: flayed.

ile, oil. 'inted (anointed) har with ashen ile, V, 305 a, 6: gave her a beating with an ashen cudgel.

ilk, ilke, same. of that ilk, III, 451, note *: having a title the same as the surname: as, Wemys of Wemys. in that ilke, I, 287, 72: in that same; III, 105, 14: at that same moment.

ilka, I, 107, 7; 302, **A** 9, 11, 12; 474, 40: each, either. ilka ane, ilkone, II, 185, 25; III, 97, 16: each one.

ilkone. See ilka.

ill, ell, ull, will.

ill-bukled, V, 276, 18: badly run down at the heel. See baucheld. (Unless ill be for old.)

ill-far'd, I, 342, 41: ill-favored.

ill-fardly, V, 115, 9: ill-favoredly, in an ugly way.

ill-wordie, V, 243, 15: unworthy.

im, am.

impale, V, 182, 5: make pale.

imy, I, 243, 7: in my.

in, IV, 464, 3; V, 277, 5, 9: an, and, if.

in o=in (in some part of ?), III, 495 b, 23, 24; IV, 19, 3; 517, 19.

in one, II, 186, 1; 187, 8; 196 e 1, 7; into ane, 184, 5, 8, 11, 18: anon, or, at once=in a single answer. In, riddle both of us into ane, the intention was, perhaps, together, simultaneously; and so, all in one, III, 4, 7; both as one, II, 187, 2.

inbearing, II, 28, 15: obtrusive, over-officious, intermeddling (with the object of thereby ingratiating oneself).

infeft with, in, I, 478, 5, 10; IV, 350, **B** b, 4, 5; V, 274, 6, 7; convey (land, money) to, put in possession of. inheft (o), IV, 349, **B** 4, 5: mistakenly for infeft.

in-fere, together. See fere.

ingle, III, 484 a, 36; V, 45 1: fire.

inheft, IV, 349, **B** 4, 5, for infeft b, to invest with a possession in fee.

inn, inne, III, 117, 11; 118, 8; 200, 6, 7; 212, 5: lodging.

i-nocked, III, 62, 132: nocked, notched.

inowe, III, 57, 13; 58, 43: enough.

instiled, III, 227, 3: styled, intitled.

'inted, V, 305 a, 6: anointed. See ile.

intil, intill, I, 68, 28; 69, 36; 302, **A** 11, IV, 171, 1: into, in.

into, I, 70, 20; 71, 29; 127, 5; 440, 13–15; IV, 263, 35: in. into his age, IV, 359, 12: at, of.

into ane, II, 184, 5, 8, 11, 18: anon, in a single answer, or simultaneously. See in one.

intoxicate, pret., II, 47, 8: intoxicated.

i-pyght, III, 63, 136: put.

ir, are.

irale (stane, as the rhyme shows the reading should be), I, 326, 9: an undetermined stone mentioned in romances.

ire, thro, II, 408, 17: seems to mean, as resenting the covering (not ballad-like). wi ire, II, 411, 10, is sufficiently incongruous.

irke with, V, 15, 14: tired, weary of.

is, III, 440, 11: has.

-is, -ys, termination of 3d *pers. pres. indic.*, he stendis louys: III, 98, 22; 101, 88.

I'se, IV, 506, 68: I am.

istow, I, 175 f., 4, 10, 16: is thou, art thou.

it (=O. Eng. his), its. defile it nest, III, 445, 32.

ith, in the.

'ith, with.

'ith, with.

ither, IV, 210 a; V, 306, 15: other.   IV, 110, 9: one another.

I wat, a wat, I wot, I wad=surely: I, 107, 1; 471, 11; and very often.   See a=I.

I wis, IV, 405, 1: probably to be taken as assuredly, since we have I wot in that sense in 7.

i-wis, i-wisse, i-wys, II, 46, 43; 265 f., 9, 26; III, 27, 104; 277, 17; 359, 84: surely, indeed.   As to *i-wis that*, III, 277, 18, 19, it is to be remembered that a superfluous *that* is common in the Percy MS.

I wist, III, 187, 32: for iwis, indeed.   Perhaps the Scottish I wat, surely, has influenced the form.

iyen, iyn, III, 57, 23, 28; 59, 58: eyen, eyes.

J

Jack, IV, 112, 4; 113, 5: insolent fellow.

iacke, III, 342, 64: (here) coat of mail, cf. 58, 59, 60. soldans iack, III, 422, 75.   An ordinary soldier's jack (III, 440, 18; 465 f., 33, 42, 49; IV, 147, 41) consisted of two folds of stout canvas, or some quilted material, with small pieces of metal enclosed.   Fairholt. Old Robin, II, 241, 21, puts a silke cote on his backe was thirteen inches folde.

jail-house, V, 300, 16: jail.

jamp, *pret.* of jump, II, 121, 21: jumped.

iapis, III, 59, 63: japes, jests, waggery, trifling.

jauel, V, 81, 11: a term of abuse, good-for-nothing, idle fellow.   Prompt. Parvulorum, gerro.   "He called the fellow ribbalde, villaine, iauel, backbiter, sclaunderer, and the childe of perdition."   Utopia, Arber, p. 53.

jaw, jawe, I, 127, 10; 128, 8; II, 21, 8; 24, 11; 29, 10–12: wave.

jawing, jawing wave, II, 223, F 7; IV, 472, 16: surging.

jawing, *n.*, IV, 462, 24: surging.

jee, I, 389, 7; IV, 476, 5: move, stir.

jelly (jolly), I, 69, 51; 298, 2; 452, 10; II, 403, 5; IV, 413, 20: handsome, pleasant, jovial.   Jamieson: "upright, worthy, excellent in its kind."

ietted, III, 199, 19; V, 86, 30: moved in state or with pride.

jimp, gimp, jump, *adj.*, I, 330, 8; 333, 6; II, 216, 18, 20; 217, 1, 3; 221, 1, 3; 225, J 1; IV, 212, 1; 272, 2: slender, slim.

jimp, *adv.*, II, 74, D 3: tightly, so as to make slender.

jo, II, 103, 5: sweetheart.

jobbing (of faces), III, 219, 14: billing (like doves).

jobbing at, I, 104 b, 10: jogging.   The at is difficult.   The old prefix means off, away, but is not separable.

Jock Sheep, John Sheephead, II, 480 a; IV, 290, 23: a man deficient in virility (?).   V, 206 a, 9: simpleton, of one who has been stultified or outwitted.

iollye, III, 278, 32: should probably be iollytë.   See enter plea.

joukd, V, 9, 12: bent forward.   See juks.

jow (of bell), II, 277, A 8: stroke.

juks, V, 110, 5: bows, obeisances.   See joukd.

jule, jewel.

jully-flowers, gilly-flowers.

jumbling, V, 102 B 13: mudding, fouling.

jumly, IV, 182, F 9: turbid.

jump, V, 267 b, 5: jimp, slender.

jumpted, IV, 519 a, 3: jumped.

justle, III, 280, 26: joust, tilt.

justler, III, 280, 31, 32: jouster, tilter.

justling, III, 279, 12, 14, 16: jousting.

K

kail, kale, colewort, made the baron like kail to a pot, IV, 86, 13: cut him up.   broth made of greens, especially of coleworts: II, 467, 41; III, 300, 12; 388, 3; IV, 500, 13.   See kell.

kaily lips, I, 302, A 10: covered with kail, and so repulsive.

kaim, kame, keem, comb.

kaivle, II, 298 f., 3, 19: lot.   See kavil.

kale.   See kail.

kame, keem, comb.

kamen, combing.

kane, I, 353, 15; 356, 56: tribute (originally a duty in the form of a part of the produce, paid by an occupant of land to his superior).

kauk, V, 116, 10: chalk.

kavil, kaivle, kevel, cavil, I, 71, 36, 38: lot.

kay, key, kine.

keach, V, 123, 17: perturbation, shaking up.

kean, *v.*, V, 110, 4: ken.

kebars, I, 332, F 6; II, 227 a: rafters.

kebbuck, IV, 323, 5: cheese.

keckle-pin, burnt like keckle-pin, II, 155, 38: that is, I suppose, like heckle-pin, the sound of the *k* being carried on from *like*.   Mr William Forbes, of Peterhead, suggests the following explanation: The pins used to hold the straw raips which hold down the thatch on cob or mud huts; being driven into the top of the walls close to the eaves, they are always dry and ready to burn.   The mass of interlaced straw is called a hackle.   Used all over East Aberdeenshire.

keeked, keekit, I, 303, D 1; 304, E 3: peeped.

keel, V, 116, 10: red chalk.

keem, kem, kemb, kame, comb.

keen, *v.*, V, 238, 18; 278, 38: ken, know.

keen, armour, II, 62, 10: no sense except for arms of offense (as in Old Eng.).

keen (of tying), II, 162, D 3: strong or hard.

keen(e), II, 45, 26; 46, 39; V, 192 f., 27, 57: bold.   spak sharp and keene, III, 394, K 3: cuttingly, poignantly.

keep, catch. See kep.

keep up, V, 114, 12: keep under custody, safe from the hands of others, lock up. See kept up.

keep(e) with, II, 411, 15; III, 36, 41: stay, live, with.

keepit a bower, II, 407, 8: frequented, lived in.

keepit, IV, 215, A 2: heeded, observed.

keist, kiest, kest, kyst, pret. of cast, I, 69, 46; 241, 3.

kell, II, 264 f., 5, 12; 364, 30; V, 161, 7: a cap of network for women's hair.

kell. lang kell, V, 110, 9, 10. See lang kell.

kelter, kelter-coat, V, 54, 20: made of kelt, black and white wool mixed and not dyed. Dillon, Fairholt's Costume in England, where a kelter-coat is cited from a will. Kelt, cloth with the knap, generally of native black wool. Jamieson.

keltit, IV, 493, 5: kelted, tucked.

kem, kemb, comb.

kemp, kempe, kempy, I, 301, 1; 302, 6, B 1; 303, C 1, 9; 309, 3, 5; II, 53 f., 25, 31, 55; III, 447 a: champion, fighting-man (A. S. cempa). kemp o the ship, V, 151 f., F 2, 4, is no doubt a corruption.

kempery(e), II, 54 f., 54, 66, 68: company of fighting men (or, if adjective, fighting).

kempy. See kemp.

ken, I, 343, 42; 345, 41; 348, 21; III, 268, 4: know. III, 266, 4: to make known.

kene, cawte and kene, III, 296, 26: wise, shrewd, or, perhaps, brave.

kenna, know not.

kep, keep, cap, cape, catch, stop, intercept: II, 322, 21; 325, 21; 407, 13; 413, 6, 8; III, 125, 34; 245, 2; 246, E 2; 436, 5, 7; IV, 480 f., 17, 18, 19; V, 230, 10, 11. she keppit him (received him) on a penknife (as he leaned over to her), II, 147, 6. she keppit Lamkin, II, 335, M 7; V, 230 b, Y 10: encountered. he kepped the table, door, wi his knee, I, 476, J 5; 481, 42; II, 91, 26; 94, 18; 271, 17: took, struck. keppit, III, 246, D 2, is an obviously wrong reading, and should be kicked; cf. 243, 2; 245, 2; 246, E 2. kepd the stane wi her knee, II, 421, 29, is absurdly taken from other ballads (and from ball-playing). pret. kept, kepd, kepped, kepit, keppit. See cap.

kepe, I, 329, 2: care for, value. kepe I be, III, 100, 80: care I to be.

keping, IV, 313, 20: meeting. The meaning is that he went to meet (come should be came) the body which was lying at the gates. There was no procession towards him.

kepping, keeping.

kept up, IV, 287, 15: shut up. See keep up.

kerches, kerchiefs.

kest, keste, pret. of cast, III, 76 f., 421, 422. See keist.

kettrin, IV, 84, 8: cateran, Highland marauder. See caterans.

kevel, kevil, I, 74 f., 3, 36; 77, 4; 80, 4-6; II, 16, 2; 301, 1; IV, 394, C 1: lot. See kavil.

key, kye.

keys, rang the keys, IV, 430, 2: keys of her spinet.

kickle, III, 230, 59 (the actual reading): not easily

managed, unsteady, Scot. kittle. (But perhaps we should read kick, since a verb would be expected.)

kiest, keist, pret. of cast, I, 74, 2; 75, 36; 80, 4; 351, 44; IV, 32, 11.

kilt, IV, 257, 3: a skirt worn by Highlanders, reaching from the belly to the knees.

kilt, kelt, tuck up: I, 341, 3, 17; 343 f., 3, 8, 16, 35; 369, 2; II, 92, 7; 461, 5; 462, 5; 471, 4. p. p. kilt, II, 423, 8; IV, 210, 7.

kin, a' kin kind, II, 114, 2: a' kin, all kind, equivalent to every. na kin thing, I, 394, 10.

kin, ken.

kind, kindly, II, 319, 7; III, 266 f., 1, 5, 21; 300, 26; IV, 501, 30: kindred, native. kindly cockward, I, 285, 24: natural, born, fool. kindly rest, V, 124, C 14: natural.

kine, what kine a man, IV, 504, 27: kind (of).

king's felon, kynggis felon, kings ffelon, III, 98, 21; 180, 16: traitor, or rebel, to the king.

kinnen, III, 370, 4: coney, rabbit.

kintra, country.

kipeng, keeping.

kipple, I, 333, 5; IV, 432, 6: couple, rafter.

kipple-roots, I, 304, F 5: the ends of couples (rafters) that rest on the top of the wall. "In rude erections the couples were rough unhewn tree-stems, which were placed with their thickest, or root, ends on the walls, the smaller ends abutting at the ridge of the roof." J. Aiken.

kirking, I, 371, 6, 12, 14: churching.

kirk-shot, IV, 359, 10: the fishings on the water where nets are shot, belonging to, or adjacent to, the kirk.

kirk-style, I, 441, 8-10; 498, 16, 24; IV, 183, 9, 11; 360, 16: the gate of the enclosure round a church, or, the stile in the church-yard wall.

kirk-toun, II, 219, 13: village in which is a parish church.

kirkyard, V, 299, 4: churchyard.

kirn, n. and v., V, 115, 6: churn.

kirtle, kirtell, kyrtell, part of a man's dress, perhaps waistcoat: III, 65, 194; 71, 299. name given to a variety of articles of female attire, explained as jacket, corsage or waist, upper petticoat, a loose upper garment, tunic or short mantle, etc. dress of silk worn under a gown, over a petticoat, I, 433, 9. gown, petticoat and kirtle, III, 273, 14. kirtle and gown, III, 215, 10; IV, 432, 7, 8.

kist, chest, I, 15, A 3; B 3; 17, D 2; III, 189, 34; IV, 485, 19; V, 115, 5: coffin.

kithe, a, III, 93, 36: of kith, of the same country, region, people. kith, kyth, and kin, II, 216, 6, 8; 252, 29; III, 93, 36.

kitt, V, 240, 14: outfit, supply.

knabby, IV, 262, 23: knobby, rough.

knack fingers (in sign of grief): IV, 418, 7; 435, 13; knak, V, 227, 5 (passage corrupted); knick, III, 455, E 1; knock, II, 312 f., 5, 6, 7: crack the finger-joints. (Elsewhere, wring, II, 315, D 7; 319, 17; III, 477, 4.) ladies crackt their fingers, II, 26, G 16.

knapped, II, 134, 8, 13: knobbed, ornamented with balls or tassels. See **naps.** golden-knobbed, II, 133, **D** 6. (knob, sometimes a tassel to the cord of a mantle.)

knapscap, napskape, IV, 7, 35; V, 251, 31: head-piece.

knaue, III, 14, 16, 17; 60, 81; 94, 50; 127, 44 (play): servant. IV, 501, 37: person of servile or low rank.

knave-bairn, I, 350, 20; II, 418, 23: male child. knave-boy, V, 235 b, after 30.

kneene, III, 362, 87: knees.

knell, v., II, 189, 23: ring.

knet, pret. of knit, III, 431, 17; IV, 31, **B** 6: knitted, knotted.

knicking fingers, III, 455, **E**: making the finger-joints crack. See **knack.**

knight-bairn, V, 236 f., 21, 28, 29: male child.

knip-knap, V, 213, 6: a knock, tap. V, 124, **C** 15: to express the sound of cracking.

knobbed. See **knapped.**

knock. See **knack.**

knocking-stane, I, 304, 10: stone mortar.

knoe. See **know.**

knop, III, 138, 9: (knap), blow.

knoppis, knobs.

know(e), knoe, II, 308 b; III, 464, 5; 466, 38; IV, 171, 4; 193, 1; 195, 1; 201, 10; 205, 22: hillock.

knowe-tap, IV, 60, **C** b 6: top of a hill.

kod, kuod, quoth.

koors, I, 353, 15: turns.

koupd. See **couped.**

kouthe, II, 499 b: known.

kow, V, 157, 11, 12: twig. See **cow.**

ky, kye, kyne, III, 464, 6, 7; 465 f., 19, 62; IV, 7, 29–32; 84, 17, 18: cows.

kyrtell. See **kirtle.**

kyst, I, 241, 3: cast.

kyth (and kin), home, country, people. See **kithe.**

kythe, II, 168, 10: be manifest, appear, pret. kythed, I, 117, 10: appeared.

L

laa, law.

lachters, lauchters, IV, 166, 14: locks.

lack, lake, adj.=laigh, low, humble. in lack o luve, II, 376, 24, 27, 30. so lack a knight as bid her ride, II, 97, 10. thought his father lack to sair, II, 408, 1 (lake, V, 235 b, 1; cf. thought father's service mean, II, 178, 2); V, 272 b, 8, 10: of mean position.

lack, lake, n. (think, hae, lack), reproach, discredit, IV, 15, 16; 518, 8. woman, lack o our kin, IV, 325, 13. had ye nae lack (reproach or fault), IV, 281, 3. what other ladies would think lack, II, 159, 22 (but here lack may=laigh, and mean beneath them, as in II, 97, 10). tooke a lake, III, 419, 2: incurred a reproach or blame? of his friends he had no lack, IV, 11, 18: corrupted from, of him his friends they had no lack (or the like). See **lauch.**

lad, in surgeon-lad, IV, 484, after 25: man. lad nor lown, IV, 304, 8, 9: should probably read, laird.

lad-bairn, II, 299, 12, 21; III, 392, 7; 395, **L** 1, 5; IV, 510, **V** 3: boy.

lad, pret. of lead, III, 75, 388.

lade, led, taken.

lader, V, 265 b, 20: leather.

laid, III, 35, 15: laid a plan. laid about, III, 329, 1: invested.

laid, laid her bye, V, 169, 6: lay down by her.

laidler, II, 503 f., 10, 11, etc.: corruptly for laidley (as in 7).

laidley, laily, laylë, layely, etc. (A. S., láðlíc), I, 312, 8, 13; 348, 14, 20; II, 503 f., 7, 32, 35; V, 214 f., 2, 3, 5, etc.: loathly, loathsome.

laigh, II, 188, 3; III, 384, 2; 397, **A** b 1; IV, 200, 9; 268, 21; V, 236, 11: low, mean. oer laigh, III, 480, 12: too low, too short. See **lack.**

laigh, leugh, n., III, 162, 49: low ground. III, 489, 10: lower part; so, leugh, 487, 6, 14, 16.

laily, laylë, layly, layelly, V, 214 f. See **laidley.**

lain, laine, layne, leane, lene, len (Icel. leyna), III, 332, 7; IV, 7 f., 30, 47; V, 250 f., 27, 40: conceal.

lain, alone. See **lane.**

laine, p. p., III, 401, 16: laid.

lair, lear (A. S., lár), II, 175, 16; 305, 15: instruction. unco lair, to learn, get: II, 118, 1; 119, 1; 174, 1; 178, 2; III, 385, 1; IV, 411, 1; unco lear, IV, 467, 1: strange lesson, applied to one who is to have an extraordinary experience; cf. English lair, IV, 466, 1. See **lear.**

lair, lear, II, 311, 1: lying-in.

laird, a landholder, under the degree of knight; the proprietor of a house, or of more houses than one. Jamieson.

lairy, IV, 22, 10: miry, boggy.

laith, loath. See **leath.**

lake, n., III, 419, 2; V, 235 b, 1; 272 b, 8, 10. See **lack.**

lake, I, 254, 8: pit, cavity. See **laigh,** n.

lake, V, 235 b, 1; 272, 8, 10=laigh, of mean position. See **lack,** adj.

lake-wake, leak-wake, lyke-wake, II, 311, 19: watching of a dead body.

lamar, lamer, lammer, II, 131, 6; 323, 24; IV, 203, 5; 204, 14: amber.

lambes woole, V, 85, 18: pulp of roasted apples mixed with ale.

lammas beds, II, 96, **J** 4, in virtue leave your: corrupt. See note, II, 100 b. Dr Davidson, correcting by sound, would read, never to leave. For lammas beds we may perhaps read, families. Cf. 87, **B** 1, that ye dinna leave your father's house.

lammer, lamer, lamar, amber. See **lamar.**

land, V, 128, 29: country (opposed to town).

land-lieutenant, IV, 517, 17. lord lieutenant, III, 492 f., 7, 11, 17. lieutenant, III, 488, 32, 33, 35, 37. See next word.

land-serg(e)ant, III, 481, 33; 482, 27; IV, 2, 9, 14: officer of the gendarmerie of the Borders, called land-lieutenant, IV, 517, 17.

landart, V, 106, **E** 1; 111, 1: belonging to the country, rural.

landen, II, 29, 17: landing.

landen span, III, 511, 16, 18: corrupted from London band, or the like.

landsman, III, 489, 44: land owner.

lane, III, 357, 51: lane, as where poor men live? (Rhymed with aye, and perhaps corrupt. 361, **C** 51, lawne.)

lane, lain, leen, lean, lone, alane, alone, annexed to the dative or genitive of the personal pronoun (as in Old Eng. him ane, hire ane), my, mine, thy, our, your, her, his, him, its: I alone, by myself, etc. my lane, I, 79, 22. thy lane, IV, 197, 8. our lane, I, 72, 20. your lane, II, 69, 1. your lone, IV, 195, 16. her lane, lean, I, 350, 10; IV, 456, 1. his lane, lean, IV, 227, 6; 345, 5. him lane, leen, I, 368, 26, 28; II, 90, 18. their lane, I, 254, c 1. its lone, I, 132, **J** 4; II, 308, 3. its leen, IV, 418, 1. it lane, II, 82, **J**; 307, 22; III, 388, 5. me ane, I, 333, 1. by my lane, I, 330, **B** 1. mine alone, alane, I, 332, **E** 1, **F** 1; III, 489, 1. him alone, III, 159, 2; cf. IV, 464, 1.

lane, IV, 281, 2: misprint for bane.

lang, at lang, IV, 318, **F** 9: at length.

lang kell, V, 110, 9, 10: coleworts not cut up and mashed. "lang kail [a tall-growing cabbage?] became extinct about 60 years ago, giving place to finer-flavored varieties." W. Forbes.

langin, she's gane langin hame, IV, 198 a, 7: perhaps simply longing, languishing; lingering would be more appropriate if the interpretation were justifiable.

lang-sought, V, 35, **B** 5: been long (and fruitlessly) seeking for some object (if the reading is right), indicating a hopeless passion.

lap, grip her in his lap, II, 325, 18: (possibly) embrace, clutch.

lap, lappe, III, 59, 70; 65, 194; 353, 12; 430 f., 15, 17: wrap, roll.

lap, *pret.* of loup, leap, I, 330, **A** 5, 7, **B** 5; 331, **C** 5, 7; III, 270, 1; V, 228, 16. lap him, III, 266, 2: the old construction of dative of the subject after a verb of motion.

lappen, *p. p.* of loup, leap.

lapperin, III, 395, **L** 4; IV, 224, 23: clotting.

lappin, IV, 510, **V** 3: covering; probably corrupted from lapperin of **L** 4, clotting.

lard, leard, V, 36, **B** 8, 9: laird.

lass-bairn, lassie-bairn, I, 350, 20; II, 301, 10, 11; IV, 418, 5: girl.

lat, I, 310, 8; 351, 37: let.

lat down, III, 281, 2, 5, 6: give over, discontinue.

late, III, 164, **b** 51: let, hindrance.

late, *pret.* of let, allow, V, 256, 13.

latten, *p. p.* of let, II, 189, 26; IV, 493 f., 7, 28, 31 (left).

lau, low.

lauch, *n.,* II, 20, 4; 385, 6; 390, 7; IV, 259, 9: laugh. IV, 327, 12: perhaps laughing-stock; but cf. lack, 325, 13, reproach.

lauch, lawhe, *v.,* IV, 121, **G** 2; V, 80, 48: laugh. *pret.* laugh, laughe, leuch, leugh, luke, lough, low, lowe, lowhe, laucht, lought.

laucht, *pret.* of laugh, II, 106, 14.

lauchter, IV, 385, 6: laugh.

lauchters, I, 74, 68, 72; 79, 25: locks.

lauchty, V, 213 a, No 33, 10: the reading in Sharpe's Ballad Book corresponding to tauchy, I, 302, **A** 10. In the copy of Sharpe used (a presentation copy), a line is drawn through the l, indicating, probably, the editor's intention to emend to tauchty or tauchy.

laue, law.

laugh, laughe, *pret.* of laugh, II, 418, 34; 420, 59; III, 287, 59.

launde, lawnde, III, 27, 105; 33, 105: plain ground in a forest; "a small park within a forest, enclosed in order to take the deer more readily, or to produce fatter venison by confining them for a time."

launsgay, III, 63, 134: a kind of lance, javelin (compound of lance and the Arabic zagaye).

lave, leve, II, 78, 11; III, 495 b, 23, 24; IV, 220, 3; 428, 6; 517, 20: rest, remainder.

lauede ablode, I, 244, 9; V, 288, 16: swam in blood.

lav(e)rock, I, 201, 3; 202, 3; 205, **F** 4; IV, 266, 16: lark.

law, I, 209 a: faith, creed.

law, Castle-law, II, 149, 4, 7; Biddess-law, III, 460, 29: hill (A. S. hlǽw).

lawhe, V, 80, 48: laugh. *pret.* lowhe.

lawin(g), III, 472, 7; IV, 151 f., **A** 2–4, **B** 5, 9, 10, etc.; 157, 5, 6: tavern-reckoning.

lawing, V, 266, 8: lying (reclining).

lawnde. See **launde.**

lax, IV, 233, 18: relief.

lay, II, 59, 25: law, faith.

lay, II, 483, 1; IV, 203 f., 6, 7, 23; V, 260, 10, 11: land not under cultivation, grass, sward. lays, IV, 224, 23: fields, plains, ground.

lay, *v.,* lie.

lay, I, 399 a, **E** 11: seems to be nonsense; probably we should read gray, as in No 248, IV, 389 f.

lay by, IV, 519, 5, 7, 11; 520, 5, 10 (lay'd=lay it): lay aside, let be, cease. lay bay, V, 275 b, 3: put aside or behind, outsail.

layelly, loathsome. See **laidley.**

laying, IV, 174, 1: lawing, reckoning.

lay-land, II, 59, 23: (Old Eng. leyland) lea land, untilled land; simply plain, ground.

laylë, loathsome. See **laidley.**

layn (withouten), III, 97, 17; 100, 81: lie (truly).

layne (Icel. leyna), IV, 7 f., 30, 47: conceal. See **lain.**

layne, *v.* (A. S. légnian), III, 297, 35, 40: lie.

layne, *v.,* II, 87, 33: lean.

lazar, -er, II, 44–46, 4, 5, 9, 11, etc.: leper.

lea, lee, lie, loe, loi, loie, loy, loo, low, lue, *v.,* I, 438, 10; II, 260, 4; 408, 23; 417, 2; 419, 52; V, 116, 2, 3; 117, 3; 220, 6; 221, 9; 242, 14; 260, 13; 272 b, 3, 7, 11; 277 f., 1, 4, 23, 31: love.

lea, lee, lie, *mentiri.*

lea, III, 457, **A** 2; IV, 100, 4; 102, **L** 6; 263, 2: leave. (so leave, IV, 94, 15, is to be sounded.)

lea, *n.* See **lee**.

lea, lee, lie lea, lie lee: IV, 26, 5; 350, **B b** after 2; 520, 2: untilled. lay lee, V, 189 b: lay waste.

leace, withouten leace, III, 27, 108, 115: falsehood.

lead, III, 460, 26: lead their horses?

lead, V, 36, 11; 117, 14; 221, 18; 268, 18: led.

lead, laid.

lead(e), I, 232, 9; V, 53, 103: vat, boiler.

leaf, loaf.

leaf, gae out under the leaf, IV, 379, 6: luff, loof, after part of a ship's bow; or here, as opposed to lee, the weather side. See **lowe**.

leak, *adj.*, V, 111, 20; 224, 26: like.

leak, *v.*, V, 242, 15: like.

leak, II, 193, 28; V, 224, 26; 228, 28:=lyke, for lyke-wake, watching of a dead body.

leak-wake, V, 228, 13, 14, 23, 24: lyke-wake, watching of a dead body. See **lake-wake, lyke-wake**.

leal, leel, leil, liel, III, 464, 12: loyal, faithful, true. I, 70, 24; 73, 34, 45, 46; II, 73, 19; III, 437, 36; IV, 212, 1; 240, 13; 283, 11; 289, 11: virginal, chaste, expers viri; so, lealest, leelest, I, 220, **A** 3; 221, **D** 6. III, 464, 3; 465, 30: veracious. V, 115, 5: upright, honest. love me leel, I, 345, 9: faithfully.

lea-lang, I, 352, 7. See **lee**, *adj.*

leall, V, 248, 4: perhaps only faithful; but possibly lief, lee (dear), leman, the final l being caught from leman.

leam, leem, *v.*, II, 410, 24: gleam.

lean, leen, his, him, IV, 345, **I** 5: lane, lone. See **lane**.

lean, leane, lene, len, *v.*, II, 403, 8 (see len); III, 330, 19; 420 f., 30, 32, 34, 52; IV, 277, 15, 17; V, 36, **B** 8, 9: conceal. II, 164, 8, 11, 14: conceal, or lie. See **lain**, to conceal.

leap, *pret.* of leap, loup, V, 227, 17. See **leepe**.

lear, II, 176, **C** 1, 2: instruction. IV, 413, 2; 414, 1; 467, 1: learning. III, 473, 24: information. See **lair**.

lear, II, 313, 25: apparently meant for lair, bed; but rhymed with white, and the reading should undoubtedly be lyke, that is, lyke-wake, as in II, 117, 16.

leard, laird. See **lard**.

lease=leash, II, 265, 19: a thong or string (as if for bringing back the deer he should kill?). I, 211, 20: a leash (of hounds), pack. III, 216, 31: a leash (of bucks), three.

leasing(e), leasynge, lesynge, leesin, I, 412, 26; III, 28, 132, 134; 359, 86; IV, 465, 22: falsehood.

leath, laith, III, 162, 54; IV, 479, 4; V, 216, 6: loath.

leaugh, leugh, lewgh, leiugh, lieugh, III, 465 f., 33, 39, 42, 49; 487, 6, 14, 16 (see **laigh**): low.

leave, gie them a' thier leave, I, 431, **D** 13, **E** 10: take leave of them all.

leave=leeve, dear, II, 414, 24. leaver, III, 362, 82.

leave (to weepe), IV, 140, 10: cease.

leave, live.

lede, III, 74, 368: leading, conduct.

ledës-man, lodesman, III, 74, 369; 88, 369: guide.

ledyt, I, 242, 11, *old imperative plural:* lead.

lee, lea, I, 100, 4; III, 171, 9; 174, 20: untilled ground, grass land, open plain, ground.

lee, lie lee, IV, 26, 5: untilled. lay lee, V, 189 b, lay waste.

lee, *adj.*, the (this, a) lee-lang, lief-lang day, I, 100, 11, 12; 440, 3; II, 96, **I** 2: (Old Eng. the leevë longë day) livelong, from A. S. léof, used like German lieb in der liebe lange tag, die liebe lange nacht. So lee, le, lei, ley, licht o the moon, I, 389, 5; II, 188 f., 4, 14, 35; 195, 37; 233, **F** 1; 374, **B** 3; 413, 7, as in die liebe sonne, der liebe mond, regen, wind, and other formulas in great variety. (lee licht o the moon is replaced, II, 103 f., 10, 12; 106, 10, by hie light, ae light.)

lee, *v.*, lie, *mentiri*.

lee, II, 256, **K** 5: live.

lee, *v.*, love. See **lea**, love.

leech, IV, 426, 11: meant for leesh, and so spelt in another copy.

leed, lied (A. S. lédén), I, 207, 18; 430, 5, 9; II, 366, 19; IV, 379, 14: talk.

leed (A. S. léod), III, 355, 3: man. *pl.* leeds, 6: people.

leed, laid.

leed, *n.*, II, 366, 37: lead.

leedginge, II, 58, 7: leeching, doctoring.

leeft, *pret.*, IV, 220, 1: lived.

leel, loyal, faithful, etc. love me leel, I, 345, 9: faithfully. See **leal**.

lee-lang. See **lee**.

leemin, II, 361, 33: gleaming.

leems, IV, 460 a, No 47: gleams; but *langs*, belongs, is the word required; cf. I, 430, 6.

leen, lean, her, your leen, him leen, IV, 291 b; 345, 9; V, 171, 2, 6: lone. See **lane**.

leepe, leap, *pret.* of leap, loup, II, 445, 76; V, 227, 17.

lees, leeze, me on thee, III, 495 a, after 7; IV, 517, 15: blessings on, commend me to. (lees me, originally leeve is me, dear is to me, my delight is.)

leese, III, 37, 75; 189, 4; 228, 17; 374, 3: lose.

leesin, IV, 465, 22: a lie. See **leasing(e)**.

leesome, I, 182–3; IV, 432, 2; 455, 18; V, 178, 1: lovely, pleasing. leesome blew the wind, IV, 410, 10: pleasantly.

leeve, leve, leave, lefe, lieve, live, *adj.*, II, 305, 13; 414, 24; V, 227, 13: lovely, dear, pleasant; *comp.* leifer, leuer, I, 328, 43; III, 24, 35; 189, **A** 9; 297, 42; 436 f., 10, 25; V, 83, 51. epithet of London, II, 265, 5, 12; 440, 14; III, 276, 1; 284, 6, 7; 330, 16; 406, 35; V, 227, 8. So, lovely London, III, 352, 1; 355, 7. lilly Londeen, IV, 485, 19. whether he were loth or lefe, III, 67, 225 (properly, him were): disagreeable or agreeable; here, unwilling or willing. For *had lever* see **leuer**.

leeve, III, 105, 15: believe.

leeve, III, 287, 62: grant.

leeze. See **lees**.

lefe, III, 28, 128: pleasing, agreeable. III, 67, 225: pleased. See **leefe**.

leffe (A. S. léfan), wolde not leffe beheynde, III, 112, 60: remain.

leg, V, 126 f., 1, 2, 5, etc.: highwayman.

legg, V, 275, 7: league.

leguays lequays, V, 217, 12, 13: likewise.

lei, ley, lei light o the moon, II, 188 f., 4, 14, 35; 195, 37. See lee, *adj.*

leifer, leifar, III, 436 f., 10, 25; IV, 196, 13: rather. See leeve.

leil. See leal.

leiugh, low. See leaugh.

leman, lemman, Old Eng. leofman, beloved (of both sexes). I, 232, 6, 7; 314, 2-4, 6; II, 271, 18; 273, 24, 400, 6; IV, 151, B 1, 2; 154, 2, 3; V, 283, 3: lover, paramour. I, 72, 30, 32; 117, 8; 254, 10; II, 73, 27, 28; 81, 40; 289, B 2, 3; V, 248, 4; 283, 12: love, mistress, loose woman.

lemanless, III, 434, 28: without lovers.

lemanry, V, 25, 4: illicit love.

len, *v.*, lean. See lend.

len, lene, III, 420 f., 30, 32, 34, 52; neither lee nor len, IV, 277, 15, 17: conceal. II, 164, 8, 11, 14: conceal, or lie. that cannot longer len, II, 403, 8: remain concealed (but the reading should probably be, I cannot). See lain, lean.

len, lene, III, 79, 40, 81; V, 283, 14: lend, give, grant.

lend, II, 229, 5, 8; III, 63 f., 153, 165; 82, 76; 85, 76; V, 49, 21: grant, give.

lend, *n.*, II, 185, 38: loan.

lend, I, 207, 19, lend ye till your pike-staff: we should no doubt read len=lean. lent, I, 223, I 4: leaned.

lende, III, 75, 395: dwell.

lene, conceal. See len.

lenger, lengre, III, 61, 105; 73, 341; 78, 443: longer.

lenght, III, 478, 17: length.

length, this length, IV, 271, A 4: for so long.

lent, *pret.*, I, 223, I 4: leaned.

lequays, likewise. See leguays.

lere (A. S. hléor), III, 57, 28: cheek, face.

lere, III, 57, 16; 77, 426: learn.

lese, leese, III, 59, 56: lose.

less (age), IV, 64 a: minor.

less o him, I, 332, G 1: smaller of him, than him.

lesse, III, 296, 25: false, falsehood.

lest, II, 81, 45 (reading in earlier MS. for rest): last.

lesynge, falsehood. See leasing(e).

let, lat (A. S. lǽtan), allow, leave. II, 54, 48; 265, 8, 15, 24; III, 58, 38: omit, fail. *pret.* late, loot, lute, lett. *p. p.* latten, letten, lotten, looten, loot (?).

let, lette (A. S. lettan), I, 334, 8; III, 110, 22, 23; 128, 75; 307, 2: hinder.

letten, *p. p.* of let, I, 87, 43; 452, 6: allowed, left.

letters, letturs, III, 99, 55 (the kyng did hit vnfold); III, 297, 36: letter.

leuch, luke, *pret.* of laugh, II, 30, K 1; 81, 33; 366, 23; IV, 272, 9.

leugh, *n.*, lower part. See laugh.

leugh, *pret.* of laugh, I, 388, A 7; II, 134, 21; III, 69, 273; 467, 60; 490, 17.

leugh, leaugh, lewgh, etc., IV, 465, 34, 38; 484 f., 8, 10: low.

leutye, lewtë, III, 64, 154, 169: loyalty, faith.

leuve, I, 17, 14: palm of the hand. See loof.

leve, lave, *m.*, II, 75, 20: rest.

leue, *v.*, III, 61, 112; 79, 76: permit, grant.

levedys, I, 334, 9: ladies.

leven, I, 324, 13; 325, 12: lawn, glade, open ground in a forest. See launde.

leuer, leifer, pleasanter, preferable, rather. had leuer, III, 24, 35; 189, A 9; 297, 42; 436 f., 10, 25; V, 83, 51. See leeve.

lewde (lye), III, 171, 8: base, vile.

lewgh, low. See leaugh.

lewte. See leutye.

ley, lea, lee, III, 109, 4; for a' his father's leys, II, 333, 11; 334, M 4; riding the leys, IV, 137, 34: land not under cultivation, simply land, plain, field. lands and ley, V, 157, 2: arable land and pasture; a common phrase in Scots conveyancing, "all and whole the lands and leas."

ley-land, I, 15, 11; 16, B 11: land lying lea, not under cultivation. See lay-land.

ley licht. See lei, lee.

leyngger, V, 80, 37: longer.

leyt, V, 80, 37: lighted.

leythe, III, 112, 62: light.

liag, V, 237, 5: leg.

libertie, lying at, II, 464, 11: possessed in one's own right, unencumbered.

liberty, lybertye, place of, II, 443, 39; 449, 44, 52: where one can fight without fear of interruption ?

liberty-wife, II, 291, 2: mistress.

licence, V, 155, C 3, make their licence free: pay the licence of an inn-keeper.

licht, I, 146, 19, 20: alight. lichted, lichtit, II, 92, 16; IV, 195, D 2; 337 b, g after 20.

lichter, I, 21 b, 8; II, 105, 10: delivered. See lighter.

lichtlie, lichtly, lightly, IV, 94, 3; 98, 8; 100, 7; 337 a, g 16: make light of, treat, or speak of, with disrespect.

lick, II, 470, 45: gratuity (of meal from the miller).

lick, III, 163, 87: take for one's self; cf. II, 470, 45.

lidder, lither, III, 464, 1: lazy. as *adv.*, 467, b 1: excessively. (A. S. lȳðre, bad.)

lie, ly, lye, I, 103, 10; III, 123, 5; 432, 17; V, 191, 5: reside, live.

lie, lee, lea, love. See lea.

lie, III, 301, E: lea.

lie, thou lie, IV, 197, 17: for thou liest, ye lie.

lied (A. S. lǽden), I, 430, 5, 9: language, talk. See leed.

lied, *pret.*, V, 220, 6: loved.

lief-lang. See lee-lang, under lee.

liel, I, 70, 24: chaste. See leal.

lien, *p. p.*, II, 135, 32: lain. she's nouther pin'd nor lien, IV, 484, after 25: has not been lying bed-rid, does not look like one who has long been confined to bed.

lierachie, III, 319, 20: hubbub. "leerach=the bottom of a dung-pit after the dung has been removed, but left in a filthy state. The word is used to signify anything in a disordered state. Hence, confusion, hubbub." Rev. Walter Gregor.

lieugh, low. See leaugh.

lieve, II, 345, 34: dear. See leeve.

life, leaf.

life, man of life, II, 244, 10: man alive (Chaucer's lives man).

lift, I, 370, 16; 440, 18; II, 26, 14: air, sky.

lift, V, 82, 37: lifted.

lig, ligg, ligge, lygge, *imperat.*, I, 328, 36; II, 437, 72; 439, 4, 7; IV, 396, 6; *inf.*, III, 212, 17: lay.

lig, ligge, lygge, I, 328, 38–41; II, 244, 6, 7: lie.

light, *pret.*, II, 46, 38; 54, 49; V, 53, 93: lighted, alighted. See lyght.

light, III, 156, 1: corruption of lith, listen.

lighter, of a bairn, I, 86 f., 7, 8, 16, 17, 24, 25, 43; II, 98, 35; 108, 12; 109, 11; 115, 23; 117, 10, 11; 118, 13; 123, 25, 26: delivered. (Icel. verða léttari, Old Eng. to lighten.) lighter a dochter, II, 132, 15 : *ellipsis of* of. See lichter.

lightly, lightlie, lyghtly(e), III, 23 ff., 11, 41, 45, 61, V, 82, 36: quickly. III, 35, 35: easily. V, 84, 3: for slight reason.

lightly, lichtlie, -ly, III, 472, 10; IV, 351, 2, 9: treat with disrespect. IV, 92, 2: slight (in love). IV, 94, 3; 98, 8; 100, 7; 103, M 1; IV, 337 a, g 16: speak disparagingly of.

like, liken, like to be dead (dee), II, 58, 7; 372, 24; III, 386, 7; 392, 6; 394, J 4; 395, M 2 (cf. L 2): in a condition, in a fair way, or likely. liker, II, 97, 22: more likely (?). See lyken.

like, III, 355, 13; 358, 60, 80; 360, 109, 111: please. III, 400, 4, (7): be pleased, satisfied.

likesome, II, 433, 5, 6, 8; 440, 23; 442, 4; 446, 89: pleasing, lovely.

lilt, I, 187 b; IV, 266, 16: to sing cheerfully. lilted, IV, 95, 3: sang, chanted.

lily, lilly, lilye, lillie, liley, lillie, lea, lee, lie, I, 325, B 11; III, 299, 8, 11; 300, 25; 301, 32, E; 435, 2; IV, 454, 6; 455, 14; 458, 7; V, 244, 16, 19; lillie leven, I, 324, 13; 325, C 12; lilly bank, brae, IV, 220, 13, 14: explained as "overspread with lilies or flowers," but clearly from A. S. léoflíc, Old Eng. lefly, etc., lovely, charming. So, lilly feet (i. e. leely), I, 130, E 13; lily leesome thing, IV, 432, 2. We have lilly Londeen, IV, 485, 19=the frequent leeve London, lovely London. See leeve, lee-lang.

limmer (French limier, a kind of hound), a term of opprobrium, or simply of dislike. II, 322, 6; III, 466, 47: wretch (*m.* or *f.*), rascal. limmer thieves, 439 f., 4, 20; 441, 34. limmer loon, IV, 146, 15, 17. of a woman, II, 219, 9: jade.

lin. See linn.

Lin, Linn, Linne, Line, Lyne, a stock ballad-locality (like Linkum): I, 78, 38; 466, 5; 478 f., 5, 10, 16, 34; II, 240, 2; 290, 19; IV, 379, 18; 381, 12; 382, 15; V,

14, 1 ff.; 182 f., 2, 11, 29; 219, 6; thro Linkum and thro Lin, II, 124, 37.

lin, III, 105, 11; 174, 15: stop.

lin'd, III, 164, 91: beat.

ling, lyng, III, 3, 6; 7, 5; 99, 53: a species of rush, or thin long grass, bent grass, Scotland ; in England, heath, furze.

lingcan, I, 299, 5: lichame, body.

linger, I, 334, 8: longer.

Linkem. See Linkum.

linkin, linken, IV, 332 b; V, 124, 4; 240, 1: tripping, walking with a light step. on a horse, II, 285, 11. linking ladie, IV, 355 b : light of movement. key gaed linking in, V, 18, b 23: passing in quickly, slipping in.

linkit his armour oer a tree, III, 270, E 7, comparing A 9; B 8; D 8, and observing the crooked carle in E 8, seems likely to be corrupt, and perhaps we should read leaned his arm out-oer. Otherwise, hung his armor, etc.

Linkum, an indefinite ballad-locality. not a bell in merry Linkum, II, 106, 21, 22. thro Linkum and thro Lin, II, 124, 37. cock crew i the merry Linkem, II, 239, B 4. a the squires in merry Linkum, IV, 432, 1.

linn, lin, lynn(e), water-course, torrent, river, pool in a river (A. S. hlynna, torrens): I, 303, D 4; II, 147, 9; 153, 24; III, 274, 1. of a mill-stream, I, 129, D 6. o'er the linne, II, 282 f., 9, 17, 18; IV, 479, 10 (= in the lynn, IV, 479, 5); II, 283, 8, 9: over the bank into.

Linnen, II, 225, D 3: Lunnon, London.

linsey, linsey-woolsey.

lint, IV, 433, 32: linen, linen mutch or cap.

lippen on me, II, 94, 10: depend. to God, III, 269, 12; to good=God, V, 243, 15: trust.

lirk, IV, 198, 2: crease, hollow.

lish, leash.

list, *n.*, III, 137, 2; 181, 16: inclination.

list, *v.*, III, 171, 9; 179, 4; 311, 19: desire, be disposed. *pret.* list, III, 171, 11. *impersonal,* me list, III, 97, 9. See lyste.

lith, lyth, I, 135, O 15, 17; 345, C 4; II, 412, 1; 413, 8: member, joint.

lith, I, 334, 7: light.

lith, lithe, lythe (Icel. hlýða), I, 334, 10; III, 22, 5; 198, 1; 411, 1: hearken.

lither, II, 54, 51; 138 f., 9, 13, 22, 23: bad. See lidder.

Little Brittaine, I, 284 f., 4, 24, 33, 37: generally understood as French Brittany, but it is inexplicable that Arthur should be reigning there. Perhaps Litle means no more in this piece than in Litle England, II, 440, 20, 22; III, 278, 34; 285, 27; Litle London, III, 285, 22; Litle Durham, III, 285 f., 29, 39, 40. All these places, it will be observed, are in the Percy MS.

live, leave.

live, V, 227, 13: dear.

live best, IV, 146, 2: are the best of those living.

lively, I, 184, 47: alive.

liuer, *adj.*, III, 180, 10: deliver, agile.

liuerance, III, 411, 8: payment for delivering.

livery-man, I, 419, 1; 421, 1: servant.

liues, II, 59, 25: 'lieves, believes.

liuor, III, 411 f., 8, 9, 10, 14: deliver, hand over, surrender.

load, III, 267, 10: loaded (with liquor).

loaden, *p. p.* of load, IV, 395, **A b** 5.

loan, lone, a common, any free or uncultivated spot where children can play or people meet, even the free spaces about a house: II, 62 a, 14, 16; 140, 1; V, 118, 2. (loan-head, IV, 285, 11, is toun-head in the original.)

locked, lockit, in a glove, II, 461, 21; 464, 6; 477, **D** 17: fastened.

lockerin, comes lockerin to your hand, IV, 213, 14; lockren, V, 258 b, 7: curling, closing as if to embrace.

loddy, IV, 70 f., **G** 4, 5, etc.: laddy.

lodder, loder, V, 283, 6, 16: louder.

lodesman. See ledesman.

lodging-maill, III, 474, 38: rent for lodging.

lodly, I, 285 f., 31, 43, 56; II, 44, 12: loathly, disgusting.

lodomy, IV, 398 f., 9, 34: laudanum.

loe, loie, loy, lou, *v.*, I, 438, 10; V, 221, 9; 260, 13; 272 b, 3, 7, 11; 277, 1, 4: love. See lea.

loffe, *n.* and *v.*, V, 79, 26, 28: love.

logie, IV, 175, **N** 11: lodge.

loie, loy, love. See loe.

lome, II, 44, 12: lame man.

lone, *n.*, II, 333, 1; 489, 17. See loan.

long, tall. Long Lankyn, Long Iamie, II, 328, 1, etc.; III, 358, 63, 65, etc.

long of, II, 436, 53; III, 98, 22: owing to, the fault of.

loo, love, II, 408, 23. *pret.* lood, II, 417, 2; 419, 52. See lea.

lood, loud.

loof, looff, lufe, luve, leuve, I, 15, 15; 16, **B** 16, **C** 16; 17, 14; 18, **F** 9; 19, 14; III, 374, 8: palm of the hand. (Icel. lófi.)

looke, IV, 503, 12: look up.

loon. See loun.

loord. See lourd.

loose, V, 300, No 191: lose.

loot, bend. See lout.

loot, *pret.* of let, I, 68, 7; 204, 19: allowed.

loot, *p. p.* (?) of let, I, 351, 49; III, 436, 13; IV, 33, 26: allowed, allowed to come.

looten, *p. p.* of let, II, 168, 8: allowed (to come). See lotten.

lope, *pret.* of loup, II, 59, 30; 434 f., 28, 47; 436, 58; III, 479, 39.

lord nor loun, III, 301, 32: man of high or low rank. In II, 159, 26, lord is a wrong reading; rogue nor loun, or the like, is required, as in 160, 20.

lordane, lurden, III, 25, 61: dolt, clodpoll, etc.

lore, lorne, III, 59, 51; V, 79, 32: lost.

loset, III, 94, 52: loosed, delivered.

loss, V, 200 a, 65; 262, No 223, 10; 277, 6: lose.

lotten, *p. p.* of let, I, 87, 38: allowed. See looten.

loudly, III, 440, 12: loud.

lough, loughe, *pret.* of laugh, II, 54, 58; 444, 48; V, 254 b, 2. See leuch, leugh.

lought, *pret.* of laugh, III, 82, 74; V, 51, 55.

loukynge, V, 283, 17: expectation, hope deferred.

loun, lown, lowne, loon, IV, 501, 36, 37: a person of low rank. laird or (nor) loun (lown), I, 69, 40, 41; 71, 32; III, 435, **F** 8; IV, 514, 12. lord nor (or) loun (lowne), III, 301, 32; 430, 13; 435, **E** 5; 436, 6, 8. IV, 11, 2; 519, **H** 2, **I** 2: rogue. often a mere term of general disparagement (as in, English loun): (of a man) II, 118, 3, 4; 140, 25; V, 171, 4; (woman) I, 100, 30; 491, **G** 24, **H** 22. fellow, without disparagement, IV, 258, 21. naughty girl, II, 419, 37. mistress, concubine, whore, II, 181 b; IV, 14, 13; 330 a, 3; 332 b; 469, 3; 519, 9; 520, 13. See lown.

loup, I, 102, **D** 3; II, 464, 1; IV, 44 f., 14, 15, 17, 23; 47, 4, 5: leap. *pret.* lap, leap, leepe, lope, loup, louped. *p. p.* loupen, luppen. loupin, V, 213, 3, has been explained as a form of leeping, heating (warming herself over the coal; cf. cowering oer a coal, I, 304, 2). We have, however, whisking ore the coal, I, 302, 4; reeking (=raiking) oer the coal, 304 **E** 3; and *across* agrees better with leaping than with heating.

loup, *pret.* of loup, II, 461, 5.

loupen, louped, *p. p.* of loup, III, 465, 27; IV, 462, 36.

lourd, loord, *pret.* and *p. p.* of lour = prefer, verb made from lever, rather. I had lourd, IV, 199, 18. I wad lourd have, IV, 7, 43. loord a had, V, 251, 36. I rather lourd it had been, II, 275 b.

lout, loot, I, 56, **B** 12; 351, 36, 48; II, 401, **C** 5: bow, bend, lean. *pret.* louted, looted. louted in, I, 331, **D** 5: bent our heads to enter? louted twafauld, threefauld, V, 242 b, 7: bent double, treble. *p. p.* louted, lootit, louten.

louten, *p. p.* of lout, II, 168, 9: bent.

love, I, 476, **J** 4: loaf.

love-clapped, II, 165, 10; 169, 8; 171, 13; 370, 8; 371, 8; IV, 392, 8; V, 277, 8: embraced lovingly, caressed.

loverd, I, 243 f., 1, 6, 17: lord.

louesome, III, 431, 30: lovely.

lov(e)ly, louelie, epithet of London: III, 199, 19; 310, 61; 352, 1; 355, 7. See leeve.

low, lowe, I, 211, 35; III, 93, 46: hill.

low, lowe, III, 435, **F** 5, 10; 436 f., 13, 20, 24, 34; IV, 47, 5; 514, 8: flame.

low, lowe, *pret.* of laugh, III, 110, 16; 112, 53; V, 78, 4. See lowhe.

lowe, doggs bite soe, III, 342, 66: a phrase for, take mean advantages.

lowe, bye lerbord or by lowe, IV, 504, 30: loof, luff, the after part of a ship's bow (Falconer, Marine Dictionary); or perhaps the weather side. See leaf.

lowhe, low, lowe, *pret.* of laugh, V, 80, 44, 46–48.

lown, IV, 304, 8, 9: must mean here a young man in a low social position, since there can be no question of her kissing a disreputable fellow. There is no proper contrast with lad, and probably we should read, laird nor lown (see **loun**).

lowse, loose, free.

loyed, V, 221, 9: loved.

lucettes, III, 297, 46: luces, pikes.

Luckenbooths, V, 162, **C** 7: a range of buildings which formerly stood in the thoroughfare of the High Street in Edinburgh, parallel to Saint Giles Church.

lue, loe, loo, lou, loie, lea, lee, lie, *v.*, love. See **lea**.

lufe, luve, leuve, loof, I, 16, **C** 16; 17, 14; 19, 14; III, 374, 8: palm of the hand.

lugs, I, 302, **A** 10; IV, 53, 11; 296, 8; V, 102, **B** 15; 103 b, 15: ears.

luid, III, 370, 19: loved.

luke, *pret.* of laugh, V, 238, 28.

lum, V, 125, 3, 9: chimney.

luppen, *p. p.* of loup, leap, I, 55, **A** 3, **B** 3; IV, 444, 26; 470, 30; 518, 8.

lurden, lordan, III, 35, 18: dolt, clodpoll.

luscan, a sturdy beggar (and thievish), III, 519 a.

lust, V, 213 a, 1: a bundle. (last, a measure, as twelve dozen hides or skins, etc. ?)

lust, III, 56, 6; 85 and 89, 446; 332, 13: inclination, disposition. thy lustës to full fyll, III, 90 b: wishes. att his owne lust, III, 332, 13: pleasure.

lute, *pret.* of lett, IV, 345, 8: allowed. V, 248, 15: let down.

luve, palm of the hand. See **loof**.

ly, lye, IV, 261, 24; V, 168 f., 1, 2, 3, etc.: live, dwell. *pret.* lyed.

lyand, lying.

lyart, IV, 7, 36: grizzled, gray.

lybertye, apoint a place of, II, 443, 39; 449, 44, 52: a place where the two can fight freely, without risk of interruption ?

lye. See **ly**.

lyed, II, 266, 28: lay, lived. See **ly**.

lygge, ligge, I, 328, 38–41: lie. See **lig**.

lygge, lay. See **lig**.

lyghte, lyght, I, 327, 21; III, 297, 33: alighted. See **light**.

lightly(e). See **lightly**.

lyke, I, 327, 22; III, 28, 121; 64, 165; 76, 417: please.

lyke, I, 506, 3, 8, 9; II, 295, 8; IV, 236, 30: lyke-wake, watching of a dead body. In II, 117, 16: simply, death-scene.

lyke-wake, I, 251, **B** 4, 5, 7; II, 282, 14; III, 495 b, 21; IV, 516 f., 1, 7, 18: watch of a dead body. dead lyke-wake, I, 251, **B** 4, 5: wake for your death. See **lyke, leak, leak-(lake-)wake**.

lyken, *participle*, IV, 511 b, **X** 6: about, at the point. See **liken**.

lynde, lyne, III, 75, 398; 91, 2; 92, 22; 93, 33; 97, 10; 98, 23; 100, 76, 78: linden, tree.

lyne. See **lynde**.

lyne. See **lin**.

lyng, III, 99, 53: heath. See **ling**.

lyon, III, 344, 33; 349, 33: the royal standard (quite out of place here).

lyste, me lyste, III, 78, 446: it would please me, I should like. See **list**.

lyth, lyth, lithe (Icel. hlýða), III, 56, 1; 63, 144, 70, 282; 71, 317: hearken.

lyth, member. See **lith**.

lyuer, III, 362, 82: leever, rather.

lyueray, III, 59, 70: present of clothes. III, 64, 161: purveyance of drink.

M

ma, III, 490, 15, 27, 29: bit, whit.

Mable, booke of, III, 422, 61: some book of predictions, like Thomas Rymer's.

made, a lie, I, 478, 25: told.

made, men, III, 406, 37: raised. made a bow o bere, V, 264 a, 2: contributed.

mae, III, 301, **E**; 349, 46; IV, 490, 27: more.

maen, mane, meen, *n.*, II, 107, 2: moan.

magger of, in the, III, 307, 1: in spite of, maugre.

maick, make, mate.

maid, may, used loosely of a young wife: II, 300, 6, 8; 307, 33; V, 227, 7. So κόρη, παρθένος, in Homer, of a young wife, and puella of married woman often.

maid *of a place*, as, maid of the Cowdenknows, IV, 200, 12, 13; 202, **J** 2, 3; 203, 8; 205, 14: the eldest daughter of the tenant or proprietor, who is generally called by the name of his farm.

maid alone, II, 149, 2: solitary, like burd-alone, I, 298, 2 (which, however, is there used of a man).

maiden, IV, 30 a: an instrument for beheading, resembling the guillotine.

maigled, IV, 41, note *: mangled.

maik. See **make**.

mail, rent. lodging-maill, III, 474, 38.

main. man o the main, is it to a man o the might, or till a man o the main, II, 403, 7, 8: main can have no sense distinct from might, and man of the might, man of the main, is simple verbiage. In **B** 4, **H** 6, we have, to a man of micht or a man of mean: man of mean cannot be wrenched into man of low degree, and we do not want that sense even if we could legitimately get it, for the antithesis is not between the man of micht and the man of mean degree, but between both these and the robber or robbers of the last half of the stanza. The stall copy, 405, 5, 6, having only grammar in mind, reads man (one) that's mean, and but for rhyme might perhaps have gone so far as, a man of means. IV, 146, 21, reads, man o mine, to avoid the difficulty. See **mean**.

main, *n.*, IV, 473, 39: moan. See **mane**.

ma-i-ntn, V, 303 a: maintain, support.

mair, IV, 21, 14: more, bigger.

mairly, IV, 59 f., d 2; e 2, g 2: a rhyme used for mair.

maist, II, 169, 7: almost.

maistly, I, 138 b, d 5: mostly, almost. See **mostly**.

make, maik, maicke, I, 127, 14; 128, 11: 129, **D** 8; 347, 23, 30; 348, 11, 17: mate, consort. I, 403, 12; II, 46, 1; IV, 344, 7; V, 184, 44: match, like; and so in, what is my lineage or what is my make, IV, 341, **D** 8.

make, III, 37, 67: for *made, p. p.*

making, IV, 208, 3: doing, deportment.

maks, V, 307 b: makes.

male, III, 63, 134; 68, 247, 255: (O. Fr. male) trunk. male-hors, III, 74, 374.

mall, with the leaden mall, III, 357, 42: mallet, hammer (referring to the weight of his stroke).

mallasin, malison.

man, V, 191, 8, 12: vassal. V, 304 b, 3: husband.

man, mane, maun, mun, I, 16, **B** 8, 9, 12–16; 146, 5, 6; V, 197, 12; 219, 29; 220, 4; 248, 12, 13: must.

mane, maen, main(e), meane, meen, I, 72, 20; 448, **A** 1, 3; etc.: moan, complaint, lament; often nothing more than utterance, enunciation, as, I, 253, 1; 394, **A** 2; 395, **C** 4; III, 489, 1.

mane, *v.*, I, 72, 23: moan. See **mean**.

maney, III, 109, 4: meny, followers. See **menë**.

mang, I, 108, 6: among.

manhood, manhead, manheed, men (man) o your, men to your, I, 108, 14; 109, 13; IV, 446 f., 14: a strange way of saying, if you are men (man) of true valor, willing to fight one by one. III, 422, 59: manly deed, exploit demanding courage.

manie, mennie, V, 270, 8: maunna, must not.

mankie, V, 173, 3: calamanco, a stuff made in the Low Countries.

manratten, manrydden (A. S. manrǽden), III, 359, 95; 362, 95: homage, vassalage.

manrent, IV, 34 b: homage, vassalage. See **manratten**.

mansworn, I, 394, 3; IV, 442, 10: perjured.

marchandise, III, 92, 22: dealing.

march-man, III, 296, 8: one who lives on the march, or border.

March-parti, Marche-partes, III, 310, 58, 67: Borderpart, -parts, Border, Borders.

marie, III, 491, 14: mare.

marie. See **mary**.

mark, II, 62 b, 11; 132, 29; IV, 202, **K** 2: murky. the mark, II, 164, 3. See **mirk**.

marke, merk, I, 394 ff., **B** 1; **C** 2; III, 68, 243, 246; 69, 270: two thirds of a pound.

marke hym, III, 297, 44: commit himself by signing the cross.

marries, IV, 487, 25: maids. See **mary**.

marrow, I, 147, 5; 148, **G** 4; 149, **I** 4; IV, 165, 13; 168, 2; V, 41, 16: (of man or woman) mate, husband, wife. IV, 165, 8, 9; **B** 2; 166, 2, 3; 167, **D** 6; 169, 5, 6; 170, **G** 3; **H** 3: match, equal in rank, equal antagonist. bear ye marrow, 169, 4: should perhaps be, be your marrow, as in 170, **G** 3.

mary, marie, marrie, marry, II, 369, 13, 15, 19, 20; 370, 13, 14, 17; 371, 14, 15, 20, 21, etc.; 390, 25; 391, 19; IV, 487, 25; 489, 26: a queen's lady, maid-of-honor (cf. III, 381 b ; 385, 18; 386, 19; etc.), maid (like abigail).

mary mild, IV, 213, 13: marigold; cf. V, 259, 5.

Mas (James Melvine), III, 471 a: Magister, Mr. Mess James Murray, V, 196, 51: see **Mess**.

masar, maser, III, 65, 175; 83, 86, 175: a drinking-vessel, of wood, especially of knotty-grained maple, often mounted with bands or rings of precious metals. See Way's note, Prompt. Parv., p. 328.

mass, in the frequent formula, when bells were rung and mass was sung and a' men bound to bed, II, 70, 21, etc.: a domestic religious service at the end of the day. evening-mass, II, 168, **A** 4.

mast, maste, III, 296 f., 22, 31; V, 79, 22: mayst.

master-man, II, 16, 2: captain of a ship. V, 191, 19: chief.

masteryes, make, III, 92, 27: do feats of skill.

mat, matt, mat he (ye) dee! wae mat fa, mat(t) worth ! = mot, in the sense of may: II, 27, 7, 10; 472, 25, 33; IV, 391, 6; 392, 9, 21; 428, 6; V, 166, 10; 306, 10. See **met**.

maught, maugt, might.

maugre, maugre in theyr teethe, III, 67, 225: in spite of.

maun, I, 16, **B** 8, 9, etc.; **C** 7–10, etc.; 17, **D** 5–7, etc.; 146, 5, 6; 183, 25, 26: must. 71, 39 in *pret.* sense. See **man, mun**.

maunna, I, 185, 25: must not. See **manie**.

mavosie, I, 465, 8: mavis, song-thrush.

maw, sea-maw, II, 360, 3; 363, 7; 365, 5; IV, 482, 6: sea-mew, gull.

maw, *v.*, I, 427, 13, 15: mow.

mawys, I, 326, 2: mavis, song-thrush.

may, mey, I, 115, **B** 1, 3, etc.; 173 f., 6, 10; III, 93, 39; 286, 45; IV, 432, 9; 515, 2: maid.

may, *optative*, frequently put after the subject, as, Christ thy speed may bee ! thou mayst sune be ! I may be dead ere morn! III, 355 f., 5, 23; 359, 87; 370, 8, 11; IV, 365, 18.

may be=is, like *can be:* II, 448, 33; 451, 100. might be = was, III, 452, 10. (So, possibly, might see, I, 434, 30.)

may gold, III, 497, 13: marigold.

mayne, strength.

maystry, mastery.

me, I, 243 f., 5, 15: men, French *on*.

me, *ethical dative*, sawe I me, etc., III, 65, 184; 68, 249; 75, 381; 79, 147; 80, 169.

meal, III, 163, 77: meal-bag.

meal, II, 230, 14, 15; 362, 36: mold, dust, earth. See **meel**.

mean, man of, I, 358, 30; II, 233, **F** 3; 400, 4, 5; 404, 6, 7; V, 36, **B** 8, 9: mere verbiage, I judge; *mean* looks like an attempt to escape from *main*, which see. (man of mean, II, 233, **F** 3, not being joined with man of might, might be understood as, man of main, or violent man.)

mean, meane, meen, *v.*, I, 426, 5; V, 246, 4, 6: moan, lament. I, 388, **A** 7, 10: bemoan, lament the state of. not to mean, V, 160, 2: not to be pitied. mean, V, 160, 1, is doubtful, but the verb corresponding to moan is to be preferred. See **mane, menyd**.

mean, *n.*, moan. See **meen**.

meany, III, 307, 3, 10: troop. See **menë**.

meaten, meeten, II, 434, 17; III, 33, 158: measured.

meathe, IV, 378, 9; 380, 17: landmark.

meatrif, III, 163, 87: abounding in food.

meckle, meikle, muckle, IV, 513, 6, 7 : much.

medder, V, 221, 11: mother.

medill-erthe, I, 327, 27. See middle-earth.

meed, I, 68, 10, 14; II, 172, 33: mood, heart, state of feeling.

meed, warld's meed, I, 108, 14; IV, 446 f., 14: seems to be corrupted from mate (make). Woreldes make is a familiar phrase in Old English, and not unfrequent in ballads.

meel, meel or mor, III, 281, 8, 10: mold, earth, ground; but perhaps an error for mede, mead. See meal.

meen, v., moan, lament. See mean, v.

meen, mean, I, 427, 5; II, 124, 39; 417, 11; III, 389, 12, 13 : lamentation. See mane.

meen, I, 222, 8; 315, 8; IV, 416, 10: moon.

meet, I, 148, F 10: (causative) pass, put, thrust in.

meet, meete, II, 46, 45: even, equal. II, 229, 13: scant, close, and so, perhaps, II, 436, 61.

meeten, meaten, II, 434, 17: measured, by measure. See met.

meiht, I, 243, 3: mayst.

meikle, meickle, mickle, muckle, I, 72, 24, 25; 86, 2, 3; 309 f., 2, 4; 330, A 3, B 3; IV, 514, 5: much, great.

meisseine, V, 132, 7: spanker, or perhaps, Fr. misaine, foresail.

mell, I, 299, 6; 304, 10; F 6; 305, 12; V, 108, B 6: mall, wooden hammer, beetle.

mell, IV, 177 b, I 7: mail.

mell, III, 172, 24: meddle.

meller's hoops, I, 304, F 5: mill-casings, the circular wooden frames which surround mill-stones.

melten (goud), IV, 471, 37: molten.

menë, menye, meany, menyie, meynë, maney, monie, III, 72, 335: followers, band.

menement, V, 242, 9, 11, 13: amendment.

menji, menji feathers in her hat, V, 163, 13: many.

mennie, manie, V, 270, 8: maunna, must not.

mensked, I, 334, 11: honored, dignified.

menyde (of hir songe), I, 326, 2: moaned, uttered, delivered. See mean.

menye, menyie, household, retinue, people: III, 91 a; IV, 127, 4, 5. See menë.

mere, IV, 493, 21: more.

meri. See mery.

merk, marke, I, 394 f., B 1, C 2: two thirds of a pound.

merk. See merkes.

merk, v., mark. merked them one, III, 297, 47: took their aim at.

merkes, III, 75, 397: distances between the bounds.

merke-soote, I, 334, 4: mark-shot, distance between the marks (cf. III, 75, 397), from bow to target, bow-shot.

merlion, merlyon, II, 45, 21, 33: merlin, the smallest of British falcons.

merrilye, III, 329, 11: in good or valiant fashion. So, nearly, IV, 477, 8.

merry (men). See mery.

merry Cock land, III, 250, 1: corruption of the merry Scotland of 249, I, J, 1; 251, M, 1; 252, O, 1.

merrys, I, 327, 22: mars, marrest.

mery, meri, merry, merrie, myrri, myrry (men), II, 386, 12; III, 66, 205; 71, 316; 73, 340; 97, 9; 114, 121, 131; 116, 2; 285 f., 30, 48; 309, 37; 330, 17; 430, 5; 431, 4; 432, 2; 433, 2; IV, 234, 39; V, 191, 4, 14: a standing phrase for followers, companions in arms.

mese, I, 328, 45: course (at table).

mese, III, 484 a, 16: mitigate.

Mess, an epithet said to be contemptuous for a priest or parish minister (as one who says, or said, mass), so Mess John,, IV, 442, 10, 12; but there is no reason to suppose disrespect in V, 196, 51. See Mas.

mestoret, V, 80, 42: needed.

met, I, 324, 3; IV, 455, 4; V, 195, 9: mat, may. See mat.

met, pret. of mete, III, 60, 73: measured. p. p. met, mete, III, 60, 72; 203, 17; IV, 465, 23; 467, 13.

methe, meat.

mett, meet.

met-yard, III, 105, 27: measuring-rod.

mey, V, 161, 9: maid. See may.

meynë, III, 27, 96; 58, 31; 61, 95, 97; 76, 419: retinue, suite, household, company, body of people. See menë.

meythe, III, 112, 59: might.

micht, v., V, 299, 4: might.

micht 'll, might well.

mickle, great, much. See meikle.

midder, mideer, mother.

middle-earth, medill-erthe, I, 327, 27; II, 59, 25: (A. S. middangeard, middaneard), earth (conceived as being the middle of the universe; see miðgarðr in Vigfusson).

middle stream, III, 125, 19: middle of the stream.

middle waist, IV, 523, 6: middle of his waist.

mid-larf, crowing a, II, 230, 5, 8: corrupt (changed by Scott to merry midnight). Taking into account the young cock crew i the merry Linkem, II, 239, B 4, midlarf may stand for some locality (suggestion of Professor Kittredge).

might be = was, III, 452, 10. See may, can.

mild, maidens mild, II, 312, 1; 314, C 1, D 1; 316, 1: meek, gentle, demure. So Mild Mary, II, 315, E 7; Mary(-ie) Mild, III, 395, M 1, 3; 396, N 1; 398 a, c 4; Mary Mile, III, 386, 5, 6, 8. Corrupted to Moil, IV, 507 b, S 2; Miles, IV, 511 a, 5. myld(e) Mary, of the Virgin, III, 97, 7, 17; 98, 35: lenient, compassionate. myld myʒth, V, 283, 13.

milk-dey, IV, 262, 26; 524, 6: dairy-woman.

mill, mille, IV, 503, 13; 505, 45; V, 221, 15, 16; 224, 25: mile.

millaine, I, 286, 42, 45: of Milan steel. See myllan.

mill-capon, II, 477 b, D 27 : a poor person who asks charity at mills from those who have grain grinding, the alms usually given being a gowpen, or handful, of meal.

millering, II, 467, 42: waste meal, sweepings of a mill (dust [which] lyes in the mill, II, 470, 43).

mill-town, mill-toun, II, 471, 18; V, 238, 29: miller's steading or place.

miln, I, 18, 11: mill.

milner, mylner, III, 85, 4; 360, 111: miller.

min. See mind.

mind, II, 216, 12, 15; 218, 13, 16: recollection. her mind she keeped, II, 72, 13: did not forget what she had promised. for changing o her min, 81, 32: seems to mean, lest she should change her mind; but the sense is not striking.

mind. mind o, on, I, 481, 26; IV, 194, 16, 9; 195, 15; 196, 17; 197, 17, etc.: remember. *pret.* mind, I, 183, 30. mind of, on, mind to, I, 470, 16; IV, 403 f., 14, 28; 437, 24: remind of. he mind't him on, V, 18, 5: remembered.

minde, ffor the maydens loue that I haue most minde, II, 58, 5: elliptical or corrupt. Comparing 59, 24 (where the MS. reads, wrongly, most meed) we see that *for* is not to be taken with *minde*. We must understand *most in mind* or *most mind to* or *of*, or, possibly, *minde* may be (from minnen, remember) *had in mind*.

minge (A. S. myndgian), III, 355, 6; 362, 72: utter. minged, II, 59, 21: didst name the name of, mention (or, perhaps, only bore in mind). myn, III, 358, 72.

minikin, V, 201 b: little, pretty little.

minion, I, 284, 12: dainty.

minnie, minny, II, 473, 16, 17; IV, 69, 16; 294, **C** 9, 10; V, 115, 9: mother. IV, 6, 15; V, 250, 14: dam.

mint to, II, 469, 31; IV, 493, 20; V, 28, 67; 238, 21: put out the hand towards, move towards. minted as, V, 9, 7: took a direction as if, made as if.

mire, myre, I, 428, 13, 14; 429, 7, 8; III, 475 b: swamp, bog. mire an moss, bog, an miery hole, IV, 22, 12; cf. 184, 5.

mirk, myrke, mark, I, 326, 16; IV, 517, 14: dark.

Mirry-land toune, III, 244, **B** 1: probably a corruption of the *merry Lincoln* of **A** 16, 17; 246, **D** 1; 251, **L** 1.

miscarry me, IV, 267, 11: get me into trouble; fail, disappoint me (?).

misgae, misgave.

misgiding, V, 117, 15: ill treatment.

misguide, misgiding, V, 117, 15; 119, 15: ill treatment.

miss, *n.*, IV, 317, **E** 5; 325, **C** 5, **D** 3: mistress, whore.

miss, *n.*, II, 465, 4: wrong or injury.

miss(e), *v.*, I, 210, 12: omit, fail. miss your Wanton slack, IV, 22, 10, 12: fail to keep him tightly reined (?).

mis-sworn, I, 395, **C** 5: mansworn, perjured.

mister, myster, III, 450 a; IV, 268, 26; 464, 15: need, requirement, an exigency. misters, III, 164, 90: sorts of.

mistkane, I, 105 a, 18, if not miswritten, seems to be simply a phonetic variation of mistane.

mith, mithe, *n.*, I, 334, 6, 7, 11: might.

mith, mithe, *v.*, II, 139, 10; IV, 493, 19: might. mith slain, II, 165, 23: might [have] slain.

mode, I, 328, 47: spirit.

modther, IV, 260, 3, 7: mother.

mody, mudie, I, 334, 10: proud, high-spirited.

mold, molde, mane of molde, I, 327, 20: earth. ouer the mold, into the Scottish mold, I, 433, 21, 23: land, country. I, 434, 37; II, 246, 7: ground.

Moll Syms, I, 126, 13; IV, 448, 7: a well-known dance tune of the sixteenth century.

mome, III, 352, 7: dolt.

monand, *n.*, II, 87, 36: moaning.

mone, I, 326, 1: moan, lamentation, complaint. See **meen**.

monie, IV, 437, 2: menie, company, suite. See **menë**.

montenans. See mountnaunce.

monty, IV, 42 a, note §: staircase. (Fr. montée.)

mood, giue me, III, 105, 23: though *give me my God* looks like a bold change, it is not improbable. We have, yeve me my savyour, in the Romaunt of the Rose, 6436, le cors nostre Seigneur, 12105, Michel. And again: For it was about Easter, at what times maidens gadded abrode, after they had taken their Maker, as they call it. Wilson, Arte of Logike, fol. 84 b. "In 1452 John Bulstone (of Norwich) bequeathed to the church of Hempstede 'j pyxte, to putte owre lord god in.'" Academy, XL, 174. (These last two citations furnished by Prof. J. M. Manly.) Again, the Breton ballad, Ervoan Camus, Revue Celtique, II, 496, st. 6, has 'she has received my God.' (Dr F. N. Robinson.) See V, 297 a.

moody-hill, moudie-hill, mould-hill, IV, 148 f., 48; 150, g, h 48: mole-hill.

mool, mools. See moul.

morn, morrow. the morn, III, 480, 18; 482, 14; 488, 19; 489, 11; IV, 517, 18: to-morrow. the morn's morning, IV, 373, 8.

mornin's gift, morning gift, II, 132, 32; 135, 28: gift made the morning after marriage.

mort, III, 307, 8; IV, 26, 8: note on the horn to announce the death of deer.

mose-water. See moss-water.

moss, muss, mose, I, 78, 32; 99, 6; III, 4, 3, 48; 440, 10; IV, 443 f., 6, 19; 445, 8: bog.

moss-water, mose-water, II, 193, 21; 195, 33; V, 224, 19: water of a peat-bog.

most, I, 328, 50: greatest.

mostly, maistly, IV, 242 b: almost.

mot, I, 473, 5: must.

mot, mote, I, 333, 2; III, 7, 9; 68, 243; 75, 394; 113, 81; IV, 137, 29; V, 82, 25, 27; 83, 44, 50, 53; 283, 3: may.

mote, III, 68, 253: meeting.

moten, molten.

mothe, mouthe, I, 334, 4, 6: for meahte (mohte), might.

mother-in-law, II, 71, 11; 72 f., 14, 15: stepmother.

mother-naked, I, 344, 33: naked as in, or coming from, the womb.

mothly, III, 148, 27: motley.

motion, III, 216, 38: proposal.

mou, moue, mow, I, 302, B 8; III, 149, 34; IV, 277, 10; V, 115, 9; 268, 18; 269, 13: mouth.

moudie-hill. See moody-hill.

moue, I, 16, C 15: put up in ricks.

mought, V, 76, 28; 83, b 25, etc.: mote, may. III, 30, 98: might, were able.

moul, mouls, mool, mools, IV, 329, A b, after 16; 330, D d 20: mould, dust, ashes (of the dead). I, 184, 10; II, 233, 6; 429, 6; IV, 492, 6; V, 210, 10: earth of a grave. See meal, II, 230, 14, 15.

mould-hill. See moody-hill.

mould-warpe, III, 420, 20: mole.

mountnaunce, montenans, I, 327, 31; III, 64, 168: amount.

mouthe. See mothe.

mow, III, 149, 34: seems to be meant for mouth (lip). But perhaps we may understand grimace (for a tyrant to make faces at). See mou.

mow, mows, IV, 224, 22; 225, 20: jest.

moyen, IV, 42 a, note: means.

mucell. See muckle.

muck, IV, 323, 6: dung.

muck the byre, IV, 293, 9; 294, C 9, 10; 295, D 9; 297, 9: carry out dung from the cow-house.

muckle, mukle, mucell, meikle, IV, 398, 6; 494, 33: big. IV, 399, 40; V, 271, 13: much.

mudie, III, 434, 27, 28: bold. See mody.

muir, moor.

mullertd, IV, 86, 12: miller.

mun, maun, man, II, 59, 20; 314, 28; IV, 343, 6: must.

mune, moon.

munt, I, 304, E 2: come to, make out.

mure, V, 202 b: moor, heath (?).

muss, III, 4, 3, 4, 8: moss, bog. See moss.

myght, welcome myght thou be, III, 65, 177: Old Eng. 2d pers. pres. ind. = mayst.

myght neuer no tyme to sleepe, III, 77, 441: probably corrupt, and to be read, no tymë slepe; but the construction is not unknown.

myȝth, n., V, 283, 13: might, power.

myld, mylde. See mild.

myle, two myle way, III, 64, 168: the time it takes to go two miles.

myllan, III, 309, 31: Milan steel. See millaine.

mylner, milner, III, 81, 4; 97, 8: miller.

myn, III, 358, 72: say. See minge.

myneyeple, III, 308, 30: corruption of manople, a gauntlet protecting the hand and the whole fore-arm (?). Skeat.

myre. See mire.

myrke, mirk, mark, I, 327, 30: dark.

myrri, myrry. See mery.

myrthës can, III, 66, 210: knows pleasant stories.

mysaunter, III, 13, 10: mischance.

myster, III, 68, 244: need, occasion. See mister.

mystery, mysterie, III, 495, B b, after 7; IV, 517, 15: craft.

N

n, carried on from preceding word to following. noo nother, no noder, III, 81, 58; 100, 80: none other. a nother, nether, III, 80, 200; V, 247, 9: an other. a naughtless, noughtless, IV, 286, 12; 287, 5: an aughtless, good for nought. a noke, V, 81, 45: an oke. they nere, they nee, III, 112, 50; 204, b 31: theyn ere, thyn ee. my nane, I, 469, 29 (but nane should probably be name). So, his nawn, her nain (nen), yer nane, as if from hisn, hern, yern, I, 469, 28; III, 269, 1; IV, 132, 13; V, 224, 24. In, an oute-horne, III, 30, 87, n seems to have been carried back, from noute (see V, 297 a). n in nant, III, 35, 24, 31, is an arbitrary prosthesis.

na, nae, no, not: I, 68 f., 12, 22, 31, 44, 51; 107, 3, 8; 310, 9, 11, 13; V, 260, 16. Frequently united with the preceding verb. hadna, I, 343, 5, 18. winna, 354, 27. canno, 368 f., 35, 37, 39. coudna, 369, 51. wadna, 394, 9, 11. shanae, 394, B 1. woudna, 396, 23, 26. shoudna, 396, 27. didna, 397, 12. kensnae, 466, 13. wasnae, 467, 34, etc., etc.

naesaid, IV, 371, 7: refused.

nags, naggs, nogs, III, 480, 11; 481, 8; 484 a, 11: notches, nicks.

nain, own. See n.

nane, nen, yer nane, my nane, etc.: own. (n, originally, carried on from mine.) See n.

nane, neen, none. I, 16, 6; 309, 12; II, 108, 13; 129, 16; 425, 3: adverbially, not, not at all. See none.

nant, III, 35, 24, 31: aunt.

naow, V, 304, 5, 12, 14: now.

napkin (-ken, -kain), I, 395, 9, 14: neckerchief. II, 108, 3; 158 f., 5, 8; 160, 4, 7; 163, 4, 6: pocket hand-kerchief. pocket-napkin, IV, 468, 2.

nappy, V, 84, 13 (of ale): strong.

naps, naps of gold were bobbing bonnie, IV, 295, 8, 9: knobs, balls, mentioned as ornaments to gloves, II, 133, D 6, golden-knobbed gloves; 134, 8, 13, siller-knapped gloves.

napskape, knapscap, IV, 7, 35; V, 251, 31: head-piece.

nar = nor, with comparative, for than: III, 112 f., 57, 69; V, 78 f., 12, 18. See nor.

nas, I, 244, 15: ne was, was not.

naught, V, 102, A 13: naughtiness.

naughtless, a naughtless lord, IV, 287, 5; a noughtless heir, 286, 12: an aughtless, oughtless, good-for-naught, impotent.

naughty, V, 267, 13: good-for-naught.

naur, II, 62 a, 15: near, or nearer.

naw = na = no.

naw, IV, 442, 2: nay. V, 296, a: not.

nawn, own. See n.

naye, withowghten naye, III, 296, 18: undeniably, truly.

ne, III, 349, 46; V, 272 b, 5, 6; 273, 16: no. III, 62, 128: not.

ne, stand ye nè aw, III, 350, 53: misprint (in original); g, stand in no awe.

nean, V, 219, 27; 220, 1; 257, 11: none.

near, neare, ner, nere, I, 101, 19; II, 183, 30; 191, 37; III, 62, 119; 111, 46; V, 224, 28: nearer.

near, IV, 446, 14⁴; 447, 14⁴: corrupt, as the repetition from the second verse shows; *while* (till) *my days are near* (to an end) would be extremely forced, in any case.

near, neer, never.

near-hand, *adj.*, IV, 197, 4, 5: near, short. *adv.*, III, 161, 36; IV, 222, 8 (near-han): near, almost.

neast, neist, nist, nest, V, 117, A 7; 216 f., 1, 5, 7, 10, 18; 242 a, 10, 12: next.

neathing, nothing.

neave, III, 123, 16, 20: fist.

neb, I, 425, A 16: beak.

nee, III, 422, 67: nigh.

needle-tack, II, 217, 5: fastening or stitch with a needle.

neen, none. See nane.

neen nae, II, 318 b, 4: need na, need not.

neerice, nurse. See nourice.

neeze, V, 222 b, 26: sneeze, snort.

neigh, *v.*, II, 54, 54, 55: nigh, approach.

neis, I, 302, B 8; IV, 247, B 12: nose.

neist, niest, I, 223, 9; 314, 5; 419 f., 1, 3, etc.: next.

nelle, V, 284, 22: ne will, will not.

nen, her nen, V, 224, 24: own. See nane.

ner, nere, III, 62, 119; 111, 46: nearer. See near.

nere, III, 113, 75: were [it] not.

nere, they nere, III, 112, 50: theyn ere, thine ear.

neshe, III, 445, 31: of delicate quality.

nest, next. See neast.

nettle-dyke, II, 463, 22: wall with nettles growing on it, or near it. Cf. II, 467, 40; 469, 42.

neuk, coat-neuk, II, 107, 4, 5: nook, corner.

new-fangle, I, 272, 9: fond of novelties, capricious, inconstant.

next, I, 412, 27; II, 45, 30, 34: nighest.

nextand, II, 94, 6. See -an.

neys, V, 80, 39: nice (ironically).

nicher, nicker, *n.* and *v.*, III, 370, 10; IV, 18, 15; 19, 13; 20, 10; 21, 11: neigh.

nicht, the, to-night.

nicked him of naye, II, 52, 12; nickd them wi nae (nay), V, 182 f., 12, 30 (clearly borrowed from the above in Percy's Reliques): refused with nay.

nicker. See nicher.

nick-nack, playd nick-nack on the wa, V, 123, 16; 124, B 14: to express the sound of successive collisions.

niddart, niddart ither wi lang braid-swords, II, 422, 49: thrust at. Jamieson, pressed hard upon. Correspondents from the North of Scotland say, notched, slashed.

nie, III, 473, 27: neigh.

nie, neigh, nigh.

niest, I, 15, B 3; 147, 5: next, nearest. come niest, IV, 485, 30: nigh to. See neist.

niffer, *n.* and *v.*, I, 203, C 10, 15; IV, 406, 24: exchange.

night-coif, III, 514, 3; 515, 1; V, 225, 4: night-cap.

night-wake, IV, 453, 3, 4: night-watch, as of a dead body, perhaps a corruption of *lyke-wake*.

nimble, nimle, wrongly for thimble, thimber, I, 332, E 2, F 2, G 2.

nine, the, III, 392, 8: the nine justices of the supreme criminal court of Scotland. Kinloch, A. S. B., p. 259.

ning, V, 165 f., 4, 12: nine. nine, 111, 26, is changed from ninge. In the older stages of the language, remarks Dr. Murray (Dialect of the Southern Counties of Scotland, p. 125), ng was often written for Latin gn, and vestiges of this substitution of the nasal for the liquid n are still found in the spoken dialect.

nip, III, 160, 18, 19: bit.

nires, norice, nurse. See nourice.

nist, nest, neast, V, 216, 10; 242 a, 10, 12: next.

nit, III, 465, 20: knit, fasten.

nit, I, 450, 2–4: nut.

nit-broun, IV, 469, 7; 470, 23, 29, etc.: nut-brown.

no, I, 86, 13; 100, 10; 108, 6, 8; 135, P 8, 10; II, 218, 12; 222, 19; III, 465, 32: not.

noble, nobellys, III, 113, 81; 126, 39; 201, 29: a gold coin of the value of one third of a pound. (Fifteen score nobles is of course exactly an hundred pound.) =20 groats, V, 76 f., 18, 19, etc.

nocked, III, 82, 132; 86, 132: notched.

noder, nother, III, 81, 58; 100, 80, no noder, noo nother=none other. See n.

nog. See nags.

noghte, not.

nolt, nout, V, 249, 4: neat, neat-cattle.

nom, III, 51 b, 13–15: take.

none, *adv.*, II, 361, 24; V, 295, 1: not at all. See nane.

none of, none of my brother, II, 11, 3, 5, 7: not at all my brother.

noo, V, 307, 11: now.

noorice. See nourice.

nor, nar, after a comparative, I, 5, C 9–18; II, 134 f., 15, 29; 268, 21; 374, 13; 409, 19; IV, 166, 12; V, 184, 49: than. nor be, II, 97, 22: than to be (if liker means more likely). too gude nor ever woud make a lie, II, 372, 26: better than, too good, to make. I doubt not nor she be, II, 390, 23,=je ne doute pas qu'elle ne soit.

not, IV, 331 b, 8: misprint for *out*.

note, notte, V, 283, 9, 19: nut.

note, III, 512, E 6: corrupt (*nut* in F 7). Some impossibility is required.

noth, nothe, I, 334, 7, 8: not.

nother. See noder.

noughtless, naughtless, IV, 286, 12; 287, 5: a noughtless=an oughtless, good-for-nothing, impotent.

noumbles, nowmbles, noumbles of the dere, of a do, III, 58, 32; 64, 172: frequently defined entrails; Palsgrave, praecordia, the numbles, as the heart, the splene, the lunges, and lyver. At least a part of the noumbles are the two muscles of the interior of the thighs of a deer: venatores nombles vocant frustum

362 GLOSSARY

carnis cervinae sectum inter femora (Ducange). See
the elaborate directions for breaking or undoing deer
in Juliana Barnes's Boke of Huntynge, and in Madden, Sir Gawayne and the Grene Kny3t, vv. 1344–
48 especially.

nourice, nourrice, noorice, nourry, nurice, nurische, nury, II, 322, 6, 13–17; 333, 5–7; III, 433, C
7; IV, 31, 7; 32, 3; 480, 5, 10, etc.: nurse.

nout, nolt, III, 460, 25, 36; IV, 246, 13; V, 116, 1:
neat cattle.

noute-horne, a, III, 26, 87: horn of neat, ox, cow
(wrongly substituted for, an oute-horne; see V, 297).

nouthe, I, 334, 5: not.

nouther, IV, 219, 8: neither.

now, V, 78 f., 5, 24, 25: new.

noy, I, 217, 7, 12: grief.

nul, nule, I, 244, 11, 13: will not.

nume, pret., III, 355, 4: took.

nurice. See nourice.

nurische, IV, 28 a, 29 a: nurse. See nourice.

nury. See nourice.

nyghtgales, I, 327, 33: nightingales.

nyll, II, 478, 4: will not.

O

O, brighter O shall, IV, 170, G 10: heard for *rose*. For
rose (which the last letter of *brighter*, the *o*, and the
first letter of *shall* make) cf. 167, 17; 169, 14; 175,
M 11.

o=of. diel o there, III, 488, 26: devil (i. e. not a
bit) of anything in that way (?) (devil be there,
489, 43).

o=on: I, 232, A 2; II, 375, 15, 16; III, 488 f., 23, 39,
45; IV, 84, 19.

ochanie, och how, IV, 103, 14; III, 392, 11: interjections of sorrow.

ocht, IV, 230, 1: aught.

ochree. See ohon.

of=on: I, 284, 14, 16: II, 59, 23; 452, 5; III, 105, 19;
309, 46 (on, 45, vppone, 42); 355, 8; 359, 89; 464, 2; IV,
503, 20. beate of mee, II, 54, 53 (?). In, put of the
pot, put of the pan, II, 118, 8, *of* is perhaps simply
an error of the scribe; we have, put on, 119, 5, 6. In,
seruyd (q. v.) hi*m* of bred, I, 241, 1, *for* is required,
and *of*, which would signify *with*, cannot stand.

officier, V, 155, D 2: officer.

o3aines, I, 192 a: against, towards.

oger, I, 202, 1: auger.

ohon ochree, III, 390, 13: exclamation of sorrow.

okerer, III, 58, 46: usurer.

old, auld, old (auld) son, of babe just born, II, 95, 11,
12; 105, 7; 107, 4, 5, 6, 17: called young son, II, 104,
12, 15; 106, 8, 10, 18, and, at II, 95, immediately after,
13, 14. See auld son. old daughter, II, 382, 1; 387,
1; 388, 15: oldest. old sister, I, 175, D 8: one older
than a second sister.

old, auld, in your fifteen year old, I, 115, 13; in fifteen
years old, I, 116, 13: of age. See aull, auld.

on=of: III, 93, 38; 132, 3; 231, 84; 296, 20; 308, 13.

on=one: V, 78 f., 7, 26, 28; 80, 52. on for on, III, 308,
21.

on, wedded on, I, 146, 24; married on, I, 497, 22: on
the strength of (to have as a dowry).

on ane, I, 334, 6: anon.

on fere, III, 98, 38: in company.

on o=on (on upon?): III, 349, 38 (calld on o); 488,
25, 27; IV, 470, 18; 517, 9. (cald of, IV, 503, 20.)

onbred, I, 415 b: incompletely grown.

one, I, 104, 6; II, 45, 28: a. of one, I, 104, 6² should
have been retained (=on a).

one, on.

onë, ony, onie, II, 58, 3: any.

ones, onys, III, 98, 23: once.

onfowghten, III, 297, 41: unfought, without fighting.

onlouping, III, 449 b: mounting (of a horse).

onthought lang, I, 478 f., 13, 47: without wearying,
entertained. See unthought lang, thinke lang.

ony, onie, onë, any.

oor, I, 133, M 6: hour.

or, I, 285, 33; 294, 10; 328, 35; 411, 17; II, 22, 13; 105,
8: before. or eir, II, 21, A 9: or or (doubling of
before).

or, II, 166, 27: than.

order, ordre, III, 66, 197, 198: rule of an order.

ordered, II, 257, 9: taken order for, made arrangements for.

orders, III, 286, 44: prepares.

ordeyn, III, 72, 326: give order for, levy.

orghie, IV, 513, H 2⁴ (to be supplied): orgeis, a
fish, large kind of ling. See V, 299 b, note on No
178.

orlange, II, 61, 8, 9, 12: perversion of eldrige.

orless, I, 141 b, S: emended to unless.

orpharë, I, 326, 9: orfevrie, goldsmith's work.

osterne, III, 412, 27: austere. See austerne.

ostler, V, 155, C 4, D 2: innkeeper.

ostler-ha, III, 270, 6: ostler-house, hostelry, inn.

ostler-house, III, 268, 4, 6, 8; 269, 4–6: hostelry.

other, pl., III, 298, 66; 335 b.

ottraunce, at, III, 90 b: to the utterance, extremity,
death.

ought, I, 294, 12: am under obligation. *pret.* and *p. p.*
III, 228, 9; 431, 30: owed.

ould, IV, 456, 9; V, 199 b, 35: would.

our, owr, ower, over, too.

oure, prep., over. See ower.

ousen, owsen, owsn, II, 192, 6: oxen.

out, he slew out, II, 383, 25; beat out, III, 151, A 4,
B 4: out and out. fight ye all out, IV, 173, 6:
through, to the last.

out into, I, 115, B 2: from within.

out of hand, II, 321, 3; III, 440, 25: forthwith.

out the gate, way, IV, 470, 21; 477, 12: along the
way.

outehorne, III, 26, 87(the original and popular reading): here, a horn blown to call out citizens to the
support of the civil authority. See Spelman's Glossary, 1687, p. 441. Cf. V, 297 a.

outlyer, I, 175 f., **D** 3, 9, 15, 21: one who lives away from men, in the woods, banished man, outlaw.

out make I, 61, **C c** 5: make out.

outmet, *p. p.*, III, 29, 158: measured out.

out-oer, -our(e), -ower, -owre, -over, I, 246, 13, 14; II, 256, **K** 1; III, 6, 19; 7, 17; 270, 13, 17: over, above. heirs out ower a' my land, II, 176, **C** 8. leand himsel outowre a tree, III, 270, **D** 8. the flower out ower (owr) them a', II, 256, **L** 1; III, 246, **D** 7. out oer her, IV, 224, 19, should perhaps be, out o' her.

outrake, III, 413, 32: excursion, outing.

outside, outsyde, II, 444, 43; 449, 48: place apart, retired.

outspeckle, IV, 7, 30; V, 250, 27: laughing-stock.

outthro, IV, 445, 20: through to the opposite side.

outwood, III, 179, 8: wood outside (of a town?).

ouer all, III, 28, 141: everywhere.

ouer goddes forbode, forbott.   See **forbode**.

ouer-by-gone, I, 326, 8: covered, set.

overthrew us, V, 134, 8: threw us over.

o-vour, II, 25, **F** 13: half owre, half way over.

ower, owre, oure, I, 16, **C** 17; 80, 1: over. ower (a window): over against.

ower, owr, our, over, too.

owerturn, owreturn, I, 332, **E, F** 7; III, 10, 21: refrain.   See **owerword**.

owes, who, IV, 205, 27: owns, whose is (who owns= wha's aucht).

owerword, owre-word, oerword, II, 254, 8, 9; 363, 14; IV, 7, 28; 482 f., 8, 11: refrain (word frequently repeated), call, cry.   See **owerturn**.

owre, II, 20, 8: or, before.

owsn, owsen, ousen, I, 465, 2; II, 175, 7, 8; 176, 8, 9; 192, 6; 194, 10: IV, 12, **C** 8; 27, 20: oxen.

owthe, III, 112, 51: out.

owtlay, III, 99, 43: outlaw.

oxe-lig, ox-leg.

oxtere, IV, 506, 6: (A. S. óhsta) arm-pit.

oyes, II, 315, 11; V, 229, 37: grandsons.

oysyd thare trawale, III, 41 a: used, carried on their operations.

P

pa, paw.

pa.   See **palle**.

Pa, III, 244, **B** 1: unintelligible and doubtless corrupt.   Percy, who supposed that Mirryland toune might be corrupted from Milan, Germ. Mailand, understands Po, although, as he observes, the Adige, not the Po, runs through Milan.

pack, IV, 69, 12: familiar.

pad, V, 114, 1: (in canting language) highway.

pae, I, 333, 3: peacock.

pakets, V, 165, 6: pockets.   (V, 306, 9, has *pouches.*)

pale (of a puncheon), II, 81, 45: tap, spigot.

pale, and the covring that these lovers had was the clouted cloak an pale, I, 305, 12: a derivation from Lat. pallium, coverlet, cloak, O. Fr. paile, palle, has

been suggested, and as to meaning would suit; but if the word were popular it should be heard of elsewhere.   Possibly an error for fale, turf, which is the bed-covering in **F** 6, p. 304; though the combination with cloak would be strange.

palle, pale, paule, pa, I, 68, 7; 333, 1; II, 139, 4; 256, **L** 4; 259, **A a** 3, b 3, **C c** 3; 483, 5: fine cloth.

pallions, III, 300, 15; IV, 500, 16: pavilions.

palmer, I, 232, 3–5, 12, **B** 1; 284, 8: pilgrim.   III, 3, 10, 11; 4, 4, 5; 180, **B** 8; 186, 10, 11, 17; 189, **A** 8, **B** 3; IV, 445, 3, 4, 20; V, 16, 9, 17: tramp, vagabond, beggar.

pannells, V, 86, 29: riding-pads or cushions.

papeioyes, I, 328, 33: popinjays.

paramour, I, 68, 4; 70, 4: in **A** 4, the word, coming between bouted flour and baken bread, should signify something eatable; **B** has attempted to make easy sense by inserting the.   Paramour as lover, lady-love, in the honest sense occurs II, 86, 19, 21; 412, 2; V, 182, 7.   the love was like paramour, II, 407, 8: like amorous passion (?).   Quite unintelligible in II, 409, 4, a red rose flower, was set about with white lilies, like to the paramour; again, 410, 2.

parand, heir and parand, II, 447, 2, 4: parand, in 4, might appear to be meant for apparent, but we have his parand and his heir, in 2.   There is more ignorance of the meaning of words in the piece.

pardon, I, 411, 8: leave of absence.

part, God, Christ haue part(e) of the (me), III, 58, 39; 329, 8: perhaps, make me an object of his care (as prendre part en=take an interest in); or, take me for his, number me among the saved.

part.   part the quick, II, 231, 9; parte our company, III, 71, 307: quit, part from.

partakers, III, 138, 7, 8: helpers.

parti, vppone a parti, III, 308, 19: aside.   March-parti, III, 310, 58: Border-side.   Marche-partes, III, 310, 67.

party, nane to party me, V, 127, 19: be of part with.

Pasch, Pasche, II, 146, 9; 147, 7: Easter.

pass for, III, 138, 15: care for.

passe vppon, V, 51, 67: pass, go, on.

passe, III, 73, 357: extent?   In 84, 357, and 88, 357, the reading is, compasse.

passage, IV, 515, 1: occurrence, incident, adventure.

passilodion, V, 71 b; 72 a: a drinking-word.

passments, IV, 343, 4: laces, trimmings for dresses.

pat, pot.

pat, patt, paut, I, 396, 20; II, 123, 29: strike the ground with the feet, stamp.   pat the ball, III, 251 **L** 1, 2: kick.   patted wi her lips, II, 83 a: struck together, smacked (?).

pat, patt, *pret.* of pit, put, I, 107, 7; 465, 2, 3; V, 218, 2.

pat-fit, I, 302, **B** 8: pot-foot.

paughty, II, 364, 21: haughty, malapert.

pauky, V, 115, 1: sly.

pautit, I, 397, **D** 9, 11: patted, struck with the foot, stamped.   See **pat**.

pavag, pauage, pawage, III, 109 f., 5, 11–13: Fr.

pavage, road-tax. See Ducange, pavagium. (passage, III, 114 f., 130, 180, 181, etc.)

paw, a slight motion. neer played paw, III, 480, 14: never stirred again.

pay, n., I, 285, 32; III, 28, 128; 59, 66: satisfaction.

pay, paye, v., I, 328, 37; II, 478, 12: satisfy, please.

pay, III, 142, 36; 161, 26; V, 105, A 5, 6; 106, E 6: beat.

payetrelle, I, 326, 9: poitrail, part of the harness on the breast of a horse.

payrelde, parelde, I, 327, 16, 17: apparelled.

peak, pick.

peak, peck.

peak-staff, pike-staff.

pean-kniff, pen-knife.

pear, peare, V, 110 f., 2, 4, 6, etc.: poor.

pearled, apron, IV, 67, 12: bordered or trimmed with lace.

pearlin, pearlins, III, 9 f., 6, 14; IV, 448 a, 2d line: pearls.

pearling, pearlin, II, 323, 6; IV, 326, 16: lace.

pearting, parting, separation.

peat, I'se gar ye dance upon a peat, V, 104 b (a threat): on a (burning) peat, make it hot for you.

pecis, III, 65, 175: vessels (of silver), probably cups.

peed, IV, 316, 14: pu'd, pulled.

peel, I, 403, 9: pool.

peel, a tower, stronghold; climbing the peel seems inappropriate at IV, 6, 4; V, 249, 4, unless the meaning be that the peel was "ransakled" for valuables (since kye would not be kept in the peel).

peeped, V, 10, 3: spoke faintly, whined.

peerls, peerls many, IV, 134, 10: poor folk (Chaucer's poraille). B 8, C 6, D 10, F 8, G 4, etc., poor folk many.

peers, pears.

peit, I, 22, 3: a peat carried to school as a contribution to the firing.

pellettes, III, 430, 12: bullets.

pendles, IV, 296, 8: pendants, ear-rings.

penned in, of windows, II, 330, G 3: fastened, perhaps pinned. See pin, v.

penny-brown, III, 281, 10: brown as a penny. penny-gray, III, 281, 8, at best would mean gray as a silver penny; but silver is called white money. It is just possible that the word is legitimate, and that, penny-brown being understood as very brown, penny-gray might come into use for very gray. Possibly penny-brown (gray) might mean dappled with brown (gray) spots.

penny-fee, -fie, I, 491, 10; IV, 444, 10: gift of a penny largess, pour-boire. (I, 490, 6, penny instead of penny-fee.) II, 469, 25, 26: simply, money.

peny, shete a peny, III, 97, 10: shoot for a penny, as 104, 6.

Perce, V, 298 a: Persia.

perelle, I, 326, 8: pearl.

perfyte, II, 72, 4; 75, 6; 78, 8: perfectly.

pestilett, III, 430, 11: pistolet.

petty toes, I, 133, L 9: pettitoes, feet (as in Winter's Tale, IV, 4), or a play upon words, little toes.

phat, III, 318, 8: what.

philabeg, IV, 234, 21; 271, 8; V, 266, 8: kilt, skirt worn by Highlanders, reaching from belly to knee.

pibrochs, IV, 298, G b 14: bagpipe airs; seems here to be meant for the pipes.

pick, pick a mill, I, 211, B 3, 4: sharpen the surface of a mill-stone when worn smooth by friction. picked a stane, II, 323, 1: dressed with a pick.

pick, pickle, I, 16, C 14; IV, 481, 5; V, 206 a, 6: a grain.

pick, n., IV, 2, 12: pitch.

pick, pict, v., 380, 20: pitch (pict, II, 28, 23, may be a misspelling).

picke, III, 358, 77: pitch (throw).

pickle, a grain. See pick.

pickle, II, 147, 12, 14; 476, 16, 17: pick, collect.

picklory, III, 132, 4: name of a cloth.

pickman, pikeman.

pict, v., II, 28, 23: pitch (probably a misspelling).

pig, I, 305, 5; IV, 206, 9: an earthen vessel, earthen pitcher.

pig-staves, V, 213 a, 1: pike-staves.

pile, o corn, I, 18, H 7: a grain.

pile, pile o the gravil green, gray, I, 350, 18, 19; pile that grows on gravel green, IV, 456, 11, 12: a fibre or blade of some velvety moss which grows on stones. See gravil.

pilk, II, 473, 16: pick, collect. See pickle.

pilleurichie. See pitleurachie.

pin, pinn, an implement for raising the fastening of a door. tirled the pin, IV, 390, 4; 415, 5. tirled at the pin, I, 470, 23; II, 141, 8; 164, 3; 471, 8; 474, I 3, etc. tirled on the pin, II, 461, 11. thirled at the pin, II, 121, 15. thrild upon a pinn, II, 138, 10, 16. twirld at the pin, IV, 390, b 4. lifted, lifted up the pin, II, 104, 14; IV, 391, 3; 415, 6. "The pin was always inside, hung by a latch, or leather point, the end of which was drawn through a small hole in the door to the outside. During the day-time, the pin was attached to a bar or sneck in such a way that when the latch was pulled the door was free to open. But at night the pin was disconnected from the door-fastening and hung loose, so that when the latch was pulled the pin rattled." W. Forbes. (See tirled.) knocked at the pin, II, 387, 10; 468, 15; upon a pin, III, 105, 12; rappit at the pin, I, 472, 17; chapped at the pin, I, 481, 29, are probably corrupted from knocked, etc., at the ring (and so, tinkled at the pin, II, 253, 3); if not, the meaning must be, knocked at the door at the place of the latch. that so priuilye knowes the pinn, I, 433, 25, implies that there was some secret connected with the pin (like, knew not the gin, IV, 446 b, 3), which it is difficult to conceive in an arrangement so simple as that described above; but it is probable that complications were employed by the cautious. See gin.

pin, gallows-pin, gallou-pine, I, 146, 25; 150, 17; III,

388, 18; V, 247, 18; hanged them out-oer a pin, III, 268, 18; hang you on a pin before my door, V, 26, 15: the projecting, or horizontal beam of the gallows? Any projection upon which a rope could be fastened.

pin, v., pin my windows in, V, 295, 5, 6: fasten. See **penned**.

pindee, II, 326, 2, of windows, pinned-ee for rhyme, or, possibly, for *in*, as penned in, II, 330, **G** 3.

pinder, pindar, pinner, III, 131 ff., **A** 1–5, etc.; **B** 1–3; II, 484, **C** 6, 7; 491 a, 5, b, 5: pounder.

pine, pyne, I, 464, 8; 470, 15, 32; 474 f., 36, 41; IV, 430 f., 4, 23; V, 219, 25: suffering, pain. Goddës, Creystys, pyne, III, 75, 391; V, 79, 18: suffering, distress, passion.

pine, I, 453, 3: (pind, poind) distrain, seize.

piner-pig, III, 385, 7: an earthen vessel for keeping money.

pingo, pingo white, IV, 213, 12: pinkie (?).

Pinnatree, The Gold, V, 141 b: name of a ship.

pinner. See **pinder**.

pint, point.

Pirie, in Pirie's chair you 'll sit, the lowest seat o hell: I, 429, 30, 31. For the derivation Sir W. D. Geddes suggests as possible le pire, which would be in the way of the Scottish "ill chiel." Professor Cappen writes: "Familiar name in doggerel lines recited by boys in their games. One boy stood back against the wall, another bent towards him with his head on the pit of the other's stomach; a third sat upon the back of the second. The boy whose head was bent down had to guess how many fingers the rider held up. The first asked the question in doggerel rhyme in which Pirie, or Pirie's chair, or hell, was the doom threatened for a wrong answer. I remember Pirie (pron. Peerie) distinctly in connection with the doom. Pirie's chair probably indicates the uncomfortable position of the second boy (or fourth, for there may have been a fourth who crouched uncomfortably on the ground below the boy bending), whose head or neck was confined in some way and squeezed after a wrong answer."

pistol-pece, III, 432, 9: pistol.

pit, I, 86, 31; 467, 17; V, 219, 10: put. pit mee down, II, 131, 4: be my death. pit back, IV, 510, **W** 3: stop the growth or development of. *pret. pat. p. p.* pitten, putten.

pith, hammer o the, II, 374, **B** 2: sounds like nonsense. The smith's anvil being of gold and his bellows-cords of silk, his hammer should be of some precious material. To say his hammer was wielded with force would be out of keeping, and very flat at best.

pitleurachie, pilleurichie, III, 320, **A** a 20, **b** 20: hubbub, discord. See **lierachie**.

pit-mirk, III, 495 a, after 7; IV, 517, 14: dark as a pit.

pitten, *p. p.* of pit, put, I, 463 f., 2, 14.

place, in place, V, 84 f., 10, 25: presence. in place, III, 422, 76: (means only) there.

plaet, *pret.*, IV, 465, 40: plaited.

plaiden, IV, 257, 3, 5: coarse woollen cloth diagonally woven.

plain fields, IV, 432 f., 2, 10, 17, 21: open fields.

plainsht, III, 360, 121: plenisht, filled.

plainstanes, IV, 152, 5: pavement.

plaow, n., V, 304, 5, 12: plough.

plat, I, 101, 19; II, 285, 20, *pret.* of plet: plaited, interfolded.

plate-jack, IV, 147, 22: a defensive upper garment laid with plates.

platen, I, 243 f., 8, 11: plates, pieces.

play-feres, III, 244, 2, 6; 245, 4, 5: play-fellows.

plea, I, 169, 7; II, 282, 2: quarrel.

plea, enter plea att my iollye, III, 278, 32. See **enter**.

plead, III, 277, 10, 12: contend.

pleasure, drink his, V, 307 a, 4: drink as much as he wishes.

plee, III, 165, 72: plea (your offer to give up your money is but a slight ground for a plea to be spared? or a slight argument to enforce the justification previously attempted?).

pleuch, pleugh, n., II, 190, 9; 194, 10: plough. IV, 196, 19; 197, 19: (of land) plough, which see.

plewed, feathers plewed with gold, II, 435, 49: not understood.

plight I lay, IV, 433, 21: the pledge I did lay? condition in which I should lie? (Very obscurely expressed stanza.)

plight, *pret.*, II, 52, 24; 364, 24; V, 50, 45: plighted.

plooky, II, 47, 14: pimpled.

plough, pleugh, pleuch, plow, IV, 194, 18, 11; 195, 18; 196, 19; 197, 19; etc. (of land): as much land as one plough will till in a year.

plucke, fyght a plucke, III, 128, 85: (blow, stroke) a bout.

plucke-buffet, they shote, III, 77, 424: at taking and giving a buffet for missing. (This supposes pluck= take, get; it may be the noun pluck, blow.)

plummet, of swords, III, 466, 40: pommel.

pock, III, 160, 5, 16; 163, 68, 74, 83: bag.

pocket-napkin, IV, 468, 2: pocket-handkerchief.

poind, *pret.*, **poinded**, *p. p.*, II, 429 b, 3; IV, 80 b; IV, 492 a, 3: distrained.

poll, lighter than the poll, IV, 434, 1 (not recognized as Scottish by any of my correspondents): boll, lintbow, the seed-pod of flax? Not probable.

poorly, IV, 444, 35: feebly. V, 10, 3; 266 b, 2: faintheartedly.

portioner, IV, 81 a: possessor of a part of a property originally divided among co-heirs. Jamieson.

portly, III, 280, 24: of imposing appearance.

pot, II, 144 f., 14, 24; 153, 22; 154 f., 17, 31, 34, 35; 474, **J** 6; IV, 181, 13; 189 f., 7, 22, 28: deep place or pool in a river.

potewer, I, 271, 6: read potener, French pautonnière, pouch, purse. "pawtenere, cassidile." Prompt. Parv. "Marsupium, a pawtenere, a powche. . . . Cassidile est pera aucupis, vel mercipium, vel sacculus, a pautenier or a pouche. Cassidile dicitur pera . . . crumena, etc. cremena, a pautener." (Way's note.)

pottinger, IV, 509 b, 13: apothecary.

pottle, V, 86, 35: a measure of two quarts.

pow, II, 476, 16: head.

powd, III, 268, 7: pulled.

powder, IV, 514, 17: dust (?).

power, above (loved), II, 286, 2: beyond (ordinary) capacity or intensity.

powther, powder.

prah, v., V, 303 a: pray.

praise, III, 204, 29: prize.

praise, V, 115, 5:=God.

praisin, III, 455, D 1: if the line is genuine, all the meaning praisin can have will be, the laudation of the queen for her generous behavior.

pran, V, 220 f., 6, 7, 9: bran.

prece, prese, prees, III, 24, 36; 67, 218: press, crowd. III, 62, 116: thick of a conflict.

pree, I, 81 a: taste. See prey.

preen, n., I, 430, 13: pin.

preen, v., I, 147, 13; III, 436, 3; V, 105, B 7: pin. See prin.

prees, prese. See prece.

preke, n., III, 112, 52. See pricke.

preke, v. See prekyd.

preker, V, 79, 13: rider.

prekyd, prycked, V, 78, 6; 80, 40: spurred, rode fast. the hors prekyd, 80, 42: ran, scampered, sped.

prese. See prece.

present, III, 199, 19: represent, act as representatives of.

presentting, wine, IV, 37, 16: holding out the cup or glass towards the person saluted.

presently, III, 400 a (7): at present.

president, III, 231, 82: precedent.

press, V, 111, 22: closet.

prest, the made them prest, III, 111, 45: ready. berdys sang preste, III, 112, 63: freely, con amore. III, 171, 10: in haste.

prestly, III, 27, 113: quickly.

pretend, I, 110, 18; V, 57, 66: purpose, design.

prevayle, III, 313, 55: avail.

prey, II, 490 b, 12–14: (prie, pree) taste.

price, III, 358, 63: estimation.

prick them to the gin, IV, 480, 4: pin to the fastening.

prick(e), pry(c)ke, preke, rod or wand, used as a mark in shooting=pricke-wand: III, 93, 28, 30; 202, 34. he cleffed the preke on three, III, 112, 52. 'have at the pryke!' 'and Y cleue the styke,' III, 90 b. a mark or butt generally, III, 29, 145. slise, cleue the wand=cleffe the preke, III, 70, 292; 75, 401.

pricked, pret., II, 266, 28: stuck.

pricke-wande, III, 93, 31: a rod set up for a mark.

prickt, p. p., I, 345, C 1: prinkt, deckt.

priefe, V, 81, 14: prove, experience, enjoy.

pril, V, 73 a: a drinking word, to which the response must be wril.

prime, pryme, I, 254, 9: the first canonical hour.

prin, n. and v., I, 345, C 1; 431, 10; II, 109, 17, 19; III, 388, 17; IV, 189, 4, 6; V, 105, B 7 (preened): pin.

prinkling, II, 386, 20: seems to be used (perhaps an error) for trinkling, trickling.

prittle, I, 59, 15: a doublet of prattle.

priving, V, 115, 8: tasting.

process, III, 164, 90: occurrences, story of occurrences.

propine, I, 79, 24: present, gift. in thy propine, I, 227 b: to be had by thee as a gift.

propose, n., V, 207 b, No 5: proposal.

proselya, the reef was o the proseyla, I, 333, 5: in other copies the roof is of beaten gold, the floor of cristal a'. The roof here might be of proseyl a', if that would help, but I know no more of proseyl than of proseyla. The nearest I can come to cristal is, porcelain.

prossed, proceed.

proue, II, 446, 81: try? Poor sense and no rhyme. The MS. reading is perhaps praie, which is, however, not preferable. Pross is a northern word for talk (Halliwell), and the corresponding verb would suit here.

prowed, proud.

Prudents, I, 471, 2, 4: black people of the Holy Land.

pruel, made her heart to pruel, II, 376, 32: to ache or shiver with fear. (Dr Davidson.) To preel in Aberdeenshire is to cool. (Principal Barbour.)

pryce, III, 63, 137: prize.

prycke, n. See pricke.

prycked, as faste as he myght ronne, III, 296, 21: sped; and so V, 80, 42. See prekyd.

pryckynge, III, 67, 229: spurring, riding briskly, should probably be rakynge; the yeomen are on foot. Cf. III, 123, 12; 180, 9, 11.

pryke, n. See pricke.

pryme, prime, III, 23, 9; 25, 72: the first canonical hour, first hour of the day.

pryse, I, 327, 16, 17: value. most(e) of pryse=most richly.

pu, pow, pull.

pudding-pricks, III, 160, 19: wooden skewers to fasten the end of a gut containing a pudding.

puggish, II, 427, 6: in a later copy, ragged. Mr Ebsworth suggests the meaning, tramper's. (puggard, thief; pugging, thieving.)

purchase, III, 203, 20: booty, prize.

purchast, p. p., III, 36, 48: acquired (perhaps, stolen).

pure, poor.

pusin, n. and v., poison.

puss-pay, V, 110, 9, 10: hare or rabbit pie (still in use: W. Walker).

put down. See putten down.

put on (intransitively), II, 92, 21; 255, 22; 278, 7; IV, 190, 25: dressed. put on him, II, 162, 12: jogged, pushed.

putten, putn, p. p. of put, I, 446, 10; 469, 3; III, 433, 3.

putten, put, down, II, 178, 39; III, 393, 15; IV, 14, 11;

66, **A** 10; **70**, 13: hanged. IV, 32, 12: put to death by violence.

putting-stane, II, 421, 28: as the stone is thrown, there is no propriety in the hitting and kepping (catching) in 29.

pyet, pyot, magpie: II, 93, 6; 148 f., 11, 13, 15, 17.

pyght, III, 296, 19: pitched (fixed in the ground the pole of).

pygrall, III, 410 b, note: paltry.

pylled, hatte, III, 179 a: (bald) that has lost the nap.

pyne, Goddes, Creystys, pyne, III, 75, 391; V, 79, 18: passion. See **pine**.

pyot. See **pyet**.

Q

quaich, V, 264 a, 3: cup or bowl (Irish cuach).

quarrelld, *p. p.*, I, 367 f., 12, 20: quarrelled with, found fault with.

quarry, IV, 26, 6: of living game, in the modern way (in an adulterated ballad). See **querry**.

quarterer, IV, 152, **B** 9, 10: lodger.

queed, II, 423, **A** 1: gueed, good is required; queed could mean only ill.

queen, quean, queyne, quen, quien, I, 69, 38, 39; 302, **A** 11; 303, **C** 6: woman. II, 141, 11; V, 272, 8, 10: concubine.

queer, quir, IV, 465, 39; V, 224, 27: choir.

queet, quit, cweet, IV, 190, 26; II, 96, **I** 3: ankle.

quen. See **queen**.

quequer, III, 112, 51: quiver.

quere, III, 250, **K** 7: inquire.

querry, quyrry, III, 307, 8; 311, 11: quarry, dead game. See **quarry**.

quest, III, 25, 69; IV, 11, 12: inquest.

questry-men, another, IV, 11, 13: men constituting a quest, inquest; but *another* raises a doubt whether we should not read *quest of*, as in 12 (ry being caught from jury, above).

queyt, III, 112, 59: quit, requite. See **quite**.

quien. See **queen**.

quiles, II, 488, 1, 2: coils, colls, cocks.

quill, IV, 213, 11: quill, the small round fold of a ruff, seems to be put for the quilled ruff; otherwise, kell, cap (or coul, night-cap, not likely).

quinë-stane, qunie-stane, V, 248, 10, 11: (quoin, coiɳ) corner-stone.

quir, queer, V, 224, 27: choir.

quirn, I, 17, 15: hand-mill.

quit, II, 283, 3: ankle. See **queet**.

quite, III, 333, 28: requite. See **queyt, quyte**.

quite, III, 431, 28: free, clear, unpunished.

qunie-stane. See **quinë-stane**.

quoif, coif, II, 279, 1: cap.

qustens, V, 217, a 15: questions.

quyrry, III, 307, 8: quarry, the slaughtered game. See **querry**.

quyte þe, III, 100, 77: acquit thyself, square the account. The other text has, quit me.

R

race, of ginger, IV, 70, **G** 3: root.

race, II, 445, 70, 72; 450, 77, 79; III, 278, 24, 29: course in justing. fetched a race, II, 454 f., 54, 58: took a run (for impetus); so I, 176, 22.

race, castle-race, II, 75, 15; 81, 43: course in the castle-grounds, or contour of the castle (?).

rache, I, 327 f., 10, 16, 51: a scenting dog.

rack, III, 472, 3, 4: ford. "A very shallow ford, of considerable breadth: Teviotdale." Jamieson.

rad, V, 192, 26: afraid.

rader, rather. V, 283, 7, 17: quicker.

rader, rider.

radly, III, 98, 24: quickly. See **rathely**.

rae, I, 350, 21; 352, 7: roe (referring to the wildness of Tam Lin).

raid, read, rede, *pret.* of ride.

raid, *n.*, IV, 520, 3: simply ride, for hunting.

raik. See **rake**.

rair, I, 256, 4: roar.

rais, raise, rase, *pret.* of rise, I, 305, 5; 327, 13; 420, 18; 422, 18; 451, 12; II, 30, 5; 92, 21; 108, 13–15; IV, 215, **A** 6.

raiths, rathes, reaths (Gael. ràidh), II, 314, 30; V, 268, 21, 22: quarters of a year.

rake, raik, reek, II, 216 f., 5, 30; 483, 1; III, 125, 27; 162, 47; 180, 9: walk, move. raking on a rowe, III, 117, 24; 123, 16; 180, 11: advancing in a line; on a rowte, III, 180, 9: in a company.

ramp, rider, IV, 198, **G** 6: wild (of manners or habits). See **rank**.

ramp, I, 302, **B** 7: spring, bounce, whisk. ramped him, I, 215 a, 7:=ramped, bounded.

randy, I, 104 a, burden of **d**: probably unmeaning, though the sense "indelicate hoyden" would suit with stanza 2.

rane, lang rane, II, 82, **C**: yarn, tedious tale.

rang, wrong.

rank (A. S. ranc, strenuus, fortis, protervus), wild, bold (turbulent), strong, violent. rank river, IV, 200, 5; 442, 4. rank robber (who robs with violence, "strong thief"): II, 223, **F** 4; 233, **F** 3; 399, 6; 400, 4; 401, **C** 6; 404, 6. rank reiver, III, 472, 6; IV, 195, **C** 3; 472, 11. rank rider, IV, 196, 4; 204, 11: rude, boisterous; but II, 434, 24; 437, 75: of spirit and courage, sturdy (stout rider, IV, 197, 3, no reference to horsemanship). ramp rider, IV, 198, **G** 6. rank Highlands, II, 93, 2, 3: rude, wild. ranke (of horses), II, 444, 59: high-fed (or used adverbially).

rankit, *pret.* and *p. p.*, V, 197, 10: drew, drawn, up in military order.

ranshakled, IV, 6, 4; V, 249, 4: ransacked.

rantan, ranten. See **ranting**.

ranted, IV, 153, **E** 4; V, 115, 1; was rantin, IV, 85, 39: of making noisy merriment.

ranting, *n.*, IV, 284, 26; 287, 1; 288, 1: raking.

ranting, rantin, rantan, ranten, laird, laddie, III, 455, **D** 1, 13; IV, 351, 1, 3 ff.; 356 f., **B** 1, 3, 4; V, 274 b,

3–6: jovial, dissipated, wanton, rakish, "fast;" we have a rantin lassie, IV, 354, **A** b 1, 2.

rap, IV, 382, 14: knock, drive. *pret.* rapped, rappit, rappet, at, with ellipsis of the door, I, 105 a, 29; IV, 444, 16, 35; V, 173, 1; 306 b, 1.

rap, II, 426, 12; IV, 352, 7; V, 161, **B** 1, 5; 274 b, 7; 302, 14: (of tears) to fall in quick succession.

rape, rope.

rarely, IV, 58, 4, 5, 7, 8, 10, 11; 358, 20, 21: rhyme-word (to which any one can assign all the sense it has). as *adj.*, IV, 154, 7: rare.

rase, *pret.* of rise. See **rais**.

rash, *n.*, IV, 75 a, b; 76, 1; 448 b, 5 (rash-bush); 524, 4, 7; V, 157, 12: rush.

rashin, V, 173, 7: rushen, of rush.

rassiecot, V, 107, 2: perhaps of no meaning, or, rush-coat.

rathely, I, 327, 13: quickly. See **radly**.

rathes, II, 314, 30. See **raiths**.

rau, row. See **rawe**.

raught, I, 434, 36: reached, delivered.

rauked, I, 69, 61: searched, rummaged. (Misprinted ranked.)

rave, reave, rive, *pret.* of rive, I, 439, 5; II, 294, 32; IV, 181, 15. See **rive**.

ravie (rave ?), V, 111, 19: rive. raving, V, 254, 14, 18, 19: tearing.

raw, green raw sea, II, 30, 6: as of weather, wet and cold; but I am informed that the singer ordinarily gave haw, as II, 28, 21.

rawe, rewe, *n.*, III, 71, 306: row.

rawstye by the roote, III, 94, 56: rusty, soiled, foul, (with blood) at the end (?).

ray, *n.* and *v.*, III, 112, 60; 201, 17; 406, 29; V, 83, b 3: array. V, 192, 34: make ready, saddle.

ray, *n.*, IV, 3, 22: track.

raye, III, 67, 230: striped cloth.

raysse, III, 295, 2: riding, raid.

reacheles on, III, 93, 38: reckless of, heedless about.

read, *pret.* of ride, IV, 457, 23; V, 166, 11; 228, 25.

read, I, 309, **B** 1; 310, **B** b: rehearse, tell.

read (of dreams), IV, 167, **D** 9, 10; 171, 11; 172, 12, etc.; 180, **C** 3; 190, 23; V, 221, 24; 224, 23; 257, 14: interpret, give an issue to.

read, reade, rede, red, redd, *n.*, II, 53, 34, 35; 182, 4: advice. See **rede**.

read, reade, red, *v.*, II, 52 f., 6, 34; III, 104, 2, 4; 105, 25: advise. read my rede, II, 186, 1: corrupted from riddle my riddle, 187, 2, 8. See **riddle**.

readilie, readylye, II, 23, **E** 7; 444, 43: (without difficulty or hesitation) certainly.

ready, V, 75, 6, 7; 81, 10: direct. readye, II, 58, 16: indubitable, certain.

reaf, reif, III, 458 b: plunder.

reak, smoke. See **reek**.

reaming, a suit o claise were o the apple reamin, IV, 176, 15: reaming=creaming, foaming, which of course gives little or no meaning. Apples were sometimes used to scent clothes.

rean, rin, run.

reap, V, 165 f., 6, 9:=ripe, search, rummage; see V, 306, 9.

reapen, *p. p.* of reap, II, 9, 26.

rear, rare.

reas, praise. See **roos**.

reas, ryse, III, 307, 5: rouse.

reast, reest, V, 256 b, 4: roost.

reaths. See **raiths**.

reave, IV, 26, 1: rob.

reave, rave, rive, *pret.* of rive, I, 442, 6; IV, 416, 18.

reavel(1)d, II, 140, 19, 20: ravelled, disordered (of hair).

reaver, rever, riever, IV, 85, 2: robber.

recher, *compar.*, V, 283, 10, 20: richer.

reck, *v.*, II, 340 b, 2d line: rock (perhaps miswritten).

recones, IV, 496 b: reckonings.

record, sma, III, 319, 22: note.

red, redd, rede, *n.*, II, 182, 4; III, 112, 58: counsel. I, 22, **B** 1; 227 a, 5: talk, tale. See **read**.

red, redd, rede, reid, *v.*, I, 329, 58; II, 59, 20; 62 a, 15; 182, 4, 6, 9, 10; 272, 6; IV, 495, 2; V, 191, 8: advise.

red, III, 163, 80: to rid, clear out. of hair, comb (see **redding-kaim**). red the question, II, 253, 18: clear up, settle.

red lan(d), I, 16, **C** 11; IV, 274, 6; V, 206 a, 5: cleared, ploughed.

red river comb, II, 216, 19, 21: corrupted, as are other versions in this passage.

redding-kaim, reeding-comb, III, 452, 8; IV, 515, 7: comb (for disentangling).

rede. See **red**.

rede, *p. p.*, III, 298, 53: read, divined, discerned.

rede, *pret.* of ride, III, 63, 134 (reden, they rode); IV, 182, **F** 5. See **read**.

redly, III, 67, 223: quickly.

reeding-comb. See **redding-kaim**.

reef, I, 333, 5: roof.

reef-tree, I, 299, 5: roof-tree, beam in the angle of a roof.

reek, reak, reik, *n.*, II, 191, 24; 193, 21; 195, 33; III, 433, **C** 6–8, **D** 12; 434, 15; 435, 14; IV, 514, 16, 20: smoke.

reek, *v.*, I, 304, **E** 3; II, 30, **L** 2; V, 152, **E** b 1: rake, range, move, turn. See **rake**.

reekit, V, 108, **B** 7: smoked, smoky.

reel, reel went round, V, 155, **C** 2: revel, riot (of merrymakers) ?

reem, II, 335, **N** 7: room.

reest, reast, IV, 189, 3, 4: roost.

reet, I, 367, 7; V, 213, 8: root.

reeve, V, 69 b: bailiff, steward. *pl.* reues.

refell, I, 110, 22: repel.

refer, message, II, 286, **C** 10: report, announce.

regulate, III, 509, 1, 7: corruption of, riddle it.

reid, *v.*, V, 200 a, after 50: advise.

reif, reiff, III, 365 b; 471, note ‡; V, 198 b, after 52: robbery.

reign, II, 8, 1: for rhyme; range ? or rein, as 9, b 1.

reik, smoke. See **reek**.

reill, reel.

reiver, rever, riever, III, 472, 6; 473, 22: robber. See reaver.

rejoyfull, IV, 173, 7: rejoicing.

remeid, II, 367, 42; 371, 13; IV, 405, 49; 428, 7: remedy.

remorse, III, 209, 10; 231, 94: compassion.

remoued, II, 58, 4: agitated.

renisht, renisht them to ride of twoe good renisht steeds, II, 52, 8; 53, 42 (42 emended from, on tow good renish, in conformity with 8): should have some such meaning as accoutred, but a derivation is not to be made out. Qy. [ha]renisht, harnessed?

renown, spake wi renown, IV, 348, 11: force of authority (of prestige), or, with the air of a person of repute.

repair, II, 163, 18: resort to? fix upon? (probably nonsense for rhyme).

require, II, 427, 6: ask for. (Other texts, inquire.)

reset, IV, 281 a: harboring.

respect, in respect, III, 364 b: considering.

rest, pret. of rest, IV, 424, 12.

restore, IV, 425, 8: restore, because the morning-gift would revert to the father and be at his disposition, no son having been born.

retour, IV, 91, note †: return.

returned, III, 356, 33: turned away.

reuelle, I, 328, 51, 52: festivity.

rever, III, 458 b; IV, 472, 11: robber. See reaver.

reues, III, 68, 254: bailiffs. See reeve.

rewe, be rewe, II, 479, 15: in a row, one after another, each of the whole class. See rawe.

rewth, III, 28, 136: pity.

ribless kiln, I, 18, F 11: the ribs of a kiln for drying grain are the cross-beams, on which were laid the "stickles," or short pieces of wood, to support a layer of straw (or hair-cloth, or bricks) on which the grain was placed. It would of course be impossible to dry grain on a ribless kiln.

rid, ried, red.

riddle, II, 184, 5, 8, 11, 18; 186, 1; 187, 2, 8; 196, e 1, 7: resolve. riddle my riddle, 187, 2, 8: resolve my dilemma. read my rede, 186, 1, is probably corrupted from riddle my riddle; cf. 187, 2, 8.

ried, ride.

rien, V, 161, 9; 162, B 6: riven.

riever, reiver, rever, IV, 84, 8; 195, C 3: robber. See reaver.

rig, rigg, riggin, ridge.

rig, rigg, of land, I, 19, 9; II, 152, 11; V, 164, 16; rig-length, III, 273, 23: a measure of land 600 feet by 15, containing 9000 square feet. Donaldson.

riggin, III, 459, 5: ridge.

right, III, 356, 19: right off, directly.

rigland, land under the plough, and so in rigs, ridges. rigland shire, II, 132, 32: a shire of such land (?).

rin, rine, rean, V, 221, 15: run.

ring, plural, II, 285, 16 f.: misprint in Scott?

ring (dancing), II, 104, 23; so, take me to the middel o the ring, V, 273, 12.

ring, knocked at the, with the, ring, II, 187, 12; 201, 2; 459, 10; III, 106, 4; 250, 11. rappit wi a, II, 462, 10. rapped on the, V, 293 b, 10. pulled at a, II, 490, D b 9. tinkled at the, II, 196 b, 4; 251, 4; 266, 7; 267, 9; 393, 11; 475, K 6: the hammer of a door-knocker. But, perhaps, in the case of tinkling, the ring may have been gently drawn up and down or struck against the projecting bow or rod of a door-handle (often wound with a spiral), an operation which, when vigorously performed, is described as risping or rasping.

ring (game), to ride at the ring, III, 448, A 3: to attempt, while at full gallop, to carry off, on the point of a rod, a ring suspended on a cross-beam resting on two upright posts. Jamieson.

ring and the ba, IV, 257, 4; 354, A b 1, 2: a game in which a ring was thrown up, and a ball was to be thrown through before the ring fell. Dr. W. Gregor. The rantin lassie plays at this, IV, 354.

ringle-tree, V, 112, B b 11: probably the huge block of wood used for scutching flax and mangling clothes. An old game-keeper tells me that he has heard the word and so understands it. When not in use for beating flax, the beetle and tree-block were used by the women to mangle their clothes after washing. W. Walker.

ripe, reap, rype, III, 160, 16; 163, 83, 84; V, 306, 9: search, rummage, clear or clean out, rifle.

rise, III, 332, 2: branch.

rise=raise: III, 513 b, 4. pret. rose, 514 a, 5. See ryse.

rise, pret. of rise, III, 369, 17.

rise, did on anchor rise so high, III, 344, 34: said of a ship in full sail; no apparent sense. (ride in B c, g, 347, 34; upon an anchor rose so high in h, 349, 34.)

rispen, fine rispen kame, II, 225, J 2: keen, sharp, risping, rasping? or, p. p., filed? (This passage is variously corrupted in different versions.)

ritted, II, 295, B b 4, 22: stuck, stabbed.

rive, rave, reave, pret. of rive, tear, V, 256, 13. p. p. II, 465, 4, 6, 8.

rive up, I, 303, 7: plough up, tear up.

riued, I, 284, 9: arrived, travelled.

river, III, 364 b: robber. See reaver.

river-comb, red, II, 216, A 19: is river a corruption of ivory? In B 2, 4, it is a tabean brirben kame. H 1, brown berry comb. J 2, fine rispen kame: fine-filed (?). All seem to be badly corrupted.

rock, roke, IV, 84, 14; 85, 4; 86, 6; 87, 4; V, 254 a, 4: distaff.

rocked, rocket, roked, II, 191, 24; 195, 33: smoked.

rod, III, 8, 21: a bier was extemporized by taking rods from bushes for spakes, spokes, or bars.

roddins, II, 408, 19, 20; 409 f., 21, 23: berries of mountain ash. (But the berries are said to grow on yonder thorn, 409, 21.)

rode, rood.

roelle-bone, I, 326; 6. royal bone, I, 466 f., 10, 33; royal ben, I, 478 f., 12, 46: interpreted variously, without satisfaction. See *rewel - boon*, Professor Skeat's note to Chaucer's Sir Thopas, v. 2068. Hertzberg suggests Reval bone, mammoth tooth, fossil ivory, imported into western Europe via Reval, Chaucer Nachlese, in Jahrbuch für Rom. und Engl. Litteratur, VIII, 164 f.; and Prof. Skeat (with a different derivation), ivory of the walrus, citing Godefroy, "rochal, ivoire de morse."

roke, III, 298, 51: reek, vapor.

roke, V, 254 a, 4: rock, distaff. See **rock**.

roked, rocket, rocked, II, 191, 24; 193, 21; 195, 33; V, 224, 19: smoked.

rom, V, 304 b, 2: room.

rood, III, 93, 28: rod (a measure).

rood, four and thirty stripes comen beside the rood, II, 59, 29: referring to the scourging of Jesus (?).

room ye roun, II, 89, 29: move round so as to make room.

roome, III, 36, 44: companye (the reading in b).

roos, rous, reas, *v.*, IV, 69, 21; 378, 2; 379, 2; 384, 2; V, 275, 2: to praise, laud, boast.

roose, *n.*, IV, 503, 19: rose.

roosing, rosin, rousing, *n.*, IV, 378, 1; 379, 1; 383, 1; V, 275, 1: praising, boasting, bragging.

root, I, 304, **F** 5: the end of a rafter, resting on a wall. ring of an auld tree-root, I, 304, **F** 4: hoops are sometimes made of tree-roots, which are very tough; the point here is the size of the fingers which such a ring would fit.

root of his sword, III, 268, 11: a blunder; see note, III, 275.

rose-garlonde, III, 75, 398: a "garland" appears to have been attached to the yerdes (397), and every shot outside of the garland was accounted a failure. The garland as the limit of allowable shots is mentioned at 93, 31. This must have been an extemporized ring of twigs in the latter case, and was so, perhaps, in the other, for it is likely that the term would become conventional, and mean, as Mr C. J. Longman suggests, nothing more than a disk with circular rings, such as survive to this day in archery targets.

rosin, V, 275, 11: boasting. See **roosing**.

rosses, roses.

rottens, rottons, I, 466, 8; V, 124, 6: rats.

roudes, II, 284, 4: haggard (*subst.*, an old wrinkled woman).

roun, rown, round, III, 199, 28; 356, 19: whisper.

rounin(g), *n.*, V, 256, 10: whispering.

round, so it went round, IV, 146, 7: so much it came to (?).

round tables, II, 343, 1: a game.

roundlie, I, 104, 6: at a good pace.

rous, roos, reas, IV, 379, 2; V, 275, 2: boast of.

rousing, *n.*, boasting. See **roosing**.

rout, *n.*, III, 160, 22: blow.

rout, *n.*, IV, 113, 3; 114, **D** 1: row, brawl, disturbance.

rout, *v.*, II, 318 a; IV, 378, 5; 380, 11: roar. IV, 6, 15; V, 250, 14: bellow.

route, rowte, rowght, III, 23, 22; 26, 88; 180, 9; 297, 33: company, band, crowd. In III, 297, 33: perhaps mêlée, affray.

routh, I, 298, 1: plenty.

row, rough.

row, rowe, I, 71, 61; 80, 33; 441, 6, 8; II, 443, 35; 448, 39; IV, 267, 9; 269 b, 9: roll. *pret.* and *p. p.* rowed, rowd, rowit, rowt, I, 441, 7, 9; IV, 274, 15; V, 106, **D** 7: rolled, wound.

rowan, rowon, rown, tree, II, 504, 18: mountain-ash.

rowe, on a, III, 67, 229; 117, 24: in a line, file.

row-footed, III, 473, 25: rough-footed.

rowght, III, 297, 33: company. ryall in rowghte, kingly among men. See **route**.

rowght, wrought.

rown, I, 312, 17, 22: rowan, mountain-ash. See **rowan**.

rown, roun, round, III, 356, 19: whisper.

rowt, *pret.*, V, 106, **D** 7: rolled. See **row**.

rowte. See **route**.

rowynde, III, 297, 33: round.

royal bone, royal ben. See **roelle-bone**.

royaltye, III, 411, 5: splendid display, or the like.

rub-chadler, rub-chandler, I, 285 f., 31, 43: rubbish-barrel. See I, 279.

rudd, *n.*, I, 272, 13, 20, 24: (redness) complexion, face.

rudd, *v.*, IV, 28, 34: redden.

rudely, III, 162, 49: sturdily.

rue, III, 220, 6: cause to rue.

rugge, I, 243, 2: back.

rule, III, 98, 32: going on, taking on, noisy bewailing.

run, IV, 289, **F** 6: issue, outcome (said to be slang).

run, red runs i the rain, II, 304, 4: gives no sense, and so of Scott's reading at this place, the red sun's on the rain. It will be observed that the day has not dawned.

run a reel, II, 108, 17: gone through, danced.

rung, I, 202, **A** 12; III, 161, 43; IV, 444, 20: staff, pike-staff.

rung (of the noise of a cannon), *n.*, IV, 52, 14: ring; appears to have been altered, for rhyme, from ring, which is in two other copies.

rusty, V, 151, **E** 6: surly.

rybybe, I, 328, 49: a stringed instrument.

ryght, straight, directly. ry3th, V, 283, 14: aright.

rynde, be rynde and rent, III, 297, 42: flayed. (rynde should perhaps be *riven*.)

rype, *v.* See **ripe**.

ryse, III, 22, 2; 23, 20: rouse. See **rise**.

rysse, I, 328, 39: probably rising ground, elevation (compare mountayne, playne, delle, hill, in 38, 40–42: not twig, brushwood).

rysyt, I, 242, 11: riseth (old *imperat. pl.*), rise.

S

s, se, as sign of the future tense. I 'se, III, 488, 19; IV, 428, 18. thou 's, 'se, IV, 3, 31; 12, **C** 6. he 's, hee 'se, II, 442, 16; IV, 146, 6. we 's, I, 467, 29; IV, 181, **D** 14. ye 'se, IV, 22, 18; 109, 7. yow 's, IV, 504, 36. they 's, IV, 486, 32. itt 's, II, 443, 22. heart 's, IV,

181, 17. Jocky Ha's, III, 487, 6. thy dinner's, III, 489, 41. (The *s* being the initial letter of sal, it would be better to write I s', etc.) *s* attached to the verb, be 's, III, 160, 9. We even find shals, I, 481, 28.

-s(-is), of the genitive, omitted, III, 97 f., 8, 23, 28; 111, 39. moder son, III, 98, 24, 27, as in A. S.

's, II, 375, 19: of his.

-s (-se), termination of the *2d pers. sing. of the pres. indic.* thou was, I, 222, **E** 11; seese þou, I, 328, 38–42; þou commes, 44. thou's welcome, III, 488, 24. shals thou, I, 481, 28. istow, 175 f., **D** 4, 10, 16. See I, 130, 5; 327, 20; 328 f., 56, 58; 341, 13; 411, 4; 413, 3; II, 54, 57; 148 f., 12, 20; 218, 8, 10, 16; III, 97, 11, 15; 99, 62; 110, 23. Etc., etc.

-s, -es, -ys, termination of *pres. indic. plur.* cods that sleeps, cheeks gars, bairns has, lies men, raches rynnys, fowles synges, I, 68, 29; 115, **C** 3; 130, **F** 11; 327, 16; 329, 59; 342, 40; 345, 39; II, 32, **P**4. So, is, was, I, 68, 27; 69, 43; 255, 3–5; 342, 30; 344, 28; II, 71, 13, 14. Etc.

saa, *pret.*, saw.

sabelline, I, 221, **D** 8, 9: sable.

sackless, sakeless, saikless, II, 145, 22, 23; 153, 19, 21; III, 437, 27; IV, 373, 9: innocent.

sad, III, 67, 215; 357, 40: steadfast, firm, stanch.

saep, *v.*, III, 269, **D** 3: soap.

saerd, *p. p.*, IV, 494, 33: served.

safe, II, 160, 4, 6, 7: save.

safeguard, V, 66, 11: riding-skirt.

safer, V, 283, 21: saffron.

safly, IV, 18, 10: softly.

saft (of sleep), III, 489, 11: lightly.

saikless. See **sackless**.

sain, I, 351, 36, 48: cross, bless. *p. p.* sained, I, 354, 26. ill sained, *pret.*, I, 350, 25. well saint, *p. p.*, III, 488, 37.

saint, III, 488, 37: blest. See **sain**.

saint, *v.*, disappear. See **sainted**.

St Mary knot(t), III, 465, 26, 27: a triple knot (see 462, note *).

sainted, saunted, I, 331, **C** 8; 333 b, 8: disappeared.

saipy-sapples, I, 303, **D** 5 (the right reading): soap-suds in which clothes have been washed (probably meaning the *strang* of V, 213, 5).

sair, sore. I, 100, 9: lamentable.

sair, sare, saer, sere, I, 301, 2; II, 71, 15; 105, 9; 408, 1, 2; IV, 248, 10; V, 105, **B** 3, 11; 239, 34: serve.

sairly, IV, 358, 19: rhyme word; *much* is all the meaning.

sait, set.

sakeless. See **sackless**.

sale, V, 228, 19: sold.

sall, shall. *pret.* sould.

sally rod, III, 252, 12: sallow, willow.

salten, *adj.*, IV, 452, 6; 475, 6: salt.

salued, III, 61, 102: greeted.

Saluter, III, 250, 3: corrupted from Sir Hugh (see other versions of the ballad).

same, alle in same, III 91 a: all, together. vppon the same, III, 361, b 33: again, after the same fashion (?).

san, sane, sayn, syne, V, 214 f., 4, 9; 221, 24; 242 a, 7; 257, 14: since.

sanchoþis, of his bryk, III, 13, 3: apparently the fork of the breeches, but the etymology is to me inexplicable.

sang, *pret.* of sing, to singe, II, 155, 37, 38.

sanna, shall not.

sarbit, II, 132, 33, 34: exclamation of sorrow.

sare, serve. See **sair**. sare a man a wear, I, 301, 2: serve, supply, a man (of) with his wear, clothing.

sark, I, 15, 8, 17; 16, **B** 8, 18, **C** 6, 18, etc.; 387 f., **A** 5, 8, 9; **B** 5, 6, 7: shirt, shift.

sarsenent, IV, 312, 8: sarcenet.

sassaray, II, 209, **E** 5: imitation of the sound of church-bells. See **céserará**.

sat, saut, I, 310, 4: salt.

sate, sit a gude sate, a silly sate, IV, 469, 8: occupy, be in, a good, pitiable, position.

sathe, I, 333, appendix 1, wrongly written (or read) for sagh (or something equivalent), saw. (th in this piece very frequent for gh.)

saugh, III, 459, 15; IV, 95, 2: willow.

saun faile, V, 297 b: assuredly.

saunted, sainted, I, 331, **C** 8; 335 b, 8: disappeared.

saut, sat, IV, 258, 26: salt.

saute, III, 327 b: assault, attack.

sauyour, see (saw) my sauyour, III, 97, 7: attended mass, or, took the sacrament.

saving tree, III, 398, **D** 4: corruption of savin tree.

saw, *v.*, I, 427, 13, 15; 428, 11: sow.

sawe, *p. p.* of see, III, 59, 60.

sawe, speech.

sawten, *v.*, *3 pl.*, III, 100, 63: assault, attack.

sawtrye, I, 328, 49: psaltery, a stringed instrument.

say, II, 87, 30: try.

say, saye, *pret.* of see, III, 111, 34; 309, 44; V, 79, 35; 80, 47.

sayn, san, sane, syne, V, 239, 34; 254, 9, 11, 13, 22; 257, 15: since, then.

sayne, I, 70, 19, *strong participle of* say. In, I yow sayne, III, 297, 46, an auxiliary, *do* or *can*, must be omitted, or else we must read *saye*, as in 32, 34, 62, 65.

scad, I, 102, 12: reflection (of the color of). In other texts, shade, shadow, I, 490, 21; 491, 20; 492, 12.

scaith, skaith, scath, *n.*, III, 162, 52, 66: hurt.

scaith, skaith, *v.*, III, 5, **D** 8; 6, 17: hurt.

scale, I, 429, 11: a drinking-vessel. (Icelandic *skál*, Danish skaal, a bowl for drinking.)

scale, III, 403 a: scatter, disperse. III, 393, 6: expel, drive away. scaling wide, III, 301, **D** 2: scattering, covering a good deal of ground.

scales, V, 211, 25, 31–34: discs worn as ornaments on the head.

scanct, I, 336 a, last line but one: shone, gleamed.

scarson, II, 434, 29: scarcely up to.

scart, I, 301, 5, 6; 303, **D** 2: scratch, scrape.

scath, scaith, *n.*, I, 284, 18: harm.

scathe, awayte me scathe, III, 66, 202; wayte me skathe, wait me scath, III, 83, 202; 86, 202: lie in wait, seek an opportunity to do me harm.

scathe away, I, 348 f., 5, 8: expel, get rid of ? See **skaith**, I, 397, 14.

scaur, Braidscaur, III, 5, **D** 2, 6: a bare and broken place on a steep hill; also, cliff, precipice. Broadspear, 6, 2, 5, is probably a corruption.

Scere-thorsday, I, 243, 1: Maundy Thursday, Thursday before Easter. (Icelandic Skíri-þorsdagr.)

schane, *pret.*, shone.

scharpper, *compar.*, V, 283, 6, 16: sharper. V, 283, 8: emend to *strenger*.

schele, **scheel**, II, 164, 2; 335, **N** 5; IV, 328, **A b**, after 7: school. See **schule**.

schet, **schette**, *pret.* of schote, shoot, III, 13 f., 13, 15.

schill. See **shill**.

scho, II, 146, 19; IV, 418, 2: she.

schon, **shon**, **shone**, V, 79, 27: shoes. See **sheen**.

schoote his horsse away, froo, III, 297, 32, 33: discarded, sent off.

schrewde (arrow), III, 13, 6: accursed, pernicious, baneful.

schule, **scheel**, **squeel**, II, 175, 16; IV, 327 f., 2, 5; 329, **D d** 7: school.

schunte besides, **beside**, III, 361, **b**, **c** 38, 41: turn aside from.

schylde, *imperat.*, V, 283, 14: shield, protect.

sckill, I, 295, 28: reason, judgment. See **skill**.

sclasps, twa lang sclasps between his eyes, IV, 489, 25: clasps. Span would answer were it not that there are but three sclasps between the shoulders. (In **L** 18, of the same ballad, II, 394, there are three women's spang (span) between his brows.) If sclasps were taken in the sense of fathom, the space between the arms extended, this would suit the shoulders well enough, but the absurd disproportion in relation to the eyes would remain. Probably yard or ell has dropped out in 25 4. (yards three in **L** 18.)

sclavin, I, 190 a: pilgrim's cloak.

scob(b), **scope**, **scoup**, II, 313, 26; 316, 10: gag.

scop, III, 138, 9: (scalp) pate, head.

scope, **scoup**, **scob**, II, 312, 29; V, 229, 33: gag.

score. See **cor**.

scorn, **skorne**, II, 105, 20; III, 113, 77: shame, humiliation, mortification. give the, this, a, scorn, III, 111, 12; 360, 23; 362, 35; 363, **D** 14; 367, 49; IV, 201, 23; 224, 24, 25; 254, 25; 357, **B** 6, 10; 358, 16; 465, 35, 36: put to shame, subject to humiliation (especially, by showing a preference as to marriage, or by slighting a woman). So, playd you the scorn, IV, 483, 25; get the scorn, III, 367, 47; IV, 221, 16; 222, 18, 19; 227, 16, 17; 228, 19; 230, 24.

scort, I, 334, 4: short.

scoup, *n.*, V, 229, 33: gag. See **scob**, **scope**.

scoup, *v.*, II, 70, 15: move hastily from one place to another, fly.

scouth, III, 161, 42: room, range.

scray, III, 116, 4, as to form suggests *scrag*, *scrog*;

but the meaning required is, branches, *branchage*, or even spray.

scread, II, 425, **A** 6: shred, bit, piece.

screeded (or **scrieded**), *pret.*, II, 212, 13: rent.

screeking, **screehing**, II, 485, 17: screeching.

screfë, **screffë**, **shryvë**, III, 111 ff., 27, 33, 38–42, etc.: sheriff.

screighed, IV, 174, 20: shrieked.

scrieded. See **screeded**.

scrime, IV, 10, 2; serime, 15, **d** 2: seem to be corrupt; possibly, crime; pursuing the crime for pursuing the criminal.

scrodeley, V, 79, 14: shrewdly, rudely, ungraciously.

scroggs, **scrogs**, III, 3, 12; 5, **C** 3; 7, **E**, **F** 11; 9, **G** 10, **H** 13; 10, **I** 5; IV, 496, 8: stunted bushes, or perhaps trees; underwood. "Scroggs, blackthorn." Halliwell, from a MS. scrogg-bush, V, 10, 4 (high enough here to hang the pair on).

scroggy, **scroggie**, IV, 174, 10; 273, 14: covered with stunted bushes; "abounding in underwood," Halliwell.

scug, to scug his deadly sin, II, 283, 22: shade, screen. (Icel. skyggja, overshadow; Dan. skygge, Swed. skugga, shade.) expiate, W. Scott.

scuttle-dishes, II, 467, 43: the larger dishes, in which things are served, in distinction from those out of which things are eaten (T. Davidson): platters.

se, sign of the future tense. See **s**.

se, *pret.* of see. See **see**.

sea-ground, I, 448, 11: bottom of the sea.

sea-maw, II, 363, 7; 365, 5; IV, 482 b, 6: gull.

seal, IV, 409, 5: (A. S. sǽl) happiness, blessing. gude seal that it sae spread, II, 420, 1: (happiness result from its spreading ?) quod faustum sit!

seale, III, 412, 24: sail.

sear, **sair**, IV, 456 f., 15, 19: sore.

sear, V, 223, 8: sure.

sear, serve. See **sair**.

search her, IV, 446, 2: look her up, see about her, overhaul (should, perhaps, be *seek*, visit).

seat, V, 274 b, 1: sight.

seck, I, 15, 15: sack.

Second person of pret. indic. without termination, thou made, thou did, thou came, etc., I, 221, **C** 9; 222, **E** 10–17; 434, 27; II, 148 f., 12, 14, 20; 218, 16. So, thou will, schall, thou 'll, well thow, I, 130, 4; 221, **C** 10, 11; III, 110, 24; 112, 48.

securly, III, 98, 34: surely.

see (*videre*), *pret.* say, saye, sey, se, see, seed. *pret.* se, see, I, 283, 1; 295, 27; II, 46, 40; 245, 27; III, 24, 47; 27, 99; 97, 19. *p. p.* se, III, 27, 102.

see, save and se(e), II, 44, 6, 15; 52 f., 10, 18, 44; III, 65, 177; IV, 198, **G** 4; 455, 4: protect (*tueri*).

see, well mot ye fare and see, III, 266, 3: as here used, *see well* would have to mean, see prosperity; but apparently there is a confusion of *well may you fare* and *God see you*, protect you (as in, save and see). In **B** 3, p. 268, *weel may ye save* might mean, may God save you, but *far better*, in the next line, is not in concatenation, and we shall be obliged to understand *weel* as good fortune. The passage must be corrupted. well may you sit and see, lady, well may you sit and say, II, 290, 15: (corrupted) nonsense.

see, sigh and see, IV, 193, 14: apparently a doublet of sigh, as *ne* of *neigh* and *nigh*, *he* of *high*.

see, *n.*, V, 283, 5, 15: sea.

seed, *pret.* of see, IV, 151, 6.

seek, seke, I, 75, 46; II, 146, 18, 20; 171, 16; III, 68, 255; V, 256 b, 14: search. I, 202, 16; 204, 11; V, 211, 19, 23: ask. socht, II, 30, 8: asked for. *partic.* seek and, seeking.

seek in, V, 180, 13, 15: ask admission.

seeke to, unto, III, 444, 5: resort to.

seel o downs, IV, 218, 12: chelidonium, celandine, mallow-wort.

seely, happy. seely court, I, 315, 12; 507 f., 2, 12: fairy court (as I, 346, 16; elfin court, 351, 30).

seen, I, 504, 7: sun.

seen, I, 183, 9, 15; II, 166, 20; 257, 30; IV, 135, 25: soon. seener, IV, 262, 31.

seen = syne, afterwards.

seene, I seene, V, 53, 105: *ellipsis of* have.

seep, II, 148, 10: ooze, leak.

seeth, III, 281, 7: sooth.

seke, III, 68, 255; 100, 76: search. See **seek.**

seke, to, III, 110, 14: at a loss.

seker, III, 67, 215: firm, resolute.

sekirlye, I, 327, 18: certainly, truly.

seld, IV, 2, 2: sold.

selerer, III, 61, 91, 93; 67, 233: the monk who has charge of the provisioning of a convent.

selke, V, 283, 21: silk.

selkie, silkie, II, 494 a: seal.

selle, I, 326, 6: saddle.

semblant, semblaunce, semblaunte, semblaunt, III, 57, 22; 79, 22; 82, 22; 85, 22: mein, look.

sembled, III, 160, 15: met. (b, asembled.)

sen, sent.

sen, II, 32, **Q** 2; 110, 2; 272, 10, 12: since.

send, sene, II, 360, 10; 365 f., (10), 17, 18: a thing sent. II, 109, 15: the messengers sent to fetch the bride.

send, *pret.*, I, 204, **D** 3: sent.

sendered, IV, 229, 12, 16: sundered, parted.

senes, IV, 315, 2; 316, 25: sends, messages. See **send.**

sent, III, 75, 384: sendeth.

sent, sent I me, III, 76, 414: assent.

sentence past, IV, 514, 6: order given.

sere, serve. See **sair.**

serre, II, 59, 29: sair, sore ? (MS. serrett).

serundad, surunded, V, 262, No 225, **A** 3; 263, 4: surrounded.

servit, II, 371, 5: (serviette) table-napkin.

seruyd him of bred and cloth, I, 241, 1: *for* would make an easier reading than *of*, which will have to be understood, on terms of (receiving food and clothing).

set, V, 80, 57: sitteth.

set, II, 168, 1; 282, 7; 463, 19, 25; III, 216, 29; IV, 135, 20; 204, 9; 331, 18: sit, become, suit. set a petticoat, IV, 331, 18: became (looked well in) the petticoat. See **become.**

set, *p. p.*, III, 37, 61: fixed, determined. See **set for,** below.

set her brest (and swom), II, 459, 8: brought her breast to a level with the water. (Elsewhere, smoothed.)

set, set a mill, I, 134, **O,** 8: to stop the machinery by turning off the water from the wheel.

set, set the monke to-fore the brest, III, 67, 223: assailed, shot at.

set (sete, and wrongly sat) a dynt on, vppon, of, III, 309, 42, 45, 46: inflicted a blow, stroke.

set by, IV, 11, 15, 20: lay aside, cease, let be.

set for, IV, 229, 12, 16: set upon, bent upon.

set them up in temper wood, IV, 222, 20: corrupt. See note, 231, **D** 20.

sete, *n.*, III, 63, 133: suit, dress.

sett, III, 340, 31: take aim.

settle by, IV, 219, 13: set you aside (?).

settled, gun, III, 341, 44: levelled, adjusted.

sevent, II, 75, 7: seventh.

several, III, 224, 13: variously.

sey, *pret.* of see, V, 80, 41.

seyn, syen, syne, then, afterwards.

seyte, neys seyte, V, 80, 39: pretty sight !

sez I, V, 304, b, 4: say(s) I.

sha, shaw, V, 267, 10: show.

shack, shake, IV, 325, 9; 326, 7: shake straw so that the corn may fall out (?).

shade, shadow, scad, I, 101, 13; 490, 21; 491, 20; 492, 12: reflection (of the color of). We have, shaddoowes *greene,* in one copy of Adam Bell, see III, 32, 48.

shaft their arrows on the wa, IV, 3, 16: so in both copies, unintelligible; corrected by Scott to sharp.

shaftmont, shathmont, I, 330 f., **A** 2, **B** 2, **C** 2; 332, **E** 2: the measure from the top of the extended thumb to the extremity of the palm, six inches. (A. S. "ix. scæfta munda." Lex. Ath.)

shake. See **shack.**

shals thou, I, 481, 28. See **s** as sign of the future tense.

shambo, II, 376, 26: shamoy, chamois.

shame, the, II, 70, 15; III, 464, 11; 466 f., 44, 52, 58: euphemism for the Devil. shame a ma, III, 490, 15, 27, 29: devil a bit.

shamefu reel, II, 110, 28: the first reel that is danced with the bride, her maiden, and two young men; called the Shame Spring or Reel, because the bride chooses the tune. Buchan.

shames death, II, 60, 41; III, 330, 14: death of shame, shameful death.

shamly, III, 80, 337: shamefully.

shane, *pret.* of sheen, shine, IV, 469 a, 11.

shank, IV, 37, **A** 6, **B** 8: the projecting point of a hill, joining it with the plain.

shapen, III, 79, 81, 85, 50: devised, ordained.

share, I, 388, **B** 7; IV, 416, 17: cutting, portion.

shathmont. See **shaftmont.**

shaw, shawe, I, 422, 3; III, 91, 1; 97, 1; V, 250, 25: wood, thicket. See **wode shawe.** In Teviotdale shawe is "a piece of ground which becomes suddenly flat at the bottom of a hill or steep bank." Jamieson. So, perhaps, V, 250, 25.

shaw, sha, show.

shay, V, 110, 8, 9: shy.

she, III, 318, 4: spurious Highland dialect, representing *he, they,* and even *Highlander,* for which she, her, hernanesell have become a nickname. (The Gaelic having no word for the neuter it, the *masc.* e and *fem.* i do duty for the absent form. i in some Highland districts is largely used in speaking of sexless objects.)

sheaf, shefe, of arrows, III, 3, 5; 62, 131: bundle of twenty-four. Cf. II, 168, 5; III, 13, 9.

shealin, shiel, shielin, shielen, shieling, shield, IV, 258, 23; 259, 17; 260, 16; 262, 27, 29; 266, 17: herdsman's hut.

shear, III, 307, 6, 8: several. (Scot. seir.)

sheave, shive, *n.,* I, 470, 32; II, 358, 27; 367, 44; V, 16, 13, 14; 18, 3, 4; 219, 25: slice.

sheave, *v.,* IV, 476, 7: slice.

sheave-wisps, V, 213, 5: wisps of straw from a sheaf, put by peasants into their shoes for more warmth.

shed, II, 116, 27; 118, 21: a piece of ground on which corn grows, so called as being separate from adjacent land.

shed by (hair), II, 129, 26, 27: parted, threw off from the face on both sides. shed back, II, 135, 39 (shook back, 135, 38).

shedd, *pret.* See **sheede.**

shee, shie, I, 68, 9, 12; III, 271, **F** 9; 384, 9: shoe.

sheed, V, 251, 36: sheet.

sheede, I, 273, 43, 44: shed, spill.

sheen, sheene, sheyne, I, 490, 7; II, 52, 5, 11; 372, **A** b 2; III, 24, 48; 91, 1; 97, 1: shining, bright, beautiful. (*bright* is also beautiful, I, 285, 25; 293, 2.) In, shawes been sheene, III, 91 and 97, 1; shadowes sheene, III, 24, 48, we must take sheene in the secondary sense, beautiful.

sheen, shene, I, 176, 2, 7, 12; II, 395, 17; IV, 380, 26; 416, 12; V, 306, 2, 3: shoes. See **schon.**

sheen, shene, *v.,* III, 392, 9, 10: shine. *pret.* shane.

sheene, *n.,* II, 183, 13: brightness, splendor (evidently a word of Percy's here).

shefe. See **sheaf.**

shend, III, 27, 114; 63, 140; 123, 13: put to shame, injure, destroy.

shent(e), *p. p.,* III, 27, 114: blamed. III, 75, 396; 123, 13: hurt, etc.

shete, shoot. shete a peny, III, 97, 10, 11: shoot for a penny-stake. *pret.* shet, III, 97, 12; shyt, III, 26, 83.

sheu, IV, 289, **F** 9: show.

sheugh, II, 238, 6; V, 108, **B** 1: trench, ditch, furrow.

shew, I, 299, a 13; II, 332, **J** 6: sew.

shewed, III, 450 b: represented.

sheyne. See **sheen.**

shie, shoe. See **shee.**

shiel, shielen, shieling, shield. See **shealin.**

shill, schill, I, 16, 1; 17, **E** 1; II, 254, 10; 382, 28; 383, 29; 386, 24; IV, 200, 2; 201, 1: shrill.

shimmerd, glittered.

shin'd, *pret.* of shine, IV, 240, 2.

shirife, shirrfe, shrife, sheriff. See **screfe.**

shirrs, shears.

shive, sheave, V, 219, 25: slice.

shock, *v.,* IV, 106 b: collide, encounter.

shoder, V, 221, 10: shoulder.

shogged, III, 332, 14: moved away.

shon, schon, shone, shoon(e), shoun, I, 69, 52; 71, 42; 73, 64; 78, 39; III, 65, 193; V, 83, 55: shoes.

shook (sword over the plain), II, 393, **K** 14: the MS. has shook, not strook, but strook must at any rate be meant (cf. 380, **A** 32). See II, 378 a.

shooled, I, 184, 10; V, 210, 10: shovelled. See **shule.**

shoon(e), shoun, shoes. See **shon.**

shoon, shoun, soon.

shoot at sun and moon, III, 201, 21; to the sun or the moon, III, 203, 18: they wish to have no mark measured, are ready to take any distance.

shope, III, 59, 64: created.

shopen, shapen, III, 82, 50: devised, ordained.

short-bread, V, 262, 22: "a thick cake of fine flour and butter, to which caraways and orange-peel are frequently added." Jamieson. (A sweet short-bread is still well known in Scotland.)

shorten her, I, 478, 14: while away the time for herself; cf. Germ. kürzen, kurzweilen. See **shortsome.**

shortlye and anone, III, 23, 10: speedily.

shortsome, *adj.,* II, 371, 2: enlivening, cheering.

shortsome, *v.,* II, 370, 13, 14: divert (while away the time, opposed to langsum). See **shorten.**

shot, o wheat, IV, 459, 2: field, patch.

shot, V, 76, 9; 127, 3: reckoning. trust me one shott, V, 15, 22.

shot, II, 256, **K** 2=schawit, looked at (?).

shot, *p. p.,* IV, 458, 3: shod.

shot-window, II, 122, 5; 141, 10; 177, 24; 230, 9; 322, 7; 357, 8; 368, 3; 375, 22; 376, 37, 40; III, 23, 22; 105, 20; IV, 135, 19; 151, 6; 153, **E** 6; 154, 11; 428, 3; 493, 12; V, 248, 8. II, 141, a princess looks out at a shot-window; II, 368, a lady draws her shot-window in her bower, harps and sings; II, 376, a knight jumps to a shot-window to escape; III, 105, Robin Hood glides out of a shot-window; IV, 135, a queen looks oer her shot-window; IV, 493, a knight goes in at a shot-window. — "Windows called shots, or shutters of timber with a few inches of glass above them." Wodrow's History, II, 286. But the shot-window of recent times is one turning on a hinge, above, and extensible at various angles by means of a perforated bar fitting into a peg or tooth. Donaldson, Jamieson's Dictionary, 1882, notes that in the west of Scotland a bow-window is called an out-shot window. A bow-window would be more convenient in some of the instances cited.

shott, V, 15, 22: reckoning (oddly used here as of an ale-house.) See **shot.**

shouir, shower, III, 385: throe, pang. See **showr.**

shoulder, looked over the left, III, 339, 7; 368, 11; 369, 13, etc.: apparently a gesture of vexation or of indignant perplexity. See the passages cited at V, 286 a.

shoun, shun, shoes. See **shon.**

shoun, soon.

shour, sure.

shourn, V, 225, 5: shoulders.

shouther, showther, shuder, I, 21 b, 3 ; 302, **A** 7; 303, 9; 331, **D** 2; 332, **F** 2; IV, 297, 10: shoulder.

showded, V, 124, **C** 15: swung.

shower. See **showr.**

shower o his best love, I, 476, **J** 4: share, or cut, of his best loaf.

showing-horne, II, 437, 78: shoeing-horn, a pun on the beggar's horn, whether as a means of sponging liquor, or of helping one to take in drink.

showne, pret., III, 37, 84: showed.

showr, shower, shouir, I, 68, 32; II, 105, 3; III, 385, 5; 386, 7: throe, paroxysm of pain.

shradds, III, 91, 1: coppices (Halliwell, perhaps conjecturally). The equivalent shard, he says, is in Yorkshire an opening in a wood. (A. S. scréadian, cut, dock ?)

shrewde, shrewed, a term of vituperation; originally, cursed. thou art a shrewed dettour, III, 61, 104; thou arte a shrewde hynde, III, 64, 164 : perhaps ironical (devilish pretty). shrewde wyle, III, 65, 181: clever.

shroggs, III, 93, 28: rods, wands (serving for prickes, marks).

shryuë, III, 70, 287: sheriff. See **screfe.**

shuder, IV, 493, 8: shoulder. See **shouther.**

shule, v., IV, 207, 20: shovel. See **shooled.**

shun, shoun, shoes.

shun, III, 357, 41: better, shunte, as in the other texts, turn off, aside. Shunte is to be understood in 43, 45, 47.

shuped, I, 204, **E** 2: shipped. (The reading may be sheeped.)

shyt, pret., III, 26, 83: shot.

shyt, imperative, III, 71, 314: shut. p. p., III, 25, 53: shut.

si, so.

siccan, sic, sick, sicke, sicken, such, such a.

siccarlie, III, 492, 27: so as to make all safe. sickerlie, III, 491, 5: securely. III, 491, 12: so as to make certain, make sure of the effect.

siccer, sicker (siccer and honestly), III, 487, 9; IV, 31, **B** 6: securely, safely.

sich, sick, n., sigh: II, 139, 6; 168, 15; 230, **C** 1.

sich, sick, v., I, 451, 12; V, 164, **D** b 10: sigh. pret. sicht, I, 73, 66; III, 453, 2. sikt, II, 241, 8. siched, I, 72, 21. sight, IV, 503 f., 6, 21, 23. pres. p. sichand,

sichan, sichin, II, 96, **I** 3, 4, 6; 471, 13; V, 41, 31; IV, 382, 6.

sichin, n., II, 286, **C** 10: sighing.

sicht, sight.

sicke, sicken, III, 367, 3; 441, 32; V, 194, 64 (sicken-like): such.

sicker. See **siccer.**

sickles of ice, ickles of ice, III, 152, 1; 154, **f** 1: icicles.

side, keeping her flocks on yon side, IV, 323, 1: ellipsis of hill, river, or the like.

side, adj., II, 122, **H** 7, 8; 407, 9; 409, 15; 466, 37, 38; 469, 38, 39; IV, 165, 15; 283, 12; 285, 4; V, 267, 4: long, and so, probably, IV, 130, 4; 134, 8. I, 80, 12, of stirrup too long, low for the foot (Icel. síðr, demissus). saddle a steed side, IV, 464, 18 : wide. wear your boots sae side, I, 428, 8; 429, 5: of boots the tops of which lap a good way over, or perhaps of boots wide at the tops; I, 430, 2. See **syde.**

side be, mother-in-law side be, II, 71, 11: seems to mean, side by, by his side. Possibly, sud, should, be.

sighan, sighend, pres. p. of sigh.

sight, sikt, pret., IV, 503 f., 6, 21, 23: sighed. See **sich**, v.

signd, IV, 288, 10: that is, sind. Sind is to wash, rinse; here she has simply wet her lips.

signots, took out the gowd signots, IV, 53, 13: ornaments, whether seals or not, attached to the ears by "grips." Three sygnets hang at a gold ring, IV, 37, 13; 38, 13, which is taken off in the latter place, and was, therefore, a finger-ring.

sike, syke, II, 238, 6; IV, 3, 28: ditch, trench (watercourse, marshy bottom with a stream in it. Jamieson.) IV, 470, 25: (perhaps) rivulet.

sikt, sighed.

sile, IV, 118, **C** 3: flow.

silkie, selkie (A. S. seolh), II, 494, 3, 4: seal.

siller-knapped (gloves), II, 134, 8, 13: ornamented with silver balls or tassels. (golden-knobbed, 133, **D** 6.)

silly. silly tin, silly twine, II, 224, 12, 17: simple, mean, of slight value. silly sisters, II, 311, 1: harmless, innocent ? silly old man, silly old woman, etc., III, 5 f., 10, 11, 20; 6 f., 9, 10; 9, **G** 9; 180 f., 3, 8, 9, 19; 271, 8 : of a "puir body," palmer, beggar. V, 129, 1; 130, 1; 131, **d** 1, **e** 1–3 : of a supposedly simple old man who turns out to be shrewd. V, 253 f., No 203, **D** 2, 8: (perhaps) spiritless, cowardly. sit a silly sate: see **sit.**

simmer, II, 261, 10 ; V, 299, 4 ; etc.: summer. simmer-dale, II, 261, 8, 9.

simple, III, 163, 72: poor, scant.

sin, III, 281, 7; IV, 260, 17: son.

sin, II, 494, 6; IV, 77, 3; 280, b 22: sun.

sin, sine, syne, I, 16, **C** 9; 17, 7; 204, **E** 3 ; II, 32, 3; 160, 4, 7; 161, 5, 7; III, 433, 11; 436, 9 (?): since (temporal and causal), then. II, 237, 6: when, as in Shakspere after verbs of remembering (Winter's Tale, v, i, 219, etc.). See **syne**, then.

sin-brunt, V, 224, 19: sun-burnt.

sinder, II, 164 f., 18, 19, 21: sunder.

sindle, II, 261, 8: seldom.

sindry, II, 344, 4: several. IV, 219, **A** 5: sundry (people).

sine, then, since. See **sin** and **syne.**

single, liverie, IV, 261, 5: dress of a plain or inferior man; IV, 334, 11, 12: dress of a private soldier. single man, sodger, soldier-lad, IV, 335, **b, c, d** 16; 337, **f, g** 15; 338, **h** after 15: private.

sinner, V, 254, 12: sooner.

sinsyne, synsyne, I, 227 b; III, 394, **J** 2; 396, **N** 2: since, afterwards.

sir, title of parson: III, 217, 49.

sit a sate, IV, 469, 8: maintain or enjoy a position. (You may live comfortably if you are well stocked with cattle, but only in a beggarly or pitiable way with nothing but beauty.) "You shall sit at an easier rent." Scott's Redgauntlet, Wandering Willie's Tale. Falstaff sits at ten pounds a week (his expenses came to that), Merry Wives, **I**, 3.

sitt, *p. p.,* III, 400, 5: seated.

sitten, sutten, *p. p.* of sit, II, 273, 37; III, 433, 4.

skail (blood), IV, 373, 13: spill.

skaith, skaeth, *n.,* I, 370, 5; II, 292 f., 8, 18: III, 162, 66: harm. gien the skaeth, II, 364, 36; IV, 465, 35, 36: done a wrong, injury.

skaith, *v.,* III, 371, 21: harm.

skaith frae, *v.,* I, 397, 14: keep from. (A. S. scéadan, Germ. scheiden, O. Eng. shed, part, divide.) See **scathe.** A skaithie in Scottish is a fence or wall to keep off wind.

skeely, skilly, III, 26, 1: skilful, intelligent.

skeigh, III, 495 b, 23, 24: shy, skittish.

skelp, V, 106, **E** 6: drub.

skerry, rocky. skerry fell, I, 325, 10: rocky hill.

skerry, skerrie, II, 494: a rock or rocky islet in the sea.

skill, sckill, skylle, reason, discernment, knowledge. a baron of sckill, I, 295, 28: reasonable, of good judgment, etc. that's but skill, I, 295, 44: reason, something right and proper. the skylle I sall þe telle wharefore, I, 328, 56: the reason why. can skill, little they can skill of their train, etc., II, 445, 62; 450, 67, 69: Icel. kunna skil, to know distinctions, have knowledge. could noe skill of the whisstill heare, IV, 506, 70: perception (that is, literally, could not hear whether there was a whistle or not). had no skill, IV, 213, 3: knew nothing of the matter, or, possibly, had no regard, felt no approbation.

skilly, skeely, II, 97, 21: intelligent, knowing, skilful.

skink, I, 190 a: pour out liquor.

skinkled, II, 183, 19: sparkled.

sklate, II, 293, 15: slate.

skomfishes, III, 433, **C** 4, 7: stifles (discomfits).

skorne, III, 113, 77: disgrace, humiliation. See **scorn.**

sky-setting, I, 351, 31: sunset.

skylle. See **skill.**

skyred, IV, 413, 12, 14: startled, blenched, shrank back.

slack, II, 116, 20; 117, 14; 313, 23; III, 181, 29; 281, 12; 363, note †; IV, 7, 27; 184, 2, 3; 467, 11; V, 250, 25; 262, 19. 1.) a gap or narrow pass between two hills. 2.) low ground, a morass. It is often not possible to determine which is intended. In III, 281, 12, the meaning is morass. Plain ground will suit III, 181, 29. Such terms vary according to locality and time. Cf. **slap.**

slacke (woe), V, 83, 44: lessen, mitigate.

slade, III, 92, 12: "a valley, ravine, plain." Halliwell. Cf. **slack, slap.**

slae, I, 450, 2: sloe.

slap, II, 120, 14; III, 185, 24, 25; V, 228, 26: a narrow pass between two hills (= slack). In III, 185, 24, 25, there is a contrast with glen, the word replacing the slack of III, 181, 29; perhaps, plain ground. IV, 300, 12: a breach in a dyke or wall.

slate, slait, of whetting a sword by passing it over a straw or the ground (Icel. sletta, to slap, or slétta, to level, smooth). has slaited on the strae, II, 273, 30. slate it on the plain, IV, 491, 11. slait it on the plain, V, 235, 32. See **strip, stroak, streak, straik, strike.**

slawe, *p. p.* of slay, III, 14, 16, 17; 71, 306. y-slaw, III, 28, 140.

slee, sly.

sleste, slist, III, 70, 292; 79, 146: sliced, split.

slet, *pret.* of slit, III, 63, 146.

slichting, slighting.

slight, III, 473, 13: demolish. we'll fecht them, we'll slight them, IV, 85, 5: make light of (?).

slipe, sleep.

slist, III, 70, 292: sliced, split.

slo, sloe, sloo, slon, I, 210, 9; III, 77, 438; 97, 8; 110, 19: slay. *pret.* sloughe, III, 308, 25. *p. p.* slo, slowe, slone, II, 479, 17; III, 35, 22; 77, 428. slawe, y-slaw.

slocken, sloken, IV, 386, 16: quench.

slode, *pret.* of slide, II, 59, 22: split.

sloe, sloo, I, 210, 9; III, 77, 438: slay. *pret.* sloughe. *p. p.* slowe, slone. See **slo.**

slogan, III, 474, 32: war-cry, gathering word of a clan. Jamieson.

sloken, slocken, III, 473, 14: quench (fire). *p. p.,* IV, 60 b, after 10 (with *ellipsis of* have).

slough-hounds, IV, 3, 15: sleuth-hounds, blood-hounds (slooth, b, 4, 15).

sloughe, *pret.* of slo, slay, III, 308, 25.

slowe, *p. p.* of slo, slay, II, 479, 17.

sma, small. of linen, I, 428, 18; 419, 3; II, 128, 5; 130, 4; 133, **D** 3; 134, 7; 269, 15; III, 7, **E** 12: of fine texture. of the blast of a horn, II, 258, 31; small, V, 83, 48: shrill, keen. of wine, I will drain it sma, IV, 476, 8: should mean, strain it fine, or, pour out in a thin stream, run it off gently; the intention seems to be, give but a small quantity.

smeek, IV, 385, 25: smoke.

smiddie, IV, 470, 18: smithy. In smiddy-bour, II, 186, 12, bour for room or workshop is strange.

smirkling, smirkling smile, IV, 117, 3: suppressed.

smit, II, 149, 2: noise, clash.

smithered, III, 268, 17: smothered.

smoldereth, III, 431, 19: smothereth.

smooth, II, 233, 14; V, 167, A 7: pass lightly over. smooth the breast for swimming, see breast.

smore, V, 37, 6: smother.

smotley, V, 79, 15: pleasantly.

snack, IV, 415, 6: quick.

snags, III, 483, 7: protruding remnants of branches hewn off.

sned, II, 274, C 19; 462, 26: cut, lop. (misprinted sued, II, 462.)

sneed, V, 165, 4, 5: snood, fillet for a maiden's hair.

sneer, IV, 18, 15; 19, 13: snort.

sneeters, V, 213, 10:=snotters, gatherings of snot.

snell, of weather, wind, frost, I, 342, 23; 344, 22; III, 435, 1; IV, 213, 17; 214, 4; V, 99, 2: sharp, keen. of a blast of a horn, III, 195, 7: keen, shrill. of talk, III, 492, 31: sharp, caustic.

snoded, tied with a snood.

snood, V, 306, 4, 5: a fillet with which a maiden's hair was bound up. See sneed.

snotters, V, 213, 10: gatherings of snot. See sneeters.

soberly, III, 487, 17: quietly, making no noise.

socht, sought, pret., I, 147, 11, 12; II, 30, 8; III, 466, 46: asked for.

sodde, pret., V, 53, 103: seethed, boiled.

solace, I, 328, 53: pleasure. solaces, III, 287, 65: merry-makings, diversions.

soldan, II, 59, 35–37: sultan, any pagan king; hence, giant. See soudan.

Soldanie, Soudonie, V, 199 b, 33; 200 b, 33: Sultan's people.

solde, I, 326, 4: should.

some, with singular, some clean white sheet, V, 294, 7.

somers, III, 67, 216, 224; 74, 374: sumpter-horses, pack-horses.

sone, at once.

sone so, I, 243, 8: as soon as.

sonsie, II, 370, 16: plump.

soom, soum, sume, swoom, II, 29, 19; III, 394, K 4; IV, 493, 9; 511 b, 4; V, 138, B 6: swim.

soon, III, 440, 13: early. soon at morn, IV, 446, 2: early in the morning.

soone, II, 446, 92: swoon.

sore, as, they mighten a had, III, 441, 26: on whatever hard terms.

sorn, IV, 464, 14: sworn.

sorners, IV, 41, note *; 81 b: sojourners, properly those who take free quarters (such may be expected to make free generally with the property of those upon whom they impose themselves); "forcible intruders, people quartering themselves on tenants, etc., masterful beggars."

sorowe, sorrow, III, 61, 96; IV, 174, 6; 241 b; V, 28, 55: sorry, sorrowful, sad.

sorraye, II, 209, 9: sorrow.

sorrowful, III, 440, 12: sorry, pitiful.

sorte, III, 128, 97: set.

souce, V, 84, 7: the head, feet and ears of swine boiled and pickled.

soud, sude, should.

soudan, sowdan, souden, soldan, I, 54, 65; V, 195, 26; 197, 5.

Soudron, V, 192, 22: Southron.

Soudronie, V, 192, 33: Southronry.

sough, sound.

sould, should.

soum, soom, sume, II, 464, 2, 3; 474, J 5; V, 237, 9: swim.

soun, make bed saft and soun, IV, 279, 31, 32: smooth. lead the bridle soun, II, 105, 14: steadily, so as not to cause a jolt by jerking it.

sound, IV, 206, 10: safe and well. sailed it sound, II, 223, F 8: safe.

sound, a sound, III, 165, 88: a-swoon.

sound, IV, 172, 12, 14; 173, 7, 10, 11: in the sleep of death.

sounded, IV, 99, 3: should probably be rounded, whispered.

souner, I, 442, 10: sounder.

soup, I, 324, B 9: sup.

sour (reek), III, 433, C 6: sharp, bitter.

souter, soutter, III, 282 a; IV, 262, 16: shoe-maker.

south, I, 334, 9: sweet.

southen, southin, II, 358, 16, 28; IV, 482 b, 2, 3, 4; 483, 9, 17, 18: southern.

southering, IV, 48, b 18: soldering (corruption of, seething).

sowdan. See soudan.

sowe, III, 41 b, line 17: to be corrected to sowter, cobbler (?).

sowens, V, 108, B 10: flummery; "oat-meal sowr'd amongst water for some time, then boiled to a consistency, and eaten with milk or butter." Herd.

sowt, III, 13, 8: sought, peered, scanned.

sowt, south.

soyt, III, 110, 23; 111, 31, 43; 112, 55; V, 79, 30: sooth.

spait, III, 473, 26; 479, 2: flood.

spak well in his mind, V, 260, 15: sounded well, suited his own thoughts.

spakes, I, 61, C c, 15: the bars of a bird-cage.

spald. See spaul.

spang, II, 394, 18: span.

spare, I, 302, A 10; 446, 10; 451, 11; III, 246, E 7: opening in a gown or petticoat.

sparks out o a weet, IV, 379, 15: rain-drops from a shower. "Spirks, spirkins, applied to drops of water in Scotland; sparks usually to fire." W. Forbes.

sparred, III, 97, 20; 99, 61: shut.

spartled, v., II, 94, 6: sprang. spartling, II, 306, 15: kicking, struggling.

spartles, n., II, 94, 4: springs.

spaul, spauld, spald, spole, III, 473, 17; V, 105, A 3, B 6; 106, D 6, E 4; 107, 3: shoulder.

spayed, spied.

speal, I, 428, 17; 430, 6, 7: another form of scale, a wooden drinking vessel.

speals, spells, II, 410, 24; V, 236, 18: chips.

spear, v., IV, 85, 1: spare.

spear, speer, speir, spier, sper, ask. See **spyrr**.

speed, prosperity, help.

speel, v., II, 73, 25: climb.

speen, IV, 287, 19; 357, **C** 8, 9: spoon.

speer, inquire. See **spyrr**.

speere, V, 15, 20: "a hole in the wall of the house, through which the family received and answered the inquiries of strangers." Ritson. This, I fear, may be conjectural. Speere, a screen (wall) between fire and door to keep off the wind is well known both in England and Scotland. But the Heir seems to be outside and could not look up at this speere.

speir, ask. See **spyrr**.

spelle, v., I, 329, 3: discourse.

spells, speals, II, 410, 24; V, 236, 18: chips.

spendyd, a spear, III, 309, 40: "spanned; hence, got ready, placed in rest." Skeat.

sper, V, 78, 5: inquire. See **spyrr**.

spier-hawk, IV, 484, 1, 2: sparrow-hawk.

spin, spine, gar your blood, IV, 84, 3, 6; V, 253, **D** 1: spirt (as in Shakspere's Henry V, iv, 2, spin in English eyes).

spird, II, 144, 12: spurred.

spite, I, 211, 27: spital.

spleen, v., III, 220, 5: regard with spleen, hatred.

spleene, n., III, 230, 70: animosity.

splent (splint), III, 473, 17: armor of overlapping plates.

splinders, II, 91, 26: splinters.

splits, II, 389, 10: strands.

sply, II, 252, 1: (perhaps miswritten) spy.

spole, III, 342, 63: (O. Fr. espaule) shoulder. See **spaul**.

sporne, v., III, 64, 161: kick.

spreckl(e)d, I, 159, 5; 160, 3: speckled.

sprente, III, 309, 32: sprang, spurted.

spring, IV, 265, 13: probably miswritten or corrupted for young, which we find in the next stanza.

spring, I, 129, 17; 130, 20; 132, 13; 135, **O** 18, **P** 18, 19; IV, 312, 4; 313, 7: quick tune.

spring (well both clear and spring), II, 198 a, last line: spring water, pure as a spring.

sprunks, fine, III, 221, 12: showily dressed women ? (Cf. prank, prink, Dan., Swed., Germ., prunk.)

spulye, n., III, 458 b: spoil.

spulyie, spuilye, spuilzie, v., III, 463 a; IV, 53, 11; 84, 5, 8: despoil.

spunk-hole, V, 213, 3 (spunk=fire): a hollow in the floor, where the fire was made, fire-place.

spurn(e), n., III, 310, 65, 66: kick. The word, though protected by rhyme and by occurring twice, is suspicious. If spurn could be taken as clash, encounter, collision, it might stand, but such a sense is forced.

spurtle, V, 92, 11, 12: stick for stirring porridge.

spylle, I, 327, 20: mar, destroy.

spyrr, spire, spier, speir, speer, spear, sper (A. S. spyrian), I, 176, 17; 325, **B** 13; 349, **G** 9; 440, 10–15; III, 98, 41; 100, 64; V, 115, 4: ask, inquire. spear at, I, 151 a, 10; IV, 328, **A b**, after 3: inquire of. I, 349, **G** 7; II, 268, 12; 272, 9, 18; 379, 12; IV, 203, 9; 205, 15: ask, request.

squar, squer, squire.

square-wright, V, 124, 3: carpenter, joiner.

squeel, schele, schule, II, 175 f., 1, 6; 306, 19; IV, 327, 8.

squier, II, 59, 30:=swire, neck.

st, as sign of the future. I 'st, II, 449, 62; III, 411, 1; 413, 36; thoust, 'st, I, 211, 29; 433, 8, 26; II, 44, 13; 442, 10; 449, 60, 61; III, 277, 4; 411, 4; 432, 7; 477, 7; V, 50, 33. shee'st, she'st, II, 442, 3; 447, 3. you'st, II, 451, 88; III, 104, 6; 412, 12. (All from English ballads.)

sta, pret. of steal, III, 464, 13, 14.

stack, I, 16, **B** 14: stalk.

stad, V, 248, 19: stood.

staen, stolen.

stage, at a, III, 98, 39: from a floor, story (?).

stage, III, 295, 3: stag.

staig, III, 301, **A a**, 3; IV, 26, 1: a young stallion.

staking, III, 138, 18: cutting into stakes (cleaving, 140, **c** 18; stacking, 140, **d** 18).

stale, stathle, I, 18, **H** 9; 19, 12: the foundation of a stack, the undermost layer of sheaves in a stack.

stale strang, V, 213, 5: urine long kept for a lye and smelling strong. (But stale may=urine as well as strang.)

stalle, in strete and stalle, III, 101, 89: station; from the contrast with street, we may infer the meaning to be, when in movement (on the road) and when stationary, or housed.

stamp o' the melten goud, IV, 471, 37: an embossed plate.

stanch, III, 364 b: check.

stand (of milk, water), I, 344, 34: a barrel set on end.

stand, briddel-(bridell-)stand, V, 228, 12, 22: suit of clothes (bridal clothes).

stand, III, 453, **A** 14; IV, 515, 13: (of a court) sit. IV, 420, 9; V, 222, 34; 269, 1: take place.

stand, IV, 152, **C** 11; stand out, III, 439, 2: stickle, scruple.

stand na, nè, no(e), awe, I, 421, 5; III, 350, 53; IV, 505, 54; 506, 69: na may be a contraction of in na. na stand in awe, I, 419, 4; stand not in awe, III, 345, 53.

standen, p. p. of stand, III, 361, b, c 64.

stane, II, 467, 56: i. e. the (stone) wall.

stane-auld, III, 9 f., 11, 12, 20: very old (Germ. stein-alt).

stane-chucking, I, 441, **E** 1: throwing the stone, as in **B** 2.

stank, IV, 47, 12, 13: (O. Fr. estanc) ditch.

stap, n. and v., I, 298, 4; II, 88, 8, 9: step.

stap, stape, stop. II, 494, 1: stop, stay, reside. will stap to die, IV, 107, 7: shrink, hesitate.

stap, I, 439, 4, 5; 440, 5, 7; 504, 7; II, 294, 31, 32; 467, 41: stuff, cram.

stare, III, 128, 104: (eyes) protrude, or, are fixed, cannot move (?).

stare (of hair), V, 66, 19: stand up.

starf, *pret.*, V, 297 b: died.

stark, I, 69, 39; III, 474, 37: strong. stark thief, III, 365 b=the English strong thief, one who uses violence. stark and stoor, II, 47, 5: in a moral sense, wanting in delicacy, rude, violent, or indecent. the wind up stark, IV, 378, 5; 380, 11: *ellipsis of* blew, came, before *up.*

starn, stern, I, 440, 18; IV, 455, 10: (Icel. stjarna), star.

start, I, 341, 5; 343, 5; 347, 3; 348, 2: spring, jump. III, 164 b, 49; 342, 64: recoil, flinch, recede. *pret.* start, stert, I, 108 b, 8; 286, 56; II, 454, 56; III, 32, 81; 64, 159; IV, 477, 16: sprang. See **stert.**

state of my lande, II, 446, 91; state of my father's lands, 451, 98: landed estate.

stathle, stale, I, 17, 12: the foundation of a stack, the undermost layer of sheaves in a stack.

staw, II, 90, 23; 184, 13: stall.

staw, *pret.* of steal, II, 76, 25; 80 f., 9, 29; IV, 12, 13; 490, 30.

stawn, *p. p.* of steal, IV, 18, 19, 20.

stay, stey, IV, 262, 23: steep.

stead(e), steed(e). See **stede.**

steal, *pret.* sta, staw. *p. p.* stawn, stowen, stown, stoun. stealed, steald, IV, 20, 16; 166, 2, 3. stelld, III, 459, 7.

stean, Marie's stean, II, 183, 19: a stone seat at the door of St. Mary's Church.

stear, steer, III, 474, 33: stir, commotion.

steck. See **steek.**

stede, steed(e), stead(e), I, 334, 7; 411, 7, 16; II, 359, 19; III, 60, 81; 74, 376; 79, 133; V, 194, 71, 72; 197, 55; 199, 71, 72: place, dwelling-place. stand in stead, steed, steede, III, 344 f., 38, 44; 349, 38; IV, 505, 45: hold good, be kept, maintained, made good.

steed, I, 298, 4: stood.

steek, steck, steik, II, 336, P 2; IV, 188, 9; 279, 19, 27; 480, 4, 5; 514, 5: stick, shut, fasten. steekit (dor an window) to the gin, IV, 480, 5: to the fastening.

steek, steik, n., II, 364, 30; IV, 483, 20: stitch with the needle. III, 397, A b 5: stitch (of pain).

steeking, n., II, 361, 26: stitching.

steel, *pret.*, I, 477, 4: stale, stole.

steer, steir, II, 21, 10, 11; 29, 13, 14: rudder.

steer, stear, II, 369, 12: disturbance.

steer, sture, I, 69, 39; 71, 31: strong, robust. (stor, big.)

steer, II, 161, 12; IV, 69, 15: disturb, meddle with (for harm).

steer, I, 251, A 13: stir, move.

steik, n., stitch. See **steek.**

steik, v., shut. See **steek.**

steir, n., rudder. See **steer.**

stell, steel.

stelld, *pret.* of steal, III, 459, 7.

stelld, IV, 110, 10: placed, planted.

stende, me stende, I, 243, 5: that people should stone.

step-minnie, II, 367 b: stepmother.

stern, starn, I, 326, 16: star.

sterne, III, 308, 30: stern (men).

stert, start, *pret.* of start, III, 66, 211: sallied. stert out of the dore, sterte (start) to an offycer, stert hym to a borde, III, 26, 81; 32, 81; 62, 120, 125: rushed. stert to foot, IV, 224, 14: sprang to their feet.

steuen, III, 94, 52: voice. vnsett steven, III, 93, 27: time not previously fixed.

stey, stay, IV, 185, 10; 264, 15: steep.

stiffe, I, 293 f., 2, 9, 11; II, 55, 67: unyielding, stanch.

still, had your still, IV, 85, 7; V, 247, 14: hold your peace.

stime, styme, I, 482, **E**; III, 163 f., 78, 91: glimpse, ray, particle of light.

Stincher, IV, 69, 6: a river of Carrick, Ayrshire. (Misprinted stincher.)

stingy, IV, 316, 17: forbidding, cross.

stint, stinte, I, 334, 8; 411, 8, 17; 412, 28: stop.

stirred, III, 162, 49: should probably be stirted (shrank, flinched). The other text has, started.

stirt, stirred.

stock, I, 419, 2; 421, 2, 4, etc.; II, 467, 56: the outer side of a bed, opposite the wall (the bed, an enclosed box, being enterable at this side only).

stock, I, 402, 5: (term of disparagement) wanting in vitality, sensibility, youth, or what not.

stogg, IV, 480, 7, 8: stick, stab.

stoll yellow, IV, 453 a, b 13: corrupt; a has, gold that is yellow.

stomach will give him, II, 447, 17: disposition will incline him. II, 450, 69: courage.

stomached, well, III, 335 b: courageous.

stonde, I, 334, 8; III, 286, 55: while, time. See **stound(e).**

stonyt, I, 242, 11: stoneth, *old plural of the imperative.*

stood, V, 269, 1: took place. stood him upon, III, 228, 11: was incumbent on. See **stand.**

stoode, my need stoode, III, 412, 16: existed.

stook, I, 485, 10: put into shocks.

stoor, stark and stoor, II, 47, 5: (store, big) in a moral sense, rude, brutal.

store, I, 328, 50: big. See **stoor.**

store, buffets store, III, 145, 8: in plenty.

store, purse of gold and store, II, 461, 23: treasure (precious things laid up). carryd the store (of constancy), V, 158, 16: the totality.

stot, stott, IV, 12, **B** 4; 26, 1; 248, 19; 519, 6; 520, 6, 7: young ox.

stoun, III, 388, 8: (stoun, stound, North of England, to smart with pain, Scott. an acute intermittent pain) a painful attack.

stoun, *p. p.* of steal, III, 453, 10; V, 221, 24. See **stowen.**

stound(e), stonde, III, 25, 68; 284, 3; 298, 55; V, 83, 42: time, point, moment of time.

stoup, II, 344, 1; V, 91, 7, 8: pitcher, can, bucket (narrower at the top than at the bottom).

stour, stoure, stowre, II, 55, 67; III, 26, 89; 298, 58; 309, 47; 441, 27: tumult, brawl, fight. stour of thy hand, III, 280, 37: turbulence, destructiveness. III, 270, 16: disturbance, commotion.

stour, II, 195, notes, **A**; IV, 470, 20: dust.

stourished, III, 520 a: read *flourished* (?), blooming. (Cf. III, 373, 4.)

stout(e), II, 282 f., 4, 17 (audacious), 18; III, 339, 5; IV, 503, 5, 7: haughty, high-mettled, bold. III, 411, 8 (traitor): audacious, unflinching. V, 36 f., 9, 10: unabashed. I, 3, 3; IV, 197, 3: sturdy.

stowen, stown, *p. p.* of steal, I, 367, 14; II, 72, 23; 79, 38; IV, 133, **H** 6, 7; 241 a. See **stoun**.

stowre, *n.* See **stour**.

stowre, *adj.*, I, 293, 2: (originally, big) strong.

stracht, straght, III, 521 b, 272, 15; V, 236, 9: straight.

strack, struck.

strae, stray, stro, II, 162, 8; 169, 19; 185, 36; 261, 15, etc. : straw.

straik, streak, streek, stroke. (a sword) oer (on) a strae (strow), II, 261, 15; V, 37, 8: pass it over a straw to give it an edge. See **streak**. straiked back hair, IV, 184, **E** 17: stroked. straik (streek) wi a (the) wan(d), II, 188, 8; IV, 46, 3; 480, 15: of a measure, to even at the top by passing a stick over.

straine, streen, the, V, 221, 24: evening of yesterday.

strait (a rope), IV, 398, 7, 25: straighten, stretch, tighten. *pret.*, of stirrups, III, 492, 27.

strait, IV, 262, 23, strait and stay: another word for *stay, stey*, steep.

straith, strath, IV, 184 a: a valley through which a river runs.

straked, streaked. straked her trouth on a wand, II, 230, 9: a symbolical act, of gently rubbing or passing the fingers over a wand, by way of giving back a lover's troth.

strand, I, 165, **M** 4; III, 460, 28; IV, 172, 15; 174, 16: stream. Sometimes hardly more than a rhyme-word. In, Scotland's strands, strand, II, 289, 7; 294, 8, strand appears to be put for country, bounds; and for nothing more definite than way, road, in he gaed in the strand, etc., II, 177, 23; 289, **B** 2; III, 3, 5; IV, 210, 1. In, stript it to the stran, II, 390, 28, stran cannot mean more than plain (ground).

strang, V, 213, 5: urine kept for a lye, and smelling strong. See **stale**.

strang, strange.

strange, V, 76, 16: backward, diffident.

strated, V, 228, 15: stretched.

stratlins, I, 368, 23: straddlings, stridings.

straucht, straught, *adj.* and *adv.*, I, 146, 14; 251, **A** 10; II, 461, 5; IV, 94, 9; 214, 1: straight.

straught, V, 199 a, after 61: stretched. See **straucht**.

stray. See **strae**.

streak, straik, of whetting a sword by passing it over a straw (cf. Germ. streichen, strike, smooth,

whet). streakd it on a strow, V, 37, 8. straiked it oer a strae, II, 261, 15. See **stroak, strike, strip, slate**.

streak, streek, I, 299, 17: stretch.

streak by, I, 454, 12: to put off, put away.

stream-tail, IV, 185, 12: the lower end of a stream as opposed to the upper. Tail-race is the name given to the stream that carries away the water after it has passed the mill. J. Aiken.

streek, straik, I, 299, 17; II, 139, 7, 12; 345, 30; V, 174, 4; 209 b, 6: stretch. streeket, streekit, strickit, *p. p.*, II, 189, 38; IV, 128, 17; 316, 25; 318, **G** 9; 319, **H** 7: stretched, laid out, as dead.

streekit. See **straik**, and **streek**.

streen, straine, the, the streen, I, 57, **C** 13; II, 30, 4; III, 396, **N** 1; IV, 47, 10, 18; V, 118, **B** 13; 221, 24; 257, 14: yestreen, yester-night.

strenger, *compar.*, V, 283, 18 (and so we should read in 8 instead of scharpper): stronger.

strickit. See **streek**.

strike, of whetting a sword, etc., on a straw, or the ground. he's struck it (rappier) in the straw, II, 249, 18. struck it (brand) ower a strow, V, 226 b, 8; (dagger) 227, 21. struck it (bran) across the plain, II, 380, 32. See **stroak, streak, strip, slate**.

strinkled, III, 4, 10; 5, **C** 6: sprinkled.

strip, of whetting a sword by passing it across straw, a stone, the ground; replaced by stroak, streak, strike, slate, draw (cf. German streifen). has striped it throw the straw, II, 159, 15. he stript it to the stroe, II, 161, 13. he's stripped it athwart the straw, II, 256, 12. he's stripd it oer a stane, II, 396, 28. has stript it to the stran, II, 390, 28. he drew it through the strae, II, 185, 36; three times thro the strae, II, 162, 8. See **stroak**, etc.

stro, stroe, strow, strae, stray, II, 131, 16: straw.

stroak, stroke, of whetting a sword by passing it over a straw. stroakd it oer a stro, strae, stray, II, 131, 16; 166, 17; 169, 19; 305, 8, 21; 306, 14. See **strip, streak, straik, strike, slate**.

stroe, stro, strow, II, 161, 13: straw.

stroke. See **stroak**.

stroke, III, 180, 13: probably corrupt; read *streke*, stretch ? (Scott. streik, streek).

stronge th(i)efe, strong thief, III, 13, 2; 67, 221; V, 77, 32; 83, 49: a thief using violence. See **stark thief**.

strook, *pret.* of strike, V, 135, b 18.

strow, stro, V, 37, 8; 226 b, 8; 227, 21: straw.

strucken, *p. p.* of strike, II, 48, 3; III, 487, 13.

stryke pantere, V, 72 b: a drinking formula, in response to fusty bandyas.

stubborn, IV, 168, 8; 169, 6, 15; 170, **G** 4, 11, **H** 3, 4, 10: seems to have its old meaning of truculent, fierce, rather than wilful, mulish. See note to **H** 3, 4, IV, 177.

stude, stede, I, 244, 15: place.

study, studie, studdy, II, 374, **A** 2, **B** 2; 375, 3: stithy, anvil.

sturdy, sturdy steel, II, 380, 15; 381, 10; 385, 4; 388, 13: stiff, rigid (stubborn, II, 393, 10).

sture, steer, I, 71, 31; 69, 39: strong, robust. (stor, big.)

sturt, II, 249, 4: trouble, anger.

stye, I, 310, 9, 11, 13: pen, den. III, 100, 76: a smaller thoroughfare, alley.

styme, I, 482, **E**. See **stime**.

styrande, III, 295, 3: stirring, dislodging. See note, 301.

stythe, I, 311, 9, 11: place.

suan, V, 277, 14: swain.

suar, III, 308, 27; 309, 42: sure, trusty.

succeed the fame, his fame, IV, 249, 9; 251, 10: corrupt for, exceed in fame, or the like. See note, IV, 254, **E** 9.

such an a, IV, 312, 12: such a.

sud, soud, suld, should.

suddled, thy suddled silks, that thou wears every day, etc., II, 186, 5, 6, 10, 11: soiled, or rumpled, creased.

suddling, suddling silks, III, 398, **C** 9: soiling, which one would not mind exposing to soiling. Perhaps we should read suddlit. See **suddled**.

suderen, V, 217, 17: southern.

suds, leave you in the suds, V, 114, 12: in difficulty, in a strait.

sugar-sops, defined in dictionaries as sugar-plums. Fletcher's Monsieur Thomas, ii, 3, "Dandle her upon my knee, and give her sugar-sops." By analogy, bits of bread or cake dipped in sugar juice.

sugh, II, 258, 34: sough, sound (of wind).

suit, V, 215, 11; 223 b, 1; 246 b, 2: sweet.

suith, III, 468, **c** 9: sooth.

sulle, sell.

sume, V, 221, 11, 12; 237, 10: swim. See **soum**.

sun-bruist, IV, 469, 9: should, perhaps, be sun-burnt, as in the following line.

sundry, II, 212, 17: asunder, apart.

sune, *adj.*, V, 256, 12: sound.

sunks, IV, 262, 29: seats.

supply, IV, 154, 13: afford help. mak him some supply, V, 196, 39, cf. 43: succor, reinforcement.

surrount, IV, 245, 3: Skene's spelling for the original serundad, surrounded.

suspitious, II, 448, 37, 38: worthy of Mrs. Malaprop, but not so easy to unriddle: in her mouth, *auspicious;* here the modern *suggestive*, significant, would suit.

suþþe, III, 514 b, 1st line: then.

sutor, I, 430, 2: shoemaker. See **souter**.

sutten, *p. p.* of sit, IV, 468, 6.

swack, IV, 415, 6: nimble.

swack, *v.*, V, 305, 5: whack.

swads, swades, V, 134, 7; 135 b, 7: "swad in the North is a pescod-shell: thence used for an empty shallow-headed fellow." Blount, in Halliwell. Also, a cant term for soldier.

swaft, swaffed, III, 511, 8, 11: swapped.

swair, swaird, laird o the Ochilberry swair, IV, 207, 27, 29; laird o Athole swaird, IV, 198, 14: sware, neck or slope of a hill. (swaird, a corruption of swair,=sward, grassland, is not likely.)

swak, III, 300, 21. See **swap**.

swap, swak, swords, with swords, III, 298, 50, 54; 299, 9; 300, 21 (swakked); 301, 30; 309, 31; 422, 73; IV, 487, 29; 500 f., 22, 35 (swakked); V, 240, 6, 9: smite.

swarmd, III, 347, g 45; IV, 505, 56, 59: climbed. (swarm, to climb a tree that has no side branches to help one.)

swarued, swerved, III, 341, 53, 56; 345, 45: climbed (=swarmd, IV, 505, 56, 59).

swat, *pret.* of swe(a)t, III, 299, 9; 300, 21; 301, 30; 309, 31. swett, III, 422, 73. swette, III, 298, 50, 54.

swathed, II, 305, 10: swaddled (as it were) in blood.

swatter, I, 135, **P** 11: flounder, splash.

sway, howsoeuer this geere will sway, III, 341, 47: whatever turn this business may take, however this affair may turn out.

swear, *pret.*, swore.

sweauen, sweuen, II, 45, 18; III, 91, 4: dream.

sweer, II, 61, 4; IV, 229, 20: slow, reluctant. III, 160, 14: reluctant (to part with money).

swerers, quest of, III, 25, 69: jurors.

swerved, III, 347, d, e, f 45: climbed. See **swarued**.

swet, swett, swette, *pret.* of swe(a)t. See **swat**.

swetter, *compar.*, V, 283, 9, 19: sweeter.

sweven, sweauen, II, 45, 18; III, 91, 4: dream.

sweythyli, V, 80, 45: swiftly.

swick, IV, 438, 12: blame.

swikele, I, 243, 4: deceptive, treacherous.

swilled, I, 287, 72: tossed about or shook, as in rinsing (but in this case to effect a mixture).

swimd, swimmed, *pret.* of swim, II, 16, 5; 24, **F** 9; IV, 129, 5; 130, **D** 9.

swinke, III, 171 f., 8, 26: labor.

swire, swyre, I, 295, 34; III, 91 a: neck. IV, 5, 2; 7, 27; V, 249, 2: "the declination of a mountain or hill, near the summit." Jamieson.

swith, II, 55, 67; 248, 18: quickly.

swither, III, 268, 17; 272, 21: trepidation.

swittert, I, 129, 11: struggled, floundered, splashed (made spasmodic motions to keep herself up).

swoghynge, *n.*, I, 327, 31: sounding.

swoom, V, 151, **F** 2: swim.

swoond, swound, *n.*, I, 434, 29; II, 105, 19; III, 373, **A** 4: swoon.

swumd, *p. p.* of swim, III, 482, 25.

swylke, I, 327, 15: such.

swyre, swire, III, 91 a: neck.

syde, I, 333, 3: (of beard) long, hanging down. I, 426, 3: of a horn worn low. See **side**.

syke, sike, II, 238, 6; IV, 3, 28: ditch, trench. IV, 470, 25: perhaps, rivulet. (water-course, marshy bottom with a stream in it. Jamieson.)

syne, sayn, san, sane, I, 17 f., **F** 2, 7; 127, 27; 347, 9; III, 437, 16, 20, 21, 24: then, afterwards. I, 204, **E** 3; V, 306 b, 1; III, 436, 9 (?): since.

synsyne, since. See **sinsyne**.

sypress, cypress, III, 148, 10; 150, b 10: crape (veil).

syre, IV, 21, 10: (sewer) drain, gutter.

syt, III, 70, 280: old contracted form of sitteth.

sythis, I, 327, 21: times.

T

tabean brirben (kame), II, 217, 2, 4: printed by Herd, Tabean birben. Jamieson conjectured for Tabean, 'made at Tabia, Italy.' Dr C. Mackay very properly remarks that Tabia was not known as a place of manufacture for combs. He suggests a Gaelic origin: taobh, a side, taobhan, sides; bior, a pin, point, prickle, the tooth of a comb; bean, a woman; whence taobhan bior bean, the side comb of a woman. Whether this is good Gaelic, I am myself unable to say; but it is a simple criticism that a woman's hair is not combed with a side-comb. The passage is undoubtedly corrupt. In IV, 471, 2, we have, a haw bayberry kame, also corrupt; bayberry was heard for whatever tabean brirben stands for. One copy had birchen, IV, 471, note to 221.

table, take vp the, III, 29, 142: take away. the tables were laid on trestles and easily handled, removed, and, as we often see in ballads, kicked over. drew her table, V, 304, 13: see explanation at V, 304 a.

tack (of needlework), II, 30, **L** 1: attachment by stitching. needle-tack, II, 217, 5.

tack, took.

tacken, taiken, IV, 515, 12: token.

tae, II, 147, 4: too.

tae, the tae,=ae, one. See **tane.**

taen, tane, tean, teyne, p. p., taken.

taiglet, taiglit, IV, 195, 4; 196, 9: tarried.

taiken, tacken, I, 396, 5, 6: token.

Tailliant, Talliant, II, 383, 22, 24, 25; 385, 23, 25, 26; 387, 17, 19, 20; 388, 16, 18, 19: Italian.

taipy-tapples, I, 303, **D** 5: misreading of saipy-sapples, which see.

tait. See **tate.**

take, V, 277, 2: talk.

take, III, 60, 72, 76; 62, 123; 65, 194; 73, 351; 110, 9: hand over, give. I, 465, 18; 472, 28; II, 108, 17; 271, 17; 273, 23; III, 110, 18; 472, 9; IV, 508, 5: deliver a blow, strike.

take on (lawing), IV, 175, **N** 4: run up (reckoning).

take road, take foot, II, 62 b, 14: make off.

take sworne, III, 340, 34; IV, 504, 34; V, 52, 73: take an oath of, put under oath.

take truce, II, 443, 39; 449, 44; III, 469 a: take trewes, pledges of good faith, for suspension of hostility. take peace, III, 278 f., 3, 6: perhaps formed upon take truce.

take up (the table), III, 29, 142: clear away (remove the boards). See **table.** take up (dogs), III, 125, 35, 36: stop, restrain, call off (?).

take with, III, 413, 47; IV, 334, 13: take up with, put up with, submit to.

takle, takyll, III, 70, 288; 75 f., 398, 404: arrow.

talbott, III, 333, 28: a species of hound.

talents.

> The talents of golde were on her head sette
> Hanged low downe to her knee,

II, 52, 17: talents probably refers to the weight or value of gold worn in massive ornaments (cf. a weight of goud hung at her chin, I, 472, 24). It is not likely that the lady wore coins.

talk, IV, 13, 12: should probably be *lack*, reproach, blame. The reading in **A** 18; **D** 5, is suspicious; lack, reproach, is in **E** 16.

talkitive, IV, 13, **D** 8: used for talkativeness.

Talliant. See **Tailliant.**

tamper ye at, keep ye up and, IV, 226, 13: seems to be corrupt, cf. 221, 17, keep ye up i temper guid. tamper may be meant for temper, in the sense of putting a machine into working order, try expedients to humor or manage you.

tane, the tane, the tither, tother, I, 253, 1; II, 104, 30; 132, 18; 190, 42; 212, 16. See **tean, ton.**

tane, taen, tean, teyne, p. p., taken. tane with me, IV, 98, 12: occupied, engrossed, captivated (seized or smitten with compassion for, love ?) tane sworn (I am), V, 52, 73: of one who has taken an oath.

tangle, I, 259 a, 11: sea-weed.

taps, V, 173, 8: tops, tips (of heather).

Targalley, V, 141, **c** 1, 2: perhaps a corruption of Turk (Turkish) galley, cf. **C, a, f, g.**

targats, targits, III, 363, note *; 371, 26, 27: tassels.

targe, III, 75, 385: "Targe or chartyr. Carta." Prompt. Parv. "quatre grosses blancs appellés targes." Ducange, targa. (Corrected from *tarpe*.)

tarlottus, tynkerris in tarlottus, III, 41 b (?).

tarnd, V, 303 a: turned.

tarpe, III, 75, 385; 80, 385: emended to *targe*.

tasse, V, 37, 9: cup (tarse in MS.).

tate, tait, teet, tet, tette, I, 86, 15; 130, **E** 14; 323, 2; II, 189, 23; 191, 18; 194, 27; 389, 16; IV, 449, 15: lock (of hair, of mane).

tattles, tittles, I, 302, **B** 7: tits, bits.

taucher, toucher, tocher, dowry. See **toucher.**

tauchy, I, 302, 10: greasy.

taul, told.

taunt, bide to taunt, II, 272, 11: endure taunting (?).

tay, tie.

tayened, tayned, V, 228, 26, 27: (tined) lost, killed.

teacht, IV, 150, **g** 25, 30: taught.

teall, tale.

tean, IV, 456 f., 5, 24; 515, 12; V, 36, 11, 15: taken. See **taen.**

tean, the tean, the eather, V, 224, 27: the one, the other. See **tane.**

tear begane this spurn, III, 310, 65: see note, 307.

tee, IV, 446, 7:=tie, 447, 7. glove tee, V, 300, 10, 16, 19.

tee, ti, I, 300, 7, 9, 15; II, 30, 4: to, too.

teem, toom, II, 169, 13; IV, 182, **F** 5: empty.

teem, I, 444, **G** b 2: pour.

teemed, II, 435, 36: allowed.

teen, teene, tithe. See **teind.**

teene, tene, I, 328, 40; III, 24, 48; 37, 63; 60, 78; 62, 128; 66, 211; 72, 329; 230, 70; 412, 22; 443, 1: injury, wrath, vexation, annoyance, grief, trouble.

teenouslye, III, 356, 21: angrily.

teet. See **tate.**

teeth, I, 305, **A** 12: tooth.

teind, teein, tiend, tene, teen, I, 342, 24; 344, 23; 350, 28; 354, 32; 452, 3; III, 504 b, 9; IV, 456, 15; 458, 16: tithe.

teindings, IV, 455, 18: tithings.

tell, till, to.

tempeng, tempen, V, 165 f., 6, 9, 10: tempting.

temper, set them up in temper wood, IV, 222, 20: corrupted, as will appear from the conclusion of the other versions. Parts of two stanzas are mixed.

tene, *v.,* III, 110, 13: do harm to.

tene, *n.* See **teene.**

tenements, V, 77, 38: holdings (whether of lands or houses does not appear here).

tenish, V, 245 a, 8: tennis.

tent, *n.,* II, 139, 11; IV, 223, 3; 390, 4: heed.

tent, *v.,* I, 74, 81; III, 478, 28: take care of, guard, watch.

tet, tette. See **tate.**

tew, V, 303 a: two.

teyne, IV, 504, 26: taken. See **taen.**

teytheyng, tythyng, V, 79, 25: tidings.

tha, then. See **tho.**

tha, V, 296 a: the.

thae, I, 369, 3; 427, 15; 447, 14; II, 190, 43; IV, 69, 12; 258, 27; 470, 28, 29: they, them, those, these.

thairbut, thairben, IV, 291, after 11: out there, in there.

thar, I, 334, 8: it is necessary (it is not necessary to hinder thee of thine errand).

that, II, 451, 93: till that.

that, *imperative particle,* anone that you tell me ! III, 27, 118. no peny that I se ! III, 58, 41; 68, 246. no ferther that thou gone ! III, 67, 219.

that, *superfluous,* I, 273, 38; 284, 7; II, 58, 6; 433, 3; 434, 16, 18; 436, 59; 437, 89; 442, 18; 444, 41; III, 276, 1; 277, 18, 19; 341, 46, 54, 57; 413, 39; IV, 503, 8; V, 48, 6. (Very common in the Percy MS., where all the above, excepting one, occur.)

that, *plur.,* that two lords, II, 130, 28, 29. See **this.**

that . . . his=whose, IV, 330, Appendix, 2.

that was her own, II, 73, 20: *that* referring to roses and ribbons, or the bridal relation, or to both.

the, thé, I, 284 f., 9, 30; III, 307 f., 3, 8, 12, 25, 28; 419 f., 14, 33; 421, 45, 65; 477, 4; 479, 38; V, 263, 7, 9, 11, 12: they.

the, thé, I, 296, 50: thee.

the day, I, 356, 56; II, 32, **Q** 2; 248, 5; 285, 14: to-day.

the morn, II, 104, 18; III, 480, 18; 482, 14; 488, 19; V, 300, 17; 307, 7: to-morrow. the morn's nicht, II, 208, **C** 9: to-morrow night.

the night, the nicht, I, 303, **C** 4; 304, **E** 4; III, 480, 18; 488, 19; V, 299 a, 1: to-night.

the streen, yestreen. See **streen.**

the, IV, 494, 29: to be corrected to *she; they* in the next line to mean the mill-people.

the, thee, then, thye, II, 164, 17; III, 67, 234; 78, 452; 113, 81; V, 76, 11; 79, 14; 82 f., 25, 27, etc.: thrive, prosper.

thee, III, 6, 20: for *thou.*

theek, I, 253, 4: thatch. *pret. and p. p.* theekit, theekd, IV, 76 f., 1, 2, 4; 458 b, 9: thatched, roofed.

theer, V, 296 a: there.

thegither, thegithar, thegether, III, 261, 3; V, 217 b, No 49, 1: together.

their. See **thir.**

then, *v.* See **the.**

there, the diel o there, III, 488, 26: seems to mean *of that;* but we have, devil be there in 43, as an equivalent phrase.

there, III, 504 a, 14; IV, 465, 25, 26; 485, 24; 510 a, 2: there is. III, 489, 9: there are (or, there is, Scottice).

there down, downwards, down.

theretoo, III, 64, 172: besides.

thes, III, 111, 34; 113, 76: thus. See **this.**

they, II, 434 f., 25, 38; 437, 78; 442 f., 19, 29: the (frequent in Percy MS.).

thick, spak thick, I, 343, 13: not articulating distinctly (from emotion).

thick, III, 35, 29: thilke, that.

thie, I, 19, 14: 330, **B** 2; 331, **C** 2, **D** 2: thigh.

thief, foul thief, V, 123, 14; 184, 44: devil.

thiggin, V, 117, 2: begging, levying supplies.

thimber, I, 330, **A** 2: (Icelandic þungbærr, heavy to bear ?) heavy, massive. Not understood and changed to nimble, nimle, I, 332, **F** 2, **G** 2, umber, I, 331, **C** 2.

think, thynk, III, 27, 98; 58, 37, 44; 60, 82: seem. me thinke, me thynke, methink, III, 81, 37; 153, c 5; 158, d 17; 321 b; V, 82, 26, 41: methinketh, methinks. See **thoghte, thouth.**

think lang (A. S. lang thyncan, seem long). thouth me nouthe lange, I, 334, 5, 9: seemed not long, amused me, impressed me pleasantly. In Scottish, personal, with substitution of *think* for *seem.* think lang, I, 370, 4; V, 115, 2: find the time wearisome, suffer from *ennui.* I think lang, I, 368, 35, 37, 39; 506, 2: long for. I 'll never think lang, IV, 257, 10: shall never be discontented. she thought (thocht) lang, I, 478, 14; II, 76, 11; 78, 14: was weary with waiting. keep frae thinking lang, I, 467, 16, 20. keep him onthought long, I, 478, 13. See **unthought lang.**

thir, their, I, 5, **C** 5; 329, 61; 482, **C** b 11; II, 78, 23, 24; 271, 21; III, 441, 34, 35; 464, 4; IV, 7, 30; 476, 4, 5; V, 115, 2; 195, 9, 10: these, those.

thirld in his ear, II, 208, 5: thrilled.

thirled at the pin, II, 121, 15: tirled, rattled.

this, *pl.,* this bonny boys, II, 81, 37; this twa, II, 158 f., 1, 19. See **that.**

this, thes, thys, III, 73, 346; 111, 34; 113, 76; IV, 210, 4; V, 283, 2: thus.

tho, III, 28, 138; 34, 7, 11; 36, 44; 111, 30: then.

thoe, III, 285, 33: they (possibly, then).

thoghte, I, 328, 50: (probably) seemed. . See **think.**

thole, thoule, I, 508, 8; II, 46, 2; 124, 38; 314, 10; IV, 17, 2; 21, 16; 278, 12; V, 229, 32: bear, suffer. (IV, 17, 2: like dree, be capable of.)

thorn, II, 27, **I** 6: dialectic variation of forn, **J** 6, *partic.* of fare: fill yourselves with good fare.

thornd, II, 110, 24: fared.

thoth, thouth, I, 334, 7, 8: though.

thother, the, III, 111, 43: tother, other.

thou, though.

thou is, thou 's, III, 483, 31; 488, 24.

thou sitts, thou rydes, III, 479, 35.

thou will, thou made, thou was, thou took, etc., *2 pers. sing.* without termination: I, 221, **C** 9–11, 222 **E** 11–17; 223, 12, 16.

thought lang, I, 370, 4; 478, 14, etc. See think lang.

thoule, II, 159, 20: suffer, put up with. See thole.

thouth, I, 334, 5, 8, 9: seemed. See think.

thouth, I, 334, 8: though. See thoth.

thowt, *n.*, V, 283, 20: thought.

thra, thrae, IV, 128, 1; 220, 2; 369 b; 446, 8; 465, 34; 470, 20; 479, 3; 518, 10; V, 197, 3, 13: dialectic variety of fra, frae, from.

thrae, I, 170, 6: through.

thrall, III, 480, 15: bondage.

thrang, V, 115, 2: intimate, familiar.

thrashes, threshes, IV, 77, b 4: thrushes, rushes.

thrashin oer his songs (of blackbird), I, 133, **M** 3, 5: repeating, or practising.

thrast, *pret.*, III, 98, 25: pressed.

thrave, I, 21, 10: twenty-four sheaves of corn, two shocks.

thraw, II, 146, 14; 147, 15; 149, 14; 283, 16; IV, 479, 8: twist, contort. *pret.* threw. *p. p.* thrawen, thrawin, thrawn, IV, 348, 6, 7; 349, b 3; 350, **B** b, after 5; V, 273, No 239, 3.

thrawin, I, 465, 12: thrown.

thrawn, twisted. See thraw.

thrawn, IV, 465, 20: ill-humoredly.

threefold oer a tree, III, 267, 9: with a double curve, over a stick.

threesome, II, 270, 30: three together.

threshes, thrashes, IV, 258 f., 5, 20: rushes.

threty, thirty.

threw, *pret.* of thraw, I, 102, 18; 492, 18; II, 111, 21; 183, 30; 185, 40; 208, 12; 286, 16; V, 262, 24: twisted, intertwined. III, 180, 10, Robin he lope, Robin he threw: may be, threw himself about, or twisted twirled, showing his suppleness.

thrien, I, 244, 18: thrice.

thrild vpon, thirled at, a pinn, II, 121, 15; 138, 10, 16: tirled, rattled. See pin.

thrill, II, 291, 27: pierce, penetrate.

thristle-cock, I, 427, 8; thristle-throat, I, 429, 8: throstle, thrush.

throch, II, 30, 6; 256, 12: through.

throly, III, 98, 25: strenuously, doggedly.

thronge, III, 25, 56: pressed, made his way.

throw, *intrans.*, fyer out of his eyen did throw, I, 211, 23: dart, shoot.

throwardlie, III, 365 a: frowardly, crossly, ill-temperedly.

throwe, III, 78, 448: space of time.

thrown, IV, 249, **F** 3: corrupted from *this road;* cf. **A** 6; **B** 7; **C** 9; **D** 6.

þrumme, III, 13, 9: the extremity of a weaver's warp, from six to nine inches long, serving to hold arrows. Cf. II, 168, 5, four-and-twenty arrows laced in a whang.

thrusty, IV, 172, 4: trusty? (rusted, 173, **K** 4.)

thurst, IV, 60 b, 6: thrust.

thryfte, euyll thryfte, III, 67, 220: ill thriving, ill speed, bad luck.

thu, V, 283, 13: thou.

thye, thigh.

thye, II, 241, 14: thrive. See the.

thys, V, 283, 2: thus. See this.

ti, I, 299, 13: to; too.

ticht. See tight.

tide, tyde, III, 299, **C** 1; 432, 15; 473, 11; V, 83, 49: time. into the tide, V, 160, 2; by the tide, 163, 4; 164, 1: at the time, now.

tidive, tidive hour, II, 257, 15: timely, early? (the hour may be early morning).

tiend, tithe. See teind.

tier, V, 151, **F** 1, should be, tree.

tift, II, 183, 17: puff, whiff.

tight, ticht, V, 151, **E** 3; 161, 2: (of a man) well built. V, 258, 4: (of a maid) neatly shaped, jimp.

till, *n.*, II, 409, 12: toil.

till, till see, II, 191, 22; till and frae, II, 71, 15: to. At III, 338 b, it is said that in **A** 66, *till* may mean *while.* Here Jamieson was followed: but there appears to be only one case to cite, in a single MS. of Barbour's Brus, where others read quhil. The remark must be withdrawn, though *while* might be offered as an emendation, since it is, for obvious reasons, far more probable than *till.*

till, *v.*, II, 54, 57: entice.

timmer, timber, wooden.

timouslie, IV, 53, 1: early.

tine, tyne, tayen, I, 16, **C** 14; II, 70, 30; 313, 21; 336, **O** 8, 9; III, 75, 398: lose. I, 324, **B** 7; IV, 454, 3; 455, 11; 458, 5: to be lost, perish. I, 115, 11: cause to perish. *pret.* and *p. p.* tint, IV, 18, 20; 127, 14; 165, 15; V, 99 **C** 4: lost.

tinye, *n.*, a little tinye, V, 51, 69: bit.

tip, tippet (of horse's mane), IV, 410, 18, 21; 413, 13: = tate, lock.

tirl at the pin, trill, rattle, at that part of the door-fastening which lifts the latch. See pin.

tit, V, 125, 9: quick pull.

tithyngus, III, 98, 40–42: tidings.

tittles and tattles, I, 302, **B** 7: tits, bits.

to, III, 110, 14, 16: two.

to, till.

tobreke, *subj.*, I, 243, 6: break, burst (apart). *p. p.* to-broke, broken up.

tocher, toucher, tougher, taucher, *n.* See toucher.

to-clouted (gowne), III, 179 a: with patches set to it.

tod, I, 355, 44; IV, 193, 11; 194, 4; 195, 9; 196, 13, etc.: fox.

toe from home, boune, IV, 504, 24: to a place away from ? (perhaps corrupt).

to-hande, III, 110, 14: two-hand, two-handed.

tolbooth, tolbuith, tollbooth, III, 482, 18; 489 f., 9, 10, 15: prison; jail. That in Edinburgh, III, 385, 12; 386, 12; 389, 14; IV, 508 b, 8; 509, 9 (Towbooth).

tolde, III, 59, 67–69; 68, 247: counted.

to-morne, I, 328, 57: to-morrow.

ton, tone, the, III, 296 f., 12, 30: the one. tone, tother, II, 53, 27, 32. the tone, the tother, II, 51, 2. See tane.

tooke, III, 405, 14: put. See take.

tooken vpon one part, III, 404, 3: engaged, enlisted, on the same side.

toom, teem, I, 72, 17; II, 124, 38; IV, 143, B 1, 3, C 6; 180, 8; V, 196, 53; 251, 30, 32; 256, 8: empty.

toomly, IV, 181, 11: empty.

toorin, I, 500, R 1–4: cooing. (Imitative, cf. Scott. curr, curroo, Germ. gurren.)

too-too, to-towe, III, 217, b, c, 41: a strong too.

top, IV, 288, E 3: should be toss, toast.

topcastle, III, 340 f., 32, 58; 344 f., 28, 46; IV, 504 f., 32, 58 (topcasaille)=top. See topps.

topps, III, 419, 15; IV, 506, 61: " Among seamen tops are taken for those round frames of board that lye upon the cross-trees, near the heads of the masts, where they get up to furle or loose the topsails." Phillips. A noble ship at III, 419, 15, has five tops.

tor (of saddle), IV, 410, 21: pommel.

tor, tore, II, 323, 11; 334, M 2; IV, 480, 8: projection or knob at the corner of old-fashioned cradles (as also, ornamental balls surmounting the backs of chairs).

torne, III, 112, 56: turn, bout.

tortyll-tre, III, 112, 56: corruptly for trystell-tre.

toss, IV, 288, E 3: toast (as a beauty). (misprinted top.)

to t', III, 439, 4: to the.

to-towe, III, 430, 1: too-too, a strong too.

toucher, tougher, taucher, n., IV, 283 f., 10, 22, 23; 285, 12, 13; 286, 11; 287, 4; 487, 30; 489, 29; V, 267, 12, 13: tocher, dowry.

toucher, v., IV, 284, 23: pay a dowry to.

touchered, V, 224, 11: dowered.

toun, town, IV, 200, 19; 201, 11; 202, K 5; 203, 13; V, 228, 27: a farmer's steading or place (or, a small collection of houses). V, 267, 7: perhaps simply house.

toun-head, V, 267, 11: centre or principal part of the town.

tour, lyin in a tour, IV, 87, 20: continuous route.

tout, I, 274, 18: backside.

touting, blowing.

tow, III, 396, N 8; 449 b; V, 125, 9: rope.

tow, III, 434, 17, 18; 435, 12: let down by a rope. V, 123, 15, 16: draw up and let down.

towbooth. See tolbooth.

toweld, II, 194, 22: twilled (?).

town. See toun.

tows, went to the, IV, 380, 8: tows=touts, drinking-bouts, fell to drinking (in contrast to Allan, who went to pray. Tows cannot be ropes; they had not gone aboard the ship).

trace, II, 479, 16: track, path, way.

trachled, V, 169, 9: tired out.

trade, II, 454, 37: should be train, as in 445, 62; 450, 67.

train, IV, 107, 1, 13, 15: company.

train(e), II, 445, 62; 450, 67: training.

traitorye, III, 411, 2: treachery.

tralled, V, 274, 10: trailed (had rather have married A. and have trailed).

trance, II, 468 f., 18, 22; V, 268, 7: passage in a house.

tranckled, I, 284, 10: travelled. (Dutch trantelen, tranten, tarde progredi; morari. Hexham, to go lazily, at a soft pace.)

trap, a doublet of trip. trip for trap, II, 328, 17: tripping.

trapand, p. p., (of horse) IV, 44, 4: treacherously dealt with.

trappin, IV, 342, 12: tape.

trattles, II, 152, 5: tattles.

travisse, II, 92, 20: (a frame for confining cavalry horses) horse's stall.

trawale, III, 41 a: travail, operations.

tray, tree (A. S. trega), injury, suffering, grief, vexation. tene and traye, I, 328, 40; tray and tene, III, 66, 218: grief and vexation. tree and teene, III, 412, 22: grief and injury. (tregan and téonan, Genesis, 2274.)

tray, try.

tread, tred, pret. of tread, II, 160, 5, 6; 165, 9; 171, 10, 12; IV, 468, 3, 4. p. p., IV, 128, 19.

treasonie, II, 344, 14: treason.

tree, tre, I, 343, 42; 345, 40; II, 218, 19; III, 23, 26; 309, 44: wood. I, 465, 2; 473, 4: pole, shaft of a cart. I, 341, 21; 344, 20; III, 25, 59; 29, 154; 63, 147; 97, 4: the cross. III, 160, 22, 25; 161, 42; 162, 55, 62; 163, 78; 267, 9; 268, 8; 270, D 8; 271, F 10: staff, straight piece of rough wood. crooked tree, III, 160, 18: bow. trenchen tree, III, 164, 91: truncheon, cudgel, staff. of (a) myghttë tre, III, 308 f., 27, 42: of strong wood. a trusti tree, III, 309, 40: perhaps shaft; but the a is likely to be of, as Professor Skeat suggests, and the meaning, of trusty wood (cf. 44, bowe made off trusti tree). horse of tree, III, 478, 13: bridge, or, at least, tree-trunk.

tree, III, 412, 22. See tray.

trenchen tree, III, 164, 91: truncheon, cudgel, staff.

trew, true, II, 384, 20, 21; III, 474, 45: trow, believe.

trews, trues, IV, 157, 18, 19; 267, 7; 272, 3; V, 165, 1; 267 a, 6; 306, 1: trousers.

treyffe, III, 113, 81: thrive.

triest, trist. See tryst.

trinkle, I, 497, 15; II, 197, 17; 209, D 7; 290, 25; 326, 11; 411, B 17; IV, 236, 5; 409, 6; 487, 27: trickle.

trip for trap, came down the stair, III, 328, 17: tripping, trip-trap (trap, a doublet of trip).

tristil-tre, III, 98, 37. See **trystell-tre**.

troule, V, 84, 13: go round (of a bowl of ale).

trow, trew, true, believe, suppose. I trow, I, 104, c 13: assuredly.

trowt, trowet, III, 110, 23, 26: troth.

truce, my petticoat, IV, 288, **E** 2: put in a trouss, tuck or fold, to shorten.

true, days of, III, 352 a: (singular of truce, trews, pledges of good faith) truce.

true, IV, 486 f., 5, 21; 491, 5: trow. See **trew**.

true-love, lover, betrothed lover (often not to be distinguished from true love), *passim*.

trues, trousers. See **trews**.

truff, II, 144 f., 14, 24: turf.

trust, II, 307, 34; 379, 4; IV, 494, 37; V, 38, 5: trow, believe, suppose (of the things one would rather not believe).

truste, III, 66, 207: trusty.

trusty tree, III, 92, 8; 116 f., 2, 21; 200, 37; V, 75, 4: an obvious corruption of trystill-tree, a tree appointed for a meeting or assemblage. (Trusty also in later copies of Adam Bell and the Gest for trysty, trystell, which see.)

trusyd, III, 13, 9: trussed, bound up.

tryst, tryste, *n.*, I, 394, **A** 1; 395, 1; IV, 2, 4, 6: appointment to meet. IV, 413, 7; 414, 3, 4: appointment for wedding. I, 326, 18: market.

tryst, tri(e)st, *v.*, I, 314, 1; II, 270, 3; 272, 4; IV, 201, 8; V, 171, 4: engage, induce, entice, to come, go with. II, 294, 13; IV, 194, 6; 198, 8; 200, 19; 201, 11; 202, **K** 5: prepare a way for coming, cause to come.

tryst, *n.* or *v.*, IV, 154, 5: appoint a place, or, appointment of a place.

trystell-tree, trysty-tre, trystyll-tre, tristil-tre, III, 69 f., 274, 286; 71, 298; 75, 387; 76, 412: a tree serving for a meeting-place (of Robin Hood's band). (In later texts, trusty.)

trysty tre, III, 26 f., 95, 98; 27, 102: tree fixed upon for rendezvous (trusty, trustie in later copies).

tu, V, 303 a: to.

tua, the tua part, V, 254 b, 4: two thirds. But twa part, V, 276, 20, seems to mean second part, half, which we have at IV, 120 **F** 7; 381, 16; that is, it is more likely that an equal share should be offered.

tul, III, 440, 25; til, to. tul a, III, 440, 13: to have.

turn, IV, 477, 14; turning o the tune, II, 249, 11; o the note, 250, 13; IV, 477, 13: refrain (owreturn, I, 332, **E, F** 7; owreword, II, 254, 8, 9). turnin o the bell, IV, 314, 19.

turn the wind wi thee, IV, 379, 6:=take the wine (i. e. wind) fra thee, V, 275, 5. (The meaning is clear, but whether turn is in actual use in the required sense I have not ascertained.)

turning. See **turn**.

tust, IV, 224, 20: tost.

twa, two. twa part, see **tua**.

twafald(-fold), oer a tree, staff, II, 461, 19; III, 268, 8: bent double over a stick. twafald ower his steed, III, 8, 18: doubled, head hanging on one side, feet on the other. See **twofold**.

twain, *v.*, part. See **twin**.

twal, twelve.

twalmon, twalmont, twelvemonth.

twalt, twelt, twelfth.

twan, *pret.* of twine, I, 256, 2.

twatling, dishes, V, 86, 36: unmeaning, nonsensical, of no account.

twaw, two.

twig, IV, 31, **B** 6: twitch, pull.

twin, twine, twyne, twin me o my make, twin babe of life, I, 129, 8; 174, 18; 175, **D** 6, 12; 177, 17; 220, **B** 3; 222, 7; II, 218, 16; IV, 179, **A** 2: deprive. twine a mantle, I, 453, 3; twine me, IV, 154, 5: part with. twin(n) with, I, 175, 4, 5, 10, 11; II, 232, 7, 10, 12; twin(e) me and my make, etc., I, 127, 14; 128, 11; 350, 15; II, 159, 12, 13 (twain); V, 178, 1: separate. gar twa loves twin (twain), etc., I, 56, **B** 9; II, 63, 22; 230, **B** 3, 6: part, *intrans.*

twine, coarse linen, duck, crash. for towel, IV, 460, No 47, 1, 2; shift (contrasted with holland), II, 224, 17. II, 27, 19, 20: canvas. I, 221, **C** 9; 504, 4: coarse stuff of some kind. Lincoln twine, III, 5, **D** 5; 8, 12; IV, 496, 10, is doubtless the Lincoln green of other versions, and so simply texture. III, 192, 10: yarn. ropes o silken twine, IV, 472, 10: twist. shoes of small corded twine, V, 301 b, 3.

twinkle, II, 409, 17; 425, **A** 7: trinkle, trickle.

twinn, *v.* See **twin**.

twinn, part in twinn, I, 432, 3: in twain, in two.

twirld, at the pin, IV, 390, b 4: tirled, rattled.

twofold oer a staff, threefold oer a tree, III, 267, 9; the body being bent double over the staff, the whole presentation is, with the staff (tree) threefold. Corruptly, III, 188, 6, two foote on a staffe, the third vpon a tree. See also **twa-fald**.

tydand, II, 433, 9: tidings.

tyde. See **tide**.

tyndes, III, 65, 186: (A. S. tind) tynes, antlers.

tyne, I, 17, 11:=tynd, harrow-tooth (harrow-pin, I, 19, 10).

tyne, *v.*, to lose, to perish. See **tine**.

tyte, his backe did from his belly tyte, III, 277, 17: quickly. A verb of the sense *fall away* may have dropped out after *did*, and is at any rate to be understood, unless *tyte* had that sense. A Scottish *tyte*, to totter, fall (tyte oer, fall over), is noted by Jamieson.

tythance, tythand(e)s, tythyng, III, 361, b, c 1; c 14, 49; 362, 93; V, 78, 5: tidings.

U

ugsome, II, 47, 15: exciting disgust or abhorrence. (Icel. uggr, fear.)

ull, I ull, V, 267, 5: will.

umber, I, 331, **C** 2: seems to be the same as thimber (I, 330, **A** 2): massive.

unbeen, my barn's unbeen, IV, 143, **A** 4: not thoroughly closed in or made tight? (been, well-provided, warm, dry and snug. A bein cask, watertight, Jamieson.) a house is beind when thoroughly dried.

vnbethought him, I, 214, **A** 17 (printed um-); II, 240, 5; V, 15, 16: bethought himself of.

unbigged, IV, 143, **A** 4: unbuilt.

unco, *adj.*, A. S. uncúð (uncouth, III, 245, 11). unco man, IV, 235, 11: unknown, strange. unco land, ground, I, 182, 1, 3; 324, 4; IV, 410, 10, 11. unco squire, V, 26 f., 25, 36: stranger. unco woman, I, 78, 26: unfriendly. unco lair (lear), II, 118, 1; 119, 1; 174, 1; 178, 2; III, 385, 1; IV, 411, 1; 467, 1: extraordinary.

unco, *adv.*, I, 370, 5: unusually, very.

uncouth, vnkowth, vnkuth, vnketh, I, 344, 25; III, 245, 11: (A. S. uncúð) unknown, strange. See unco.

vnder, Grenwich, III, 358, 78: perhaps, below, further down the Thames.

vnder hand, shott it vnder hand, III, 199, 29; 202, 33; shot under his hand, III, 204, 26: Dr Furnivall and Mr C. J. Longman suggest, putting the bow horizontally, in which case you shoot with the arrow under the left hand, instead of beside it, as in shooting with the bow vertical. Ascham speaks of an underhand shaft, but without defining it: "The underhande [shafte] must have a small breste, to go cleane awaye oute of the bowe; the forehande muste have a bigge breste, to bere the great myght of the bowe." Toxophilus, 1545, ed. Arber, p. 126. And again, as cited by Dr W. Hand Browne, of Johns Hopkins University: "Men doubt yet, in looking at the mark, what way is best, above or beneth hys hand"; "a byg brested shafte for hym that shoteth *under hande*, bycause it will hobble." Upon which Dr Browne remarks, "As he is here speaking only of taking aim, under-hand shooting would seem to be done when the archer raised his bow high, and looked at the mark under the arrow-hand."

under night, I, 100, 1: in the night.

vndergoe, II, 59, 33: undertake.

undertaking, be your, IV, 152, 6; 153, **D** 7: will undertake, manage for you.

vnfaine, III, 355, 14: not glad.

unfriends, III, 470 b: enemies.

vngoodly, III, 322 a: unhandsome.

vnhappie, V, 82, 29: ill-conditioned, having bad tricks.

unhappy, IV, 64 a: mischievous.

unhappy, V, 86, 32: unlucky (as speaking inopportunely). (The on of horson occasioned the omission of un-.)

unkensome, III, 495 **B** b 7: not to be known.

unkent, IV, 435, 12: unknown.

vnketh, vnkouth, vnkuth, III, 56, 6; 57, 18; 66, 209; 79, 6, 18; 82, 6, 18; 85, 6: uncouth, unknown, stranger.

vnmackley, II, 59, 30: misshapen. (Scott. makly, well proportioned. mackerly, Northumberland, shapely. Halliwell.)

vnneth, unneath, III, 73, 358; **171**, 17: with difficulty, scarcely.

vnready, V, 81, 10: indirect, or, attended with difficulties.

unright(e), I, 294, 7; III, 339, 5; IV, 503, 5: wrong.

unruly, IV, 383, 1: should probably be unseally, as in IV, 378, 1.

unseally, IV, 378, 1: unlucky.

vnsett, III, 358, 71: surrounded, invested. (A. S. ymbsettan.)

unshemly, V, 215, 14: unseemly.

unthought, unthocht, onthought lang, haud, keep, I, 478, 13; 482, **C** b 16, 20; II, 139, 3; III, 492, 5; IV, 260, 10: keep from thinking long, wearying, from *ennui*. See think lang.

vnthrift, V, 81, 16: spendthrift.

until, untill, I, 221, **D** 3, 4; III, 488, 35, 36: unto, to.

unto, IV, 170, 11; 467, 11; V, 262, 19: into, in.

vnto the same, I, 284, 12: after the same fashion.

vntyll, gates shut them vntyll, III, 25, 52: to, against.

vnwieldie, V, 82, 29: unmanageable.

vowsed, uowsed, V, 79, 14: used, practised.

vp chaunce, III, 57, 18; 66, 209: on, for, the chance.

up stark, IV, 378, 5; 380, 11: (came, blew) up strong, as still common, with the like ellipsis, V, 51, 68; **56**, 45.

upgive, V, 193, 59: avow, acknowledge, own up.

vpon, vppon, I, 271, 2; 433, 15, 16: on. stay upon, wait upon, III, 450 b: for.

upper hand, II, 245, 29: upper tier, above.

upricht, I, 473, 3: right out.

upstart, II, 54, 56: sprang up.

us, I us gar, V, 267, 12: shall, will. See **s**, sign of future.

used, V, 85, 23: frequented. used him in her company, IV, 98, **F** 6: accustomed him to.

vtter, III, 361, b, c 52: outer.

utuer, IV, 506, 59. See beame.

V

vain, streams proud and vain, IV, 204, 8: repetition of proud in the sense of fierce, etc.

valiant (of ladies), V, 119, 1: of worth, estimation.

value (of an hour), IV, 514, 15, 16: amount.

value, va(l)low, *v.*, II, 162, **E** 2: think important, make ado about, stick. vallow not the feed, IV, 36, 3: value, care not for the feud which will ensue; cf. **B** 3.

vance, spak wi a vance, IV, 465, 30: seems to be meant for vaunt. It is hardly probable that the plural of the old Scottish and English avant, vaunt (*with avants*) can be intended.

vanitie, IV, 300, 2, is nonsense.

vawward, III, 284, 14; vanward, III, 285, 21, 34; **333**, 27: vanguard, van.

veiwe, vew, vewe, III, 92, 15: yew.

velvaret, IV, 369, 1: meant for velvet; not velveret.

venie (?), III, 219 b, note: vein.

venison, II, 59, 38: hunting (prerogative of).

vension, III, 196, d 4: venison.

vepan, weapon.

verament, III, 308, 26; 333, 26: truly.

vessell, *pl.*, III, 65, 175, 179, 191: vessels.

vew, your vew, V, 86, 40: sight of you.

vew, vewe, veiwe, III, 92, 15; 105, 27; 362, 78: yew. (The v is not for u. The word is pronounced vewe in Cheshire.)

vild, V, 53, 102: vile.

virgus, I, 420, 13: verjuice, a kind of vinegar (green juice).

virr, I, 183, 16: vigor.

virtue, in virtue leave your lammas beds, II, 96, **J** 4: corrupt. Cf. **B** 1. Dr Davidson suggests, never tae leave your lammie's, lambkin's beds (lammie's, innocent).

vo, vou, woe.

vogie, IV, 176, 11: vain, merry; no longer have you cause for self-gratulation, to be demonstratively joyful.

vones, I, 334, 6: dwellest.

voss. a voss o, IV, 224, 8, 12: comparing **G** 8, 10, 21, **K** 22, the voice of, this last seems to be meant. Otherwise, a corruption of, it was a (cf. **A** 11; **C** 15; **D** 17; **E** 19; **H** 11).

votes, IV, 114, **C** 2: for voters? probably a corruption.

vou 's me, V, 271, 16, 17, wo is me!

vouch it safe, III, 75, 381: grant, bestow (safe corrected from halfe).

voued, *pret.*, V, 268, 17: viewed.

vour. o vour, II, 25, **F** 13: half owre, as in **C** 18.

vow, wow, IV, 133 f., 12, 15; 136, 21; V, 118, **C** 11: exclamation of surprise, emphasis, or admiration.

voyded, III, 26, 79: made off.

vue, *v.*, V, 265, 17: view.

vyld, wild.

vytouten nay, I, 334, 4: without, beyond, denial.

W

wa, wae, IV, 448 a, 3d st.: wo.

waaf, II, 72, 2: waif.

wad, *n.*, II, 63, 23; 172, 31, 32: pledge, in security. I, 340, 2; 343, 2; II, 376, 39; III, 455, 10: forfeit.

wad. I wad, I, 130, **F** 14, 15, 20: I wot, in a weak sense, assuredly, truly. See a=I, and **wat**.

wad, wade, I, 71, 55, 56; 74, 76, 77; III, 465, 30; V, 299, 2: would. See **wads**.

wad, wade, *v.*, IV, 18, 17; 185, 7; 384, 5; 385, 2, 7; 386, 2; V, 219, 23; 275 b, 6; 300, 14: wager. IV, 432, 4, 5: engage (to fight).

wadded, I, 272, 11: of woad color, blue.

wadded, V, 261, 6: wedded.

wadding, wadin, II, 131 f., 11, 16, 19, 20; IV, 470, 15–17: wedding.

wade, wad, *pret.* of wide, wade, II, 97, 12, 13; 283, 4; 461, 10; IV, 68, 6; 190, 27, 28; 438, 13; 455, 9.

waders, IV, 188, 20: miscopied by Skene for mideers, mothers.

wadin. See **wadding**.

wads, II, 133, **D** 4, 5, 6: wishes (wad, would, treated as a present tense).

wae, wa, I, 69, 48; 127, 28; 169, 3; 217, 3, 6; V, 306, 10: wo.

wae, *adj.*, I, 367, 11; II, 70, 25; 89, 36; 129, 17: unhappy.

wael, IV, 443, 5: choice. See **wale**.

waely, IV, 59, d 3: a rhyme-word for wae, sad.

waesome, IV, 369 b: woful.

waft, I, 420, 15, 16; 422, 12, 13: weft, woof.

wafu, woful.

wainless, II, 72, 8: homeless (without a wane, habitation).

wair, II, 472, 24: bestow. See **war**.

wait, I wait, a wait, wate, IV, 128, 16, 17; 169, 3; 371, 2, 3, 5; 447, 6, 17; 470, 17; 510, **W** 2; 515, 12, 15; 517, 20: I wot, know, indeed. See **wat**, and a=I.

wait, IV, 456, 7:=wite, blame.

wait, wayte, III, 57, 18; 66, 209; 83, 202; 86, 202; 412, 21: watch, lie in wait, seek an opportunity, to do.

waith, steed, V, 176, 18: waif, stray, wandering.

waitmen, II, 424, 3: waiting-men (or possibly, wight men, strong men).

wake, II, 327, 2, 4, 5: aperture, way. (Icel. vök, aperture, especially one cut in ice, or remaining in water not completely frozen over; passage cut for ships in ice; Swed. vak, hole in ice; Dutch vak, empty space. "In Norfolk, when the 'broads' are mostly frozen over, the spaces of open water are called wakes." Wedgwood.)

wake, I, 107, 5; IV, 446, 5; 447, 5: watch (people set to watch me), but the reading at I, 107; IV, 447, is probably wrong; cf. I, 108, **B** 4. See **wane**.

wake, IV, 141, 12: merry-making, sport.

wake, *v.*, V, 277, 2: walk.

wake, III, 88, 340, is an original misprint.

waken, I, 433, 24: waking.

wakerife. See **waukrife**.

wald, walde, I, 334, 6: would.

wale, wael, walle, IV, 265, **A** b 10; 477, 19; V, 256 a, 2: choice.

wale, weil, wile, wyle, I, 428, 14; IV, 169, 5; 300, 12; 461, 19; V, 105, **B** 1: choose.

wale wight, I, 490, 13. See **wall wight**.

walker, I, 272, 14: fuller.

wall, I, 387, 2, 4; 440, 4, 6; V, 206 a, 3: well, spring. The water at St Johnston's wall was fifty fathom deep, II, 21, 14: an alleged deep place in the Tay; cf. 24, 14, there's a brig at the back o Sanct John's toun, it's fifty fadom deep.

wall, green wall sea, green wall wave, V, 275 b, 7, 8: apparently wave, despite tautology; cf. II, 22, 15, green-waved sea. (haw sea, IV, 379, 10; 380, 19. Prof. Murison informs me that when Mrs Murison sings the ballad mechanically, or without attention, she invariably sings haw.)

walle, V, 256 a, 2: wale, choice. See **wale**.

wallourt. See **wallowt**.

wallowd, II, 392, 10: rolled over (?).

wallowit, II, 361, 32: withered.

wallowt, IV, 127, 3: drooped, grew pallid. was wallourt, IV, 138, **M**: (misspelt) was pallid.

wall-wight, II, 123, 15; 403, 9; III, 10, 23; IV, 392, 11, 12; V, 37, 6; 41, 29, 32 (all from Buchan's ballads): explained by Donaldson as waled wight, picked strong men. Donaldson cites *weild wightman* from Semple of Beltrees. See **well wight, wale wight men**, I, 490, 13.

wallwood, swine, II, 299, 16: wild-wood, compare II, 144, 3, wild-wood steer (unhallowed swine, II, 154, 10).

walting, IV, 312, 8: welting, edging.

waly, IV, 21, 13: fine large.

waly, wallie, wally, II, 363, 1, line 1; IV, 109 f., 5, 8; 293, **A** 1, 2, 7, 9 (oh and a waly); V, 195, 8; 197, 9, 10, 11: exclamation of admiration. O braw wallie, IV, 296, **F** 1: literally, O good, lucky! or, O good luck! but, as before, an exclamation of admiration.

waly, wally, II, 363, 1, line 3; IV, 92, 1, 3; 94, 1; 95, 1, etc.: interjection of lamentation (probably A. S. wá lá!). the wally o 't, IV, 290, **D b** 1: sorrow, pity of it! waly 's my love! V, 208, 1, 2, etc.

wamb(e), wame, II, 130, 2; 183, 24; 189, 27; 195, 33; III, 437, 23: womb. See **weam**.

wan, one.

wan, dark-colored, pallid, colorless, white. II, 92, ., 4, 9; 97, 11; 144, 13; 147, 10; 150, 14: dark-colored. II, 74, **E** 6; 79, 28; 185, 33; 187, 16; 399, 2: pallid. wan water (as contrasted with wine), II, 70, 17; 74, **D** 7; 75, 10; 92, 4; 96, **J** 7, 8: colorless. far got ye that water that washes ye so wan, II, 191, 23: white (ye wad never be so white, 24).

wan, wane, *pret.* of win, I, 73, 53; II, 21, 4; 123, 22; III, 474, 32; IV, 180, 7. he wan free, V, 300, 11: got free.

wan, *p. p.* of win, IV, 385, 26.

wand, II, 146, 13; 147, 14; 150, **E** 9; 151, **G** 4: of (willow) twigs. staff made of the wand, II, 118, 22 (very nearly verbiage): made of a rod.

wane, I, 334, 7; III, 63, 148: habitation. in my bower there is a wane, IV, 446, 5: wane, says Jamieson, denotes not only a dwelling (Old Eng. wone), but "different apartments in the same habitation;" if so, in my house there is a room, is the sense here. wan, in the wake there is a wan, IV, 447, 5: should at least be, in the wane there is a wake, as the rhyme shows, and as we have at 446, 5. In, at the wake there is a wane, I, 107, 5, wane was meant by Scott to be understood as a collection of people (wheen). See **wake**.

wane, III, 309, 36: "quantity, multitude; a single arrow out of a vast quantity." Skeat (quantity as in Chaucer's wone, see **wheen**). This is to me quite unsatisfactory, but I have no better interpretation to offer. Wain, in the sense of a vehicle for a missile, ballista, catapult, would be what is wanted, but I have not succeeded in finding a case.

wanhappy, IV, 386, 1: unlucky.

wanna, did not win, go.

wannelld, III, 488, 38: was unsteady, staggered. (A. S. wancol, North Eng. wankle, unstable, Germ. wankeln.)

wannle, IV, 491, 32: agile, vigorous, strong.

wanny, II, 261, 8, 9: small wand, rod.

want, IV, 196, 3; 268, 17, 22; 357, **B** 7; 358, 17: do without, dispense with. sae soon as we 've wanted him, IV, 359, 12: had to do without. III, 513 b, 2, *pret.*: wanted.

wanton, III, 452, 1; 453, 1: free and easy, frolicsome. (rantin, 455, 1.) Cf. Wanton Brown (a horse), IV, 17, 1, etc.

wantonlie, -ly, III, 488, 27; 490, 14: gaily, merrily. rode, lap, wantonly, IV, 146 f., 8, 38: in easy, spirited style.

wap, horse will gie his head a wap, I, 182 f., 8, 14: throw, toss.

wap, *n.*, coost a wap on horse's nose, IV, 21, 9: noose.

wap, *v.*, wrap, lap. wap cloth into ship's side, II, 27, 19: stuff. roun ship's side, 20: wrap. wap halter oer horse's nose, IV, 17, 4: lap, twine, perhaps throw.

wap, *v.*, throw. wappin corn and hay oer to horse, IV, 21, 18: throwing. wappit wings, II, 139 f., 7, 12, 22: beat, flapped.

war, ware. be war, ware, a, of, on, I, 273, 37; II, 46, 37; III, 66, 213; 109, 4; 296, 20; 307, 10: be aware, have a sight of. was war wher, III, 98, 39.

war, waur, I, 388, **A** 10; 420, 12, 13; 466, 22; II, 417, 6, 9; V, 193, 48: worse.

war, waur, I, 132, **I** 1; 149, **I** 1; 331, **B** 8: were.

war, ware, wair, I, 431, 3; 478, 7; II, 418, 22; 472, 24; V, 142, 11: expend, bestow. ware my dame's cauf's skin on thee, IV, 7, 31; V, 250, 29: apply, use, my wife's (mother's) whip.

waran, warran, warrand, warraner, warrant, III, 430, 15; 435, **F** 7; 436, 5, 7: sponsor for, security. III, 405, 7; IV, 310, 4 (cf. **warn**): safeguard.

ward, warde, III, 404 b; 470 b: defence. III, 72, 332, 337; 449 a; IV, 11, 18: prison, confinement. enter himself in ward, III, 447 b: voluntarily go into confinement.

ward, IV, 446, 1: *corrupt*. See **weird**.

warde, II, 273, 25; 340 b, line 8: forewarn, advise.

warden, I, 161, 4; V, 209 a, 4: guardian, tutor.

warden, IV, 317, **F** 3, 4: facing, edging (cf. the walting, welting, of 312, **A** 8).

warden pies, III, 216, 35: made of large pears called wardens.

wardle, I, 127, 14; V, 214 f., 1, 6: world. wardle's make, see **warld**.

ware, V, 169, 11: sea-weed, alga marina (used for manure).

ware, V, 306, 2, 3: were.

ware, *pret.*, V, 221, 20: wore.

ware. See **war**.

warison, waryson, III, 100, 74; 297, 43: reward.

warld, world. warld's make, I, 129, 8; 348, 17; 351 f., 40, 54; 353, **H** 12; wardle's make, I, 127, 14; warldly, worldly, make, mate, I, 344, 30; II, 118, 6, 7; world's make, I, 128, 11; 348, 11; wordlye make, II, 86, 18, 20: world's, earthly, mate, consort. world's mait, I, 508, 9.

warldly. See warld.

warlock, II, 220, 11, 12; 223 f., 8, 14; IV, 472 f., 24, 25: wizard.

warn, IV, 309, 2, 6: surety, safeguard. Cf. warran, IV, 310, 4, and see waran.

warn, p. p., IV, 445 b, 2, No 8: warnd (as 446, b 2).

warp, v., I, 312, 8; II, 503, 7: curl, twist.

warran, warrand. See waran.

warraner. See waran.

warsle, n., I, 438, A 1: wrestle.

warsle, warsel, v., I, 438, A 2; 439, 2; 440, 3; 441, 1–3: wrestle. warsled, I, 56, 14: wrestled, struggled, bestirred herself.

warslin, a-warslin, I, 440, 1, 2: a-wrestling.

warwolf, I, 311, 15, 16: werewolf, man-wolf, man transformed into a wolf.

waryson. See warison.

wa's, ways.

was. See wash.

wash. pres. was, I, 494, 7; III, 111, 41. pret. weesh, wish, wush. p. p. washen (I, 304, E 5; II, 111, 10; V, 102, B 15), wushen, which see.

wast, west.

waste, I, 349, F 9: seems to be nonsense (ride expected).

wat, wate, wait, watt, weet, wet, wit, wite, wyte, wis, wot, know. I wat, wate, a wat, a wite, etc., frequently nothing more than assuredly, indeed: II, 159, 11, 13, 15, 16, 19, 23; 160, 10–16, 18, 19; 161, 12, 13, 17; III, 199, 23; 464 f., 10, 15, 34; 466, 43; IV, 175, M 7; 359, 4, 5, 7, etc.; 470, 17; V, 300, 2. pret. wist. p. p. wist, west.

wat, pret. of weet, weit, to wet, I, 17, D 6; II, 21, 12, 13; 23 f., D 7, F 10, etc.; IV, 424, 5. p. p., I, 55, B 7; II, 23, E 8.

wate, knew. See wat, wait.

wate, pret. of wite, blame, II, 273, 25.

water, water-side, IV, 7, 25; V, 250, 24, 25: "the banks of a river, in the mountainous districts of Scotland the only inhabitable parts." Scott.

water-cherry, II, 186, 18: perhaps a species of cherry used as a cosmetic.

water-gate, IV, 510, 6; V, 250, 12: street leading to the water, way along the water.

water-kelpy, IV, 185, 10: water-sprite.

water-side. See water.

water-sluice. bored nine holes in her water-sluice, V, 142, f 5, should mean in the gate or valve of some vent for water; bored a watery sluice, or aperture for water, g 6, is a more rational reading.

water-stoups, V, 91, 7, 8: water-buckets or pitchers.

wather, wither, wuther, V, 107, 3, 5: wether.

watt, III, 199, 23: know. See wat.

waught, I, 299, 14: draught.

wauk, walk.

wauk, II, 139, 5, 13: watch, be awake.

wauken, II, 139, 11, 13: waken. pret. waukenit, II, 79, 38: awoke.

wauken(e)d at, II, 162, 12: tried to waken; perhaps, chid, expostulated with.

waukrife, wakerife, IV, 389 b: watchful, wakeful.

waur, war, I, 5, 13, 18; 422, 17; 475, 44; 476, J 6; II, 421, 26; IV, 26, 4, 5: worse.

waur, I, 147, C 1; II, 61, 9; IV, 417, 5, 10: were.

wavers wi the wind, II, 266, B 1: is as restless, changeable (?).

wawis, IV, 196, 19: walls.

way, I, 4, A 13, 16; B 8, 9; 5, D 4, 9; V, 283, 7, 17: the Milky Way.

way. would I way or would I wight, I, 77, 13; 78, 42: nonsense. See weight. Motherwell conjectures, would I away, or would I wait. See wee.

waylawaye, alas.

ways, IV, 196, 15: in a direction.

wayte, wait, III, 57, 18; 66, 209; 83, 202; 86, 202; 412, 21: look out for ; watch, lie in wait, seek an opportunity, to do. pret. wayted, III, 72, 331: lay in wait for.

waythmen, III, 41 a: hunters. See wight-men.

we, V, 302 a, 13: with.

we an E an O me, we an E an O an O me, V, 275 a, 9, 10: these words have been treated as interjections. It is possible that they are corrupted from something like, were a' foald in a yeir to me, III, 370, 9; cf. II, 465, 9.

wea, see your body wea, V, 226 b, 7:=wae, suffering ? (strange expression, see II, 305, 7, you red and blue.)

wead, would.

weal, III, 310, 60: "clench so as to leave marks, mark with wales"(?). "Perhaps read wringe and wayle." Skeat.

weame, IV, 505, 56: belly. See wamb(e), weme.

wean, II, 136 a, 16; III, 253, R; 397, A b 2: wee an, little one, child.

wear. sare a man a wear, I, 301, 2: sair, supply, a man, of, with, his wear, clothing.

wear, pret., V, 221, 21: wore.

Wearie, I, 55 f., 3, 4, 6, etc.: the Devil.

wearied, wearit. See wearyd.

wearifu, V, 115, 7: tiresome, vexatious, cursed.

wearin's wa, I, 333, 6: wearing his way, growing less and less, slowly vanishing.

weary fa, IV, 389 b: a curse befall.

weary, wearie, I, 310, 16; II, 131 f., 11, 16; 231, 1; III, 319, 24; IV, 56, A 3, B 3; 57, C 3, 6; 133, G 6; V, 16, 1, 2, 5, 8; 192, 25: sad, unhappy, distressed. IV, 44, 6; 290, B c 5; 359, 6; 480, 3: vexatious, hateful, horrid, cursed.

weary, weary high hat, III, 184, 13: monstrously, deucedly.

wearyd, wearied, wearit, III, 261 f., 8, 10; IV, 128, 5; 132, 8: troubled, afflicted.

wearyin for me in, V, 155, 6: longing to have me indoors.

weate, III, 341, 47: corrupt. Possibly, I weate, wit, know.

weather, IV, 213, 17, 18: storm of rain or snow.

wed, wedd(e), wad, III, 66, 214; 71, 298; 110, 7, 8, 12, 13; 356, 34: pledge, fine, forfeit (ley a wed, 110, 7, 8, = leffe, leave a wed, 12, 13). sette to wedde, III, 59, 54: put in pledge.

wed, v., I, 481, 42: wager. See wad.

wed, proudest wed, III, 4, 5: proudest dressed (from wede).

wede, weed, II, 28, 28; III, 61, 97; 74, 368, 371; IV, 212, 2, 7; 213, 10, 15; V, 306, 13: clothing, garment.

wee, I, 163, J 1, 2, etc.; 164, K 1, 2, etc.: little. I, 203, 5; IV, 412, 15; 413, 18; 421, 25: short time.

wee. would I wee or would I way, I, 77, 12; 78, 41: would I (stay) wi (him) or (go) away, is all the meaning this can have. Motherwell conjectures, would I wait or would I away. See way.

weed. See wede.

weel, well. See well.

weel. the weel gae wi his body, IV, 129, 21, 23–25: prosperity.

weel, well. weel fa! good luck befall, I, 388, B 5. for my weel, II, 461, 8; 466, 24: well, advantage (461, 9, for my better). Euphemism for God: weel met thee save! I, 324, 3 (MS. thou); well met ye (you) save! IV, 455, 4; V, 195, 9; well (weel, weill) may ye (you) save! IV, 195, 13; 198 f., G 4, 21. So III, 268, 3¹, originally; the far better in the line following, is nonsense.

weel, weil, IV, 517, 19: a pot, deep place, or whirl-pool in a river.

weel that was her own, II, 73, 20: seems to mean that the roses and ribbons were indeed hers by right.

weel-busked, hat, IV, 199, 9: handsomely adorned.

weel-fared, weel-fart, weil-faurit, etc.: well-fa-vored. See fared.

weel-worst, V, 214 a, 1: very worst.

ween, II, 132, 21: whimper, whine, lament.

ween, heigh a ween and oh a ween (where a may be I), II, 504, 27: exclamation of distress.

weep, n., V, 241 a, 4, 5: weeping, tears.

weer, I, 72 f., 6, 61: weird, fortune.

weer, war. See weir.

weesh, pret. of wash, V, 213, 6.

weet, II, 293, 13: know.

weet, n., III, 160, 6; IV, 379, 15: rain, shower of rain.

weet, weit, v., III, 401, 7: wet.

weetie, weety, IV, 197, 9, 17; 258, 25: rainy.

weighed more, II, 455, 57: made more account.

weight, IV, 224, 23: wight, strong.

weight, was he weel or was he weight, I, 80, 9: non-sense; weight would be wight, strong, etc., which has no pertinency. The same of, would I way or would I wight, 77, 13. See way.

weil, weel, IV, 182, G 8: a pot, deep place, or whirl-pool in a river. weil-head, II, 153, 17: vortex of a whirlpool.

weil, wile, V, 10, 2: wale, choose. See wale.

weil=well, very. See well.

weir, weer, were, III, 480, 9; 491, 6; IV, 432, 14; V, 183, 21: war.

weir, bot weir, I, 140 N: without doubt. (Pinker-ton.)

weir-window, wire-window, IV, 44, 10; 46, 11, 7: seems to be a window grated with iron bars.

weird, wierd, weer, n., I, 69, 42, 47; 71, 37; 72 f., 6, 61; 77, 6; 309, B 1; 482, E: fate, fortune, destiny.

weird, v., I, 311, 3: destine.

weird, I, 107, 1: the reading at this place is com-pounded from, weird her a grit sin, IV, 445, 1, and ward her in a great sin, IV, 446, 1; the reading of IV, 445, would mean, destined, put her in the way of, a great sin; ward in of the other text does not give an easy sense, and ward is perhaps a corruption of weird.

weirdless, III, 391, H 3: unlucky.

weit, I, 140, N (Pinkerton): know.

welde, III, 112, 52: would.

well, euphemism for God. See weel.

well, III, 112, 48: will.

well, the well o wine gaed in, IV, 428, 16: perhaps wale, choice, the best; but since the wine was poi-soned, this must be meant ironically.

well, weel, weil, very, right. well good, II, 46, 43; III, 132, 5; 478 f., 15, 34; V, 49, 11: very good. weil gaucy, V, 152, 3. well warst, V, 180, 14, 16; 214 a, 1: very worst. well faire mayde, II, 439, 3, 8, should perhaps be well-fared.

well and wellsome, II, 159, 16: should probably be wae and waesome (sad and woful).

well o Spa, IV, 286, 6: a spring to the west of Aber-deen.

well or wae, was he well or was he wae, I, 80, 8: whether he liked or disliked. (The passage is vari-ously corrupted, and the original reading probably nowhere preserved.)

well-a-woo, III, 77, 438: a variety of well-a-way. (A. S. wá-lá-wá.)

well-bespoke, V, 149, 9–11: well spoken.

well-strand, I, 165, M 4; IV, 172, 15; 174, 16: stream from a spring.

well-wight, III, 3 f., 12, 16, 21; 487, 5, 7; IV, 165, 7; 222, 9 (wiel-wight); 428, 4: very strong, sturdy, stal-wart; but, sometimes, brave, see III, 4, 16. See wall-wight.

welt, pret. of wield, III, 74, 366: disposed of.

welth(e), III, 77, 436: either, simply, his money, or, more probably, his well-being, his palmy days; so III, 287, 65. III, 295, 5, 6; 296, 15, (rich) booty.

weme (of ring), III, 412, 21: belly, hollow. See weame.

wen, III, 200, 3: win, get, go. V, 256, 7: pret. of win.

wend, III, 38, 104: gone (gone, b).

wend, went, V, 80, 42; 81, 14: weened.

wenion, with a, III, 138, 11: wanion, a curse, bad luck (waniand, waning (of the moon). Skeat).

wenking, winking.

went. See wend.

were, I, 334, 11: war. See **weir**.

were, vulgar English, he were, II, **4, 2; 8, 8.**

werne, II, 139, 23: were.

werre, I, 327, 20: worse.

werryed, I, 273, 37: worried.

werschepyd, III, 109, 3: showed respect to.

west, *p. p.*, III, 113, 70: wist.

west-airt lands, II, 73, 30: western. See **airt**.

westlan, westlin, westryn, II, 258, 34; III, 431, 20; 435, **E** 7; IV, 240, 18: western.

wet, wete, III, 63, 141; 70, 287; 112, 50: know.

wether, I, 210, 14; III, 430, 2; 432, 19 (perhaps= whether): whither.

wex, weks, *n.*, V, 283, 11, 21: **wax**.

weynde, III, 297, 41: wend, go.

wha, who.

wha 's (whae 's) aught. See **aucht**.

whall, white as whall, II, 478, 7: that is, whale's bone.

whang, I, 19, 11; II, 168, **A** 5: thong. In II, 217, 1, 3, lace his middle with a whang, the reading should no doubt be *band* as in other versions.

whang (of cheese), V, 115, 8: slice.

whar, whaur, I, 164, **K** 1, 3, **L** 1, 5: where.

whas, whose.

what an a, whaten a, whatna, whattna, whatten, I, 169, **B** 4; 203, **C** 18; 441, 19; II, 195, 34; III, 433, 2; 434, 2; 453, 12, 13; V, 162, **C** 2: what sort ? what (in particular) ? what a ! So, what for a ? V, 160, 3; what like a ? V, 163, 5; 164, **E b** 2.

wheder, III, 57, 11: whither.

wheen, a wheen blackguards, IV, 67, 5, 6: number, pack, etc.

whether, II, 455, 62; III, 92, 26: which of the two.

whether, whither.

whew, whue, whute, III, 440, 10: whistle.

whidderand, whithering, V, 191, 16: (of arrows) whizzing, moving with a whiz.

whight. See **wight**.

whikety whack, V, 304, 9: whick-whack (whick, doublet of whack).

while, the other, I, 414, 18: the remaining time, henceforth (?).

while, I, 232, **A** 2: for a while.

while, whyll(*e*), II, 223, **F** 1, 2; III, 201, 23, 31; 298, 50, 54; 309, 47: till.

whiles, I, 115, **B** 1; **C** 1; 131, **G** 9; 256, 2; II, 470, 59: at times.

whiles, whilest, whileste, whilste, whyllys, the whyles, III, 87, 278; 107 b, 7; 357, 38, 45; 358, 83; 361, b, c 38, 43, c 41: while.

whilk, IV, 373, 10; 476, 1: which.

whin, whun, win, fun, II, 116, 10, 18; 117, 4, 12; 360, 5, 7: furze.

whirpled, V, 106, **E** 5: evidently whipped, stripped (but I have not found the word elsewhere).

whistling (of ladies moving), II, 386, 19: whisking.

white bookes, III, 357, 58: clear of oppressive charges.

white bread, II, 88, 15, 16, 22, 23: wheat bread, as in 89, 4; 92, 5, 6 (white meal is contrasted with corn and oats, II, 88, 17, 18). So 96, **J** 5, 6; fite bread, whit bread, V, 220 f., 6, 7, 9.

white-fish, II, 129, 8; IV, 436, 10, 18, 19; V, 122, 1; 124, 1; 274, 10 (fait fish): haddock, cod, ling, etc., as distinguished from gray-fish, coal-fish; in Banff, as opposed to salmon, trout, herring.

white-fisher, IV, 436, 18, 19: one who fishes for haddock, cod, etc. (as distinguished from salmon).

white-land, IV, 213, 14: wheat-land.

white meal and gray, II, 261, 12; IV, 494, 29; V, 238, 29: oat-meal as distinguished from barley-meal (oat-meal and grey, II, 462, 30). But white meal, II, 88, 17, 18, being contrasted with corn (oats), must there be wheat.

white money, monie, I, 464, 7; 471, 11, 12; 473, 12; II, 352 f., **E** 5, 7; 473, 7, 8, 14; 475, 13, 14; 476, 10, 13; III, 389, 17, 18, 20, 22: silver.

white rigs, IV, 131, 14: of grain (to distinguish from crops which remain green).

whithering, whidderand, V, 191, 16; 199 b, 16: whizzing.

who would, III, 163, 87: if one would.

whorle, V, 116, 10; 118, 4; 119, 7; 120, 5: the fly of a spinning-rock.

whue. See **whute**.

whummil, I, 255, 2: wimble, gimlet.

whun, fun, III, 5, **D** 7; 6, 12: whin, furze. See **whin**.

whunnie, IV, 69, 22: covered with whins, furze.

whute, fute, whue, whew, *n.* and *v.*, III, 125, 29–31: whistle. 126 **B, b** 29–31, whues.

why, V, 264, 5: whey.

whyles, the whyles, III, 70, 278: while. See **whiles**.

whyll(*e*), till. See **while**.

whyllys, III, 309, 37: while. See **whiles**.

wiald, wield.

wicht. See **wight**.

wicker, wigger, III, 125, 20; 126 f., b, d–f: willow. (Wycker, osier. Palsgrave. Swed. and Dan. dialects, vikker, vægger, willow. Skeat.)

wicker, IV, 31, 6: twist.

wid, IV, 456, 15: would.

wide, I, 55 f., **B** 4, 6, 8; II, 88, 5; 94, 3; 96, **I** 5; IV, 424, 11: wade. (Spelt *wade*, but rhymed with -ide, II, 462, 7; 465, 19; III, 493, 14.) *pres. p.* widen, IV, 68, 6. *pret.* wade, wad. *p. p.* wooden.

widifu, widdifu, widifau, widdefu, IV, 84, 7, 10, 11, 13; 85, 3; V, 253 f., No 203, **D** 2, 8: one qualified to fill a widdie or halter.

widna, widne, would not.

wiel-wight, IV, 222, 9: bold, stanch. See **well-wight**.

wierd. See **weird**.

wigger. See **wicker**.

wight, wyght, wicht, whight, I, 330 f., **A** 3, **B** 3, **C** 3; 333, 4; II, 409, 16; III, 63, 152; 414, 49: strong; but also, denoting bodily activity, brisk, as III, 117, 20; III, 63, 148, of John, who has shot well. III, 27, 97; 65, 195; 75, 389; 78, 448, Adam Bell, Clim, and William, and Robin Hood's men are wight young men. III, 91 f., 6, 8, Guy of Gisborne is a wight yeoman: sturdy. See **well-wight**. wighty, III, 94, 48, has perhaps caught the y from the word following. See **wighty**.

wightdom, III, 488, 26: weight.

wightlye, II, 58, 10: with vigor, or briskness.

wight-men, II, 433, 7: waith-men, hunters. (Icel. veiði-maðr, Germ. weidmann.) See **waythmen**.

wightsmen, IV, 432, 1: wechtsmen, winnowers. wecht is "an instrument for winnowing corn, made of sheep's skin, in the form of a sieve, but without holes."

wighty, III, 32, 45, 50; 94, 48; 362, 70:=wight, strong. See **wight**.

wil, IV, 472 f., 24, 25: wild, perhaps vile.

wild, I, 334, 6: would.

wild-fire, III, 281, 12: ignis fatuus. (slack here is marsh.)

wild-wood swine, steer, drunk as, II, 144, 3, 4; 368, 7: a popular comparison like, drunk as a dog.

wile, vile.

wilfull, III, 92, 24, wilfull of my way: (Scottish will, Icel. villr) astray, lost ; *and of my morning tyde* may be that he does not know the hour, or, he has lost his time as well as his road. See **will**.

wile, wyle, weil, wale, I, 428, 13; 429, 7, 8; II, 344, 12 ; IV, 287, 14 ; V, 127, 20, 21; 157, 9: choose.

will, *pret.* wald, walde, wad, wade, wild, wid, wud.

will, would, *ellipsis of.* as muckle guid canvas as wrap the ship a' roun, II, 28, 22. there's nane come, win, II, 89, 34; 99 b, 34. So, II, 26, 11; 375, 23; IV, 131, 13; 379, 11; 380, 7; 381, 8, 10; 382, 13; V, 177, 9; 184, 38; 276, 14.

will, V, 16, 10, 15, 20: bewildered, at a loss what to do. will of his way, V, 70 b: lost, astray. See **wilfull**.

willinglye, I, 272, 22: at will, freely.

williwa, IV, 19, **C** 6: wellaway, interjection of (affected) reluctance.

willy, willow.

wilsome, IV, 235, 3: erratic, intricate.

win, I, 72, 22, 23: whin, furze, gorse. See **whin**.

win, wynne, won, wonne, hay, III, 295, 1; 299, **B** 1, **C** 1; V, 243, 1: dry by airing.

win, wine, wynne, wen, won, make your way, arrive. III, 71, 314; IV, 314, 15: get, go. IV, 189, 2, 4, 6: arrive, get there. win down, I, 481, 39. win frie, III, 453, 11. lat me win in, II, 148, 25: get in. win up, I, 368 f., 34, 36, 44, 47: get up. win on, I, 388, **A** 7: go on, keep on. win through, Î, 21 b, 4: transitively, allow, cause, to pass through. win to, I, 466, 13; V, 262, 17: get to, arrive at. *pret.* wan. *p. p.* wone, wan, win, wine, wen.

win, *p. p.* of win, I, 101, 15; IV, 189, 15; 220, 3; 446, 17; 467, 8, 9.

win your love aff me, II, 207, **B** 2: detach your love from me.

wine, *p. p.* of win, V, 276, 22.

winder, I, 430, 1: wonder, wondrous. See **wonder**.

windie, II, 362, 3: window.

windling sheet, III, 245, **B** 13: winding-sheet.

winking, II, 463, 16: with eye closed as if blind.

winn, in your barn, IV, 323, 6: do harvest work generally, dry corn, etc., by exposing to the air. (unless meant for winna, winnow.)

winna, IV, 326, 7: winnow.

winna, winnë, will not.

winten, V, 248, 7: (wanting) without.

winter, wynter, III, 58, 47; 64, 162; 285, 20: year(s).

wir, I, 217, 9: our.

wire-window. See **weir-window**.

wis, I, 217, 9: us.

wis, you wis, IV, 233, 13: know.

wis, III, 319, 20, 24; V, 206 a, No 2, 4: **was**.

wish, *pret.* of wash, V, 36, 14.

wiss, *n.*, I, 420, 12; II, 194, 8: wish.

wiss, wis, *v.*, I, 22, 6, 8; 217, 3; III, 453, 3; IV, 168, **E** 15; 169, 12; 461, 8, 9: wish. *pret.* wist, II, 423, **A** 1; III, 434, 20; V, 248, 18.

wiss, I wiss, III, 223, 10: perhaps for I wot (not i-wiss). wist, III, 187, 32; 222, 34: know. (I wist, 187, 32=assuredly.)

wist, *pret.* of wiss, wish. See **wiss**.

wiste, wist, *pret.* of wat, etc., I, 243, 6; 334, 6; 368, 23; 413, 37. *p. p.* west, III, 113, 70.

wit, witt, *n.*, III, 393, 22, 23; 419, 8, 12; IV, 509 a, 11; 512, 16, 17: knowledge, information.

wit, wite, wyte, I, 334, 6; II, 307, 34; III, 67, 230; 385, 15, 16; 396, **M** 8; IV, 98, 2; 221, 5; 508, 10, 11; 513, 6, 7; V, 81, 7; 82, 23: know. *p. p.* wit, IV, 98, 2.

wite, I wite, II, 160, 18; IV, 260, 12; 277, 5: I know= indeed. See **wat, wyte**.

wite, wyte, witt, *n.*, I, 350, 12; II, 145, 25; 146, 8; 312, 30; IV, 33, 28; 127, 1; 207, 21; V, 171, 5; 247, 11: blame.

wite, wyte, *v.*, I, 397, 13; II, 271, 19; 273, 25; III, 357, 53: blame. *pret.* wate, II, 273, 25.

with, I, 334, 7: wit, know (orthography doubtful).

with, wyth, III, 297, 42; 358, 75; 434, 23: by.

with that, II, 478, 5; III, 76, 414; V, 298 a: on condition that.

wither, wather, V, 105, **B** 7, 8: wether.

witherlands, witherlins, IV, 378, 5; 380, 11: (-lins, -lingis as in Scottish backlingis, backlins, English sidelins, sidelong; -lands a corruption of -lins) in a contrary, unwished-for, direction.

withershins, II, 318 a, 2: (M. H. Germ. widersinnes) in the wrong direction, in a direction contrary to the usual, or the desired (contrary to the course of the sun, often, but not necessarily here).

within me, lept, III, 127, Play 12: inside of my guard (?).

withouten, withowghten, I, 425, **f** 9, 10; III, 272, 6; 296, 18: without. See **wythowtten**.

witt, knowledge. See **wit**.

witt, *n.*, blame, V, 247, 11. See **wite**.

witted, V, 132, 2: minded.

witter, I, 399, **A b** 8:=wittering, information.

wittering, I, 394, 8: information, indication.

witty, III, 131, 3: corruption of wight, wighty.

wo, woo, woe, II, 59, 33; 86, 16; 139, 20; III, 23, 23; 27, 101; 70, 297; 97, 19: sad, unhappy. a woe ses me, II, 504, 27: exclamation of distress; perhaps corruption of, woe is.

wobs, I, 305 a, A 3: webs (of cloth).

wod, wode, mad. See wood.

wode, III, 54, 3: went.

wode, V, 283, 9, 19: wood.

wode-shawe. grene-wode shawe, greenwood shaw, III, 57, 14; 70, 284; IV, 427, 1: thicket of the wood. (wood-shaw is of rather frequent occurrence and Halliwell cites, under the shawe of the wood, Morte d'Arthur, I, 374).

wodewale, woodwele, woodweele, I, 326, 2; III, 91, 2: wood-lark (?).

woe. See wo.

wol, v., V, 283, 1, etc.: will.

wolt, v., V, 283, 4: wilt.

wolwarde, III, 77, 442: with skin against wool, that is wearing a woolen fleece directly against the skin.

won, wone, one.

won, I, 18, I 1; 174, 1; 246, 1; 299, 6, 17; II, 419, 44, 51; III, 71, 315; IV, 19, C 5; 26, 15: dwell.

won, wonne, win, hay, III, 293 a; IV, 432, 1; 499, 1: dry by airing.

won, win, I, 464, 15; 506, 7; II, 89, 32; 140, 22; 172, 24; 256, K 2; 407, 12; IV, 242 a; 259, 21, 23: get, go, come, arrive. II, 316, 3, 7; IV, 115, D 9: gain, earn. (spelt one, IV, 284, 23; corrected to win.) p. p. wone, V, 276, 20. See wun.

wonder, III, 411, 2: bewilderment? disaster?

wonder, V, 283, 1: wondrous. See winder.

wone, III, 98, 15: number, plenty.

wone, withowtyn, withowt wone, V, 78 f., 9, 23: fail.

wonige, I, 334, 7: dwelling. Qy. wonninge?

wonynge, wonning, III, 63, 148; 86, 148: dwelling.

woo, wool.

woo. See wo.

wood, woode, wode, wod, wud, I, 242, 7; 244, 9; 328, 51; 348, 12, 18; II, 183, 26; 242, 30; 245, 27; V, 80, 42: mad.

woodcock(e), III, 199, 27; 201, 31: tropically, fool (from the bird's reputation for folly). (A proverb, perhaps.)

wooden, p. p. of wide, wade, I, 324, B 6.

woodweele, wodewale, III, 91, 2 (MS. woodweete): woodwale, woodlark? (generally explained as woodpecker; sometimes as thrush, red-breast).

woon, won, v., III, 146, 16: dwell.

woone, III, 358, 77: domicile.

woot, V, 82, 26, 41: wolt, wilt.

word, att a, I, 411, 9: in short.

wordie, III, 269, 12: worthy.

wordlye make, II, 86, 18, 20: earthly mate, consort. See warld.

wordy, IV, 135, 16: worthily.

worrie, worry, v., (of smoke, flame) III, 434, 15; 435, 14; 437, 24; IV, 514, 20: choke.

worselaid, V, 217, H 2: wrestled.

worset, worset lace, III, 11, J 1: worsted; lace must be meant for web; it cannot mean cord, and seems quite out of place.

worth, wat sal worth of, I, 334, 11: come, come to pass. wo the worth, worth the! III, 65, 189; 70, 296; 400, 1: come, be, to thee. woe worth you, wae worth ye, II, 245, 27; V, 247, 10; 248, 11. wae mat worth, IV, 236, 28; 428, 6; V, 166, 10; 306, 10: may wo come to.

wou, I, 244, 13: how.

wouche, III, 308, 26: (A. S. wóh, Scott. wouch) evil, harm.

would, ellipsis of, II, 375, 23; IV, 131, 13; V, 177, 9; 184, 38; etc. See will.

wound, pret., II, 148, 4; IV, 15, 19; 392, 19: wounded.

wow, I, 101, 20; 299, 8, 10, 12; II, 260 f., 1, 11, 14: exclamation of distress. IV, 65, 1; V, 272 a, 9: exclamation of admiration, sorrowful surprise. II, 282 2; IV, 271, A 3, 4, 7, 9; V, 197, 6: of confirmation, (vow!). See vow.

wrack, ruin.

wrack, V, 122, 11: mischief! devil!

wraft, I, 424, b 12, 13: waft (woof) misspelt.

wraikit, III, 427, note ‡: wrecked, destroyed.

wraith, wroth.

wraith, I, 134, N 15; III, 505, 12: apparition.

wreck, sea-wreck, IV, 442, 7: whatever is thrown up by the sea.

wreke, p. p., I, 243, 6: avenged.

wril, V, 73 a: a drinking-word, in response to pril.

wrist, III, 179, 4; 181, 16; 188, 3: ankle, instep. (Icel. rist, instep, ristar-liðr, instep-joint; Germ. rist, instep or wrist; fotwerst, fotwriust, hondriust, Richthofen, Altfriesisches Wörterbuch.)

writer, writter, IV, 131, 18; 135, 25: scrivener. IV, 180, D 2, 3; 181, 3; V, 256 a, 2, 3: attorney (?).

writhe of, III, 413, 34: (pret. of writhe, twist) twisted off.

writs (things written), papers.

writter. See writer.

wrobbe, I, 326, 4: wrabbe, warble? or Scottish wrable, warble, wriggle? J. A. H. Murray.

wrocht, wrought.

wrocken, wroken, p. p., III, 91, 3: avenged.

wrongeous, II, 129, 25: unjust.

wrought, p. p., II, 46, 40: rought, recked.

wrought, pret., I, 286, 51: raught, reached.

wrthe, I, 243, 5: worthy.

wruched, I, 286, 47: thrown up (ruck, a heap, to gather in heaps); perhaps, thrown ashore as wrack (Icelandic rek, originally vrek, reki, originally vreki, a thing drifted ashore).

wrye, I, 326, 4: twist.

wud, II, 249, 19: mad. See wood.

wud, I, 78, 53: would.

wuddie, IV, 69, 18: widdie, withy, a rope of willow-twigs.

wuman, V, 304 b, 1, 2: woman.

wun, n., II, 315, E 6: wind.

wun, *v.*, II, 190, 4, 10: win, gain. See **won**.

wundouten nay, I, 334, 9: without, beyond contradiction, truly.

wus, V, 304 b, 1: was.

wush, *pret.* of wash, III, 386, 20; IV, 166, **C** 7. *p. p.* wushen, I, 490, 22.

wuther, V, 304 b, 3, 4: wether.

wyght, *adj.*, strong, sturdy, active. See **wight**.

wyȝth, *n.*, V, 283, 14: wight.

wyld, III, 307, 6: (like Germ. wild) deer; or, perhaps, an adjective with noun to be supplied, of which there are several cases in the ballad.

wyle, choose. See **wile**.

wyled, they wyled the bonny lassie by, IV, 205, 26: the meaning cannot be that they (a troop of gentlemen) enticed the lassie aside. Mr. Forbes suggests, very plausibly, wyled (waled, took) their way past the lassie.

wyliecot, V, 107, 2: under-vest.

wynd, alley, lane.

wynke, III, 77, 441: shut the eyes.

wynne, III, 296, 22: joy, pleasure.

wynne, *v.* See **win**.

wynter, **winter**, III, 58, 47; 64, 162; 285, 20: year(s).

wyse in, V, 156, **B** after 16: show the way in (?), let in.

wystly, III, 76, 410: observingly, thoughtfully.

wyte, I wyte, I, 332, **G** 3; II, 376, 25; IV, 32 f., 6, 17, 19, 27; 136, 13; 278, 21; 410, 25; V, 299 b, 1, 300, 14, 17, 18: (I know) indeed, assuredly. II, 307, 34: I know, simply. See **wit, wyte**.

wyte, *n.* and *v.*, blame. See **wite**.

wyth, with, III, 297, 42; 358, 75; 434, 23: by.

wythe, I, 334, 11: wight, strong. (Orthography questionable.)

wythowtten, drede, III, 296, 8: without, beyond doubt. withowghten naye, 296, 18: beyond denial. wythowghten (withouten) stryffe (strife), 295, 2; 299, **B** 2: beyond contestation. See **withouten**.

X

xal, I, 242, 8, 9; III, 13 f., 7, 10–12, 14: shall.

xalt, III, 13 f., 9, 16, 17: shalt.

xul, *sing.* and *pl.*, III, 13, 4, 12: shall.

xuld, I, 415 b: should.

Y

(See also under ȝ, at the end of **G** and **I**.)

y, first y, III, 3, 15: ae, one. See **a, ae**.

yad, III, 483, 5, 9: jade, mare.

yae, I, 446, 8, 9: ae, only. II, 183, 17: every. See **a, ae**.

yard, **yerde**, I, 287, 63; III, 75, 397: rod, stick.

yard o stane, I, 466, **B** 23: perhaps, garden stane, something being meant equivalent to the fountain stane of **A** 23, at which the lady was christened.

yare, ȝare, II, 261, 6; III, 98, 24: ready.

yate, **yeat**, **yett**, I, 68 f., 23, 69; II, 336, **P** 2; III, 268, 15; V, 28, 60: gate. ȝates, ȝatis, III, 99, 61, 62.

yatid, I, 334, 10: granted. (A. S. géatan).

ychon, III, 101, 88: each one.

ydrawe, III, 91 a: drawn.

ydyght, idyght, III, 62, 131, 132: prepared, made, fabricated, adjusted. III, 75, 392: made ready.

yeaman. See **yeman**.

yeard-fast, yird-fast, II, 88, 11; 94, 8; 97, 15: fixed firmly in the earth.

yearl, II, 191; 20: earl. See **yerl**.

yeat, IV, 68, **D** 1: gate. See **yate**.

yebent, III, 308, 25: bent.

yede, yeede, yeed, yed, ȝede, yode, yod, *pret.* of gang, gae, go, I, 211, 37; III, 73, 346; 76, 408; 83 and 86, 160; 99, 60; 110, 18; 163, 69: went.

yee, III, 297, 39: eye.

yeen, I, 333, 2: towards, on.

ye feth, i faith.

yeff, yeffe, V, 79 f., 17, 51, 53, 54: if.

yeffell, III, 109, 6; 111, 34: evil, ill.

yeffor. See **yeuer**.

yeft, III, 70, 295: gift.

yeldyde, surrendered.

yellow-fit, yellow-foot[ed].

yeman, yeaman, III, 22, 4; 24, 43; 25, 51; 28, 121; 30, 165, 170; 56, 1, 3, etc.: yeoman.

yemanr(e)y, yemenrey, yeomanry, yeomandree, yeomandrie, yeomendry, III, 58, 45; 110, 23; 113, 83; 123, 19; 157, 31; 186, 14; 192, 23; 204, 31: class or company of yeomen; what is in accordance with a yeoman's principles, idea or character.

yend, III, 110, 17: yond, yon.

yenoughe, enough.

yeomanry, yeomandrie, etc. See **yemanr(e)y**.

ye'r, V, 306 b, 2: ye are.

yerde. See **yard**.

yerl, yerle, yerlle, yirl, yearl, III, 298, 52, 60; 308, 19; 309, 33; IV, 298, **G c** 11: 354, 7: earl.

yerly, III, 307, 7: early.

yerning, I, 334, 10: desire.

ye'se, ye shall. See **s**.

yestreen, II, 20, 7; 21, 7; 22, 6; 23, 7, etc.; V, 299 a, 1: yesterday even, yesternight. See **streen**.

yet, yett, I, 204, 11; 207, 20; 465, 11, 15; 472, 17, 18, 21; III, 269, 11; 270, 15: gate. See **yate**.

yett-pin, IV, 483 b: bolt, or latch, of a gate.

yeuer, yeffor, III, 113, 82; V, 79, 33; 80, 52: ever.

ygeve, V, 298 a: given.

yield, IV, 514, 9: grant, concede.

yill, III, 449, 8; IV, 481, 6; V, 99, 9: ale.

yird-fast. See **yeard-fast**.

yirl, IV, 69, 9: earl. See **yerl**.

ylk a, I, 328, 45: each, every. See **ilka**.

ylke, III, 61, 95: same. See **ilk**.

yll, with grete, III, 26, 90: in much distress.

ymet, III, 85, 72: measured.

ympe tree, I, 216 a: a grafted fruit tree; here, perhaps, apple, see I, 340 a.

ynowe, III, 113, 80: enough.

yo, V, 296 a: you.

yo, V, 296 a: your.

yode, **yod**, **youd**, *pret.* of gang, gae, go, I, 333, 1; II, 138, 12; 265, 9; 483, 7; III, 110, 25: went. good, III, 464, 4. gude, V, 153, 1. See **yede**.

yolden, III, 282 b: surrendered.

yon, such a blast as yon, III, 4, 7: that.

yonders, III, 187, b 13; 193, b 17; 259, 16, 17; 264, **A** b, c 17: yonder.

yont, I, 431, 3; II, 82, 51: beyond. lie yond, yont, II, 82, 49; 168, 12; IV, 345, 11; 494, 40: further off.

you, **yowe**, IV, 195 f., 1, 4, 10, 12, 17; 198, **F** 6; 206, 1; 261, 20: ewe.

youd, II, 138, 12: went. See **yode**.

young son, of a babe just born, I, 183 f., 32, 45, 47; II, 89, 35; 91, 30, 33, 35, **D** 29; 92, 22; 93, 9–12, etc.; called auld son, being the oldest because the only one, I, 184, 3, 8, 9. See **auld son, old son**.

yowe-bucht. See **bucht**.

yowre, V, 78 f., 7, 15: our. (But *owre* twelve times in the same piece, *howre* six.)

y-slaw, *p. p.* of slay, III, 28, 140.

SOURCES OF THE TEXTS

OF THE ENGLISH AND SCOTTISH BALLADS

MANUSCRIPTS.

MS. B. 14. 39, Library of Trinity College, Cambridge, 13th century. Recently recovered (see V, 288). (No 23.)

Rawlinson MS. D. 328, 15th century (before 1445). Bodleian Library. (No 1.)

MS. F. f. 5. 48, Library of the University of Cambridge, c. 1450. (No 119, a.)

One leaf of MS. in Bagford Ballads, vol. i, art. 6, British Museum, c. 1450. (No 119, b.)

Sloane MS. 2593, British Museum, c. 1450. (Nos 22, 115.)

MS. E. e. 4. 35, Library of the University of Cambridge, C. 1500. (No 121.)

Rawlinson MS. C. 813, beginning of the sixteenth century. Bodleian Library. (No 111.)

Cotton MS. Cleopatra, C. iv., British Museum, c. 1550. (No 161, **A, a.**)

MS. Ashmole 48, Bodleian Library, Oxford, 1550, or later. (No 162.)

MS. in York Minster Library, 16th century. (No 167, **C,** IV, 503.)

Cotton MS. Vespasian, A. xxv, British Museum, end of 16th century. (No 178.)

Harleian MS. 293, leaf 52, British Museum, about 1620. (No 161 **A, b.**)

Percy MS., British Museum, Additional MSS, 27879, c. 1650.

Philiphaugh MS. of No 305, Edinburgh, 1689–1708 (?). Not now accessible : printed by Aytoun. A supposed transcript extant among the Philiphaugh papers is not older than 1848. (V, 191.)

Fly-leaf of a volume printed at Edinburgh, 1670. Laing MSS, Div. II, 358, Library of the University of Edinburgh. (Fragment, V, 202 b.)

Elizabeth Cochrane's Songbook, Collection of Songs English and Scots, 1730 (?). Harvard College Library. (Nos 5, **E,** I, 76 ; 76, **A,** II, 215 ; 144, **B,** III, 195 ; 293, **A,** V, 160.)

Mrs Cockburn's MS. of No 305, used by Scott, and described by him as "apparently of considerable antiquity." Edinburgh. Not now accessible. (V, 191.)

Bishop Percy's papers. MS. copies of ballads from

Rev. P. Parsons of Wye, Miss Fisher of Carlisle, Principal Robertson of Edinburgh, the Dean of Derry, George Paton of Edinburgh, Rev. Robert Lambe of Norham, Roger Halt, the Duchess Dowager of Portland, and others. In all about 33. 1766–80. Harvard College Library.

David Herd's MSS, two volumes folio, the second volume duplicating a portion of the first. 1776. British Museum, Additional MSS, 22311–12. (See Mr H. L. D. Ward's Catalogue of Romances, I, 531.*)

MSS of Mrs Brown of Falkland. 1783–1801.

(1) Jamieson-Brown MS., mostly taken down from the mouth of Mrs Brown by Professor Scott of Aberdeen about 1783. Laing MSS, Library of the University of Edinburgh.

(2) William Tytler's Brown MS. Fifteen ballads, with the airs : thirteen being revisions of pieces in (1). Presented by Mrs Brown to W. Tytler in 1783. Described by Anderson in a letter to Percy, Nichols's Illustrations, VII, 176 ff. The MS. has disappeared, but, excepting one, all the pieces it contained are substantially known from (1) or other sources.

(3) Alexander Fraser Tytler's Brown MS. Nine ballads sent A. F. T. by Mrs Brown in 1800 ; with the airs. Anderson, as above, VII, 179 f. Aldourie Castle, Inverness-shire.

Sir Walter Scott's collection, Abbotsford. 1783–1830.

(1) Small folio without title, Library, L 2 (Catalogue, p. 57). Two fragments.

(2) 'Scottish Songs,' 1795. Library, N 3 (Catalogue, p. 104). Seven ballads with airs and three fragments. All the ballads appear to be Mrs Brown's copies altered.

(3) Letters addressed to Sir Walter Scott, 1796–1831. Ballads enclosed have in most cases been removed, but some seven remain.

(4) 'Scotch Ballads, Materials for Border Minstrelsy,' a folio volume made up at a recent date from detached pieces to the number of above eighty.

(5) 'North Country Ballads' in a quarto volume

---

* Mr Macmath drew up for the Edinburgh Bibliographical Society a bibliography of Scottish Popular Ballads in Manuscript (Session 1891-2, and a supplement, 1893-4), which may be advantageously consulted for details, as I myself have found.

with the title 'Miscellanea Curiosa,' Library B 5 (Catalogue, p. 15).

(6) 'Miscellanies,' a folio with one ballad and a fragment.

Glenriddell MS., 1791. In vol. XI of Robert Riddell's collection of Scottish Antiquities. (There is an earlier transcript of one of the ballads in vol. VIII.) Library of the Society of Antiquaries of Scotland.

MS. described by Scott as the 'collection of an old lady's complete set of ballads.' In two portions, the first in 53 pages, on paper of 1805-6-7; the second in 10 pages, on paper of 1818. Contains thirty-two popular ballads and gives the titles of others known to the compiler. Obtained by Skene of Rubislaw in the north of Scotland (but obviously not so early as 1802-3 as endorsed by Scott on the cover of the Skene MS.), turned over to Scott by Skene, and in 1823 by Scott to C. K. Sharpe. In the possession of Mr Macmath.

Skene MS., nine separate quires, amounting in all to 125 pages, and containing thirty-six pieces. Almost all of these are found in the Old Lady's Collection, from which they appear to have been transcribed, but with misreadings and changes. 118 pages in the possession of Mr Alexander Allardyce of Edinburgh; the remainder in the possession of Mr Macmath.

Pitcairn's MSS, 1817-25. Three volumes in the writing of Robert Pitcairn; partly from printed sources. In the possession of the representatives of Mr James L. Mansfield, Edinburgh.

Charles Kirkpatrick Sharpe's Collection (besides the Old Lady's MS. and the Skene MS.). (1) 'Songs,' 12mo, in Sharpe's handwriting. (2) MS. of 32 pages, small 4to, on paper of 1822, not in Sharpe's hand. (3) MS. of 12 pages, on paper of 1820, not in Sharpe's hand. (4) An independent transcript by Sharpe of the pieces entitled by Scott 'North Country Ballads.' (5) Letters from Motherwell to Sharpe, enclosing ballads. (6) Single copies of ballads, not in Sharpe's hand. All in the possession of Mr Macmath.

Motherwell's MS., 1825 and after. A folio, almost entirely in Motherwell's hand, containing, besides some pieces not indexed, 228 indexed ballads. Most of these are from the West of Scotland, but not a few were given Motherwell by Buchan and are duplicates of copies which occur in Buchan's MSS. In the possession of Mr Malcolm Colquhoun Thomson, Glasgow.

Motherwell's Note-Book, c. 1826-27. A small octavo containing various memoranda referring to ballads, including the whole, or a portion, of several copies. Formerly in the possession of Mr J. Wylie Guild.

Kinloch MSS, 1826 and after. Seven volumes, the fourth being an interleaved (printed) copy of Kinloch's Ancient Scottish Ballads with additions and variations. Vols I, II, III, VII, are almost wholly in Kinloch's hand; V, VI are mostly in the writing of James Beattie, John Hill Burton, and Joseph Robertson. Harvard College Library.

Peter Buchan's MSS, about 1828. Two volumes, folio. British Museum, Additional MSS, 29408-9. For a description, see Mr Ward's Catalogue of Romances, etc., I, 537.

Mr. David Scott of Peterhead possesses a volume entirely in Buchan's writing "which contains all [the ballads] that Buchan ever collected except some 'high-kilted' ones in another volume." [The two volumes here mentioned are now in the Child Memorial Library of Harvard University. The "high-kilted" volume is entitled 'Secret Songs of Silence.']

Joseph Robertson's MSS, 1829-32. Four small note-books, one entitled 'Journal of Excursions;' another, 'Adversaria'; also an annotated copy of The New Deeside Guide [1832]. In the possession of Dr Robertson's representatives.

John Hill Burton's MSS, 1829-30. Mostly in the Kinloch collection, but his daughter, Mrs Rodger, Aberdeen, has a small volume containing portions of two ballads.

Alexander Laing of Brechin's MS., 1829-35. 'Ancient Ballads and Songs, etc., etc., from the recitation of old people; never published, 1829.' Three ballads and a fragment. Harvard College Library.

Robert White's Papers, 1829 and after. Ballads selected from his *collectanea* by Mr White of Newcastle-on-Tyne. Harvard College Library.

British Museum, Additional MSS, 20094. 1829. (No. 4.)

Campbell MSS, 1830 or earlier. 'Old Scottish Songs collected in the counties of Berwick, Roxburgh, Selkirk and Peebles.' 2 volumes. Collector unknown. At Marchmont House, Berwickshire.

'Scottish Songs and Ballads,' copied probably before 1830, by a granddaughter of Lord Woodhouselee, mostly from print or from A. F. Tytler's Brown MS., but containing two or three versions of popular ballads not found elsewhere.

Harris MS. Ballads learned by Amelia Harris in her childhood from an old nurse in Perthshire (the last years of the 18th century); taken down by her daughter, who has added a few of her own collecting. With an appendix of airs. Harvard College Library.

Joseph Robertson. An interleaved and annotated copy of The New Deeside Guide [1832] (of which J. R. was the author).

Gibb MS., 1860. Twenty-one ballads written down from the recitation of his mother by Mr James Gibb of Joppa, representing the form in which ballads were recited about the beginning of the century in Angus and Mearns. Harvard College Library.

David Louden's MS., 1873. Contains four popular ballads derived from reciters in Haddingtonshire. Harvard College Library.

Murison MS., about 1873. Some forty pieces collected by Mrs A. F. Murison in Old Deer, among which there are several traditional popular ballads. Harvard College Library.

A few detached ballads collected by Dr Alexander Laing of Newburgh-on-Tay. About 1873.

Findlay MSS. Two volumes, the first (only) containing several ballads and many fragments gathered from recitation by Rev. William Findlay, of Saline, Fifeshire, 1865–85. In the hands of the collector.

Macmath MS. Ballads and songs recently collected by Mr Macmath. In the possession of the collector.

"Common Place Book filled with a collection of Old Ballads of the 17th century," a MS. formerly belonging to J. Payne Collier, now in the British Museum. Contains thirty ballads written in a forged hand of the 19th century, some of the pieces being also spurious. Nos 8 C, 137, 168 are in this MS.

Communications, noted in their places, of a single ballad or of several ballads, taken down or remembered by friends or correspondents in Europe and America, and several taken down by myself. [Child MSS, Harvard College Library.]

PRINTED SOURCES.

A Gest of Robyn Hode. Fragment without printer's name or date, but of the end of the 15th or beginning of the 16th century : the eleventh and last piece in a volume the other contents of which are nine pieces printed by Walter Chepman and Andrew Myllar — three of these purporting to be printed at Edinburgh in 1508 — and one other piece the printer of which is also unascertained. Advocates' Library, Edinburgh.

A Lytell Geste of Robyn Hode, etc. Wynken de Worde, London, n. d. (1492–1534). Library of the University of Cambridge.

Three fragments (one of which was attributed to Wynken de Worde by Ritson). Douce, Bodleian Library.

A Mery Geste of Robyn Hoode, etc. London, Wyllyam Copland, n. d. (1549–69). British Museum.

A Merry Iest of Robin Hood, etc. London, Printed for Edward White, n. d. (1577–1612). Bodleian Library. The sources of the later Robin Hood ballads may more conveniently be entered here, than in regular course. Articles n. d. may of course not be in strict chronological order.

Broadside copies in the Wood, Pepys, Douce, Roxburghe, and Rawlinson collections.

Martin Parker, A True Tale of Robbin Hood. London, 1634 (?). British Museum, C. 39, a. 52. — The same. By Clark, Thackeray, and Passinger. London, 1686. Bodleian Library.

Robin Hoods Garland; or Delightful Songs, Shewing the noble Exploits of Robin Hood, and his Yeomendrie. With new Edditions and Emendations. London, Printed for W. Gilbertson, at the Bible in Giltspur-street without Newgate, 1663. (17 ballads.) Wood, Bodleian Library.

Robin Hoods Garland. Containing his merry Exploits, and the several Fights which he, Little John, and Will. Scarlet had, upon several occasions. Some

of them never before Printed. [London,] Printed for F. Coles, T. Vere, and J. Wright. 1670. (16 ballads.) Douce, Bodleian Library.

Robin Hood's Garland. Printed by C. Dicey in Bow Church Yard, n. d. (before 1741).*

Robin Hood's Garland, without place or printer. 1749. Percy Papers, Harvard College Library.

Robin Hood's Garland. Printed by W. & C. Dicey, in St. Mary Aldermary Church Yard, Bow Lane, Cheapside, and sold at the Warehouse in Northampton, n. d. (c. 1753).*

The English Archer . . . Robin Hood. Paisley, printed by John Neilson for George Caldwell, Bookseller, near the Cross, 1786.*

The English Archer, or . . . Robin Hood. York, printed by N. Nickson in Feasegate, n. d.*

Robin Hood's Garland. Printed by L. How in Peticoat Lane, n. d.*

Robin Hood's Garland. London, J. Marshall & Co., Aldermary Churchyard, n. d. Harvard College Library.

Robin Hood's Garland. London. R. Marshall, in Aldermary Church Yard, Bow Lane, n. d. Harvard College Library.

Captain Delany's Garland. In a collection of folio sheet-ballads mostly dated 1775. Edinburgh (?). British Museum, 1346. m. 7. (9.)

Robin Hood's Garland. York, T. Wilson and R. Spence, n. d.*

Robin Hood's Garland. Preston, Printed and sold by W. Sergent, n. d.*

Robin Hood's Garland. Wolverhampton, Printed and sold by J. Smart, n. d.*

Adventures of . . . Robin Hood. Falkirk, Printed and sold by T. Johnston, 1808.*

The History of Robin Hood and the Beggar. Aberdeen. A. Keith (1810–35).*

Adam Bell, Clim of the Clough, and William of Cloudesly. Two fragments of an edition by John Byddell. London, 1536. Library of the University of Cambridge.

A fragment by a printer not identified, formerly in the possession of J. Payne Collier. (No 116.)

Adambel, Clym of the cloughe, and Wyllyam of cloudesle. William Copeland, London, n. d. (1562–69. See Arber, Transcript, V, 25). British Museum.

Adam Bell, Clim of the Clough, and William of Cloudesle. London, Printed by James Roberts, 1605.*

[Thomas Ravenscroft.] Deuteromelia, or, The Second Part of Musicks Melodie or Melodius Musicke, etc. London, 1609.

[Thomas Ravenscroft.] Melismata, Musicall Phansies, fitting the Court, Cittie, and Countrey Humours. London, 1611.

Thomas Deloney. Pleasant History of John Winchcomb, in his younger years called Jacke of Newberie : reprint of the 9th edition, of London, 1633, by J. O. Halliwell. London, 1859.

* Bodleian Library, Oxford.

The History of the Houses of Douglas and Angus, written by Master David Hume of Godscroft. Edinburgh, 1644.

Broadsides: mostly of the second half of the 17th century.

Wood, Rawlinson, Douce collections. Bodleian Library. Here from the originals.

Pepys collection. Magdalen College Library, Cambridge. Mostly from the originals.

Roxburghe collection. British Museum. Here sometimes from originals, sometimes from The Roxburghe Ballads, Ballad Society. Vols I, II, edited by William Chappell, London, 1871–80. Vols IV–VII, edited by J. W. Ebsworth, 1883–93.

Bagford Collection. British Museum. Here from the Bagford Ballads, Ballad Society, edited by J. W. Ebsworth, 2 vols. Hertford, 1878.

Osterley Park Library, British Museum, c. 39, k. 6 (60). 1690(?).

Laing (Scottish) Broadsides, c. 1700. In the possession of Lord Rosebery.

A Scottish Broadside formerly in the possession of J. Maidment, c. 1700. (No 162.) Harvard College Library.

"Ballard's Collection" (so cited by Percy).

Pepys Penny Merriments. Magdalen College Library, Cambridge.

The King's Pamphlets. British Museum, 669. f. 20, 55. 1657.

Wit Restord, in several select poems not formerly publisht. London, 1658 (in Facetiæ, Musarum Deliciæ, 1656, Wit Restord, 1658, and Wits Recreations, 1640. 2 vols. London, 1817).

Wit and Drollery, Jovial Poems. Corrected and amended, with New Additions. London, 1682.

Wit and Mirth, or, Pills to Purge Melancholy, being a collection of the best Merry Ballads and Songs, etc., [with airs]. London. [Ed. by Henry Playford,] four editions, London, 1699–1714, 5 vols. ; [ed. by T. D'Urfey,] 6 vols. London, I–V, 1719, VI, 1720.

True Love Requited, or, The Bayliff's Daughter of Islington. Printed and sold in Aldermary Churchyard, Bow Lane, "1700 or a little later."

A Collection of Old Ballads, corrected from the best and most ancient copies extant. With introductions historical, critical, or humorous. 3 vols. London, I, II, 1723 ; III, 1725.

Allan Ramsay. The Ever Green, being a collection of Scots Poems, wrote by the ingenious before 1600. 2 vols. Edinburgh, 1724.

Allan Ramsay. The Tea-Table Miscellany, or a collection of Choice Songs, Scots and English. (Vol. I, Edinburgh, 1724 ; vol. II, 172–? ; vol. III, 1727. 3 vols in one, Dublin, 1729; London, 1733. 9th edition, enlarged with a fourth volume, London, 1740. 11th edition, four volumes in one, London, 1750. David Laing's notes in the Musical Museum, ed. 1853, pp. 108* f., 382*, 393* f.) London, 1733, 3 vols in one; 1763, 4 vols in one.

W. Thomson. Orpheus Caledonius, or, a Collection of the best Scotch Songs. [London, 1725.] 1 vol. fol. Orpheus Caledonius, or, a Collection of Scots Songs. 2 vols, 8°, London, 1733.

Gill Morrice. An Ancient Scottish Poem, 2d ed. Robert & Andrew Foulis, 1755.

Young Waters. An Ancient Scottish Poem, never before printed. Robert & Andrew Foulis, Glasgow, 1755.

Edom of Gordon. An Ancient Scottish Poem, never before printed. Robert & Andrew Foulis, Glasgow, 1755.

Letter of Thomas Gray, June, 1757? (Gray's Works, ed. Gosse, II, 316. London, 1884.)

Thomas Percy. Reliques of Ancient English Poetry : consisting of Old Heroic Ballads, Songs, and other pieces of our Earlier Poets, together with some few of later date. 3 vols. London, 1765, 1767, 1775. 4th ed., 1794, ostensibly edited by Percy's nephew, with restoration of some original readings.

Garlands, etc., of the second half of the 18th century :

The Brown Girl's Garland. British Museum. 11621 c. 3. (10.)

The Duke of Gordon's Garland. British Museum. 11621 c. 2. (15.) Also, Harvard College Library.

The Glasgow Lasses Garland. British Museum. 11621 c. 3. (68.)

The Jovial Rake's Garland. (No 104.) Bodleian Library.

Lord Roslin's Daughter's Garland. (No 46.)

Lovely Jenny's Garland. (No 91.)

Sir James the Rose's Garland. Harvard College Library.

The Rambler's Garland. B. M. 11621 c. 4. (57.)

A chap-book of Four New Songs and a Prophecy. 1745? (Here from The Scots Musical Museum, 1853, IV, 458.)

The Merry Cuckold and Kind Wife. Broadside. Printed and Sold at the Printing Office in Bow Church-Yard, London.

Five Excellent New Songs. Edinburgh, 1766. B. M. 11621. b. 6. (8.)

The Duke of Gordon's Daughter, 1775, in a collection of folio ballads. B. M. 1346. m. 8.

Sir James the Rose, stall-tract of about 1780. Abbotsford Library.

The Duke of Gordon's Daughter. C. McLachlan, Dumfries, 1785 (?).

Lord Douglas Tragedy, stall-copy of 1792.

[David Herd.] The Ancient and Modern Scots Songs, Heroic Ballads, etc., now first collected into one body from the various Miscellanies wherein they formerly lay dispersed, containing likewise a great number of Original Songs from Manuscripts never before published. Edinburgh, 1769.

[David Herd.] Ancient and Modern Scottish Songs, Heroic Ballads, etc., collected from memory, tradition and ancient authors. The second edition. 2 vols. Edinburgh, 1776.

John Pinkerton. Scottish Tragic Ballads. London, 1781.

John Pinkerton. Select Scotish Ballads. 2 vols. (vol. I, Tragic Ballads ; vol. II, Comic Ballads). London, 1783.

[Joseph Ritson.] A Select Collection of English Songs, with their Original Airs, and a historical essay on the Origin and Progress of National Song. 3 vols. London, 1783. (The second edition, with Additional Songs, and occasional Notes. By Thomas Park. 3 vols. London, 1813.)

[Joseph Ritson.] " The Bishopric Garland, or Durham Minstrel. Being a choice collection of Excellent Songs relating to the above county. Stockton, 1784. A new edition, corrected, 1792." Reprinted by J. Haslewood in, Northern Garlands, edited by the late Joseph Ritson, Esq. London, 1810.

[George Caw.] The Poetical Museum. Containing Songs and Poems on almost every subject. Mostly from periodical publications. Hawick, 1784.

James Johnson. The Scots Musical Museum, in six volumes. Consisting of Six Hundred Scots Songs, with proper Basses for the Piano Forte, etc. Edinburgh, [1787–1803]. (Second Edition, 1839.) Third Edition, with copious Notes and Illustrations of the Lyric Poetry and Music of Scotland, by the late William Stenhouse, [and] with additional Notes and Illustrations [by David Laing]. 4 vols. Edinburgh and London, 1853.

[Joseph Ritson.] Ancient Songs, from the time of King Henry the Third to the Revolution. London, 1790. (" Printed, 1787 ; dated 1790 ; published 1792." Second Edition. Ancient Songs and Ballads from the Reign of King Henry the Second to the Revolution. Collected by Joseph Ritson, Esq. 2 vols. London, 1829.)

Joseph Ritson. Pieces of Ancient Popular Poetry : from authentic manuscripts and old printed copies. London, 1791. 2d ed., London, 1833.

[Joseph Ritson.] " The Northumberland Garland, or Newcastle Nightingale. A matchless collection of Famous Songs. Newcastle, 1793." Reprinted by J. Haslewood in, Northern Garlands, edited by the late Joseph Ritson, Esq. London, 1810.

[Joseph Ritson.] Scotish Song. In two volumes. London, 1794.

[Joseph Ritson.] Robin Hood : A Collection of all the Ancient Poems, Songs, and Ballads, now extant, relative to that celebrated English Outlaw. To which are prefixed Historical Anecdotes of his Life. In two volumes. London, 1795. (Second edition, London, 1832.)

[J. Currie.] The Works of Robert Burns, with an Account of his Life, etc. 4th ed., 4 vols. London, 1803.

John Leyden. The Complaynt of Scotland, written in 1548. With a Preliminary Dissertation and Glossary. Edinburgh, 1801.

Walter Scott. Minstrelsy of the Scottish Border :

consisting of Historical and Romantic Ballads collected in the Southern Counties of Scotland, with a few of modern date, founded upon local tradition. 3 vols. Vols I, II, Kelso, 1802 ; vol. III, Edinburgh, 1803. 2d ed., Edinburgh, 1803 ; 3d, 1806 ; 4th, 1810. 4 vols, edited by J. G. Lockhart, with airs. Edinburgh, 1833.

The Edinburgh Magazine, or, Literary Miscellany. Edinburgh, 1803.

The Scots Magazine, vol. LXV, 1803 ; vol. LXXX, 1817 ; vol. LXXXIX, 1822. Edinburgh.

The Sporting Magazine, vol. XXV. London, 1805.

Robert Jamieson. Popular Ballads and Songs from Tradition, Manuscripts, and Scarce Editions ; with translations of similar pieces from the Ancient Danish Language, and a few Originals by the Editor. 2 vols. Edinburgh, 1806.

John Finlay. Scottish Historical and Romantic Ballads, chiefly ancient. 2 vols. Edinburgh, 1808.

R. H. Cromek. Remains of Nithsdale and Galloway Song : with Historical and Traditional Notices relative to the manners and customs of the Peasantry. London, 1810.

R. H. Cromek. Select Scottish Songs, Ancient and Modern ; with Critical Observations and Biographical Notices, by Robert Burns. 2 vols. London, 1810.

Gammer Gurton's Garland, or, The Nursery Parnassus. London, 1810.

John Bell. Rhymes of Northern Bards, being a curious collection of Old and New Songs and Poems peculiar to the counties of Newcastle upon Tyne, Northumberland, and Durham. Edited by John Bell, Jun. Newcastle upon Tyne, 1812.

[John Fry.] Pieces of Ancient Poetry from unpublished manuscripts and scarce books. Bristol, 1814.

H. Weber, R. Jamieson, W. Scott. Illustrations of Northern Antiquities, etc. Edinburgh, 1814.

Sir Egerton Brydges. Restituta, vol. I. London. 1814.

Alexander Campbell. Albyn's Anthology, or, a select collection of the Melodies and Local Poetry peculiar to Scotland and the Isles, hitherto unpublished. 2 vols. 1816, 1818.

R. H. Cromek. Reliques of Robert Burns. 4th ed. London, 1817.

James Hogg. The Jacobite Relics of Scotland, being the Songs, Airs, and Legends of the adherents to the House of Stuart. 2 vols. Edinburgh, 1819–21.

R. A. Smith. The Scotish Minstrel, a selection from the Vocal Melodies of Scotland, ancient and modern. 6 vols. Edinburgh, [1820–24].

John Struthers. The British Minstrel, a selection of Ballads, ancient and modern, etc. 2 vols. London, 1822.

Robert Trotter. Lowran Castle, or, The Wild Boar of Curridoo, with other Tales, illustrative of the Superstitions, Manners, and Customs of Galloway. Dumfries, 1822.

[Alexander Laing.] Scarce Ancient Ballads, many never before published. Aberdeen, 1822.

Alexander Laing. The Thistle of Scotland, a selection of Ancient Ballads, with notes. Aberdeen, 1823.

[Charles Kirkpatrick Sharpe.] A Ballad Book. Edinburgh, 1823.] Reprinted by E. Goldsmid, Edinburgh, 1883.

Davies Gilbert. Some Ancient Christmas Carols, with the Tunes to which they were formerly sung in the West of England. Together with two ancient Ballads, a Dialogue, etc. 2d edition. London, 1823.

William Hone. Ancient Mysteries. London, 1823.

[James Maidment.] A North Countrie Garland. Edinburgh, 1824. Reprinted by E. Goldsmid. Edinburgh, 1884.

The Common-Place Book of Ancient and Modern Ballad and Metrical Legendary Tales. An original selection, including many never before published. Edinburgh, 1824.

John Mactaggart. The Scottish Gallovidian Encyclopedia, or, the original, antiquated, and natural Curiosities of the South of Scotland. London, 1824.

David Webster. A Collection of curious Old Ballads and Miscellaneous Poetry. Edinburgh, 1824.

The Gentleman's Magazine. Vol. XCV, Part I. London, 1825.

Peter Buchan. Gleanings of Scotch, English, and Irish scarce old Ballads chiefly tragical and historical, etc. Peterhead, 1825.

Allan Cunningham. The Songs of Scotland, ancient and modern, with an introduction and notes, historical and critical, etc. 4 vols. London, 1825.

Stall copies, etc., mostly of uncertain date :

The Song of Bewick and Grahame. B. M. 11621. e. 1. (4.)

Bewick and Graham's Garland. M. Angus & Son, Newcastle.

A Jolly Book of Garlands collected by John Bell in Newcastle. Abbotsford Library.

Curious Tracts, Scotland. B. M. 1078. m. 24. A collection made by J. Mitchell at Aberdeen in 1828.

The Unfortunate Weaver, etc. (for No 25). Greenock, [1810]. B. M. 11621. b. 7. (43.)

Stall or chap-book copies by M. Randall & C. Randall, Stirling ; John Sinclair, Dumfries ; W. Fordyce, Newcastle ; T. Johnston, Falkirk ; P. Buchan, Peterhead ; Aberdeen, printed for the booksellers.

Recent Broadsides of Catnach, Pitts, Such.

Peggy Irvine. Stall-copy printed by J. Morren, Cowgate, Edinburgh.

Robert Chambers. The Popular Rhymes of Scotland, with illustrations, chiefly collected from oral sources. Edinburgh, 1826, 1870.

George R. Kinloch. Ancient Scottish Ballads, recovered from tradition and never before published, with notes, historical and explanatory, and an appendix containing the airs of several of the ballads. London and Edinburgh, 1827.

[George R. Kinloch.] The Ballad Book. Edinburgh, 1827. Reprinted by E. Goldsmid. Edinburgh, 1885.

Thomas Lyle. Ancient Ballads and Songs, chiefly from tradition, manuscripts, and scarce works, etc. London, 1827.

William Motherwell. Minstrelsy, Ancient and Modern, with an historical introduction and notes. Glasgow, 1827. (A copy with MS. entries by Motherwell).

Peter Buchan. Ancient Ballads and Songs of the North of Scotland, hitherto unpublished, with explanatory notes. 2 vols. Edinburgh, 1828.

The Paisley Magazine, or, Literary and Antiquarian Miscellany. Paisley, 1828.

Robert Chambers. The Scottish Ballads, collected and illustrated. Edinburgh, 1829.

Sir N. H. Nicolas. History of the Battle of Agincourt. 2d ed. London, 1832.

[Joseph Robertson.] The New Deeside Guide, by James Brown. Aberdeen, [1832].

Andrew Picken. Traditionary Stories of Old Families. 2 vols. London, 1833.

William Sandys. Christmas Carols, Ancient and Modern, including the most popular in the West of England, and the airs to which they are sung, etc. London, 1833.

William Sandys. Christmastide, its history, festivities, and carols. London, [18—].

Sir Cuthbert Sharpe. The Bishoprick Garland, or a collection of Legends, Songs, Ballads, etc., belonging to the county of Durham. London, 1834.

The Universal Songster, or, Museum of Mirth, forming the most complete, extensive, and valuable collection of Ancient and Modern Songs in the English language. 3 vols. London, 1834.

The Songs of England and Scotland. 2 vols. London, 1835.

Fisher's Drawing-Room Scrap-Book. London, 1835.

[E. V. Utterson.] A Little Book of Ballads. [Printed for the Roxburghe Club.] Newport, 1836.

J. E. Tyler. Henry of Monmouth, or, Memoirs of the Life and Character of Henry the Fifth. 2 vols. London, 1838.

The Loving Ballad of Lord Bateman. Illustrated by George Cruikshank. London, 1839.

Sir N. H. Nicolas. The Poetical Works of Robert Burns. Aldine Edition. 3 vols. London, 1839.

J. O. Halliwell. The Nursery Rhymes of England, collected principally from oral tradition. London, 1842 (Vol. IV of the Percy Society Publications). 4th ed., 1846 ; 5th ed., 1853.

Alexander Whitelaw. The Book of Scottish Song ; collected and illustrated with historical and critical notices, etc. (Glasgow, 1844.) Glasgow, Edinburgh, and London, 1855.

Alexander Whitelaw. The Book of Scottish Ballads ; collected and illustrated with historical and critical notices. Glasgow, Edinburgh, and London. [1844] 1845.

J. O. Halliwell. Nugæ Poeticæ. Select Pieces of Old English Popular Poetry, illustrating the manners and arts of the fifteenth century. London, 1844.

R. Chambers. Twelve Romantic Scottish Ballads, with the original airs. Edinburgh, 1844.

[James Maidment.] A New Book of Old Ballads. Edinburgh, 1844.

T. Wright and J. O. Halliwell. Reliquiæ Antiquæ. Scraps from Ancient Manuscripts. 2 vols. London, 1845.

The New Statistical Account of Scotland, vol. V. Edinburgh and London, 1845.

James Henry Dixon. Scottish Traditional Versions of Ancient Ballads. (Vol. XVII of the Percy Society Publications.) London, 1845.

James Henry Dixon. Ancient Poems, Ballads, and Songs of the Peasantry of England, taken down from oral recitation, and transcribed from private manuscripts, rare broadsides, and scarce publications. (Vol. XVII of the Percy Society Publications.) London, 1846.

M. A. Richardson. The Borderer's Table Book, or, Gatherings of the Local History and Romance of the English and Scottish Border. 8 vols. Newcastle-upon-Tyne and London, 1846.

James Paterson and Charles Gray. The Ballads and Songs of Ayrshire, illustrated with sketches historical, traditional, narrative, and biographical. 2 series. Ayr, 1846, 1847.

Frederick Sheldon. The Minstrelsy of the English Border, being a collection of Ballads, ancient, remodelled, and original, founded on well known Border legends. London, 1847.

John Matthew Gutch. A Lytyll Geste of Robin Hode, with other Ancient and Modern Ballads and Songs relating to this celebrated yeoman, etc. 2 vols. London, 1847.

The Scottish Journal. Vol. II, 1848.

The Edinburgh Topographical, Traditional, and Antiquarian Magazine. [Sept.–Dec. 1848.] Edinburgh, 1849.

J. O. Halliwell. Popular Rhymes and Nursery Tales; a sequel to the Nursery Rhymes of England. London, 1849.

J. O. Halliwell. Ballads and Poems respecting Hugh of Lincoln. Brixton Hill, 1849.

Abraham Hume. Sir Hugh of Lincoln, or, an examination of a curious tradition respecting the Jews, with a notice of the Popular Poetry connected with it. London, 1849.

Notes and Queries. London, 1850–.

Proceedings of the Society of Antiquaries of Scotland. Vol. I, 1852.

J. S. Moore. The Pictorial Book of Ancient Ballad Poetry of Great Britain, historical, traditional, and romantic, etc. London, 1853.

John Miller. Fly-Leaves, or Scraps and Sketches, literary, biographical, and miscellaneous. The Second Series. London, 1855.

William Chappell. Popular Music of the Olden Time. A collection of Ancient Songs, Ballads, and Dance Tunes, illustrative of the National Music of England, etc. 2 vols. London, [1855–59].

Jabez Allies. The British, Roman, and Saxon Antiquities and Folk-lore of Worcestershire. 2d ed. London, " 1856 " [1852?].

Robert Bell. Ancient Poems, Ballads, and Songs of the Peasantry of England, taken down from oral recitation, and transcribed from private manuscripts, rare broadsides, and scarce publications. London, 1857.

William E. Aytoun. The Ballads of Scotland. 2 vols. Edinburgh and London, 1858; 2d ed., revised and augmented, 1859.

James Maidment. Scotish Ballads and Songs. Edinburgh, London, and Glasgow, 1859.

R. Chambers. The Romantic Scottish Ballads : their Epoch and Authorship. London and Edinburgh, 1859.

Thomas Hughes. The Scouring of the White Horse. Cambridge [England], 1859.

Joshua Sylvester. A Garland of Christmas Carols, ancient and modern, including some never before given in any collection. London, 1861.

Mary (Wilson) Gordon. Christopher North. A Memoir of John Wilson. 2 vols. Edinburgh, 1862.

William Allingham. The Ballad Book. A selection of the choicest British Ballads. London, 1865.

Robert Hunt. Popular Romances of the West of England. First Series. London, 1865.

M. H. Mason. Nursery Rhymes and Country Songs, both tunes and words from tradition. London, n. d. [c. 1877].

William Henderson. Notes on the Folk-Lore of the Northern counties of England and the Borders. With an Appendix by S. Baring-Gould. London, 1866 ; new ed., 1879.

Llewellyn Jewitt. The Ballads and Songs of Derbyshire, with illustrative notes and examples of the original music, etc. London and Derby, 1867.

John W. Hales and Frederick J. Furnivall. Bishop Percy's Folio Manuscript. Ballads and Romances. 3 vols and a supplement. London, 1867–68.

James Maidment. Scotish Ballads and Songs, Historical and Traditionary. 2 vols. Edinburgh, 1868.

W. H. Logan. A Pedlar's Pack of Ballads and Songs, with illustrative notes. Edinburgh, 1869.

Robert Chambers. Popular Rhymes of Scotland. New edition. London and Edinburgh, [1870].

Wm. Henry Husk. Songs of the Nativity, being Christmas Carols, Ancient and Modern, several of which appear for the first time in a collection. London, [187–?].

Salopian Shreds and Patches. Vol. I. Shrewsbury, 1875.

Jahrbuch für Romanische u. Englische Sprache und Literatur. Vol. XV. Leipzig, 1876.

W. Christie. Traditional Ballad Airs, arranged and harmonized, etc., from copies obtained in the counties of Aberdeen, Banff, and Moray, etc. Edited, with the words for singing and with illustrative notes. 2 vols. Edinburgh, vol. I, 1876; vol. II, 1881.

Suffolk Notes and Queries, in The Ipswich Journal, 1877–78.

H. R. Bramley and J. Stainer. Christmas Carols, New and Old. London, [187–?].

Folk-Lore Record. Vol. II. London, 1879.

Francis Hindes Groome. In Gipsy Tents. Edinburgh, 1880.

The Leisure Hour, February 14, 1880. London.

Walter W. Skeat. Specimens of English Literature, from the Ploughmans Crede to the Shepherdes Calender, etc. 3d ed. Oxford, 1880.

A Ballad Book. By Charles Kirkpatrick Sharpe, Esq. 1823. Reprinted with Notes and Ballads from the unpublished MSS of Charles Kirkpatrick Sharpe, Esq., and Sir Walter Scott, Bart. Edited by the late David Laing. Edinburgh and London, 1880.

Aungervyle Society's Publications. A Garland of Old Historical Ballads. Edinburgh, 1881.

B. Harris Cowper. The Apocryphal Gospels. 5th ed. London, 1881.

J. C. Bruce and J. Stokoe. Northumbrian Minstrelsy. A collection of the Ballads, Melodies and Small-Pipe Tunes of Northumbria. Newcastle-upon-Tyne, 1882.

A. Nimmo. Songs and Ballads of Clydesdale. Edinburgh and Glasgow, 1882.

G. A. Sala. 'Sir Hugh,' in Illustrated London News, October 21, 1882. (Repeated in Living London, 1883.)

Charlotte Sophia Burne. Shropshire Folk-Lore, a sheaf of gleanings edited from the collections of Georgina F. Jackson. London, 1883–6.

Wm W. Newell. Games and Songs of American Children. New York, 1883.

Edmund Venables. A Walk through Lincoln Minster. Lincoln, 1885.

W. H. Long. A Dictionary of the Isle of Wight Dialect, and of Provincialisms used, . . . with illustrative anecdotes and tales, etc. London and Newport, 1886.

Transactions of The New Shakspere Society, 1880–86. London, 1886.

A. H. Bullen. Carols and Poems from the 15th century to the present time. London, 1886.

Letters from and to Charles Kirkpatrick Sharpe, Esq. Ed. by Alexander Allardyce. 2 vols. Edinburgh and London, 1888.

Mrs Graham R. Tomson. Ballads of the North Countrie. London, 1888.

S. Baring-Gould and H. Fleetwood Sheppard. Songs and Ballads of the West. A collection made from the mouths of the People. 4 parts. London, [1889 (?)–91].

The Monthly Chronicle of North-Country Lore and Legend. Vol. III. Newcastle-on-Tyne and London, 1889.

The Folk-Lore Journal. Vols VI, VII. London, 1888–9.

James Raine, Jr. A volume of English Miscellanies, illustrating the history and language of the Northern Counties of England. Surtees Society, No 85. Durham, 1890.

Blackwood's Magazine. Vol. CXLVII. Edinburgh, 1890.

Margaret Warrender. Walks near Edinburgh. Edinburgh, 1890.

Longman's Magazine. Vol. XVII. London, 1890.

Journal of the Gypsy-Lore Society. Vol. II. London, 1890–91.

Frank Kidson. Traditional Tunes. A collection of Ballad Airs, chiefly obtained in Yorkshire and the South of Scotland, together with their appropriate words from broadsides or from oral tradition. Oxford, 1891.

Lucy E. Broadwood and J. A. Fuller Maitland. English County Songs, words and music. London and New York, 1893.

County Folk-Lore. Printed Extracts. No 2. Suffolk. Collected and edited by the Lady Eveline Camilla Gurdon. Folk-Lore Society. London, 1893.

The Journal of American Folk-Lore. Vol. VII. Boston, 1894.

H. A. Kennedy. Professor Blackie: his Sayings and Doings. London, 1895.

Francis Hindes Groome. Two Suffolk Friends. Edinburgh and London, 1895.

INDEX OF PUBLISHED AIRS OF ENGLISH AND SCOTTISH POPULAR BALLADS

WITH AN APPENDIX OF SOME AIRS FROM MANUSCRIPT

THE oldest book of airs here referred to is Thomson's Orpheus Caledonius, ed. 1733. Earlier music-books or manuscript notations were used in great number by Chappell, Rimbault, and others, and the results are accessible through their works as cited below. The same air will frequently be found to have been repeated in successive publications. Undoubtedly the cases in which the original air of the older ballads has been preserved are but few.

Of the airs from manuscript some are very likely to have been published already ; the ascertaining of the fact would have cost considerable labor, and was not demanded for a list which avowedly includes repetitions from printed books. The earliest noted down are, I suppose, the five from the Abbotsford MS. entitled " Scottish Songs," which appear to have been derived from William Tytler's unrecovered Brown MS. This lost MS. was obtained by William Tytler in 1783, and contained fifteen ballads with the melodies as written down by Professor Scott from Mrs Brown's singing ; of which melodies it is said : " Being then but a mere novice in music, he added in the copy such musical

notes as he supposed might give some notion of the air, or rather lilts, to which they were sung." Twenty-three airs are given from the Harris Ballad-MS. as sung by Mrs Amelia Harris to her children about 1830. Miss Jane Harris, one of them, says that the airs are to be " orally and directly traced from my great father's (Rev. P. Duncan, Tibbermore) manse from 1745." Six airs are from a MS. of Charles Kirkpatrick Sharpe written on paper with a watermark of 1822. The remaining airs are very recent communications from various duly registered sources, and were all but a very few seemingly written down within a year or two.

The compilation of the list of printed airs was undertaken for me by my constant friend Mr William Walker, of Aberdeen. Some additions have been made. Mr Walker also furnished me with several melodies from the north of Scotland. Revision of the manuscript airs was required in some cases to correct obvious errors of notation, and this was performed for me by Mr W. R. Spalding, of Harvard College, who has not gone beyond the amendment of self-evident errors of transcribers.

ABBREVIATED INDICATIONS OF BOOKS REFERRED TO

Baring-Gould. S. Baring-Gould, English Minstrelsie. Edinburgh, 1895–. 8 vols (7 published.)

Baring-Gould, S. Baring-Gould and Sheppard, Songs and Ballads of the West. London, [1889–91]. Four parts.

Barsanti. Francis Barsanti, A Collection of Old Scots Tunes. Edinburgh, [1742?].

Bramley. H. R. Bramley and J. Stainer, Christmas Carols, New and Old. London, [187–?].

Broadwood. L. E. Broadwood and J. A. F. Maitland, English County Songs. London, 1893.

Bruce. J. C. Bruce and J. Stokoe, Northumbrian Minstrelsy. Newcastle-upon-Tyne, 1882.

Burne. Charlotte Sophia Burne, Shropshire Folk-Lore. London, 1883–6.

Campbell. Alexander Campbell, Albyn's Anthology. Edinburgh, 1816, 1818. 2 vols.

Chambers. Robert Chambers, Twelve Romantic Scottish Ballads. Edinburgh, 1844.

Chappell. W. Chappell, Popular Music of the Olden Time. London, [1855, 1859]. 2 vols.

Christie. W. Christie, Traditional Ballad Airs. Edinburgh, 1876, 1881. 2 vols.

Cruikshank. The Loving Ballad of Lord Bateman. London, 1839.

Dauney. Wm. Dauney, Ancient Scottish Melodies, from a Manuscript of the reign of King James VI. Edinburgh, 1838.

Gilbert. Davies Gilbert, Some Ancient Christmas Carols, with the tunes. London, 1823.

Gordon. Mrs. Gordon, Christopher North, A Memoir of John Wilson. Edinburgh, 1862. 2 vols.

Graham. G. F. Graham, The Songs of Scotland. Edinburgh, [1854–56]. 3 vols.

Husk. Wm. Henry Husk, Songs of the Nativity. London, [187– ?].

Jewitt. Llewellyn Jewitt, The Ballads and Songs of Derbyshire. London and Derby, 1867.

Johnson. James Johnson, The Scots Musical Museum. Edinburgh and London, [1787–1803]. 6 vols.

Journal. Journal of American Folk-Lore. Vol. VIII. Boston and New York, 1895.

Kidson. Frank Kidson, Traditional Tunes. Oxford, 1891.

Kinloch. G. R. Kinloch, Ancient Scottish Ballads, Appendix. London and Edinburgh, 1827.

Mason. M. H. Mason, Nursery Rhymes and Country Songs. London, n. d. [1877].

Motherwell. Wm. Motherwell, Minstrelsy Ancient and Modern, Appendix. Glasgow, 1827.

Rimbault. Edward F. Rimbault, Musical Illustrations of Bishop Percy's Reliques of Ancient English Poetry. London, 1850.

Rimbault, C. E. F. Rimbault. (Chappell's Christmas Carols.) A Collection of Old Christmas Carols with the tunes to which they are sung. London, n. d.

Rimbault, G. E. F. Rimbault, Musical Illustrations of the Robin Hood Ballads, in J. M. Gutch's Robin Hood Garlands and Ballads. London, 1850. 2 vols, the second.

Ritson, A. [Joseph Ritson,] Ancient Songs. London, 1790.

Ritson, E. [Joseph Ritson,] A Select Collection of English Songs. London, 1783. 3 vols. Cited by pages of 2d ed., 1813.

Ritson, S. [Joseph Ritson,] Scotish Song. London, 1794. 2 vols.

Sandys, C. C. W. Sandys, Christmas Carols, Ancient and Modern. London, 1833.

Sandys, C. T. W. Sandys, Christmastide, its history, festivals, and carols. London, [18—?].

Scott. Walter Scott, Minstrelsy of the Scottish Border. Edinburgh, 1833. 4 vols.

Smith, R. R. A. Smith, The Scotish Minstrel. Edinburgh, [1820–24]. 6 vols.

Smith, S. J. Stafford Smith, Musica Antiqua : a Collection of Music from the 12th till the 18th Century. London, 1812. 2 vols.

Sussex. Sussex Songs, arranged by H. F. Birch Reynardson. London, [1891?].

Thomson, G. George Thomson, The Select Melodies of Scotland, etc. [1793–1841. 6 vols. fol.] London, [1822–25]. 6 vols. 8vo.

Thomson, W. W. Thomson, Orpheus Caledonius, or, A Collection of Scots Songs. 2d ed. London, 1733. 2 vols.

INDEX

[The figures in the left-hand column refer to the numbers of the ballads in this collection.]

BALLAD AIRS FROM MANUSCRIPT

3 C. THE FAUSE KNIGHT UPON THE ROAD.

Miss M. MACMATH.

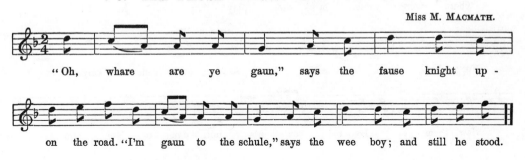

"Oh, whare are ye gaun," says the fause knight up - on the road. "I'm gaun to the schule," says the wee boy; and still he stood.

9 G. THE FAIR FLOWER OF NORTHUMBERLAND.

SHARPE MS.

10 Bc. THE TWA SISTERS.

ABBOTSFORD MS. "SCOTTISH SONGS."

There was twa sis - ters in a bour, Ed - in-bor-ough, Ed-in-borough; There was twa sis - ters in ae bour, Stir - ling for ay. There was twa sis - ters in ae bour, There came a . . knight to be their wooer, Bon - ny St. John - ston stands up - on Tay.

10 W. THE TWA SISTERS.

T. LUGTEN, KELSO.

There were three la - dies play - ing at the ba,

Nor - ham, down by Nor - ham, And oot cam a knight to

view them a,' By the bon - nie mill - dams o Nor - ham.

10. THE TWA SISTERS.

MRS HARRIS AND OTHERS.

11 C. THE CRUEL BROTHER.

HARRIS MS.

12 D. LORD RANDAL.

Received from J. F. CAMPBELL (of Islay).
"Transcribed by G. E. JOHNSTONE."

Oh, where hae ye been, Lord

I hae been to the wild wood, mith-er

For I'm

12 P. LORD RANDAL.

Miss M. Macmath.

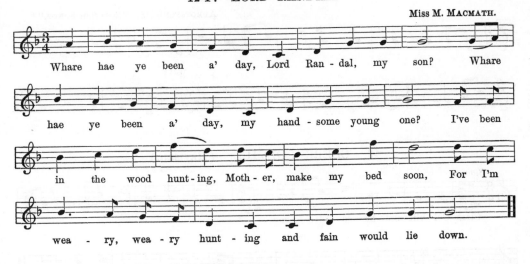

Whare hae ye been a' day, Lord Ran-dal, my son? Whare
hae ye been a' day, my hand-some young one? I've been
in the wood hunt-ing, Moth-er, make my bed soon, For I'm
wea-ry, wea-ry hunt-ing and fain would lie down.

17 I. HIND HORN.

Miss M. Macmath.

She gave him a gay gold ring, hey lil-le-lu and how lo lan, and
he gave her a far bet-ter thing, Wi my hey down and a he did-dle down-ie.

20 Ja. THE CRUEL MOTHER.

Mrs Harris and others.

40. THE QUEEN OF ELFAN'S NOURICE.

W. Walker, Aberdeen. *

* "Perhaps an improvised adaptation of a pibroch tune."

42. CLERK COLVILL.

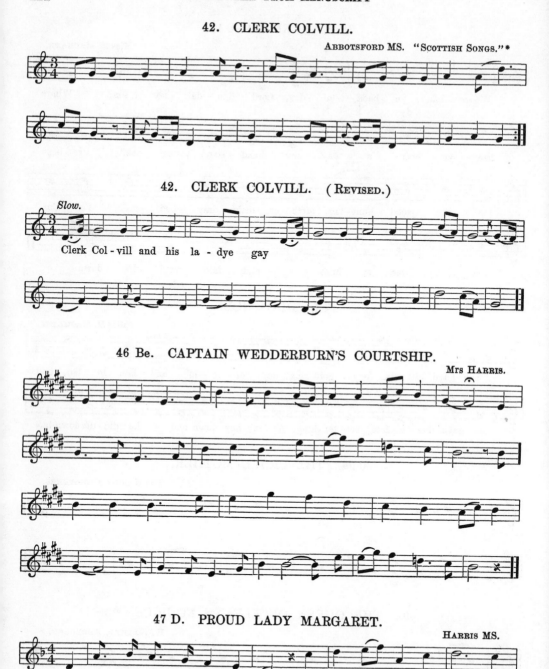

ABBOTSFORD MS. "SCOTTISH SONGS."*

42. CLERK COLVILL. (REVISED.)

Slow.

Clerk Col-vill and his la-dye gay

46 Be. CAPTAIN WEDDERBURN'S COURTSHIP.

MRS HARRIS.

47 D. PROUD LADY MARGARET.

HARRIS MS.

*Also noted in Glenriddell's hand in the fly-leaf at the end of Vol. I of his copy of Herd, 1776, in the Signet Library.

W. MACMATH.

53. YOUNG BEICHAN.

Mrs HARRIS.

58 J. SIR PATRICK SPENS.

Mrs HARRIS.

61. SIR COLIN.

Mrs HARRIS.

63 E. CHILD WATERS.

Mrs HARRIS.

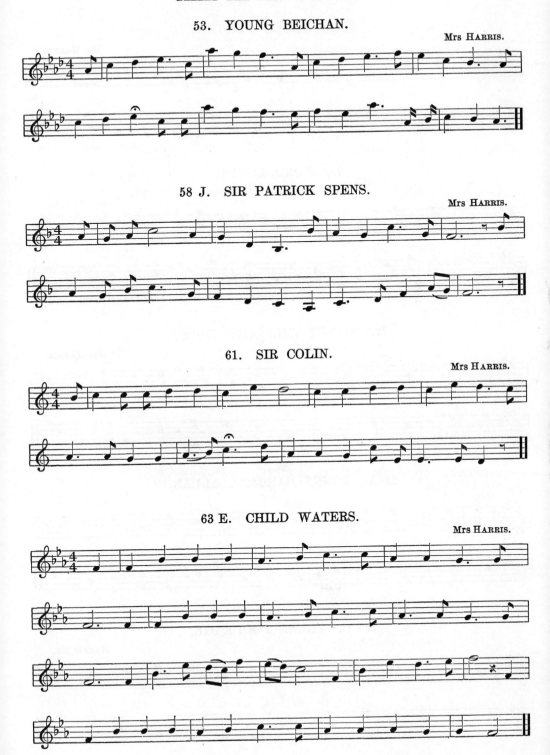

68 C. YOUNG HUNTING.

Mrs HARRIS.

75. LORD LOVEL.

As sung in Aberdeen above forty years ago.

W. WALKER.

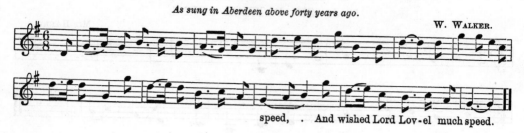

speed,   .   And wished Lord Lov-el much speed.

77. SWEET WILLIAM'S GHOST.

Mrs HARRIS.

84 A. BONNY BARBARA ALLAN.

Mrs HARRIS.

89 C. FAUSE FOODRAGE.

HARRIS MS.

95 L. THE MAID FREED FROM THE GALLOWS.

Miss E. M. Backus, North Carolina.

97 Ab. BROWN ROBIN.

Abbotsford MS, "Scottish Songs."

98 B. BROWN ADAM.

Mrs Harris.

99 A. JOHNIE SCOT.

ABBOTSFORD MS., "SCOTTISH SONGS."

99 O. JOHNIE SCOT.

Miss M. MACMATH.

Out then spak his auld fai-ther, And a blythe auld man was he, sayin, "I'll

send five hun-ner o my brisk young men, To bear John-ie com-pa-nie."

100 J. WILLIE O WINSBURY.

Miss M. MACMATH.

There was a lass in the north coun-trie, And her cloth-ing it was the

green; And she's looked ower her fa-ther's cas-tle wa', For to

see her fa-ther's ships sail in, in, For to see her fa-ther's ships on sea.

106. THE FAMOUS FLOWER OF SERVING–MEN.

Mrs HARRIS.

114 G. JOHNIE COCK.

Mrs Harris.

157 I. GUDE WALLACE.

Sharpe MS.

161 (V, 243). THE BATTLE OF OTTERBURN.

Sharpe MS.

It was a-bout the Lam-mes time When moor-land men do win their hay,

Brave Earl Doug-lass in ar-mer bright, Marchd to the Bor-der with-out de-lay.

163. THE BATTLE OF HARLAW.

W. Walker, "from a residenter in the Garioch."

wi   a

164.   KING HENRY FIFTH'S CONQUEST OF FRANCE.

Mrs Harris.

164 (V, 245).   KING HENRY FIFTH'S CONQUEST OF FRANCE.

Sharpe MS.

Chorus. . . . .

169 C.   JOHNIE ARMSTRONG.

Sharpe MS.

169.   JOHNIE ARMSTRONG.

Mrs Harris.

173 J. MARY HAMILTON.

Mrs HARRIS.

182 D. THE LAIRD O LOGIE.

Mrs HARRIS.

222 (V, 261). BONNY BABY LIVINGSTON.

SHARPE MS.

Bon - ny An - ny Liv - ie - ston Went out to see the play,

By came the Laird of Glen - lion And took her quite a - way.

226 H. LIZIE LINDSAY.

As sung by George Mitchell, Edgell Castle, Forfarshire.

W. WALKER.

228 C. GLASGOW PEGGIE.

Miss M. MacMath.

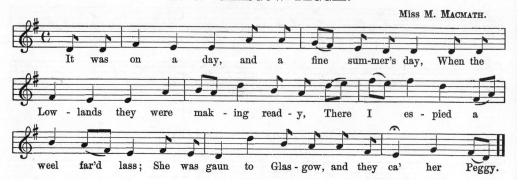

It was on a day, and a fine sum-mer's day, When the
Low - lands they were mak - ing read - y, There I es - pied a
weel far'd lass; She was gaun to Glas - gow, and they ca' her Peggy.

235 E. THE EARL OF ABOYNE.

Mrs Harris.

247 b. LADY ELSPAT.

Abbotsford MS., "Scottish Songs."

247 b. LADY ELSPAT. (Revised.)

How brent is . . your brow, my la - dy Els - pat; How . . gold -
en yel - low is your hair! Of a' the . . maids in . . fair . . . .
Scot - land There . . is . . none like . . la - dy Els - pat fair.

250 E (V, 302). ANDREW BARTIN.

Miss L. P. HASKELL, South Carolina.

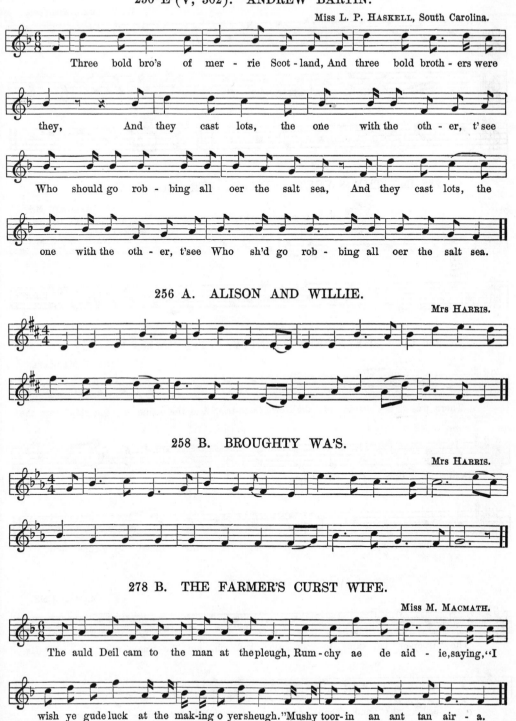

Three bold bro's of mer - rie Scot - land, And three bold broth - ers were

they, And they cast lots, the one with the oth - er, t'see

Who should go rob - bing all oer the salt sea, And they cast lots, the

one with the oth - er, t'see Who sh'd go rob - bing all oer the salt sea.

256 A. ALISON AND WILLIE.

Mrs HARRIS.

258 B. BROUGHTY WA'S.

Mrs HARRIS.

278 B. THE FARMER'S CURST WIFE.

Miss M. MACMATH.

The auld Deil cam to the man at the pleugh, Rum - chy ae de aid - ie, saying, "I

wish ye gude luck at the mak - ing o yer sheugh." Mushy toor - in an ant tan air - a.

281. THE KEACH I THE CREEL.

W. Walker, Aberdeen.

286 Ba. THE SWEET TRINITY. (The Golden Vanity.)

Macmath MS.

From a copy in the handwriting of P. S. Fraser (slightly corrected).

286 Cg. THE SWEET TRINITY. (The Golden Vanity.)

Miss M. Macmath.

There was a ship of the North Coun-trie, And the name of the ship was the

Gold - en Trin - i - tie; She was sail - ing in the Low - lands

low, low, low, She was sail - ing in the Low - Lands low.

299 D (V, 306). TROOPER AND MAID.

Macmath MS.

The troop-er lad cam to oor gate, And oh, but he was wea - ry; He

rap - ped at and chap - ped at, Syne called for his kind dear - y.

INDEX OF BALLAD TITLES

———◆———

Ladin.

Lettish.

Lithuanian.

Magyar.

TITLES OF COLLECTIONS OF BALLADS, OR OF BOOKS CONTAINING BALLADS,

WHICH ARE VERY BRIEFLY CITED IN THIS WORK

Albanian.

Camarda, D. Appendice al saggio di grammatologia comparata sulla lingua albanese. Prato, 1866.

de Grazia, Demetrio. Canti popolari albanesi tradizionali nel mezzogiorno d'Italia, riordinati, tradotti, e illustrati da ——. Noto, 1889.

de Rada, Girolamo. Rapsodie d' un poema albanese raccolte nelle colonie del Napoletano, tradotte da —— e per cura di lui e di Niccolò Jeno de' Coronei ordinate e messe in luce. Firenze, 1866.

Breton.

Luzel, F. M. Gwerziou Breiz-Izel. Chants populaires de la Basse-Bretagne. 2 vols. Lorient, 1868-74.

—— Soniou Breiz-Izel. Chansons populaires de la Basse-Bretagne. 2 vols. Paris, 1890.

Quellien, N. Chansons et danses des Bretons. Paris, 1889.

Taylor, Tom. Ballads and Songs of Brittany, translated from the Barsaz-Breiz of Vicomte Hersart de la Villemarqué. London and Cambridge, 1865.

Villemarqué, Le Vicomte Hersart de la. Barzaz Breiz, chants populaires de la Bretagne. 6e éd. Paris, 1867.

Catalan.

Cansons de la terra. Cants populars catalans, colleccionats per Francesch Pelay Briz y Candi Candi. Barcelona, I, 1866; II, F. P. Briz y Joseph Saltó, 1867; III-V, F. P. Briz, 1871, 1874, 1877.

Milá y Fontanals, Manuel. Romancerillo catalan. Canciones tradicionales. Segunda edicion, refundida y aumentada. Barcelona, 1882.

—— Observaciones sobre la poesia popular, con muestras de romances catalanes inéditos, por——. Barcelona, 1853.

Miscelánea folk-lórica per los Srs Almirall, Arabia, et cet. Barcelona, 1887.

Danish.

Abrahamson, Nyerup og Rahbek. Udvalgte Danske Viser fra Middelalderen; efter A. S. Vedels og P. Syvs trykte Udgaver og efter haandskrevne Samlinger, udgivne paany af ——. Kjøbenhavn, 1812-14. 5 vols.

Berggreen, A. P. Danske Folke-Sange og Melodier. 2d ed. Kjøbenhavn, 1860. 3d ed. med et Tillæg af islandske og færøiske. Kjøbenhavn, 1869.

Boisen, P. O. Nye og gamle Viser, af og fra danske Folk, samlede og udgivne af ——. 10th ed. Kjøbenhavn, 1875.

Borrow, George. Romantic Ballads, translated from the Danish, etc. London, 1826.

Brage og Idun, et nordisk Fjærdingårsskrift, udgivet af Frederik Barfod. København, 1839-42. 4 vols and 1 haefte.

Dansk Kirketidende. Kjøbenhavn, 1846-.

Feilberg, Henning Frederik. Fra Heden. Haderslev, 1862.

Grimm, W. C. Altdänische Heldenlieder, Balladen und Märchen, übersetzt von ——. Heidelberg, 1811. Zusätze und Verbesserungen, in Drei altschottische Lieder. Heidelberg, 1813.

Grundtvig, Svend. Engelske og skotiske Folkeviser med oplysende Anmærkninger, fordanskede. Kjøbenhavn, 1842-6.

—— Danmarks gamle Folkeviser, udgivne af ——. I-V (first half). Kjøbenhavn, 1853-78. V, completed by Axel Olrik, 1890.

—— Danske Ridderviser, efter Forarbeider af Svend Grundtvig udgivne af Axel Olrik. 1 Bind, 1, 2 Hæfte. København, 1895-96.

—— Folkelæsning. Danske Kæmpeviser og Folkesange fra Middelalderen, fornyede i gammel Stil. Kjøbenhavn, 1867.

—— Gamle danske Minder i Folkemunde : Folkeæventyr, Folkeviser, Folkesagn, samlede og udgivne af ——. Kjøbenhavn, 1854. Ny Samling, 1857.

Kristensen, E. T. Gamle jyske Folkeviser, samlede af Folkemunde (100 Gamle jyske F.; Gamle Viser i Folkemunde). Vols. I, II, X, XI, of Jyske Folkeminder. Kjøbenhavn, 1871-76, '89, '91.

—— Skattegraveren. 12 half-yearly parts. Kolding, 1884-89.

—— Efterslæt til Skattegraveren. Kolding, 1890.

Nyerup, Rasmus. Almindelig Morskabslæsning i Danmark og Norge. Kjøbenhavn, 1816.

Nyerup, R., og Rasmussen, P. Udvalg af danske Viser fra Midten af det 16de Aarhundrede til henimod Midten af det 18de. 2 vols. Kjøbenhavn, 1821.

Prior, R. C. Alexander. Ancient Danish Ballads, translated from the originals. 3 vols. London, Edinburgh and Leipzig, 1860.

Madsen, Jens. Folkeminder fra Hanved Sogn ved Flensborg, samlede og udgivne af ——. Kjøbenhavn, 1870.

Oehlenschläger, A. G. Gamle danske Folkeviser, utgivne af ——. Kjøbenhavn, 1840.

Olrik, Axel. Danske Ridderviser, efter Forarbeider af Svend Grundtvig udgivne af ——. 1 Bind, 1, 2 Hæfte. København, 1895.

Pontoppidan, Erik. Everriculum fermenti veteris, seu residuae in Danico orbe cum paganismi tum papismi reliquiae in apricum prolatae. Hafniae, 1736.

Rahbek, K. L. Læsning i blandede Æmner. Et Maanedsskrift af ——. 4 vols. Kjøbenhavn, 1821–23.

Rask, H. K. Morskabslæsning for den danske Almue, udgivet af ——. Kjøbenhavn, 1839–46. 4 vols.

[Sandvig, Berthel Christian.] Levninger af Middelalderens Digtekunst. Kjøbenhavn, 1780, 1784. 2 Hefter.

—— Beskrivelse over Møen. Kjøbenhavn, 1776.

Syv, Peder. Et Hundrede udvalde Danske Viser om allehaande merkelige Krigs-Bedrivt og anden selsom Eventyr. . . . Forøgede med det Andet Hundrede Viser om Danske Konger, Kæmper og Andre. Kjøbenhavn, 1695.

[Vedel, A. S.] Et hundrede vduaalde danske Viser. Ribe, 1591. Kjøbenhavn, 1632, 1643, 1671. Christiania, 1664.

—— Tragica, eller gamle danske historiske Elskoffs Viser. Kjøbenhavn, 1657.

Dutch, Flemish and Frisian.

Alberdingk-Thijm, J. A. Gedichten uit de verschillende Tijdperken der Noord- en Zuid-nederlandsche Literatuur, verzameld, naar Tijdsorde gerangschikt en toegelicht door ——. 2 vols. Amsterdam, 1850–52.

—— and L. J. Oude en nieuwere Kerstliederen. Amsterdam, 1852.

Antwerpener Liederbuch vom Jahre 1544. Herausgegeben von Hoffmann von Fallersleben. Hannover, 1855. (Horae Belgicae, studio atque opera Henrici Hoffmann Fallerslebensis, XI.)

Baecker, Louis de. Chants historiques de la Flandre, 400–1650. Lille, 1855.

Coussemaker, E. de. Chants populaires des Flamands de France. Gand, 1856.

Dykstra, W., and van der Meulen, T. G. In Doaze fol alde Snypsnaren. Oarde en folle formeardere Druk. Frjentsjer, 1882.

Fétis, François Joseph. Histoire générale de la Musique. 5 vols. Paris, 1869–76.

Hoffmann von Fallersleben. Niederländische Volkslieder. Gesammelt und erläutert. Zweite Ausgabe. Hannover, 1856.

Le Jeune, J. C. W. Letterkundig Overzigt en Proeven van de nederlandsche Volkszangen sedert de XVde Eeuw. Door ——. 's Gravenhage, 1828.

Lootens, Adolphe, and Feys, J. M. E. Chants populaires flamands, avec les airs notés, et poesies populaires diverses, recueillis à Bruges. Bruges, 1879.

Snellaert, F. A. Oude en nieuwe Liedjes, bijeen verzameld door ——. Tweede vermeerderde Uitgave. Gent, 1864.

Nederlandsch Liederboek, uitgegeven door het Willems-Fonds. 2 vols. Gent, 1891–92.

van Paemel, L., publisher. Oude Liedekens in Bladeren. Te Gend, by L. van Paemel, Boekdrukker op den Brabanddam.

Volkskunde. Tijdschrift voor nederlandsche Folklore, onder Redactie van Pol de Mont en Aug. Gittée. Gent, 1888–.

Willems, J. F. Oude vlæmsche Liederen. Gent, 1848.

Esthonian.

Dorpater Jahrbücher für Litteratur, Statistik und Kunst, besonders Russlands. 5 vols. Riga, Dorpat and Leipzig, 1833–36.

Fosterländskt Album. Utgifvet af H. Kellgren, R. Tengström, K. Tigerstedt. Helsingfors, I, II, 1845; III, 1847.

Hurt, Jakob. Vana Kannel. Alte Harfe. Vollständige Sammlung alter estnischer Volkslieder. Dorpat, 1875–86. (Erste, Zweite Sammlung, Dorpat, 1886.)

Neus, H. Ehstnische Volkslieder. Urschrift und Uebersetzung. Neval, 1850.

Rosenplänter, J. H. Beiträge zur genauern Kenntniss der ehstnischen Sprache. Herausgegeben von ——. 5 parts. Pernau, 1813–25.

Färöe.

Antiquarisk Tidsskrift, udgivet af det Kongelige Nordiske Oldskrift-Selskab. 7 vols. Kjøbenhavn, 1845–64.

Fugloyarbók. MS. collection, by Hans Hansson, of ballads of Fuglø : now included in Grundtvig and Block's Føroyja kvæði.

Grundtvig, Svend, and Block, Jörgen. Føroyja kvæði. Corpus Carminum Færoensium. MS. Royal Library, Copenhagen. 16 vols.

Hammershaimb, V. U. Færöiske Kvæder, samlede og besörgede ved ——. 2 vols. København, 1851, 1855.

Hammershaimb, V. U. Færøsk Anthologi. 2 vols. København, 1891 [1886–91].

Lyngbye, Hans Christian. Færøiske Qvæder om Sigurd Fofnersbane og hans Æt. Med et Anhang. Samlede og oversatte af ——. Randers, 1822.

Nyeste Skilderie af Kjøbenhavn. Udgivet, redigeret og forlagt af S. Soldin. Attende Aargang. Kjøbenhavn, 1821.

Svabo, Jens Kristjan. MS. 3 vols in Royal Library at Copenhagen: now included in Grundtvig and Block's Føroyja kvæði.

Finnish.

Finsk Tidskrift för Vitterhet, Vetenskap, Konst och Politik. Utgifven af C. G. Estlander. Vol. X. Helsingfors, 1881.

[Lönnrot, Elias.] Kanteletar, taikka Suomen kansan wanhoja lauluja ja wirsiä. [The Harp, or, The Finnish People's old Songs and Lays.] 2d ed. Helsingfors, 1864.

Schröter, H. R. von. Finnische Runen. Upsala, 1819. 2d ed., by G. H. v. Schröter. Stuttgart, 1834.

Flemish. See Dutch.

French and Provençal.

"Airs de Cour, comprenans le Trésor des Trésors, la Fleur des Fleurs, et Eslite des chansons amoureuses. Poictiers, 1607."

Almanach de Boulogne-sur-Mer pour 1863. Boulogne, 1863.

Almanach des Traditions populaires. [E. Rolland.] Paris, 1882.

[Ampère, J. J., and others.] Bulletin du Comité de la Langue, de l'Histoire et des Arts de la France, 1852–1857. Paris, 1854–60.

—— Instructions relatives aux Poésies Populaires de la France [rédigées par J. J. Ampère]. Extrait du Bulletin du Comité de la Langue, de l'Histoire, et des Arts de la France. Paris, 1853. [Vol. I, pp. 217–279, of the above.]

Arbaud, Damase. Chants populaires de la Provence, recueillis et annotés par ——. 2 vols. Aix, 1862–1864.

Atger, Aimé. Poésies populaires en Langue d' oc, recueillis par ——. Montpellier, 1875. (Extrait de la Revue des Langues romanes, t. VI.)

Aycard, Marie. Ballades et chants populaires de la Provence. Paris, 1826.

Basselin, Olivier. Vaux-de-vire d'Olivier Basselin, suivis d'un choix d'anciens vaux-de-vire, de bacchanales et de chansons, etc. Publiés par Louïs du Bois. Caen, 1821.

—— Vaux-de-vire d'Olivier Basselin et Jean le Houx, suivis d'un choix d'anciens vaux-de-vire et d'anciennes chansons normandes, etc. Nouv. éd. revue par P. L. Jacob [Paul Lacroix]. Paris, 1858.

Beauquier, Charles. Chansons populaires recueillies en Franche-Comté. Paris, 1894.

Beaurepaire, Eugène de. Étude sur la poésie populaire en Normandie, et spécialement dans l'Avranchin. Avranches et Paris, 1856.

Bladé, J. F. Poésies populaires en langue française, recueillies dans l'Armagnac et l'Agenais. Paris, 1879.

—— Poésies populaires de la Gascogne. 3 vols. Paris, 1881–82.

Bosquet, Amélie. La Normandie romanesque et merveilleuse. Paris and Rouen, 1845.

Buchon, Max. Noëls et chants populaires de la Franche-Comté. Salins, 1863.

Bujeaud, Jérome. Chants et chansons populaires des provinces de l'Ouest, Poitou, Saintonge, Aunis et Angoumois, avec les airs originaux. 2 vols. Niort, 1866.

Bulletin du Comité, etc. See Ampère, J. J.

Bulletin de Folklore. Société de Folklore Wallon. Tome II. Liége, 1893.

Champfleury [= Jules Fleury]. Chansons populaires des provinces de France. Paris, 1860.

Combes, Anacharsis. Chants populaires des Pays Castrais. Castres, 1862.

Le Chroniqueur du Périgord et du Limousin. Revue historique, artistique et religieuse, sous la direction de M. Armand de Siorac. Première année. Périgueux, 1853.

Dardy, L'abbé Léopold. Anthologie populaire de l'Albret. I. Poésies gasconnes. Agen, 1891.

Daudet, Alphonse. Numa Roumestan. Mœurs parisiennes. Paris, 1881.

Daymard, Joseph. Collection de vieilles chansons recueillies par M. Daymard, ingénieur civil à Serignac. In Bulletin de la Société des Études littéraires, scientifiques et artistiques du Lot. T. IV, 2e fascicule. Cahors, 1878.

—— Vieux chants populaires recueillis en Quercy, etc. Cahors, 1889.

Decombe, L. Chansons populaires recueillies dans le département d'Ille-et-Vilaine. Rennes, 1884.

de Gaspé, Philippe Aubert. Les anciens Canadiens. 2 vols. Québec, 1887.

Fleury, Jean. Littérature orale de la Basse-Normandie. Paris, 1883.

Gagnon, Ernest. Chansons populaires du Canada, recueillies et publiées avec annotations, etc. 2e éd. Québec, 1880.

Gasté, A. Chansons normandes du XVe siècle, publiées pour la première fois sur les MSS de Bayeux et de Vire. Caen, 1866.

[Gothier, J.] Recueil de crâmignons populaires français et wallons. Liége, 1882.

Guillon, Ch. Chansons populaires de l'Ain. Paris, 1883.

Haupt, Moriz. Französische Volkslieder zusammengestellt von —— und aus seinem Nachlass herausgegeben. Leipzig, 1877.

Laforest, Pierre. Limoges au XVII⁰ siècle. Limoges, 1862.

Laroche, Pierre (" P. Fagot "). Folk Lore de Lauragnais. 7 parts. Albi, 1891–94.

Legeay, Georges. Noëls anciens. Société générale de Libraire catholique. Paris and Bruxelles, n. d. (1875?).

Le Héricher, Édouard. Littérature populaire de Normandie. Avranches, 1884.

[Lovell, J.] Recueil de chansons canadiennes et françaises. Montréal, 1859.

Malo, Charles. Les chansons d'autrefois, vieux chants populaires de nos pères. Recueillis et annotés par ——. Paris, 1861.

Mélusine. Recueil de mythologie, littérature populaire, traditions et usages. Publié par MM. H. Gaidoz et E. Rolland. Paris, 1878–.

Meyrac, Albert. Traditions, coutumes, légendes et contes des Ardennes. Charleville, 1890.

Moncaut, Cénac. Littérature populaire de la Gascogne. Contes, mystères, chansons historiques, satiriques, sentimentales, rondeaux, recueillis dans l'Astarac, le Pardiac, le Béarn, et le Bigorre. Paris, 1868.

Le Moniteur Universel. Paris, 1853.

Montel, Achille, and Lambert, Louis. Chansons populaires du Languedoc. Paris, 1880.

Nerval, Gérard de (= Gérard Labrunie). La Bohème galante. Paris, 1866.

—— Les Filles du Feu. Paris, 1867.

—— Les Faux Saulniers. Œuvres Complètes, t. IV. Paris, 1868.

—— Chansons et ballades populaires du Valois, recueillies par ——. Paris, 1885.

Noëlas, Frédéric. Essai d'un romancero forézien. In Annales de la Société imperiale d'Agriculture, Industrie, Sciences, Arts et Belles-lettres du département de la Loire, t. IX. St.-Étienne, 1865.

Pineau, Léon. Le folk-lore du Poitou. Paris, 1892.

Poésies populaires de la France. MS. 6 vols. Bibliothèque Nationale, Paris. 1852. [A copy of this MS. is in the Library of Harvard College.]

Pouvillon, Émile. Nouvelles réalistes. Paris, 1878.

Puymaigre, Le comte [Théodore] de. Chants populaires recueillis dans le pays Messin, mis en ordre et annotés par ——. Metz et Paris, 1865. Nouvelle édition, augmentée de notes et de pièces nouvelles. 2 vols. Paris, 1881.

Questionnaire de folk-lore, publié par la Société du Folk-Lore Wallon. Liége, 1891.

Revue critique d'histoire et de littérature. Paris, 1866–.

Revue des Deux Mondes. Paris, 1849, 1854.

Revue des Provinces de l'Ouest, histoire, littérature, sciences et arts. Année I–VI. Nantes, 1853–57.

Revue des langues romanes. Montpellier et Paris, 1870–.

Revue des traditions populaires. Société des Traditions Populaires. Paris, 1886–.

Rolland, Eugène. Recueil de chansons populaires. 6 vols. Paris, 1883–90.

Romania. Recueil trimestriel, consacré à l'étude des langues et des littératures romanes. Publié par Paul Meyer et Gaston Paris. Paris, 1872–.

Rondes et chansons populaires, illustrées, avec musique. Paris, 1876.

Smith, Victor. Chansons populaires du Velay et du Forez. Chants de Pauvres en Forez et en Velay. Noëls du Velay et du Forez. See Romania.

—— Vieilles chansons recueillies en Velay et en Forez. (Extrait de la Romania, t. VII.) Paris, 1878.

Socard, Alexis. Noëls et cantiques imprimés à Troyes, depuis le XVII⁰ siècle jusqu'à nos jours. Paris, Troyes and Reims, 1865.

Soleville, Emmanuel. Chants populaires du Bas-Quercy, recueillis et notés. Paris, 1889.

Souvestre, Émile. Les Derniers Paysans. Paris, 1871.

Tarbé, P. Romancero de Champagne. Collection des Poètes de Champagne antérieurs au XVI⁰ siècle. Vols XX–XXIV. Rheims, 1863, 1864.

Terry, Léonard, and Chaumont, Léopold. Recueil d'airs de crâmignons et de chansons populaires à Liége. Liége, 1889. (Extrait du t. V de la 2⁰ série du Bulletin de la Société liégoise de Littérature wallonne.)

La Tradition. Revue générale des contes, légendes, chants, usages, traditions et arts populaires. Paris, 1887–.

Vaugeois, J. F. Gabriel. Histoire des antiquités de la ville de l'Aigle et de ses environs, etc. L'Aigle, 1841.

Wallonia. Recueil de Littérature orale, croyances et usages traditionnels. Fondé par O. Colson, Jos. Defrecheux et G. Willame. Liége, 1893–.

Wolff, O. L. B. Altfranzösische Volkslieder. Leipzig, 1831.

Frisian. See Dutch.

Gaelic.

Campbell, J. F. Leabhar na Feinne. Heroic Gaelic Ballads collected in Scotland chiefly from 1512 to 1871. Arranged by ——. London, 1872.

German.

Alemannia. Zeitschrift für Sprache, Litteratur und Volkskunde des Elsasses und Oberrheins (E., O. und Schwabens). Herausgegeben von A. Birlinger. Bonn, 1873–90. Zeitschrift für Sprache, Kunst und Altertum, besonders des alemannisch-schwäbischen Gebiets, fortgeführt von F. Pfaff. Bonn, 1892–.

Baumgarten, P. A. Aus der volksmässigen Ueberlieferung der Heimat. Linz, 1869.

Becker, Karl. Rheinischer Volksliederborn. Auswahl der edelsten und schönsten Volkslieder mit ihren Melodien der verschiedenen Gegenden der Rheinlande. Neuwied a/Rhein, [1892].

[Birlinger, Anton.] Schwäbische Volks-Lieder. Beitrag zur Sitte und Mundart des schwäbischen Volkes. Freiburg im Breisgau, 1864.

—— Schwäbisch - Augsburgisches Wörterbuch. München, 1864.

—— and Crecelius, W. Deutsche Lieder. Festgruss an L. Erk. Heilbronn, 1876.

Blätter für pommersche Volkskunde. Herausgegeben von D. Knoop und Dr. A. Haas. Stettin, 1892–.

Böckel, Otto. Deutsche Volkslieder aus Oberhessen. Marburg, 1885.

Böhme, Franz M. Altdeutsches Liederbuch. Volkslieder der Deutschen nach Wort und Weise, aus dem 12. bis zum 17. Jahrhundert, gesammelt und erläutert von ——. Leipzig, 1877.

—— Deutscher Liederhort . . . von Ludwig Erk . . . nach Erk's handschriftlichem Nachlasse und auf Grund eigener Sammlung neubearbeitet und fortgesetzt. 3 vols. Leipzig, 1893–94.

Börner, W. Volkssagen aus dem Orlagau, u. s. w. Altenburg, 1838.

[Brentano, Clemens.] Godwi oder Das steinerne Bild der Mutter. Ein verwilderter Roman von Maria. 2 vols. Bremen, 1801–02.

Briefe Goethes und der bedeutendsten Dichter seiner Zeit an Herder. Herausgegeben von Heinrich Düntzer und F. G. von Herder. Besonderer Abdruck aus der Sammlung Aus Herders Nachlass. Frankfurt am Main, 1858.

Bragur. Ein litterarisches Magazin der deutschen und nordischen Vorzeit. Herausgegeben von F. D. Gräter (und anderen). 8 vols. Leipzig, 1791–1805.

Büsching, Johann Gustav. Wöchentliche Nachrichten für Freunde der Geschichte, Kunst und Gelahrtheit des Mittelalters. 4 vols. Breslau, I, II, 1816; III, 1817; IV, 1819.

—— and von der Hagen, F. H. Sammlung deutscher Volkslieder, mit einem Anhange flammländischer und französischer, nebst Melodien. Berlin, 1807.

Deutsches Museum. [H. C. Boie and C. K. W. von Dohm.] 26 vols. Leipzig, 1776–88.

Ditfurth, Franz Wilhelm, Freiherr von. Fränkische Volkslieder, aus dem Munde des Volkes selbst gesammelt und herausgegeben von ——. Erster Theil, Geistliche Lieder ; Zweiter Theil, Weltliche Lieder. Leipzig, 1855.

—— Deutsche Volks- und Gesellschaftslieder des 17. und 18. Jahrhunderts. Wort und Weise gesammelt und herausgegeben von ——. Nördlingen, 1872.

Düntzer, Heinrich, and von Herder, F. G. Briefe Goethes und der bedeutendsten Dichter seiner Zeit an Herder. Besonderer Abdruck aus der Sammlung Aus Herders Nachlass. Frankfurt a. M., 1858.

Elwert, A. Ungedrukte Reste alten Gesangs nebst

Stücken neurer Dichtkunst. Giesen und Marburg, 1784.

Erk, Ludwig. Neue Sammlung deutscher Volkslieder mit ihren eigenthümlichen Melodien. Berlin, 1841–45. (Vols. I, II, in 6 Hefte, and Vol. III, 1st Heft.)

—— Deutscher Liederhort. Auswahl der vorzüglichern deutschen Volkslieder aus der Vorzeit und der Gegenwart mit ihren eigenthümlichen Melodien. Berlin, 1856. For new edition see Böhme, Franz M.

—— and Irmer, Wilhelm. Die deutschen Volkslieder mit ihren Singweisen. Gesammelt und herausgeben von ——. Zweite Ausgabe in Einem Bande. Leipzig, 1843.

Erlach, Friedrich Karl, Freiherr von. Die Volkslieder der Deutschen. Eine vollständige Sammlung der vorzüglichen deutschen Volkslieder von der Mitte des fünfzehnten bis in die erste Hälfte des neunzehnten Jahrhunderts. Herausgegeben und mit den Bemerkungen und Hinweisungen versehen, wo die verschiedenen Lieder aufgefunden werden können. 5 vols. Mannheim, 1834–36.

Eschenburg, Johann Joachim. Denkmäler altdeutscher Dichtkunst, beschrieben und erläutert. Bremen, 1799.

Fiedler, Eduard. Volksreime und Volkslieder in Anhalt-Dessau. Gesammelt und herausgegeben von ——. Dessau, 1847.

Firmenich, J. M. Germaniens Völkerstimmen. Sammlung der deutschen Mundarten in Dichtungen, Sagen, Mährchen, Volksliedern, u. s. w. 3 vols. and Nachträge. Berlin, [1843]–67.

Forster, Georgius. Frische Liedlein. Nürnberg, 1552, 1560.

Frankfurter Liederbuch. Lieder Büchlein, darin begriffen sind zweyhundert vnd sechtzig allerhand schöner weltlicher Lieder, u. s. w. Frankfurt a. M., 1584.

Frischbier, H., and Sembrzycki, J. Hundert ostpreussische Volkslieder in hochdeutscher Sprache. Leipzig, 1893.

Frommann, G. Karl. Die deutschen Mundarten. Eine Monatschrift [Vierteljahrsschrift] für Dichtung, Forschung und Kritik. Begründet von J. A. Pangkofer, fortgesetzt von ——. 6 vols. Nürnberg, 1854–57; Nördlingen, 1858–59. 7th vol., Halle, 1877 (Zeitschrift, u. s. w.).

[Herder, J. G. v.] Volkslieder. Erster Theil. Leipzig, 1778. Zweiter Theil. Volkslieder (nebst untermischten andern Stücken). Leipzig, 1779.

Herrmann, E., and Pogatschnigg, D. Deutsche Volks-Lieder aus Kärnten. Gesammelt u. ausgewählt von ——. Salon-Ausgabe. Graz, 1884.

Hoffmann von Fallersleben, and Richter, Ernst. Schlesische Volkslieder mit Melodien. Aus dem Munde des Volks gesammelt und herausgegeben von ——. Leipzig, 1842.

Hruschka, Alois, and Toischer, Wendelin. Deutsche

Volkslieder aus Böhmen. 3 Lieferungen. Prag, 1888–89.

Jahn, Ulrich. Volkssagen aus Pommern und Rügen. Gesammelt und herausgegeben von ——. Stettin, 1886.

Kind, Friedrich. Auserwählte Unterhaltungen. 10 vols. Wien, 1827.

Knoop, Otto. Volkssagen, Erzählungen, Aberglauben, Gebräuche und Märchen aus dem östlichen Hinterpommern. Posen, 1885.

Köhler, Joh. Aug. Ernst. Volksbrauch, Aberglauben, Sagen, und andre alte Ueberlieferungen im Voigtlande. Leipzig, 1867.

Körner, Ph. Max. Historische Volkslieder aus dem sechzehnten und siebenzehnten Jahrhundert, nach den in der k. Hof- und Staatsbibliothek zu München vorhandenen fliegenden Blättern gesammelt und herausgegeben von ——. Mit einem Vorworte von J. A. Schmeller. Stuttgart, 1840.

Kretzschmer, Andreas. Deutsche Volkslieder mit ihren Original-Weisen. Unter Mitwirkung des Herrn Professor Dr. Massmann in München, des Herrn von Zuccalmaglio in Warschau, und mehrerer anderer Freunde der Volks-Poesie, nach handschriftlichen Quellen herausgegeben und mit Anmerkungen versehen von ——. Erster Theil. Berlin, 1840.

Kurz, Heinrich. Aeltere Dichter. Schlacht- und Volkslieder der Schweizer. In einer Auswahl herausgegeben von ——. Zurich, 1860.

Lemke, Elisabeth. Volksthümliches in Ostpreussen. 2 pts. Mohrungen, 1884–87.

Lewalter, Johann. Deutsche Volkslieder in Niederhessen aus dem Munde des Volkes gesammelt. 5 Hefte. Hamburg, 1890–94.

von Liliencron, R. Die historischen Volkslieder der Deutschen vom 13. bis 16. Jahrhundert. Gesammelt und erläutert von ——. 4 vols and Nachtrag. Leipzig, 1865–69.

[Longard, J. B.] Altrheinländische Mährlein und Liedlein, grosse und kleine, hübsche und reine, zarte und feine, so man von alters her in rheinischen Landen aller Enden hört singen und pfeifen. Zu besserer Gedächtniss und seinen Landsleuten zu Nutz und Frommen ganz treulich und fleissiglich gesammelt und in dies Büchlein gebracht durch einen Liebhaber teutscher Poeterei. Coblenz, 1843.

Lütolf, Alois. Sagen, Bräuche und Legenden aus den fünf Orten Lucern, Uri, Schwyz, Unterwalden und Zug. Lucern, 1865.

Meier, Ernst. Deutsche Kinder-Reime und Kinder-Spiele aus Schwaben. Aus dem Volksmunde gesammelt und herausgegaben von ——. Tübingen, 1851.

—— Schwäbische Volks-Lieder. Mit ausgewählten Melodien. Aus mündlicher Ueberlieferung gesammelt von ——. Berlin, 1855.

Meinert, Joseph Georg. [Der Fylgie.] Alte teutsche

Volkslieder in der Mundart des Kuhländchens. Herausgegeben und erläutert von ——. Erster Band. Wien und Hamburg, 1817.

Mittler, Franz Ludwig. Deutsche Volkslieder. Sammlung von ——. Marburg und Leipzig, 1855. 2ᵉ Ausg. Frankfurt am Main, 1865.

Montanus. See Vincenz von Zuccalmaglio.

Müllenhof, Karl. Sagen, Märchen und Lieder der Herzogthümer Schleswig-Holstein und Lauenburg. Kiel, 1845.

Müller, Alfred. Volkslieder aus dem Erzgebirge. Annaberg, 1883.

Mündel, Curt. Elsässische Volkslieder. Strassburg, 1884.

Münsterische Geschichten. Sagen und Legenden, nebst einem Anhange von Volksliedern und Sprüchwörtern. Münster, 1825.

Neocorus. Johann Adolfis, genannt Neocorus, Chronik des Landes Dithmarschen. Aus der Urschrift herausgegeben von Prof. F. C. Dahlmann. 2 vols. Kiel, 1827.

Der neuen Preussischen Provinzial-Blätter andere Folge. Herausgegeben von Dr. A. Hagen. Band III. Königsberg, 1853.

Nicolai, Friedrich. Eyn feyner kleyner Almanach vol schönerr echterr liblicher Volckslieder, lustigerr Reyen vnndt kleglicherr Mordgeschichte, gesungen von Gabriel Wunderlich weyl. Benkelsengerrn zu Dessaw, herausgegeben von Daniel Seuberlich, Schusterrn tzu Ritzmück ann der Elbe. Erster Jahrgang, Berlynn vnndt Stettynn, 1777. Zweiter Jargang, 1778. Verlegts Friedrich Nicolai.

Niederdeutsche Volkslieder, gesammelt und herausgegeben vom Vereine für niederdeutsche Sprachforschung, Heft 1. Die niederdeutschen Liederbücher von Uhland und de Bouck. Hamburg, 1883.

[Norrenberg, P.] Niederrheinische Volkslieder, im alten Mühlgau gesammelt von Dr. Hans Zurmühlen. Zweite Ausgabe von: Des Dülkener Fiedlers Liederbuch. Viersen, 1875. Leipzig, 1879.

Pailler, Wilhelm. Weihnachtlieder aus Oberösterreich. Gesammelt und herausgegeben von ——. Innsbruck, 1881.

Parisius, Ludolf. Deutsche Volkslieder mit ihren Singweisen, geistliche Lieder und Balladen, in der Altmark und im Magdeburgischen aus Volksmunde gesammelt von ——. Erstes Heft. Magdeburg, 1879.

Paudler, A. Nordböhmische Volkslieder. Böhm.-Leipa, 1877.

Peter, Anton. Volksthümliches aus Osterreichisch-Schlesien. Gesammelt und herausgegeben von ——. 3 vols. Troppau, 1865–73.

Pogatschnigg, V., and Herrmann, Emanuel. Deutsche Volks-Lieder aus Kärnten. Gesammelt von ——. 2 vols. Graz, 1869.

Pröhle, Heinrich. Weltliche und geistliche Volks-lieder und Volksschauspiele. Mit einer Musikbei-lage. Aschersleben, 1855.

Reifferscheid, Alexander. Westfälische Volkslieder, in Wort und Weise, mit Klavier-begleitung und liedervergleichenden Anmerkungen. Heilbronn, 1879.

Richter, L., and Marschner, A. E. Alte und neue Volks-Lieder, mit Bildern und Singweisen. Her-ausgegeben von ——. Leipzig, n. d.

Rochholz, Ernst Ludwig. Schweizersagen aus dem Aargau. Gesammelt und erläutert von ——. 2 vols. Aarau, 1856.

Rosegger, Petri Kettenfeier, and Heuberger, Richard. Volkslieder aus Steiermark, mit Melodieen. Pest, 1872.

Schade, Oskar. Bergreien. Eine Liedersammlung des XVI. Jahrhunderts, nach dem Exemplare der Groszherzoglichen Bibliothek zu Weimar her-ausgegeben von ——. Weimar, 1854.

Scherer, Georg. Deutsche Volkslieder. Gesammelt von ——. 2ᵉ Auflage. Leipzig, 1851.

—— Deutsche Volkslieder mit ihren eigenthümli-chen Singweisen. Gesammelt und herausgegeben von ——. Stuttgart, Heft I, 1854; Heft II, 1855.

—— Jungbrunnen. Die schönsten deutschen Volkslieder, gesammelt von ——. (Dritte Auflage der "Deutschen Volkslieder".) Berlin, 1875.

Scleicher, Aug. Volksthümliches aus Sonneberg im Meininger Oberlande. Weimar, 1858.

Schlossar, Anton. Deutsche Volkslieder aus Steier-mark. Innsbruck, 1881.

Schmeller, J. A. Die Mundarten Bayerns gramma-tisch dargestellt. München, 1821.

[Schmid, C. H., and Dyck, J. G.] Taschenbuch für Dichter und Dichterfreunde. Achte Abtheilung, 1778. Leipzig, 1774–81 (12 Abtheilungen).

Schmitz, Jacob H. Sitten und Sagen, u. s. w., des Eifler Volkes, herausgegeben von ——. 2 vols. Trier, 1856, 1858.

Schröer, K. J. Ein Ausflug nach Gottschee. Bei-trag zur Erforschung der Gottscheewer Mundart. Wiener Akademie. Sitzb. d. Phil.-hist. Cl., LX, 1868. Wien, 1869.

Schuster, Fried. Wilhelm. Siebenbürgisch-sächs-ische Volkslieder, Sprichwörter, Räthsel, Zauber-formeln und Kinder-Dichtungen. Hermannstadt, 1865.

Schweizerblätter. Eine Monatschrift, herausgegeben von A. Henne und I. I. Reithard. II. Jahrgang, St. Gallen, 1833.

Seckendorff, Leo, Freiherr von. Musenalmanach für das Jahr 1808. Regensburg.

Seuffert, Bernhard. Maler Müller. Im Anhang, Mittheilungen aus Müller's Nachlass. Berlin, 1877.

Simrock, K. Die geschichtlichen deutschen Sagen, aus dem Munde des Volkes und deutscher Dichter. Frankfurt am Main, 1850.

Simrock, K. Die deutschen Volkslieder. Gesam-melt von ——. Frankfurt am Main, 1851.

Spee, Johannes. Volksthümliches vom Niederrhein. 2 Hefte. Köln, 1875.

Tobler, Ludwig. Schweizerische Volkslieder. 2 vols. Frauenfeld, 1882–84.

Tschischka, F., and Schottky, J. M. Oesterrei-chische Volkslieder, mit ihren Singweisen. Gesam-melt und herausgegeben durch ——. Zweite ver-besserte und vermehrte Auflage, besorgt von Franz Tschischka. Pesth, 1844. (1ᵉ Auflage, 1818.)

Uhland, Ludwig. Alte hoch- und niederdeutsche Volkslieder, in fünf Büchern, herausgegeben von ——. 2 Abtheilungen. Stüttgart und Tübingen, 1844–45.

Walter, Wilibald. Sammlung deutscher Volkslieder welche noch gegenwärtig im Munde des Volkes leben und in keiner der bisher erschienenen Samm-lungen zu finden sind. Herausgegeben von ——. Leipzig, 1841.

Wittstock, Heinrich. Sagen und Lieder aus dem Nösner Gelände. Bistritz, 1860.

Wolf, Adam. Volkslieder aus dem Egerlande. Ge-sammelt und herausgegeben von ——. Eger, 1869.

Wolfram, Ernst H. Nassauische Volkslieder nach Wort und Weise aus dem Munde des Volks ge-sammelt, u. s. w. Berlin, 1894.

Wunderhorn. Des Knaben Wunderhorn. Alte deutsche Lieder gesammelt von L. Achim v. Arnim und Clemens Brentano. 3 vols. Heidel-burg : I, 1806; II, III, 1808. Erster Theil, Zweite Auflage, 1819.

—— Des Knaben Wunderhorn. Alte deutsche Lieder gesammelt von L. A. von Arnim und Clemens Brentano. Vierter Theil, nach A. v. Arnim's handschriftlichen Nachlass herausgegeben von Ludwig Erk. Berlin, 1857.

—— Des Knaben Wunderhorn. Alte deutsche Lieder gesammelt von L. A. v. Arnim und Clemens Brentano. Neu bearbeitet von Anton Birlinger und Wilhelm Crecelius. Vol. I, Wiesbaden, 1874; II, Wiesbaden und Leipzig, 1876.

Zacher's Zeitschrift. See Zeitschrift für deutsche Philologie.

Zarnack, August. Deutsche Volkslieder mit Volk-weisen für Volksschulen, nebst einer Abhandlung über das Volkslied. Erster Theil, Berlin, 1818; Zweiter Theil, Berlin, 1820.

Zeitschrift für deutsche Philologie herausgegeben von Ernst Höpfner und Julius Zacher (von Hugo Gering). Halle, 1869–.

Zuccalmaglio, A. Wilhelm von. Deutsche Volkslie-der mit ihren Original-Weisen. Unter Mitwir-kung des Herrn Professor Dr. E. Baumstark und meherer anderer Freunde der Volks-Dichtung, als Forsetzung des A. Kretzschmer'schen Werkes, gesammelt und mit Anmerkungen versehen. Zwei-ter Theil, Berlin, 1840.

[Zuccalmaglio, Vincenz von.] Die deutschen Volks-

feste. Ein Beitrag zur vaterländischen Sitten-
geschichte, von Montanus. Iserlohn und Elberfeld,
1854.

Gipsy.
Wlislocki, H. v. Volksdichtungen der siebenbürgischen und südungarischen Zigeuner. Wien, 1890.

Icelandic.
Grundtvig, Svend, and Sigurðsson, Jón. Íslenzk
Fornkvæði. Kjøbenhavn, I, 1854–58 ; II, 1859–85.

Italian.
Alexander, Francesca. Roadside Songs of Tuscany,
translated and illustrated by ——; and edited by
John Ruskin, 10 parts. New York, 1885 [1884–85].
Archivio per lo studio delle tradizioni popolari. Ri-
vista trimestrale, diretta da G. Pitrè e S. Salo-
mone-Marino. Palermo, 1882–.
Barbi, Michele. Poesia popolare pistoiese. Firenze,
1895.
Bernoni, Dom Giuseppe. Canti popolari veneziani,
raccolti da ——. Venezia, 1872.
—— Nuovi canti popolari veneziani, raccolti da
——. Venezia, 1874.
—— Tradizioni popolari veneziane, raccolte da
——. Venezia, 1875.
Biblioteca di letteratura popolare italiana, publicata
per cura di Severino Ferrari. 1 vol., and 2 fascicoli of a 2ᵈ. Firenze, 1882–83.
Bolognini, Nepomuceno. Usi e costumi del Tren-
tino. Le Leggende del Trentino. Rovereto, 1885–
89. *In* Annuario della Società degli Alpinisti Tri-
dentini, XI–XIV.
Bolza, Giambattista. Canzoni. popolari comasche,
raccolte e publicate colle melodie. (Sitzungsbe-
richte der Phil.-Hist. Classe der Kaiserl. Akademie,
LIII, 637–95.) Wien, 1867.
La Calabria. Rivista di letteratura popolare. Diretta da Luigi Bruzzano. Monteleone, 1888–.
Casetti, Antonio, and Imbriani, Vittorio. Canti
popolari delle provincie meridionali. 2 vols.
Torino, etc., 1871–72.
Dalmedico, Angelo. Canti del popolo veneziano, per
la prima volta raccolti ed illustrati da ——. 2ᵈ ed.
Venezia, 1857.
D' Ancona, Alessandro. La poesia popolare italiana.
Livorno, 1878.
De Nino, Antonio. Saggio di canti popolari sabi-
nesi, illustrati da ——. Rieti, 1869.
Ferraro, Giuseppe. Canti popolari monferrini, raccolti ed annotati dal Dr. ——. Torino, Firenze,
1870.
—— Nuova raccolta di canti popolari monferrini,
per ——. Estratto dalla Rivista Europea. Firenze,
1875.
—— Canti popolari di Ferrara, Cento e Pontelagoscuro, raccolti per cura del Prof. ——. Ferrara, 1877.

Ferraro, Giuseppe. Canti popolari del Basso Mon-
ferrato, raccolti ed annotati da ——. Palermo,
1888.
—— Canti popolari in dialetto logudorese, raccolti
per cura di ——. Torino, 1891.
Gianandrea, Antonio. Canti popolari marchigiani,
raccolti e annotati dal Prof. ——. Roma, Torino,
Firenze, 1875.
Giannini, Giovanni. Canti popolari della Montagna
Lucchese, raccolti e annotati da ——. Torino,
1889.
Giornale di filologia romanza. Diretto da Ernesto
Monaci. 4 vols. Roma, 1878–83.
Guerrini, Olindo. Alcuni canti popolari romagnoli,
raccolti da ——. Bologna, 1880.
Ive, Antonio. Canti popolari istriani, raccolti a
Rovigno ed annotati da ——. Roma, Torino,
Firenze, 1877.
Kaden, Woldemar. Italiens Wunderhorn. Volks-
lieder aus allen Provinzen der Halbinsel und Sicili-
ens in deutscher Uebertragung. Stuttgart, 1878.
Kopisch, August. Agrumi. Volksthümliche Poesieen
aus allen Mundarten Italiens und seiner Inseln.
Gesammelt und übersetzt. Berlin, 1838.
Marcoaldi, Oreste. Canti popolari inediti umbri,
liguri, piceni, piemontesi, latini, raccolti e illus-
trati da ——. Genova, 1855.
Mazzatinti, Giuseppe. Canti popolari umbri raccolti
a Gubbio e illustrati da ——. Bologna, 1883.
Nannarelli, Fabio. Studio comparativo sui canti
popolari di Arlena. Roma, 1871.
Nigra, Costantino. Canzoni popolari del Piemonte
in Rivista Contemporanea, Vols. XII, XIII, XV,
XX, XXIV, XXXI. Torino, 1858–62.
—— Canti popolari del Piemonte, pubblicati da
——. Torino, 1888.
Nuove Effemeridi Siciliani. 2ᵈ serie, I. Palermo,
1875.
Oesterreichische Wochenschrift für Wissenschaft,
Kunst, und öffentliches Leben, I. Wien, 1863.
Pitrè, Giuseppe. Studi di poesia popolare. Palermo,
1872.
—— Canti popolari siciliani, raccolti ed illustrati
da ——. Preceduti da uno studio critico dello
stesso autore. 2 vols. Palermo, 1870–71.
—— —— Secunda edizione, interamente rifusa. 2
vols. Palermo, 1891.
La Rassegna settimanale di politica, scienze, lettere
ed arti. Vol. III. Roma, 1879.
Ricordi, Giulio. Canti popolari lombardi, raccolti,
etc. Fasc. I. Canti milanesi. Milano, [1857].
Righi, Ettore Scipione. Saggio di canti popolari
veronesi, per cura di ——. Verona, [1863].
La Rivista Europea. Firenze, 1869–76.
Rivista Contemporanea. Vols. XII, XIII, XV, XX,
XXIV, XXXI. Torino, 1858–62. See Nigra, C.
Rivista di filologia romanza, diretta da L. Manzoni,
E. Monaci, E. Stengel. 2 vols. Imola and Roma,
1872–75.

Rivista di Letteratura popolare diretta da G. Pitrè e Francesco Sabatini. 4 fascicoli. Roma, 1877–79.

Rivista delle Tradizioni popolari italiane, diretta da Angelo de Gubernatis. II. Roma, 1894.

Salomone-Marino, Salvatore. Leggende popolari siciliane in poesia, raccolte ed annotate da ——. Palermo, 1880.

Tigri, Giuseppe. Canti popolari toscani, raccolti e annotati da ——. 2ᵈ ed. Firenze, 1860.

Trifone Nutricati-Briganti, A. Intorno ai canti e racconti popolari del Luccese. Wien [Lecce], 1873.

Vigo, Lionardo. Canti popolari siciliani raccolti e illustrati da ——. Catania, 1857.

—— Raccolta amplissima di canti popolari siciliani. 2ª ed. Catania, 1870–74.

Visconti, P. E. Saggio de' canti popolari della provincia Marittima e Campagna. Roma, 1830.

Widter und Wolf. Volkslieder aus Venetien. Gesammelt von Georg Widter, herausgegeben von Adolf Wolf. Wien, 1864. (Akademie der Wissenschaften, Phil.-hist. Classe, Sitzungsberichte, XLVI.)

Wolff, O. L. B. Egeria. Sammlung italienischer Volkslieder . . . begonnen von Wilhelm Mueller, vollendet, u. s. w., von ——. Leipzig, 1829.

Ladin.

Flugi, Alfons von. Die Volkslieder des Engadin. Nebst einem Anhange engadinischer Volkslieder im Original und in deutscher Uebersetzung. Strassburg, 1873.

Lettish.

Dorpater Jahrbücher für Litteratur, Statistik und Kunst, besonders Russlands. 5 vols. Riga und Dorpat, 1833–36.

Tielemann, G. T. Livona. Ein historisch-poetisches Taschenbuch für die deutsch-russischen Ostseeprovinzen. 2 vols. Riga und Dorpat, 1812, 1816.

Ulmann, Karl. Lettische Volkslieder übertragen im Versmaass der Originale. Riga, 1874.

Lithuanian.

Bartsch, Christian. Dainu Balsai. Melodieen litauischer Volkslieder, u. s. w. Heidelberg. Erster Theil, 1886 ; Zweiter Theil, 1889.

Beiträge zur Kunde Preussens. 7 vols. Königsberg, 1818–24.

Bezzenberger, Adalbert. Litauische Forschungen. Beiträge zur Kenntniss der Sprache und des Volkstumes der Litauer. Göttingen, 1882.

Leskien, A., and Brugman, K. Litauische Volkslieder und Märchen. Strassburg, 1882.

Nesselmann, G. H. F. Littauische Volkslieder, gesammelt, kritisch bearbeitet und metrisch übersetzt von ——. Berlin, 1853.

Rhesa, L. J. Dainos oder Litthauische Volkslieder, gesammelt, übersetzt, u. s. w., von ——. Königsberg, 1825 ; Neue Auflage, verbessert von Fried. Kurschat, Berlin, 1843.

Magyar.

Aigner, Ludvig. Ungarische Volksdichtungen, übersetzt und eingeleitet von ——. 2ᵉ Auflage. Budapest, [1879].

Arany, J. Koszorú, 1864. Szépirodalmi sátalános miveltség terjesztö hetilap. Szerkeszti ——. Pest, 1863–.

Arany, Lázló, and Gyulai, Pál. Magyar népköltési gyüjtemény. Uj folyam. [Collection of Magyar Popular Poetry. New Series.] Pest, I, II, 1872; III, 1882.

Erdélyi, János. Népdalok és mondák : a Kisfaludy-Társaság megbizásábul szerkeszti és kiadja. [Popular Songs and Tales collected and edited at the instance of the Kisfaludy Society.] 3 vols. Pest, 1846–48.

Herrmann, Anton. Ethnologische Mitteilungen aus Ungarn. Zeitschrift für die Volkskunde der Bewohner Ungarns und seiner Nebenländer. Budapest, 1887–96.

Kálmány, Lájos. Koszorúk az Alföld vad virágaiból. [Garlands from Alföld Fieldflowers.] Aradon, 1877–78. 2 vols.

Kertbeny [= K. M. Benkert]. Ausgewählte ungarische Volkslieder. Darmstadt, 1851.

Kríza, János. Vadrózsák. Székely népköltési gyüjtemény, szerkeszti ——. [Wild Roses. A collection of Szekler popular poetry, edited by ——.] vol. I. Kolozsvártt, 1863.

Ungarische Revue. Mit Unterstützung der Ungarischen Akademie der Wissenschaften herausgegeben von Paul Hunfalvy und Gustav Heinrich. Leipzig, etc., 1881–.

Norwegian.

Bugge, Sophus. Gamle norse Folkeviser, samlede og udgivne af ——. Kristiania, 1858.

Landstad, M. B. Norske Folkeviser, samlede og udgivne af ——. Christiania, 1853.

Lindeman, L. M. Ældre og nyere norske Fjeldmelodier, samlede og bearbeidede for Pianoforte. Kristiania, 1853–67. 3 vols and 1 hefte. Ny revideret udgave. 2 vols. Kristiania, 1878 (?).

Moe, J. M., and Mortenson, Ivar. Norske Fornkvæde og Folkevisur, tilskipade ved ——. I. Kristiania, 1877.

Norske Universitets- og Skole-Annaler. Kristiania, 1834–.

Nytaarsgave for Illustreret Nyhedsblads Abonnenter, udgivet af P. Botten-Hansen. Christiania, 1860.

Portuguese and Galician.

Almeida-Garrett. Romanceiro pelo Visconde de Almeida-Garrett. 3 vols. Lisboa, 1863. [4ᵃ ed. of

vol. I, Romances da renascença : 2ª ed. of vols
II, III, Romances cavalherescos antigos.]

Azevedo, Alvaro Rodrigues de. Romanceiro do
Archipelago da Madeira, colligido e publicado por
——. Funchal, 1880.

Bellermann, Christ. Fr. Portugiesische Volkslieder
und Romanzen, portugiesisch und deutsch, mit
Anmerkungen herausgegeben von ——. Leipzig,
1864.

Braga, Theophilo. Romanceiro geral, colligido da
tradição por ——. Coimbra, 1867.

—— Cantos populares do Archipelago Açoriano.
Publicados e annotados por ——. Porto, 1869.

—— Amplições ao Romanceiro das Ilhas dos
Açores, in Revista Lusitana, I, 99 ff.

Coelho, F. A. Romances populares e rimas infantis
portuguezes. In Zeitschrift für romanische Philologie, III, 1879.

Hardung, Victor Eugenio. Romanceiro portuguez,
coordinado, annotado e acompanhado d'uma introducção e d'um glossario. 2 vols. Leipzig, 1877.

Iglesia, Antonio de la. El idioma gallego, su antigüedad y vida. 3 vols. La Coruña, 1886.

Revista Lusitana. Archivo de estudos philologicos
e ethnologicos relativos a Portugal, publicado por
J. Leite de Vasconcellos. Porto, 1887–92. 2 vols.

Rodrigues de Azevedo. See Azevedo.

Roméro, Sylvio. Cantos populares do Brazil, colligido pelo Dr. ——, acompanhados de introducção
e notas comparativas por Theophilo Braga. 2 vols.
Lisboa, 1883.

Veiga, Estacio da. Romanceiro do Algarve. Lisboa, 1870.

Romaic (and Italian Greek).

Arabantinos, Panagiotes. Συλλογὴ δημῴδων ᾀσμάτων
τῆς Ἠπείρου. Athens, 1880.

Bartholdy, J. L. S. Bruchstücke zur näheren Kent-
niss des heutigen Griechenlands, u. s. w. Erster
Theil. Berlin, 1805.

Chasiotes, G. Chr. Συλλογὴ τῶν κατὰ τὴν Ἤπειρον
δημοτικῶν ᾀσμάτων. Athens, 1866.

Δελτίον τῆς Ἱστορικῆς καὶ Ἐθνολογικῆς Ἑταιρίας τῆς
Ἑλλάδος. 4 vols. Athens, 1883–92.

Eulampios, K. Ὁ Ἀμάραντος, ἤτοι τὰ ῥόδα τῆς ἀναγεν-
νηθείσης Ἑλλάδος. St Petersburg, 1843.

Fauriel, C. Chants populaires de la Grèce moderne.
2 vols. Paris, 1824–25.

Garnett, Lucy M. J. Greek Folk-Songs from the
Turkish Provinces of Greece, literal and metrical
translation by ——. Classified, revised and edited
by J. S. Stuart Glennie. London, 1885.

Jeannaraki, Anton. Ἄσματα Κρητικά. Leipzig, 1876.

Joannides, Sab. Ἱστορία καὶ στατιστικὴ Τρ[α]πεζοῦντος,
καὶ τῆς περὶ ταύτην χώρας. Constantinople, 1870.

Kanellakes, K. N. Χιακὰ Ἀνάλεκτα. Athens, 1890.

Kind, Theodor. Anthologie neugriechischer Volkslieder. Im Original, mit deutscher Uebersetzung.
Leipzig, 1861.

Legrand, Émile. Recueil de chansons populaires
grecques. Paris, 1874.

Lemercier, N. Chants héroiques des montagnards
et matelots grecs, traduits en vers français. Paris,
1824.

Manousos, Antonios. Τραγούδια ἐθνικὰ συναγμένα καὶ
διασαφηνισμένα ὑπὸ ——. 2 parts. Corcyra, 1850.

Marcellus, Marie Louis de. Chants du peuple en
Grèce. 2 vols. Paris, 1851.

Νεοελληνικὰ Ἀνάλεκτα, περιοδικῶς ἐκδιδόμενα ὑπὸ τοῦ
φιλολογικοῦ συλλόγου Παρνασσοῦ. Athens, I, 1870–72;
II, 1874–81.

Oikonomides, Athanasios K. Τραγούδια τοῦ Ὀλύμπου
συλλεγέντα ὑπὸ ——. Athens, 1881.

Πανδώρα. Σύγγραμμα περιοδικόν. Athens, [1850]–72.

Passow, A. Carmina popularia Graeciae recentioris.
Leipzig, 1860.

Φιλολογικὸς Συνέκδημος. Σύγγραμμα περιοδικὸν ὑπὸ λογίων
ἀνδρῶν συντασσόμενον. Athens, 1849.

Sakellarios, Athanasios A. Τὰ Κυπριακά. III. Athens, 1868.

Schmidt, B. Griechische Märchen, Sagen und
Volkslieder. Leipzig, 1877.

Sheridan, C. B. The Songs of Greece, from the
Romaic text edited by M. C. Fauriel, with additions, translated by ——. London, 1825.

Tommaséo, N. Canti popolari toscani, corsi, illirici,
greci. 4 vols. Venezia, 1841–42.

Zampelios, Spuridion. Ἄσματα δημοτικὰ τῆς Ἑλλάδος.
Corcyra, 1852.

Ζωγραφεῖος Ἀγών, ἤτοι Μνημεῖα τῆς ἑλλ. ἀρχαιότητος
ζῶντα ἐν τῷ νῦν Ἑλληνικῷ λαῷ. Vol. I. Constantinople, 1891.

Comparetti, Domenico. Saggi dei dialetti greci dell'
Italia meridionale, raccolti ed illustrati da ——.
Pisa, 1866.

Morosi, Giuseppe. Studi sui dialetti greci della
terra d' Otranto, preceduto da una raccolta dei
canti, etc. Lecce, 1870.

[Pellegrini, Astorre.] Canti popolari dei Greci di
Cargese (Corsica). Bergamo, 1871.

Roumanian.

Alecsandri, Vasile. Poesiĭ populare ale Românilor,
adunate şi întocmite de ——. Bucuresci, 1866.

—— Ballades et chants populaires de la Roumanie
(principautés danubiennes) recueillis et traduits
par ——. Paris, 1855.

Marienescu, At. Marianu. Poesia popurala, Balade;
culese si corese de ——. Pest'a, 1859.

Mironu, Pompiliu. Balade populare Române, adunate
de ——. Iassi, 1870.

Möckesch, S. Romänische Dichtungen ins Deutsche
übersetzt von ——. Hermannstadt, 1851.

Murray, E. C. Grenville. The National Songs and
Legends of Roumania. London, 1859.

Schuller, J. K. Romänische Volkslieder, metrisch
übersetzt und erläutert von ——. Hermannstadt,
1859.

Stanley, Henry. Rouman Anthology, or, Selections of Rouman Poetry, Ancient and Modern, being a collection of the National Ballads of Moldavia and Wallachia, etc., with an appendix containing translations of the poems, notes, etc. Hertford, 1856.

Slavic.

Ahacel, Matija, and Korytko, Emil. Slovénske pésmi krajnskiga naróda. [Slovenian Songs of the Carniola people.] 5 parts. Laibach, 1839–44.

Altmann, Julius. Die Balalaika. Russische Volkslieder, gesammelt und in's Deutsche übertragen von ——. Berlin, 1863.

Antonovič, Vl., and Dragomanov, M. Istoričeskija pěsni malorusskago naroda. [Historical Poems of the Malorussians.] 2 vols. Kiev, 1874–5.

Bartoš, František. Nové národní písně moravské. Za doplněk sbirky Sušilovy. [New popular Moravian Songs. Supplement to Sušil's collection.] Brünn, 1882.

—— Národní písně moravské v nově nasbírané. [Popular Moravian songs newly collected.] Brünn, 1889.

Bezsonov, P. Kalěki perechožie. Sbornik stichov i izslědovanie. [Travelling Pilgrims. Collection of Religious Songs, with an Investigation.] 2 vols. Moscow, 1861–4.

Bodenstedt, Friedrich. Die poetische Ukraine. Stuttgart, 1845.

Bogišić, V. Narodne pjesme, iz starijih najviše primorskih zapisa. [Popular Songs from old Collections, mainly from the Littoral.] 2 parts. Belgrad, 1878.

Bowring, John. Wýbor z básnictwi českého. Cheskian Anthology. London, 1832.

Bowring, John. Narodne srpske pjesme. Servian Popular Poetry, translated by ——. London, 1827.

Buslaev, T. J. Istoričeskie očerki. [Historical Sketches.] 2 vols. St. Petersburg, 1861.

Carrara, Francesco. Canti del popolo dalmata. Zara, 1849.

Chodźko, A. Les chants historiques de l'Ukraine. Paris, 1879.

[Czeczot, Jan.] Piosnki wieśniacze znad Dźwiny. [Peasant Songs from the Dvina Country.] Książeczka trzecia (third pamphlet). Wilna, 1840.

Čelakowský, F. L. Slowanské národní písně. [Slavic Popular Songs.] 3 Parts. Prague, 1822–7.

Danilov, Kirša. Drevnija rossijskija stichotvorenija, sobrannyja ——. [Old Russian Poems, collected by ——. Ed. K. Kalajdovič.] Moscow, 1818; 3ᵈ ed. Moscow, 1878.

Davidović, S. N. Srpske narodne pjesme iz Bosne (Ženske). [Serbian Popular Songs from Bosnia.] Pantchevo, 1884.

Dozon, A. Bǔlgarski narodni pěsni. [Chansons populaires bulgares inédites.] Paris, 1875.

von Düringsfeld, Ida. Böhmische Rosen. Czechische Volkslieder, übersetzt von ——. Breslau, 1851.

Erben, K. J. Pjsně národnj w Čechách. [Popular Songs in Bohemia.] 3 vols. Prague, 1842–5.

—— Prostonárodní české písně a říkadla. [Popular Bohemian Songs and Saws.] Prague, 1864.

—— Kytice z básní. [Anthology of Fables.] Prague, 1871.

Fedorowski, M. Lud okolic Żarek, Siewierza i Pilicy. [The Peasantry in Żarki, Siewierz and Pilica.] 2 vols. Warsaw, 1888–9.

Goetze, P. von. Serbische Volkslieder in 's deutsche übertragen von ——. St. Petersburg and Leipzig, 1827.

—— Stimmen des russischen Volks in Liedern. Gesammelt und übersetzt von ——. Stuttgart, 1828.

Golovackij, Jakov F. Narodnyja pěsni galickoj i ugorskoj Rusi. [Popular Songs in Galician and Hungarian Ruthenia.] 3 parts in 4 vols. Moscow, 1878–9.

Grudziński, Stephan. "Lenore" in Polen, eine litterarhistorische Abhandlung. Bochnia, 1890.

Grün, Anastasius. [Graf Anton Alexander.] Volkslieder aus Krain. Leipzig, 1850.

Hapgood, Isabel Florence. The Epic Songs of Russia. New York, 1886.

Haupt, Leopold, and Schmaler, Johann Ernst. Pjesnički hornych a delnych Łužiskich Serbow. Volkslieder der Wenden in der Ober- und Nieder-Lausitz. 2 parts. Grimma, 1841, 1843.

Hilferding, A. F. Onežskija byliny. [Bylinas from Onega.] St Petersburg, 1873.

Hiltebrandt, Peter A. Sbornik pamjatnikov narodnago tvorčestva v sěvero-zapadnom kraě. Izdanie redakcii Vilenskago Věstnika. [Collection of Monuments of the Popular Creation in the North-West. Edited by the Vilenski Věstnik.] Wilna, 1866.

Hrvatske narodne pjesme što se pjevaju po Istri i Kvarnerskih Otocih, preštampane iz "Naše Sloge." [Croatian Popular Songs sung in Istria and the Quarnero Islands, reprinted from "Naše Sloge."] Triest, 1879.

Jakuškin, P. Narodnyja russkija pěsni iz sobranija ——. [Russian Popular Songs from the Collection of ——.] St Petersburg, 1865.

Kapper, Siegfried. Die Gesänge der Serben. 2 vols. Leipzig, 1852.

Karadžić, Vuk Stefanović. Srpske narodne pjesme. [Serbian Popular Songs.] 5 vols. Vienna, 1841–65.

—— Srpske narodne pjesme iz Hercegovine (Ženske). [Serbian Popular Songs from Hercegovina.] Vienna, 1866.

Kętrzyński, W. O Mazurach. [The Mazuri.] Posen, 1872.

Kirěevskij, P. V. Pěsni sobrannyja P. V. Kirěevskim. [Songs collected by P. V. K.; edited by

P. A. Bezsonov and others. 2ᵈ ed., 10 parts. Moscow, 1868–75.

Kolberg, Oskar. Pieśni ludu polskiego. [Songs of the Polish Peasantry.] (1ˢᵗ vol. of Lud.) Warsaw, 1857.

—— Lud, jego zwyczaje, sposób życia, mowa, podania, prsysłowia, obrzędy, gusta, zabawy, pieśni, muzyka i tańce. [The Peasantry : their customs, manner of life, speech, traditions, saws, rites, tastes, amusements, songs, music and dances.] Cracow, 1865–89. Vols II–XXII. (Krakowskie, 5–8; Poznańskie, 9–15 ; Lubelskie, 16–17; Kieleckie, 18–19 ; Łęczyckie, 22.)

—— Mazowsze. Obraz etnograficzny. [The Mazovians. An ethnographical Sketch.] 4 vols. Cracow, 1885–88.

—— Pokucie. Obraz etnograficzny. [Pokucie, ethnographical Sketch.] 4 vols. Cracow, 1882–89.

Kollár, Jan. Národnié zpievanky, čili pjsně světské Slováků v Uhrách. [Popular Songs or Worldly Songs of the Slovaks in Hungary.] 2 vols. Buda, 1834–85.

Konopka, Józef. Pieśni ludu krakowskiego. [Songs of the Cracow Peasantry.] Cracow, 1840.

Kozłowski, Kornel. Lud. Pieśni, podania, baśnie, zwyczaje i przesądy ludu z Mazowsza Czerskiego. [The Peasantry. Songs, Traditions, Fables, Habits and Prejudices of the Peasantry in Mazowia, near Czersk.] Warsaw, 1869.

Krasić, V. Srpske narodne pjesme, starijeg i novijeg vremena. [Serbian Popular Songs of ancient and modern times.] Pantchevo, 1880.

Kupčanko, G. I. Sbornik pěsen bukovinskago naroda. Sostavil A. Lonačevskij. [Collection of Songs of the People of the Bukowina. Arranged by A. L.] Kiev, 1875.

Kurelac, Fran. Jačke ili narodne pěsme prostoga i neprostoga puka hrvatskoga na Ugrih. [Popular Songs of the Masses of the Croatian Populace in Hungary.] Agram, 1871.

Lewestam, F. H. Polnische Volkssagen und Märchen. Aus dem Polnischen des K. W. Woycicki, von ——. Berlin, 1839.

Lipiński, J. J. Piosnki ludu wielkopolskiego. [Songs of the Peasantry in Great Poland.] Posen, 1842.

Maksimovič, Michail. Ukrainskija narodnyja pěsni. [Popular Songs of the Ukraine.] Moscow, 1834.

—— Sbornik ukrainskich pěsen'. [Collection of Songs of the Ukraine.] Kiev, 1849.

Marjanović, Luka. Hrvatske narodne pjesme. [Croatian Popular Songs.] Agram, 1864.

Mažuranić, Stjepan. Hrvatske narodne pjesme. [Croatian Popular Songs.] Seng, 1876.

Metlinskij, Ambrosius. Narodnyja južnorusskija pěsni. [Popular South Russian Songs.] Kiev, 1854.

Mickiewicz, Adam. Dzieła. Wydanie zupełne przez dzieci autora dokonane. [Works. Complete edition, edited by the author's children.] 6 vols. Paris, 1880.

Mikulićić, F. Narodne pripovietke i pjesme iz hravtskoga primorja. [Popular Tales and Songs from the Croatian Littoral.] Porte Rè, 1876.

Miladinov, D. L. K. Bŭlgarski narodni pěsni. [Bulgarian Popular Songs.] Agram, 1861 ; Sophia, 1891.

Pauli, Żegota. Pieśni ludu polskiego w Galicyi. [Songs of the Polish Peasantry in Galicia.] Lemberg, 1838.

—— Pieśni ludu ruskiego w Galicyi. [Songs of the Ruthenian Peasantry in Galicia.] 2 vols. Lemberg, 1839–40.

Pellegrini, Ferdinando de. Saggio di una versione di canti popolari slavi. Torino, 1846.

Periodičesko spisanie na bŭlgarskoto knižovno družestvo v Srědec. [Periodical Journal of the Bulgarian Literary Society.] Sophia, 1882.

Petranović, J. B. Srpske narodne pjesme iz Bosne (Ženske). [Serbian Popular Songs in Bosnia (women's songs).] Serajevo, 1867.

—— Srpske narodne pjesme iz Bosne i Hercegovine. [Serbian Popular Songs from Bosnia and Hercegovina.] Belgrad, 1867.

Plohl-Herdvigov, R. F. Hrvatske narodne pjesme i pripoviedke. [Croatian Popular Songs and Tales.] Warasdin, 1868.

Prace filologiczne. [Philological Memoirs.] Warsaw, 1885–.

Przyjaciel ludu, czyli tygodnik potrzebnych i pożytecznych wiadomości. [Friend of the Peasantry, or, Weekly of Necessary and Useful Knowledge.] Leszno, 1834–39.

Rajković, Djordje. Srpske narodne pesme (Ženske). [Serbian Popular Songs (women's songs)]. Neusatz, 1869.

Ralston, W. R. S. The Songs of the Russian People, as illustrative of Slavonic Mythology and Russian Social Life. London, 1872.

Rambaud, A. La Russie épique, étude sur les chansons héroïques de la Russie. Paris, 1876.

Roger, Julius. Pieśni ludu polskiego w Górnym Szlązku. [Songs of the Polish Peasantry in Upper Silesia.] Breslau, 1863.

Romanov, E. Bělorusskij sbornik. [White-Russian Collection.] 5 parts. Kiev, Vitebsk, 1886–91.

Rosen, Georg. Bulgarische Volksdichtungen, gesammelt und ins Deutsche übertragen von ——. Leipzig, 1879.

Rybnikov, P. N. Pěsni sobrannyja ——. [Songs collected by P. N. R. Edited by P. Bezsonov and others.] 4 vols. I, II, Moscow, 1861, '62 ; III, Petrozavodsk, 1864 ; IV, St Petersburg, 1867.

Sacharov, J. Pěsni russkago naroda. [Songs of the Russian People.] 5 vols. St Petersburg, 1838–39.

—— Skazanija russkago naroda. [Utterances of

the Russian People.] 2 vols. St Petersburg, 1841–49.

Sbornik za narodni umotvorenija, nauka i knižnina, izdava ministerstvoto na narodnoto prosvěštenie. [Collection of the National Creations, Science and Literature, edited by the Ministry of Public Instruction.] 11 vols. Sofia, 1889–94.

Šejn, P. V. Bělorusskija narodnyja pěsni. [White Russian Popular Songs.] St Petersburg, 1874.

—— Russkija narodnyja pěsni. [Russian Popular Songs.] Moscow, 1870.

—— Materialy dlja izučenija byta i jazyka russkago naselenija sěvero-zapadnago kraja. [Materials for learning the State and Language of the Russian Population in the North-West.] 3 parts. St Petersburg, 1887–93.

Stojanović, M. Pučke pripoviedke i pjesme. [Popular Tales and Songs.] Agram, 1867.

Štúr, Ludevít. O národních písních a pověstech plemen slovanských. [On the Popular Songs and Tales of the Slavic Nations.] Prague, 1853.

Sumlork, W. S. [= Krolmus]. Staročeské powěsti, zpěwy, etc. [Old-Bohemian Tales, Songs, etc.] 3 vols. Prague, 1845–51.

Sušil, František. Moravské národní písně. [Moravian Popular Songs.] 2ᵈ ed. Brünn, 1860.

Swoboda, W. A. Sbírka českých národních písní. [Collection of Bohemian Popular Songs.] Prague, 1845.

Talvj [T. A. L. von Jakob Robinson]. Volkslieder der Serben, metrisch übersetzt und historisch eingeleitet. Neue umgearbeitete und vermehrte Auflage. 2 vols. Leipzig, 1853.

—— Historical View of the Languages and Literature of the Slavic Nations, with a sketch of their Popular Poetry. New York, 1850.

Trudy etnografičesko-statističeskoj ekspedicii v zapadno-russkij kraj, narjažennoj Imperatorskim Russkim Geografičeskim Obščestvom. Jugo-zapadnyj otděl. [Memoirs of the Ethnographic-statistical Expedition in the West-Russian region, under the auspices of the Russian Imperial Geographical Society, South-West Division.] 7 vols. St Petersburg, 1872–77.

Valjavec, M. K. Narodne pripovjesti u Varaždinu i okolici. [Popular Tales in and about Warasdin.] 2d ed. Agram, 1890.

Verković, Stefan J. Narodne pesme makedonski Bugara. [Popular Songs of the Macedonian Bulgarians.] Belgrad, 1860.

Vraz, Stanko. Narodne pěsni ilirske, koje se pěvaju po štajerskoj, krajnskoj, korušskoj, i zapadnoj strani ugàrske. [Popular Illyrian Songs, sung in Styria, Carniola, Carinthia, and West-Hungary.] Agram, 1839.

Vuk. See Karadžić.

Waldau, Alfred. Böhmische Granaten. Czechische Volkslieder, übertragen von ——. Prague, 1858. Zweiter Band. Prague, 1860. 2 vols.

Waldbrühl, Wilhelm von [A. W. F. von Zuccalmaglio]. Slawische Balalaika. Leipzig, 1843.

Wasilewski, L. Jagodne. Zarys etnograficzny. [Ethnological Sketch.] Warsaw, 1889.

Wenzig, Joseph. Bibliothek slavischer Poesien, in deutscher Uebertragung. Prague, 1875.

—— Westslawischer Märchenschatz. Ein Charakterbild der Böhmen, Mähren und Slowacken in ihren Märchen, Sagen, Geschichten, Volksgesängen und Sprüchwörtern. Leipzig, 1857.

—— Slawische Volkslieder übersetzt von ——. Halle, 1830.

Wisła, Miesięcznik geograficzno-etnograficzny. [Vistula. Geographic-ethnographical Monthly.] Ed. by Jan Karłowicz. Warsaw, 1887.

Wojcicki, K. W. Klechdy. Starożytne podania i powieści ludowe. [Klechdy. Old Traditions and Stories of the Peasantry.] 2 vols. Warsaw. 1851–52.

—— Pieśni Ludu Biało-Chrobatów, Mazurów i Rusi znad Bugu. [Songs of the Peasantry, the White Croatians, Mazurs and Ruthenians near the Bug.] Warsaw, 1836.

Wollner, Wilhelm. Untersuchungen über die Volksepik der Grossrussen. Leipzig, 1879.

Zapolskij, M. Bělorusskaja svad'ba i svadebnyja pěsni. [White Russian Wedding and Wedding Songs.] Kiev, 1888.

Zawiliński, R. Z powieści i pieśni górali beskidowych. [Stories and Songs of the Bieskid Mountaineers.] Warsaw, 1889.

Zbiór wiadomości do antropologii krajowéj. [Collection of Facts bearing on native Anthropology.] Cracow, 1877–.

Z Oleska, Wacław (Zaleski) Pieśni polskie i ruskie ludu galicyjskiego. [Polish and Ruthenian Songs of the Galician peasantry.] Lemberg, 1833.

Spanish.

de los Rios, José Amador. Historia crítica de la literatura española. 7 vols. Madrid, 1861–65.

—— Romanzen Asturiens, aus dem Volksmunde zum ersten Mal gesammelt und herausgegeben von ——. In Jahrbuch für romanische und englische Literatur, III. Leipzig, 1863.

Depping y Galiano. Romancero castellano ó coleccion de antiguos romances populares de los Españoles, publicada con una introduccion y notas por G. R. Depping. Nueva edicion, con las notas de D. Antonio Alcala-Galiano. 3 vols. Leipsique, 1844–46.

Duran, Agustin. Romancero General, ó, coleccion de romances castellanos anteriores al siglo XVIII, recogidos, ordenados, clasificados y anotados por ——. 2 vols. Madrid, 1849–51.

El Folk-Lore Frexnense y Bético-Extremeño. Fregenal, 1883–84.

Grimm, J. Silva de romances viejos, publicada por Jacobo Grimm. Vienna, 1815.

Marin, Francisco Rodriguez. Cantos populares españoles, recogidos, ordenados é ilustrados por ——. 5 vols. Sevilla, 1882–83.

de Ochoa, Eugenio. Tesoro de los romanceros y cancioneros españoles, históricos, caballerescos, moriscos y otros, recogidos y ordenados por ——. Paris, 1838.

de Puymaigre, Le comte (Théodore). Les vieux auteurs castillans. 2 vols. Paris and Metz, 1861–62.

Pidal, Juan Menendez. Poesía popular. Coleccion de los viejos romances que se cantan por los Asturianos, et cét. Madrid, 1885.

Recuerdos y Bellezas de España. 10 vols. [Madrid, 1842–65.]

Wolf, F. J., y Hofmann, C. Primavera y Flor de Romances, ó, coleccion de los mas viejos y mas populares romances castellanos, publicada con una introduccion y notas por ——. 2 vols. Berlin, 1856.

Swedish.

Afzelius, Arv. Aug. Svenska Folk-Visor från Forntiden, samlade och utgifne af Er. Gust. Geijer och Arv. Aug. Afzelius. 3 vols. Stockholm, 1814–16.

—— Svenska Folkvisor, utgifna af E. G. Geijer och A. A. Afzelius. Ny betydligt tillökad Upplaga, utgifven af R. Bergström och L. Höijer. 3 vols. Stockholm, 1880.

—— Svenska Folkets Sago-Häfder, till Läsning för Folket. Andra Upplagan. 5 parts. Stockholm, 1844–53.

Album utgifvet af Nyländingar. 8 numbers. Helsingfors, 1860–81.

Aminson. See Bidrag.

Arwidsson, Adolf Iwar. Svenska Fornsånger. 3 vols. Stockholm, 1834–42.

Atterbom, P. D. A. Poetisk Kalender för 1816. Upsala.

Axelson, Maximilian. Vandring i Wermlands Elfdal och Finnskogar. Stockholm, [1852].

—— Vesterdalarne, dess Natur, Folklif och Fornminnen. Stockholm, 1855.

Berggreen, A. P. Svenske Folke-Sange og Melodier. 2ᵈ ed. Kjøbenhavn, 1861. Vol. III of his Folke-Sange og Melodier, fædrelandske og fremmede. 11 vols. 2ᵈ ed. Kjøbenhavn, 1860–71.

Bidrag till Södermanlands äldre Kulturhistoria. Utgifna af H. Aminson (Häfte 1–5); Häfte 6 af J. Wahlfisk. Strengnäs and Stockholm (Häfte 6, Upsala), 1877–86.

"Borgström, F. L. Folkvisor upptecknade i Vermland och Dalsland, 1845. Kristinehamn, 1875 " ?

Djurklou, G. Ur Nerikes Folkspråk och Folklif. Anteckningar, o. s. v., utgifne af ——. Örebro, 1860.

Dybeck, Richard. Swenska Wisor, upteknade och samlade af ——. 2 Hefts. Stockholm, n. d.

—— Runa. En Skrift (Läsning) för Fäderneslandets Fornvänner. 10 parts in 3 vols. Stockholm, [1842]–50.

—— —— En Skrift för Nordens Fornvänner. Stockholm, 1865–74. 2ᵃ Samlingen, 1874.

Fagerlund, Lars Wilhelm. Anteckningar om Korpo och Houtskärs Socknar. Helsingfors, 1878. In Bidrag till Kännedom af Finlands Natur och Folk, utgifna af Finska Veterskaps-Societeten. Hæfte 28.

1500- och 1600-Talens Visböcker, utgifna af Adolf Noreen och Henrik Schück. Harald Oluffsons Visbok. Första Häftet. Stockholm, 1884. Bröms Gyllenmär's Visbok, Första Häftet. Stockholm, 1885.

Hazelius, Artur. Ur de nordiska Folkens Lif. Skildringar. Utgifna af ——. Stockholm, 1882. In his Bidrag til vår Odlings Häfder. Stockholm, 1881–85.

Hofberg, Herman. Nerikes gamla Minnen. Örebro, 1868.

Lagus, Ernst. Nyländska Folkvisor, ordnade och utgifna af ——. Helsingfors, 1887 ——. In Nyland. Samlingar utgifna af Nyländska Afdelningen, III.

Nicolovius [Nils Loven]. Folklifwet i Skytts Härad i Skåne, Barndomsminnen. Lund, 1847.

Nyare Bidrag till Kännedom om de svenska Landsmålen ock svenskt Folklif. Tidskrift. Stockholm, 1879.

[Öberg, Theodor.] Filikromen. Hittills otryckta skämtsamma Sånger (ord och musik), samlade och utgifna af Axel I. Ståhl. 1–9. Stockholm, 1850–65.

Rancken, Oskar. Några Prof af Folksång och Saga i det svenska Österbotten. Helsingfors, 1874. (Separat afdrag ur Finska Fornminnes-Föreningens Tidskrift, Årgång 1.)

Svenska Fornminnesföreningens Tidskrift. Stockholm, 1871–.

Werner, Hilder. Westergötlands Fornminnen. Anteckningar af ——. Stockholm, [1868].

Westergötlands Fornminnesförenings Tidskrift. Häfte 1–3, Lund, 1869–77; Häfte 4–7, Stockholm, 1888–93.

Wigström, Eva. Folkvisor från Skåne. In Artur Hazelius, Ur de nordiska Folkens Lif.

—— Folkdiktning, Visor, sägner, sagor, o. s. v., samlad och upptecknad i Skåne af ——. Köbenhavn, 1880.

—— Andra Samlingen. Folkdiktning, Visor, Folktro, Sägner, o. s. v., samlad och upptecknad i Skåne af ——. Göteborg, 1881.

—— Skånska Visor, Sagor och Sägner, samlade och utgifa af ——. Lund, 1880.

INDEX OF MATTERS AND LITERATURE

force from Carlisle castle by Sir Walter Scott, laird of Buccleuch, III, 469–74; his extraordinary and proverbial rapacity, 471.

Armstrongs, their strength, III, 363; ravage both the English and the Scottish border, 364 a. See under Family Names.

Arngosk, Lady of, ballad, IV, 241 ff.

Arrow, bearing, III, 29, 202, 341; broad, III, 29, 160, 176, 199, 202, 341; IV, 505 f.; letter sent on an arrow-head, III, 223 f., 231; V, 241 a; arrow shot to determine place for grave, I, 185 (?); III, 106; to show where a wife is to be sought, II, 499.

Arthour and Merlin, romance of, IV, 479 b.

Arthur, King, I, 257–67, 271–3, 283–91, 289–91, 293–6; his custom of not dining until he had had or heard of an adventure, I, 257, 263; III, 51, and n. So Robin Hood, III, 51.

Arthur a Bland, tanner of Nottingham, kinsman of Little John, III, 137; the tune, 133, and n.

Arthur a Bradley, a ballad, III, 215, 217.

Arthur's seat shall be my bed, song, IV, 105.

Artificial curiosities, wand with three singing living lavrocks sitting thereon, etc., I, 201 f., 205, 503; III, 501 b; IV, 450 b.

Artiga, V, 4 f.

Atamulc, story of, V, 13.

Athelbrus, steward of King Ailmar, and tutor of Horn and his comrades, I, 188 f.

Atherly. See John of Atherly.

Athulf, Horn's faithful friend, I, 188, 190.

Les Aubrays, Lizandré, Breton knight, kills a Moor by receiving him on the point of his sword as the Moor leaps in the air, II, 378; III, 276.

Audam and Doorkhaunee, Afghan poem, I, 98.

Augur (wimble) bore, lady first seen, or courted, through an, I, 202, B, 205, F, 206, H; first and only sight, I, 255.

Auld Man = Devil, I, 18, I.

Auld Robin Gray, a play, V, 88.

Die Ausgleichung, I, 265.

Austerities vowed by actors in tragic stories, as tributes of grief, penances, etc., II, 156 f., 159, 162 f., 165 f., 175, 177, 179, 258, 318 f.; IV, 97, 360, 433; V, 223 a.

Austrrfki, I, 460 n.

The Avowynge of King Arthur, metrical romance, I, 209.

Ayrer's plays, V, 24 f., 97.

Baba-Yaga, I, 484 a.

Baffling malice with ready answers, I, 20–22, 485; III, 496; IV, 440.

Bahome, Bee Hom, II, 318 f.

Baillie Lunnain, Gaelic tale, I, 191 n.

Balcanqual, II, 337.

Balewise, bæliwis, I, 67 n.

Balfour, John, called Burly, IV, 106 f.

Bandello, Novelle, I, 269; II, 42; III, 258; V, 23 n.

Banier, Sir (= Sir Beduer, Bedewere?), I, 295.

La Barbe Bleue, I, 47.

Barberine, A. de Musset, I, 269.

Y Bardd Glas Keraint, II, 136, 511.

Der Bärenhäuter, tale, I, 198.

Barnard, Bernard, Barnet, Burnett, Burnard, Lord, II, 244–8, 251 f., 256–8, 266–74.

Barnsdale, III, 50 f.

Barrel spiked, punishment of rolling or dragging in, II, 343; IV, 30 n., 32; V, 48.

Barton, Sir Andrew, maintained by the English to be a pirate, III, 335 f., 339, 345, 352; IV, 503; his dangerous "beams," III, 337, and n., 338, 340 f., 344 f., 349; IV, 504 f.; his ship brass within and steel without, III, 340, 344, 349; IV, 504; and magnificently ornamented, III, 340, 342; boasts that he once salted thirty heads of the Portuguese, and sent them home to eat with bread, IV, 505; 300 crowns (500 angels) tied about his middle, when his body is thrown overboard, to secure burial, III, 342; IV, 506.

Basile, Il Pentamerone, I, 269, 461 n.; II, 127; V, 48.

Bastars de Buillon, Li, romance, V, 6.

Bathing for recovering human shape, I, 308, 338, and n.; II, 505; III, 505; V, 39 f.

The Battle of Harlaw, of Hara Law, a tune; The Battle of Hardlaw, a pibroch, III, 318. See Harlaw.

Beating of daughters, I, 192; II, 435; V, 237 a.

Beaumont and Fletcher, Knight of the Burning Pestle, I, 105; II, 199, 243, 457 n.; V, 201 f.; The Spanish Curate, I, 239 n.; Monsieur Thomas, II, 10, 243; III, 294, 331; Bonduca, II, 243; V, 202; The Pilgrim, II, 457; The Two Noble Kinsmen, II, 506 b; V, 133, 202; Philaster, III, 129.

Beauty and the Beast, La Belle et la Bête, tale, I, 308, 313 f.

Becket, Gilbert, romantic story of, I, 457 f.

Becket, Thomas, stands by his votaries, I, 505 a.

Beeldwit, I, 67.

Beggar (palmer), Hind Horn changes clothes with, I, 189, 191 f., 202–7; Robin Hood, III, 178–82, 184; Little John, III, 188; Wallace, III, 271, 273; other disguises as beggar or pilgrim, V, 2, 4, 5, 279 f.; beggar who receives girl's favors turns out to be a person of high degree, V, 109 ff., 116 ff., 305 a.

The Beggar and the Five Muffins, Eastern story, V, 281.

Beggar and Robin Hood, III, 156, 159; beggar (beggars) and Little John, III, 188 f.

Beggar's dress and equipment, II, 436 f. (61, 78).

Die beiden Fürsten, Turkish tale, I, 10.

Beket. See Becket.

Le Bel Inconnu, Libeaus Desconeus, I, 308; II, 51, 510 b.

Bele Ydoine, romance, IV, 482 a.

Belewitte, I, 67.

La Belle et la Bête, I, 308 n., 313 f.

Bellerophon's sons and Sarpedon, III, 20.

Bells, numerous, on horses, I, 320 n.; V, 290 a; on every lock of horse's mane, I, 323; II, 189, 191, 344; IV, 410, 413; mane and tail, II, 194; twenty-four on horse's mane, II, 183, 185; hung at every corner of a ship, IV, 462 a; bell sewed to every stitch of a cap for a (supposed) dead girl, III, 364; IV, 483; bells ring of themselves, I, 173, 231; III, 235, 244, 519 f.; bells rung backward as an alarm, III, 26; girl sold for a new church-bell, I, 91 f.

Belly-blind. See Billie Blind.

Beloe's Oriental Apologues, V, 97.

Benbow, Admiral, V, 147.

Benediction in church, merman's (human) wife must not stay till, or expose herself to, I, 366; nix flies from, ib., n.

Bengwill, Benwall, Brangwill, Lord, I, 62, 76, 78; II, 253.

Béowulf, I, 50, 54 n.; II, 56.

Der Berghüter und seine kluge Tochter, Transylvanian tale, I, 8.

Berkeley, Witch of, V, 298 a.

Bernabò Visconti and the Abbot, tale of Sacchetti, I, 406.

142 f.; bride assigned by dying man to his brother, I, 376, 378, and n.; she will not give her troth to two brothers, I, 376, 378, and n.; bride, wife, whose bridegroom, husband, has died is put off with false explanations, I, 376-9, 381, 383-87; bride carried off by lover on the day she was to wed a rival, IV, 218, 230; V, 260 f.

Bridegroom caressing bride while taking her home killed by her brother, I, 142; bridegroom killed on his way to fetch the bride, I, 386; bridegroom drowned on the way to his wedding, IV, 179-183, 189 f.; V, 257; lover drowned on his way to visit his mistress, IV, 185.

Brome, brome on hill, song, I, 390.

The broom blooms bonny and says it is fair, I, 450.

The Broom of Cowden Knowes, O the broome, the bonny bonny broome, tune, IV, 192, 208.

Brother's consent to a sister's marriage, importance of obtaining, I, 142; brother whose consent has not been asked kills his sister as she is riding to or from the wedding, I, 145-50; brother flogs to death unmarried sister who has had a child, II, 102.

Brown, Andrew, his services to James VI, III, 442-6.

Brown bride despised for her complexion, II, 182-97; brown girl rejected for this reason, V, 167 f. See also I, 120, 133 (**M** 10), 135 (1).

Brown Robin, II, 305 f., 368, 371, 418.

Bruce, David. See David Bruce.

Die Bruck zu Karidol, I, 267, and n.

Buccleuch, Sir Walter Scott of, rescue of Kinmont Willie, III, 469 ff. See under Family Names.

Bulat and Ivan, tsar's son, Russian tale, V, 46.

Bunion Bay, I, 24, 57.

Burden, burden-stem, I, 7 n., 484 a; II, 204 n.

Burial, gold bound round bodies thrown into the water, to secure, II, 14; III, 342; IV, 502 b, 506 a; V, 245.

Buridan and the Queen of France, tale, IV, 502.

Burlow-beanie, a variety of Billy Blin (here a loathly fiend, with seven heads), I, 286 f.

Burnet, Burnett. See under Family Names.

Burning, penalty for incontinence (in Danish ballads, for incest), II, 41, 43 f., 46-8, 113-125; III, 508 b; V, 292 b.

Burns, Robert, author of Kellyburnbraes, V, 107; his Hallowe'en, V, 286 a.

Butler, Sir John, his murder and the ballad thereon, III, 327 ff.

Buttons bursting, as a consequence of violent emotion, II, 186; IV, 101, 302; waistcoat bursted, IV, 185; stays, gown and all, IV, 320.

By Lands-dale, hey ho, song, III, 54.

Byliny, Russian popular epics, I, 200 (II, 499 f.); II, 15, and n., 502; III, 122, 501 b; IV, 463, 497 a, 499 a; V, 2; Bulgarian, IV, 463.

Byron, Child Harold's Pilgrimage, III, 91; IV, 36.

Caberstaing, Guillems de, story of, V, 33.

Cæsarian operation, three and five wives die successively thereof, II, 309 f.; six sisters (and the seventh doomed) 311-16, V, 227-9; in the case of Queen Jane, III, 373-6; V, 245 f.; in Danish ballad, I, 83.

Cæsarius Heisterbacensis, Dialogus Miraculorum, I, 197, 237.

Calaf, Prince, Persian story, I, 417.

Calender, tale of the Second, I, 402.

Campbell. See under Family Names.

Campbell, Bonny James, ballad, IV, 142.

La caña del riu de arenas, Catalan story, I, 125.

Cane (walking rod), ridiculously introduced. See the commonplace of mantle and cane (under Commonplaces); also, IV, 190, 421; V, 16 f.

Car, Ker, Captain, III, 424-7, 430-2.

Caradawc, I, 265; V, 289 a. See Carados.

Carados (Briebras, Brisié Bras), I, 258, 261 n., 263-5; Caradawc Vreichvras, 265; variations of the name Carados, I, 264 n.; V, 289 a.

Carduino (Le Bel Inconnu), Italian romance, I, 308.

Carevič i ego Sluga, The Prince and his Servant, Russian tale, V, 281.

Carl Blind, surnamed Bavís, I, 67, 95.

Carl Hood, old, I, 67, 92, 95, and n., 489; IV, 443 f.

Carl of Carlile, rhymed tale, I, 290 n., 301 n., 316; V, 289 a.

Caskets, riddle of the three, I, 13.

Cassilis. See under Family Names.

Catharine I., Empress of Russia, III, 383.

Cawfield, Archie of, ballad, III, 484 ff.

Ce qui plaît aux Dames, Voltaire's tale, I, 292.

The Ceabharnach, West Highland tale, III, 507.

Le Centi Novelle Antiche, V, 34.

Chains of gold, servants in waiting wear, I, 410.

Chambers, Robert, his contention that Lady Wardlaw was the author of Sir Patrick Spens and other ballads, II, 20 n.

Champion, diminutive, successful against huge and dangerous antagonist in judicial combat, II, 35-37, 37 n., 38, 39 ?, 43 n., 45 f. See Child-champion.

Change of clothes with beggar, palmer, I, 189, 191, 192, 202-207; III, 157, 179, 181 f., 184, 188, 271, 273 f.

Change of parts of man and woman in different versions of the same or a similar tale, I, 142, 187, 455, Nos 17, 53; 298; II, 236, 349, 426; IV, 186; V, 34, 296.

Charcoal-burners, III, 109; V, 6, 70 f., 75, and n.

Charlemagne's Journey to Jerusalem, I, 274-9; III, 503 b.

Charles the Fifth (emperor) and a broom-maker; and a peasant; Belgian stories, V, 74.

Charles the Great and the charcoal-burner, rhymed tale, V, 70 f.

Charm: knight obliges lady to go off with him by sticking a charm in her sleeve, I, 57; charm or rune employed to induce sleep, I, 28, 48, 55, 391.

Charrois de Nymes, Li, chanson de geste, V, 298 a.

Charter of peace sought by outlaws, III, 27.

Chastity, or fidelity in love, tests of, I, 258-71, 507 a; II, 502; III, 503; IV, 454 a; V, 212 f., 289 a.

Arch, sword and garland in Amadis which test the fact and the measure of faithful love, I, 267.

(Talking) bed, blankets, pillows, rug, sheets, I, 64 f., 68, 70.

Bridge in the younger Titurel which cannot be passed by knight or lady faulty in matter of love, I, 267.

Brook which tests virginity, I, 269.

Chair, golden, in which none but a maid will sit till bidden, I, 72 f.; can sit, 75.

Crown that exposes the infidelity of husbands, I, 266 f.

Cup from which no man or woman can drink who has been false to love, I, 264.

Cup of tears in Palmerin of England which tests the best knight and most faithful lover, I, 267.

Flowers (lotus, rose) or evergreen which keep fresh as long as wife or man and wife are faithful, I, 268.

Glove as test of virtue of man or woman, I, 266.

Mallet, David, and his Margaret's Ghost, II, 199 f.; V, 294 a.

Malleus Maleficarum, I, 489; III, 18.

Malory's King Arthur (Morte Darthur), I, 257 n.; IV, 456 a; V, 289 b; 298 a.

Man in danger of his life dressed by landlady as woman and set to baking, IV, 151–4; man preparing to hang himself finds money, leaves the rope, with which the owner of the money hangs himself, V, 13; man who flies from home on account of enormous crime, in his desperation commits his relations to miserable fates, I, 169 f., 445; man who has assaulted maid, to marry her, if bachelor, be hanged, if married, II, 460 f., 464 (466), 469, 471, 474 f.; IV, 493.

Mandeville, Sir John, his (fictitious) Voyage and Travel, I, 308; III, 501; V, 209.

Les Manteaux, Caylus, I, 257.

Der Mantel of Heinrich von dem Türlîn, I, 259 f.

Le Mantel Mautaillié, fabliau, I, 257.

Mantle and costumes enclosed between two nut-shells, I, 260, and n., 271.

Mantle, as chastity chest. See The Boy and the Mantle, No 29, I, 257 ff., etc. ; Gaelic ballad of the mantle, I, 261 f.; V, 289 a ; the mantle of Karodes, I, 261.

Mantle Rhymes, see Skikkju Rímur, I, 264 n.

Már fights when both his hands are off, IV, 502 a.

Margaret Twynstoun, Twinslace, Vinstar, Weiksterne, frees her lover, Wemyss of Logie, condemned to death, by taking him through the royal bedchamber and letting him down from a window, III, 449 f., 452–5.

Margaret's Ghost, David Mallet, II, 199 f.; V, 294 a.

Le Mari Confesseur, conte of La Fontaine, III, 258.

Marie de France, Lai del Freisne, II, 67 f. ; Lanval, II, 510 ; Guigemar, IV, 377 ; Yonec, V, 39.

Marineo, Lucio, I, 238.

Maríu saga, I, 98; III, 52 n., 240.

Markenfield (Martinfield), Thomas, III, 418–22; knows every banner, whether any man he has laid eyes on is friend or foe, can speak any language, and has the gift of prophecy, 419 f.

Marko Kraljević, II, 357; III, 499 a, 507 b; IV, 463 b.

Marr, house of, IV, 157.

Marramiles, one of Arthur's knights, I, 279, 284, 287.

Marriage ceremony interrupted by lover, who takes the bride, IV, 412–14.

Marriage, forced, justified as happiest, IV, 244.

Marriage: maid to wait, lover absent, seven (eight, nine) years and not marry, I, 189 f., 192–4, 459, 502 b ; maid and man parting, neither to marry for seven years, I, 191 n., 464 f., 473, 477, 480; II, 508; IV, 461; man gives his troth to woman to marry no other for seven years, I, 469 f. ; man parting with his wife engages her not to marry again for seven years, I, 195 f., 198, 200 n., 462 (three cases) ; for three, five, six, eight, nine or twelve years, nine years and nine days, year month and day, I, 194, 197, 199, 200 (and 499), 461 ; Epirot and Albanian custom of betrothing or marrying early in youth and parting for long periods, I, 502.

Marriage, second, of wife prevented by sudden (often miraculous) return of husband, I, 194–200, 502 f. ; II, 499 b ; III, 501; IV, 450 b ; V, 210 b ; betrothed maid arrests marriage of lover to another woman, I, 502 f.

Marriage-contract, seigneur miraculously conveyed home on the eve of his wife's marrying identifies himself by producing one half of his marriage-contract, which fits the other half left with his wife, II, 499 b.

Marriages, unequal : serving man preferred by Lord Arundel's daughter to Lord Phenix, II, 441–55 ; lady refuses nine gentlemen for servant-lad, ploughman, IV, 172 f., 522 ; V, 255 ; Earl of Wigton's daughter marries footman, IV, 292–9 ; V, 270 ; lady of birth and fame loves a kitchenboy, IV, 403–8 ; V, 277 f.

Martial, Epigrams, IV, 186.

Mary, Mild, II, 309, 315 ; Mary Mild, Myle, Moil, II, 72; III, 386, 395 f., 398 a ; IV, 507 f., 510 f. ; Mary Miles (corruptly), IV, 511 ; maidens mild, II, 312, 314, 316 ; V, 227.

Masenžny Dzjadok, White Russian tale, V, 281.

Mass, forced, exacted by Robin Hood, III, 192, 199, 202, 228.

Massinger, The Picture, I, 269.

Matthew, apocryphal Gospel of, I, 271 ; II, 1, 2 n., 7.

Matthew Paris, Chronica Majora, II, 37, 143 ; III, 235, 241, 519.

Matilda Fitzwalter, Maid Marian, III, 56 n., 214, 218, 519.

Matildas, three, popularly supposed to have been persecuted by King John, III, 519.

Maximilian II (Emperor) and a charcoal-burner, Bohemian tale, V, 75.

Maxwells: affray with the Johnstones, III, 485 ; feuds with the Johnstones, IV, 34–8 ; Lord Maxwell kills Sir James Johnstone, IV, 35 ; Lord Maxwell's Last Goodnight, ballad, IV, 34 ff. See under Family Names.

May-game, III, 44–46.

Meilyr, story of, in Giraldus Cambrensis, his ability to expose lies, I, 320 n.

Meisterlieder der Kolmarer Handschrift, I, 269, 270.

Meldrum, Squire, III, 306 n.

Mellerstain, Laird of, ballad, IV, 281 f.

Mélusine, romance, V, 226 a.

Mem and Zin, Kurdish poem, I, 98.

Memering, Mimmering, Mimmer, Mimecan, smallest of men, champion of Gunild, II, 34–8.

La menta y'l Gaitx, Catalan tale, II, 510.

Merfolk apt to be ferocious, I, 366 n. (see 365 b, 366 a).

Merlin, Roman de Merlin, I, 257 n.; II, 113; IV, 454 a (English prose romance) ; (in Arthour and Merlin), IV, 479 b.

Mermaid, sight of, bad omen for ships, II, 19, 29 f., 32, 510 b ; V, 149–52; one has betrayed seven ships, II, 19.

Mermaiden affects man with some mortal ailment, I, 387–9 (probably incited thereto by his inconstancy : see I, 372).

Merman entering church, all the images turn their backs; when woman who has perforce been the merman's consort enters church, everything in it bows, I, 365.

Merman takes maid (princess) to the sea-bottom, where she lives some eight years and has children ; hearing the bells of home, she longs to go to her mother and is allowed to pay her a visit, taking her children with her; merman comes for her, she refuses to return ; merman says they must divide the children, three and three each, and half of the seventh, I, 364 f.; merman tears the children to pieces and hangs himself, 366. See Dwarf-king.

Merman's human wife, allowed to visit her mother, must not bow when the priest pronounces the holy name, or make an offering, I, 364 ; must not stay for the benediction, 366.

Message (deceptive) from dying man or woman to father,

Sheet, sark, smock (for the dead), one half cambric, the other needle work, one side of beaten gold, the other needle work, one half silk, the other cambric, I, 506 ; II, 358 f., 362, 366 ; IV, 471, 485.

The Shepherd and the King, broadside ballad, V, 73.

Shepherd's daughter (pretended) persists in marrying a knight whom the king has adjudged to her, II, 459–76 ; makes him think her a beggar's brat, carl's daughter, 462–4, 466 f., 469–73, 476.

Sheriff and outlaws (especially the Sheriff of Nottingham and Robin Hood), III, 26, 28, 57, 63–6, 70–3, 93 f., 97 f., 100 f., 111–13, 117–19, 157, 180–7, 222–4.

Ship, in a bad storm, promised that gold shall be her hire if she will behave well, gold nails for iron, IV, 379 f. ; V, 276 ; silver and gold bolts driven in for iron and oak wanting, IV, 381 f. ; leaking badly, silken cloath and canvass stuffed in to calk her, II, 27 ; wrapped round with feather beds and canvass, or canvass, and pitched, II, 28 ; IV, 379–82 ; V, 276.

Ships, intelligent and talking, IV, 376–80 ; V, 275 f. ; race of, forty-five, fifty-three, twenty-one ships, and all wrecked but one, IV, 378–82 ; V, 275 f. ; splendid ships, I, 72, 312, 474 ; II, 13, 30, 217 f. ; III, 340 ; IV, 472 ; V, 285 ; ships stopped or endangered ; sinful parties, or other persons determined by lot, being thrown into sea, or put out of the ship, or confessing, or vowing offerings, or a captive being released, the voyage proceeds, I, 244–6 ; II, 13–16, 510 a ; IV, 452, 463 a ; V, 220 a, 288 a, 292 a ; ship stopped by serpents till a holy man whose instruction they desire shall be delivered to them ; he throws himself in, the ship moves on, II, 13 f. n.

Shirt, custom of maid's making one for her betrothed, V, 284 ; significance of a man's making such a request, 284 ; shirt demanded by Elfin Knight, I, 7 ; V, 284.

Shoes slacked to run, II, 115, 177, 257, 313, 379, 395 ; IV, 398 ; cast off to run, II, 125, 212, 287.

Shooting from boy's (man's) head of apple, nut, chessman, coin, and similar feats, III, 16–21.

Shooting under hand, III, 199, 202, 204.

Shoulder, looking over the left shoulder, I, 100 (twice), 103, 464, 490 (left collar-bane), 492 ; III, 259, 263 f., 339, 368 f., 413, 465, 488 ; IV, 11, 13, 15, 17 f., 20, 52, 135, 445, 518–20. (See V, 286 a.)

Shovell, Sir Cloudesley (" Shawfield "), V, 147.

Shrift saves a ship endangered by a storm, II, 15 ; sinner thrown overboard to save a ship taken to heaven by the Virgin for the shrift he has made, II, 16.

Shukasaptati, Seventy Tales of a Parrot, I, 11 n., 12 n., 13, 268 n., 270, and n. ; V, 289 a.

Sibilla, wife of Charles the Great, suspected of unfaithfulness, various forms of the story, II, 40 f.

Siddhi-Kür, I, 402.

Side, Armstrongs of the, especially Jock o the Side, III, 475 ff.

Sidney's admiration of the song of Percy and Douglas, III, 305.

Le sifflet enchanté, Le sifflet qui parle, tale, I, 493 b ; II, 498 b ; III, 499 a.

Sigrdrifumál, I, 392.

Sigurðarkviða Fáfnisbana, III, II, 127.

Simon, Simond, Peter, a noble gunner employed by Lord Howard against Andrew Barton, III, 339, 341–5, 348–50 ; IV, 503, 505–7.

Simon the Foundling, Servian hero, V, 295 a.

Sinadab, story of, V, 12.

Der singende Knochen, tale, I, 125.

Das singende springende Löweneckerchen, tale, I, 307 n.

Sinkarib, Histoire de, et de ses deux Visirs, Persian tale, I, 11 n.

Sir Bevis of Hamptoun, romance, II, 499, 506, 513 ; III, 520 ; the French romance, II, 511.

Sir Broninge, knight, I, 210.

Sir Eger, Sir Grahame, and Sir Gray-Steel, romance, I, 209.

Sir Eglamour of Artois, romance, I, 209 ; II, 511 a.

Sir Egrabell, I, 210.

Sir Gawayn and the Green Knight, romance, I, 257 n.

Sir Gowther, II, 303.

Sir Hugh, ballad of A. Cunningham, II, 260.

Sir Isumbras, romance, II, 513 a.

Sir James the Ross, A Historical Ballad, by Michael Bruce, IV, 156. See Rose.

Sir Olaf (Oluf), and the elf, I, 374–8 ; poisoned by the elf for inconstancy, 375 ; is run through with a sword for refusing to consort with elves, 375 ; is struck by elf to whom he has declined to plight himself (being already betrothed) and dies in a day, 375 f. ; may choose between living with the elves and dying, 377.

Sir Orpheo, Orfeo, romance, I, 216, 340, 504 a ; II, 128.

Sir Perceval, English romance, II, 51. See Perceval.

Sir Ryalas, I, 212 f.

Sir Triamour, romance, II, 41 ; V, 176.

Sir Tristrem, romance, I, 67, 317, 487 a ; II, 127.

Sisibe, wife of Sigmundr, falsely accused of adultery, II, 41.

Sister comes every Saturday to comb the head of a brother who has been transformed into a worm, I, 315 ; the same, by sister changed to a mackerel, 316.

Sister hunted to death by rival in love, V, 158.

Sisters (sister) killed or maltreated by robbers who turn out to be their brothers, I, 171–7 ; Russian ballad, II, 499 a.

Skelton, John, Against the Scottes, Chorus de Dis, IV, 499 a ; Colyn Cloute, V, 100 ; perhaps author of a Robin Hood pageant, III, 519 b.

Skikkju Rímur, or Mantle Rhymes, Icelandic, I, 259, 261 n., 264 n.

Skuin over de groenelands heide, III, 502.

Slangen og den lille Pige, Danish tale, I, 307.

Slaughter in large numbers of relations of lady-love by lover : six or seven brothers and father and other kinsmen, I, 89 ; father, eleven brothers, seven brothers-in-law, 91 ; father and six brothers, 92 ; six brothers, 94 n. ; father and seven brothers, 101 f. ; six or seven brothers, II, 170, and n. (eighteen thousand assailants, I, 91 ; fourteen of father's best men, I, 100, 108).

Sleep, induced by charms, runes, I, 28, 48, 55, 391 f. ; by runes written on sheets of a bed, 391 ; by a letter inserted between sheet and coverlet, by an enchanted feather, by runes written on cushions, 392 ; by a soporific pillow, I, 393 ; by sleep-thorns, -pins, I, 392 f. ; III, 506 ; IV, 459 ; by strewing broom-blossoms at a man's head and feet (on his neck), I, 394 f. ; by magic of some sort, V, 2 ; by music, see Music.

Sleep : man in deep (unnatural) sleep cannot be roused by maid at a critical moment ; servant afterwards repeats to him what has occurred, I, 307, and n.

Sleep you, wake you, the formula, II, 240, 513 a ; III, 514 a ; V, 201 b, 225 b.

Sword and ring laid before maid ' to stick him wi the brand or wed him wi the ring,' II, 469; IV, 493; V, 28, 238.

Swords, Adelring, Sudevind, and others of superexcellent quality, II, 34, 35, and n., 50.

Swords, two in a scabbard, II, 133, 135, 245, 251, 256, 258; IV, 477.

Sworn brethren, IV, 146 f.

Syntipas, V, 13 f.

Table, drawing a, explained, V, 304 a.

Table jumped, kicked or thrown over, under the effect of exciting events or information, table furniture broken to flinders or hurled into fire, etc., I, 65, 217, 457 n., 465, 472, 475 f., 481, 502 a, b; II, 35, 94, 127 f., 128 n., 132, 205, 271, 273, 312 f., 511 b; III, 509 a; IV, 316, 345, 462, 508; V, 219, 271, 287 b, 292 b. In Slavic ballads, bride jumps over four tables (and knocks over a fifth); husband, hearing news, jumps nine, I, 502 b; II, 511 b; III, 509 a; person jumps seven and touches the eighth, V, 287 b.

Tales cited without title: —

　Albanian, V, 47.

　Armenian (= King John and Bishop), IV, 459 b; tale or ballad, I, 490 a.

　Breton, III, 504 a, 506 b, 507 a.

　Esthonian, I, 308.

　Gypsy (Transylvanian, etc.), IV, 459 b; V, 60.

　Lithuanian, II, 499 b, 511 a.

　Magyar, IV, 459 b; V, 60, 216 a.

　Romaic, I, 97, 337, 401, 437, 461 n.; II, 127, 511 a; V, 39.

　Roumanian, I, 85, 401.

　Slavic, I, 124 f., 308, 401 f., 417, 484 a, 499 b, 507, 513 a; III, 52 n., 513 b; IV, 439 b, 440 b, 459 b; V, 2 f., 6, 46 f., 60, 74, 107, 241, 279.

Talismans: ring with stone which by change of color, or breaking, signifies unfaithfulness of giver, I, 192, 201–7; II, 318 f.; V, 210 f.; by rusting or dimming shows that giver is dead, I, 201; ring which protects the wearer from all bodily harm, assures superiority in fight, doubles strength, keeps from sickness and captivity, I, 189, 190 f., 201 n.; V, 287 b; gold-embroidered handkerchief, gold melting shows that giver is dead, I, 201; ring, sword, chain, which will stanch blood or prevent blood from being drawn, II, 61, 318 f.; V, 183 f.; the protective power of the ring conditional upon the wearer when in danger thinking of his leman, I, 189; with his keeping faith, 190 f.

Talking Bird, Singing Tree, and Yellow Water, Arabian tale, I, 311.

The Talking Dish, Chinese drama, I, 126.

Tam o Lin, Tom a Lin, Tammy Linn, etc., popular verses about, I, 340; III, 505 b.

Tarlton's Jests, IV, 495 a.

Tarn Wadling. See Tearne Wadling.

Tasks and problems, difficult or impossible, I, 7–13, 15–20, 418, 484 f.; II, 495 f.; III, 496 a; IV, 439 f.; V, 205 f.; impossible tasks propounded by man as condition of love or marriage, offset by others preliminary, equally difficult, proposed by woman, I, 7 f., 15–19, 484 f.; II, 495 f.; III, 496 a; IV, 439 f.; V, 205 f., 284 (an Elphin knight gives the tasks, I, 15–17; an auld man, 18 f. (I), who represents the devil; a dead lover, IV, 439 f., and the devil expressly, V, 283; the maid would have been carried off had she failed). Similar requisitions, not conditional to marriage, met in the same way, I, 10, 13; in Babylonian Talmud, V, 284; similar performances, ostensibly undertaken, to show the absurdity of a demand, I, 10, 11; an assertion offset by another of the same extravagance, 13; tasks in which no one of the only possible procedures is allowed, I, 8 f., 418; problems ingeniously solved, I, 12 f.; tasks propounded by one king to another, king rescued from attack or from a forfeit by the sagacity of his minister or minister's daughter, I, 11 f.; wife won by doing riddling tasks, Siberian-Turkish tale, I, 418; dead lover propounds tasks to his truelove; if she had not "answered" well she must have gone away with him, IV, 439 f.

Taubenliebe, Albanian tale, I, 338.

Tausend und eine Nacht, I, 11 n., 12, 269; V, 13.

Tay, water of, I, 127, 129; II, 21, 24, 96, 314, 462, 465, 471; III, 271; IV, 98, 100, 143 f., 193.

Tchînavar, the bridge, II, 235.

Tearne Wadling, I, 294.

Tears destroy the peace of the dead, II, 228, 234–7, 512 f.; III, 513 b; IV, 474 b; V, 62, 294.

Tegau Eurvron, wife of Caradawc Vreichvras, I, 265.

Teind (teene), tribute: teind taken of fairies by the fiend at stated periods, I, 328, 339, 342, 344–6, 350, 353; III, 505 a; IV, 456, 458; V, 215 b.

Telfer, Jamie, ballad, IV, 4 ff.

Tell, William, III, 16 f., 18 n.; IV, 496 b; his apple-shot, III, 13, 21 n.; his name, 19 n., 21 n.

Tennis-balls in the ballad of Henry V, authorities, III, 321 f.; parallel in Pseudo-Callisthenes, 322.

Testament, oral, or last wishes, of dying person, will good things to friends and ill things to the author of death, I, 143–50, 153–6, 158–60, 162 f., 166, 496–501; II, 498 b; III, 499; IV, 449; V, 208 f.; without animosity to author of death, I, 144, 156; other testaments, where there is no occasion for animosity, I, 144, 496 b; V, 291 b; parodies of these testaments, I, 144 b; III, 499 b; V, 208 b, 286; bequest of sorrow to wife and children and a curse to·mother by a man who had been instigated by her to kill brother or father, I, 169 f.

Testament of fox, robin, ass, dog, etc., I, 144 b; V, 208 b, 286.

Tests (molten lead or gold, burning with red-hot iron, cutting off little finger, etc.) to determine the reality of a woman's apparent death, II, 359, 361, 364–7; III, 517 b; IV, 485; V, 3, 6; other tests, III, 517 b. See Chastity.

Thales solves riddles, I, 13 n.

Thedel von Walmoden, poem and tale, I, 199 n.

Ther wer three ravns, a tune, IV, 126 n., 454.

Thetis, Proteus and Nereus made submissive by maintaining a firm hold through their various transformations, I, 337, 338 n.

Thévenot, I, 240.

Thirty pieces for which Jesus was sold, legends concerning, I, 243 f.; history of, before birth of Jesus, 243.

Þiðriks saga, I, 49, 94 n.; II, 35 n., 41; III, 16; V, 243 b.

Thom of Lyn, a dance, I, 336.

Thomas, Gospel of, II, 7.

Thomas Cantipratensis, Bonum Universale, II, 235, 513 a.

Thomas of Erceldoune, Thomas the Rhymer, I, 317–19, 321 f., 335, 340; his prophecies, 317; Thomas of Erceldoune and Ogier le Danois, 319, and n., 320 n., 340; V, 290 a.

BIBLIOGRAPHY

[The Bibliography which follows is intended to supplement the two special lists already provided, (1) the Sources of the Texts (pp. 397–404, above), and (2) the List of Books of Ballads, etc. (pp. 455–468, above). In some instances, however, the repetition of a title already entered in one of these lists has seemed to be necessary.]

Aasen, Ivar. Norsk Ordbog med dansk Forklaring. Omarbeidet og forøget Udgave af en ældre "Ordbog over det norske Folkesprog." Christiania, 1873.

Abend Zeitung auf das Jahr 1819. (Herausgegeben von T. Hell und F. Kind [and others]. Dresden, Dresden and Leipzig, Leipzig, 1805–57.) [See II, 348.]

Aberdeen. A view of the Diocese of Aberdeen. (MDCCXXXII.) In Joseph Robertson, Collections for a history of the shires of Aberdeen and Banff, III, 67–652. Aberdeen, 1843. (Spalding Club, Publications, 9.)

Aberdeen Herald and Weekly Free Press. Aberdeen, 1806–.

The Aberdeen Magazine. Aberdeen, 1831–32. 2 vols.

Aboyne, Records of. See Huntly, Marquis of.

The Academy. A monthly Record of Literature, Learning, Science, and Art. [Continued as] A weekly Review of Literature, Science, and Art. London, 1869–.

Achilles Tatius. De Clitophontis et Leucippes Amoribus libri viii Graece et Latine. Textum recognovit C. G. Mitscherlich. Biponti, 1792. (Christ. Guil. Mitscherlich. Scriptores erotici Graeci, I.)

Acta Comparationis Litterarum Universarum. Összehasonlitó irodalomtörténelmi lapok, etc. Edited by S. Brassai and H. Meltzl v. Lomnitz. Kolozsvárt, etc. 1877–83. 12+ vols.

Acta Sanctorum quotquot toto orbe coluntur, vel a catholicis scriptoribus celebrantur. Antverpiae, Venetiis, Bruxellis, Parisiis, Romae. 1643–1894. Vols. I–LXIII.

Acts of the Parliaments of Scotland. [Edinburgh,] 1844, '14–24. 11 vols. General Index and Supplement, 1875.

Adam of Cobsam. The Wright's Chaste Wife, a merry tale. Ed. by F. J. Furnivall. London, 1865. (Early English Text Society, 12.)

Adam de la Halle. Li gieux de Robin et de Marion, c'Adans fist. In L. J. N. Monmerqué et Francisque Michel, Théatre Français au Moyen Age, pp. 102–135. Paris, 1842.

Adam of Usk. Chronicon Adae de Usk, A. D. 1377–1404. Ed., with a translation and notes, by Edward M. Thompson. London, 1876.

Adam, E. See Torrent of Portyngale.

Adams, Ernest. The Vernacular Names of Insects. II. In Transactions of the London Philological Society, 1859, pp. 84–96.

Adamson, [Henry]. The Muses Threnodie; or Mirthfull Mournings on the death of Master Gall. New edition. ... Explanatory notes: King James's charter of confirmation: an account of Gowrie's conspiracy. ... Compiled from authentic records. By J. Cant. Perth, 1774.

Addison, Joseph. [Criticism of The Hunting of the Cheviot (Chevy Chace).] In The Spectator, Nos 70, 74. 1711.

Adgar, [Willame]. Marienlegenden nach der Londoner Handschrift Egerton 612 zum ersten Mal vollständig hrsg. von Carl Neuhaus. Heilbronn, 1886. (W. Foerster, Altfranzösische Bibliothek, 9.)

Adolfi, Johann (genannt Neocorus). Chronik des Landes Dithmarschen. Aus der Urschrift herausgegeben von F. C. Dahlmann. Kiel, 1827. 2 vols.

Adrian and Ritheus. In J. M. Kemble, Salomon and Saturnus, pp. 198–211.

Ælfric. De vetere et de novo Testamento. In C. W. M. Grein, Bibliothek der angelsächsischen Prosa, I. Cassel und Göttingen, 1872.

Aelian. Claudii Aeliani De Animalium Natura libri xvii, Varia Historia, Epistolae, Fragmenta, ex recognitione Rudolphi Hercheri. Lipsiae, 1864–66. 2 vols.

Æsop. Μύθων Αἰσωπείων Συναγωγή. Ἐν Παρισίοις, 1810. In Adamantios Koraes, Πάρεργα Ἑλληνικῆς Βιβλιοθήκης, 2.

Afanas'ev, A. N. Narodnyja russkija legendy. [Popular Russian Legends.] Moscow, 1859.

—— Narodnyja russkija skazki. [Popular Russian Tales.] Moscow. 8 parts. Izdanie vtoroe vnov' peresmotrĕnnoe, K. Soldatenkova. Moscow, 1873. 4 vols. (Second edition, corrected.)

—— Poetičeskija vozzrĕnija Slavjan na Prirodu. [Poetic Views of the Slavonians about Nature.] Moscow, 1865–69. 3 vols.

Afzelius, Arvid August. Swenska Folkets Sago-Häfder, eller Fäderneslandets Historia, sådan hon lefwat och till en del ännu lefwer i Sägner, Folksånger och andra Minnesmärken. Stockholm, 1844–53. 5 vols.

Aimoinus. Aimoini monachi Floriacensis Historia Francorum. In A. et F. Du Chesne, Historiae Francorum Scriptores, III, 1–124. Lutetiae Parisiorum, 1641.

Aiol et Mirabel und Elie de Saint Gille. Zwei altfranzösische Heldengedichte, mit Anmerkungen und Glossar und einem Anhang: die Fragmente des mittelniederländischen Aiol, herausgegeben von Prof. Dr. J. Verdam in Amsterdam. Zum ersten Mal herausgegeben von Dr. Wendelin Foerster. Heilbronn, 1876–82.

Albericus Trium Fontium. See Leibnitz.

Albertus Magnus. De Mineralibus. In Beati Alberti Magni Ratisbonensis Episcopi Opera quae hactenus haberi potuerunt. In lucem edita studio et labore R. A. P. F. Petri Iammy. Lugduni, 1651. 21 vols. II, 210–272.

Alemannia. Zeitschrift für Sprache, Litteratur und Volkskunde des Elsasses und Oberrheins (E., O. und Schwabens;
Zeitschrift für Sprache, Kunst und Altertum besonders
des alemannisch-schwäbischen Gebiets). Herausgegeben
von Dr. Anton Birlinger (von Fridrich Pfaff). Bonn, 1873-.

[Alexander the Great.] Kyng Alisaunder. *In* Henry
Weber, Metrical Romances, I, 1-327.

—— Lambert li Tors et Alexandre de Bernay. Li Romans d'Alixandre. Nach Handschriften der königlichen
Büchersammlung zu Paris hrsg. von Heinrich Michelant.
Stuttgart, 1846. (Bibliothek des Litterarischen Vereins
in Stuttgart, 13.)

—— Lamprecht, *der Pfaffe*. Alexander, Gedicht des
zwölften Jahrhunderts. Urtext und Uebersetzung von
Heinrich Weismann. Frankfurt, 1850. 2 vols.

—— Ulrich von Eschenbach. Alexander, hrsg. v. Wendelin Toischer. Tübingen, 1888. (Bibl. d. Litt. Ver. in
Stuttgart, 183.)

—— See Meyer, Paul.

Alexis, Willibald. See Hohenhausen, Elise von.

Alfonso X, *the Wise*. Las siete partidas, cotejadas con
varios codices antiguos por la Real Academia de la Historia. Madrid, 1807. 3 vols.

—— See Cronica de España.

Allardyce, Alexander. See Sharpe, Charles Kirkpatrick.

Allatius, Leo. De templis Graecorum recentioribus, ad
Ioannem Morinum; de narthece ecclesiae veteris . . . ;
nec non de Graecorum hodie quorundam opinationibus,
ad Paullum Zacchiam. Coloniae Agrippinae, 1645.

[Allen, Thomas.] History of the County of Lincoln.
London and Lincoln, 1834. 2 vols.

Almanach des Traditions populaires. [Edited by Eugène
Rolland.] Paris, 1882-84.

Alpenburg, Johann Nepomuk von. Deutsche Alpensagen.
Wien, 1861.

Alphonsus a Spina. Fortalicium Fidei contra fidei Christianae hostes. [Bernhard Richel ? Basle, *cir.* 1475.]

Altdeutsche Blätter. See Haupt, Moriz, and Hoffmann,
Heinrich [von Fallersleben]. Leipzig, 1836-40. 2 vols.

Altenglische Bibliothek. Herausgegeben von Eugen Kölbing. Heilbronn, 1883-90. 5 vols.

Altfranzösische Bibliothek. Herausgegeben von Wendelin
Foerster. Heilbronn, Leipzig, 1879-92. 13 vols.

Altpreussische Monatschrift zur Spiegelung des provinziel-
len Lebens in Literatur, Kunst, Wissenschaft und Industrie, hrsg. v. R. Reicke und E. Wichert. Königsberg,
1864-.

Altswert. Meister Altswert, herausgegeben von W. Holland und A. Keller. Stuttgart, 1850. (Bibliothek des
Litterarischen Vereins in Stuttgart, 21.)

Amadas et Ydoine. Poëme d'aventures, publié par C. Hippeau. Paris, 1863.

Amadis de Gaula. Dell' Historia di Amadis di Gavla Libri
Qvattro. Nuouamente tradotti della lingua Spagnuola
nella lingua Italiana. Venetia, 1609.

—— Le 1er-8e Livre d'Amadis de Gaule, mis en François
par Nicolas de Herberay : Le 9e-13e Livre [by various
translators]. Anvers, 1573, '72-73. 13 livr. in 3 vols.

—— I Qvattro Libri di Amadis di Gavla, ove si racconta
. . . l' historia de' suoi strenui e ualorosi gesti. Tradotti pur hora di lingua Spagnuola nella nostra buona
Italiana. Venetia, 1552.

Amador de los Rios, José. Historia crítica de la literatura
española. Madrid, 1861-65. 7 vols.

Amador de los Rios, José. Historia social, política y reli-
giosa de los Judíos da España y Portugal. Madrid, 1875-
76. 3 vols.

—— Romanzen Asturiens aus dem Volksmunde zum
ersten Mal gesammelt und herausgegeben von ——. *In*
Jahrbuch für romanische und englische Literatur, III,
268-91. 1861.

Amelung, Arthur, and Jänicke, Oskar. Ortnit und die
Wolfdietriche nach Müllenhoff's Vorarbeiten herausge-
geben von ——. *In* Deutsches Heldenbuch, III, IV.
Berlin, 1871, '73. 2 vols.

Amer, M. V. See Genesi de Scriptura.

American Journal of Philology. Edited by Basil L. Gildersleeve. Baltimore, 1880-.

Aminson, Henrik. See Bidrag till Södermanlands äldre
Kulturhistoria.

Amis and Amiloun. Zugleich mit der altfranzösischen
Quelle hrsg. von Eugen Kölbing. Heilbronn, 1884. (Altenglische Bibliothek, 2.)

Amis e Amilun. *In* Amis and Amiloun, hrsg. v. E. Kolbing,
pp. 109-187.

Amis et Amiles und Jourdains de Blaivies. Zwei altfranzösische Heldengedichte des kerlingischen Sagenkrieses,
hrsg. v. Konrad Hofmann. 2e Auflage. Erlangen, 1882.

Amyot, Thomas. See Taming of a Shrew.

Les Anciens Poëtes de la France. See Guessard, F.

d'Ancona, Alessandro. La poesia popolare italiana. Studj.
Livorno, 1878.

—— Sacre rappresentazioni dei secoli XIV, XV e XVI.
Firenze, 1872. 3 vols.

—— See Comparetti, Domenico. See Sercambi, Giovanni.

Anderson, Joseph. See Low, George.

Anderson, William. Genealogy and Surnames : with some
heraldic and biographical notices. Edinburgh, 1865.

Andresen, Hugo. See Wace.

Angelo de Tummulillis. See Tummulillis, Angelo de.

Anglia. Zeitschrift für englische Philologie. Herausgegeben von Richard Wülker [and others]. Halle, 1877-.

Anglo-Saxon Chronicle. See Earle, John.

Anketell, Rev. John. Poems. Dublin, 1793. [See III,
307.]

Annales archéologiques. See Didron, A. N.

Annales Monastici. See Luard, H. R.

Annales Placentini ab Anno MCCCCI usque ad
MCCCCLXIII ab Antonio de Ripalta patricio Placentino conscripti, ac deinde continuati ab Alberto de Ripalta
ejus filio usque ad annum MCCCCLXXXIV. Nunc
primum in lucem proferuntur e msto codice Placentino.
In Lodovico Antonio Muratori, Rerum Italicarum Scriptores, XX, 869-978. Mediolani, 1731.

Annals of Burton. *In* H. R. Luard, Annales Monastici, I,
181-414.

Annals of Winchester. *In* H. R. Luard, Annales Monastici,
II, 3-125.

Annuario della Società degli Alpinisti Tridentini, vols XI-
XIV. Rovereto, 1885-9.

Anonymi De Antiquitatibus Constantinopolitanis. *In* A.
Banduri, Imperium Orientale, t. I, pars iii, lib. 1-3.
Venetiis, 1729.

Anstis, John. The Register of the Most Noble Order of the
Garter, with notes, and an introduction by the editor.
London, 1724.

Anthologia Graeca ad fidem codicis olim Palatini nunc Pari-
sini ex apographo Gothano edita. Curavit, epigrammata

in codice Palatino desiderata et annotationem criticam adiecit Fridericus Jacobs. Lipsiae, 1813–17. 3 vols in 4.

Antiquarisk Tidskrift, utgivet af det Kongelige Nordiske Oldskrift-Selskab. Kjøbenhavn, 1845–64. 10 vols.

The Antiquary. A Magazine devoted to the study of the past. London, 1880–.

Antiquiteter i Thorskinge. Fornminnet eller Kummel-Runan, tolkande Systersveket Bröllopps-dagen. Götheborg, 1836. [See I, 493 b.]

Antoninus Liberalis. Transformationes. In Anton Westermann, Μυθόγραφοι, 1843, pp. 200–38.

Anvár-i Suhailí. See Pilpay.

Anzeiger für deutsches Alterthum und deutsche Litteratur. Unter Mitwirkung von Karl Müllenhoff und Wilhelm Scherer hrsg. von Elias Steinmeyer. Berlin, 1876–.

Anzeiger für Kunde des deutschen Mittelalters (der teutschen Vorzeit). See Mone's Anzeiger.

Apollodorus. Apollodori Atheniensis Bibliothecae libri tres et fragmenta. Curis secundis illustravit Chr. G. Heyne. Gottingae, 1803.

Apollonius Rhodius. Apollonii Argonautica. Emendavit, apparatum criticum et prolegomena adiecit R. Merkel. Scholia vetera e codice Laurentiano edidit Henricus Keil. Lipsiae, 1854.

Apollonius of Tyre. Appollonius Tyrus. Appolonius von Tiria. In Griseldis. Apollonius von Tyrus. Aus Handschriften herausgegeben von Carl Schröder. Leipzig, 1873.

—— Historia Apollonii Regis Tyri. Recensuit et praefatus est Alexander Riese. Lipsiae, 1871.

—— Kynge Apollyn of Thyre. Printed by Wynkyn de Worde, 1510. Reproduced in facsimile by E. W. Ashbee. London, 1870.

Arabian Nights. The Arabian Nights Entertainments; revised from the Arabic. [With] a selection of new tales now first translated from the Arabic originals, by Jonathan Scott. London, 1811. 6 vols.

—— Tausend und Eine Nacht. Arabische Erzählungen. Deutsch von M. Habicht, F. H. von der Hagen und Carl Schall. Breslau (1ᵗᵉˢ Bdchn, Stuttgart, 6ᵗᵒ Aufl., 1881), 1840. 15 Bdchn.

—— The Thousand and One Nights, commonly called The Arabian Nights' Entertainments; transl. by Edward William Lane. London, 1841. 3 vols.

Arany, János. See Koszorú.

Arber, Edward. A Transcript of the Registers of the Company of Stationers of London. 1554–1640 A. D. Vols I–IV, London, 1875–77; vol. V, Birmingham, 1894. 5 vols.

d'Arbois de Jubainville, H., et Loth, J. Cours de littérature celtique. Paris, 1883–95. 8 vols.

Archæologia, or, Miscellaneous Tracts relating to Antiquity. Published by the Society of Antiquaries. London, 1804–.

Archæologia Cambrensis. A Record of the Antiquities of Wales and its Marches, and the Journal of the Cambrian Archæological Association. London, 1846–.

Archæologia Scotica. See Society of Antiquaries of Scotland.

Archæological Review. London, 1888–90. 4 vols.

Archiv für Litteraturgeschichte, herausgegeben von Dr Richard Gosche (Bd I–II; von Dr. Franz Schnorr von Carolsfeld, Bd III–XV). Leipzig, 1870–87. 15 vols.

Archiv für slavische Philologie. Unter Mitwirkung von A. Leskien und W. Nehring hrsg. v. V. Jagić. Berlin, 1876–.

Archiv für das Studium der neueren Sprachen und Lite-

raturen. Eine Vierteljahrschrift. Herausgegeben von Ludwig Herrig und Heinrich Viehoff [and others]. Bd I–V, Elberfeld und Iserlohn, 1846–49. Bd VI–. Braunschweig, 1849–.

Archiv für wissenschaftliche Kunde von Russland. Herausgegeben von A. Erman. Berlin, [1841]–67. 25 vols.

Archivio per lo studio delle tradizioni popolari. Rivista trimestrale, diretta da G. Pitrè e S. Salomone-Marino. Palermo, Torino, 1882–.

Arda Viraf. The Book of Arda Viraf. The Pahlavi text prepared by Destur Hoshangji Jamaspji Asa, revised and collated with further MSS, with an English translation and introduction, and an appendix containing the texts and translations of the Gosht-i Fryano and Hadokht-nask, by Martin Haug, assisted by E. W. West. Bombay, London, 1872.

Arentsschildt, L. von. Albion und Erin. In Liedern von Th. Moore, Lord Byron, P. B. Shelley, Th. Campbell, J. Thomson; und aus Th. Percy's "Ueberreste altengl. Dichtkunst." Im Versmasse der Originale übertragen von ——. Mit beigedrucktem Originaltext. Mainz, 1851.

—— Völkerstimmen. Portugal, Spanien, Italien, Schottland, England. Hannover, 1847.

Aretin, Johann Christoph von. Geschichte der Juden in Baiern. Landshut, 1803.

Arkiv för nordisk Filologi. Udgivet under Medvirkning af Sophus Bugge [et al.] ved Gustav Storm, I–IV; genom Axel Kock, V–. Christiania, Lund, 1883–.

Armana prouvençau. Avignon, 1855–.

Armstrong, Robert Bruce. The History of Liddesdale, Eskdale, Ewesdale, Wauchopedale, and the Debateable Land. Edinburgh, 1883.

—— Notes on a Feud between the Elliots and the Scotts during the years 1564, 1565, and 1566. In Proceedings of the Society of Antiquaries of Scotland, XV, 93–100 (1880–81). 1881.

Árnason, Jón. Icelandic Legends, collected by ——. Translated by George E. J. Powell and Eiríkr Magnússon. London, 1864. Second Series, London, 1866.

—— Íslenzkar þjóðsögur og Æfintýri. Leipzig, 1862–4. 2 vols.

Arnaud, Camille. Ludus Sancti Jacobi. Fragment de mystère provençal découvert et publié par ——. Marseille, 1858.

Arndt, Ernst Moritz. Blütenlese aus Altem und Neuem. Leipzig, 1857.

Arnim, Ludwig Achim von. Tröst Einsamkeit, alte und neue Sagen und Wahrsagungen, Geschichten und Gedichte. Herausgegeben von ——. (Also with the title, Zeitung für Einsiedler.) Heidelberg, 1808.

Arnold, Edwin. Indian Idylls, from the Sanskrit of the Mahâbhârata. Boston, 1883.

Arnold, T. See Henry of Huntingdon.

[Arrom, Cecilia d'.] La Gaviota; novela de costumbres, por Fernan Caballero. London, 1868.

—— Lágrimas, novela de costumbres contemporaneas, por Fernan Caballero. Madrid, 1858.

Arthour and Merlin: a metrical romance. Now first edited from the Auchinleck MS. [by W. B. D. D. Turnbull]. Edinburgh, 1838. (Abbotsford Club, Publications, 12.)

Arthur, King. See Malory, Sir Thomas. See (Le) Morte Arthur. See Arthour and Merlin.

Asbjørnsen, Peter Christian. Juletræet for 1850. En Samling af norske Folke- og Børne-Eventyr. Christiania, 1850. Juletræet for 1851. Norske Eventyr og Folke-Sagn. Christiania, 1851. Juletræet, 1866. Norske Folke- og Børne-Eventyr. Andet Oplag. Christiania, 1866.

Asbjørnsen, Peter Christian. Norske Folke-Eventyr. Ny Samling. Med Bidrag fra Jørgen Moes Reiser og Optegnelser. Christiania, 1871. Anden Udgave. Kjøbenhavn, 1876.

—— Norske Huldre-Eventyr og Folkesagn. Christiania, 1845–48. Same. Anden forøgede Udgave. I. Christiania, 1859.

—— and Moe, Jørgen. Norske Folkeeventyr. Anden forøgede Udgave. Christiania, 1852.

Ascham, Roger. Toxophilus, 1545. Carefully edited by Edward Arber. London, 1868. (Edward Arber, English Reprints, 1868, No. 7.)

Ashton, John. See Skelton, John.

Ásmundarson, Valdimar. See Fornaldarsögur Norðrlanda.

Assende, Diederic van. See Floire et Blanceflor.

Asser, Joannes. Annales Rerum Gestarum Ælfredi Magni, auctore Asserio Menevensi, recensuit Franciscus Wise. Oxonii, 1722.

Astley, Thomas, publisher. A new General Collection of Voyages and Travels. London, 1745–47. 4 vols.

The Athenæum. Journal of Literature, Science and the Fine Arts. London, 1828–.

Aue, K. Verzeichniss zweier Samlungen deutscher Volkslieder und Volksspiele auf fliegenden Blättern. In Mone's Anzeiger, VIII, 354–80. 1839.

Auersperg, Graf von. See Grün, Anastasius.

[Aulnoy, Marie Catherine Jumelle de Berneville, Comtesse d'.] Les Contes des Fées. Par Madame D****. Nouv. éd. Paris, 1774. 4 vols.

—— Mémoires de la Cour d'Espagne. In La Cour et la Ville de Madrid. Deuxième partie. La Haye, 1691. 2 pts.

Das Ausland: ein Tageblatt für Kunde des geistigen und sittlichen Lebens der Völker. München, Stuttgart (with varying title), 1828–.

Ausonius. Epigrammata. In D. Magni Ausonii Burdigalensis Opera ex doctorum virorum emendatione. Basiliae, 1781.

Axelson, Maximilian. Vandring i Wermlands Elfdal och Finnskogar. Stockholm, [1852].

—— Vesterdalarne, dess Natur, Folklif och Fornminnen. Under Vandringar derstädes tecknade. Stockholm, 1855.

Axon, William E. A. Lancashire Gleanings. Manchester and London, 1883.

Ayrer, Jakob. Dramen, herausgegeben von Adelbert von Keller. Stuttgart, 1865. 5 vols. (Bibliothek des Litterarischen Vereins in Stuttgart, 76–80.)

Baader, Bernhard. Neugesammelte Volkssagen aus dem Lande Baden und den angrenzenden Gegenden. Karlsruhe, 1859.

—— Teutsche Volkssagen (und Mährchen). Aus mündlicher Ueberlieferung mitgetheilt von ——. In Mone's Anzeiger, IV, 162–4, 306–12, 406–11; V, 174–7, 318–22, 413–15; VI, 68–71, 173–5, 304–10, 394–400; VII, 51–55, 221–7, 362–71, 471–80; VIII, 60–66, 176–86, 303–15, 530–40. 1835–39.

Babcock, W. H. The London Ballads. In Folk-Lore Journal, VII, 27–35. 1889.

Babucke, Heinrich. See Josef.

Bacon, Francis. Essays and Colours of Good and Evil. With notes and a glossarial index by W. Aldis Wright. London, 1871.

Bäckström, P. O. Svenska Folkböcker. Sagor, legender och äfventyr, efter äldre upplagor och andra källor utgifne, jemte öfversigt af svensk folkläsning från äldre till närvarande tid. Stockholm, 1845–48. 2 vols.

The Bagford Ballads. Edited, with introduction and notes, by Joseph Woodfall Ebsworth. Hertford, 1878. 2 vols. (Ballad Society.)

Baillie, Robert. The Letters and Journals of Robert Baillie, A. M., Principal of the University of Glasgow. M. DC. XXXVII. – M. DC. LXII. [Edited by David Laing.] Edinburgh, 1841–42. 3 vols. (Bannatyne Club.)

Bain, Joseph. See Maitland, Richard.

Baissac, C. Le folk-lore de l'Île-Maurice; texte créole et traduction française. Paris, 1888. (Les littératures populaires de toutes les nations, 27.)

Balderic. Historia Hierosolymitana Baldrici Archiepiscopi. In Migne, Patrologia, CLXVI, 1061–1152. 1854.

Balfour, J. See Sharpe, C. K.

The Ballad Minstrelsy of Scotland, romantic and historical: with notes and introduction on the ballad poetry of Scotland. London and Glasgow, 1871.

Ballesteros, José Pérez. Cancionero popular gallego y en particular de la provincia de la Coruña por ——, con un prólogo del ilustre mitógrafo portugués Theóphilo Braga. Madrid, 1885–86. 3 vols. (Folk-lore Español. Biblioteca de las Tradiciones populares Españolas, VII, IX, XI. Director: Antonio Machado y Álvarez.)

Bandello, Matteo. Novelle. [Ed. by Gaetano Poggiali.] London, 1791–93. 9 tom. 4 pt.

Banduri, Anselm. Imperium Orientale, sive Antiquitates Constantinopolitanae. Venetiis, 1729. 2 vols. (Byzantinae Historiae Scriptores, Graece et Latine, 23, 24.)

Bannatyne, Richard. Journal of the Transactions in Scotland, during the contest between the adherents of Queen Mary and those of her son, 1570–1573. Edinburgh, 1806.

Barack, Karl August. See Zimmerische Chronik.

Barącz, X. Sadok. Bajki, fraszki, podania, przysłowia i pieśni na Rusi. [Fables, jests, traditions, saws and songs.] Tarnopol, 1866.

Barbazan, Étienne de. Fabliaux et contes des poètes françois des XI, XII, XIII, XIV et XVᵉ siècles; nouvelle édition, augmentée par M. Méon. Paris, 1808. 4 vols.

Barbi, Michele. Maggi della montagna pistoiese. In Archivio per lo studio delle tradizioni popolari, VII, 97–113. 1888.

Barclay, Alexander. Certayne Egloges of Alexander Barclay, Priest. Whereof the first three conteyne the miseryes of Courtiers and Courtes of all princes in generall, Gathered out of a Booke named in Latin, Miseriæ Cvrialivm, compiled by Eneas Siluius Poet and Oratour. An. Do. 1570. Manchester, 1885. (Spenser Society Publications, 39.)

Barfod, F. See Brage og Idun.

Baring-Gould, Sabine, and Sheppard, Henry Fleetwood. Songs and Ballads of the West. A collection made from the mouths of the people. Harmonised and arranged for voice and pianoforte. London, [1889 ?–91].

Baróti, Ludwig. See Grünn, Karl.

Barry, Edward. Thèse de littérature sur les vicissitudes et les transformations du cycle populaire de Robin Hood. Paris, 1832.

Barry, George. History of the Orkney Islands. 2nd ed., with corrections and additions by James Headrick. London, 1808.

Barry, George Augustus. Letter . . . concerning Bessie Bell and Mary Gray. *In* Archæologia Scotica, II, 108–110. 1822.

Bartholdy, Jakob L. Salomon. Bruchstücke zur nahern Kenntniss des heutigen Griechenlands, gesammelt auf einer Reise von J. L. S. Bartholdy im Jahre 1803–1804. Erster Theil. Berlin, 1805.

Bartsch, Karl. Altfranzösische Romanzen und Pastourellen. Leipzig, 1870. Also with the title, Romances et pastourelles françaises des XIIᵉ et XIIIᵉ siècles.

—— Gedicht auf den Zauberer Virgilius. *In* Germania, IV, 237–40. 1859.

—— Meisterlieder der Kolmarer Handschrift. Stuttgart, 1862. (Bibl. d. Litt. Ver. in Stuttgart, 68.)

—— Sagen, Märchen und Gebräuche aus Meklenburg. Wien, 1879–80. 2 vols.

—— See Germania. See Herzog Ernst.

—— See Kudrun. See Nibelungenlied.

—— See Reinfrid von Braunschweig.

Basile, Giambattista. Il Pentamerone; ouero, Lo Cvnto de li Cvnte, trattenemiento de li peccerille di Gian Alesio Abbatvtis. Napoli, 1674.

—— Der Pentamerone; oder, Das Märchen aller Märchen. Aus dem Neapolitanischen übertragen v. Felix Liebrecht. Nebst einer Vorrede v. Jacob Grimm. Breslau, 1846. 2 vols.

Basnage [Jacques de Beauval]. Histoire des Juifs depuis Jésus-Christ. La Haye, 1716–[1726]. 15 vols.

Basset, René. Contes populaires berbères. Paris, 1887. (Collection de contes et de chansons populaires, 12.)

—— Le prêt miraculeusement remboursé. *In* Revue des traditions populaires, IX, 14–31, 1894.

Li Bastars de Buillon; poëme du XIVᵉ siècle, publié pour la première fois par Aug. Scheler. Bruxelles, 1877.

Baumgarten, P. Amand. Aus der volksmässigen Ueberlieferung der Heimat. Linz, 1864.

Beamont, William. Annals of the Lords of Warrington for the first five centuries after the Conquest. [Manchester,] 1872. 2 pts. (Chetham Society, 86, 87.)

Beaujeu, Renaud de. See Bel Inconnu.

Beaumanoir, Philippe de Remi, sire de. Œuvres poétiques de ——, publiées par Hermann Suchier. Paris, 1884–85. 2 vols. (Société des anciens textes français.)

—— The romance of Blonde of Oxford and Jehan of Dammartin. By Philippe de Reimes, a trouvère of the thirteenth century. Edited, from the unique MS. in the Imperial Library in Paris, by M. Le Roux de Lincy. London, 1858. (Camden Society.)

Beaumont, Francis, and Fletcher, John. Works. With notes and a biographical memoir by the Rev. Alexander Dyce. London, 1843–46. 11 vols.

Beaumont, Madame Leprince de. Les contes de fées. Préface de Mery. Paris, 1865.

Bech, F. See Hartmann von Aue.

Bechstein, Ludwig. Märchenbuch, 32. Aufl. Leipzig, 1879.

Bechstein, Reinhold. See Tristan.

Bedae Collectanea et Flores. *In* Salomon and Saturnus, ed. Kemble, pp. 322–26.

Bédier, Joseph. Les fabliaux: études de littérature populaire et d'histoire littéraire du moyen âge. Paris, 1893. (Bibl. de l'école des hautes études, 98.) 2ᵉ éd., 1895.

Begbie, Peter James. Supernatural Illusions. London, 1851. 2 vols.

Behrnauer, Walter F. A. Die Vierzig Veziere oder weisen Meister. Ein altmorgenländischer Sittenroman, zum ersten Male vollständig aus dem Türkischen übertragen. Leipzig, 1851.

Beiträge zur Geschichte der deutschen Sprache und Literatur. Herausgegeben von Hermann Paul und Wilhelm Braune (von E. Sievers). Halle, 1874–.

Beiträge zur Kunde Preussens. Königsberg, 1818–24. 7 vols.

Bekker, Immanuel. See Codinus.

—— See Crestien de Troyes.

—— See Floire et Blancefleur.

Le Bel Inconnu: ou Giglain, fils de Messire Gauvain, par Renauld de Beaujeu. Publié d'après le manuscrit unique de Londres par C. Hippeau. Paris, 1860.

Belgisch Museum voor de Nederduitsche Tael- en Letterkunde; uitgeven op last der Maetschappy tot Bevordering der Nederduitsche Tael- en Letterkunde, door J. F. Willems. Gent, 1837–46. 10 vols.

Bell, Robert. Early Ballads illustrative of history, traditions, and customs. London, 1856.

Beloe, William. Miscellanies, consisting of Poems, Classical Extracts, and Oriental Apologues. London, 1795. 3 vols.

Benecke, G. F. See Wirnt von Gravenberg.

Benfey, Theodor. [Review of] Garcin de Tassy, La poésie philosophique et religieuse chez les Persans. *In* Göttingische Gelehrte Anzeigen, 1861, pp. 677–80.

—— Göthe's Gedicht: Legende (Werke, 1840, I, 200) und dessen indisches Vorbild. *In* Orient und Occident, I, 719–32. 1862.

—— Die kluge Dirne. Die indischen Märchen von den klugen Räthsellösern und ihre Verbreitung über Asien und Europa. *In* Das Ausland, XXXII, 457–61, 486–89, 511–15, 567–71, 589–94. Stuttgart and Augsburg, 1859.

—— See Orient und Occident.

—— See Pantschatantra.

Benoît de Sainte-More. Extrait de l'estoire e la généalogie des dux qui unt esté par ordre en Normendie. *In* Chroniques Anglo-Normandes. Recueil d'extraits et d'écrits relatifs a l'histoire de Normandie et d'Angleterre pendant les XIᵉ et XIIᵉ siècles. Publié par Francisque Michel. Rouen, 1836. 3 vols. I, 167–303.

Benzel, E. See Vastovius.

Berceo, Gonzalo de. Poesias de don Gonzalo de Berceo. *In* Thomas Antonio Sanchez. Coleccion de poesias castellanas anteriores al siglo XV. Illustradas con algunas notas e indice de voces antiquadas. Vol. II. Madrid, 1780.

Berger, Arnold E. See Orendel.

Bergh, Laurent Phillipe Charles van den. De nederlandsche Volksromans. Eene Bijdrage tot de Geschiedenis onzer Letterkunde. Amsterdam, 1837.

—— Proeve van een kritisch Woordenboek der nederlandsche Mythologie. Utrecht, 1846.

Berlin Academy. Abhandlungen der Akademie. Aus den Jahren 1804–. Berlin, 1815–.

—— Monatsberichte der königlich Preussischen Akademie der Wissenschaften. Berlin, 1856–81. Continued as Sitzungsberichte der . . . Akademie, etc., 1882–.

Bernay, Alexandre de. See Alexander the Great.

Bernoni, Giuseppe. Fiabe e novelle popolari veneziane. Venezia, 1873.

Bernoni, Giuseppe. Tradizioni popolari veneziane. Venezia, 1875–78. 7 parts.

Berntsen, Kl. Folke-Æventyr. Odense, 1873–83. 2 collections.

Bertrand, Nicolas. Bertrandi opus de Tholosanorum gestis ab urbe condita cunctis mortalibus apprime dignum conspectibus. Tholose, 1515.

Beuter, Pere Anton. Coronica general de toda España. Valencia, 1604.

Beves of Hamtoun. The romance of Sir Beves of Hamtoun. Edited from six manuscripts and the old printed copy, with introduction, notes, and glossary, by Eugen Kölbing. London, 1885–94. (Early English Text Society, Extra Series, 46, 48, 65.)

—— Sir Beves of Hamtoun; a metrical romance. Now first edited from the Auchinleck MS. Edinburgh, 1838. (Maitland Club.)

Bezzenberger, Adalbert. Litauische Forschungen. Beiträge zur Kenntniss der Sprache und des Volkstumes der Litauer. Göttingen, 1882.

Biagi, Guido. Le novelle antiche, con una introduzione sulla storia esterna del testo del Novellino. Firenze, 1880. (Raccolta di Opere Inedite o Rare di ogni secolo della Letteratura Italiana, [1].)

Biblioteca de Autores Españoles, desde la formacion del lenguaje hasta nuestros dias. M[anuel] Rivadeneyra, impresor-editor. Madrid, 1860–1880. 71 vols.

La Bibliothèque Bleue. Liége, 1787. 3 vols.

Bibliothèque universelle des Romans, ouvrage périodique, dans lequel on donne l'analyse raisonnée des romans anciens & modernes, françois, ou traduits dans notre langue; avec des anecdotes & des notices historiques & critiques concernant les auteurs ou leurs ouvrages; ainsi que les mœurs, les usages du temps, les circonstances particulières & relatives, & les personnages connus, déguisés ou emblématiques. Paris, 1775–1789. 112 vols.

Bidpaï. See Pilpay.

Bidrag till Södermanlands äldre Kulturhistoria utgifna af Henrik Aminson. Stockholm, 1877–. (Södermanlands Fornminnesförening.)

Binder, Eugen. Weiteres zu Bürgers 'Kaiser und Abt.' In Zeitschrift für vergleichende Literaturgeschichte, N. F., V, 466–9. 1892.

Binder, W. Schwäbische Volkssagen, Geschichten und Mährchen. Stuttgart, 1845. 2 vols.

[Bikez,] Biquet, Robert. Le Lai du Cor. Restitution critique par Dr. Fredrik Wulff. Lund, 1888.

Birch, Thomas. Memoirs of the Reign of Queen Elizabeth from the year 1581. London, 1754. 2 vols.

Birlinger, Anton. Aus Schwaben. Sagen, Legenden, Aberglauben, Sitten, Rechtsbräuche, Ortsneckereien, Lieder, Kinderreime. Wiesbaden, 1874. 2 vols.

—— Legende von den Jakobsbrüdern. In Alemannia, XIII, 42–45. 1885.

—— Schwäbisch-augsburgisches Wörterbuch. München, 1864. [Supplementheft to Sitzungsberichte of Munich Academy.]

—— Zum Volksliede. In Germania, V, 372–5. 1860.

—— See Alemannia.

—— and Buck, M. R. Volksthümliches aus Schwaben. 1ter bd. Sagen, Märchen, Volksaberglauben, von A. Birlinger und M. R. Buck. 2ter bd. Sitten und Gebräuche, von A. Birlinger. Freiburg im Breisgau, 1861–2. 2 vols.

Birrel, Robert. The Diarey of Robert Birrel, Burges of Edinburghe. Containing divers passages of staite, and uthers memorable accidents. Frome the 1532 zeir of our redemptione, till ye beginning of the zeir 1605. In John Graham Dalyell, Fragments of Scotish History, II. Edinburgh, 1798.

[Björner, Erik Julius.] Nordiska Kämpa Dater, i en sagoflock samlade om forna kongar och hjältar [etc.]. Volumen historicum, continens variorum in orbe hyperboreo antiquo regum, heroum et pugilum res praeclare et mirabiliter gestas. Stockholmiae, 1737.

Blaas, C. M. Volksthümliches aus Niederösterreich. In Germania, XXV, 426–31. 1880.

Black, William. Three Feathers. A novel. 6th ed. London, 1885.

Black, William Henry. The Life and Martyrdom of Thomas Beket, from the series of Lives and Legends by Robert of Gloucester. London, 1845. (Percy Society.)

Blackwell, I. A. See Northern Antiquities.

Blackwood's Edinburgh Magazine. Edinburgh, 1817–.

Bladé, Jean-François. Contes populaires de la Gascogne. Paris, 1886. 3 vols. (Les littératures populaires de toutes les nations, 19–21.)

—— Contes et proverbes populaires recueillis en Armagnac. Paris, 1867.

Blätter für literarische Unterhaltung. Leipzig, 1830–76, 1880–.

Blätter für pommersche Volkskunde. Monatsschrift für Sage und Märchen, Sitte und Brauch, Schwank und Streich, Lied, Rätsel und Sprachliches in Pommern. Herausgegeben von D. Knoop und Dr. A. Haas. Stettin, 1893–.

Blaeu, Willem Janszoon or Janssen. Het Licht der Zeevaert, daerinne claerlijck beschreven ende afgebeeldet werdē alle de custen ende havenen, vande Westersche, Noordsche, Oostersche ende Middelandsche Zee'n. Amsterdam, 1623–25. 2 books.

Blakhal, Gilbert. A Breiffe Narration of the Services done to three Noble Ladyes. 1631–1649. Aberdeen, 1844. (Spalding Club, 11.)

Blind Harry. See Henry the Minstrel.

Blind, Karl. Scottish, Shetlandic, and Germanic Water Tales. In Contemporary Review, XL, 186–208, 399–423, 534–63. 1881.

Blonde of Oxford. See Beaumanoir.

Der Blut-Prozess von Tisza Eszlár in Ungarn . . . nach den amtlichen, stenographischen Protocollen aus dem Ungarischen übertragen. New York, 1883.

[Bodmer, J. J.] Altenglische Balladen. [1tes bdchn.] Altenglische und altschwäbische Balladen. 2tes bdchn. Zürich u. Winterthur, Zürich, 1780–81. 2 vols.

Boece, Hector. Scotorum historiae a prima gentis origine. [Paris, 1526.]

Böckel, Otto. Zur Lenorensage. In Germania, XXXI, 117–18. 1886.

Böhmer, Eduard. See Romanische Studien.

Böttiger, C. A. Ilithyia oder die Hexe, ein archäologisches Fragment nach Lessing. In his Kleine Schriften, 1850, I, 61–92.

—— Die Jungfernprobe in der Drachenhöhle zu Lanuvium. In his Kleine Schriften, 1850, I, 178–82.

—— Kleine Schriften archäologischen und antiquarischen Inhalts, hrsg. v. Julius Sillig. 2te Ausg. Leipzig, 1850. 3 vols.

Bohlin, Karl. Folktoner från Jämtland upptecknade år 1880 af ——. Stockholm, 1883. (Nyare Bidrag till Kännedom om de svenska Landsmålen ock svenskt Folklif, II, 10.)

Bolognini, N. Usi e Costumi del Trentino. Le Leggende del Trentino. Rovereto, 1885–89. (Extracts from Annuario della Società degli Alpinisti Tridentini, XI–XIV.)

Bolte, Johannes. Zu dem Märchen von den sieben Grafen. *In* Zeitschrift des Vereins für Volkskunde, III, 61–67.
—— See Köhler, Reinhold.

Le Bon Sens. Carcassone, Aug. 10, 1878. [Newspaper.]

Bondeson, August. Halländska Sagor. Lund, 1880. (Boksamling utgifven af de Skånska Landskapens Historiska och Arkeologiska Förening.)
—— Svenska Folksagor från Skilda Landskap. Stockholm, [1882.]

Bongi, S. See Doni.

The Booke of the Universall Kirk of Scotland. *In* Acts and Proceedings of the General Assemblies of the Kirk of Scotland, from the year 1560 [to 1618]. Collected from the most authentic manuscripts. [Ed. by Thomas Thomson.] Edinburgh, 1839–45. 3 pts. and appendix, 4 v. (Pt I, Bannatyne Club, 69; pts II and III, Maitland Club, 49.)

Borde, Andrew. The fyrst boke of the Introduction of Knowledge, ed. by F. J. Furnivall. London, 1870. (Early English Text Society, Extra Series, 10.)

[Borrow, George.] Danish and Norwegian Literature. *In* Foreign Quarterly Review, VI, 48–87. 1830.
—— Targum, or, Metrical Translations from thirty languages and dialects. St Petersburg, 1835.

Bosanske narodne pripovjedke. Skupio i na svietlo izdao zbor redovničke omladine bosanske u Djakovu. Sissek, 1870.

Bosquet, Amélie. La Normandie romanesque et merveilleuse: traditions, légendes et superstitions populaires. Paris and Rouen, 1845.

Bothe, Friedrich Heinrich. Frühlings-Almanach. Berlin, 1804.
—— Janus: Geschichte, Literatur und Kunst, herausg. von ——. Zürich, 1837.
—— Volkslieder, nebst untermischten andern Stücken. Berlin, 1795.

Boucherie, Anatole. See Renaut.

Bouchier, John. See Froissart, Jean.

Bouck, Joseph Ludewig de. See Uhland, L.

Bourbon, Étienne de. See Étienne de Bourbon.

Bower, Walter. Continuation of Fordun. See Fordun.

Brachet, Auguste. Les chansons populaires de la Touraine. *In* Revue critique, 1866, II, 125–127.

Bradley, Henry. (The Name of) Robin Hood. *In* The Academy, XXIV, 184, 384. 1883.

Braga, Theophilo. As adivinhas populares. *In* Era Nova, 1881, pp. 241–55.
—— Amplições ao Romanceiro das Ilhas dos Açores. *In* Revista Lusitana, I, 99–116.
—— Contos tradicionaes do povo portuguez, com um estudo sobre a novellistica geral. Porto, [1883]. 2 vols.
—— See Vaz, João.

Brage og Idun, et nordisk Fjaerdingårsskrift, udgivet af Frederik Barfod. København, 1839–42. 5 vols.

Brand, John. Observations on Popular Antiquities, arranged and revised, with additions, by Henry Ellis. London, 1813. 2 vols.

Brand, John. Popular Antiquities of Great Britain, edited, with very large corrections and additions, by W. Carew Hazlitt. London, 1870. 3 vols.

Brandl, Alois. See Thomas of Erceldoune.

Brandt, C. J. Romantisk Digtning fra Middelalderen. København, 1869–77. 3 vols.

Brassai, S. See Acta Comparationis.

Brathwait, Richard. Barnabæ Itinerarium; or, Drunken Barnaby's Four Journeys to the North of England: in Latin and English Metre . . . now at last made public . . . by Richard Brathwait. With a life of the author, copious notes, and index. York, 1852.
—— A Strappado for the Diuell, with an introduction by J. W. Ebsworth. Boston (Lincolnshire), 1878.

Braune, Wilhelm. See Paul, Hermann.

Bravonius. See Florentius Wigorniensis.

Bray, Mrs. A. E. Traditions, Legends, Superstitions and Sketches of Devonshire on the borders of the Tamar and the Tavy; in a series of letters to Robert Southey. London, 1838. 3 vols.
—— The Borders of the Tamar and the Tavy. London, 1879. 2 vols. [A new ed. of the preceding.]

[Brentano, Clemens.] Godwi oder Das steinerne Bild der Mutter. Ein verwilderter Roman von Maria. Bremen, 1801–02. 2 vols.

Brewer, E. Cobham. A Dictionary of Miracles, imitative, realistic and dogmatic. London, 1884.

Brewer, J. S., [and others]. Letters and Papers, foreign and domestic, of the reign of Henry VIII. London, 1862–. 14 vols. (Calendars of State Papers.)
—— See Giraldus Cambrensis.

British Bibliographer. See Brydges, Sir Egerton.

Briz, Francesch Pelay. See Roig, Jaume.

Broadwood, Lucy E., and Maitland, J. A. Fuller. English County Songs, Words and Music. London and New York, 1893.

Brock, Edmund. See Furnivall, Frederick James.

Brockhaus, H. See Kathā sarit sāgara.

Brome, Richard. A Joviall Crew: or, The Merry Beggars. 1652. *In* The Dramatic Works of Richard Brome, III, 341–452. London, 1873.

Bromton, Johannes. Chronicon ab A. D. 588 usque A. D. 1198. *In* Roger Twysden, Historiae Anglicanae Scriptores X, London, 1652, cols. 721–1284.

Brontë, Emily. Wuthering Heights. *In* Wuthering Heights, and Agnes Gray. By Ellis and Acton Bell [Emily and Anne Brontë]. Leipzig, 1851. 2 vols.

Browne, James. A History of the Highlands and of the Highland Clans; with an extensive selection from the hitherto inedited Stuart Papers. New ed. London, etc., 1852–53. 4 vols.

Browne, William. The Whole Works of ——, now first collected and edited by W. Carew Hazlitt. [London,] 1868–9. 2 vols. (Roxburghe Library.)

Bruce, John Collingwood, and Stokoe, John. Northumbrian Minstrelsy. A collection of the Ballads, Melodies, and small-pipe Tunes of Northumbria. Newcastle-upon-Tyne, 1882. (Society of Antiquaries of Newcastle-upon-Tyne.)

Bruce, Michael. Poems on several Occasions. New ed. Edinburgh, 1807.
—— Works, edited by Alexander B. Grosart. Edinburgh and London, 1865.

Brugman, Karl. Litauische Märchen, übersetzt von K.

Brugman, mit Anmerkungen von W. Wollner. *In* A. Leskien u. K. Brugman, Litauische Volkslieder und Märchen, pp. 349–578. Strassburg, 1882.

Brugmann, K. See Indogermanische Forschungen.

Brunet, Charles. See Mélusine. See Herbert.

Brunet, Jacques Charles. Manuel du libraire et de l'amateur de livres. . . . Cinquième édition originale entièrement refondue et augmentée d'un tiers par l'auteur. Paris, 1860–65. 6 vols.

—— Supplement . . . par MM. P. Deschamps et G. Brunet. Paris, 1878, '80. 2 vols.

Bruns, Paul Jakob. Beiträge zur kritischen Bearbeitung unbenutzter alter Handschriften, Drucke und Urkunden. Braunschweig, 1802–03. 3 Stücke.

Bruzzano, Luigi. See Calabria.

Brydges, Sir Egerton, and Haslewood, Joseph. The British Bibliographer. London, 1810–14. 4 vols.

Brynjúlfsson, G. G. See Tristan.

Buchanan, George. Rerum Scoticarum Historia. Edimburgi, 1582.

Buchanan, Robert. Ballad Stories of the Affections; from the Scandinavian. London, [187–].

Buchon, J. A. Collection des chroniques nationales françaises, écrites en langue vulgaire du 13e au 16e siècle. Paris, 1826, '24–28. 47 vols.

—— Chroniques étrangères relatives aux expéditions françaises pendant le XIIIe siècle. Paris, 1840.

Buck, M. R. See Birlinger, Anton.

Bürger, Gottfried August. Briefe von und an Gottfried August Bürger. Ein Beitrag zur Literaturgeschichte seiner Zeit. Aus dem Nachlasse Bürger's und anderen meist handschriftlichen Quellen herausgegeben von Adolf Strodtmann. Berlin, 1874. 4 vols.

Büsching, Johann Gustav. Erzählungen, Dichtungen, Fastnachtsspiele und Schwänke des Mittelalters. Erster Band. Breslau, 1814.

—— Wöchentliche Nachrichten für Freunde der Geschichte, Kunst und Gelahrtheit des Mittelalters. Breslau, 1816–19. 4 vols.

—— Volks-sagen, Märchen und Legenden. Neue Auflage. Leipzig, 1820.

—— und von der Hagen, Friedrich Heinrich. Buch der Liebe. Berlin, 1809. 1er Bd. [No more published.]

—— Deutsche Gedichte des Mittelalters. Berlin, 1808.

Bugge, Sophus. Bidrag til den nordiske Balladedigtnings Historie. *In* Det Philologisk-historiske Samfunds Mindeskrift i Anledning af dets femogtyveaarige Virksomhed 1854–1879, pp. 64–92. Kjøbenhavn, 1879.

—— Harpens Kraft. Et Bidrag til den nordiska Balladedigtnings Historie. *In* Arkiv för nordisk Filologi, VII, 97–141. 1891.

—— Studien über das Beowulfepos. *In* Beiträge zur Geschichte der deutschen Sprache und Literatur, XII, 1–112, 360–75. 1886–7.

—— See Edda Sæmundar.

Bugiel, Włodzimierz. Tło ludowe "Balladyny." Studjum folklorystyczne. *In* Wisła, VII, 339–61, 557–80, 665–85. 1893.

Bullen, A. H. Carols and Poems from the fifteenth century to the present time. London, 1886.

Bulletin de la Classe des Sciences historiques, philologiques et politiques (de la Classe historico-philologique) de l'Académie Impériale des Sciences de Saint-Pétersbourg. St Pétersbourg, 1844–59. 16 vols.

Bulletin de Folklore. Organe de la Société du Folklore Wallon. Directeur: Eugène Monseur. Vol. I, 1891–92; Vol. II, 1893–95. Liége, Bruxelles, Paris, etc. 2 vols.

Bulletin de la Société des Études littéraires, scientifiques et artistiques du Lot. IV. Cahors, [1877 ?] 1878.

Burn, Richard. See Nicolson, Joseph.

Burnet, Gilbert. The History of the Reformation of the Church of England. Oxford, 1829. 4 vols. 7 pts.

Burnouf, Eugène. Introduction à l'histoire du Buddhisme indien. Paris, 1844.

Burns, Robert. The life and works of ——. Edited by Robert Chambers. Edinburgh, 1851. 4 vols.

—— The Works of ——, with his Life, by Allan Cunningham. London, 1834. 8 vols.

Burton, John Hill. The History of Scotland, from Agricola's invasion to the extinction of the last Jacobite insurrection. 2d ed. Edinburgh and London, 1873. 8 vols. and index vol.

—— Narratives from Criminal Trials in Scotland. London, 1852. 2 vols.

—— See (The) Register of the Privy Council of Scotland.

Buslaev, T. J. Istoričeskie očerki. [Historical Sketches.] St Petersburg, 1861. 2 vols.

Butler, Alban. The Lives of the Fathers, Martyrs, and other principal Saints. London, 1812–13. 12 vols.

Butler, Samuel. Hudibras. *In his* Poetical Works, Aldine ed. London, 1835. 2 vols.

Byron. George Gordon Noel, Lord. Childe Harold's Pilgrimage. *In his* Works, VIII. London, 1832.

Cabala, sive Scrinia Sacra, Mysteries of State and Government: in Letters of illustrious Persons . . . in the reigns of King Henry the Eighth [etc.]. London, 1663.

Caballero, Fernan, *pseudon.* See Arrom, Cecilia d'.

Le Cabinet des Fées, ou Collection choisie des contes des fées, et autres contes merveilleux. [Ed. C. J. Mayer.] Genève, 1787–89. 41 vols.

Caesarius Heisterbacensis. Dialogus Miraculorum. Textum recognovit Josephus Strange. Coloniae, Bonnae et Bruxellis, 1851. 2 vols.

La Calabria. Rivista di letteratura popolare, diretta da Luigi Bruzzano. Monteleone, 1888–.

Calder, Robert. See The Scotch Presbyterian Eloquence.

Calderwood, David. The History of the Kirk of Scotland. Edinburgh, 1842–49. 8 vols. (Wodrow Society, 5.)

Calendar of State Papers, Foreign Series, of the reign of Elizabeth [1558–1577] preserved in the State Paper Department of Her Majesty's Public Record Office. Edited by the Rev. Joseph Stevenson [vols. I–VII] and Allan James Crosby [VIII–XI]. London, 1863–80. 11 vols. (Master of the Rolls. Calendar of State Papers.)

Calendar of the State Papers, relating to Scotland, preserved in the State Paper Department of Her Majesty's Public Record Office. By Markham John Thorpe. London, 1858. 2 vols. (Master of the Rolls. Calendar of State Papers. The Scottish Series.)

Calendarium Rotulorum Patentium in Turri Londinensi. [London,] 1802. (Record Commission.)

Callisthenes, *pseudon.* Pseudo-Callisthenis Historiam fabulosam ex tribus codicibus nunc primum edidit, itinerarium Alexandri et indices adjecit Carolus Müller. *In* Arriani Anabasis et Indica, ed. F. Dübner. Parisiis, 1846.

Cambrian Journal. See Archæologia Cambrensis.

Camden, William. Britannia, sive florentissimorum regnorum Angliae, Scotiae, Hiberniae . . . chorograpica descriptio. London, 1607.

Camden, William. Britannia, or, A chorographical description of Great Britain and Ireland. Transl. by Edmund Gibson. 4th ed. London, 1772. 2 vols.

Campbell, Alexander. Albyn's Anthology, or A select collection of the melodies and local poetry peculiar to Scotland and the Isles hitherto unpublished. The modern Scotish and English verses adapted to the Highland, Hebridean and Lowland melodies, written by Walter Scott, Esq., and other living poets of the first eminence. Edinburgh, 1816, '18. 2 vols.

Campbell, Lord Archibald. Waifs and Strays of Celtic Tradition. Series initiated and directed by ——. Argyllshire Series, Nos. 1–5. London, 1889–95. 5 vols.

Campbell, J. F. Popular Tales of the West Highlands, orally collected. With a translation. Edinburgh, 1860–62. 4 vols.

Campbell, John Gregorson. The Fians, or, Stories, Poems and Traditions of Fionn and his warrior band. London, 1891. (Waifs and Strays of Celtic Tradition, Argyllshire Series, 4.)

Campeu Charlymaen. See Charlemagne.

Cant, J. See Adamson, Henry.

Cantipratensis, Thomas. See Thomas Cantipratensis.

Cantù, Cesare. Documenti alla Storia Universale. Vol. V, No xiv. Delle canzone e della poesia popolare e nazionale. Torino, 8th ed., 1858.

Capgrave, John. The Chronicle of England. Ed. by F. C. Hingeston. London, 1858. (Rolls Series.)

—— Liber de Illustribus Henricis. Ed. by F. C. Hingeston. London, 1858. (Rolls Series.)

Carbonell, Pere Miguel. Chroniques de Espāya. Barcelona, 1547.

Cardonne, D. D. Mêlanges de littérature orientale. La Haye, 1788. See also Pilpay.

Carduino. I cantari di Carduino, giuntovi quello di Tristano e Lancielotto quando combattettero al Petrone di Merlino. Poemetti cavallereschi pub. per cura di Pio Rajna. Bologna, 1873. (Scelta di curiosità letterarie inedite o rare, 135.)

Carew, Richard. The Survey of Cornwall. London, 1602.

Carleton, William. Traits and Stories of the Irish Peasantry. 10th ed. London, [1854]. 2 vols.

Carlyle, T. J. The Debateable Land. Read before the Dumfriesshire and Galloway Natural History and Antiquarian Society. Dumfries, 1868.

Carmi, Maria. Canti popolari Emiliani. In Archivio per lo studio delle tradizioni popolari, XII, 175–96. 1893.

Carmichael, A. A. Deirdire. In Transactions of the Gaelic Society of Inverness, XIII, 241–57 (1886–87). 1888.

Carnel, l'abbé. Noels dramatiques des Flamands de France publiés par ——. Paris, 1856 ?

Carnoy, Henry. Contes picards, merveilleux ou plaisants (Romania, tome VIII). In Contes Français, Deuxième partie. Paris, 1885. (Collection de contes et de chansons populaires, 8.)

—— Contes, petites légendes [etc.], recueillis à Warloy-Baillon ou à Mailly. In Romania, VIII, 222–63.

—— and Menu, Henri. Chansons populaires de la Picardie. In La Tradition, IV, 346–49 ; V, 117–18, 186–87, 210 ; VI, 28. 1891–92.

Caro, J. See Horn.

Carrer, Luigi. Prose e poesie. Venezia, 1837–38. 4 vols.

Carrington, Evelyn. Lord Ronald in Italy. In The Antiquary, III, 154–7. 1881.

Carruthers, Robert. Abbotsford Notanda, or, Sir Walter Scott and his factor. Appended to Chambers, Robert, Life of Sir Walter Scott. Edinburgh and London, 1871, pp. 109–196.

Cary, Robert. Memoirs of the Life of Robert Cary, Baron of Leppington and Earl of Monmouth. Written by himself, and now published from an original Manuscript in the Custody of John Earl of Corke and Orrery. With some explanatory notes. London, 1759.

Časopis. See Společnost, etc.

Cassel, Paulus. Der Schwan in Sage und Leben. 2te Ausg. Berlin, 1863. In his Hierozoicon. Die Thierwelt in Heiliger Schrift, Legende und Sage, I.

Cassel, Selig (afterwards Paulus). Zum Armen Heinrich Hartmanns von Aue. In Weimarisches Jahrbuch, I, 408–78. 1854.

Castrén, M. Alexander. Reiseerinnerungen aus den Jahren 1838–1844, hrsg. v. A. Schiefner. St Petersburg, 1853. In his Nordische Reisen und Forschungen, 9 vols, 1853–56, vol. I.

Cavalcaselle, G. B. See Crowe, Joseph Archer.

Cavendish, William, first Duke of Newcastle. See The Varietie.

Caylus, Anne Claude Philippe, comte de. Histoire du vaillant chevalier Tiran le Blanc. In Œuvres Badines, I, II. Amsterdam, etc., 1787.

—— Nouveaux Contes Orientaux. In Œuvres Badines, VII, p. 283–VIII. Amsterdam, etc., 1787.

—— Œuvres Badines complettes du comte de Caylus. Amsterdam, etc., 1787. 12 vols.

Cederschiöld, Gustaf. Fornsögur Suðrlanda. Isländska bearbetningar af främmande romaner från medeltiden. Efter gamla handskrifter utgifna. Lund, 1876–82. In Acta Universitatis Lundensis : Lunds Universitets Årsskrift, vols XIII–XV, XVIII.

—— and Wulff, F. A. Versions nordiques du fabliau français Le Mantel Mautaillié. Lund, 1877.

Cedrenus, Georgius. Georgius Cedrenus, Ioannis Scylitzae ope ab Immanuele Bekkero suppletus et emendatus. In Corpus Scriptorum Historiae Byzantinae, XXXIII, XXXIV. Bonnae, 1838, '39. 2 vols.

The Celtic Magazine. Inverness, 1876–88. 13 vols.

Cénac-Moncaut, Justin Édouard Mathieu. Contes populaires de la Gascogne. Paris, 1861.

—— Littérature populaire de la Gascogne. Contes, mystères, chansons historiques, satiriques, sentimentales, rondeaux, recueillis dans l'Astarac, le Pardiac, le Béarn et le Bigorre. Texte patois avec la traduction en regard et la musique des principaux chants. Paris, 1868.

Les Cent Nouvelles Nouvelles. Avec introduction et notes par Thomas Wright. Paris, 1858–57. 2 vols.

Cerquand, J. F. Légendes et récits populaires du pays basque. In Bulletin de la Société des Sciences, Lettres et Arts de Pau, IIe Série, IV, 233–289 ; V, 183–260 ; VI, 450–531 ; XI, 101–294. Pau, 1875, '76, '77, '82.

Ceruti, Antonio. See Charlemagne.

Chabaneau, Camille. Les biographies des troubadours en langue provençale. Toulouse, 1885. Extrait du tome X de l'Histoire générale de Languedoc, édition Éd. Privat.

Chabaneau, Charles. Sainte Marie Madeleine dans la littérature provençale. In Revue des Langues Romanes, XXIII, 105–115 ; XXIV, 53–63 ; XXV, 105–32, 157–88 ; XXVI,

105–33; XXVII, 105–20, 261–8; XXVIII, 5–23, 53–7; XXIX, 261–83; XXXI, 5–14. 1883–87.

Chalmers, George. See Lindsay, Sir David.

Chalmers, James. Notices of the Life and Writings of William Hamilton, of Bangour, Esq.; and a chronological list of his poems. *In* Archæologia Scotica, III, 255–66.

Chalmers, Robert. See Jātaka.

Chamberlain, Mrs. Edith L. A Glossary of West Worcestershire words; with glossic notes by Thomas Hallam. London, 1882. (English Dialect Society, 36.)

Chamberlain's Accounts of the Town of Nottingham. *In* Records of the Borough of Nottingham. A series of extracts from the archives of the corporation. Ed. by W. H. Stevenson. London, 1882–89. 4 vols.

Chambers, Robert. The Book of Days. A miscellany of Popular Antiquities in connection with the Calendar. Edinburgh, 1863–64. 2 vols.; reprinted, Philadelphia, 1863–64. 2 vols.

—— Domestic Annals of Scotland. Edinburgh and London, 1858–61. 3 vols.

—— Life of Sir Walter Scott. With Abbotsford Notanda by Robert Carruthers. London and Edinburgh, 1871.

—— The Popular Rhymes of Scotland, with illustrations, chiefly collected from oral sources. Edinburgh, 1826.

—— Popular Rhymes of Scotland. New [third] Edition. London and Edinburgh, [1870].

—— The Romantic Scottish Ballads: their epoch and authorship. London and Edinburgh, 1859. *In his* Edinburgh Papers.

—— See Burns, Robert.

Chambers, William. Exploits and Anecdotes of the Scottish Gypsies, with traits of their origin, character, and manners. [Reprinted from the edition of 1821.] Edinburgh, 1886.

Chanson de Roland. See Charlemagne.

Chappell, William. David Mallet and the Ballad of William and Margaret. *In* The Antiquary, I, 8–9. 1880.

—— Popular Music of the Olden Time; a collection of Ancient Songs, Ballads and Dance Tunes, illustrative of the National Music of England. London, [1855–59]. 2 vols.

—— See Johnson, Richard.

—— See Roxburghe Ballads.

Charlemagne, an Anglo-Norman Poem of the twelfth Century, now first published, with an introduction and a glossarial index, by Francisque Michel. London, 1836.

—— Campeu Charlymaen. *In* R. Williams and G. H. Jones, Selections from the Hengwrt MSS preserved in the Peniarth Library, II, 1–118. London, 1892.

—— The English Charlemagne Romances, ed. by Sidney J. Herrtage [and others]. London, 1879–87. 12 pts. (Early English Text Society, Extra Series, 34–41, 43–45, 50.)

—— Karl Meinet, zum ersten Mal herausgegeben durch Adelbert von Keller. Stuttgart, 1858. (Bibliothek des Litterarischen Vereins in Stuttgart, 45.)

—— Karls des Grossen Reise nach Jerusalem und Constantinopel. Ein altfranzösisches Gedicht des XI. Jahrhunderts, herausgegeben von Eduard Koschwitz. Heilbronn, 1880. (Altfranzösische Bibliothek, 2.) 3d ed., 1895.

—— Sechs Bearbeitungen des altfranzösischen Gedichts von Karl des Grossen Reise nach Jerusalem und Constantinopel. Herausgegeben von Eduard Koschwitz. Heilbronn, 1879.

Charlemagne. Il viaggio di Carlo Magno in Ispagna per conquistare il cammino di S. Giacomo. Testo di lingua inedito, pubblicato per cura di Antonio Ceruti. Bologna, 1871. 2 vols. (Scelta di curiosità letterarie inedite o rare dal secolo XIII, etc., 123, 124.)

—— See Karlamagnus Saga.

Châtelain de Coucy. L'histoire du Châtelain de Coucy et de la dame de Fayel. Publiée et mise en François par G. A. Crapelet. Paris, 1829.

Chaucer, Geoffrey. The Canterbury Tales of Chaucer. To which are added, an essay upon his language and versification; an introductory discourse, and notes. In four volumes (Vol. V containing a glossary). [Ed. by Thomas Tyrwhitt.] London, 1775–78. 5 vols.

—— The Canterbury Tales of Chaucer; with an essay on his language and versification, an introductory discourse, notes, and a glossary by Tho. Tyrwhitt. London, 1830. 5 vols.

—— The Canterbury Tales. A new text with illustrative notes. Edited by Thomas Wright. London, 1848. (Percy Society, 25.)

—— Poetical Works. Edited by Richard Morris. With memoir by Sir Harris Nicolas. London, 1891. 6 vols. (The Aldine edition of the British Poets.)

Chaucer Society. Originals and Analogues. See Furnivall, F. J., and others, editors.

Chénier, M. J. Les miracles. Conte. *In his* Œuvres, Paris, 1826, '24–26, 5 vols, III, 259–285.

Chestre, Thomas. See Launfal.

Chełchowski, Stanisław. Powieści i opowiadania ludowe z okolic Przasnysza. Warszawa, 1889–90. Część 1, 2. (Bibljoteka "Wisły," 3, 6.)

Chetham Miscellanies. [Manchester,] 1851–78. 6 vols. (Chetham Society, 24, 37, 57, 83, 96, 103.)

Chettle, Henry. See Munday, Anthony.

Le Chevalier au Cygne et Godefroid de Bouillon, poëme historique. Publication commencée par M. le Baron de Reiffenberg et achevée par M. A. Borgnet. Bruxelles, 1846–1854. 3 vols.

Li Chevaliers as Deus Espees, zum ersten Mal hrsg. v. Wendelin Foerster. Halle, 1877.

Child, Francis James. English and Scottish Ballads. Boston, 1857–58. 8 vols.

—— See Spenser, Edmund.

Chladenius, Carl Gottfried Theodor. Materialien zur Grossenhayner Stadtchronik. Pirna, [1788].

Chodzko, Alexandre. Contes des paysans et des pâtres slaves. Paris, 1864.

—— Specimens of the Popular Poetry of Persia, as found in the adventures and improvisations of Kurroglou, the bandit-minstrel of northern Persia; and in the songs of the people inhabiting the shores of the Caspian Sea. Orally collected and translated, with philological and historical notes. London, 1842. (Oriental Translation Fund of Great Britain and Ireland, 56.)

Choice notes from Notes and Queries. Folk-Lore. London, 1859.

Choix de petites pièces, etc. See Le Roi et le Meunier.

Chourmouzis, M. Κρητικά. 'Εν 'Αθήναις, 1842.

Chrestien de Troyes. See Crestien de Troyes.

Chronicle of Aberdeen. MCCCCXCI-MDXCV. *In* Miscellany of the Spalding Club, Aberdeen, 1841–52, 5 vols, II, 29–70.

Chronicon de Lanercost. MCCI-MCCCXLVI. [Ed. by

Joseph Stevenson.] Edinburgi, 1839. (Maitland Club, 46.)

Chronicon Novaliciense. *In* G. H. Pertz, Monumenta Germaniae Historica, Scriptores, VII, 73–133. Hannoverae, 1846.

Chronicon Nurembergense. See Nuremberg Chronicle.

Les Chroniques de Normandie. Rouen, 1487. [See I, 198.]

Le Chroniqueur de Périgord et du Limousin : revue historique, artistique, et religieuse, sous la direction (1ʳᵉ année) de M. A. de Siorac ; 2ᵉ–4ᵉ année de par MM. de Moursin, Lapeyre, [and others]. Périgueux, 1853–56.

Chudjakov, I. A. Velikorusskija skazki. [Great Russian tales.] Moscow, 1860–2. 3 pts.

Churchill, Awnsham and John. Collection of Voyages and Travels. Some now first Printed from Original Manuscripts. Others Translated out of Foreign Languages, and now first Published in English. London, 1704. 4 vols. Continued by other editors, London, 1732–47. 4 vols. 8 in all.

Church-wardens' accounts of Croscombe, Pilton, Yatton, Tintinhull, Morebath and St. Michael's, Bath. A. D. 1349–1560. Ed. by Bishop Hobhouse. [London], 1890. (Somerset Record Society, 4.)

Cinthio, Giraldi. See Giraldi Cinthio.

La Civiltà Cattolica. Serie 1–7, Roma (vols I, II, Napoli), 1850–70. Serie 8–, Firenze, 1871–. [See III, 242, and note.]

Clavers, the Despot's Champion. A Scots biography. By a Southern. London, 1889.

Cleasby, Richard, and Vigfusson, Gudbrand. An Icelandic-English dictionary based on the MS. collections of the late Richard Cleasby, enlarged and completed by Gudbrand Vigfusson. Oxford, 1874.

Cligés. See Crestien de Troyes.

Clodd, Edward. The Philosophy of Rumpelstiltskin. *In* Folk-Lore Journal, VII, 135–61. 1889. (Cf. Folk-Lore, I, 272–4. 1890.)

Clouston, W. A. The Barrin' o' the Door. *In* The Athenæum, No 3412, March 18, 1893, pp. 346–47.

—— Originals and Analogues of some of Chaucer's Canterbury Tales. See Furnivall, F. J.

—— Popular Tales and Fictions, their migrations and transformations. Edinburgh and London, 1887. 2 vols.

Clyne, Norval. Ballads from Scottish History. Edinburgh, 1863.

—— The Romantic Scottish Ballads and the Lady Wardlaw Heresy. Aberdeen, 1859.

Cober, Gottlieb. Der aufrichtige Cabinet-Prediger. . . . Aufs neue herausgegeben von M. H. Lange. Halle, 1854. 2 pts.

Codinus, Georgius, Curopalata. Georgii Codini Excerpta de Antiquitatibus Constantinopolitanis, ex recognitione Immanuelis Bekkeri. Bonnae, 1843. (Corpus Scriptorum Historiae Byzantinae, 45.)

Coelho, F. Adolpho. Contos populares portuguezes. Lisboa, 1879.

—— Romances populares e rimas infantís portuguezes. *In* Zeitschrift für romanische Philologie, III, 61–72 ; 193–99. 1879.

Coggeshall, Ralph de. Radulphi de Coggeshall Chronicon Anglicanum. *In* Radulphi de Coggeshall Chronicon Anglicanum, De Expugnatione Terrae Sanctae libellus, Thomas Agnellus de morte et sepultura Henrici regis Angliae junioris, Gesta Fulconis filii Warini, Excerpta ex

Otiis Imperialibus Gervasii Tilburiensis. Ex codicibus manuscriptis edidit Josephus Stevenson. London, 1875. (Rolls Series.)

Colburn, and others, editors. The New Monthly Magazine. London, 1814–. [See II, 494 b.]

Cole, Charles Augustus. Memorials of Henry the Fifth. London, 1858. (Rolls Series.)

Collé, Charles. La Partie de Chasse de Henri IV, comédie. *In* Répertoire Général du Théâtre Français, LXIV, 334–436. Paris, 1818. 67 vols.

A Collection of Seventy-nine Black-Letter Ballads and Broadsides printed in the reign of Queen Elizabeth, between the years 1559 and 1597. London, 1867, '70.

Colleville, Vicomte de. Vieilles chansons. *In* La Tradition, VI, 207–16, 308–11, 372–75 ; VII, 39–43, 89–92. 1892–93.

Collier, John Payne. A Book of Roxburghe Ballads. London, 1847.

—— Five Old Plays, forming a Supplement to the Collections of Dodsley and others. London, 1833.

—— The History of English Dramatic Poetry to the time of Shakespeare : and Annals of the Stage to the Restoration. London, 1831. 3 vols.

—— Household books of John, Duke of Norfolk, and Thomas, Earl of Surrey : temp. 1481–1490. London, 1844. (Roxburghe Club.)

—— Shakespeare's Library : a collection of the Romances, Novels, Poems and Histories used by Shakespeare. London, [1843]. 2 vols.

—— See Dodsley, R.; Guilpin, E.; Henslowe, P.; Stubbes, P.

Collin de Plancy, Jacques. Légendes des saintes images de Notre-Seigneur, de la Sainte Vierge et des Saints. Paris, [1862]. (Bibliothèque des Légendes.)

Colshorn, Carl und Theodor. Märchen und Sagen. Hannover, 1854.

Columna luĭ Traĭan. Revista mensuala pentru istoriă, linguistică şi psicologia poporana. Director, B. P. Hasdeŭ. Noua seria. Bucharest, 1876–.

Colvil, Samuel. The Whiggs Supplication ; or, the Scotch Hudibras, a mock poem. London, 1710. Glasgow, 1751. St Andrews, 1796.

Comparetti, Domenico. Novelline popolari italiane. Vol. I. Torino, *etc.*, 1875. *In* Comparetti, Dom., ed d' Ancona, Alessandro, Canti e racconti del popolo italiano. Torino, *etc.* 1870–91. 9 vols. VI.

—— Saggi dei dialetti greci dell' Italia meridionale. Pisa, 1866.

—— and d' Ancona, Alessandro. Canti e racconti del popolo italiano. Torino, etc., 1870–91. 9 vols.

The Complaining Lover's Garland. [British Museum, 11621. c. 3 (39). See V, 229 b.]

Complaynt of Scotland, written in 1548. With a preliminary dissertation [by John Leyden] and glossary. Edinburgh, 1801.

The Complaynt of Scotlande vyth ane Exortatione to the Thre Estaits to be vigilante in the Deffens of their Public veil, 1549. [Etc.] Re-edited from the originals, with Introduction and Glossary, by James A. H. Murray. London, 1872–[73]. (Early English Text Society, Extra Series, 17, 18.)

I Complementi della Chanson d'Huon de Bordeaux. See Huon de Bordeaux. Complementi, etc.

The Complete Collection of Old and New English and Scotch Songs, 1735. [British Museum. See V, 296 b.]

Comte de Poitiers, Roman du. Publié pour la première fois d'après le manuscrit unique de l'Arsenal, par Francisque Michel. Paris, 1831.

The Contemporary Review. London, 1866-.

Contes à rire, ou récréations françoises. Nouvelle édition, corrigée et augmentée. Paris, 1781. 3 vols.

Li Contes dou Roi Flore, etc. See Roi Flore.

Contes et fables indiennes de Bidpaï et de Lokman. See Pilpay.

Conybeare, John Josias. See Octavian.

Cooper, William Durrant. See Udall, Nicholas.

Coray. See Koraes.

Corpus Scriptorum Historiae Byzantinae. Editio emendatior et copiosior, consilio B. S. Niebuhrii, etc. Bonnae, 1828-78. 49 vols.

Corvisieri, Costantino. See Tummulillis, Angelo de.

Coryat, Thomas. Coryat's Crudities. London, 1611. 1 vol.
— Same. London, 1776. 3 vols.

Cosmos. Revue enclycopédique hebdomadaire des progrès des sciences et de leurs applications aux arts et à l'industrie. Paris, 1852-64-67-70. 37 vols.

Cosquin, Emmanuel. Contes populaires de Lorraine, comparés avec les contes des autres provinces de France et des pays étrangers. Paris, [1886]. 2 vols.

Coster, Charles de. See Eulenspiegel.

Couldrette, La. See Mélusine.

County Folk-Lore. Printed Extracts, No. 2. Suffolk. Collected and edited by the Lady Eveline Camilla Gurdon, with introduction by Edward Clodd. London, 1893. (Folk-Lore Society.)

Coventry Mysteries, ed. Halliwell. See Halliwell, J. O. Ludus Coventriae.

Cowell, E. B. See Jātaka.

Cox, Captain. See Furnivall, F. J. Captain Cox, etc.

Cox, Rev. Sir George W. The Mythology of the Aryan Nations. London, 1870. 2 vols.

Cox, J. C. Three Centuries of Derbyshire Annals. London, 1890. 3 vols.

Craig-Brown, T. The History of Selkirkshire ; or, Chronicles of Ettrick Forest. Edinburgh, 1886. 2 vols.

Crane, Thomas Frederick. Italian Popular Tales. [With a bibliography.] Boston, 1885.
— See Jacques de Vitry.

Cranstoun, James. See Montgomerie, Alexander.

Crapelet, G. A. See Châtelain de Coucy.

Crawfurd, David. Memoirs of the affairs of Scotland, containing a full account of the Revolution in that Kingdom begun in 1567. London, 1706. [See III, 424 b, note.]

Creichton, John. The Memoirs of Captain John Creichton, from his own materials, drawn up and digested by Jonathan Swift. First printed in 1731. London, 1827. In Autobiography. A Collection of the most instructive and amusing lives ever published, written by the parties themselves. With brief introductions, and compendious sequels carrying on the narrative to the death of each writer. London, 1826-32. 33 vols. Vol. XI.

Creizenach, Wilhelm. Judas Ischarioth in Legende und Sage des Mittelalters. In Beiträge zur Geschichte der deutschen Sprache und Literatur, II, 177-207. 1876.

Crestien de Troyes. Christian von Troyes Cligés. Textausgabe, mit Einleitung und Glossar herausgegeben von W. Foerster. Halle, 1888. (Romanische Bibliothek, 1.)
— Des Chrestien von Troyes Erec und Enide. Her-

ausgegeben von Immanuel Bekker. In Zeitschrift für deutsches Alterthum, X, 373-550. Berlin, 1856.

Crestien de Troyes. Perceval, etc. See Perceval le Gallois.

Cronica de España. Las quatro partes enteras de la Cronica de España que mando componer el serenissimo rey don Alonso llamado el Sabio. . . . Vista y emendada por F. Docāpo. Zamora, 1541.

Crosby, Allan James. See Calendar of State Papers.

Croscombe Church-wardens' accounts. See Church-wardens' accounts of Croscombe, etc.

Croston, James. County Families of Lancashire and Cheshire. London, 1887.

Crowe, Joseph Archer, and Cavalcaselle, Giovanni Battista. A new History of Painting in Italy from the second to the sixteenth century. Drawn up from fresh materials and recent researches in the archives of Italy ; as well as from personal inspection of the works of art scattered throughout Europe. London, 1864-66. 3 vols.

Crown Garland of Golden Roses. See Johnson, Richard.

Dei Çukasaptati (Textus simplicior), aus dem Sanskrit übersetzt von Richard Schmidt. Kiel, 1894.
— See also Tuti-nameh.

Curiositäten der physisch-literarisch-artistisch-historischen Vor- und Mitwelt; zur angenehmen Unterhaltung für gebildete Leser. [Ch. Aug. Vulpius, herausgeber.] Weimar, 1811-23. 10 vols.

Cursor Mundi (The Cursur o the World): A Northumbrian poem of the XIVth century, in four versions. Ed. by Richard Morris. London, 1874-93. 3 vols. (Early English Text Society, 57, 59, 62, 66, 68, 99, 101.)

Curtin, Jeremiah. Myths and Folk-lore of Ireland. Boston, 1890.

Curtze, L. Volksüberlieferungen aus dem Fürstenthum Waldeck. Nebst einem Idiotikon. Arolsen, 1860.

Cutts, Edward L. Scenes and Characters of the Middle Ages. London, [1872].

Dahlmann, F. C. See Adolfi, Johann.

Dalyell, John Graham. Fragments of Scotish History. Edinburgh, 1798. See Birrel, Robert.
[——] Scotish Poems of the Sixteenth Century. Edinburgh, 1801. 2 vols.
— See Lindsay, Robert.

Dames, M. Longworth. Balochi Tales. In Folk-Lore, III, 517-28; IV, 195-206. 1892-93.

Dania. Tidsskrift for Folkemål og Folkeminder, udgivet for Universitets-jubilæets Danske Samfund af Otto Jespersen og Kristoffer Nyrop. København, 1890-.

Daniel von Blumenthal. Initium carminis hactenus inediti de Daniele Blumenthal eqvite Tabulae Rotundae. In Symbolae ad Literaturam Teutonicam Antiquiorem, pp. 461-480. Havniae, 1787.

Daniel, Gabriel. Histoire de France, depuis l'établissement de la monarchie françoise dans les Gaules, par le père G. Daniel, de la Compagnie de Jesus. Nouvelle édition. Paris, 1755-57. 17 vols.

Danske Samlinger for Historie, Topographi, Personal- og Literatur-historie. Kjøbenhavn, 1865-70. 6 vols.

Dardy, Léopold, L'Abbé. Anthologie populaire de l'Albret (sud-ouest de l'Agenais ou Gascogne landaise). I, Poésies gasconnes. II, Contes populaires. Agen, 1891. 2 vols.

Dasent, George Webbe. Popular Tales from the Norse; with an essay on the origin and diffusion of popular tales. 2d edition. Edinburgh, 1859. [A translation of the collection of Asbjørnsen and Moe.]

[Dati, Carlo Roberto.] Prose fiorentine, raccolte dallo Smarrito Academico della Crusca. Firenze, 1716–45. 4 pts. in 17 vols.

Dauney, William. Ancient Scotish Melodies, with an introductory enquiry illustrative of the history of the music of Scotland. Edinburgh, 1838. (Bannatyne Club, 62.)

D'Avenant, Sir William. Works. Consisting of those which were formerly printed, and those which he design'd for the press. London, 1673. 3 pts.

—— Dramatic Works. With prefatory memoir and notes. [By James Maidment and W. H. Logan.] Edinburgh, 1872–74. 5 vols. (Dramatists of the Restoration.)

The Dean of Lismore's Book. See Lismore.

Decourdemanche, J. A. See Nasr-Eddin Hodja.

Decurtins, Caspar. Märchen aus dem Bündner Oberlande, gesammelt und nach den Räto-Romanischen erzählt. Chur, 1874. In Jecklin, Dietrich, Volksthümliches aus Graubünden. 1ᵉʳ theil, Zürich. 2ᵉʳ, 3ᵉʳ theil, Chur. 1874–78. 3 pts. I, 97–136.

The Deeside Guide, descriptive and traditionary. Aberdeen, etc., 1889.

Delaborde, H. F. See Guillaume le Breton.

Delamer, Henry, Lord. The Case of William Earl of Devonshire. In his Works, London, 1694, pp. 563–82.

Delitiae Poetarum Scotorum hujus aevi Illustrium. [Ed. by Arthur Johnston.] Amsterdami, 1637.

Delrio, Martin. Disquisitionum Magicarum libri sex, quibus continetur accurata curiosarum artium, et vanarum superstitionum confutatio, utilis Theologis, Jurisconsultis, Medicis, Philologis. Auctore Martino Delrio Societatis Jesu presbytero. . . . Moguntiae, 1624.

Δελτίον τῆς Ἱστορικῆς καὶ Ἐθνολογικῆς Ἑταιρίας τῆς Ἑλλάδος. Athens, 1883–92. 4 vols.

Demaundes Joyous. In Salomon and Saturnus, ed. Kemble, pp. 285–301.

The Denham Tracts. A Collection of Folklore by Michael Aislabie Denham, and reprinted from the original tracts and pamphlets printed by Mr. Denham between 1846 and 1859. Edited by Dr. James Hardy. London, [1891] 1892–95. 2 vols. (Folklore Society, 29, 35.)

de Nino, Antonio. Usi abruzzesi, Usi e costumi abruzzesi, descritti da ——. Firenze, 1879–91. 5 vols.

Dennys, N. B. The Folk-lore of China, and its affinities with that of the Aryan and Semitic races. London and Hongkong, 1876.

D'Esclot, Bernat. Chronique de Pierre III et expédition française de 1285. (Texte catalan inédit.) Cronica del Rey en Pere e dels seus antecessors passats. In J. A. C. Buchon. Chroniques étrangères relatives aux expéditions françaises pendant le XIIIᵉ siècle, pp. 565–736. Paris, 1840.

Desportes, Henri. Le mystère du sang chez les Juifs de tous les temps. Préface d'Édouard Drumont. Paris, 1889.

Destriché, Mme. Coutumes et superstitions de Maine. In Revue des Traditions Populaires, I, 55–56. 1886.

Deutsches Heldenbuch. See Heldenbuch.

Deutsches Museum. [Edited by Heinrich Christian Boie and Christian Konrad Wilhelm von Dohm.] Leipzig, 1776–88. 26 vols.

—— Zeitschrift für Literatur, Kunst und öffentliches Leben. Herausgegeben von Robert Prutz (Wilhelm Wolfsohn, Karl Frenzel). Verantwortlicher Redacteur: Heinrich Brockhaus. Leipzig, 1851–67. 34 vols.

Diago, Francisco. Historia de los victoriosissimos antiguos Condes de Barcelona. Barcelona, 1603.

Diceto, Ralph de. Abbreviationes. In Radulfi de Diceto Decani Lundoniensis Opera Historica. The Historical Works of Master Ralph de Diceto, Dean of London. Edited from the original manuscripts by William Stubbs. I, 3–263. London, 1876. (Rolls Series.)

Dickson, Robert. Introduction of the Art of Printing into Scotland. Aberdeen, 1885.

Didron, Adolphe Napoléon, ainé. Annales archéologiques. Paris, 1844–81. 28 vols.

Diederic van Assende. See Floire et Blanceflor.

Dietrich von Bern. Saga Điðriks konungs af Bern. Fortælling om kong Thidrik af Bern og hans kæmper, i norsk bearbeidelse fra det trettende aarhundrede efter tydske kilder. Utgivet af C. R. Unger. Christiania, 1853.

—— Sagan om Didrik af Bern. Efter svenska handskrifter utgifven af Gunnar Olof Hyltén-Cavallius. Stockholm, 1850–54.

Dietrich, Anton. Russische Volksmärchen, ins Deutsche übersetzt. Mit einem Vorwort von Jacob Grimm. Leipzig, 1831.

Dietrich's Flucht. In Deutsches Heldenbuch, II, 55–215.

Digby Mysteries, ed. by F. J. Furnivall. London, 1882. (New Shakspere Society, Series VII, 1.)

Dimock, J. F. See Giraldus.

Dinaux, Arthur. Trouvères, jongleurs et ménestrels du nord de la France et du midi de la Belgique. Paris, Bruxelles, 1837–63. 4 vols.

Diurnal of remarkable Occurrents that have passed within the country of Scotland since the death of King James the Fourth till the year MDLXXV. [Ed. by Thomas Thomson.] Edinburgh, 1833. (Bannatyne Club, 45.)

Dixon, James Henry. Ancient Poems, Ballads, and Songs of the Peasantry of England, taken down from oral recitation, and transcribed from private manuscripts, rare broadsides and scarce publications. London, 1846. (Percy Society, 17.)

Djurklou, G. Ur Nerikes Folkspråk och Folklif. Anteckningar utgifne till Fornvänners Ledning. Örebro, 1860.

Długosz, J. Historiae Polonicae libri XII, cum praefatione H. L. B. ab Huyssen. Lipsiae, 1711–12. 2 vols.

Dobeneck, Friedrich Ludwig Ferdinand von. Des deutschen Mittelalters Volksglauben und Heroensagen. Hrsg. u. mit einer Vorrede begleitet von Jean Paul. Berlin, 1815. 2 vols.

Dobrovol'skij, V. N. Smolenskij etnografičeskij sbornik, I. [Smolensk Ethnographical Collection.] St Petersburg, 1891.

Dobšinský, P. Prostonárodnie slovenské povesti. Usporiadal a vydáva ——. [Popular Slovak Tales. Arranged and edited by ——.] Turč. Sv. Martin, 1880–83. 8 parts.

Le Doctrinal de Sapience. See Roye, Guy de.

Dodsley, Robert. The Modern British Drama. London, 1811. 5 vols.

—— A Select Collection of Old Plays. New edition, with additional notes and corrections, by J. Reed, O. Gilchrist, and the editor [J. P. Collier]. London, 1825–27. 12 vols.

—— A Select Collection of Old English Plays. Ed. by W. Carew Hazlitt. London, 1874–76. 15 vols.

Doenniges, Wilhelm. Altschottische und altenglische Volks-

balladen, nach den Originalen bearbeitet. Nebst einem
Nachwort über den alten Minstrelgesang. München,
1852.

Döring, [Heinrich]. Brittischer Balladenschatz in metri-
scher Uebersetzung, mit beigefügtem Original. 2te Aufl.
Leipzig, 1858.

Dolopathos. See Herbert. See Johannes de Alta Silva.

Doncieux, George. La belle dans la tour. Text critique.
In Mélusine, V, 265–71. 1891.

—— Le cycle de Sainte Marie-Madeleine dans la chanson
populaire. *In* Revue des Traditions populaires, VI, 257–
76, 474–76 (appendice), 604 (erratum). 1891.

Doni, Antonio Francesco. I Marmi del Doni, academico
peregrino. Vinegia, 1552–53. 4 pts.

—— Novelle, colle notizie sulla vita dell' autore raccolte
da Salvatore Bongi. Lucca, 1852.

Doon de Maience. Chanson de geste publiée pour la première fois d'après les manuscrits de Montpellier et de Paris
par M. A. Pey. Paris, 1859. (*In* François Guessard,
Les anciens Poëtes de la France, etc., II.)

Dorpater Jahrbücher für Litteratur, Statistik und Kunst,
besonders Russlands. Riga und Dorpat (Leipzig), 1833–
36. 5 vols.

Douce, Francis. Illustrations of Shakspeare and of Ancient Manners. London, 1807. 2 vols.

Douglas, Gavin. Palice of Honour. *In* Poetical Works of
Gavin Douglas with Memoir, Notes, and Glossary, by John
Small, I, 1–81. Edinburgh and London, 1874. 4 vols.

Douglas, [Sir] Robert. The Peerage of Scotland, containing
an Historical and Genealogical Account of the Nobility
of that Kingdom, from their Origin to the present Generation: collected from the Public Records, and Ancient
Chartularies of this nation, the Charters, and other Writings of the Nobility, and the Works of our best Historians. Illustrated with Copper-Plates. By Robert Douglas, Esq. Edinburgh, 1764.

—— Second edition. Revised and corrected, with a continuation to the present period, by John Philip Wood,
Esq. With engravings of arms of the peers. Edinburgh,
1813. 2 vols.

Douhet, Jules, comte de. Dictionnaire des legendes du
Christianisme, ou collection d'histoires apocryphes et mer-
veilleuses, etc. Par M. le comte de Douhet. Publié par
M. l'abbé Migne. Paris, 1855. (J. P. Migne, Encyclo-
pédie théologique, 3e série, XIV.)

Dow, Daniel. Collection of Ancient Scots Music, [c. 1776].
[See III, 318 b.]

Dozon, Auguste. Contes albanais recueillis et traduits par
——. Paris, 1881. (Collection de contes et chansons
populaires, 3.)

Dragomanov, M. Malorusskija narodnyja predanija i raz-
skazy. [Malorussian Popular Traditions and Stories.]
Kiev, 1876.

Drayton, Michael. The Poly-Olbion; a chorographicall
Description of Great Britain. Reprinted from the ed. of
1622. [Manchester,] 1889–90. 3 pts. (Spenser Society,
New Series, 1–3.)

Drummond, William, of Hawthornden, The Poems of.
Glasgow, 1832. (Maitland Club.)

Drumont, Édouard. La France Juive. Essai d'histoire
contemporaine. Nouvelle éd. Paris, 1887. 2 vols.

Drunken Barnaby. See Brathwait, Richard.

Dryden, John. Miscellany Poems. 3rd ed. London, 1702–
08. 5 pts.

Dryden, John. Same. 4th ed. London, 1716. 6 pts.

Dsanglun oder der Weise und der Thor. Aus dem Tibeti-
schen übersetzt und mit dem Original-texte herausgegeben von I. J. Schmidt. St Petersburg, 1843. 2 pts.

Ducange. Du Fresne, Charles, Seigneur du Cange. Glossarium Mediae et Infimae Latinitatis ... cum Supplementis
D. P. Carpenterii et Additamentis Adelungii et aliorum
digessit G. A. L. Henschel. Parisiis, 1840–50. 7 vols.

Du Chesne, André. Histoire d'Angleterre, d'Escosse, et
d'Irlande. Seconde édition reveuë et augmentée jusques
à présent. Paris, 1634.

—— et François. Historiae Francorum scriptores coae-
tanei ab ipsius gentis origine ad Pipinum usque regem.
Opera ac studio Andreae Du Chesne geographi regii
(Tom I, II). Opera ac studio filij post patrem Francisci
Duchesne (Tom III–V). Lutetiae Parisiorum, 1636–49.
5 vols.

Des Dülkener Fiedlers Liederbuch. See Zürmuhlen, Hans.

Düntzer, Heinrich. See Goethe.

Dufilhol, Louis Antoine. See Kérardven, J.

Dugdale, Sir William. The Antiquities of Warwickshire
illustrated, from Records, Leiger-Books, Manuscripts,
Charters, Evidences, Tombes, and Armes: beautified with
Maps, Prospects, and Portraictures. The Second Edition,
in Two Volumes, Printed from a Copy corrected by the
Author himself, and with the Original Copper Plates.
The whole revised, augmented, and continued down to
this present Time, By William Thomas. London, 1730.
2 vols.

—— The Baronage of England, or An Historical Account
of the Lives and most Memorable Actions of Our English
Nobility In the Saxons time, to the Norman Conquest;
And from thence, of those who had their rise before the
end of King Henry the Third's Reign. Deduced From
Publick Records, Antient Historians, and other Authorities. London, 1675–76. 2 vols.

—— Monasticon Anglicanum: a history of the abbies and
other monasteries, hospitals, frieries, and cathedral and
collegiate churches, with their dependencies, in England
and Wales; also of all such Scotch, Irish, and French
monasteries as were in any manner connected with religious houses in England. Originally published in Latin
by Sir William Dugdale, Kt., Garter Principal King at
Arms. A new edition, by John Caley, Henry Ellis, and
the Rev. Bulkeley Bandinel. London, 1817–30. 6 vols
in 8.

Du Méril, Édélestand. Histoire de la poésie scandinave.
Prolégomènes. Paris, 1839.

—— Poésies populaires latines du Moyen Age. Paris and
Leipzig, 1847.

—— See Floire et Blanceflor.

The Dumfries Magazine. Dumfries, 1825–26. 3 vols.

Dunbar, William. Poems, now first collected. With notes
and a memoir by David Laing. Edinburgh, 1834. 2
vols.

—— Poems, ed. by John Small. Introduction by Æ. J. G.
Mackay. Edinburgh and London, 1893 [1884–93]. 3
vols. (Scottish Text Society, 2, 4, 16, 21, 29.)

Dunlop, John Colin. The History of Fiction, being a critical account of the most celebrated Prose works of Fiction,
from the earliest Greek Romances to the Novels of the
present Day. London, 1814. 3 vols.

—— History of Prose Fiction. New ed., by Henry Wilson.
London, 1888. 2 vols. (Bohn's Standard Library.)

Dunlop, John Colin. John Dunlop's Geschichte der Prosa-
dichtungen, oder Geschichte der Romane, Novellen, Märchen u. s. w. Aus dem Englischen übertragen und viel-
fach vermehrt und berichtigt, so wie mit einleitender
Vorrede, ausführlichen Anmerkungen und einem vollstän-
digen Register versehen, von Felix Liebrecht. Berlin,
1851.

Duplessis, G. See Le Marchant, Jehan.

Duran, Agustin. Romancero General, ó coleccion de romances castellanos anteriores al siglo XVIII, recogidos,
ordenados, clasificados y anotados. Madrid, 1849, '51. 2
vols. (Biblioteca de autores españoles, 10, 16.)

Dybeck, Richard, editor. Runa. En skrift för Fäderneslandets Fornvänner. [Later series with the title] Runa.
En skrift för Nordens Fornvänner. Stockholm, 1842-74.

Dyce, Alexander. See Beaumont and Fletcher.
—— See Greene, Robert. See Peele, George.
—— See Skelton, John. See Webster, John.

Dyck, Johann Gottfried. See Taschenbuch für Dichter.

Earle, John. Two of the Saxon Chronicles parallel with
supplementary extracts from the others. Edited, with
introduction, notes, and a glossarial index. Oxford, 1865.

Eastwick, Edward B. The Anvár-i Suhailí. See Pilpay.

Eberhard, A. See Planudes.

Ebsworth, Joseph Woodfall. See Bagford. See Roxburghe.
—— See Brathwait, Richard.

Echard, Laurence. The History of England. From the
First Entrance of Julius Cæsar and the Romans, to the
Conclusion of the Reign of King James the Second, and
the Establishment of King William and Queen Mary
upon the Throne, in the year 1688. 3d ed. London,
1720.

Die Edda. Eine Sammlung altnordischer Götter- und Heldenlieder. Herausgegeben von Hermann Lüning. Zürich, 1859.

Edda Sæmundar. Norrœn Fornkvæði. Islandsk Samling
af folkelige Oldtidsdigte om Nordens Guder og Heroer
almindelig kaldet Sæmundar Edda hins Fróða. Udgiven
af S. Bugge. Christiania, 1867.

Edda Sæmundar hinns Fróda. Edda rhythmica seu anti-
qvior, vulgo Sæmundina dicta. Hafniae, 1787-1828. 3 pts.

Edda Snorra Sturlusonar. Edda Snorronis Sturlaei. Hafniae, 1848-87. 3 vols.

Edinburgh Evening Courant. Edinburgh, 1705-. [News-
paper.]

Egeria. See Wolff, O. L. B.

Eichhorn, C. Äldre svenska Folkvisor, meddelade och
belysta af ——. In Svenska Fornminnesföreningens
Tidskrift (1873-74), II, 69-78. 1875.

Eilhart von Oberge. Herausgegeben von Franz Lichtenstein. Strassburg, London, 1877. (Quellen und Forschungen zur Sprach- und Culturgeschichte der germanischen Völker, 19.)

Eisenmenger, Johann Andreas. Johann Andreä Eisenmen-
gers Professors der Orientälischen Sprachen bey der
Universität Heydelberg Entdecktes Judenthum Oder
Gründlicher und Wahrhaffter Bericht Welchergestalt
Die verstockte Juden die Hochheilige Drey-Einigkeit
Gott Vater Sohn und Heil. Geist erschrecklicher Weise
lästern und verunehren, [etc.] Königsberg, 1711. 2 pts.

Ekkehardus Sangallensis I. Ekkehardi Primi Waltharius.
Edidit Rudolfus Peiper. Berolini, 1873.

Elie de Saint Gille. See Aiol et Mirabel.

Ellis, Frederick Startridge. The Huth Library. A catalogue of the printed books, manuscripts, autograph letters,
and engravings, collected by Henry Huth, with collations
and bibliographical descriptions. London, 1880. 5 vols.

Ellis, George. Specimens of Early English Metrical Ro-
mances, to which is prefixed an historical introduction,
on the rise and progress of romantic composition in
France and England. London, 1805.
—— —— A new edition, revised by J. O. Halliwell.
London, 1868. (Bohn's Antiquarian Library.)

Ellis, [Sir] Henry. Original Letters, Illustrative of English
History; including numerous royal letters. From auto-
graphs in the British Museum, and one or two other col-
lections. With notes and illustrations. First Series.
Second Edition. London, 1825. 3 vols.
—— See Brand, John.
—— See Dugdale, Sir William.
—— See Fabyan, Robert.

Elmham, Thomas de. Liber Metricus de Henrico Quinto.
In C. A. Cole. Memorials of Henry the Fifth, King of
England. London, 1858.
—— Thomae de Elmham Vita et Gesta Henrici Quinti,
Anglorum regis. E codicibus MSS. vetustis descripsit, et
primus luci publicae dedit Tho. Hearnius. Oxonii, 1727.

Elphinstone, Mountstuart. An Account of the kingdom
of Caubul, and its dependencies in Persia, Tartary, and
India; comprising a view of the Afghaun nation, and a
history of the Dooraunee monarchy. London, 1815.

The Ely Volume; or, the Contributions of our Foreign
Missions to science and human well-being. By Thomas
Laurie, D. D. Second edition, revised. Boston, 1885.

Encyclopedia Republicana. Revista de sciencias e littera-
tura ao alcance de todas as intelligencias. Collaborada
por Affonso de Sousa [and others]. Lisboa, 1882.

Enenkel, Jansen. Aus Jansen Enenkels Weltbuche. In
Friedrich Heinrich von der Hagen, Gesammtabenteuer,
II, 487-650; III, CXXVIII — CLXVI. Stuttgart and
Tübingen, 1850.

Engelhardt, Christian Moriz. See Staufenberg.

Engelien, August, and Lahn, W. Der Volksmund in der
Mark Brandenburg. Sagen, Märchen, Spiele, Sprichwörter und Gebräuche. Berlin, 1868.

Engelische Comedien vnd Tragedien, das ist: Sehr schöne
. . . Comedi vnd Tragedi Spiel, sampt dem Pickelhering,
welche . . . von den Engelländern in Deutschland . . .
agiret vnd gehalten worden vnd zuvor nie im Druck auss-
gangen, etc., 1620.

Englische Studien, hrsg. v. E. Kölbing. Heilbronn (later
Leipzig), 1877-.

The English Charlemagne Romances. Ed. by S. J. Herrtage. See Charlemagne.

English Historical Review. London, 1886-.

Enrique. See Oliva.

Era Nova. Rivista do movimento contemporaneo. Lisbon,
1880-1881.

Erec et Enide. See Crestien de Troyes.

The Erl of Tolous and the Emperes of Almayn. Eine englische Romanze aus dem Anfange des 15. Jahrhunderts,
nebst litterarischer Untersuchung über ihre Quelle, die
ihr verwandten Darstellungen und ihre geschichtliche
Grundlage, herausgegeben von Gustav Lüdtke. Berlin,
1881. (Sammlung englischer Denkmäler in kritischen
Ausgaben, 3.)

Erman, A. See Archiv für wissenschaftliche Kunde, etc.

Ernault, Émile. Les contes bretons et les publications populaires. *In* Mélusine, IV, 20–21, 138–39, 1888.

—— Gaidoz, Henri; Luzel, F. M., and Rolland, E. Chansons populaires de la Basse-Bretagne. *In* Mélusine, III, 77–83, 161–63, 184–86, 208–10, 260–62, 327–28, 350–52, 393–95, 421–22, 477–78, 570–73; IV, 299–303, 329–30, 357–58, 379, 404–05, 425–26, 452–53, 471–73, 501; V, 83–84, 188–89, 213–15, 255–56, 272–84, 305–08; VI, 66–69, 91–92, 105–07, 165–67, 252–56; VII, 5–12, 62–63, 125–33, 183–89, 203–05, 256–62. 1886–95.

Erythraeus,. Janus Nicius [= Gian Vittorio Rossi]. Erythraei Exempla. [Cologne ?] [Rome ?], 1663.

Eschenbach, Ulrich von. See Alexander the Great.

Eschenbach, Wolfram von. Wolfram's von Eschenbach Parzival und Titurel. Herausgegeben von Karl Bartsch. Leipzig, 1870–71. 3 pts. (Deutsche Classiker des Mittelalters, begründet von Franz Pfeiffer, 9–11.)

Eschenburg, Johann Joachim. Denkmäler altdeutscher Dichtkunst, beschrieben und erläutert. Bremen, 1799.

Escherny, François-Louis, comte d'. Mélanges de littérature, d'histoire, de morale et de philosophie. . . . Paris, 1811. 3 vols.

Estienne, Henri. Apologie pour Hérodote. [Satire de la Société au XVIᵉ siècle.] Nouvelle édition, faite sur la première et augmentée de remarques par P. Ristelhuber. Avec trois tables. Paris, 1879. 2 vols.

Estlander, C. G. See Finsk Tidskrift.

Ethnologische Mitteilungen aus Ungarn. Zeitschrift für die Volkskunde der Bewohner Ungarns und seiner Nebenländer. Redigirt und herausgegeben von Anton Herrmann. Vols. I–V. Budapest, 1887–96. (Vol. II redigirt von A. Herrmann u. L. Katona.)

Étienne de Bourbon. Anecdotes historiques, légendes et apologues tirés du recueil inédit d'——. Publiés par A. Lecoy de la Marche. Paris, 1877. (Société de l'Histoire de France.)

Etnografičeskoe Obozrěnie (N. ʿA. Jančuk). Moscow, 1889–.

Etnografičeski Sbornik. i–vi, 4 tom. St Petersburg, 1853–64.

Ettmüller, Ludwig. See Orendel und Brîde.

—— See Oswald.

Études Romanes dédiées à Gaston Paris le 29 Décembre 1890 (25ᵉ anniversaire de son doctorat ès lettres) par ses élèves français et ses élèves étrangers des pays de langue française. Paris, 1891.

Eulenspiegel. La légende d'Ulenspiegel par Ch. de Coster. Ouvrage illustré, *etc.* Paris, 1868.

—— Charles de Coster. La légende et les aventures héroïques, joyeuses et glorieuses d'Ulenspiegel et de Lamme Goedzak au pays de Flandres et ailleurs. Bruxelles, 1893.

—— Dr. Thomas Murners Ulenspiegel. Herausgegeben von J. M. Lappenberg. Leipzig, 1854.

—— Howleglas. Edited by Frederic Ouvry. [Privately printed.] London, 1867.

Eulogium Historiarum sive Temporis: Chronicon ab orbe condito usque ad Annum Domini M.CCC.LXVI., a monacho quodam Malmesburiensi exaratum. Accedunt continuationes duae quarum una ad annum M.CCCC.XIII., altera ad annum M.CCCC.XC. perducta est. Edited by Frank Scott Haydon. London, 1858–63. 3 vols. (Rolls Series.)

Eustache le Moine. Roman d'Eustache le Moine, pirate fameux du XIIIᵉ siècle. Publié pour la première fois d'après un manuscrit de la Bibliothèque Royale par Francisque Michel. Paris, Londres, 1834.

Εὐσταθίου πρωτονωβελεσίμου τοῦ Μακρεμβολίτου τῶν καθ' Ὑσμίνην καὶ Ὑσμινίαν λόγοι ια'. Eustathii Macrembolitae protonobilissimi de Hysmines et Hysminiae Amoribus libri xi. Recensuit Isidorus Hilberg. Vindobonae, 1876.

Eustathius. Commentarii ad Homeri Iliadem, ad fidem exempli Romani editi. Lipsiae, 1827–30. 4 vols.

Evans, D. Silvan. See Stephens, Thomas.

Evans, Thomas. Old Ballads, Historical and Narrative, with some of modern date. Now first collected, and reprinted from rare Copies and MSS. With notes. London, 1784. 2 vols.

Evax. De gemmis scriptum Evacis regis Arabum olim a poeta quodam non infoeliciter carmine redditum et nunc primum in lucem editum opera et studio D. Henrici Rantzovii. Witebergae, 1574.

[Exchequer Rolls.] Rotulorum Originalium in Curia Scaccarii Abbreviatio. [London], 1805–10. 2 vols. (Record Commission.)

The Exchequer Rolls of Scotland. Rotuli Scaccarii Regum Scotorum. Edinburgh, 1878–97. 16 vols.

Ey, August. Harzmärchenbuch, oder Sagen und Märchen aus dem Oberharze. Stade, 1862.

Eyering, Eucharius. Proverbiorum Copia. Etlich viel Hundert Lateinischer und Teutscher schönen und lieblicher Sprichwörter, etc. Eissleben, 1601–3. 3 pts.

Eyssenhardt, Franciscus. Historia Miscella. Berolini, 1869.

Fabriano, Mambrino Roseo da. See Sferamundi.

Fabricius, Johann Albert. Codex Pseudepigraphus Veteris Testamenti, collectus, castigatus, testimoniisque censuris et animadversionibus illustratus. 2d ed. Hamburgi, 1722, '23. 2 vols.

Fabyan, Robert. The New Chronicles of England and France. In Two Parts. Named by himself the Concordance of Histories. Reprinted from Pynson's edition of 1516. A biographical and literary preface, and an index, by Henry Ellis. London, 1811.

Facetiæ. Musarum Deliciæ: or the Muses Recreation, conteining severall pieces of poetique wit. By Sr J. M. and Ja: S. 1656. and Wit Restor'd, in severall select poems, not formerly publisht. 1658. Also Wit's Recreations, selected from the finest fancies of moderne muses. With A thousand out-landish proverbs, printed from edition 1640. . . . To which are now added memoirs of Sir J. Mennis and Dr. J. Smith with a preface. [Edited by T. Park.] London, 1817. 2 vols. See Wit and Drollery.

Fagerlund, Lars Wilhelm. Anteckningar om Korpo och Houtskärs Socknar. Sommarstudier. *In* Bidrag till Kännedom af Finlands Natur och Folk, utgifna af Finska Vetenskaps-Societaten, XXVIII. Helsingfors, 1878.

Fagot, P. See Laroche, Pierre.

Fairholt, Frederick W. Lord Mayors' Pageants: being collections towards a history of these annual celebrations, with specimens of the descriptive pamphlets published by the city poets. London, 1843, '44. 2 parts. (Percy Society, 10.)

—— Costume in England, a History of Dress to the end of the Eighteenth Century. 3d ed. Enlarged and thoroughly revised by the Hon. H. A. Dillon. London, 1885. 2 vols.

Falconer, William. An Universal Dictionary of the Marine:

or, a copious explanation of the technical terms and phrases employed in the construction, equipment, furniture, machinery, movements, and military operations of a ship. Illustrated with variety of original designs of shipping, in different situations; together with separate views of their masts, sails, yards, and rigging. To which is annexed a translation of the French sea-terms and phrases, collected from the works of Mess. Du Hamel, Aubin, Saverien, &c. London, 1769.

The Famous Victories of Henry the Fifth. Containing The Honourable Battell of AGIN-COURT. As it was acted by the Kinges Majesties Servants. *In* [John Nichols,] Six Old Plays, on which Shakspeare founded his [etc.], I, 317–375. London, 1779.

Fastnachtspiele aus dem fünfzehnten Jahrhundert. See Keller, Adelbert von.

Favart, Charles Simon. La Fée Urgèle. Comédie en quatre actes, melée d'ariettes. Paris, 1765.

Faye, Andreas. Norske Folke-Sagn. 2d ed. Christiania, 1844.

Federer, Charles A. See Flodden Field.

Fedorowski, M. Lud okolic Żarek, Siewierza i Pilicy. [The Peasantry in Żarki, Siewierz and Pilica.] Warsaw, 1888–89. 2 vols. (Bibljoteka "Wisły," 1, 2.)

Feifalik, Julius. Zwei böhmische Volksbücher zur Sage von Reinfrit von Braunschweig; *and* Nachtrag zu der Abhandlung über zwei böhmische Volksbücher, etc. *In* Sitzungsberichte der Philosophisch-Historischen Classe der Kaiserlichen Akademie der Wissenschaften, XXIX, 83–97, XXXII, 322–331, Jahrg. 1858, '59. Wien, 1859.

—— See Kindheit Jesu.

Fenn, Sir John. See Paston Letters.

Ferguson, William. The Great North of Scotland Railway. A Guide. Edinburgh, 1881.

Ferrari, Severino. Canti popolari in San Pietro Capofiume. *In* Archivio per lo studio delle tradizioni popolari, VII, 387–403; VIII, 105–12; X, 413–18. 1888–91.

—— Canzoni ricordate nell' Incatenatura del Bianchino. *In* Giornale di Filologia Romanza, III, No 7, pp. 51–88. 1880.

Ferrario, Giulio. Storia ed analisi degli antichi romanzi di cavalleria e dei poemi romanzeschi d' Italia, con dissertazioni sull' origine, sugl' instituti, sulle cerimonie de' cavalieri, sulle corti d' amore, sui tornei, sulle giostre ed armature de' paladini, sull' invenzione e sull' uso degli stemmi, ecc. Milano, 1828–29. 4 vols.

Ferraro, Giuseppe. Saggio di canti popolari raccolti a Pontelagoscuro (Provincia di Ferraro, a. 1875). *In* Rivista di Filologia Romanza, II, 193–220. 1876.

—— XVI canti popolari della Bassa Romagna. *In* Rivista di letteratura popolare, I, 55–68. 1877.

—— Spogliature di canti popolari parmigiani e monferrini. *In* Archivio per lo studio delle tradizioni popolari, VIII, 322–33, 496–504; IX, 267–74. 1889–90.

Ferumbras. Sir Ferumbras. Edited from the unique paper MS. about 1380 A. D., in the Bodleian Library (Ashmole MS. 33) by Sidney J. Herrtage. London, 1879. (The English Charlemagne Romances, I; Early English Text Society, Extra Series, 34.) See, also, Fierabras.

Fickler, Johann Baptist. Theologia juridica, seu jus civile theologicum. Dilling, 1575.

Fiedler, Eduard. Geschichte der volksthümlichen schottischen Liederdichtung. Zerbst, 1846. 2 vols.

Fierabras. Chanson de geste. Publiée pour la première fois d'après les manuscrits de Paris, de Rome et de Londres par MM. A. Krœber et G. Servois. Paris, 1860. (F. Guessard, Les anciens Poëtes de la France, 4.) See, also, Ferumbras.

Figlia del Re di Dacia, Novella della. Testo inedito del buon secolo della lingua [con prefazione del Alessandro Wesselofsky]. Pisa, 1866. (Collezione di antiche scritture italiane inedite o rare.)

Fillon, Benjamin. L'histoire véridique des grandes et exécrables voleries et subtilités de Guillery, depuis sa naissance jusqu'à la juste punition de ses crimes. Fontenay, 1848.

—— et Rochebrune, Octave de. Poitou et Vendée. Études historiques et artistiques. Niort, 1887. 2 vols.

Finamore, Gennaro. Storie popolari abruzzesi in versi. *In* Archivio per lo studio delle tradizioni popolari, I, 83–92, 206–222. 1882.

—— Tradizioni popolari abruzzesi. Torino, Palermo, 1894. (G. Pitrè, Curiosità popolari tradizionali, 13.)

Finlay, John. Scottish Historical and Romantic Ballads, chiefly ancient; with explanatory notes and a glossary. Edinburgh, 1808. 2 vols.

Finsk Tidskrift för Vitterhet, Vetenskap, Konst ock Politik, utgifven af C. G. Estlander, *etc.* Helsingfors, 1876–.

Firdusi. Le Livre des Rois par Abou'lkasim Firdousi, publié, traduit et commenté par M. Jules Mohl. Paris, 1838–68. 6 vols. (Collection Orientale. Manuscrits inédits de la Bibliothèque Royale traduits et publiés par ordre du Roi.)

Fischart, Johann. Erneuwerte Beschreibung der wol gedenckwürdigen Alten vnd warhafften verwunderlichen Geschicht von Herrn Petern v. Stauffenberg, genant Diemringer ausz der Orttenau bei Rhein, . . . erneuwert vnnd an den tag gebracht durch I. F. Strassburg, 1588.

Fitchett, John. Bewsey, a poem. Warrington, 1796.

Fittis, Robert S. *In* The Perthshire Antiquarian Miscellany. Perth, 1875. [See IV, 359.]

Fitz Warine, Fulk. The history of Fulk Fitz Warine, an outlawed baron in the reign of King John. Edited from a manuscript preserved in the British Museum, with an English translation and explanatory and illustrative notes, by Thomas Wright. . . . London, 1885. (Warton Club.)

Flateyjarbók. En Samling af norske Konge-Sagaer med indskudte mindre Fortællinger om Begivenheder i og udenfor Norge, samt Annaler. Udgiven efter offentlig Foranstaltning. Christiania, 1860, '62, '68. 3 vols.

Fleck, Konrad. Flore und Blanscheflur. See Floire et Blanceflor.

Fletcher, John. See Beaumont, Francis.

—— Shakespeare and Fletcher. The Two Noble Kinsmen. Edited by the Rev. Walter W. Skeat. Cambridge [Eng.], 1875.

Flodden Field, The Ballad of. A Poem of the XVIth Century. Edited by Charles A. Federer. Manchester, 1884.

—— The Battle of. A poem of the Sixteenth Century. With the various readings [etc.], by Henry Weber. Edinburgh and London, 1808.

Floire et Blanceflor. Poèmes du XIIIe siècle, publiés d'après les manuscrits, avec une introduction, des notes et un glossaire, par M. Édélestand du Meril. Paris, 1856.

—— Der Roman von Flore und Blanceflor, Altfranzösisch. Herausgegeben von Hrn. [I.] Bekker. Berlin, K. Akademie der Wissenschaften, Philologische und historische Abhandlungen aus dem Jahre 1844, pp. 1–41. Berlin, 1846.

Floire et Blanceflor. Der Roman von Flore und Blancheflor. Neugriechisch. Herausgegeben von Hrn. [I.] Bekker. Berlin, K. Akademie der Wissenschaften, Philologische und historische Abhandlungen aus dem Jahre 1845, pp. 127–180. Berlin, 1847.

—— Flore und Blanscheflur. Eine Erzählung von Konrad Fleck. Herausgegeben von Emil Sommer. Quedlinburg and Leipzig, 1846. (Bibliothek der gesammten deutschen National-Literatur, 12.)

—— Flores och Blanzeflor. En Kärleks-dikt från Medeltiden. Efter gamla handskrifter af Gustaf Edv. Klemming. Stockholm, 1844.

—— Floris ende Blancefloer door Diederic van Assende. Mit Einleitung, Anmerkungen und Glossar herausgegeben von Hoffmann von Fallersleben. *In his* Horae Belgicae, III. Lipsiae, 1836.

—— Floris ende Blancefloer. Med inleiding en aanteekeningen door Dr H. E. Moltzer. Groningen, 1879. (Moltzer and te Winkel, Bibliotheek van middelnederlandsche Letterkunde, 23.)

—— Floris and Blauncheflur. Mittelenglisches Gedicht aus dem 13. Jahrhundert. Nebst litterarischer Untersuchung und einem Abriss über die Verbreitung der Sage in der europäischen Litteratur herausgegeben von Emil Hausknecht. Berlin, 1885. (Sammlung englischer Denkmäler in kritischen Ausgaben, 5.)

—— Floyris. See Steinmeyer, Elias.

Flore. See Roi Flore (Li Contes dou).

Flore, Jeanne. Comptes amoureux par Mad. Jeanne Flore, touchant la punition que faict Venus de ceux qui contemnent et meprisent le vray amour. Paris, 1543.

Florell, Otto. See Krohn, Kaarle.

Florentius Wigorniensis. Chronicon ex chronicis, ab adventu Hengesti et Horsi in Britanniam usque ad annum M.C.XVII, etc. Ad fidem codicum manuscriptorum edidit, brevique adnotatione passim illustravit Benjamin Thorpe. . . . Londini, 1848, '49. 2 vols. (English Historical Society.)

Flügel, Ewald. Liedersammlungen des XVI. Jahrhunderts, besonders aus der Zeit Heinrich's VIII. *In* Anglia, XII, 225–72, 585–97. 1889.

—— Neuenglisches Lesebuch. I. Band. Die Zeit Heinrichs VIII. Halle a. S., 1895.

Foerster, Wendelin. See Aiol et Mirabel.

—— See Altfranzösische Bibliothek.

—— See Chevaliers, Li, as Deus Espees.

—— See Crestien de Troyes.

—— See Elie de Saint Gille.

—— See Richars li Biaus.

[Folengo, Theophilo.] Orlandino di Limerno Pittocco. Londra, 1775. *Also*, Vinegia, 1550.

Folk-Lore; a quarterly Review of Myth, Tradition, Institution, and Custom. London, 1890-. (Folk-Lore Society.)

El Folk-Lore Andaluz. Órgano de la Sociedad de este nombre. Sevilla, 1882–83.

Folk-Lore Español. See Machado.

El Folk-Lore Frexnense y Bético-Extremeño. Órgano temporal de las Sociedades de este nombre. Fregenal, 1883–84.

Folk-Lore Journal. Vols I–VII. London, 1883–89. 7 vols. (Folk-Lore Society.)

The Folk-Lore Record. Vols I–V. London, 1878–82. 5 vols. (Folk-Lore Society.)

The Fond Mother's Garland, n. d. (but earlier than 1776). [See IV, 60 a.]

Forbes, John. Cantus. Songs and Fancies. 2d ed. Aberdeen, 1666. 3d ed., 1682.

Ford, Robert. Auld Scots Ballants. Paisley and London, 1889.

Fordun, Joannes de. Chronica Gentis Scotorum. Ed. by William F. Skene. Chronicle of the Scottish Nation, translated from the Latin text by F. J. H. Skene. Edinburgh, 1871–72. 2 vols. (The Historians of Scotland. Edin., 1871–80. 10 vols. 1, 4.)

—— Scotichronicon Genuinum, una cum ejusdem Supplemento ac Continuatione : ed. Tho. Hearnius. Oxonii, 1722. 5 vols.

—— Scotichronicon, cum supplementis et continuatione Walteri Boweri. Praefixa est ad historiam Scotorum Introductio brevis, cura Walteri Goodall. Edinburgi, 1759. 2 vols.

Foreign Quarterly Review. I–XXXVII. London, 1827–46.

Fornaldar Sögur Norðrlanda, eptir gömlum handritum utgefnar af C. C. Rafn. Kaupmannahöfn, 1829–30. 3 vols.

Fornaldarsögur Norðrlanda. Valdimar Ásmundarson hefir búið undir prentun. Texta-útgáfa. Reykjavík, 1885–89. 3 vols.

Fornmanna Sögur, eptir gömlum handritum útgefnar að tilhlutun hins Norræna Fornfræða Fèlags. [Edited by Egilsson, Guðmundarson, Rafn, and others.] Kaupmannahöfn, 1825–37. 12 vols.

Fornsögur Suðrlanda. See Cederschiöld, Gustaf.

Fornsvenskt Legendarium. See Stephens, George.

The Forsaken Lover's Garland. [Newcastle ? 1750 ?] British Museum, 11621. e. 1. See V, 109 b.]

Fortalicium Fidei. See Alphonsus a Spina.

Forty Vezirs. See Gibb, E. J. W. ; Behrnauer, W.

The Four Elements, The Interlude of. An early Moral Play. Ed. by James Orchard Halliwell. London, 1848. (Percy Society, 22.)

Fox, John. Acts and Monuments of matters most speciall and memorable, happening in the Church, with an universall Historie of the same, etc. . . . Also with the title, The Booke of Martyrs. London, 1641. 3 vols.

Franck, Melchior. Fasciculus Quodlibeticus. Nürnberg, 1611. [See V, 290 b.]

Franzisci, Franz. Cultur-Studien über Volksleben, Sitten und Bräuche in Kärnten. Nebst einem Anhang : Märchen aus Kärnten. Wien, 1879. (Grillparzer-Literatur-Verein in Wien.)

Fraser, Sir William. The Book of Carlaverock. Memoirs of the Maxwells, Earls of Nithsdale, Lords Maxwell and Herries. Edinburgh, 1873. 2 vols.

—— The Douglas Book. Edinburgh, 1885. 4 vols.

Fredegarius. Chronicon. *In* A. du Chesne, Historiae Francorum Scriptores Coaetanei, I, 740–779. Lutetiae Parisiorum, 1636.

Freiligrath, Ferdinand. Neue Gedichte. Stuttgart, 1887.

—— Zwischen den Garben. Eine Nachlese älterer Gedichte. Stuttgart and Tübingen, 1849.

Fricke, Richard. Die Robin-Hood-Balladen. Ein Beitrag zum Studium der englischen Volksdichtung. Braunschweig, 1883.

Fritslar, Hermann von. Das Heiligenleben. *In* Franz Pfeiffer, Deutsche Mystiker des vierzehnten Jahrhunderts, I, 3–258. Leipzig, 1845.

Froissart, Jean. Chroniques de Froissart. 15 vols. Paris, 1824–26. *In* J. A. Buchon, Collection des chroniques nationales françaises, écrites en langue vulgaire du treizième au seizième siècle ; avec notes et éclaircissements, XI–XXV.

—— Here begynnith the firste volum of Syr John Froissart : of the Cronycles of Englande, Fraunce, Spayne, Portyngale, Scotlande, Bretaine, Flaunders : and other places adioynynge. Translated oute of Frenche into oure materall Englysshe tongue, by John Bouchier knyghte, lorde Berners : At the cōmaundement of oure moste hyghe redouted soueraygne lorde kynge Henrye the viij. kynge of Englande, Fraunce, and Irelande, defendour of the faith : and of the church of Engelande and also of Irelande in earth the supreme heade. London, 1523–25. 2 vols.

Frommann, G. Karl. Die Deutschen Mundarten. Monatsschrift (Vierteljahrsschrift, Zeitschrift) für Dichtung, Forschung und Kritik. Herausgegeben von——. Nürnberg, 1854–57 ; Nördlingen, 1858–59 ; Halle, 1877. 7 vols.

Froude, James Anthony. The English in Ireland in the Eighteenth Century. London, 1872–74. 3 vols.

—— Reign of Elizabeth. Vols VII–XII *of his* History of England from the Fall of Wolsey to the Death of Elizabeth. New York, 1870. 12 vols.

Fulk Fitz Warine. See Fitz Warine, Fulk.

Fuller, William. Brief Discovery of the True Mother of the Pretended Prince of Wales, known by the name of Mary Grey. London, 1696.

Furnivall, Frederick James. Captain Cox, his Ballads and Books ; or, Robert Laneham's Letter. London, 1871. (Ballad Society.)

—— Early English Poems and Lives of Saints (with those of the wicked birds Pilate and Judas). Copied and edited from manuscripts in the library of the British Museum. Berlin, 1862. (Philological Society, 2.)

—— See Adam of Cobsam.

—— See Borde, Andrew.

—— See Digby Mysteries.

—— See Generides.

—— See (Le) Morte Arthur.

—— See Percy MS.

—— See Stubbes, Phillip.

—— Brock, Edmund, and Clouston, William Alexander. Originals and Analogues of some of Chaucer's Canterbury Tales. London, 1872–87. (Chaucer Society.)

Fussesbrunnen, Konrad von. Die Kindheit Jesu. Herausgegeben von Karl Kochendörffer. Strassburg and London, 1881. (Quellen und Forschungen zur Sprach- und Culturgeschichte der germanischen Völker, 43.)

Gaal, Georg. See Stier, A.

Gadde, A. (*aus Gloddow*). Volkslieder aus Hinterpommern. *In* Zeitschrift für Volkskunde, III, 187–89, 224–27. 1891.

Gaelic Society of Dublin. Transactions. I. Dublin, 1808.

—— of Inverness. Transactions. Inverness, 1872–.

Gaidoz, Henri. Le coq cuit qui chante. *In* Mélusine, VI, 25–27 (cf. 23–24). 1892.

—— Les deux arbres entrelacés. *In* Mélusine, IV, 62, 85–91, 142.

Gaidoz, Henri. Le folk-lore aux États-Unis et trois nouvelles revues de folk-lore. *In* Mélusine, IV, 206–11. 1888.

—— Le suicide. *In* Mélusine, IV, 11–14.

—— See Ernault, Émil.

—— See Mélusine.

—— See Perdrizet, P. F. See Revue Celtique.

—— and Rolland, E. [and others]. Les noyés. *In* Mélusine, II, 250–55, 333, 453 ; III, 72, 141, 215. 1885–86.

Gaimar, Geoffroi. Extrait de la Chronique de Geoffroi Gaimar. *In* F. Michel, Chroniques Anglo-Normandes, I, 1–64. Rouen, 1836.

—— Lestorie des Engles solum la translacion Maistre Geffrei Gaimar. Edited by the late Sir Thomas Duffus Hardy and Charles Trice Martin. London, 1888–89. 2 vols. (Rolls Series.)

Gairdner, James. See Paston Letters.

Galerent, Roman de. See Renaut.

Galien. Histoire des nobles prouesses et vaillances de Gallien Restauré. Troyes, n. d.

Galland, L., and Cardonne, D. D. See Pilpay.

Gamelyn. The Tale of Gamelyn from the Harleian MS. No 7334, collated with six other MSS. Edited with notes and a glossarial index by the Rev. Walter W. Skeat. Oxford, 1884. (Clarendon Press Series.)

Gammer Gurton's Needle. *In* Robert Dodsley, A Select Collection of Old English Plays, II, 1–83. London, 1825. (III, 164–256, ed. W. Carew Hazlitt, London, 1876.)

Garcin de Tassy, Joseph Héliodore. La poésie philosophique et religieuse chez les Persans. Le langage des Oiseaux. (Extrait de la Revue Contemporaine, t. XXIV, 93ᵉ livraison.) Paris, 1856.

Gardiner, Samuel Rawson. History of England from the accession of James I to the outbreak of the Civil War, 1603–1642. London, 1883–84. 10 vols.

—— History of the Great Civil War, 1642–1649. London, 1886, '89, '91. 3 vols.

Garnier de Pont Sainte Maxence. La Vie de Saint Thomas le Martyr, Archevêque de Canterbury. Publiée et précédée d'une introduction par C. Hippeau. Paris, 1859.

Gaspé, Philippe Aubert de. Les anciens Canadiens. (2ᵉ éd., Québec, 1864. 1 vol.) Québec, 1877. 2 vols.

Gaster, Moritz. Beiträge zur vergleichenden Sagen- und Märchenkunde. Bukarest, 1883. (Separat-abdruck aus der Monatschrift für Geschichte und Wissenschaft des Judenthums, 29–30 Jahrgang, 1880–81.)

Gaucher de Dourdans. See Gautier de Doulens.

Gautier d'Aupais ; Le Chevalier à la Corbeille : fabliaux du XIIIᵉ siècle. Publiés pour la première fois d'après deux manuscrits par Francisque Michel. Paris, 1835.

Gautier de Coincy. Les Miracles de la Sainte Vierge. Publiés par l'abbé Poquet. Avec une introduction, des notes explicatives et un glossaire, accompagnés de nombreuses miniatures. Paris, 1857.

Gautier de Doulens (Gaucher de Dourdans). Conte du Graal. *In* Potvin's Perceval. See Perceval.

Gautier, Léon. Les épopées françaises, étude sur les origines et l'histoire de la littérature nationale. Paris, 1865, '67, '68. 3 vols. 2ᵉ éd., 1878–94. 4 vols.

Gawayne. See Madden, Sir Frederic.

Gayangos, Pascual de. Libros de Caballerias, con un discurso preliminar y un catálogo razonado. Madrid, 1857. (Biblioteca de Autores Españoles.)

—— See Oliva. See Gran Conquista.

Gebhart, J. Oesterreichisches Sagenbuch. Pest, 1862.

Die Gegenwart. Wochenschrift für Literatur, Kunst und öffentliches Leben. Berlin, 1872-.

Geiger, L. See Zeitschrift für vergleichende Litteratur.

—— See Vierteljahrsschrift für Kultur, u. s. w.

[Geijer, Erik Gustav.] See Iduna.

Geiler, Johann, von Kaisersberg. Trostspiegel. In Das irrig Schaf. Sagt von Kleinmütikeit und Verzweiflung. Gebrediget, und gedeütscht durch ——. Strassburg, [1510?]. 7 pts.

Generides. A Royal Historie of the excellent knight Generides. Edited from the unique MS. of John Tollemache, Esq., M. P., of Peckforton Castle, South Cheshire, and Helmingham Hall, Suffolk, by Frederick J. Furnivall. Hertford, 1865. (Roxburghe Club.)

Generydes, a Romance in seven-line stanzas. Edited from the unique paper MS. in Trinity College, Cambridge (about 1440 A. D.), by W. Aldis Wright. London, 1878 ['73-78]. (Early English Text Society, 55, 70.)

Genesi de Scriptura. Compendi historial de la Biblia que ab lo títol de Genesi de Scriptura trelladá del provençal a la llengua catalana Mossen Guillem Serra en l'any M.CCCCLI, y ara ha fet estampar per primera vegada En Miquel Victoriá Amer. Barcelona, 1873. (Biblioteca Catalana.)

Genest, John. Some Account of the English Stage, from the Restoration in 1660 to 1830. Bath, 1832. 10 vols.

Genovefa. See Seuffert, Bernhard.

The Gentleman's Magazine; or, Monthly Intelligencer, 1731-35. The Gentleman's Magazine and Historical Chronicle, 1736-1807. New Series, 1808-33; 1834-56; 1856-65; 1866-67; 1868-. London, 1731-.

Gentleman's Magazine Library: being a classified collection of the chief contents of the Gentleman's Magazine from 1731-1868. Edited by G. L. Gomme. London, 1883-.

Geoffrey of Monmouth. Galfredi Monumetensis de Origine et Gestis Regum Britanniae libri XII. In [Hieronymus Commelinus,] Rerum Britannicarum Scriptores Vetustiores ac Praecipui, pp. 1-92. Heidelbergae, 1587.

George a Green. The History of George a Green, Pindar of the Town of Wakefield. In William J. Thoms, A Collection of Early Prose Romances, II. London, 1828.

Georgeakis, G., et Pineau, Léon. Le Folk-Lore de Lesbos. Paris, 1894. (Les littératures populaires de toutes les nations, 31.)

Georgius Cedrenus. See Cedrenus.

Georgius Codinus. See Codinus.

Gérard de Nevers. See Gibert de Montreuil.

Gerhard, Wilhelm. Minstrelklänge aus Schottland rhythmisch verdeutscht. Leipzig, 1853.

—— Wila. Serbische Volkslieder und Heldenmährchen. Leipzig, 1828. 2 pts.

Gering, Hugo. Íslendzk Æventýri. Isländische Legenden, Novellen und Märchen. Halle, 1882-83. 2 vols.

Germania. Vierteljahrsschrift für deutsche Alterthumskunde. Herausgegeben von F. Pfeiffer (later, by Karl Bartsch, and others). Stuttgart and Wien, 1856-92. 37 vols.

—— See Hagen, Friedrich Heinrich von der.

Gervase of Tilbury. Des Gervasius von Tilbury Otia Imperialia. In einer Auswahl neu herausgegeben und mit Anmerkungen begleitet von Felix Liebrecht. Ein Beitrag zur deutschen Mythologie und Sagenforschung. Hannover, 1856.

Gervasius Monachus Dorobornensis (sive Cantuariensis).

Chronica de tempore Regum Angliae, Stephani, Hen. II. et Ricardi I. In Roger Twysden, Historiae Anglicanae Scriptores X, col. 1338-1627. Londini, 1652.

Gesner, J. M. See Orpheus.

Gesta Romanorum. Gesta Romanorum, das älteste Mährchen- und Legendenbuch des christlichen Mittelalters zum ersten Male vollständig aus dem Lateinischen in's Deutsche übertragen, aus gedruckten und ungedruckten Quellen vermehrt, mit Anmerkungen und einer Abhandlung über den wahren Verfasser und die bisherigen Ausgaben und Uebersetzungen desselben versehen, von Dr. Johann Georg Theodor Grässe. Dresden und Leipzig, 1842.

—— Gesta Romanorum. Von Hermann Oesterley. Berlin, 1872.

—— or, entertaining Moral Stories. Translated from the Latin with preliminary observations and copious notes by the Rev. Charles Swan. London, 1824. 2 vols.

—— The old English Versions of the Gesta Romanorum. Edited for the first time from manuscripts in the British Museum and University Library, Cambridge, with an introduction and notes, by Sir Frederic Madden. London, 1838. (Roxburghe Club.)

—— The Early English Versions, re-edited by Sidney J. H. Herrtage. London, 1879. (Early English Text Society.)

Giannini, Alfredo. Canzoni del contado di Massa Lunense. In Archivio per lo studio delle tradizioni popolari, VIII, 273-86. 1889.

Giannini, Giovanni. Saggio di canti popolari della mentagna lucchese. In Archivio per lo studio delle tradizioni popolari, VI, 355-67. 1887.

Gibb, E. J. W. The History of the Forty Vezirs, or the story of the Forty Morns and Eves, written in Turkish by Sheykh-Zāda, done into English. London, 1886.

Gibert de Montreuil. Roman de la Violette, ou de Gérard de Nevers, en vers, du XIIIᵉ siècle. Publié pour la première fois d'après deux manuscrits de la Bibliothèque Royale, par Francisque Michel. Paris, 1834.

Gibson, Edmund. See Camden, William.

Gibson, William Sidney. Dilston Hall; or, Memoirs of the Right Hon. James Radcliffe, Earl of Derwentwater, a martyr in the Rebellion of 1715. London, 1850.

Gilchrist, O. See Dodsley, Robert.

Gildersleeve, Basil L. See American Journal of Philology.

Gilmour, Sir John. The Decisions of the Lords of Council and Session, from July, 1601, to July, 1666. Edinburgh, 1701. (In A Collection of Decisions of the Lords of Council and Session, pt. I.)

Giornale di Filologia romanza. Diretto da Ernesto Monaci. Vols. I-IV. Roma, 1878-83.

Giornale Storico della Letteratura italiana. Torino, 1883-.

Giovanni, Ser. See Pecorone.

Giraldi Cinthio, Giovanbattista. De gli Hecatommithi Parte prima(-seconda, nella quale si contengono tre Dialoghi della uita ciuile). Monte Regale. 1565.

Giraldus [de Barri] Cambrensis. Opera. Vols I-IV, edited by J. S. Brewer; vols V-VII, edited by J. F. Dimock; vol. VIII, edited by G. F. Warner. London, 1861-91. 8 vols. (Speculum Ecclesiae, vol. IV, 1873. Itinerarium Kambriae, vol. VI, 1868.) (Rolls Series.)

Giraud, Charles. See Perrault, Charles.

Gittée, Aug. See Volkskunde.

—— and de Mont, Pol. Mijn man komt thuis. In Volkskunde, II, 49-58; V, 20-21. 1889, 1892.

[Gladwin, F.] See Tuti-nameh.

Gliński, A. J. Bajarz polski. Baśni powieści i gawędy ludowe. Wilno, 1862. 4 vols. (3d ed., 1881.)

Gobius, Johannes, *Junior*. Scala Celi. Ulm, 1480.

Godefridus Viterbensis. Pantheon Gotfridi Viterbiensis, de universo Veteri et Novo Testamento; de omnibus aetatibus et temporibus seculorum, etc. *In* Johann Pistorius, Rerum Germanicarum Scriptores aliquot insignes . . . , II, 8–392. Ratisbonae, 1726.

Godefroid de Bouillon. See Chevalier au Cygne.

Godfrey of Viterbo. See Godefridus Viterbensis.

Goedeke, Karl. Deutsche Dichtung im Mittelalter. Zweite Ausgabe, vermehrt um Buch XII: Niederdeutsche Dichtung, von Hermann Oesterley. Dresden, 1871.

—— Elf Bücher deutscher Dichtung. Von Sebastian Brant (1500) bis auf die Gegenwart. Aus den Quellen. Mit biographisch-literarischen Einleitungen und mit Abweichungen der ersten Drucke. Leipzig, 1849. 2 pts.

—— Grundriss zur Geschichte der deutschen Dichtung aus den Quellen. Bd. I, II, Hannover, 1859. Bd. III, Abt. 1, 2, Dresden, 1881. 3 vols. in 4.

—— See Reinfrît von Braunschweig.

—— See Sachs, Hans.

Goedsche, Herrmann. Schlesischer Sagen-, Historien- und Legendenschatz. Meissen, 1840 [1839–40].

Göngu-Hrólfs Saga. *In* Fornaldar Sögur, ed. C. C. Rafn, III, 235–364, Kaupmannahöfn, 1830. *Also in* Fornaldar Sögur, ed. V. Ásmundarson, III, 143 ff., Reykjavík, 1889.

Goethe. Briefe Goethe's und der bedeutendsten Dichter seiner Zeit an Herder. Herausgegeben von Heinrich Düntzer u. F. G. von Herder. Frankfurt a. M., 1858.

—— Goethe's Lyrische Gedichte. Erläutert von Heinrich Düntzer. Zweite, neu bearbeitete Auflage. Leipzig, 1874, '75, '77. 3 vols. (Erläuterungen zu den deutschen Klassikern, XVII–XIX.)

Göttinger Musenalmanach für 1785. Göttingen, 1785. [See I, 410.]

Göttingische Gelehrte Anzeigen. Unter Aufsicht der Königlichen Gesellschaft der Wissenschaften. Göttingen, 1852–.

Goetze, E. See Sachs, Hans.

Golden Legend. See Legenda Aurea.

Goldoni, Carlo. Opere teatrali. Venezia, 1788–95. 44 vols.

Goldsmith, Oliver. Essays. London, 1765.

Gomme, George Laurence. English Traditional Lore: to which is added Customs of Foreign Countries and Peoples. *In* The Gentleman's Magazine Library: being a classified collection of the chief contents of the Gentleman's Magazine from 1731 to 1868. London, 1885.

—— See Hickathrift, Thomas.

Gonzenbach, Laura. Sicilianische Märchen. Aus dem Volksmund gesammelt. Mit Anmerkungen Reinhold Köhler's und einer Einleitung herausgegeben von Otto Hartwig. Leipzig, 1870. 2 pts.

Gordon, Alexander. The History of Peter the Great, Emperor of Russia. To which is prefixed a short general history of the country, from the rise of that monarchy: and an account of the author's life. By Alexander Gordon·of Achintoul, Esq.; several years a Major-General in the Czar's service. Aberdeen, 1755. 2 vols.

Gordon, James. History of Scots Affairs from MDCXXXVII to MDCXLI. By James Gordon, parson of Rothiemay. Aberdeen, 1841. 3 vols. (Spalding Club, 1, 3, 5.)

Gordon, Mary (Wilson). 'Christopher North.' A Memoir of John Wilson. Edinburgh, 1862. 2 vols.

Gordon, Sir Robert, of Gordonstoun, Baronet. A Genealogical History of the Earldom of Sutherland, from its origin to the year 1630; with a continuation to the year 1651. Published from the Original Manuscript. Edinburgh, 1813.

Gordon, William. The History of the Ancient, Noble, and Illustrious Family of Gordon, from their first Arrival in Scotland, in Malcolm III.'s Time, to the year 1690. Together with the History of the most remarkable Transactions in Scotland, from the Beginning of Robert I. his Reign, to that year 1690, containing the space of about 400 years. By Mr. William Gordon of Old Aberdeen. Edinburgh, 1726–27. 2 vols.

Gosche's Archiv. See Archiv für Litteraturgeschichte.

Gottfried von Strassburg. See Tristan.

Gottlund, C. A. Otava, 1832. [See V, 288 a.]

Gottschalk, Friedrich. Deutsche Volksmärchen. Leipzig, 1846. 2 vols.

Gower, John. Confessio Amantis. Edited and collated with the best manuscripts by Dr. Reinhold Pauli. London, 1857. 3 vols.

Gowther, Sir. Syr Gowghther. *In* E. V. Utterson, Select Pieces of Early Popular Poetry, I, 157–190. London, 1825.

Gozzi, Carlo. Turandot. Fiaba chinese teatrale tragicomica in cinque atti. *In his* Opere edite ed inedite (Venezia, 1801–02, 14 vols.), II, 3–108. Venezia, 1801.

Grässe, Johann Georg Theodor. Beiträge zur Literatur und Sage des Mittelalters. Dresden, 1850.

—— Die grossen Sagenkreise des Mittelalters. Dresden and Leipzig, 1842.

—— Der Sagenschatz des Königreichs Sachsen. Zum ersten Male in der ursprünglichen Form aus Chroniken, mündlichen und schriftlichen Ueberlieferungen und anderen Quellen gesammelt und herausgegeben. Zweite verbesserte und sehr vermehrte Auflage. Mit einem Anhange: Die Sagen des Herzogthums Sachsen-Altenburg. . . . Dresden, 1874. 2 vols.

—— See Gesta Romanorum. See Legenda Aurea.

Gräter, F. D. See Idunna und Hermode.

Grätz, H. Geschichte der Juden von den ältesten Zeiten bis auf die Gegenwart. Aus den Quellen neu bearbeitet. Leipzig [etc.], 1853–75.

Graf, Arturo. Miti, leggende e superstizioni del medio evo. Torino, 1892–93. 2 vols.

—— La leggenda del Paradiso Terrestre. Lettura fatta nella R. Università di Torino addi 11 Novembre, 1878. Torino, etc., 1878.

—— See Huon de Bordeaux.

Grafton, Richard. Grafton's Chronicle; or, History of England. London, 1809. 2 vols.

Graham, George Farquhar. The Popular Songs of Scotland with their appropriate melodies, arranged by G. F. Graham and others. Illustrated by critical and other notices. Glasgow, 1887.

Graham's Illustrated Magazine. Philadelphia, September, 1858. 18[38?]–.

La Gran Conquista de Ultramar, que mandó escribir el rey Don Alfonso el Sabio; illustrada con notas críticas y un glosario por Don Pascual de Gayangos. Madrid, 1858. *In* Biblioteca de Autores Españoles.

Le Grand Parangon des Nouvelles Nouvelles recueillies par

Nicolas de Troyes, publié pour la première fois et précédé d'une introduction par Émile Mabille. Bruxelles and Paris, 1866.

Grandmaison, C. See Huon.

Grant. Ane Account of the Rise and Offspring of the name of Grant. [Extracted by Charles Harcourt Chambers from a MS. History of the Grants.] London, 1876.

Grant, Mrs Anne MacVicar. Essays on the Superstitions of the Highlanders of Scotland: to which are added translations from the Gaelic [etc.]. New York, 1813. 2 vols.

Graser, Bernhard. De veterum re navali. Berolini, 1864.

Graves, Alfred Perceval. Irish Songs and Ballads. 3d ed. London, 1882.

Gray, Charles. See Paterson, James.

Gray, Sir Thomas. Scalachronica, by Sir Thomas Gray of Heton, Knight. A chronicle of England and Scotland from A. D. MLXIV to A. D. MCCCLXII. Now first printed from the unique manuscript with an introduction and notes [by Joseph Stevenson]. Edinburgh, 1836. (Maitland Club, 40.)

de Grazia, Demetrio. Canti popolari albanesi tradizionali nel mezzogiorno d'Italia. Riordinati, tradotti e illustrati. Noto, 1889.

Green Knight. Syr Gawayn and the Grene Knyȝt. In Sir F. Madden, Syr Gawayne, pp. 3–92. London, 1839. (Bannatyne Club, 64.)

Greene, Robert. Life and Complete Works in Prose and Verse. For the first time collected and edited by the Rev. Alexander B. Grosart. [London], 1881–86. 15 vols.

—— and Peele, George. The Dramatic and Poetical Works of ——. With memoirs of the Authors and notes by the Rev. Alexander Dyce. London, 1887.

Gregor, Walter. Notes on the Folk-Lore of the North-East of Scotland. London, 1881. (Folk-Lore Society, 7.)

—— Some Folk-Tales and Word-Jingles from Aberdeen and Banff Shires. In Folk-Lore Journal, III, 269–74.

Gregory, Donald. History of the Western Highlands and Isles of Scotland, from A. D. 1493 to A. D. 1625: with a brief introductory sketch from A. D. 80 to A. D. 1493. Edinburgh, 1836; 2d ed., London, 1881.

Grein, C. W. M. See Ælfric. See Hildebrandslied.

Grimm, Albert Ludwig. Deutsche Sagen und Märchen für die Jugend. 2te Aufl. Leipzig, 1872.

Grimm, Jacob. Deutsche Mythologie. 2te Ausg. Göttingen, 1844. 2 vols. 4te Ausg., besorgt v. E. H. Meyer. Berlin, 1875–78. 3 vols.

—— Deutsche Rechtsalterthümer. 2te Ausg. Göttingen, 1854.

—— Gedanken über Mythos, Epos und Geschichte. Mit altdeutschen Beispielen. 1813. In his Kleinere Schriften, IV, 74–85. Berlin, 1869.

—— Kleinere Schriften. Berlin, 1864–71. 5 vols.

—— and Wilhelm. Altdeutsche Wälder, herausgegeben durch die Brüder Grimm. Cassel, 1813–16. 3 vols.

—— and Wilhelm. Deutsche Sagen. Herausgegeben von den Brüdern Grimm. Berlin, 1816–18. 2 vols.

—— and Wilhelm. Kinder- und Hausmärchen. Gesammelt durch die Brüder Grimm. I-II Band, Grosse Ausg., 7e Aufl. III Band, 3e Aufl. Göttingen, 1857, '56. 3 vols.

—— and Schmeller, Andreas. Lateinische Gedichte des X. und XI. Jh. Göttingen, 1838.

Grimm, Wilhelm. Drei altschottische Lieder in Original und Uebersetzung aus zwei neuen Sammlungen. Nebst einem Sendschreiben an Herrn Professor F. D. Gräter von

W. C. Grimm. Angehängt sind Zusätze und Verbesserungen zu den Altdänischen Heldenliedern, Balladen und Märchen. Heidelberg, 1813.

—— Kleinere Schriften. Herausgegeben von Gustav Hinrichs. Berlin, 1881–87. 4 vols.

Gröber's Zeitschrift. See Zeitschrift für romanische Philologie.

Groome, Francis Hindes. Two Suffolk Friends. Edinburgh and London, 1895.

Groote, E. von. See Tristan.

Grosart, Alexander B. See Bruce, M.; Greene, R.; Nashe, T.

Grudziński, Stephan. "Lenore" in Polen. Eine litterarhistorische Abhandlung. Bochnia, 1890.

Grün, Anastasius. [pseudon. for Anton. Alexander, Graf von Auersperg.] Robin Hood. Ein Balladenkranz nach altenglischen Volksliedern. Stuttgart, 1864.

Grünbaum, Max. Jüdischdeutsche Chrestomathie. Zugleich ein Beitrag zur Kunde der hebräischen Literatur. Leipzig, 1882.

Grünn, Karl, and Baróti, Ludwig. Deutsche Volksballaden aus Südungarn. In Ethnologische Mitteilungen aus Ungarn, II, 198–204. 1892.

Grundtvig, Nikolai Frederik Severin. Idunna. En Nytaarsgave for 1811. Kiøbenhavn, [1811].

Grundtvig, Svend. Danske Folkeæventyr, efter utrykte Kilder gjenfortalte. Anden Udgave. Kjøbenhavn, 1881.

—— Danske Folkeæventyr, fundne i Folkemunde og gjenfortalte. Ny Samling. Kjøbenhavn, 1878.

—— Elveskud, dansk, svensk, norsk, færøsk, islandsk, skotsk, vendisk, bømisk, tysk, fransk, italiensk, katalonsk, spansk, bretonsk Folkevise, i Overblik. Kjøbenhavn, 1881. Særtryk af Danmarks gamle Folkeviser, 4de (og 2de) Del.

—— Engelske og Skotske Folkeviser, med oplysende Anmærkninger fordanskede. Kjøbenhavn, 1842–46. 4 Hefter.

—— Folkelæsning. Danske Kæmpeviser og Folkesange fra Middelalderen, fornyede i gammel Stil. Med 6 Melodier. Ved Udvalget for Folkeoplysnings Fremme. Kjøbenhavn, 1867.

Gruter, Janus. Inscriptiones Antiquae totivs orbis Romani in absolutissimum corpus redactae, etc. Amstelaedami, 1707. 2 pts.

de Gubernatis, Angelo. La Mythologie des Plantes, ou les légendes du règne végétal. Paris, 1878, '82. 2 vols.

—— Le novelline di Santo Stefano, raccolte da ——, e precedute da una introduzione sulla parentela del mito con la novellina. (Estratto dalla Rivista Contemporanea Nazionale Italiana.) Torino, 1869.

—— Zoölogical Mythology; or, the Legends of Animals. London, 1872. 2 vols.

—— See Rivista delle Tradizioni, etc.

Guessard, François. Les Anciens Poëtes de la France. Nouvelle Série de la Bibliothèque Elzévirienne. Publiée sous les auspices de S. E. M. le Ministre de l'Instruction Publique et des Cultes. Paris, 1858–70. [Vols I-X.]

Guest, Lady Charlotte. See Mabinogion.

Gützlaff, Karl Friedrich August. Geschichte des chinesischen Reiches von den ältesten Zeiten bis auf den Frieden von Nanking. Hrsg. von K. F. Neumann. Stuttgart, etc., 1847.

Gueulette, Thomas Simon. Les milles et un quart d'heure. Contes tartares. Genève, 1787. 3 vols. (Cabinet des Fées, 21, 22, 23.)

Guilielmus Armoricus. See Guillaume le Breton.

Guilielmus Malmesburiensis. Willielmi Monachi Malmesburiensis de Gestis Regum Anglorum libri v. *In* Rerum Anglicarum Scriptores post Bedam praecipui. [Ed. by Sir Henry Savile.] Pp. 7–174. Francofurti, 1501.

—— Willelmi Malmesbiriensis Monachi de Gestis Regum Anglorum libri quinque; Historiæ Novellæ libri tres. Edited from manuscripts by William Stubbs. London, 1887–89. 2 vols. (Rolls Series.)

Guilielmus Neubrigensis. Historia sive Chronica Rerum Anglicarum, libris quinque. E codice MS. pervetusto . . . studio atque industria Thomae Hearnii. Oxonii, 1719. 3 vols.

Guillaume le Breton. Chronique et Philippide. *In* Œuvres de Rigord et de Guillaume le Breton, historiens de Philippe-Auguste. Publiées pour la Société de l'Histoire de France par H. François Delaborde. Paris, 1882, '85. 2 vols.

Guillaume d'Orange. See Jonckbloet, W. J. A.

Guillaume de Palerne. Publié d'après le manuscrit de la Bibliothèque de l'Arsenal à Paris par H. Michelant. Paris, 1876. (Société des anciens textes français.)

[Guilpin, Edward.] Skialetheia. Or, A shadowe of Truth in certaine Epigrams and Satyres. At London, 1598. *In* John Payne Collier, Miscellaneous Tracts Temp. Eliz. & Jac. I, No 4. [London, 1870.]

Die Gull-Þóris Saga oder Þorskfirðinga Saga. Herausgegeben von Dr. Konrad Maurer. Leipzig, 1858.

Gunnlaugssaga Ormstungu. Mit Einleitung und Glossar herausgegeben von E. Mogk. Halle, 1886. (Altnordische Texte, herausgegeben von E. Mogk, 1.)

Gurdon, the Lady Eveline Camilla. See County Folk-Lore.

Gutch, John Mathew. The Robin Hood Garlands and Ballads, with the tale of The Lytell Geste. A collection of all the poems, songs, and ballads relating to this celebrated yeoman; to which is prefixed his history and character, deduced from documents hitherto unrevised. London, 1850. 2 vols. [See, also, p. 403, above.]

Gyllenmär, Bröms. Visbok. See Visböcker.

Haas, A. See Blätter für pommersche Volkskunde.

Habicht, M. See Arabian Nights.

Hagen, A. See Neue Preussische Provinzial-Blätter.

Hagen, Friedrich Heinrich von der. Germania. Neues Jahrbuch der Berlinischen Gesellschaft für Deutsche Sprach- und Alterthumskunde. Berlin, Leipzig, 1836–53. 10 vols.

—— Gesammtabenteuer. Hundert altdeutsche Erzählungen: Ritter- und Pfaffen-Mären, Stadt- und Dorfgeschichten, Schwänke, Wundersagen und Legenden von Jacob Appet, u. s. w. . . . meist zum erstenmal gedruckt und herausgegeben. Stuttgart and Tübingen, 1850. 3 vols.

—— Heldenbuch. Altdeutsche Heldenlieder aus dem Sagenkreise Dietrichs von Bern und der Nibelungen. Meist aus einzigen Handschriften zum erstenmal gedruckt oder hergestellt. Leipzig, 1855. 2 vols.

—— Minnesinger. Deutsche Liederdichter des zwölften, dreizehnten und vierzehnten Jahrhunderts. Leipzig, 1838. 4 pts.

—— See Arabian Nights.

—— See Tausend und Ein Tag.

—— and Büsching, Johann Gustav. Buch der Liebe. Berlin, 1809. 1 Bd. [No more published.]

Hagen, F. H. von der, and Büsching, J. G. Deutsche Gedichte des Mittelalters. Berlin, 1808.

—— and Primisser, A. Der Helden Buch in der Ursprache. Berlin, 1820–25. 2 pts.

Hahn, Johann Georg von. Griechische und albanesische Märchen. Gesammelt, übersetzt und erläutert. Leipzig, 1864. 2 pts. See Pio, Jean.

Hahn, Karl August. Das alte Passional. Neue Ausgabe. Frankfurt a.-M., 1857.

—— See Titurel.

—— See Ulrich von Zatzikhoven.

Hales, John W. See Percy MS.

Hall, Andrew. Interesting Roman Antiquities recently discovered in Fife. 1823. [See II, 378.]

Hall, Edward. Hall's Chronicle; containing the History of England during the reign of Henry the Fourth, and the succeeding Monarchs, to the end of the reign of Henry the Eighth. London, 1809.

Hall, Fitzedward. See Lindsay, Sir David; Wilson, H. H.

Hall, Spencer Timothy. The Forester's Offering. London, 1841. 2 pts.

Hallam, Henry. The Constitutional History of England from the accession of Henry VII. to the death of George II. Paris, 1827. 4 vols.

Halliwell-Phillipps, James Orchard. Ballads and Poems respecting Hugh of Lincoln. Brixton Hill, 1849. *In* Contributions to Early English Literature. London, 1849.

—— Descriptive notices of Popular English Histories. London, 1848. (Percy Society, 23.)

—— A Dictionary of Archaic and Provincial Words, Obsolete Phrases, Proverbs, and Ancient Customs, from the fourteenth century. London, 1847. 2 vols.

—— The Early Naval Ballads of England. London, 1841. (Percy Society, 2.)

—— Illustrations of the Fairy Mythology of A Midsummer Night's Dream. London, 1845. (Shakespeare Society, [26].)

—— Ludus Coventriae, a collection of Mysteries represented at Coventry on the feast of Corpus Christi. London, 1841. (Shakespeare Society, 4.)

—— The Nursery Rhymes of England, collected principally from Oral Tradition. London, 1842. (Percy Society, 4.)

—— The Nursery Rhymes of England, obtained principally from Oral Tradition. Second edition, with alterations and additions. London, 1843.

—— Palatine Anthology, a collection of Ancient Poems and Ballads, relating to Lancashire and Cheshire. (For Private Circulation only.) London, 1850.

—— Popular Rhymes and Nursery Tales: a sequel to the Nursery Rhymes of England. London, 1849.

—— The Thornton Romances. The early English metrical romances of Perceval, Isumbras, Eglamour, and Degrevant. Selected from manuscripts at Lincoln and Cambridge. London, 1844. (Camden Society, 30.)

—— See Ellis, George.

—— See Four Elements.

—— See Lady Bessy.

—— See Torrent of Portugal. See Sir Triamour.

Haltrich, Joseph. Deutsche Volksmärchen aus dem Sachsenlande in Siebenbürgen. Berlin, 1856. 2te, vermehrte Aufl., Wien, 1877. 3te, vermehrte Aufl., Wien, 1882.

[Hamilton, William.] Poems on Several Occasions. [Published without name.] Glasgow, 1748.

Hamilton, William. Poems on Several Occasions. By William Hamilton of Bangour, Esquire. Edinburgh, 1760.

—— The Poems and Songs of William Hamilton of Bangour; collated with the MS. volume of his poems, and containing several pieces hitherto unpublished; with illustrative notes and an account of the life of the author. By James Paterson. Edinburgh, 1850.

Hammer-[Purgstall], Joseph von. Geschichte der schönen Redekünste Persiens, mit einer Blüthenlese aus zweihundert persischen Dichtungen. Wien, 1818.

Hampson, R. T. Medii Aevi Kalendarium; or, dates, charters, and customs of the Middle Ages, with calendars from the tenth to the fifteenth century; and an alphabetical digest of obsolete names of days: forming a glossary of the dates of the Middle Ages, with tables and other aids for ascertaining dates. London, 1841. 2 vols.

Hapgood, Isabel Florence. The Epic Songs of Russia, with an introductory note by Francis J. Child. New York, 1886.

Hardwick, Charles. Traditions, Superstitions, and Folk-Lore (chiefly Lancashire and the North of England), their affinity to others in widely-distributed localities, their Eastern origin and mythical significance. Manchester and London, 1872.

Hardy, James. See Denham Tracts.

Hardy, R. Spence. A Manual of Budhism in its modern development; translated from Singhalese MSS. London and Edinburgh, 1860.

Hardy, Sir Thomas Duffus. Descriptive Catalogue of Materials relating to the History of Great Britain and Ireland, to the end of the reign of Henry VII. London, etc., 1862–71. 3 vols. (Rolls Series.)

—— See Gaimar, Geoffroi.

Harland, John. Ballads and Songs of Lancashire, chiefly older than the 19th century. London, 1865.

—— Ballads and Songs of Lancashire. Ancient and Modern. 3d edition, corrected, revised, and enlarged by T. T. Wilkinson. London, 1882.

Harper's New Monthly Magazine. New York, 1850–.

Hartland, Edwin Sidney. Fairy Births and Human Midwives. In The Archæological Review, IV, 328–43. 1889.

—— The Legend of Perseus, a study of tradition in story, custom and belief. London, 1894–96. 3 vols.

Hartmann von Aue. Herausgegeben von Fedor Bech. Dritter Theil: Iwein. Leipzig, 1869.

Hartshorne, Charles Henry. Ancient Metrical Tales, printed chiefly from original sources. London, 1829.

Hartwig, O. See Gonzenbach, Laura.

Hasdeŭ, B. P. See Columna luĭ Traian.

Haslewood, Joseph. See Brydges, Sir Egerton.

—— See Painter, William.

Haug, Martin, and West, E. W. See Arda Viraf.

Haupt, Moriz. See Pyramus und Thisbe.

—— und Hoffmann, Heinrich [von Fallersleben]. Altdeutsche Blätter. Leipzig, 1836–40. 2 vols.

Haupt's Zeitschrift. See Zeitschrift für deutsches Alterthum.

Hausknecht, Emil. See Floire et Blanceflor.

Havercamp, S. See Josephus.

The Hawkins' Voyages during the reigns of Henry VIII, Queen Elizabeth, and James I. Ed. by C. R. Markham. London, 1878. (Hakluyt Society.)

Haxthausen, August, Freiherr von. Transkaukasia. Andeutungen über das Familien- und Gemeindeleben und die socialen Verhältnisse einiger Völker zwischen dem Schwarzen und Kaspischen Meere. Reiseerinnerungen und gesammelte Notizen. Leipzig, 1856. 2 pts.

Haydon, Frank Scott. See Eulogium Historiarum.

Hazlitt, William Carew. Hand-Book to the Popular, Poetical, and Dramatic Literature of Great Britain, from the invention of printing to the Restoration. London, 1867.

—— Remains of the Early Popular Poetry of England; collected and edited, with introductions and notes. London, 1864–66. 4 vols. (Library of Old Authors.)

—— Shakespeare Jest-Books; reprints of the early and very rare jest-books supposed to have been used by Shakespeare. Edited, with introduction and notes. London, 1864. 3 vols. (Old English Jest-Books, I–III.)

—— See Brand, John.

—— See Browne, William.

—— See Dodsley, Robert.

—— See Warton, Thomas.

Headrick, James. See Barry, George.

Hearne, Thomas. See Elmham, Thomas de.

—— See Fordun, Joannes de.

—— See Guilielmus Neubrigensis.

—— See Langtoft, Pierre de.

—— See Leland, John.

—— See Otterbourne.

—— See Robert of Gloucester.

—— See Titus Livius.

Gli Hecatommithi di M. Giovanbattista Giraldi Cinthio nobile Ferrarese. Nel Monte Regale appresso Lionardo Torrentino. MDLXV. 2 parts.

Heinrich Julius, Herzog von Braunschweig. Die Schauspiele des Herzogs Heinrich Julius von Braunschweig nach alten Drucken und Handschriften herausgegeben von Dr. Wilhelm Ludwig Holland. Stuttgart, 1855. (Bibliothek des Litterarischen Vereins in Stuttgart.)

Heinrich von dem Türlîn. Diu Crône, hrsg. v. Gottlob H. F. Scholl. Stuttgart, 1852. (Bibl. d. Litt. Ver. in Stuttgart, 27.)

—— Der Mantel. See Warnatsch, Otto.

Heinrich von Freiberg. See Tristan.

Heinrich von Neustadt. Apollonius. Von Gotes Zuokunft. Im Auszuge, mit Einleitung, Anmerkungen und Glossar herausgegeben von Joseph Strobl. Wien, 1875.

Heinrich, Gustav. Ungarische Volksballaden. In Ungarische Revue, 1883, pp. 138–161, 755–66.

Heinz der Kellner. See Turandot.

Heldenbuch. Deutsches Heldenbuch.

Teil I. Biterolf und Dietlieb, herausgegeben von Oskar Jänicke. Laurin und Walberan, mit Benutzung der von Franz Roth gesammelten Abschriften und Vergleichungen. Berlin, 1866.

Teil II. Alpharts Tod, Dietrichs Flucht, Rabenschlacht, herausgegeben von Ernst Martin. Berlin, 1866.

Teil III, IV. Ortnit und die Wolfdietriche, nach Müllenhoff's Vorarbeiten herausgegeben von Arthur Amelung und Oskar Jänicke. Berlin, 1871–73.

Teil V. Dietrichs Abenteuer von Albrecht von Kemenaten, nebst den Bruchstücken von Dietrich und Wenezlan, herausgegeben von Julius Zupitza. Berlin, 1870.

—— See Hagen, F. H. von der.

Heliodorus. Ἡλιοδώρου Αἰθιοπικῶν βιβλία δέκα. Hieronymi Commelini opera. [Heidelberg,] 1596.

Helmold. Helmoldi Presbyteri Chronica Slavorum ex recensione I. M. Lappenbergii in usum scholarum ex

Monumentis Germaniae Historicis recudi fecit Georgius Heinricus Pertz. Hannoverae, 1868. (Scriptores Rerum Germanicarum.)

Helwig, Christopher. Erster (Ander) Theil jüdischer Historien, oder Thalmudischer, Rabbinischer, wunderbarlicher Legenden. Durch Christophorum Helvicum. Giessen, 1612. 2 parts.

Henderson, William. Notes on the Folk-Lore of the Northern Counties of England and the Borders. A new edition, with many additional notes. London, 1879. (Folk-Lore Society, Publ., 2.)

Hengwrt MSS. Selections from the Hengwrt MSS preserved in the Peniarth Library. Edited by R. Williams (and J. H. Jones). London, 1876 ['74–76]–92. 2 vols.

Henne, Anton. Alte Volkssagen aus der Schweiz. In Schweizerblätter, II, 28–31, 106–08, 184–88, 229–32, 303–10. St. Gallen, 1833.

—— See Schweizerblätter.

Henry of Huntingdon. Henrici Archidiaconi Huntendunensis Historia Anglorum. The History of the English, by Henry, Archdeacon of Huntingdon, from A. C. 55 to A. D. 1154, in eight books. Edited by Thomas Arnold. London, 1879. (Rolls Series.)

Henry the Minstrel. The Actis and Deidis of the illustere and vailȝeand Campioun Schir William Wallace, Knicht of Ellerslie, by Henry the Minstrel, commonly known as Blind Harry. Edited by James Moir. Edinburgh and London, 1889 [1885–89]. (Scottish Text Society, 6, 7, 17.)

Henryson, Robert. Robene and Makyne. In The Poems and Fables of Robert Henryson, now first collected. With notes and a memoir of his life. By David Laing. Edinburgh, 1865.

Henslowe, Philip. The Diary of Philip Henslowe, from 1591 to 1609. Printed from the original manuscript preserved at Dulwich College. Edited by J. Payne Collier. . . . London, 1845. (Shakespeare Society, [28].)

Herberay, Nicolas de. See Amadis de Gaula.

Herbert. Li romans de Dolopathos. Publié pour la première fois en entier . . . par Charles Brunet et Anatole de Montaiglon. Paris, 1856. (Bibliothèque Elzévirienne).

Herbert, Edward, Lord Herbert of Cherbury. The Life and Raigne of King Henry the Eighth. London, 1649.

Hercher, R. See Aelian.

Hereward. De gestis Herwardi Saxonis. In Chroniques Anglo-Normandes, publiés par Francisque Michel, II, 1–98. Rouen, 1836.

Héricault, Charles d'. See Moland, Louis.

Hermannus Contractus. Chronicon, una cum ejus vita et continuatione a Bertholdo, ejus discipulo, scripta. Subjicitur Chronicon Petershusanum ineditum. Ex MSS. codicibus collegit, notis et observationibus illustravit, P. Aemilianus Ussermann. In J. P. Migne, Patrologiae Cursus Completus, CXLIII, cols 55–380. Parisiis, 1853.

Hermann von Fritslar. See Fritslar, Hermann von.

Herodotus. Herodoti Musae. Textum ad Gaisfordii editionem recognovit, perpetua tum Fr. Creuzeri tum sua annotatione instruxit, commentationem de vita et scriptis Herodoti, tabulas geographicas indicesque adiecit Io. Christ. Fel. Baehr. Lipsiae, 1830–35. 5 vols.

Herrig's Archiv. See Archiv für das Studium der neueren Sprachen und Literaturen.

Herrmann, Anton; Wlislocki, Heinrich von, and Köhler, Reinhold. Beiträge zur Vergleichung der Volkspoesie. In Ethnologische Mitteilungen aus Ungarn, I, 12–19, 34–49, 63–77, 90–95, 165–67, 203–15, 292–308, 312–18, 319–23. 1887–89.

Herrmann, Anton. See Ethnologische Mitteilungen aus Ungarn.

Herrtage, Sidney J. See Charlemagne.

—— See Ferumbras.

—— See Gesta Romanorum.

Hertz, Wilhelm. Deutsche Sagen im Elsass. Stuttgart, 1872.

—— Die Rätsel der Königin von Saba. In Zeitschrift für deutsches Alterthum, XXVII, 1–33. 1883.

—— Spielmanns-Buch. Novellen in Versen aus dem zwölften und dreizehnten Jahrhundert. Stuttgart, 1886.

—— Der Werwolf. Beitrag zur Sagengeschichte. Stuttgart, 1862.

Hertzberg, Wilhelm. Nachlese zu Chaucer. In Jahrbuch für romanische und englische Literatur, VIII, 129–69. 1867.

Herzog Ernst. Hrsg. v. Karl Bartsch. Wien, 1869.

Hesychius. De Originibus Urbis Constantinopoleos. In Hesychii Milesii Opuscula Duo [etc.] recognovit . . . Io. Conradus Orellius, pp. 59–73. Lipsiae, 1820.

Hexham, Henry. A copious Engliscg and Netherduytch Dictionarie, composed out of our best English Authours. With an Appendix of the names of all kind of Beasts, Fowles, Birds, Fishes, Hunting, and Hawking. As also a compendious Grammar for the Instruction of the Learner. Het Groot Woorden-Boeck, gestelt in 't Engelsch ende Nederduytsch [etc.]. Rotterdam, 1660.

Heyne, Chr. G. See Apollodorus.

Heywood, Thomas. The Hierarchie of the Blessed Angells. Their Names, orders and Offices. The fall of Lucifer with his Angells. Written by Tho: Heywood. London, 1635.

Heywood, Thomas. See Lady Bessy.

Hibbert, Samuel. A Description of the Shetland Islands, comprising an account of their geology, scenery, antiquities, and superstitions. Edinburgh, 1822.

Hickathrift, Thomas. The History of Thomas Hickathrift. Printed from the earliest extant copies, and edited, with an introduction, by George Laurence Gomme. London, 1885. (Villon Society. Chap - Books and Folk-Lore Tracts. First Series, 1.)

Higden, Ranulphus. Polychronicon Ranulphi Higden Monachi Cestrensis; together with the English translations of John Trevisa and of an unknown writer of the fifteenth century. (Vols I, II, edited by Churchill Babington; vols III–IX, by Joseph Rawson Lumby.) London, 1865–86. 9 vols. (Rolls Series.)

Hilberg, I. See Eustathius.

Hildebrandslied. Dasz Hildebrandslied, herauszgegeben von Al. Vollmer und K. Hofmann. Leipzig, 1850.

—— Das Hildebrandslied nach der Handschrift von Neuem herausgegeben, kritisch bearbeitet und erläutert nebst Bemerkungen über die ehemaligen Fulder Codices der Kasseler Bibliothek, von C. W. M. Grein. 2te Auflage. Kassel, 1880.

Hingeston, F. C. See Capgrave, John.

Hinrichs, G. See Grimm, W.

Hins, Eugène. Légendes chrétiennes de l'Oukraine. In Revue des Traditions Populaires, II, 401–8; 509–21; III, 318–26, 444–51; IV, 35–37, 116–23. 1887–89.

Hippeau, C. See Amadas et Ydoine.

—— See Garnier.

—— See Le Bel Inconu.

Hippeau, C. See Messire Gauvain.

Hiseley, Jean Joseph. Recherches critiques sur l'histoire de Guillaume Tell. Lausanne, 1843. (Société d'Histoire de la Suisse Romande, Mémoires, tom. II, livre 3.)

Histoire des Ducs de Normandie, etc. See Michel, Francisque.

Histoire Littéraire de la France. Par des Religieux Benedictins de la Congregation de S. Maur; continuée par des Membres de l'Institut. Paris, 1733–1893. 31 vols.

Historia de Enrique, fi de Oliva. See Oliva.

Historia de Preliis. See Leo.

Historia Miscella. Franciscus Eyssenhardt recensuit. Berolini, 1869.

[Historical Manuscripts Commission.] The Royal Commission on Historical Manuscripts. Reports. London, 1874–.

Historical and Traditional Tales in Prose and Verse, connected with the South of Scotland. Original and Select. [By William Mackenzie?] Kirkcudbright, 1843.

Historie of King James the Sext. See James VI.

The History of the Feuds and Conflicts among the Clans, in the northern parts of Scotland, and in the Western Isles. From the year M.XXXI. unto M.DC.XIX. Now first published, from a manuscript, wrote in the Reign of King James VI. Glasgow, M.DCC.LXIV. Re-printed, 1818. In Miscellanea Scotica, I, iii. Glasgow, 1818.

Hobhouse, Bishop. See Church-wardens' accounts, etc.

Hoccleve, Thomas. See Occleve, Thomas.

Hocker, N. Frouwa und der Schwan. In Zeitschrift für deutsche Mythologie, I, 305–10. 1853.

—— Volkslieder von der Mosel. In Zeitschrift für deutsche Mythologie, I, 250–52. 1853.

Höpfner, Ernst. See Zeitschrift für deutsche Philologie.

Hofberg, Herman. Nerikes gamla Minnen, sådana de ännu qvarlefva i fornlemningar, fornfynd, aflefvor af medeltidens kyrkliga konst, folklif, sånger, sägner, folkspråk, m.m. Ett bidrag till faderneslandets fornkännedom, konst- och odlings-historia. Örebro, 1868.

Hoffmann von Fallersleben, August Heinrich. Horae Belgicae. Hannoverae, etc. 1833–62. 12 pts.

—— Niederländische Volkslieder. 2ᵗᵉ Ausg. In his Horae Belgicae, II. Hannover, 1856.

—— Unsere volksthümlichen Lieder. 2ᵗᵉ Auflage. Leipzig, 1859.

—— Fundgruben für Geschichte deutscher Sprache und Litteratur. Breslau, 1830–37. 2 pts.

—— See Floire et Blanceflor.

—— See Haupt, Moriz.

—— See Weimarisches Jahrbuch. See Wernher.

Hofmann, Konrad. Zur Gudrun. In Sitzungsberichte der k. bayerischen Akademie der Wissenschaften, 1867, Bd II, pp. 205–30, 357–74.

—— See Amis et Amiles.

—— See Hildebrandslied.

—— See Joufrois. See Jourdains de Blaivies.

Hohenhausen, Elise von; Alexis, Willibald, and Lüdemann, Wilhelm von. Historische und romantische Balladen der Schottischen Grenzlande, von Walter Scott, Esq. Aus dem Englischen und Schottischen übersetzt von ——. Zwickau, 1826–27. 7 Bdchn. [I, II, by E. von H.; III–V, by W. A.; VI, VII, by W. von L.]

Holder, Alfred. See Saxo Grammaticus.

Holinshed, Raphael or Ralph. Holinshed's Chronicles of England, Scotland and Ireland. London, 1807–08. 6 vols.

Holland, W. L. See Altswert.

—— See Heinrich Julius.

Holmboe, C. A. See Norske Universitets- og Skole-Annaler.

Holtzmann, Adolf. Der grosse Wolfdieterich. Heidelberg, 1865.

Home, John. Douglas, a Tragedy. In Works, now first collected. To which is prefixed an Account of his Life and Writings. By Henry Mackenzie. I, 287–385. Edinburgh and London, 1822. 3 vols.

Hondorff, Andreas. Promptuarium Exemplorum. Das ist Historien vnd Exempelbuch nach Ordnung vnd Disposition der heiligen zehen Gebott Gottes, ausz heiliger Schrifft vnd andern bewerten vnd glaubwirdigen, Geistlichen vnd Weltlichen, alten vnd newen Scribenten, mit allem fleisz zusammen getragen. Frankfurt am Main, 1574. (Grässe.)

—— Promptvarivm Exemplorum. Historien vnd Exempelbuch. Darinnen ordentlich nach den heiligen Zehen Geboten Gottes allerley gute vnd böse Exempel von Tugenden vnd Lastern rechtem brauch vnd missbrauch derselben Gebot Gottes begriffen werden. Zum spiegel des Menschlichen lebens vnd warhafftiger Busse aus heiliger Schrifft vnd bewerten Scribenten menniglich zu gut zusammen verfasset durch Andream Hondorff. Nun aber mit vielen newen Historien vnd Titteln auffs new vermehret . . . durch Vincentium Sturmium. Leipzig, 1586.

Hone, William. Ancient Mysteries described, especially the English Miracle Plays. London, 1823.

—— The Every-Day Book, and Table Book; or, Everlasting Calendar of popular amusements, sports, pastimes, ceremonies, manners, customs, and events, etc. London, 1841. 3 vols.

—— Table Book. Vol. III of the Every-Day Book and Table Book. London, 1841.

Horn. The Geste of Kyng Horn. In J. Ritson, Ancient Engleish Metrical Romanceës, II, 91–155. London, 1802.

—— The Geste of Kyng Horn. In F. Michel, Horn et Rimenhild, pp. 257–339. Paris, 1845.

—— Horn Childe and Maiden Rimnild. In F. Michel, Horn et Rimenhild, pp. 339–393. Paris, 1845.

—— Horn Childe and Maiden Rimnild. [Ed. by] J. Caro. In Englische Studien, XII, 323–366. Heilbronn, 1889.

—— Francisque Michel. Horn et Rimenhild. Recueil de ce qui reste des pöemes relatifs à leurs aventures composés en françois, en anglais et en écossois dans les treizième, quatorzième, quinzième et seizième siècles. Publié d'après les manuscrits de Londres, de Cambridge, d'Oxford et d'Edinburgh. Paris, 1845. (Bannatyne Club, 85.)

—— King Horn, etc., from a MS. in the Cambridge University Library. Ed., with notes and a glossary, by J. R. Lumby. London, 1866. (Early English Text Society, 13.)

—— King Horn. In Mätzner, Altenglische Sprachproben, I, i, 207–31. 1867.

—— Horstmann, Carl. King Horn nach Ms. Laud 108. In Archiv für das Studium der neueren Sprachen und Literaturen, L, 39–58. 1872.

—— King Horn. Untersuchungen zur mittelenglischen Sprach- und Litteraturgeschichte von Theodor Wissmann. Strassburg and London, 1876. (Quellen und Forschungen zur Sprach- und Culturgeschichte der germanischen Völker, 16.)

—— Das Lied von King Horn. Mit Einleitung, Anmerkungen und Glossar herausgegeben von Dr. Theodor Wissmann. Strassburg and London, 1881. (Quellen und Forschungen zur Sprach- und Culturgeschichte der germanischen Völker, 45.)

Horstmann, Carl. Altenglische Legenden. Kindheit Jesu. Geburt Jesu. Barlaam und Josaphat. St. Patrik's Fegefeuer. Aus den verschiedenen MSS. zum ersten Male herausgegeben. Paderborn, 1875.

—— Sammlung altenglischer Legenden, grösstentheils zum ersten Male herausgegeben. Heilbronn, 1878.

—— Altenglische Legenden. Neue Folge. Mit Einleitung und Anmerkungen herausgegeben. Heilbronn, 1881.

—— Altenglische Marienlegenden aus MS. Vernon zum ersten Mal herausgegeben von ——. In Archiv für das Studium der neueren Sprachen und Literaturen, LVI, 221–236. 1876.

—— See Horn.

—— See Lydgate, John.

—— See Wade, Laurence.

Household Books of John, Duke of Norfolk and Thomas, Earl of Surrey; temp. 1481–1490. From the original Manuscripts in the Library of the Society of Antiquaries, London. Edited by J. Payne Collier, Esq., F.S.A. London, 1844. (Roxburghe Club, 61.)

Howitt, William and Mary. The Literature and Romance of Northern Europe: constituting a complete history of the literature of Sweden, Denmark, Norway and Iceland. London, 1852. 2 vols.

Howleglas. Ed. by F. Ouvry. [Privately printed.] London, 1867. See also Eulenspiegel.

Hudibras. See Butler, Samuel.

Hudson, John. See Josephus.

Hughes, Thomas. The Ashen Faggot, a tale for Christmas. In Macmillan's Magazine, V, 234–52. 1862.

Hume, Abraham. Sir Hugh of Lincoln: or, an examination of a curious tradition respecting the Jews, with a notice of the popular poetry connected with it. London, 1849.

—— Review of. In The Athenaeum, 1849, pp. 1269–71.

Hume, David, of Godscroft. The History of the Houses of Douglas and Angus. Written by Master David Hume of Godscroft. Edinburgh, 1644.

Hunfalvy, P. See Ungarische Revue.

Hunt, Robert. Popular Romances of the West of England; or, the Drolls, Traditions, and Superstitions of Old Cornwall. First and Second Series. London, 1865, 2 vols.; [2d ed., 1871,] 1 vol.; 3d ed., revised and enlarged, 1881, 1 vol.

Hunter, Joseph. Critical and Historical Tracts. London, 1849–52. 5 nos.

—— The Great Hero of the ancient Minstrelsy of England "Robin Hood." His period, real character, etc., investigated and perhaps ascertained. London, 1852. (Mr. Hunter's Critical and Historical Tracts, No 4.)

—— New Illustrations of the Life, Studies, and Writings of Shakespeare. Supplementary to all the editions. London, 1845. 2 vols.

Hunter, William. Biggar and the House of Fleming. An account of the Biggar District, archæological, historical, and biographical. 2d edition. Edinburgh and Biggar, 1867.

Huntly, Marquis of. The Records of Aboyne, 1230–1681. Edited by ——. Aberdeen, 1894. (New Spalding Club.)

Huon de Bordeaux, chanson de geste. Publiée pour la première fois d'après les manuscrits de Tours, de Paris et de Turin par MM. F. Guessard et C. Grandmaison. Paris, 1860. (Les Anciens Poëtes de la France.)

Huon de Bordeaux. I Complementi della Chanson d'Huon de Bordeaux. Pubblicati da A. Graf. I. Auberon. Halle, 1878.

Hurtado, L. See Palmerin of England.

Hurwitz, Hyman. Hebrew Tales. Selected and translated from the writings of the ancient Hebrew sages. New-York, 1847.

—— Sagen der Hebräer. Aus den Schriften der alten hebräischen Weisen. Nebst einer Abhandlung über den Ursprung, den Geist und Werth des Talmuds. Aus dem Englischen des ——. Zweite durchgesehene Auflage. Leipzig, 1828.

Hutchinson, William. A View of Northumberland with an Excursion to the Abbey of Mailross in Scotland. Anno 1776. Newcastle, 1778. 2 vols.

Huth Library. See Ellis, Frederick Startridge.

Hutten, J. G. See Plutarchus.

Hyde, Douglas. Beside the Fire: a collection of Irish Gaelic Folk Stories. Edited, translated, and annotated. With additional notes by Alfred Nutt. London, 1890.

Hyltén-Cavallius, G. O. See Dietrich von Bern.

—— and Stephens, George. Svenska Folk-Sagor och Äfventyr. Efter muntlig Öfverlemning samlade och utgifna af ——. Första Delen. Stockholm, 1844.

Icelandic Legends. See Árnason, Jón.

Ideler, Julius Ludwig. Die Sage von dem Schuss des Tell. Eine historisch-kritische Abhandlung. Berlin, 1836.

Iduna. En Skrift för den Nordiska Fornålderns Älskare. [By Erik Gustav Geijer.] Häfte 1–10, and Musik-bilagor. Stockholm, 1811–24. 4 vols and Atlas.

Idunna und Hermode. Eine Alterthumszeitung. Herausgegeben von F. D. Gräter. Jahrg. I, II, Breslau, 1812–13; III, IV, Schillingsfürst und Dinkelsbühl, 1814–15; IV, Halle, 1816. 5 vols.

Iglesia, Antonio de la. El idioma gallego, su antigüedad y vida. La Coruña, 1886. 3 vols. (Biblioteca gallega, [4–6].)

Ignaurès. See Renaut.

Iken, Johann Gottfried Ludwig. See Tuti-nameh.

Illgen, Christian Friedrich. See Zeitschrift für die historische Theologie.

Illustrations of Northern Antiquities. See Weber, Henry, and Jamieson, R.

Illustreret Nyhedsblad, ugentlige Efterretninger om Nutidens vigtigste Begivenheder og Personligheder. Christiania, 1852–66. 15 vols.

Imbriani, Vittorio. La novellaja fiorentina. Fiabe e novelline stenografate in Firenze dal dettato popolare. Ristampa, accresciuta di molte novelle inedite, di numerosi riscontri e di note, nelle quali è accolta integralmente la Novellaja Milanese dello stesso raccoglitore. Livorno, 1877.

—— La novellaja Milanese. Bologna, 1872. Also in his La novellaja Fiorentina. Livorno, 1877.

Indogermanische Forschungen. Zeitschrift für indogermanische Sprach- und Altertumskunde. Herausg. von Karl Brugmann und Wilhelm Streitberg. Strassburg, 1894–.

Ingledew, C. J. Davison. The Ballads and Songs of Yorkshire, transcribed from private manuscripts, rare broadsides, and scarce publications; with notes and a glossary. London, 1860.

Das Inland. Eine Wochenschrift. Dorpat, 1836–63.

The International Folk-Lore Congress, 1891. Papers and Transactions. Edited by Joseph Jacobs and Alfred Nutt. London, 1892.

Iōannidēs, Sab. Ἱστορία καὶ στατιστικὴ Τρ[α]πεζοῦντος καὶ τῆς περὶ ταύτην χώρας ὡς καὶ τὰ περὶ τῆς ἐνταῦθα ἑλληνικῆς γλώσσης. Constantinople, 1870.

Ipomydon. The Lyfe of Ipomydon. In Henry Weber, Metrical Romances of the thirteenth, fourteenth, and fifteenth Centuries, II, 279–365. Edinburgh, 1810.

The Ipswich Journal. [Newspaper.] 1877–78.

Íslendíngar Sögur. Eptir gömlum handritum útgefnar at tilhlutun hins Konúngliga Norræna Fornfræða Fèlags. [Ed. by Þ. Guðmundsson and Þ. Helgason.] Kaupmanna-höfn, 1829, ’30. 2 vols.

—— udgivne efter gamle Haandskrifter af det Kongelige Nordiske Oldskrift-Selskab. [Ed. by Rafn and others.] Kjöbenhavn, 1843–75. 3 vols.

d'Istria, Dora. La nationalité albanaise d'après les chants populaires. In Revue des Deux Mondes, 2ᵉ période, LXIII, 382–418. 1866.

Jacob, P. L., Bibliophile. See Lacroix, Paul.

Jacob, P. W. Hindoo Tales: or, the Adventures of Ten Princes, freely translated from the Sanscrit of the Dasakumaracharitam. London, 1873.

Jacobs, Friedrich. See Anthologia Graeca.

Jacobs, Joseph. See International Folk-Lore Congress.

—— See Painter, William.

Jacobus a Voragine. See Legenda Aurea.

Jacottet, E. Contes populaires des Bassoutos (Afrique du Sud) recueillis et traduits. Paris, 1895. (Collection de contes et chansons populaires, 20.)

Jacques de Vitry. The Exempla or Illustrative Stories from the Sermones Vulgares of Jacques de Vitry. Edited, with introduction, analysis, and notes, by Thomas Frederick Crane. London, 1890. (Folk Lore Society, 26.)

Jäklin. See Jecklin, Dietrich.

Jänicke, Oskar. See Heldenbuch.

——; Steinmeyer, Elias; Wilmanns, Wilhelm. Altdeutsche Studien. Der Ritter von Staufenberg. Das jüngere Gedicht vom Riesen Sigenot. Zur Geschichte des Eckenliedes. Berlin, 1871.

Jagić, V. Die christlich-mythologische Schicht in der russischen Volksepik. In Archiv für slavische Philologie, I, 82–133. 1876.

—— and Köhler, Reinhold. Aus dem südslavischen Märchenschatz. In Archiv für slavische Philologie, I, 267–89; II, 614–41; V, 17–79. 1876–81.

—— See Archiv für slavische Philologie.

Jahn, Ulrich. Volkssagen aus Pommern und Rügen. Stettin, 1886.

Jahrbuch für romanische und englische Literatur herausgegeben von Adolf Ebert (vols I–V), von Ludwig Lemcke (vols VI–XV). Berlin (vols I–III), Leipzig (vols IV–XV), 1859–76.

Jahrbücher der Königlichen Akademie gemeinnütziger Wissenschaften. Neue Folge. Erfurt, 1860–.

—— für wissenschaftliche Kritik. Herausgegeben von der Societät für wissenschaftliche Kritik zu Berlin. Stuttgart, Tübingen, Berlin, 1827–46.

James, M. R. See Jessopp, Augustus.

James VI, King of Scotland. The Historie and Life of King James the Sext: being an account of the affairs of

Scotland, from the year 1566, to the year 1596; with a short continuation to the year 1617. [Edited by Thomas Thomson.] Edinburgh, 1825. (Bannatyne Club, Publications, 13.)

Jameson, Mrs. Anna. Sacred and Legendary Art. 3d edition. London, 1857. 2 vols.

Jamieson, John. An Etymological Dictionary of the Scottish Language. A new edition, carefully revised and collated, with the entire Supplement incorporated, by John Longmuir and David Donaldson. Paisley, 1877–82. 4 vols.

Jamieson, Robert. Illustrations of Northern Antiquities. See Weber, Henry.

—— List of Desiderata of Popular Ballads. In The Scots Magazine, LXV, 697–701. 1803.

—— Popular Ballads and Songs, from tradition, manuscripts, and scarce editions; with translations of similar pieces from the ancient Danish language, and a few originals by the editor. Edinburgh, 1806. 2 vols.

Jančuk, N. A. See Etnografičeskoe Obozrênie.

The Jātaka, or, Stories of the Buddha's former Births. Translated from the Pāli by various hands under the editorship of Professor E. B. Cowell. Vol. I, translated by Robert Chalmers. Vol. II, translated by W. H. D. Rouse, Cambridge, [Eng.,] 1895.

Jean de Paris. Histoire de Jean de Paris, roi de France. In Le Roux de Lincy, Nouvelle Bibliothèque Bleue, ou légendes populaires de la France, pp. 97–151. Paris, 1843. See, also, Jehan de Paris.

Jeanroy, Alfred. Les origines de la poésie lyrique en France au moyen-âge. Études de littérature française et comparée. Thèse présentée à la Faculté des Lettres de Paris. Paris, 1889.

Jecklin (Jäklin), Dietrich. Volksthümliches aus Graubünden. Theil I, Zürich, 1874; Theil II, Chur, 1876; Theil III, Cur, 1878.

Jehan d'Arras. See Mélusine.

Jehan de Paris. Le romant de Jehan de Paris, roy de France, revu pour la première fois sur deux manuscrits de la fin du quinzième siècle par M. Anatole de Montaiglon. Paris, 1867. See, also, Jean de Paris.

Jehan et Blonde = Blonde of Oxford. See Beaumanoir.

Jeitteles, Adalbert. Zur Charakteristik des deutschen Volksliedes in Steiermark. In Archiv für Litteraturgeschichte, IX, 356–404. 1880.

Jervise, Andrew. Epitaphs and Inscriptions . . . in the North East of Scotland. 1875. [See IV, 322.]

Jespersen, Otto. See Dania.

Jessopp, Augustus, and James, M. R. The Life and Miracles of St William of Norwich by Thomas of Monmouth. Cambridge, [Eng.], 1896.

Johannes de Alta Silva. Dolopathos, sive de rege et septem sapientibus. Herausgegeben von Hermann Oesterley. Strassburg and London, 1873.

Johnson, James. The Scots Musical Museum, in six volumes. Consisting of six hundred Scots songs, with proper basses for the piano forte, &c. Humbly dedicated to the Society of Antiquaries of Scotland. In this publication the original simplicity of our ancient national airs is retained unincumbered with useless accompaniments and graces depriving the hearers of the sweet simplicity of their native melodies. Edinburgh, [1787–1803]. 6 vols.

—— The Scots Musical Museum; consisting of upwards of six hundred songs, with proper basses for the pianoforte originally published by James Johnson; and now accompanied with copious notes and illustrations of the lyric poetry and music of Scotland, by the late William Stenhouse. With additional notes and illustrations [by David Laing]. New edition, in four volumes. Edinburgh and London, 1853. 4 vols.

Johnson, Richard. The Crown Garland of Golden Roses. From the edition of 1612; edited by W. Chappell. London, 1842. Part II, from the edition of 1659.. London, 1845. (Percy Society, 6, 15.)

Johnston, Arthur. Arturi Ionstoni Scoti Poemata Omnia. Middelb[urg], Zeland, 1642.

—— Delitiae Poetarum Scotorum hujus aevi illustrium. Amsterdami, 1637. 2 pts.

Johnston, Robert. Historia rerum Britannicarum, ut et multarum Gallicarum, Belgicarum, et Germanicarum, . . . ab anno 1572 ad annum 1628. Amstelaedami, 1655.

Johnstone, James. The Robbing of the Nunnery; or, The Abbess outwitted; a danish Ballade, translated into english in the style of the sixteenth century. Kjøbenhavn, 1786. [See I, 250.]

Jonckbloet, W. J. A. Guillaume d'Orange. Chansons de geste des XIe et XIIe siècles. La Haye, 1854. 2 vols.

—— See Lancelot.

Jones, Edward. The Bardic Museum, of primitive British literature; and other admirable rarities; forming the second volume of the Musical, Poetical, and Historical Relicks of the Welsh Bards and Druids: drawn from authentic documents of remote antiquity; (with great pains now rescued from oblivion,) and never before published: [etc.] By Edward Jones, Bard to the Prince. London, 1802.

—— Musical and Poetical Relicks of the Welsh Bards: preserved by tradition, and authentic manuscripts, from very remote antiquity; never before published [etc.]. By Edward Jones, Bard to the Prince. . . . The third edition, augmented and corrected by the author, with additional plates. London, 1808. 2 vols.

Jones, G. H. Campeu Charlymaen. See Charlemagne.

Jonson, Ben. The Gipsies Metamorphosed. In Works, VI, 71–118. (London, 1756, 7 vols.)

—— Timber, or Discoveries made upon men and matter. Edited by F. E. Schelling. Boston, 1893.

Jordan, J. P. Ueber kleinrussische Volkspoesie. In Blätter für literarische Unterhaltung, 1840, pp. 1001–03, 1013–15.

Josef. Gedicht von den sieben Todsünden, in fortlaufenden Auszügen und Inhaltsangabe zum ersten Male nach der Handschrift bekannt gemacht von Dr. [Heinrich] Babucke, Rektor des Königl. Progymnasiums zu Norden. [1874.]

Josephus, Flavius. Antiquitatum Judaicarum libri xx. In Flavii Josephi quae' reperiri potuerunt Opera Omnia, Graece et Latine, cum notis et nova versione Joannis Hudsoni. Diligenter recensuit . . . Sigebertus Havercampus. I. Amstelaedami, etc., 1726.

—— De Antiquitate Judaeorum contra Apionem libri ii. In Flavii Josephi Opera Omnia (as above), II, 436–496.

Joufrois. Altfranzösisches Rittergedicht, zum ersten Mal herausgegeben von Konrad Hofmann und Franz Muncker. Halle a. S., 1880.

Jourdains de Blaivies. In Amis et Amiles und Jourdains de Blaivies. Zwei altfranzösische Heldengedichte der kerlingischen Sagenkreises. Nach der Pariser Handschrift

zum ersten Male herausgegeben von Konrad Hofmann. Zweite vermehrte und verbesserte Auflage. Erlangen, 1882.

The Journal of American Folk-Lore, edited by Franz Boas, T. Frederick Crane, J. Owen Dorsey: W. W. Newell, general editor. Boston and New York, 1888–. (American Folk-Lore Society.)

Journal Asiatique. Paris, 1822–.

Journal des Savan(t)s. Paris, 1816–.

Jovial Crew. See Brome, Richard.

Jubinal, Achille. Mystères inédits du quinzième siècle, publiés pour la première fois, d'après le MSS. unique de la Bibliothèque Ste.-Geneviève. Paris, 1837. 2 vols.

—— Nouveau recueil de contes, dits, fabliaux et autres pièces inédites des XIIIe, XIVe et XVe siècles pour faire suite aux collections Legrand d'Aussy, Barbazan et Méon, mis au jour pour la première fois. D'après les MSS. de la Bibliothèque du Roi. Paris, 1839–42. 2 vols.

Jülg, Bernhard. Mongolische Märchen-Sammlung. Die neun Märchen des Siddhi-Kûr nach der ausführlicheren Redaction und die Geschichte des Ardschi-Bordschi Chan. Mongolisch mit deutscher Uebersetzung und kritischen Anmerkungen hrsg. von ——. Innsbruck, 1868.

Julia, Antonio. Storie popolari Acresi. In La Calabria, Oct. 15, 1888, pp. 5–8.

Julius Valerius. Latin version of Pseudo-Callisthenes, in C. Müller's edition. See Callisthenes.

Kačanovskij, Vlad. Pamjatniki bolgarskago narodnago tvorčestva. [Monuments of Bulgarian National Creation.] St Petersburg, 1882.

Kaiser Octavianus. See Octavian.

Kaiserchronik. Der Keiser und der Kunige Buoch, oder die sogenannte Kaiserchronik. . . . Zum ersten Male herausgegeben von Hans Ferd. Massmann. Quedlinburg and Leipzig, 1849–54. 3 pts. (Bibliothek der gesammten deutschen National-Literatur von der ältesten bis auf die neuere Zeit, Bd. IV, Abth. 1–3.)

Kalewala, das National-Epos der Finnen, nach der zweiten Ausgabe ins Deutsche übertragen von Anton Schiefner. Helsingfors, 1852.

Kálidása. Raghuvansa Kálidásae Carmen Sanskrite et Latine edidit Adolphus Fridericus Stenzler. London, 1832. (Oriental Translation Fund.)

Kalilah and Dimnah. See Pilpay.

Karadschitsch, Wuk Stephanowitsch. Volksmärchen der Serben. Gesammelt und herausgegeben von ——. Ins Deutsche übersetzt von dessen Tochter Wilhelmine. Mit einer Vorrede von Jacob Grimm. Nebst einem Anhange von mehr als tausend serbischen Sprichwörtern. Berlin, 1854.

Karajan, Theodor Georg von. Frühlingsgabe für Freunde älterer Literatur. Wien, 1839.

—— Der Schatzgräber, Beiträge für ältere deutsche Literatur. Leipzig, 1842.

Karl Meinet, zum ersten Mal herausgegeben durch Adelbert von Keller. Stuttgart, 1858. (Bibliothek des litterarischen Vereins in Stuttgart, 45.)

Karlamagnus Saga ok Kappa hans. Fortællinger om Keiser Karl Magnus og hans Jævninger. I norsk Bearbeidelse fra det trettende Aarhundrede. Utgivet af C. R. Unger. Christiania, 1860.

Karłowicz, Jan. Systematyka pieśni ludu polskiego. In Wisła, III, 253–78, 531–43; IV, 156–65, 393–425.

Karłowicz, Jan. Les deux arbres entrelacés. *In* Mélusine, V, 39–41. 1890.

Kathā sarit sāgara. Die Mährchensammlung des Sri Somadeva Bhatta aus Kaschmir. Erstes bis fünftes Buch. Sanskrit und Deutsch. Herausgegeben von Dr. Hermann Brockhaus. Leipzig, 1839.

—— or, Ocean of the Streams of Story, translated from the original Sanskrit by C. H. Tawney. Calcutta, 1880–84 ['87]. 2 vols. 14 fasc. (Asiatic Society of Bengal. Bibliotheca Indica. New Series.)

Kaye, Sir John William. The Life and Correspondence of . . . Sir J. Malcolm . . . from unpublished Letters and Journals. London, 1856. 2 vols.

Kayser, C. L. See Philostratus.

Keightley, Thomas. The Fairy Mythology; illustrative of the Romance and Superstition of various Countries. London, 1833. 2 vols.

Keil, H. See Apollonius.

Keller, Heinrich Adelbert von. Altfranzösische Sagen gesammelt von H. A. von Keller. Tübingen, 1839, '40. 2 vols. 2te Auflage. Heilbronn, 1876. 1 vol.

—— Fastnachtspiele aus dem fünfzehnten Jahrhundert. Stuttgart, 1853. 3 parts. (Bibliothek des Litterarischen Vereins in Stuttgart, 28, 29, 30.) Also, Nachlese, 1858. (No 46.)

—— See Altswert.

—— See Ayrer, Jacob.

—— See Karl Meinet.

—— See Sachs, Hans.

Kemble, John Mitchell. Codex Diplomaticus aevi Saxonici. Londini, 1839–48. 6 vols. (English Historical Society.)

—— The Dialogue of Salomon and Saturnus, with an historical introduction. London, 1848. (Ælfric Society.)

Kennedy, Historical Account of the noble Family of. Edinburgh, 1849. [See IV, 64.]

Kennedy, Howard Angus. Professor Blackie, his sayings and doings. A biographical sketch, by his nephew. London, 1895.

Kérardven, J. [*pseud.* for Louis Antoine Dufilhol]. Guionvac'h. Études sur la Bretagne. Deuxième édition. Paris, 1835.

Kern, J. Urban. Schlesische Sagen-Chronik. Ein Album ausgewählter Balladen, Romanzen und Legenden Schlesiens. Breslau, 1840.

Kętrzyński, W. O Mazurach. [The Mazuri.] Posen, 1872.

Keyser, R. See Olafs Saga.

—— See Strengleikar.

K[illinger], K[arl] von. Erin. Auswahl vorzüglicher irischer Erzählungen mit lebensgeschichtlichen Nachrichten von ihren Verfassern und Sammlung der besten irischen Volkssagen, Mährchen und Legenden. Stuttgart and Tübingen, 1847–49. 6 vols.

Kind, Friedrich. Auserwählte Unterhaltungen. Wien, 1827. 10 vols.

Die Kindheit Jesu. Gedicht des zwölften Jahrhunderts. Herausgegeben von Julius Feifalik. Wien, 1859.

—— von Konrad von Fussesbrunnen. Herausgegeben von Karl Kochendörffer. Strassburg, London, 1881. (Quellen and Forschungen, 43.)

Kingscote, Georgiana, and Naṭeça Çāstrī. Tales of the Sun; or, Folklore of Southern India. Collected by Mrs. Howard Kingscote and Paṇḍit Naṭésá Sástrî. London, 1890.

Kirchhof, Hans Wilhelm. Wendunmuth. Herausgegeben von Hermann Oesterley. Tübingen, 1869. 5 vols. (Bibliothek des Litterarischen Vereins in Stuttgart, 95–99.)

Kirk, Robert. The secret Commonwealth of Elves, Fauns, and Fairies. A study in folk-lore and psychical research. The text by Robert Kirk, M. A., Minister of Aberfoyle, A. D. 1691. The comment by Andrew Lang, M. A., A. D. 1893. London, 1893. (Bibliothèque de Carabas, 8.)

Kirkton, James. The secret and true History of the Church of Scotland, from the Restoration to the year 1678. By the Rev. Mr. Kirkton. To which is added, an account of the murder of Archbishop Sharp, by James Russell, an actor therein. Edited from the MSS. by Charles Kirkpatrick Sharpe. Edinburgh, 1817.

Kittredge, George Lyman. Sir Orfeo. *In* American Journal of Philology, VII, 176–202. 1886.

Klee, Gotthold Ludwig. Zur Hildesage. Leipzig, 1873.

Klemming, G. E. See Floire et Blanceflor.

Klöden, Karl Friedrich. Diplomatische Geschichte des Markgrafen Waldemar von Brandenburg. Unmittelbar nach den Quellen dargestellt. Berlin, 1844–45. 4 pts.

Knighton, Henry. Henrici Knighton Canonici Leycestrensis Chronica de Eventibus Angliae a tempore Regis Edgari usque mortem Regis Ricardi Secundi. *In* [Roger Twysden,] Historiae Anglicanae Scriptores X, ii, cols 2311–2743. Londini, 1652.

Knoop, D. See Blätter für pommersche Volkskunde.

Knoop, Otto. Volkssagen, Erzählungen, Aberglauben, Gebräuche und Märchen aus dem östlichen Hinterpommern. Posen, 1885.

Knortz, Karl. Lieder und Romanzen Alt-Englands. Deutsch von Karl Knortz. Cöthen, 1872.

—— Schottische Balladen. Deutsch von Karl Knortz. Halle, 1875.

Knowles, James Hinton. Folk-Tales of Kashmir. London, 1888. (Trübner's Oriental Series.)

Knox, John. The History of the Reformation in Scotland. Edited by David Laing. *In* The Works of John Knox. Collected and edited by David Laing. Vols I–II. Edinburgh, 1846–48. 2 vols. (Wodrow Society.)

Knust, Hermann. Mittheilungen aus dem Eskurial. Tübingen, 1879. (Bibliothek des Litterarischen Vereins in Stuttgart, 141.)

Knyghton. See Knighton.

Koberstein, A. Ueber die in Sage und Dichtung gangbare Vorstellung von dem Fortleben abgeschiedener menschlicher Seelen in der Pflanzenwelt. *In* Weimarisches Jahrbuch, I, 73–100. 1854. Nachtrag by R. Köhler, pp. 479–83.

Koch, John. Die Siebenschläferlegende, ihr Ursprung und ihre Verbreitung. Eine mythologisch-literaturgeschichtliche Studie. Leipzig, 1883.

Koch, Max. See Zeitschrift für vergleichende Litteratur.

Kochendörffer, Karl. See Kindheit Jesu.

Kock, Axel. See Arkiv för nordisk Filologi.

Köffinger, Johann Paul. See Koloczaer Codex.

Köhler, Johann August Ernst. Volksbrauch, Aberglauben, Sagen und andre alte Ueberlieferungen im Voigtlande, mit Berücksichtigung des Orlagau's und des Pleissnerlandes. Ein Beitrag zur Kulturgeschichte der Voigtländer. Leipzig, 1867.

Köhler, Reinhold. Le conte de la reine qui tua son sénéchal. *In* Romania, XI, 581–84. 1882.

Köhler, Reinhold. [On] Cosquin, Contes populaires lorrains. *In* Zeitschrift für romanische Philologie, II, 350–51. 1878.

—— Die Erde als jungfräuliche Mutter Adams. *In* Germania, VII, 476–80. 1862.

—— Italienische Novellen. *In* Jahrbuch für romanische und englische Literatur, XII, 347–52, 407–14. 1871.

—— Italienische Volksmärchen. *In* Jahrbuch für romanische und englische Literatur, VIII, 241–70. 1867.

—— Nasr-eddin's Schwänke. *In* Orient und Occident, I, 431–48. 1862.

—— Die Pehlevi-Erzählung von Gôsht-i Fryânô und der kirgisische Büchergesang 'Der Lerche.' *In* Zeitschrift der deutschen morgenländischen Gesellschaft, XXIX, 633–36. 1876.

—— [Review of] Alexander Reifferscheid, Westfälische Volkslieder, Heilbronn, 1879. *In* Anzeiger für deutsches Alterthum, VI, 263–75. 1880.

—— Sainte Tryphine et Hirlande. *In* Revue Celtique, I, 222–25. 1870–72.

—— Ueber J. F. Campbell's Sammlung gälischer Märchen. *In* Orient and Occident, II, 98–126, 294–331, 486–506, 677–90; III, 348–52 (Nachtrag). 1864–65.

—— Vergleichende Anmerkungen. *Prefixed to* Karl Warnke's edition of Marie de France, Halle, 1885. See Marie de France.

—— Vom Fortleben der Seelen in der Pflanzenwelt. *In* Weimarisches Jahrbuch, I, 479–83. 1854.

—— Der weisse, der rothe und der schwarze Hahn. *In* Germania, XI, 85–92. 1866.

—— Zu der Erzählung Adams von Cobsam 'The Wright's Chaste Wife.' *In* Jahrbuch für romanische und englische Literatur, VIII, 44–64. 1867.

—— Zu F. Wolf's Proben portugiesischer und catalanischer Volksromanzen. *In* Jahrbuch für romanische und englische Literatur, III, 56–63. Nachwort von Ferd. Wolf, III, 63–73. 1861.

—— Zu von der Hagens Gesammtabenteuer Nr. LXIII. *In* Germania, XIV, 269–71. 1869.

—— Zu den von Laura Gonzenbach gesammelten sicilianischen Märchen. Nachträge aus dem Nachlasse Reinhold Köhlers, herausgegeben von J. Bolte. *In* Zeitschrift des Vereins für Volkskunde, VI, 58–78, 161–175. 1896.

—— Zum Fabliau vom Stadtrichter von Aquileja. *In* Jahrbuch für romanische und englische Literatur, XI, 231–32. 1870.

—— Zwei und vierzig alte Rätsel und Fragen. *In* Weimarisches Jahrbuch, V, 329–56. 1856.

—— See Gonzenbach, Laura.

—— See Herrmann, Anton.

—— See Jagić, V.

—— See Kreutzwald, Friedrich.

—— See Luzel, F. M.

—— See Meyer, Gustav.

Kölbing, Eugen. Kleine Beiträge zur Erklärung und Textkritik englischer Dichter. I. *In* Englische Studien, III, 92–105. 1880.

—— Riddarasögur. Parcevals saga, Valvers þáttr, Ívents saga, Mírmans saga. Zum ersten Mal herausgegeben und mit einer literarhistorischen Einleitung versehen. Strassburg, 1872.

—— See Altenglische Bibliothek.

—— See Amis and Amiloun.

—— See Beves of Hamtoun.

Kölbing, Eugen. See Englische Studien.

—— See Tristan.

König Rother. See Rother.

Königshofen, Jacob Twinger von. Chronik. Die älteste Teutsche, so wol Allgemeine, als insonderheit Elsassische u. Strassburgische Chronicke, von Jacob Twinger von Königshofen, anjetzo zum ersten mal heraus- u. m. histor. Anmerk. in Truck gegeben von Joh. Schiltern. Strassburg, 1698.

Kolberg, Oskar. Lud. Jego zwyczaje, sposób życia, mowa, podania, przysłowia, obrzędy, gusła, zabawy, pieśni, muzyka i tańce. [The Peasantry : their customs, manner of life, speech, traditions, saws, rites, tastes, amusements, songs, music and dances.] Vols I–IV, Warsaw ; V–XXII, Cracow. 1857–89.

—— Mazowsze. Obraz etnograficzny. [The Mazovians. An ethnographical Sketch.] Cracow, 1885–88. 4 vols.

—— Pokucie. Obraz etnograficzny. [Pokucie. Ethnographical Sketch.] Cracow, 1882–89. 4 vols.

Koloczaer Codex altdeutscher Gedichte. Herausgegeben von Johann Nep[omuk] Grafen Mailáth und Johann Paul Köffinger. Pesth, 1817.

Konrad von Fussesbrunnen. See Fussesbrunnen, Konrad von.

Konrad von Würzburg. Die Mähre von der Minne oder die Herzmähre, nach acht Handschriften herausgegeben von Franz Roth. Frankfurt am Main, 1846.

Koraes. See Æsop.

Koschwitz, Eduard. Karls des Grossen Reise nach Jerusalem und Constantinopel. Ein altfranzösisches Gedicht des XI. Jahrhunderts. Heilbronn, 1880. (Altfranzösische Bibliothek, 2.)

—— Sechs Bearbeitungen des altfranzösischen Gedichts von Karl des Grossen Reise nach Jerusalem und Constantinopel. Heilbronn, 1879.

—— Ueberlieferung und Sprache der Chanson du Voyage de Charlemagne à Jérusalem et à Constantinople. Eine kritische Untersuchung. Heilbronn, 1876.

Kosegarten, J. G. See Tuti-nameh.

Kostomarov. See Kuśelev-Bezborodko.

Koszorú. Szépirodalmi s Átalános miveltség terjesztö Hetilap. Szerkeszti Arany János. Pest, 1863–65. 5 vols.

Kozłowski, Kornel. Lud. Pieśni, podania, baśnie, zwyczaje i przesądy ludu z Mazowsza Czerskiego. [The Peasantry. Songs, traditions, fables, habits and prejudices of the peasantry in Mazowia near Czersk.] Warsaw, 1869.

Krainz, Johann. Mythen und Sagen aus dem steirischen Hochlande. Gesammelt und herausgegeben von Johann Krainz. Bruck a. d. Mur, 1880.

—— Sagen aus Steiermark. Wien, [1880].

Krantz, Albertus. Saxonia. Francofurti, 1621.

Krauss, Friedrich S. Sagen und Märchen der Südslaven. Zum grossen Teil aus ungedruckten Quellen. Leipzig, 1883–84. 2 vols. (Sagen und Märchen der Südslaven in ihrem Verhältnis zu den Sagen und Märchen der übrigen indogermanischen Völkergruppen von Dr. Friedrich S. Krauss, I, II.)

Krek, Bogomil. Ein Beitrag zur Literatur des Lenorenstoffes. *In* Archiv für slavische Philologie, X, 356–59. 1887.

—— Ein neuer Beitrag zur Litteratur des Lenorenstoffes. (Aus der slavischen Volkspoesie.) *In* Magazin für die Litteratur des In- und Auslandes, CXII, 629–32, 650–54. 1887.

Kreutzwald, Friedrich. Ehstnische Märchen. Aufgezeichnet von Friedrich Kreutzwald. Aus dem Ehstnischen übersetzt von F. Löwe. Nebst einem Vorwort von Anton Schiefner und Anmerkungen von Reinhold Köhler und Anton Schiefner. Halle, 1869.

Kristni-Saga, sive Historia Religionis Christianae in Islandiam introductae; nec non Þattr af Isleifi Biskupi, sive narratio de Isleifo Episcopo; ex manuscriptis Legati Magnaeani cum interpretatione Latina, notis, chronologia, tabulis genealogicis, [etc.]. Hafniae, 1773.

Kroeber, A. See Fierabras.

Krohn, Julius. Das Lied vom Mädchen, welches erlöst werden soll. (Uebersetzt aus Virittäjä, II, 36–50.) *Appended to* Kaarle Krohn. Histoire du traditionisme en Esthonie. Traduite par Otto Florell. Helsingfors, 1891. [See V, 231–33.]

Krohn, Kaarle. Die geographische Verbreitung estnischer Lieder. Kuopio, 1892.

—— See Krohn, Julius.

Krolmus. See Sumlork.

Kudrun. Herausgegeben von Karl Bartsch. 2te Auflage. Leipzig, 1867. (Deutsche Classiker des Mittelalters. Mit Wort- und Sacherklärungen. Herausgegeben von Franz Pfeiffer, 2.)

Kuhn, Adalbert. Märkische Sagen und Märchen nebst einem Anhange von Gebräuchen und Aberglauben. Berlin, 1843.

—— Sagen, Gebräuche und Märchen aus Westfalen, u. s. w. Leipzig, 1859. 2 pts.

—— Todte soll man nicht beweinen. *In* Zeitschrift für deutsche Mythologie, I, 62–63. 1853.

—— Wodan. *In* Zeitschrift für Deutsches Alterthum, V, 472–494. 1845.

Kuhn, Ernst. See Literatur-Blatt, etc.

Kuinoel, C. T. See Propertius.

Kulda, Beneš Method. Moravské národní pohádky, povĕsti, obyčeje a povĕry. Prague, 1874–75. 2 vols.

Kurz, Heinrich. See Waldis, Burkhard.

Kuŝelev-Bezborodko, Grigorij. Pamjatniki starinnoj russkoj literatury. [Monuments of the older Russian Literature.] Ed. Nikolaj Kostomarov. St Petersburg, 1860–62. 4 pts.

Labrunie, Gérard. See Nerval, Gérard de.

Lach-Szyrma, K. Pamiętnik naukowy służący za ciąg dalszy ćwiczeń. Warsaw, 1819.

La Chaussée, [Pierre Claude] Nivelle de. Œuvres de Nivelle de la Chaussée, de l'Académie Françoise. Nouvelle édition, corrigée et augmentée de plusieurs pièces qui n'avoient point encore paru. Paris, 1777. 5 vols.

—— Supplément aux Œuvres de Nivelle de la Chaussée. Amsterdam, 1778.

[Lacroix, Paul.] Dissertations bibliographiques par P. L. Jacob, bibliophile. Paris, 1864.

—— Mœurs, usages et costumes au moyen âge et à l'époque de la renaissance. Troisième édition. Paris, 1873.

Lacroix. See Pétis de la Croix.

Lady Bessy. The most pleasant song of Lady Bessy [etc.]. With notes by Thomas Heywood. Privately printed. London, 1829.

—— The most pleasant song of Lady Bessy; and how she married king Henry the Seventh, of the house of Lancaster. Edited by James Orchard Halliwell, Esq. London, 1847. (Percy Society, 20.)

Lafon, Jean Bernard, *called* Mary Lafon. Histoire littéraire du Midi de la France. Paris, 1882.

La Fontaine, Jean de. Œuvres complètes de La Fontaine. Nouvelle édition, très-soigneusement revue sur les textes originaux avec un travail de critique et d'érudition, aperçus d'histoire littéraire, vie de l'auteur, notes et commentaires, bibliographie, etc., par M. Louis Moland. Paris, 1872–76. 7 vols. (Chefs-d'œuvre de la Littérature française, 33–39.)

Laforest, Pierre. Limoges au XVIIe siècle. Limoges, 1862. (Études sur les anciennes Provinces de France.)

Lageniensis. *Pseudon. for* John O'Hanlon. Irish Folk Lore: traditions and superstitions of the country; with humorous tales. By "Lageniensis." Glasgow and London, [1870].

Lahn, W. See Engelien, August.

Laing, Alexander. The Donean Tourist: giving an account of the battles, castles, gentlemen's seats, families, with their origin, armorial ensigns, badges of distinction, carefully selected from the best authorities, and interspersed with anecdotes, and ancient national ballads, &c. &c. &c. Aberdeen, 1828.

Laing, David. Collection of ancient Scottish Prophecies, in alliterative verse. Reprinted from Waldegrave's edition, 1603 (and collated with Hart's, 1615). Edinburgh, 1833. (Bannatyne Club, 44.)

—— Early Metrical Tales; including the history of Sir Egeir, Sir Gryme, and Sir Gray-Steill. Edinburgh, 1826.

—— The Scots Musical Museum. See Johnson, James.

—— Select Remains of the Ancient Popular Poetry of Scotland. Edinburgh, 1822.

—— See Baillie, Robert.

—— See Dunbar, William.

—— See Henryson, Robert.

—— See Knox, John.

—— See Roswall and Lillian.

—— See Wyntown, Andrew.

Laistner, Ludwig. Ruodlieb-Märchen in Russland. *In* Zeitschrift für deutsches Alterthum, XXIX, 443–65. 1885.

Lambert li Tors. See Alexander the Great.

Lambert, L. See Montel, A.

Lammert, G. Volksmedizin und medizinischer Aberglaube in Bayern und den angrenzenden Bezirken, begründet auf die Geschichte der Medizin und Cultur. Mit historischer Einleitung und einer lithographirten Tafel. Würzburg, 1869.

Lammikin: an Old Scotch Ballad. Aberdeen, Lewis and James Smith, 1862. [See II, 320 a.]

Lamprecht, Pfaffe. See Alexander the Great.

Lancelot. Roman van Lancelot (XIIIe eeuw). Naar het (eenig-bekende) handschrift der Koninklijke Bibliotheek, op gezag van het gouvernement, uitgegeven door Dr. W. J. A. Jonckbloet. 's Gravenhage, 1846–49. 2 pts.

Landau, Marcus. Die Quellen des Decamerone. Wien, 1869.

Landgraf, Gustav. See Leo.

Landsberger, Julius. See Syntipas.

Lane, Edward William. See Arabian Nights.

Laneham, Robert. Letter to Humfrey Martin, in F. J. Furnivall, Captain Cox. London, 1871. (The Ballad Society.)

Lang, Andrew. At the Sign of the Ship. *In* Longman's Magazine, XVII, 215–23. 1890.

Lang, Andrew. The Mystery of "The Queen's Marie." *In* Blackwood's Edinburgh Magazine, CLVIII, 381–90. 1895.

—— See Kirk, Robert.

Lange, M. H. See Cober, Gottlieb.

Langland, William. The Vision of William concerning Piers the Plowman, in three parallel texts. Edited with preface, notes, and a glossary by W. W. Skeat. Oxford, 1886. 2 vols. (Clarendon Press.)

Langtoft, Pierre de. Peter Langtoft's Chronicle (as illustrated and improv'd by Robert of Brunne) from the Death of Cadwalader to the end of K. Edward the First's Reign. Transcrib'd and now first publish'd, from a MS. in the Inner-Temple Library, by Thomas Hearne. Oxford, 1725. 2 vols.

—— The Chronicle of Pierre de Langtoft, in French verse, from the earliest period to the death of King Edward I. Ed. by Thomas Wright. London, 1866–68. 2 vols. (Rolls Series.)

Lanval. See Launfal.

Lappenberg, J. M. See Eulenspiegel.

—— See Helmold.

Larivey, Pierre de. See Louveau, Jean.

Larminie, Wm. West-Irish Folk-Tales and Romances. Collected and translated. London, 1893.

Laroche, Pierre [P. Fagot, *pseudon.*]. Folklore du Lauraguais. Albi, 1891–94. 7 pts.

Launfal. Thomas Chestre, Launfal. *In* Joseph Ritson, Ancient Engleish Romanceës, I, 170–215. London, 1802.

—— Lai de Lanval. *In* Poésies de Marie de France. Publiées par B. de Roquefort, I, 202–250. Paris, 1820.

Laurie, Thomas. See (The) Ely Volume.

Laurin. Ein tirolisches Heldenmärchen aus dem Anfange des XIII. Jahrhunderts herausgegeben von Karl Müllenhoff. Berlin, 1874.

Law, Robert. Memorialls, or, the Memorable Things that fell out within this island of Brittain from 1638 to 1684. By the Rev. Mr. Law. Edited from the MS. by Charles Kirkpatrick Sharpe, Esq. Edinburgh, 1818.

Layland, John. See Leland, John.

Laʒamons Brut, or Chronicle of Britain. Now first published . . . by Sir F. Madden. London, 1847. 3 vols. (Society of Antiquaries of London.)

Lea, Henry Charles. El Santo Niño de la Guardia. *In* The English Historical Review, IV, 229–50. 1889.

—— Superstition and Force. Essays on the wager of law, the wager of battle, the ordeal, torture. Third edition, revised. Philadelphia, 1878.

Le Braz, A. La légende de la mort en Basse-Bretagne : croyances, traditions et usages des Bretons armoricains. Avec une introduction de L. Marillier. Paris, 1893.

Lecoy de la Marche, A. See Étienne de Bourbon.

Le Duc, Philibert. Les nöels bressans de Bourg, de Pont-de-Vaux et des paroisses voisines, augmentés de plusieurs couplets inédits ; suivis de six nöels bugistes, de trois anciens nöels français, et des airs en musique ; corrigés sur les premières éditions, traduits et annotés. Bourg-en-Bresse, 1845.

Lefèvre, André. See Perrault, Charles.

Legenda Aurea. Jacobi a Voragine Legenda Aurea, vulgo Historia Lombardica dicta. Ad optimorum librorum fidem recensuit Dr. Th. Graesse. Editio secunda. Lipsiae, 1850.

Legrand, Émile. Chansons populaires recueillies en Octobre

1876 à Fontenay-le-Marmion, arrondissement de Caen (Calvados). *In* Romania, X. 365–96. 1881.

Legrand, Émile. Recueil de contes populaires grecs, traduits sur les textes originaux. Paris, 1881. (Collection de chansons et de contes populaires, 1.)

Le Grand d'Aussy, Pierre Jean Baptiste. Fabliaux ou contes du XIIe et du XIIIe siècle, traduits ou extraits d'après divers manuscrits du tems ; avec des notes historiques et critiques, et les imitations qui ont été faites de ces contes depuis leur origine jusqu'à nos jours. Paris, 1779–81. 4 vols.

—— Fabliaux, ou contes, fables et romans du XIIe et du XIIIe siècle. Troisième édition. Paris, 1829. 5 vols.

Leibnitz, Gottfried Wilhelm von. Chronicon Alberici, monachi Trium Fontium. *In* Godefridi Guilielmi Leibnitii Accessiones Historicae, quibus utilia superiorum temporum historiis illustrandis scripta monumentaque nondum hactenus edita inque iis scriptores diu desiderati continentur. Tom. II. Hannoverae, 1698.

Leigh, Egerton. Ballads and Legends of Cheshire. London, 1867.

The Leisure Hour. London, 1852–. [Magazine.]

Leite de Vasconcellos, José. Tradições populares de Portugal, colligidas e annotadas. Porto, 1882. (Bibliotheca Ethnographica Portugueza, 1.)

—— Versão portugueza do romance popular de Jean Renaud. *In* Romania, XI, 585–86. 1882.

—— See Revista Lusitana.

Leland, *or* Layland, John. Lelandi Joannis antiquarii de rebus Britannicis Collectanea. Cum Thomae Hearnii praefatione, notis et indice ad editionem primam. [*Also with the title* Leland's Collectanea in six volumes.] Editio altera. Londini, 1770. 6 vols.

Le Marchant, Jehan. Le livre des miracles de Notre-Dame de Chartres écrit en vers au XIIIe siècle. Publié pour la première fois, d'après un manuscrit de la Bibliothèque de Chartres, avec une préface, un glossaire et des notes. Par M. G. Duplessis. Chartres, 1855.

Lemcke, Ludwig. See Jahrbuch für romanische und englische Literatur.

Lemke, Elisabeth. Völksthümliches in Ostpreussen. Mohrungen, 1884–87. 2 pts.

Lengert, O. Die schottische Romanze Roswall and Lillian. *In* Englische Studien, XVI, 321–56 ; XVII, 341–77. 1891–92.

Leo. Die Vita Alexandri Magni des Archipresbyters Leo (Historia de Preliis). Nach der Bamberger und ältesten Münchener Handschrift zum erstenmal herausgegeben von Dr. Gustav Landgraf. Erlangen, 1885.

Lerch, P. Bericht über: 'Resumé de l'ouvrage kourde d'Ahmed Effendi Khani, fait et traduit par A. Jaba.' *In* Bulletin de la classe des sciences historiques, philologiques et politiques de l'Académie impériale des Sciences de St.-Pétersbourg, XV, 161–171. 1858.

Le Roux de Lincy, A. J. V. Nouvelle Bibliothèque Bleue, ou Légendes populaires de la France. Paris, 1843.

—— See Beaumanoir.

—— See Wace.

Leskien, A. See Brugman, Karl.

Lesley, John (Bishop of Ross). De Origine, Moribus et Rebus Gestis Scotorum libri decem. E quibus septem veterum Scotorum res in primis memorabiles contractius, reliqui vero tres posteriorum regum ad nostra tempora historiam, quae huc usque desiderabatur, fusius explicant.

Accessit nova et accurata regionum et insularum Scotiae, cum vera ejusdem topographia tabula, descriptio. Authore Joanne Leslaeo, Episcopo Rossensi. Romae, M.D.LXXVIII. Nunc denuô recus. Anno Domini, 1675.

Lesley, John. The History of Scotland, from the death of King James I. in the year M.CCCC.XXXVI, to the year M.D.LXI. Edinburgh, 1830. (Bannatyne Club, 39.)

Lespy, V. Proverbes du pays de Béarn, enigmes et contes populaires. Montpellier, 1876. (Publications spéciales de la Societé pour l'Étude des Langues Romanes, 2.)

Lewalter, Johann. Deutsche Volkslieder. In Niederhessen aus dem Munde des Volkes gesammelt, mit einfacher Klavierbegleitung, geschichtlichen und vergleichenden Anmerkungen herausgegeben. Hamburg, 1890 - 94. 5 Hfte.

Lewestam, Friedrich Heinrich. Polnische Volkssagen und Märchen. Aus dem Polnischen des K. W. Woycicki. Berlin, 1839.

Lewis, Matthew Gregory. Tales of Wonder, written and collected by ——. London, 1801. 2 vols.

Lexandre, A. Le pèlerinage de Mireille. Portraits et paysage de la Provence. Paris, 1864.

Lexer, Matthias. Kärntisches Wörterbuch. Mit einem Anhange: Weihnacht-Spiele und Lieder aus Kärnten. Leipzig, 1862.

Leyden, John. See Complaynt of Scotland.

Leyser, Hermann. Buridan und die Königin von Frankreich. In Zeitschrift für deutsches Alterthum, II, 362–70. 1842.

Libros de Caballerias, con un discurso preliminar y un catálogo razonado por Don Pascual de Gayangos. Madrid, 1857. (Biblioteca de Autores Españoles.)

Lichtenstein, Franz. See Eilhart.

Liebrecht, Felix. Beiträge zur Novellenkunde mit besonderem Bezug auf die ältere deutsche Litteratur. In Germania, I, 257–72. 1856.

—— Bishop Percy's Folio Manuscript. Edited by Hales and Furnivall. [Review.] In Göttingische Gelehrte Anzeigen, 1868, pp. 1881–1920.

—— Review of Child, Ballads, Pt. I. In Englische Studien, IX, 444–48. 1886.

—— Review of: Decameron von Heinrich Steinhöwel, hrsg. v. A. von Keller. In Jahrbuch für romanische und englische Literatur, IV, 106–13. 1862.

—— Ein sicilisches Volkslied [Scibilia nobili]. In Zeitschrift für deutsche Philologie, IX, 53–64. 1878.

—— Vlämische Märchen und Volkslieder. In Germania, XIV, 84–96. 1869.

—— Zur Volkskunde. Alte und neue Aufsätze. Heilbronn, 1879.

—— Zur Zimmerischen Chronik. In Germania, XIV, 385–405. 1869.

—— See Basile.

—— See Dunlop, John Colin.

—— See Gervase of Tilbury.

Lieder für fröhliche Gesellschaften. Hamburg, 1790.

Lights of Canopus. See Pilpay.

Lindblom, C. G. Antiquiteter i Thorskinge. Fornminnet eller Kummel-Runan, tolkande Systersveket Bröllopsdagen. Götheborg, 1836. [See I, 493 b.]

Lindsay, Sir David. The Historie of ane nobil and wailʒeand sqvyer, William Meldrum, vmqvhyle laird of Cleische and Bynnis. Compylit be Sir David Lyndesay of the Mont, alias, Lyoun King of Armes. [Reprint of the edition of 1594.] Edited by F. Hall. London, 1868. (Early English Text Society, 35.)

Lindsay, Sir David. The Poetical Works of Sir David Lindsay of the Mount, Lion King at Arms under James V. A new edition, corrected and enlarged: with a life of the author, prefatory dissertations, and an appropriate glossary. By George Chalmers. London, 1806. 3 vols.

Lindsay, Robert, of Pitscottie. The Cronicles of Scotland. Published from several old manuscripts [by J. G. Dalyell]. Edinburgh, 1814. 2 vols.

Linhagens. See Livros de Linhagens.

Lismore. The Dean of Lismore's Book, a selection of Ancient Gaelic Poetry from a MS. collection made by Sir James M'Gregor, Dean of Lismore, in the beginning of the sixteenth century. Edited with a translation and notes by T. M'Lauchlan, and an introduction and notes by W. F. Skene. Edinburgh, 1862.

Literatur-Blatt für orientalische Philologie, unter Mitwirkung von Dr. Johannes Klatt in Berlin herausgegeben von Prof. Dr. Ernst Kuhn in München. Vols. I–III. Leipzig, 1883–1887.

Livius, Titus (Foro-Juliensis). See Titus Livius.

Livona. See Tielemann, G. T.

Os livros de Linhagens. In Portugaliae monumenta historica a saeculo octavo post Christum usque ad quintumdecimum, jussu Academiae Scientiarum Olisiponensis edita. (Olisipone, 1856-.) Scriptores, vol. I, fascic. ii. Olisipone, 1860.

Llorente, Juan Antonio. Histoire critique de l'Inquisition d'Espagne, depuis l'époque de son établissement par Ferdinand V jusqu'au règne de Ferdinand VII. Traduite de l'espagnol, sur le manuscrit et sous les yeux de l'auteur, par Alexis Pellier. Seconde édition. Paris, 1818. 4 vols.

Lobeck, Christian August. Aglaophamus, sive de theologiae mysticae Graecorum causis libri tres. Regimontii Prussorum, 1829. 2 vols.

Loeb, Isidore. Un mémoire de Laurent Ganganelli sur la calomnie du meurtre rituel. In Revue des Études juives, XVIII, 179–211. 1889.

Loève - Veimars, Adolphe. Ballades, légendes et chants populaires de l'Angleterre et de l'Écosse, par Walter-Scott, Thomas Moore, Campbell et les anciens poètes; publiés et précédés d'une introduction par A. Loève-Veimars. Paris, 1825.

—— Popular Ballads and Songs, from tradition, manuscripts, and scarce editions. Paris, 1825.

Löwe, F. See Kreutzwald, F.

Logan, W. H. See D'Avenant, Sir William.

Loiseleur-Deslongchamps, A. Essai sur les fables indiennes; suivi du Roman des Sept Sages de Rome. Paris, 1838.

—— See (Les) Mille et Un Jours.

The London Magazine, Vol. IV. London, 1821. [See IV, 415.]

London Philological Society. Transactions. London, 1854-.

The London and Westminster Review. London, 1836–40. [See III, 42 a.]

The Longing Maid's Garland, composed of five delightful new songs. N. p., n. d. [In a volume (of garlands) formerly belonging to Heber and now in Harvard College Library: 25252, 6. See the note at V, 129.]

Longmuir, John. See Jamieson, John.

Lorris, Guillaume de. See Rose, Roman de la.

Loth, J. See d'Arbois de Jubainville.

—— See Mabinogion.

Louveau, Jean, and Larivey, Pierre de, *translators*. Les Facétieuses Nuits de Straparole. Paris, 1857. 2 vols.

Loven, Nils. See Nicolovinus.

Lover, Samuel. Legends and Stories of Ireland. New edition, complete in one volume. London, [1860].

Low, George. A Tour through the Islands of Orkney and Schetland, containing hints relative to their ancient, modern, and natural history collected in 1774. With illustrations from drawings by the author, and with an introduction by Joseph Anderson. Kirkwall, 1879.

Luard, Henry Richards. Annales Monastici, edited by ——. London, 1864–69. 5 vols. (Rolls Series.)

—— *editor*. Lives of Edward the Confessor. I. La Estoire de Seint Aedward le Rei. II. Vita Beati Edvardi Regis et Confessoris. III. Vita Æduuardi regis qui apud Westmonasterium requiescit. London, 1858. (Rolls Series.)

—— See Paris, Matthew.

Lubbock, Sir John. The Origin of Civilization and the Primitive Condition of Man. Mental and social condition of savages. Fourth edition, with numerous additions. London, 1882.

Lucian. Περὶ πένθους. De Luctu. *In* Luciani Samosatensis Opera, Graece et Latine, VII, 206–219. Biponti, 1790.

Ludus Sancti Jacobi. See Arnaud, Camille.

Ludwig Salvator, Archduke. Die Balearen geschildert in Wort und Bild. [Privately printed.] Leipzig, 1871. [New ed.] Würzburg and Leipzig, 1897. 2 vols.

Lüdemann, Wilhelm von. See Hohenhausen, Elise von.

Lüdtke, Gustav. See (The) Erl of Tolous.

Lüning, Hermann. See Edda.

Lütolf, Alois. Heimdall und Wilhelm Tell. *In* Germania, VIII, 208–16. 1863.

—— Sagen, Bräuche und Legenden aus den fünf Orten Lucern, Uri, Schwyz, Unterwalden und Zug. Lucern, 1865.

Lumby, J. R. See Horn. See Higden.

Lumsden, Henry William. Memorials of the Families of Lumsdaine, Lumisden, or Lumsden. Edinburgh, 1889.

—— Matthew. Genealogy of the Family of Forbes. Written in 1580. Inverness, 1819. Reprinted, 1883.

Lundell, J. A. See Nyare Bidrag.

Lusse, D. See Recueil des romans historiques, etc.

Luther, Martin. Tischreden oder Colloquia so er in vielen Jahren gegen gelahrten Leuten, auch fremden Gästen und seinen Tischgesellen geführet, in Auswahl für das deutsche Volk. Wohlfeile und veränderte zweite Auflage. Berlin, 1877.

Luttrell, Narcissus. A brief Historical Relation of State Affairs from September, 1678, to April, 1714. Oxford, 1857. 6 vols.

Luzel, François Marie. Contes populaires de la Basse-Bretagne. Paris, 1887. 3 vols. (Les littératures populaires de toutes les nations, 24–26.)

—— Contes populaires des Bretons armoricains. Koadalan. *In* Revue Celtique, I, 106–131. *With* Observations, by Reinhold Köhler, 132–134. 1870–72.

—— De l'authenticité des chants du Barzaz-Breiz de M. de la Villemarqué. Paris, 1872.

—— Jannic aux deux sous. Conte breton. *In* Revue des traditions populaires, III, 474–83. 1888.

—— Le prince blanc. *In* Revue des traditions populaires, I, 278–89. 1886.

—— La princesse enchantée. Conte breton. *In* Annuaire de la Société des Traditions populaires, II, 53–57. 1887.

—— See Ernault, Émile.

Lydgate, John. Kalender in Versen, von Dan John Lydgate. [Hrsg. v.] C. Horstmann. *In* Archiv für das Studium der neueren Sprachen und Litteraturen, LXXX, 114–135. 1888.

Lyle, Thomas. Ancient Ballads and Songs, chiefly from tradition, manuscripts, and scarce works; with biographical and illustrative notices, including original poetry. London, 1827.

Lyngbye, H. C. Den underbare Harpe. En færøisk Vise med Oversættelse. *In* Nyeste Skilderie af Kjøbenhavn, XVIII, 997–1004. 1821.

Lysons, Daniél. The Environs of London: being an historical account of the towns, villages, and hamlets within twelve miles of that capital; interspersed with biographical anecdotes. London, 1792–1811. 6 vols.

Lysons, Daniel and Samuel. Cumberland. *In* Magna Brittania, being a concise Topographical Account of the several counties of Great Britain. Vol. IV. London, 1816.

Mabille, Émil. See Le Grand Parangon, etc.

Mabillon, Jean. Annales Ordinis S. Benedicti Occidentalium Monachorum Patriarchae. In quibus non modo res monasticae, sed etiam ecclesiasticae historiae non minima pars continetur. Editio prima Italica a quamplurimis mendis, quae in Parisiensem irreperant, ad auctoris mentem expurgata. . . . Lucae, 1739–45. 6 vols.

The Mabinogion. From the Llyfr Coch o Hergest, and other ancient Welsh manuscripts, with an English translation and notes, by Lady Charlotte Guest. London, [1838–49]. 3 vols.

—— From the Welsh of the Llyfr Coch o Hergest (The Red Book of Hergest) in the library of Jesus College, Oxford. Translated, with notes, by Lady Charlotte Guest. London, 1877.

—— traduits en entier pour la première fois en français. Avec un commentaire explicatif et des notes critiques. Par J. Loth. Paris, 1889. 2 vols. (Cours de la Littérature Celtique par H. d'Arbois de Jubainville et par J. Loth, 3, 4.)

Macaire: ein altfranzösisches Gedicht herausgegeben von Adolf Mussafia. Wien, 1864. (Altfranzösische Gedichte aus venezianischen Handschriften, herausgegeben von Adolf Mussafia, 2.)

—— chanson de geste. Publiée d'après le manuscrit unique de Venise, avec un essai de restitution en regard par M. F. Guessard. Paris, 1866. (Les Anciens Poëtes de la France, 9.)

[Macbain, Alexander.] The Hero Tales of the Gael. *In* The Celtic Magazine, XIII, 1–7, 69–77, 129–38, 185–89, 280–87, 319–26, 351–59, 424–30, 512–16, 563–66. 1887–88.

Macdonald, W. B., of Rammerscales. Ten Scottish Songs rendered into German by ——. Scottish and German. Edinburgh, 1854. [See note, V, 303 f.]

MacFarren, G. A. See Oxenford, John.

M'Gregor, Sir James. See Lismore.

Machado y Álvarez, Antonio. Folk-lore español. Biblioteca de las tradiciones populares españolas. Sevilla, [1883-]86. 11 vols. (Vols. I–IV entitled, Folk-lore.)

Machyn, Henry. The Diary of Henry Machyn, citizen and merchant-taylor of London, from A. D. 1550 to A. D. 1563. Edited by John Gough Nichols. London, 1848. (Camden society, 42.)

MacInnes, Donald. Folk and Hero Tales. Collected, edited, and translated by the Rev. D. MacInnes. With notes by the editor and Alfred Nutt. London, 1890. (Waifs and Strays of Celtic tradition, Argyllshire Series, 2.)

MacInnes, Donald. *The Same.* London, 1890. (Folk-Lore Society, Publications, 25.)

Mackay, Æ. J. G. See Dunbar, William.

Mackay, Charles. Songs of Scotland. The Book of Scottish Songs. London, [1857].

Mackenzie, Sir George. The Science of Herauldry treated as a part of the Civil Law and Law of Nations. Edinburgh, 1680.

[Mackenzie, William?] Historical and traditional Tales in Prose and Verse, connected with the South of Scotland. Original and select. Kirkcudbright, 1843.

M'Lauchlan, T. See Lismore.

Macmillan's Magazine. Edited by D. Masson (Sir G. Grove, John Morley). Cambridge, 1859–.

Macpherson, D. See Wyntown, Andrew.

MacRitchie, David. Ancient and Modern Britons: a retrospect. London, 1884. 2 vols.

—— The Finn-Men of Great Britain. *In* The Archæological Review, IV, 1–26, 107–129. 1889.

—— British Dwarfs. *Ib.*, 184–207.

Mactaggart, John. The Scottish Gallovidian Encyclopedia, or, the original, antiquated, and natural curiosities of the South of Scotland. London, 1824.

Madden, Sir Frederic. Syr Gawayne. A Collection of Ancient Romance-poems, by Scotish and English authors, relating to that celebrated knight of the Round Table, with an introduction, notes, and a glossary. London, 1839. (Bannatyne Club, 64.)

—— See Gesta Romanorum.

—— See Laȝamons Brut.

Madsen, Jens. Folkeminder fra Hanved Sogn ved Flensborg. Kjøbenhavn, 1870.

Mätzner, Eduard. Altenglische Sprachproben nebst einem Wörterbuche, unter Mitwirkung von Karl Goldbeck. Berlin, 1867–.

Magazin für die Literatur des Auslands. Berlin, 1832–78; Leipzig, 1879–80. Das Magazin für die Literatur des In- und Auslands. Leipzig, 1881–87; Dresden, 1888–90. Das Magazin für Litteratur. Berlin, 1891–. (Begründet von Joseph Lehmann. Herausg. von E. Engel; F. Hirsch, and others.)

Le Magasin Pittoresque, publié, depuis sa fondation, sous la direction de M. Édouard Charton. Paris, 1833–76. 44 ann.

Maginn, William. Chevy Chase . . . idem Latine redditum. *In* Blackwood's Edinburgh Magazine, VI, 199–201; VII, 323–29. 1820.

Magus saga Jarls. See Cederschiöld, Fornsögur Suðrlanda.

Magnússon, Eiríkr. See Árnason, Jón.

Mahā-bhārata. Cited by book, chapter, and verse of the edition published at Bombay by the Gana patakṛṣṇājī Press, Çaka era 1799 (= A. D. 1877–78).

—— See Arnold, Edwin.

[Maidment, James.] A Book of Scotish Pasquils. 1568–1715. Edinburgh, 1868.

—— See D'Avenant, Sir William.

Mailáth, János Nepomuk, Graf. See Koloczaer Codex.

Maitland, J. A. Fuller. See Broadwood, Lucy E.

Maitland, Richard. The Poems of Sir Richard Maitland of Lethingtoun, Knight. With an appendix of selections from the poems of Sir John Maitland Lord Thirlestane,

and of Thomas Maitland. [Edited by Joseph Bain.] Glasgow, 1830. (Maitland Club.)

Major (*or* Mair), John. Historia Maioris Britanniae, tam Anglię ꝗ Scotię, per Ioannē Maiorem, nomine quidem Scotum, professione autem Theologum, e veterum monumentis concinnata. [Paris,] 1521.

Mallet, Paul Henri. Histoire de Dannemarc. Troisième édition, revue, corrigée et considérablement augmentée. Genève, 1787–88. 9 vols.

—— See Northern Antiquities.

Malleus Maleficarum, maleficas et earum haeresin framea conterens, ex variis auctoribus compilatus. Lugduni. 1620. 3 vols.

Malory, Sir Thomas. [La Morte Darthur.] The Byrth, Lyf, and Actes of Kyng Arthur, [etc.]. With an introduction and notes, by Robert Southey, Esq. Printed from Caxton's Edition, 1485. London, 1817. 2 vols.

—— La Mort d'Arthure. The history of King Arthur and of the knights of the Round Table. Compiled by Sir Thomas Malory, Knt. Edited from the text of the edition of 1634, with introduction and notes, by Thomas Wright. Second edition. London, 1865–66. 3 vols.

—— Le Morte Darthur by Syr Thomas Malory. The original edition of William Caxton now reprinted and edited with an introduction and glossary by H. Oskar Sommer. With an essay on Malory's prose style by Andrew Lang. London, 1889–91. 3 vols.

Malverne, Johannes. A continuation of the Polychronicon. *In* Polychronicon Ranulphi Higden Monachi Cestrensis. Edited by Joseph Rawson Lumby, Vol. IX. London, 1886. (Rolls Series.)

Mandeville, Sir John. The Voiage and Travaile of Sir John Maundevile, Kt. Which Treateth of the Way to Hierusalem; and of marvayles of Inde, With other Ilands and Countryes. Now publish'd entire from an Original MS. in the Cotton Library. London, 1725.

Marchant, Jehan le. See Le Marchant.

Mango, Fr. Poesie popolare infantile in Calabria. *In* Archivio per lo studio delle tradizioni popolari, I, 234–42, 389–96. 1882.

Mannhardt, Wilhelm. Mythologische Forschungen aus dem Nachlasse von Wilhelm Mannhardt. Herausgegeben von Hermann Patzig, mit Vorreden von Karl Müllenhoff und Wilhelm Scherer. Strassburg and London, 1884. (Quellen und Forschungen zur Sprach- und Culturgeschichte der germanischen Völker, 51.)

—— Wald- und Feldkulte. Berlin, 1875–77. 2 pts.

—— See Zeitschrift für deutsche Mythologie.

Manni, Domenico Maria. Istoria del Decamerone di Giovanni Boccaccio. Firenze, 1742.

Mannyng, Robert (of Brunne). See Langtoft, Pierre de.

Mapes, Walter. De Nugis Curialium distinctiones quinque. Edited from the unique manuscript in the Bodleian Library at Oxford, by Thomas Wright. London, 1850. (Camden Society, 50.)

Marbach, Gotthard Oswald. See Volksbücher.

Marées, Adolph von. Alt-englische und schottische Dichtungen der Percyschen Sammlung, übersetzt von ——. Berlin, 1857.

Marelle, Charles. Contes et chantes populaires françaises. *In* Archiv für das Studium der neueren Sprachen, LVI, 187–220, 281–310. 1876.

Marie de France, Die Lais der. Herausgegeben von Karl Warnke. Mit vergleichenden Anmerkungen von Reinhold Köhler. Halle, 1885. (Suchier, Bibliotheca Normannica.)

Marie de France, Poésies de. Publiées d'après les manuscrits de France et d'Angleterre, . . . par B. de Roquefort. Paris, 1820. 2 vols.

Marienlegenden. [Edited by Franz Pfeiffer.] Stuttgart, 1846.

Marineo, Lucio. Obra compuesta por Lucio Marineo Siculo Coronista de sus Majestades de las cosas memorables de España. Alcalá de Henares, 1539.

Markham, Clements R. Narratives of the Rites and Laws of the Incas. Translated from the original Spanish manuscripts, and edited, with Notes and an Introduction. London, 1873. (Hakluyt Society.)

—— See Hawkins' Voyages, The.

Marshall, Rev. William. Historic Scenes in Perthshire. Edinburgh, 1879. [See IV, 359.]

Martin, C. T. See Gaimar.

Martinengo-Cesaresco, Evelyn. Essays in the Study of Folk-Songs. London, 1886.

Mason, M. H. Nursery Rhymes and Country Songs, both tunes and words from tradition. With illustrations by Miss E. M. S. Scannell. Collected and arranged by ——. London, 1877.

Maspons y Labrós, Francisco. Lo Rondallayre. Quentos populars catalans, coleccionats per ——. 1ª, 2ª, 3ª série. Barcelona, 1871, '72, '74.

Massinger, Philip. Plays. With notes critical and explanatory by William Gifford. 2d ed. London, 1813. 4 vols.

Massmann, Hans Ferdinand. Denkmäler deutscher Sprache und Literatur aus Handschriften des 8ten bis 16ten Jahrhunderts. München, etc., 1828.

—— Deutsche Gedichte des zwölften Jahrhunderts und der nächstverwandten Zeit. Herausgegeben von H. F. Massmann. Quedlinburg and Leipzig, 1837. 2 pts. (Bibliothek der gesammten deutschen National-Literatur, Bd III, Th. i, ii.)

—— See Kaiserchronik.

Masson, David. See (The) Register of the Privy Council of Scotland.

Matthäi, C. F. von. See Syntipas.

Matthew Paris. See Paris, Matthew.

Maurer, Konrad [von]. Isländische Volkssagen der Gegenwart. Leipzig, 1860.

—— See Die Gull-Þóris Saga.

Mayer, C. J. See Cabinet des Fées.

Mazzatinti, Giuseppe. Storie popolari umbre. In Giornale di Filologia Romanza, IV, 63–72. 1882.

Medicus, Oberst. Badische Volkssagen. In Mone's Anzeiger, III, 87–93, 145–49, 255–60, 363–67. 1834.

Meier, Ernst. Deutsche Sagen, Sitten und Gebräuche aus Schwaben. Stuttgart, 1852. 2 pts.

—— Deutsche Volksmärchen aus Schwaben. Aus dem Munde des Volks gesammelt. Stuttgart, 1852.

Meisner, H. See Ein niederrheinischer Bericht, u. s. w.

Melander, Otho (Dionysius Melander). Iocorum atque Seriorum, tum novorum, tum selectorum, atque imprimis memorabilium centuriae aliquot. Francofurti, 1617.

Meltzl von Lomnitz, Hugo. See Acta Comparationis.

Mélusine. Recueil de Mythologie, Littérature populaire, Traditions et Usages. Publié par H. Gaidoz et E. Rolland (par H. Gaidoz). Paris, 1878–.

Mélusine. Geschichte von der edlen und schönen Melusina, welche ein Meerwunder und des Königes Helmas Tochter war. Leipzig, 1838. (Marbach, Volksbücher, 3.)

Mélusine. Mellusine: poème relatif a cette fée poitevine composé dans le quatorzième siècle par Couldrette, publié pour la première fois d'après les manuscrits de la Bibliothèque Impériale par Francisque Michel. Niort, 1854.

—— Mélusine, par Jehan d'Arras. Nouvelle édition, conforme à celle de 1478, revue et corrigée avec une préface par M. Ch. Brunet. Paris, 1854. (Bibliothèque Elzévirienne.)

—— The Romans of Partenay, or of Lusignen: otherwise known as the Tale of Melusine. Translated from the French of La Coudrette (about 1500–1520 A. D.). Edited from a unique manuscript in the Library of Trinity College, Cambridge, by the Rev. Walter W. Skeat. London, 1866. (Early English Text Society, 22.)

Mémoires de la Cour d'Espagne. La Haye, 1691. [See V, 34.]

Menghini, M. Canzoni popolari romane. In Sabatini, F., Il Volgo di Roma, 1890, I, 75 ff.

Mennes, Sir John. See Wit and Drollery.

—— See Facetiae.

Mennung, Albert. Der Bel Inconnu des Renaut de Beaujeu in seinem Verhältnis zum Lybeaus Disconus, Carduino und Wigalois. Eine litterar-historische Studie. Halle, 1890.

Mensa Philosophica. In hoc Opusculo tractatur de his quibus vtimur in mensa. De naturis rerum videlicet cibi et potus. De questionibus mensalibus varijs ac iocundis quibus in mensa recreamur. deq3 conditionibus eorum quibus in mensa conuersamur phylosophice hilariterq3 procedit. quare merito appellatur. Mensa Philosophica. Colonie, [c. 1500].

Menu, Henri. See Carnoy, Henry.

Menzel, Wolfgang. Odin. In his Zur Deutschen Mythologie, I. Stuttgart, 1855.

Méon, Dominique Martin. Nouveau recueil de fabliaux et contes inédits, des poètes français des XIIᵉ, XIIIᵉ, XIVᵉ et XVᵉ siècles. Paris, 1823. 2 vols.

—— See Barbazan, Étienne de.

Méril, du. See du Méril.

Merkel, R. See Apollonius.

Merlin; or, the early History of King Arthur: a prose romance (about 1450–1460 A. D.). Edited from the unique MS. in the University Library, Cambridge, by Henry B. Wheatley. With an introduction by D. W. Nash. London, 1865–66–69. 3 pts. (Early English Text Society, 10, 21, 36.)

—— See Arthour and Merlin.

Messire Gauvain, ou la Vengeance de Raguidel: poème de la Table Ronde par le trouvère Raoul, publié et precédé d'une introduction par C. Hippeau. Paris, 1862.

Meung, Jean de. See Rose, Roman de la.

Meyer, Gustav. Albanische Märchen, übersetzt von ——, mit Anmerkungen von Reinhold Köhler. In Archiv für Litteraturgeschichte, XII, 92–148. 1884.

Meyer, Kuno. See Zeitschrift für celtische Philologie.

Meyer, Nicolaus, and Mooyer, Ernst Friedrich. Altdeutsche Dichtungen. Aus der Handschrift herausgegeben. Quedlinburg and Leipzig, 1833.

Meyer, Paul. Alexandre le Grand dans la littérature française du moyen âge. Paris, 1886. 2 vols. (Bibliothèque Française du Moyen Age, 4, 5.)

Meyer, Paul. [Review of] Comparetti, Saggi dei dialetti greci dell' Italia meridionale, 1866. *In* Revue Critique, 1866, II, 300–2.

—— See Romania.

Meyer von Knonau. See White Book.

Meyrac, Albert. Traditions, coutumes, légendes et contes des Ardennes. Comparés avec les traditions, légendes et contes de divers pays. (Préface par M. P. Sébillot.) Charleville, 1890.

Michaud, Joseph. Histoire des Croisades. Quatrième édition, revue, corrigée et augmentée. Paris, 1825–29. 6 vols.

Michel, Francisque. Chroniques Anglo-Normandes. Recueil d'extraits et d'écrits relatifs à l'histoire de Normandie et d'Angleterre pendant les XIᵉ et XIIᵉ siècles; publié, pour la première fois, d'après les manuscrits de Londres, de Cambridge, de Douai, de Bruxelles et de Paris. Rouen, 1836–40. 3 vols.

—— Les Chroniques de Normandie, publ. pour la première fois d'après deux manuscrits de la Bibliothèque du Roi, à Paris, par ——. Rouen, 1839.

—— Histoire des ducs de Normandie et des rois d'Angleterre, publiée en entier, pour la première fois, d'après deux manuscrits de la Bibliothèque du Roi; suivie de la relation du Tournoi de Ham, par Sarrazin, trouvère du XIIIᵉ siècle, et précédée d'une introduction. Paris, 1840. (Société de l'histoire de France.)

—— Horn et Rimenhild. Recueil de ce qui reste des poèmes relatifs a leurs aventures composés en françois, en anglois et en écossois dans les treizième, quatorzième, quinzième et seizième siècles. Publié d'après les manuscrits de Londres, de Cambridge, d'Oxford et d'Edinburgh. Paris, 1845. (Bannatyne Club. Publ., 85.)

—— Hugues de Lincoln. Recueil de ballades anglo-normande et écossoises relatives au meurtre de cet enfant par les Juifs en MCCLV. Publié avec une introduction et des notes. Paris, 1834.

—— See Charlemagne.

—— See Comte de Poitiers, Roman du.

—— See Eustache le Moine.

—— See Gibert de Montreuil.

—— See Mélusine.

—— See Monmerqué, Louis Jean Nicolas.

—— See Renaut.

—— See Tristan.

—— See Violette, Roman de la.

Michelant, Henri. See Alexander the Great.

—— See Guillaume de Palerne.

Mickiewicz, Adam. Dzieła. Wydanie zupełne przez dzieci autora dokonane. [Works. Complete edition, edited by the author's children.] Paris, 1880. 6 vols.

Migne, Jacques Paul. Patrologiae Cursus Completus, seu Bibliotheca Universalis . . . omnium SS. Patrum, [etc.]. Parisiis, 1844–64. 221 vols.

—— See Douhet, Jules, comte de.

Mijatovies, Madam Csedomille. Serbian Folk-Lore. Popular Tales selected and translated. Edited, with an introduction, by the Rev. W. Denton. London, 1874.

Miklosich, Franz. Märchen und Lieder der Zigeuner der Bukowina. *In* Ueber die Mundarten und die Wanderungen der Zigeuner Europa's, pt IV–V. Wien, 1874.

—— Ueber die Mundarten und die Wanderungen der Zigeuner Europa's. Wien, 1872–80. 12 pts. in 4 vols. (Separatdruck aus dem 21(–23, 25–27, 30–31) Bande der

Denkschriften der Philosophisch-historischen Classe der Kaiserlichen Akademie der Wissenschaften.)

Mikulićić, F. Narodne pripovietke i pjesme iz hravtskoga primorja. [Popular Tales and Songs from the Croatian Littoral.] Porte Rè, 1876.

Milá y Fontanals, Manuel. Observaciones sobre la poesia popular, con muestras de romances catalanes inéditos. Barcelona, 1853.

—— Romancerillo catalan : canciones tradicionales. Segunda edicion, refundida y aumentada. Barcelona, 1882.

Milenowsky, J. Volks-Märchen aus Böhmen. Breslau, 1853.

Les Mille et Un Jours. Contes persans, traduits en français par Pétis de Lacroix, suivis de plusieurs autres recueils de contes traduits des langues orientales. Nouvelle édition, accompagnée de notes et de notices historiques par A. Loiseleur-Deslongchamps; publiée sous la direction de M. L. Aimé-Martin. Paris, 1840. (Panthéon Littéraire. Littérature Orientale. Romans.)

Milne, [Adam]. A Description of the Parish of Melrose. Edinburgh, 1743. [See III, 306 a, note.]

Miracles de Notre-Dame de Chartres. See Le Marchant, Jehan.

Miracles de Nostre Dame par Personnages. See Paris, Gaston.

The Mirror of Literature, Amusement, and Instruction, vols I–XXXVIII. London, 1823–41. New Series, I–VIII, 1842–45. [See III, 45 a.]

Miscelánea Folk-Lórica por los Srs. Almirall, Arabia, Bosch de la Trinxeria, Brú, Cortils y Vieta, Gomis, Maspons y Labrós, Roca y Cusi, Segura (Pbre.) y Vidal de Valenciano (G.). Barcelona, 1887. (Associació d'Excursions Catalana. Folk-Lore Catalá, IV.)

Miscellanea Scotica. A collection of tracts relating to the History, Antiquities, Topography, and Literature of Scotland. Glasgow, 1818–19. 4 vols.

The Miscellany of the Spalding Club. [Edited by John Stuart.] Aberdeen, 1841–52. 5 vols.

Missale ad' usum insignis et praeclarae Ecclesiae Sarum. Burntisland and London, 1861–67. 2 pts.

Mistral, Frederi. Mirèio pouèmo prouvençau de ——; emé la traducioun literalo en regard. Paris, 1872.

Mitchell, George. The Ballad, Lizzie Lindsay, written from memory by George Mitchell, at Mrs. Dawson Rowley's request, 1891. Brighton, privately printed, 1895.

Mitchell, James. The Scotsman's Library; being a collection of anecdotes and facts illustrative of Scotland and Scotsmen. Edinburgh, Dublin, and London, 1825.

Mitscherlich, C. W. See Achilles Tatius.

Möbius, T. See Vigfússon, G.

Moe, Jørgen. See Asbjørnsen, Peter Christian.

Mogk, E. Mythologie. *In* H. Paul, Grundriss der germanischen Philologie, Strassburg, 1889–93, I, 982–1138.

—— See Gunnlaugssaga.

Mohl, Jules. See Firdusi.

Moir, James. See Henry the Minstrel.

Moisant de Brieux, [Jacques]. Origines de quelque coutumes anciennes et de plusieurs façons de parler triviales. Avec une introduction biographique et littéraire par M. E. de Beaurepaire, un commentaire et une table analytique par M. G. Garnier, et un portrait de l'auteur gravé par M. L. de Merval. Caen, 1874. 2 vols.

Moland, Louis. See La Fontaine.

—— and d'Héricault, Charles. Nouvelles françoises en

prose du XIII⁰ siècle. Publiées d'après les manuscrits avec une introduction et des notes. Paris, 1856. (Bibliothèque Elzévirienne.)

Moltzer, H. E. See Floire et Blanceflor.

Moncaut, J. É. M. Cénac. Littérature populaire de la Gascogne. Contes, mystères, chansons historiques, satiriques, sentimentales, rondeaux, recueillis dans l'Astarac, le Pardiac, le Béarn, et le Bigorre. Paris, 1868. See Cénac.

Mone, Franz Joseph. Räthselsammlung. *In* Mone's Anzeiger, VII, 32–50, 258–68, 371–84. 1838.

—— Zweite Räthselsammlung. *Ib.*, VIII, 217–29, 315–26. 1839.

—— Uebersicht der niederländischen Volks - Literatur älterer Zeit. Tübingen, 1838.

Mone's Anzeiger. Anzeiger für Kunde des deutschen Mittelalters (der teutschen Vorzeit). Nürnberg, 1832–34 ; Karlsruhe, 1835–39. (1, 2, H. v. Aufsess ; 3, Aufsess u. Mone ; 4–8, Franz Joseph Mone.)

Monmerqué, Louis Jean Nicolas. See Renaut.

—— and Michel, Francisque. Théâtre français au moyen âge. Publié d'après les manuscrits de la Bibliothèque du Roi. Paris, 1842.

Monseur, Eugène. Contes. L'os qui chante. *In* Bulletin de Folklore. Organe de la Société du Folklore Wallon, I, 39–51, 89–149 ; II, 219–41, 245–51. 1891–95.

Mont, Pol de. De Sage van Lenore. *In* Volkskunde, II, 129–35. 1889.

—— See Gittée, Aug.

—— See Volkskunde.

Montaiglon, Anatole de, and Raynaud, Gaston. Recueil général et complet des fabliaux des XIII⁰ et XIV⁰ siècles imprimés ou inédits. Publiés d'après les manuscrits. (Tom. I, par M. A. de Montaiglon ; tom. II–VI, par MM. A. de Montaiglon et Gaston Raynaud.) Paris, 1872–90. 6 vols.

—— See Herbert.

—— See Jehan de Paris.

Monteiro, Henriqueta. See Pedroso, Consiglieri.

Montel, A., and Lambert, L. Chants populaires du Languedoc. *In* Revue des Langues Romanes, VI, 476–555 ; VII, 236–312 ; IX, 138–92, 317–44 ; X, 169–188, 281–302 ; XI, 73–87 ; XII, 14–29, 235–67 ; XIV, 73–92. 1874–78.

Montgomerie, Alexander. Poems. Edited by James Cranstoun. Edinburgh and London, 1887 [1886–87]. (Scottish Text Society.)

The Monthly Chronicle of North-Country Lore and Legend. Newcastle-on-Tyne and London, 1887–91.

The Monthly Magazine and British Register. London, 1796–1826.

Mooyer, E. F. See Meyer, Nicolaus.

Moraes, Francisco de. See Palmerin of England.

More, Sir Thomas. Utopia. Originally printed in Latin, 1516. Translated into English by Ralph Robinson. His second and revised edition, 1556 : preceded by the title and epistle of his first edition, 1551. Carefully edited by Edward Arber. London, 1869. (Arber, English Reprints, 14.)

Morel-Fatio, A. See Sanchez, Climente.

Morlini, Girolamo. Hieronymi Morlini Parthenopei Novellae, Fabulae, Comoedia. Editio tertia, emendata et aucta. Lutetiae Parisiorum, 1855. (Bibliothèque Elzévirienne.)

Morosi, Giuseppe. Studi sui dialetti greci della terra d'Otranto. Preceduta da una raccolta di canti, leggende, proverbi e indovinelli nei dialetti medisimi. Lecce, 1870.

Morris, Mowbray. Claverhouse. London, 1887. (English Worthies. Edited by Andrew Lang.)

Morris, Richard. See Cursor Mundi.

—— See Chaucer, Geoffrey.

Le Morte Arthur. Edited from the Harleian MS. 2252 by F. J. Furnivall. London and Cambridge, 1864.

Morte Darthur. See Malory, Sir Thomas.

Moyen de parvenir, Le. See Verville, F. B. de.

Moysie, David. Memoirs of the Affairs of Scotland. By ——. M.D.LXXVII. – M.DC.III. From early manuscripts. [Edited by James Dennistoun.] (Edinburgh, 1830. (Maitland Club, 3.)

Müllenhoff, Karl. Sagen, Märchen und Lieder der Herzogthümer Schleswig-Holstein und Lauenburg. Kiel, 1845.

—— See Laurin.

—— See Zeitschrift für deutsches Alterthum.

—— and Scherer, Wilhelm. Denkmäler deutscher Poesie und Prosa aus dem VIII–XII Jahrhundert. Berlin, 1864. 2ᵗᵉ Ausg. Berlin, 1873.

Müller, C. See Callisthenes.

Müller, Friedrich. Siebenbürgische Sagen. Gesammelt und mitgetheilt von ——. Kronstadt, 1857.

—— Siebenbürgische Sagen. Gesammelt und herausgeben von ——. Zweite veränderte Auflage. Wien, 1885. (Siebenbürgisch-deutsche Volks-Bücher, 1.)

Müller, Peter Erasmus. Sagabibliothek, med Anmærkninger og indledende Afhandlinger. Kiøbenhavn, 1817–20. 3 vols.

—— See Saxo Grammaticus.

Müller, Wilhelm. Zur Symbolik der deutschen Volkssage. *In* G. Schambach und W. Müller, Niedersächsische Sagen und Märchen, pp. 373–424. Göttingen, 1855.

—— Egeria. See Wolff, O. L. B.

Mündel, Curt. See Stöber, August.

Münsterische Geschichten. Sagen und Legenden, nebst einem Anhange von Volksliedern und Sprüchwörtern. Münster, 1825.

[Muir, Rev. Dr John ?] Mill o' Tifty's Annie, a Buchan Ballad, with Introduction, etc. Peterhead, 1872. [See IV, 301.]

Munch, J. S. See Saga.

Muncker, F. See Joufrois.

Munday, Anthony. The Downfall of Robert Earl of Huntington. *In* Five Old Plays, forming a Supplement to the Collections of Dodsley and others. Edited by J. Payne Collier. London, 1833.

—— See Palmerin of England.

—— and Chettle, Henry. The Death of Robert Earl of Huntington. *In* Five Old Plays, forming a supplement to the Collections of Dodsley and others. Edited by J. Payne Collier. London, 1833.

Munich Academy. Sitzungsberichte der königl. bayer. Akademie der Wissenschaften. München, 1860–.

Munthe, Åke W:son. Folkpoesi från Asturien. *In* Upsala Universitets Årsskrift 1887, '91. Språkvetenskapliga Sällskapets i Upsala Förhandlingar, 1885–88, pp. 105–26 ; 1888–91, pp. 1–32. Upsala, 1888, '91.

Muratori, Lodovico Antonio. Rerum Italicarum Scriptores ab anno aerae Christianae quingentesimo ad millesimumquingentesimum. Mediolani, 1723–51. 25 vols. Ab anno M ad annum MDC. Florentiae, 2 vols. 1748–70.

Murner, Thomas. Dr. Thomas Murners Ulenspiegel. Herausgegeben von J. M. Lappenberg. Leipzig, 1854.

Murray, James Augustus Henry. The Dialect of the Southern Counties of Scotland: its pronunciation, grammar, and historical relations. With an appendix and a linguistical map of Scotland. London, 1873. (Philological Society.)

Murray, James Augustus Henry. See Complaynt of Scotland.

—— See Thomas of Erceldoune.

Murray, John. Handbook for Travellers in Scotland. London, etc., 1868.

Musarum Deliciae. See Facetiae.

Musenalmanach. Göttingen, 1771–95.

Musical Museum. See (The) Scots Musical Museum.

Mussafia, Adolf. Altfranzösische Gedichte aus venezianischen Handschriften. Wien, 1864.

—— Studien zu den mittelalterlichen Marienlegenden. In Vienna Akad., Phil.-hist. Classe, Sitzungsberichte, CXIII, 917–94; CXV, 5–92. 1886–87.

—— Sulla leggenda del legno della Croce. In Wiener Akad., Sitzungsberichte, Phil.-hist. Classe, LXIII, 165–216. 1869.

—— See Macaire.

—— See Prise de Pampelune.

Mylne, Robert. Ane Catalogue of the Books, Manuscripts and Pamphlets belonging to Robert Mylne, Wryter in Ed^r, 1709. [Advocates Library.]

The Myvyrian Archaiology of Wales, collected out of Ancient Manuscripts. [Edited by Owen Jones, Edward Williams, and William Owen Pughe.] London, 1801–07. 3 vols.

Nairne, Carolina Oliphant, Baroness. Life and Songs of the Baroness Nairne, with a Memoir and Poems of Caroline Oliphant, the younger. Edited by the Rev. Charles Rogers. With a portrait and other illustrations. Third edition, enlarged. London, 1872.

Nakhshabî. See Tuti-Nameh.

Nannucci, Vincenzio. Manuale della letteratura del primo secolo della lingua italiana. Firenze, 1837–39. 3 vols.

Napier, James. Old Ballad Folk-Lore. In The Folk-Lore Record, II, 92–126. 1879.

Napier, Mark. Memorials and Letters illustrative of the life and times of John Graham of Claverhouse, Viscount of Dundee. Edinburgh, 1859–62. 3 vols.

—— Montrose and the Covenanters, their characters and conduct, illustrated from private letters and other original documents hitherto unpublished, embracing the time of Charles the First, from the rise of the troubles in Scotland, to the death of Montrose. London, 1838. 2 vols.

Nardo-Cibele, Angela. Canti ed orazioni bellunesi. In Archivio per lo studio delle tradizioni popolari, XIV, 209–17, 345–49. 1895.

Nashe, Thomas. Strange Newes of the Intercepting certaine Letters. In vol. II of his Complete Works, ed. by Alexander B. Grosart. London, 1883–85. 6 vols. (The Huth Library.)

Nasr-Eddin Hodja. Les Plaisanteries de Nasr-Eddin Hodja. Traduites du turc par J. A. Decourdemanche. Paris, 1876. (Bibliothèque Orientale Elzévirienne, 5.)

Naṭêśa Sâstrî [Naṭeça Çāstrī]. Folklore in Southern India. By Paṇḍit S. M. Naṭêśa Sâstrî. Bombay, 1884, '86, '88. 3 pts.

—— See Kingscote, G.

Naumann, Robert. See Serapeum.

Neckam, Alexander. Alexandri Neckam De Naturis Rerum libri duo. With the poem of the same author, De

Laudibus Divinae Sapientiae. Edited by Thomas Wright. London, 1863. (Rolls Series.)

Neh Manzer, ou Les Neuf Loges. Conte traduit du persan. Gênes, 1806.

Neocorus, pseudon. See Adolfi, Johann.

Νεοελληνικὰ ἀνάλεκτα περιοδικῶς ἐκδιδόμενα ὑπὸ τοῦ Φιλολογικοῦ Συλλόγου Παρνασσοῦ. Athens, 1871, '74–81. 2 vols.

Nerucci, Gherardo. Storie e cantari, ninne-nanne e indovinelle del Montale nel circondario di Pistoja. In Archivio per lo studio delle tradizioni popolari, II, 503–28; III, 39–56. 1883–84.

Nerval, Gérard de, pseud. for Gérard Labrunie. La Bohème Galante. Nouvelle édition. Paris, 1866.

Der Neuen Preussischen Provinzial-Blätter andere Folge. Im Namen der Alterthums-Gesellschaft Prussia herausgegeben von Dr. A. Hagen. Königsberg, 1852-57. 12 vols.

Neuhaus, Carl. See Adgar.

Neumann, K. F. See Gützlaff, K. F. A.

Neus, H. Ueber die Volkslieder der Esthen. In Dorpater Jahrbücher, V, 217–32. 1836.

The New British Songster, a Collection of Songs, Scots and English, with Toasts and Sentiments for the Bottle. Falkirk, 1785. [See note, I, 414.]

The New Statistical Account of Scotland. See Statistical Account of Scotland.

Newell, William Wells. See Journal of American Folk-Lore.

Das Nibelungenlied. Herausgegeben von Karl Bartsch. Zweite Auflage. Leipzig, 1869. (Franz Pfeiffer, Deutsche Classiker des Mittelalters, 3.)

Nichols, John. Illustrations of the Literary History of the Eighteenth Century. Consisting of Authentic Memoirs and Original Letters of Eminent Persons. (Vols VII, VIII by John Bowyer Nichols.) London, 1817-58. 8 vols.

—— Illustrations of the Manners and Expences of Antient Times in England, in the fifteenth, sixteenth, and seventeenth centuries, deduced from the accompts of churchwardens, and other authentic documents, collected from various parts of the kingdom. With explanatory notes, London, 1797.

—— See The Famous Victories, etc.

Nichols, John Gough. See Machyn, Henry.

Nicolas de Troyes. See Le Grand Parangon des Nouvelles Nouvelles.

Nicolas, Sir [Nicholas] Harris. The History of the Battle of Agincourt, and of the expedition of Henry the Fifth into France: to which is added, the Roll of the Men at Arms in the English Army. 2^d edition. London, 1832. 2 pts.

—— A History of the Royal Navy, from the earliest times to the wars of the French Revolution. London, 1847. 2 vols.

Nicolaysen, N. See Norsk Magasin.

Nicolovius, pseudon. for Nils Loven. Folklifwet i Skytts Härad i Skåne wid början af detta århundrade: Barndomsminnen. Utgifne af ——. Lund, 1847.

Nicolson, Joseph, and Burn, Richard. The History and Antiquities of the counties of Westmoreland and Cumberland. London, 1777. 2 vols.

Ein niederrheinischer Bericht über den Orient. [Ed. by] Röhricht und Meisner. In Zeitschrift für deutsche Philologie, XIX, 1-5. Halle, 1887.

Nigra, C. Il Moro Saracino, canzone popolare piemontese. In Romania, XIV, 231–73. 1885.

—— Versions piémontaises de la chanson populaire de Renaud. In Romania, XI, 391-98. 1882.

de Nino, Antonio. Saggio di canti popolari sabinesi illustrati da——. Rieti, 1869.

—— Usi abruzzesi, descritti da——. Vol. I. Usi e costumi abruzzesi descritti da——. Vols. II–V. Firenze, 1879–91. 5 vols.

Nisami (aus Gendsch). Die sieben Gestalten oder Schönheiten. *In* J. von Hammer-Purgstall, Geschichte der schönen Redekünste Persiens, 114–117. Wien, 1818.

Nivelle de la Chaussée, Pierre Claude. See La Chaussée.

Nordisk Tidskrift för Vetenskap, Konst och Industri. Utgifven af Letterstedtska Föreningen. . . . Stockholm, etc. 1878-.

Noreen, Adolf. See Visböcker.

[Norrenberg, P.] See Zurmühlen, Hans, *pseud.* Des Dülkener Fiedlers Liederbuch.

Norsk Magasin. Skrifter og Optegnelser angaaende Norge og forfattede efter Reformationen. Samlede og udgivne af N. Nicolaysen. Christiania, 1858–70. 3 vols.

Norske Universitets- og Skole-Annaler. Udgif. af C. A. Holmboe (and others). Christiania, 1834-.

Northern Antiquities, translated from the French of M. Mallet by Bishop Percy. New edition by I. A. Blackwell. London, 1847.

Nostradamus, Caesar de. L'Histoire et Chronique de Provence. Lyon, 1614.

Notes and Queries. London, 1850-.

Nottingham, Records of. See Stevenson, W. H.

Nouveaux contes à rire, et aventures plaisantes de ce tems, ou récréations françoises. Nouvelle édition augmentée et corrigée. Cologne, 1709.

Novelistas anteriores á Cervantes. *In* Biblioteca de Autores Españoles, III.

Nuremberg Chronicle = Chronicon Nurembergense. [Hartmann Schedel.] Liber chronicarum cu[m] figuris et ymagĭbus ab inicio mundi. Nuremberge, 1493.

Nutricati-Briganti, A. Trifone. Intorno ai canti e racconti popolari del Leccese. Wien (?), 1873.

Nutt, Alfred. The Finn-Men of Britain. *In* Archæological Review, IV, 232. 1889.

—— The Marriage of Sir Gawain and the Loathly Damsel. *In* The Academy, XLI, 425–26. 1892. Cf. Old Irish and the Spoken Language (by the same), XXXVI, 254–55. 1889.

—— See International Folk-Lore Congress.

—— See MacInnes, Donald.

Nyare Bidrag till Kännedom om de svenska Landsmålen ock svenskt Folklif. Tidskrift utgifven genom J. A. Lundell. Stockholm, 1879-.

Nyerup, Rasmus. Almindelig Morskabslæsning i Danmark og Norge igjennem Aarhundreder. Kjøbenhavn, 1816.

—— See Symbolae ad Literaturam Teutonicam.

Nyeste Skilderie af Kjøbenhavn. Kjøbenhavn, 1804–30.

Nyland. Samlingar utgifna af Nyländska Afdelningen. Helsingfors, 1884–89. 4 Häfter.

Nyrop, Kristoffer. Kludetræet. En sammenlignende Undersøgelse. *In* Dania, I, 1–32. København, 1890.

—— Navnets Magt. En folkepsykologisk Studie. København, 1887.

—— See Dania.

Occleve, Thomas. De Regimine Principum. A poem written in the reign of Henry IV. Edited for the first time by Thomas Wright. London, 1860. (Roxburghe Club, 79.)

Ochoa, Eugenio de. Tesoro de los romanceros y cancioneros españoles, históricos, caballerescos, moriscos y otros, recogidos y ordenados por——. Paris, 1838. (Coleccion de los Mejores Autores Españoles, 16.)

Octavian. Kaiser Octavianus. *In* Karl Simrock, Die deutschen Volksbücher, II, 241–424. Frankfurt a. M., 1845.

—— The Romance of Octavian, Emperor of Rome, abridged from a manuscript in the Bodleian Library. [By John Josias Conybeare.] Oxford, 1809.

—— The Romance of Octavian, Emperor of Rome. Abridged from a Manuscript in the Bodleian Library (circa 1250). By the Rev. J. J. Conybeare. And Edited with Additional Notes by E. M. Goldsmid. Edinburgh, 1882. (Aungervyle Society, I, 8, 9.)

—— Zwei mittelenglische Bearbeitungen der Sage, herausgegeben von Dr. Gregor Sarrazin. Heilbronn, 1885. (Altenglische Bibliothek, 3.)

O'Curry, Eugene. On the Manners and Customs of the Ancient Irish. A series of lectures delivered by the late ——. Edited, with an introduction, appendices, etc., by W. K. Sullivan. London, 1873. 3 vols.

Oehlenschläger, Adam Gottlob. Samlede Digte. Kiøbenhavn, 1823.

Oesterley, Hermann. See Gesta Romanorum.

—— See Goedeke, Karl.

—— See Kirchhof, Hans Wilhelm, Wendunmuth.

—— See Johannes de Alta Silva.

—— See Pauli, Johann.

Oesterreichische Wochenschrift für Wissenschaft, Kunst und öffentliches Leben. Vol. I. Wien, 1863.

Ogier de Danemarche. See Raimbert de Paris.

O'Grady, Standish H. Silva Gadelica (I–XXXI). A collection of tales in Irish, with extracts illustrating persons and places. Edited from MSS and translated. London, 1892. 2 vols.

O'Hanlon, John. Irish Folk-lore Mythology. *In* The Gentleman's Magazine and Historical Review, CCXIX, 281–91, 417–26, 564–76, 697–707. London, 1865.

—— See Lageniensis, *pseudon.*

Ohle, R. Shakespeares Cymbeline und seine romanischen Vorläufer. Berlin, 1890.

Olafs saga hins Helga. En kort Saga om Kong Olaf den Hellige fra anden Halvdeel af det tolfte Aarhundrede. Efter et gammelt Pergaments-Haandskrift i Universitets-Bibliotheket i Upsala, . . . udgivet af R. Keyser og C. R. Unger. Christiania, 1849.

Oliphant, C. O. See Nairne, Baroness.

Oliva. Historia de Enrique, fi de Oliva, rey de Jerusalen y emperador de Constantinopla. Sevilla, 1498.

—— Historia de Enrrique fi de Oliua rey de Iherusalem, emperador de Constantinopla. (Segun el ejemplar único de la Biblioteca Imperial de Viena.) [Edited by Pascual de Gayangos.] Madrid, 1871. (Sociedad de Bibliófilos Españoles, 8.)

Oluffson, Harald. Visbok. See Visböcker.

Once a Week. London, 1859–65. 13 vols. [Magazine.]

Orain, Adolphe. See Rolland, Eugène.

The Order of Combats for Life in Scotland. *In* The Miscellany of the Spalding Club, II, no xiv, pp. 381–90. Aberdeen, 1842. (Spalding Club, Publications, 6.)

Ordnance Survey of Scotland. Southampton, [1861–93].

Orelli, J. C. See Hesychius.

Orendel, ein deutsches Spielmannsgedicht. Mit Einleitung

und Anmerkungen herausgegeben von Arnold E. Berger. Bonn, 1888.

Orendel und Brîde, eine Rûne des deutschen Heidenthums, umgedichtet im zwölften Jahrhundert zu einem befreiten Jerusalem. Herausgegeben von Ludwig Ettmüller. Zürich, 1858.

Orfeo. Sir Orfeo, ein englisches Feenmärchen aus dem Mittelalter. Mit Einleitung und Anmerkungen herausgegeben von Dr. Oscar Zielke. Breslau, 1880.

Orient und Occident, insbesondere in ihren gegenseitigen Beziehungen. Forschungen und Mittheilungen. Eine Vierteljahrsschrift herausgegeben von Theodor Benfey. Göttingen, 1862–66. 3 vols.

Originals and Analoges of some of Chaucer's Canterbury Tales. Chaucer Society, London. 1872–92. 6 parts.

Orpheus de Lapidibus. In Ὀρφέως Ἅπαντα. Orphei Argonautica, Hymni, Libellus de Lapidibus, et Fragmenta. Cum notis H. Stephani et Andr. Christ. Eschenbachii. Textum ad codd. MSS. et editiones veteres recensuit. . . . Io. Matthias Gesnerus, curante Ge. Christo. Pp. 295–353. Lipsiae, 1764.

Ortnit und die Wolfdietriche, nach Müllenhoffs Vorarbeiten herausgegeben von Arthur Amelung und Oskar Jänicke. In Deutsches Heldenbuch, III, IV. Berlin, 1871–73. 2 vols.

Ortoli, J. B. Frédéric. Les contes populaires de l'île de Corse. Paris, 1883. (Les Littératures populaires de toutes les Nations, 16.)

Oswald. Sant Oswaldes Leben. Ein Gedicht aus dem zwölften Jahrhundert. Herausgegeben von Ludwig Ettmüller. Zürich, 1835.

Otterbourne, Thomas. Duo Rerum Anglicarum Scriptores Veteres, viz. Thomas Otterbourne et Johannes Whethamstede ab origine gentis Britannicae usque ad Edvardum IV. E Codicibus MSS. antiquis nunc primus eruit T. Hearnius. Oxonii, 1732. 2 vols.

Ouville, Antoine Le Metel, sieur d'. L'élite des Contes du sieur d'Ouville. Première partie. Augmenté en cette édition. Seconde partie. Dernière edition revûë et augmentée. Rouen, 1699. 2 pts.

—— L'élite des Contes du sieur d'Ouville. La Haye, 1703. 2 vols.

—— L'élite des Contes du sieur d'Ouville. Avec introduction et notes par P. Ristelhuber. Paris, 1876.

Ouvry, Frederic. See Howleglas.

Oxenford, John. Old English Ditties, selected from W. Chappell's Popular Music of the Olden Time; with a new introduction: the long ballads compressed and occasionally new words written by John Oxenford (vol. II, by J. O. and Nathalia Warren); the symphonies and accompaniments by G. A. MacFarren. London, n. d. 2 vols.

P. Fagot, pseudon. for Laroche, Pierre.

Painter, William. The first(–second) tome of the Palace of Pleasure, beautified, adorned, and well furnished with pleasant histories and excellent novels. Edited by Joseph Haslewood. London, 1813. 2 vols.

—— The Palace of Pleasure. Now again edited for the fourth time, by Joseph Jacobs. London, 1890. 3 vols.

The Paisley Magazine. Paisley, [1828].

Palanus. L'histoire de Palanus, comte de Lyon, mise en lumière, jouxte le manuscrit de la Bibliothèque de l'Arsenal, par Alfred de Terrebasse. Lyon, 1833.

The Palatine Anthology. See Halliwell-Phillipps, J. O.

Palgrave, Sir Francis. See (The) Parliamentary Writs.

Palmeirim de Inglaterra, Cronica de, 1ᵃ e 2ᵃ parte, por Francisco de Moraes. [Etc.] Lisboa, 1786. 3 vols.

Palmerin of England, by Francisco de Moraes. [Translated by A. Munday, corrected by Robert Southey.] London, 1807. 4 vols.

Palsgrave, John. L'Éclaircissement de la Langue Française par Jean Palsgrave, suivi de la Grammaire de Gilles du Guez, publiés pour la première fois en France par F. Génin. Paris, 1852. (Collection de documents inédits sur l'histoire de France.)

Panciatichi, Lorenzo. Cicalata decima in lode della Frittura. In Carlo Roberto Dati, Prose Fiorentine, raccolte dallo Smarrito Accademico della Crusca. Parte terza, Volume secondo, contenente cose giocose. Pp. 177–203. Firenze, 1741.

Πανδώρα. Σύγγραμμα περιοδικὸν ἐκδιδόμενον δὶς τοῦ μηνός. Σύντακται, Ἀ. Ρ. Ῥαγκαβῆς, Κ. Παπαρρηγόπουλος, Ν. Δραγούμης, κλ. Athens, [1850]–72. 22 vols.

Pantschatantra : fünf Bücher indischer Fabeln, Märchen und Erzählungen. Aus dem Sanskrit übersetzt, mit Einleitung und Anmerkungen, von Theodor Benfey. Leipzig, 1859. 2 pts.

Panzer, Friedrich. Bayerische Sagen und Bräuche. Beitrag zur deutschen Mythologie. München, 1848–55. 2 vols.

Pap, Gyula. Palóc Népköltemények. Sárospatak, 1865. [Palozische Volksdichtungen.]

Parcerisa, F. J. Recuerdos y bellezas de España. En laminas dibujadas del natural y litografiadas por ——, acompañadas de texto (por J. M. Quadrato, P. Piferrer y F. Pi y Margall, P. de Madrazo). Madrid, 1842–65. 10 vols.

Parcevals Saga. See Riddarasögur.

Paris, Gaston. Le Carmen de prodicione Guenonis et la légende de Roncevaux. In Romania, XI, 465–518. 1882.

—— La chanson du Pèlerinage de Charlemagne. In Romania, IX, 1–50. 1880.

—— Chants populaires du Piémont. In Journal des Savants, 1889, pp. 526–45, 611–621, 666–75.

—— La femme de Salomon. In Romania, X, 436–43 (cf. VII, 462). 1880.

—— Histoire poétique de Charlemagne. Paris, 1865.

—— Jakemon Sakesep, auteur du roman du Châtelain de Couci. In Histoire Littéraire de la France, XXVIII, 352–90. Paris, 1881.

—— Lais inédits de Tyolet, de Guingamor, de Doon, du Lecheor et de Tydorel. In Romania, VIII, 29–72. 1879.

—— Le roman du Châtelain de Couci. In Romania, VIII, 343–73 (= Hist. litt., XXVIII, 352–90). 1879.

—— La légende du Châtelain de Couci dans l'Inde. In Romania, XII, 359–63. 1883.

—— Versions inédites de la chanson de Jean Renaud. In Romania, XI, 97–108. 1882.

—— Nouvelles versions de la chanson de Renaud. In Romania, XII, 114–17. 1883.

—— Le Roman de la Geste de Monglane. In Romania, XII, 1–13. 1883.

—— Romans en vers du cycle de la Table Ronde. In Histoire Littéraire de la France, XXX, 1–270. Paris, 1888.

—— See Romania.

—— and Robert, Ulysse. Miracles de Nostre Dame par

Personnages. Publiés d'après le manuscrit de la Bibliothèque Nationale. Paris, 1876–93. 8 vols. (Société des Anciens Textes Français.)

Paris, Gaston, [and others]. Les transformations. *In* Revue des traditions populaires, I, 98–105. 1886.

Paris, Matthew. Matthaei Parisiensis, Monachi Sancti Albani, Chronica Majora. Edited by Henry Richards Luard. London, 1872–83. 7 vols. (Rolls Series.)

Parish, William Douglas, and Shaw, William Francis. A Dictionary of the Kentish Dialect and Provincialisms in use in the county of Kent. London, 1887. (English Dialect Society, Publications, Series C, 54.)

Park, T. See Facetiae.

The Parliamentary Writs and Writs of Military Summons, together with the Records and Muniments relating to the suit and service due and performed to the King's High Court of Parliament and the councils of the realm, or affording evidence of attendance given at parliaments and councils. Collected and edited by Sir Francis Palgrave. [London], 1827–34. 2 vols in 4. (Record Commission.)

Parrot, Henry. Laquei ridiculosi, or Springes for Woodcocks. London, 1613.

Partenay, The Romans of. See Mélusine.

Paston Letters. Original Letters, written during the reigns of Henry VI, Edward IV, and Richard III, by various persons of rank or consequence. Ed. by John Fenn. A new edition, by A. Ramsay. London, 1840–41. 2 vols.

—— 1422–1509 A. D. A new edition: containing upwards of four hundred letters, etc., hitherto unpublished. Edited by James Gairdner. London, 1872, '74, '75. 3 vols. (Edward Arber, Annotated Reprints.)

Paterson, James. See Hamilton, William.

[Paterson, James, and Gray, Charles.] The Ballads and Songs of Ayrshire, illustrated with sketches, historical, traditional, narrative, and biographical. Ayr, 1846.

Paton, W. R. Holy Names of the Eleusinian Priests. *In* International Folk-lore Congress, 1891. Papers and Transactions, pp. 202–14.

Patten, Robert. The History of the late Rebellion: with original papers, and the characters of the principal noblemen and gentlemen concern'd in it. The second edition, with large additions. London, 1717. The fourth edition, London, 1745.

Patten, William. The Expedition into Scotlāde. *In* J. G. Dalyell, Fragments of Scotish History, IV. Edinburgh, 1798.

Patzig, Hermann. Zur Geschichte der Herzmäre. (Wissenschaftliche Beilage zum Programm des Friedrichs-Gymnasiums zu Berlin. Ostern, 1891. Progr. No 54.) Berlin, 1891.

—— See Mannhardt, Wilhelm.

Paul, Hermann. Grundriss der germanischen Philologie. Strassburg, 1889–93. 2 vols.

—— and Braune, Wilhelm. Beiträge zur Geschichte der deutschen Sprache und Literatur. Herausgegeben von —— (von E. Sievers). Halle, 1874–.

Paul, J. B. See Registrum, etc.

Pauli, Johann. Schimpf und Ernst, von Johannes Pauli. Herausgegeben von Hermann Oesterley. Stuttgart, 1866. (Bibliothek des Litterarischen Vereins in Stuttgart, 85.)

Pauli, Reinhold. See Gower, John.

Paulus Diaconus. Pauli Warnefridi Diaconi Forojuliensis De Gestis Langobardorum. *In* J. P. Migne, Patrologiae Cursus Completus, XCV, cols 433–672. Parisiis, 1851.

Peacock, Mabel. The Name of Robin Hood. *In* The Academy, XXIV, 231. 1883.

Il Pecorone di ser Giovanni Fiorentino nel quale si contengono cinquanta novelle antiche belle d' invenzione e di stile. Milano, 1804. 2 tom.

Pedroso, Consiglieri. Portuguese Folk-Tales. Transl. by Henriqueta Monteiro. With an introduction by W. R. S. Ralston. London, 1882. (Folk-Lore Society, Publ., 9.)

Peele, George. Works. Collected and edited, with some account of his life and writings, by the Rev. Alexander Dyce. ... Second edition, with additions, in two volumes [and a supplement]. London, 1829–39. 3 vols.

Pegge, Samuel. An Alphabet of Kenticisms, Containing 600 Words and Phrases in a great measure peculiar to the Natives and Inhabitants of the County of Kent [etc.]. London, 1876. (English Dialect Society, Series C, 3.)

Peiper, R. See Ekkehardus.

Pelay Briz. See Briz.

Pellier, Alexis. See Llorente, Juan Antonio.

Pennant, Thomas. A Tour in Scotland: MDCCLXIX. London, 1772. Fourth ed., London, 1776. Part II, London, 1776.

Pepys, Samuel. Diary and Correspondence of ——, from his MS. cypher in the Pepysian Library, with a Life and Notes by Richard Lord Braybrooke. Deciphered, with additional notes, by Rev. Mynors Bright. London, 1875–79. 6 vols.

—— Edited by Henry B. Wheatley. London, 1893–96. 8 vols.

Perceforest. La tres elegante, Delicieuse, Mellifiue et tres playsante Histoire du tres Noble Victorieux et excellentissime Roy Perceforest, Roy de la grant Bretaigne, fundateur du franc Palais et du Temple du Souverain Dieu [etc.]. 1531–32. (Earlier ed., 1528.) 6 vols in 3.

—— La dilettevole historia del valorosiss. Parsaforesto Re della gran Bretagna: con i gran fatti del valente Gadiffero re di Scotia. ... Nuovamente traslato di francese in lingua italiana. Vinegia, 1558. 6 pts in 7 vols.

Perceval le Gallois, ou le Conte du Graal; publié par Ch. Potvin. 1ᵉ partie: le roman en prose, I. 2ᵉ partie: le poème de Chrestien de Troyes, et des ses continuateurs, II–VI. Mons, 1866–71. 6 vols. (Société des Bibliophiles Belges, 21.)

Perceval. The romance of Sir Perceval of Galles. *In* J. O. Halliwell, The Thornton Romances. London, 1844.

—— See Eschenbach, Wolfram von.

Percy MS. Bishop Percy's Folio Manuscript. Edited by John W. Hales and Frederick J. Furnivall. London, 1867–68. 4 vols.

Percy, Thomas (Bishop of Dromore). Reliques of Ancient English Poetry: consisting of Old Heroic Ballads, Songs, and other Pieces of our earlier Poets (chiefly of the Lyric kind), ... Together with some few of later Date. First ed., London, 1765. Second ed., London, 1767. Third ed., London, 1775. Fourth ed., London, 1794. 3 vols.

—— Reliques of Ancient English Poetry. Edited, with a general introduction, additional prefaces, notes, etc., by Henry B. Wheatley. London, 1876–77. 3 vols.

—— See Northern Antiquities.

Perdrizet, P. F., and Gaidoz, H. La mensuration du cou. *In* Mélusine, VI, 225–27. 1893.

Peringskiöld, J. See Wilkina Saga.

Periodičesko spisanie na bŭlgarskoto knižovno družestvo v Srědec. [Periodical Journal of the Bulgarian Literary Society.] Sophia, 1882-.

Perrault, Charles. Les contes des fées en prose et en vers de ——. Deuxième édition, revue et corrigée sur les éditions originales et précédée d'une lettre critique par Ch. Giraud. Lyon, 1865.

—— Les contes de ——. Contes en vers : Histoires ou contes du temps passé (Contes de ma mère Loye). Avec deux essais sur la Vie et les Œuvres de Perrault et sur la mythologie dans ses Contes, des notes et variantes et une notice bibliographique, par André Lefèvre. Paris, 1875.

Perthshire Antiquarian Miscellany. Perth, 1875. [See IV, 359.]

Pertz, Georg Heinrich. Monumenta Germaniae Historica inde ab anno Christi quingentesimo usque ad annum millesimum et quingentesimum, edidit —— (edidit Societas aperiendis Fontibus Rerum Germanicarum Medii Aevi). Hannoverae, 1872–96. 30 vols.

Peter, Anton. Volksthümliches aus Osterreichisch-Schlesien. Troppau, 1865–73. 3 vols.

Pétis de la Croix, François. Les Mille et un Jour, contes persans. Genève, 1787. (Cabinet des Fées, 14, 15.)

—— Les Mille et un Jours, contes persans, traduits en français par Pétis de Lacroix, suivis de plusieurs autres recueils de contes traduits des langues orientales. Nouv. éd., accompagnée de notes et de notices historiques par A. Loisleur-Deslongchamps ; publiée sous la direction de M. L. Aimé-Martin. Paris, 1840.

Petitot, Émile. Traditions indiennes du Canada nord-ouest. Paris, 1886. (Les litt. pop. de toutes les nations, 23.)

Pez, B. See Potho.

Pfannenschmid, H. Der mythische Gehalt der Tellsage. In Germania, X, 1–40. 1865.

Pfeiffer, Franz. Deutsche Mystiker des vierzehnten Jahrhunderts. Leipzig, 1845–57. 2 vols.

—— Marienlegenden. Stuttgart, 1846.

—— See Fritslar.

—— See Germania.

—— See Wirnt von Gravenberg.

Phelps, William Lyon. The Beginnings of the English Romantic Movement. Boston, 1893.

Phillips, Edward. The New World of Words : or, Universal English Dictionary [etc.]. Compiled by ——. The Seventh Edition, revised, corrected, and improved. By J. K., Philobibl. London, 1720.

Φιλολογικὸς Συνέκδημος. Σύγγραμμα περιοδικὸν ὑπὸ λογίων ἀνδρῶν συντασσόμενον. Athens, 1848–49.

Det Philologisk-historiske Samfunds Mindeskrift i Anledning af dets femogtyveaarige Virksomhed 1854–79. Kjøbenhavn, 1879.

Philostratus, Flavius. Τὰ ἐς τὸν Τυανέα Ἀπολλώνιον. In Flavii Philostrati Opera auctiora edidit C. L. Kayser, I, 1–344. Lipsiae, 1870.

Picken, Andrew. Traditionary Stories of old Families, and legendary illustrations of family history. With notes, historical and biographical. London, 1833. 2 vols.

Pidal, José. See Sanchez, T. A.

Pilpay. The Anvár-i Suhailí ; or, the Lights of Canopus ; being the Persian version of the Fables of Pilpay ; or, the book "Kalílah and Damnah," rendered into Persian by Husain Vá'iz U'l-Káshifí : literally translated into prose and verse, by Edward B. Eastwick. Hertford, 1854.

Pilpay. Les contes et fables indiennes de Bidpaï et de Lokman. Traduites d'Ali-Tchélébi-ben-Saleh, auteur turc. Ouvrage commencé par feu M. Galland, continué et fini par M. Cardonne. In Le Cabinet des Fées, XVII–XVIII, pp. 1–231. Genève, 1787.

—— The Fables of Pilpay. London, 1818.

Pindar. Πινδάρου Ὀλύμπια Νέμεα Πύθια Ἴσθμια. Pindari Olympia, Nemea, Pythia, Isthmia. Una cum Latina omnium versione carmine lyrico per Nicolaum Sudorium. Oxonii, 1697.

Pineau, Léon. La chanson de Renaud. Essai de littérature populaire comparée. In Revue des Traditions Populaires, XI, 66–82. 1896.

—— Le Folk-Lore du Poitou. Avec notes et index. Paris, 1892. (Collection de Contes et de Chansons Populaires, 18.)

—— See Georgeakis, G.

Pinkerton, John. Ancient Scotish Poems, never before in print. With large notes and a Glossary. Prefixed are an essay on the Origin of Scottish Poetry [etc.]. London, 1786. 2 vols.

—— A general Collection of the best and most interesting Voyages and Travels, in all parts of the World ; many of which are now first translated into English. Digested on a new plan. Vols I–VI, Philadelphia, 1810–12. Vols VII–XVII, London, 1811–14. 17 vols.

—— The History of Scotland from the accession of the House of Stuart to that of Mary. With appendixes of original papers. London, 1797. 2 vols.

—— Select Scotish Ballads. London, 1783. 2 vols.

Pio, Jean. Νεοελληνικὰ Παραμύθια, contes populaires grecs publiés d'après les manuscrits du Dr. J. G. de Hahn et annotés par ——. Copenhague, 1879.

Pistorius, Johann. Rerum Germanicarum Scriptores Aliquot insignes, . . . primum collectore Joanne Pistorio Nidano, tribus tomis, in lucem producti, nunc denuo recogniti, . . . editione tertia emendatiori et locupletiori ad usus publicos reducti, curante Burcardo Gotthelff. Struvio . . . Ratisbonae, 1726. 3 vols.

Pitcairn, Robert. Criminal Trials in Scotland, from A. D. M.CCCC.LXXXVIII to A. D. M.DC.XXIV, embracing the entire reigns of James IV. and V., Mary Queen of Scots, and James VI. Compiled from the original records and MSS., with historical notes and illustrations. Edinburgh, 1833. 3 vols. (Bannatyne Club, Publications, 42.)

Pitrè, Giuseppe. Biblioteca delle tradizioni popolari siciliane. Palermo, 1870–89. 18 vols.

—— Curiosità popolari trazidionali. Palermo ; Torino, Palermo, 1885–95. 14 vols.

—— Fiabe, novelle e racconti popolari siciliani. Raccolti ed illustrati da ——. Con discorso preliminare, grammatica del dialetto e delle parlate siciliane, saggio di novelline albanesi di Sicilia, e glossario. Palermo, 1875. 4 vols. (In his Biblioteca delle Tradizioni Popolari Siciliane, 4–7.)

—— Novelle popolari toscane. In Archivio per lo studio delle tradizioni popolari, I, 35–69, 183–205, 520–40 ; II, 157–72. 1882–83.

—— Saggi di critica letteraria. Palermo, 1871.

—— Studi di poesia popolare. Palermo, 1872.

—— See Archivio.

—— See Rivista di Letteratura Popolare.

Planudes. Vita Aesopi. In Alfred Eberhard, Fabulae Romanenses Graece conscriptae. I, 225–310. Lipsiae, 1872.

Platen, Graf von. Gesammelte Werke. Stuttgart and Tübingen, 1847. 5 vols.

Ploennies, Luise von. Reise-Erinnerungen aus Belgien. Berlin, 1845.

Ploennies, Maria von. Die Sagen Belgiens. Köln, 1846.

Ploennies, Wilhelm von. Zwei Odenwälder Märchen. *In* Zeitschrift für deutsche Mythologie, II, 373–84. 1855.

Plohl-Herdvigov, R. F. Hrvatske narodne pjesme i pripoviedke. [Croatian Popular Songs and Tales.] Warasdin, 1868.

Ploix, Charles. L'os qui chante. *In* Revue des Traditions populaires, VIII, 129–43. 1893.

Plot, Robert. The Natural History of Staffordshire. Oxford, 1686.

Plutarchus. Ἑπτὰ Σοφῶν συμποσίον. Septem Sapientum Convivium. *In* Plutarchi Chaeronensis quae supersunt omnia. Opera Joannis Georgii Hutten. VIII, 1–53. Tubingae, 1796.

Poggiali, Gaetano. See Bandello, Matteo.

Polidori, Filippo Luigi. See Tristan.

Polites, N. G. Τὸ δημοτικόν ᾆσμα περὶ τοῦ νεκροῦ ἀδελφοῦ. Ἀπόσπασμα ἐκ τοῦ Δελτίου τῆς Ἱστορικῆς καὶ Ἐθνολογικῆς Ἑταιρίας τῆς Ἑλλάδος. Athens, 1885.

Polo, Marco. The book of Ser Marco Polo, the Venetian, concerning the kingdoms and marvels of the East. Newly translated and edited, with notes, by Colonel Henry Yule. With maps and other illustrations. London, 1871. 2 vols.

Polychronicon. See Higden, Ralph.

Polydore Vergil. See Vergil, Polydore.

[Pontoppidan, Erik.] Everriculum Fermenti Veteris Seu Residuae in Danico Orbe cum Paganismi tum Papismi Reliqviae in apricum prolatae, Opusculum Restituendo suae, aliqva ex parte, integritati Christianismo Velificaturum. Hafniae, 1736.

Popov, A. V. Mongol'skaja christomatija. Kasan, 1836.

Popular Tales of Hindoostan. Story I. *In* Asiatic Journal, XI, 206–14. 1833.

Poquet, A. E. See Gautier de Coincy.

Porteous, ——. Extracts from a History of the Parishes of Monivaird and Strowan. *In* Archæologia Scotica, II, 65–75. 1822.

Portugaliae Monumenta Historica a saeculo octavo post Christum usque ad quintumdecimum; jussu Academiae Scientiarum Olisiponensis Edita. Olisipone, 1856–.

Potho. Pothonis Presbyteri et Monachi Prunveningensis Ord. S. Ben. Liber de miraculis Sanctae Dei Genetricis Mariae. *In* Ven. Agnetis Blannbekin, Quae sub Rudolpho Habspurgico et Alberto I. Austriacis Impp. Wiennae floruit, Vita et Revelationes Auctore Anonymo Ord. FF. Min. è Celebri Conv. S. Crucis Wiennensis, ejusdum Virg. Confess. Accessit Pothonis Presbyteri et Monachi celeberr. Monast. Prunveningensis, nunc Priflingensis, prope Ratisbonam, Ord. S. B. qui seculo Christi XII. claruit, Liber de Miraculis Sanctae Dei genitricis Mariae. Utrumque Opusculum ex MSS. Codd. primùm edidit R. P. Bernardus Pez, Benedictinus et Bibliothecarius Mellicensis. Viennae, 1731.

Potvin, Charles. See Perceval le Gallois.

Pouvillon, Émile. Nouvelles réalistes. Paris, 1878.

Powell, F. York. See Vigfússon, G.

Powell, George E. J., and Magnússon, Eiríkr. Icelandic Legends. Collected by Jón Arnason, translated by George E. J. Powell and Eiríkr Magnússon. London, 1864. Second Series. London, 1866.

Prace filologiczne, wydawane przez J. Baudouina de Courtenay, J. Karłowicza, A. A. Kryńskiego i L. Malinowskiego. Vols I–V. Warsaw, 1885–95. 5 vols.

Praetorius, Johann. Alectryomantia, seu Divinatio Magica cum Gallis Gallinaceis peracta, heîc secundùm varias suas species producta & unà cum curiositate, (cui obiter insperguntur multiplices motus, praestigiarum praetextus, cucuritio pullorum, gallinarumq; praesagitionum origo, ciconiarum latibulum hyemale, Fridericus Caesar, Longidormius, Pülsterus Sondershusanus, Blocksberga, Sagae portium, Pallio-vectura, &c.) diris debitis devota per M. Johannem Praetorium, P. L. C. Francofurti & Lipsiae, 1680.

Prato, Stanislas. Psyché. Références. *In* Bulletin de Folklore, Organe de la Société du Folklore Wallon, I, 316–35. 1892.

Pratt, John Burnett. Buchan. 3d ed. Aberdeen, 1870.

Price, Richard. See Warton, Thomas.

Price, Thomas, The Literary Remains of. Llandovery, 1854–55. 2 vols.

Prideaux, W. F. Anglo-Irish Ballads. *In* Notes and Queries, 6th Ser., XII, 223–25.

Primisser, A. See Hagen, F. H. von der.

La Prise de Pampelune: ein altfranzösisches Gedicht herausgegeben von Adolf Mussafia. Wien, 1864. (Altfranzösische Gedichte aus venezianischen Handschriften, I.)

Procopius. Procopii Cæsariensis V. I. Ἀνέκδοτα. Arcana Historia, qui est liber nonus Historiarum. Ex bibliotheca Vaticana Nicolaus Alemannus protulit, Latinè reddidit, notis illustravit. Nunc primùm in lucem prodit triplici indice locupletata. Lugduni, 1623.

Pröhle, Heinrich. Gottfried August Bürger. Sein Leben und seine Dichtungen. Leipzig, 1856.

—— Kinder- und Volksmärchen. Gesammelt von ——. Leipzig, 1853.

—— Märchen für die Jugend. Mit einer Abhandlung für Lehrer und Erzieher. Halle, 1854.

Propertius, Sextus. Sexti Aurelii Propertii Opera Omnia ex editione Ch. Th. Kuinoelis cum notis et interpretatione in usum Delphini. Londini, 1822. 2 vols.

Prutz, R. See Deutsches Museum.

Prym, Eugen, and Socin, Albert. Kurdische Sammlungen. Erzählungen und Lieder in den Dialekten des Ṭûr 'Abdîn und von Bohtan. Gesammelt, herausgegeben und übersetzt. St Petersburg, 1887–90. 2 pts.

—— Syrische Sagen und Märchen, aus dem Volksmunde gesammelt und übersetzt. Göttingen, 1881. *In their* Der neu-aramäische Dialekt des Ṭûr 'Abdîn. Zweiter Teil.

Przyjaciel ludu, czyli tygodnik potrzebnych i pożytecznych wiadomości. [Friend of the Peasantry, or, Weekly of Necessary and Useful Knowledge.] Leszno, 1834–39.

Pujades, Gerónimo. Crónica universal del Principado de Cataluña, escrita a principios del siglo XVII. Barcelona, 1829–32. 8 vols.

Puymaigre, Théodore, comte de. Les vieux auteurs castillans. Paris and Metz, 1861–62. 2 vols.

Pyramus und Thisbe. Herausgegeben von Moriz Haupt. *In* Zeitschrift für deutsches Alterthum, VI, 504–17. 1848.

Quadrilogus, the First. Vita et processus S. Thomae Cantuariensis super libertate ecclesiastica. *In* J. P. Migne, Patrologiae Cursus Completus, CXC, cols. 346–352. Paris, 1854.

Quellen und Forschungen zur Sprach- und Culturgeschichte der germanischen Völker. Herausgegeben von B. ten Brink und W. Scherer [and others]. Strassburg and London, 1874–.

Questionnaire de Folklore, publié par la Société du Folklore Wallon. Liége, 1891.

Questions enigmatiques, recreatiues, & propres pour deuiner, & y passer le temps aux veillées des longues nuicts. Auec les responces subtiles, & autres propos ioyeux. Lyon, 1619. [1568.] [See Weimarisches Jahrbuch, V, 339.]

Radloff, Wilhelm. Proben der Volkslitteratur der nördlichen türkischen Stämme, gesammelt und übersetzt. St Petersburg, 1885–86. 2 pts.

—— Proben der Volkslitteratur der türkischen Stämme Süd-Sibiriens, gesammelt und übersetzt. St. Petersburg, 1866–72. 4 pts.

Radulphus de Coggeshall. See Coggeshall, Ralph de.

Radulphus de Diceto. See Diceto, Ralph de.

Rafn, C. C. See Fornaldar Sögur Norðlanda.

—— See Fornmanna Sögur.

—— See Íslendínga Sögur.

Rahbek, Knud Lyne. Læsning i blandede Æmner. Et Maanedsskrift af ——. Kjøbenhavn, 1821–23. 4 vols.

Raimbert de Paris. La Chevalerie Ogier de Danemarche par ——. Poëme du XII siècle. Publié pour la première fois d'après le Ms. de Marmoutier et le Ms. 2729 de la Bibliothèque du Roi [par J. Barrois]. Paris, 1842. 2 vols. (Romans des Douze Pairs de France, 8, 9.)

Raine, James. See Taylor, George.

Rajna, Pio. Le fonti dell' Orlando Furioso. Ricerche e studii. Firenze, 1876.

—— Le origine dell' epopea francese indagate da ——. Firenze, 1884.

—— Ricerche intorno ai Reali di Francia. Seguite dal libro delle Storie di Fioravante e dal cantare di Bovo d' Antona. In I Reali di Francia, vol. I. Bologna, 1872. (Collezione di Opere Inedite o Rare dei primi tre Secoli della Lingua, pubblicata per cura della R. Commissione pe' Testi di Lingua nelle Provincie dell' Emilia.)

—— Uggeri il Danese nella letteratura romanzesca degl' Italiani. In Romania, II, 153–69; III, 31–77; IV, 398–436. 1873–75.

—— See Carduino.

Ralph de Coggeshall. See Coggeshall, Ralph de.

Ralph de Diceto. See Diceto, Ralph de.

Ralston, W. R. S. Beauty and the Beast. In The Nineteenth Century, IV, 990–1012. 1878.

—— Russian Folk-Tales. London, 1873.

—— The Songs of the Russian People, as illustrative of Slavonic mythology and Russian social life. London, 1872.

Rambaud, Alfred. La Russie épique. Étude sur les chansons héroïques de la Russie, traduites ou analysées pour la première fois. Paris, 1876.

Rampini, Charles. The Burning of Frendraught. In The Scottish Review, X, 143–63. 1887.

Ramsay, A. See Paston Letters.

Ramsay, Allan. A New Miscellany of Scots Sangs. London, 1727.

—— Poems. Edinburgh, 1721.

—— The Tea-Table Miscellany. See p. 400 b, above.

Rantzau, H. von. See Evax.

Raoul, le Trouvère. See Messire Gauvain ou la vengeance de Raguidel.

Rapin-Thoyras, Paul de. Histoire d'Angleterre. La Haye, 1724–27. 10 vols.

Rask, Hans Kristian. Morskabslæsning for den danske Almue. Kjøbenhavn, 1839–46.

Rassegna Napolitana. Vol. II. Napoli, 1895. [See V, 303 b.]

La Rassegna Settimanale di Politica, Scienze, Lettere ed Arti. Roma, 1879–81. 3 nos.

Raszmann, August. Die deutsche Heldensage und ihre Heimat. Hannover, 1857–58. 2 vols.

Rathery, E. J. B. Des chansons populaires et historiques en France. In Le Moniteur Universel, feuilletons of March 19, April 23, 27, May 27, June 15, Aug. 26, 27, 1853.

Ravenscroft, Thomas. Pammelia: Musick's Miscellanie, or mixed varietie of pleasant roundelayes, [etc.]. London, 1609.

Raynaud, Gaston. See Montaiglon, Anatole de.

Razzi, Serafino. Giardino d' essempi, overo Fiori delle vite de' Santi. Venice, 1720.

Reading, William. See Socrates.

Li Reali di Francia, nei quali si contiene la generazione degli imperadori, re, principi, baroni e paladini con la bellissima istoria di Buovo di Antona. Edizione per la prima volta purgata da infiniti errori. Venezia, 1821.

I Reali di Francia, nei quali si contiene la generazione degli imperatori, re, duchi, principi, baroni e paladini di Francia colle grandi imprese e battaglie da loro date, cominciando da Costantino Imperatore sino ad Orlando, Conte d' Anglante. Palermo, 1888.

—— See Rajna, Pio.

Recueil de crâmignons populaires français et wallons. Liège, 1882.

Recueil de romances historiques, tendres et burlesques tant anciennes que modernes, avec les airs notés. Par M. D. L[usse]. Paris, 1767. 2 vols.

Recuerdos y Bellezas de España. See Parcerisa, F. J.

Recull de eximplis e miracles, gestes e faules e altres ligendes ordenades per A–B–C, tretes de un manuscrit en pergami del començament del segle XV, ara per primera volta estampades. [Barcelona, 1880–88?] 2 vols. (Biblioteca Catalana.)

Reed, J. See Dodsley, R.

The Register of the Privy Council of Scotland. Edited and abridged by John Hill Burton (vols I, II; by David Masson, vols III–XIII). Edinburgh, 1877–96. 13 vols. (Published by the authority of the Lords Commissioners of her Majesty's Treasury, under the direction of the Lord Clerk Register of Scotland.)

Registrum Magni Sigilli Regum Scotorum. Vol. I. 1306–1424 [ed. by T. Thomson], [London,] Record Commission, 1814. [Vols II–IX], 1424–1651, ed. by J. B. Paul and J. Maitland Thomson. Edinburgh, 1882–97.

Reicke, R. See Altpreussische Monatschrift.

Reid, Mayne. The Scalp-Hunters; or, Romantic Adventures in Northern Mexico. London, 1851. 3 vols.

Reiffenberg, Baron de. See Chevalier au Cygne.

Reinfrid von Braunschweig, herausgegeben von Karl Bartsch. Tübingen, 1871. (Bibliothek des Litterarischen Vereins in Stuttgart, 109.)

Reinfrît von Braunschweig. Von Karl Gödeke. Hannover, 1851. (Archiv des histor. Vereins für Niedersachsen, 1849.)

Reinisch Simon Leo. Sprachen von Nord-Ost-Afrika. Bd I, Die Barea-Sprache. Bd. II, III, Die Nuba-Sprache. Wien, 1874–79. 3 vols.

Reinsch, Robert. Die Pseudo-Evangelien von Jesu und Maria's Kindheit in der romanischen und germanischen Literatur. Mit Mittheilungen aus Pariser und Londoner Handschriften versehen. Halle, 1879.

Reithard, J. J. See Schweizerblätter.

Remi, Philippe de. See Beaumanoir.

Renart le Contrefait, Le roman de. (Nach der Handschrift der k. k. Hofbibliothek Nr 2562; früher, Hohendorf, fol. 39.) Von Ferdinand Wolf. Wien, 1861. (Denkschriften der Philosophisch-historischen Classe der Kaiserlichen Akademie der Wissenschaften, XII.)

Renaud de Beaujeu. See Bel Inconnu.

Renaut. Lai d'Ignaurès, en vers, du XII⁰ siècle, par Renaut, suivi des lais de Melion et du Trot, en vers, du XIII⁰ siècle, publiés pour la première fois d'après deux manuscrits uniques, par L.- J.- N. Monmerqué et Francisque Michel. Paris, 1832.

Renaut. Le Roman de Galerent, comte de Bretagne, par le trouvère Renaut. Publié pour la première fois d'après le manuscrit unique de la Bibliothèque Nationale par Anatole Boucherie. Montpellier, 1888. (Société pour l'Étude des Langues Romanes, Publications Spéciales, 14.)

Renier, Rodolfo. See Sercambi, Giovanni.

Répertoire général du Théâtre Français. Paris, 1818. 67 vols.

Resen, Peder. Descriptio et illustratio Samsoae Insulae Maris Balthici praemissa uti specimen Theatri Daniae sive potius Atlantis Danici sequentibus annis munificentia augustissimi regis Christiani V. in lucem prodituri (etc.). Hafniae, 1675.

The Retrospective Review. London, 1820-26. 14 vols. Second Series. London, 1827-28.. 2 vols.

Revista Ibérica de Ciencias, Politica, Literatura, Artes é Instruccion Pública. [Edited by F. de P. Canelejas.] Vols I-VI. Madrid, 1861-65.

Revista Lusitana. Archivo de estudos philologicos e ethnologicos relativos a Portugal, publicado por J. Leite de Vasconcellos. Porto, 1887-92. 12 vols.

Revue Celtique. Dirigée par H. Gaidoz (and others). Paris, 1870-.

Revue Critique d'Histoire et de Littérature. Paris, 1866-.

Revue des Études Juives. Publication trimestrielle de la Société des Études Juives. Paris, 1880-.

Revue des Langues Romanes. Publiée par la Société pour l'Étude des Langues Romanes. Montpellier, 1870-.

Revue des Provinces. Rédacteur en chef E. Fournier. [Continuation of La Décentralization Littéraire et Scientifique.] Vols III-XI. Paris, 1864-66.

Revue des Traditions Populaires. Paris, 1886-. (Société des Traditions Populaires.)

Rhesa, L. J. Ueber litthauische Volkspoesie. In Beiträge zur Kunde Preussens, I, 507-24. 1818.

Rhŷs, John. History of Charlemagne, translated by——. [From the Red Book of Hergest.] In E. Koschwitz, Sechs Bearbeitungen des altfranzösischen Gedichts von Karl des Grossen Reise nach Jerusalem und Constantinopel, I, 19-39. Heilbronn, 1879.

—— Lectures on the Origin and Growth of Religion as illustrated by Celtic Heathendom. The Hibbert Lectures, 1886. London, 1888.

Richard Coer de Lion. In Henry Weber, Metrical Romances of the thirteenth, fourteenth, and fifteenth Centuries, II, 1-278. Edinburgh, 1810.

Richars li Biaus. Zum ersten Male herausgegeben von Dr. Wendelin Foerster. Wien, 1874.

Richter, Jean Paul. See Dobeneck.

Richthofen, Karl Freiherr von. Altfriesisches Wörterbuch. Göttingen, 1840.

Riddarasögur. See Kölbing, Eugen.

Ridpath, George. The Border History of England and Scotland, deduced from the earliest times to the union of the two crowns. Revised and published by the author's brother, the Rev. Philip Ridpath. A New Edition. Berwick, 1848.

Riese, Alexander. See Apollonius of Tyre.

Rigord. Œuvres de Rigord et de Guillaume le Breton, historiens de Philippe-Auguste, publiées par H. F. Delaborde. Paris, 1882-85. 2 vols. (Société de l'histoire de France.)

Riley, Henry Thomas. See Walsingham, Thomas.

Ringel, J. See Stöber, August.

Rischka, Robert. Verhältnis der polnischen Sage "Walgierz Wdały" zu den deutschen Sagen von "Walther v. Aquitanien." Brody, [1880].

Ristelhuber, P. See Ouville.

—— See Estienne, Henri.

Ritson, Joseph. Ancient Engleish Metrical Romanceës, selected and publish'd by ——. London, 1802. 3 vols.

—— Ancient Songs, from the time of King Henry the Third to the Revolution. London, 1790.

—— The North-Country Chorister: an unparalleled variety of excellent songs. In Northern Garlands edited by the late Joseph Ritson, Esq. London, 1810.

—— Robin Hood: a collection of all the Ancient Poems, Songs, and Ballads, now extant relative to that celebrated English Outlaw. London, 1832. 2 vols.

Ritter von Staufenberg. See Staufenberg.

Rivadeneyra, M. See Biblioteca de Autores Españoles.

Rivista Contemporanea, etc. Torino, 1854-69.

La Rivista Europea. Firenze, 1869-76.

Rivista di Filologia Romanza. Diretta da L. Manzone, E. Monaci, E. Stengel. Vols I, II. Imola and Roma, 1872-76.

Rivista di Letteratura Popolare, diretta da G. Pitrè, F. Sabatini. Roma, etc., 1877-79.

Rivista delle Tradizioni Popolari Italiane, diretta da Angelo de Gubernatis. Roma, 1893-94. 2 vols.

Robert of Gloucester. See Black, W. H.

Robert of Gloucester's Chronicle. Transcrib'd, and now first publish'd, from a MS. in the Harleyan Library by Thomas Hearne, M. A. To which is added, besides a Glossary and other Improvements, a Continuation (by the Author himself) of this Chronicle from a MS. in the Cottonian Library. Oxford, 1724. 2 vols.

Robert le Diable. In La Bibliothèque Bleue, I. Liége, 1787. Bibliothèque Bleue. Paris, [1862].

—— Roberte the Deuyll. A Metrical Romance from an Ancient Illuminated Manuscript. [Ed. by I. Herbert.] London, 1798.

—— Le roman de Robert le Diable en vers, d'après les manuscrits de la Bibliothèque du Roi par G. S. Trebutien. Paris, 1837.

Robert, A. C. M. Fables Inédites des XII⁰, XIII⁰ et XIV⁰ siècles, et fables de La Fontaine rapprochées de celles de tous les auteurs qui avoient, avant lui, traité les mêmes sujets, précédés d'une notice sur les fabulistes. . . . Paris, 1825. 2 vols.

Robert, Ulysse. See Paris, Gaston.

Robertson, James Craigie. Materials for the History of Thomas Becket Archbishop of Canterbury. (Vols I–VI. Vol. VII ed. by J. C. R. and J. Brigstocke Sheppard.) London, 1875–85. 7 vols. (Rolls Series.)

Robertson, Joseph. Collections for a History of the Shires of Aberdeen and Banff. Aberdeen, 1843. (Spalding Club, Publications, 9.)

—— Illustrations of the Topography and Antiquities of the Shires of Aberdeen and Banff. Aberdeen, 1847–69. 4 vols. (Spalding Club, Publications, 16, 28, 31, 36.)

Robin Hood. In Edinburgh Review, LXXXVI, 122–38. 1847.

Robinson, Theresa A. L. von Jakob. See Talvj.

Robson, John. Three Early English Metrical Romances. With an introduction and glossary. Edited from a MS. in the possession of J. I. Blackburne, Esq., M. P. London, 1842. (Camden Society, [18].)

—— The Scottish Field. [Manchester,] 1855. (In Chetham Miscellanies, 2.)

Roby, John. Traditions of Lancashire. London, 1879. 2 vols.

Rochebrune, Octave de. See Fillon, Benjamin.

Rochholz, Ernst Ludwig. Aargauer Sagen und Legenden. In Zeitschrift für deutsche Mythologie, II, 225–54. 1855.

—— Alemmanisches Kinderlied und Kinderspiel aus der Schweiz. Gesammelt und sitten- und sprachgeschichtlich erklärt. Leipzig, 1857.

—— Deutscher Unsterblichkeitsglaube. Deutscher Glaube und Brauch im Spiegel der heidnischen Vorzeit. Erster Band. Berlin, 1867. [2 vols. in 1.]

—— Altdeutsches Bürgerleben. Deutscher Glaube und Brauch im Spiegel der heidnischen Vorzeit. Zweiter Band. Berlin, 1867. [2 vols. in 1.]

—— Naturmythen. Neue Schweizersagen gesammelt und erläutert. Leipzig, 1862.

—— Schweizersagen aus dem Aargau. Gesammelt und herausgegeben von ——. 2 vols. Aarau, 1856.

—— Tell als Zauberschütze. In Germania, XIII, 39–58. 1868.

—— Tell und Gessler in Sage und Geschichte. Nach urkundlichen Quellen. Heilbronn, 1877.

Röhricht, R., and Meisner, H. Ein niederrheinischer Bericht über den Orient. In Zeitschrift für deutsche Philologie, XIX, 1–86. Halle, 1886.

Röthe, G. See Zeitschrift für deutsches Alterthum.

Rogers, Charles. See Nairne, Carolina Oliphant, Baroness.

Rohde, Erwin. Der griechische Roman und seine Vorläufer. Leipzig, 1876.

Roi Flore (Li Contes dou) et de la bielle Jehane. In Nouvelles Françoises en prose du XIIIᵉ siècle, publiées d'après les manuscrits, avec une introduction et des notes par MM. L. Moland et C. d'Héricault. Pp. 85–157. Paris, 1856.

Le Roi et le Meunier. In Choix de petites pièces du théâtre anglais, traduites des originaux [en prose, par Patu]. Londres et Paris, 1756. 2 vols.

Roig, Jaume. Lo libre de les dones ó de conçells mòlt profitosos y saludables aixi pera regiment y ordre de ben viurer, com pera augmentar la devoció á la puritat de la Concepció de la Sacratíssima Verge María, fet per lo magnifich Mestre Jaume Roig y donat novament á llum segons la edició de 1735 per Francesch Pelay Briz. Barcelona, 1865.

Rolland, Eugène. Chansons de la Bretagne. In Almanach des Traditions populaires, I, 65–112. 1882.

—— Faune populaire de la France. (Noms vulgaires, dictons, proverbes, contes et superstitions.) Paris, 1877–82. 5 vols.

——, Orain, Adolphe, and others. Les chansons populaires en Haute-Bretagne. In Mélusine, II, 296–307, 388–92, 433–41; III, 134; IV, 45, 112, 189, 305–6, 377. 1885–89.

—— See Almanach.

—— See Ernault, Émile.

—— See Gaidoz, H.

—— See Mélusine.

Roman de la Rose. See Rose, Roman de la.

Roman de Violette. See Gibert de Montreuil.

Romania. Recueil trimestriel consacré a l'Étude des Langues et des Littératures Romanes. Publié par Paul Meyer et Gaston Paris. Paris, 1872–.

Romanische Studien. Hrsg. v. Eduard Böhmer. Iᵉʳ–VIᵉʳ Bd. Strassburg, etc., 1875 ['71]–85.

Rondini, Druso. Canti popolari marchigiani inediti (raccolti a Fossombrone). In Archivio per lo Studio delle tradizioni popolari, VI, 469–71; VII, 169–92, 531–46; VIII, 185–92, 401–14. 1887–89.

Roquefort, B. de. See Marie de France.

Rose, Roman de la. The Romaunt of the Rose. In The Poetical Works of Geoffrey Chaucer, edited by Richard Morris. London, 1891. 6 vols. VI, 1–234.

Rosen, Georg. See Tuti-nameh.

Rosenöl, oder Sagen und Kunden des Morgenlandes aus arabischen, persischen und türkischen Quellen. Stuttgart and Tübingen, 1813. 2 vols.

Rosenplänter, Joh. Heinr. Beiträge zur genauern Kenntniss der esthnischen Sprache. Pernau, 1813–32. 20 Hefte.

Rossi. See Erythraeus.

Rost, Reinhold. See Wilson, H. H.

Roswall and Lillian. A Pleasant History of Roswall and Lillian. Edinburgh, 1663. [A reprint; edited by David Laing. Edinburgh, 1822.]

Roth, F. See Konrad von Würzburg.

Rother. König Rother. Herausgegeben von Heinrich Rückert. Leipzig, 1872. (Karl Bartsch, Deutsche Dichtungen des Mittelalters, 1.)

Rotuli Parliamentorum; ut et Petitiones, et Placita in Parliamento. [London, 176–.] 6 vols.

Rotulorum Originalium in Curia Scaccario Abbreviatio. [London,] 1805, '10. 2 vols. (Record Commission.)

Rouse, W. H. D. See Jātaka.

The Roxburghe Ballads. Vols I–III, with short notes by William Chappell. London (Vol. I), Hertford, 1871–80. Vols IV–VIII, pt II, edited, with special introductions and notes, by J. Woodfall Ebsworth. Hertford, 1883–96. (Ballad Society.)

[Roxby, Robert.] The Lay of the Reedwater Minstrel, illustrated with notes, historical and explanatory. By a son of Reed. Newcastle, 1809; also, 1832.

La Royalle Couronne des Roys d'Arles. [By Jean Baptiste] Bovis. Avignon, 1641.

Roye, [Guy de]. Doctrinal de Sapience. [Lyons, 1490?]

Rua, Giuseppe. Novelle del "Mambriano" del Cieco da Ferrara, esposte ed illustrate. Torino, 1888.

Rudčenko, I. I. Narodnyja južnorusskija skazki. Kiev, 1869–70. 2 pts.

Russ, Melchior. Melchior Russen, Ritters von Lucern, Eidgenössische Chronik; geschrieben im Jahre 1482, und zum Erstenmale herausgegeben 1832 von J. Schneller. Bern, 1834[-38].

[Russell, John Fuller.] Christmas and Christmas Carols. London, [1847].

Ruthven, Patrick. A Relation of the Death of David Rizzi. Together with an account of David Rizzi, faithfully translated from Geo. Buchanan's History of Scotland. London, 1699.

Rymer, Thomas, and Sanderson, Robert. Foedera, Conventiones, Literae, et cujuscunque generis Acta Publica, [etc.]. Accurante Thoma Rymer. Editio Secunda, denuo summa fide collata et emendata studio Georgii Holmes. London, 1727. 20 vols.

Sabatini, Francesco. Il Volgo di Roma. Raccolta di tradizioni e costumanze popolari, a cura di ——. Vols I, II. Roma, 1890.

—— See Rivista di Letteratura Popolare.

Sacchetti, Franco. Novelle. Firenze, 1860. 2 vols.

—— Le Novelle di ——. Recate a buona lezione e dichiarate con note. [Ed. by Eugenio Camerini.] Milano, 1876.

Sacharov, J. Skazanija russkago naroda. [Utterances of the Russian People.] St Petersburg, 1841-49. 2 vols.

Sachs, C. Beiträge zur Kunde alt-französischer, englischer und provenzalischer Literatur aus französischen und englischen Bibliotheken. Berlin, 1857.

Sachs, Hans. Dichtungen von Hans Sachs. Herausgegeben: erster Theil von Karl Goedeke; zweiter, dritter Theil von Julius Tittmann. Leipzig, 1870-71. 3 pts. (K. Goedeke und J. Tittmann. Deutsche Dichter des sechzehnten Jahrhunderts. Mit Einleitungen und Worterklärungen. Vols IV-VI.)

—— Herausgegeben von Adelbert von Keller und E. Goetze. (Vols I-XII, von A. von Keller; vols XIII, XIV, von A. von Keller und E. Goetze; vols XV-XXIII, von E. Goetze.) Tübingen and Stuttgart, 1870-95. 23 vols. (Bibliothek des litterarischen Vereins in Stuttgart, 102-106, 110, 115, 121, 125, 131, 136, 140, 149, 159, 173, 179, 181, 188, 191, 193, 195, 201, 207.)

Sächsische Gesellschaft der Wissenschaften. Abhandlungen der Philologisch-historischen Classe. 1850-.

Sæmund. See Edda.

Saga. Et Fjerdingaars-Skrift, utgivet af J. S. Munch. Christiania, 1816-20. 3 vols.

Sagen aus Baden und der Umgegend. Carlsruhe, 1834.

The Sailing Trade. Glasgow, Printed by J. and M. Robertson, Saltmarket, 1801. [See V, 148 b.]

St. Helen's, Churchwardens' Accounts of. See Ward, J.

Saint Oswald. See Oswald.

Sakellarios, Athanasios A. Τὰ Κυπριακά, ἤτοι πραγματεία περὶ γεωγραφίας, ἀρχαιολογίας, στατιστικῆς, ἱστορίας, μυθολογίας, καὶ διαλέκτου τῆς Κύπρου. Athens, 1855-68. 3 vols.

[Sakesep, Jakemon.] L'histoire du Châtelain de Coucy et de la Dame de Fayel, publiée d'après le manuscrit de la Bibliothèque du Roi, et mise en françois par G. A. Crapelet, imprimeur. Paris, 1829. See, also, Paris, Gaston.

Salman und Morolf. See Vogt, Friedrich.

Salomon and Saturn. The Dialogue of Salomon and Saturnus; with an historical introduction by John M. Kemble. London, 1848. (Ælfric Society.)

Salomone-Marino, Salvatore. Leggende popolari siciliane in poesia, raccolte ed annotate da ——. Palermo, 1880.

Salomone-Marino, Salvatore. See Archivio.

Salvadori, G. Storie popolari toscane. In Giornale di Filologia Romanza, II, 194-204. 1879.

Samson the Fair. Sagann af Samsone fagra. In Erik Julius Björner, Nordiska Kämpa Dater. Stockholmiae, 1737.

Sanchez, Climente. El Libro de Exenplos por A. B. C. de Climente Sanchez, Archidiacre de Valderas. A. Morel-Fatio, in Romania, VII, 481-526. Paris, 1878.

Sanchez, Tomas Antonio. Coleccion de poesias castellanas anteriores al siglo XV. Ilustradas con algunas notas e indice de voces antiquadas. Madrid, 1779-90. 4 vols.

—— Poetas castellanos anteriores al siglo XV. Coleccion hecha por Don Tomas Antonio Sanchez, continuada por Don Pedro José Pidal, considerablemente aumentada é ilustrada, á vista de los códices y manuscritos antiguos, por Don Florencio Janer. Madrid, 1864. (Biblioteca de Autores Españoles.)

Sanderson, Robert. See Rymer, Thomas.

Sandvig, Berthel Christian. Omstændelig og tilforladelig Beskrivelse over Øen Møen. . . . Tilligemed en . . . Fortegnelse over Landsdommerne i Sielland og Møen. Kiøbenhavn, 1776.

—— See Symbolae ad Literaturam Teutonicam Antiqviorem.

Il sangue cristiano nei riti ebraici della moderna sinagoga, rivelazioni di Neofito ex rabbino, monaco greco, per la prima volta pubblicate in Italia. Versione dal greco del professore N. F. S. Segue un' appendice storica sopra lo stesso argomento. Prato, 1883.

Sarrazin, Gregor. See Octavian.

[Sarum Missal.] Missale ad usum insignis et praeclarae ecclesiae Sarum. Burntisland and London, 1861-67. 2 pts.

Savile, Sir Henry. See Guilielmus Malmesburiensis.

Saxby, Jessie M. Edmondstone. Folk-Lore from Unst, Shetland. In The Leisure Hour, 1880, pp. 75-77, 108-10, 198-200, 246-48, 342-43.

Saxo Grammaticus. Danica Historia libris xvi . . . conscripta. [Editio Philippi Loniceri.] Francofurti ad Moenum, 1576.

—— Danorum regum heroumque Historie. [Ed. by Christiern Pedersen.] Basileae, 1534.

—— Saxonis Grammatici Historiae Danicae lib. xvi. Steph. Joan. Stephanius recognovit, notisque illustravit. Sorae, 1644.

—— Saxonis Grammatici Gesta Danorum, herausgegeben von Alfred Holder. Strassburg, 1886.

—— Saxonis Grammatici Historia Danica. Recensuit et commentariis illustravit Dr. Petrus Erasmus Müller. Opus morte Mülleri interruptum absolvit Mag. Joannes Matthias Velschow. Havniae, 1839, '58. 2 pts in 3 vols. (Part II contains Prolegomena et Notas Uberiores.)

Sayce, A. H. See Smith, George.

Sbornik za narodni umotvorenija, nauka i knižnina. Sofia, 1889-.

Scala Celi. See Gobius, Johannes, Junior.

Scalachronica. See Gray, Sir Thomas.

Schade, Oskar. Liber de infantia Mariae et Christi Salvatoris ex codice Stuttgartensi descripsit et enarravit ——. Halis Saxonum, 1869.

—— Narrationes de vita et conversatione beatae Mariae Virginis et de pueritia et adolescentia Salvatoris ex codice Gissensí edidit ——. Halis Saxonum, 1870.

Schade, Oskar. Volkslieder aus Thüringen. In und um Weimar gesammelt von ——. *In* Weimarisches Jahrbuch, III, 241–328. 1855.

—— Ueber das Volkslied vom Betler. *Ib.*, 465–69.

—— See Weimarisches Jahrbuch.

Schall, C. See Arabian Nights.

Schambach, Georg, and Müller, Wilhelm. Niedersächsische Sagen und Märchen. Aus dem Munde des Volkes gesammelt und mit Anmerkungen und Abhandlungen herausgegeben. Göttingen, 1855.

Schedel, Hartmann. See Nuremberg Chronicle.

Scheler, Aug. See Bastars de Buillon.

Schelling, F. E. See Jonson, Ben.

Schenkl, Karl. Zur deutschen Märchenkunde. *In* Germania, XI, 450–52. 1866.

[Schérer, Jean Benoît.] Anecdotes intéressantes et secrètes de la cour de Russie, tirées de ses archives ; avec quelques anecdotes particulières aux différens peuples de cet empire. Publiées par un voyageur qui a séjourné treize ans en Russie. Londres, 1792. 6 vols.

Scherer, Wilhelm. See Müllenhoff, Karl.

—— See Quellen und Forschungen.

Schiefner, Anton. Awarische Texte, hrsg. von ——. St Petersburg, 1873. (Mém. de l'Acad. des Sciences.)

—— See Castrén, M. A.

—— See Kalewala.

—— See Kreutzwald, Friedrich.

Schiller. Turandot, Prinzessin von China. Ein tragikomisches Mährchen nach Gozzi. *In* Schillers Sämmtliche Werke, V, 139–242. Stuttgart and Tübingen, 1844.

Schischmánov, Ivan D. Der Lenorenstoff in der bulgarischen Volkspoesie. *In* Indogermanische Forschungen, IV, 412–48. 1894.

Schjøtt, Julie. Vise om Caroline Mathilde. *In* Dania, II, 275–82. 1893.

Schlagintweit, Emil. Buddhism in Tíbet illustrated by literary documents and objects of religious worship. With an account of the Buddhist systems preceding it in India. Leipzig, London, 1863.

[Schlegel, Christian Hieronymus Justus.] Reisen in mehrere russische Gouvernements in den Jahren 178*, [etc.–1833]. 10 Bdchn : I, II, IV–X, Meiningen, 1819, '18–34 ; III, Erfurt and Gotha, 1818.

Schlegel, Gustave. Uranographie chinoise, ou, preuves directes que l'astronomie primitive est originaire de la Chine, et qu'elle a été empruntée par les anciens peuples occidentaux a la sphère chinoise. Publié par l'Institut Royal pour la Philologie, la Géographie et l'Ethnologie des Indes-Orientales Néerlandaises à la Haye. La Haye, Leyde, 1875. 2 pts in 1 vol.

Schleicher, August. Litauische Märchen, Sprichworte, Räthsel und Lieder. Gesammelt und übersetzt von ——. Weimar, 1857.

—— Volkstümliches aus Sonneberg im Meininger Oberlande. Weimar, 1858.

Schmeller, Andreas. Bayerisches Wörterbuch. Stuttgart and Tübingen, 1827, '28, '36, '37. 4 pts.

—— Die Mundarten Bayerns. Beygegeben ist eine Sammlung von Mundart-Proben, d. i. kleinen Erzählungen, Gesprächen, Sing - Stücken, figürlichen Redensarten u. dergl. in den verschiedenen Dialekten des Königreichs, nebst einem Kärtchen zur geographischen Uebersicht dieser Dialekte. München, 1821.

—— See Grimm, Jacob.

Schmid, Christian Heinrich. See Taschenbuch für Dichter.

Schmid, Reinhold. Die Gesetze der Angelsachsen. In der Ursprache mit Uebersetzung, Erläuterung und einem antiquarischen Glossar herausgegeben. Zweite, völlig umgearbeitete und vermehrte Auflage. Leipzig, 1858.

Schmidt, Bernhard. Griechische Märchen, Sagen und Volkslieder. Leipzig, 1877.

—— Das Volksleben der Neugriechen und das hellenische Alterthum. Leipzig, 1871.

Schmidt, Erich. Charakteristiken. Berlin, 1886.

Schmidt, F. W. V. See Straparola, Giovanfrancesco.

Schmidt, I. J. See Dsanglun.

Schmidt, Richard. See Çukasaptati.

Schmitz, Jacob H. Sitten und Sagen, Lieder, Sprüchwörter und Räthsel des Eifler Volkes. Vol. I. Sitten und Bräuche, Lieder, u. s. w. Vol. II. Sagen und Legenden. Trier, 1856–58. 2 vols.

Schneller, Christian. Märchen und Sagen aus Wälschtirol. Ein Beitrag zur deutschen Sagenkunde. Gesammelt von ——. Innsbruck, 1867.

Schneller, J. See Russ, Melchior.

Schönemann, C. P. C. Hundert Merkwürdigkeiten, u. s. w. See Staufenberg.

Schönhuth, Ottmar. Die Burgen, Kloster, Kirchen und Kapellen Badens und der Pfalz mit ihren Geschichten, Sagen und Märchen. Illustrirt unter Leitung von A. v. Bayer, herausgegeben von ——. Lahr, [1865]. 2 vols.

Schönwerth, Fr. Aus der Oberfalz. Sitten und Sagen. Augsburg, 1857, '58, '59. 3 pts.

Schöpflin, Johann Daniel. Alsatia illustrata. Colmariae, 1751, '61. 2 vols.

Schofield, W. H. Studies on the Libeaus Desconus. *In* Studies and Notes in Philology and Literature, published under the direction of the Modern Language Departments of Harvard University, IV. Boston, 1896.

Scholl, G. H. F. See Heinrich von dem Türlîn.

Schoppner, A. Sagenbuch der Bayerischen Lande. Aus dem Munde des Volkes, der Chronik und der Dichter herausgegeben von ——. München, 1852, '53. 3 vols.

Schorbach, Karl. Jüngere Drucke des Ritter von Staufenberg. *In* Zeitschrift für deutsches Altertum, XL, 123–25. 1896.

Schott, Arthur and Albert. Walachische Mährchen, herausgegeben von ——. Mit einer Einleitung über das Volk der Walachen und einem Anhang zur Erklärung der Märchen. Stuttgart and Tübingen, 1845.

Schröder, Edward. Zwei altdeutsche Rittermären : Moriz von Craon, Peter von Staufenberg. Neu herausgegeben. Berlin, 1894.

—— See Zeitschrift für deutsches Alterthum.

Schröder, Carl. See Apollonius of Tyre.

Schubart, Henriette. Schottische Lieder und Balladen von Walter Scott. Uebersetzt von ——. Leipzig und Altenburg, 1817.

Schück, Henrik. See Visböcker.

Schütze, Johann Friedrich. Holsteinisches Idiotikon : ein Beitrag zur Volkssittengeschichte. Hamburg, etc., 1800–06. 4 pts in 2 vols.

Schulenburg, Wilibald von. Wendische Volkssagen und Gebräuche aus dem Spreewald. Leipzig, 1880.

Schulz, Alwin. Das höfische Leben zur Zeit der Minnesinger. Leipzig, 1879–80. 2 vols.

Schupp, Balthasar. Schriften. Franckfurt, 1701. [See I, 408.]

Schwarzer, Jos. Visionslegende. *In* Zeitschrift für deutsche Philologie, XIII, 338–51. 1881.

Schweizerblätter. Eine Monatschrift. Herausgegeben von Dr A. Henne, von Sarzans, und J. J. Reithard, von Küssnacht. 2er Jahrg. St. Gallen, 1833.

Scogin's Jests. The merry Jests, and witty Shifts of Scogin. (Scoggin's Jests.) [Reprinted from ed. of 1626.] *In* W. Carew Hazlitt, Shakespeare Jest-Books, II, 37–161. London, 1864.

Scot, Reginald. The Discovery of Witchcraft : proving, That the Compacts and Contracts of Witches and Devils and all Infernal Spirits or Familiars, are but Erroneous Novelties and Imaginary Conceptions. In sixteen books. London, 1665.

The Scotch Presbyterian Eloquence ; or, The foolishness of their teaching discovered from their books, sermons and prayers ; and some remarks on Mr. Rule's late vindication of the Kirk. [Jacob] Curate [i. e. Robert Calder ?]. London, 1692.

Scotichronicon. See Fordun, Joannes de.

The Scots Magazine. Edinburgh, 1739–1803.

The Scots Musical Museum. See Johnson, James.

The Scotsman. [A periodical.] Edinburgh, 1865–.

Scott, Jonathan. See Arabian Nights.

Scott, Sir Walter. The History of Scotland. London, 1830, 1831. 2 vols. London, 1837, 1840. 2 vols. (Dionysius Lardner, Cabinet Cyclopædia, 13, 14.)

—— Illustrations of Northern Antiquities. See Weber, Henry.

—— Poetical Works. Edinburgh, [1833–34]. 12 vols.

—— Schottische Lieder und Balladen von ——. Uebersetzt von Henriette Schubart. Leipzig und Altenburg, 1817.

—— Tales of a Grandfather. History of Scotland. Boston, 1861. 6 vols.

—— See Hohenhausen, Elise von.

—— See Sir Tristrem.

—— See Swift, Jonathan.

The Scottish Journal of Topography, Antiquities, Traditions, etc. Edinburgh, 1847–48. 2 vols.

The Scottish Review : a quarterly journal of social progress and general literature. Nos 1–41. Glasgow, [1853–63].

The Scottish Review. London and Paisley, 1883–.

Sébillot, Paul. Contes populaires de la Haute-Bretagne. Paris, 1880. 2e série, Paris, 1881. 3e série, Paris, 1882.

—— Gargantua dans les traditions populaires. Paris, 1883. (Les Littératures Populaires de toutes les Nations, 12.)

—— Littérature orale de la Haute-Bretagne. Paris, 1881. (Les Littératures Populaires de toutes les Nations, 1.)

—— Traditions et superstitions de la Haute-Bretagne. Paris, 1882. 2 vols. (Les Littératures Populaires de toutes les Nations, 9, 10.)

Sédaine, Michel Jean. Le Roi et le Fermier. *In his* Œuvres Choisies, Vol. I, No IV. Paris, 1813.

Seidemann, Johann Karl. Zu Bürgers Ballade ' Der Kaiser und der Abt.' *In* Archiv für Litteraturgeschichte, IX, 423–24. 1880.

Šejn, P. V. Materialy dlja izučenija byta i jazyka russkago naselenija sěvero-zapadnago kraja. [Materials for learning the State and Language of the Russian Population in the North-West.] St Petersburg, 1887–93. 3 pts.

Selden, John. Titles of Honor. The Second Edition. London, 1631.

A Selection of Scots Songs. Harmonized, improved with simple and adapted graces. By Peter Urbani, Professor of Music. Edinburgh, [c. 1794].

Semevskij, M. I. Slovo i Dělo. 3d ed. St Petersburg, 1885. [See III, 382 b, note.]

Seneca, Lucius Annaeus. L. Annaei Senecae pars prima sive opera philosophica quae recognovit M. N. Bouillet.... *In* Omnia opera quae vulgo extant sub nomine L. A. Senecae philosophica declamatoria et tragica. Parisiis, 1827–31. 6 vols. (N. E. Lemaire, Bibliotheca Classica Latina.)

Sénecé, Antoine Bauderon de. Œuvres Choisies. Nouvelle édition. Publiée par MM. Émile Chasles et P. A. Cap. Précédée d'une monographie de la famille Bauderon de Senescey par M. Émile Chasles. Paris, 1855.

Sepp, Johannes Nepomuk. Altbayerischer Sagenschatz zur Bereicherung der indogermanischen Mythologie. München, 1876.

Serapeum. Zeitschrift für Bibliothekwissenschaft, Handschriftenkunde und ältere Litteratur. Im Vereine mit Bibliothekaren und Litteraturfreunden herausgegeben von Dr. Robert Naumann. Leipzig, 1840–70. 31 vols.

Sercambi, Giovanni. Novelle [ed. by Alessandro d' Ancona]. Bologna, 1871. (Scelta di curiosità letterarie, 119.)

—— Novelle inedite, tratte dal codice Trivulziano cxciii per cura di Rodolfo Renier. Torino, 1889.

Sermones Parati. See Histoire Littéraire de la France, XXVIII, 382–84. Paris, 1829.

Serra, Guillem. See Genesi de Scriptura.

Servius, Maurus Honoratus. Pub. Virgilii Maronis Bucolicorum Eclogae x, Georgicorum libri iiii, Aeneidos libri xii. Et in ea, Mauri Servii Honorati grammatici commentarii. Parisiis, 1600.

Servois, G. See Fierabras.

Seuffert, Bernhard. Die Legende von der Pfalzgräfin Genovefa. Habilitationsschrift. Würzburg, 1877.

—— Maler Müller. Berlin, 1877. 2te Ausgabe, Berlin, 1881.

The Seven Sages, in English verse, edited from a manuscript in the Public Library of the University of Cambridge by Thomas Wright. London, 1845. (Percy Society, Publications, 16.)

Seven Wise Masters. The History of the Seven Wise Masters of Rome. Now newly corrected, better explained in many places, and enlarged with many pretty pictures, lively expressing the full history. London, 1673.

Sferamundi. Della historia del Principe Sferamvndi Figliuolo di Don Rogello di Grecia, Di nuovo tradotta dalla lingua Spagnuola nella Italiana. Per M. Mambrino Roseo da Fabriano. Venetia, 1610. 6 pts.

Shakspere, William. See Fletcher, John.

[Sharp, Sir Cuthbert.] Memorials of the Rebellion of 1569. London, 1840.

Sharpe, Charles Kirkpatrick. A Historical Account of the belief in Witchcraft in Scotland. London, Glasgow, 1884.

—— Letters from and to Charles Kirkpatrick Sharpe, Esq. Edited by Alexander Allardyce. With a Memoir by the Rev. W. K. R. Bedford. London, 1888. 2 vols.

—— A Memorial of the Conversion of Jean Livingston, Lady Waristoun. With an Account of her carriage at her Execution, July, 1600. [By J. Balfour ? Edited by C. K. Sharpe.] Edinburgh, 1827.

—— See Kirkton, James.

—— See Law, Robert.

Shaw, William Francis. See Parish, William Douglas.

Sheppard, H. F. See Baring-Gould, Sabine.

Sherwood, Clarence. Die neu-englischen Bearbeitungen der Erzählung Boccaccios von Ghismonda und Guiscardo. [Berlin dissertation.] Berlin, 1892.

Shukasaptati. See Çukasaptati.

Siarkowski, Ks. Materyały do etnografii ludu polskiego z okolic Kielc. In Zbiór Wiadomości, etc. Cracow, 1879, III, pt. II.

Siddhi-Kûr. See Jülg, Bernhard.

Sidney, Sir Philip. An Apologie for Poetrie. 1595. Carefully edited by Edward Arber. London, 1868. (English Reprints, 4.)

Sievers, E. See Beiträge, etc.

Sigibertus Gemblacensis. Chronographia. Edidit D. Ludowicus Conradus Bethmann. In G. H. Pertz, Scriptores, VI, 268-535. Auctarium : Roberti de Monte Cronica, 475-535. Hannoverae, 1844. (Monumenta Germaniae Historica.)

Sillig, J. See Böttiger, C. A.

Simrock, Karl. Das deutsche Kinderbuch. Altherkömmliche Reime, Lieder, Erzählungen, Uebungen, Räthsel und Scherze für Kinder gesammelt von ——. Zweite vermehrte Auflage. Frankfurt am Main, 1857.

—— Deutsche Märchen, erzählt von ——. Stuttgart, 1864.

—— Die deutschen Volksbücher. See Volksbücher.

—— Die geschichtlichen deutschen Sagen, aus dem Munde des Volks und deutscher Dichter. Frankfurt am Main, 1850.

—— Der gute Gerhard und die dankbaren Todten. Ein Beitrag zur deutschen Mythologie und Sagenkunde. Bonn, 1856.

Sinclair, Sir John. The Statistical Account of Scotland. Drawn up from the communications of the ministers of the different parishes. Edinburgh, 1791-99. 21 vols.

Singer, S. Sagengeschichtliche Parallelen aus dem babylonischen Talmud. In Zeitschrift des Vereins für Volkskunde, II, 293-301. 1892.

Siperis de Vinevaux. Lhystoire plaisäte & recreatiue faisät mention des prouesses et vailläces du noble Syperis de Vineuaulx. Et de ses dixsept filz. Nouuellement imprimee. Paris, n. d. [Reprinted, Paris, 1842, in] Collection de Poésies, Romans, Chroniques &ᵉ, publiée d'après d'anciens manuscrits et d'après des éditions des XVᵉ et XVIᵉ siecles. 14ᵉ livraison.

[Sir Gowther.] Sir Gowghter. In E. V. Utterson, Select Pieces of Early Popular Poetry, London, 1825, I, 157-190. [Later ed. by Karl Breul, Oppeln, 1886.]

Sir Orfeo. See Orfeo.

Sir Triamour. The Romance of Syr Tryamoure, from a manuscript preserved in the University Library, Cambridge. Edited by James Orchard Halliwell. London, 1846. (Percy Society, 16.)

—— Syr Tryamour. In [Edward Vernon Utterson,] Select Pieces of Early Popular Poetry, I, 1-72. London, 1825.

—— Sir Triamore. In Bishop Percy's Folio Manuscript, Ballads and Romances. Edited by John W. Hales and Frederick J. Furnivall. II, 78-135. London, 1868.

Sir Tristrem. See Tristan.

Six Old Plays. See (The) Famous Victories, etc.

Skeat, Walter W. An Etymological Dictionary of the English Language. Oxford, 1882.

—— See Fletcher, John.

—— See Gamelyn.

—— See Langland, William.

Skeat, Walter W. See Mélusine.

Skelton, John. A Ballade of the Scottysshe Kinge. Written by John Skelton, poet laureate to King Henry the Eighth. Reproduced in facsimile with an historical and bibliographical introduction by John Ashton. London, 1882.

—— Poetical Works of. With notes, and some account of the author and his writings, by the Rev. Alexander Dyce. London, 1843. 2 vols.

Skene, F. J. H. See Fordun.

Skene, W. F. See Lismore.

Small, Andrew. Interesting Roman Antiquities recently discovered in Fife, ascertaining the site of the great battle fought betwixt Agricola and Galgacus, with the discovery of the position of five Roman towns, and of the site and names of upwards of seventy Roman forts: also observations regarding the Ancient Palaces of the Pictish Kings in the town of Abernethy, and other local antiquities. Edinburgh, 1823.

Small, George. See Tuti-nameh.

Small, John. See Douglas, Gavin.

—— See Dunbar, William.

Smith, Alexander. A new History of Aberdeenshire. Edited by ——. Aberdeen, etc., 1875. 2 pts.

Smith, George. The Chaldean Account of Genesis. Containing the description of the creation, the fall of man, the deluge, the tower of Babel, the times of the patriarchs, and Nimrod; Babylonian fables, and legends of the Gods; from the cuneiform inscriptions. Third edition. London, 1876. New ed., revised, with additions, by A. H. Sayce. London, 1880.

Smith, James. See Facetiae. See Wit and Drollery.

Smith, R. A. The Scotish Minstrel, a Selection from the Vocal Melodies of Scotland, ancient and modern, arranged for the voice and pianoforte by ——. Vols I-III, third edition; vols IV-VI, second edition. Edinburgh, [1820-24].

Smith, Victor. Chants de pauvres en Forez et en Velay. In Romania, II, 455-76. 1873.

—— Chants du Velay et du Forez. Ib. III, 365-70; IV, 108-18, 437-52; X, 581-87. 1874-80.

—— Vieilles chansons recueillies en Velay et en Forez. Ib. VII, 52-84. 1878.

—— Chants populaires du Velay et du Forez. Ib. VIII, 410-21; IX, 288-93; X, 194-211. 1879-81.

—— Un mariage dans le Haut-Forez: usages et chants. Ib. IX, 547-70. 1880.

[Snegirev, J.] Russkie prostonarodnye prazdniki. [Russian Popular Festivals.] Moscow, 1837-39. 4 vols.

Snorri Sturluson. See Edda.

Société des Traditions Populaires. Annuaire. Paris, 1886-94.

Society of Antiquaries, London. See Archaeologia.

Society of Antiquaries of Scotland. Archaeologia Scotica: or Transactions of the Society of Antiquaries of Scotland. Edinburgh, 1792-1890. 5 vols.

—— Proceedings. Edinburgh, 1852-.

Socin, Albert. See Prym, Eugen.

—— and Stumme, Hans. Der arabische Dialekt der Houwāra des Wād Sūs in Marokko. Leipzig, 1894. (Abhandlungen der phil.-hist. Classe der Königl. Sächsischen Gesellschaft der Wissenschaften, vol. XV.)

Socrates. Socratis Scolastici Historia Ecclesiastica. Henrico Valesio Interprete. In Eusebii Pamphili, Socratis Scholastici, Hermiae Sozomeni, Theodoriti et Evagrii, item

Philostorgii et Theodori Lectoris quae extant Historiae Ecclesiasticae, [ed. Gul. Reading]. II, 1–396. Cantabrigiae, 1720.

Soldatenkov, K. See Afanas'ev, A. N.

Somadeva. See Kathā sarit sāgara.

Sommer, Emil. Sagen, Märchen und Gebräuche aus Sachsen und Thüringen. Gesammelt von ——. Halle, 1846.

—— See Floire et Blanceflor.

Sommer, H. Oskar. See Malory, Sir Thomas.

Sonnerat, Pierre. Voyage aux Indes Orientales et à la Chine, fait depuis 1774 jusqu'en 1781. Paris, 1782. 2 vols.

Sousa, Affonso de. See Encyclopedia Republicana.

Southey, Robert. Lives of the British Admirals, with an introductory view of the Naval History of England. (Vols I–IV; continued by Robert Bell, vol. V.) London, 1833–40. 5 vols. (D. Lardner, Cabinet Cyclopædia, 70–74.)

—— The Pilgrim to Compostella: being the legend of a cock and a hen to the honour and glory of Santiago. A Christmas tale. In his Works, VII, 239–294 (vol. II of Ballads and Metrical Tales). London, 1842.

—— Poetical Works. Collected by himself. London, 1838–44. 10 vols.

—— See Malory, Sir Thomas.

—— See Palmerin of England.

Souvestre, Émile. Les derniers paysans. Paris, 1871.

—— Les récits de la muse populaire. La fileuse. In Revue des Deux Mondes, XIX année, nouvelle période, t. II, pp. 102–133. 1849.

Sozonovič, I. Lenora Bjurgera i rodstvennye ej sjužety v narodnoj poezii evropejskoj i russkoj. [Bürger's Lenore and the related matter in European and Russian popular poetry.] Warsaw, 1893.

Spalding, John. Memorialls of the Trubles in Scotland and in England. A. D. 1624–A. D. 1645. [Edited by John Stuart.] Aberdeen, 1850, '51. 2 vols. (Spalding Club, Publications, 20, 22.)

Spalding Club. See Miscellany.

The Spectator. London, 1711–14.

Spee, Johannes. Volksthümliches vom Niederrhein. Gesammelt von ——. Köln, 1875.

Spelman, Sir Henry. Glossarium Archaiologicum, continens Latino-Barbara, peregrina, obsoleta, and novatae significationis vocabula [etc.]. Editio tertia. Londini, 1787.

Spenser, Edmund. Poetical Works. The text carefully revised, and illustrated with notes, original and selected, by Francis J. Child. Boston, 1855. 5 vols.

Společnost vlastenského musea v čechách. Casopis. Prague, 1827–.

The Sporting Magazine. London, 1793–1870.

Spottiswood (Spotswood), John, Archbishop of St Andrews. The History of the Church of Scotland, beginning the year of our Lord 203 and continued to the end of the reign of King James the VI. London, 1655. 2d ed., London, 1666.

Sprenger, J. See Malleus Maleficarum.

Stallbaum, J. G. See Eustathius.

State Papers. British and Foreign State Papers. (1812–1890.) Compiled by the Librarian and Keeper of the Papers, Foreign Office. London, 1841–1879. 82 vols.

Stationers' Registers. See Arber, Edward.

Statistical Account of Scotland. See Sinclair, Sir John.

Statistical Account of Scotland. The New Statistical Account of Scotland. By the ministers of the respective parishes. Edinburgh and London, 1845. 15 vols.

The Statutes of the Realm. Printed by command of his Majesty King George the Third, in pursuance of an address of the House of Commons of Great Britain. From Original Records and Authentic Manuscripts. London, 1810–21. 8 vols. (Record Commission.)

Staufenberg. Der Ritter von Staufenberg. In Altdeutsche Studien, by Jänicke, and others. See Jänicke, Oskar.

—— Die Legende vom Ritter Herrn Peter Diemringer von Staufenberg in der Ortenau. (Friedr. Culemann.) In Hundert Merkwürdigkeiten der Herzoglichen Bibliothek zu Wolfenbüttel. Für Freunde derselben aufgezeichnet von C. P. C. Schönemann. Und Legende vom Ritter Herrn Peter Diemringer von Staufenberg in Ortenau. Hannover, 1849.

—— Der Ritter von Stauffenberg, ein Altdeutsches Gedicht, herausgegeben nach der Handschrift der öffentlichen Bibliothek zu Strassburg . . . von Christian Moriz Engelhardt. Strassburg, 1823. 1 vol. and atlas.

—— See Fischart, Johann.

—— See Schröder, Edward.

Staveley, Thomas. The Romish Horseleech; or, An impartial Account of the intolerable Charge of Popery to this Nation [etc.]. London, 1769.

Steevens, George. See Tollet, George.

Stefanović, D. K. Srpske narodne pripovjedke. Neusatz, 1871.

Steinmeyer, Elias. Trirer Bruchstücke. I. Floyris. In Zeitschrift für deutsches Alterthum, XXI, 307–331. 1877.

—— See Anzeiger (Zeitschrift) für deutsches Alterthum.

—— See Jänicke, Oskar.

Stenhouse, William. The Scots Musical Museum. See Johnson, James.

Stenzler, Adolf Friedrich. See Kālidāsa.

—— See Yâjnavalkya's Gesetzbuch.

Stephanius, Steph. Joan. See Saxo Grammaticus.

Stephens, George. Ett forn-svenskt Legendarium, innehällande Medeltids Kloster-sagor om Helgon, Påfvar och Kejsare ifrån det I:sta till det XIII:de Århundradet. Efter gamla Handskrifter af ——. Stockholm, 1847, '58, '74. 3 vols.

—— The old Popular Ballads and Songs of Sweden. In Foreign Quarterly Review, XXV, 26–48; XXVI, 29–56. 1840–41.

—— See Hyltén-Cavallius, G. O.

Stephens, Thomas. The Literature of the Kymry: being a critical essay on the History of the Language and Literature of Wales during the twelfth and two succeeding centuries; containing numerous specimens of ancient Welsh poetry in the original and accompanied with English translations. Second edition, edited, with the author's additions and corrections, by the Rev. D. Silvan Evans. With a life of the author by B. T. Williams. London, 1876.

Stern, Ludw. Chr. Die gälische Ballade vom Mantel in Macgregors Liederbuche. In Zeitschrift für celtische Philologie, I, 294–326. 1896.

—— See Zeitschrift für celtische Philologie.

Stevenson, Joseph. See Calendar of State Papers.

—— See Coggeshall, Ralph de.

—— See Chronicon de Lanercost.

Stevenson, Joseph. See Gray, Sir Thomas.

Stevenson, W. H. See Chamberlain's Accounts, etc.

—— Records of the Borough of Nottingham, being a series of Extracts from the Archives of the Corporation of Nottingham. London, 1882–89. 4 vols.

Stewart, Alexander. 'Twixt Ben Nevis and Glencoe : the natural history, legends, and folk-lore of the West Highlands. Edinburgh, 1885.

Stewart, W. Grant. The Popular Superstitions and Festive Amusements of the Highlanders of Scotland. Edinburgh, 1823.

Stiefel, A. Ludwig. Ueber die Quelle der Turandot-Dichtung Heinz des Kellners. In Zeitschrift für vergleichende Litteraturgeschichte, Neue Folge, VIII, 257–261. 1895.

Stier, A. Ungarische Volksmärchen. Nach der aus Georg Gaals Nachlass herausgegebenen Urschrift übersetzt von ——. Pesth, [1857].

Stimming, Albert. [Review of] Theodor Wissmann, King Horn : Untersuchungen, 1876. In Englische Studien, I, 351–62. 1877.

Stobbe, Otto. Die Juden in Deutschland während des Mittelalters in politischer, socialer und rechtlicher Beziehung. Braunschweig, 1866.

Stodart, Robert Riddle. Scottish Arms, being a collection of Armorial Bearings A. D. 1370–1678; reproduced in facsimile from contemporary manuscripts. With heraldic and genealogical notes. Edinburgh, 1881. 2 vols.

Stöber, August. Die Sagen der Elsasses, zum ersten Male getreu nach der Volksüberlieferung, den Chroniken und andern gedruckten und handschriftlichen Quellen, gesammelt und erläutert von ——. Mit einer Sagenkarte von J. Ringel. St. Gallen, 1852.

—— Neue Ausgabe, besorgt von Curt Mündel. Strassburg, 1892, '96. 2 pts.

Stojanović, M. Pučke pripoviedke i pjesme. [Popular Tales and Songs.] Agram, 1867.

Stokes, Whitley. The Marriage of Sir Gawain. In The Academy, XLI, 399. 1892.

—— Mythological Notes. In Revue Celtique, I, 256–62; II, 197–203.

—— The Prose Tales in the Rennes Dindšenchas. In Revue Celtique, XV, 272–336, 419–84; XVI, 31–83, 135–67, 269–312. 1894–95.

Stokoe, John. See Bruce, John Collingwood.

Storm, Gustav. Sagnkredsene om Karl den Store og Didrik af Bern hos de nordiske Folk. Et Bidrag til Middelalderens Litterære Historie. Kristiania, 1874. (Norske Historiske Forening.)

—— See Arkiv för nordisk Filologi.

Stow, John. Annales, or, a Generall Chronicle of England. Begun by —— : continved and augmented with matters forraigne and domestique, ancient and moderne, vnto the end of this present yeere, 1631, by Edmvnd Howes, Gent. Londini. 1631.

—— A Survey of the Cities of London and Westminster brought down from the year 1633 . . . to the present time by J. Strype. London, 1720. 2 vols.

Strange, J. See Caesarius Heisterbacensis.

Straparola, Giovanfrancesco. Les Facétieuses Nuits de Straparole. Traduites par Jean Louveau et Pierre de Larivey. Paris, 1857. 2 vols.

—— Die Märchen des Straparola. Aus dem Italiänischen, mit Anmerkungen von Dr. Friedr. Wilh. Val. Schmidt. Berlin, 1817. (Märchen-Saal. Sammlung alter Märchen, mit Anmerkungen ; herausgegeben von Dr. Friedr. Wilh. Val. Schmidt, 1.)

Straparola, Giovanfrancesco. Le Piacevoli Notti di M. Giovanfrancesco Straparola da Caravagio, nelle qvali si contengono le fauole con i loro enimmi da dieci donne, & da duo giouani raccontate, cosa dilettevole, et rara, ne mai piu data in luce. In Venetia, 1560. 2 bks.

Streitberg, Wilhelm, and Brugmann, Karl. See Indogermanische Forschungen.

Strengleikar eða Lioðabok. En Samling af romantiske Fortællinger efter bretoniske Folkesange (Lais). . . . Udgivet af R. Keyser og C. R. Unger. Christiania, 1850.

Strodtmann, Adolf. Briefe von und an G. A. Bürger. See Bürger, G. A.

Strohal, R. Hrvatskih narodnih pripoviedaka. Knjiga I. Na Rieci, 1886.

Struve, B. G. See Pistorius, J.

Strype, John. See Stow, John.

Stuart, John. See Miscellany of the Spalding Club.

—— See Spalding, John.

Stubbes, Phillip. The Anatomie of Abuses : contayning a discoverie, or briefe summarie, of such notable vices and imperfections, as now raigne in many Christian countreyes of the worlde, but (especiallie) in a verie famous ilande called Ailgna, [etc.]. Made dialogue-wise by Phillip Stubbes. . . . London, 1583. In John Payne Collier, Miscellaneous Tracts temp. Eliz. & Jac. I, 11 [London, 1870].

—— Phillip Stubbes's Anatomy of the Abuses in England in Shakspere's youth, A. D. 1583. [Etc.] Edited by Frederick J. Furnivall. London, 1877–79, '82. 2 pts. (New Shakspere Society, Series VI, nos 4, 6, 12.)

Stubbs, William. The Constitutional History of England in its origin and development. Oxford, 1874. 3 vols.

—— See Diceto, Ralph de.

—— See Guilielmus Malmesburiensis.

Studies and Notes in Philology and Literature. Published under the Direction of the Modern Languages Departments of Harvard University. Boston, 1892–.

Stumme, Hans. See Socin, Albert.

Štúr, Ludevít. O národních písních a pověstech plemen slovanských. [On the Popular Songs and Tales of the Slavic Nations.] Prague, 1853.

Sturm, V. See Hondorff, A.

Suchier, H. See Beaumanoir.

Sullivan, W. K. See O'Curry, Eugene.

Sumlork, W. S. [= Krolmus]. Staročeské powěsti, zpěwy, etc. [Old-Bohemian Tales, Songs, etc.] Prague, 1845–51. 3 pts. in 2 vols.

Sutermeister, Otto. Kinder- und Hausmärchen aus der Schweiz. Gesammelt und herausgegeben von ——. Zweite, mit Zusätzen, Erläuterungen und literarischen Nachweisen vermehrte Auflage. Aarau, 1873.

Svenska Fornminnesförening. Tidskrift. Stockholm, 1871–.

Swan, Charles. See Gesta Romanorum.

Swift, Jonathan. Tale of a Tub. In Works, with notes and a life of the author by Sir Walter Scott, X, 1–216. Edinburgh, 1824.

Swynnerton, Charles. The Adventures of the Panjáb hero Rájá Rasálu and other folk-tales of the Panjáb. Collected and compiled from original sources. Calcutta, 1884.

—— Four Legends of King Rasálu of Sialkot. In Folk-Lore Journal, I, 129–152. 1883.

Swynnerton, Charles. Indian Nights' Entertainment; or, Folk-Tales from the Upper Indus. London, 1892.

[Sydow, Friedrich Wilhelm von, *editor*.] Thüringen und der Harz, mit ihren Merkwürdigkeiten, Volkssagen und Legenden. Historisch-romantische Beschreibung aller in Thüringen und auf dem Harz vorhanden gewesenen und noch vorhandenen Schlösser, Burgen, Klöster, merkwürdigen Kirchen und anderer Gebäude, Fabrikorter, Bergwerke, Ruinen, Höhlen, Denkmäler, malerischen Gegenden und sonst beachtenswerther Gegenstände aus dem Reiche der Geschichte und Natur. Sondershausen, 1839–44. 8 vols.

Symbolae ad Literaturam Teutonicam antiqviorem ex codicibus manu exaratis, qvi Havniae asservantur, editae sumptibus Petri Friderici Suhm. [By Berthel Christian Sandvig and Rasmus Nyerup.] Havniae, 1787.

Syntipas. Syntipae philosophi Persae Fabulae LXII. Graece et Latine. Ex duobus codicibus Mosquensibus primum edidit . . . Christianus Fridericus Matthaei [etc.]. Lipsiae, 1781.

—— Die Fabeln des Sophos. Syrisches Original der griechischen Fabeln des Syntipas in berichtigtem vocalisirtem Texte zum ersten Male vollständig mit einem Glossar herausgegeben nebst literarischen Vorbemerkungen und einer einleitenden Untersuchung über das Vaterland der Fabel von Dr. Julius Landsberger. Posen, 1859.

Syrku, P. Zur mittelalterlichen Erzählungsliteratur aus dem Bulgarischen. *In* Archiv für slavische Philologie, VII, 78–98. 1884.

Taine, Henri. Les origines de la France contemporaine. Paris, 1876–94. 6 vols.

Tales of a Parrot. See Tuti-nameh.

Talvj, *pseudon. for* Therese A. L. v. Jakob Robinson. Versuch einer geschichtlichen Charakteristik der Volkslieder germanischer Nationen. Leipzig, 1840.

—— Historical View of the Languages and Literature of the Slavic Nations; with a sketch of their popular poetry. By Talvj. With a preface by Edward Robinson. New York, 1850.

Taming of a Shrew. The old Taming of a Shrew, upon which Shakespeare founded his comedy. Reprinted from the edition of 1594, and collated with the subsequent editions of 1596 and 1607. Edited by Thomas Amyot. London, 1844. (Shakespeare Society, 25.)

Tamlane: an old Scottish Border Ballad. Aberdeen, 1862.

Tarbé, Prosper. Poètes de Champagne antérieurs au siècle de François Ier. Proverbes champenois avant le XVIe siècle [etc.]. Reims, 1851.

Tarlton's Jests, 1611. *In* W. Carew Hazlitt, Shakespeare Jest-Books, II, 190–260. London, 1864.

Taschenbuch für Dichter und Dichterfreunde. [Edited by Christian Heinrich Schmid and Johann Gottfried Dyck.] Leipzig, 1774–1781. 12 pts.

Tausend und Eine Nacht. See Arabian Nights.

Tausend und Ein Tag. Morgenländische Erzählungen. Aus dem Persischen, Türkischen und Arabischen nach Petits de la Croix, Galland, Cardonne, Chawis und Cazotte, dem Grafen Caylus und Anderen, übersetzt von F. H. von der Hagen. Prenzlau, 1827–29. 10 vols. Bd. XI, zweite wohlfeilere Ausgabe. Prenzlau, 1836.

La Tavola Ritonda. See Tristan.

Tawney, C. H. See Kathā sarit sāgara.

Taylor, Elizabeth. The Braemar Highlands: their Tales, Traditions, and History. Edinburgh, 1869.

Taylor, George. A Memoir of Robert Surtees, Esq., M. A., F. S. A. A new edition, with additions, by the Rev. James Raine. Durham, London, Edinburgh, 1852. (Surtees Society, 24.)

Taylor, James. The great Historic Families of Scotland. London, 1887. 2 vols.

Taylor, Richard. See Warton, Thomas.

Tea-Table Miscellany. See Ramsay, Allan.

Temme, J. D. H. Die Volkssagen der Altmark. Mit einem Anhange von Sagen aus den übrigen Marken und aus dem Magdeburgischen. Gesammelt von ——. Berlin, 1839.

Temple, Richard Carnac. The Legends of the Panjâb. Bombay and London, 1883–86. 3 vols.

ten Brink, B. See Quellen und Forschungen.

Tendlau, Abraham M. Das Buch der Sagen und Legenden jüdischer Vorzeit. Nach den Quellen bearbeitet nebst Anmerkungen und Erläuterungen von ——. Zweite vermehrte Auflage. Stuttgart, 1845.

Terrebasse, Alfred de. See Palanus.

Tettau, Wilhelm [Johann Albert], Freiherr von. Ueber einige bis jetzt unbekannte Erfurter Drucke aus dem 15. Jahrhundert. Ein Beitrag zur Bibliographie der älteren deutschen Literatur und zur vergleichenden Sagenkunde von Wilh. Freih. v. Tettau. *In* Jahrbücher der Königlichen Akademie gemeinnütziger Wissenschaften zu Erfurt. Neue Folge. Heft VI, 171–328. Erfurt, 1870.

te Winkel, J. See Floire et Blanceflor.

Teza, Emilio. L' Avvelenatrice, canzone boema. *In* Atti e Memorie della R. Accademia di Scienze, Lettere ed Arti in Padova. Anno ccxcii (1890–91). Nuova Serie, vol. VII, pp. 227–238. Padova, 1891.

—— I tre Banditi, canzone scozzese del cinque-cento. *In* Atti e Memorie della R. Accademia di Scienze, Lettere ed Arti in Padova. Anno ccxcv (1893–94). Nuova Serie, vol. X, pp. 113–38. Padova, 1894.

Thackeray, William Makepeace. Little Billee. *In* Works, vol. XXI. London, 1879.

Theal, George McCall. Kaffir Folk-Lore; or, a selection from the Traditional Tales current among the people living on the eastern border of the Cape Colony. With copious explanatory notes. London, 1882.

Thedel von Walmoden. Des edeln gestrengen weitberühmten und streitbaren Helden Thedel Unverfährt von Walmoden tapfere männliche und ritterliche Thaten und wunderbarliche Geschichten. *In* Karl Simrock, Die deutschen Volksbücher, IX, 397–426. Frankfurt a. M., 1856.

—— See Thym, Georg.

Theophanes Isaurus, the Confessor. Theophanis Chronographia. Ex recensione Ioannis Classeni. Bonnae, 1833, '41. 2 vols. (Corpus Scriptorum Historiae Byzantinae. Editio emendatior et copiosior. XXXVIII, XXXIX.)

Thévenot, Jean de. Relation d'un voyage fait au Levant. Dans laquelle il est curieusement traité des états sujets au Grand Seigneur, des mœurs, religions, forces, gouuernemens, politiques, langues, et coustumes des habitans de ce grand empire. [Pt. I.] Rouen, 1765. Suite du Voyage de Levant. Seconde partie. Paris, 1774.

Thiele, J. M. Danmarks Folkesagn. Samlede af ——. Kiøbenhavn, 1843–60. 3 pts.

Thierry, Augustin. Histoire de la Conquête de l'Angleterre par les Normands, de ses causes et de ses suites jusqu'à nos jours, en Angleterre, en Écosse, en Irlande et sur le Continent. Troisième édition, entièrement revue et augmentée. Paris, 1830. 4 vols.

Thiers, Jean Baptiste. Traité des superstitions selon l'Écriture Sainte, les décrets des conciles et les sentimens des SS. Pères et des théologiens. Seconde édition. Paris, 1697.

—— Traité des superstitions selon l'Écriture Sainte, les décrets des conciles et les sentimens des saints Pères et des théologiens. In [J. F. Bernard,] Cérémonies et coutumes religieuses de tous les peuples du monde. Nouvelle édition, entièrement conforme a celle de Holland. Paris, 1807-10. 12 vols. Tom. XI, 27-168. 1810.

Thilo, Johann Carl. Codex apocryphus Novi Testamenti e libris editis et manuscriptis . . . collectus, recensitus, notisque et prolegomenis illustratus. Lipsiae, 1832.

Thomas Cantipratensis. Bonum Universale. [With the title] Th. Cantipratani Miraculorum et exemplorum mirabilium sui temporis libri duo: . . . opera G. Colvenerii. Douay, 1605, 1624.

Thomas of Erceldoune. The Romance and Prophecies of ——. Printed from five manuscripts; with illustrations from the prophetic literature of the 15th and 16th centuries. Edited, with introduction and notes, by James A. H. Murray. . . . London, 1875. (Early English Text Society, [61].)

—— Thomas of Erceldoune, herausgegeben von Alois Brandl. Berlin, 1880. (Sammlung englischer Denkmäler in kritischen Ausgaben, 2.)

Thomas of Monmouth. See Jessopp, Augustus.

Thomas, Martha Carey. Sir Gawayne and the Green Knight. A comparison with the French Perceval, preceded by an investigation of the author's other works and followed by a characterization of Gawain in English poems. Zürich, 1883.

Thomas, William. See Dugdale, Sir William.

Thompson, Edward Maunde. The Eikon Basilike and a Book of Ballads. In The Academy, XXVII, 170. 1885.

—— See Adam of Usk.

Thoms, William J. A Collection of Early Prose Romances. London, 1828, '27. 3 vols.

Thomson, George. Thomson's Collection of the Songs of Burns, Sir Walter Scott, Bart., and other eminent lyric poets ancient and modern, united to the Select Melodies of Scotland, and of Ireland and Wales, with symphonies and accompaniments. . . . London, 1822-25. 6 vols. [See above, V, 406 b.]

Thomson, J. M. See Registrum Magni Sigilli.

Thomson, Thomas. See Booke of the Universall Kirk of Scotland.

—— See Diurnal of Remarkable Occurrents.

—— See James VI.

Thornton Romances. The Early English Metrical Romances of Perceval, Isumbras, Eglamour, and Degrevant. Selected from manuscripts at Lincoln and Cambridge. Edited by James Orchard Halliwell. London, 1844. (Camden Society, 30.)

Thorpe, Benjamin. See Florentius.

Thorpe, Markham John. See Calendar of the State Papers, etc.

Thorpe, T. B. Reminiscences of the Mississippi. In Harper's New Monthly Magazine, XII, 25-41. 1856.

Thüringen und der Harz. See Sydow, F. W. von.

Thym, Georg. Des edlen gestrengen, weitberümbten, vnd streitbaren Heldes Thedel Vnnorferden von Walmoden, tapfferer, menlicher, vnd ritterlicher Thaten, [etc.]. Auffs fleissigste in Reim gebracht durch M. Georgium Thym von Zwickaw, Schulmeister zu Wernigerode. Magdeburg, [1558].

Thym, Georg. Georg Thyms Gedicht Thedel von Wallmoden. Herausgegeben von Paul Zimmermann. Halle a. S., 1887. (Braune, Neudrucke deutscher Litteraturwerke des XVI. und XVII. Jahrhunderts, 72.)

Tibullus, Albius. Opera omnia ex editione I. G. Huschkii cum notis et interpretatione in usum Delphini [etc.]. Londini, 1822.

Tieck, Ludwig von. Deutsches Theater, herausgegeben von ——. Berlin, 1817. 2 vols.

Tielemann, G. T. Livona. Ein historisch - poetisches Taschenbuch für die deutsch-russischen Ostsee-Provinzen. Riga und Dorpat, 1812, '16. 2 vols.

Timoneda, Juan de. El Patrañuelo. In Novelistas Anteriores á Cervantes. Biblioteca de Autores Españoles, III, 129-165. Madrid, 1846.

The Tinker and Farmer's Daughter's Garland. [British Museum, 11621. a. 6 (34). See V, 109 b.]

Tischendorf, Constantin. Evangelia apocrypha, adhibitis plurimis codicibus Graecis et Latinis maximam partem primum consultis atque ineditorum copia insignibus edidit ——. Lipsiae, 1853.

Tisza Eszlár. See Blut-Prozess, etc.

Tittmann, J. See Sachs, Hans.

Titurel. Der jüngere Titurel, herausgegeben von K. A. Hahn. Quedlinburg and Leipzig, 1842. (Bibliothek der gesammten deutschen National-Literatur von der ältesten bis auf die neuere Zeit, 24.)

Titus Livius Foro-Juliensis. Vita Henrici Quinti, Regis Angliae. Accedit sylloge epistolarum, a variis Angliae principibus scriptarum. E codicibus calamo exaratis descripsit ediditque Tho. Hearnius. Oxonii, 1716.

Töppen, M. Aberglauben aus Masuren, mit einem Anhange enthaltend: Masurische Sagen und Mährchen. Zweite durch zahlreiche Zusätze und durch den Anhang erweiterte Auflage. Danzig, 1867.

Toischer, Wendelin. See Alexander the Great.

Tollet, George. Mr. Tollet's Opinion concerning the Morris Dancers upon his Window. In The Plays of William Shakspeare, to which are added notes by Samuel Johnson and George Steevens, VIII, 596-606. London, 1793. 15 vols.

Tomson, Graham R. Ballads of the North Countrie, edited with introduction and notes. London, 1888.

Tonndorf, Max. Rauf Coilyear. Ein mittelschottisches Gedicht. Litterarische, sprachliche und metrische Untersuchungen. [Halle dissertation.] Halle a. S., 1893.

Torfason (Torfæus), Þormóðr. Historia Hrolfi Krakii inter potentissimos in ethnicismo Daniae reges celeberrimi . . . a fabulis, in quantum fieri potuit, vindicata, cumque aliis historicis imprimis Saxone Grammatico diligenter collata. Havniae, 1705.

—— Historia Rerum Norvegicarum, [etc.]. Hafniae, 1711. 4 pts.

Torrent of Portugal. An English Metrical Romance. Now first published from an unique manuscript of the fifteenth century, preserved in the Chetham Library at Manchester. Edited by James Orchard Halliwell. London, 1842.

Torrent of Portyngale. Edited by E. Adam. London, 1887. (Early English Text Society.)

Tors, Lambert li. See Alexander the Great.

Totā Kahānī. See Tuti-nameh.

Toubin, Charles. Jean-Denis le vigneron. Histoire jurassienne. *In* Revue des Deux Mondes, XXIV° année, 2° série de la nouvelle période, t. VII, pp. 459–91. 1854.

Touti Nameh. See Tuti-nameh.

La Tradition. Revue générale des contes, legendes, chants, usages, traditions et arts populaires. Paris, 1887-.

Train, Joseph Karl von. Die wichtigsten Thatsachen aus der Geschichte der Juden in Regensburg. *In* Zeitschrift für die historische Theologie, VII, iii, 39–138. Leipzig, 1837.

Trebutien, G. S. See Robert le Diable.

Treichel, A. Sagen aus Westpreussen. *In* Zeitschrift für Volkskunde, II, 143–44. 1890.

Trench, Richard Chenevix. Poems. London and Cambridge, 1865.

Trevisa, John. See Higden, R.

Triamour. See Sir Triamour.

Tristan. The poetical Romances of Tristan in French, in Anglo-Norman, and in Greek composed in the XII and XIII centuries, edited by Francisque Michel. London, 1835–39. 3 vols.

—— Eilhart von Oberge. Herausgegeben von Franz Lichtenstein. Strassburg, London, 1877. (Quellen und Forschungen zur Sprach- und Culturgeschichte der germanischen Völker, 19.)

—— Tristan von Meister Gotfrit von Strassburg mit der Fortsetzung des Meisters Ulrich von Turheim. In zwei Abtheilungen herausgegeben von E. von Groote. Berlin, 1821.

—— Tristan und Isolt. *In* Gottfrieds von Strassburg Werke, aus den bessten Handschriften mit Einleitung und Wörterbuch herausgegeben durch Friedr. Heinr. von der Hagen. Breslau, 1823. 2 vols. Vol. I.

—— Gottfried von Strassburg. Tristan. Herausgegeben von Reinhold Bechstein. Leipzig, 1869. 2 vols.

—— Heinrichs von Friberg Fortsetzung von Gottfrieds Tristan. *In* Gottfrieds von Strassburg Werke. Herausgegeben durch Friedr. Heinr. von der Hagen. II, 3–98. Breslau, 1823.

—— Heinrich von Freiberg. Tristan. Herausgegeben von Reinhold Bechstein. Leipzig, 1877. (Deutsche Dichtungen des Mittelalters. Mit Wort- und Sacherklärungen. Herausgegeben von Karl Bartsch. V.)

—— Fortsetzung von Meister Ulrich von Turheim. *In* Tristan von Meister Gotfrit von Strassburg mit der Fortsetzung des Meisters ——. In zwei Abtheilungen herausgegeben von E. von Groote. Pp. 333–390. Berlin, 1821.

—— Saga af Tristram ok Ísönd, samt Möttuls Saga, udgivne af det Kongelige Nordiske Oldskrift-Selskab. [Ed. by G. G. Brynjúlfsson.] Kjöbenhavn, 1878.

—— Tristrams Saga ok Ísondar. Mit einer literarhistorischen Einleitung, deutscher Uebersetzung und Anmerkungen zum ersten Mal herausgegeben von Eugen Kölbing. *In* Die nordische und die englische Version der Tristan-Sage. Herausgegeben von Eugen Kölbing. 2 vols. Erster Theil. Heilbronn, 1878.

—— La Tavola Ritonda o l' istoria di Tristano, testo di lingua citato dagli accademici della Crusca ed ora per la prima volta pubblicato secondo il codice della Mediceo-Laurenziana per cura e con illustrazioni di Filippo-Luigi Polidori. Bologna, 1864, '65. 2 pts. (Collezione di opere inedite o rare dei primi tre secoli della lingua,

pubblicata per cura della R. Commissione pe' Testi di Lingua nelle Provincie dell' Emilia.)

Tristan. Sir Tristrem. Mit Einleitung, Anmerkungen und Glossar herausgegeben von Eugen Kölbing. *In* Die nordische und die englische Version der Tristan-Sage. Herausgegeben von Eugen Kölbing. 2 vols. Zweiter Theil. Heilbronn, 1882.

—— Sir Tristrem, a metrical Romance of the Thirteenth Century. Edited from the Auchinleck MS. by Walter Scott. 3d ed. Edinburgh, 1811.

—— Sir Tristrem. *In* Walter Scott, Poetical Works, vol. V. Edinburgh, 1833.

Tristrem. See Tristan.

Troyes, Nicolas de. See (Le) Grand Parangon des Nouvelles Nouvelles.

Trudy etnografičesko-statističeskoj ekspedicii v zapadnorusskij kraj, snarjažennoj Imperatorskim Russkim Geografičeskim Obščestvom. Jugo-zapadnyj otděl. [Memoirs of the Ethnographic-statistical Expedition in the West-Russian region, under the auspices of the Russian Imperial Geographical Society, South-West Division.] St Petersburg, 1872–77. 7 vols.

Trueba, Antonio de. Cuentos populares. Leipzig, 1866. (F. A. Brockhaus, Coleccion de autores españoles, 19.)

Tschudius, Aegidius. Aegidii Tschudii gewesenen Land-Ammanns zu Glarus Chronicon Helveticum. . . . Nunmehro zum Ersten mahl herausg. von Johann Rudolff Iselin. Basel, 1734, '36. 2 vols.

Tudor, John R. The Orkneys and Shetland, their past and present state. London, 1883.

Tummulillis, Angelo de. Notabilia Temporum, a cura di Costantino Corvisieri. Livorno, 1890. (*In the series* Fonti per la Storia d' Italia.)

Turandot. Von Heinz dem Kellner. *In* F. H. von der Hagen. Gesammtabenteuer, III, 175–185. Stuttgart and Tübingen, 1850.

Turnbull, W. B. D. D. See Arthour and Merlin.

The Turnip-Sack Garland, containing three excellent new songs. N. p., n. d. [In a volume (of garlands) formerly belonging to Heber, and now in Harvard College Library, 25252.6. See the note at V, 129.]

[Tuti-nameh.] The Totā Kahānī; or, Tales of a Parrot, translated from Saiyid Ḥaidar Bakhsh's Hindūstānī version of Muḥammad Ḳādirī's Persian abridgement of Nakhshabī's Tūtī Nāma, by George Small. London, 1875.

—— The Tooti-Nameh, or Tales of a Parrot, in the Persian language with an English translation [by F. Gladwin]. Calcutta and London, 1801.

—— Touti Nameh. Eine Sammlung persischer Mährchen von Nechschebi. Deutsche Uebersetzung von Carl Jakob Ludwig Iken. Mit einem Anhange von demselben, und von J. G. L. Kosegarten. Stuttgart, 1822.

—— Das Papagaienbuch. Eine Sammlung orientalischer Erzählungen. Nach der türkischen Bearbeitung zum ersten Male übersetzt von Georg Rosen. Leipzig, 1858. 2 pts.

Twinger, Jacob. See Königshofen.

Two old Historical Scots Poems, giving an account of the Battles of Harlaw and the Reid-Squair. Glasgow, Robert Foulis, 1748. [See III, 316 a, note.]

[Twysden, Roger.] Historiae Anglicanae Scriptores X. Ex vetustis manuscriptis nunc primum in lucem editi. Londini, 1652. 2 vols.

Tyler, James Endell. Henry of Monmouth, or, Memoirs of

the Life and Character of Henry the Fifth, as Prince of Wales and King of England. London, 1838. 2 vols.

Tyrwhitt, Thomas. See Chaucer, Geoffrey.

Tytler, Patrick Fraser. History of Scotland. Edinburgh, 1828–43. 9 vols.

Udall, Nicholas. Apophthegmes that is to saie, prompte, quicke, wittie and sentencious saiynges of certain Emperours, Kynges, Capitaines, Philosophiers and Oratours, as well Grekes, as Romaines. . . . First gathered and compiled in Latine by the ryght famous clerke Maister Erasmus of Roterodame. And now translated into Englysche by N. Udall. Londini, 1542.

—— Ralph Roister Doister, a comedy, by ——. And the Tragedie of Gorboduc, by Thomas Norton and Thomas Sackville. With introductory memoirs. Edited by William Durrant Cooper. London, 1847. (Shakespeare Society, 34.)

Uhland, Ludwig. Schriften zur Geschichte der Dichtung und Sage. Stuttgart, 1865–73. 8 vols.

—— Zum schwäbischen Sagenkunde. III. Bodman. In Pfeiffer's Germania, IV, 35–96. 1859.

—— and Bouck, Joseph Ludewig de. Die niederdeutschen Liederbücher von ——. Herausgegeben von der germanistischen Section des Vereins für Kunst und Wissenschaft in Hamburg. In Niederdeutsche Volkslieder. Heft I. Hamburg, 1883. (Verein für Niederdeutsche Sprachforschung.)

Ulenspiegel. See Eulenspiegel.

Ulrich von Eschenbach. See Alexander the Great.

Ulrich von Turheim. See Tristan.

Ulrich von Zatzikhoven. Lanzelet. Herausgegeben von K. A. Hahn. Frankfurt a. M., 1845.

Ulrich, Johann Caspar. Johan Caspar Ulrichs, Pfarrers zum Frauen-Münster in Zürich, Sammlung Jüdischer Geschichten, welche sich mit diesem Volk in dem XIII. und folgenden Jahrhunderten bis auf MDCCLX. in der Schweitz von Zeit zu Zeit zugetragen. Zur Beleuchtung der allgemeinen Historie dieser Nation herausgegeben. Basel, 1768.

Ulster Ballads. [British Museum, 1162, k. 6. See V, 216 a.]

Ungarische Revue, mit Unterstützung der Ungarischen Akademie der Wissenschaften herausgegeben von P. Hunfalvy, [etc.]. Leipzig, Berlin, Wien, 1881–95.

Unger, Carl Richard. Mariu Saga. Legender om Jomfru Maria og hendes Jertegn. Efter gamle Haandskrifter udgivne af C. R. Unger. Christiania, 1871 ['67–'71]. (Norsk Oldskriftselskab, Samlinger, 11, 12, 14, 16.)

—— See Dietrich von Bern.

—— See Karlamagnus Saga.

—— See Olafs Saga.

—— See Strengleikar.

The Universal Magazine. New Series. London, 1804–14. 21 vols.

Upsala Universitets Årsskrift. See Munthe, Å. W:son.

Urbani, Peter. See Selection of Scots Songs.

Ursinus, August Friedrich. Balladen und Lieder altenglischer und altschottischer Dichtart. Herausgegeben von ——. Berlin, 1777.

Ussermann, E. See Hermannus.

[Utterson, Edward Vernon.] Select Pieces of Early Popular Poetry: re-published principally from early printed copies, in the black letter. London, 1825. 2 vols.

Valerius Maximus. Facta Dictaque Memorabilia ex editione Joannis Kappii. Londini, 1823. 3 vols.

Valjavec, M. K. Narodne priprovjesti u Varaždinu i okolici. [Popular Tales in and about Warasdin.] 2d ed. Agram, 1890.

The Varietie. In The Country Captain and The Varietie, two Comedies written by a person of honour. [William Cavendish, first Duke of Newcastle.] London, 1649. 2 pts.

Varnhagen, Hermann. Zu mittelenglischen Dichtungen. VIII. Lay le Freine. In Anglia, III, 415–25. 1880.

Vasari, Georgio. Vite de' piu' eccellenti pittori, scultori e architetti. Illustrate con note. Milano, 1807–11. 16 vols.

Vasconcellos. See Leite de Vasconcellos, José.

Vastovius, Joannes. Vitis Aquilonia, sive Vitae sanctorum regni Sueo-gothici, emendavit ac notis illustravit Er. Benzelius filius. Upsaliae, 1708.

Vaugeois, J. F. Gabriel. Histoire des antiquités de la ville de l'Aigle et de ses environs [etc.] L'Aigle, 1841.

Vaz, João. Villa Nova de Gaia, romance por ——. Publicado segundo a edição de 1630 e acompanhado de um estudo sobre a transformação do romance anonymo no romance com fórma litteraria por Theophilo Braga. Coimbra, 1868.

Veckenstedt, Edmund. Wendische Sagen, Märchen und abergläubische Gebräuche. Gesammelt und nacherzählt von ——. Graz, 1880.

—— See Zeitschrift für Volkskunde.

Veitch, John. The original Ballad of the Dowie Dens. In Blackwood's Edinburgh Magazine, CXLVII, 739–46. 1890. [Republished in his Border Essays, Edinburgh and London, 1896, pp. 55–79.]

Velschow, J. M. See Saxo Grammaticus.

Vergil, Polydore. Polydori Vergilii Vrbinatis Anglicae Historiae Libri vigintiseptem. Basileae, 1570.

Vernaleken, Theodor. Alpensagen. Volksüberlieferungen aus der Schweiz, aus Vorarlberg, Kärnten, Steiermark, Salzburg, Ober- und Niederösterreich. Wien, 1858.

—— Mythen und Bräuche des Volkes in Oesterreich. Als Beitrag zur deutschen Mythologie, Volksdichtung und Sittenkunde. Wien, 1859.

—— Oesterreichische Kinder- und Hausmärchen, treu nach mündlicher Ueberlieferung. Wien, 1864.

[Verville, François Béroalde de.] Le moyen de parvenir. Nouvelle édition. Londres, 1786. 3 vols.

Vesselofsky, A. See Wesselofsky, A.

Vicars, John. Account of the Siege of Gloucester. In his Jehovah-Jireh, God in the Mount: or, England's Parliamentarie-Chronicle. London, 1644–46. 4 pts. I, 401.

Viehoff, H. See Archiv für das Studium, u. s. w.

Vienna Academy. Denkschriften der kaiserlichen Akademie der Wissenschaften. Philosophisch-historische Classe. Wien, 1850–.

—— Kaiserliche Akademie der Wissenschaften. Sitzungsberichte der Philosophisch - historischen Classe. Wien, 1848–.

Vierteljahrsschrift für Kultur und Litteratur der Renaissance. Herausgegeben von Dr. Ludwig Geiger. Berlin, 1886–87. 2 vols.

Vigfússon, Guðbrandr. See Cleasby, Richard.

—— and Möbius, Theodor. Fornsögur: Vatnsdælasaga Hallfreðarsaga Flóamannasaga, herausgegeben von ——. Leipzig, 1860.

Vigfússon, Guðbrandr, and Powell, F. York. Corpus Poeticum Boreale : the Poetry of the Old Northern tongue from the earliest times to the thirteenth century, edited, classified and translated with introduction, excursus, and notes. Oxford, 1883. 2 vols.

Villanis, P. Otto canzoni popolari Zaratine. *In* Archivio per lo studio delle tradizioni popolari, XI, 32–39. 1892.

Villemarqué, Hersart de la. Les romans de la Table Ronde et les contes des anciens Bretons. Troisième édition revue et considérablement modifiée. Paris, 1860.

Vilmar, August Friedrich Christian. Handbüchlein für Freunde des deutschen Volkliedes. Zweite Auflage. Marburg in Hessen, 1868. Dritte vermehrte Auflage. Marburg, 1886.

Vincent of Beauvais. Speculum Historiale Vincentii. [Venetiis,] 1494.

—— Speculum Morale Vincentii. [Venetiis, 1493.]

—— Incipit speculū naturale Vincentij beluacēſs fratris ordinis p̄dicatorum. [Strassburg ?], [1473]. 2 vols.

Vinson, Julien. Le folk-lore du pays basque. Paris, 1883. (Les Littératures Populaires de toutes les Nations, 15.)

—— See Webster, Wentworth.

Violette. Roman de la Violette. See Gibert de Montreuil.

Viollet le Duc, Emmanuel Louis Nicolas. Ancien théâtre françois, ou, collection des ouvrages dramatiques les plus remarquables depuis les mystères jusqu'à Corneille, publié avec des notes et éclaircissements par M. ——. Paris, 1854–57. 10 vols.

Virgilius. *In* William J. Thoms, A Collection of Early Prose Romances, London, 1828, II.

Virginal [= Dietrich und seine Gesellen]. *In* Dietrichs Abenteuer, herausgegeben von Julius Zupitza, pp. 1–200. Berlin, 1870. (Deutsches Heldenbuch, V.)

Visböcker. Bröms Gyllenmärs Visbok. Första häftet. *In* 1500- och 1600-talens Visböcker, utgifna af Adolf Noreen och Henrik Schück. II. Stockholm, 1885. (Skrifter utgifna af Svenska Literatursällskapet.)

—— Bröms Gyllenmärs Visbok. *In* Nyare Bidrag till Kännedom om de svenska Landsmålen ock svenskt Folklif. Stockholm, 1887.

—— Harald Oluffsons Visbok. Första häftet. *In* 1500- och 1600-talens Visböcker, utgifna af Adolf Noreen och Henrik Schück. I. Stockholm, 1884. (Skrifter utgifna af Svenska Literatursällskapet.)

Vischer, Wilhelm. Die Sage von der Befreiung der Waldstädte nach ihrer allmälichen Ausbildung. Nebst einer Beilage : Das älteste Tellenschauspiel. Leipzig, 1867.

Visentini, Isaia. Fiabe mantovane raccolte da ——. Torino-Roma, 1879. *In* D. Comparetti ed Alessandro d' Ancona, Canti e racconti del popolo italiano, VII.

Vitry, Jacques de. See Jacques de Vitry.

Vocal Music, or, The Songsters Companion, containing a new and choice Collection of the greatest variety of Songs, Cantatas, &c., with the music prefixt to each, together with an alphabetical Index of the whole. [London,] Printed for Robert Horsfield, at N. 22, in Ludgate Street. n. d.

Voetius, Gisbertus. Selectae disputationes theologicae. Ultrajecti, 1648–69. 5 vols.

Vogl, Johann Nepomuk. Die ältesten Volksmärchen der Russen. Wien, 1841.

Vogt, Friedrich. Die deutschen Dichtungen von Salomon und Markolf, herausgegeben von Friedrich Vogt. I. Band. Salman und Morolf. Halle, 1880.

Vogt, Friedrich. Zur Salman-Morolfsage. *In* Beiträge zur Geschichte der deutschen Sprache und Literatur, VIII, 313–23. 1882.

Volksbücher. 1–34, herausgebeben von G. O. Marbach. 38, von O. Wigand. 37, 39–50, von O. L. B. Wolff. Leipzig, 1838[–49]. 52 nos.

—— Die deutschen Volksbücher. Gesammelt und in ihrer ursprünglichen Echtheit wiederhergestellt von Karl Simrock. Frankfurt a. M., 1845–56. 9 vols.

Volkskunde. Tijdschrift voor nederlandsche Folklore, onder Redactie van Pol de Mont en Aug. Gittée. Gent, 1888–.

Vollmer, A. See Hildebrandslied.

Voltaire, François Marie Arouet de. Ce qui plaît aux dames. *In* Œuvres Completes. Contes. T. XIV, 33–48. [Kehl ?], 1785. (Société Littéraire-typographique.)

—— Recueil des lettres de M. de Voltaire 1765–1766. *In* Œuvres Completes. Tom. LXXVII. [Kehl ?], 1785. (Société Littéraire-typographique.)

Vonbun, F. J. Die Sagen Vorarlbergs. Nach schriftlichen und mündlichen Ueberlieferungen gesammelt und erläutert von Dr ——. Innsbruck, 1858.

Voretzsch, Carl. Ueber die Sage von Ogier dem Dänen und die Entstehung der Chevalerie Ogier. Halle a. S., 1891.

Vuk. See Karadschitsch, Wuk Stephanowitsch.

Vulpius, Ch. Aug. See Curiositäten.

W., C. H. Unterhaltende Räthsel-spiele in Fragen und Antworten, gesammelt von C. H. W. Merseburg, 1824.

Wace, Robert. Le roman de Brut. Publié pour la première fois d'après les manuscrits des bibliothèques de Paris avec un commentaire et des notes par Le Roux de Lincy. Rouen, 1836–38. 2 vols.

—— Maistre Wace's Roman de Rou et des Ducs de Normandie. Nach den Handschriften von neuem herausgeben von Dr. Hugo Andresen. Heilbronn, 1877–79. 2 vols.

Wackernagel, Wilhelm. Sagen und Märchen aus dem Aargau. *In* Zeitschrift für deutsches Alterthum, III, 35–37. 1842.

Wade, Laurence. Thomas Beket, epische Legende, von Laurentius Wade (1497), nach der einzigen Hs. im Corp. Chr. Coll. Cambr. 278, p. 1 ff., hrsg. v. C. Horstmann. *In* Englische Studien, III, 409–469. 1880.

Wager, William. A very mery and pythie Commedie, called The longer thou livest, the more foole thou art. London, [1580 ?].

Wagner, Joseph Maria. Deutsche Volkslieder aus Oesterreich. Gesammelt und mitgetheilt von ——. *In* Deutsches Museum, 1862, II, 756–70, 799–810.

Wagner, Wilhelm. Medieval Greek Texts : being a collection of the earliest compositions in vulgar Greek prior to the year 1500. Edited, with prolegomena and critical notes by, . . . with an essay on the Greek version of Appollonius of Tyre, by M. A. Ch. Gidel. London, Berlin, 1870. Pt. I. (Philological Society.)

Waifs and Strays of Celtic Tradition. See Campbell, Lord Archibald.

Waldau, Alfred. Böhmisches Märchenbuch. Deutsch von ——. Prag, 1860.

Waldis, Burkhard. Esopus. Herausgegeben und mit Erläuterungen versehen von Heinrich Kurz. Leipzig, 1862. 2 pts. (Deutsche Bibliothek. Sammlung seltener Schriften der älteren deutschen National-Literatur. Herausgegeben von Heinrich Kurz. 1, 2.)

Wallonia. Recueil de littérature orale, croyances et usages traditionnels fondé par O. Colson, Jos. Defrecheux et G. Willame. Liége, 1893–.

Walpole, Horace. A Catalogue of the Royal and Noble Authors of England: with lists of their works. Second ed. London, 1759. 2 vols.

Walsingham, Thomas. Thomae Walsingham, quondam monachi S. Albani, Historia Anglicana. Edited by Henry Thomas Riley. London, 1863, '64. 2 vols. (Rolls Series.)

Waltharius. See Ekkehardus Sangallensis I.

Ward, Henry Leigh Douglas. Catalogue of Romances in the Department of Manuscripts in the British Museum. London, 1883, '93. 2 vols.

Ward, J. Extracts from the Churchwardens Accompts of the Parish of St Helen's in Abington, Berkshire. In Archaeologia, I, 13–25. 3d ed. 1804.

Wardrop, Marjory. Georgian folk tales, translated by ——. London, 1894. (Grimm Library, 1.)

Warnatsch, Otto. Der Mantel. Bruchstück eines Lanzelet-romans des Heinrich von dem Türlin, nebst einer Abhandlung über die Sage vom Trinkhorn und Mantel und die Quelle der Krone, herausgegeben von ——. Breslau, 1883. (K. Weinhold, Germanistische Abhandlungen, 2.)

Warner, G. F. See Giraldus.

Warner, William. Albions England. A continved Historie of the same Kingdome, from the originals of the first inhabitants thereof: With the most chiefe Alterations and Accidents there hapning, vnto, and in the happie Raigne of our now most Soueraigne Lord King Iames. Not barren in varietie of Inventive and Historicall Inter-mixtures. First penned and published by —— and now reuised, and newly enlarged a little before his Death. Whereunto is also newly added an Epitome of the whole Historie of England. London, 1612.

Warnke, Karl. See Marie de France.

Warren, N. See Oxenford, John.

Warrens, Rosa. Schottische Volkslieder der Vorzeit. Im Versmass des Originals übertragen von ——. Hamburg, 1861.

Warton, Thomas. The History of English Poetry, from the close of the Eleventh Century to the commencement of the Eighteenth Century. From the edition of 1824. Superintended by the late Richard Price. [Edited by Richard Taylor.] London, 1840. 3 vols.

—— History of English Poetry from the Twelfth to the close of the Sixteenth century. With a preface by Richard Price, and notes variorum. Edited by W. Carew Hazlitt. London, 1871. 4 vols.

Wasilewski, Zygmunt. Jagodne (wieś w powiecie łukow-skim, gminie Dąbie), zarys etnograficzny. Warsaw, 1889. (Bibljoteka "Wisły," IV.)

Weber, A. Ueber eine Episode im Jaîmini-Bhârata. In Berlin Akad., Monatsberichte aus dem Jahre 1869, pp. 10–48.

Weber, Henry. Metrical Romances of the Thirteenth, Fourteenth, and Fifteenth Centuries: published from ancient manuscripts. With an introduction, notes, and a glossary. Edinburgh, 1810. 3 vols.

—— See Flodden Field.

——, Jamieson, R., and Scott, Walter. Illustrations of Northern Antiquities, from the earlier Teutonic and Scandinavian Romances; being an Abstract of the Book of Heroes, and Nibelungen Lay; with translations of metrical tales, from the Old German, Danish, Swedish, and

Icelandic Languages; with notes and dissertations. Edinburgh, 1814.

Webster, John. Works, with some account of the author and notes. By the Rev. Alexander Dyce. New ed., revised and corrected. London, etc., 1859.

Webster, Wentworth. Basque Legends, collected, chiefly in the Labourd, by Rev. ——. With an essay on The Basque Language by M. Julien Vinson. London, 1877. 2d ed., London, 1879.

Wedgwood, Hensleigh. A Dictionary of English Etymology. London, 1859–65. 3 vols.

The Weekly Magazine, or, Edinburgh Amusement. Edinburgh, 1768[–79]. Vols I–XIV.

Weimarisches Jahrbuch für deutsche Sprache, Litteratur und Kunst. Herausgegeben von Hoffmann von Fallersleben und Oskar Schade. Hannover, 1854–57. 6 vols.

Weinhold, Karl. Die deutschen Frauen in dem Mittelalter. Ein Beitrag zu den Hausalterthümern der Germanen. Wien, 1851. 2te Aufl., 1882.

—— Weihnacht-Spiele und Lieder aus Süddeutschland und Schlesien. Mit Einleitungen und Erläuterungen. Mit einer Musikbeilage. Neue Ausgabe. Wien, 1875.

—— See Zeitschrift des Vereins für Volkskunde.

Weismann, Heinrich. See Alexander the Great.

Welcker, Friedrich Gottlieb. Kleine Schriften. Bonn, 1844–61. 4 pts. Fünfter Theil, herausgegeben von Otto Lüders. Elberfeld, 1867.

Wells Convocation Records. In First Report of the Royal Commission on Historical Manuscripts. Pp. 106–8. London, 1874.

Wendunmuth. See Kirchhof, Hans Wilhelm.

Wenzig, Joseph. Westslawischer Märchenschatz. Ein Charakterbild der Böhmen, Mährer und Slowaken in ihren Märchen, Sagen, Geschichten, Volksgesängen und Sprüchwörtern. Deutsch bearbeitet von ——. Mit Musikbeilagen. Leipzig, 1857. (Carl B. Lorck's Hausbibliothek, 61.)

Werner, Friedrich Ludwig Zacharias. Der vierundzwanzigste Februar. Eine Tragödie in Einem Akt. Zweite Auflage. Leipzig, 1819.

Werner, Hilder. Westergötlands Fornminnen. Anteckningar af ——. Stockholm, [1868].

Wernher, der Pfaffe. Maria. In Fundgruben für Geschichte deutscher Sprache und Litteratur. Hrsg. von Dr. Heinrich Hoffmann. II, 145–212. Breslau, 1837.

Wesselofsky, Alexander. Beiträge zur Erklärung des russischen Heldenepos. In Archiv für slavische Philologie, IX, 282–91. 1886.

—— Neue Beiträge zur Geschichte der Salomonssage. In the same, VI, 393–411, 548–90. 1882.

—— Slavjanskija skazanija o Solomoně i Kitovrasě. St Petersburg, 1872.

—— See Figlia del Re di Dacia.

Wessén, C. J. De paroecia Kärna. Upsala, 1836.

West, E. W. See Arda Viraf.

Westergötlands Fornminnesförenings Tidskrift. Lund, etc. 1869–.

Westermann, A. See Antoninus Liberalis.

Wharton, Henry. Anglia Sacra, sive Collectio Historiarum, partim antiquitus, partim recenter scriptarum, de archiepiscopis et episcopis Angliae, a prima fidei Christianae susceptione ad annum MDXL. Londini, 1691. 2 parts.

Wheatley, Henry B. See Merlin.

Wheatley, Henry B. See Percy, Thomas.

Whitaker, Thomas Dunham. An History of the original Parish of Whalley and Honor of Clitheroe, in the Counties of Lancaster and York. London, 1818.

The White Book of Obwalden. Das weisse Buch des Archivs von Obwalden, [hrsg. in] Geschichtsfreund, XIII, 66 ff., durch Gerold Meyer von Knonau. [Brixen,] 1867.

White, Robert. History of the Battle of Otterburn, fought in 1388 ; with memoirs of the warriors who engaged in that memorable conflict. London, 1857.

Wichert, E. See Altpreussische Monatschrift.

Wickerhauser, Moriz. Die Papageimärchen, erzählt von ——. Leipzig, 1858.

Widter, Georg, and Wolf, Adam. Volksmärchen aus Venetien. Gesammelt und hrsg. von —— u. ——. Mit Nachweisen und Vergleichungen verwandter Märchen von Reinhold Köhler. In Jahrbuch für romanische und englische Literatur, VII, 1–36, 121–154, 249–290. 1866.

Wigalois. See Wirnt von Gravenberg.

Wigamur. Hie vacht sich an das pŭch Wigamurs des ritters mit dem adler, der bey kŭnig Artus was, vnd an der tafelrunde sass, gar ain schönes. In Friedrich Heinrich von der Hagen und Johann Gustav Büsching, Deutsche Gedichte des Mittelalters, I. Berlin, 1808.

Wigand, O. See Volksbücher.

Wild, Charles. An Illustration of the Architecture and Sculpture of the Cathedral Church of Lincoln. London, 1819.

Wilkina Saga, eller Historien om Konung Thiderich af Bern och hans Kämpar; samt Niflunga Sagan, . . . sive Historia Wilkinensium, Theoderici Veronensis, ac Niflungorum. Ex MSS. codicibus lingvae veteris Scandicae in hodiernam Svecicam atque Latinam translata, opera Johannis Peringskiold. Stockholmis, 1715.

Wilkinson, T. T. See Harland, John.

Willems, Jan Frans. Oude vlaemsche Liederen ten deele met de Melodiën uitgegeven door ——. Gent, 1848.

—— Sproken (Fabliaux). In Belgisch Museum, X, 51–98. 1846.

—— See Belgisch Museum.

William of Malmesbury. See Guilielmus Malmesburiensis.

Williams, Benjamin. Henrici Quinti, Angliae Regis, Gesta, ad fidem codicum manuscriptorum recensuit, chronicam traduxit, notisque illustravit ——. Londini, 1850. (English Historical Society.)

Williams, R. Campeu Charlymaen. See Charlemagne.

—— See Hengwrt MSS.

Wilmanns, Wilhelm. See Jänicke, Oskar.

Wilmotte, M. La belle dans la tour. In Bulletin de Folklore, II, 34–44. 1893.

Wilson, Sir Daniel. Memorials of Edinburgh in the Olden Time. New edition. Edinburgh, 1872.

Wilson, Henry. See Dunlop, J. C.

Wilson, Horace Hayman. Essays, Analytical, Critical, and Philological, on subjects connected with Sanskrit Literature. By the late H. H. Wilson. Collected and edited by Dr. Reinhold Rost. In three volumes. London, 1864, '65. (Being vols III–V of the Works of Horace Hayman Wilson, edited by Dr. Reinhold Rost and Fitzedward Hall. London, 1864–77. 9 vols.)

Wilson, Thomas. The Rule of Reason, conteinyng the Arte of Logique. Sette furthe in Englishe, and newly corrected by ——. London, 1553.

Winkel. See te Winkel.

Wirnt von Gravenberg. Wigalois, der Ritter mit dem Rade. Hrsg. v. G. F. Benecke. 1er druck. Berlin, 1819. 2 vols.

—— Wigalois. Hrsg. v. Franz Pfeiffer. Leipzig, 1847. (Dichtungen des deutschen Mittelalters, 6.)

Wirth, Albrecht. Danae in christlichen Legenden. Wien, 1892.

Wise, F. See Asser.

Wisła, miesięcznik gieograficzno-etnograficzny. Warsaw, 1887–.

Wissmann, Theodor. King Horn. Untersuchungen zur mittelenglischen Sprach- und Litteraturgeschichte. Strassburg and London, 1876. (Quellen und Forschungen zur Sprach- und Culturgeschichte der germanischen Völker, 16.) See, also, Horn.

Wit and Drollery, Joviall Poems : corrected and much amended, with additions. By Sir F. M., Ja. S., Sir W. D., J. D., and the most refined wits of the Age. London, 1661. Corrected and amended, with new additions. London, 1682.

—— See Facetiae.

Wlislocki, Heinrich von. Märchen und Sagen der Bukowinaer und Siebenbürger Armenier. Aus eigenen und fremden Sammlungen übersetzt von ——. Hamburg, 1891.

—— Märchen und Sagen der transilvanischen Zigeuner. Gesammelt und aus unedirten Origintexten übersetzt von ——. Berlin, 1886.

—— Volksdichtungen der siebenbürgischen und südungarischen Zigeuner. Gesammelt und aus unedirten Originaltexten übersetzt von ——. Wien, 1890.

—— Volkstümliches zum Armen Heinrich. In Zeitschrift für deutsche Philologie, XXIII, 217–25. 1890.

—— Zu Bürgers 'Kaiser und Abt.' In Zeitschrift für vergleichende Litteraturgeschichte, N. F., IV, 106–12. 1891.

—— See Herrmann, Anton.

Wodrow, Robert. The History of the Sufferings of the Church of Scotland, from the Restauration to the Revolution : collected from the publick records, original papers, and manuscripts of that time, and other well attested narratives. Edinburgh, 1721, '22. 2 vols.

Wöchentliche Nachrichten. See Büsching, J. G.

Wöste, Friedrich. De witte Swâne (Volksmärchen aus dem Grafschaft Mark). In Zeitschrift für deutsche Mythologie, III, 46–50. 1855.

Wójcicki, K. W. Klechdy. Starożytne podania i powieści ludowe. [Klechdy. Old Traditions and Stories of the Peasantry.] Warsaw, 1851–52. 2 vols.

—— Polnische Volkssagen und Märchen. Aus dem Polnischen des K. W. Woycicki von Friedrich Heinrich Lewestam. Berlin, 1839.

Wolf, Ferdinand. Le roman de Renart le Contrefait (nach der Handschrift der k. k. Hofbibliothek Nr. 2562, früher Hohendorf, Fol. 39). Wien, 1861. (Aus dem XII. Bande der Denkschriften der philosophisch-historischen Classe der Kaiserlichen Akademie der Wissenschaften.)

—— Ueber die beiden wiederaufgefundenen niederländischen Volksbücher von der Königinn Sibille und von Huon von Bordeaux. In Denkschriften der k. Akad. der Wissenschaften, Phil.-hist. Classe, VIII, 180–282. Wien, 1857.

—— Ueber die Lais, Sequenzen und Leiche. Ein Beitrag zur Geschichte der rhythmischen Formen und Singweisen der Volkslieder und der volksmässigen Kirchen- und Kunstlieder im Mittelalter. Heidelberg, 1841.

Wolf, Ferdinand. Ueber die neuesten Leistungen der Franzosen für die Herausgabe ihrer National-Heldengedichte insbesondere aus dem fränkisch-karolingischen Sagenkreise; nebst Auszügen aus ungedruckten oder seltenen Werken verwandten Inhalts. Ein Beitrag zur Geschichte der romantischen Poesie. Wien, 1833.

—— Ueber eine Sammlung spanischer Romanzen in fliegenden Blättern auf der Universitäts-Bibliothek zu Prag. Nebst einem Anhang über die beiden für die ältesten geltenden Ausgaben des Cancionero de romances. Wien, 1850.

—— See Köhler, R., Zu F. Wolf's Proben, u. s. w.

Wolf, Johannes Wilhelm. Beiträge zur deutschen Mythologie. Göttingen, 1852, '57. 2 pts.

—— Deutsche Hausmärchen. Wohlfeile Ausgabe. Göttingen, 1858.

—— Deutsche Märchen und Sagen. Gesammelt und mit Anmerkungen begleitet. Herausgegeben von ——. Leipzig, 1845.

—— Hessische Sagen. Herausgegeben von ——. Leipzig, 1853.

—— Niederländische Sagen. Gesammelt und mit Anmerkungen begleitet. Herausgegeben von ——. Leipzig, 1843.

—— See Zeitschrift für deutsche Mythologie.

Wolfdietrich. In F. H. von der Hagen, Heldenbuch, I, 71–151, 163–166, 199–278. Leipzig, 1855.

—— Der grosse Wolfdieterich. Herausgegeben von Adolf Holtzmann. Heidelberg, 1865.

—— Wolfdietrich A. Bearbeitet von Arthur Amelung. In Ortnit und die Wolfdietriche nach Müllenhoffs Vorarbeiten herausgegeben von Arthur Amelung und Oskar Jänicke, I, 79–163. Berlin, 1871. (Deutsches Heldenbuch, 3ter Teil.)

—— Wolfdietrich B. Bearbeitet von Oskar Jänicke. In Ortnit und die Wolfdietriche nach Müllenhoffs Vorarbeiten herausgegeben von Arthur Amelung und Oskar Jänicke, I, 165–301. Berlin, 1871. (Deutsches Heldenbuch, 3ter Teil.)

Wolff, O. L. B. Egeria. Raccolta di poesie italiane popolari, cominciata da Guglielmo Müller, dopo la di lui morte terminata e pubblicata da O. L. B. Wolff. Lipsia, 1829. *Also with the title:* Sammlung italienischer Volkslieder, aus mündlicher Ueberlieferung und fliegenden Blättern, begonnen von Wilhelm Müller, vollendet, nach dessen Tode herausgegeben und mit erläuternden Anmerkungen versehen von Dr. O. L. B. Wolff. Leipzig, 1829.

—— Halle der Völker. Sammlung vorzüglicher Volkslieder der bekanntesten Nationen. Grösstentheils zum ersten Male metrisch in das Deutsche übertragen. Frankfurt a. M., 1847. Frankfurt a. M. and Hamburg, 1857. 2 vols.

—— Hausschatz der Volkspoesie. Sammlung der vorzüglichsten u. eigenthümlichsten Volkslieder aller Länder und Zeiten in metrischen deutschen Uebersetzungen. 4te Auflage. Leipzig, 1853.

—— See Volksbücher.

Wollner, Wilhelm. Anmerkungen. In Leskien und Brugman, Litauische Volkslieder und Märchen, 1882, pp. 511–76.

—— Der Lenorenstoff in der slavischen Volkspoesie. In Archiv für slavische Philologie, VI, 239–69. 1882.

—— Untersuchungen über die Volksepik der Grossrussen.

Mit einem Anhange: Analyse einiger der wichtigeren grossrussischen Volksepen. A. Die älteren Helden. B. Die Helden von Kiev. Leipzig, 1879.

Wood, John Philip. See Douglas, Robert.

Woycicki, K. W. See Wójcicki.

Wright, Thomas. Essays on Archæological Subjects, and on various questions connected with the history of Art, Science, and Literature in the Middle Ages. London, 1861. 2 vols.

—— A History of Domestic Manners and Sentiments in England during the Middle Ages. With illustrations from the illuminations in contemporary manuscripts and other sources, drawn and engraved by F. W. Fairholt. London, 1862.

—— Influence of Mediæval upon Welsh Literature. The story of the Cort Mantel. In Archaeologia Cambrensis, 3d Series, IX, 7–40. 1863.

—— Political Poems and Songs relating to English History, composed during the period from the Accession of Edw. III. to that of Ric. III. London, 1859, '61. 2 vols. (Rolls Series.)

—— Queen Elizabeth and her Times, a series of Original Letters, selected from the inedited private correspondence of the Lord Treasurer Burghley, the Earl of Leicester, the Secretaries Walsingham and Smith, Sir Christopher Hatton, and most of the distinguished persons of the period. London, 1838. 2 vols.

—— A Selection of Latin Stories from Manuscripts of the Thirteenth and Fourteenth Centuries: a contribution to the history of fiction during the middle ages. London, 1842. (Percy Society, 8.)

—— Songs and Ballads, with other short Poems, chiefly of the reign of Philip and Mary. Edited from a Manuscript in the Ashmolean Museum. London, 1860. (Roxburghe Club, 78.)

—— Songs and Carols printed from a Manuscript in the Sloane Collection in the British Museum. London, 1836.

—— Songs and Carols from a manuscript in the British Museum ·of the Fifteenth Century. London, 1856. (Warton Club, 4.)

—— See Cent Nouvelles Nouvelles.

—— See Chaucer, Geoffrey.

—— See Fitz Warine, Fulk.

—— See Langtoft, Pierre de.

—— See Malory, Sir Thomas.

—— See Mapes, Walter.

—— See Neckam, Alexander.

—— See Occleve, Thomas.

—— See Seven Sages.

Wright, W. Aldis. See Bacon, Francis.

—— See Generydes.

Wucke, C. L. Sagen der mittleren Werra nebst den angrenzenden Abhängen des Thüringer Waldes und der Rhön. Salzungen, 1864. 2 vols.

Wülker, Richard. See Anglia.

Würzburg, Konrad von. See Konrad von Würzburg.

Wulff, Fredrik A. Recherches sur les sagas de Mágus et de Geirard et leurs rapports aux épopées françaises. Lund, [1873]. (Lunds Universitäts Årsskrift, X. 1873.)

—— See Bikez, Robert.

—— See Cederschiöld, G.

Wuttke, Karl Friedrich Adolf. Der deutsche Volksaberglaube der Gegenwart. Zweite, völlig neue Bearbeitung. Berlin, 1869.

Wyntown, Andrew. Ðe Orygynale Cronykil of Scotland, be Androw of Wyntown, priowr of Sanct Serfis Ynche in Loch Levyn. Now first published, with notes, a glossary, etc. by David Macpherson. London, 1795. 2 vols.

—— The Orygynale Cronykil of Scotland. By Androw of Wyntoun. Edited by David Laing. Edinburgh, 1872–79. 3 vols. (The Historians of Scotland, 2, 3, 9.)

Yacoub Artin Pacha. Contes populaires inédits de la vallée du Nil traduits de l'Arabe parlé par S. E. ——. Paris, 1895. (Les Littératures Populaires de toutes les Nations, 32.)

Yâjnavalkya's Gesetzbuch. Sanskrit und Deutsch herausgegeben von Dr. Adolf Friedrich Stenzler. Berlin, London, 1849.

Yule, Henry. See Polo, Marco.

Zacher's Zeitschrift. See Zeitschrift für deutsche Philologie.

Zamarski, R. Podania i baśni ludu w Mazowszu. Warsaw, 1852.

[Zambrini, Francesco.] Collezione di leggende inedite scritte nel buon secolo della lingua toscana. Bologna, 1855. 2 vols.

Zapol'skij, M. Bělorusskaja svad'ba, i svadebinyja pěsni. [White-Russian Weddings and Wedding Songs.] Kiev, 1888.

Zatzikhoven, Ulrich von. See Ulrich von Zatzikhoven.

Zawiliński, R. Z powieści i pieśni górali beskidowych. [Stories and Songs of the Beskid Mountaineers.] Warsaw, 1889.

Zbiór wiadomości do antropologii krajowéj wydawany staraniem komisyi Antropologicznéj Akademii Umiejętności. Cracow, 1877–.

Zeitschrift der Deutschen Morgenländischen Gesellschaft, hrsg. unter der verantwortlichen Redaction des Prof. Dr. R. Anger, Bd. V, VI; des Prof. Dr. A. Brockhaus, Bd. VII–XIX; des Prof. Dr. L. Krehl, Bd. XX–XXVII; des Prof. Dr. O. Loth, Bd. XXVIII–XXXIII; des Prof. Dr. E. Windisch, Bd. XXXIV–. Leipzig, 1847–.

Zeitschrift des Vereins für Volkskunde. Neue Folge der Zeitschrift für Völkerpsychologie und Sprachwissenschaft. Herausg. von Karl Weinhold. Berlin, 1891–.

Zeitschrift für celtische Philologie. Herausgegeben von Kuno Meyer und L. Chr. Stern. Halle a. S., 1896–.

Zeitschrift für deutsche Mythologie und Sittenkunde. 4 vols. Herausgegeben, I, II, von J. W. Wolf, III, IV, von W. Mannhardt. Göttingen, 1853–59.

Zeitschrift für deutsche Philologie. Herausgegeben von Dr. Ernst Höpfner u. Dr. Julius Zacher (I–XIX; XXI–, v. Hugo Gering). Halle, 1869–.

Zeitschrift für deutsches Alterthum, I–XVI, 1841–73, hrsg. von Moriz Haupt; XVII, XVIII, von K. Müllenhoff u. E. Steinmeyer; XIX–XXII, von E. Steinmeyer; XXIII–, von E. Schröder und G. Röthe. From XIX, Z. f. d. A. und deutsche Litteratur. I–IX, Leipzig, IX–, Berlin, 1841–.

Zeitschrift für die historische Theologie. In Verbindung mit der Historisch-theologischen Gesellschaft zu Leipzig, herausgegeben von D. Christian Friedrich Illgen [and others]. Leipzig; Hamburg and Gotha; Gotha, 1832–75. 45 vols.

Zeitschrift für romanische Philologie. Herausgegeben von Dr. Gustav Gröber. Halle, 1877–.

Zeitschrift für vergleichende Litteraturgeschichte (und Renaissance-Litteratur). Herausgegeben von Dr. Max Koch (and Dr L. Geiger). Berlin, 1887 ['86–87]–93; Weimar und Berlin, 1894; Weimar, 1895–.

Zeitschrift für Volkskunde, u. s. w., herausgegeben von Dr. Edmund Veckenstedt. Vols I–IV. Leipzig, 1888–92.

Ziehnert, Widar. Sachsen's Volkssagen, Balladen, Romanzen und Legenden. Neue Auflage. Nebst einem Anhang, enthaltend: die hinterlassenen Gedichte des Verfassers. Annaberg, 1851. (Vierte Aufl., 1881.)

Zielke, Oscar. See Orfeo.

Zimmer, Heinrich. [Review of] Nutt, Alfred, Studies on the Legend of the Holy Grail. In Göttingische Gelehrte Anzeigen, 1890, pp. 488–528.

Zimmerische Chronik. Herausgegeben von Karl August Barack. Zweite verbesserte Auflage. Freiburg i. B. and Tübingen, 1881–82. 4 vols.

Zimmermann, Paul. See Thym, Georg.

Zingerle, Ignaz V. Das goldene Horn. In Pfeiffer's Germania, V, 101. 1860.

—— Sitten, Bräuche und Meinungen des Tiroler Volkes. Gesammelt und herausgegeben von ——. Zweite vermehrte Auflage. Innsbruck, 1871.

—— and Joseph. Kinder- und Hausmärchen aus Tirol. Gesammelt durch die Brüder Zingerle, herausgegeben von Ignaz Vinc. Zingerle. Zweite vermehrte Auflage. Gera, 1870.

—— and Joseph. Tirols Volksdichtungen. Gesammelt durch die Brüder Ignaz u. Joseph Zingerle. Innsbruck, 1852, '54. 2 vols.

—— and Joseph. Zwei Märchen aus Tirol. In Zeitschrift für deutsche Mythologie, II, 364–73. 1855.

Zingerle, Joseph. Volkslieder aus Passeier. In Zeitschrift für deutsche Mythologie, I, 341–44. 1853.

Ζωγραφεῖος Ἀγών. Constantinople, 1891. (Ἑλληνικὸς Φιλολογικὸς Σύλλογος.)

Zunz, [Leopold]. Die synagogale Poesie des Mittelalters. Berlin, 1855. (Index. Berlin, 1889.)

Zupitza, Julius. Kleine Bemerkungen. In Anglia, III, 369–72. 1880.

—— Die mittelenglischen Bearbeitungen der Erzählung Boccaccios von Ghismonda und Guiscardo. In Vierteljahrsschrift für Kultur und Litteratur der Renaissance, I, 63–102. Berlin, 1886.

—— See Heldenbuch.

Zurmühlen, Dr. Hans, pseud. for Norrenberg, P. Des Dülkener Fiedlers Liederbuch. Herausgegeben von ——. Viersen, 1875.

—— Niederrheinische Volkslieder. Im alten Mühlgau gesammelt von ——. (Zweite Ausgabe von "Des Dülkener Fiedlers Liederbuch.") Leipzig, 1879.

TO BE CORRECTED IN THE PRINT

I, 2 b, note, 6th line from below. *Read* II, 175.
 3 b, 12th line. *Read* 2 I.
 9 b, 3d line from below. *Read* Karadžić's.
 11 a, note *, 3d line. *Read* 48th and 49th.
 14 a, 10th line from below. *Read* I.
 24 b, 5th line from below. *Read* 2d.
 29 a, 2d paragraph, 8th line. *Read* De (Mörners sang).
 36 b. [On the names cf. Bugge, Helge-Digtene i den Ældre Edda, deres Hjem og Forbindelser (second series of his Studier over de nordiske Gude- og Heltesagn), Kjøbenhavn, 1896, p. 271.]
 39 a, 1st line. *Read* contributed by Hoffmann.
 94. [See Bugge's discussion of the Scandinavian and the English ballads, Helge-Digtene i den Ældre Edda, pp. 283 ff.]
 113 a, 2d paragraph, 5th line. *Read* Reifferscheid.
 124, note †, 4th line. *Read* Lettish ballad.
 154 a, lines 1, 2. *Read* Reifferscheid.
 217 b, 11th line. *Read* early.
 239 a, last line but one of text. *Read* circumstance.
 250 b, last paragraph, 4th line. *Read* II, 366.
 267 b, note †. *Read* Altswert.
 270 a, note *, 5th line. *Read* I, 152.
 281 a, note †, second line. *Read* Ásmundur.
 339 b, 2d paragraph. *Read* Lanval.
 392 b, 2d paragraph, last line but one. *Read* des.
 393 b, 3d line. *Read* Gianandria.
 393 b, 3d paragraph, 23d line. *Read* No 20, p. 16.
 401 a, last paragraph, Pellegrini. *Exchange* p. 37, p. 93.
 418 a, 9th line. *Read* Asbjørnsen.
 424 b, 16th line. *Read* garland *instead of* broadside.
 457 a, line 20. *Read* H 42.
 487 a, 41 a, 16th line. *Read* II, 29.
 488 a, 2d paragraph, 3d line. *Read* kiego, II, 21.
 493 b, 124 a, 5th line. *Read* Tielemann.
 499 a, 2d paragraph, last line. *Read* blindness and.
II, 39, note †, 3d line. *Read* c. 49.
 81, 45⁴. *Read* (*according to earlier MS.*) lest.
 102 b, 13th line. *Read* B, C, G, H, K, M.
 137 b, 2d paragraph, line 3. *Read* G 11.
 137 b, 2d paragraph, line 6. *Read* D 21.
 205 b, notes, 4th line. *Read* I, 159.
 215 a, 2d paragraph, 5th line. *Read* 1882.
 227 f. [See Bugge's discussion of 'Fæstemanden i

Graven' and related ballads, etc., in his Helge-Digtene i den Ældre Edda, deres Hjem og Forbindelser, pp. 206 ff.]
 236 b, 2d paragraph, 4th line. *Read* II, 84.
 244 b, 2d line. *Read* 26, 27.
 346 a, 4th paragraph, line 4. *Read* 1875.
 424 b, last line but three of preface. *Drop* 83, E 32.
 502 a, No 29, line 3. *For* Erox *read* Evax.
 510 a, No 57, 2d paragraph. *For* R. Köhler *read* L. Laistner.
 512 a, No 68, 1st line ; 515 a, last line. *Read* Norsk.
III, 9 H, 4¹. *Read* browen.
 16 a, last line. *Read* No 119.
 19 a, notes, first line. *Read* X, 5.
 41, note §, 2d line. *Read* I, vii f.
 51 b, 5th line. *Read* No 119.
 241 a, 6th line of notes. *Read* 1765.
 242 a, note †, 3d line. *Read* 1873.
 352 a, 2d line. *Read* ed. 1720.
 366 b, note ‡. *Read* ed. 1873.
 373 a, 3d line. *Read* ed. 1777, II, 54 f.
 427, note *. *Read* Dalyell.
 499 b, p. 156 b, etc., 5th and 6th lines. *Read* Koritko, Part III, p. 47.
 501 b, 4th paragraph, 1st line. *Read* I, 503 a.
 501 b, 6th paragraph, 2d line. *Read* 572.
 517 b, 22d line. *Read* 69. 23d line. *Read* 659.
 520 a, 1st line. *Read* El Penitente.
IV, 62 b, 3d paragraph, 8th line. *Read* J a, b.
 162, note ‖, last line but two. *Read* next ballad.
 165 b. [On the Scandinavian ballad see Bugge, Helge-Digtene, pp. 295–7.]
 187 a, 9th line. *Read* 386.
 268, 19¹. *Read* Now she 's.
 401 b, 2d line. *Read* Hind Horn.
 410, 23¹, garned. *Read* gazed (*as in the original MS.*).
 441 a, 4th paragraph, last line. *Read* Fedorowski.
 459 b, 3d paragraph, 4th line. *Read* VIII, 109.
 482 a, No 96, 2d paragraph, 1st line. *Read* Doncieux.
V. Advertisement. 3d paragraph, 2d line. *Read* Saline.
 8 b, note †. *Read* note by Pinkerton.
 13 b, line 15. *Read* Jours.
 32 a, lines 4, 6. *Read* Böhme.

34 b, note †. *Read* Harland . . . ed. 1882.

36, 3³. *Read* petticoats.

40 b, 7th line. *Read* I, 67.

65 a, 3d line. *Read* Χιακὰ.

65 a, 8th and 9th lines. *Read* 1857, I, 409.

88 b, 3d paragraph, 3d line. *Read* Genest.

98 a, **B**, 2d line. *Read* 20th August.

99, 9³. *Read* Now since.

108, **B**, 10¹. *Read* year (*twice*).

121 a, 2d paragraph, line 2. *Read* May 18.

147, 4⁴. *Read* man who.

151, **F**, 1³. *Read* nor tree.

168 a, 2d line of notes. *Drop* **B**.

180, 2⁸. *Read* Ye sleep, ye wake, ye.

203 a, 9th, 10th line from below. *Read* p. 80, No 73 **C**.

210 b, No 17, Romaic. *Read* Manousos, II, 103 ; but the ballad has been cited II, 215, where it more properly belongs.

214 b, 3². *Drop* ea, *remnant of a correction of reading.*

215, 14⁸. *Read* An a' the fish came.

215 b, No 39, **D** a, 12². *Read* aft her gates.

219, 17⁴. *Read* Has he.

220 a, No 56, 2d line. *Read* Dardy.

221, 20⁴. *Read* gell *as in the MS.*

222 a, 31¹. *Bracket this line.*

222 b, 115, **B**, 4⁴. *Drop.*

225 b, note to No 80, 10th line. *Read* Yule's (Marco Polo).

227 b, 7⁴. *Read* Ther.

231 b, 2d paragraph, 4th line. *Read* II, 265.

234 a, No 96, 1st paragraph. *Drop the last sentence.*

235 b, **D**, 1². *Read* An a.

240 a, No 132. *Read* P. 154.

241 a, **U**, first line. *Read* 1892.

243 b, 3⁴. *Read* hes.

246 a, 3¹. *Read* Her father.

247 a, 11³. *Read* bare the bran.

249, note *. *Read* R. R. Stodart.

251 b, 5th line. *Drop.*

255 a, 314. *Read* 214.

256 b, 13⁴. *Drop* she.

257 a, 10⁶. *Read* rins our my.

262, No 223, *MSS have at* 13², with : 18¹, over.

262, No 225, P. 249, last line but one, *say* added later by Sharpe.

264 a, 24³. *Read* Thee.

265 b, 6³. *Read* onye thing that.

270 a, line 8. *Drop* 7⁴. O come.

275 a, last line but 4. *Read* Skene.

275 a, 1¹. *Probably* bonny Lothen.

276, 12⁸. *Read* gin we.

277, 7¹. *Probably* mony fair.

279 a, 17⁴. *Drop.*

279 b, No 266, 4th line. *Read* V, III, 104.

281 a, last line of 3d paragraph. *Read* **I** †.

Trivial Corrections of Spelling.

I, 492 a, 5¹. *Read* better.

II, 104, 19¹,². *Read* pat.

III, 9, **H** 8⁴. *Read* brume.

IV, 105, 11¹. *Read* Martinmass.

267, 10². *Read* convoyd.

268, 18³. *Read* Altho.

V, 33 b, line 16. *Read* turpiter.

35, **A**, 4⁴. *Read* go sae.

36, 14¹. *Read* tean.

98, **B**, 2¹. *Read* win.

99, 8⁴. *Read* doun.

103 b, **B**, c, 1⁴. *Read* and letee. 15¹. *Read* friar.

108, **B**, 4¹. *Read* jumpet. 6¹. *Read* a'.

110, 4², 12². *Read* misstres.

111, 22². *Read* Hony.

116 a, **A**, title. *Read* Shiperd.

116 a, 2². *Read of* . . . nead.

116 a, 2⁸. *Read* whelk.

116 b, 3². *Read* loued.

117, 7⁴. *Read* follouing.

117 b, 13¹. *Read* gentilmen.

121 a, 2d paragraph, l. 5. *Read* i the. l. 9. *Read* wi.

125, 5¹. *Read* a dream.

140, e, 8². *Read* an thrice.

147, 10⁸. *Read* I am.

153 a, 1². *Read* drinkin'.

153 b, 4th line of preface. *Read* Kiltie.

153 b, 6⁸. *Read* cuningly.

165, 1⁴. *Read* Tartan-trues.

197, 10⁸. *Read* muntit.

208, 8¹. *Read* cam.

209 b, line 16. *Read* Roñnal (*whatever that may mean*).

215 a, 11³. *Read* daugh[t]er.

217 a, 17². *Read* divell.

217 b, No 49, 1¹. *Read* two.

218 a, 6¹. *Read* on my.

219 b, 28¹. *Read* count[r]y.

220 b, 5¹. *Read* saddel.

223 a, p. 148, 21¹, 22¹. *Read* h'm.

223 b, 8⁸. *Read* marrey (?).

224, 12¹. *Read* He'se (?).

224, 12⁸. *Read* marrage. 16⁸. smaa.

224, 17⁵. *Read* got (?).

225 a, p. 219. *Insert,* 11². gate.

227, 7⁸. *Perhaps,* monning.

228, 19¹. *Read* Mukkel. 20¹. ribbins.

228, 22⁸. *Read* gei, *or* gee. 26⁸. an she.

228, 26⁴. *Read* att. 28². milk-whit.

229, 31². *Read* hee. 33¹. *Perhaps* daughters.

235 b, **D**, 5⁸. *Read* k[n]ight.

236 b, 20². *Read* frie.

241 b, 5¹. *Read* one.

242 a, 8⁴. *Read* Belou. 15². baked leak.

243 a, 16⁴.　*Read* smodderd.

247 b, 21².　*Read* Nor.　23³.　fra.

247 b, 1².　*Read* call.　1⁴.　halld.

247 b, 2².　*Read* merrey.

248, 3³.　*Read* Edom.　11³.　t[a]ne.

248, 13³.　*Read* Bat.　19¹.　an of.

248, 22⁴.　*Read* gett.　Last line, *add* 17¹.　Her.

249 b, 8².　*Read* weel.

256 a, 2².　*Read* get.　7¹.　forder.

256 b, 14².　*Read* narrou.

260, No 221, 3¹.　*Read perhaps*, Lamendall.

261 b, 11¹.　*Read* But.

265 a, 11¹.　*Read* S[i]r.　13².　ouer.

265 a, 17¹.　*Read* milk-whit.　18³.　came.

265 b, 4⁴.　*Read* Healend.

266 b, 5¹.　*Read* rode.

267 b, 5².　*Read* middell.

269, 1³.　*Read* marriage.　16³.　hunder.

271 a, 6⁴.　*Read* welcom.　13².　wer.

271 a, 16³.　*Read* horses.

271 b, 5th line.　*Read* carrlis.　3⁴.　welcome.

273 a, 13⁴.　*Read, perhaps*, haae.

275 a, 12³.　*Read* mach.

276 a, 15¹.　*Read* tuenty.

277 a, 2³.　*Read* forestes.

277 b, 8¹.　*Read* clapet.

278 a, 25¹.　*Read* ouer.

278 b, 31³.　*Read, perhaps*, eair.　32¹.　sayes.

Appendix

[This essay is reprinted from the *Publications of the Modern Language Association of America,* Vol. XXI, No. 4, pp. 755-807 (New Series, Vol. XIV, No. 4), 1906.]

PROFESSOR CHILD AND THE BALLAD

In the course of his insistence upon the necessity of a continued recognition of the popular ballad as a distinct literary type, Professor Gummere points out the value of a collection of Professor Child's critical remarks on the ballad and an attempt to determine their general drift.[1] Such is the purpose of the present paper. Aside from the article in the *Universal Cyclopædia,* Professor Child's comments are mere *obiter dicta,* based upon no underlying principle and forming no part of a set purpose. They are, therefore, not easy to classify; the attempt to reduce them to order can be only partially successful, and any arrangement must appear more or less arbitrary. Yet some arrangement has seemed advisable and they have been roughly grouped under the following headings: (1) Authorship and Transmission; (2) Subject-Matter; (3) Technique; (4) A Comparison of the *Ballads* of 1857–1859 and *The English and Scottish Popular Ballads* of 1882–1898; (5) A Collection of General Comments upon Specific Ballads; (6) Summary.

[1] *Modern Philology,* I, 377 f.

I.

In that article in the *Universal Cyclopœdia* which Professor Child "wished to be neither quoted nor regarded as final," [1] but which must here be combined with other tentative or fragmentary statements, he defined the *popular ballad* as " a distinct and very important species of poetry. Its historical and natural place," he said, " is anterior to the appearance of the poetry of art, to which it has formed a step, and by which it has been regularly displaced, and, in some cases, all but extinguished. Whenever a people in the course of its development reaches a certain intellectual and moral stage, it will feel an impulse to express itself, and the form of expression to which it is first impelled is, as is well known, not prose, but verse, and in fact narrative verse. The condition of society in which a truly national or popular poetry appears explains the character of such poetry. It is a condition in which the people are not divided by political organization and book-culture into markedly distinct classes, in which consequently there is such community of ideas and feelings that the whole people form an individual. Such poetry, accordingly, while it is in its essence an expression of our common human nature, and so of universal and indestructible interest, will in each case be differenced by circumstances and idiosyncrasy. On the other hand, it will always be an expression of the mind and heart of the people as an individual, and never of the personality of individual men. The fundamental characteristic of popular ballads is therefore the absence of subjectivity and of self-consciousness. Though they do not 'write themselves,' as William Grimm has said, though a man and not a people has composed them, still the author counts for nothing, and it

---

[1] Professor Gummere in *Modern Philology*, i, 378.

is not by mere accident, but with the best reason, that they have come down to us anonymous. Hence, too, they are extremely difficult to imitate by the highly civilized modern man, and most of the attempts to reproduce this kind of poetry have been ridiculous failures.

"The primitive ballad, then, is popular, not in the sense of something arising from and suited to the lower orders of a people. As yet, no sharp distinction of high and low exists, in respect to knowledge, desires, and tastes. An increased civilization, and especially the introduction of book-culture, gradually gives rise to such a division; the poetry of art appears; the popular poetry is no longer relished by a portion of the people, and is abandoned to an uncultivated or not over-cultivated class—a constantly diminishing number."

But "the popular ballad is not originally the product or the property of the lower orders of the people. Nothing, in fact, is more obvious than that many of the ballads of the now most refined nations had their origin in that class whose acts and fortunes they depict—the upper class— though the growth of civilization has driven them from the memory of the highly polished and instructed, and has left them as an exclusive possession to the uneducated. The genuine popular ballad had its rise in a time when the distinctions since brought about by education and other circumstances had practically no existence. The vulgar ballads of our day, the 'broadsides' which were printed in such large numbers in England and elsewhere in the six- teenth century or later, belong to a different genus; they are products of a low kind of *art*, and most of them are, from a literary point of view, thoroughly despicable and worthless.

"Next it must be observed that ballads which have been handed down by long-repeated tradition have always departed considerably from their original form. If the transmission has been purely through the mouths of unlearned people, there is less probability of willful change, but once in the hands of professional singers there is no amount of change which they may not undergo. Last of all comes the modern editor, whose so-called improvements are more to be feared than the mischances of a thousand years. A very old ballad will often be found to have resolved itself in the course of what may be called its propagation into several distinct shapes, and each of these again to have received distinct modifications. When the fashion of verse has altered, we shall find a change of form as great as that in the *Hildebrandslied*, from alliteration without stanza to stanza with rhyme. In all cases the language drifts insensibly from ancient forms, though not at the same rate with the language of every-day life. The professional ballad-singer or minstrel, whose sole object is to please the audience before him, will alter, omit, or add, without scruple, and nothing is more common than to find different ballads blended together.

"There remains the very curious question of the origin of the resemblances which are found in the ballads of different nations, the recurrence of the same incidents or even of the same story, among races distinct in blood and history, and geographically far separated." It is not necessary to go back to a common ancestry to explain these resemblances. "The incidents of many ballads are such as might occur anywhere and at any time ; and with regard to agreements that can not be explained in this way we have only to remember that tales and songs were the chief social amusement of all classes of people in all the nations of Europe during the Middle Ages, and that new stories would be eagerly sought for by those whose business it was to furnish this amusement, and be rapidly spread among the fraternity. A great effect was undoubtedly produced by the crusades, which both brought the chief European nations into closer intercourse and made them acquainted with the East, thus facilitating the interchange of stories and greatly enlarging the stock."

This account of authorship and transmission may be illustrated and supplemented by *obiter dicta* from *The English and Scottish Popular Ballads.* "The author counts for nothing;" the ballad is essentially anonymous: that Expliceth quod Rychard Sheale means merely that *The Hunting of the Cheviot* (162) "was of course part of his stock as minstrel; the supposition that he was the author is preposterous in the extreme." [1]

Ballads are at their best when "the transmission has been purely through the mouths of unlearned people," when they have come down by domestic tradition, through knitters and weavers. *Glasgerion* (67, B) "is mainly of good derivation (a poor old woman in Aberdeenshire)." [2] And "no Scottish ballads are superior in kind to those recited in the last century by Mrs Brown, of Falkland." [3] Yet even upon Mrs Brown printed literature may have had some influence: in *Fause Foodrage* (89), "the resemblance in the verse in A 31, 'The boy stared wild like a gray gosehawke,' to one in 'Hardyknute,' 'Norse een like gray goss-hawk stared wild,' struck Sir Walter Scott as suspicious," and "it is quite possible that Mrs Brown may unconsciously have adopted this verse from the tiresome and affected Hardyknute, so much esteemed in her day." [4] A literary treatment of a ballad theme may affect the traditional versions of that ballad. In the case of *Child Maurice* (83) "the popularity of the play [Home's *Douglas*] seems to have given vogue to the ballad. The sophisticated copy passed into recitation, and may very likely have more or less infected those which were repeated from earlier tradi-

[1] III, 303.   [2] II, 136.   [3] I, vii.   [4] II, 296.

tion." [1] A whole ballad may even be completely derived from print, and yet, in the course of time, revert to the popular form. Of this same ballad, *Child Maurice*, "Mr Aytoun considers that E is only the copy printed in the middle of the last century purged, in the process of oral transmission, of what was not to the popular taste, 'and altered more.' There is no doubt that a copy learned from print may be transformed in this way, but it is certain that old tradition does not come to a stop when a ballad gets into print." [2]

Not only the possible influence of print is to be taken into account; much depends on the material to which the reciter was exposed and upon his selection. "It will not . . . . help the ballad [*Young Bearwell* (302)] much that it was not palmed off on Buchan in jest or otherwise, or even if it was learned from an old person by Mr Nicol in his youth. The intrinsic character of the ballad remains, and old people have sometimes burdened their memory with worthless things." [3] Editors were not the only interpolators; of *The Twa Sisters* (10), A, a, 11–13, need not have been written, but "might easily be extemporized by any singer of sufficiently bad taste." [4] The varying memory of reciters, too, was a cause of unintentional change. Thus "Mrs Brown was not satisfied with A b [of *Bonny Baby Livingston* (222)], which Jamieson had taken down from her mouth, and after a short time she sent him A a. The verbal differences are considerable. We need not suppose that Mrs Brown had heard two 'sets' or 'ways,' of which she blended the readings; the fact seems to be that, at the time when she recited to Jamieson, she was not in good

---

[1] II, 263. An old woman (the reciter of E) knew *Chield Morice* as a child, but later learned *Gil Morice* which began to be more fashionable. II, 264.

[2] II, 464, n.　　　　　[3] V, 178.　　　　　[4] I, 119.

condition to remember accurately."[1] In general, however, the folk memory is remarkable for its tenacity. "Most of the [Danish] versions [of *Earl Brand* (7)] from recitation are wonderful examples and proofs of the fidelity with which simple people 'report and hold' old tales: for, as the editor has shown, verses which never had been printed, but which are found in old manuscripts, are now met with in recited copies; and these recited copies, again, have verses that occur in no Danish print or manuscript, but which nevertheless are found in Norwegian and Swedish recitations, and, what is more striking, in Icelandic tradition of two hundred years' standing."[2]

The ballad does not remain in the possession of the simple folk, or of reciters of Mrs Brown's instinctive good taste. Its best fortune is then perhaps to fall into the hands of children, like *The Maid Freed From the Gallows* (95), of which "F had become a children's game, the last stage of many old ballads."[3] Again, "it is interesting to find the ballad [*The Twa Brothers* (49)] still in the mouths of children in American cities,—in the mouths of the poorest, whose heritage these old things are."[4] *Sir Hugh* (155) in the form of *Little Harry Hughes and the Duke's Daughter,* was heard, says Mr Newell, "from a group of colored children, in the streets of New York city," and traced "to a little girl living in one of the cabins near Central Park."[5]

Less happy is the fate of the ballad when it falls into the hands of professional singers,—the Minstrel Ballad is to be considered presently,—or when it falls into the hands of amateurs of various sorts, who corrupt and debase it. *Hind Etin* (41) "has suffered severely by the accidents of

---

[1] IV, 231.

[2] I, 89. See also the comment on Apollodorus and the Cretan fairy-tale, I, 337, quoted, p. 774, below.

[3] II, 346.   [4] I, 435.   [5] Quoted, III, 254.

tradition. A has been not simply damaged by passing through low mouths, but has been worked over by low hands. Something considerable has been lost from the story, and fine romantic features, preserved in Norse and German ballads, have been quite effaced." [1] Of *The Clerk's Twa Sons o Owsenford* (72) "D has some amusing dashes of prose, evidently of masculine origin. [Examples follow]. We have here a strong contrast with both the blind-beggar and the housemaid style of corruption; something suggesting the attorney's clerk rather than the clerk of Owsenford, but at least not mawkish." [2] The "blind beggar" is, of course, Buchan's collector, and whether he or the editor was responsible for the corruptions is not always clear. The blind beggar himself, however, comes in for special condemnation in the comment on *The Bent Sae Brown* (71): "The introduction and conclusion, and some incidental decorations, of the Scottish ballad will not be found in the Norse, but are an outcome of the invention and the piecing and shaping of that humble but enterprising rhapsodist who has left his trail over so large a part of Buchan's volumes." [3] In *Brown Robin* (97) "the story undoubtedly stops at the right point in A, with the escape of the two lovers to the wood. The sequel in C is not at all beyond the inventive ability of Buchan's blind beggar, and some other blind beggar may have contrived the cane and the whale, the shooting and the hanging, in B." [4] As type of the housemaid style of corruption may, perhaps, stand *Lizie Lindsay* (226). "Leezie Lindsay from a maid-servant in Aberdeen," wrote Jamieson to Scott of A b. [5] And, "in his preface to B, Kinloch remarks that the ballad is very popular in the North, 'and few milk-maids in that quarter but can chaunt it.'" [6]

---

[1] I, 360.　　[2] II, 173.　　[3] II, 170.　　[4] II, 368.
[5] IV, 255, n.　[6] IV, 255.

" Ballads of this description [a young lord o the Hielands, pretending that he is the son of an auld shepherd and an auld dey, persuades a young lady of Edinburgh to fly with him to the Highlands, where he at length reveals his identity]—ballads of this description are peculiarly liable to interpolation and debasement, and there are two passages, each occurring in several versions, which we may, without straining, set down to some plebeian improver." [1]

Not mere corruption, but serving-man authorship, even, is suggested for *Tom Potts* (109): "Such events [unequal matches] would be celebrated only by fellows of the yeoman or of the foot-boy, and surely in the present case the minstrel was not much above the estate of the serving-man. Lord Jockey's reckless liberality throughout, and Lord Phoenix's in the end, is a mark of the serving-man's ideal nobleman." [2] Again as mere corrupter, rather than author, appears the ostler in one version of *Bewick and Graham* (211). In the 1833 edition of *The Border Minstrelsy* "deficiencies were partly supplied and some different readings adopted 'from a copy obtained by the recitation of an ostler in Carlisle.'" g "is shown by internal evidence to be the ostler's copy. Both copies [g and h] were indisputably derived from print, though h may have passed through several mouths. g agrees with b—f closely as to minute points of phraseology which it is difficult to believe that a reciter would have retained. It looks more like an immediate, though faulty, transcript from print." [3] Contrasting styles are suggested in the comment on *The Broomfield Hill* (43): "The editor [of the broadside, "differing as to four or five words only from F"] remarks that A is evidently taken from F; from which it is clear that the pungent buckishness of the broadside does not necessarily make an impression.

[1] IV, 256. Cf. B 10, D 10, E 19; F 11; E 10, F 6.
[2] II, 441.   [3] IV, 144.

A smells of the broom ; F suggests the groom." [1] Perhaps not to be classed with these non-professional corrupters or interpolaters is the bänkelsänger who is responsible for one of the German versions of *Lady Isabel and the Elf Knight* (4): "M smacks decidedly of the bänkelsänger, and has an appropriate moral at the tail: *animi index cauda!*" [2] Perhaps he is to be regarded as a humble sort of minstrel; to the comments on this class we may now turn our attention.

It does not appear from Professor Child's remarks whether he thought of the minstrel as composing his ballads,—or making them over,—orally or in writing. Perhaps we are to suppose that he followed now one method, now the other. Rychard Sheale may be supposed to have affixed his "expliceth" to his written copy of Chevy Chase; yet it is "*quod* Rychard Sheale" as if the manuscript had been written by another from his singing. But whether the ballad passed through the minstrel's mouth or through his hands, it received some peculiar and characteristic modifications. Thus *The Boy and the Mantle* (29), *King Arthur and King Cornwall* (30), and *The Marriage of Sir Gawain* (31) "are clearly not of the same rise, and not meant for the same ears, as those which go before. They would come down by professional rather than by domestic tradition, through minstrels rather than knitters and weavers. They suit the hall better than the bower, the tavern or public square better than the cottage, and would not go to the spinning-wheel at all. An exceedingly good piece of minstrelsy 'The Boy and the Mantle' is, too; much livelier than most of the numerous variations on the somewhat overhandled theme." [3] *Crow and Pie* (111), likewise, "is not a purely popular ballad, but rather of that kind which,

[1] I, 391.   [2] I, 34.   [3] I, 257.

for convenience, may be called the minstrel-ballad. It has, however, popular features, and markedly in stanzas 13, 14," [1] —the damsel's demanding the name of the man who has wronged her, a feature found in *The Bonny Hind* (50) and its continental parallels.[2] The term *minstrel* may, perhaps, be more loosely used in the passage which describes *The Rising in the North* (175) as "the work of a loyal but not unsympathetic minstrel;" [3] in the statement concerning *Northumberland Betrayed by Douglas* (176), that "the ballad-minstrel acquaints us with circumstances concerning the surrender of Northumberland;" [4] and in the statement to the effect that, in the case of *Tom Potts* (109), "the minstrel was not much above the estate of the serving-man." [5]

We may now attempt to construct an account of the vicissitudes to which the ballad was subject when, in the course of transmission, it sometimes found its way into writing and into print. Version B of *The Hunting of the Cheviot* (162) "is a striking but by no means a solitary example of the impairment which an old ballad would suffer when written over for the broadside press. This very seriously enfeebled edition was in circulation throughout the seventeenth century, and much sung . . . . despite its length. It is declared by Addison, in his appreciative and tasteful critique . . . . to be the favorite ballad of the common people of England." [6] Similarly, in the case of *Sir Andrew Barton* (167), "a collation of A and B will show how ballads were retrenched and marred in the process of preparing them for the vulgar press." [7] "B begins vilely, but does not go on so ill. The forty merchants coming 'with fifty sail' to King Henry on a mountain top . . . . requires to be taken indulgently." [8] Though a broadside differs

[1] II, 478.   [2] Cf. I, 444 f.   [3] III, 403.   [4] III, 410.
[5] II, 441.   [6] III, 305.   [7] III, 334.   [8] III, 334, n.

widely from a true ballad, it is not to be supposed that,— at least in the examples included by Professor Child,— some general traits or special features peculiar to the popular or traditional matter or manner did not survive. Thus, although the ballad of *The Twa Knights* (268) "can have had no currency in Scotland, and perhaps was known only through print," yet "a similar one is strictly traditional in Greece, and widely dispersed, both on the mainland and among the islands." [1] Again, there are two broadsides of *King John and the Bishop* (45), which Professor Child does not include, "both inferior even to B, and in a far less popular style." [2] There are, then, degrees of departure from the popular style. There are degrees of departure from the popular matter, also, and the broadside preserves sometimes but a single popular feature. Version M of *Young Beichan* (53) "was probably a broadside or stall copy, and is certainly of that quality, but preserves a very ancient traditional feature." [3] The broadside version of *The Broomfield Hill* (43) is distinguished by a "pungent buckishness," which is not found in A, and which "suggests the groom." [4] A broadside may itself become tradition. The English version of *Lord Thomas and Fair Annet* (73) "is a broadside of Charles the Second's time. . . . This copy has become traditional in Scotland and Ireland. The Scottish traditional copy . . . . is far superior, and one of the most beautiful of our ballads, and indeed of all ballads." [5] The tradition lives, even after a ballad has found its way into print, and may influence and modify later versions of the printed form. Of *Prince Heathen* (104) "the fragment A . . . . is partly explained by B, which is no doubt some stall-copy, reshaped from tradition." [6] Of *The Baffled Knight*

[1] v, 21.   [2] i, 404.   [3] i, 455.   [4] i, 391.
[5] ii, 180.   [6] ii, 424.

(112) " E is, in all probability, a broadside copy modified by tradition." [1]   In origin, in any case, the broadsides in *The English and Scottish Popular Ballads* are popular.[2]   " There is a Scottish ballad [similar to *The Baffled Knight*] in which the tables are turned. . . .   This, as being of comparatively recent, and not of popular, but of low literary origin, cannot be admitted here." [3]

" Last of all comes the modern editor," and from Professor Child's comments and skilful undoing of much of their work one might put together fairly complete accounts of the methods of Percy, Scott, Jamieson, Buchan, and the rest.   We are concerned, however, not so much with the editors as with the results of their editing, with the kinds of change that the ballad suffered in their hands.   It was often lengthened, in many cases by the combination of several versions.   Thus Scott's version of *Tam Lin* (39, I), " as he himself states, was compounded of the Museum copy, Riddell's, Herd's, and ' several recitals from tradition.' " [4]   Of this use of materials from recitation examples are very numerous.   Ballads were lengthened also by the interpolation of new stanzas.   After Scott's edition, in the *Minstrelsy*, of *The Twa Sisters* (10), " Jamieson followed . . . . with a tolerably faithful, though not, as he says, *verbatim*,[5] publication of his copy of Mrs Brown's ·ballad,

---

[1] II, 480.

[2] The comparison of broadsides with traditional versions is instructive. See I, A, a, b, c ; 10, A, a ; 45, B ; 53, L, M ; 73, D ; 104, B, 112, E (and II, 491) ; 110, A ; 145, C ; 151 ; 152 ; 153 ; 162, B ; 167, B ; 268.   Much of the later Robin Hood poetry looks like " char-work done for the petty press" (III, 42).   *Robin Hood Rescuing Will Stutly* (141) "is a ballad made for print, with little of the traditional in the matter and nothing in the style" (III, 185).

[3] II, 480.   [4] I, 335.

[5] " Jamieson was not always precise in the account he gave of the changes he made in his texts" (IV, 255).   Cf. also I, 138.

somewhat marred, too, by acknowledged interpolations." [1]
King Henry (32) was increased by Jamieson's interpolations
from twenty-two to thirty-four stanzas.[2] Scott's version of
Fair Annie (62, A) " was obtained ' chiefly from the recitation of an old woman,' but we are not informed who supplied
the rest. Herd's fragment, D, furnished stanzas 2–6, 12,
17, 19. A doubt may be hazarded whether stanzas 8–10
came from the old woman." [3] Interpolation and combination are here both illustrated. Scott's later edition of *Tam
Lin* (39) " was corrupted with eleven new stanzas, which
are not simply somewhat of a modern cast as to diction, as
Scott remarks, but of a grossly modern invention, and
as unlike popular verse as anything can be." [4] Of his
version of *Jellon Grame* (90) Scott says : " ' Some verses
are apparently modernized.' " " The only very important
difference between Scott's version and Mrs Brown's is its
having four stanzas of its own, the four before the last two,
which are evidently not simply modernized, but modern." [5]

But the editor did not merely combine or interpolate ;
more vaguely, he " improved." Version E of *The Fair
Flower of Northumberland* (9), " a traditional version from
the English border, has unfortunately been improved by
some literary pen." [6] Or he " retouched," [7] or " altered," [8]
or " emended." Scott confesses to some emendation of
Kinmont Willy (186) ; " it is to be suspected that a great
deal more emendation was done than the mangling of
reciters rendered absolutely necessary. One would like, for
example, to see stanzas 10–12 and 31 in their mangled
condition." [9] In general, no changes or additions are " in
so glaring contrast with the groundwork as literary emenda-

---

[1] Stanzas 20, 21, 27, etc. I, 119. Cf. II, 83.
[2] I, 297.　　　　[3] II, 63 f.　　　　[4] I, 335.　　　　[5] II, 302.
[6] I, 112.　　　　[7] IV, 5.　　　　[8] I, 138.　　　　[9] III, 472.

tions of traditional ballads." [1]   "Variations," also, are to be
noted : inaccuracies in *The Fire of Frendraught* (196) are
acknowledged by Motherwell ; "the implication is, or should
be, that these variations are of editorial origin." [2]   Of *Sweet
William's Ghost* (77, A and B), "Percy remarks that the
concluding stanza seems modern.   There can be no doubt
that both that and the one before it are modern ; but, to the
extent of Margaret's dying on her lover's grave, they are
very likely to represent original verses not remembered
in form." [3]

Certain general results of transmission, of whatever kind,
are to be noted. As a ballad passes from one country to
another the nationality of the hero may be changed. In
Hugh Spencer's Feats in France (158) "Hugh is naturally
turned into a Scotsman in the Scottish version, C." [4] The
hero's name is not more stable than his nationality. "In
the course of transmission [of *John Thomson and the Turk*
(266)], as has ever been the wont, names were changed, and
also some subordinate circumstances." [5] Again, "the actual
name of the hero of a ballad affords hardly a presumption
as to who was originally the hero." [6] Even the part that
he plays the hero may exchange with another character.
"Robin Hood's rescue of Little John, in Guy of Gisborne,
after quarrelling with him on a fanciful provocation, is a
partial offset for Little John's heart-stirring generosity in
this ballad. [*Robin Hood and the Monk* (119).] We have
already had several cases of ballads in which the principal
actors exchange parts." [7] The ballad, again, is not constant
in its attachment to one locality, and "the topography of
traditional ballads frequently presents difficulties, both because it is liable to be changed, wholly, or, what is more

---

[1] II, 428.   [2] IV, 39. Cf. II, 317.   [3] II, 226.   [4] III, 276.
[5] V, 2.   [6] II, 19.   [7] III, 96.

embarrassing, partially, to suit a locality to which a ballad has been transported, and again because unfamiliar names, when not exchanged, are exposed to corruption." [1] Thus, "in the ballad which follows this [*Rare Willie Drowned in Yarrow* (215)], a western variety of the same story, Willie is drowned in the Clyde." [2]

The corruption of names is but one phase of the change to which all unfamiliar ballad diction is exposed. "At every stage of oral transmission we must suppose that some accidental variations from what was delivered would be introduced, and occasionally some wilful variations. Memory will fail at times; at times the listener will hear amiss, or will not understand, and a perversion of sense will ensue, or absolute nonsense,—nonsense which will be servilely repeated, and which repetition may make more gross. . . . Learned words do not occur in ballads; still an old native word will be in the same danger of metamorphosis. But, though unfamiliarity naturally ends in corruption, mishearing may have the like effect where the original phrase is in no way at fault. . . .

"It must be borne in mind, however, that as to nonsense the burden of proof rests always upon the expositor. His personal inability to dispose of a reading is not conclusive; his convictions may be strong, but patience and caution are his part and self-restraint as to conjectures." [3]

In transmission, then, and even in the best of it, the ballad ordinarily fares but ill, "departs from the original form," becomes less typically ballad; and, generally speaking, the older it is, the earlier it is caught and fixed in print, the better. Professor Child has thus special praise for those Robin Hood ballads which "have come down to us in comparatively ancient form." [4] *Robin Hood's Death* (120, B)

---

[1] IV, 156. [2] IV, 178. [3] V, 309. [4] III, 42.

is "in the fine old strain." [1] *Robin Hood and the Beggar* (134, II), "by far the best of the Robin Hood ballads of the secondary, so to speak cyclic, period," is "a composition of some antiquity," [2] *Thomas Rymer* (37) "is an entirely popular ballad as to style, and must be of considerable age." [3] One is not to expect in a late or modern ballad the excellence found in an early or ancient one. *Robin Hood's Chase* (146) "is a well-conceived ballad, and only needs to be older." [4] *Walter Lesly* (296) is "a late, but life-like and spirited ballad." [5] *The Hunting of the Cheviot* (162, B) "is a striking . . . . example of the impairment which an old ballad would suffer when written over for the broadside press." [6] Version M of *Young Beichan* (53) "was probably a broadside or stall copy, and is certainly of that quality, but preserves a very ancient traditional feature." [7] The "ridiculous ballad" of *John Thomson and the Turk* (266) finds a place in the collection because it is "a seedling from an ancient and very notable story." [8] *The Knight's Ghost* (265) "has not a perceptible globule of old blood in it, yet it has had the distinction of being more than once translated as a specimen of Scottish popular ballads." [9] Scott's later edition of *Tam Lin* (39) "was corrupted with eleven new stanzas, which are not simply somewhat of a modern cast as to diction, as Scott remarks, but of a grossly modern invention, and as unlike popular verse as anything can be." [10] Scott's version of *Jellon Grame* (90) has four stanzas of its own, "which are evidently not simply modernized. but modern." [11] Certain stanzas in version B b of *Archie o Cawfield* (188) "are indifferent modern stuff." [12] The "modern

---

[1] III, 103. [2] III, 159. [3] I, 320. [4] III, 206.
[5] V, 168. [6] III, 305. [7] I, 455. [8] V, 1.
[9] IV, 437. [10] I, 335. [11] II, 302. [12] III, 486.

ballad" on the subject of *The Heir of Linne* (267) is "an inexpressibly pitiable ditty."[1]

Certain counterfeits, imitations, or "spurious" ballads, wholly or almost wholly the work of editors or modern writers, are included in Professor Child's collection. *Robin Hood and the Tinker* (127) is a "contemptible imitation of imitations."[2] Buchan's version of *Young Waters* (94) is, for the most part, "a counterfeit of the lowest description. Nevertheless it is given in an appendix ; for much the same reason that thieves are photographed."[3] *Young Ronald* (304) is an example of the "spurious" ballad, and the reasons for its inclusion are given at some length. "If any lover of ballads should feel his understanding insulted by the presentation of such a piece as this, I can have no quarrel with him. There is certainly much in it that is exasperating. . . . In this and not a very few other cases, I have suppressed disgust, and admitted an actually worthless and manifestly — at least in part — spurious ballad, because of a remote possibility that it might contain relics, or be a debased representative, of something genuine and better. Such was the advice of my lamented friend, Grundtvig, in more instances than those in which I have brought myself to defer to his judgment."[4] For the same reason is included *The Laidley Worm of Spindleston Heughs:* "This composition of Mr. Lamb's—for nearly every line of it is his[5]—is not only based on popular tradition, but evidently preserves some small fragments of a popular ballad, and for this reason is given in an Appendix."[6]

---

[1] v, 12. Cf. also I, 35, IV, 10, 142, 401, for passages condemned as "modern."

[2] III, 140.   [3] II, 342.   [4] v, 182.

[5] Communicated by the Rev. Mr Lamb to Hutchinson "with this harmless preamble : 'a song 500 years old, made by the old Mountain Bard, Duncan Frasier, living on Cheviot, A. D. 1270.'"

[6] I, 308.

II.

From what has been said it is clear that, as a rule, the ballad is at its best, is most typically ballad, when its subject-matter is of purely popular origin. The *Gest* and the earliest Robin Hood ballads "are among the best of all ballads," and Robin Hood "is absolutely a creation of the popular muse. The earliest mention we have of him is as the subject of ballads." [1] "Absolutely a creation of the popular muse" would seem to imply that the ballad is not,—or that these ballads at least are not,—based either upon a formless popular tradition or upon definite prose tales. Local traditions follow the ballad, as attempts to explain it; they do not supply the story. "In places where a ballad has once been known, the story will often be remembered after the verses have been wholly or partly forgotten, and the ballad will be resolved into a prose tale, retaining, perhaps, some scraps of verse, and not infrequently taking up new matter, or blending with other traditions. Naturally enough, a ballad and an equivalent tale sometimes exist side by side." [2]

The existence of foreign traditional parallels is one evidence of popular origin. *The Bent Sae Brown* (71) has close resemblances with Norse ballads; "but the very homeliness of the Scottish ballad precludes any suspicion beyond tampering with tradition. The silliness and fulsome vulgarity of Buchan's versions often enough make one wince or sicken. . . . But such correspondences with foreign ballads as we witness in the present case are evidence of a genuine traditional foundation." [3] Less complete, yet even more striking, are the foreign versions of the theme of *Tam Lin* (39).

---

[1] III, 42.   [2] I, 46; examples follow.   [3] II, 170, n.

"This fine ballad stands by itself, and is not, as might have been expected, found in possession of any people but the Scottish. Yet it has connections, through the principal feature in the story, the retransformation of Tam Lin, with Greek popular tradition older than Homer." [1] " We come . . . . surprisingly near to the principal event of the Scottish ballad in a Cretan fairy-tale . . . . [1820–1830]." And this " Cretan tale does not differ from the one repeated by Apollodorus from earlier writers a couple of thousand years ago more than two versions of a story gathered from oral tradition in these days are apt to do. Whether it has come down to our time from mouth to mouth through twenty-five centuries or more, or whether, having died out of the popular memory, it was reintroduced through literature, is a question that cannot be decided with certainty; but there will be nothing unlikely in the former supposition to those who bear in mind the tenacity of tradition among people who have never known books." [2] *The Suffolk Miracle* (272) has " impressive and beautiful" [3] European parallels, and therefore finds a place in Professor Child's collection. Other debased or counterfeit or spurious ballads are present for the same reason, or because, like *Tam Lin*, they contain some purely popular or traditional feature. Certain features are expressly declared to be popular or to be common in ballads; among these are the quibbling oaths and the unbosoming oneself to an oven or stove, in *The Lord of Lorn and the False Steward* (271); [4] the miraculous harvest in *The Carnal and the Crane* (55); [5] the childbirth in the wood in *Leesome Brand* (15) and in *Rose the Red and White Lily* (103); [6] the presence of three ladies, " that the youngest may be preferred to the others;" the unpardonable "offence

---

[1] I, 336. [2] I, 337. [3] V, 59. [4] V, 48.
[5] II, 7. [6] II, 416.

given by not asking a brother's assent to his sister's marriage" in *The Cruel Brother* (11);[1] the testament in *The Cruel Brother, Lord Randal, Edward*, etc.;[2] the riddles in *Riddles Wisely Expounded* (1), etc.;[3] and certain stanzas in *Crow and Pie* (111).[4] "Heroic sentiment" is a characteristic of the earlier Robin Hood ballads; in the later it is gone.[5] It may be that in his appreciation of certain other features Professor Child is thinking not merely of their excellence but of their peculiarly popular quality as well. Thus he speaks of "the fine trait of the ringing of the bells without men's hands, and the reading of the books without man's tongue,"[6] in *Sir Hugh* (155); and thinks that "perhaps the original conception [of *The Twa Sisters* (10)] was the simple and beautiful one which we find in English B and both the Icelandic ballads, that the king's harper, or the girl's lover, takes three locks of her yellow hair to string his harp with."[7]

The ballad does not always go to ancient tradition, or draw upon the stock of popular themes and motives; occasionally, in more modern times, it tells the story of some actual occurrence; it is based on fact. But the balladist feels himself under no obligation of loyalty to the fact. "A strict accordance with history should not be expected, and indeed would be almost a ground of suspicion ["or a pure accident"]. Ballad singers and their hearers would be as indifferent to the facts as the readers of ballads are now; it is only editors who feel bound to look closely into such matters."[8] In *Johnie Armstrong* (169) "the ballads treat facts with the customary freedom and improve upon them greatly."[9] *Bonny John Seton* (198) "is accurate as to the date, not commonly a good sign for such things."[10] "A ballad

[1] I, 142.   [2] Examples, I, 143.   [3] I, 1.   [4] II, 478.
[5] III, 159.   [6] III, 235.   [7] I, 121. [8] II, 19.
[9] III, 366.   [10] IV, 51.

taken down some four hundred years after the event will be apt to retain very little of sober history." [1] Yet, in the case of *The Hunting of the Cheviot* (162), at least, "the ballad can scarcely be a deliberate fiction. The singer is not a critical historian, but he supposes himself to be dealing with facts; he may be partial to his countrymen, but he has no doubt that he is treating of a real event." [2] Part of *The Earl of Westmoreland* (177) "has an historical substratum, though details are incorrect." [3] In *Northumberland Betrayed by Douglas* (176) "the ballad-minstrel acquaints us with circumstances concerning the surrender of Northumberland which are not known to any of the historians." [4] Local tradition would seem to be even less authentic than the ballad; "in such cases" as *The Coble o Cargill* (242) it "seldom means more than a theory which people have formed to explain a preëxisting ballad." [5]

We have already seen how a ballad derived from print tends to revert to the popular form; the same tendency is evident in the ballad derived from a romance. Of *Gude Wallace* (157) "Blind Harry's Wallace . . . . is clearly the source." "But the portions of Blind Harry's poem out of which these ballads were made were perhaps themselves composed from older ballads, and the restitution of the lyrical form may have given us something not altogether unlike what was sung in the fifteenth, or even the fourteenth, century." [6] *Thomas Rymer* (37) is derived from the romance, yet it is "an entirely popular ballad as to style." [7] These are the only cases where Professor Child admits without question the derivation of a ballad from a romance; in other cases, where ballad and romance tell the same story, he insists that the possibility of the priority of the ballad must

---

[1] III, 317. [2] III, 304. [3] III, 417. [4] III. 410,
[5] IV, 359. [6] III, 265 f. [7] I, 320.

be considered. Thus the ballad of *Hind Horn* (17) has close affinity with the later English romance, but no filiation. "And were filiation to be accepted, there would remain the question of priority. It is often assumed, without a misgiving, that oral tradition must needs be younger than anything that was committed to writing some centuries ago; but this requires in each case to be made out; there is certainly no antecedent probability of that kind."[1] *Fair Annie* (62) is not derived from the lay; they "have a common source, which lies further back, and too far for us to find."[2] In *Gil Brenton* (5) "the artifice of substituting waiting-woman for bride has been thought to be derived from the romance of Tristan. . . . Grundtvig truly remarks that a borrowing by the romance from the popular ballad is as probable a supposition as the converse."[3] The ballad does sometimes go to the romance for details. Thus, in *The Earl of Westmoreland* (177) "what follows [stanza 15] is pure fancy work, or rather an imitation of stale old romance."[4] *The Kitchie-Boy* (252) is a modern adaptation of King Horn, but, "in the particular of the hero's having his choice of two women, it is more like the *gest* of 'King Horn,' or 'Horn Childe and Maiden Rimnild;' but an independent invention of the Spanish lady is not beyond the humble ability of the composer of 'The Kitchie-Boy.'"[5] In the "worthless and manifestly—at least in part—spurious ballad" of *Young Ronald* (304), "the nicking with nay and the giant are borrowed from romances."[6] Though the *Gest*, finally, "as to all important considerations, is eminently original, absolutely so as to the conception of Robin Hood, some traits and incidents, as might be expected, are taken from what we may call the general stock of mediæval

[1] I, 193. [2] II, 67. [3] I, 67. [4] III,
[5] IV, 401. [6] V, 182.

fiction." [1] Thus "Robin Hood will not dine until he has some guest that can pay handsomely for his entertainment. . . . This habit of Robin's seems to be a humorous imitation of King Arthur, who in numerous romances will not dine till some adventure presents itself." [2]

Not only from ancient tradition, from fact, from romance or the sources of romance may the ballad derive its subject-matter; it may also turn back upon itself, and as late ballads counterfeit or imitate the style of earlier ones, so late ballads go to earlier ones for their subject-matter as well. Thus *The Battle of Otterburn* (161) "is likely to have been modernized from . . . . a predecessor." [3] Part of *The King's Disguise, and Friendship with Robin Hood* (151) "is a loose paraphrase, with omissions, of the seventh and eighth fits of the Gest." [4] *The Brown Girl* (295) "recalls 'Lord Thomas and Fair Annet,' 'Sweet William's Ghost,' 'Clerk Saunders,' 'The Unquiet Grave,' 'Bonny Barbara Allen,' and has something of all of them. . . . Still it is not deliberately and mechanically patched together (as are some pieces in Part VIII), and in the point of the proud and unrelenting character of the Brown Girl it is original." [5] "Deliberately and mechanically put together" were the pieces of Part VIII which follow. *Auld Matrons* (249) "was made by someone who had acquintance with the first fit of 'Adam Bell.' The anonymous 'old wife' becomes 'auld Matrons;' Inglewood, Ringlewood. The conclusion is in imitation of the rescues in Robin Hood ballads." [6] *Henry Martyn* (250) "must have sprung from the ashes of 'Andrew Barton,' of which name Henry Martyn would be no extraordinary corruption." [7] *The Kitchie-Boy* (252) is "a modern 'adaptation' of 'King Horn'. . . . from which

[1] III, 49 f. [2] III, 51. [3] III, 293. [4] III, 220.
[5] V, 166. [6] IV, 391. [7] IV, 393.

A 33, 34, B 47, D 7, 8, are taken outright."[1] The first half of *Willie's Fatal Visit* (255) "is a medley of 'Sweet William's Ghost,' 'Clerk Saunders,' and 'The Grey Cock,'"[2] Of *Broughty Wa's* (258), "Stanza 9, as it runs in b, is a reminiscence of 'Bonny Baby Livingston,' and 13 recalls 'Child Waters,' or 'The Knight and the Shepherd's Daughter.'"[3] A large part of *The New-Slain Knight* (263) "is imitated or taken outright from very well known ballads."[4] Like some of these later ballads the *Gest of Robyn Hode* goes back to earlier ballads for its subject-matter. "The Gest is a popular epic, composed from several ballads by a poet of a thoroughly congenial spirit. No one of the ballads from which it was made up is extant in a separate shape, and some portions of the story may have been of the compiler's own invention. The decoying of the sheriff into the wood, stanzas 181–204, is of the same derivation as the last part of Robin Hood and the Potter, No 121, Little John and Robin Hood exchanging parts; the conclusion, 451–56, is of the same source as Robin Hood's Death, No 120."[5] Some of the Middle-English forms "may be relics of the ballads from which this little epic was made up; or the whole poem may have been put together as early as 1400, or before."[6] It is noteworthy that the *Gest* was composed *from*, not *of*, several ballads; it was not made up of unchanged ballads, "deliberately and mechanically put together."

The motives or features characteristic of subject-matter derived from pure popular tradition have already been noted; we may now note those traits which Professor Child declares or implies to be not characteristic of such subject-matter. Extravagance would seem to be one of these: the extravagance of *Hughie Grame* (191, A, 16) "it is to be

---

[1] IV, 401.   [2] IV, 415.   [3] IV, 423.   [4] IV, 434.
[5] III, 49.   [6] III, 40.

hoped is a corruption." [1] In *Mary Hamilton* (173) "there are not a few spurious passages. Among these are the extravagance of the queen's bursting in the door, F 8; the platitude,[2] of menial stamp, that the child, if saved, might have been an honor to the mother, D 10, L 3, O 4,"[3] Exaggeration is another non-traditional trait: "It is but the natural course of exaggeration that the shepherd, having beaten Robin Hood, should beat Little John. This is descending low enough, but we do not see the bottom of this kind of balladry here"[4] [*Robin Hood and the Shepherd* (165)]. *Robin Hood and Queen Katherine* (145) is "a very pleasant ballad, with all the exaggeration." [5] The true ballad is not prosaic: in *Fause Foodrage* (89) "the . . . . king kills his successful rival on his wedding-day. According to the prosaic, not at all ballad-like, and evidently corrupted account in A, there is a rebellion of nobles four months after the marriage, and a certain False Foodrage takes it upon himself to kill the king." [6] The true ballad is not over-refined: in *The Braes of Yarrow* (214, C, 2) "the brothers have taken offence because their sister was not regarded as his equal by her husband, which is perhaps too much of a refinement for ballads, and may be a perversion." [7] The true ballad is not cynical: *The Twa Corbies* sounds "something like a cynical variation of the tender little English ballad," [8] and it is not printed as a ballad in Professor Child's collection. The true ballad is not sophisticated: it was the influence of the play, Home's *Douglas*, that gave vogue to the ballad, *Child Maurice* (83), and "the sophisticated copy passed into recitation." [9] The true ballad is not sentimental: in *Mary Hamilton* (173), "there are not a few spurious

---

[1] IV, 10. [2] Cf. III, 225. [3] III, 381.
[4] III, 165. [5] III, 197. [6] II, 296.
[7] IV, 161. [8] I, 253. Cf. also III, 258. [9] II, 263.

passages," among them, "the sentimentality of H 3, 16." [1]
Jamieson published *Child Waters* (63, B a) with "the addition of three sentimental stanzas to make Burd Ellen die
just as her enduring all things is to be rewarded." [2]   The
true ballad does not append a moral : a German version of
Lady Isabel and the Elf-Knight (4) "smacks decidedly of the
bänkelsänger, and has an appropriate moral at the tail." [3]
A certain degree of probability or naturalness is to be
expected of the true ballad story : in *Jellon Grame* (90),
"one day, when the boy asks why his mother does not take
him home, Jellon Grame (very unnaturally) answers, I slew
her, and there she lies : upon which the boy sends an arrow
through him." [4]   Finally, the plot of the true ballad is not
trite.   In *Child Owlet* (291) "the chain of gold in the first
stanza and the penknife below the bed in the fourth have a
false ring, and the story is of the tritest.   The ballad seems
at best to be a late one, and is perhaps mere imitation." [5]

III.

It is clear that to Professor Child's mind it was necessary
that the ballad should tell a story.   "The word *ballad* in
English signifies a narrative song, a short tale in lyric
verse." [6]   Thus the English versions of *Geordie* (209) are
said to be mere 'goodnights,' whereas "the Scottish ballads
have a proper story, with a beginning, middle, and end, and
(save one late copy), a good end, and they are most certainly
. . . . independent of the English." [7]   *Dugall Quin* (294) is
a "little ballad, which has barely story enough to be so

[1] III, 381.   [2] II, 83.   [3] I, 34.   [4] II, 302.   [5] v, 156 f.
[6] *Universal Cyclopædia*, "Ballad Poetry." The lyrical element is of
equal importance ; see p. 790, below.
[7] IV, 126.

called." [1]   To the "English 'ditty' (not a traditional ballad)
. . . . there is very little story." [2]

Necessary as the story is, however, it is seldom completely
told in the ballad; something is left to the hearers' imagination. Sometimes the close of the story is omitted: "it is
not said (except in the spurious portions of E) that the lady
was carried back by her husband, but this may perhaps be
inferred from his hanging the gypsies. In D and K we
are left uncertain as to her disposition." [3]   Transitions are
usually abrupt,—"abrupt even for a ballad" in *Willie's
Lady* (6) from stanza 33 to stanza 34. [4]   Jamieson, in printing *The Bonny Birdy* (82), introduced several stanzas 'to fill
up chasms.'   "But the chasms, such as they are, are easily
leapt by the imagination, and Jamieson's interpolations are
mere bridges of carpenter's work." [5]   Of *Sir Patrick Spens*
(58), "Percy's version [A] remains, poetically, the best. It
may be a fragment, but the imagination easily supplies all
that may be wanting; and if more of the story, or the whole,
be told in H, the half is better [6] than the whole." [7]   These
abrupt transitions do not, then, result in incoherence, which
accompanies corruption and is a sign of degeneracy. Thus
The Carnal and the Crane (55) "had obviously been trans-
mitted from mouth to mouth before it was fixed in its
present incoherent and corrupted form by print." [8]   *Young
Bearwell* (302) is "one of not a few flimsy and unjointed
ballads found in Buchan's volumes, the like of which is
hardly to be found elsewhere." [9]   After an attempt to make
the story of *The White Fisher* (264) hang together, Professor

[1] v, 165.
[2] iv, 192. [The Broom of Cowdenknows (217)].
[3] iv, 63. [The Gypsie Laddie (200)].
[4] i, 82.   [5] ii, 260.
[6] Surely better *as ballad*. Cf. p. 796, below.
[7] ii, 18.   [8] ii, 7.   [9] v, 178.

Child concludes : " But we need not trouble ourselves much to make these counterfeits reasonable. Those who utter them rely confidently upon our taking folly and jargon as the marks of genuineness." [1] Coherence, on the contrary, is a characteristic of the true ballad, an important phase of ballad excellence. " I am persuaded that there was an older and better copy of this ballad [*Bewick and Graham* (211)] than those which are extant. The story is so well composed, proportion is so well kept, on the whole, that it is reasonable to suppose that certain passages (as stanzas 3, 4, 50) may have suffered some injury." [2] Introductions, not closely connected with the ballad story, are not characteristic. "The narrator in the Ever Green poem reports at second hand : as he is walking, he meets a man who, upon request, tells him the beginning and the end. Both pieces have nearly the same first line. The borrowing was more probably on the part of the ballad, for a popular ballad would be likely to tell its tale without preliminaries." [3]

Brevity is a characteristic of the true ballad, and it may be, in this respect, profitably contrasted with Buchan's versions. Version C of *Brown Adam* (98) " has the usual marks of Buchan's copies, great length, vulgarity, and such extravagance and absurdity as are found in stanzas 23, 26, 29." [4] " Buchan, who may generally be relied upon to produce a longer ballad than anybody else, has ' Young Waters' in thirty-nine stanzas, ' the only complete version which he had ever met.' " [5] His version of *The Gay Goshawk* (96, G) is " vilely dilated and debased," [6] and that of *Jellon Grame* (90, C) " has nearly the same incidents as B, diluted and vulgarized in almost twice as many verses." [7]

The action is seldom carefully localized : the compiler of

[1] IV, 435.   [2] IV, 145.   [3] III, 317.   [4] II, 373.
[5] II, 342.   [6] II, 355.   [7] II, 302.

A Gest of Robyn Hode was careless of geography.[1] The New England copy of *Archie o Cawfield* (188, F) " naturally enough, names no places." "The route in C is not described[2] there is no reason, if they start from Cafield (see 23), why they should cross the Annan, the town being on the eastern side. All difficulties are escaped in D by giving no names."[2] The attention given to the setting in some of the Robin Hood ballads is, then, exceptional. Of *Robin Hood and the Monk* (119), " the landscape background of the first two stanzas has often been praised, and its beauty will never pall. It may be called landscape or prelude, for both eyes and ears are addressed, and several others of these woodland ballads have a like symphony or setting : Adam Bell, Robin Hood and the Potter, Guy of Gisborne, even the much later ballad of The Noble Fisherman. It is to be observed that the story of the outlaw Fulk Fitz Warine, which has other traits in common with Robin Hood ballads, begins somewhat after the same fashion."[3]

In dealing with the supernatural the way of the true ballad is to omit description or explanation. In *James Harris* (243), " to explain the eery personality and proceedings of the ship-master, E—G, with a sort of vulgar rationalism, turn him into the devil. . . . D (probably by the fortunate accident of being a fragment) leaves us to put our own construction upon the weird seaman ; and, though it retains the homely ship-carpenter, is on the whole the most satisfactory of all the versions."[4] In *Johnie Scot* (99) " the champion is described in A 31 as a gurious (grugous, gruous ?) ghost ; in H 27 as a greecy (frightful) ghost ; in L 18 he is a fearsome sight, with three women's spans between his brows and three yards between his shoulders ; in the Abbotsford copy of A, 29, 30, a grisly sight, with a

---

[1] III, 51.   [2] III, 486.   [3] III, 95.   [4] IV, 362.

span between his eyes, between his shoulders three and three, and Johnie scarcely reaching his knee. These points are probably taken from another and later ballad, which is perhaps an imitation, and might almost be called a parody, of Johnie Soot." [1] Ghosts, though not thought sufficiently strange to demand special treatment, should, nevertheless, "have a fair reason for walking. . . . In popular fictions, the motive for their leaving the grave is to ask back plighted troth, to be relieved from the inconveniences caused by the excessive grief of the living, to put a stop to the abuse of children by stepmothers, to repair an injustice done in the flesh, to fulfil a promise; at the least, to announce the visitant's death." [2]

Turning now from technique,—from treatment of plot, of setting, of the supernatural,—to style in the narrower sense, we find that the comments are again largely in the way of pointing out flaws, or traits which are not characteristic of the true ballad, and which are due to the peculiar conditions of ballad transmission. From such negative comments may be inferred, again, the stylistic marks of the true ballad. Thus, in the first place, ballad style is artless and homely. In *Andrew Lammie* (233):

> Her bloom was like the springing flower
> > That hails the rosy morning,
> With innocence and graceful mein
> > Her beauteous form adorning.

and

> ' No kind of vice eer staind my life,
> > Or hurt my virgin honour ;
> My youthful heart was won by love,
> > But death will me exoner' (C, 2, 42).

are " not homely enough." [3] Moreover,

---

[1] II, 378.   [2] V, 59.   [3] IV, 301, n.

> 'At Fyvie's yetts there grows a flower,
>   It grows baith braid and bonny;
>   There's a daisie in the midst o it,
>   And it's ca'd by Andrew Lammie' (A, 1.).

"the mystical verses with which A and B begin are also not quite artless." [1]   The ninth stanza of *The New-Slain Knight* (263) "is pretty, but not quite artless." [2]   In the true ballad the conceit is out of place.   Scott's version (C) of *Thomas Rymer* (37) closes with two satirical stanzas not popular in style.   " 'The repugnance of Thomas to be debarred the use of falsehood when he should find it convenient,' may have, as Scott says, 'a comic effect,' but is, for a ballad, a miserable conceit." [3]   In *The Mother's Malison* (216), A 8^{1-2}, C 10^{1-2},

> Make me your wrack as I come back,
>   But spare me as I go,

the conceit (from Martial) "does not overwell suit a popular ballad." [4]   The literary manner is thus to be contrasted with the popular.   In *Edward* (13) "the word 'brand,' in the first stanza, is possibly more literary than popular; further than this the language is entirely fit." [5]   Of *Earl Brand* (7) "A a has suffered less from literary revision than . . . . A c." [6]   This revision may be illustrated by the following stanza:

> To a maiden true he'll give his hand,
> To the king's daughter o fair England,
> To a prize that was won by a slain brother's hand,

which c substitutes for a 32:

> This has not been the death o ane,
> But it's been that of fair seventeen.

Of *The Fair Flower of Northumberland* (9) " E, a traditional

---

[1] IV, 301, n.   [2] IV, 434.   [3] I, 320, n.
[4] IV, 186.   [5] I, 167.   [6] I, 88.

version from the English border, has unfortunately been improved by some literary pen." [1] These improvements consist in part of descriptions of the lady's states of mind ; [2] for example :

> To think of the prisoner her heart was sore,
> Her love it was much but her pity was more.

> The words that he said on her fond heart smote,
> She knew not in sooth if she lived or not.

> She looked to his face, and it kythed so unkind
> That her fast coming tears soon rendered her blind.
>
> (Sts. 3, 9, 10.)

Jamie Telfer (190) "was retouched for the Border Minstrelsy, nobody can say how much. The 36th stanza is in Hardy-knute style." [3]

Of *Hughie Grame* (191), B, 3, 8, "are obviously, as Cromek says, the work of Burns, and the same is true of 10^{3-4}." [4] *The Famous Flower of Serving-Men* (106), an "English broadside, which may be reasonably believed to be formed upon a predecessor in the popular style, [5] was given in Percy's *Reliques*, . . , 'from a written copy containing some improvements (perhaps modern ones).' These improvements are execrable in style and in matter, so far as there is new matter, but not in so glaring contrast with the groundwork as literary emendations of traditional ballads." [6] Such contrast is found in the "hack-rhymester lines" in *Bewick and Graham* (211, 7^3, 19^2), which are "not up to the mark of the general style." [7] Similarly, *King Henry* (32) "as pub-

---

[1] I, 112.   [2] [The true ballad has little to say of mental states.]
[3] IV, 5. The stanza reads :

> But he's taen aff his gude steel cap,
> And thrice he's waved it in the air ;
> The Dinlay snaw was neer mair white
> Nor the lyart locks of Harden's hair.

[4] IV, 10.   [5] II, 430.   [6] II, 428.   [7] IV, 145.

lished by Jamieson . . . . is increased by interpolation to thirty-four stanzas [from twenty]. 'The interpolations will be found enclosed in brackets,' but a painful contrast of style of itself distinguishes them." [1]   Editorial changes are, however, in some cases confined to slight verbal variations, where the contrast is less evident or painful.[2]

Yet, in spite of its artless, homely, and non-literary style, the ballad is not without conventions of its own. Most striking of these is the use of "commonplaces" or passages which recur in many ballads, like :

> When bells were rung and mass was sung,
> And a' men bound to bed ;

or,

> O whan he came to broken briggs
>   He bent his bow and swam,
> An whan he came to the green grass growin
>   He slackd his shoone and ran.[3]

Another convention is the complete repetition of the message by the messenger. Thus in *Fair Mary of Walling-ton* (91, A) "the stanza which should convey . . . . part of the message is wanting, but may be confidently supplied from the errand-boy's repetition." [4]   Another form of repetition occurs in the narration of similar incidents by different ballads. "There is a general resemblance between the rescue of Robin Hood in stanzas 61–81 and that of William of Cloudesly in Adam Bell, 56–94, and the precaution suggested by Much in the eighth stanza corresponds to the warning given by Adam in the eighth stanza of the other ballad. There is a verbal agreement in stanzas 71 of the first and 66 of the second. Such agreements or repetitions are numerous in the Robin Hood ballads, and in other traditional ballads, where similar situations occur." [5]

---

[1] I, 297.   [2] Cf. II, 83, 317 ; IV, 39.
[3] See the *Index of Matters and Literature*, V, 474 f.
[4] II, 309, n.   [5] III, 96.

In the course of degeneration, ballads retain, but distort, the commonplace. Thus in *Lord Thomas and Lady Margaret* (261) " B 14[3, 4] is a commonplace, which, in inferior traditional ballads, is often, as here, an out-of-place. B 15, 16 is another commonplace, of the silly sort." [1] " Hacknied commonplaces " occur in *Auld Matrons* (249), stanzas 2–5 ; [2] " frippery commonplaces," in *The White Fisher* (264), stanzas 2, 7, 8, 12.[3]

Turning now to the emotional qualities of ballad style, we find that the ghost ballad, in spite (or perhaps because) of the absence of special treatment noted above, is, at its best, " impressive." The scene at the grave in *Sweet William's Ghost* (77 C 11–13) " may be judged grotesque, but is not trivial or unimpressive. These verses may be supposed not to have belonged to the earliest form of the ballad, and one does not miss them from A, but they cannot be an accretion of modern date." [4] In *The Wife of Usher's Well* (79) " there is no indication that the sons come back to forbid obstinate grief, as the dead often do. But supplying a motive would add nothing to the impressiveness of these verses. Nothing that we have is more profoundly affecting." [5] *The Suffolk Miracle* (272) is to be contrasted with the continental versions, " one of the most remarkable tales and one of the most impressive and beautiful ballads of the European continent." [6] *Bewick and Graham* (211), in spite of certain defects, " is a fine-spirited ballad as it stands, and very infectious." [7] *Walter Lesly* (296) is " a late, but lifelike and spirited ballad." [8] *The Wee Wee Man* (38) is an " extremely airy and sparkling little ballad." [9] *Andrew Lammie* (233) " is a homely ditty, but the gentleness and fidelity of Annie under the brutal behavior of her family are genuinely pathetic, and justify the remarkable popularity

---

[1] IV, 426. [2] IV, 391. [3] IV, 435. [4] II, 227. [5] II, 238.
[6] V, 59. [7] IV, 145. [8] V, 168. [9] I, 329.

which the ballad has enjoyed in the north of Scotland." [1] Contrasted with the cynical *Twa Corbies* of Scott's Minstrelsy is *The Three Ravens* (26), a "tender little English ballad." [2] In the *Gest*: "Nothing was ever more felicitously told, even in the best *dit* or *fabliau*, than the 'process' of Our Lady's repaying the money which had been lent on her security. Robin's slyly significant welcome to the monk upon learning that he is of Saint Mary Abbey, his professed anxiety that Our Lady is wroth with him because she has not sent him his pay, John's comfortable suggestion that perhaps the monk has brought it, Robin's incidental explanation of the little business in which the Virgin was a party, and request to see the silver in case the monk has come upon her affair, are beautiful touches of humor, and so delicate that it is all but brutal to point them out." [3] The tales which are cited as parallels to *Queen Eleanor's Confession* (156) all "have the cynical Oriental character, and, to a healthy taste, are far surpassed by the innocuous humor of the English ballad." [4] While we need not question the substantial genuineness of *Fause Foodrage* (89), "we must admit that the form in which we have received it is an enfeebled one, without much flavor or color." [5] *The Suffolk Miracle* (272) preserves the story only in a "blurred, enfeebled, and disfigured shape." [6] Version B of the *Cheviot* (162) is "very seriously enfeebled." [7]

The lyrical quality,—the fact that the ballad was made to be sung,—must not be lost sight of. "Fair Annie's fortunes have not only been charmingly sung, as here [in the ballad of *Fair Annie* (62)] ; they have also been exquisitely *told* in a favorite lay of Marie de France." [8] The superior lyrical quality of *The Bonny Birdy* (82) "makes up for its inferiority [to *Little Musgrave* (81)] as a story, so that on

---

[1] IV, 301. [2] I, 253. [3] III, 53. [4] III, 258.
[5] II, 296. [6] V, 59. [7] III, 305. [8] II, 67.

the whole it cannot be prized much lower than the noble English ballad." [1] Thus lyrical quality is to be regarded as no less significant than plot as a trait of the true ballad. *The Queen of Elfan's Nourice* (40), "after the nature of the best popular ballad, forces you to chant and will not be read." [2] Even *The Jolly Pindar of Wakefield* (124) "is thoroughly lyrical, . . . and was pretty well sung to pieces before it ever was printed." [3] "It is not . . . . always easy to say whether an isolated stanza belonged to a ballad or a song;" [4] and Professor Child speaks even of the whole of *Bessy Bell and Mary Gray* (201) as "this little ballad, or song." [5] Of *Lord Lovel* (75) he says: "It can scarcely be too often repeated that such ballads as this were meant only to be sung, not at all to be recited. . . . 'Lord Lovel' is especially one of those which, for their due effect, require the support of a melody, and almost equally the comment of a burden. No burden is preserved in the case of 'Lord Lovel,' but we are not to infer that there never was one. The burden, which is at least as important as the instrumental accompaniment of modern songs, sometimes, in these little tragedies, foreshadows calamity from the outset, sometimes . . . . is a cheerful-sounding formula, which in the upshot enhances by contrast the gloom of the conclusion. 'A simple but life-like story, supported by the burden and the air, these are the means by which such old romances seek to produce an impression.'" [6] *The Elfin Knight* (2 A) "is the only example, so far as I remember, which our ballads afford of a burden of this kind, one that is of greater extent than the stanza with which it was sung, though this kind of burden seems to have been common enough with old songs and carols." [7]

[1] II, 260.   [2] I, 358.   [3] III, 129.
[4] V, 201.   [5] IV, 75.   [6] II, 204, n.
[7] I, 7. See the foot-note for Professor Child's longest discussion of the burden.

IV.

The English and Scottish Popular Ballads of 1882–1898 has naturally superseded the *English and Scottish Ballads* of 1857–1859, and Professor Child himself shared the general tendency to underestimate the real value of the earlier collection. It was of course made on a different plan; its limits were not so clearly defined, and it did not attempt to give every version of every known ballad. Many of the sources, moreover, were not yet open. One is, then, surprised to find that, of the three hundred and five ballads printed in the later collection, only ninety are new; and these are, for the most part, unimportant additions to the body of ballad literature. They are distributed as follows: 15 in volume I, 16 in II, 11 in III, 25 in IV, 23 in V. Thus 59 of the 90 occur in the last three volumes; of these there is not one of first importance. Of the remaining 31 not more than 10 can be regarded as really valuable additions, though such an estimate must of necessity be based more or less upon personal impression. Some of these were already accessible, in Buchan's versions, or elsewhere: *Willie's Lyke-Wake* (25), *Lizie Wan* (51), *The King's Dochter Lady Jean* (52), *Brown Robyn's Confession* (57), *Fair Mary of Waltington* (91). These, doubtless, were omitted because of the nature of their subject-matter; it was only in the later collection that Professor Child "had no discretion." [1] Other important ballads were not yet accessible, or not yet discovered: *St. Stephen and Herod* (22), *The Laily Worm and the Machrel of the Sea* (36), *The Queen of Elfan's Nourice* (40), *The Unquiet Grave* (78), *The Great Silkie of Sule Skerry* (113). Of the ten, only four are included in Professor Gummere's collection. The main addition of the later collection is thus rather in the way of

---

[1] *Sheath and Knife* (16), also, was accessible but omitted.

new versions of important ballads, or of more authentic versions based directly upon the manuscripts; in the citation of a larger number of foreign parallels; and, generally, in the matter contained in the introductions.

The *Ballads* contained 115 pieces which do not appear in the later collection. The nature of such material, since it is excluded from the "complete" *English and Scottish Popular Ballads,* is significant as throwing some additional light upon Professor Child's conception. In many cases the reason for exclusion is made clear by Professor Child himself, in comments in the earlier or in the later collection. Of the whole group of lays and romances contained in Book I of the *Ballads,* he says: "Some of the longer pieces in this book are not of the nature of ballads, and require an apology. They were admitted before the limits of the work had been determined with exactness."[1] If such pieces as these do not fulfil the lyrical requirement of the true ballad, others cannot fulfil the requirement of plot, and the songs of the *Ballads,* like *A Lyke Wake Dirge, Fair Helen of Kirconnel,* or *The Lowlands of Holland*[2] find no place in the later collection. The *Ballads* contains also translations from the Danish, and the original and translation of a modern Greek parallel of the Lenore story; these are naturally not included in *The English and Scottish Popular Ballads.*

The later collection is much more chary of the admission of broadsides or sheet-ballads: in many cases they are relegated to introductions or appendices; in many more, omitted.

---

[1] *Ballads,* I, xi, n. "Certain short romances which formerly stood in the First Book, have been dropped from this second Edition [1860], in order to give the collection a homogeneous character." *Ballads* [1860], I, xii.

[2] "A song," II, 317. (Where merely volume and page are given the reference is still to the later collection; references to the earlier are preceded by the word *Ballads.*)

William Guiseman is cited merely, under *Brown Robin's Confession* (57), as "a copy, improved by tradition, of the 'lament' in 'William Grismond's Downfal,' a broadside of 1650." [1] *The Lament of the Border Widow*, which occurs in Book VI of the *Ballads*, "shows broader traces of the sheet-ballad," and is quoted in the introduction to No 106 for "those who are interested in such random inventions (as, under pardon, they must be called)." [2] Of *The Lady Isabella's Tragedy* Professor Child says in the later collection: "Though perhaps absolutely the silliest ballad that ever was made, and very far from silly sooth, the broadside was traditionally propagated in Scotland without so much change as is usual in such cases." [3] Even in the *Ballads* one finds this comment: "The three following pieces [*The Spanish Virgin, Lady Isabella's Tragedy, The Cruel Black*] are here inserted merely as specimens of a class of tales, horrible in their incidents but feeble in their execution, of which whole dreary volumes were printed and read about two centuries ago. They were all of them, probably, founded on Italian novels." [4] Although the *Ballads* includes *Macpherson's Rant*, it is declared "worthy of a hangman's pen." [5] A number of tales which employ a highly artificial stanza, such as *The Fray of Suport, The Raid of the Reidswire*, or *The Flemish Insurrection*, do not find their way into the later collection.

Traces of the modern editor or author become less common in the later collection. Versions "modernized and completed by Percy" (Book I, Nos. 1b and 5b) are excluded. The cynical *Twa Corbies* appears only in the introduction to *The Three Ravens;* and Motherwell's edition, declared already in the *Ballads* to be a "modernized version," [6] does not appear at all. Motherwell's *Bonnie*

---

[1] II, 16. [2] II, 429. [3] v, 34, n.
[4] *Ballads*, III, 360. [5] *Ballads*, VI, 263. [6] *Ballads*, III, 61.

George Campbell suffers a like fate, and this, we infer, because "Motherwell made up his 'Bonnie George Campbell' from B, C, D."[1] As, no doubt, not merely modernized but modern, *Sir Roland* is excluded. "This fragment, Motherwell tells us, was communicated to him by an ingenious friend, who remembered having heard it sung in his youth. He does not vouch for its antiquity, and we have little or no hesitation in pronouncing it a modern composition."[2] Similarly, *Lady Anne* "is on the face of it a modern composition, with extensive variations, on the theme of the popular ballad."[3] It is printed in the appendix to No 20. *Earl Richard* is "an entirely modern composition, excepting only the twenty lines of Herd's fragment."[4] Of *Auld Maitland* Professor Child says: "Notwithstanding the authority of Scott and Leyden, I am inclined to agree with Mr Aytoun, that this ballad is a modern imitation, or if not that, a comparatively recent composition. It is with reluctance that I make for it the room it requires."[5] The essential anonymity of the ballad, in Professor Child's final conception, naturally excludes pieces like Henryson's *Robene and Makyne* and *The Bludy Serk*, which had found their way into the *Ballads*.[6]

There are but few instances of definite praise, as ballads, of pieces included in the earlier collection and excluded from the later. *The Children in the Wood* is said to be "perhaps the most popular of all English ballads. Its merit is attested by the favor it has enjoyed with so many generations, and was vindicated to a cold and artificial age by the kindly pen of Addison."[7] We must not forget,

---

[1] IV, 142.   [2] *Ballads*, I, 341.   [3] I, 218, n.   [4] *Ballads*, III, 293.
[5] *Ballads*, VI, 220. Cf. Mr Andrew Lang's plea for *Auld Maitland*, *Folk-Lore*, XIII, 191 ff.
[6] See also the comments on the Rev. Mr Lamb's *Laidley Worm of Spindleston Heugh*, *Ballads*, I, 386, and cf. p. 772, above.
[7] *Ballads*, III, 128.

however, that Professor Child was fifty years nearer the
kindly pen of Addison. The cold and artificial age, moreover, was also sentimental and moral; and why, with it,
this ballad was so popular, a single stanza will show:

> You that executors be made,
>   And overseers eke
> Of children that be fatherless,
>   And infants mild and meek;
> Take you example by this thing,
>   And yield to each his right,
> Lest God with such like miserye
>   Your wicked minds requite (vv. 153 ff.).

The Blind Beggar's Daughter of Bednall's Green is said to
be printed from a modern broadside, yet it is characterized
as " this favorite popular ballad." [1] *The Nutbrowne Maid* is
"this matchless poem," "this beautiful old ballad." [2] Yet,
clearly, it is not a popular ballad at all.

On the whole, it is not difficult to see why the 115
ballads are excluded from the later collection; and one gets
the impression that, had Professor Child chosen to enforce the
conception of the ballad which he already had in mind, most
of them would have been excluded from the earlier collection as well. This impression is deepened by an examination
of the comments scattered through the *Ballads*.

He already regarded the ballad as inimitable: [3] " The
exclusion of the ' Imitations'. . . . may possibly excite the
regret of a few. . . . Whatever may be the merit of the pro-
ductions in question, they are never less likely to obtain
credit for it, than when they are brought into comparison
with their professed models." [4] Again, *Sir Patrick Spence*,
" if not ancient, has been always accepted as such by the
most skilful judges, and is a solitary instance of a successful

---

[1] *Ballads*, IV, 161.   [2] *Ballads*, IV, 143 f.
[3] Cf. p. 757, above.   [4] *Ballads*, V, iv.

imitation, in manner and spirit, of the best specimens of authentic minstrelsy." [1]

Professor Child had already fallen foul of the editors, and their alterations and interpolations.[2] It is interesting to see how, in many cases, he anticipated the corrections and comments made possible, for the later collection, by access to the manuscripts. Of *The Child of Elle* he says: "So extensive are Percy's alterations and additions, that the reader will have no slight difficulty in detecting the few traces that are left of the genuine composition." [3] Compare: "So much of Percy's 'Child of Elle' as was genuine, which, upon the printing of his manuscript, turned out to be one fifth." [4] Again, Percy acknowledges interpolations, which " might with some confidence be pointed out. Among them are certainly most, if not all, of the last twelve stanzas of the Second Part, which include the catastrophe to the story." [5] In Percy, he says in the later collection, *Sir Cawline* " is extended to nearly twice the amount of what is found in the manuscript, and a tragical turn is forced upon the story." [6] Again: " We have given *Gil Morrice* as it stands in the *Reliques* (iii. 132,) degrading to the margin those stanzas which are undoubtedly spurious." [7] The stanzas thus degraded turned out to be actually spurious.[8] Condemnation of Buchan is scattered throughout the *Ballads*. Thus: " Some resolution has been exercised, and much disgust suppressed, in retaining certain pieces from Buchan's collections, so strong is the suspicion that, after having been procured from very inferior sources, they were tampered with by the editor." [9] Again: " One uncommonly tasteless stanza [41, A, 53], the interpolation of some nursery-maid,[10]

---

[1] *Ballads*, III, 148–149.   [2] Cf. p. 767, above.   [3] *Ballads*, III, 225.
[4] I, 88.   [5] *Ballads*, III, 173.   [6] II, 56.
[7] *Ballads*, II, 30.   [8] II, 275.   [9] *Ballads*, I, ix, n.
[10] Cf. p. 762, above.

is here omitted. Too many of Buchan's ballads have suffered in this way, and have become both prolix and vulgar."[1] Even in the *Ballads* Professor Child placed "no confidence in any of Allan Cunningham's *souvenirs* of Scottish song,"[2] and his early suspicions[3] of the character of Cunningham's version of Gil Brenton are confirmed in the later collection.[4] *King Henry*, printed in the earlier collection "without the editor's [Jamieson's] interpolations,"[5] appears in the same form in the later, except that stanza 14 is printed in small type, as not being in the Jamieson-Brown MS. Again, in *The Bonny Birdy*, "the lines supplied by Jamieson have been omitted."[6] There is an interesting comment on these lines in the later collection.[7]

Professor Child was already aware that change of nationality was accompanied by change of the scene of action.[8] He quoted Scott's account of the locality of *The Douglas Tragedy* [= *Earl Brand* (7, B)], and added: "After so circumstantial a description of the scene, ... the reader may be amused to see the same story told in various Scandinavian ballads, with a no less plausible resemblance to actual history. This, as has already been pointed out under *Guy of Warwick* and *Kempion*,[9] is an ordinary occurrence in the transmission of legends."[10]

He noted, too, the tendency of ballads to combine: "The natural desire of men to hear more of characters in whom they have become strongly interested, has frequently stimu-

---

[1] *Ballads*, I, 306 n.   [2] *Ballads*, II, 220.   [3] *Ballads*, I, 270.
[4] See I, 62, and, for the omitted couplets, I, 80–81.
[5] *Ballads*, I, 265.   [6] *Ballads*, II, 22.
[7] II, 260. See, also, the comments on Jamieson's *Child Rowland and Burd Ellen*, *Ballads*, I, 416, and *English and Scottish Popular Ballads*, v. 201, n.
[8] Cf. p. 769, above.   [9] *Ballads*, I, 256.   [10] *Ballads*, II, 115.

lated the attempt to continue successful fictions." [1] *Sweet William's Ghost* is often made the sequel to other ballads. [2]

So far as subject-matter is concerned, we find in the *Ballads* the same conception of the relation of ballad and fact. *Jane Shore* "adheres to matter of fact with a fidelity very uncommon," [3] and this is, perhaps, one reason why it does not find a place in the later collection. [4] We may contrast, on the other hand, the two statements in regard to the relation of *Hind Horn* and the romance: "Metrical romances . . . . are known in many cases to have been adapted for the entertainment of humbler hearers, by abridgment in the form of ballads." He regards *Hind Horn* as a case of this sort. [5]

Style and plot, finally, are a test of genuineness: "I cannot assent to the praise bestowed by Scott on *The Outlaw Murray*. The story lacks point and the style is affected— not that of the unconscious poet of the real *traditional* ballad." [6] Though there without comment, it is placed at the very end of the later collection.

From a comment like this it is obvious that Professor Child already had in mind the conception of "a real *traditional* ballad," a "specimen of authentic minstrelsy." [7] Although he admitted to the earlier collection lays, romances, songs, broadsides and sheet-ballads, as well as modern or modernized compositions, yet he was aware that all these differed from the true ballad. This true ballad, he conceived, was inimitable, in matter and manner. In transmission it might suffer, from the invention of a nursery-maid, from Buchan's beggar, from a "hangman's pen," from the modern editors. It drew its subject-matter from fact (to which it

---

[1] *Ballads*, II, 64.   [2] *Ballads*, II, 45.   [3] *Ballads*, VII, 194.
[4] Cf. the comment on *The Hunting of the Cheviot*, *Ballads*, VII, 25.
[5] *Ballads*, IV, 17.   For the later comment, see p. 777, above.
[6] *Ballads*, VI, 22.   [7] *Ballads*, III, 148–149.

was not loyal), from romances, from other ballads. In quality the subject-matter was not "horrible." In style the true ballad was not feeble in execution, not prolix and vulgar, and not affected. The earlier conception was not as complete as the later, and it was by no means so rigorously enforced. In regard to specific compositions, there was, as is to be expected, some change of opinion. But the significant fact is that for at least forty years Professor Child retained without essential change his conception of the traditional ballad as a distinct literary type.

V.

We may now bring together the passages in which Professor Child declared certain ballads to be of the true "popular" or "traditional" type. The fewness of such passages is at first surprising, yet it clearly formed no part of a set purpose to include in his introductions estimates of this kind, and such "appreciations" seem to have been either spontaneous,—springing, as in the case of *Johnie Cock,* from his delight in the ballad with which he was concerned,—or intended, as in the case of *Edward,* as answer to his predecessors' doubts of authenticity. On ballads like *Lord Randal, Babylon, Hind Horn, Clerk Saunders, Fair Margaret and Sweet William,* there is no such comment. It would seem, no doubt, in such cases obviously unnecessary. Nevertheless the list is fairly representative. We have examples of the Domestic Ballad,—tragic, in *Earl Brand* (7), *Edward* (13), *Old Robin of Portingale* (80), *Little Musgrave* (81), *The Bonny Birdy* (82); not tragic, in *Child Waters* (63), *Young Beichan* (53), *Queen Eleanor's Confession* (156): we have examples of the Supernatural Ballad,—transformation, in *The Laily Worm and the Machrel of the Sea* (36); fairy, in *Thomas Rymer* (37); ghost, in *The Wife of Usher's Well* (79): we have examples of the Border Ballad in *Captain Car* (178 F) and *Jock o the Side* (187): of the Outlaw Ballad in *Johnie Cock* (114), the Robin Hood ballads, 117–121: of the Heroic Ballad in *King Estmere* (60), *Sir Aldingar* (59), *Sir Patrick Spens* (58 A).

Johnie Cock (114): "This precious specimen of the unspoiled traditional ballad." III, 1.

Edward (13): "The word 'brand,' in the first stanza, is possibly more literary than popular; further than this the language is entirely fit. The affectedly antique spelling in Percy's copy has given rise to vague suspicions concerning tbe authenticity of the ballad, or of the language: but as spelling will not make an old ballad, so it will not unmake one. We have, but do not need, the later traditional copy to prove the other genuine. 'Edward' is not only unimpeachable, but has ever been regarded as one of the noblest and most sterling specimens of the popular ballad." I, 167.

The Laily Worm and the Machrel of the Sea (36): "Somewhat mutilated, and also defaced, though it be, this ballad has certainly never been retouched by a pen, but is pure tradition. It has the first stanza in common with 'Kemp Owyne,' and shares more than that with 'Allison Gross.' But it is independent of 'Allison Gross,' and has a far more original sound." I, 315.

Earl Brand (7) .... "has preserved most of the incidents of a very ancient story with a faithfulness unequalled by any ballad that has been recovered from English oral tradition." I, 88.

The Wife of Usher's Well (79): "A motive for the return of the wife's three sons is not found in the fragments which remain to us. . . . But supplying a motive would add nothing to the impressiveness of these verses. Nothing that we have is more profoundly affecting." II, 238.

Thomas Rymer (37): "B . . . . has been corrupted here and there, but only by tradition." I, 317.

"The fairy adventures of Thomas and of Ogier have the essential points in common, and even the particular trait that the fairy is taken to be the Virgin. The occurrence of this trait again in the ballad, viewed in connection with the general similarity of the two, will leave no doubt that the ballad had its source in the romance. Yet it is an entirely popular ballad as to style,[1] and must be of considerable age, though the earliest version (A) can be traced at furthest only into the first half of the last century." I, 319 f.

---

[1] "Excepting the two satirical stanzas with which Scott's version (C) concludes."

Captain Car (178) : "F is purely traditional and has one fine stanza not found in any of the foregoing :

> Out then spake the lady Margaret,
> As she stood on the stair ;
> The fire was at her goud garters,
> The lowe was at her hair." III, 429.

Queen Eleanor's Confession (156) : "There is reason to question whether this [F] and the other recited versions are anything more than traditional variations of printed copies. The ballad seems first to have got into print in the latter part of the seventeenth century, but was no doubt circulating orally sometime before that, for it is in the truly popular tone." III, 255.

Robin Hood and the Tanner (126) : "The sturdy Arthur a Bland is well hit off, and, bating the sixteenth and thirty-fifth stanzas, the ballad has a good popular ring. There is corruption at 8^3, 12^3, and perhaps 13^3." III, 137.

The earliest Robin Hood ballads (117–121) "are among the best of all ballads, and perhaps none in English please so many and please so long." III, 42.

Robin Hood and the Monk (119) : "Too much could not be said in praise of this ballad, but nothing need be said. It is very perfection in its kind ; and yet we have others equally good, and beyond doubt should have had more, if they had been written down early, as this was, and had not been left to the chances of tradition. Even writing would not have saved all, but writing has saved this (in large part), and in excellent form." III, 95.

Child Waters (63) : "This charming ballad, which has perhaps no superior in English, and if not in English perhaps nowhere." II, 84. ("Caution is imperative where so much ground is covered, and no man should be confident that he can do absolute justice to poetry in a tongue that he was not born to ; but foreign poetry is as likely to be rated too high as to be undervalued." II, 84, n.)

Jock o the Side (187) : "The ballad is one of the best in the world, and enough to make a horse-trooper of any young borderer, had he lacked the impulse." III, 477.

Sir Patrick Spens (58, A) : "This admired and most admirable ballad." "It would be hard to point out in ballad poetry, or other, happier or more refined touches than the two stanzas in A which portray the bootless waiting of the ladies for the return of the seafarers." II, 17 f.[1]

Young Beichan (53) : "A favorite ballad and most deservedly." I, 455.

King Estmere (60) : "While we cannot but be vexed that so distinguished a ballad, not injured much, so far as we can see, by time, should

---

[1] See also the comment in the *Ballads*, quoted p. 804, below.

not come down to us as it came to Percy, our loss must not be exaggerated. The changes made by the editor, numerous enough, no doubt, cannot be very material until we approach the end. Stanzas 63–66 are entirely suspicious, and it may even be questioned whether the manuscript contained a word that is in them." II, 49.

Little Musgrave and Lady Barnard (81) : "The noble English ballad." II, 260.

The Bonny Birdy (82) : "A fine ballad upon the same theme." II, 243.

Old Robin of Portingale (80) : "This fine ballad." II, 240.

Sir Aldingar (69) : "This ballad, one of the most important of all that the Percy manuscript has saved from oblivion." II, 33.

Robin Hood's Death (120) : "B, though found only in late garlands, is in the fine old strain." III, 103.

Certain ballads are expressly condemned as not "traditional" or "popular" :

Robin Hood Rescuing Will Stutly (141) : "This is a ballad made for print, with little of the traditional in the matter and nothing in the style. It may be considered as an imitation of the Rescue of the Three Squires." III, 185.

Robin Hood's Birth, Breeding, etc. (149) : "The jocular author of this ballad, who would certainly have been diverted by any one's supposing him to write under the restraints of tradition. . . ." III, 214.

The Lovely Northerne Lasse (217, Appendix) : "There is an English 'ditty' (not a traditional ballad) . . . . which was printed in the first half of the seventeenth century. It is here given in an appendix." IV, 192.

To these may be added a few examples of less specific condemnation :

The Earl of Mar's Daughter (270) : A Scandinavian ballad and this "are, perhaps, on a par, for barrenness and folly, but the former may claim some age and vogue, the Scottish ballad neither." V, 39.

The Drunkard's Legacy (267, Appendix) : "The modern ballad . . . . used by Percy was 'The Drunkard's Legacy,' an inexpressibly pitiable ditty." V, 12.

John Thomson and the Turk (266) : "This ridiculous ballad." V, 1.

Robin Hood and the Tinker (127) : "The fewest words will best befit this contemptible imitation of imitations." III, 140.

Robin Hood and Maid Marian (150) : "This foolish ditty." III, 218.

Robin Hood and the Valiant Knight (153) : "Written, perhaps, because it was thought that authority should in the end be vindicated against outlaws, which may explain why this piece surpasses in platitude everything that goes before." III, 225.

The Suffolk Miracle (272): "This piece could not be admitted here on its own merits. At the first look, it would be classed with the vulgar prodigies printed for hawkers to sell and for Mopsa and Dorcas to buy. It is not even a good specimen of its kind." v, 58.

We may add from the *Ballads* half-a-dozen examples of specific praise :

The Lass of Lochroyan [76, D][1] : "This beautiful piece." *Ballads*, II, 98.

The Queen's Marie [173, I] : "Jamieson and Kinloch have each published a highly dramatic fragment of this terrible story." *Ballads*, III, 107.

The Lochmaben Harper [192, A] : "This fine old ballad . . . . has the genuine ring of the best days of minstrelsy. On account of its excellence, we give two versions." *Ballads*, VI, 3.

Earl Richard [68, J] : "This gloomy and impressive romance." *Ballads*, III, 3.

Chevy-Chace [162, A] : "Addison's papers in the *Spectator* . . . . evince so true a perception of the merits of this ballad [162, B], shorn as it is of the most striking beauties of the grand original, that we cannot but deeply regret his never having seen the ancient and genuine copy ('The noble ballad,' 162, A ; *Ballads*, VII, 27), which was published by Hearne only a few days after Addison died." *Ballads*, VII, 43.

Sir Andrew Barton [167, A] : "This noble ballad." *Ballads*, VII, 56.

Sir Patrick Spence [58, A] : "If not ancient, has been always accepted as such by the most skilful judges, and is a solitary instance of a successful imitation, in manner and spirit, of the best specimens of authentic minstrelsy." *Ballads*, III, 149.

VI.

We are now in position to attempt a summary of Professor Child's conception of the popular ballad. He regarded it as a distinct species of poetry, which precedes the poetry of art, as the product of a homogeneous people, the expression of our common human nature, of the mind and heart of the people, never of the personality of an individual man, devoid, therefore, of all subjectivity and self-consciousness.

[1] The numbers in brackets are those affixed to the ballads in the later collection.

Hence the author counts for nothing; hence, too, the ballad is difficult to imitate and most attempts in this way are ridiculous failures. In transmission the ballad regularly departs from the original form, least in the mouths of unlearned people, more in the hands of professional singers or editors. It is at its best when it has come down by a purely domestic tradition, yet even so it is sometimes influenced by printed literature; and much depends on the experience and selection of the reciters, and on their varying memory, which is, however, ordinarily remarkable for its tenacity. Less fortunate is the ballad when it passes through low mouths or hands, suffering corruption of various kinds,—in the style of the attorney's clerk, or the housemaid or the serving-man, or ostler, or blind beggar. In the hands of the *bänkelsänger* or of the minstrel, the ballad departs still further from its original form. Or, rewritten for the broadside press, it is seriously enfeebled, or retrenched and marred, though it may retain some original features, and there are thus degrees of departure from the original matter and manner. The broadside may, in turn, become tradition. It is, so far as it appears in Professor Child's later collection, always founded on tradition, and this tradition lives after the composition of the broadside, and may influence the later versions of the printed form. Last comes the modern editor, and by him the ballad is sometimes lengthened,—by combination of different versions, by interpolation of new stanzas, always more or less unlike the popular style; or it is sometimes "improved," or retouched, or emended, or altered,— changed to something in glaring contrast to the groundwork. Some results of the vicissitudes of transmission are, the change of the hero's nationality, of his name, of his rôle; change of the scene of action; corruption of diction resulting in perversion of sense or in nonsense; introduction of learned words. The ballad thus suffers in transmission, and is at its best when it is early caught and fixed in print. It is sometimes counterfeited or imitated, and counterfeits are included in the later collection for contrast, for much the same reason that thieves are photographed, or because they may contain relics of something genuine or better.

Of the Subject-Matter of the ballad, the sources may be, and in the best instances are, purely popular, consisting of material which appears only in popular literature. Professor Child mentions no instance where a prose tale is the source of a ballad, but the ballad, he says, may sometimes be resolved into a prose tale. Popular origin is attested by foreign parallels in folk-literature. Of such literature certain features or themes are characteristic, such as the quibbling oath, the miraculous harvest, the childbirth in the wood, the testament, the riddle, heroic sentiment, etc. The source may, again, be an actual occurrence, in which case the ballad, while not deliberate fiction, is yet not loyal to the fact. Or the source may be a romance, or the source of a romance, in which case oral tradition may be older than written, the ballad older than the romance. Or the source may be earlier ballads, mechanically and deliberately put together in later ones, made over and assimilated in the *Gest of Robin Hood*. In the course of transmission certain features appear which are not characteristic of popular literature; the subject-matter of the true ballad does not deal in extravagance, or exaggeration, or platitude; it is not prosaic, over-refined, cynical, sophisticated, sentimental, unnatural, trite, or moral, though the "pungent buckishness" of the broadside, and the gay cynicism of the minstrel, are foreign to it.

So far as Technique is concerned, the ballad must have plot. The story may not be completely told; conclusion, transitions, and preliminaries may be omitted; but the result is not nonsense, the ballad is not incoherent. At its best it is, however, brief. It is careless of geography, and, except in some,—and some of the best,—of the Robin Hood ballads, it touches Setting lightly. In dealing with the Supernatural it does not attempt to explain the action or to describe supernatural figures; ghosts, however, do not walk without reason.

In Style the ballad is artless and homely, and in it the conceit, and literary or learned words and phrases, are out of place. Yet it has certain conventions of its own, such as the "commonplace," the repetition of a message by a messenger, the verbally similar treatment of similar incidents as they occur in different ballads. Emotionally, the ghost ballad is impressive and affecting; and, in general, the ballad may be infectious, or spirited and life-like, or pathetic, or tender, or humorous, or vigorous and not lacking in color or flavor. It is essentially lyrical, and its lyrical quality is not less essential than plot. Often it absolutely requires the support of a melody and the comment of a burden. This burden sometimes foreshadows the calamity, sometimes enhances by contrast the gloom of the conclusion. It is usually less than the stanza with which it was sung; and, unlike the refrain, it was sung, not after the stanza, but with it. It is sometimes of different metre, sometimes not. The absence of the burden is in no case proof that it never existed.

WALTER MORRIS HART.